Deviant Behavior

A TEXT-READER IN
THE SOCIOLOGY OF DEVIANCE

SECOND EDITION

Deviant Behavior

A TEXT-READER IN
THE SOCIOLOGY OF DEVIANCE

SECOND EDITION

Delos H. Kelly

CALIFORNIA STATE UNIVERSITY, LOS ANGELES

ST. MARTIN'S PRESS
NEW YORK

cover design: Meryl Levavi
text design: Judith Woracek

Acknowledgments

"Conceptions of Deviant Behavior: The Old and the New" by Jack P. Gibbs. *Pacific Sociological Review,* 9:1 (Spring, 1966), pp. 9–11. Copyright © 1966 by the Pacific Sociological Association. Reprinted by permission of Sage Publications, Inc.
Selections from *Outsiders* by Howard S. Becker. Reprinted with permission of Macmillan Publishing Company. Copyright © 1963 by The Free Press, a Division of Macmillan Publishing Company.
Selection from *The Legislation of Morality* by Troy Duster. Reprinted with permission of Macmillan Publishing Company. Copyright © 1970 by The Free Press, a Division of Macmillan Publishing Company.
"The 'Discovery' of Child Abuse" by Stephen J. Pfohl. *Social Problems,* 24:3 (February, 1977), pp. 310–323. Reprinted by permission of the author and The Society for the Study of Social Problems.
Selection from *The Manufacture of Madness* by Thomas S. Szasz. Reprinted by permission of Harper & Row, Publishers, Inc. Copyright © 1970 by Thomas S. Szasz, Trustee.
Selection from *The Rules of the Sociological Method* by Emile Durkheim, translated by Sarah A. Solovay and John H. Mueller, edited by George E.G. Catlin. Reprinted with permission of Macmillan Publishing Company. Copyright © 1938 by George E.G. Catlin, renewed in 1966 by Sarah A. Solovay, John H. Mueller, and George E.G. Catlin.
"The Functions of Deviance in Groups" by Robert A. Dentler and Kai T. Erikson. *Social Problems,* 7:2 (Fall, 1959), pp. 98–107. Reprinted by permission of the authors and The Society for the Study of Social Problems.
"Culture Conflict and Crime" by Thorsten Sellin. A report of the Subcommittee on Delinquency of the Committee on Personality and Culture, *Social Science Research Council Bulletin* 41 (New York, 1938). Reprinted by permission.

Acknowledgments and copyrights continue at the back of the book on pages 843–846, which constitute an extension of the copyright page.

To Jane, Brett Alan, and Erin Lynn

Preface

Some anthologies dealing with the subject of deviance emphasize the ways in which society responds to deviant behavior. Others, by examining why certain individuals violate the social norm, focus on the motivational element. And a few trace the evolution of deviant categories. *Deviant Behavior* has been designed to integrate and balance these concerns in a single volume—to explore, through carefully selected readings, the ramifications of deviance for both the individual (the *actor*) and for society.

Part One considers the ways society defines deviance and the deviant. Of particular interest is the role that specific individuals—especially those who hold political power or who serve as enforcers of the law—play in the labeling of actors and acts as deviant. It will become clear to the reader that no individual and no behavior is inherently deviant: it is society's perception of an actor or an act as deviant that affixes the label. Deviance, in other words, is in the eye of the beholder.

Why does socially prohibited behavior occur—and persist, despite society's efforts to eliminate or discourage it? How can we make sense of deviance? Sociologists approach these questions from a number of different theoretical perspectives. Part Two presents readings by major theorists representing the most important of these perspectives. The introduction to the section furnishes students with the theoretical framework upon which to build an understanding and an appreciation of these key thinkers.

Part Three follows the evolving *career* of the social deviant: it traces the steps by which he or she becomes identified by society as a deviant. It depicts, for example, the efforts of relatives to cope with the increasingly bizarre behavior of a family member. Frequently, of course, attempts to manage the deviant at home fail, and the family turns to institutions and agencies of social control for help. The couple in the article by Marian Radke Yarrow and others, "The Psychological Meaning of Mental Illness in the Family," exemplifies such an eventuality, as a woman responds to the growing awareness that her husband can no longer be counted upon to act rationally.

Once deviants have been institutionalized, their career is determined, to a great extent, by their experiences within the institution. Part Four explores the workings of several people-processing and people-changing facilities—ranging from juvenile court to mental hospital—to examine how such structures deal with clients and how clients, in turn, adapt their behavior and their self-concept to their surroundings.

For certain types of deviance, institutional controls are far less significant than the traditions and norms of deviant subcultures. Part Five examines the ways in which such norms shape the career of the religious cultist, the prostitute, the road hustler, and others.

Finally, Part Six analyzes the processes by which deviant categories, actors, and structures can be altered or transformed. The first two selections offer contemporary accounts of how selected deviant conceptions and categories have actually undergone significant changes. Clearly, if the underlying content of the prevailing images changes, then so, too, must the picture of deviance change. Thus activities that may have been seen as "deviant" at one point in time may now be perceived as "acceptable" or even "normal" by various audiences. Adler and Adler's research on "tinydopers" (i.e., marijuana-smoking children between the ages of 0–8 years) offers an excellent illustration of this process. The next two readings describe various personal and institutional barriers that confront those who desire to move from a deviant to a nondeviant status—in particular, society's reluctance to accept as "normal" anyone who has borne the stigma of deviance. The remaining three pieces outline specific ways in which deviant organizations, decision makers, and structures could be controlled, sanctioned, or perhaps even rehabilitated.

Overall, then, this book explores the establishment and maintenance of deviant categories; the motivations behind deviant behavior; the identification as deviant of individuals and of particular segments of society, by formal and informal means; the effects of institutionalization upon the deviant; and the efforts of deviants, to eradicate the label society has placed upon them. Analysis is also given to the ways in which deviant categories and structures can be altered.

I would like to thank several people for their help in preparing the second edition of this book, particularly my editors Walter Kossmann and Richard Steins. I am grateful as well for the solid contributions of Steve Gordon and John Johnson. The efforts of Sharon Edwards should also be acknowledged.

Delos H. Kelly
Pasadena, California

Contents

Introduction
Deviant Conceptions and Categories

Deviant Behavior

A TEXT-READER IN
THE SOCIOLOGY OF DEVIANCE

SECOND EDITION

/ General Introduction

We all carry in our minds images of deviance and the deviant. To some, deviants are murderers and rapists. Others would include in the list prostitutes, child molesters, wife beaters, and homosexuals. With regard to the motivations behind deviant behavior, some of us would place the blame on the family, while others would emphasize genetic or social factors, especially poverty.

CREATING DEVIANCE

Regardless of what kinds of behavior we consider deviant or what factors we believe cause deviance, we must recognize that deviance *and* the deviant emerge out of a continuous process of interaction among people. For deviance to become a public fact, however, several conditions need to be satisfied: (1) some deviant category (e.g., mores and laws) must exist; (2) a person must be viewed as violating the category; and (3) someone must attempt to enforce the violation of the category. If the individual demanding enforcement is successful in his or her efforts to label the violator, the social deviant has been created.

The Creation of Deviant Categories

As far as deviant categories are concerned, relatively little attention has been focused on their evolution. Formal and informal codes of conduct are generally accepted as "givens," and investigators concentrate on the examination of *why* the categories are violated and *how* they are enforced. An approach of this kind is inadequate, however, particularly in view of the fact that new categories are continually evolving and old ones are being modified. Obviously, as the definitions or categories of deviance change, the picture of deviance must also be altered. The rapidly changing content of the laws governing marijuana provides an example. If there are no penalties for possessing and smoking marijuana, one cannot be formally charged and processed for doing so.

In studying deviance, then, a central question needs to be raised:

How (and why) do *acts* become defined as deviant?[1] Providing answers to this question requires an examination of how deviance is defined, how the definitions are maintained, and how violators of the definitions are processed and treated. What is entailed is both a historical and an ongoing analysis of those legislative and political processes that affect the evolution, modification, and enforcement of deviant categories. Central focus must be placed on those who possess the power and resources not only to define deviance but to apply a label of deviance to a violator and to make the label stick. These processes are highlighted in Part 1 and will be evident in the discussion of the "conflict model" in Part 2.

Reactions to Violators of Deviant Categories

In terms of the *actor*, an equally important question can be asked. How (and why) do violators of various types of deviant categories (mores, laws, and regulations) become labeled as deviant? Answering this question requires an examination of the interaction occurring between an *actor* and an *audience*. A simple paradigm (Figure 1) can illustrate how the deviant is reacted to and thus socially created. This paradigm can be applied to most of the selections in this volume.

The Interactional Paradigm: A young man (the social *actor*) is seen smoking marijuana (the *act*, a violation of a deviant category) by a police officer (a social *audience*, an enforcer of the deviant category) and is arrested. The youth's deviation thus becomes a matter of public record, and a deviant career is initiated—a career that may be solidified and perpetuated by legal and institutional processing. Another officer, however, might ignore the offense. In the first case, then, the violator is initially labeled as a "deviant," while in the second he is not. Figure 1 indicates that not only is audience response critical, but it depends on several factors. The example also helps to

Figure 1 / Interactional Paradigm

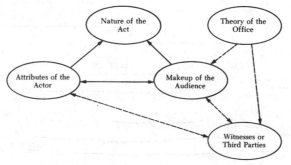

Figure 2 / Organizational Paradigm

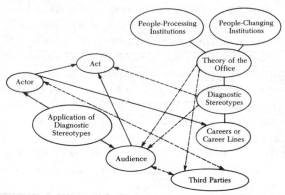

underscore the fact that there is nothing inherently deviant about any act or actor—their meanings are derived from the interpretations *others* place on them. Hence the notion that "deviance lies in the eyes of the beholder." This example can be extended by considering the fourth element of the paradigm: *third parties, or witnesses.* Specifically, a young man may be observed smoking marijuana by a peer, and the peer may choose to ignore the offense. Another peer, however, not only may consider the act illegal or deviant but may decide to do something about it. The peer lacks the power to arrest; he can, however, bring in third parties in an effort to create a shared attitude toward the smoker—namely, that he is a "criminal" or "deviant." The peer may turn to other peers, and they may decide to call the police and have the smoker arrested. If this happens, the person's "deviance" becomes a public fact.

Thus, the label "deviant" is a status conferred on a person by an observer or observers. Although an understanding of this process requires an examination of the way the four basic elements of the paradigm interact with one another, such an examination is not sufficient. An awareness of the *theory of the office* that a particular agent or audience operates out of is also necessary, especially if the occupant of the office is an agent of social control. The preceding example, as well as the "organizational paradigm" highlighted in Figure 2, can be used to illustrate this requirement. This paradigm represents a refinement of the "interactional paradigm" described in Figure 1. Here I am focusing on the audience, particularly in terms of how an institution expects certain outcomes on the part of its agents. This paradigm will be generally applied throughout this volume.

The Organizational Paradigm: Although it might be assumed that the police officer in our examples operates on the basis of his or her own initiative, this is frequently far from the truth. The officer, like any institutional agent concerned with the processing (through the courts) or rehabilitating (in correctional facilities) of clients, is guided and generally constrained by a theory of the office, or "working ideology." The officer, through informal (contacts with other officers) and formal (police academies) socialization experiences, learns how to identify and classify deviants or suspected deviants. These institutional, or "diagnostic," stereotypes (Scheff, 1966) comprise a basic ingredient of a department's official perspective. The officer, for example, learns how to recognize the "typical" case of child molestation, runaway, or rape. These "normal crimes" (Sudnow, 1965), or "social type designations," not only help the officer make sense out of events; they also provide criteria upon which a suspect can be initially identified, classified, and then selected out to play the role of the deviant.

An institution's stereotypes are basic to the *rate production process*—the creation of a body of institutional statistics. If, for example, a police chief feels that homosexual behavior is morally wrong or criminal, not only will this one individual's conception become embedded within the theory of the office, but the officers will be required to zero in on such activity. This response will produce a set of crime statistics exhibiting an unusually high arrest rate for homosexual exchanges. Similarly, if a police chief formally or informally communicates to his departmental personnel that blacks, Mexicans, Indians, and other minorities constitute the "real" deviants, delinquents, and criminals, such people will be disproportionately selected out to play the role of the deviant—that is, they will become more vulnerable to institutional processing. This, too, will produce a set of statistics reflecting a heavy concentration of these individuals. The statistics can, in turn, serve as justification for heavy and continued surveillance in areas containing such groups. Examples of this phenomenon abound.

If we are to approach an understanding of what causes deviance, and particularly of the ways in which institutional careers arise and are perpetuated, then we need initially to analyze and dissect the existing structure of the institutions of social control. To obtain an understanding of how institutions operate requires, as suggested by Figure 2, sensitization to several basic organizational elements and processes: (1) the institution's theory of the office, (2) the content of the institutional stereotypes embedded within the theory of the office and used to identify clients for typing and processing, (3) the existing careers or career lines (and associated role expectations) into which the identified clients are placed, (4) the socialization of institutional agents and their application of diagnostic stereotypes to clients, and (5) the effects of institutional typing and processing, from the perspectives of both the client and the institution.

UNDERSTANDING DEVIANCE

In the discussion of the creation of deviance it was argued that some deviant category must exist, a person must be viewed as violating the category, and someone must make a demand for enforcement. Thus far, too, the focus has been upon the evolution and change of deviant categories, as well as on the interactional aspects—how and why violators of categories may be reacted to. Missing from this analysis, however, is a concern for the motivational aspects—the reasons why people may violate deviant categories. This concern has been generally ignored by the labeling or interactionist proponents. Their main interest revolves around examining audience reactions and the impact of those reactions on people. Implicit in such a stand is the idea that the reasons for behavior are relatively unimportant. If, however, we are to approach a more complete understanding of deviance from a dynamic perspective, attention must also be given to motivation. Such a view provides us with an opportunity continually to analyze how behavior and labels interact with each other.

Violations of Deviant Categories

Traditionally, writers have concentrated on trying to explain why people may violate various types of deviant categories. Some have spent their time trying to explain group or structural rates of deviance, while others have concentrated on those processes by which individuals learn culture and traditions. These efforts have produced many schools of thought, each with its own set of assumptions. The "anomie" theorists, for example, argue that blocked opportunity can produce a tendency toward deviation. The "conflict" theorists, by contrast, contend that the powerless may consciously violate the laws formulated by the powerful. Understanding deviance, then, requires that we investigate those reasons why people may violate deviant categories and by their violations bring upon themselves a particular labeling. The selections in Part 2 offer some representative attempts to explore this question.

BECOMING DEVIANT

With regard to the process of becoming deviant, an initial distinction can be made between private and public settings. A husband may violate a particular set of expectations by acting strangely. The wife may try to make sense out of such behavior by rationalizing it away or neutralizing it. She may argue to herself and others that her husband has experienced some personal setbacks and that the peculiar behavior will pass. At this stage the wife is trying to develop a counterdefinition of the situation, and she is also refusing to impute a deviant label to her spouse. The husband's behavior may grow increasingly violent, though, to the point where the wife finds it necessary to bring in agents of social control. She may call the police (third parties) or ultimately have her husband committed to a mental institution. If this should happen, not only have the wife's tolerance limits been exceeded but her attempts at various strategies of *accommodation* (such as neutralization or rationalization) have failed. The husband may then be typed as, for example, a schizophrenic and processed in accordance with the establishment's expectations of what the schizophrenic career should entail. The patient is expected, thereafter, to live up to his institutional role—to accept the label and act accordingly. The case of McMurphy in *One Flew Over the Cuckoo's Nest* (Kesey, 1962) describes what may happen when a patient protests against his assigned label. Because McMurphy rejects the "sick role," he becomes embroiled in a running battle with Big Nurse, the institution's agent. In our example, a similar situation may evolve with respect to the husband's response: he may repudiate the institutional tag, he may try to ignore it, or he may accept it. His response, like the responses of observers, is frequently difficult to predict.

In private settings, attempts may be made to regulate and control behavior, and these efforts may be successful. However, once third parties or social-control agents (such as the police or psychiatrists) are called in, the individual is frequently on his or her way to becoming an institutional deviant—that is, the organizational paradigm becomes operative, not only from the institution's viewpoint but from the actor's perspective. In particular, if a mental institution is involved, the client becomes viewed as a "mental patient"; this label becomes the patient's *master status* (Becker, 1963), and people will then react to the person on the basis of the label rather than regarding him as sane or "normal." The changing of one's status, or the *status degradation ceremony* (Garfinkel, 1956), also affects the views others have of the "deviant" (one's public identity), as well as how the actor views himself (one's personal identity). The change frequently affects the person's self-esteem (how one views self, positively or negatively, relative to others on selected criteria).

INSTITUTIONAL AND NONINSTITUTIONAL CAREERS

An important distinction should be made between *institutional* and *noninstitutional* careers. A noninstitutional career is one that a person pursues primarily as a matter of choice. The individual takes an active role in structuring and presenting a specific image of self to others. The bookie, gambler, con artist, nudist, skid row alcoholic, and homosexual provide examples. Such individuals generally progress through some semblance of a career: once they gain entry or exposure, they begin to learn the existing culture and traditions. The bookie, for instance, may start out as a runner, "learn the ropes," and then move into other phases of the bookmaking operation. Similarly, if the skid row alcoholic wants to become an accepted member of the "bottle gang culture," he will become familiar with the norms prevalent among the skid row inhabitants, particularly norms that relate to the procurement and consumption of alcohol. Violations of the normative code frequently cause a person to be excluded from the group (Rubington, 1973). As with the sanctioning of "deviants" by "nondeviants," the "labeled deviants" have ways of punishing those who deviate from their own code.

Institutional careers, by contrast, involve those in which the individual plays a relatively passive role. Here, the career is initiated and perpetuated by some socializing or social-control institution; this process was briefly noted in the discussion of how one becomes deviant. The careers of the "school misfit," mental patient, delinquent, and criminal are of this type. The major difference between institutional careers and noninstitutional careers concerns the role of the actor, particularly in the matter of choice and in the means of gaining entry. Once the institutional career begins, though, the mental patient, like the skid row alcoholic, is expected to learn and act in accordance with the existing subculture and its traditions.

Institutional and noninstitutional careers are not always mutually exclusive. Frequently, a degree of overlap exists between the two. The skid row alcoholic, for example, may be arrested and sent to an alcoholic ward, where his or her behavior becomes subject to institutional control. Similarly, the prostitute may be arrested and taken to jail. In both instances the activities become a matter of institutional knowledge and record. A secret homosexual, by contrast, may never directly experience the effects of institutional processing.

The Effects of Institutional and Noninstitutional Careers

The distinction between institutional and noninstitutional careers provides a backdrop against which a person's reactions can be assessed. How, for example, is a person likely to respond to institutional typing and processing as a deviant? Will he or she reject or accept the institutional label? Answering these questions requires a consideration of how the "status degradation ceremony" affects an actor's personal and public identity. If the deviant rejects the label, a discrepancy (or *identity crisis*) occurs between one's personal and public identities—that is, between one's view of oneself as normal and the institution's view of one as a deviant. Obviously, unless some personal gain can be realized, such as the enhancement of one's prestige or status in the eyes of others, most persons will reject a deviant label imputed to them. Maintaining an image of self that is at odds with the institution's is not without its costs, though, and eventually the individual may come to accept the label and bring his or her behavior into line with institutional expectations. Lemert (1951) argues that *acceptance of the label* is a critical step on the way to secondary or *career* deviance. Not only do some individuals change their view of self—for instance, from that of "normal" to that of "schizophrenic"—but they often change their mode of dress, mannerisms, and circle of acquaintances. Acceptance of the label, it should be noted, is an important precondition to being certified as being "sane" or "rehabilitated" by institutions.

Involvement in noninstitutional careers or activities affects not only the participants but other members of society as well. The covert gay teacher, for example, engages in sexual activity that some would consider deviant, and a discrepancy may evolve between her personal and public identities. Privately she may view herself as gay and a normal female, but publicly she is viewed and responded to as a heterosexual teacher. As with the institutional deviant, however, an identity crisis may arise. She may decide to "come out" and admit her sexual preference to others. Such a strategy is not without its costs. She may be ostracized by her family, friends, and acquaintances; and, more than likely, she will be either discriminated against on her job or fired. In view of these possibilities, she may decide to keep her sexual preference hidden and perhaps become involved in a gay subculture. Such involvement can provide her with a degree of social support, as well as appropriate rationalizations to legitimize her way of life. Still, she (and other noninstitutional deviants) is aware that she not only is engaging in potentially discrediting behavior but must operate in a society in which there are many hostile elements.

CHANGING DEVIANCE

Identity problems do not cease when one leaves an institution or decides to "go straight." Public or known ex-deviants, whether of the institutional or noninstitutional variety, continue to be viewed as deviants. What Simmons (1969) calls a "lingering of traces" quite frequently occurs, especially among those who carry an institutionally bestowed label. Institutions, it has been pointed out, are most efficient in assigning deviant labels; they are notoriously inefficient when it comes to removing labels and their associated stigma (Goffman, 1963). Former deviants must continue to bear the brunt of the label—with the result that their behavioral patterns are much less likely to change.

The probability of rehabilitating someone who does not view his or her activity or career as deviant is poor. Many noninstitutional deviants—such as prostitutes, gamblers, and homosexuals—feel little need to "repent"; they believe that the pressures on them and the difficulties they experience result from the intolerance of society. In fact, many of these individuals feel strongly that it is society that should be rehabilitated. On the other hand, some noninstitutional deviants—as well as some institutional deviants, such as mental patients, criminals, and delinquents—may try to transform their "deviant" identity. If they do, they can expect to encounter certain barriers. Job applications, for example, frequently require prospective employees to list any arrests, convictions, or periods of institutionalization—circumstances that bar entry into many occupations. Such roadblocks can produce feelings of frustration and inferiority. What many ex-deviants soon realize is that even if they change, they will still be effectively discriminated against because of past activities or involvement with stigmatizing institutions. They also learn very quickly that the social and political establishment is virtually unchanging—that the burden of change falls upon *them*.

SUMMARY AND ORGANIZATION OF THIS VOLUME

This book explores the subject of deviance in a number of ways—by focusing in turn on society, on the individual, and on institutions of control and rehabilitation. Part 1 describes how deviant categories evolve and how people who violate these categories become defined as social deviants. Part 2 analyzes why people may elect to violate deviant categories—violations that initiate the defining or labeling process. Part 3 deals with the deviant career, particularly as it arises in private, noninstitutional settings. Part 4 describes how careers may become initiated and perpetuated by institutions, while Part 5 examines the rise and furtherance of noninstitutional careers. Finally, Part 6 discusses how conceptions, careers, and organizational structures may be altered. Throughout, a major focus is on the impact that involvement in institutional as well as noninstitutional activities and careers has upon actors, audiences, and third parties.

Note

1. For an excellent discussion of questions such as these, see particularly Ronald L. Akers, "Problems in the Sociology of Deviance: Social Definitions and Behavior." *Social Forces,* 46 (June 1968), 455–465.

References

Becker, Howard S. *Outsiders: Studies in the Sociology of Deviance.* New York: Free Press, 1963.

Garfinkel, Harold. "Conditions of Successful Degradation Ceremonies." *American Journal of Sociology,* 61 (March 1956), 420–424.

Goffman, Erving, *Stigma: Notes on the Management of Spoiled Identity.* Englewood Cliffs. N.J.: Prentice-Hall, 1963.

———. "The Moral Career of the Mental Patient," *Psychiatry,* 22 (1959), 123–142.

Kesey, Ken. *One Flew Over the Cuckoo's Nest.* New York: Viking, 1962.

Lemert, Edwin. *Social Pathology.* New York: McGraw-Hill, 1951.

Rubington, Earl. "Variations in Bottle-Gang Controls." In Earl Rubington and Martin S. Weinberg, eds., *Deviance: The Interactionist Perspective.* New York: Macmillan, 1973.

Scheff, Thomas J. "Typification in the Diagnostic Practices of Rehabilitation Agencies." In Marvin B. Sussman, ed., *Sociology and Rehabilitation.* Washington, D.C.: American Sociological Association, 1966.

Simmons, J.L. *Deviants.* Berkeley. Glendessary, 1969.

Sudnow, David. "Normal Crimes: Sociological Features of the Penal Code," *Social Problems,* 12 (Winter 1965), 255–270.

Part 1 / Creating Deviance

As noted in the general introduction, approaching an understanding of deviance requires an examination of several inter-related factors. An initial concern involves the way in which the subject matter is to be approached, viewed, and subsequently defined. Does the theorist or researcher, for example, conceptualize and define deviance and the deviant in individual terms, or does he or she invoke some type of structural view? Similarly, is there something inherently deviant about certain acts or actors, or do their meanings derive from the interpretations and reactions of others? If the latter, then not only should the student of deviance be aware that a specific image is being advanced (i.e., the notion that deviance and the deviants are social constructs), but he or she must also recognize the need to examine the evolution of deviant categories, and the ways in which violators of the categories may be perceived and responded to. As noted earlier, for deviance to become a social fact, a person must be viewed as violating some deviant category and thereafter labeled as deviant by a social observer.

The initial two selections in this part introduce, in a general way, the major conceptual and definitional issues in the field of deviance. Some important tools are also introduced. The selections that follow offer illustrations of how the concepts are utilized. In addition, more systematic attention is given to the basic processes involved in the construction of the social deviant: (1) the creation of deviant categories, and (2) the reactions to violators of deviant categories.

Conceptions, Images, and Entrepreneurs

The idea that deviant categories can be viewed as social constructs represents a particular image of deviance. Such a view also suggests the possibility of competing conceptions. Jack P. Gibbs, in "Conceptions of Deviant Behavior: The Old and the New," acknowledges these points but stresses that the prevailing conceptions continue to dominate. How one comes to "think about" a specific phenomenon influences the definitions that are developed, as well as the theory or

11

explanation that may result. For example, in the area of deviance, do we locate pathological or deviant-producing stimuli within the actor or do we look elsewhere, perhaps to society in general? Gibbs maintains that the former viewpoint is favored in the fields of crime and deviance. Historically, the dominant conception has been one of individual pathology. Gibbs then proceeds to compare what he terms the "older conceptions" (e.g., the idea that deviants or criminals possess some *internal* trait that distinguishes them from nondeviants) with the "new conception" (i.e., the view that the essential characteristic of a deviant or deviant act is *external* to the actor and the act). This new perspective emphasizes the *character of the reaction* that a specific act or actor may elicit. If the responses are of a certain kind, deviance comes into being. Gibbs then offers several criticisms of the new conception. Is, for example, this perspective intended to be a substantive theory of deviant behavior, or is it primarily a definitional/conceptual treatment of it? Even if the perspective is viewed as an explanatory framework, Gibbs maintains that several questions have not been answered adequately. "Why," for example, "is the act in question considered deviant and/or criminal in some societies but not in others?"

The Gibbs piece sensitizes one to the fact that the underlying images and conceptions of deviance have changed, and also helps to highlight the manner in which social observers—either individually or collectively—ascribe meaning to the actions of others. Thus, deviance is very much a product of initiative on the part of observers. Logically, then, the reactors and decision-makers must become the object of direct study. What, for example, can we say about the content of their conceptions and belief systems? The selection by Howard S. Becker, "Moral Entrepreneurs: The Creation and Enforcement of Deviant Categories," adds some refinements to these issues. Becker also provides an excellent general overview of how deviant categories, particularly rules, evolve. Central to his analysis is the role of *moral entrepreneurs,* whom he categorizes into *rule creators* and *rule enforcers.* Rule creators are individuals who see some "evil" in society and feel that the evil can be corrected only by legislating against it. Frequently their efforts result in the passage of a new law—that is, the creation of a new deviant category. Becker offers several interesting examples that describe this legislative-political phenomenon. He argues that a successful crusade not only will result in "the creation of a new set of rules" but will often give rise to "a new set of enforcement agencies and officials." It becomes the function of these officials to enforce the new rules. Becker concludes his analysis by offering several comments relating to rule enforcers. He contends, for example, that enforcers are concerned primarily with enforcing the law and not its contents; they are also interested in justifying their own position in the organization, as well as in gaining respect from their clients. Many of these same notions can be applied to several subsequent selections, especially those that deal with institutional incarceration and deviance.

Deviant Categories and Actors

Quite clearly, in cases where the moral entrepreneurs and their crusades succeed, society is often confronted with a new deviant category and a corresponding enforcement or social-control apparatus. Becker's general discussion of the dynamics behind the passage of various laws (e.g., the Eighteenth Amendment and sexual psychopath laws) offers illustrations of this. Troy Duster, in "The Legislation of Morality: Creating Drug Laws," presents a more in-depth account of how specific laws, or deviant categories, were created. His focus is primarily on the Harrison Narcotics Act of 1914.

Duster argues initially that there is often an intertwining between law and morality. He then proceeds to document his case. He begins by noting that, even though in recent times the public has been concerned primarily with LSD and marijuana, it is the drug opium that has dominated our conception of narcotics. Not only was morphine, an opium-based pain reliever, widely used during the Civil War, and for some years afterward, but there were no state or federal laws regulating the sale and distribution of the drug. Pharmacists sold it at will. Duster estimates that 3 percent of the population was probably addicted to morphine around the turn of the century; this began to produce alarm among members of the medical profession. During this period, heroin, a morphine derivative, was also produced. Unlike morphine, heroin was at first thought to be nonaddictive. Five years after it was discovered in 1898, serious warnings about heroin's addictive features appeared in an American medical journal. However, the warnings spread slowly, and heroin, like morphine, became very popular. In fact, Duster states that, during the period from 1865 to 1900, addiction was probably eight times greater than it is today. If he is correct, then why is addiction today viewed as being of far greater moral, legal, and social significance?

Duster hypothesizes that the major factor accounting for the differing conceptions of addiction has been the dramatic shift of addicts from one social category to another. Although most people today believe that addiction is mainly a lower-class problem, this has not always been the case. In fact, up until 1914, the middle and upper classes had the largest numbers of addicts. As, Duster's quotes from medical journals show, lower-class addicts were regarded as mental and moral defectives, while upper-class addicts were equated with ministers, judges, and senators. A similar shift occurred with respect to age (i.e., from predominantly middle-aged to the young) and sex (i.e., from predominantly female to male). Associated with these shifts and changing moral interpretations were attempts, primarily by doctors, to have laws passed that would regulate the manufacture and distribution of narcotics. Many states did pass individual laws. On the national level, Congress ratified the Harrison Narcotics Act in 1914.

Stephen J. Pfohl, in "The 'Discovery' of Child Abuse," provides another historical account of how conceptions of behavior can change rather dramatically during a short period of time. Pfohl focuses primarily on the social and organizational factors that led to the initial deviant labeling of "child beating" and its subsequent criminalization. In spite of various reform efforts to deal with child neglect and cruelty (e.g., the crusades by the Society for the Prevention of Cruelty to Children and the founding of juvenile courts), Pfohl notes that, prior to the early 1960s, there were no fixed deviant labels related to child abuse. The public's attitude was generally one of tolerance for parents; apparently, agencies were unwilling to upset the traditional balance of power between parent and child. The "discovery" of abuse, as well as its perception as a social problem, awaited what Pfohl terms "a coalition of organized interests."

The coalition itself was forged out of the medical profession, and the actual leaders were pediatric radiologists. Why did the radiologists "see" abuse first? Pfohl cites several factors that impeded the recognition of abuse by physicians. For example, it is contended that doctors were unaware of the possibility of "abuse" as a diagnosis, were unwilling to believe that parents would injure their children, were fearful of the legal liability that might have ensued if the norm of confidentiality was violated, and were reluctant to become involved with the criminal justice system. These barriers were generally irrelevant to the radiologists. Pfohl claims that the factors behind the "discovery" have to do with the nature of the radiological specialty itself. Traditionally, pediatric radiology has been viewed as a marginal specialty; however, with the "discovery" of abuse, radiologists not only became involved with the important task of patient diagnosis but, by doing so, enhanced their status and prestige within organized medicine. Other factors that hastened the defining of abuse as deviant included the opportunity on the part of the radiologists to form a coalition with other, more prestigious specialties (i.e., pediatrics and psychodynamically oriented psychiatry), as well as the creation of an acceptable label (i.e., the "battered child syndrome"). Pfohl concludes by noting how the label was accepted and disseminated.

The selections by Duster and Pfohl illustrate how, as a result of changing perceptions, behavior not only may become increasingly defined as deviant but may become criminalized. When this occurs, we can speak of the creation of deviant or criminal categories. And once the categories are in place, we can begin to analyze how others react to the violators of the categories. Thomas S. Szasz, in "The Manufacture of Witches," offers an account of this. He begins by drawing several parallels between mental illness and witchcraft. Of significance is his statement that men who believed in witchcraft manufactured witches, ascribing the role of witch to these women. Szasz notes that some women, for a combination of reasons, did assume the role voluntarily; most, however, did so involuntarily. The same applies to mental patients. Most do not choose their role—rather, they are defined and treated against their will.

At this point, Szasz distinguishes more clearly between the voluntary and involuntary patient. The involuntary patient, for example, is handled by an institutional psychiatrist, while the voluntary patient is treated by a contractual psychiatrist. Further, the institutional psychiatrist is a bureaucrat whose services are paid for by some private or public organization. The contractual psychiatrist, by contrast, is a private entrepreneur whose services are paid for by the client. The most important social characteristic of the institutional psychiatrist is the use of force and fraud. The contractual psychiatrist avoids the use of such tactics. Szasz maintains that the typical patient seen by an institutional psychiatrist is a poor or lower-class person, either in trouble or else accused of such. Szasz ends by charging that institutional psychiatry itself is an abuse, and also takes sociologists to task for their tendency to use the term "deviance" in a rather wholesale, nondiscriminatory fashion. Many of Szasz's contentions find support in Scheff and Culver's research in Part 4.

1 / Conceptions of Deviant Behavior: The Old and the New

JACK P. GIBBS

The ultimate end of substantive theory in any science is the formulation of empirical relations among classes of phenomena, e.g., X varies directly with Y, X is present if and only if Y is present. However, unless such propositions are arrived at by crude induction or sheer intuition, there is a crucial step before the formulation of a relational statement. This step can be described as the way the investigator comes to perceive or "think about" the phenomena under consideration. Another way to put it is the development of a "conception."

There is no clear-cut distinction between, on the one hand, a conception of a class of phenomena and, on the other, formal definitions and substantive theory. Since a conception emphasizes the predominant feature of a phenomenon, it is not entirely divorced from a definition of it; but the former is not identical with the latter. Thus, for example, the notion of exploitation looms large in the Marxian conception of relations among social classes; but exploitation is or may be only one feature of class relations, and it does not serve as a formal definition of them. Further, in certain fields, particularly the social sciences, a conception often not only precedes but also gives rise to operational definitions. As the case in point, if an operational definition of social class relies on the use of "reputational technique," the investigator's conception of social class is in all probability non-Marxian.

What has been said of the distinction between definitions and conceptions holds also for the relation between the latter and substantive theory. A conception may generate a particular theory, but it is not identical with it. For one thing, a conception contains definitional elements and is therefore partially tautological, which means that in itself a conception is never a clear-cut empirical proposition. Apart from its tautological character, a conception is too general to constitute a testable idea. Nonetheless, a conception may generate substantive theory, and it is certainly true that theories reflect conceptions. Durkheim's work is a classic illustration. His theory on suicide clearly reflects his view of society and social life generally.

In a field without consensus as to operational definitions and little in the way of systematic substantive theory, conceptions necessarily occupy a central position. This condition prevails in most of the social sciences. There, what purport to be definitions of classes of phenomena are typically general and inconsistent to the point of lacking empirical applicability (certainly in the operational sense of the word). Moreover, what passes for a substantive theory in the social sciences is more often than not actually a loosely formulated conception. These observations are not intended to deride the social sciences for lack of progress. All fields probably go through a "conceptions" stage; it is only more apparent in some than in others.

Of the social sciences, there is perhaps no better clear cut illustration of the importance of conceptions than in the field identified as criminology and the study of deviant behavior. As we shall see, the history of the field can be described best in terms of changing conceptions of crime, criminals, deviants, and deviation. But the purpose of this paper is not an historical account of major trends in the field. If it is true that conceptions give rise to formal definitions and substantive theory, then a critical appraisal of conceptions is important in its own right. This is all the more true in the case of criminology and the study of deviant behavior, where conceptions are frequently confused with substantive theories, and the latter so clearly reflect the former.

OLDER CONCEPTIONS

In recent years there has been a significant change in the prevailing conception of deviant behavior and deviants. Prior to what is designated here as the "new perspective," it commonly was assumed that there is something inherent in deviants which distinguishes them from non-deviants.[1] Thus, from Lombroso to Sheldon, criminals were viewed as biologically distinctive in one way or another.[2] The inadequacies of this conception are now obvious. After decades of research, no biological characteristic which distinguishes criminals has been discovered, and this generalization applies even to particular types of criminals (e.g., murderers, bigamists, etc.). Consequently, few theorists now even toy with the notion that all criminals are atavistic, mentally defective, constitutionally inferior. But the rejection of the biological conception of crime stems from more than research findings. Even casual observation and mild logic cast doubt on the idea. Since legislators are not geneticists, it is difficult to see how they can pass laws in such a way as to create "born criminals." Equally important, since most if not all "normal" persons have violated a law at one time or another,[3] the assertion that criminals are so by heredity now appears most questionable.

Although the biological conception generally has been rejected, what is here designated as the analytic conception of criminal acts largely has escaped criticism. Rather than view criminal acts as nothing more or less than behavior contrary to legal norms, the acts are construed as somehow injurious to society. The shift from the biological to the analytical conception is thus from the actors to the characteristics of their acts, with the idea being that some acts are inherently "criminal" or at least that criminal acts share intrinsic characteristics in common.

The analytical conception is certainly more defensible than the biological view, but it is by no means free of criticism. Above all, the "injurious" quality of some deviant acts is by no means conspicuous, as witness Durkheim's observation:

> ... there are many acts which have been and still are regarded as criminal without in themselves being harmful to society. What social danger is there in touching a tabooed object, an impure animal or man, in letting the sacred fire die down, in eating certain meats, in failure to make the traditional sacrifice over the grave of parents, in not exactly pronouncing the ritual formula, in not celebrating holidays, etc.?[4]

Only a radical functionalism would interpret the acts noted by Durkheim as literally injuring society in any reasonable sense of the word. The crucial point is that, far from actually injuring society or sharing some intrinsic feature in common, acts may be criminal or deviant because and only because they are proscribed legally and/or socially. The proscription may be irrational in that members of the society cannot explain it, but it is real nonetheless. Similarly, a law may be "arbitrary" in that it is imposed by a powerful minority and, as a consequence, lacks popular support and is actively opposed. But if the law is consistently enforced (i.e., sanctions are imposed regularly on violators), it is difficult to see how it is not "real."

The fact that laws may appear to be irrational and arbitrary has prompted attempts to define crime independently of legal criteria, i.e., analytically. The first step in this direction was Garofalo's concept of natural crime—acts which violate prevailing sentiments of pity and probity.[5] Garofalo's endeavor accomplished very little. Just as there is probably no act which is contrary to law universally, it is equally true that no act violates sentiments of pity and probity in all societies. In other words, cultural relativity defeats any attempt to compile a list of acts which are crimes universally. Also, it is hard to see why the violation of a rigorously enforced traffic regulation is not a crime even though unrelated to sentiments of pity and probity. If it is not a crime, what is it?

The search for an analytic identification of crime continued in Sellin's proposal to abandon legal criteria altogether in preference for "conduct norms."[6] The rationale for the proposal is simple. Because laws vary and may be "arbitrary" in any one society, a purely legal definition of crime is not suited for scientific study. But Sellin's observations on the arbitrariness of laws apply in much the same way to conduct norms. Just as the content of criminal law varies from one society to the next and from time to time, so does the content of extra-legal norms. Further, the latter may be just as arbitrary as criminal laws. Even in a highly urbanized society such as the United States, there is evidently no rationale or utilitarian reason for all of the norms pertaining to mode of dress. True, there may be much greater conformity to conduct norms than to some laws, but the degree of conformity is hardly an adequate criterion of the "reality" of norms, legal or extra-legal. If any credence whatever can be placed in the Kinsey report, sexual taboos may be violated frequently and yet remain as taboos. As a case in point, even if adultery is now common in the United States, it is significant that the participants typically attempt to conceal their acts. In brief, just as laws may be violated frequently and are "unreal" in that sense, the same applies to some conduct norms; but in neither case do they cease to be norms. They would cease to be norms if and only if one defines deviation in terms of statistical regularities in behavior, but not even Sellin would subscribe to the notion that normative phenomena can or should be defined in statistical terms.

In summary, however capricious and irrational legal and extra-legal norms may appear to be, the inescapable conclusion is that some acts are criminal or deviant for the very simple reason that they are proscribed.

THE NEW CONCEPTION

Whereas both the pathological and the analytical conception of deviation assume that some intrinsic feature characterizes deviants and/or deviant acts, an emerging perspective in sociology flatly rejects any such assumption. Indeed, as witness the following statements by Kitsuse, Becker, and Erikson, exactly the opposite position is taken.

Kitsuse:
Forms of behavior *per se* do not differentiate deviants from non-deviants; it is the responses of the conventional and conforming members of

the society who identify and interpret behavior as deviant which sociologically transform persons into deviants.[7]

Erikson:

From a sociological standpoint, deviance can be defined as conduct which is generally thought to require the attention of social control agencies—that is, conduct about which 'something should be done.' Deviance is not a property *inherent in* certain forms of behavior; it is a property *conferred upon* these forms by the audiences which directly or indirectly witness them. Sociologically, then, the critical variable in the study of deviance is the social *audience* rather than individual *person*, since it is the audience which eventually decides whether or not any given action or actions will become a visible case of deviation.[8]

Becker:

From this point of view, deviance is *not* a quality of the act a person commits, but rather a consequence of the application by others of rules and sanctions to an 'offender.' The deviant is one to whom that label has successfully been applied; deviant behavior is behavior that people so label.[9]

The common assertion in the above statements is that acts can be identified as deviant or criminal only by reference to the character of reaction to them by the public or by the official agents of a politically organized society. Put simply, if the reaction is of a certain kind, then and only then is the act deviant. The crucial point is that the essential feature of a deviant or deviant act is *external* to the actor and the act. Further, even if the act or actors share some feature in common other than social reactions to them, the feature neither defines nor completely explains deviation. To take the extreme case, even if Lombroso had been correct in his assertion that criminals are biologically distinctive, the biological factor neither identifies the criminal nor explains criminality. Purely biological variables may explain why some persons commit certain acts, but they do not explain why the acts are crimes. Consequently, since criminal law is spatially and temporally relative, it is impossible to distinguish criminals from noncriminals (assuming that the latter do exist, which is questionable) in terms of biological characteristics. To illustrate, if act X is a crime in society A but not a crime in society B, it follows that, even assuming Lombroso to have been correct, the anatomical features which distinguish the criminal in society A may characterize the non-criminal in society B. In both societies some persons may be genetically predisposed to commit act X, but the act is a crime in one society and not in the other. Accordingly, the generalization that all persons with certain anatomical features are criminals would be, in this instance, false. True, one may assert that the "born criminal" is predisposed to violate the laws of his own society, but this assumes either that "the genes" know what the law is or that the members of the legislature are geneticists (i.e., they deliberately enact laws in such a way that the "born criminal" will violate them). Either assumption taxes credulity.

The new perspective of deviant behavior contradicts not only the biological but also the analytical conception. Whereas the latter seeks to find something intrinsic in deviant or, more specifically, criminal acts, the new conception denies any such characterization. True, the acts share a common denominator—they are identified by the character of reaction to them—but this does not mean that the acts are "injurious" to society or that they are in any way inherently abnormal. The new conception eschews the notion that some acts are deviant or criminal in all societies. For that matter, the reaction which identifies a deviant act may not be the same from one society or social group to the next. In general, then, the new conception of deviant behavior is relativistic in the extreme.

. . .

Notes

1. Throughout this paper crime is treated as a sub-class of deviant behavior. Particular issues may be discussed with reference to crime, but on the whole the observations apply to deviant behavior generally.

2. Although not essential to the argument, it is perhaps significant that the alleged biological differentiae of criminals have been consistently viewed as "pathological" in one sense or another.

3. See Edwin H. Sutherland and Donald R. Cressey, *Principles of Criminology*, 6th ed., Chicago: J.B. Lippincott, 1960, p. 39.

4. Emile Durkheim, *The Division of Labor in Society*, trans. George Simpson, Glencoe, Illinois: The Free Press, 1949, p. 72.

5. Raffaele Garofalo, *Criminology*, Boston: Little, Brown, & Co., 1914, Chapter I.

6. Thorsten Sellin, *Culture Conflict and Crime*, New York: Social Science Research Council, Bulletin 41, 1938.

7. John I. Kitsuse, "Societal Reaction to Deviant Behavior: Problems of Theory and Method," *Social Problems*, 9 (Winter, 1962), p. 253.

8. Kai T. Erikson, "Notes on the Sociology of Deviance," *Social Problems*, 9 (Spring, 1962), p. 308.

9. Howard S. Becker, *Outsiders*, New York: The Free Press of Glencoe, 1963, p. 9.

2 / Moral Entrepreneurs: The Creation and Enforcement of Deviant Categories

HOWARD S. BECKER

RULE CREATORS

The prototype of the rule creator, but not the only variety as we shall see, is the crusading reformer. He is interested in the content of rules. The existing rules do not satisfy him because there is some evil which profoundly disturbs him. He feels that nothing can be right in the world until rules are made to correct it. He operates with an absolute ethic; what he sees is truly and totally evil with no qualification. Any means is justified to do away with it. The crusader is fervent and righteous, often self-righteous.

It is appropriate to think of reformers as crusaders because they typically believe that their mission is a holy one. The prohibitionist serves as an excellent example, as does the person who wants to suppress vice and sexual delinquency or the person who wants to do away with gambling.

These examples suggest that the moral crusader is a meddling busybody, interested in forcing his own morals on others. But this is a one-sided view. Many moral crusades have strong humanitarian overtones. The crusader is not only interested in seeing to it that other people do what he thinks right. He believes that if they do what is right it will be good for them. Or he may feel that his reform will prevent certain kinds of exploitation of one person by another. Prohibitionists felt that they were not simply forcing their morals on others, but attempting to provide the conditions for a better way of life for people prevented by drink from realizing a truly good life. Abolitionists were not simply trying to prevent slave owners from doing the wrong thing; they were trying to help slaves to achieve a better life. Because of the importance of the humanitarian motive, moral crusaders (despite their relatively single-minded devotion to their particular cause) often lend their support to other humanitarian crusades. Joseph Gusfield has pointed out that:

The American temperance movement during the 19th century was a part of a general effort toward the improvement of the worth of the human being through improved morality as well as economic conditions. The mixture of the religious, the equalitarian, and the humanitarian was an outstanding facet of the moral reformism of many movements. Temperance supporters formed a large segment of movements such as sabbatarianism, abolition, woman's rights, agrarianism, and humanitarian attempts to improve the lot of the poor. . . .

In its auxiliary interests the WCTU revealed a great concern for the improvement of the welfare of the lower classes. It was active in campaigns to secure penal reform, to shorten working hours and raise wages for workers, and to abolish child labor and in a number of other humanitarian and equalitarian activities. In the 1880's the WCTU worked to bring about legislation for the protection of working girls against the exploitation by men.[1]

As Gusfield says,[2] "Moral reformism of this type suggests the approach of a dominant class toward those less favorably situated in the economic and social structure." Moral crusaders typically want to help those beneath them to achieve a better status. That those beneath them do not always like the means proposed for their salvation is another matter. But this fact—that moral crusades are typically dominated by those in the upper levels of the social structure—means that they add to the power they derive from the legitimacy of their moral position, the power they derive from their superior position in society.

Naturally, many moral crusades draw support from people whose motives are less pure than those of the crusader. Thus, some industrialists supported Prohibition because they felt it would provide them with a more manageable labor force.[3] Similarly, it is sometimes rumored that Nevada gambling interests support the opposition to attempts to legalize gambling in California because it would cut so heavily into their business, which depends in substantial measure on the population of Southern California.[4]

The moral crusader, however, is more concerned with ends than with means. When it comes to drawing up specific rules (typically in the form of legislation to be proposed to a state legislature or the Federal Congress), he frequently relies on the advice of experts. Lawyers, expert in the drawing of acceptable legislation, often play this role. Government bureaus in whose jurisdiction the problem falls may also have the necessary expertise, as did the Federal Bureau of Narcotics in the case of the marihuana problem.

As psychiatric ideology, however, becomes increasingly acceptable, a new expert has appeared—the psychiatrist. Sutherland, in his discussion of the natural history of sexual psychopath laws, pointed to the psychiatrist's influence.[5] He suggests the following as the conditions under which the sexual psychopath law, which provides that a person "who is diagnosed as a sexual psychopath may be confined for an indefinite period in a state hospital for the insane,"[6] will be passed.

First, these laws are customarily enacted after a state of fear has been aroused in a community by a few serious sex crimes committed in quick succession. This is illustrated in Indiana, where a law was passed following three or four sexual attacks in Indianapolis, with murder in two. Heads of families bought guns and watch dogs, and the supply of locks and chains in the hardware stores of the city was completely exhausted. . . .

A second element in the process of developing sexual psychopath laws is the agitated activity of the community in connection with the fear. The attention of the community is focused on sex crimes, and people in the most varied situations envisage dangers and see the need of and possibility for their control. . . .

The third phase in the development of those sexual psychopath laws has been the appointment of a committee. The committee gathers the many conflicting recommendations of persons and groups of persons, attempts to determine "facts," studies procedures in other states, and makes recommendations, which generally include bills for the legislature. Although the general fear usually subsides within a few days, a committee has the formal duty of following through until positive action is taken. Terror which does not result in a committee is much less likely to result in a law.[7]

In the case of sexual psychopath laws, there usually is no government agency charged with dealing in a specialized way with sexual deviations. Therefore, when the need for expert advice in drawing up legislation arises, people frequently turn to the professional group most closely associated with such problems:

In some states, at the committee stage of the development of a sexual psychopath law, psychiatrists have played an important part. The psychiatrists, more than any others, have been the interest group back of the laws. A committee of psychiatrists and neurologists in Chicago wrote the bill which became the sexual psychopath law of Illinois; the bill was sponsored by the Chicago Bar Association and by the state's attorney of Cook County and was enacted with little opposition in the next session of the State Legislature. In Minnesota all the members of the governor's committee except one were psychiatrists. In Wisconsin the Milwaukee Neuropsychiatric Society shared in pressing the Milwaukee Crime Commission for the enactment of a law. In Indiana the attorney-general's committee received from the American Psychiatric Association copies of all the sexual psychopath laws which had been enacted in other states.[8]

The influence of psychiatrists in other realms of the criminal law has increased in recent years.

In any case, what is important about this example is not that psychiatrists are becoming increasingly influential, but that the moral crusader, at some point in the development of his crusade, often requires the services of a professional who can draw up the appropriate rules in an appropriate form. The crusader himself is often not concerned with such details. Enough for him that the main point has been won; he leaves its implementation to others.

By leaving the drafting of the specific rule in the hands of others, the crusader opens the door for many unforeseen influences. For those who draft legislation for crusaders have their own interests, which may affect the legislation they prepare. It is likely that the sexual psychopath laws drawn by psychiatrists contain many features never intended by the citizens who spearheaded the drives to "do something about sex crimes," features which do however reflect the professional interests of organized psychiatry.

THE FATE OF MORAL CRUSADES

A crusade may achieve striking success, as did the Prohibition movement with the passage of the Eighteenth Amendment. It may fail completely, as has the drive to do away with the use of tobacco or the anti-vivisection movement. It may achieve great success, only to find its gains whittled away by shifts in public morality and increasing restrictions imposed on it by judicial interpretations; such has been the case with the crusade against obscene literature.

One major consequence of a successful crusade, of course, is the establishment of a new rule or set of rules, usually with the appropriate enforcement machinery being provided at the same time. I want to consider this consequence at some length later. There is another consequence, however, of the success of a crusade which deserves mention.

When a man has been successful in the enterprise of getting a new rule established—when he has found, so to speak, the Grail—he is out of a job. The crusade which has occupied so much of his time, energy, and passion is over. Such a man is likely, when he first began his crusade, to have been an amateur, a man who engaged in a crusade because of his interest in the issue, in the content of the rule he wanted established. Kenneth Burke once noted that a man's occupation may become his preoccupation. The equation is also good the other way around. A man's preoccupation may become his occupation. What started as an amateur interest in a moral issue may become an almost full-time job; indeed, for many reformers it becomes just this. The success of the crusade, therefore, leaves the crusader without a vocation. Such a man, at loose ends, may generalize his interest and discover something new to view with alarm, a new evil about which something ought to be done. He becomes a professional discoverer of wrongs to be righted, of situations requiring new rules.

When the crusade has produced a large organization devoted to its cause, officials of the organization are even more likely than the individual crusader to look for new causes to espouse. This process occurred dramatically in the field of health problems when the National Foundation for Infantile Paralysis put itself out of business by discovering a vaccine that eliminated epidemic poliomyelitis. Taking the less constraining name of The National Foundation, officials quickly discovered other health problems to which the organization could devote its energies and resources.

The unsuccessful crusade, either the one that finds its mission no longer attracts adherents or the one that achieves its goal only to lose it again, may follow one of two courses. On the one hand, it may simply give up its original mission and concentrate on preserving what remains of the organization that has been built up. Such, according to one study, was the fate of the Townsend Movement.[9] Or the failing movement may adhere rigidly to an increasingly less popular mission, as did the Prohibition Movement. Gusfield has described present-day members of the WCTU as "moralizers-in-retreat."[10] As prevailing opinion in the United States becomes increasingly anti-temperance, these women have not softened their attitude toward drinking. On the contrary, they have become bitter at the formerly "respectable" people who no longer will support a temperance movement. The social class level from which WCTU members are drawn has moved down from the upper-middle class to the lower-middle class. The WCTU now turns to attack the middle class it once drew its support from, seeing this group as the locus of acceptance of moderate drinking. The following quotations from Gusfield's interviews with WCTU leaders give some of the flavor of the "moralizer-in-retreat":

> When this union was first organized, we had many of the most influential ladies of the city. But now they have got the idea that we ladies who are against taking a cocktail are a little queer. We have an undertaker's wife and a minister's wife, but the lawyer's and the doctor's wives shun us. They don't want to be thought queer.
>
> We fear moderation more than anything. Drinking has become so much a part of everything—even in our church life and our colleges.
>
> It creeps into the official church boards. They keep it in their iceboxes. . . . The minister here thinks that the church has gone far, that they are doing too much to help the temperance cause. He's afraid that he'll stub some influential toes.[11]

Only some crusaders, then, are successful in their mission and create, by creating a new rule, a new group of outsiders. Of the successful, some find they have a taste for crusades and seek new problems to attack. Other crusaders fail in their attempt and either support the organization they have created by dropping their distinc-

tive mission and focusing on the problem of organizational maintenance itself or become outsiders themselves, continuing to espouse
and preach a doctrine which sounds increasingly queer as time goes
on.

RULE ENFORCERS

The most obvious consequence of a successful crusade is the creation
of a new set of rules. With the creation of a new set of rules we often
find that a new set of enforcement agencies and officials is established. Sometimes, of course, existing agencies take over the administration of the new rule, but more frequently a new set of rule
enforcers is created. The passage of the Harrison Act presaged the
creation of the Federal Narcotics Bureau, just as the passage of the
Eighteenth Amendment led to the creation of police agencies charged
with enforcing the Prohibition Laws.

With the establishment of organizations of rule enforcers, the
crusade becomes institutionalized. What started out as a drive to
convince the world of the moral necessity of a new rule finally becomes an organization devoted to the enforcement of the rule. Just as
radical political movements turn into organized political parties and
lusty evangelical sects become staid religious denominations, the
final outcome of the moral crusade is a police force. To understand,
therefore, how the rules creating a new class of outsiders are applied
to particular people we must understand the motives and interests of
police, the rule enforcers.

Although some policemen undoubtedly have a kind of crusading
interest in stamping out evil, it is probably much more typical for the
policeman to have a certain detached and objective view of his job. He
is not so much concerned with the content of any particular rule as he
is with the fact that it is his job to enforce the rule. When the rules are
changed, he punishes what was once acceptable behavior just as he
ceases to punish behavior that has been made legitimate by a change
in the rules. The enforcer, then, may not be interested in the content of
the rule as such, but only in the fact that the existence of the rule
provides him with a job, a profession, and a *raison d'être*.

Since the enforcement of certain rules provides justification for his
way of life, the enforcer has two interests which condition his
enforcement activity: first, he must justify the existence of his position
and, second, he must win the respect of those he deals with.

These interests are not peculiar to rule enforcers. Members of all
occupations feel the need to justify their work and win the respect of
others. Musicians, as we have seen, would like to do this but have

difficulty finding ways of successfully impressing their worth on customers. Janitors fail to win their tenants' respect, but develop an ideology which stresses the quasi-professional responsibility they have to keep confidential the intimate knowledge of tenants they acquire in the course of their work.[12] Physicians, lawyers, and other professionals, more successful in winning the respect of clients, develop elaborate mechanisms for maintaining a properly respectful relationship.

In justifying the existence of his position, the rule enforcer faces a double problem. On the one hand, he must demonstrate to others that the problem still exists: the rules he is supposed to enforce have some point, because infractions occur. On the other hand, he must show that his attempts at enforcement are effective and worthwhile, that the evil he is supposed to deal with is in fact being dealt with adequately. Therefore, enforcement organizations, particularly when they are seeking funds, typically oscillate between two kinds of claims. First, they say that by reason of their efforts the problem they deal with is approaching solution. But, in the same breath, they say the problem is perhaps worse than ever (though through no fault of their own) and requires renewed and increased effort to keep it under control. Enforcement officials can be more vehement than anyone else in their insistence that the problem they are supposed to deal with is still with us, in fact is more with us than ever before. In making these claims, enforcement officials provide good reason for continuing the existence of the position they occupy.

We may also note that enforcement officials and agencies are inclined to take a pessimistic view of human nature. If they do not actually believe in original sin, they at least like to dwell on the difficulties in getting people to abide by rules, on the characteristics of human nature that lead people toward evil. They are skeptical of attempts to reform rule-breakers.

The skeptical and pessimistic outlook of the rule enforcer, of course, is reinforced by his daily experience. He sees, as he goes about his work, the evidence that the problem is still with us. He sees the people who continually repeat offenses, thus definitely branding themselves in his eyes as outsiders. Yet it is not too great a stretch of the imagination to suppose that one of the underlying reasons for the enforcer's pessimism about human nature and the possibilities of reform is that fact that if human nature were perfectible and people could be permanently reformed, his job would come to an end.

In the same way, a rule enforcer is likely to believe that it is necessary for the people he deals with to respect him. If they do not, it will be very difficult to do his job; his feeling of security in his work will be lost. Therefore, a good deal of enforcement activity is devoted not to the actual enforcement of rules, but to coercing respect from the people the enforcer deals with. This means that one may be labeled as deviant not because he has actually broken a rule, but because he has shown disrespect to the enforcer of the rule.

Westley's study of policemen in a small industrial city furnishes a good example of this phenomenon. In his interview, he asked policemen, "When do you think a policeman is justified in roughing a man up?" He found that "at least 37% of the men believed that it was legitimate to use violence to coerce respect."[13] He gives some illuminating quotations from his interviews:

> Well, there are cases. For example, when you stop a fellow for a routine questioning, say a wise guy, and he starts talking back to you and telling you you are no good and that sort of thing. You know you can take a man in on a disorderly conduct charge, but you can practically never make it stick. So what you do in a case like that is to egg the guy on until he makes a remark where you can justifiably slap him and, then, if he fights back, you can call it resisting arrest.

> Well, a prisoner deserves to be hit when he goes to the point where he tries to put you below him.

> You've gotta get rough when a man's language becomes very bad, when he is trying to make a fool of you in front of everybody else. I think most policemen try to treat people in a nice way, but usually you have to talk pretty rough. That's the only way to set a man down, to make him show a little respect.[14]

What Westley describes is the use of an illegal means of coercing respect from others. Clearly, when a rule enforcer has the option of enforcing a rule or not, the difference in what he does may be caused by the attitude of the offender toward him. If the offender is properly respectful, the enforcer may smooth the situation over. If the offender is disrespectful, then sanctions may be visited on him. Westley has shown that this differential tends to operate in the case of traffic offenses, where the policeman's discretion is perhaps at a maximum.[15] But it probably operates in other areas as well.

Ordinarily, the rule enforcer has a great deal of discretion in many areas, if only because his resources are not sufficient to cope with the volume of rule-breaking he is supposed to deal with. This means that he cannot tackle everything at once and to this extent must temporize with evil. He cannot do the whole job and knows it. He takes his time, on the assumption that the problems he deals with will be around for a long while. He establishes priorities, dealing with things in their turn, handling the most pressing problems immediately and leaving others for later. His attitude toward his work, in short, is professional. He lacks the naive moral fervor characteristic of the rule creator.

If the enforcer is not going to tackle every case he knows of at once, he must have a basis for deciding when to enforce the rule, which persons committing which acts to label as deviant. One criterion for selecting people is the "fix." Some people have sufficient political influence or know-how to be able to ward off attempts at enforcement, if not at the time of apprehension then at a later stage in the process. Very often, this function is professionalized; someone performs the job on a full-time basis, available to anyone who wants to hire him. A professional thief described fixers this way:

> There is in every large city a regular fixer for professional thieves. He has no agents and does not solicit and seldom takes any case except that of a professional thief, just as they seldom go to anyone except him. This centralized and monopolistic system of fixing for professional thieves is found in practically all of the large cities and many of the small ones.[16]

Since it is mainly professional thieves who know about the fixer and his operations, the consequence of this criterion for selecting people to apply the rules to is that amateurs tend to be caught, convicted, and labeled deviant much more frequently than professionals. As the professional thief notes:

> You can tell by the way the case is handled in court when the fix is in. When the copper is not very certain he has the right man, or the testimony of the copper and the complainant does not agree, or the prosecutor goes easy on the defendant, or the judge is arrogant in his decisions, you can always be sure that someone has got the work in. This does not happen in many cases of theft, for there is one case of a professional to twenty-five or thirty amateurs who know nothing about the fix. These amateurs get the hard end of the deal every time. The coppers bawl out about the thieves, no one holds up his testimony, the judge delivers an oration, and all of them get credit for stopping a crime wave. When the professional hears the case immediately preceding his own, he will think, "He should have got ninety years. It's the damn amateurs who cause all the heat in the stores." Or else he thinks, "Isn't it a damn shame for that copper to send that kid away for a pair of hose, and in a few minutes he will agree to a small fine for me for stealing a fur coat?" But if the coppers did not send the amateurs away to strengthen their records of convictions, they could not sandwich in the professionals whom they turn loose.[17]

Enforcers of rules, since they have no stake in the content of particular rules themselves, often develop their own private evaluation of the importance of various kinds of rules and infractions of them. This set of priorities may differ considerably from those held by the general public. For instance, drug users typically believe (and a few policemen have personally confirmed it to me) that police do not consider the use of marihuana to be as important a problem or as dangerous a practice as the use of opiate drugs. Police base this conclusion on the fact that, in their experience, opiate users commit other crimes (such as theft or prostitution) in order to get drugs, while marihuana users do not.

Enforcers, then, responding to the pressures of their own work situation, enforce rules and create outsiders in a selective way. Whether a person who commits a deviant act is in fact labeled a deviant depends on many things extraneous to his actual behavior: whether the enforcement official feels that at this time he must make some show of doing his job in order to justify his position, whether the misbehaver shows proper deference to the enforcer, whether the "fix" has been put in, and where the kind of act he has committed stands on the enforcer's list of priorities.

The professional enforcer's lack of fervor and routine approach to dealing with evil may get him into trouble with the rule creator. The rule creator, as we have said, is concerned with the content of the rules that interest him. He sees them as the means by which evil can be stamped out. He does not understand the enforcer's long-range approach to the same problems and cannot see why all the evil that is apparent cannot be stamped out at once.

When the person interested in the content of a rule realizes or has called to his attention the fact that enforcers are dealing selectively with the evil that concerns him, his righteous wrath may be aroused. The professional is denounced for viewing the evil too lightly, for failing to do his duty. The moral entrepreneur, at whose instance the rule was made, arises again to say that the outcome of the last crusade has not been satisfactory or that the gains once made have been whittled away and lost.

Notes

1. Joseph R. Gusfield, "Social Structure and Moral Reform: A Study of the Woman's Christian Temperance Union," *American Journal of Sociology*, LXI (November, 1955), 223.

2. *Ibid.*

3. See Raymond G. McCarthy, editor, *Drinking and Intoxication* (New Haven and New York: Yale Center of Alcohol Studies and The Free Press of Glencoe, 1959), pp. 395–396.

4. This is suggested in Oscar Lewis, *Sagebrush Casinos: The Story of Legal Gambling in Nevada* (New York: Doubleday and Co., 1953), pp. 233–234.

5. Edwin H. Sutherland, "The Diffusion of Sexual Psychopath Laws," *American Journal of Sociology*, LVI (September, 1950), 142–148.

6. *Ibid.*, p. 142.

7. *Ibid.*, pp. 143–145.

8. *Ibid.*, pp. 145–146.

9. Sheldon Messinger, "Organizational Transformation: A Case Study of a Declining Social Movement," *American Sociological Review*, XX (February, 1955), 3–10.

10. Gusfield, *op. cit.*, pp. 227–228.

11. *Ibid.*, pp. 227, 229–230.

32 / HOWARD S. BECKER

12. See Ray Gold, "Janitors Versus Tenants: A Status-Income Dilemma," *American Journal of Sociology*, LVII (March, 1952), 486–493.

13. William A. Westley, "Violence and the Police," *American Journal of Sociology*, LIX (July, 1953), 39.

14. *Ibid.*

15. See William A. Westley, "The Police: A Sociological Study of Law, Custom, and Morality" (unpublished Ph.D. dissertation, University of Chicago, Department of Sociology, 1951).

16. Edwin H. Sutherland (editor), *The Professional Thief* (Chicago: University of Chicago Press, 1937), pp. 87–88.

17. *Ibid.*, pp. 91–92.

3 / The Legislation of Morality: Creating Drug Laws

TROY DUSTER

INTRODUCTION

The relationship between law and morality is both complicated and subtle. This is true even in a situation where a society is very homogeneous and where one might find a large degree of consensus about moral behavior. Those who argue that law is simply the empirical operation of morality are tempted to use homogeneous situations as examples. In discussing this relationship, Selznick asserts that laws are secondary in nature.[1] They are secondary in the sense that they obtain their legitimacy in terms of some other more primary reference point.

> The distinctively legal emerges with the development of secondary rules, that is, rules of authoritative determination. These rules, selectively applied, "raise up" the primary norms and give them a legal status.... The appeal from an *asserted* rule, however coercively enforced, to a justified rule is the elementary legal act. This presumes at least a dim awareness that some reason lies behind the impulse to conform, a reason founded not in conscience, habit, or fear alone, but in the decision to uphold an authoritative order. The rule of legal recognition may be quite blunt and crude: the law is what the king or priest says it is. But this initial reference of a primary norm to a ground of obligation breeds the complex elaboration of authoritative rules that marks a developed legal order.[2]

The most primary of reference points is, of course, the moral order. One can explain why he does something for just so long, before he is driven to a position where he simply must assert that it is "right" or "wrong." With narcotics usage and addiction, the issue in contemporary times is typically raised in the form of a moral directive, irrespective of the physiological and physical aspects of addiction. The laws concerning narcotics usage may now be said to be a secondary set held up against the existing primary or moral view of drugs. However, the drug laws have been on the books for half a century, during which time, as we shall see, this country has undergone a remarkable transformation in its moral interpretation of narcotics usage. Clearly,

33

if we want to understand the ongoing relationship between the law and morality, we are misled by assuming one has some fixed relationship to the other. To put it another way, if a set of laws remains unchanged while the moral order undergoes a drastic transformation, it follows that the relationship of law to morality must be a changing thing, and cannot be static. If narcotics law was simply the empirical element of narcotics morality, a change in the moral judgment of narcotics use should be accompanied by its counterpart in the law, and vice versa. As Selznick points out:

> In recent years, the great social effects of legal change have been too obvious to ignore. The question is no longer *whether* law is a significant vehicle of social change but rather *how* it so functions and what special problems arise.[3]

Selznick goes on to suggest explorations into substantive problems of "change." The connection of law to change is clearly demonstrable. If a society undergoes rapid technological development, new social relationships will emerge, and so too, will a set of laws to handle them. The gradual disintegration of the old caste relationships in India has been and will be largely attributable to the development of new occupations which contain no traditional forms regulating how one caste should respond to another.

The relationship of law to morality is not quite so clear. It is more specific, but more abstract. The sociological study of the narcotics problem is critical to discussion of this relationship, because it provides a specific empirical case where one can observe historically the interplay between the two essential components. More than any other form of deviance, the history of drug use contains an abundance of material on both questions of legislation and morality, and of the relationship between them.

BACKGROUND AND SETTING

Despite the public clamor of the 1960s about LSD and marijuana, the drug that has most dominated and colored the American conception of narcotics is opium. Among the most effective of painkillers, opium has been known and used in some form for thousands of years. Until the middle of the nineteenth century, opium was taken orally, either smoked or ingested. The Far East monopolized both production and consumption until the hypodermic needle was discovered as an extremely effective way of injecting the drug instantly into the bloodstream. It was soon to become a widely used analgesic. The first hypodermic injections of morphine, an opiun derivative used to relieve pain, occurred in this country in 1856.[4]

Medical journals were enthusiastic in endorsing the new therapeutic usages that were possible, and morphine was the suggested remedy for an endless variety of physical sufferings. It was during the Civil War, however, that morphine injection really spread extensively. Then wholesale usage and addiction became sufficiently pronounced so that one could speak of an American problem for the first time.[5] Soldiers were given morphine to deaden the pain from all kinds of battle injuries and illnesses. After the war, ex-soldiers by the thousands continued using the drug, and recommending it to friends and relatives.

Within a decade, medical companies began to include morphine in a vast number of medications that were sold directly to consumers as household remedies. This was the period before governmental regulation, and the layman was subjected to a barrage of newspaper and billboard advertisements claiming cures for everything from the common cold to cholera. "Soothing Syrups" with morphine often contained no mention of their contents, and many men moved along the path to the purer morphine through this route.

It is not surprising that many persons became dependent on these preparations and later turned to the active drug itself when accidentally or otherwise they learned of its presence in the "medicine" they had been taking. . . . The peak of the patent medicine industry was reached just prior to the passage of the Pure Food and Drug Act in 1906.[6]

It must be remembered that there were no state or federal laws concerning the sale and distribution of medicinal narcotic drugs during this period under discussion, and pharmacists sold morphine simply when it was requested by a customer. There is no way to accurately assess the extent of addiction at that time, nor is there now, for that matter. However, there are some informed estimates by scholars who have studied many facets of the period. Among the better guesses many will settle for is that from 2 to 4 per cent of the population was addicted in 1895.[7] Studies of pharmaceutical dispensaries, druggists, and physicians' records were carried out in the 1880s and 1890s which relate to this problem. The widespread use of morphine was demonstrated by Hartwell's survey of Massachusetts druggists in 1888,[8] Hull's study of Iowa druggists in 1885,[9] Earle's work in Chicago in 1880,[10] and Grinnell's survey of Vermont in 1900.[11] The methodological techniques of investigation do not meet present-day standards, but even if certain systematic biases are assumed, the 3 per cent figure is an acceptable guess of the extent of addiction.

The large numbers of addicts alarmed a growing number of medical men. The American press, which had been so vocal in its denunciation of the sensational but far less common opium smoking in opium dens in the 1860s and 1870s, was strangely if typically silent on morphine medication and its addicting effects. Just as the present-day press adroitly avoids making news of very newsworthy government proceedings on false advertising (an issue in which there may also be some question of the accomplice), newspapers of that time did not want to alienate the advertisers, because they were a major source of revenue. Nonetheless, the knowledge of the addicting qualities of morphine became more and more common among a sizable minority of physicians.

It was in this setting, in 1898, that a German pharmacological researcher named Dreser produced a new substance from a morphine base, diacetylmorphin, otherwise known as heroin. The medical community was enthusiastic in its reception of the new drug. It had three times the strength of morphine, and it was believed to be free from addicting qualities. The most respectable medical journals of Germany and the United States carried articles and reports lauding heroin as a cure for morphine addiction.[12]

Within five short years, the first definitive serious warnings about the addicting qualities of heroin appeared in an American medical journal.[13] The marvelous success of heroin as a painkiller and sedative, however, made the drug popular with both physician and patient. It should be remembered that one did not need a prescription to buy it. The news of the new warnings traveled slowly, and heroin joined morphine as one of the most frequently used pain remedies for the ailing and suffering.

From 1865 to 1900, then, addiction to narcotics was relatively widespread. This is documented in an early survey of material by Terry and Pellens, a treatise which remains the classic work on late nineteenth- and early twentieth-century problems of addiction.[14] In proportion to the population, addiction was probably eight times more prevalent then than now, despite the large increase in the general population.

It is remarkable, therefore, that addiction is regarded today as a problem of far greater moral, legal, and social significance than it was then. As we shall see directly, the problem at the turn of the century was conceived in very different terms, treated in a vastly different manner, and located in opposite places in the social order.

The first task is to illustrate how dramatic and complete was the shift of addicts from one social category to another during a critical twenty-year period. The second task is to examine the legal activity which affected that shift. Finally, the task will be to examine the changing moral judgments that coincided with these developments.

It is now taken for granted that narcotic addicts come primarily from the working and lower classes. . . . This has not always been true. The evidence clearly indicates that the upper and middle classes predominated among narcotic addicts in the period up to 1914. In 1903, the American Pharmaceutical Association conducted a study of selected communities in the United States and Canada. They sent out mailed questionnaires to physicians and druggists, and from the responses, concluded that

> while the increase is most evident with the lower classes, the statistics of institutes devoted to the cure of habitues show that their patients are principally drawn from those in the higher walks of life. . . .[15]

From a report on Massachusetts druggists published in 1889 and cited by Terry and Pellens, the sale of opium derivatives to those of higher incomes exceeded the amount sold to lower-income persons.[16] This is all the more striking if we take into account the fact that the working and lower classes comprised a far greater percentage of the population of the country in 1890 than they do today. (With the 1960 census figures, the population of the United States becomes predominantly white collar for the first time in history.) In view of the fact that the middle-class comprised proportionately less of the population, the incidence of its addiction rate can be seen as even more significant.

It was acknowledged in medical journals that a morphine addict could not be detected as an addict so long as he maintained his supply.[17] Some of the most respectable citizens of the community, pillars of middle-class morality, were addicted. In cases where this was known, the victim was regarded as one afflicted with a physiological problem, in much the same way as we presently regard the need of a diabetic for insulin. Family histories later indicated that many went through their daily tasks, their occupations, completely undetected by friends and relatives.[18]

There are two points of considerable significance that deserve more careful consideration. The first is the fact that some friends and relatives could and did know about an addiction and still did not make a judgment, either moral or psychological, of the person addicted. The second is that the lower classes were not those primarily associated with morphine or heroin usage in 1900.

The moral interpretation of addiction in the twentieth century is especially interesting in view of the larger historical trend. Western man has, on the whole, developed increasing tolerance and compassion for problems that were previously dogmatically treated as moral issues, such as epilepsy, organic and functional mental disorders, polio, diabetes, and so on. There was a time when most were convinced that the afflicted were possessed by devils, were morally evil, and inferior. Both medical opinion and literature of the eighteenth and nineteenth centuries were replete with the moral interpretation of

countless physiological problems which have now been reinterpreted in an almost totally nonmoral fashion. The only moral issue now
attendant to these questions is whether persons suffering should receive treatment from physicians. Even venereal diseases, which retain a stigma, are unanimously conceived as physiological problems
that should be treated physiologically irrespective of the moral conditions under which they were contracted.

The narcotic addict of the 1890s was in a situation almost the reverse of those suffering from the above problems. His acquaintances
and his community could know of his addiction, feel somewhat sorry
for his dependence upon *medication,* but admit him to a position of
respect and authority. If the heroin addict of 1900 was getting a will-
ful thrill out of his injection, no one was talking about either the will-
ful element or the thrill, not even the drug companies. If the thrill
was to be had, there was no reason for manufacturers not to take
advantage of this in their advertisements. They had no moral com-
punctions about patently false claims for a cure, or about including
an opium derivative without so stating on the label.

Despite the fact that all social classes had their share of addicts,
there was a difference in the way lower class addicts were regarded.
This difference was exacerbated when legislation drove heroin underground, predominantly to the lower classes. Writing in the *American Journal of Clinical Medicine* in 1918, G. Swaine made an arbitrary social classification of addicts, about which he offered the following distinction:

> In Class one, we can include all of the physical, mental and moral defec-
> tives, the tramps, hoboes, idlers, loaders, irresponsibles, criminals, and
> denizens of the underworld. . . . In these cases, morphine addiction is a
> vice, as well as a disorder resulting from narcotic poisoning. These are the
> "drug fiends." In Class two, we have many types of good citizens who have
> become addicted to the use of the drug innocently, and who are in every
> sense of the word "victims." Morphine is no respecter of persons, and the
> victims are doctors, lawyers, ministers, artists, actors, judges, congress-
> men, senators, priests, authors, women, girls, all of who realize their condi-
> tions and want to be cured. In these cases, morphine-addiction is not a
> vice, but, an incubus, and, when they are cured they stay cured.[19]

This may seem to jump ahead of the task of this section, which is
simply to portray as accurately as possible the dramatic shift of addicts from one social category to another during this period. However, the shift itself carried with it more than a description. These were
the beginnings of moral interpretations for the meaning of that shift.
By 1920, a medical journal reported cases treated at Riverside Hospital in New York City in the following manner:

> Drug addicts may be divided into two general classes. The first class is
> composed of people who have become addicted to the use of drugs

through illness, associated probably with an underlying neurotic temperament. The second class, which is *overwhelmingly in the majority* [italics mine], is at the present time giving municipal authorities the greatest concern. These persons are largely from the underworld, or channels leading directly to it. They have become addicted to the use of narcotic drugs largely through association with habitues and they find in the drug a panacea for the physical and mental ills that are the result of the lives they are leading. Late hours, dance halls, and unwholesome cabarets do much to bring about this condition of body and mind. . . . [20]

Whereas in 1900 the addict population was spread relatively evenly over the social classes (with the higher classes having slightly more), by 1920, medical journals could speak of the "overwhelming" majority from the "unrespectable" parts of society. The same pattern can be seen with the shift from the predominantly middle-aged to the young, and with the shift from a predominance of women to an overwhelming majority of men.

In a study reported in 1880 and cited by Terry and Pellens, addiction to drugs was said to be "a vice of middle life, the larger number, by far, being from 30 to 40 years of age."[21] By 1920, Hubbard's study of New York's clinic could let him conclude that:

Most, in fact 70 per cent of the addicts in our clinic, are young people . . . the one and only conclusion that we can arrive at, is that acquirements of this practice—drug addiction—is incident to propinquity, bad associates, taken together with weak vacillating dispositions, making a successful combination in favor of the acquirement of such a habit.[22]

A report of a study of addiction to the Michigan State Board of Health in 1878 stated that, of 1,313 addicts, 803 were females, 510 males.[23] This is corroborated by Earle's study of Chicago, reported in 1880:

Among the 235 habitual opium-eaters, 169 were found to be females, a proportion of about 3-to-1. Of these 169 females, about one-third belong to that class known as prostitutes. Deducting these, we still have among those taking the different kinds of opiates, 2 females to 1 male.[24]

Similarly, a report by Hull in 1885 on addiction in Iowa lists the distribution by sex as two-thirds female, and Terry's research in Florida in 1913 reported that 60 per cent of the cases were women.[25] Suddenly, as if in magical correspondence to the trend cited above on social class and age, the sex distribution reversed itself, and in 1914, McIver and Price report that 70 per cent of the addicts at Philadelphia General Hospital were males.[26] A governmental report to the Treasury Department in 1918 found addicts about equally divided between both sexes in the country, but a 1920 report for New York conclusively demonstrated that males were by then the predominant sex among drug addicts. Hubbard's report indicated that almost 80 per cent of the New York Clinic's population of addicts were male.[27] The Los Angeles Clinic had a similar distribution for 1920 and 1921. The picture is clear. Taking only the three variables of age, sex, and social class into account, there is a sharp and remarkable transformation to be noticed in the two-decade period at the turn of the century. Let us examine now the legal turn of events of the period.

Prior to 1897, there was no significant legislation in any state concerning the manufacture or distribution of narcotics. As we have seen, the medical profession was becoming increasingly aware of the nature of morphine addiction when heroin was discovered in 1898. The alarm over the common practice of using morphine for a myriad of ills was insufficient to stem the tide of the great enthusiasm with which physicians greeted heroin. Nonetheless, a small band of dedicated doctors who had been disturbed by the widespread ignorance of morphine in the profession (warnings about addiction did not appear in medical texts until about 1900) began to agitate for governmental intervention and regulation.[28]

From 1887 to 1908, many states passed individual laws aimed at curbing some aspect of the distribution of narcotics. Opium smoking was a favorite target of most of these laws, a development occasioned by the more concentrated treatment given this issue in the American press. Nonetheless, many of the state legislatures listened to medical men who insisted on the need for more control on the widespread distribution of the medicinally used opium derivatives. New York's state legislature passed the first comprehensive piece of legislation in the country concerning this problem in 1904, the Boylan Act.

As with many other problems of this kind, the lack of uniform state laws meant that control was virtually impossible. There is great variety in the law-making ability of each state, and sometimes it seems as though each state reviews the others carefully in order not to duplicate the provisions of their laws. If New York wanted registration of pharmacists, Massachusetts would want the registration of the central distributing warehouses, Illinois might want only physician's prescriptions, and so forth. It soon became clear that only national and even international centralized control would be effective.

At the request of the United States, an international conference on opium was called in early 1909. Among countries accepting the invitation to this convention held in Shanghai were China, Great Britain, France, Germany, Italy, Russia, and Japan. Prior to this time, there had been a few attempts at control by individual nations in treaties, but this was the first concerted action on a truly international level. The major purpose of this first conference, as well as two other international conventions that were called within the next four years, was to insure that opium and related drugs be distributed only for expressly medical purposes, and ultimately distributed to the consumer through medical channels. The conferences called for regulation of the traffic at ports of entry, especially, but also tried to deal with the complicated problem of mail traffic. The handful of nations represented at the first Shanghai conference recognized the need for obtaining agreement and compliance from every nation in the world. The United States found itself in the embarrassing position of being the only major power without any control law covering distribution of medicinal narcotics within its borders. (The 1909 federal law was directed at opium smoking.) It was very much as a direct result of participation in the international conventions, then, that this country found itself being pressed for congressional action on the problem.

In this climate of both internal and international concern for the medicinal uses of the opium derivatives, Congress passed the Harrison Narcotic Act, approved December 17, 1914.

The Harrison Act stipulated that anyone engaged in the production or distribution of narcotics must register with the federal government and keep records of all transactions with drugs. This was the first of the three central provisions of the act. It gave the government precise knowledge of the legal traffic, and for the first time, the various uses and avenues of distribution could be traced.

The second major provision required that all parties handling the drugs through either purchase or sale pay a tax. This was a critical portion, because it meant that enforcement would reside with the tax collector, the Treasury Department, and more specifically, its Bureau of Internal Revenue. The Bureau set up a subsidiary organization to deal with affairs related to surveillance of activities covered by the new law. The immediate task was to insure that drugs were registered and passed through legitimate channels, beginning with importation and ending with the consumer. Since everyone was required to keep a record, the Bureau could demand and survey documentary material at every stage of the market operation.

Finally, the third major provision of the Harrison Act was a subtle "sleeper" that was not to obtain importance until the Supreme Court made a critical interpretation in 1919. This was the provision that unregistered persons could purchase drugs only upon the prescription of a physician, and that such a prescription must be for legitimate medical use. It seemed innocent enough a provision, one that was clearly included so that the physician retained the only control over the dispensation of narcotics to the consumer. As such, the bill was designed by its framers to place the addict completely in the hands of the medical profession.

It is one of those ironic twists that this third provision, intended for one purpose, was to be used in such a way as to thwart that purpose. As a direct consequence of it, the medical profession abandoned the drug addict. The key revolved around the stipulation that doctors could issue a prescription only to addicts for *legitimate* medical purposes. The decision about what is legitimate medical practice rests ultimately outside the medical profession in the moral consensus which members of society achieve about legitimacy. Even if the medical profession were to agree that experimental injections of a new drug on a random sample of babies would do most to advance medical science, the moral response against experimentation would be so strong as to destroy its claim to legitimacy. Thus, it is only in arbitrary and confined hypothetical instances that we can cogently argue that the medical profession determines legitimate practice.

So it was that the germ of a moral conception, the difference between good and evil or right and wrong, was to gain a place in the exercise of the new law.

Since the Harrison Act said nothing explicitly about the basis upon which physicians could prescribe narcotics for addicts, the only theoretical change that was forseeable was the new status of the prescription at the drug counter. All sales were to be registered, and a signed prescription from a physician was required. But when the physician became the only legal source of the drug supply, hundreds of thousands of law-abiding addicts suddenly materialized outside of doctors' offices. It was inconceivable that the relatively small number of doctors in the country could so suddenly handle over half a million new patients in any manner, and certainly it was impossible that they might handle them individually. The doctor's office became little more than a dispensing station for the addict, with only an infinitesimal fraction of addicts receiving personal care. In most cases, this was simply a continuation of the small number who had already been under regular care.

In New York City for example, it was impossible for a doctor with even a small practice to do anything more than sign prescriptions for his suddenly created large clientele. The government agents were alarmed at what they regarded as cavalier treatment of the prescription by the medical profession, and were concerned that the spirit and intent of the new drug law were being violated. They decided to prosecute some physicians who were prescribing to addicts en masse. They succeeded in convicting them, and appeals took the cases up to the Supreme Court. In a remarkable case (Webb vs. U.S., 1919) the Supreme Court made a decision that was to have far-reaching effects on the narcotics traffic, ruling that:

> a prescription of drugs for an addict "not in the course of professional treatment in the attempted cure of the habit, but being issued for the purpose of providing the user with morphine sufficient to keep him comfortable by maintaining his customary use" was not a prescription in the

meaning of the law and was not included within the exemption for the doctor-patient relationship.[29]

Doctors who continued to prescribe to addicts on anything but the most personal and individual basis found themselves faced with the real, demonstrated possibility of fines and prison sentences. As I have indicated, there were hundreds of thousands of addicts, and only a few thousand physicians to handle them. If there were thirty or forty addicts outside a doctor's office waiting for prescriptions, *or even waiting for a chance to go through withdrawal,* the Supreme Court decision and the Treasury Department's actions made it almost certain that the doctor would turn them away. A minority of doctors, some for humanitarian reasons, some from the profit-motive of a much higher fee, continued to prescribe. Scores of them were arrested, prosecuted, fined, imprisoned, and set forth as an example to others. The addict found himself being cut off gradually but surely from all legal sources, and he began to turn gradually but surely to the welcome arms of the black marketeers.

And so it was that the law and its interpretation by the Supreme Court provided the final condition and context for a moral reassessment of what had previously been regarded as a physiological problem. The country could begin to connect all addicts with their new-found underworld associates, and could now begin to talk about a different class of men who were consorting with criminals. The step was only a small one to the imputation of criminal intent. The bridge between law and morality was drawn.

Notes

1. Philip Selznick, "Sociology of Law" (mimeographed, Center for the Study of Law and Society, University of California, Berkeley), April, 1965. Prepared for the *International Encyclopedia of the Social Sciences.*
2. *Ibid.*
3. *Ibid.,* p.23.
4. Charles E. Terry and Mildred Pellens, *The Opium Problem* (New York: Bureau of Social Hygiene, 1928), p. 66.
5. *Ibid.,* p. 69.
6. *Ibid.,* p.75.
7. Marie Nyswander, *The Drug Addict as a Patient* (New York: Grune & Stratton, 1956), 1–13.
8. B. H. Hartwell, "The Sale and Use of Opium in Massachusetts," *Annual Report Massachusetts State Board of Health,* 1889.
9. Terry and Pellens, *op. cit.,* p. 17.
10. C. W. Earle, "The Opium Habit," *Chicago Medical Review,* 2 (1880), 442–90.
11. A. P. Grinnell, "A Review of Drug Consumption and Alcohol as Found in Proprietary Medicine." *Medical Legal Journal,* 1905, pp. 426–589.
12. A much longer list of references is cited by Terry and Pellens, *op. cit.,* and the following are only a small but representative portion: H. Dreser, the man credited with the discovery of heroin, writing of his own findings in an Abstract to the *Journal*

of the American Medical Association, 1898; two reports by M. Manges in the *New York Medical Journal,* November 26, 1898 and January 20, 1900.

13. G. E. Pettey, "The Heroin Habit, Another Curse," *Alabama Medical Journal,* 15 (1902–1903), 174–180.

14. Terry and Pellens, *op. cit.*

15. E. G. Eberle, "Report of Committee on Acquirement of Drug Habits," *American Journal of Pharmacology,* October, 1903, p. 481.

16. Terry and Pellens, *op.cit.,* p. 468.

17. C. S. Pearson, "A Study of Degeneracy as Seen Among Addicts," *New York Medical Journal,* November 15, 1919, pp. 805–808.

18. For example, cf T.S. Blair, "Narcotic Drug Addiction as Regulated by a State Department of Health," *Journal of the American Medical Association,* 72 (May 17, 1919), 1442–44.

19. G. D. Swaine, "Regarding the Luminal Treatment of Morphine Addiction," *American Journal of Clinical Medicine,* 25 (August,1918), 611.

20. Terry and Pellens, *op. cit.,* p. 499.

21. *Ibid.,* p. 475.

22. S. D. Hubbard, "The New York City Narcotic Clinic and Differing Points of View on Narcotic Addiction," *Monthly Bulletin of the Department of Health, City of New York,* February, 1920.

23. Terry and Pellens, *op. cit.,* p. 11.

24. Earle, *op. cit.*

25. Terry and Pellens, *op. cit.,* pp. 470–471.

26. J. McIver and G. E. Price, "Drug Addiction," *Journal of the American Medical Association,* 66 (February 12, 1916), 477.

27. Hubbard, *op. cit.*

28. Nyswander, *op. cit.*

29. Alfred R. Lindesmith, *The Addict and the Law* (Bloomington: Indiana University Press, 1965), p. 6.

4 / The "Discovery" of Child Abuse

STEPHEN J. PFOHL

Despite documentary evidence of child beating throughout the ages, the "discovery" of child abuse as deviance and its subsequent criminalization are recent phenomena. In a four-year period beginning in 1962, the legislatures of all fifty states passed statutes against the caretaker's abuse of children. This paper is a study of the organization of social forces which gave rise to the deviant labeling of child beating and which promoted speedy and universal enactment of criminal legislation. It is an examination of certain organized medical interests, whose concern in the discovery of the "battered child syndrome" manifestly contributed to the advance of humanitarian pursuits while covertly rewarding the groups themselves.

The structure of the present analysis is fourfold: First, an historical survey of social reaction to abusive behavior prior to the formulation of fixed labels during the early sixties, focussing on the impact of three previous reform movements. These include the nineteenth-century "house-of-refuge" movement, early twentieth-century crusades by the Society for the Prevention of Cruelty to Children, and the rise of juvenile courts. The second section concentrates on the web of cultural values related to the protection of children at the time of the "discovery" of abuse as deviance. A third section examines factors associated with the organizational structure of the medical profession conducive to the "discovery" of a particular type of deviant label. The fourth segment discusses social reaction. Finally, the paper provides a sociological interpretation of a particular social-legal development. Generically it gives support for a synthesis of conflict and labeling perspectives in the sociology of deviance and law.

THE HISTORY OF SOCIAL REACTION: PREVENTATIVE PENOLOGY AND "SOCIETY SAVING"

The purposeful beating of the young has for centuries found legitimacy in beliefs of its necessity for achieving disciplinary, educational

45

or religious obedience (Radbill, 1968). Both the Roman legal code of "Patria Patistas" (Shepard, 1965), and the English common law (Thomas, 1973), gave guardians limitless power over their children who, with chattel-like status, had no legal right to protection.

The common law heritage of America similarly gave rise to a tradition of legitimized violence toward children. Legal guardians had the right to impose any punishment deemed necessary for the child's upbringing. In the seventeenth century, a period dominated by religious values and institutions, severe punishments were considered essential to the "sacred" trust of child-rearing (Earle, 1926:119–126). Even in the late eighteenth and early nineteenth centuries, a period marked by the decline of religious domination and the rise of rationalism and a proliferation of statutes aimed at codifying unacceptable human behavior, there were no attempts to prevent caretaker abuse of children. A major court in the state of North Carolina declared that the parent's judgment of need for a child's punishment was presumed to be correct. Criminal liability was said to exist only in cases resulting in "permanent injury" (*State v. Pendergass*, in Paulsen, 1966b:686).

I am not suggesting that the American legal tradition failed to recognize any abuse of discipline as something to be negatively sanctioned. A few cases resulting in the legal punishment of parents who murdered their children, have been recorded. But prior to the 1960s sociolegal reactions were sporadic, and atypical of sustained reactions against firmly labeled deviance.

Beginning in the early nineteenth century, a series of three reform movements directed attention to the plight of beaten, neglected and delinquent children. These included the nineteenth century "house-of-refuge" movement, the turn of the century crusades by the Society for the Prevention of Cruelty to Children and the early twentieth century rise of juvenile courts. Social response, however, seldom aimed measures at ameliorating abuse or correcting abusive parents. Instead, the child, rather than his or her guardians, became the object of humanitarian reform.

In each case the primary objective was not to save children from cruel or abusive parents, but to save society from future delinquents. Believing that wicked and irresponsible behavior was engendered by the evils of poverty and city life, these movements sought to curb criminal tendencies in poor, urban youths by removing them from corrupt environments and placing them in institutional settings. There they could learn order, regularity and obedience (Rothman, 1970). Thus, it was children, not their abusive guardians, who felt the weight of the moral crusade. They, not their parents, were institutionalized.

The "House of Refuge" Movement

Originating in the reformist dreams of the Jacksonian era, the so-called "House of Refuge Movement" sought to stem the social pathologies of an industrializing nation by removing young people, endangered by "corrupt urban environments," to institutional settings. Neglect statutes providing for the removal of the young from bad home lives were originally enacted to prevent children from mingling freely with society's dregs in alm houses or on the streets. In 1825, the first statute was passed and the first juvenile institution, the New York House of Refuge, was opened. Originally privately endowed, the institution soon received public funds to intervene in neglectful home situations and transplant children to a controlled environment, where they shared a "proper growing up" with other vagrant, abandoned and neglected youths as well as with delinquents who had violated criminal statutes. Similar institutions were established in Philadelphia and Boston a year later, in New Orleans in 1845, and in Rochester and Baltimore in 1849.

The Constitutionality of the neglect statutes, which formed the basis for the House of Refuge Movement, was repeatedly challenged on the grounds that it was really imprisonment without due process. With few exceptions court case after court case upheld the policy of social intervention on the Aristotelian principle of "parens patriae." This principle maintained that the State has the responsibility to defend those who cannot defend themselves, as well as to assert its privilege in compelling infants and their guardians to act in ways most beneficial to the State.

The concept of preventive penology emerged in the wording of these court decisions. A distinction between "delinquency" (the actual violation of criminal codes) and "dependency" (being born into a poor home with neglectful or abusive parents) was considered irrelevant for "child saving." The two were believed to be intertwined in poverty and desolation. If not stopped, both would perpetuate themselves. For the future good of both child and society, "parens patriae" justified the removal of the young before they became irreparably tainted (Thomas, 1972:322–323).

The underlying concept of the House of Refuge Movement was that of preventive penology, not child protection. This crusade registered no real reaction against child beating. The virtue of removing children from their homes was not to point up abuse or neglect and protect its victims, it was to decrease the likelihood that parental inadequacies, the "cause of poverty," would transfer themselves to the child and hence to the next generation of society (Giovannoni, 1971:652). Thus, as indicated by Zalba (1966), the whole nineteenth century movement toward institutionalization actually failed to differentiate between abuse and poverty and therefore registered no social reaction against beating as a form of deviance.

Mary Ellen, the SPCC, and a Short-Lived Social Reaction

The first period when public interest focussed on child abuse occurred in the last quarter of the nineteenth century. In 1875, the Society for the Prevention of Cruelty to Animals intervened in the abuse case of a nine-year-old girl named Mary Ellen who had been treated viciously by foster parents. The case of Mary Ellen was splashed across the front pages of the nation's papers with dramatic results. As an outgrowth of the journalistic clamor, the New York Society for the Prevention of Cruelty to Children was formed. Soon incorporated under legislation that required law enforcement and court officials to aid agents of authorized cruelty societies, the NYSPCC and other societies modeled after it undertook to prevent abuse.

Though the police functions of the anti-cruelty societies represented a new reaction to abuse, their activities did not signify a total break with the society-saving emphasis of the House of Refuge Movement. In fact, three lines of evidence suggest that the SPCC enforcement efforts actually withheld a fixed label of deviancy from the perpetrators of abuse, in much the same manner as had the House of Refuge reforms. First, the "saving" of the child actually boosted the number of children placed in institutions, consequently supporting House of Refuge activities (Thomas, 1972:311). Second, according to Falks (1970:176), interorganizational dependency grew between the two reform movements; best evidenced by the success of SPCC efforts in increasing public support to childcare institutions under the auspices of House of Refuge groups. Finally, and perhaps most convincingly, natural parents were not classified as abusers of the great majority of the so-called "rescued children." In fact, the targets of these savings missions were cruel employers and foster or adopted parents (Giovannoni, 1971:653). Rarely did an SPCC intervene against the "natural" balance of power between parents and children. The firmness of the SPCC's alleged social action against abuse appears significantly dampened by its reluctance to shed identification with the refuge house emphasis on the "industrial sins of the city" and to replace it with a reaction against individuals.

The decline of the SPCC movement is often attributed to lack of public interest, funding problems, mergers with other organizations and the assumption of protection services by public agencies (Felder,

1971: 187). Its identification with the House of Refuge Movement also contributed to its eventual demise. More specifically, the House of Refuge emphasis on the separation of child from family, a position adopted and reinforced by the SPCC's activities, came into conflict with perspectives advocated by the newly-emerging professions of social work and child psychology (Kadushen, 1967:202f). Instead of removing the child from the home, these new interests emphasized efforts to unite the family (Thomas, 1972). This latter position, backed by the power of professional expertise, eventually undercut the SPCC's policy of preventive policing by emphasizing the protection of the home.

The erosion of the SPCC position was foreshadowed by the 1909 White House Conference on Children. This Conference proclaimed that a child should not be removed from his or her home for reasons of poverty alone, and called for service programs and financial aid to protect the home environment. Yet, the practice of preventive policing and institutionalization did not vanish, due, in part, to the development of the juvenile court system. The philosophy and practice of this system continued to identify abuse and neglect with poverty and social disorganization.

The Juvenile Court and the Continued Shadow of Abuse

The founding of the first juvenile court in Illinois in 1899 was originally heralded as a major landmark in the legal protection of juveniles. By 1920, courts were established in all but three states. Nonetheless, it is debatable that much reform was accomplished by juvenile court legislation. Coalitions of would-be reformers (headed by various female crusaders and the commissioners of several large public reformatories) argued for the removal of youthful offenders from adult institutions and advocated alteration of the punitive, entrepreneurial and sectarian "House of Refuge" institutions (Fox, 1970:1225–29). More institutions and improved conditions were demanded (Thomas, 1972:323). An analysis of the politics of juvenile court legislation suggests, however, that successful maneuvering by influential sectarian entrepreneurs resulted in only a partial achievement of reformist goals (Fox, 1970:1225–26). Legislation did remove juveniles from adult institutions. It did not reduce the House of Refuge Movement's control of juvenile institutions. Instead, legislation philosophically supported and financially reinforced the Movement's "society-saving" operation of sectarian industrial schools (Fox, 1970:1226–27).

The channeling of juvenile court legislation into the "society-saving" mold of the House of Refuge Movement actually withheld a deviant label from abusive parents. Even the reformers, who envisioned it as a revolution in child protection, did not see the court as protection from unfit parents. It was meant instead to prevent the development of "lower class" delinquency (Platt, 1969) and to rescue "those less fortunate in the social order" (Thomas, 1972:326). Again, the victims of child battering were characterized as pre-delinquents, as part of the general "problem" of poverty. These children, not their guardians, were the targets of court action and preventive policies. The courts, like the House of Refuge and SPCC movements before them, constrained any social reaction which would apply the label of deviant to parents who abused their children.

SOCIAL REACTION AT MID-CENTURY: THE CULTURAL SETTING FOR THE "DISCOVERY" OF ABUSE

The Decline of Preventative Penology

As noted, preventative penology represented the philosophical basis for various voluntary associations and legislative reform efforts resulting in the institutionalization of neglected or abused children. Its primary emphasis was on the protection of society. The decline of preventative penology is partially attributed to three variables: the perceived failure of "institutionalization," the impact of the "Great Depression" of the 1930's, and a change in the cultural meaning of "adult vices."

In the several decades prior to the discovery of abuse, the failure of institutionalization to "reorder" individuals became increasingly apparent. This realization undermined the juvenile courts' role in administering a pre-delinquency system of crime prevention. Since the rise of juvenile courts historically represented a major structural support for the notion of preventative penology, the lessening of its role removed a significant barrier to concern with abuse as an act of individual victimization. Similarly, the widespread experience of poverty during the Great Depression weakened other beliefs in preventative penology. As impersonal economic factors impoverished a great number of citizens of good moral credentials, the link between poverty and immorality began to weaken.

Another characteristic of the period immediately prior to the discovery of abuse was a changing cultural awareness of the meaning of adult vice as indices of the future character of children. "Parental immoralities that used to be seen as warnings of oncoming criminality in children [became] acceptable factors in a child's homelife" (Fox, 1970:1234). Parental behavior such as drinking, failing to provide a Christian education, and refusing to keep a child busy with useful labor, were no longer classified as unacceptable nor deemed symptoms of immorality transmitted to the young. Hence, the saving of society from the tainted young became less of a mandate, aiding the perception of social harm against children as "beings" in themselves.

Advance of Child Protection

Concurrent with the demise of "society-saving" in the legal sphere, developments in the fields of child welfare and public policy heightened interest in the problems of the child as an individual. The 1909 White House Conference on Children spawned both the "Mother's Aid" Movement and the American Association for the Study and Prevention of Infant Mortality. The former group, from 1910 to 1930, drew attention to the benefits of keeping children in the family while pointing out the detrimental effects of dehumanizing institutions. The latter group then, as now, registered concern over the rate of infant deaths.

During the first half of the twentieth century, the Federal Government also met the issue of child protection with legislation that regulated child labor, called for the removal of delinquent youths from adult institutions, and established, in 1930, a bureaucratic structure whose purpose revolved around child protection. The Children's Bureau of HEW immediately adopted a "Children's Charter" promising every child a home with love and security plus full-time public services for protection from abuse, neglect, exploitation or moral hazard (Radbill, 1968:15).

Despite the growth of cultural and structural dispositions favoring the protection and increased rights of children, there was still no significant attention given to perpetrators of abuse, in the courts (Paulsen, 1966:710), in the legislature (DeFrancis, 1967:3), or by child welfare agencies (Zalba, 1966). While this inactivity may have been partly caused by the lack of effective mechanisms for obtaining data on abuse (Paulsen, 1966:910), these agencies had little social incentive for interfering with an established power set—the parent over the child. As a minority group possessing neither the collective awareness nor the elementary organizational skills necessary to address their grievances to either the courts or to the legislators, abused and neglected children awaited the advocacy of some other organized interest. This outside intervention would not, however, be generated by that sector of "organized helping" most closely associated with the protective needs of children—the growing web of child welfare bureaucracies at State and Federal levels. Social work had identified its professional advance with the adoption of the psychoanalytic model of casework (Zalba, 1966). This perspective, rather than generating a concern with political inequities internal to the family, focused instead on psychic disturbances internal to its members. Rather than challenging the strength of parents, this served to reinforce the role of powerful guardians in the rearing of young.

Nor would advocacy come from the public at large. Without organized labeling interests at mid-century, child abuse had not become an issue publicly regarded as a major social problem. In fact, a fairly general tolerance for abuse appeared to exist. This contention is supported by the findings of a nationwide study conducted by NORC during the period in which laws against abuse were actually being adopted (Gil & Nobel, 1969). Despite the wide-scale publicizing of abuse in this "post-discovery" period, public attitudes remained lenient. Data revealed a high degree of empathy with convicted or suspected perpetrators (Gil, 1970:63–67). These findings are understandable in light of cultural views accepting physical force against children as a nearly universally applied precept of intrafamilial organization (Goode, 1971). According to the coordinator of the national survey, "Culturally determined permissive attitudes toward the use of physical force in child rearing seem to constitute the common core of all physical abuse of children in American society" (Gil, 1970:141).

While the first half of the twentieth century is characterized by an increasing concern for child welfare, it developed with neither an organizational nor attitudinal reaction against child battering as a specific form of deviance. The "discovery" of abuse, its definition as a social problem and the socio-legal reaction against it, awaited the coalition of organized interest.

THE ORGANIZATION OF SOCIAL REACTION AGAINST THE "BATTERED CHILD SYNDROME"

What organization of social forces gave rise to the discovery of abuse as deviance? The discovery is not attributable to any escalation of abuse itself. Although some authors have recently suggested that the increasing nuclearization of the family may increase the victimization of its offspring (Skolnick & Skolnick, 1971), there has never been any evidence that, aside from reporting inflation due to the impact of new laws, battering behavior was actually increasing (Eads, 1972). The attention here is on the organizational matrix encouraging a recognition of abuse as a social problem. In addressing this issue I will examine factors associated with the organizational structure of the medical profession leading to the discovery of abuse by pediatric radiologists rather than by other medical practitioners.

The "discovery" of abuse by pediatric radiology has often been described chronologically (Radbill, 1968:15; McCoid, 1965:2–5; Thomas, 1972:330). John Caffey (1946) first linked observed series of long bone fractures in children with what he termed some "unspecific origin." Although his assumption was that some physical disturbance would be discovered as the cause of this pattern of "subdural hematoma," Coffey's work prompted a series of further investigations into various bone injuries, skeletal trauma, and multiple fractures in young children. These research efforts led pediatric radiology gradually to shift its diagnosis away from an internal medical explication toward the ascription of social cause.

In subsequent years it was suggested that what was showing up on x-rays might be the results of various childhood accidents (Barmeyer et al., 1951), of "parental carelessness" (Silverman, 1953), of "parental conduct" (Bakwin, 1956), and most dramatically, of the "indifference, immaturity and irresponsibility of parents" (Wooley & Evans, 1955). Surveying the progression of this research and reviewing his own investigations, Coffey (1957) later specified "misconduct and deliberate injury" as the primary etiological factors associated with what he had previously labelled "unspecific trauma." The discovery of abuse was on its way. Both in scholarly research (McCoid, 1966:7) and journalistic outcry (Radbill, 1968:16), the last years of the fifties showed dramatically increased concern for the beaten child.

Why did pediatric radiologists and not some other group "see" abuse first? Legal and social welfare agents were either outside the scene of abusive behavior or inside the constraining vision of psychoanalytically committed casework. But clinicians, particularly hospital physicians and pediatricians, who encountered abused children more immediately, should have discovered "abuse" before the radiologists.

Four factors impeded the recognition of abuse (as it was later labeled). First, some early research maintained that doctors in emergency room settings were simply unaware of the possibilities of "abuse" as a diagnosis (Bain, 1963; Boardman, 1962). While this may be true, the massive symptoms (blood, burns, bruises) emergency room doctors faced far outweighed the lines appearing on the x-ray screens of radiologic specialists. A second line of evidence contends that many doctors were simply psychologically unwilling to believe that parents would inflict such atrocities on their own children (Elmer, 1960; Fontana, Donovan, Wong, 1963; Kempe et al., 1963). This position is consistent with the existing cultural assumptions pairing parental power with parental wisdom and benevolence. None-theless, certain normative and structural elements within profession-al medicine appear of greater significance in reinforcing the physi-cian's reluctance to get involved, even diagnostically. These factors are the "norm of confidentiality between doctor and client" and the goal of professional autonomy.

The "norm of confidentiality" gives rise to the third obstacle to a diagnosis of abuse: the possibility of legal liability for violating the confidentiality of the physician-patient relationship (Boardman, 1962). Interestingly, although some research connotes doctors' con-cern over erroneous diagnosis (Braun, Braun & Simonds, 1963), phy-sicians primarily view the parent, rather than the child, as their real patient. On a strictly monetary level, of course, it is the parent who contracts with the doctor. Additional research has indicated that, particularly in the case of pediatricians, the whole family is viewed as one's clinical domain (Bucher & Strauss, 1961:329). It is from this vantage point that the impact of possible liability for a diagnostic dis-closure is experienced. Although legal liability for a diagnosis of abuse may or may not have been the risk (Paulsen, 1967b:32), the belief in such liability could itself have contributed to the narrowness of a doctor's diagnostic perceptions (McCoid, 1966:37).

A final deterrent to the physician's "seeing" abuse is the reluc-tance of doctors to become involved in a criminal justice process that would take both their time (Bain, 1963:896) and ability to guide the consequences of a particular diagnosis (Boardman, 1962:46). This de-terrent is particularly related to the traditional success of organized medicine in politically controlling the consequences of its own per-formance, not just for medical practitioners but for all who come in contact with a medical problem (Freidson, 1969:106; Hyde *et al.*, 1954).

The political control over the consequences of one's profession would be jeopardized by the medical diagnosis of child abuse. Doc-tors would be drawn into judicial proceedings and subordinated to a role as witnesses. The outcome of this process would be decided by criminal justice standards rather than those set forth by the medical profession. Combining this relatively unattractive alternative with the obvious and unavoidable drain on a doctor's financial earning time, this fourth obstacle to the clinician's discovery of abuse is sub-stantial.

Factors Conducive to the Discovery of Abuse by Pediatric Radiology

Why didn't the above factors inhibit the discovery of abuse by pediat-ric radiologists as well as by clinicians? First it must be recognized that the radiologists in question (Caffey, Barmeyer, Silverman, Wooley and Evans) were all researchers of children's x-rays. As such, the initial barrier becomes irrelevant. The development of diagnostic categories was a consequence rather than a pre-condition of the medical mission. Regarding the psychological denial of parental responsibility for atrocities, it must be remembered that the dramatic character of a beating is greatly reduced by the time it reaches an x-ray laboratory. Taken by technicians and developed as black and white prints, the radiologic remnants of abuse carry with them little of the horror of the bloody assault.

With a considerable distance from the patient and his or her family, radiologists are removed from the third obstacle concerning legal liabilities entailed in violating the doctor-patient relationship. Unlike pediatricians, radiologists do not routinely regard the whole family as one's clinical domain. Of primary importance is the individual whose name or number is imprinted on the x-ray frames. As such, fears about legal sanctions instigated by a parent whom one has never seen are less likely to deter the recognition of abuse.

Given the irrelevance of the first three obstacles, what about the last? Pediatric radiologists are physicians, and as such would be expected to participate in the "professional control of consequences" ethos. How is it that they negotiate this obstacle in favor of public recognition and labelling of abuse?

The Discovery: An Opportunity for Advancement Within the Medical Community

To ask why the general norm of "professional control of consequences" does not apply equally to radiologists as to their clinical counterparts is to confuse the reality of organized medicine with its image. Although the medical profession often appears to outsiders as a separate and unified community within a community (Goode, 1957), and although medical professionals generally favor the maintenance of this image (Glaser, 1960), it is nonetheless more adequately described as an organization of internally competing segments, each striving to advance its own historically derived mission and future importance (Bucher & Strauss, 1961). In analyzing pediatric radiology as one such segment, several key variables facilitated its temporary parting with the dominant norms of the larger medical community. This parting promoted the elevation of its overall status within that community.

The first crucial element is that pediatric radiology was a marginal specialty within organized medicine. It was a research-oriented subfield in a profession that emphasized face-to-face clinical interaction. It was a safe intellectual endeavor within an overall organization which placed a premium on risky pragmatic enterprise. Studies of value orientations among medical students at the time of the "discovery" of abuse have suggested that those specialties which stress "helping others," "being of service," "being useful," and "working with people" were ranked above those which work "at medical problems that do not require frequent contact with patients" (Cahalan, 1957). On the other hand, intellectual stimulation afforded very little prestige. Supporting this conclusion was research indicating that although forty-three percent of practicing physicians selected "close patient relations" as a mandate of their profession, only twenty-four percent chose "research" as worthy of such an evaluation (Philips, 1964). Pairing this ranking system with the profession's close-knit, "fraternity-like" communication network (Hall, 1946), one would expect research-oriented radiologists to be quite sensitive about their marginal evaluation by colleagues.

Intramedical organizational rankings extend along the lines of risk-taking as well as patient-encounters. Here, too, pediatric radiologists have traditionally ranked lower than other medical specialties. Becker's (1961) study of medical student culture suggests that the most valued specialties are those which combine wide experiences with risk and responsibility. These are most readily "symbolized by the possibility of killing or disabling patients in the course of making a mistake" (Freidson, 1969:107). From this perspective, it is easy to understand why surgery and internal medicine head the list of the most esteemed specialties. Other research has similarly noted the predominance of surgeons among high elected officials of the American Medical Association (Hall, 1946). Devoid of most risk taking, little involved in life or death decisions, pediatric radiologists are again marginal to this ethos of medical culture.

The "discovery" of child abuse offered pediatric radiologists an alternative to their marginal medical status. By linking themselves to the problem of abuse, radiologists became indirectly tied into the crucial clinical task of patient diagnosis. In addition, they became a direct source of input concerning the risky "life or death" consequences of child beating. This could represent an advance in status, a new basis for recognition within the medical profession. Indeed, after initial documentation of abuse, literature in various journals of radiology, roentgenology and pediatrics, articles on this topic by Wooley and Evans (1955) and Gwinn, deWin and Peterson (1961) appeared in the *Journal of the American Medical Association*. These were among the very few radiologic research reports published by that prestigious journal during the time period. Hence, the first factor conducive to the radiological discovery of abuse was a potential for intraorganizational advance in prestige.

(2.) The Discovery: An Opportunity for Coalition Within the Medical Community

A second factor encouraging the discovery of abuse by relatively low-status pediatric radiologists concerns the opportunity for a coalition of interests with other more prestigious segments within organized medicine. The two other segments radiologists joined in alliance were pediatrics and psychodynamically oriented psychiatry. By virtue of face-to-face clinical involvements, these specialties were higher ranking than pediatric radiology. Nevertheless each contained a dimension of marginality. Pediatrics had attained valued organizational status several decades prior to the discovery of abuse. Yet, in an age characterized by preventive drugs and treatments for previously dangerous or deadly infant diseases, it was again sliding toward the margins of the profession (Bucher & Strauss, 1961). Psychodynamic psychiatry (as opposed to its psychosomatic cousin) experienced marginality in dealing with non-physical problems.

For both pediatrics and psychodynamic psychiatry, links with the problem of abuse could partially dissipate the respective marginality of each. Assuming a role in combatting the "deadly" forces of abuse could enlarge the "risky" part of the pediatric mission. A symbolic alliance of psychodynamic psychiatry with other bodily diagnostic and treatment specialties could also function to advance its status. Neither of these specialties was in a position to "see" abuse before the radiologists. Pediatricians were impeded by the obstacles discussed above. Psychiatrists were blocked by the reluctance of abusive parents to admit their behavior as problematic (Steele & Pollock, 1968). Nonetheless, the interests of both could perceivably be advanced by a coalition with the efforts of pediatric radiologists. As such, each represented a source of potential support for pediatric radiologists in their discovery of abuse. This potential for coalition served to reinforce pediatric radiology in its movement toward the discovery of abuse.

(3.) The Discovery: An Opportunity for the Application of an Acceptable Label

A crucial impediment to the discovery of abuse by the predominant interests in organized medicine was the norm of controlling the consequences of a particular diagnosis. To diagnose abuse as social deviance might curtail the power of organized medicine. The management of its consequences would fall to the extramedical interests of formal agents of social control. How is it then, that such a diagnosis by pediatric radiology and its endorsement by pediatric and psychiatric

specialties, is said to have advanced these specialties within the organization of medicine? Wasn't it more likely that they should have
received criticism rather than acclaim from the medical profession?

By employing a rather unique labelling process the coalition of discovery interests were able to convert the possible liability into a discernible advantage. The opportunity of generating a medical, rather
than socio-legal label for abuse provided the radiologists and their
allies with a situation in which they could both reap the rewards associated with the diagnosis and avoid the infringement of extra-medi-
cal controls. What was discovered was no ordinary behavior form but
a "syndrome." Instead of departing from the tradition of organized
medicine, they were able to idealize its most profound mission. Possessing a repertoire of scientific credibility, they were presented
with the opportunity "to label as illness what was not previously labeled at all or what was labeled in some other fashion, under some
other institutional jurisdiction" (Freidson, 1971:261).

The symbolic focal point for the acceptable labeling of abuse was
the 1962 publication of an article entitled "The Battered Child Syndrome" in the Journal of the American Medical Association (Kempe
et al., 1962). This report, representing the joint research efforts of a
group of radiologic, pediatric, and psychiatric specialists, labelled
abuse as a "clinical condition" existing as an "unrecognized trauma"
(Kempe, 1962:17). It defined the deviance of its "psychopathic" perpetrators as a product of "psychiatric factors" representing "some
defect in character structure" (Kempe, 1962:24). As an indicator of
prestige within organized medicine, it is interesting to note that the
position articulated by these labellers was endorsed by the editorial
board of the AMA in that same issue of *JAMA*.

As evidenced by the AMA editorial, the discovery of abuse as a new
"illness" reduced drastically the intra-organizational constraints on
doctors' "seeing" abuse. A diagnostic category had been invented
and publicized. Psychological obstacles in recognizing parents as capable of abuse were eased by the separation of normatively powerful
parents from non-normatively pathological individuals. Problems associated with perceiving parents as patients whose confidentiality
must be protected were reconstructed by typifying them as patients
who needed help. Moreover, the maintenance of professional autonomy was assured by pairing deviance with sickness. This last statement is testimony to the power of medical nomenclature. It was evidenced by the fact that (prior to its publication) the report which
coined the label "battered child syndrome" was endorsed by a Children's Bureau conference which included social workers and law enforcement officials as well as doctors (McCoid, 1965:12).

The Generation of the Reporting Movement

The discovery of the "battered child syndrome" was facilitated by the opportunities for various pediatric radiologists to advance in medical prestige, form coalitions with other interests, and invent a professionally acceptable deviant label. The application of this label has been called the child abuse reporting movement. This movement was well underway by the time the 1962 Children's Bureau Conference confirmed the radiological diagnosis of abuse. Besides foreshadowing the acceptance of the sickness label, this meeting was also the basis for a series of articles to be published in *Pediatrics* which would further substantiate the diagnosis of abuse. Soon, however, the reporting movement spread beyond intraorganizational medical maneuvering to incorporate contributions from various voluntary associations, governmental agencies, as well as the media.

Extramedical responses to the newly discovered deviance confirmed the recognition of abuse as an illness. These included reports by various social welfare agencies which underscored the medical roots of the problem. For instance, the earliest investigations of the problem by social service agents resulted in a call for cooperation with the findings of radiologists in deciding the fate of abusers (Elmer, 1960:100). Other studies called for "more comprehensive radiological examinations" (Boardman, 1962:43). That the problem was medical in its roots as well as consequences was reinforced by the frequent referral of caseworkers to themselves as "battered child therapists" whose mission was the "curing" of "patients" (Davoren, 1968). Social welfare organizations, including the Children's Division of the American Humane Association, the Public Welfare Association, and the Child Welfare League, echoed similar concerns in sponsoring research (Children's Division, 1963; DeFrancis, 1963) and lobbying for "treatment based" legislative provisions (McCoid, 1965).

Not all extramedical interests concurred with treatment of abusers as "sick." Various law enforcement voices argued that the abuse of children was a crime and should be prosecuted. On the other hand, a survey of thirty-one publications in major law journals between 1962–1972 revealed that nearly all legal scholars endorsed treatment rather than punishment to manage abusers. Lawyers disagreed, however, as to whether reports should be mandatory and registered concern over who should report to whom. Yet, all concurred that various forms of immunity should be granted reporters (Paulsen, 1967a; DeFrancis, 1967). These are all procedural issues. Neither law enforcers nor legal scholars parted from labelling abuse as a problem to be managed. The impact of the acceptable discovery of abuse by a respected knowledge sector (the medical profession) had generated a stigmatizing scrutiny bypassed in previous eras.

The proliferation of the idea of abuse by the media cannot be underestimated. Though its stories were sensational, its credibility went unchallenged. What was publicized was not some amorphous set of muggings but a "syndrome." Titles such as "Cry rises from beaten babies" (*Life,* June 1963), "Parents who beat children" (*Saturday Evening Post,* October 1962), "The shocking price of parental anger" (*Good Housekeeping,* March 1964), and "Terror struck children" (*New Republic,* May 1964) were all buttressed by an awe of scientific objectivity. The problem had become "real" in the imaginations of professionals and laymen alike. It was rediscovered visually by ABC's "Ben Casey," NBC's "Dr. Kildare," and CBS's "The Nurses," as well as in several other television scripts and documentaries (Paulsen, 1967b: 488–89).

Discovered by the radiologists, substantiated by their colleagues, and distributed by the media, the label was becoming widespread. Despite this fact, actual reporting laws were said to be the cooperative accomplishments of zealous individuals and voluntary associations (Paulsen, 1967b:491). Who exactly were these "zealous individuals"?

Data on legislative lobbyists reveal that, in almost every state, the civic committee concerned with abuse legislation was chaired by a doctor who "just happened" to be a pediatrician (Paulsen, 1967b:491). Moreover, "the medical doctors who most influenced the legislation frequently were associated with academic medicine" (Paulsen, 1967b:491). This information provides additional evidence of the collaborative role of pediatricians in guiding social reaction to the deviance discovered by their radiological colleagues.

Lack of Resistance to the Label

In addition to the medical interests discussed above, numerous voluntary associations provided support for the movement against child abuse. These included the League of Women Voters, Veterans of Foreign Wars, the Daughters of the American Republic, the District Attorneys Association, Council of Jewish Women, State Federation of Womens Clubs, Public Health Associations, plus various national chapters of social workers (Paulsen, 1967b,495). Two characteristics emerge from an examination of these interests. They either have a professional stake in the problem or represent the civic concerns of certain upper-middle class factions. In either case the labelers were socially and politically removed from the abusers, who in all but one early study (Steele and Pollock), were characterized as lower class and minority group members.

The existence of a wide social distance between those who abuse and those who label, facilitates not only the likelihood of labelling but nullifies any organized resistance to the label by the "deviant" group itself. Research findings which describe abusers as belonging to no outside-the-family associations or clubs (Young, 1964) or which portray them as isolates in the community (Giovannoni, 1971) reinforce the conclusion. Labelling was generated by powerful medical interests and perpetuated by organized media, professional and upper-middle class concerns. Its success was enlarged by the relative powerlessness and isolation of abusers, which prevented the possibility of organized resistance to the labelling.

THE SHAPE OF SOCIAL REACTION

I have argued that the organizational advantages surrounding the discovery of abuse by pediatric radiology set in motion a process of labelling abuse as deviance and legislating against it. The actual shape of legislative enactments has been discussed elsewhere (De-Francis, 1967; Paulsen, 1967a). The passage of the reporting laws encountered virtually no opposition. In Kentucky, for example, no one even appeared to testify for or against the measure (Paulsen, 1967b, 502). Any potential opposition from the American Medical Association, whose interests in autonomous control of the consequences of a medical diagnosis might have been threatened, had been undercut by the radiologists' success in defining abuse as a new medical problem. The AMA, unlikely to argue against conquering illness, shifted to support reporting legislation which would maximize a physician's diagnostic options.

The consequences of adopting a "sick" label for abusers is mirrored in two findings: the low rate of prosecution afforded offenders and the modification of reporting statutes so as exclusively to channel reporting toward "helping services." Regarding the first factor, Grumet (1970:306) suggests that despite existing laws and reporting statutes, actual prosecution has not increased since the time of abuse's "discovery." In support is Thomas (1972) who contends that the actual percentage of cases processed by family courts has remained constant during the same period. Even when prosecution does occur, convictions are obtained in only five to ten per cent of the cases (Paulsen, 1966b). And even in these cases, sentences are shorter for abusers than for other offenders convicted under the same law of aggravated assault (Grumet, 1970:307).

State statutes have shifted on reporting from an initial adoption of the Children's Bureau model of reporting to law enforcement agents, toward one geared at reporting to child welfare or child protection agencies (DeFrancis, 1970). In fact, the attention to abuse in the early sixties has been attributed as a factor in the development of specialized "protective interests" in states which had none since the days of the SPCC crusades (Eads, 1969). This event, like the emphasis on abuser treatment, is evidence of the impact of labelling of abuse as an "illness."

References

Bain, Katherine
  1963 "The physically abused child." Pediatrics 31(June): 895–897.
Bakwin, Harry
  1956 "Multiple skeletal lesions in young children due to trauma." Journal of Pediatrics 49(July): 7–15.
Barmeyer, G. H., L. R. Anderson and W. B. Cox
  1951 "Traumatic periostitis in young children." Journal of Pediatrics 38(Feb): 184–90.
Becker, Howard S.
  1963 The Outsiders, New York: The Free Press.
Becker, Howard S. et al.
  1961 Boys in White. Chicago: University of Chicago Press.
Boardman, Helen
  1962 "A project to rescue children from inflicted injuries." Journal of Social Work 7(January): 43–51.
Braun, Ida G., Edgar J. Braun and Charlotte Simonds
  1963 "The mistreated child." California Medicine 99(August): 98–103.
Bremner, R.
  1970 Children and Youth in America: A Documentary History. Vol. I Cambridge, Mass: Harvard University Press.
Bucher, Rue and Anselm Strauss
  1961 "Professions in process." American Journal of Sociology 66(January): 325–334.
Caffey, John
  1946 "Multiple fractures in the long bones of infants suffering from chronic subdural hematoma." American Journal of Roentology 56(August): 163–173.
  1957 "Traumatic lesions in growing bones other than fractures and lesions: clinical and radiological features." British Journal of Radiology 30(May): 225–238.
Cahalan, Don
  1957 "Career interests and expectations of U.S. medical students." 32: 557–563.

Chambliss, William J.
1964 "A sociological analysis of the law of vagrancy." Social Problems 12(Summer): 67–77.
Children's Division
1963 Child Abuse—Preview of a Nationwide Survey. Denver: American Humane Association (Children's Division).
Davoren, Elizabeth
1968 "The role of the social worker." Pp. 153–168 in Ray E. Helfer and Henry C. Kempe (eds.), The Battered Child. Chicago: University of Chicago Press.
De Francis, Vincent
1963 "Parents who abuse children." PTA Magazine 58(November): 16–18.
1967 "Child abuse—the legislative response." Denver Law Journal 44(Winter): 3–41.
1970 Child Abuse Legislation in the 1970's. Denver: American Humane Association.
Eads, William E.
1969 "Observations on the establishment of child protection services in California." Stanford Law Review 21(May): 1129–1155.
Earle, Alice Morse
1926 Child Life in Colonial Days. New York: Macmillan.
Elmer, Elizabeth
1960 "Abused young children seen in hospitals." Journal of Social Work 3(October): 98–102.
Felder, Samuel
1971 "A lawyer's view of child abuse." Public Welfare 29: 181–188.
Folks, Homer
1902 The Case of the Destitute, Neglected and Delinquent Children. New York: Macmillan.
Fontana, V., D. Donovan and R. Wong
1963 "The maltreatment syndrome in children." New England Journal of Medicine. 269(December): 1389–1394.
Fox, Sanford J.
1970 "Juvenile justice reform: an historical perspective." Stanford Law Review 22(June): 1187–1239.
Freidson, Eliot J.
1968 "Medical personnel: physicians." Pp. 105–114 in David L. Sills (ed.), International Encyclopedia of the Social Sciences. Vol. 10. New York: Macmillan.
1971 The Profession of Medicine: A Study in the Sociology of Applied Knowledge. New York: Dodd, Mead and Co.
Gil, David
1970 Violence Against Children. Cambridge, Mass.: Harvard University Press.
Gil, David and John H. Noble
1969 "Public knowledge, attitudes and opinions about physical child abuse." Child welfare 49(July): 395–401.

Giovannoni, Jeanne
 1971 "Parental mistreatment." Journal of Marriage and the Family 33(November): 649–657.
Glaser, William A.
 1960 "Doctors and politics." American Journal of Sociology 66(November); 230–245.
Goode, William J.
 1957 "Community within a community: the profession." American Sociological Review 22(April): 194–200.
 1971 "Force and violence in the family." Journal of Marriage and the Family 33(November): 424–436.
Grumet, Barbara R.
 1970 "The plaintive plaintiffs: victims of the battered child syndrome." Family Law Quarterly 4(September): 296–317.
Gusfield, Joseph R.
 1963 Symbolic Crusade. Urbana, Ill.: University of Illinois Press.
Gwinn, J. J., K. W. Lewin and H. G. Peterson
 1961 "Roetenographic manifestations of unsuspected trauma in infancy." Journal of the American Medical Association 181(June): 17–24.
Hall, Jerome
 1952 Theft, Law and Society. Indianapolis: Bobbs-Merrill Co.
Hall, Oswald
 1946 "The informal organization of medicine." Canadian Journal of Economics and Political Science 12(February): 30–41.
Hyde, D. R., P. Wolff, A. Gross and E. L. Hoffman
 1954 "The American Medical Association: power, purpose and politics in organized medicine." Yale Law Journal 63(May): 938–1022.
Kadushin, Alfred
 1967 Child Welfare Services. New York. Macmillan.
Kempe, C. H., F. N. Silverman, B. F. Steele, W. Droegemuller and H. K. Silver
 1962 "The battered-child syndrome." Journal of the American Medical Association. 181(July): 17–24.
Lemert, Edwin M.
 1974 "Beyond Mead: the societal reaction to deviance." Social Problems 21(April): 457–467.
McCoid, A. H.
 1965 "The battered child syndrome and other assaults upon the family." Minnesota Law Review 50(November): 1–58.
Paulsen, Monrad G.
 1966 "The legal framework for child protection." Columbia Law Review 66(April): 679–717.
 1967 "Child abuse reporting laws: the shape of the legislation." Columbia Law Review 67(January): 1–49.
Philips, Bernard S.
 1964 "Expected value deprivation and occupational preference." Sociometry 27(June): 15–160.

Platt, Anthony M.
   1969   The Child Savers: The Invention of Juvenile Delinquency. Chicago: University of Chicago Press.
Quinney, Richard
   1970   The Social Reality of Crime. Boston: Little Brown.
Radbill, Samuel X.
   1968   "A history of child abuse and infanticide." Pp. 3–17 in Ray E. Helfer and Henry C. Kempe (eds.), The Battered Child. Chicago: University of Chicago Press.
Rothman, David J.
   1971   The Discovery of the Asylum: Social Order and Disorder in the New Republic. Boston: Little Brown.
Shepard, Robert E.
   1965   "The abused child and the law." Washington and Lee Law Review 22(Spring): 182–195.
Silverman, F. N.
   1965   "The roentgen manifestation of unrecognized skeletal trauma in infants." American Journal of Roentgenology, Radium and Nuclear Medicine 69(March): 413–426.
Skonick, Arlene and Jerome H. Skolnick
   1971   The Family in Transition. Boston: Little Brown.
Steele, Brandt and Carl F. Pollock
   1968   "A psychiatric study of parents who abuse infants and small children." Pp. 103–147 in Ray E. Helfer and Henry C. Kempe (eds.), The Battered Child. Chicago: University of Chicago Press.
Sutherland, Edwin H.
   1950   "The diffusion of sexual psychopath laws." American Journal of Sociology 56(September): 142–148.
Thomas, Mason P.
   1972   "Child abuse and neglect: historical overview, legal matrix and social perspectives." North Carolina Law Review 50(February): 293–349.
Woolley, P. V. and W. A. Evans Jr.
   1955   "Significance of skeletal lesions in infants resembling those of traumatic origin." Journal of the American Medical Association 158(June): 539–543.
Young, Leontine
   1964   Wednesday's Children: A Study of Child Neglect and Abuse. New York: McGraw-Hill.
Zalba, Serapio R.
   1966   "The abused child. I. A survey of the problems." Social Work 11(October): 3–16.

5 / The Manufacture of Witches

THOMAS S. SZASZ

> . . . was there ever any domination which did not appear natural to those who possessed it?
>
> —*John Stuart Mill*[1]

The concept of mental illness is analogous to that of witchcraft. In the fifteenth century, men believed that some persons were witches, and that some acts were due to witchcraft. In the twentieth century, men believe that some people are insane, and that some acts are due to mental illness. Nearly a decade ago, I tried to show that the concept of mental illness has the same logical and empirical status as the concept of witchcraft; in short, that witchcraft and mental illness are imprecise and all-encompassing concepts, freely adaptable to whatever uses the priest or physician (or lay "diagnostician") wishes to put them.[2] Now I propose to show that the concept of mental illness serves the same social function in the modern world as did the concept of witchcraft in the late Middle Ages; in short, that the belief in mental illness and the social actions to which it leads have the same moral implications and political consequences as had the belief in witchcraft and the social actions to which it led.

Henry Sigerist, dean of American medical historians, has written that "In the changing attitude towards witchcraft, modern psychiatry was born as a medical discipline."[3] This view has been interpreted to mean that people thought to be witches were actually mentally sick, and that instead of being persecuted for heresy they should have been treated for insanity.

Although I agree with Sigerist and other medical historians that psychiatry developed as the persecution of witches declined and disappeared, my explanation differs radically from theirs. They say it happened because of the gradual realization that persons supposed to be heretics were actually mentally sick. I say it happened because of the transformation of a religious ideology into a scientific one: medicine replaced theology; the alienist, the inquisitor; and the insane, the witch. The result was the substitution of a medical massmovement for a religious one, the persecution of mental patients replacing the persecution of heretics.

Men who believed in witchcraft created witches by ascribing this role to others, and sometimes even to themselves. In this way they literally manufactured witches whose existence as social objects then proved the reality of witchcraft. To claim that witchcraft and witches did not exist does not mean, of course, that the personal conduct exhibited by alleged witches or the social disturbances attributed to them did not exist. In the days of the witch-hunts, there were, indeed, people who disturbed or upset others—for example, men whose religious beliefs and practices differed from those of the majority, or women who, as midwives, assisted at the delivery of stillborn infants. Such men and women were often accused of witchcraft and persecuted as witches. The point is that *these* witches did not choose the role of witch; they were defined and treated as witches against their will; in short, the role was *ascribed* to them. As far as the accused witches were concerned—they would have elected, had they been given a choice, to be left alone by the holders of Church and State power.

To be sure, once the social role of witch had been established by the irresistible combination of authoritative opinion, widespread propaganda, and popular credulity, it happened occasionally that people claimed to be witches. They declared that they experienced the ideas and feelings characteristic of witches; and they openly proclaimed their deviant status to gain their particular ends (which might have been to impart meaning to their lives or to commit a kind of indirect suicide). *These* witches chose the role they were playing; they were defined and treated as witches voluntarily; in short, they *assumed* the role of witch.

In the past, men created witches; now they create mental patients. But, again, it is important to keep in mind that to claim that mental diseases and insane patients do not exist does not mean that the personal conduct exhibited by persons classified as mentally sick, or certain kinds of social disturbances attributed to them, do not exist. In our day, there are, indeed, individuals who break the law, or flout the conventions of morality and society—for example, men who use heroin, or women who neglect their newborn infants. Such men and women are often accused of mental illness (by being classified as "addicts" or "post-partum psychotics"), and persecuted as mental patients (by means of involuntary hospitalization and treatment).* The point is that *these* mental patients do not choose the role of mental

---

*The mental patient, especially if so defined against his will, is perhaps best viewed as a "deviant," either of society as a whole, or of a smaller group, typically the family. The individual who differs from his peers, who disturbs or scandalizes his family or society, is often branded as insane; sometimes he need not even play a deviant role but is declared mad nevertheless. Such psychiatric derogation fulfills important needs for the "mentally healthy" members of the group.

patient; they are defined and treated as mental patients against their will; in short, the role is *ascribed* to them. As far as the accused mental patients are concerned—they would elect, were they given a choice, to be left alone by the holders of Medical and State power.

In other words, if our aim is to see things clearly, rather than to confirm popular beliefs and justify accepted practices, then we must sharply distinguish three related but distinct classes of phenomena: first, *events* and *behaviors*, such as the birth of a stillborn baby, or a mother's rejection of her healthy infant; second, their *explanations* by means of religious or medical concepts, such as witchcraft or mental illness; third, their *social control*, justified by the religious or medical explanations, utilizing theological or therapeutic interventions, such as burning witches at the stake or hospitalizing the insane against their will.

One may accept the reality of an event or a behavior, but reject its generally accepted explanation and methods of social control. Indeed, the most passionate disputes in both religion and science have centered not on whether or not particular events were real, but on whether or not their explanations were true and the actions used to suppress them good. The true believers in witchcraft thus maintained that human problems were caused by witches and that burning them at the stake was good; whereas those opposed to this theory regarded the explanation as false and the measures justified by it as evil. The true believers in mental illness similarly maintain that human problems are caused by madmen and that incarcerating them in mental hospitals is good; whereas those opposed to this theory regard the explanation as false and the measures justified by it as evil.*

The social role of mental patient having been established by the still irresistible combination of authoritative opinion, widespread propaganda, and popular credulity, it happens occasionally that people claim to be mentally ill. They say that they experience the ideas and feelings characteristic of mentally ill persons; and they openly proclaim their deviant status to gain their particular ends (which might be to escape military service or some other obligation or to injure themselves and their families). Of course, individuals may also define themselves as mentally ill in order to secure the psychiatric

---

*Since people abhor unexplained events and unsolved problems, they tend to embrace blindly—rather than examine critically and, if necessary, reject—global explanations, such as those of witchcraft and mental illness. No doubt this is why the belief in witchcraft and the remedial practices of the Theological State were not simply abandoned, but were replaced by the belief in madness and the remedial practices of the Therapeutic State. The mythology of mental illness and the repressive measures it justifies will perhaps also not be abandoned until they can be replaced by another belief system and a social institution based on it. Let us hope that the change, when it comes, will be an improvement.

assistance they need and want. As a rule, such persons know that they are not physically ill and that their illness is metaphoric. They assume the role of mental patient as the price they must pay to obtain the services of an expert whose clients are socially defined in this way. The concept of mental illness is, however, neither necessary nor useful for the practice of contractual psychotherapy.[4] Indeed, "psychotherapy patients" are often "treated" by nonmedical therapists, such as psychologists and social workers. *Most of what is written in this book does not pertain to these patients, their therapists, or to the relationship between them.*

Although individuals occasionally assumed the role of witch voluntarily, in historical studies of the witch-hunts it is rightly taken for granted that the witch was cast into her role involuntarily, and that the institution responsible for her situation was the Inquisition. I shall proceed similarly in the present study. Although individuals occasionally assume the role of mental patient voluntarily, I shall presume that the mental patient is cast into his role involuntarily, and that the organization responsible for his situation is Institutional Psychiatry. To clearly distinguish between the voluntary and involuntary patient, I usually refer to the victim of the psychiatric relationship as the "involuntary patient," to his oppressor as the "institutional psychiatrist," and to the system authorizing and embodying their interaction as "Institutional Psychiatry."

The most important economic characteristic of Institutional Psychiatry is that the institutional psychiatrist is a bureaucratic employee, paid for his services by a private or public organization (not by the individual who is his ostensible client); its most important social characteristic is the use of force and fraud. In addition to the commitment procedure and the long-term incarceration of the "insane," the interventions of the institutional psychiatrist include such diverse measures as the examination of defendants to determine their sanity or fitness to stand trial, of employees to determine their fitness for a job, of applicants to college, medical school, or psychoanalytic institutes to determine their suitability for admission to these institutions, of the histories of deceased persons to determine their "testamentary capacity," and so forth.[5] Psychiatrists employed by state mental hospitals, college health services, military organizations, courts, prisons, and others in similar positions are, according to this definition, institutional psychiatrists.

The most important economic characteristic of Contractual Psychiatry is that the contractual psychiatrist is a private entrepreneur, paid for his services by his client; its most important social characteristic is the avoidance of force and fraud (and the existence of legal penalties for their use). The relationship between contractual psychiatrist and patient is <u>based on contract, freely entered into by both,</u> and, <u>in general, freely terminable by both</u> (except where the therapist relinquishes some of his options in this regard). The contract consists of an exchange of psychiatric services for money.[6] In short, <u>whereas the institutional psychiatrist imposes himself on his "patients," who do not pay him, do not want to be his patients, and are not free to reject his "help"</u>—the contractual psychiatrist offers himself to his patients, <u>who must pay him, must want to be his patients, and are free to reject his help.</u>

<u>Like the typical European witch in the fifteenth century, the typical American mental patient today is usually a poor person in trouble or accused of making trouble, who is declared mentally ill against his will.</u> Such a person may accept the role <u>or may try to repudiate it; the institutional psychiatrist confronted with him may try to keep him confined in his role, and perhaps in a hospital, for a long time,</u> or may release him after a relatively brief period of incarceration. In any case, the psychiatric authorities are in full control of the relationship.

For an illustration of the way being poor and unwanted predisposes a person to being cast into the role of mental patient, the following example, culled at random from the newspapers, should suffice. "Attorneys representing welfare clients testified . . . before the State Board of Social Welfare that 'on six or seven occasions within the past two years, relief recipients who threatened trouble for [New York] city Department of Welfare caseworkers were sent to Bellevue psychiatric ward.' "[7]

For an illustration of the way being accused of troublemaking predisposes a person to being cast into the role of mental patient, consider these examples. In 1964, a total of 1,437 individuals "under complaint or indictment before the criminal courts of Massachusetts were committed . . . for pretrial observation of their mental status."[8] In plain English, 1,437 persons were treated—for a shorter or longer time—as if they were mentally sick, simply because they had been charged with an offense. This is about double the number so committed eight years earlier. Moreover, of the 1,437 persons committed for temporary observation (usually for two months), 224, or about one sixth, were recommitted for an indefinite period of incarceration. In 1964, in the Manhattan Criminal Court alone, 1,388 defendants were committed for pretrial psychiatric examinations; of these, one fourth were recommitted for an indefinite period of incarceration.[9]

<u>I cite these reports</u> *not* <u>as examples of the unfortunate abuses of the mental hospital system in need of correction by an enlightened citizenry, but rather as characteristic</u> examples of a pervasive psychiatric pattern of harassment, intimidation, and degradation, authenti-

cating the right of certain social authorities to cast individuals, especially from the lower socioeconomic classes, into the role of mental patient. To maintain that a social institution suffers from certain "abuses" is to imply that it has certain other desirable or good uses. This, in my opinion, has been the fatal weakness of the countless exposés—old and recent, literary and professional—of private and public mental hospitals.[10] My thesis is quite different: Simply put, it is that there are, and can be, no abuses of Institutional Psychiatry, because Institutional Psychiatry *is*, itself, an abuse; similarly, there were, and could be, no abuses *of* the Inquisition, because the Inquisition was, itself, an abuse. Indeed, just as the Inquisition *was* the characteristic abuse of Christianity, so Institutional Psychiatry is the characteristic abuse of Medicine.

In other words, it is reasonable and useful to speak of the uses and abuses of such complex human enterprises as Religion and Medicine (or Science and Law). But it is unreasonable and misleading to speak of the uses and abuses of institutions (whether they be religious, medical, political, or still other) which, because of their characteristic and indispensable methods, we deem incompatible with our standards of human decency and morality. Clearly, what is compatible or incompatible with one's standard of human decency or morality varies from time to time and from person to person. While it flourished, the Inquisition did not offend the sensibilities of most people—though individually men did all they could to stay out of its clutches. In the same way, Institutional Psychiatry does not now offend the sensibilities of most people—though individually men do all they can to stay out of its clutches.

Resting squarely on the moral judgment that Institutional Psychiatry *is* an abuse of both the human personality and the healing relationship, I want it to be clearly understood that in describing its operations, I shall be illustrating its uses, not its abuses. I shall thus try to show that if Institutional Psychiatry is harmful to the so-called mental patient, this is not because it is liable to abuse, but rather because harming persons categorized as insane is its essential function: Institutional Psychiatry is, as it were, designed to protect and uplift the group (the family, the State), by persecuting and degrading the individual (as insane or ill).

Although I have used the sociological approach to deviance in this study, I have, whenever possible, avoided calling witches and mental patients "deviants." Words have lives of their own. However much sociologists insist that the term• "deviant" does not diminish the worth of the person or group so categorized, the implication of inferiority adheres to the word. Indeed, sociologists are not wholly exempt from blame: They describe addicts and homosexuals as deviants, but never Olympic champions or Nobel Prize winners. In fact, the term is rarely applied to people with admired characteristics, such as great wealth, superior skills, or fame—whereas it is often applied to those with despised characteristics, such as poverty, lack of marketable skills, or infamy.

For this reason, I repudiate the tacit assumption inherent in designating mental patients as deviants: that, because such persons differ, or are alleged to differ, from the majority, they are *ipso facto* sick, bad, stupid, or wrong, whereas the majority are healthy, good, wise, or right. The term "social deviants" for individuals incriminated as mentally ill is unsatisfactory for another reason: it does not make sufficiently explicit—as the terms "scapegoat" or "victim" do—that majorities usually categorize persons or groups as "deviant" in order to set them apart as inferior beings and to justify their social control, oppression, persecution, or even complete destruction.

Roles, it is well to remember, are social artifacts. Role-deviance, therefore, has meaning only in the context of specific social customs and laws. The criminal is deviant because he breaks the law; the homosexual because most people are heterosexuals; the atheist because most people believe, or say they believe, in God. Although departure from a statistical norm of behavior is an important criterion of social deviance, it is not the only criterion. A person may be considered deviant not only because his conduct differs from a socially observed norm, but also because it differs from a morally professed ideal. Thus, although a happy marriage is probably more the exception than the rule, the unmarried or unhappily married person is often considered psychologically abnormal and socially deviant. In earlier days, when masturbation was no doubt just as prevalent as it is at present, psychiatrists considered the practice both a symptom and a cause of insanity.

Social deviance is thus a term naming a vast category. Which kinds of social deviance are regarded as mental illnesses? The answer is, those that entail personal conduct not conforming to psychiatrically defined and enforced rules of mental health. If narcotics-avoidance is a rule of mental health, narcotics ingestion will be a sign of mental illness; if even-temperedness is a rule of mental health, depression and elation will be signs of mental illness; and so forth.

However obvious this may be, its implications for our understanding of mental illness and Institutional Psychiatry are vastly unappreciated. The fact is that every time psychiatrists formulate a new rule of mental health, they create a new class of mentally sick individuals—just as every time legislators enact a new restrictive law, they create a fresh category of criminals.

Notes

1. John Stuart Mill, *The Subjection of Women*, p. 229.
2. Thomas S. Szasz, *The Myth of Mental Illness*.
3. Henry Sigerist, Introduction, in Gregory Zilboorg, *The Medical Man and the Witch During the Renaissance*, pp. ix-x.
4. See Thomas S. Szasz, *The Ethics of Psychoanalysis*.
5. See Thomas S. Szasz, *Law, Liberty, and Psychiatry*, and *Psychiatric Justice*.
6. See Thomas S. Szasz: Psychotherapy: A sociocultural perspective, *Comprehensive Psychiat.*, 7: 217–223 (Aug.), 1966.
7. John P. Callahan, Welfare clients called coerced, *New York Times*, July 22, 1967, p. 22.
8. A. Louis McGarry, Competency for trial and due process via the state mental hospital. *Amer. J. Psychiat.*, 122: 623–630 (Dec.), 1965.
9. Edith E. Asbury, Faster mental examinations ordered for defendants here, *New York Times*, July 8, 1967, p. 26.
10. For a sampling, see Anton Pavlovich Chekhov, Ward No. 6, in *Seven Short Stories by Chekhov*, pp. 106–157; Mary Jane Ward, *The Snake Pit;* Frank L. Wright, Jr., *Out of Sight, Out of Mind;* Lois Wille, The mental health clinic, Expressway to asylum, *Chicago Daily News*, Mar. 26, 1962; 11 times 12? Youth flunks mental exam, ibid., Mar. 27, 1962; Misfiled card saves salesman from mental hospital, ibid., Mar. 28, 1962; Why refugee asked for ticket to Russia, ibid., Mar. 29, 1962; S. J. Micciche, Bridgewater holds colony of lost men, *Boston Globe*, Feb. 20, 1963; Some jailed 40 years for truancy, ibid.; Consultant psychiatrist, The scandal of the British mental hospital, *Manchester Guardian*, Mar. 19, 1965; Norman Shrapnel, Mental hospitals disclosures appall MP, ibid., Mar. 20, 1965; Sylvia Wilson, The Cinderellas (Letters), ibid., Mar. 30, 1965; D. J. Harvey, Typical conditions (Letters), ibid., March 30, 1965.

Part 2 / Understanding Deviance: Theories and Perspectives

    In Part 1 I introduced a specific concern for the ways in which deviant categories arise, as well as the ways in which violators of existing categories may be reacted to. Missing from this introduction was a concern for *why* actors may exhibit behavior in violation of established norms, rules, regulations, and laws—violations that may ultimately result in their being initially labeled as deviants. I have argued previously that if we are to approach a more complete understanding of deviance in terms of social processes, we not only must analyze the creation of deviant categories and the reactions to violators of categories; we must also examine the motivations for deviance. The selections in this part represent some of the major attempts to do so.

    Explanations of the motivations for deviance have taken various forms. Some observers would place the blame on a defective family structure or arrested personality adjustment; others would emphasize such conditions as poverty or racism; and there are proponents of the thesis that individuals are born deviant. It should be recognized, however, that no single factor can adequately explain why actors commit deviant acts. For example, what we generally find in the area of delinquency research is that a combination of family, school, and peer variables seems to make the most sense in providing motivations for youth crime and deviance.

    The actual attempts at understanding or explaining can, for our purposes, be roughly grouped into seven categories: (1) functionalist, (2) culture conflict, (3) cultural transmission, (4) anomie, (5) conflict theory, (6) control-commitment, and (7) interactionist. Of these particular approaches, it should be noted that functionalism, culture conflict, control-commitment theory, and anomie are basically structural. Some who use this model seek to explain why crime and deviance exist in the social system, while others analyze societal-structural conditions that seem to produce pressures toward deviation. The cultural transmission view is concerned primarily with how, through social-psychological-symbolic processes, actors learn existing cultures and traditions. The conflict theorists, by contrast, investigate how the powerful influence the creation of deviant categories, and point out, as well, the frequent application of such categories to the less powerful. Finally, the interactionists analyze the labeling ceremony and its impact on individuals. While each of the above approaches explicitly emphasizes certain underlying themes, concepts, or processes, there is frequently an implied or direct overlap among the various models. Such linkages are evident in the discussions of each model that follows.

The Functionalist Perspective

Social scientists who use a functionalist model contend that deviance is an integral part of any social system and that such behavior satisfies some societal need. In terms of sociological analysis, advocates of this model maintain that deviance serves the important function of demarcating and maintaining current boundaries of acceptable behavior. These particular conceptions are embedded in Emile Durkheim's work.

In his statement "The Normal and the Pathological," Durkheim argues that crime not only is present in all societies but serves a useful function for the collective conscience, particularly in maintaining the social system. And while forms and definitions of criminal and deviant behavior (i.e., the *collective types* or deviant categories) may vary from society to society, such behaviors do provide members with a basis for punishing violators of the prevailing normative codes. Punishment serves as an important reminder to others that certain behaviors are acceptable while others are not. Thus, achievement of an understanding of deviance and its categories requires an examination of the prevailing definitions of conformity.

A somewhat similar position has been advanced by Robert A. Dentler and Kai T. Erikson. In "The Functions of Deviance in Groups," they focus on social groups, especially with regard to the way in which deviance affects groupings or collectivities. They postulate that (1) groups tend to induce, sustain, and permit deviant behavior; (2) deviant behavior functions in enduring groups to help maintain group equilibrium; and (3) groups will resist any trend toward alienation of a member whose behavior is deviant. Dentler and Erikson attempt to substantiate their propositions by analyzing Quaker work projects and Army basic training units. One gains an understanding, from their study, of the ways in which various types of deviant activity actually affect group stability and maintenance.

It should be noted that Durkheim, and Dentler and Erikson, make no real attempt to explain why actors engage in activities that may result in their being labeled as deviants. The next perspective, however, considers the question of motivation more directly; in so doing, it enters the realm of social-psychological, or interactional, processes, particularly those aspects concerned with the inculcation of values and traditions within members of a society.

The Culture Conflict Perspective

A basic premise underlying this perspective is the notion that, because socializing influences and experiences vary a great deal, people are frequently confronted with conflicting definitions of a situation. Furthermore, if they act in accordance with their own values, they may be defined as deviants by those who are operating from a different set of values.

These ideas are elaborated upon by Thorsten Sellin. In "The Conflict of Conduct Norms," he argues that actors are members of numerous groups and are, therefore, exposed to many different sets of conduct norms and values. Among those who migrate from one society to another, the sense of cultural conflict may be particularly severe. Migrants frequently find themselves constrained and regulated by a new and unfamiliar set of values. Sellin cites, as an example, the case in which a father kills the seducer of his daughter. In Sicily, killing a seducer is acceptable; in the United States it is considered murder. A lack of consensus with respect to existing norms, then, not only may give rise to cultural conflicts of various types but may result in the application of deviant labels to those who violate deviant categories.

J. Mark Watson, in "Outlaw Motorcyclists: An Outgrowth of Lower Class Cultural Concerns," provides another illustration of the culture conflict model. Watson focuses on outlaw motorcyclists—a subculture that he, as a participant-observer, studied over a period of three years. He initially describes the biker subculture and the associated outlaw lifestyle. Of interest are the ways in which the outlaw bikers view the world and themselves. Not only do they tend to see the world as "hostile, weak, and effeminate," but they also generally view themselves as "outsiders." Watson concludes with an analysis of how the biker subculture, in its operation, compares with a typology of "focal concerns" (e.g., the emphasis that is placed on "trouble," "toughness," "smartness," and "excitement") developed by Walter Miller. For example, trouble not only is a major theme but serves important functions for the group (e.g., it provides an opportunity for demonstrating masculinity and helps to enforce group solidarity). The selection gives an excellent feel for how a particular subculture operates in a larger, dominant culture—a culture that possesses the power and resources to tag people as "outsiders."

Cultural Transmission Theory

A central tenet underlying the cultural transmission model is the idea that one learns cultural traditions and values through symbolic communication with others. Probably the most famous representatives of this position are Edwin H. Sutherland and Donald R. Cressey.

In "Differential Association Theory," they seek to explain the ways in which deviant, and particularly criminal, behavior arises. Central to their analysis is the notion that as we learn to become conformists, we must also learn to become criminals. Basic to this learning process is the concept of social interaction, whereby actors, relating to one another in small, intimate groups, become socialized into the ways of the existing cultures and traditions. As part of socialization, one may learn that violation of the law is unacceptable, or one may be taught that it is acceptable, even desirable. Sutherland and Cressey argue that it is those individuals who have learned that violation is acceptable who will engage in criminal activities. Another important point concerns the *content* of learning. Individuals learn not only the appropriate "motives, drives, rationalizations, and attitudes" for committing crimes but the specific techniques for doing so.

The next selection, by Gresham M. Sykes and David Matza, also relates directly to cultural transmission theory, especially to those aspects dealing with the content of learning—that is, definitions of legal codes and rationalizations. In "Techniques of Neutralization: A Theory of Delinquency," Sykes and Matza argue that juveniles do not really reject middle-class values. Rather, because the existing normative structure has a certain flexibility, actors can "bend" the laws to fit their needs. Also basic to this thesis is the idea that when actors contemplate the commission of a delinquent or criminal act, they must come to grips with any immediate or potential threats to their identity. Developing an effective system of "neutralization" or rationalization is one way of accomplishing this. Sykes and Matza assert, moreover, that an attitude of self-justification is necessary not only before the commission of the offense; rationalization is operative during and after the act as well. The writers make the additional point that we all use rationalizations, whether we are involved in deviant activities or not.

Several of the articles discussed thus far (e.g., the one by Sutherland and Cressey) have been concerned rather directly with the way in which socialization processes may bring about behavior that can be labeled as deviant. However, with one notable exception (Watson's theory), none of these writers has systematically examined the conditions that may lead to an exploration of nonconformist adaptations. The next perspective offers a more specific attempt to do so.

Anomie or Opportunity Theory

Those who subscribe to anomie theory are concerned primarily with the social conditions that may produce a strain toward deviation. Of particular focus is the way actors posture themselves relative to the existing social structure. Robert K. Merton's article "Social Structure and Anomie" represents what many consider the classic study, within anomie theory, of the emergence of deviant behavior.

Basic to Merton's explanation is the contention that any society can be characterized in terms of its structure, particularly its goals and its means. A well-integrated society, he reasons, displays a balance between these elements. In such a society, when people want to obtain societal goals, they will use the appropriate institutionalized means for doing so. American society, according to Merton, does not maintain this sort of balance. It is a society in which emphasis is placed almost exclusively on the achievement of goals—regardless of the methods used to attain them. Those affected the most by the imbalance are the *lower classes.* Most members of the lower classes accept the American dream of attaining success; when they attempt to realize their goals through legitimate means, however, they find themselves blocked, mainly because they do not possess the necessary resources. They may substitute other means—for instance, stealing or robbing. Merton refers to these individuals as "innovators." He argues, further, that when there is a disjunction between goals and means, the result may be cultural chaos, or *anomie.* In this situation, predictability and regulation of behavior become tenuous.

Richard A. Cloward and Lloyd E. Ohlin, in "Differential Opportunity and Delinquent Subcultures," extend Merton's theory by incorporating the notion of *illegitimate opportunity structures;* they also make a significant contribution to the literature on the formation of deviant subcultures. The authors argue specifically that, just as there are differentials in access to legitimate means (Merton), so there are differentials in access to illegitimate means (Sutherland and Cressey). What this means is that illegitimate avenues are not necessarily open or freely available to those unable to obtain goals through legitimate channels. Not everyone, for instance, can become a successful con artist or embezzler. Cloward and Ohlin substantiate their thesis by showing how status-deprived, lower-class males learn the necessary skills associated with a particular type of criminal activity. Whether a specific activity or subculture evolves, however, is a function of the existing structure of the neighborhood, especially the relative availability of legitimate and illegitimate opportunity structures. For example, in a setting that exhibits a high degree of integration, or interplay, between legitimate and illegitimate structures, a criminal subculture is likely to evolve. Such a subculture furnishes the deprived with a source of material gain and provides them with a setting in which they can become socialized into the ways of an existing culture and traditions.

Although several of the statements thus far have offered hypotheses as to why deviance exists in a social system—and why actors commit deviant acts—none has provided an overall framework that can be used to understand how deviant categories arise, why they are violated, and how they are enforced. (The major exception is Becker's general statement in Part 1.) The next perspective addresses these concerns in a more systematic, integrated manner.

Conflict Theory

Conflict theorists study groups, particularly the ways in which their interests and needs influence the definitions, laws, and policies that evolve. William J. Chambliss, in "A Sociological Analysis of the Law of Vagrancy," provides an interesting account of how selected vagrancy laws came into being. He focuses initially on those social conditions that produced the first full-fledged vagrancy law. This statute, passed in England in 1349, was a partial outgrowth of the Black Death that struck England in 1348. Probably the most significant economic effect produced by this pestilence was the decimation of the labor force. Not only did at least 50 percent of the population die but, and equally important, the English economy was dependent on a cheap source of labor. Even prior to the Black Death, obtaining an adequate supply of cheap labor was becoming a problem. It was in conditions such as these that the first vagrancy laws emerged. Chambliss maintains that the statutes were actually designed for one express purpose: to force laborers to accept employment under conditions favorable to the landowners. The laws also effectively curtailed the geographical mobility of laborers. In time, such curtailment was no longer necessary. However, the statutes were not eliminated or negated; rather, they underwent some notable alterations. For example, a modification passed in England in 1530 shifted society's focus from laborers to criminals. Chambliss ends by presenting a general discussion of vagrancy laws in the United States—many of which are adoptions of English laws.

Jeffrey H. Reiman, in "A Radical Perspective on Crime," offers another, more contemporary statement on the conflict model. Like Chambliss, he maintains that laws and the associated criminal justice system operate in such a manner as to support the established social and economic order. Concentrating on the individual wrongdoer, Reiman argues, is a particularly effective way of attaining this end. By blaming the individual, the criminal justice system not only diverts our attention away from the possible evils of the social order but acquits society of any criminality or injustice. Further, Reiman argues that various types of social arrangements actually sustain and benefit from the perpetuation of the ideology of individual failure or blame. Reiman uses portions of Cloward and Ohlin's theory to buttress his case. For example, even though people are encouraged to succeed, many do fail, and especially those from the lower classes. As Reiman puts it: ". . . many are called but few are chosen." Involvement in criminal activities does offer an outlet for those experiencing failure and frustration. Thus, not only is society structured in such a way as to actually produce crime, but those who "reap the benefits of the competition for success" (i.e., those who enjoy a high standard of living) do not have to pay for the costs of this competition. The bill is paid for by the poor. In fact, the affluent, Reiman argues, deny that they benefit from an economic system that produces a high degree of suffering and frustration for the poor.

This bias against the poor is also manifested in other ways. Reiman speaks specifically of the bonuses associated with such a bias. For example, an image is conveyed that the real threat to a decent society comes from the poor. Another important bonus for the powerful is that the bias generates persistent hostility toward the poor. Reiman then notes some of the indignities that the poor suffer at the hands of the welfare system and its agents. Aid, instead of being viewed as an act of justice, is perceived as an act of charity. Many of these points, I might add, will be elaborated on in Part 6, particularly in my discussion of the need to rehabilitate institutions and social systems.

Control-Commitment Theory

A central feature of control theory is the view that various levels and types of societal commitment, when coupled with other factors, are often important precursors to the commission of deviant acts. Scott Briar and Irving Piliavin offer a representative statement of this position.

In "Delinquency, Situational Inducements, and Commitment to

Conformity," Briar and Piliavin argue that most juvenile crime is sporadic in nature, as are most of the situationally induced stimuli. Whether youth deviance emerges or not is a function of an individual's degree and type of commitment relative to impinging stimuli. The actor must also evaluate the risk element—that is, consequences which may result from the commission of a delinquent act. Thus the potential deviant (or delinquent actor) must weigh the situationally induced stimuli, his or her commitments, and the risk element. Throughout, Briar and Piliavin not only generally underscore the problematic nature of predicting involvement in deviance; they also give the actor central theoretical focus. It is he or she who must assess the situation. The model developed by these writers suggests several interesting possibilities with respect to predicting motivation. How, for example, will a juvenile with a low stake in conformity respond to peer pressure to commit an illegal act, particularly when the assessed risk element is low? How would the youth with a high stake in conformity respond? As an illustration, what we frequently find in the area of delinquency research is that juveniles with a low degree of school commitment—independent of such selection factors as sex, class, and race—are more apt to become involved in youth deviance and crime; they are also more likely to drop out or become truant.

Travis Hirschi, in "A Control Theory of Delinquency," provides another statement on control theory. Like Briar and Piliavin, he notes that control theorists assume that delinquency will result when an actor's bond to society is weakened or broken. He then proceeds to discuss and analyze the various elements that comprise the bond of society, particularly as they relate to the question of motivation. For example, the "commitment" element—the major component of Briar and Piliavin's perspective—refers to the idea that most people invest a great deal of time and energy in conventional lines of activity (e.g., educational and occupational pursuits). When deviant behavior is contemplated, the risks of such deviation must be considered. The guiding assumption is that involvement in deviance or crime would jeopardize one's investments. Hirschi concludes with a section on "belief," another major element of the bond to society. The underlying premise is that society is characterized by a common value system. If this is correct—and if, further, one retains some type of allegiance to established values—then a basic question presents itself: "Why does a man violate the rules in which he believes?" Hirschi, in his attempt to answer this question, rejects the view that an actor must rationalize or neutralize his or her behavior. Hirschi prefers, instead, the notion that the weakness of one's beliefs can be used to explain motivation. When a person's belief in the validity of norms is weakened, the probability of delinquency and deviance increases.

The last perspective to be considered in this section—the interactionist view—is not specifically concerned with the evolution of deviant categories or their violation. Rather, this model explores the ways in which people who violate deviant categories (for whatever reasons) are responded to by formal and informal agents of social control. In this respect, definitional and interactional processes are given central focus. As explicated and refined by the interactional and organizational paradigms in the general introduction, this perspective is applied systematically throughout the remainder of this volume.

The Interactionist, Societal Reactions, or Labeling Perspective

Individuals who subscribe to the interactionist, or labeling, school examine those social and psychological, or interactional, processes that take place among actors, audiences, and third parties, particularly in terms of their impact on the personal and social-public identity of the actor. The main concern of these proponents, then, is definitional processes and products, and their effects.

Edwin M. Lemert, in "Primary and Secondary Deviation," is concerned with the "sequence of interaction" that takes place between actors and audiences—especially those aspects that ultimately give rise to secondary or career deviance. Central to this process are the actor's perceptions and reactions to the negative social reactions he or she encounters. Quite often the actor's response to negative sanctions (or punishments) leads to the application of additional penalties. This type of reciprocal relationship, and its gradual deterioration, can reach the point at which the deviant actually accepts the imputed status or label. The acceptance of this particular status and associated label frequently results in other significant changes. The deviant may, for example, buy new clothes and change his or her speech, posture, and mannerisms to fit the new role.

Howard S. Becker has explored the concept of career, the major orienting focus of this volume, in some depth. He also introduces some important analytical distinctions. In "Career Deviance," he argues that public labeling is generally the most crucial step in building a long-term deviant career. Not only does being branded a deviant affect one's continued social participation, but it frequently produces notable changes in the actor's self-image. The most drastic change, however, seems to occur with respect to the actor's public identity—that is, how others view him or her. All of a sudden, in the eyes of others he or she has become a different person; this new status can be effectively referred to as a *master status*. In offering an important distinction between master and subordinate statuses, Becker argues that master statuses assume a certain priority and appear to override most other status considerations.

The status of a deviant is one such status. In relating to a deviant, people will frequently respond to the label and not to the individual. Treatment of an actor in this fashion—as if he or she is generally deviant and not specifically deviant—can serve as a self-fulfilling prophecy whereby attempts are made to mold the actor into the image others have of him or her. Deliberate attempts may be made, for example, to exclude the deviant from any meaningful social intercourse. The actor may respond negatively to such treatment, and, over time, exclusion and its associated reactions can actually give rise to more deviance. The treatment situation, Becker claims, is especially likely to produce such a result. Many of these processes, as well as those described by Lemert, will become even more evident in my discussion of the initiation and perpetuation of deviant careers, particularly those careers that are subject to institutional processing (Part 4).

functional

6 / The Normal and the Pathological

EMILE DURKHEIM

Crime is present not only in the majority of societies of one particular species but in all societies of all types. There is no society that is not confronted with the problem of criminality. Its form changes; the acts thus characterized are not the same everywhere; but, everywhere and always, there have been men who have behaved in such a way as to draw upon themselves penal repression. If, in proportion as societies pass from the lower to the higher types, the rate of criminality, i.e., the relation between the yearly number of crimes and the population, tended to decline, it might be believed that crime, while still normal, is tending to lose this character of normality. But we have no reason to believe that such a regression is substantiated. Many facts would seem rather to indicate a movement in the opposite direction. From the beginning of the [nineteenth] century, statistics enable us to follow the course of criminality. It has everywhere increased. In France the increase is nearly 300 per cent. There is, then, no phenomenon that presents more indisputably all the symptoms of normality, since it appears closely connected with the conditions of all collective life. To make of crime a form of social morbidity would be to admit that morbidity is not something accidental, but, on the contrary, that in certain cases it grows out of the fundamental constitution of the living organism; it would result in wiping out all distinction between the physiological and the pathological. No doubt it is possible that crime itself will have abnormal forms, as, for example, when its rate is unusually high. This excess is, indeed, undoubtedly morbid in nature. What is normal, simply, is the existence of criminality, provided that it attains and does not exceed, for each social type, a certain level, which it is perhaps not impossible to fix in conformity with the preceding rules.[1]

Here we are, then, in the presence of a conclusion in appearance quite paradoxical. Let us make no mistake. To classify crime among the phenomena of normal sociology is not to say merely that it is an inevitable, although regrettable phenomenon, due to the incorrigible wickedness of men; it is to affirm that it is a factor in public health, an integral part of all healthy societies. This result is, at first glance,

85

surprising enough to have puzzled even ourselves for a long time. Once this first surprise has been overcome, however, it is not difficult to find reasons explaining this normality and at the same time confirming it.

In the first place crime is normal because a society exempt from it is utterly impossible. Crime, we have shown elsewhere, consists of an act that offends certain very strong collective sentiments. In a society in which criminal acts are no longer committed, the sentiments they offend would have to be found without exception in all individual consciousnesses, and they must be found to exist with the same degree as sentiments contrary to them. Assuming that this condition could actually be realized, crime would not thereby disappear; it would only change its form, for the very cause which would thus dry up the sources of criminality would immediately open up new ones.

Indeed, for the collective sentiments which are protected by the penal law of a people at a specified moment of its history to take possession of the public conscience or for them to acquire a stronger hold where they have an insufficient grip, they must acquire an intensity greater than that which they had hitherto had. The community as a whole must experience them more vividly, for it can acquire from no other source the greater force necessary to control these individuals who formerly were the most refractory. For murderers to disappear, the horror of bloodshed must become greater in those social strata from which murderers are recruited; but, first it must become greater throughout the entire society. Moreover, the very absence of crime would directly contribute to produce this horror; because any sentiment seems much more respectable when it is always and uniformly respected.

One easily overlooks the consideration that these strong states of the common consciousness cannot be thus reinforced without reinforcing at the same time the more feeble states, whose violation previously gave birth to mere infraction of convention—since the weaker ones are only the prolongation, the attenuated form, of the stronger. Thus robbery and simple bad taste injure the same single altruistic sentiment, the respect for that which is another's. However, this same sentiment is less grievously offended by bad taste than by robbery; and since, in addition, the average consciousness has not sufficient intensity to react keenly to the bad taste, it is treated with greater tolerance. That is why the person guilty of bad taste is merely blamed, whereas the thief is punished. But, if this sentiment grows stronger, to the point of silencing in all consciousnesses the inclination which disposes man to steal, he will become more sensitive to the offenses which, until then, touched him but lightly. He will react against them, then, with more energy; they will be the object of greater opprobrium, which will transform certain of them from the simple moral faults that they were and give them the quality of crimes. For example, improper contracts, or contracts improperly executed, which only incur public blame or civil damages, will become offenses in law.

Imagine a society of saints, a perfect cloister of exemplary individuals. Crimes, properly so called, will there be unknown; but faults which appear venial to the layman will create there the same scandal that the ordinary offense does in ordinary consciousnesses. If, then, this society has the power to judge and punish, it will define these acts as criminal and will treat them as such. For the same reason, the perfect and upright man judges his smallest failings with a severity that the majority reserve for acts more truly in the nature of an offense. Formerly, acts of violence against persons were more frequent than they are today, because respect for individual dignity was less strong. As this has increased, these crimes have become more rare; and also, many acts violating this sentiment have been introduced into the penal law which were not included there in primitive times.[2]

In order to exhaust all the hypotheses logically possible, it will perhaps be asked why this unanimity does not extend to all collective sentiments without exception. Why should not even the most feeble sentiment gather enough energy to prevent all dissent? The moral consciousness of the society would be present in its entirety in all the individuals, with a vitality sufficient to prevent all acts offending it—the purely conventional faults as well as the crimes. But a uniformity so universal and absolute is utterly impossible; for the immediate physical milieu in which each one of us is placed, the hereditary antecedents, and the social influences vary from one individual to the next, and consequently diversify consciousnesses. It is impossible for all to be alike, if only because each one has his own organism and that these organisms occupy different areas in space. That is why, even among the lower peoples, where individual originality is very little developed, it nevertheless does exist.

Thus, since there cannot be a society in which the individuals do not differ more or less from the collective type, it is also inevitable that, among these divergences, there are some with a criminal character. What confers this character upon them is not the intrinsic quality of a given act but that definition which the collective conscience lends them. If the collective conscience is stronger, if it has enough authority practically to suppress these divergences, it will also be more sensitive, more exacting; and, reacting against the slightest deviations with the energy it otherwise displays only against more considerable infractions, it will attribute to them the same gravity as formerly to crimes. In other words, it will designate them as criminal.

Crime is, then, necessary; it is bound up with fundamental conditions of all social life, and by that very fact it is useful, because these conditions of which it is a part are themselves indispensable to the normal evolution of morality and law.

Indeed, it is no longer possible today to dispute the fact that law and morality vary from one social type to the next, nor that they change within the same type if the conditions of life are modified. But, in order that these transformations may be possible, the collective sentiments at the basis of morality must not be hostile to change, and consequently must have but moderate energy. If they were too strong, they would no longer be plastic. Every pattern is an obstacle to new patterns, to the extent that the first pattern is inflexible. The better a structure is articulated, the more it offers a healthy resistance to all modification; and this is equally true of functional, as of anatomical, organization. If there were no crimes, this condition could not have been fulfilled; for such a hypothesis presupposes that collective sentiments have arrived at a degree of intensity unexampled in history. Nothing is good indefinitely and to an unlimited extent. The authority which the moral conscience enjoys must not be excessive; otherwise no one would dare criticize it, and it would too easily congeal into an immutable form. To make progress, individual originality must be able to express itself. In order that the originality of the idealist whose dreams transcend his century may find expression, it is necessary that the originality of the criminal, who is below the level of his time, shall also be possible. One does not occur without the other.

Nor is this all. Aside from this indirect utility, it happens that crime itself plays a useful role in this evolution. Crime implies not only that the way remains open to necessary changes but that in certain cases it directly prepares these changes. Where crime exists, collective sentiments are sufficiently flexible to take on a new form, and crime sometimes helps to determine the form they will take. How many times, indeed, it is only an anticipation of future morality—a step toward what will be! According to Athenian law, Socrates was a criminal, and his condemnation was no more than just. However, his crime, namely, the independence of his thought, rendered a service not only to humanity but to his country. It served to prepare a new morality and faith which the Athenians needed, since the traditions by which they had lived until then were no longer in harmony with the current conditions of life. Nor is the case of Socrates unique; it is reproduced periodically in history. It would never have been possible to establish the freedom of thought we now enjoy if the regulations prohibiting it had not been violated before being solemnly abrogated. At that time, however, the violation was a crime, since it was an offense against sentiments still very keen in the average conscience.

And yet this crime was useful as a prelude to reforms which daily became more necessary. Liberal philosophy had as its precursors the heretics of all kinds who were justly punished by secular authorities during the entire course of the Middle Ages and until the eve of modern times.

From this point of view the fundamental facts of criminality present themselves to us in an entirely new light. Contrary to current ideas, the criminal no longer seems a totally unsociable being, a sort of parasitic element, a strange and unassimilable body, introduced into the midst of society.[3] On the contrary, he plays a definite role in social life. Crime, for its part, must no longer be conceived as an evil that cannot be too much suppressed. There is no occasion for self-congratulation when the crime rate drops noticeably below the average level, for we may be certain that this apparent progress is associated with some social disorder. Thus, the number of assault cases never falls so low as in times of want.[4] With the drop in the crime rate, and as a reaction to it, comes a revision, or the need of a revision in the theory of punishment. If, indeed, crime is a disease, its punishment is its remedy and cannot be otherwise conceived; thus, all the discussions it arouses bear on the point of determining what the punishment must be in order to fulfil this role of remedy. If crime is not pathological at all, the object of punishment cannot be to cure it, and its true function must be sought elsewhere.

Notes

1. From the fact that crime is a phenomenon of normal sociology, it does not follow that the criminal is an individual normally constituted from the biological and psychological points of view. The two questions are independent of each other. This independence will be better understood when we have shown, later on, the difference between psychological and sociological facts.

2. Calumny, insults, slander, fraud, etc.

3. We have ourselves committed the error of speaking thus of the criminal, because of a failure to apply our rule (*Division du travail social*, pp. 395–96).

4. Although crime is a fact of normal sociology, it does not follow that we must not abhor it. Pain itself has nothing desirable about it; the individual dislikes it as society does crime, and yet it is a function of normal physiology. Not only is it necessarily derived from the very constitution of every living organism, but it plays a useful role in life, for which reason it cannot be replaced. It would, then, be a singular distortion of our thought to present it as an apology for crime. We would not even think of protesting against such an interpretation, did we not know to what strange accusations and misunderstandings one exposes oneself when one undertakes to study moral facts objectively and to speak of them in a different language from that of the layman.

7 / The Functions of Deviance in Groups

ROBERT A. DENTLER
KAI T. ERIKSON

Although sociologists have repeatedly noted that close similarities exist between various forms of social marginality, research directed at these forms has only begun to mark the path toward a social theory of deviance. This slow pace may in part result from the fact that deviant behavior is too frequently visualized as a product of organizational failure rather than as a facet of organization itself.

Albert Cohen has recently attempted to specify some of the assumptions and definitions necessary for a sociology of deviant behavior (3). He has urged the importance of erecting clearly defined concepts, devising a homogeneous class of phenomena explainable by a unified system of theory, and developing a sociological rather than a psychological framework—as would be the case, for example, in a central problem which was stated: "What is it about the structure of social systems that determines the kinds of criminal acts that occur in these systems and the way in which such acts are distributed within the systems?" (3, p. 462). Cohen has also suggested that a theory of deviant behavior should account simultaneously for deviance and conformity; that is, the explanation of one should serve as the explanation of the other.

In this paper we hope to contribute to these objectives by presenting some propositions about the sources and functions of deviant behavior in small groups. Although we suspect that the same general processes may well characterize larger social systems,[1] this paper will be limited to small groups, and more particularly to enduring task and primary groups. Any set of propositions about the functions of deviance would have to be shaped to fit the scope of the social unit chosen for analysis, and we have elected to use the small group unit in this exploratory paper primarily because a large body of empirical material dealing with deviance in groups has accumulated which offers important leads into the study of deviance in general.

With Cohen, we define deviance as "behavior which violates institutionalized expectations, that is, expectations which are shared and recognized as legitimate within a social system" (3, p. 462). Our

90

guiding assumption is that deviant behavior is a reflection not only of the personality of the actor, but the structure of the group in which the behavior was enacted. The violations of expectation which the group experiences, as well as the norms which it observes, express both cultural and structural aspects of the group. While we shall attend to cultural elements in later illustrations, our propositions are addressed primarily to the structure of groups and the functions that deviant behavior serves in maintaining this structure.

PROPOSITION ONE

Our first proposition is that *groups tend to induce, sustain, and permit deviant behavior*. To say that a group *induces* deviant behavior, here, is to say that as it goes through the early stages of development and structures the range of behavior among its members, a group will tend to define the behavior of certain members as deviant. A group *sustains* or *permits* this newly defined deviance in the sense that it tends to institutionalize and absorb this behavior into its structure rather than eliminating it. As group structure emerges and role specialization takes place, one or more role categories will be differentiated to accommodate individuals whose behavior is occasionally or regularly expected to be deviant. It is essential to the argument that this process be viewed not only as a simple group adjustment to individual differences, but also as a requirement of group formation, analogous to the requirement of leadership.

The process of role differentiation and specialization which takes place in groups has been illuminated by studies which use concepts of sociometric rank. Riecken and Homans conclude from this evidence: "The higher the rank of a member the closer his activities come to realizing the norms of the group . . . and there is a tendency toward 'equilibration of rank' " (11, p. 794). Thus the rankings that take place on a scale of social preference serve to identify the activities that members are expected to carry out: each general rank represents or contains an equivalent role which defines that member's special relationship to the group and its norms. To the extent that a group ranks its members preferentially, it distributes functions differentially. The proposition, then, simply notes that group members who violate norms will be given low sociometric rank; that this designation carries with it an appropriate differentiation of the functions that such members are expected to perform in respect to the group; and that the roles contained in these low-rank positions become institutionalized and are retained in the structure of the group.

The most difficult aspect of this proposition is the concept of *induc-*

tion of deviance. We do not mean to suggest that the group creates the motives for an individual's deviant behavior or compels it from persons not otherwise disposed toward this form of expression. When a person encounters a new group, two different historical continuities meet. The individual brings to the group a background of private experience which disposes him to certain patterns of conduct; the group, on the other hand, is organized around a network of role priorities to which each member is required to conform. While the individual brings new resources into the group and alters its potential for change and innovation, the group certainly operates to rephrase each member's private experience into a new self-formula, a new sense of his own needs.

Thus any encounter between a group and a new member is an event which is novel to the experience of both. In the trial-and-error behavior which issues, both the functional requirements of the group and the individual needs of the person will undergo certain revisions, and in the process the group plays an important part in determining whether those already disposed toward deviant behavior will actually express it overtly, or whether those who are lightly disposed toward deviating styles will be encouraged to develop that potential. Inducing deviance, then, is meant to be a process by which the group channels and organizes the deviant possibilities contained in its membership.

The proposition argues that groups induce deviant behavior in the same sense that they induce other group qualities like leadership, fellowship, and so on. These qualities emerge early and clearly in the formation of new groups, even in traditionless laboratory groups, and while they may be diffusely distributed among the membership initially they tend toward specificity and equilibrium over time. In giving definition to the end points in the range of behavior which is brought to a group by its membership, the group establishes its boundaries and gives dimension to its structure. In this process, the designation of low-ranking deviants emerges as surely as the designation of high-ranking task leaders.

PROPOSITION TWO

Bales has written:

> The displacement of hostilities on a scapegoat at the bottom of the status structure is one mechanism, apparently, by which the ambivalent attitudes toward the ... "top man" ... can be diverted and drained off. These patterns, culturally elaborated and various in form, can be viewed as particular cases of mechanisms relevant to the much more general problem of equilibrium (2, p. 454).

This comment provides a bridge between our first and second propositions by suggesting that deviant behavior may serve important functions for groups—thereby contributing to, rather than disrupting, equilibrium in the group. Our second proposition, accordingly, is that *deviant behavior functions in enduring groups to help maintain group equilibrium.* In the following discussion we would like to consider some of the ways this function operates.

Group Performance. The proposition implies that deviant behavior contributes to the maintenance of optimum levels of performance, and we add at this point that this will particularly obtain where a group's achievement depends upon the contributions of all its members.

McCurdy and Lambert devised a laboratory task which required full group participation in finding a solution to a given problem (7). They found that the performance of their groups compared unfavorably with that of individual problem-solvers, and explained this by noting the high likelihood that a group would contain at least one member who failed to attend to instructions. The group, they observed, may prove no stronger than its weakest member. The implication here, as in the old adage, seems to be that the group would have become correspondingly stronger if its weakest link were removed. Yet this implication requires some consideration: to what extent can we say that the inattentive member was acting in the name of the group, performing a function which is valuable to the group over time? To what extent can we call this behavior a product of group structure rather than a product of individual eccentricity?

As roles and their equivalent ranks become differentiated in a group, some members will be expected to perform more capably than others; and in turn the structure of the group will certainly be organized to take advantage of the relative capabilities of its members—as it demonstrably does in leadership choice. These differentials require testing and experimentation: the norms about performance in a group cannot emerge until clues appear as to how much the present membership can accomplish, how wide the range of variation in performance is likely to be, and so on. To the extent that group structure becomes an elaboration and organization of these differentials, certainly the "weak link" becomes as essential to this process as the high-producer. Both are outside links in the communication system which feeds back information about the range of group performance and the limits of the differentiated structure.

As this basis for differentiation becomes established, then, the group moves from a state in which pressure is exerted equally on all members to conform to performance norms, and moves toward a state in which these norms become a kind of anchor which locates the center of wide variations in behavior. The performance "mean" of a group is of course expected to be set at a level dictated by "norms"; and this mean is not only achieved by the most conforming members, but by a balance of high and low producers as well. It is a simple calculation that the loss of a weak link, the low producer, would raise the mean output of the group to a point where it no longer corresponded to original norms unless the entire structure of the group shifted as compensation. In this sense we can argue that neither role differentiation nor norm formation could occur and be maintained without the "aid" of regular deviations.

Rewards. Stated briefly, we would argue that the process of distributing incentives to members of the group is similarly dependent upon the recurrence of deviant behavior. This is an instance where, as Cohen has urged, an explanation of conformity may lead to an explanation of deviance. Customarily, conformance is rewarded while deviance is either unrewarded or actively punished. The rewards of conformity, however, are seen as "rewarding" in comparison to other possible outcomes, and obviously the presence of a deviant in the group would provide the continual contrast without which the reward structure would have little meaning. The problem, then, becomes complex: the reward structure is set up as an incentive for conformity, but depends upon the outcome that differentials in conformity will occur. As shall be pointed out later, the deviant is rewarded in another sense for his role in the group, which makes it "profitable" for him to serve as a contrast in the conventional reward structure. Generally speaking, comparison is as essential in the maintenance of norms as is conformity: a norm becomes most evident in its occasional violation, and in this sense a group maintains "equilibrium" by a controlled balance of the relations which provide comparison and those which assure conformity.

Boundaries. Implicit in the foregoing is the argument that the presence of deviance in a group is a boundary-maintaining function. The comparisons which deviance makes possible help establish the range in which the group operates, the extent of its jurisdiction over behavior, the variety of styles it contains, and these are among the essential dimensions which give a group identity and distinctiveness. In Quaker work camps, Riecken found that members prided themselves on their acceptance of deviations, and rejected such controls as ridicule and rejection (10, pp. 57–67). Homans has noted that men in the Bank Wiring Group employed certain sanctions against deviant behavior which were felt to be peculiar to the structure of the group (5). A group is distinguished in part by the norms it creates for handling deviance and by the forms of deviance it is able to absorb and contain. In helping, then, to give members a sense of their group's distinctiveness, deviant behavior on the group's margins provides an important boundary-maintaining function.

PROPOSITION THREE

Kelley and Thibault have asserted:

> It is common knowledge that when a member deviates markedly from a group standard, the remaining members of the group bring pressures to bear on the deviate to return to conformity. If pressure is of no avail, the deviate is rejected and cast out of the group. The research on this point is consistent with common sense (6, p. 768).

Apparently a deviating member who was *not* rejected after repeated violations would be defined as one who did not deviate markedly enough. While there is considerable justification to support this common-sense notion, we suggest that it overattends to rejection and neglects the range of alternatives short of rejection. The same focus is evident in the following statement by Rossi and Merton:

> What the individual experiences as estrangement from a group tends to be experienced by his associates as repudiation of the group, and this ordinarily evokes a hostile response. As social relations between the individual and the rest of the group deteriorate, the norms of the group become less binding for him. For since he is progressively seceding from the group and being penalized by it, he is the less likely to experience rewards for adherence to . . . norms. Once initiated, this process seems to move toward a cumulative detachment from the group (2, p. 270).

While both of the above quotations reflect current research concerns in their attention to the group's rejection of the individual and his alienation from the group, our third proposition focuses on the common situation in which the group works to prevent elimination of a deviant member. *Groups will resist any trend toward alienation of a member whose behavior is deviant.* From the point of view of the group majority, deviants will be retained in the group up to a point where the deviant expression becomes critically dangerous to group solidarity. This accords with Kelley and Thibault's general statement, if not with its implication; but we would add that the point at which deviation becomes "markedly" extreme—and dangerous to the group—cannot be well defined in advance. This point is located by the group as a result of recurrent interaction between conforming members who respect the central norms of the group and deviating members who test its boundaries. This is the context from which the group derives a conception of what constitutes "danger," or what variations from the norm shall be viewed as "marked."

From the point of view of the deviant, then, the testing of limits is an exercise of his role in the group; from the point of view of the group, pressures are set into motion which secure the deviant in his "testing" role, yet try to assure that his deviation will not become pronounced enough to make rejection necessary. Obviously this is a delicate balance to maintain, and failures are continually visible. Yet there are a great many conditions under which it is worth while for the group to retain its deviant members and resist any trend which might lead the majority membership and other deviant members to progressive estrangement.

ILLUSTRATIONS OF PROPOSITIONS

Each of the authors of this paper has recently completed field research which illuminates the propositions set forth here. Dentler studied the relative effectiveness of ten Quaker work projects in influencing conformity with norms of tolerance, pacifism, democratic group relations, and related social attitudes (4). One interesting sidelight in this study was the finding that while all ten groups were highly solidary, those with relatively higher numbers of sociometric isolates exhibited higher degrees of favorable increased conformity.

Case study of five of the ten groups, using interviews and participant observation, revealed that the two groups achieving the greatest favorable changes in tolerance, democratism, pacifism, and associated attitudes not only had the highest proportions of social isolates, but some of the isolates were low-ranking deviants. Of course none of the groups was without at least one isolate and one deviant, and these roles were not always occupied by the same member. But in the two high-change groups low-rank deviants were present.

In one group, one of these members came from a background that differed radically from those of other members. Although these were cooperative living and work projects, this member insisted upon separately prepared special food and complained loudly about its quality. Where three-fourths of the group members came from professional and managerial families, and dressed and acted in conformity with upper-middle-class standards, this deviant refused to wear a shirt to Sunday dinner and often came to meals without his shoes. He could not hold a job and lost two provided by the group leader during the first two weeks of the program.

His social and political attitudes also differed radically from group norms, and he was often belligerently assertive of his minority perspectives. He had no allies for his views. In an interview one of the group's leaders described the group's response to this deviant:

At first we didn't know how to cope with him though we were determined to do just that. After he came to Sunday dinner in his undershirt, and after he smashed a bowl of food that had been fixed specially for him—as usual— we figured out a way to set down certain firm manners for him. There were some rules, we decided, that no one was going to violate. We knew he was very new to this kind of life and so we sought to understand him. We never rejected him. Finally, he began to come to terms; he adapted, at least enough so that we can live with him. He has begun to conform on the surface to some of our ways. It's been very hard to take that he is really proud of having lost his first two jobs and is not quiet about it. Things have gone better since we made a birthday cake for him, and I feel proud of the way our group has managed to handle this internal problem.

The same group sustained another deviant and even worked hard to retain him when he decided to leave the group. Here a group leader discusses group relations with this member:

X left our group after the first four weeks of the eight-week program. He had never been away from home before although he was about 21 years old. He couldn't seem to adjust to his job at the day camp, and he just couldn't stand doing his share of the housework and cooking. This lack of doing his share was especially hard on us, and we often discussed privately whether it would be good for him to relieve him of any household chores. We decided that wouldn't be right, but we still couldn't get him to work. Funny, but this sort of made housework the center of our group life. We are proud that no one else has shirked his chores; there is no quibbling now. . . . Anyway, X kept being pressured by his mother and brother to come home, but we gave him tremendous support. We talked it all out with him. We let him know we really wanted him to stay. This seemed to unify our group. It was working out the problem of X that seemed to unify our group. It was working out the problem of X that seemed to help us build some group standards. He began to follow some of our standards but he also stayed free to dissent. His mother finally forced him to come home.

In the second high-change group, there were also two extreme deviants. Here a group leader comments on one of them:

I've never got over feeling strongly antagonistic toward K. K has been a real troublemaker and we never really came to terms with him or controlled him significantly. He is simply a highly neurotic, conflicted person as far as life in our group goes. Personally, I've resented the fact that he has monopolized Z, who without him would have been a real contributor but who has become nothing more than a sort of poor imitation of K. After we had been here about half the summer, incidentally, a professional came out from staff headquarters and after observing our meetings he asked why K hadn't been dismissed or asked to leave the group early in the summer. But K didn't leave, of course, and most of us wouldn't want him to leave.

Finally a group leader described the reaction to the departure of its second deviant, who was repeatedly described in interviews as "kind of obnoxious":

On the night N was upstairs talking with your interviewer, the group got together downstairs suddenly to talk about getting up a quick party, a farewell party for him. In 15 minutes, like a whirlwind, we decorated the house and some of the fellows wrote a special song of farewell for N. We also wrote a last-minute appeal asking him to stay with the group and people ran about asking, "What are you doing for N?" There seemed to be a lot of guilt among us about his leaving. We felt that maybe we hadn't done enough to get him more involved in the life of our group. I think there was some hidden envy too. After he had left, a joke began to spread around that went like this: If you leave now maybe we'll have a party for you.

The group with the lowest amount of change during the summer contained two low-ranking members, one of whom deviated from the group's norms, occasionally, but no evidence came to light to indicate that this group achieved the same intensity in social relationships or the same degree of role differentiation as did groups with more extremely deviant members. Members of this low-change group reflected almost without exception the views expressed in this typical quotation:

Objectively, this is a good, congenial group of individuals. Personally they leave me a little cold. I've been in other project groups, and this is the most congenial one I've been in; yet, I don't think there will be any lasting friendships.

All these quotations reflect strong impressions embodied in our observational reports. Taken as a whole they illustrate aspects of our three postulates. While this material does not reveal the sense in which a group may induce deviance—and this is perhaps the most critical proposition of all—it does show how groups will make great efforts to keep deviant members attached to the group, to prevent full alienation. By referring to our findings about attitude change we have hoped to suggest the relevance of deviance to increasing conformity, a functional relationship of action and reaction.

In 1955–6, Erikson participated in a study of schizophrenia among basic trainees in the U. S. Army, portions of which have been published elsewhere (1). Through various interview and questionnaire techniques, a large body of data was collected which enabled the investigators to reconstruct short histories of the group life shared by the future schizophrenic and his squad prior to the former's hospitalization. There were eleven subjects in the data under consideration. The bulk of the evidence used for this short report comes from loosely structured interviews which were conducted with the entire squad in attendance, shortly after it had lost one of its members to the psychiatric hospital.

The eleven young men whose breakdown was the subject of the

interviews all came from the north-eastern corner of the United States, most of them from rural or small-town communities. Typically, these men had accumulated long records of deviation in civilian life: while few of them had attracted psychiatric attention, they had left behind them fairly consistent records of job failure, school truancy, and other minor difficulties in the community. Persons in the community took notice of this behavior, of course, but they tended to be gently puzzled by it rather than attributing distinct deviant motives to it.

When such a person enters the service, vaguely aware that his past performance did not entirely live up to expectations current in his community, he is likely to start negotiating with his squad mates about the conditions of his membership in the group. He sees himself as warranting special group consideration, as a consequence of a deviant style which he himself is unable to define; yet the group has clear-cut obligations which require a high degree of responsibility and coordination from everyone. The negotiation seems to go through several successive stages, during which a reversal of original positions takes place and the individual is fitted for a role which is clearly deviant.

The first stage is characteristic of the recruit's first days in camp. His initial reaction is likely to be an abrupt attempt to discard his entire "civilian" repertoire to free himself for adoption of new styles and new ways. His new uniform for daily wear seems to become for him a symbolic uniform for his sense of identity: he is, in short, overconforming. He is likely to interpret any gesture of command as a literal moral mandate, sometimes suffering injury when told to scrub the floor until his fingers bleed, or trying to consciously repress thoughts of home when told to get everything out of his head but the military exercise of the moment.

The second stage begins shortly thereafter as he fails to recognize that "regulation" reality is different from the reality of group life, and that the circuits which carry useful information are contained within the more informal source. The pre-psychotic is, to begin with, a person for whom contacts with peers are not easy to establish, and as he tries to find his way into these circuits, looking for cues to the rhythm of group life, he sees that a fairly standard set of interaction techniques is in use. There are ways to initiate conversation, ways to impose demands, and so on. Out of this cultural lore, then, he chooses different gambits to test. He may learn to ask for matches to start discussion, be ready with a supply of cigarettes for others to "bum," or he may pick up a local joke or expression and repeat it continually. Too often, however, he misses the context in which these interaction cues are appropriate, so that his behavior, in its over-literal simplicity, becomes almost a caricature of the sociability rule he is trying to follow. We may cite the "specialist" in giving away cigarettes:

> I was out of cigarettes and he had a whole pack. I said, "Joe, you got a smoke?" He says "yes," and Jesus, he gave me about twelve of them. At other times he used to offer me two or three packs of cigarettes at a time when I was out.

Or the "specialist" in greetings:

> He'd go by you in the barracks and say, "What do you say, Jake?" I'd say, "Hi, George, how are you?" and he'd walk into the latrine. And he'd come by not a minute later, and it's the same thing all over again, "What do you say, Jake?" It seemed to me he was always saying "hi" to someone. You could be sitting right beside him for ten minutes and he would keep on saying it.

These clumsy overtures lead the individual and the group into the third stage. Here the recruit, almost hidden from group view in his earlier overconformity, has become a highly visible group object: his behavior is clearly "off beat," anomalous; he has made a presentation of himself to the squad, and the squad has had either to make provisions for him in the group structure or begin the process of eliminating him. The pre-psychotic is clearly a low producer, and in this sense he is potentially a handicap. Yet the group neither exerts strong pressures on him to conform nor attempts to expel him from the squad. Instead, he is typically given a wide license to deviate from both the performance and behavior norms of the group, and the group in turn forms a hard protective shell around him which hides him from exposure to outside authorities.

His duties are performed by others, and in response the squad only seems to ask of him that he be at least consistent in his deviation—that he be consistently helpless and consistently anomalous. In a sense, he becomes the ward of the group, hidden from outside view but the object of friendly ridicule within. He is referred to as "our teddy bear," "our pet," "mascot," "little brother," "toy," and so on. In a setting where having buddies is highly valued, he is unlikely to receive any sociometric choices at all. But it would be quite unfortunate to assume that he is therefore isolated from the group or repudiated by it: an accurate sociogram would have the deviant individual encircled by the interlocking sociometric preferences, sheltered by the group structure, and an important point of reference for it.

The examples just presented are weak in that they include only failures of the process described. The shell which protected the deviant from visibility leaked, outside medical authorities were notified, and he was eventually hospitalized. But as a final note it is interesting to observe that the shell remained even after the person for whom it was erected had withdrawn. Large portions of every squad interview were devoted to arguments, directed at a psychiatrist, that the departed member was not ill and should never have been hospitalized.

DISCUSSION

The most widely cited social theories of deviant behavior which have appeared in recent years—notably those of Merton and Parsons (8; 9)—have helped turn sociologists' attention from earlier models of social pathology in which deviance was seen as direct evidence of disorganization. These newer models have attended to the problem of how social structures exert pressure on certain individuals rather than others toward the expression of deviance. Yet the break with the older social disorganization tradition is only partial, since these theories still regard deviance from the point of view of its value as a "symptom" of dysfunctional structures. One aim of this paper is to encourage a functional approach to deviance, to consider the contributions deviant behavior may make toward the development of organizational structures, rather than focusing on the implicit assumption that structures must be somehow in a state of disrepair if they produce deviant behavior.

Any group attempts to locate its position in social space by defining its symbolic boundaries, and this process of self-location takes place not only in reference to the central norms which the group develops but in reference to the *range* of possibilities which the culture makes available. Specialized statuses which are located on the margins of the group, chiefly high-rank leaders and low-rank deviants, become critical referents for establishing the end points of this range, the group boundaries.

As both the Quaker and Army illustrations suggest, deviant members are important targets toward which group concerns become focused. Not only do they symbolize the group's activities, but they help give other members a sense of group size, its range and extent, by marking where the group begins and ends in space. In general, the deviant seems to help give the group structure a visible "shape." The deviant is someone about whom something should be done, and the group, in expressing this concern, is able to reaffirm its essential cohesion and indicate what the group is and what it can do. Of course the character of the deviant behavior in each group would vary with the group's general objectives, its relationship to the larger culture, and so on. In both the Quaker groups and Army squads, nurturance was a strong element of the other members' reaction to their deviant fellow. More specifically in the Army material it is fairly sure that the degree of helplessness and softness supplied by the pre-psychotic introduced emotional qualities which the population—lacking women and younger persons—could not otherwise afford.

These have been short and necessarily limited illustrations of the propositions advanced. In a brief final note we would like to point out how this crude theory could articulate with the small group research tradition by suggesting one relatively ideal laboratory procedure that might be used. Groups composed of extremely homogeneous members should be assigned tasks which require group solution but which impose a high similarity of activity upon all members. If role differentiation occurs, then, it would be less a product of individual differences or the specific requirements of the task than a product of group formation. We would hypothesize that such differentiation would take place, and that one or more roles thus differentiated would be reserved for deviants. The occupants of these deviant roles should be removed from the group. If the propositions have substance, the group—and this is the critical hypothesis—would realign its members so that these roles would become occupied by other members. While no single experiment could address all the implications of our paradigm, this one would confront its main point.

This paper, of course, has deliberately neglected those group conditions in which deviant behavior becomes dysfunctional: it is a frequent group experience that deviant behavior fails to provide a valued function for the structure and helps reduce performance standards or lower levels of interaction. We have attempted here to present a side of the coin which we felt was often neglected, and in our turn we are equally—if intentionally—guilty of neglect.

Summary

This paper has proposed the following interpretations of deviant behavior in enduring primary and task groups:

1. Deviant behavior tends to be induced, permitted, and sustained by a given group.

2. Deviant behavior functions to help maintain group equilibrium.

3. Groups will resist any trend toward alienation of a member whose behavior is deviant.

The substance of each proposition was discussed heuristically and illustrated by reference to field studies of deviant behavior in Quaker work projects and Army basic training squads. A laboratory test was suggested as one kind of critical test of the paradigm. The aim of the presentation was to direct attention to the functional interdependence of deviance and organization.

References

1. Artiss, Kenneth L., ed., *The Symptom as Communication in Schizophrenia* (New York: Grune and Stratton, 1959).
2. Bales, Robert F., "The Equilibrium Problem in Small Groups," in *Small Groups*, A. Paul Hare, et al., eds. (New York: Knopf, 1955), 424–456.
3. Cohen, Albert K., "The Study of Social Disorganization and Deviant

Behavior," in *Sociology Today*, Robert K. Merton, et al., eds. (New York: Basic Books, 1959), 461–484.

4. Dentler, Robert, *The Young Volunteers* (Chicago: National Opinion Research Center Report, 1959).
5. Homans, George W., *The Human Group* (New York: Harcourt, Brace, 1950).
6. Kelley, Harold H., and John W. Thibault, "Experimental Studies of Group Problem Solving and Process," in *Handbook of Social Psychology*, Vol. II, Gardner Lindzey, ed. (Cambridge: Addison-Wesley, 1954), 759–768.
7. McCurdy, Harold G., and Wallace E. Lambert, "The Efficiency of Small Human Groups in the Solution of Problems Requiring Genuine Cooperation," *Journal of Personality*, 20 (June, 1952), 478–494.
8. Merton, Robert K., *Social Theory and Social Structure*, rev. ed. (Glencoe: Free Press, 1957).
9. Parsons, Talcott, *The Social System* (Glencoe: Free Press, 1951), 256–267, 321–325; and Talcott Parsons, Robert F. Bales and Edward A. Shils, *Working Papers in the Theory of Action* (Glencoe: Free Press, 1953), 67–78.
10. Riecken, Henry, *Volunteer Work Camp* (Cambridge: Addison-Wesley, 1952), 57–67.
11. Riecken, Henry, and George W. Homans, "Psychological Aspects of Social Structure," in *Handbook of Social Psychology*, Vol. II. Gardner Lindzey, ed. (Cambridge: Addison-Wesley, 1954), 786–832.

Note

1. One of the authors (Erikson) is currently preparing a paper which deals with the broader implications of the problems discussed here.

*culture
conflict*

8 / The Conflict of Conduct Norms

THORSTEN SELLIN

CULTURE CONFLICTS AS CONFLICTS OF CULTURAL CODES

. . . There are social groups on the surface of the earth which possess complexes of conduct norms which, due to differences in the mode of life and the social values evolved by these groups, appear to set them apart from other groups in many or most respects. We may expect conflicts of norms when the rural dweller moves to the city, but we assume that he has absorbed the basic norms of the culture which comprises both town and country. How much greater is not the conflict likely to be when Orient and Occident meet, or when the Corsican mountaineer is transplanted to the lower East Side of New York. Conflicts of cultures are inevitable when the norms of one cultural or subcultural area migrate to or come in contact with those of another.

Conflicts between the norms of divergent cultural codes may arise

1. when these codes clash on the border of contiguous culture areas;
2. when, as may be the case with legal norms, the law of one cultural group is extended to cover the territory of another; or
3. when members of one cultural group migrate to another.[1]

Speck, for instance, notes that "where the bands popularly known as Montagnais have come more and more into contact with Whites, their reputation has fallen lower among the traders who have known them through commercial relationships within that period. The accusation is made that they have become less honest in connection with their debts, less trustworthy with property, less truthful, and more inclined to alcoholism and sexual freedom as contacts with the frontier towns have become easier for them. Richard White reports in 1933 unusual instances of Naskapi breaking into traders' store houses."[2]

Similar illustrations abound in the works of the cultural anthropologists. We need only to recall the effect on the American

104

Indian of the culture conflicts induced by our policy of acculturation by guile and force. In this instance, it was not merely contact with the white man's culture, his religion, his business methods, and his liquor, which weakened the tribal mores. In addition, the Indian became subject to the white man's law and this brought conflicts as well, as has always been the case when legal norms have been imposed upon a group previously ignorant of them. Maunier[3] in discussing the diffusion of French law in Algeria, recently stated: "In introducing the *Code Penal* in our colonies, as we do, we transform into offenses the ancient usages of the inhabitants which their customs permitted or imposed. Thus, among the Khabyles of Algeria, the killing of adulterous wives is ritual murder committed by the father or brother of the wife and not by her husband, as elsewhere. The woman having been sold by her family to her husband's family, the honor of her relatives is soiled by her infidelity. Her father or brother has the right and the duty to kill her in order to cleanse by her blood the honor of her relatives. Murder in revenge is also a duty, from family to family, in case of murder of or even in case of insults to a relative: the vendetta, called the *rekba* in Khabylian, is imposed by the law of honor. But these are crimes in French law! Murder for revenge, being premeditated and planned, is assassination, punishable by death! . . . What happens, then, often when our authorities pursue the criminal, guilty of an offense against public safety as well as against morality: public enemy of the French order, but who has acted in accord with a respected custom? The witnesses of the assassination, who are his relatives, or neighbors, fail to lay charges against the assassin; when they are questioned, they pretend to know nothing; and the pursuit is therefore useless. A French magistrate has been able to speak of the conspiracy of silence among the Algerians; a conspiracy aiming to preserve traditions, always followed and obeyed, against their violation by our power. This is the tragic aspect of the conflict of laws. A recent decree forbids the husband among the Khabyles to profit arbitrarily by the power given him according to this law to repudiate his wife, demanding that her new husband pay an exorbitant price for her—this is the custom of the *lefdi*. Earlier, one who married a repudiated wife paid nothing to the former husband. It appears that the first who tried to avail himself of the new law was killed for violating the old custom. The abolition of the ancient law does not always occur without protest or opposition. That which is a crime was a duty; and the order which we cause to reign is sometimes established to the detriment of 'superstition'; it is the gods and the spirits, it is believed, that would punish any one who fails to revenge his honor."

When Soviet law was extended to Siberia, similar effects were observed. Anossow[4] and Wirschubski[5] both relate that women among the Siberian tribes, who in obedience to the law, laid aside their veils were killed by their relatives for violating one of the most sacred norms of their tribes.

We have noted that culture conflicts are the natural outgrowth of processes of social differentiation, which produce an infinity of social groupings, each with its own definitions of life situations, its own interpretations of social relationships, its own ignorance or misunderstanding of the social values of other groups. The transformation of a culture from a homogeneous and well-integrated type to a heterogeneous and disintegrated type is therefore accompanied by an increase of conflict situations. Conversely, the operation of integrating processes will reduce the number of conflict situations. Such conflicts within a changing culture may be distinguished from those created when different cultural systems come in contact with one another, regardless of the character or stage of development of these systems. In either case, the conduct of members of a group involved in the conflict of codes will in some respects be judged abnormal by the other group.

THE STUDY OF CULTURE CONFLICTS

In the study of culture conflicts, some scholars have been concerned with the effect of such conflicts on the conduct of specific persons, an approach which is naturally preferred by psychologists and psychiatrists and by sociologists who have used the life history technique. These scholars view the conflict as internal. Wirth[6] states categorically that a culture "conflict can be said to be a factor in delinquency only if the individual feels it or acts as if it were present." Culture conflict is mental conflict, but the character of this conflict is viewed differently by the various disciplines which use this term. Freudian psychiatrists[7] regard it as a struggle between deeply rooted biological urges which demand expression and the culturally created rules which give rise to inhibitive mechanisms which thwart this expression and drive them below the conscious level of the mind, whence they rise either by ruse in some socially acceptable disguise, as abnormal conduct when the inhibiting mechanism breaks down, or as neuroses when it works too well. The sociologist, on the other hand, thinks of mental conflict as being primarily the clash between antagonistic conduct norms incorporated in personality. "Mental conflict in the person," says Burgess in discussing the case presented by Shaw in The Jack-Roller, "may always be explained in terms of the conflict of divergent cultures."[8]

If this view is accepted, sociological research on culture conflict and its relationships to abnormal conduct would have to be strictly limited to a study of the personality of cultural hybrids. Significant studies could be conducted only by the life-history case technique applied to persons in whom the conflict is internalized, appropriate control groups being utilized, of course. . . .

The absence of mental conflict, in the sociological sense, may, however, be well studied in terms of culture conflict. An example may make this clear. A few years ago a Sicilian father in New Jersey killed the sixteen-year-old seducer of his daughter, expressing surprise at his arrest since he had merely defended his family honor in a traditional way. In this case a mental conflict in the sociological sense did not exist. The conflict was external and occurred between cultural codes or norms. We may assume that where such conflicts occur violations of norms will arise merely because persons who have absorbed the norms of one cultural group or area migrate to another and that such conflict will continue so long as the acculturation process has not been completed. . . . Only then may the violations be regarded in terms of mental conflict.

If culture conflict may be regarded as sometimes personalized, or mental, and sometimes as occurring entirely in an impersonal way solely as a conflict of group codes, it is obvious that research should not be confined to the investigation of mental conflicts and that contrary to Wirth's categorical statement that it is impossible to demonstrate the existence of a culture conflict "objectively . . . by a comparison between two cultural codes"[9] this procedure has not only a definite function, but may be carried out by researchers employing techniques which are familiar to the sociologist.

The emphasis on the life history technique has grown out of the assumption that "the experiences of one person at the same time reveals the life activities of his group" and that "habit in the individual is an expression of custom in society."[10] This is undoubtedly one valid approach. Through it we may hope to discover generalizations of a scientific nature by studying persons who (1) have drawn their norms of conduct from a variety of groups with conflicting norms, or (2) who possess norms drawn from a group whose code is in conflict with that of the group which judges the conduct. In the former case alone can we speak of mental or internal culture conflict; in the latter, the conflict is external.

If the conduct norms of a group are, with reference to a given life situation, inconsistent, or if two groups possess inconsistent norms, we may assume that the members of these various groups will individually reflect such group attitudes. Paraphrasing Burgess, the experiences of a group will reveal the life activities of its members. While these norms can, no doubt, be best established by a study of a sufficient number of representative group members, they may for some groups at least be fixed with sufficient certainty to serve research purposes by a study of the social institutions, the administration of justice, the novel, the drama, the press, and other expressions of group attitudes. The identification of the groups in question having been made, it might be possible to determine to what extent such conflicts are reflected in the conduct of their members. Comparative studies based on the violation rates of the members of such groups, the trends of such rates, etc., would dominate this approach to the problem.

In conclusion, then, culture conflict may be studied either as mental conflict or as a conflict of cultural codes. The criminologist will naturally tend to concentrate on such conflicts between legal and nonlegal conduct norms. The concept of conflict fails to give him more than a general framework of reference for research. In practice, it has, however, become nearly synonymous with conflicts between the norms of cultural systems or areas. Most researches which have employed it have been done on immigrant or race groups in the United States, perhaps due to the ease with which such groups may be identified, the existence of more statistical data recognizing such groupings, and the conspicuous differences between some immigrant norms and our norms.

Notes

1. This is unfortunately not the whole story, for with the rapid growth of impersonal communication, the written (press, literature) and the spoken word (radio, talkie), knowledge concerning divergent conduct norms no longer grows solely out of direct personal contact with their carriers. And out of such conflicts grow some violations of custom and of law which would not have occurred without them.

2. Speck, Frank G. "Ethical Attributes of the Labrador Indians." *American Anthropologist*. N. S. 35:559–94. October–December 1933. P. 559.

3. Maunier, René, "La diffusion du droit français en Algérie." Harvard Tercentenary Publications, *Independence, Convergence, and Borrowing in Institutions, Thought, and Art*. Cambridge: Harvard University Press. 1937. Pp. 84–85.

4. Anossow, J. J. "Die volkstümlichen Verbrechen im Strafkodex der USSR." *Monatsschrift für Kriminalpsychologie und Strafrechtsreform*. 24: 534–37. September 1933.

5. Wirschubski, Gregor. "Der Schutz der Sittlichkeit im Sowjetstrafrecht." *Zeitschrift für die gesamte Strafrechtswissenschaft*. 51: 317–28. 1931.

6. Wirth, Louis. "Culture Conflict and Misconduct." *Social Forces*. 9: 484–92. June 1931. P. 490. Cf. Allport, Floyd H. "Culture Conflict versus the Individual as Factors in Delinquency." *Ibid*. Pp. 493–97.

7. White, William A. *Crimes and Criminals*. New York: Farrar & Rinehart. 1933. Healy, William. *Mental Conflict and Misconduct*. Boston: Little, Brown & Co. 1917. Alexander, Franz and Healy, William. *Roots of Crime*. New York: Alfred A. Knopf. 1935.

8. Burgess, Ernest W. in Clifford R. Shaw's *The Jack-Roller*. Chicago: University of Chicago Press. 1930. Pp. 184–197, p. 186.

9. Wirth, Louis. *Op. cit*. P. 490. It should be noted that Wirth also states that culture should be studied "on the objective side" and that "the sociologist is not primarily interested in personality but in culture."

10. Burgess, Ernest W. *Op. cit*. P. 186.

culture conflict

9 / Outlaw Motorcyclists: An Outgrowth of Lower Class Cultural Concerns

J. MARK WATSON

INTRODUCTION

Walter Miller's (1958) typology of focal concerns of lower class culture as a generating milieu for gang delinquency is by most standards a classic in explaining gang behavior among juvenile males. Its general heuristic value is here demonstrated by the striking parallel between this value system and that of adult outlaw motorcyclists.

The reader may remember Miller's general schema, which concerned the strain between the value system of youthful lower class males and the dominant, middle-class value system of those in a position to define delinquent behavior. Miller, by describing these values (he used the term "focal concerns"), anticipated conflict theory, without directly pointing out the conflicting values of the middle class definers of delinquent behavior. Although there have been some disagreements surrounding details of Miller's description of the functioning of adolescent gangs, the basic focal concerns described in the typology have been relatively free of criticism as to their validity in describing the values of young lower class males. Some questions have been raised about the degree to which these values actually are in contrast with those of middle class adolescents, however (see, for example, Short et al., 1963). Because the typology itself is contained in the discussion of biker values, it will not be discussed separately here.

METHODOLOGY

The findings of the paper are based on my 3 years of participant observation in the subculture of outlaw motorcyclists. Although I am not a member of any outlaw clubs, I am or have been acquainted with members and officers of various clubs, as well as more loosely

109

organized groups of motorcyclists for 10 years. I am myself a motor-cycle enthusiast, which facilitated a natural entry into the biker scene. I both build and ride bikes and gained direct access to local biker groups by frequenting places where bikers congregate to work on their bikes. Building a bike gave me legitimation and access to local biker groups and eventually led to contact with other bikers, including outlaws. Groups observed varied from what could be classi-fied as clubs to loose-knit groups of associated motorcyclists. Four groups were studied in depth. Two small local groups in middle Ten-nessee were subjects of direct participation. Here they are given the fictional names of the Brothers and the Good Old Boys. In addition, one regional group from North Carolina, given the fictional name of Bar Hoppers, was studied through interviews with club officers and members. One national-level group, one of the largest groups of out-law motorcyclists, was extensively observed and interviewed, pri-marily at regional and national events. This group is given the fiction-al name of the Convicts. Additional information was also gathered by attempting to interview at regional and national events members and officers of a wide range of clubs. This was easily done by simply looking at club "colors" (patches) and seeking out members of clubs that were not already represented in the study. This technique was used primarily to check for the representativeness of behavior, val-ues, beliefs, and other characteristics observed in in-depth studies of the four clubs mentioned above. Another source of validation of con-clusions was extensive use of biker literature such as magazines and books by or about bikers. These are listed in the bibliography.

Data were collected by means of interviews conducted from Janu-ary 1977 to March 1980. Interviews were informally administered in the sense that no formal interview schedule was used. Instead, bikers were queried in the context of what would pass for normal conversa-tion. Extensive observations of behavior were made while directly participating in the activities of the groups, everyday events such as hanging out and from building bikes to "runs," (trips), swap meets, and cult events, such as speed week at Daytona Beach, Florida, and the National Motorcycle Drag Championships at Bowling Green, Kentucky. Such events led to contact with bikers from all over the United States, inasmuch as these events attract a national sample of dedicated bikers, including the whole range of types from simple en-thusiasts to true outlaws. Notes and impressions were taken at night and/or after the events. Groups and individuals were generally not aware that they were being studied, although I made no attempt to hide my intentions. Some bikers who came to know me were curious about a university professor participating in such activities and ac-cordingly were told that a study was being conducted. This honesty was prompted by fear of being suspected of being a narcotics agent.

Such self-revelation was rarely necessary as the author affected the clothing and jargon of bikers and was accepted as such. Frequent invitations to engage in outrageous and illegal behavior (e.g., drug use and purchase of stolen parts) that would not be extended to outsiders were taken as a form of symbolic acceptance. My demeanor and extensive association with lower class gangs in adolescence combined with the type of mechanical skills necessary to build bikes mentioned earlier may have contributed to an ability to blend in. Reactions to self-revelation, when necessary, generally ranged from amazement to amusement. I suspect that, as is true with the general population, most bikers had no idea what a sociologist was, but the presence of a professor in their midst was taken as a sort of legitimation for the group.

Observations and conclusions were cross-checked on an on-going basis with a group of five biker informants whom I knew well, including members of the Brothers, Good Old Boys, and the Convicts who lived in the mid-Tennessee area. Informants were selected on the basis of several criteria. First, informants had to know and be known well enough by me to establish a trusting relationship. This limited informants to local bikers found in my area of residence. As mentioned above, outlaw motorcyclists are not particularly trusting, and this obstacle had to be overcome. Second, informants had to be articulate enough to communicate such concepts as values. Most bikers are not particularly articulate, so this criterion eliminated many members of local groups whom I knew well. Third, informants had to have extensive experience in biker subculture. Consequently, informants were limited to bikers who had traveled and lived in a wide geographic area and had experience wider than that represented by the mid-South region. Consequently, informants were generally older than the typical biker population, varying in age from the early 30s to the mid-40s. Three of the informants were former or current owners of custom motorcycle shops that catered to biker clientele. All were what might be defined as career bikers. Finally, all informants had to possess enough objectivity about the biker lifestyle to be willing to read and comment on the author's conclusions. Many of these conclusions, though valid and objective, one hopes, are not particularly flattering to participants in the outlaw motorcyclists subculture. One informant was lost because of obvious antagonism generated by some conclusions. In addition, conversations with hundreds of unsuspecting bikers were held in order to ascertain the generalizability of observations. The latter technique involved appearing to be ignorant or confused and simply asking for a definition of the situation, for example, "What's happening?" or, "What are they doing?" or even venturing an evaluation such as, "That's stupid; Why do they do that?" all in order to elicit a response from an observer of some act. It must be kept in mind that research conducted with this kind of deviant subculture can be dangerous. Because many outlaws do not welcome scrutiny and carefully avoid those whom they feel may not be trusted, which includes most nonbikers, I remained as unobtrusive as possible. Consequently, the methodology was adapted to the setting. Generally, I felt my presence was accepted. Throughout the study I sensed no change in the cyclists' behavior over time by my presence. This acceptance can be symbolized by my receiving a nickname (Doc) and eventually being defined as an expert in a certain type of obsolete motorcycle (the Harley-Davidson 45-cubic-inch side-valve model). I assumed the role of an inside outsider.

THE BIKER SUBCULTURE

We may locate outlaw bikers in the general spectrum of bikers as the most "outrageous" (their own term, a favorite modifier indicating something distinctively appealing to their own jaded sense of values) on the continuum of bikers, which extends from housewives on mopeds to clubs that actually engage in illegal behavior with a fair degree of frequency, thus the term "outlaws" (Thompson, 1967:9). Outlaws generally adopt certain symbols and lead a lifestyle that is clearly defined and highly visible to other bikers. Symbols include extensive tattooing, beard, dirty jeans, earrings, so-called stroker caps and quasi-military pins attached, engineer's boots, and cut-off jackets with club emblems, called "colors," sewn on the back. Weapons, particularly buck knives and guns of any sort, and chains (motorcycle or other types) are favorite symbols as well (Easyriders, November, 1977:28, 29, 55). By far the most important symbol, however, is the Harley-Davidson V-twin motorcycle.[1] It should be kept in mind that many other motorcyclists affect these symbols, although they are by no means outlaws. Outlaws almost always belong to clubs, whereas many motorcyclists who do not belong to the clubs use them as reference groups and attempt to imitate some aspects of their behavior. These symbols and the basic lifestyle are generalizable to a wide range of bikers and may even be found among British and European bikers, with the exception of the Harley-Davidson motorcycle (Choppers, April 1980:12).

OUTLAW LIFESTYLE

For the outlaw, his lifestyle takes on many of the characteristics of dedication to a religious sect (Watson, 1979). This lifestyle is in many respects a lower class variation of bohemian, "dropout" subcultures. Such similarities include frequent unemployment and disdain for cleanliness, orderliness, and other concerns of conventional culture. For example, I have observed bikes being built and stored in living rooms or kitchens, two non-essential rooms in the subculture. This is apparently a common practice. Parts may be stored in an oil bath in the bathtub, also a nonessential device. The biker and other bohemian subcultures may appear similar on the basis of casual observations, but some outlaw biker values are strikingly different from the beatnik or hippy subcultures of the 1950s and 1960s. Other bohemian subcultures emphasized humanistic values, whereas the outlaw bikers' values emphasize male dominance, violence, force, and racism (Easyriders, October 1977:15). Although individual freedom and choice are also emphasized, the clubs actually suppress individual freedom, while using the value to defend their lifestyle from outsiders. For example, when the Convicts take a club trip called a "run," all members must participate. Those whose bikes are "down" for repairs are fined and must find a ride in a truck with the women. Many club rules require members to follow orders as prescribed by club decisions upon threat of violence and expulsion. Club rules generally include a constitution and bylaws that are surprisingly elaborate and sophisticated for groups of this nature. Many club members express pride in their written regulations. It seems likely that the basic format is borrowed from that developed by the Hell's Angels (Thompson, 1967:72). Most club decisions are made in a democratic way, but minority rights are not respected. Once such a decision is made, it is imperative to all members, with risk of physical retribution for failure to conform. Typical rules include care of colors, which are to never touch the ground or be washed. They are treated essentially as a flag. Other rules mentioned above and below have to do with following group decisions without dissent and such requirements as defending club honor through unanimous participation in avenging affronts to other clubs' members. Club rules may be enforced by self-appointed committees or by formally designated sergeants at arms or enforcers. One informant expressed it this way: "They'll take your bike, your old lady, and stomp the shit out of you if you make 'em look bad." This particular expression related to some prospective "probate" members and their failure to live up to club rules requiring violent reactions to challenges to club honor. The observation came from a retired club member when I queried him about an almost surreal conflict over the wearing of a club symbol by a nonmember.

Use of mind-altering drugs is another area of overlap between biker and bohemian subcultures. Outlaw bikers will take or drink almost anything to alter their consciousness (Easyriders, May 1978:24, 25).

The groups studied regularly used "uppers," "downers," and marijuana but rarely used hallucinogens. One informant explained that the latter "fuck you up so you can't ride, so we don't use it much." Apparently, one can ride on uppers, downers, or when drunk but not when hallucinating. Curiously enough, the most commonly used drug is alcohol taken in the rather mild form of beer (though in great quantity). Where there are outlaw bikers one will usually find drugs, but one will almost always find beer.

Outsider status, the use of drugs, and the seeking of cheap rent result in frequent overlap between outlaw bikers and other bohemian types, in both territory and interpersonal relations. The bikers usually tolerate the other bohemians, because the latter share an interest in and serve as a source of supply of, or customers for, drugs. Bikers, however, view them with contempt because they are not masculine enough. Hippies, dopers, and fairies are similar types as far as bikers are concerned. Masculinity as a dominant value is expressed in many ways, including toughness and a general concern with looking mean, dirty, and "outrageous." When asked about a peripheral member of a local group, one informant replied, "He's a hippy, but he don't ride. We put up with him because he has good dope. I feel sorry for him because he's just a fucked-up puke."

Some other biker-associated values include racism, concern with Nazism, and in-group superiority. "Righteousness" is achieved through adherence to these values. One celebrity member of the Brothers had been convicted of killing a young black man in a street confrontation. He is reported to have jumped bail and lived with a Nazi couple in South America, where he worked as a ranch hand. This particular member spoke some German and frequently spouted racist and Nazi doctrine. A typical righteous outlaw belongs to a club, rides an American-made motorcycle, is a white male, displays the subculture's symbols, hates most if not all nonwhites and Japanese motorcycles, works irregularly at best, dresses at all times in dirty jeans, cut-off denim jacket, and engineer's boots, drinks beer, takes whichever drugs are available, and treats women as objects of contempt.

OUTLAW BIKER WORLD VIEW AND SELF-CONCEPT

The outlaw biker generally views the world as hostile, weak, and effeminate. Perhaps this view is a realistic reaction to a working-class socialization experience. However, the reaction contains certain elements of a self-fulfilling prophecy. Looking dirty, mean, and generally undesirable may be a way of frightening others into leaving one alone, although, in many senses such an appearance arouses anger, hostility, and related emotions in the observer and results in the persecution that such qualities are intended to protect one from.

Bikers tend to see the world in terms of here and now. They are not especially hostile toward most social institutions such as family, government, and education. Most of the local group members had finished high school and had been employed from time to time, and some had been college students. Some were veterans, and nearly all had been married more than once. Few had been successful in these endeavors, however. They are generally not capable of establishing the temporal commitments necessary for relating to such institutions. For example, marriages and similar relationships rarely last more than a few years, and education requires concentrated effort over a time span that they are generally not willing or in many cases not capable of exerting. Most of them drift from one job to another or have no job at all. Simply keeping up with where the informants were living proved to be a challenge. I frequently had a call from a local biker relating that he was "on his way over" only to find that he did not arrive at all or arrived hours or days later. I have been on runs that were to depart in the early morning and that did not in fact depart until hours later. The biker's sense of time and commitment to it is not only lower class, but more typical of preliterate societies. The result is frequent clashes with bureaucratically organized institutions, such as government and economy, which are oriented toward impulse control, commitment, and punctuality, and failure in organizations that require long-term commitments or interpersonal relations, such as family and education.

A similar view of regulation causes frequent conflicts. Bikers are not basically violent but are impulsive. Regulations that conflict with their impulses are ignored. Attempts to enforce such regulations (generally by law enforcement officers) are viewed not as legal regulation but as unreasonable demands (harassment). Of course, this impulsiveness can be destructive and self-defeating. I have seen bikers destroy engines they spent hundreds of dollars on by simply overrevving them. I have also seen doors, jukeboxes, bike gas tanks, and other items destroyed in an impulsive moment—sometimes in rage, sometimes in humor, or out of boredom. Bikers demand freedom to follow these impulses, which often involve behavior defined by the observer as outrageous. Occasionally bikers reinforce this conception by conforming to the stereotype and deliberately shocking more conventional people, especially if they feel their social space is being invaded. An illustrative incidence occurred in 1978 at the National Championship Drag Races, an event for motorcycles in Bowling

Green, Kentucky. An area of a local amusement park was designated "for bikers only." This area was clearly marked with large signs. Occasionally local citizens and outraged tourists insisted on driving through to see the scene. Bikers had begun "partying" and engaging in heavy drinking, drug use, and generally impulsive behavior, including frequent male and female nudity, which occasioned some notice but no shock to other bikers. However, when outsiders drove through, they were deliberately exposed to substantial nudity and what were no doubt interpreted as obscene and disgusting displays by those viewing them. The result was that the city of Bowling Green declined future events of that nature. The races have been held elsewhere in subsequent years.

Outlaw bikers generally view themselves as outsiders. I have on occasion invited local bikers to settings that would place them in contact with members of the middle class. Their frequent response is that they would "not fit in" or would "feel out of place." Basically, they seem to feel that they cannot compete with what sociologists define as the middle class although I have never heard the term used by bikers. Outlaws see themselves as losers, as symbolized by tatoos, patches, and even their humor, which portrays them as ignorant. "One percenter" is a favorite patch, referring to its wearers as the most deviant fraction of the biker fraternity. In effect, the world that they create for themselves is an attempt to suspend the rules of competition that they cannot win by and create a world where one does not compete but simply exists (Montgomery, 1976, 1977). Pretense and self-importance are ways to lose acceptance quickly in such a situation. One does not compete with or "put down" a fellow biker, for he is a "brother."

It is not that bikers are uniformly hostile toward the outside world; they are indifferent toward, somewhat threatened by, and contemptuous of it.

MILLER'S FOCAL CONCERNS AS EXPRESSED IN OUTLAW BIKER CULTURE

Trouble

Trouble is a major theme of the outlaw biker culture as illustrated by the very use of the term "outlaw." The term refers to one who demonstrates his distinctiveness (righteousness) by engaging in outrageous and even illegal behavior. Trouble seems to serve several purposes in this subculture. First, flirting with trouble is a way of demonstrating masculinity—trouble is a traditionally male prerogative.

Trouble also enforces group solidarity through emphasizing the out-sider status of the outlaw, a status that can be sustained only by the formation of counterculture. Given the outlaw biker's world view and impulsiveness, trouble comes without conscious effort. Trouble may come over drug use, stolen bikes or parts, possession of firearms, or something as simple as public drunkenness. Some of the local bik-ers whom I knew well had prison records for manslaughter (defined as self-defense by the subjects), receiving stolen property, drug pos-session, statutory rape, and assault on an officer. All saw these sen-tences as unjust and claimed that the behavior was justifiable or that they were victims of a case of overzealous regulation of everyday ac-tivities or deliberate police harassment.

Trouble used to take the form of violence between biker clubs and groups (Easyriders, April 1979:13, 41). Most of this activity was gen-erated by issues of club honor involving the stealing of women or perceived wrongs by members of other clubs. The general motiva-tion for this activity seemed to be an opportunity to demonstrate toughness (see below). The only open conflict that I saw was an inci-dent, mentioned earlier, between the Brothers and the Convicts over the right of the other groups to wear a one percenter badge as part of their club colors. In recent years most groups have abandoned the practice of interclub violence and emphasize instead the conflict between group members and police. An issue that is a current exam-ple of this conflict and that therefore serves this unifying purpose is the mandatory helmet laws in many states and the related attempts of the federal Department of Transportation to regulate modifica-tion by owners of motorcycles (Supercycle, May 1979:4, 14–15, 66).

Organized reaction to trouble in the sense of attempts to regulate motorcycles and motorcyclists is probably as close to political aware-ness and class consciousness as bikers come. Outlaw types, however, generally have little to do with these activities, partly because they view them as hopeless and partly because they correctly perceive their support and presence at such activities as unwelcome and poor public relations.

Toughness

In addition to trouble, toughness is at the heart of the biker emphasis on masculinity and outrageousness. To be tough is to experience trouble without showing signs of weakness. Therefore, the objective of trouble is to demonstrate the masculine form of toughness. Bikers have contempt for such comforts as automobiles or even devices that increase biking comfort or safety such as eye protection, helmets, windshields, farings or even frames with spring rear suspension (a so-called hardtail is the preferred frame). Bikers wear denim or leather, but the sleeves are generally removed to show contempt for the danger of "road rash," abrasions caused by contact with the road surface at speed, which protective material can prevent. Part of toughness is the prohibition against expressing love for women and children in any but a possessive way. Women are viewed with contempt and are regarded as a necessary nuisance (generally referred to as "cunts," "whores," or "sluts"), as are children ("rug rats"). Curiously, bikers seem to attract an adequate supply of women despite the poor treatment they receive from them in such a situation. One informant expressed his contempt for women this way, "Hell, if I could find a man with a pussy, I wouldn't fuck with women. I don't like 'em. They're nothing but trouble." When asked about the female's motivation for participation in the subculture, one (male) informant stated simply "they're looking for excitement." The women attracted to such a scene are predictably tough and hard-bitten themselves. Not all are unattractive, but most display signs of premature aging typical of lower class and deviant lifestyles. All work to keep up their mate and his motorcycle. I must admit that my interviews with biker women were limited lest my intentions be misinterpreted. I could have hired some of them under sexual pretenses, as many may be bought, but ethical and financial considerations precluded this alternative. My general impression is that these women generally come from lower class families in which the status of the female is not remarkably different from that they currently enjoy. Being a biker's "old lady" offers excitement and opportunities to engage in exhibitionist and outlandish behavior that in their view contrasts favorably with the lives of their mothers. Many are mothers of illegitimate children before they resort to bikers and may view themselves as fallen women who have little to lose in terms of respectability. Most seem to have fairly low self-concepts, which are compatible with their status as bikers' old ladies.

Of course, the large, heavy motorcycles bikers ride are symbolic of their toughness as well. Not everyone can ride such a machine because of its sheer weight. Many models are "kick start," and require some strength and skill just to start. A certain amount of recklessness is also used to express toughness. To quote Bruce Springsteen: "It's a death trap, a suicide rap" (Springsteen, 1976), and the ability to ride it, wreck it, and survive demonstrates toughness in a very dramatic way. An example of my experience in this regard may be illuminating. Although I had ridden motorcycles for years, I became aware of the local biker group while building my first Harley-Davidson. Full acceptance by this group was not extended until my first and potentially fatal accident, however. Indeed, local bikers who had only vaguely known me offered the gift of parts and assistance in reconstructing my bike and began to refer to me by a new nickname, "Doc." I sensed and was extended a new degree of acceptance after demonstrating my "toughness" by surviving the accident. Toughness, in this sense, is a combination of stupidity and misfortune, and hardly relates to any personal virtue.

Smartness

On this characteristic, biker values seem to diverge from general lower class values as described by Miller. The term "dumb biker" is frequently used as a self-description. Given the choice of avoiding, outsmarting, or confronting an opponent, the biker seems to prefer avoidance or confrontation. Confrontation gives him the opportunity to demonstrate toughness by generating trouble. Avoidance is not highly valued, but no one can survive all the trouble he could generate, and the stakes are frequently the highest—life itself or at least loss of freedom. The appearance of toughness and outlandishness mentioned above make confrontation a relatively infrequent occurrence, as few outsiders will challenge a group of outlaw bikers unless the issue is of great significance. Smartness, then, does not seem to be an emphasized biker value or characteristic. Gambling on outsmarting an opponent is for low stakes such as those faced by the adolescents Miller studied.

Excitement

One of the striking things about the outlaw lifestyle is its extremes. Bikers hang out at chopper (motorcycle) shops, clubhouses, or bars during the day, except when they are in prison or jail, which is not uncommon. Places frequented by bikers are generally located in lower class neighborhoods. A clubhouse, for example, is generally a rented house which serves as a headquarters, party location, and place for members to "crash" when they lack more personal accommodations. They are not unlike a lower class version of a fraternity house. Outlaws tend to designate bars as their own. This involves taking over bars to the exclusion of their usual lower or working-class clientele. Such designations are frequently short-lived as the bars may be closed as a public nuisance or the proprietor may go out of business for economic or personal reasons as a result of the takeover. I know of at least one such bar that was burned by local people to rid the neighborhood of the nuisance. Its owner relocated the business some 40 miles away.

Local bikers who worked generally had unskilled and semi-skilled jobs, which are dull in themselves. Examples include laborers, factory workers, construction workers, and hospital orderlies. Many do not work regularly, being supported by their women.[2] In any case, most of their daylight hours are spent in a deadly dull environment, where the most excitement may be a mechanical problem with a bike. Escape from this dull lifestyle is dramatic in its excesses. Drugs, alcohol, and orgiastic parties are one form of escape. Other escapes include the run or simply riding the bikes for which the subculture is named. Frequently both forms of escape are combined, and such events as the Daytona and Sturgis runs are remarkable, comparing favorably to Mardi Gras as orgiastic events. Living on the edge of trouble, appearing outlandish, fierce, and tough, itself yields a form of self-destructive excitement, especially when it can be used to outrage others. Unlike the situation that Miller studied, excitement and trouble rarely seem to center around women, as their status among bikers is even lower than in the lower class in general. I have never seen a conflict over a woman among bikers and am struck by the casual manner in which they move from one biker to another. The exchange of women seems to be the male's prerogative, and women appear to be traded or given away as casually as pocket knives are exchanged among old men. I have on occasion been offered the use of a female for the duration of a run. This offer was always made by the male and was made in the same manner that one might offer the use of a tool to a neighbor. (I have never been offered the loan of a bike, however.) The low regard for women combined with the traditional biker's emphasis on brotherhood seem to minimize conflicts over women. Those conflicts that do occur over women seem to occur between clubs and are a matter of club honor rather than jealousy or grief over the loss of a relationship.

Fate

Because bikers do not emphasize smartness to the extent that Miller perceived it among the lower class, the role of fate in explaining failure to succeed is somewhat different for them. In Miller's analysis fate was a rationalization used when one was outsmarted. The biker's attitude toward fate goes much deeper and could be described as figuratively and literally fatalistic. The theme of death is central to their literature and art.[3] A biker who becomes economically successful or who is too legitimate is suspect. He is no longer one of them. He has succeeded in the outside and in a sense has sold out. His success alone shows his failure to subscribe to the basic values that they hold. He is similar to a rich Indian—no longer an Indian but a white man with red skin. Members of local groups, the Brothers and the Good Old Boys, came and went. Membership fluctuated. Few members resigned because of personal difficulty. However, many former members were still around. The single characteristic that they all shared was economic success. Although these former members tend-'ed to be older than the typical member, many current members were as old or older. Success in small businesses were typical. Some former members had been promoted to lower management positions in local factories and related businesses, apparently were no longer comfortable in their former club roles, and so resigned. Some kept their bikes, others exchanged them for more respectable touring bikes, and others sold their bikes. In any case, although some maintained limited social contact and others participated in occasional weekend runs, their success appeared to make them no longer full participants in group activities and resulted ultimately in their formal resignation from the clubs. Bikers basically see themselves as losers and affect clothing, housing, and other symbols of the embittered and dangerous loser. They apparently no longer dream the unrealistic adolescent dreams of the "big break." Prison and death are seen as natural concomitants of the biker lifestyle. Fate is the grim reaper that so often appears in biker art.

Autonomy

Autonomy in the form of freedom is central to the outlaw biker expressed philosophy and in this respect closely parallels the lower class themes outlined by Miller. A studied insistence that they be left alone by harassing law enforcement agencies and overregulating bureaucrats is a common theme in biker literature and personal expressions. The motorcycle itself is an individual thing, begrudgingly including an extra seat for an "old lady" or "down" brother. Ironically, the outlaw biker lifestyle is so antisocial vis-à-vis the wider society that it cannot be pursued individually. A lone outlaw knows he is a target, an extremely visible and vulnerable one. Therefore, for purposes of self-protection, the true outlaw belongs to a club and rarely makes a long trip without the company of several brothers.

Outlaw clubs are themselves both authoritarian and democratic. Members may vote on issues or at least select officers,[4] but club policy and rules are absolute and may be enforced with violence (Choppers, March 1978:36–39). Antisocial behavior associated with the outlaw lifestyle itself frequently results in loss of autonomy. Most prisons of any size not only contain a substantial biker population but may contain local (prison) chapters of some of the larger clubs (Life, August 1979:80–81). Easyriders, a biker magazine, regularly contains sections for pen pals and other requests from brothers in prison (Easyriders, October 1977:16–19, 70). So, although autonomy in the form of the right to be different is pursued with a vengeance, the ferocity with which it is pursued ensures its frequent loss.

Miller noted an ambivalent attitude among lower class adolescents toward authority: they both resented it and sought situations in which it was forced on them. The structure of outlaw clubs and the frequent incarceration that is a result of their lifestyle would seem to be products of a similar ambivalence. Another loss of autonomy that Miller noted among lower class gangs was a dependence on females that caused dissonance and was responsible for lower class denigration of female status. Outlaws take the whole process a step further, however. Many of their women engage in prostitution, topless waitressing, or menial, traditionally female labor. Some outlaws live off the income of several women and in this sense are dependent on them but only in the sense that a pimp is dependent on his string of girls. From their point of view, the females see themselves as protected by and dependent on the male rather than the other way around.

CONCLUSION

Miller's typology of lower class focal concerns appears to be a valid model for analyzing outlaw biker cultures, just as it was for analyzing some forces behind juvenile gang delinquency. Although there are some differences in values and their expression, the differences are basically those occurring by the transferring of the values from street-wise adolescents to adult males. Both groups could be described as lower class, but my experiences with bikers indicate a working-class family background with downward mobility. A surprising proportion of the bikers interviewed indicated respectable working-class or lower middle-class occupations for their fathers. Examples included postal worker, forestry and lumber contractor, route sales business owner, and real estate agency owner. They are definitely not products of multigenerational poverty. I would classify them as nonrespectable working-class marginals.

The study is presented primarily as an ethnographic description of a difficult and sometimes dangerous subculture to study, which when viewed from the outside appears as a disorganized group of deviants but when studied carefully with some insider's insights is seen to have a coherent and reasonably consistent value system and a life-style based on that value system.

Notes

1. A favorite T-shirt observed at cult events is one saying, "If you ain't a Harley rider, you ain't shit!"
2. Outlaw bikers sometimes support themselves by dealing in drugs, bootleg liquor, and prostitution of their women.
3. Of the fiction in the entire 1977 issue of Easyriders, 40% of the articles concerned themselves with death.
4. Officer selection may be based on many processes, some of which would hardly be recognized as democratic by those outside the subculture. Leaders are popularly selected, however. Physical prowess may be the basis of selection, for example.

References

Choppers
1978 "Club profile: Northern Indiana Invaders M/C." (March):36.
Choppers
1980 "Mailbag." (April):12.
Easyriders
1977 "Gun nut report." (February):28, 29, 55.
Easyriders
1977 "Gang wars are a thing of the past." (April):13, 41.
Easyriders
1977 "Man is the ruler of woman." (October):15.
Easyriders
1977 "Jammin in the joint." (October):16–19 (Also "Mail call").
Easyriders
1978 "The straight dope on Quaaludes." (May):24–25.
Gordon, Robert A., Short, Jr., James F., Cartwright, Desmond, and Strodt-beck, Fred
1963 "Values and gang delinquency." American Journal of Sociology 69:109–128.
Life
1979 "Prison without stripes." (1979):80–81.
Miller, Walter B.
1958 "Lower Class culture as a generating milieu for gang delinquen-cy." Journal of Social Issues 14:5–19.
Montgomery, Randall
1976 "The outlaw motorcycle subculture." Canadian Journal of Crimi-nology and Corrections 18.
Montgomery, Randall
1979 "The outlaw motorcycle subculture II." Canadian Journal of Crim-inology and Corrections 19.
Springsteen, Bruce
1975 "Born to run." Columbia Records.

Supercycle
    1979   "On reserve." (May):14–15, 66.
Thompson, Hunter
    1967   Hell's Angels: a strange and terrible saga. New York: Random
           House.
Watson, John M.
    1979   "Righteousness on two wheels: bikers as a secular sect." Unpub-
           lished paper read at the Southwestern Social Science Association,
           March 1979.

cultural transmission

10 / Differential Association Theory

EDWIN H. SUTHERLAND
DONALD R. CRESSEY

THE PROBLEM FOR CRIMINOLOGICAL THEORY

If criminology is to be scientific, the heterogeneous collection of "multiple factors" known to be associated with crime and criminality should be organized and integrated by means of explanatory theory which has the same characteristics as the scientific theory in other fields of study. That is, the conditions which are said to cause crime should always be present when crime is present, and they should always be absent when crime is absent. Such a theory or body of theory would stimulate, simplify, and give direction to criminological research, and it would provide a framework for understanding the significance of much of the knowledge acquired about crime and criminality in the past. Furthermore, it would be useful in control of crime, provided it could be "applied" in much the same way that the engineer "applies" the scientific theories of the physicist.

There are two complementary procedures which may be used to put order into criminological knowledge, to develop a causal theory of criminal behavior. The first is logical abstraction. Negroes, urban-dwellers, and young adults all have comparatively high crime rates. What do they have in common that results in these high crime rates? Research studies have shown that criminal behavior is associated, in greater or lesser degree, with the social and personal pathologies, such as poverty, bad housing, slum-residence, lack of recreational facilities, inadequate and demoralized families, mental retardation, emotional instability, and other traits and conditions. What do these conditions have in common which apparently produces excessive criminality? Research studies have also demonstrated that many persons with those pathological traits and conditions do not commit crimes and that persons in the upper socioeconomic class frequently violate the law, although they are not in poverty, do not lack recreational facilities, and are not mentally retarded or emotionally unstable. Obviously, it is not the conditions or traits themselves which

125

cause crime, for the conditions are sometimes present when criminality does not occur, and they also are sometimes absent when
criminality does occur. A causal explanation of criminal behavior can
be reached by abstracting, logically, the mechanisms and processes
which are common to the rich and the poor, the Negroes and the
whites, the urban- and the rural-dwellers, the young adults and the old
adults, and the emotionally stable and the emotionally unstable who
commit crimes.

In arriving at these abstract mechanisms and processes, criminal
behavior must be precisely defined and carefully distinguished from
noncriminal behavior. The problem in criminology is to explain the
criminality of behavior, not behavior, as such. The abstract mechanisms and processes common to the classes of criminals indicated
above should not also be common to noncriminals. Criminal behavior
is human behavior, has much in common with noncriminal behavior,
and must be explained within the same general framework used to
explain other human behavior. However, an explanation of criminal
behavior should be a specific part of a general theory of behavior. Its
specific task should be to differentiate criminal from noncriminal
behavior. Many things which are necessary for behavior are not for
that reason important to the criminality of behavior. Respiration, for
instance, is necessary for any behavior, but the respiratory process
cannot be used in an explanation of criminal behavior, for it does not
differentiate criminal behavior from noncriminal behavior.

The second procedure for putting order into criminological knowledge is differentiation of levels of analysis. This means that the problem is limited to a particular part of the whole situation, largely in
terms of chronology. The causal analysis must be held at a particular
level. For example, when physicists stated the law of falling bodies,
they were not concerned with the reasons why a body began to fall
except as this might affect the initial momentum. It made no difference to the physicist whether a body began to fall because it was
dropped from the hand of an experimental physicist or rolled off the
edge of a bridge because of vibration caused by a passing vehicle.
Also, a round object would have rolled off the bridge more readily
than a square object, but this fact was not significant for the law of
falling bodies. Such facts were considered as exsisting on a different
level of explanation and were irrelevant to the problem with which
the physicists were concerned.

Much of the confusion regarding criminal behavior is due to a
failure to define and hold constant the level of explanation. By analogy, many criminologists would attribute some degree of causal
power to the "roundness" of the object in the above illustration.
However, consideration of time sequences among the conditions as-

sociated with crime and criminality may lead to simplicity of statement. In the heterogeneous collection of factors associated with criminal behavior, one factor often occurs prior to another factor (in much the way that "roundness" occurs prior to "vibration," and "vibration" occurs prior to "rolling off a bridge"), but a theoretical statement about criminal behavior can be made without referring to those early factors. By holding the analysis at one level, the early factors are combined with or differentiated from later factors or conditions, thus reducing the number of variables which must be considered in a theory.

A motion picture several years ago showed two boys engaged in a minor theft; they ran when they were discovered; one boy had longer legs, escaped, and became a priest; the other had shorter legs, was caught, committed to a reformatory, and became a gangster. In this comparison, the boy who became a criminal was differentiated from the one who did not become a criminal by the length of his legs. But "length of legs" need not be considered in a criminological theory, for there is no significant relationship between criminality and length of legs; certainly many persons with short legs are law-abiding, and some persons with long legs are criminals. The length of the legs does not determine criminality and has no necessary relation to criminality. In the illustration, the differential in the length of the boys' legs may be observed to be significant to subsequent criminality or noncriminality only to the degree that it determined the subsequent experiences and associations of the two boys. It is in these experiences and associations, then, that the mechanisms and processes which are important to criminality or noncriminality are to be found. A "one-level" theoretical explanation of crime would be concerned solely with these mechanisms and processes, not with the earlier factor, "length of legs."

TWO TYPES OF EXPLANATIONS OF CRIMINAL BEHAVIOR

Scientific explanations of criminal behavior may be stated either in terms of the processes which are operating at the moment of the occurrence of crime or in terms of the processes operating in the earlier history of the criminal. In the first case, the explanation may be called "mechanistic," "situational," or "dynamic"; in the second, "historical" or "genetic." Both types of explanation are desirable. The mechanistic type of explanation has been favored by physical and biological scientists, and it probably could be the more efficient type of explanation of criminal behavior. However, criminological explanations of the mechanistic type have thus far been notably unsuccessful, perhaps largely because they have been formulated in connection with the attempt to isolate personal and social pathologies among criminals. Work from this point of view has, at least, resulted in the conclusion that the immediate determinants of criminal behavior lie in the person-situation complex.

The objective situation is important to criminality largely to the extent that it provides an opportunity for a criminal act. A thief may steal from a fruit stand when the owner is not in sight but refrain when the ower is in sight; a bank burglar may attack a bank which is poorly protected but refrain from attacking a bank protected by watchmen and burglar alarms. A corporation which manufactures automobiles seldom violates the pure food and drug laws, but a meat-packing corporation might violate these laws with great frequency. But in another sense, a psychological or sociological sense, the situation is not exclusive of the person, for the situation which is important is the situation as defined by the person who is involved. That is, some persons define a situation in which a fruit-stand owner is out of sight as a "crime-committing" situation, while others do not so define it. Furthermore, the events in the person-situation complex at the time a crime occurs cannot be separated from the prior life experiences of the criminal. This means that the situation is defined by the person in terms of the inclinations and abilities which he has acquired. For example, while a person could define a situation in such a manner that criminal behavior would be the inevitable result, his past experiences would, for the most part, determine the way in which he defined the situation. An explanation of criminal behavior made in terms of these past experiences is an historical or genetic explanation.

The following paragraphs state such a genetic theory of criminal behavior on the assumption that a criminal act occurs when a situation appropriate for it, as defined by the person, is present. The theory should be regarded as tentative, and it should be tested by the factual information presented in the later chapters and by all other factual information and theories which are applicable.

GENETIC EXPLANATION OF CRIMINAL BEHAVIOR

The following statements refer to the process by which a particular person comes to engage in criminal behavior.

1. *Criminal behavior is learned.* Negatively, this means that criminal behavior is not inherited, as such; also, the person who is not already trained in crime does not invent criminal behavior, just as a person does not make mechanical inventions unless he has had training in mechanics.

2. *Criminal behavior is learned in interaction with other persons in a process of communication*. This communication is verbal in many respects but includes also "the communication of gestures."

3. *The principal part of the learning of criminal behavior occurs within intimate personal groups*. Negatively, this means that the impersonal agencies of communication, such as movies and newspapers, play a relatively unimportant part in the genesis of criminal behavior.

4. *When criminal behavior is learned, the learning includes (a) techniques of committing the crime, which are sometimes very complicated, sometimes very simple; (b) the specific direction of motives, drives, rationalizations, and attitudes*.

5. *The specific direction of motives and drives is learned from definitions of the legal codes as favorable or unfavorable*. In some societies an individual is surrounded by persons who invariably define the legal codes as rules to be observed, while in others he is surrounded by persons whose definitions are favorable to the violation of the legal codes. In our American society these definitions are almost always mixed, with the consequence that we have culture conflict in relation to the legal codes.

6. *A person becomes delinquent because of an excess of definitions favorable to violation of law over definitions unfavorable to violation of law*. This is the principle of differential association. It refers to both criminal and anticriminal associations and has to do with counteracting forces. When persons become criminal, they do so because of contacts with criminal patterns and also because of isolation from anticriminal patterns. Any person inevitably assimilates the surrounding culture unless other patterns are in conflict; a southerner does not pronounce *r* because other southerners do not pronounce *r*. Negatively, this proposition of differential association means that associations which are neutral so far as crime is concerned have little or no effect on the genesis of criminal behavior. Much of the experience of a person is neutral in this sense, e.g., learning to brush one's teeth. This behavior has no negative or positive effect on criminal behavior except as it may be related to associations which are concerned with the legal codes. This neutral behavior is important especially as an occupier of the time of a child so that he is not in contact with criminal behavior during the time he is so engaged in the neutral behavior.

7. *Differential associations may vary in frequency, duration, priority, and intensity*. This means that associations with criminal behavior and also associations with anticriminal behavior vary in those respects. "Frequency" and "duration" as modalities of associations are obvious and need no explanation. "Priority" is assumed to be important in the sense that lawful behavior developed in early childhood may persist throughout life, and also that delinquent be-

havior developed in early childhood may persist throughout life. This tendency, however, has not been adequately demonstrated, and priority seems to be important principally through its selective influence. "Intensity" is not precisely defined, but it has to do with such things as the prestige of the source of a criminal or anticriminal pattern and with emotional reactions related to the associations. In a precise description of the criminal behavior of a person, these modalities would be rated in quantitative form and a mathematical ratio [would] be reached. A formula in this sense has not been developed, and the development of such a formula would be extremely difficult.

8. *The process of learning criminal behavior by association with criminal and anticriminal patterns involves all of the mechanisms that are involved in any other learning.* Negatively, this means that the learning of criminal behavior is not restricted to the process of imitation. A person who is seduced, for instance, learns criminal behavior by association, but this process would not ordinarily be described as imitation.

9. *While criminal behavior is an expression of general needs and values, it is not explained by those general needs and values, since noncriminal behavior is an expression of the same needs and values.* Thieves generally steal in order to secure money, but likewise honest laborers work in order to secure money. The attempts by many scholars to explain criminal behavior by general drives and values, such as the happiness principle, striving for social status, the money motive, or frustration, have been, and must continue to be, futile, since they explain lawful behavior as completely as they explain criminal behavior. They are similar to respiration, which is necessary for any behavior, but which does not differentiate criminal from noncriminal behavior.

It is not necessary, at this level of explanation, to explain why a person has the associations he has; this certainly involves a complex of many things. In an area where the delinquency rate is high, a boy who is sociable, gregarious, active, and athletic is very likely to come in contact with the other boys in the neighborhood, learn delinquent behavior patterns from them, and become a criminal; in the same neighborhood the psychopathic boy who is isolated, introverted, and inert may remain at home, not become acquainted with the other boys in the neighborhood and not become delinquent. In another situation, the sociable, athletic, aggressive boy may become a member of a scout troop and not become involved in delinquent behavior. The person's associations are determined in general context of social organization. A child is ordinarily reared in a family; the place of residence of the family is determined largely by family income; and the delinquency rate is in many respects related to the rental value of the houses. Many other aspects of social organization affect the kinds of associations a person has.

The preceding explanation of criminal behavior purports to explain the criminal and noncriminal behavior of individual persons. As indicated earlier, it is possible to state sociological theories of criminal behavior which explain the criminality of a community, nation, or other group. The problem, when thus stated, is to account for variations in crime rates and involves a comparison of the crime rates of various groups or the crime rates of a particular group at different times. The explanation of a crime rate must be consistent with the explanation of the criminal behavior of the person, since the crime rate is a summary statement of the number of persons in the group who commit crimes and the frequency with which they commit crimes. One of the best explanations of crime rates from this point of view is that a high crime rate is due to social disorganization. The term *social disorganization* is not entirely satisfactory, and it seems preferable to substitute for it the term *differential social organization.* The postulate on which this theory is based, regardless of the name, is that crime is rooted in the social organization and is an expression of that social organization. A group may be organized for criminal behavior or organized against criminal behavior. Most communities are organized for both criminal and anticriminal behavior, and, in that sense the crime rate is an expression of the differential group organization. Differential group organization as an explanation of variations in crime rates is consistent with the differential association theory of the processes by which persons become criminals.

11 / Techniques of Neutralization: A Theory of Delinquency

GRESHAM M. SYKES
DAVID MATZA

As Morris Cohen once said, one of the most fascinating problems about human behavior is why men violate the laws in which they believe. This is the problem that confronts us when we attempt to explain why delinquency occurs despite a greater or lesser commitment to the usages of conformity. A basic clue is offered by the fact that social rules or norms calling for valued behavior seldom if ever take the form of categorical imperatives. Rather, values or norms appear as *qualified* guides for action, limited in their applicability in terms of time, place, persons, and social circumstances. The moral injunction against killing, for example, does not apply to the enemy during combat in time of war, although a captured enemy comes once again under the prohibition. Similarly, the taking and distributing of scarce goods in a time of acute social need is felt by many to be right, although under other circumstances private property is held inviolable. The normative system of a society, then, is marked by what Williams has termed *flexibility;* it does not consist of a body of rules held to be binding under all conditions.[1]

This flexibility is, in fact, an integral part of the criminal law in that measures for "defenses to crimes" are provided in pleas such as non-age, necessity, insanity, drunkenness, compulsion, self-defense, and so on. The individual can avoid moral culpability for his criminal action—and thus avoid the negative sanctions of society—if he can prove that criminal intent was lacking. *It is our argument that much delinquency is based on what is essentially an unrecognized extension of defenses to crimes, in the form of justifications for deviance that are seen as valid by the delinquent but not by the legal system or society at large.*

These justifications are commonly described as rationalizations. They are viewed as following deviant behavior and as protecting the individual from self-blame and the blame of others after the act. But there is also reason to believe that they precede deviant behavior and make deviant behavior possible. It is this possibility that Sutherland mentioned only in passing and that other writers have failed to exploit from the viewpoint of sociological theory. Disapproval flowing from internalized norms and conforming others in the social environment is neutralized, turned back, or deflected in advance. Social controls that serve to check or inhibit deviant motivational patterns are rendered inoperative, and the individual is freed to engage in delinquency without serious damage to his self-image. In this sense, the delinquent both has his cake and eats it too, for he remains committed to the dominant normative system and yet so qualifies its imperatives that violations are "acceptable" if not "right." Thus the delinquent represents not a radical opposition to law-abiding society but something more like an apologetic failure, often more sinned against than sinning in his own eyes. We call these justifications of deviant behavior techniques of neutralization; and we believe these techniques make up a crucial component of Sutherland's "definitions favorable to the violation of law." It is by learning these techniques that the juvenile becomes delinquent, rather than by learning moral imperatives, values, or attitudes standing in direct contradiction to those of the dominant society. In analyzing these techniques, we have found it convenient to divide them into five major types.

① THE DENIAL OF RESPONSIBILITY

Insofar as the delinquent can define himself as lacking responsibility for his deviant actions, the disapproval of self or others is sharply reduced in effectiveness as a restraining influence. As Justice Holmes has said, even a dog distinguishes between being stumbled over and being kicked, and modern society is no less careful to draw a line between injuries that are unintentional, i.e., where responsibility is lacking, and those that are intentional. As a technique of neutralization, however, the denial of responsibility extends much further than the claim that deviant acts are an "accident" or some similar negation of personal accountability. It may also be asserted that delinquent acts are due to forces outside of the individual and beyond his control such as unloving parents, bad companions, or a slum neighborhood. In effect, the delinquent approaches a "billiard ball" conception of himself in which he sees himself as helplessly propelled into new situations. From a psychodynamic viewpoint, this orientation toward one's own actions may represent a profound alienation from self, but it is important to stress the fact that interpretations of responsibility are cultural constructs and not merely idiosyncratic beliefs. The similarity between this mode of justifying illegal behavior assumed by the delinquent and the implications of a "sociological" frame of reference or a "humane" jurisprudence is readily apparent.[2] It is not the validity of this orientation that concerns us here, but its function of deflecting blame attached to violations of social norms and its relative independence of a particular personality structure.[3] By learning to view himself as more acted upon than acting, the delinquent prepares the way for deviance from the dominant normative system without the necessity of a frontal assault on the norms themselves.

THE DENIAL OF INJURY

A second major technique of neutralization centers on the injury or harm involved in the delinquent act. The criminal law has long made a distinction between crimes which are *mala in se* and *mala prohibita*—that is, between acts that are wrong in themselves and acts that are illegal but not immoral—and the delinquent can make the same kind of distinction in evaluating the wrongfulness of his behavior. For the delinquent, however, wrongfulness may turn on the question of whether or not anyone has clearly been hurt by his deviance, and this matter is open to a variety of interpretations. Vandalism, for example, may be defined by the delinquent simply as "mischief"—after all, it may be claimed, the persons whose property has been destroyed can well afford it. Similarly, auto theft may be viewed as "borrowing," and gang fighting may be seen as a private quarrel, an agreed upon duel between two willing parties, and thus of no concern to the community at large. We are not suggesting that this technique of neutralization, labeled the denial of injury, involves an explicit dialectic. Rather, we are arguing that the delinquent frequently, and in a hazy fashion, feels that his behavior does not really cause any great harm despite the fact that it runs counter to law. Just as the link between the individual and his acts may be broken by the denial of responsibility, so may the link between acts and their consequences be broken by the denial of injury. Since society sometimes agrees with the delinquent, e.g., in matters such as truancy, "pranks," and so on, it merely reaffirms the idea that the delinquent's neutralization of social controls by means of qualifying the norms is an extension of common practice rather than a gesture of complete opposition.

THE DENIAL OF THE VICTIM

Even if the delinquent accepts the responsibility for his deviant actions and is willing to admit that his deviant actions involve an injury or hurt, the moral indignation of self and others may be neutralized by an insistence that the injury is not wrong in light of the circumstances. The injury, it may be claimed, is not really an injury; rather, it is a form of rightful retaliation or punishment. By a subtle alchemy the delinquent moves himself into the position of an avenger and the victim is transformed into a wrong-doer. Assaults·on homosexuals or suspected homosexuals, attacks on members of minority groups who are said to have gotten "out of place," vandalism as revenge on an unfair teacher or school official, thefts from a "crooked" store owner—all may be hurts inflicted on a transgressor, in the eyes of the delinquent. As Orwell has pointed out, the type of criminal admired by the general public has probably changed over the course of years and Raffles no longer serves as a hero;[4] but Robin Hood, and his latter-day derivatives such as the tough detective seeking justice outside the law, still capture the popular imagination, and the delinquent may view his acts as part of a similar role.

To deny the existence of the victim, then, by transforming him into a person deserving injury is an extreme form of a phenomenon we have mentioned before, namely, the delinquent's recognition of appropriate and inappropriate targets for his delinquent acts. In addition, however, the existence of the victim may be denied for the delinquent, in a somewhat different sense, by the circumstances of the delinquent act itself. Insofar as the victim is physically absent, unknown, or a vague abstraction (as is often the case in delinquent acts committed against property), the awareness of the victim's existence is weakened. Internalized norms and anticipations of the reactions of others must somehow be activated if they are to serve as guides for behavior; and it is possible that a diminished awareness of the victim plays an important part of determining whether or not this process is set in motion.

④ THE CONDEMNATION OF THE CONDEMNERS

A fourth technique of neutralization would appear to involve a condemnation of the condemners or, as McCorkle and Korn have phrased it, a rejection of the rejectors.[5] The delinquent shifts the focus of attention from his own deviant acts to the motives and behavior of those who disapprove of his violations. His condemners, he may claim, are hypocrites, deviants in disguise, or impelled by personal spite. This orientation toward the conforming world may be of particular importance when it hardens into a bitter cynicism directed against those assigned the task of enforcing or expressing the norms of the dominant society. Police, it may be said, are corrupt, stupid, and brutal. Teachers always show favoritism and parents always "take it out" on their children. By a slight extension, the rewards of conformity—such as material success—become a matter of pull or luck, thus decreasing still further the stature of those who stand on the side of the law-abiding. The validity of this jaundiced viewpoint is not so important as its function in turning back or deflecting the negative sanctions attached to violations of the norms. The delinquent, in effect, has changed the subject of the conversation in the dialogue between his own deviant impulses and the reactions of others; and by attacking others, the wrongfulness of his own behavior is more easily repressed or lost to view.

THE APPEAL TO HIGHER LOYALTIES

Fifth, and last, internal and external social controls may be neutralized by sacrificing the demands of the larger society for the demands of the smaller social groups to which the delinquent belongs, such as the sibling pair, the gang, or the friendship clique. It is important to note that the delinquent does not necessarily repudiate the imperatives of the dominant normative system, despite his failure to follow them. Rather, the delinquent may see himself as caught up in a dilemma that must be resolved, unfortunately, at the cost of violating the law. One aspect of this situation has been studied by Stouffer and Toby in their research on the conflict between particularistic and universalistic demands, between the claims of friendship and general social obligations, and their results suggest that "it is possible to classify people according to a predisposition to select one or the other horn of a dilemma in role conflict."[6] For our purposes, however, the most important point is that deviation from certain norms may occur not because the norms are rejected but because others' norms, held to be more pressing or involving a higher loyalty, are accorded precedence. Indeed, it is the fact that both sets of norms are believed in that gives meaning to our concepts of dilemma and role conflict.

The conflict between the claims of friendship and the claims of law, or a similar dilemma, has of course long been recognized by the social scientist (and the novelist) as a common human problem. If the juvenile delinquent frequently resolves his dilemma by insisting that he must "always help a buddy" or "never squeal on a friend," even when it throws him into serious difficulties with the dominant social order, his choice remains familiar to the supposedly law-abiding. The delinquent is unusual, perhaps, in the extent to which he is able to see the fact that he acts in behalf of the smaller social groups to which he belongs as a justification for violations of society's norms, but it is a matter of degree rather than of kind.

"I didn't mean it." "I didn't really hurt anybody." "They had it coming to them." "Everybody's picking on me." "I didn't do it for myself." These slogans or their variants, we hypothesize, prepare the juvenile for delinquent acts. These "definitions of the situation" represent tangential or glancing blows at the dominant normative system rather than the creation of an opposing ideology; and they are extensions of patterns of thought prevalent in society rather than something created *de novo*.

Techniques of neutralization may not be powerful enough to fully shield the individual from the force of his own internalized values and the reactions of conforming others, for as we have pointed out, juvenile delinquents often appear to suffer from feelings of guilt and shame when called into account for their deviant behavior. And some delinquents may be so isolated from the world of conformity that techniques of neutralization need not be called into play. Nonetheless, we would argue that techniques of neutralization are critical in lessening the effectiveness of social controls and that they lie behind a large share of delinquent behavior. Empirical research in this area is scattered and fragmentary at the present time, but the work of Redl,[7] Cressey,[8] and others has supplied a body of significant data that has done much to clarify the theoretical issues and enlarge the fund of supporting evidence. Two lines of investigation seem to be critical at this stage. First, there is need for more knowledge concerning the differential distribution of techniques of neutralization, as operative patterns of thought, by age, sex, social class, ethnic group, etc. On a priori grounds it might be assumed that these justifications for deviance will be more readily seized by segments of society for whom a discrepancy between common social ideals and social practice is most apparent. It is also possible, however, that the habit of "bending" the dominant normative system—if not "breaking" it— cuts across our cruder social categories and is to be traced primarily to patterns of social interaction within the familial circle. Second, there is need for a greater understanding of the internal structure of techniques of neutralization, as a system of beliefs and attitudes, and its relationship to various types of delinquent behavior. Certain techniques of neutralization would appear to be better adapted to particular deviant acts than to others, as we have suggested, for example, in the case of offenses against property and the denial of the victim. But the issue remains far from clear and stands in need of more information.

In any case, techniques of neutralization appear to offer a promising line of research in enlarging and systematizing the theoretical grasp of juvenile delinquency. As more information is uncovered concerning techniques of neutralization, their origins, and their consequences, both juvenile delinquency in particular and deviation from normative systems in general may be illuminated.

Notes

1. Cf. Robin Williams, Jr., *American Society,* New York: Knopf, 1951, p. 28.
2. A number of observers have wryly noted that many delinquents seem to show a surprising awareness of sociological and psychological explanations for their behavior and are quick to point out the causal role of their poor environment.
3. It is possible, of course, that certain personality structures can accept some techniques of neutralization more readily than others, but this question remains largely unexplored.
4. George Orwell, *Dickens, Dali, and Others,* New York: Reynal, 1946.
5. Lloyd W. McCorkle and Richard Korn, "Resocialization Within Walls," *The Annals of the American Academy of Political and Social Science,* 293 (May, 1954), pp. 88–98.
6. See Samuel A. Stouffer and Jackson Toby, "Role Conflict and Personality," in *Toward a General Theory of Action,* edited by Talcott Parsons and Edward A. Shils, Cambridge, Mass.: Harvard University Press, 1951, p. 494.
7. See Fritz Redl and David Wineman, *Children Who Hate,* Glencoe, Ill.: The Free Press, 1956.
8. See D. R. Cressey, *Other People's Money,* Glencoe, Ill.: The Free Press, 1953.

anomie

12 / Social Structure and Anomie

ROBERT K. MERTON

There persists a notable tendency in sociological theory to attribute the malfunctioning of social structure primarily to those of man's imperious biological drives which are not adequately restrained by social control. In this view, the social order is solely a device for "impulse management" and the "social processing" of tensions. These impulses which break through social control, be it noted, are held to be biologically derived. Nonconformity is assumed to be rooted in original nature.[1] Conformity is by implication the result of a utilitarian calculus or unreasoned conditioning. This point of view, whatever its other deficiencies, clearly begs one question. It provides no basis for determining the nonbiological conditions which induce deviations from prescribed patterns of conduct. In this paper, it will be suggested that certain phases of social structure generate the circumstances in which infringement of social codes constitutes a "normal" response.[2]

The conceptual scheme to be outlined is designed to provide a coherent, systematic approach to the study of socio-cultural sources of deviate behavior. Our primary aim lies in discovering how some social structures *exert a definite pressure* upon certain persons in the society to engage in noncomformist rather than conformist conduct. The many ramifications of the scheme cannot all be discussed; the problems mentioned outnumber those explicitly treated.

Among the elements of social and cultural structure, two are important for our purposes. These are analytically separable although they merge imperceptibly in concrete situations. The first consists of culturally defined goals, purposes, and interests. It comprises a frame of aspirational reference. These goals are more or less integrated and involve varying degrees of prestige and sentiment. They constitute a basic, but not the exclusive, component of what Linton aptly has called "designs for group living." Some of these cultural aspirations are related to the original drives of man, but they are not determined by them. The second phase of the social structure defines, regulates, and controls the acceptable modes of achieving these goals. Every social group invariably couples its scale of desired ends with moral or in-

139

stitutional regulation of permissible and required procedures for attaining these ends. These regulatory norms and moral imperatives do not necessarily coincide with technical or efficiency norms. Many procedures which form the standpoint of *particular individuals* would be most efficient in securing desired values, e.g., illicit oil-stock schemes, theft, fraud, are ruled out of the institutional area of permitted conduct. The choice of expedients is limited by the institutional norms.

To say that these two elements, culture goals and institutional norms, operate jointly is not to say that the ranges of alternative behaviors and aims bear some constant relation to one another. The emphasis upon certain goals may vary independently of the degree of emphasis upon institutional means. There may develop a disproportionate, at times, a virtually exclusive, stress upon the value of specific goals, involving relatively slight concern with the institutionally appropriate modes of attaining these goals. The limiting case in this direction is reached when the range of alternative procedures is limited only by technical rather than institutional considerations. Any and all devices which promise attainment of the all important goal would be permitted in this hypothetical polar case.[3] This constitutes one type of cultural malintegration. A second polar type is found in groups where activities originally conceived as instrumental are transmuted into ends in themselves. The original purposes are forgotten, and ritualistic adherence to institutionally prescribed conduct becomes virtually obsessive.[4] Stability is largely ensured while change is flouted. The range of alternative behaviors is severely limited. There develops a tradition-bound, sacred society characterized by neophobia. The occupational psychosis of the bureaucrat may be cited as a case in point. Finally, there are the intermediate types of groups where a balance between culture goals and institutional means is maintained. These are the significantly integrated and relatively stable, though changing, groups.

An effective equilibrium between the two phases of the social structure is maintained as long as satisfactions accrue to individuals who conform to both constraints, viz., satisfactions from the achievement of the goals and satisfactions emerging directly from the institutionally canalized modes of striving to attain these ends. Success, in such equilibrated cases, is twofold. Success is reckoned in terms of the product and in terms of the process, in terms of the outcome and in terms of activities. Continuing satisfactions must derive from sheer *participation* in a competitive order as well as from eclipsing one's competitors if the order itself is to be sustained. The occasional sacrifices involved in institutionalized conduct must be compensated by socialized rewards. The distribution of statuses and roles through competition must be so organized that positive incentives for conformity to roles and adherence to status obligations are provided *for every position* within the distributive order. Aberrant conduct, therefore, may be viewed as a symptom of dissociation between culturally defined aspirations and socially structured means.

Of the types of groups which result from the independent variation of the two phases of the social structure, we shall be primarily concerned with the first, namely, that involving a disproportionate accent on goals. This statement must be recast in a proper perspective. In no group is there an absence of regulatory codes governing conduct, yet groups do vary in the degree to which these folkways, mores, and institutional controls are effectively integrated with the more diffuse goals which are part of the culture matrix. Emotional convictions may cluster about the complex of socially acclaimed ends, meanwhile shifting their support from the culturally defined implementation of these ends. As we shall see, certain aspects of the social structure may generate countermores and antisocial behavior precisely because of differential emphases on goals and regulations. In the extreme case, the latter may be so vitiated by the goal-emphasis that the range of behavior is limited only by considerations of technical expediency. The sole significant question then becomes, which available means is most efficient in netting the socially approved value?[5] The technically most feasible procedure, whether legitimate or not, is preferred to the institutionally prescribed conduct. As this process continues, the integration of the society becomes tenuous and anomie ensues.

Thus, in competitive athletics, when the aim of victory is shorn of its institutional trappings and success in contests becomes construed as "winning the game" rather than "winning through circumscribed modes of activity," a premium is implicitly set upon the use of illegitimate but technically efficient means. The star of the opposing football team is surreptitiously slugged; the wrestler furtively incapacitates his opponent through ingenious but illicit techniques; university alumni covertly subsidize "students" whose talents are largely confined to the athletic field. The emphasis on the goal has so attenuated the satisfactions deriving from sheer participation in the competitive activity that these satisfactions are virtually confined to a successful outcome. Through the same process, tension generated by the desire to win in a poker game is relieved by successfully dealing oneself four aces, or, when the cult of success has become completely dominant, by sagaciously shuffling the cards in a game of solitaire. The faint twinge of uneasiness in the last instance and the surreptitious nature of public delicts indicate clearly that the institutional rules of the game are *known* to those who evade them, but that the emotional supports of these rules are largely vitiated by cultural exaggeration of the success-goal.[6] They are microcosmic images of the social macrocosm.

Of course, this process is not restricted to the realm of sport. The process whereby exaltation of the end generates a *literal demoralization*, i.e., a deinstitutionalization, of the means is one which characterizes many[7] groups in which the two phases of the social structure are not highly integrated. The extreme emphasis upon the accumulation of wealth as a symbol of success[8] in our own society militates against the completely effective control of institutionally regulated modes of acquiring a fortune.[9] Fraud, corruption, vice, crime, in short, the entire catalogue of proscribed behavior, becomes increasingly common when the emphasis on the *culturally induced* success-goal becomes divorced from a coordinated institutional emphasis. This observation is of crucial theoretical importance in examining the doctrine that antisocial behavior most frequently derives from biological drives breaking through the restraints imposed by society. The difference is one between a strictly utilitarian interpretation which conceives man's ends as random and an analysis which finds these ends deriving from the basic values of the culture.[10]

Our analysis can scarcely stop at this juncture. We must turn to other aspects of the social structure if we are to deal with the social genesis of the varying rates and types of deviate behavior characteristic of different societies. Thus far, we have sketched three ideal types of social orders constituted by distinctive patterns of relations between culture ends and means. Turning from these types of *culture patterning*, we find five logically possible, alternative modes of adjustment or adaptation *by individuals* within the culture-bearing society or group.[11] These are schematically presented in the following table, where (+) signifies "acceptance," (−) signifies "elimination," and (±) signifies "rejection and substitution of new goals and standards."

		Culture goals	Institutionalized means
I.	Conformity	+	+
II.	Innovation	+	−
III.	Ritualism	−	+
IV.	Retreatism	−	−
V.	Rebellion[12]	±	±

Our discussion of the relation between these alternative responses and other phases of the social structure must be prefaced by the observation that persons may shift from one alternative to another as they engage in different social activities. These categories refer to role adjustments in specific situations, not to personality *in toto*. To treat the development of this process in various spheres of conduct would introduce a complexity unmanageable within the confines of this paper. For this reason, we shall be concerned primarily with economic activity in the broad sense, "the production, exchange, distribution, and consumption of goods and services" in our competitive society, wherein wealth has taken on a highly symbolic cast. Our task is to search out some of the factors which exert presure upon individuals to engage in certain of these logically possible alternative responses. This choice, as we shall see, is far from random.

In every society, Adaptation I (conformity to both culture goals and means) is the most common and widely diffused. Were this not so, the stability and continuity of the society could not be maintained. The mesh of expectancies which constitutes every social order is sustained by the modal behavior of its members falling within the first category. Conventional role behavior oriented toward the basic values of the group is the rule rather than the exception. It is this fact alone which permits us to speak of a human aggregate as comprising a group or society.

Conversely, Adaptation IV (rejection of goals and means) is the least common. Persons who "adjust" (or maladjust) in this fashion are, strictly speaking, *in* the society but not *of* it. Sociologically, these constitute the true "aliens." Not sharing the common frame of orientation, they can be included within the societal population merely in a fictional sense. In this category are *some* of the activities of psychotics, psychoneurotics, chronic autists, pariahs, outcasts, vagrants, vagabonds, tramps, chronic drunkards, and drug addicts.[13] These have relinquished, in certain spheres of activity, the culturally defined goals, involving complete aim-inhibition in the polar case, and their adjustments are not in accord with institutional norms. This is not to say that in some cases the source of their behavioral adjustments is not in part the very social structure which they have in effect repudiated nor that their very existence within a social area does not constitute a problem for the socialized population.

This mode of "adjustment" occurs, as far as structural sources are concerned, when both the culture goals and institutionalized procedures have been assimilated thoroughly by the individual and imbued with affect and high positive value, but where those institutionalized procedures which promise a measure of successful attainment of the goals are not available to the individual. In such instances, there results a two-fold mental conflict insofar as the moral obligation for adopting institutional means conflicts with the pressure to resort to illegitimate means (which may attain the goal) and inasmuch as the individual is shut off from means which are both legitimate *and* effective. The competitive order is maintained, but the frustrated and handicapped individual who cannot cope with this order drops out. Defeatism, quietism, and resignation are manifested in escape mechanisms which ultimately lead the individual to "escape" from the requirements of the society. It is an expedient which arises from continued failure to attain the goal by legitimate measures and from an inability to adopt the illegitimate route because of internalized prohibitions and institutionalized compulsives, *during which process the supreme value of the success-goal has as yet not been renounced.* The conflict is resolved by eliminating *both* precipitating elements, the goals and means. The escape is complete, the conflict is eliminated, and the individual is associated.

Be it noted that where frustration derives from the inaccessibility of effective institutional means for attaining economic or any other type of highly valued "success," that Adaptations II, II, and V (innovation, ritualism, and rebellion) are also possible. The result will be determined by the particular personality, and thus, the *particular* cultural background, involved. Inadequate socialization will result in the innovation response whereby the conflict and frustration are eliminated by relinquishing the institutional means and retaining the success-aspiration; an extreme assimilation of institutional demands will lead to ritualism wherein the goal is dropped as beyond one's reach but conformity to the mores persists; and rebellion occurs when emancipation from the reigning standards, due to frustration or to marginalist perspectives, leads to the attempt to introduce a "new social order."

Our major concern is with the illegitimacy adjustment. This involves the use of conventionally proscribed but frequently effective means of attaining at least the simulacrum of culturally defined success,—wealth, power, and the like. As we have seen, this adjustment occurs when the individual has assimilated the cultural emphasis on success without equally internalizing the morally prescribed norms governing means for its attainment. The question arises, Which phases of our social structure predispose toward this mode of adjustment? We may examine a concrete instance, effectively analyzed by Lohman,[14] which provides a clue to the answer. Lohman has shown that specialized areas of vice in the near north side of Chicago constitute a "normal" response to a situation where the cultural emphasis upon pecuniary success has been absorbed, but where there is little access to conventional and legitimate means for attaining such success. The conventional occupational opportunities of persons in this area are almost completely limited to manual labor. Given our cultural stigmatization of manual labor, and its correlate, the prestige of white collar work, it is clear that the result is a strain toward innovational practices. The limitation of opportunity to unskilled labor and the resultant low income cannot compete *in terms of conventional stan-*

dards of achievement with the high income from organized vice.

For our purposes, this situation involves two important features. First, such antisocial behavior is in a sense "called forth" by certain conventional values of the culture *and* by the class structure involving differential access to the approved opportunities for legitimate, prestige-bearing pursuit of the culture goals. The lack of high integration between the means-and-end elements of the cultural pattern and the particular class structure combine to favor a heightened frequency of antisocial conduct in such groups. The second consideration is of equal significance. Recourse to the first of the alternative responses, legitimate effort, is limited by the fact that actual advance toward desired success-symbols through conventional channels is, despite our persisting open-class ideology,[15] relatively rare and difficult for those handicapped by little formal education and few economic resources. The dominant pressure of group standards of success is, therefore, on the gradual attenuation of legitimate, but by and large ineffective, strivings and the increasing use of illegitimate, but more or less effective, expedients of vice and crime. The cultural demands made on persons in this situation are incompatible. On the one hand, they are asked to orient their conduct toward the prospect of accumulating wealth and on the other, they are largely denied effective opportunities to do so institutionally. The consequences of such structural inconsistency are psychopathological personality, and/or antisocial conduct, and/or revolutionary activities. The equilibrium between culturally designated means and ends becomes highly unstable with the progressive emphasis on attaining the prestige-laden ends by any means whatsoever. Within this context, Capone represents the triumph of amoral intelligence over morally prescribed "failure," when the channels of vertical mobility are closed or narrowed[16] *in a society which places a high premium on economic affluence and social ascent for* all *its members.*[17]

This last qualification is of primary importance. It suggests that other phases of the social structure besides the extreme emphasis on pecuniary success must be considered if we are to understand the social sources of antisocial behavior. A high frequency of deviate behavior is not generated simply by "lack of opportunity" or by this exaggerated pecuniary emphasis. A comparatively rigidified class structure, a feudalistic or caste order, may limit such opportunities far beyond the point which obtains in our society today. It is only when a system of cultural values extols, virtually above all else, certain *common* symbols of success *for the population at large* while its social structure rigorously restricts or completely eliminates access to approved modes of acquiring these symbols *for a considerable part of the same population* that antisocial behavior ensues on a considerable scale. In other words, our egalitarian ideology denies by implication the existence of noncompeting groups and individuals in the pursuit of pecuniary success. The same body of success-symbols is held to be desirable for all. These goals are held to *transcend class lines*, not to be bounded by them, yet the actual social organization is such that there exist class differentials in the accessibility of these *common* success-symbols. Frustration and thwarted aspiration lead to the search for avenues of escape from a culturally induced intolerable situation; or unrelieved ambition may eventuate in illicit attempts to acquire the dominant values.[18] The American stress on pecuniary success and ambitiousness for all thus invites exaggerated anxieties, hostilities, neuroses, and antisocial behavior.

This theoretical analysis may go far toward explaining the varying correlations between crime and poverty.[19] Poverty is not an isolated variable. It is one in a complex of interdependent social and cultural variables. When viewed in such a context, it represents quite different states of affairs. Poverty as such, and consequent limitation of opportunity, are not sufficient to induce a conspicuously high rate of criminal behavior. Even the often mentioned "poverty in the midst of plenty" will not necessarily lead to this result. Only insofar as poverty and associated disadvantages in competition for the culture values approved for *all* members of the society are linked with the assimilation of a cultural emphasis on monetary accumulation as a symbol of success is antisocial conduct a "normal" outcome. Thus, poverty is less highly correlated with crime in southeastern Europe than in the United States. The possibilities of vertical mobility in these European areas would seem to be fewer than in this country, so that neither poverty *per se* nor its association with limited opportunity is sufficient to account for the varying correlations. It is only when the full configuration is considered, poverty, limited opportunity, and a commonly shared system of success symbols, that we can explain the higher association between poverty and crime in our society than in others where rigidified class structure is coupled with *differential class symbols of achievement*.

In societies such as our own, then, the pressure of prestige-bearing success tends to eliminate the effective social constraint over means employed to this end. "The-end-justifies-the-means" doctrine becomes a guiding tenet for action when the cultural structure unduly exalts the end and the social organization unduly limits possible recourse to approved means. Otherwise put, this notion and associated behavior reflect a lack of cultural coordination. In international relations, the effects of this lack of integration are notoriously apparent. An emphasis upon national power is not readily coordinated with an inept organization of legitimate, i.e., internationally defined and accepted, means for attaining this goal. The result is a tendency toward the abrogation of international law, treaties become scraps of paper, "undeclared warfare" serves as a technical evasion, the bombing of civilian populations is rationalized,[20] just as the same societal situation induces the same sway of illegitimacy among individuals.

The social order we have described necessarily produces this "strain toward dissolution." The pressure of such an order is upon outdoing one's competitors. The choice of means within the ambit of institutional control will persist as long as the sentiments supporting a competitive system, i.e., deriving from the possibility of outranking competitors and hence enjoying the favorable response of others, are distributed throughout the entire system of activities and are not confined merely to the final result. A stable social structure demands a balanced distribution of affect among its various segments. When there occurs a shift of emphasis from the satisfactions deriving from competition itself to almost exclusive concern with successful competition, the resultant stress leads to the breakdown of the regulatory structure.[21] With the resulting attenuation of the institutional imperatives, there occurs an approximation of the situation erroneously held by utilitarians to be typical of society generally wherein calculations of advantage and fear of punishment are the sole regulating agencies. In such situations, as Hobbes observed, force and fraud come to constitute the sole virtues in view of their relative efficiency in attaining goals—which were for him, of course, not culturally derived.

It should be apparent that the foregoing discussion is not pitched on a moralistic plane. Whatever the sentiments of the writer or reader concerning the ethical desirability of coordinating the means-and-goals phases of the social structure, one must agree that lack of such coordination leads to anomie. Insofar as one of the most general functions of social organization is to provide a basis for calculability and regularity of behavior, it is increasingly limited in effectiveness as these elements of the structure become dissociated. At the extreme, predictability virtually disappears and what may be properly termed cultural chaos or anomie intervenes.

This statement, being brief, is also incomplete. It has not included an exhaustive treatment of the various structural elements which predispose toward one rather than another of the alternative responses open to individuals; it has neglected, but not denied the relevance of, the factors determining the specific incidence of these responses; it has not enumerated the various concrete responses which are constituted by combinations of specific values of the analytical variables; it has omitted, or included only by implication, any consideration of the social functions performed by illicit responses; it has not tested the full explanatory power of the analytical scheme by examining a large number of group variations in the frequency of deviate and conformist behavior; it has not adequately dealt with rebellious conduct which seeks to refashion the social framework radically; it has not examined the relevance of cultural conflict for an analysis of culture-goal and institutional-means malintegration. It is suggested that these and related problems may be profitably analyzed by this scheme.

Notes

1. E.g., Ernest Jones, *Social Aspects of Psychoanalysis*, 28, London, 1924. If the Freudian notion is a variety of the "original sin" dogma, then the interpretation advanced in this paper may be called the doctrine of "socially derived sin."
2. "Normal" in the sense of a culturally oriented, if not approved, response. This statement does not deny the relevance of biological and personality differences which may be significantly involved in the *incidence* of deviate conduct. Our focus of interest is the social and cultural matrix; hence we abstract from other factors. It is in this sense, I take it, that James S. Plant speaks of the "normal reaction of normal people to abnormal conditions." See his *Personality and the Cultural Pattern*, 248, New York, 1937.
3. Contemporary American culture has been said to tend in this direction. See André Siegfried, *America Comes of Age*, 26–37, New York, 1927. The alleged extreme(?) emphasis on the goals of monetary success and material prosperity leads to dominant concern with technological and social instruments designed to produce the desired result, inasmuch as institutional controls become of secondary importance. In such a situation, innovation flourishes as the *range of means* employed is broadened. In a sense, then, there occurs the paradoxical emergence of "materialists" from an "idealistic" orientation. Cf. Durkheim's analysis of the cultural conditions which predispose toward crime and innovation, both of which are aimed toward efficiency, not moral norms. Durkheim was one of the first to see that "contrairement aux idées courantes le criminel n'apparait plus comme un être radicalement insociable, comme une sorte d'elément parasitaire, de corps étranger et inassimilable, introduit au sein de la société; c'est un agent régulier de la vie sociale." See *Les Règles de la Méthode Sociologique*, 86–89, Paris, 1927.
4. Such ritualism may be associated with a mythology which rationalizes these actions so that they appear to retain their status as means, but the dominant pressure is in the direction of strict ritualistic conformity, irrespective of such rationalizations. In this sense, ritual has proceeded farthest when such rationalizations are not even called forth.
5. In this connection, one may see the relevance of Elton Mayo's paraphrase of the title of Tawney's well-known book. "Actually the problem *is not that of the sickness of an acquisitive society; it is that of the acquisitiveness of a sick society.*" *Human Problems of an Industrial Civilization*, 153, New York, 1933. Mayo deals with the process through which wealth comes to be a symbol of social achievement. He sees this as arising from a state of anomie. We are considering the unintegrated monetary-success goal as an element in producing anomie. A complete analysis would involve both phases of this system of interdependent variables.
6. It is unlikely that interiorized norms are completely eliminated. Whatever residuum persists will induce personality tensions and conflict. The process involves a certain degree of ambivalence. A manifest rejection of the institutional norms is coupled with some latent retention of their emotional correlates. "Guilt feelings," "sense of sin," "pangs of conscience" are obvious manifestations of this unrelieved tension; symbolic adherence to the nominally repudiated values or rationalizations constitute a more subtle variety of tensional release.
7. "Many," and not all, unintegrated groups, for the reason already mentioned. In groups where the primary emphasis shifts to institutional means, i.e., when the range of

alternatives is very limited, the outcome is a type of ritualism rather than anomie.

8. Money has several peculiarities which render it particularly apt to become a symbol of prestige divorced from institutional controls. As Simmel emphasized, money is highly abstract and impersonal. However acquired, through fraud or institutionally, it can be used to purchase the same goods and services. The anonymity of metropolitan culture, in conjunction with this peculiarity of money, permits wealth, the sources of which may be unknown to the community in which the plutocraft lives, to serve as a symbol of status.

9. The emphasis upon wealth as a success-symbol is possibly reflected in the use of the term "fortune" to refer to a stock of accumulated wealth. This meaning becomes common in the late sixteenth century (Spenser and Shakespeare). A similar usage of the Latin *fortuna* comes into prominence during the first century B.C. Both these periods were marked by the rise to prestige and power of the "bourgeoisie."

10. See Kingsley Davis, "Mental Hygiene and the Class Structure," *Psychiatry*, 1928, 1: esp. 62–63; Talcott Parsons, *The Structure of Social Action*, 59–60, New York, 1937.

11. This is a level intermediate between the two planes distinguished by Edward Sapir; namely, culture patterns and personal habit systems. See his "Contribution of Psychiatry to an Understanding of Behavior in Society," *Amer. J. Sociol.*, 1937, 42:862–870.

12. This fifth alternative is on a plane clearly different from that of the others. It represents a *transitional* response which seeks to *institutionalize* new procedures oriented toward revamped cultural goals shared by the members of the society. It thus involves efforts to *change* the existing structure rather than to perform accommodative actions *within* this structure, and introduces additional problems with which we are not at the moment concerned.

13. Obviously, this is an elliptical statement. These individuals may maintain some orientation to the values of their particular differentiated groupings within the larger society or, in part, of the conventional society itself. Insofar as they do so, their conduct cannot be classified in the "passive rejection" category (IV). Nels Anderson's description of the behavior and attitudes of the bum, for example, can readily be recast in terms of our analytical scheme. See *The Hobo*, 93–98, *et passim*, Chicago, 1923.

14. Joseph D. Lohman, "The Participant Observer in Community Studies," *Amer. Sociol. Rev.*, 1937, 2:890–898.

15. The shifting historical role of this ideology is a profitable subject for exploration. The "office-boy-to-president" stereotype was once in approximate accord with the facts. Such vertical mobility was probably more common then than now, when the class structure is more rigid. (See the following note.) The ideology largely persists, however, possibly because it still performs a useful function for maintaining the *status quo*. For insofar as it is accepted by the "masses," it constitutes a useful sop for those who might rebel against the entire structure, were this consoling hope removed. This ideology now serves to lessen the probability of Adaptation V. In short, the role of this notion has changed from that of an approximately valid empirical theorem to that of an ideology, in Mannheim's sense.

16. There is a growing body of evidence, though none of it is clearly conclusive, to the effect that our class structure is becoming rigidified and that vertical mobility is declining. Taussig and Joslyn found that American business leaders are being *increasingly* recruited from the upper ranks of our society. The Lynds have also found a "diminished chance to get ahead" for the working classes in Middletown. Manifestly, these objective changes are not alone significant; the individual's subjective evaluation of the situation is a major determinant of the response. The extent to which this change in opportunity for social mobility has been recognized by the least advantaged classes is still conjectural, although the Lynds present some suggestive materials. The writer suggests that a case in point is the increasing frequency of cartoons which observe in a tragi-comic vein that "my old man says everybody can't be President. He says if ya can get three days a week steady on W.P.A. work ya ain't doin' so bad either." See F. W. Taussig and C. S. Joslyn, *American Business Leaders*, New York, 1932; R. S. and H. M. Lynd, *Middletown in Transition*, 67 ff., chap. 12, New York, 1937.

17. The role of the Negro in this respect is of considerable theoretical interest. Certain elements of the Negro population have assimilated the dominant caste's values of pecuniary success and social advancement, but they also recognize that social ascent is at present restricted to their own caste almost exclusively. The pressures upon the Negro which would otherwise derive from the structural inconsistencies we have noticed are hence not identical with those upon lower class whites. See Kingsley Davis, *op. cit.*, 63; John Dollard, *Caste and Class in a Southern Town*, 66 ff., New Haven, 1936; Donald Young, *American Minority Peoples*, 581, New York, 1932.

18. The psychical coordinates of these processes have been partly established by the experimental evidence concerning *Anspruchsniveaus* and levels of performance. See Kurt Lewin, *Vorsatz, Willie und Bedurfnis*, Berlin, 1926; N. F. Hoppe, "Erfolg und Misserfolg," *Psychol. Forschung*, 1930, 14:1–63; Jerome D. Frank, "Individual Differences in Certain Aspects of the Level of Aspiration," *Amer. J. Psychol.*, 1935, 47:119–128.

19. Standard criminology texts summarize the data in this field. Our scheme of analysis may serve to resolve some of the theoretical contradictions which P. A. Sorokin indicates. For example, "not everywhere nor always do the poor show a greater proportion of crime . . . many poorer countries have had less crime than the richer countries . . . . The [economic] improvement in the second half of the nineteenth century, and the beginning of the twentieth, has not been followed by a decrease of crime." See his *Contemporary Sociological Theories*, 560–561, New York, 1928. The crucial point is, however, that poverty has varying social significance in different social structures, as we shall see. Hence, one would not expect a linear correlation between crime and poverty.

20. See M. W. Royse, *Aerial Bombardment and the International Regulation of War*, New York, 1928.

21. Since our primary concern is with the socio-cultural aspects of this problem, the psychological correlates have been only implicitly considered. See Karen Horney, *The Neurotic Personality of Our Time*, New York, 1937, for a psychological discussion of this process.

13 / Differential Opportunity and Delinquent Subcultures

RICHARD A. CLOWARD
LLOYD E. OHLIN

THE AVAILABILITY OF ILLEGITIMATE MEANS

Social norms are two-sided. A prescription implies the existence of a prohibition, and *vice versa*. To advocate honesty is to demarcate and condemn a set of actions which are dishonest. In other words, norms that define legitimate practices also implicitly define illegitimate practices. One purpose of norms, in fact, is to delineate the boundary between legitimate and illegitimate practices. In setting this boundary, in segregating and classifying various types of behavior, they make us aware not only of behavior that is regarded as right and proper but also of behavior that is said to be wrong and improper. Thus the criminal who engages in theft or fraud does not invent a new way of life; the possibility of employing alternative means is acknowledged, tacitly at least, by the norms of the culture.

This tendency for proscribed alternatives to be implicit in every prescription, and *vice versa*, although widely recognized, is nevertheless a reef upon which many a theory of delinquency has foundered. Much of the criminological literature assumes, for example, that one may explain a criminal act simply by accounting for the individual's readiness to employ illegal alternatives of which his culture, through its norms, has already made him generally aware. Such explanations are quite unsatisfactory, however, for they ignore a host of questions regarding the *relative availability* of illegal alternatives to various potential criminals. The aspiration to be a physician is hardly enough to explain the fact of becoming a physician; there is much that transpires between the aspiration and the achievement. This is no less true of the person who wants to be a successful criminal. Having decided that he "can't make it legitimately," he cannot simply choose among an array of illegitimate means, all equally available to him. As we have noted earlier, it is assumed in the theory of anomie that access to conventional means is differentially distributed, that some individuals, because of their social class, enjoy certain advantages that are denied to those elsewhere in the class structure. For example, there are variations in the degree to which members of various classes are fully exposed to and thus acquire the values, knowledge, and skills that facilitate upward mobility. It should not be startling, therefore, to suggest that there are socially structured variations in the availability of illegitimate means as well. In connection with delinquent subcultures, we shall be concerned principally with differentials in access to illegitimate means within the lower class.

Many sociologists have alluded to differentials in access to illegitimate means without explicitly incorporating this variable into a theory of deviant behavior. This is particularly true of scholars in the "Chicago tradition" of criminology. Two closely related theoretical perspectives emerged from this school. The theory of "cultural transmission," advanced by Clifford R. Shaw and Henry D. McKay, focuses on the development in some urban neighborhoods of a criminal tradition that persists from one generation to another despite constant changes in population.[1] In the theory of "differential association," Edwin H. Sutherland described the processes by which criminal values are taken over by the individual.[2] He asserted that criminal behavior is learned, and that it is learned in interaction with others who have already incorporated criminal values. Thus the first theory stresses the value systems of different areas; the second, the systems of social relationships that facilitate or impede the acquisition of these values.

Scholars in the Chicago tradition, who emphasized the processes involved in learning to be criminal, were actually pointing to differentials in the availability of illegal means—although they did not explicitly recognize this variable in their analysis. This can perhaps best by seen by examining Sutherland's classic work, *The Professional Thief.* "An inclination to steal," according to Sutherland, "is not a sufficient explanation of the genesis of the professional thief."[3] The "self-made" thief, lacking knowledge of the ways of securing immunity from prosecution and similar techniques of defense, "would quickly land in prison; . . . a person can be a professional thief only if he is recognized and received as such by other professional thieves." But recognition is not freely accorded: "Selection and tutelage are the two necessary elements in the process of acquiring recognition as a professional thief. . . . A person cannot acquire recognition as a professional thief until he has had tutelage in professional theft, *and tutelage is given only to a few persons selected from the total population.*" For one thing, "the person must be appreciated by the professional thieves. He must be appraised as having an adequate equipment of wits, front, talking-ability, honesty, reliability, nerve and determination." Furthermore, the aspirant is judged by high standards of performance, for only "a very small percentage of those who start on this process ever reach the stage of professional thief. . . ." Thus motivation and pressures toward deviance do not fully account for deviant behavior any more than motivation and pressures toward conformity account for conforming behavior. The individual must have access to a learning environment and, once having been trained, must be allowed to perform his role. Roles, whether conforming or deviant in content, are not necessarily freely available; access to them depends upon a variety of factors, such as one's socioeconomic position, age, sex, ethnic affiliation, personality characteristics, and the like. The potential thief, like the potential physician, finds that access to his goal is governed by many criteria other than merit and motivation.

What we are asserting is that access to illegitimate roles is not freely available to all, as is commonly assumed. Only those neighborhoods in which crime flourishes as a stable, indigenous institution are fertile criminal learning environments for the young. Because these environments afford integration of different age-levels of offender, selected young people are exposed to "differential association" through which tutelage is provided and criminal values and skills are acquired. To be prepared for the role may not, however, ensure that the individual will ever discharge it. One important limitation is that more youngsters are recruited into these patterns of differential associations than the adult criminal structure can possibly absorb. Since there is a surplus of contenders for these elite positions, criteria and mechanisms of selection must be evolved. Hence a certain proportion of those who aspire may not be permitted to engage in the behavior for which they have prepared themselves.

Thus we conclude that access to illegitimate roles, no less than access to legitimate roles, is limited by both social and psychological factors. We shall here be concerned primarily with socially structured differentials in illegitimate opportunities. Such differentials, we contend, have much to do with the type of delinquent subculture that develops.

LEARNING AND PERFORMANCE STRUCTURES

Our use of the term "opportunities," legitimate or illegitimate, implies access to both learning and performance structures. That is, the individual must have access to appropriate environments for the acquisition of the values and skills associated with the performance of a particular role, and he must be supported in the performance of the role once he has learned it.

Tannenbaum, several decades ago, vividly expressed the point that criminal role performance, no less than conventional role performance, presupposes a patterned set of relationships through which the requisite values and skills are transmitted by established practitioners to aspiring youth:

> It takes a long time to make a good criminal, many years of specialized training and much preparation. But training is something that is given to people. People learn in a community where the materials and the knowledge are to be had. A craft needs an atmosphere saturated with purpose and promise. The community provides the attitudes, the point of view, the philosophy of life, the example, the motive, the contacts, the friendships, the incentives. No child brings those into the world. He finds them here and available for use and elaboration. The community gives the criminal his materials and habits, just as it gives the doctor, the lawyer, the teacher, and the candlestick-maker theirs.[4]

Sutherland systematized this general point of view, asserting that opportunity consists, at least in part, of learning structures. Thus "criminal behavior is learned" and, furthermore, it is learned "in interaction with other persons in a process of communication." However, he conceded that the differential-association theory does not constitute a full explanation of criminal behavior. In a paper circulated in 1944, he noted that "criminal behavior is partially a function of opportunities to commit [i.e., to perform] specific classes of crime, such as embezzlement, bank burglary, or illicit heterosexual intercourse." Therefore, "while opportunity may be partially a function of association with criminal patterns and of the specialized techniques thus acquired, it is not determined entirely in that manner, and consequently differential association is not the sufficient cause of criminal behavior."[5]

To Sutherland, then, illegitimate opportunity included conditions favorable to the performance of a criminal role as well as conditions favorable to the learning of such a role (differential associations). These conditions, we suggest, depend upon certain features of the social structure of the community in which delinquency arises.

We believe that each individual occupies a position in both legitimate and illegitimate opportunity structures. This is a new way of defining the situation. The theory of anomie views the individual primarily in terms of the legitimate opportunity structure. It poses questions regarding differentials in access to legitimate routes to success-goals; at the same time it assumes either that illegitimate avenues to success-goals are freely available or that differentials in their availability are of little significance. This tendency may be seen in the following statement by Merton:

> Several researches have shown that specialized areas of vice and crime constitute a "normal" response to a situation where the cultural emphasis upon pecuniary success has been absorbed, but where there is little access to conventional and legitimate means for becoming successful. The occupational opportunities of people in these areas are largely confined to manual labor and the lesser white-collar jobs. Given the American stigmatization of manual labor *which has been found to hold rather uniformly for all social classes*, and the absence of realistic opportunities for advancement beyond this level, the result is a marked tendency toward deviant behavior. The status of unskilled labor and the consequent low income cannot readily compete *in terms of established standards of worth* with the promises of power and high income from organized vice, rackets and crime. . . . [Such a situation] leads toward the gradual attenuation of legitimate, but by and large ineffectual, strivings and the increasing use of illegitimate, but more or less effective, expedients.[6]

The cultural-transmission and differential-association tradition, on the other hand, assumes that access to illegitimate means is variable, but it does not recognize the significance of comparable differentials in access to legitimate means. Sutherland's "ninth proposition" in the theory of differential association states:

> *Though criminal behavior is an expression of general needs and values, it is not explained by those general needs and values since non-criminal behavior is an expression of the same needs and values.* Thieves generally steal in order to secure money, but likewise honest laborers work in order to secure money. The attempts by many scholars to explain criminal behavior by general drives and values, such as the happiness principle, striving for social status, the money motive, or frustration, have been and must continue to be futile since they explain lawful behavior as completely as they explain criminal behavior.[7]

In this statement, Sutherland appears to assume that people have equal and free access to legitimate means regardless of their social position. At the very least, he does not treat access to legitimate means as variable. It is, of course, perfectly true that "striving for social status," "the money motive," and other socially approved drives do not fully account for either deviant or conforming behavior. But if goal-oriented behavior occurs under conditions in which there are socially structured obstacles to the satisfaction of these drives by legitimate means, the resulting pressures, we contend, might lead to deviance.

The concept of differential opportunity structures permits us to unite the theory of anomie, which recognizes the concept of differentials in access to legitimate means, and the "Chicago tradition," in which the concept of differentials in access to illegitimate means is implicit. We can now look at the individual, not simply in relation to one or the other system of means, but in relation to both legitimate and illegitimate systems. This approach permits us to ask, for example, how the relative availability of illegitimate opportunities affects the resolution of adjustment problems leading to deviant behavior. We believe that the way in which these problems are resolved may depend upon the kind of support for one or another type of illegitimate activity that is given at different points in the social structure. If, in a given social location, illegal or criminal means are not readily available, then we should not expect a criminal subculture to develop among adolescents. By the same logic, we should expect the manipulation of violence to become a primary avenue to higher status only in areas where the means of violence are not denied to the young. To give a third example, drug addiction and participation in subcultures organized around the consumption of drugs presuppose that persons can secure access to drugs and knowledge about how to use them. In some parts of the social structure, this would be very difficult; in others, very easy. In short, there are marked differences from one part of the social structure to another in the types of illegitimate adaptation that are available to persons in search of solutions to problems of adjustment arising from the restricted availability of legitimate means.[8] In this sense, then, we can think of individuals as being located in two opportunity structures—one legitimate, the other illegitimate. Given limited access to success-goals by legitimate means, the nature of the delinquent response that may result will vary according to the availability of various illegitimate means.[9]

VARIETIES OF DELINQUENT SUBCULTURE

As we have noted, there appear to be three major types of delinquent subculture typically encountered among adolescent males in lower-class areas of large urban centers. One is based principally upon criminal values; its members are organized primarily for the pursuit of material gain by such illegal means as extortion, fraud, and theft. In the second, violence is the keynote; its members pursue status ("rep") through the manipulation of force or threat of force. These are the "warrior" groups that attract so much attention in the press. Finally, there are subcultures which emphasize the consumption of drugs. The participants in these drug subcultures have become alienated from conventional roles, such as those required in the family or the occupational world. They have withdrawn into a restricted world in which the ultimate value consists in the "kick." We call these three subcultural forms "criminal," "conflict," and "retreatist," respectively.[10]

These shorthand terms simply denote the *principal* orientation of each form of adaptation from the perspective of the dominant social order; although one can find many examples of subcultures that fit accurately into one of these three categories, subcultures frequently appear in somewhat mixed form. Thus members of a predominantly conflict subculture may also on occasion engage in systematic theft; members of a criminal subculture may sometimes do combat in the streets with rival gangs. But this should not obscure the fact that these subcultures tend to exhibit essentially different orientations.

The extent to which the delinquent subculture organizes and controls a participant's allegiance varies from one member to another. Some members of the gang are almost totally immersed in the perspectives of the subculture and bring them into play in all their contacts; others segregate this aspect of their lives and maintain other roles in the family, school, and church. The chances are relatively slight, however, that an adolescent can successfully segregate delinquent and conforming roles for a long period of time. Pressures emanate from the subculture leading its members to adopt unfavorable attitudes toward parents, school teachers, policemen, and other adults in the conventional world. When he is apprehended for delinquent acts, the possibility of the delinquent's maintaining distinctly separate role involvements breaks down, and he is confronted with the necessity of choosing between law-abiding and delinquent styles of life. Since family, welfare, religious, educational, law-enforcement, and correctional institutions are arrayed against the appeal of his delinquent associates, the decision is a difficult one, frequently requiring either complete acceptance or complete rejection of one or the other system of obligations.[11]

At any one point in time, however, the extent to which the norms of the delinquent subculture control behavior will vary from one member to another. Accordingly, descriptions of these subcultures must be stated in terms of the fully indoctrinated member rather than the average member. Only in this way can the distinctiveness of delinquent styles of life be made clear. It is with this understanding that we offer the following brief empirical characterizations of the three main types of delinquent subculture.

The Criminal Pattern

The most extensive documentation in the sociological literature of delinquent behavior patterns in lower-class culture describes a tradition which integrates youthful delinquency with adult criminality.[12]

In the central value orientation of youths participating in this tradition, delinquent and criminal behavior is accepted as a means of achieving success-goals. The dominant criteria of in-group evaluation stress achievement, the use of skill and knowledge to get results. In this culture, prestige is allocated to those who achieve material gain and power through avenues defined as illegitimate by the larger society. From the very young to the very old, the successful "haul"—which quickly transforms the penniless into a man of means—is an ever-present vision of the possible and desirable. Although one may also achieve material success through the routine practice of theft or fraud, the "big score" remains the symbolic image of quick success.

The means by which a member of a criminal subculture achieves success are clearly defined for the aspirant. At a young age, he learns to admire and respect older criminals and to adopt the "right guy" as his role-model. Delinquent episodes help him to acquire mastery of the techniques and orientation of the criminal world and to learn how to cooperate successfully with others in criminal enterprises. He exhibits hostility and distrust toward representatives of the larger society. He regards members of the conventional world as "suckers," his natural victims, to be exploited when possible. He sees successful people in the conventional world as having a "racket"—e.g., big businessmen have huge expense accounts, politicians get graft, etc. This attitude successfully neutralizes the controlling effect of conventional norms. Toward the in-group the "right guy" maintains relationships of loyalty, honesty, and trustworthiness. He must prove himself reliable and dependable in his contacts with his criminal associates although he has no such obligations toward the out-group of noncriminals.

One of the best ways of assuring success in the criminal world is to cultivate appropriate "connections." As a youngster, this means running with a clique composed of other "right guys" and promoting an apprenticeship or some other favored relationship with older and successful offenders. Close and dependable ties with income-producing outlets for stolen goods, such as the wagon peddler, the junkman, and the fence, are especially useful. Furthermore, these intermediaries encourage and protect the young delinquent in a criminal way of life by giving him a jaundiced perspective on the private morality of many functionaries in conventional society. As he matures, the young delinquent becomes acquainted with a new world made up of predatory bondsmen, shady lawyers, crooked policemen, grafting politicians, dishonest businessmen, and corrupt jailers. Through "connections" with occupants of these half-legitimate, half-illegitimate roles and with "big shots" in the underworld, the aspiring criminal validates and assures his freedom of movement in a world made safe for crime.

The Conflict Pattern[13]

The role-model in the conflict pattern of lower-class culture is the "bopper" who swaggers with his gang, fights with weapons to win a wary respect from other gangs, and compels a fearful deference from the conventional adult world by his unpredictable and destructive assaults on persons and property. To other gang members, however, the key qualities of the bopper are those of the successful warrior. His performance must reveal a willingness to defend his personal integrity and the honor of the gang. He must do this with great courage and displays of fearlessness in the face of personal danger.

The immediate aim in the world of fighting gangs is to acquire a reputation for toughness and destructive violence. A "rep" assures not only respectful behavior from peers and threatened adults but also admiration for the physical strength and masculinity which it symbolizes. It represents a way of securing access to the scarce resources for adolescent pleasure and opportunity in underprivileged areas.

Above all things, the bopper is valued for his "heart." He does not "chicken out," even when confronted by superior force. He never defaults in the face of a personal insult or a challenge to the integrity of his gang. The code of the bopper is that of the warrior who places great stress on courage, the defense of his group, and the maintenance of honor.

Relationships between bopping gang members and the adult world are severely attenuated. The term that the bopper uses most frequently to characterize his relationships with adults is "weak." He is unable to find appropriate role-models that can designate for him a structure of opportunities leading to adult success. He views himself as isolated and the adult world as indifferent. The commitments of adults are to their own interests and not to his. Their explanations of why he should behave differently are "weak," as are their efforts to help him.

Confronted by the apparent indifference and insincerity of the adult world, the ideal bopper seeks to win by coercion the attention and opportunities he lacks and cannot otherwise attract. In recent years the street-gang worker who deals with the fighting gang on its own "turf" has come to symbolize not only a recognition by conventional adult society of the gang's toughness but also a concession of opportunities formerly denied. Through the alchemy of competition between gangs, this gesture of attention by the adult world to the "worst" gangs is transformed into a mark of prestige. Thus does the manipulation of violence convert indifference into accommodation and attention into status.

The Retreatist Pattern

Retreatism may include a variety of expressive, sensual, or consummatory experiences, alone or in a group. In this analysis, we are interested only in those experiences that involve the use of drugs and that are supported by a subculture. We have adopted these limitations in order to maintain our focus on subcultural formations which are clearly recognized as delinquent, as drug use by adolescents is. The retreatist preoccupation with expressive experiences creates many varieties of "hipster" cult among lower-class adolescents which foster patterns of deviant but not necessarily delinquent conduct.

Subcultural drug-users in lower-class areas perceive themselves as culturally and socially detached from the life-style and everyday preoccupations of members of the conventional world. The following characterization of the "cat" culture, observed by Finestone in a lower-class Negro area in Chicago, describes drug use in the more general context of "hipsterism."[14] Thus it should not be assumed that this description in every respect fits drug cultures found elsewhere. We have drawn heavily on Finestone's observations, however, because they provide the best descriptions available of the social world in which lower-class adolescent drug cultures typically arise.

The dominant feature of the retreatist subculture of the "cat" lies in the continuous pursuit of the "kick." Every cat has a kick—alcohol, marijuana, addicting drugs, unusual sexual experiences, hot jazz, cool jazz, or any combination of these. Whatever its content, the kick is a search for ecstatic experiences. The retreatist strives for an intense awareness of living and a sense of pleasure that is "out of this world." In extreme form, he seeks an almost spiritual and mystical knowledge that is experienced when one comes to know "it" at the height of one's kick. The past and the future recede in the time perspective of the cat, since complete awareness in present experience is the essence of the kick.

The successful cat has a lucrative "hustle" which contrasts sharply with the routine and discipline required in the ordinary occupational tasks of conventional society. The many varieties of the hustle are characterized by a rejection of violence or force and a preference for manipulating, persuading, outwitting, or "conning" others to obtain resources for experiencing the kick. The cat begs, borrows, steals, or engages in some petty con-game. He caters to the illegitimate cravings of others by peddling drugs or working as a pimp. A highly exploitative attitude toward women permits the cat to view pimping as a prestigeful source of income. Through the labor of "chicks" engaged in prostitution or shoplifting, he can live in idleness and concentrate his entire attention on organizing, scheduling, and experiencing the esthetic pleasure of the kick. The hustle of the cat is secondary to his interest in the kick. In this respect the cat differs from his fellow delinquents in the criminal subculture, for whom income-producing activity is a primary concern.

The ideal cat's appearance, demeanor, and taste can best be characterized as "cool." The cat seeks to exhibit a highly developed and sophisticated taste for clothes. In his demeanor, he struggles to reveal a self-assured and unruffled manner, thereby emphasizing his aloofness and "superiority" to the "squares." He develops a colorful, discriminating vocabulary and ritualized gestures which express his sense of difference from the conventional world and his solidarity with the retreatist subculture.

The word "cool" also best describes the sense of apartness and detachment which the retreatist experiences in his relationships with the conventional world. His reference group is the "society of cats," and "elite" group in which he becomes isolated from conventional society. Within this group, a new order of goals and criteria of achievement are created. The cat does not seek to impose this system of values on the world of the squares. Instead, he strives for status and deference within the society of cats by cultivating the kick and the hustle. Thus the retreatist subculture provides avenues to success-goals, to the social admiration and the sense of well-being or oneness with the world which the members feel are otherwise beyond their reach.

Notes

1. See esp. C. R. Shaw, *The Jack-Roller* (Chicago: University of Chicago Press, 1930); Shaw, *The Natural History of a Delinquent Career* (Chicago: University of Chicago Press, 1931); Shaw *et al.*, *Delinquency Areas* (Chicago: University of Chicago Press, 1940); and Shaw and H. D. McKay, *Juvenile Delinquency and Urban Areas* (Chicago: University of Chicago Press, 1942).

2. E. H. Sutherland, ed., *The Professional Thief* (Chicago: University of Chicago Press, 1937); and Sutherland, *Principles of Criminology*, 4th Ed. (Philadelphia: Lippincott, 1947).

3. All quotations on this page are from *The Professional Thief*, pp. 211–13. Emphasis added.

4. Frank Tannenbaum, "The Professional Criminal," *The Century*, Vol. 110 (May-Oct. 1925), p. 577.

5. See A. K. Cohen, Alfred Lindesmith, and Karl Schuessler, eds., *The Sutherland Papers* (Bloomington, Ind.: Indiana University Press, 1956), pp. 31–35.

6. R. K. Merton, *Social Theory and Social Structure*, Rev. and Enl. Ed. (Glencoe, Ill.: Free Press, 1957), pp. 145–46.

7. *Principles of Criminology*, *op. cit.*, pp. 7–8.

8. For an example of restrictions on access to illegitimate roles, note the impact of racial definitions in the following case: "I was greeted by two prisoners who were to be .

my cell buddies. Ernest was a first offender, charged with being a 'hold-up' man. Bill, the other buddy, was an older offender, going through the machinery of becoming a habitual criminal, in and out of jail. . . . The first thing they asked me was, 'What are you in for?' I said, 'Jack-rolling.' The hardened one (Bill) looked at me with a superior air and said, 'A hoodlum, eh? An ordinary sneak thief. Not willing to leave jack-rolling to the niggers, eh? That's all they're good for. Kid, jack-rolling's not a white man's job.' I could see that he was disgusted with me, and I was too scared to say anything." (Shaw, *The Jack-Roller, op. cit.*, p. 101).

9. For a discussion of the way in which the availability of illegitimate means influences the adaptations of inmates to prison life, see R. A. Cloward, "Social Control in the Prison," *Theoretical Studies of the Social Organization of the Prison*, Bulletin No. 15 (New York: Social Science Research Council, March 1960), pp. 20–48.

10. It should be understood that these terms characterize these delinquent modes of adaptation from the reference position of conventional society; they do not necessarily reflect the attitudes of members of the subcultures. Thus the term "retreatist" does not necessarily reflect the attitude of the "cat." Far from thinking of himself as being in retreat, he defines himself as among the elect.

11. Tannenbaum summarizes the community's role in this process of alienation by the phrase "dramatization of evil" (Frank Tannenbaum, *Crime and the Community* [New York: Columbia University Press, 1938], pp. 19–21). For a more detailed account of this process, see Chap. 5, *infra*.

12. See esp. C. R. Shaw, *The Jack Roller* (Chicago: University of Chiago Press, 1930); Shaw, *The Natural History of a Delinquent Career* (Chicago: University of Chicago Press, 1940); Shaw and H. D. McKay, *Juvenile Delinquency and Urban Areas* (Chicago: University of Chicago Press, 1942); E. H. Sutherland, ed., *The Professional Thief (Chicago: University of Chicago Press, 1937)*; Sutherland, *Principles of Criminology*, 4th ed. (Philadelphia: J. P. Lippincott Co., 1947); and Sutherland, *White Collar Crime* (New York: Dryden Press, 1949).

13. For descriptions of conflict groups, see Harrison Salisbury, *The Shook-up Generation* (New York: Harper & Bros., 1958); *Reaching the Unreached*, a Publication of the New York City Youth Board, 1952; C. K. Myers, *Light the Dark Streets* (Greenwich, Conn.: Seabury Press, 1957); Walter Bernstein, "The Cherubs Are Rumbling," *The New Yorker*, Sept. 21, 1957; Sam Glane, "Juvenile Gangs in East Side Los Angeles," *Focus*, Vol. 29 (Sept. 1959), pp. 136–41; Dale Kramer and Madeline Karr, *Teen-Age Gangs* (New York: Henry Holt, 1953); S. V. Jones, "The Cougars—Life with a Brooklyn Gang," *Harper's*, Vol. 209 (Nov. 1954), pp. 35–43; P. C. Crawford, D. I. Malamud, and J. R. Dumpson, *Working with Teen-Age Gangs* (New York Welfare Council, 1950); Dan Wakefield, "The Gang That Went Good," *Harper's*, Vol. 216 (June 1958), pp. 36–43.

14. Harold Finestone, "Cats, Kicks and Color," *Social Problems*, Vol. 5 (July 1957), pp. 3–13.

14 / A Sociological Analysis of the Law of Vagrancy

WILLIAM J. CHAMBLISS

With the outstanding exception of Jerome Hall's analysis of theft[1] there has been a severe shortage of sociologically relevant analyses of the relationship between particular laws and the social setting in which these laws emerge, are interpreted, and take form. The paucity of such studies is somewhat surprising in view of widespread agreement that such studies are not only desirable but absolutely essential to the development of a mature sociology of law.[2] A fruitful method of establishing the direction and pattern of this mutual influence is to systematically analyze particular legal categories, to observe the changes which take place in the categories and to explain how these changes are themselves related to and stimulate changes in the society. This chapter is an attempt to provide such an analysis of the law of vagrancy in Anglo-American Law.

LEGAL INNOVATION: THE EMERGENCE OF THE LAW OF VAGRANCY IN ENGLAND

There is general agreement among legal scholars that the first full fledged vagrancy statute was passed in England in 1349. As is generally the case with legislative innovations, however, this statute was preceded by earlier laws which established a climate favorable to such change. The most significant forerunner to the 1349 vagrancy statute was in 1274 when it was provided:

> Because that abbies and houses of religion have been overcharged and sore grieved, by the resort of great men and other, so that their goods have not been sufficient for themselves, whereby they have been greatly hindered and impoverished, that they cannot maintain themselves, nor such charity as they have been accustomed to do; it is provided, that none shall come to eat or lodge in any house of religion, or any other's foundation than of his own, at the costs of the house, unless he be required by the governor of the house before his coming hither.[3]

Unlike the vagrancy statutes this statute does not intend to curtail the movement of persons from one place to another, but is solely designed to provide the religious houses with some financial relief from the burden of providing food and shelter to travelers.

The philosophy that the religious houses were to give alms to the poor and to the sick and feeble was, however, to undergo drastic change in the next fifty years. The result of this changed attitude was the establishment of the first vagrancy statute in 1349 which made it a crime to give alms to any who were unemployed while being of sound mind and body. To wit:

> Because that many valiant beggars, as long as they may live of begging, do refuse to labor, giving themselves to idleness and vice, and sometimes to theft and other abominations; it is ordained, that none, upon pain of imprisonment shall, under the colour of pity or alms, give anything to such which may labour, or presume to favour them towards their desires; so that thereby they may be compelled to labour for their necessary living.[4]

It was further provided by this statute that:

> ... every man and woman, of what condition he be, free or bond, able in body, and within the age of threescore years, not living in merchandize nor exercising any craft, nor having of his own whereon to live, nor proper land whereon to occupy himself, and not serving any other, if he in convenient service (his estate considered) be required to serve, shall be bounded to serve him which shall him require. . . . And if any refuse, he shall on conviction by two true men, . . . be commited to gaol till he find surety to serve.
>
> And if any workman or servant, of what estate or condition he be, retained in any man's service, do depart from the said service without reasonable cause or license, before the term agreed on, he shall have pain of imprisonment.[5]

There was also in this statute the stipulation that the workers should receive a standard wage. In 1351 this statute was strengthened by the stipulation:

> And none shall go out of the town where he dwelled in winter, to serve the summer, if he may serve in the same town.[6]

By 34 Ed. 3 (1360) the punishment for these acts became imprisonment for fifteen days and if they "do not justify themselves by the end of that time, to be sent to gaol till they do."

A change in official policy so drastic as this did not, of course, occur simply as a matter of whim. The vagrancy statutes emerged as a result of changes in other parts of the social structure. The prime-mover for this legislative innovation was the Black Death which struck England about 1348. Among the many disastrous consequences this had upon the social structure was the fact that it decimated the labor force. It is estimated that by the time the pestilence had run its course at least fifty per cent of the population of England had died from the plague. This decimation of the labor force would necessitate rather drastic innovations in any society but its impact was heightened in England where, at this time, the economy was highly dependent upon a steady supply of cheap labor.

Even before the pestilence, however, the availability of an adequate supply of cheap labor was becoming a problem for the landowners. The crusades and various wars had made money necessary to the lords and, as a result, the lord frequently agreed to sell the serfs their freedom in order to obtain the needed funds. The serfs, for their part, were desirous of obtaining their freedom (by "fair means" or "foul") because the larger towns which were becoming more industrialized during this period could offer the serf greater personal freedom as well as a higher standard of living. This process is nicely summarized by Bradshaw:

> By the middle of the 14th century the outward uniformity of the manorial system had become in practice considerably varied . . . for the peasant had begun to drift to the towns and it was unlikely that the old village life in its unpleasant aspects should not be resented. Moreover the constant wars against France and Scotland were fought mainly with mercenaries after Henry III's time and most villages contributed to the new armies. The bolder serfs either joined the armies or fled to the towns, and even in the villages the free men who held by villein tenure were as eager to commute their services as the serfs were to escape. Only the amount of "free" labor available enabled the lord to work his demesne in many places.[7]

And he says regarding the effect of the Black Death:

> . . . in 1348 the Black Death reached England and the vast mortality that ensued destroyed that reserve to labor which alone had made the manorial system even nominally possible.[8]

The immediate result of these events was of course no surprise: Wages for the "free" man rose considerably and this increased, on the one hand, the landowner's problems and, on the other hand, the plight of the unfree tenant. For although wages increased for the personally free laborers, it of course did not necessarily add to the standard of living of the serf, if anything it made his position worse because the landowner would be hard pressed to pay for the personally free labor which he needed and would thus find it more and more difficult to maintain the standard of living for the serf which he had heretofore supplied. Thus the serf had no alternative but flight if he chose to better his position. Furthermore, flight generally meant both freedom and better conditions since the possibility of work in the new weaving industry was great and the chance of being caught small.[9]

It was under these conditions that we find the first vagrancy statutes emerging. There is little question but that these statutes were designed for one express purpose: to force laborers (whether personally free or unfree) to accept employment at a low wage in order to insure the landowner an adequate supply of labor at a price he could afford to pay. Caleb Foote concurs with this interpretation when he notes:

> The anti-migratory policy behind vagrancy legislation began as an essential complement of the wage stabilization legislation which accompanied the breakup of feudalism and the depopulation caused by the Black Death. By the Statutes of Labourers in 1349–1351, every able-bodied person without other means of support was required to work for wages fixed at the level preceding the Black Death; it was unlawful to accept more, or to refuse an offer to work, or to flee from one country to another to avoid offers of work or to seek higher wages, or go give alms to able-bodied beggars who refused to work.[10]

In short, as Foote says in another place, this was an "attempt to make the vagrancy statutes a substitute for serfdom."[11] This same conclusion is equally apparent from the wording of the statute where it is stated:

> Because great part of the people, and especially of workmen and servants, late died in pestilence; many seeing the necessity of masters, and great scarcity of servants, will not serve without excessive wages, and some rather willing to beg in idleness than by labour to get their living: it is ordained, that every man and woman, of what condition he be, free or bond, able in body and within the age of threescore years, not living in merchandize, (etc.) be required to serve. . . .

The innovation in the law, then, was a direct result of the aforementioned changes which had occurred in the social setting. In this case these changes were located for the most part in the economic institution of the society. The vagrancy laws were designed to alleviate a condition defined by the lawmakers as undesirable. The solution was to attempt to force a reversal, as it were, of a social process which was well underway; that is, to curtail mobility of laborers in such a way that labor would not become a commodity for which the landowners would have to compete.

Statutory Dormancy: A Legal Vestige

In time, of course, the curtailment of the geographical mobility of laborers was no longer requisite. One might well expect that when the function served by the statute was no longer an important one for society, the statutes would be eliminated from the law. In fact, this has not occurred. The vagrancy statutes have remained in effect since 1349. Furthermore, as we shall see in some detail later, they were taken over by the colonies and have remained in effect in the United States as well.

The substance of the vagrancy statutes changed very little for some time after the first ones in 1349–1351 although there was a tendency to make punishments more harsh than originally. For example, in 1360 it was provided that violators of the statute should be imprisoned for fifteen days,[12] and in 1388 the punishment was to put the offender in the stocks and to keep him there until "he find surety to return to his service."[13] That there was still, at this time, the intention of providing the landowner with labor is apparent from the fact that this statute provides:

> ... and he or she which use to labour at the plough and cart, or other labour and service of husbandry, till they be of the age of 12 years, from thenceforth shall abide at the same labour without being put to any mistery or handicraft: and any covenant of apprenticeship to the contrary shall be void.[14]

The next alteration in the statutes occurs in 1495 and is restricted to an increase in punishment. Here it is provided that vagrants shall be "set in stocks, there to remain by the space of three days and three nights, and there to have none other sustenance but bread and water; and after the said three days and nights, to be had out and set at large, and then to be commanded to avoid the town."[15]

The tendency to increase the severity of punishment during this period seems to be the result of a general tendency to make finer distinctions in the criminal law. During this period the vagrancy statutes appear to have been fairly inconsequential in either their effect as a control mechanism or as a generally enforced statute.[16] The processes of social change in the culture generally and the trend away from serfdom and into a "free" economy obviated the utility of these statutes. The result was not unexpected. The judiciary did not apply the law and the legislators did not take it upon themselves to change the law. In short, we have here a period of dormancy in which the statute is neither applied nor altered significantly.

A SHIFT IN FOCAL CONCERN

Following the squelching of the Peasant's Revolt in 1381, the services of the serfs to the lord ". . . tended to become less and less exacted, although in certain forms they lingered on till the seventeenth century. . . . By the sixteenth century few knew there were any bondmen in England . . . and in 1575 Queen Elizabeth listened to the prayers of almost the last serfs in England . . . and granted them man-umission."[17]

In view of this change we would expect corresponding changes in the vagrancy laws. Beginning with the lessening of punishment in the statute of 1503 we find these changes. However, instead of remaining dormant (or becoming more so) or being negated altogether, the vagrancy statutes experienced a shift in focal concern. With this shift the statutes served a new and equally important function for the social order of England. The first statute which indicates this change was in 1530. In this statute (22 H. 8. c. 12 1530) it was stated:

> If any person, being whole and mighty in body, and able to labour, be taken in begging, or be vagrant and can give no reckoning how he lawfully gets his living; . . . and all other idle persons going about, some of them using divers and subtle crafty and unlawful games and plays, and some of them feigning themselves to have knowledge of . . . crafty sciences . . . shall be punished as provided.

What is most significant about this statute is the shift from an earlier concern with laborers to a concern with *criminal* activities. To be sure, the stipulation of persons "being whole and mighty in body, and able to labour, be taken in begging, or be vagrant" sounds very much like the concerns of the earlier statutes. Some important differences are apparent however when the rest of the statute includes those who ". . . can give no reckoning how he lawfully gets his living"; "some of them using divers subtil and unlawful games and plays." This is the first statute which specifically focuses upon these kinds of criteria for adjudging someone a vagrant.

It is significant that in this statute the severity of punishment is increased so as to be greater not only than provided by the 1503 statute but the punishment is more severe than that which had been provided by *any* of the pre-1503 statutes as well. For someone who is merely idle and gives no reckoning of how he makes his living the offender shall be:

> . . . had to the next market town, or other place where they [the constables] shall think most convenient, and there to be tied to the end of a cart naked, and to be beaten with whips throughout the same market town or other place, till his body be bloody by reason of such whipping.[18]

But, for those who use "divers and subtil crafty and unlawful games and plays," etc., the punishment is ". . . whipping at two days together in manner aforesaid."[19] For the second offense, such persons are:

> . . . scourged two days, and the third day to be put upon the pillory from nine of the clock till eleven before noon of the same day and to have one of his ears cut off.[20]

And if he offend the third time "... to have like punishment with whipping, standing on the pillory and to have his other ear cut off."

This statute (1) makes a distinction between types of offenders and applies the more severe punishment to those who are clearly engaged in "criminal" activities, (2) mentions a specific concern with categories of "unlawful" behavior, and (3) applies a type of punishment (cutting off the ear) which is generally reserved for offenders who are defined as likely to be a fairly serious criminal.

Only five years later we find for the first time that the punishment of death is applied to the crime of vagrancy. We also note a change in terminology in the statute:

> and if any ruffians ... after having been once apprehended ... shall wander, loiter, or idle use themselves and play the vagabonds ... shall be eftfoons not only whipped again, but shall have the gristle of his right ear clean cut off. And if he shall again offend, he shall be committed to gaol till the next sessions; and being there convicted upon indictment, he shall have judgments to suffer pains and execution of death, as a felon, as an enemy of the commonwealth.[21]

It is significant that the statute now makes persons who repeat the crime of vagrancy a felon. During this period then, the focal concern of the vagrancy statutes becomes a concern for the control of felons and is no longer primarily concerned with the movement of laborers.

These statutory changes were a direct response to changes taking place in England's social structure during this period. We have already pointed out that feudalism was decaying rapidly. Concomitant with the breakup of feudalism was an increased emphasis upon commerce and industry. The commercial emphasis in England at the turn of the sixteenth century is of particular importance in the development of vagrancy laws. With commercialism came considerable traffic bearing valuable items. Where there were 169 important merchants in the middle of the fourteenth century there were 3,000 merchants engaged in foreign trade alone at the beginning of the sixteenth century.[22] England became highly dependent upon commerce for its economic support. Italians conducted a great deal of the commerce of England during this early period and were held in low repute by the populace. As a result, they were subject to attacks by citizens and, more important, were frequently robbed of their goods while transporting them. "The general insecurity of the times made any transportation hazardous. The special risks to which the alien merchant was subjected gave rise to the royal practice of issuing formally executed covenants of safe conduct through the realm."[23]

Such a situation not only called for the enforcement of existing laws but also called for the creation of new laws which would facilitate the control of persons preying upon merchants transporting goods. The vagrancy statutes were revived in order to fulfill just such a purpose. Persons who had committed no serious felony but who were suspected of being capable of doing so could be apprehended and incapacitated through the application of vagrancy laws once these laws were refocused so as to include ". . . any ruffians . . . [who] shall wander, loiter, or idle use themselves and play the vagabonds. . . ."[24]

The new focal concern is continued in 1 Ed. 6. c. 3 (1547) and in fact is made more general so as to include:

> Whoever man or woman, being not lame, impotent, or so aged or diseased that he or she cannot work, not having whereon to live, shall be lurking in any house, or loitering or idle wandering by the highway side, or in streets, cities, towns, or villages, not applying themselves to some honest labour, and so continuing for three days; or running away from their work; every such person shall be taken for a vagabond. And . . . upon conviction of two witnesses . . . the same loiterer (shall) be marked with a hot iron in the breast with the letter V, and adjudged him to the person bringing him, to be his slave for two years. . . .

Should the vagabond run away, upon conviction, he was to be branded by a hot iron with the letter S on the forehead and to be thenceforth declared a slave forever. And in 1571 there is modification of the punishment to be inflicted, whereby the offender is to be "branded on the chest with the letter V" (for vagabond). And, if he is convicted the second time, the brand is to be made on the forehead. It is worth noting here that this method of punishment, which first appeared in 1530 and is repeated here with somewhat more force, is also an indication of a change in the type of person to whom the law is intended to apply. For it is likely that nothing so permanent as branding would be applied to someone who was wandering but looking for work, or at worst merely idle and not particularly dangerous *per se*. On the other hand, it could well be applied to someone who was likely to be engaged in other criminal activities in connection with being "vagrant."

By 1571 in the statute of 14 Ed. c. 5 the shift in focal concern is fully developed:

> All rogues, vagabonds, and sturdy beggers shall . . . be committed to the common goal . . . he shall be grievously whipped, and burnt thro' the gristle of the right ear with a hot iron of the compass of an inch about. . . . And for the second offense, he shall be adjudged a felon, unless some person will take him for two years in to his service. And for the third offense, he shall be adjudged guilty of felony without benefit of clergy.

And there is incuded a long list of persons who fall within the statute: "proctors, procurators, idle persons going about using subtil, crafty and unlawful games or plays; and some of them feigning themselves to have knowledge of . . . absurd sciences . . . and all fencers, bearwards, common players in interludes, and minstrels . . . all juglers, pedlars, tinkers, petty chapmen . . . and all counterfeiters of licenses, passports and users of the same." The major significance of this statute is that it includes all the previously defined offenders and adds some more. Significantly, those added are more clearly criminal types, counterfeiters, for example. It is also significant that there is the following qualification of this statute: "Provided also, that this act shall not extend to cookers, or harvest folks, that travel for harvest work, corn or hay."

That the changes in this statute were seen as significant is indicated by the following statement which appears in the statute:

> And whereas by reason of this act, the common goals of every shire are like to be greatly pestered with more number of prisoners than heretofore hath been, for that the said vagabonds and other lewd persons before recited shall upon their apprehension be committed to the said goals; it is enacted. . . .[25]

And a provision is made for giving more money for maintaining the gaols. This seems to add credence to the notion that this statute was seen as being significantly more general than those previously.

It is also of importance to note that this is the first time the term *rogue* has been used to refer to persons included in the vagrancy statutes. It seems, *a priori*, that a "rogue" is a different social type than is a "vagrant" or a "vagabond"; the latter terms implying something more equivalent to the idea of a "tramp" whereas the former (rogue) seems to imply a more disorderly and potentially dangerous person.

The emphasis upon the criminalistic aspect of vagrants continues in Chapter 17 of the same statute:

> Whereas divers *licentious* persons wander up and down in all parts of the realm, to countenance their *wicked behavior;* and do continually assemble themselves armed in the highways, and elsewhere in troops, *to the great terror* of her majesty's true subjects, *the impeachment of her laws,* and the disturbance of the peace and tranquility of the realm; and whereas many outrages are daily committed by these dissolute persons, and more are likely to ensue if speedy remedy be not provided. (Italics added.)

With minor variations (e.g., offering a reward for the capture of a vagrant) the statutes remained essentially of this nature until 1743. In 1743 there was once more an expansion of the types of persons included such that "all persons going about as patent gatherers, or gatherers of alms, under pretense of loss by fire or other casualty; or going about as collectors for prisons, gaols, or hospitals; all persons playing of betting at any unlawful games; and all persons who run away and leave their wives or children . . . all persons wandering abroad, and lodging in alehouses, barns, outhouses, or in the open air, not giving good account of themselves," were types of offenders added to those already included.

By 1743 the vagrancy statutes had apparently been sufficiently reconstructed by the shifts of concern so as to be once more a useful instrument in the creation of social solidarity. This function has apparently continued down to the present day in England and the changes from 1743 to the present have been all in the direction of clarifying or expanding the categories covered but little has been introduced to change either the meaning or the impact of this branch of the law.

We can summarize this shift in focal concern by quoting from Halsbury. He has noted that in the vagrancy statutes:

> . . . elaborate provision is made for the relief and incidental control of destitute wayfarers. These latter, however, form but a small portion of the offenders aimed at by what are known as the Vagrancy Laws, . . . many offenders who are in no ordinary sense of the word vagrants, have been brought under the laws relating to vagrancy, and the great number of the offenses coming within the operation of these laws have little or no relation to the subject of poor relief, but are more properly directed towards the prevention of crime, the preservation of good order, and the promotion of social economy.[26]

Before leaving this section it is perhaps pertinent to make a qualifying remark. We have emphasized throughout this section how the vagrancy statutes underwent a shift in focal concern as the social setting changed. The shift in focal concern is not meant to imply that the later focus of the statutes represents a completely new law. It will be recalled that even in the first vagrancy statute there was reference to those who "do refuse labor, giving themselves to idleness and vice and sometimes to theft and other abominations." Thus the possibility of criminal activities resulting from persons who refuse to labor was recognized even in the earliest statute. The fact remains, however, that the major emphasis in this statute and in the statutes which followed the first one was always upon the "refusal to labor" or "begging." The "criminalistic" aspect of such persons was relatively unimportant. Later, as we have shown, the criminalistic potential becomes of paramount importance. The thread runs back to the earliest statute but the reason for the statutes' existence as well as the focal concern of the statutes is quite different in 1743 than it was in 1349.

VAGRANCY LAWS IN THE UNITED STATES

In general, the vagrancy laws of England, as they stood in the middle eighteenth century, were simply adopted by the states. There were some exceptions to this general trend. For example, Maryland restricted the application of vagrancy laws to "free" Negroes. In addition, for *all* states the vagrancy laws were even more explicitly concerned with the control of criminals and undesirables than had been the case in England. New York, for example, explicitly defines prostitutes as being a category of vagrants during this period. These exceptions do not, however, change the general picture significantly and it is quite appropriate to consider the U.S. vagrancy laws as following from England's of the middle eighteenth century with relatively minor changes. The control of criminals and undesirables was the *raison d'être* of the vagrancy laws in the U.S. This is as true today as it was in 1750. As Caleb Foote's analysis of the application of vagrancy statutes in the Philadelphia court shows, these laws are presently applied indiscriminately to persons considered a "nuisance." Foote suggests that ". . . the chief significance of this branch of the criminal law lies in its quantitative impact and administration usefulness."[27] Thus it appears that in America the trend begun in England in the sixteenth, seventeenth and eighteenth centuries has been carried to its logical extreme and the laws are now used principally as a mechanism for "clearing the streets" of the derelicts who inhabit the "skid rows" and "Bowerys" of our large urban areas.

Since the 1800's there has been an abundant source of prospects to which the vagrancy laws have been applied. These have been primarily those persons deemed by the police and the courts to be either actively involved in criminal activities or at least peripherally involved. In this context, then, the statutes have changed very little. The functions served by the statutes in England of the late eighteenth century are still being served today in both England and the United States. The locale has changed somewhat and it appears that the present day application of vagrancy statutes is focused upon the arrest and confinement of the "down and outers" who inhabit certain sections of our larger cities but the impact has remained constant. The lack of change in the vagrancy statutes, then, can be seen as a reflection of the society's perception of a continuing need to control some of its "suspicious" or "undesirable" members.[28]

A word of caution is in order lest we leave the impression that this administrative purpose is the sole function of vagrancy laws in the U.S. today. Although it is our contention that this is generally true it is worth remembering that during certain periods of our recent history, and to some extent today, these laws have also been used to control the movement of workers. This was particularly the case during the depression years and California is of course infamous for its use of vagrancy laws to restrict the admission of migrants from other states.[29] The vagrancy statutes, because of their history, still contain germs within them which make such effects possible. Their main purpose, however, is clearly no longer the control of laborers but rather the control of the undesirable, the criminal and the "nuisance."

DISCUSSION

The foregoing analysis of the vagrancy laws has demonstrated that these laws were a legislative innovation which reflected the socially perceived necessity of providing an abundance of cheap labor to landowners during a period when serfdom was breaking down and when the pool of available labor was depleted. With the eventual breakup of feudalism the need for such laws eventually disappeared and the increased dependence of the economy upon industry and commerce rendered the former use of the vagrancy statutes unnecessary. As a result, for a substantial period the vagrancy statutes were dormant, undergoing only minor changes and, presumably, being applied infrequently. Finally, the vagrancy laws were subjected to considerable alteration through a shift in the focal concern of the statutes. Whereas in their inception the laws focused upon the "idle" and "those refusing to labor" after the turn of the sixteenth century and emphasis came to be upon "rogues," "vagabonds," and others who were suspected of being engaged in criminal activities. During this period the focus was particularly upon "road men" who preyed upon citizens who transported goods from one place to another. The increased importance of commerce to England during this period made it necessary that some protection be given persons engaged in this enterprise and the vagrancy statutes provided one source for such protection by refocusing the acts to be included under the statutes.

Comparing the results of this analysis with the findings of Hall's study of theft we see a good deal of correspondence. Of major importance is the fact that both analyses demonstrate the truth of Hall's assertion that "The functioning of courts is significantly related to concomitant cultural needs, and this applies to the law of procedure as well as to substantive law."[30]

Our analysis of the vagrancy laws also indicates that when changed social conditions create a perceived need for legal changes that these alterations will be effected through the revision and refocusing of existing statutes. This process was demonstrated in Hall's analysis of theft as well as in our analysis of vagrancy. In the case of vagrancy the laws were dormant when the focal concern of the laws was shifted so as to provide control over potential criminals. In the case of theft the laws were re-interpreted (interestingly, by the courts and not by the legislature) so as to include persons who were transporting goods for a merchant but who absconded with the contents of the packages transported.

It also seems probable that when the social conditions change and previously useful laws are no longer useful there will be long periods when these laws will remain dormant. It is less likely that they will be officially negated. During this period of dormancy it is the judiciary which has principal responsibility for *not* applying the statutes. It is possible that one finds statutes being negated only when the judiciary stubbornly applies laws which do not have substantial public support. An example of such laws in contemporary times would be the "Blue Laws." Most states still have laws prohibiting the sale of retail goods on Sunday yet these laws are rarely applied. The laws are very likely to remain but to be dormant unless a recalcitrant judge or a vocal minority of the population insists that the laws be applied. When this happens we can anticipate that the statutes will be negated.[31] Should there arise a perceived need to curtail retail selling under some special circumstances, then it is likely that these laws will undergo a shift in focal concern much like the shift which characterized the vagrancy laws. Lacking such application the laws will simply remain dormant except for rare instances where they will be negated.

This analysis of the vagrancy statutes (and Hall's analysis of theft as well) has demonstrated the importance of "vested interest" groups in the emergence and/or alteration of laws. The vagrancy laws emerged in order to provide the powerful landowners with a ready supply of cheap labor. When this was no longer seen as necessary and particularly when the landowners were no longer dependent upon cheap labor nor were they a powerful interest group in the society the laws became dormant. Finally a new interest group emerged and was seen as being of great importance to the society and the laws were then altered so as to afford some protection to this group. These findings are thus in agreement with Weber's contention that "status groups" determine the content of the law.[32] The findings are inconsistent, on the other hand, with the perception of the law as simply a reflection of "public opinion" as is sometimes found in the literature.[33] We should be cautious in concluding, however, that either of these positions is necessarily correct. The careful analysis of other laws, and especially of laws which do not focus so specifically upon the "criminal," are necessary before this question can be finally answered.

In conclusion, it is hoped that future analyses of changes within the legal structure will be able to benefit from this study by virtue of (1) the data provided and (2) the utilization of a set of concepts (innovation, dormancy, concern and negation) which have proved useful in the analysis of the vagrancy law. Such analyses should provide us with more substantial grounds for rejecting or accepting as generally valid the description of some of the processes which appear to characterize changes in the legal system.

Notes

1. Hall, J., *Theft, Law and Society* (Bobbs-Merrill, 1939). See also, Alfred R. Lindesmith, "Federal Law and Drug Addiction," *Social Problems*, Vol. 7, No. 1, 1959, p. 48.

2. See, for examples, Rose, A., "Some Suggestions for Research in the Sociology of Law," *Social Problems*, Vol. 9, No. 3, 1962, pp. 281–283, and Geis, G., "Sociology, Criminology, and Criminal Law," *Social Problems*, Vol. 7, No. 1, 1959, pp. 40–47. *For a more complete listing of most of the statutes dealt with in this report the reader is referred to Burn*, The History of the Poor Laws. *Citations of English statutes should be read as follows: 3 Ed. 1. c. 1. refers to the third act of Edward the first, chapter one, etc.*

3. 3 Ed. 1. c. 1.

4. 35 Ed. 1. c. 1.

5. 23 Ed. 3.

6. 25 Ed. 3 (1351).

7. Bradshaw, F., *A Social History of England*, p. 54.

8. *Ibid.*

9. *Ibid.*, p. 57.

10. Foote, C., "Vagrancy Type Law and Its Administration," *Univ. of Pennsylvania Law Review* (104), 1956, p. 615.

11. *Ibid.*

12. 34 Ed. 3 (1360).

13. 12 R. 2 (1388).

14. *Ibid.*

15. 11 H. & C. 2 (1495).

16. As evidenced for this note the expectation that ". . . the common gaols of every shire are likely to be greatly pestered with more numbers of prisoners than heretofore . . ." when the statutes were changed by the statute of 14 Ed. c. 5 (1571).

17. Bradshaw, *op. cit.*, p. 61.

18. 22 H. 8. c. 12 (1530).

19. *Ibid.*

20. *Ibid.*

21. 27 H. 8. c. 25 (1535).

22. Hall, *op. cit.*, p. 21.

23. *Ibid.*, p. 23.

24. 27 H. 8. c. 25 (1535).

25. 14 E., c. 5. (1571).

26. Earl of Halsbury, *The Laws of England* (Butterworth & Co., Bell Yard, Temple Bar, 1912), pp. 606–607.

27. Foote, *op. cit.*, p. 613. Also see in this connection, Irwin Deutscher; "The Petty Offender," *Federal Probation*, XIX, June, 1955.

28. It is on this point that the vagrancy statutes have been subject to criticism. See for example, Lacey, Forrest W., "Vagrancy and Other Crimes of Personal Condition," *Harvard Law Review* (66), p. 1203.

29. *Edwards v. California,* 314 S. 160 (1941).

30. Hall, *op. cit.,* p. XII.

31. Negation, in this instance, is most likely to come about by the repeal of the statute. More generally, however, negation may occur in several ways including the declaration of a statute as unconstitutional. This later mechanism has been used even for laws which have been "on the books" for long periods of time. Repeal is probably the most common, although not the only, procedure by which a law is negated.

32. M. Rheinstein, *Max Weber on Law in Economy and Society* (Harvard University Press, 1954).

33. Friedman, N., *Law in a Changing Society* (Berkeley and Los Angeles: University of California Press, 1959).

conflict

15 / A Radical Perspective on Crime

JEFFREY H. REIMAN

THE IMPLICIT IDEOLOGY OF CRIMINAL JUSTICE

Every criminal justice system conveys a subtle, yet powerful message in support of established institutions. It does this for two interconnected reasons.

First, because it concentrates on *individual* wrongdoers. This means that *it diverts our attention away from our institutions, away from consideration of whether our institutions themselves are wrong or unjust or indeed "criminal."*

Second, because the criminal law is put forth as the *minimum neutral ground rules* for any social living. We are taught that no society can exist without rules against theft and violence, and thus the criminal law is put forth as politically neutral, as the minimum requirements of *any* society, as the minimum obligations that any individual owes his fellows to make social life of any decent sort possible. Thus, it not only diverts our attention away from the possible injustice of our social institutions, but *the criminal law bestows upon those institutions the mantle of its own neutrality.* Since the criminal law protects the established institutions (e.g., the prevailing economic arrangements are protected by laws against theft, etc.), attacks on those established institutions become equivalent to violations of the minimum requirements for any social life at all. In effect, *the criminal law enshrines the established institutions as equivalent to the minimum requirements for* any *decent social existence—and it brands the individual who attacks those institutions as one who has declared war on all organized society and who must therefore be met with the weapons of war.*

This is the powerful magic of criminal justice. By virtue of its focus on *individual* criminals, it diverts us from the evils of the *social* order. By virtue of its presumed neutrality, it transforms the established social (and economic) order from being merely *one* form of

178

society open to critical comparison with others into *the* conditions of *any* social order and thus immune from criticism. Let us look more closely at this process.

What is the effect of focusing on individual guilt? Not only does this divert our attention from the possible evils in our institutions, but it puts forth half the problem of justice as if it were the *whole* problem. To focus on individual guilt is to ask whether or not the individual citizen has fulfilled his obligations to his fellow citizens. *It is to look away from the issue of whether his fellow citizens have fulfilled their obligations to him.*

To look only at individual responsibility is to look away from social responsibility. To look only at individual criminality is to close one's eyes to social injustice and to close one's ears to the question of whether our social institutions have exploited or violated the individual. *Justice is a two-way street—but criminal justice is a one-way street.*

Individuals owe obligations to their fellow citizens because their fellow citizens owe obligations to them. Criminal justice focuses on the first and looks away from the second. *Thus, by focusing on individual responsibility for crime, the criminal justice system literally acquits the existing social order of any charge of injustice!*

This is an extremely important bit of ideological alchemy. It stems from the fact [that] the same act can be criminal or not, unjust or just, depending on the conditions in which it takes place. Killing someone is ordinarily a crime. But if it is in self-defense or to stop a deadly crime, it is not. Taking property by force is usually a crime. But if the taking is just retrieving what has been stolen, then no crime has been committed. Acts of violence are ordinarily crimes. But if the violence is provoked by the threat of violence or by oppressive conditions, then, like the Boston Tea Party, what might ordinarily be called criminal is celebrated as just. This means that when we call an act a crime *we are also making an implicit judgment about the conditions in response to which it takes place.* When we call an act a crime, we are saying that the conditions in which it occurs are not themselves criminal or deadly or oppressive or so unjust as to make an extreme response reasonable or justified, that is, to make such a response noncriminal.

This means that when the system holds an individual responsible for a crime, *it is implicitly conveying the message that the social conditions in which the crime occurred are not responsible for the crime,* that they are not so unjust as to make a violent response to them excusable. The criminal justice system conveys as much by what it does not do as by what it does. By holding the individual responsible, *it literally acquits the society of criminality or injustice.*

Judges are prone to hold that an individual's responsibility for a violent crime is diminished if it was provoked by something that might lead a "reasonable man" to respond violently and that criminal responsibility is eliminated if the act was in response to conditions so intolerable that any "reasonable man" would have been likely to respond in the same way. In this vein, the law acquits those who kill or injure in self-defense and treats lightly those who commit a crime when confronted with extreme provocation. The law treats leniently the man who kills his wife's lover and the woman who kills her brutal husband, even when neither has acted directly in self-defense. By this logic, when we hold an individual completely responsible for a crime, we are saying that the conditions in which it occurred are such that a "reasonable man" should find them tolerable. In other words, by focusing on individual responsibility for crimes, *the criminal justice system broadcasts the message that the social order itself is reasonable and not intolerably unjust.*

Thus the criminal justice system serves to focus moral condemnation on individuals and to deflect it away from the social order that may have either violated the individual's rights or dignity or literally pushed him or her to the brink of crime. This not only serves to carry the message that our social institutions are not in need of fundamental questioning, but it further suggests that the justice of our institutions is obvious, not to be doubted. Indeed, since it is deviations from these institutions that are crimes, the established institutions become the implicit standard of justice from which criminal deviations are measured.

This leads to the second way in which a criminal justice system always conveys an implicit ideology. It arises from the presumption that the criminal law is nothing but the politically neutral minimum requirements of any decent social life. What is the consequence of this?

Obviously, as already suggested, this presumption transforms the prevailing social order into justice incarnate and all violations of the prevailing order into injustice incarnate. This process is so obvious that it may be easily missed.

Consider, for example, the law against theft. It does indeed seem to be one of the minimum requirements of social living. As long as there is scarcity, any society—capitalist or socialist—will need rules preventing individuals from taking what does not belong to them. But the law against theft is more: it is a law against stealing what individuals *presently* own. *Such a law has the effect of making present property relations a part of the criminal law.*

Since stealing is a violation of law, this means that present property relations become the implicit standard of justice against which criminal deviations are measured. Since criminal law is thought of as the minimum requirements of any social life, this means that present property relations become equivalent to the minimum requirements of *any* social life. And the criminal who would alter the present property relations becomes nothing less than someone who is declaring war on all organized society. The question of whether this "war" is provoked by the injustice or brutality of the society is swept aside. Indeed, this suggests yet another way in which the criminal justice system conveys an ideological message in support of the established society.

Not only does the criminal justice system acquit the social order of any charge of injustice, it specifically cloaks the society's own crime-producing tendencies. I have already observed that by blaming the individual for a crime, the society is acquitted of the charge of injustice. I would like to go further now and argue that by blaming the individual for a crime, the society is acquitted of the charge of complicity in that crime! This is a point worth developing, since many observers have maintained that modern competitive societies such as our own have structural features that tend to generate crime. Thus, holding the individual responsible for his or her crime serves the function of taking the rest of society off the hook for their role in sustaining and benefiting from social arrangements that produce crime. Let us take a brief detour to look more closely at this process.

Cloward and Ohlin argue in their book *Delinquency and Opportunity*[1] that much crime is the result of the discrepancy between social goals and the legitimate opportunities available for achieving them. Simply put, in our society everyone is encouraged to be a success, but the avenues to success are open only to some. The conventional wisdom of our free enterprise democracy is that anyone can be a success if he or she has the talent and the ambition. Thus, if one is not a success, it is because of their own shortcomings: laziness or lack of ability or both. On the other hand, opportunities to achieve success are not equally open to all. Access to the best schools and the best jobs is effectively closed to all but a few of the poor and begins to open wider only as one goes up the economic ladder. The result is that many are called but few are chosen. And many who have taken the bait and accepted the belief in the importance of success and the belief that achieving success is a result of individual ability must cope with the feelings of frustration and failure that result when they find the avenues to success closed. Cloward and Ohlin argue that one method of coping with these stresses is to develop alternative avenues to success. Crime is such an alternative. Crime is a means by which people who believe in the American dream pursue it when they find the traditional routes barred. Indeed, it is plain to see that the goals pursued by most criminals are as American as apple pie. I suspect that one of the reasons that American moviegoers enjoy gangster films—movies in which gangsters such is Al Capone, Bonnie and Clyde, or Butch Cassidy and the Sundance Kid are the heroes, as distinct from police and detective films whose heroes are defenders of the law—is that even where they deplore the hero's methods, they identify with his or her notion of success, since it is theirs as well, and respect the courage and cunning displayed in achieving that success.

It is important to note that the discrepancy between success goals and legitimate opportunities in America is not an aberration. It is a structural feature of modern competitive industrialized society, a feature from which many benefits flow. Cloward and Ohlin write that

> ... a crucial problem in the industrial world ... is to locate and train the most talented persons in every generation, irrespective of the vicissitudes of birth, to occupy technical work roles. ... Since we cannot know in advance who can best fulfill the requirements of the various occupational roles, the matter is presumably settled through the process of competition. But how can men throughout the social order be motivated to participate in this competition? ...
>
> One of the ways in which the industrial society attempts to solve this problem is by defining success-goals as potentially accessible to all, regardless of race, creed, or socioeconomic position.[2]

But since these universal goals are urged to encourage a competition to weed out the best, there are necessarily fewer openings than seekers. And since those who achieve success are in a particularly good position to exploit their success to make access for their own children easier, the competition is rigged to work in favor of the middle and upper classes. As a result, "many lower-class persons ... are the victims of a contradiction between the goals toward which they have been led to orient themselves and socially structured means of striving for these goals."[3]

> [The poor] experience desperation born of the certainty that their position in the economic structure is relatively fixed and immutable—a desperation made all the more poignant by their exposure to a cultural ideology in which failure to orient oneself upward is regarded as a moral defect and failure to become mobile as proof of it.[4]

The outcome is predictable. "Under these conditions, there is an acute pressure to depart from institutional norms and to adopt illegitimate alternatives."[5]

In brief, this means that the very way in which our society is structured to draw out the talents and energies that go into producing our high standard of living has a costly side effect: it produces crime. But by holding individuals responsible for this crime, those who enjoy that high standard of living can have their cake and eat it. They can reap the benefits of the competition for success and escape the responsibility of paying for the costs of that competition. By holding the poor crook legally and morally guilty, the rest of society not only passes the costs of competition on to the poor, but they effectively deny that they (the affluent) are the beneficiaries of an economic system that exacts such a high toll in frustration and suffering.

Willem Bonger, the Dutch Marxist criminologist, maintained that competitive capitalism produces egotistic motives and undermines compassion for the misfortunes of others and thus makes human beings literally *more capable of crime*—more capable of preying on their fellows without moral inhibition or remorse—than earlier cultures that emphasized cooperation rather than competition.[6] Here again, the criminal justice system relieves those who benefit from the American economic system of the costs of that system. By holding criminals morally and individually responsible for their crimes, we can forget that the motives that lead to crime—the drive for success at any cost, linked with the beliefs that success means outdoing others and that violence is an acceptable way of achieving one's goals—are the same motives that powered the drive across the American continent and that continue to fuel the engine of America's prosperity.

David Gordon, a contemporary political economist, maintains "that nearly all crimes in capitalist societies represent perfectly *rational* responses to the structure of institutions upon which capitalist societies are based."[7] That is, like Bonger, Gordon believes that capitalism tends to provoke crime in all economic strata. This is so because most crime is motivated by a desire for property or money and is an understandable way of coping with the pressures of inequality, competition, and insecurity, all of which are essential ingredients of capitalism. Capitalism depends, Gordon writes,

> . . . on basically competitive forms of social and economic interaction and upon substantial inequalities in the allocation of social resources. Without inequalities, it would be much more difficult to induce workers to work in alienating environments. Without competition and a competitive ideology, workers might not be inclined to struggle to improve their relative income and status in society by working harder. Finally, although rights of property are protected, capitalist societies do not guarantee economic security to most of their individual members. Individuals must fend for themselves, finding the best available opportunities to provide for themselves and their families . . . Driven by the fear of economic insecurity and by a competitive desire to gain some of the goods unequally distributed throughout the society, many individuals will eventually become "criminals."[8]

To the extent that a society makes crime a reasonable alternative for a large number of its members from all classes, that society is itself not very reasonably or humanely organized and bears some degree of responsibility for the crime it encourages. Since the criminal law is put forth as the minimum requirements that can be expected of any "reasonable man," its enforcement amounts to a denial of the real nature of the social order to which Gordon and the others point. Here again, by blaming the individual criminal, the criminal justice system serves implicitly but dramatically to acquit the society of its criminality.

THE BONUS OF BIAS

We turn now to consideration of the additional ideological bonus that is derived from the criminal justice system's bias against the poor. This bonus is a product of the association of crime and poverty in the popular mind. This association, the merging of the "criminal classes" and the "lower classes" into the "dangerous classes," was not invented in America. The word "villain" is derived from the Latin *villanus*, which means a farm servant. And the term "villein" was used in feudal England to refer to a serf who farmed the land of a great lord and who was literally owned by that lord.[9] In this respect, our present criminal justice system is heir to a long and hallowed tradition.

The value of this association was already seen when we explored the "average citizen's" concept of the Typical Criminal and the Typical Crime. It is quite obvious that throughout the great mass of middle America, far more fear and hostility are directed toward the predatory acts of the poor than the rich. Compare the fate of politicians in recent history who call for tax reform, income redistribution, prosecution of corporate crime, and any sort of regulation of business that would make it better serve American social goals with that of politicians who erect their platform on a call for "law and order," more police, less limits on police power, and stiffer prison sentences for criminals—and consider this in light of what we have already seen about the real dangers posed by corporate crime and business-as-usual.

In view of all that has been said already, it seems clear that Americans have been systematically deceived as to what are the greatest dangers to their lives, limbs and possessions. The very persistence with which the system functions to apprehend and punish poor crooks and ignore or slap on the wrist equally or more dangerous individuals is testimony to the sticking power of this deception. That Americans continue to tolerate the gentle treatment meted out to white-collar criminals, corporate price fixers, industrial polluters, and political-influence peddlers, while voting in droves to lock up more poor people faster and longer, indicates the degree to which they harbor illusions as to who most threatens them. It is perhaps also part of the explanation for the continued dismal failure of class-based politics in America. American workers rarely seem able to forget their differences and unite to defend their shared interests against the rich whose wealth they produce. Ethnic divisions serve this divisive function well, but undoubtedly the vivid portrayal of the poor— and, of course, the blacks—as hovering birds of prey waiting for the opportunity to snatch away the workers' meager gains serves also to deflect opposition away from the upper classes. A politician who promises to keep their communities free of blacks and their prisons full of them can get their votes even if the major portion of his or her policies amount to continuation of favored treatment of the rich at their expense. Surely this is a minor miracle of mind control.

The most important "bonus" derived from the identification of crime and poverty is that it paints the picture that the threat to decent middle Americans comes from those below them on the economic ladder, not those above. For this to happen the system must not only identify crime and poverty, but *it must also fail to reduce crime so that it remains a real threat.* By doing this, it deflects the fear and discontent of middle Americans, and their possible opposition, away from the wealthy. The two politicians who most clearly gave voice to the discontent of middle Americans in the post-World War II period were George Wallace and Spiro Agnew. Is it any accident that their politics were extremely conservative and their anger reserved for the poor (the welfare chiselers) and the criminal (the targets of law and order)?

There are other bonuses as well. For instance, if the criminal justice system functions to send out a message that bestows legitimacy on present property relations, the dramatic impact is mightily enhanced if the violator of the present arrangements is propertyless. In other words, the crimes of the well-to-do "redistribute" property among the haves. In that sense, they do not pose a symbolic challenge to the larger system in which some have much and many have little or nothing. If the criminal threat can be portrayed as coming from the poor, then the punishment of the poor criminal becomes a morality play in which the sanctity of legitimacy of the system in which some have plenty and others have little or nothing is dramatically affirmed. It matters little who the poor criminals really rip off.

What counts is that middle Americans come to fear that those poor criminals are out to steal what they own.

There is yet another and, I believe, still more important bonus for the powerful in America, produced by the identification of crime and poverty. It might be thought that the identification of crime and poverty would produce sympathy for the criminals. My suspicion is that it produces or at least reinforces the reverse: *hostility toward the poor.*

Indeed, there is little evidence that Americans are very sympathetic to criminals or poor people. I have already pointed to the fact that very few Americans believe poverty to be a cause of crime. Other surveys find that most Americans believe that police should be tougher than they are now in dealing with crime (83 percent of those questioned in a 1972 survey); that courts do not deal harshly enough with criminals (75 percent of those questioned in a 1969 survey); that a majority of Americans would like to see the death penalty for convicted murderers (57 percent of those questioned in November 1972); and that most would be more likely to vote for a candidate who advocated tougher sentences for law-breakers (83 percent of those questioned in a 1972 survey).[10] Indeed, the experience of Watergate seems to suggest that sympathy for criminals begins to flower only when we approach the higher reaches of the ladder of wealth and power. For some poor ghetto youth who robs a liquor store, five years in the slammer is our idea of tempering justice with mercy. When a handful of public officials try to walk off with the U.S. Constitution, a few months in a minimum security prison will suffice. If the public official is high enough, resignation from office and public disgrace tempered with a $60,000-a-year pension is punishment enough.

My view is that since the criminal justice system—in fact and fiction—deals with *individual legal* and *moral guilt,* the association of crime with poverty does not mitigate the image of individual moral responsibility for crime, the image that crime is the result of an individual's poor character. My suspicion is that it does the reverse: it generates the association of poverty and individual moral failing and thus *the belief that poverty itself is a sign of poor or weak character.* The clearest evidence that Americans hold this belief is to be found in the fact that attempts to aid the poor are regarded as acts of charity rather than as acts of justice. Our welfare system has all the demeaning attributes of an institution designed to give handouts to the undeserving and none of the dignity of an institution designed to make good on our responsibilities to our fellow human beings. If we acknowledged the degree to which our economic and social institutions themselves breed poverty, we would have to recognize our own responsibilities toward the poor. If we can convince ourselves that the poor are poor because of their own shortcomings, particularly moral shortcomings like incontinence and indolence, then we need acknowledge no such responsibility to the poor. Indeed, we can go further and pat ourselves on the back for our generosity and handing out the little that we do, and of course, we can make our recipients go through all the indignities that mark them as the undeserving objects of our benevolence. By and large, this has been the way in which Americans have dealt with their poor.[11] It is a way that enables us to avoid asking the question of why the richest nation in the world continues to produce massive poverty. It is my view that this conception of the poor is subtly conveyed by the way our criminal justice system functions.

Obviously, no ideological message could be more supportive of the present social and economic order than this. It suggests that poverty is a sign of individual failing, not a symptom of social or economic injustice. It tells us loud and clear that massive poverty in the midst of abundance is not a sign pointing toward the need for fundamental changes in our social and economic institutions. It suggests that the poor are poor because they deserve to be poor, or at least because they lack the strength of character to overcome poverty. When the poor are seen to be poor in character, then economic poverty coincides with moral poverty and the economic order coincides with the moral order—as if a divine hand guided its workings, capitalism leads to everyone getting what they morally deserve!

If this association takes root, then when the poor individual is found guilty of a crime, the criminal justice system acquits the society of its responsibility not only for crime *but for poverty as well.*

With this, the ideological message of criminal justice is complete. The poor rather than the rich are seen as the enemies of the mass of decent middle Americans. Our social and economic institutions are held to be responsible for neither crime nor poverty and thus are in need of no fundamental questioning or reform. The poor are poor because they are poor of character. The economic order and the moral order are one. And to the extent that this message sinks in, the wealthy can rest easily—even if they cannot sleep the sleep of the just.

Thus, we can understand why the criminal justice system creates the image of crime as the work of the poor and fails to stem it so that the threat of crime remains real and credible. The result is ideological alchemy of the highest order. The poor are seen as the real threat to decent society. The ultimate sanctions of criminal justice dramatically sanctify the present social and economic order, and *the poverty of criminals makes poverty itself an individual moral crime!*

Such are the ideological fruits of a losing war against crime whose distorted image is reflected in the criminal justice carnival mirror and widely broadcast to reach the minds and imaginations of America.

Notes

1. Richard A. Cloward and Lloyd E. Ohlin, *Delinquency and Opportunity: A Theory of Delinquent Gangs* (New York: The Free Press, 1960), esp. pp. 77–107.

2. Ibid., p. 81.

3. Ibid., p. 105.

4. Ibid., p. 107.

5. Ibid., p. 105.

6. Willem Bonger, *Criminality and Economic Conditions,* abridged and with an introduction by Austin T. Turk (Bloomington, Indiana: Indiana University Press, 1969), pp. 7–12, 40–47. Willem Adriaan Bonger was born in Holland in 1876 and died by his own hand in 1940 rather than submit to the Nazis. His *Criminalité et conditions économiques* first appeared in 1905. It was translated into English and published in the United States in 1916. Ibid., pp. 3–4.

7. David M. Gordon, "Capitalism, Class and Crime in America," *Crime and Delinquency* (April 1972), p. 174.

8. Ibid., p. 174.

9. William and Mary Morris, *Dictionary of Word and Phrase Origins,* II (New York: Harper & Row, 1967), p. 282.

10. *Sourcebook,* pp. 203, 204, 223, 207; see also p. 177.

11. Historical documentation of this can be found in David J. Rothman, *The Discovery of the Asylum: Social Order and Disorder in the New Republic* (Boston: Little, Brown, 1971); and in Frances Fox Piven and Richard A. Cloward, *Regulating the Poor: The Functions of Public Welfare* (New York: Pantheon, 1971), which carries the analysis up to the present.

16 / Delinquency, Situational Inducements, and Commitment to Conformity

SCOTT BRIAR
IRVING PILIAVIN

In recent years a theory of delinquency, the delinquent subculture thesis, has been advanced which has had an enormous influence on delinquency prevention and control programs throughout the United States. In the present paper we will show: first, that the sub-culture thesis, and the general class of theories of which it is a part, are unable to account satisfactorily for crucial aspects of the phenomena of delinquency; and second, that these phenomena can be better explained by an alternative class of formulations currently categorized as social control theories, when these theories are modified in ways suggested below.

The subculture theory of delinquency along with some of the theories it is intended to supersede—such as psychoanalytic theory and the adolescent rebellion thesis—belong to the class of what may be termed motivational theories of delinquency. These theories regard the illegal acts of delinquents as the product of some enduring disposition or combination of dispositions unique to these youths. While motivational theories differ widely on the nature and precise etiology of these dispositions, they follow a common logic regarding the development of these dispositions and their role in delinquent behavior. In brief, these dispositions are seen as: (1) deriving from certain interpersonal and/or social conditions which delinquents experience; (2) essentially permanent aspects of the personality and/or value framework of delinquent boys; and (3) forces which propel them into illegal behavior.

Despite their numerous differences, however, all motivational theories of delinquency have incurred common problems. First, the etiological factors they postulate do not operate uniformly. That is, many boys subjected to experiences which presumably should give rise to delinquency-producing dispositions do not acquire them. Second, many boys who exhibit these dispositions do not appear among identified delinquents. Third, the great majority of identified delinquents apparently become law-abiding in late adolescence and early adulthood—a fact which motivational theories of delinquency cannot explain, with their assumptions of the enduring nature of delinquency-producing dispositions. Fourth, even if we grant, despite the above problems,[1] that delinquent behavior is in some fashion and to some degree a product of enduring dispositions, we still face the unexplained fact that only a small portion of boys who are members of delinquent gangs or who are designated delinquent by juvenile courts have those characteristics predicted for them by contemporary motivational theories of delinquency. Finally, motivational theories of delinquency do not account for the well documented fact that the vast majority of boys engage in delinquent behavior to some degree.

To avoid the above problems, defenders of these theories have (1) indicated that various factors may mitigate the influence of delinquency-producing dispositions, (2) suggested that forces other than those so far identified may also lead boys to commit illegal acts, and (3) argued that the delinquent behavior of so-called non-delinquents is accidental, prankish, or otherwise understandable in terms not applicable to true delinquents.[2] These arguments, however, imply a cumbersome multi-factor theory of delinquency whose obvious defects have led some theorists to doubt whether etiological explanations of the phenomena are in fact possible.[3]

SITUATIONALLY INDUCED MOTIVES TO DEVIATE

Those who argue for a radical distinction between delinquent and non-delinquent traits attempt to justify it on the basis of the apparent differentials in the frequency of various types of delinquent activity among "delinquents" (or a particular class of delinquents) and "non-delinquents." Having established such differentials, these theorists argue that the infractions of "delinquents" are different in origin from those of "non-delinquents." More concise and less questionable, however, is the assumption that the delinquent acts of both non-delinquents and delinquents are conditioned largely by common factors. This assumption provides the basic premise for the formulation to follow.

Because delinquent behavior is typically episodic, purposive, and confined to certain situations,[4] we assume that the motives for such behavior are frequently episodic, oriented to short-term ends, and confined to certain situations. That is, rather than considering delinquent acts as solely the product of long-term motives deriving from conflicts or frustrations whose genesis is far removed from the arenas in which the illegal behavior occurs, we assume these acts are prompted by short-term situationally induced desires experienced by all boys to obtain valued goods, to portray courage in the presence of, or be loyal to peers, to strike out at someone who is disliked, or simply to "get kicks."[5]

The influence of currently experienced situations on individuals' attitudes and behaviors has been emphasized in numerous sociological and social-psychological studies. In brief, these studies indicate that situational factors can confront actors with conflicts, opportunities, pressures, and temptations which may influence the actors' actions and views. Many of these studies, especially those conducted under "real-life" conditions, have focused on highly patterned situations of long duration, such as the social structure of an industrial plant, a hospital ward, or a housing project.[6] On the other hand, several theoretical writings,[7] material from some case studies,[8] and a large number of experimental studies in social psychology indicate that situationally induced stimuli of relatively short duration also can affect, to varying extents, the values and behaviors of those exposed to these stimuli. In the words of Lewin:

> It is a simple fact, but still not sufficiently recognized in psychology and sociology, that the behavior of a person depends above all upon his momentary position. Often, the world looks very different before and after an event which changes the region in which a person is located.[9]

But even granting that short-term situationally induced stimuli can influence individuals, we question whether or not such stimuli are sufficient to effect deviant behavior. There is some evidence to suggest that they are. Cressey, for example, has shown that the criminal violation of financial trust can be viewed as a narrow goal-oriented response to a situationally induced financial problem:

> Trusted persons become trust violators when they conceive of themselves as having a financial problem which is nonsharable, have the knowledge or awareness that this problem can be secretly resolved by violation of the position of financial trust, and are able to apply to their own conduct in the situation verbalizations which enable them to adjust their conceptions of themselves as trusted persons with their conceptions of themselves as users of the entrusted funds or property.[10]

Additional support for the notion that situationally induced stimuli of short duration can lead to illegal behavior is provided by self-reports from gang members:

> When we were shoplifting we always made a game of it. For example we might gamble on who could steal the most caps in a day, or who could steal

in the presence of a detective and then get away. This was the best part of the game. . . . It was the fun I wanted, not the hat.[11]

I was walkin' uptown with a couple of friends, and we run into Magician and them there. They asked us if we wanted to go to a fight, and we said "Yes." When they asked me if I wanted to go to a fight, I couldn't say, "No." I mean I could say, "No," but for old-time's sake, I said, "Yes."[12]

You see, man, it's not that I'm against anyone else, I'm just "all for me." Our stealing did have a utilitarian motive. Sometimes we stole something we actually liked and wanted and stealing always proved we had guts. . . . [But] most of the time I didn't even have stealing on my mind. . . .

What have we done? We're just trying to have some fun. We don't want to be like those middle class guys. We are no mamma's boys.[13]

Thus, there is considerable basis for assuming that the immediate situation in which a youth finds himself can play an important role in his decision to engage in delinquent behavior. Obviously, however, this is not to say that the situation offering inducement or pressure to a youth to deviate will necessarily lead him to take such action. For one thing, situationally induced motives vary in intensity. Furthermore, their expression depends on a variety of contingencies, such as the ease with which the motivated behavior can be carried out, the risks involved, and the press or attractiveness of other activities.[14] Finally, whether or not the motives to deviate are situationally induced, the behavioral expression of them depends on the degree to which the individuals experiencing the motives also experience constraints against the behavior.

CONSTRAINTS ON DEVIANCE: THE CONCEPT OF COMMITMENT

Three dominant views can be identified in motivational theories of delinquency regarding (1) the nature of the influences which constrain individuals from engaging in delinquent behavior, and (2) the conditions under which these influences are neutralized.

In delinquent sub-culture theories, the basic constraint against the exercise of deviant motives is allegiance to the dominant values of the larger society. Depending on the particular theorist, a youth's freedom from this constraint entails allegiance to an oppositional system of values by means of either a type of reaction-formation,[15] a more or less rational process of decision-making,[16] or socialization to a cultural tradition differing from that of the larger society.[17]

A second type of constraint involves internalization of parental prohibitions and demands—in other words, the development of a super-ego. Freedom from this constraint is seen largely as the product of parental failure to socialize children properly. Such failure may result from a variety of conditions, ranging from parental failure to articulate conventional values to lack of the kind of familial atmosphere in which such values, even if articulated, can be incorporated by children.[18]

There are, however, important limitations in these two formulations of the constraining influences on deviant behavior. For one thing, empirical studies have failed to find a strong oppositional or autonomous value system among delinquent gang youth as predicted by delinquent sub-culture theorists.[19] Moreover, considerable evidence indicates that moral concerns, such as would be expected from the operation of the super-ego, are neither the only nor necessarily the major factors in constraining persons from engaging in or legitimizing illegal behavior.[20]

A third formulation of the constraints against delinquency, deriving from the writings of social control theorists, overcomes these limitations to some extent. This formulation stresses the importance of social institutions such as the family, the school, and law enforcement as instruments of control on the delinquent motives of boys. Presumably all boys are subject to these motives;[21] however, they express them in overt behavior only when, for whatever reason, the controlling potential of these institutions is not realized. A considerable literature has developed attempting to specify the conditions under which this occurs. Thus the absence of family controls has been linked to parental rejection, ineffectuality, and neglect;[22] and the deficiency of controls within the school has been traced, among other things, to its failure to be oriented to the capabilities and interests of students.[23] But while social control theory can account for much delinquency, it, too, suffers limitations, since the nature of the processes by which social control is exercised and the sequential patterning of these processes have not been specified. Thus, for example, social control theories are ambiguous regarding the relationship between "inner controls" and external (or social) controls; moreover, they are unable to account for some of the phenomena of delinquency, such as the eventual conventionalization of many delinquent boys.

These problems can be eliminated by viewing the central processes of social control as "commitments to conformity." By this term we mean not only fear of the material deprivations and punishments which might result from being discovered as an offender but also apprehension about the deleterious consequences of such a discovery on one's attempts to maintain a consistent self image, to sustain valued relationships, and to preserve current and future statuses and activities. A youth with strong commitments to conformity is less likely to engage in deviant acts than is one for whom these commitments are minimal, given that both [youths] experience motives to deviate in the same degree. The cumulative strength of one's various commitments is not to be equated with motives to deviate. Commitment refers instead to the *probability* that such motives will be acted upon when they are experienced. Even persons with strong commitments to conformity experience motives to engage in criminal acts, and they may perform such acts when their commitments do not appear to be threatened (for example, under conditions of low visibility) or when the motives to deviate are very strong.

The role of commitments of the type discussed here is not new to sociological or psychological discussion. For example, Goode has stated that interpersonal commitments are fundamentally important in understanding conformity within modern urban society:

> ... In a secularized society, with perhaps weak commitment to norms or role emotion, role or norm conformity may depend far more on the greater sensitivity of ego to alter's response that it does in other types of societies. This is not to assert that high sensitivity is inversely correlated with high intensity of role commitment or emotion. Rather when there is low intensity there must be a correlative increase of sensitivity to "alter opinion" or to "community opinion" (outsiders related to alter and ego) if role obligations are to be met generally.[24]

A more general formulation of the concept of commitment has been put forth recently by Becker:

> First, the individual is in a position in which his decision with regard to some particular line of action has consequences for other interests and activities not necessarily related to it. Second, he has placed himself in that position by his own prior actions. A third element is present though so obvious as not to be apparent: the committed person must be aware ... (of these other interests) and must recognize that his decision in this case will have ramifications beyond it.[25]

The applicability of this formulation for socially disapproved as well as conventional behaviors is suggested by one of Becker's examples:

> A middle class girl can find herself committed to a consistently chaste line of behavior by the sizable bit of her reputation that middle class culture attaches to virginity for females. A girl who is a member of a social class where virginity is less valued could not be committed in this way; and except for a few puritanical enclaves in our society, boys cannot acquire commitments of this kind at all, for male virginity has little value. . . .[26]

If commitments to, or stakes in, conformity play an important role in determining a youth's capability for deviance, they also are significant in at least two other respects. First, they affect the stance the youth takes vis-à-vis adult authority figures. The boy with high commitments to conformity is by definition committed to maintaining and achieving desired statuses as well as to obtaining the approval of those whose love and protection he regards as important. Those aims, however, will also lead this youth to defer to the judgments of adult authorities, to accord these adults respect during social intercourse, and to be fearful, contrite, and ashamed when they confront him with his misdeeds. The low stake boy, however, is less likely to manifest these attributes. Because the disapproval of these adults entails less cost for him than for the high stake youth, he is not as constrained to defer to or show respect for adults.

Secondly, stakes in conformity will influence the youth's choice of friends. Those boys who have high stakes will tend not to befriend peers whose stakes are low since the latter are more likely to "get into trouble." Boys with low stakes, on the other hand, will tend to avoid those who are "chicken" and to seek out those with congruent interests and freedom to act. These processes are not different logically from those involved in the formation of most youth groups. Just as athletes, daters, and music lovers cluster together,[27] so do those with similar commitments to conformity.[28]

Acquiring or losing stakes in conformity does not take place only through a sudden or cataclysmic event, nor is it an irreversible process. Boys who for a considerable period have had high commitments to maintaining a conventional appearance, and whose deviance is rare and circumspect, may, for a variety of reasons, gradually have these commitments reduced and become more active and visible in their illegal activities. Conversely, many of those whose stakes in conformity have been low may encounter experiences which serve to increase their stakes, leading them in turn to more conventional be-

SOME BASES FOR COMMITMENTS TO CONFORMITY

A variety of conditions can serve as bases for the development of commitments to conformity, including, among others, belief in God, affection for conventionally behaving peers, occupational aspirations, ties to parents, desire to perform well in school, and fear of the material deprivations and punishments associated with arrest. Among the most important, if not, in fact, the most important of these conditions is the relationship of the youth to his parents. In most families, parental sanctions and the withdrawal of love implied in their use are effective instruments for maintaining parental authority. Because of his dependence on and affection for his parents, the child conforms to their expectations in order to obtain their approval. In some families, however, parents fail to exercise authority. The punitive parent who does not reward conformity with affection thereby may undermine the basis for voluntary compliance by his child.[29] The parent who is overwhelmed by current responsibilities and problems may ignore his children, leaving them to fend for themselves and to define alone their relations with the outside world. Some parents who love their children and who are loved by them may caution their children against many things but then fail to enforce these expectations. They thus behave toward their children more as friends and siblings than as authorities, and their desires, therefore, are compromised because control is not exercised. Finally, some parents are unable to be effective authorities because they lack the economic and social statuses which their children equate with legitimate authorities.[30] The unemployed male, for example, may be seen as inferior not only by his peers but by his children, thus undermining his claim to parental authority. These examples obviously do not exhaust the various conditions which can lead children to develop autonomy from parental expectations. Moreover, these conditions do not necessarily represent steady states. Parents who are fully able to cope with infants and toddlers may be far less capable of dealing with more active, less dependent, and more perceptive school-age children. Also, a variety of crises and tragedies may vitiate parents' competence to operate as adult authorities, regardless of the adequacy with which they formerly performed these tasks.

It is likely that failure to develop conformity commitments through the desire to satisfy parental expectations reduces the probability that the youth will develop such commitments in other social contexts. As a case in point, the desire to achieve in school is in many instances the product of parents' expectations that their child perform well in the classroom and of the child's concern for fulfilling these expectations.[31] Should either or both of these conditions be lacking, then the chances of developing commitments based on academic aspirations are reduced. Similar considerations hold in the conformity commitments arising from fear of the consequences of arrest. Most youth regard arrest as a fearful experience because they believe, among other things, that (1) it can alter their public image adversely, and (2) it exposes them to punishment, deprivation, and the moral indignation of parents, friends, and officials. Those youths, then, whose behavior is not governed by parental evaluations, lack an important basis for developing concern about the consequences of arrest.

Nevertheless, the failure of children to develop commitments to conformity through a desire to fulfill parental expectations need not necessarily preclude the development of such commitments in other ways. For example, the desire to achieve in school, which can provide a potent incentive for conventional behavior, may develop in response to praise from teachers, respect from friends, and the anticipation of future pay-offs for school achievement, even in the absence of strong commitments to perform in accord with parental expectations. Furthermore, loss of commitments in arenas outside the home may precede and lead to loss of commitments within the family. Again, using the school as an example, some youths with high commitments to parental expectations may nevertheless be disinterested in and perform poorly in school or may be apprehended as offenders. If as a result they experience severe and enduring parental criticism, their commitments to parental authority may diminish.

CONGRUENCE WITH EMPIRICAL DATA ON DELINQUENCY

As noted above, little evidence is available which provides a direct test of the basic propositions in the model presented here. However, we can examine the congruence between this model and what is known empirically about delinquency. Obviously, even if considerable congruence is found, it cannot be interpreted as a demonstration of the validity of these propositions; nevertheless, it does suggest their plausibility.

First, the conditions for lack of commitment to conformity are more prevalent among lower class than middle class youth. "The lower class individual is more likely to have been exposed to punishment, lack of love, and a general atmosphere of tension and aggression since early childhood."[32] Furthermore, his parents devote less time to supervising his activities,[33] are less trusting of him,[34] and are less likely to be viewed by him as legitimate authorities.[35] Consequently, and consistent with empirical findings, the lower class youth, lacking these bases for commitment, will engage in more frequent, more visible, and more severely punished delinquent behavior than their middle class peers.

Second, since this formulation does not regard delinquent acts as the product of enduring motives, nor as completely determined by stable characteristics of boys and their situations, it is consistent with the observation that delinquent behavior is an episodic and typically noncompulsive activity.[36]

Third, the present framework can account for the fact that virtually all middle class and lower class boys engage in some delinquent activities and that some middle class boys are serious delinquents while many lower class boys are not. As indicated earlier, even boys with strong commitments to their parents' expectations, who perform well and aspire to good performance in school, and who fear the punishments associated with arrest and detention will commit delinquent acts if the rewards are sufficient, visibility is low, and the act can be rationalized or justified so as not to denigrate the youth's self-image.[37] Furthermore, in some middle class families, parent–child relationships are not always so benign as to rule out the possibility that parental authority will fail to be acknowledged. Nor are lower class parents uniformly so punishing, rejecting, or incapable that they fail, even in high delinquency areas, to be effective authority figures vis-à-vis their children. Similar considerations apply to children's commitments to academic performance and fear of the consequences ensuing from arrest and detention.

Fourth, this formulation explains the evident reduction in delinquent activities among late adolescents and young adults. Specifically, during these years some delinquents obtain jobs; others marry; and for all, the penalties for offending behavior greatly increase. Such events increase commitments to conformity. Furthermore, insofar as employment takes boys off the streets and provides them with money, they are less likely to experience motives to commit illegal acts for gain.

Fifth, the group nature of many delinquent activities and the norms of these groups are not nearly as compelling as some theorists have assumed.[38] This is not to suggest that the expectations of gang members do not influence individuals considerably, nor that those delinquent gang members with more than minimal commitments to conformity will not forego these commitments on occasion in response to the demands of their peers. On the other hand, adolescents in general frequently give priority to peer expectations over those emanating from other sources.[39] What is distinctive about delinquent gang members is that a greater proportion of their activities involve illegal acts. This can be accounted for by the argument that members of delinquent gangs, at the time of their recruitment, already lack strong commitments to conformity.[40]

Sixth, the model provides a conceptual basis for understanding the hostile and/or coolly indifferent and unconcerned demeanor which many delinquent boys display toward adult authority figures such as teachers, police, and correctional workers.[41] The boy with a high stake in conformity is by definition committed to meeting conventional expectations in order to maintain and achieve desired statuses as well as to obtain the approval of those whose love and protection he regards as important. These aims, however, will also lead this youth to defer to the judgments of adult authorities, to accord these adults respect during social intercourse and to be fearful, contrite and ashamed when they confront him with his misdeeds. The low stake boy, however, is less likely to manifest these attributes. Because the approval of these adults carries for him less significance than for the high stake youth, he is not as constrained to defer to or show respect for adults.[42]

Finally, the present model permits a more complete explanation of the phenomenon known as secondary deviance. The theory of secondary deviance holds that the experience of being labeled and treated as a deviant has self-fulfilling consequences.

> [Branding and] treating a person as though he were generally deviant . . . sets in motion several mechanisms which conspire to shape the person in the image people have of him.
>
> Put . . . generally, the point is that the treatment of deviants denies them the ordinary means of carrying on the routines of everyday life open to most people. Because of this denial the deviant must of necessity develop illegitimate routines.[43]

Secondary deviance theory, however, has not been able to account for the fact that many boys who are labeled delinquent by the courts apparently do not continue their deviant behavior. An explanation of this phenomenon consistent with the thesis of this paper is that the effects of labeling a youth delinquent are a function of his pre-existing commitments to conformity. For the high stake boy, arrest is likely to lead to a reconfirmation of conventional behavior. He will "toe the line" more rigorously in order to (1) regain and maintain the respect and affection of those who expect him to behave conventionally and (2) increase his chances of achieving conventional goals. For the low stake boy, however, arrest may remove one of the few remaining constraints against his exercise of deviant behavior. That is, for the boy who is not committed to parental expectations of conformity and who has little interest in school achievement, etc., one of the few bases for his conformity may be his fear of the experiences he will go through during arrest, trial, and incarceration. But typically these experiences are not as depriving as anticipated, and in encountering them the low stake boys may find they need not be feared. For these boys, then, this source of commitment to conformity has, in effect, been reduced, and the probability of their committing further delinquencies is enhanced.

CONCLUSION

The formulation presented in this paper is essentially a probabilistic one. It views delinquency as the product of commitments to conformity, situationally induced motives to deviate, and a variety of contingencies. This framework is consistent with the empirical data on delinquency and, in fact, accounts for some aspects of this phenomena—such as its presence among most youth and its decline in early adulthood—which are not accounted for by other theoretical models.

For example, one implication of Cloward and Ohlin's delinquent sub-culture thesis is that lower class boys will reduce their delinquent activities if they perceive that opportunities for employment will be provided them when they become adults. In our view, however, employment opportunities do not become a salient influence on the day to day behavior of delinquent boys until they develop commitments and needs that make full-time work a valued activity. Moreover, such commitments ordinarily do not occur until late adolescence and early adulthood. Younger boys, those in the age group with the highest rate of delinquent behavior, are not affected by job market conditions; rather, their behavior is influenced, as we have argued above, by more mundane situational considerations. For these boys, therefore, it is necessary to provide bases for conformity commitments which are more immediately relevant than future employment opportunities. While a variety of such bases could be developed, one suggestion by way of example would involve the use of money wages to boys on the condition that they keep out of trouble. The effectiveness of such wages would not depend on long-term efforts by professionals in order to develop boys' aspirations and alleviate their interpersonal problems; consequently, if such wages are effective at all, their impact should be immediate. In any event, the idea of paying boys to conform is sufficiently intriguing to merit study and experimentation.

Notes

1. Presumably these problems can be dealt with by the introduction of additional factors which either augment or constrain the influence of those factors considered basic to the development of delinquent-producing dispositions and/or the operation of the dispositions themselves. However, to our knowledge, no systematic effort has been made to identify these ancillary conditions and their operation.

2. This interpretation is not shared by Bloch and Niederhoffer who, in acknowledging the universality of delinquent behavior, attribute it to adolescent identity crisis. But as Cloward and Ohlin point out, this view of delinquency fails to account for apparent differentials in illegal activities among various identifiable adolescent sub-groupings. Herbert Bloch and Arthur Niederhoffer, *The Gang: A Study in Adolescent Behavior* (New York: Philosophical Library, 1958), p. 17; Richard A. Cloward and Lloyd E. Ohlin, *Delinquency and Opportunity* (Glencoe Ill.: The Free Press, 1960), pp. 50–55.

3. David Matza, *Delinquency and Drift* (New York: John Wiley & Sons, 1964), pp. 33–67.

4. Borrowing from Kohn and Williams, we define a situation as ". . . a series of interactions, located in space and time, and perceived by the participants as an event: in this usage 'situation' is a delimiting term, cutting out from the flow of experience a

particular series of interpersonal actions which are seen by the participants as a describable event, separable from preceding and succeeding events, constraining the participants to act in particular ways and having its own unique consequences." Melvin L. Kohn and Robin M. Williams, "Situational Patterning in Intergroup Relations," *American Sociological Review*, 21 (April 1956), p. 164.

5. We are suggesting here that the situations which delinquents find tempting and exciting are similar, in spirit, to those which attract the non-delinquent. As Matza has pointed out, the teen-age culture is "a conventional version of the delinquent tradition. Here we find an emphasis on fun and adventure: a disdain for scholastic effort; the more or less persistent involvement in 'tolerated' status offenses like drinking, gambling, occasional truancy, 'making out' in the sense of sexual conquest, driving cars before the appropriate age, smoking, swearing, and staying out late. . . . Aggression is considerably tempered, but there is a persistent concern with the credentials on [sic] masculinity and femininity." David Matza, "Subterranean Traditions of Youth," *Annals of the American Academy of Political and Social Science*, 338 (November 1961), p. 116.

6. See for example: Leon Festinger, Stanley Schachter, and Kurt Back, *Social Pressures in Informal Groups* (New York: Harper, 1950); Morton Deutsch and Mary E. Collins, *Interracial Housing: A Psychological Evaluation of a Social Experiment* (Minneapolis: Univ. of Minnesota Press, 1951); Neal Gross, Ward S. Mason, Alexander W. McEachern, *Explorations in Role Analysis* (New York: John Wiley & Sons, 1958); Kurt Lewin, Ronald Lippett, and Ralph K. White, "Patterns of Aggressive Behavior in Experimentally Created 'Social Climates,' " *Journal of Social Psychology*, 10 (1939), pp. 271–299; Seymour Lieberman, "The Effects of Changes in Roles on the Attitudes of Role Occupants," *Human Relations*, 9 (1950), pp. 385–403; Alvin Gouldner, *Patterns of Industrial Bureaucracy* (Glencoe, Ill.: The Free Press, 1954); Peter G. Garabedian, "Social Roles and Processes of Socialization in the Prison Community," *Social Problems*, 11 (Fall 1963), pp. 139–152; Alfred Stanton and Morris Schwartz, *The Mental Hospital* (New York: Basic Books, 1954); Peter Blau, "Structural Effects," *American Sociological Review*, 25 (1960), pp. 178–193.

7. Kurt Lewin, *Field Theory in Social Science* (New York: Harper & Brothers, 1951); George C. Homans, *Social Behavior: Its Elementary Forms* (New York: Harcourt, Brace and World, 1961), pp. 46–47, 51–82.

8. Gouldner, op. cit., pp. 83–85; Kohn and Williams, op. cit., pp. 164–174.

9. Lewin, op. cit., p. 137.

10. Donald R. Cressey, "The Criminal Violation of Financial Trust," *American Sociological Review*, 15 (December 1950), p. 742.

11. Clifford R. Shaw, "Juvenile Delinquency—A Group Tradition," *Bulletin of the State University of Iowa*, No. 23, N.S. No. 700, 1933, p. 8.

12. Lewis Yablonsky, *The Violent Gang* (New York: Macmillan, 1962), p. 13.

13. Comments of an ex-gang leader as quoted in Sophia M. Robison, *Juvenile Delinquency* (New York: Holt, Rinehart and Winston, 1960), pp. 134–137.

14. It should be emphasized, however, that while many situational contingencies of this sort fall in the class of phenomena often considered "accidental," these events do not occur randomly. For example, boys living in slums are more likely to encounter experiences which can evoke motives to deviate in certain ways than are their middle class counterparts. To illustrate: the slum youth is more likely to find drunks sleeping in doorways, to see wares displayed in open counters on the sidewalk, to meet adult criminals, and to come under police surveillance than is the youth living in a middle class neighborhood.

15. Albert K. Cohen, *Delinquent Boys: The Culture of the Gang* (Glencoe, Ill.: The Free Press, 1955).

16. Richard A. Cloward and Lloyd E. Ohlin, op. cit., *passim.*

17. Walter Miller, "Lower Class Culture as a Generating Milieu of Gang Delinquency," *Journal of Social Issues*, 14, No. 3 (1958), pp. 5–19.

18. Kate Friedlander, *The Psychoanalytic Approach to Juvenile Delinquency* (New York: International Universities Press, 1947).

19. Robert A. Gordon, James F. Short, Jr., Desmond S. Cartwright, and Fred L. Strodtbeck, "Values and Gang Delinquency: A Study of Street-Corner Groups," *American Journal of Sociology*, 69 (1963), pp. 109–128.

20. Solomon Rettig and Harve E. Rawson, "The Risk Hypothesis in Predictive Judgements of Unethical Behavior," *Journal of Abnormal and Social Psychology,* 66 (March 1963), pp. 243–248; Helen Merrell Lynd, *On Shame and the Search for Identity* (New York: Harcourt, Brace, and Co., 1958); David P. Ausubel, "Relationships Between Shame and Guilt in the Socializing Process," *Psychological Review,* 62 (1955), pp. 378–390; Justin Aronfreed, "The Nature, Variety, and Social Patterning of Moral Responses to Transgression," *Journal of Abnormal and Social Psychology,* 63 (1961), pp. 223–240.

21. However, it must be admitted that the nature of these motives is not well articulated by social control theorists.

22. F. Ivan Nye, *Family Relationships and Delinquent Behavior* (New York: John Wiley & Sons, 1958); William McCord and Joan McCord, *Origins of Crime* (New York: Columbia University Press, 1959).

23. Jackson Toby and Marcia L. Toby, *Low School Status as a Predisposing Factor in Subcultural Delinquency* (New Brunswick, N.J.: Rutgers University, no date, mimeographed); Cohen, op. cit., pp. 112–116.

24. William J. Goode, "Norm Commitment and Conformity to Role-Status Obligations," *American Journal of Sociology,* 66 (November 1960), pp. 246–258.

25. Howard S. Becker, "Notes on the Concept of Commitment," *American Journal of Sociology,* 66 (July 1960), pp. 35–36. See also Howard S. Becker, "Personal Change in Adult Life," *Sociometry,* 27 (1964), p. 40–53.

26. Becker, "Notes on the Concept of Commitment," op. cit., p. 39.

27. James S. Coleman, *The Adolescent Society* (New York: The Free Press, 1962), pp. 173–219.

28. This argument derives from that of Merton and Lazersfeld on value homophyly. Paul F. Lazersfeld and Robert K. Merton, "Friendship as Social Process" in Monroe Berger, Theodore Abel, and Charles H. Page (eds.), *Freedom and Control in Modern Society* (New York: Van Nostrand, 1954), pp. 18–66.

29. While the threat of severe physical punishment and material deprivation can constrain the child's behavior at home, it is not as likely to control his behavior in other social contexts as less severe parental sanctions. Moreover, severe punishment may lower the child's reliance on parental guidance. Albert Bandura and Richard H. Walters, *Adolescent Aggression* (New York: Ronald Press, 1959); Albert Bandura and Richard H. Walters, *Social Learning and Personality Development* (New York: Holt, Rinehart and Winston, 1963).

30. Donald G. McKinley, *Social Class and Family Life* (New York: The Free Press, 1964), pp. 92–93, 152–191.

31. David C. McClelland, John W. Atkinson, Russell A. Clark, and Edgar L. Lowell, *The Achievement Motive* (New York: Appleton-Century-Crofts, 1953); McKinley, op. cit., p. 96.

32. Seymour Martin Lipset, "Democracy and Working-Class Authoritarianism," *American Sociological Review,* 24 (August 1959), p. 495. See, too, Urie Bronfenbrenner, "Socialization and Social Class Through Time and Space," in Eleanor E. Maccoby, Thomas M. Newcomb, and E. L. Hartley (eds.), *Readings in Social Psychology* (New York: Holt, 1958), pp. 400–425, and Genevieve Knupfer, "Portrait of the Underdog," *Public Opinion Quarterly,* 11 (Spring 1947), pp. 103–114.

33. Eleanor E. Maccoby, "Effects Upon Children of Their Mothers' Working," in Norman W. Bell and Ezra Vogel (eds.), *A Modern Introduction to the Family* (Glencoe, Ill.: The Free Press, 1960), pp. 521–533.

34. Ivan Nye, "Adolescent-Parent Adjustment—Socio-Economic Level as a Variable," *American Sociological Review,* 16 (June 1951), pp. 341–349; George Psathas, "Ethnicity, Social Class, and Adolescent Independence from Parental Control," *American Sociological Review,* 22 (August 1957), pp. 415–23.

35. McKinley, op. cit., pp. 92–93, 156–157; Albert Reiss, "Delinquency as the Failure of Personal and Social Controls," *American Sociological Review,* 16 (April 1951), pp. 196–207.

36. David Matza, op. cit., pp. 22, 26–30.

37. Sykes and Matza have pointed out that such "techniques of neutralization" are used by so-called confirmed delinquents. Their use by other youths who offend seems

therefore quite probable. [Gresham M. Sykes and David Matza, "Techniques of Neutralization: A Theory of Delinquency," *American Sociological Review*, 22 (December 1957), pp. 664–670.] Moreover, as Matza points out in *Delinquency and Drift* (op. cit., pp. 90–91), "the delinquent by using these techniques of neutralization, is able to consider himself not responsible for his acts, a self-conception which is confirmed, perhaps surpassed by views held in certain quarters of conventional society." In this way, the delinquent is able to preserve an image of himself as an essentialy law-abiding person who is being treated unfairly. This at least suggests that the delinquent does not necessarily see himself as more delinquent than the so-called non-delinquent.

38. Matza, op. cit., pp. 38–40.

39. James S. Coleman, *The Adolescent Society* (New York: The Free Press, 1961), pp. 138–141, 172; Joseph Stone and Joseph Church, *Childhood and Adolescence* (New York: Random House, 1957), pp. 288–292.

40. Albert Cohen considers this possibility but rejects it in favor of the notion that the offenses of delinquent gang members are group compelled. No empirical evidence is given, however, for his conclusions. Albert K. Cohen, op. cit., pp. 31–32.

41. Irving Piliavin and Scott Briar, "Police Encounters with Juveniles," *American Journal of Sociology*, 70 (September, 1964), pp. 206–214; Frederic M. Thrasher, *The Gang*, abridged edition (Chicago: University of Chicago Press, 1963), pp. 270–273.

42. It is important to note in this regard that delinquents do respect and work well for some teachers and that they do not hate all policemen. The attributes of liked and respected officials are discussed in Carl Werthman and Irving Piliavin, "Delinquency and Alienation from Authority" (in process).

43. Howard S. Becker, *Outsiders* (New York: The Free Press, 1963), pp. 34–35.

Control
Commitment

17 / A Control Theory of Delinquency

TRAVIS HIRSCHI

Control theories assume that delinquent acts result when an individual's bond to society is weak or broken. Since these theories embrace two highly complex concepts, the *bond* of the individual to *society*, it is not surprising that they have at one time or another formed the basis of explanations of most forms of aberrant or unusual behavior. It is also not surprising that control theories have described the elements of the bond to society in many ways, and that they have focused on a variety of units as the point of control. . . .

ELEMENTS OF THE BOND

Attachment

In explaining conforming behavior, sociologists justly emphasize sensitivity to the opinion of others.[1] Unfortunately, . . . they tend to suggest that man *is* sensitive to the opinion of others and thus exclude sensitivity from their explanations of deviant behavior. In explaining deviant behavior, psychologists, in contrast, emphasize insensitivity to the opinion of others.[2] Unfortunately, they too tend to ignore variation, and, in addition, they tend to tie sensitivity inextricably to other variables, to make it part of a syndrome or "type," and thus seriously to reduce its value as an explanatory concept. The psychopath is characterized only in part by "deficient attachment to or affection for others, a failure to respond to the ordinary motivations founded in respect or regard for one's fellows";[3] he is also characterized by such things as "excessive aggressiveness," "lack of superego control," and "an infantile level of response."[4] Unfortunately, too, the behavior that psychopathy is used to explain often becomes part of the *definition* of psychopathy. As a result, in Barbara Wootton's words: "[The psychopath] is. . . *par excellence*, and without shame or qualification, the model of the circular process by which mental abnormality is inferred from anti-social behavior while anti-social behavior is explained by mental abnormality."[5]

The problems of diagnosis, tautology, and name-calling are avoided if the dimensions of psychopathy are treated as causally and therefore problematically interrelated, rather than as logically and therefore necessarily bound to each other. In fact, it can be argued that all of the characteristics attributed to the psychopath follow from, are effects of, his lack of attachment to others. To say that to lack attachment to others is to be free from moral restraints is to use lack of attachment to explain the guiltlessness of the psychopath, the fact that he apparently has no conscience or superego. In this view, lack of attachment to others is not merely a symptom of psychopathy, it *is* psychopathy; lack of conscience is just another way of saying the same thing; and the violation of norms is (or may be) a consequence.

For that matter, given that man is an animal, "impulsivity" and "aggressiveness" can also be seen as natural consequences of freedom from moral restraints. However, since the view of man as endowed with natural propensities and capacities like other animals is peculiarly unpalatable to sociologists, we need not fall back on such a view to explain the amoral man's aggressiveness.[6] The process of becoming alienated from others often involves or is based on active interpersonal conflict. Such conflict could easily supply a reservoir of *socially derived* hostility sufficient to account for the aggressiveness of those whose attachments to others have been weakened.

Durkheim said it many years ago: "We are moral beings to the extent that we are social beings." This may be interpreted to mean that we are moral beings to the extent that we have "internalized the norms" of society. But what does it mean to say that a person has internalized the norms of society? The norms of society are by definition shared by the members of society. To violate a norm is, therefore, to act contrary to the wishes and expectations of other people. If a person does not care about the wishes and expectations of other people—that is, if he is insensitive to the opinion of others—then he is to that extent not bound by the norms. He is free to deviate.

The essence of internalization of norms, conscience, or superego thus lies in the attachment of the individual to others.[8] This view has several advantages over the concept of internalization. For one, explanations of deviant behavior based on attachment do not beg the question, since the extent to which a person is attached to others can be measured independently of his deviant behavior. Furthermore, change or variation in behavior is explainable in a way that it is not when notions of internalization or superego are used. For example, the divorced man is more likely after divorce to commit a number of deviant acts, such as suicide or forgery. If we explain these acts by reference to the superego (or internal control), we are forced to say that the man "lost his conscience" when he got a divorce; and, of course, if he remarries, we have to conclude that he gets his conscience back.

This dimension of the bond to conventional society is encountered in most social control-oriented research and theory. F. Ivan Nye's "internal control" and "indirect control" refer to the same element, although we avoid the problem of explaining changes over time by locating the "conscience" in the bond to others rather than making it part of the personality.[9] Attachment to others is just one aspect of Albert J. Reiss's "personal controls"; we avoid his problems of tautological empirical *observations* by making the relationship between attachment and delinquency problematic rather than definitional.[10] Finally, Scott Briar and Irving Piliavin's "commitment" or "stake in conformity" subsumes attachment, as their discussion illustrates, although the terms they use are more closely associated with the next element to be discussed.[11]

Commitment

"Of all passions, that which inclineth men least to break the laws, is fear. Nay, excepting some generous natures, it is the only thing, when there is the appearance of profit or pleasure by breaking the laws, that makes men keep them."[12] Few would deny that men on occasion obey the rules simply from fear of the consequences. This rational component in conformity we label commitment. What does it mean to say that a person is committed to conformity? In Howard S. Becker's formulation it means the following:

> First, the individual is in a position in which his decision with regard to some particular line of action has consequences for other interests and activities not necessarily [directly] related to it. Second, he has placed himself in that position by his own prior actions. A third element is present though so obvious as not to be apparent; the committed person must be aware [of these other interests] and must recognize that his decision in this case will have ramifications beyond it.[13]

The idea, then, is that the person invests time, energy, himself, in a certain line of activity—say, getting an education, building up a business, acquiring a reputation for virtue. When or whenever he considers deviant behavior, he must consider the costs of this deviant behavior, the risk he runs of losing the investment he has made in conventional behavior.

If attachment to others is the sociological counterpart of the superego or conscience, commitment is the counterpart of the ego or common sense. To the person committed to conventional lines of action, risking one to ten years in prison for a ten-dollar holdup is stupidity, because to the committed person the costs and risks obviously exceed ten dollars in value. (To the psychoanalyst, such an act exhibits failure to be governed by the "reality-principle.") In the sociological control theory, it can be and is generally assumed that the decision to commit a criminal act may well be rationally determined—that the actor's decision was not irrational given the risks and costs he faces. Of course, as Becker points out, if the actor is capable of in some sense calculating the costs of a line of action, he is also capable of calculational errors: ignorance and error return, in the control theory, as possible explanations of deviant behavior.

The concept of commitment assumes that the organization of society is such that the interest of most persons would be endangered if they were to engage in criminal acts. Most people, simply by the process of living in an organized society, acquire goods, reputations, prospects that they do not want to risk losing. These accumulations are society's insurance that they will abide by the rules. Many hypotheses about the antecedents of delinquent behavior are based on this premise. For example, Arthur L. Stinchcombe's hypothesis that "high school rebellion . . . occurs when future status is not clearly related to present performance"[14] suggests that one is committed to conformity not only by what one has but also by what one hopes to obtain. Thus "ambition" and/or "aspiration" play an important role in producing conformity. The person becomes committed to a conventional line of action, and he is therefore committed to conformity.

Most lines of action in a society are of course conventional. The clearest examples are educational and occupational careers. Actions thought to jeopardize one's chances in these areas are presumably avoided. Interestingly enough, even nonconventional commitments may operate to produce conventional conformity. We are told, at least, that boys aspiring to careers in the rackets or professional thievery are judged by their "honesty" and "reliability"—traits traditionally in demand among seekers of office boys.[15]

Involvement

Many persons undoubtedly owe a life of virtue to a lack of opportunity to do otherwise. Time and energy are inherently limited: "Not that I would not, if I could, be both handsome and fat and well dressed, and a great athlete, and make a million a year, be a wit, a bon vivant, and a lady killer, as well as a philosopher, a philanthropist, a statesman, warrior, and African explorer, as well as a 'tone-poet' and saint. But the thing is simply impossible."[16] The things that William

James here says he would like to be or do are all, I suppose, within the realm of conventionality, but if he were to include illicit actions he would still have to eliminate some of them as simply impossible.

Involvement or engrossment in conventional activities is thus often part of a control theory. The assumption, widely shared, is that a person may be simply too busy doing conventional things to find time to engage in deviant behavior. The person involved in conventional activities is tied to appointments, deadlines, working hours, plans, and the like, so the opportunity to commit deviant acts rarely arises. To the extent that he is engrossed in conventional activities, he cannot even think about deviant acts, let alone act out his inclinations.[17]

This line of reasoning is responsible for the stress placed on recreational facilities in many programs to reduce delinquency, for much of the concern with the high school dropout, and for the idea that boys should be drafted into the army to keep them out of trouble. So obvious and persuasive is the idea that involvement in conventional activities is a major deterrent to delinquency that it was accepted even by Sutherland: "In the general area of juvenile delinquency it is probable that the most significant difference between juveniles who engage in delinquency and those who do not is that the latter are provided abundant opportunities of a conventional type for satisfying their recreational interests, while the former lack those opportunities or facilities."[18]

The view that "idle hands are the devil's workshop" has received more sophisticated treatment in recent sociological writings on delinquency. David Matza and Gresham M. Sykes, for example, suggest that delinquents have the values of a leisure class, the same values ascribed by Veblen to *the* leisure class: a search for kicks, disdain of work, a desire for the big score, and acceptance of aggressive toughness as proof of masculinity.[19] Matza and Sykes explain delinquency by reference to this system of values, but they note that adolescents at all class levels are "to some extent" members of a leisure class, that they "move in a limbo between earlier parental domination and future integration with the social structure through the bonds of work and marriage."[20] In the end, then, the leisure of the adolescent produces a set of values, which, in turn, leads to delinquency.

Belief

Unlike the cultural deviance theory, the control theory assumes the existence of a common value system within the society or group whose norms are being violated. If the deviant is committed to a value system different from that of conventional society, there is, within the context of the theory, nothing to explain. The question is, "Why does a man violate the rules in which he believes?" It is not, "Why do men differ in their beliefs about what constitutes good and desirable conduct?" The person is assumed to have been socialized (perhaps imperfectly) into the group whose rules he is violating; deviance is not a question of one group imposing its rules on the members of another group. In other words, we not only assume the deviant *has* believed the rules, we assume he believes the rules even as he violates them.

How can a person believe it is wrong to steal at the same time he is stealing? In the strain theory, this is not a difficult problem. (In fact, . . . the strain theory was devised specifically to deal with this question.) The motivation to deviance adduced by the strain theorist is so strong that we can well understand the deviant act even assuming the deviator believes strongly that it is wrong.[21] However, given the control theory's assumptions about motivation, if both the deviant and the nondeviant believe the deviant act is wrong, how do we account for the fact that one commits it and the other does not?

Control theories have taken two approaches to this problem. In one approach, beliefs are treated as mere words that mean little or nothing if the other forms of control are missing. "Semantic dementia," the dissociation between rational faculties and emotional control which is said to be characteristic of the psychopath, illustrates this way of handling the problem.[22] In short, beliefs, at least insofar as they are expressed in words, drop out of the picture; since they do not differentiate between deviants and nondeviants, they are in the same class as "language" or any other characteristic common to all members of the group. Since they represent no real obstacle to the commission of delinquent acts, nothing need be said about how they are handled by those committing such acts. The control theories that do not mention beliefs (or values), and many do not, may be assumed to take this approach to the problem.

The second approach argues that the deviant rationalizes his behavior so that he can at once violate the rule and maintain his belief in it. Donald R. Cressey had advanced this argument with respect to embezzlement,[23] and Sykes and Matza have advanced it with respect to delinquency.[24] In both Cressey's and Sykes and Matza's treatments, these rationalizations (Cressey calls them "verbalizations," Sykes and Matza term them "techniques of neutralization") occur prior to the commission of the deviant act. If the neutralization is successful, the person is free to commit the act(s) in question. Both in Cressey and in Sykes and Matza, the strain that prompts the effort at neutralization also provides the motive force that results in the subsequent deviant act. Their theories are thus, in this sense, strain theories. Neutralization is difficult to handle within the context of a theory that adheres closely to control theory assumptions, because in the control theory there is no special motivational force to account for the neutralization. This difficulty is especially noticeable in Matza's later treatment of this topic, where the motivational component, the "will to delinquency," appears *after* the moral vacuum has been created by the techniques of neutralization.[25] The question thus becomes: Why neutralize?

In attempting to solve a strain-theory problem with control-theory tools, the control theorist is thus led into a trap. He cannot answer the crucial question. The concept of neutralization assumes the existence of moral obstacles to the commission of deviant acts. In order plausibly to account for a deviant act, it is necessary to generate motivation to deviance that is at least equivalent in force to the resistance provided by these moral obstacles. However, if the moral obstacles are removed, neutralization and special motivation are no longer required. We therefore follow the implicit logic of control theory and remove these moral obstacles by hypothesis. Many persons do not have an attitude of respect toward the rules of society; many persons feel no moral obligation to conform regardless of personal advantage. Insofar as the values and beliefs of these persons are consistent with their feelings, and there should be a tendency toward consistency, neutralization is unnecessary; it has already occurred.

Does this merely push the question back a step and at the same time produce conflict with the assumption of a common value system? I think not. In the first place, we do not assume, as does Cressey, that neutralization occurs in order to make a specific criminal act possible.[26] We do not assume, as do Sykes and Matza, that neutralization occurs to make many delinquent acts possible. We do not assume, in other words, that the person constructs a system of rationalizations in order to justify commission of acts he *wants* to commit. We assume, in contrast, that the beliefs that free a man to commit deviant acts are *unmotivated* in the sense that he does not construct or adopt them in order to facilitate the attainment of illicit ends. In the second place, we do not assume, as does Matza, that "delinquents concur in the conventional assessment of delinquency."[27] We assume, in contrast, that there is *variation* in the extent to which people believe they should obey the rules of society, and, furthermore, that the less a person believes he should obey the rules, the more likely he is to violate them.[28]

In chronological order, then, a person's beliefs in the moral validity of norms are, for no teleological reason, weakened. The probability that he will commit delinquent acts is therefore increased. When and if he commits a delinquent act, we may justifiably use the weakness of his beliefs in explaining it, but no special motivation is required to explain either the weakness of his beliefs or, perhaps, his delinquent act.

The keystone of this argument is of course the assumption that there is variation in belief in the moral validity of social rules. This assumption is amenable to direct empirical test and can thus survive at least until its first confrontation with data. For the present, we must return to the idea of a common value system with which this section was begun.

The idea of a common (or perhaps better, a single) value system is consistent with the fact, or presumption, of variation in the strength of moral beliefs. We have not suggested that delinquency is based on beliefs counter to conventional morality; we have not suggested that delinquents do not believe delinquent acts are wrong. They may well believe these acts are wrong, but the meaning and efficacy of such beliefs are contingent on other beliefs and, indeed, on the strength of other ties to the conventional order.[29]

Notes

1. Books have been written on the increasing importance of interpersonal sensitivity in modern life. According to this view, controls from within have become less important than controls from without in *producing* conformity. Whether or not this observation is true as a description of historical trends, it is true that interpersonal sensitivity has become more important in *explaining* conformity. Although logically it should also have become more important in explaining nonconformity, the opposite has been the case, once again showing that Cohen's observation that an explanation of conformity should be an explanation of deviance cannot be translated as "an explanation of conformity has to be an explanation of deviance." For the view that interpersonal sensitivity currently plays a greater role than formerly in producing conformity, see William J. Goode, "Norm Commitment and Conformity to Role-Status Obligations," *American Journal of Sociology*, LXVI (1960), 246–258. And, of course, also see David Riesman, Nathan Glazer, and Rouel Denney, *The Lonely Crowd* (Garden City, New York: Doubleday, 1950), especially Part I.

2. The literature on psychopathy is voluminous. See William McCord and Joan McCord, *The Psychopath* (Princeton: D. Van Nostrand, 1964).

3. John M. Martin and Joseph P. Fitzpatrick, *Delinquent Behavior* (New York: Random House, 1964), p. 130.

4. *Ibid.* For additional properties of the psychopath, see McCord and McCord, *The Psychopath*, pp. 1–22.

5. Barbara Wootton, *Social Science and Social Pathology* (New York: Macmillan, 1959), p. 250.

6. "The logical untenability [of the position that there are forces in man 'resistant to socialization'] was ably demonstrated by Parsons over 30 years ago, and it is widely recognized that the position is empirically unsound because it assumes [!] some universal biological drive system distinctly separate from socialization and social context—a basic and intransigent human nature" (Judith Blake and Kingsley Davis, "Norms, Values, and Sanctions," *Handbook of Modern Sociology*, ed. Robert E. L. Faris [Chicago: Rand McNally, 1964], p. 471).

7. Emile Durkheim, *Moral Education*, trans. Everett K. Wilson and Herman Schnurer (New York: The Free Press, 1961), p. 64.

8. Although attachment alone does not exhaust the meaning of internalization, attachments and beliefs combined would appear to leave only a small residue of "internal control" not susceptible in principle to direct measurement.

9. F. Ivan Nye, *Family Relationships and Delinquent Behavior* (New York: Wiley, 1958), pp. 5–7.

10. Albert J. Reiss, Jr., "Delinquency as the Failure of Personal and Social Controls," *American Sociological Review*, XVI (1951), 196–207. For example, "Our observations show ... that delinquent recidivists are less often persons with mature ego ideals or nondelinquent social roles" (p. 204).

11. Scott Briar and Irving Piliavin, "Delinquency, Situational Inducements, and Commitment to Conformity," *Social Problems*, XIII (1965), 41–42. The concept "stake in conformity" was introduced by Jackson Toby in his "Social Disorganization and Stake in Conformity: Complementary Factors in the Predatory Behavior of Hoodlums," *Journal of Criminal Law, Criminology and Police Science*, XLVIII (1957), 12–17. See also his "Hoodlum or Business Man: An American Dilemma," *The Jews*, ed. Marshall Sklare (New York: The Free Press, 1958), pp. 542–550. Throughout the text, I occasionally use "stake in conformity" in speaking in general of the strength of the bond to conventional society. So used, the concept is somewhat broader than is true for either Toby or Briar and Piliavin, where the concept is roughly equivalent to what is here called "commitment."

12. Thomas Hobbes, *Leviathan* (Oxford: Basil Blackwell, 1957), p. 195.

13. Howard S. Becker, "Notes on the Concept of Commitment," *American Journal of Sociology*, LXVI (1960), 35–36.

14. Arthur L. Stinchcombe, *Rebellion in a High School* (Chicago: Quadrangle, 1964), p. 5.

15. Richard A. Cloward and Lloyd E. Ohlin, *Delinquency and Opportunity* (New York: The Free Press, 1960), p. 147, quoting Edwin H. Sutherland, ed., *The Professional Thief* (Chicago: University of Chicago Press, 1937), pp. 211–213.

16. William James, *Psychology* (Cleveland: World Publishing Co., 1948), p. 186.

17. Few activities appear to be so engrossing that they rule out contemplation of alternative lines of behavior, at least if estimates of the amount of time men spend plotting sexual deviations have any validity.

18. *The Sutherland Papers*, ed. Albert K. Cohen et al. (Bloomington: Indiana University Press, 1956), p. 37.

19. David Matza and Gresham M. Sykes, "Juvenile Delinquency and Subterranean Values," *American Sociological Review*, XXVI (1961), 712–719.

20. *Ibid.*, p. 718.

21. The starving man stealing the loaf of bread is the image evoked by most strain theories. In this image, the starving man's belief in the wrongness of his act is clearly not something that must be explained away. It can be assumed to be present without causing embarrassment to the explanation.

22. McCord and McCord, *The Psychopath*, pp. 12–15.

23. Donald R. Cressey, *Other People's Money* (New York: The Free Press, 1953).

24. Gresham M. Sykes and David Matza, "Techniques of Neutralization: A Theory of Delinquency," *American Sociological Review*, XXII (1957), 664–670.

25. David Matza, *Delinquency and Drift* (New York: Wiley, 1964), pp. 181–191.

26. In asserting that Cressey's assumption is invalid with respect to delinquency, I do not wish to suggest that it is invalid for the question of embezzlement, where the problem faced by the deviator is fairly specific and he can reasonably be assumed to be an upstanding citizen. (Although even here the fact that the embezzler's nonsharable financial problem often results from some sort of hanky-panky suggests that "verbalizations" may be less necessary than might otherwise be assumed.)

27. *Delinquency and Drift*, p. 43.

28. This assumption is not, I think, contradicted by the evidence presented by Matza against the existence of a delinquent subculture. In comparing the attitudes and actions of delinquents with the picture painted by delinquent subculture theorists, Matza emphasizes—and perhaps exaggerates—the extent to which delinquents are tied to the conventional order. In implicitly comparing delinquents with a super-

moral man, I emphasize—and perhaps exaggerate—the extent to which they are not tied to the conventional order.

29. The position taken here is therefore somewhere between the "semantic dementia" and the "neutralization" positions. Assuming variation, the delinquent is, at the extremes, freer than the neutralization argument assumes. Although the possibility of wide discrepancy between what the delinquent professes and what he practices still exists, it is presumably much rarer than is suggested by studies of articulate "psychopaths."

18 / Primary and Secondary Deviation

EDWIN M. LEMERT

SOCIOPATHIC INDIVIDUATION

The deviant person is a product of differentiating and isolating processes. Some persons are individually differentiated from others from the time of birth onward, as in the case of a child born with a congenital physical defect or repulsive appearance, and as in the case of a child born into a minority racial or cultural group. Other persons grow to maturity in a family or in a social class where pauperism, begging, or crime are more or less institutionalized ways of life for the entire group. In these latter instances the person's sociopsychological growth may be normal in every way, his status as a deviant being entirely caused by his maturation within the framework of social organization and culture designated as "pathological" by the larger society. This is true of many delinquent children in our society.[1]

> It is a matter of great significance that the delinquent child, growing up in the delinquency areas of the city, has very little access to the cultural heritages of the larger conventional society. His infrequent contacts with this larger society are for the most part formal and external. Quite naturally his conception of moral values is shaped and molded by the moral code prevailing in his play groups and the local community in which he lives . . . the young delinquent has very little appreciation of the meaning of the traditions and formal laws of society. . . . Hence the conflict between the delinquent and the agencies of society is, in its broader aspects, a conflict of divergent cultures.

The same sort of gradual, unconscious process which operates in the socialization of the deviant child may also be recognized in the acquisition of socially unacceptable behavior by persons after having reached adulthood. However, with more verbal and sophisticated adults, step-by-step violations of societal norms tend to be progressively rationalized in the light of what is socially acceptable. Changes of this nature can take place at the level of either overt or covert behavior, but with a greater likelihood that adults will preface overt behavior changes with projective symbolic departures from society's norms. When the latter occur, the subsequent overt changes may appear to be "sudden" personality modifications. However, whether these changes are completely radical ones is to some extent a moot point. One writer holds strongly to the opinion that sudden and dramatic shifts in behavior from normal to abnormal are seldom the case, that a sequence of small preparatory transformations must be the prelude to such apparently sudden behavior changes. This writer is impressed by the day-by-day growth of "reserve potentialities" within personalities of all individuals, and he contends that many normal persons carry potentialities for abnormal behavior, which, given proper conditions, can easily be called into play.[2]

Personality Changes Not Always Gradual

This argument is admittedly sound for most cases, but it must be taken into consideration that traumatic experiences often speed up changes in personality.[3] Nor can the "trauma" in these experiences universally be attributed to the unique way in which the person conceives of the experience subjectively. Cases exist to show that personality modifications can be telescoped or that there can be an acceleration of such changes caused largely by the intensity and variety of the social stimulation. Most soldiers undoubtedly have entirely different conceptions of their roles after intensive combat experience. Many admit to having "lived a lifetime" in a relatively short period of time after they have been under heavy fire in battle for the first time. Many generals have remarked that their men have to be a little "shooted" or "blooded" in order to become good soldiers. In the process of group formation, crises and interactional amplification are vital requisites to forging true, role-oriented group behavior out of individuated behavior.[4]

The importance of the person's conscious symbolic reactions to his or her own behavior cannot be overstressed in explaining the shift from normal to abnormal behavior or from one type of pathological behavior to another, particularly where behavior variations become systematized or structured into pathological roles. This is not to say that conscious choice is a determining factor in the differentiating process. Nor does it mean that the awareness of the self is a purely conscious perception. Much of the process of self-perception is doubtless marginal from the point of view of consciousness.[5] But however it may be perceived, the individual's self-definition is closely connected with such things as self-acceptance, the subordination of minor to major roles, and with the motivation involved in learning the skills, techniques, and values of a new role. *Self-definitions or self-realizations are likely to be the result of sudden perceptions and they*

*are especially significant when they are followed immediately by
overt demonstrations of the new role they symbolize.* The self-
defining junctures are critical points of personality genesis and in the
special case of the atypical person they mark a division between two
different types of deviation.

Primary and Secondary Deviation

There has been an embarrassingly large number of theories, often
without any relationship to a general theory, advanced to account for
various specific pathologies in human behavior. For certain types of
pathology, such as alcoholism, crime, or stuttering, there are almost as
many theories as there are writers on these subjects. This has been
occasioned in no small way by the preoccupation with the origins of
pathological behavior and by the fallacy of confusing *original* causes
with *effective* causes. All such theories have elements of truth, and the
divergent viewpoints they contain can be reconciled with the general
theory here if it is granted that original causes or antecedents of
deviant behaviors are many and diversified. This holds especially for
the psychological processes leading to similar pathological behavior,
but it also holds for the situational concomitants of the initial aberrant
conduct. A person may come to use excessive alcohol not only for a
wide variety of subjective reasons but also because of diversified
situational influences, such as the death of a loved one, business
failure, or participating in some sort of organized group activity calling
for heavy drinking of liquor. Whatever the original reasons for violating the norms of the community, they are important only for certain
research purposes, such as assessing the extent of the "social problem" at a given time or determining the requirements for a rational
program of social control. From a narrower sociological viewpoint the
deviations are not significant until they are organized subjectively
and transformed into active roles and become the social criteria for
assigning status. The deviant individuals must react symbolically to
their own behavior aberrations and fix them in their sociopsychological patterns. The deviations remain primary deviations or symptomatic and situational as long as they are rationalized or otherwise dealt
with as functions of a socially acceptable role. Under such conditions
normal and pathological behaviors remain strange and somewhat
tensional bedfellows in the same person. Undeniably a vast amount of
such segmental and partially integrated pathological behavior exists
in our society and has impressed many writers in the field of social
pathology.

Just how far and for how long a person may go in dissociating his
sociopathic tendencies so that they are merely troublesome adjuncts

of normally conceived roles is not known. Perhaps it depends upon the number of alternative definitions of the same overt behavior that he can develop; perhaps certain physiological factors (limits) are also involved. However, if the deviant acts are repetitive and have a high visibility, and if there is a severe societal reaction, which, through a process of identification is incorporated as part of the "me" of the individual, the probability is greatly increased that the integration of existing roles will be disrupted and that reorganization based upon a new role or roles will occur. (The "me" in this context is simply the subjective aspect of the societal reaction.) Reorganization may be the adoption of another normal role in which the tendencies previously defined as "pathological" are given a more acceptable social expression. The other general possibility is the assumption of a deviant role, if such exists; or, more rarely, the person may organize an aberrant sect or group in which he creates a special role of his own. *When a person begins to employ his deviant behavior or a role based upon it as a means of defense, attack, or adjustment to the overt and covert problems created by the consequent societal reaction to him, his deviation is secondary.* Objective evidences of this change will be found in the symbolic appurtenances of the new role, in clothes, speech, posture, and mannerisms, which in some cases heighten social visibility, and which in some cases serve as symbolic cues to professionalization.

Role Conceptions of the Individual
Must Be Reinforced by Reactions of Others

It is seldom that one deviant act will provoke a sufficiently strong societal reaction to bring about secondary deviation, unless in the process of introjection the individual imputes or projects meanings into the social situation which are not present. In this case anticipatory fears are involved. For example, in a culture where a child is taught sharp distinctions between "good" women and "bad" women, a single act of questionable morality might conceivably have a profound meaning for the girl so indulging. However, in the absence of reactions by the person's family, neighbors, or the larger community, reinforcing the tentative "bad-girl" self-definition, it is questionable whether a transition to secondary deviation would take place. It is also doubtful whether a temporary exposure to a severe punitive reaction by the community will lead a person to identify himself with a pathological role, unless, as we have said, the experience is highly traumatic. Most frequently there is a progressive reciprocal relationship between the deviation of the individual and the societal reaction, with a compounding of the societal reaction out of the minute accretions in the deviant behavior, until a point is reached where ingrouping and outgrouping between society and the deviant is manifest.[6] At this point a stigmatizing of the deviant occurs in the form of name calling, labeling, or stereotyping.

The sequence of interaction leading to secondary deviation is roughly as follows: (1) primary deviation; (2) social penalties; (3) further primary deviation; (4) stronger penalties and rejections; (5) further deviation, perhaps with hostilities and resentment beginning to focus upon those doing the penalizing; (6) crisis reached in the tolerance quotient, expressed in formal action by the community stigmatizing of the deviant; (7) strengthening of the deviant conduct as a reaction to the stigmatizing and penalties; (8) ultimate acceptance of deviant social status and efforts at adjustment on the basis of the associated role.

As an illustration of this sequence the behavior of an errant schoolboy can be cited. For one reason or another, let us say excessive energy, the schoolboy enagages in a classroom prank. He is penalized for it by the teacher. Later, due to clumsiness, he creates another disturbance and again he is reprimanded. Then, as sometimes happens, the boy is blamed for something he did not do. When the teacher uses the tag "bad boy" or "mischief maker" or other invidious terms, hostility and resentment are excited in the boy, and he may feel that he is blocked in playing the role expected of him. Thereafter, there may be a strong temptation to assume his role in the class as defined by the teacher, particularly when he discovers that there are rewards as well as penalties deriving from such a role. There is, of course, no implication here that such boys go on to become delinquents or criminals, for the mischief-maker role may later become integrated with or retrospectively rationalized as part of a role more acceptable to school authorities.[7] If such a boy continues this unacceptable role and becomes delinquent, the process must be accounted for in the light of the general theory of this volume. There must be a spreading corroboration of a sociopathic self-conception and societal reinforcement at each step in the process.

The most significant personality changes are manifest when societal definitions and their subjective counterpart become generalized. When this happens, the range of major role choices becomes narrowed to one general class.[8] This was very obvious in the case of a young girl who was the daughter of a paroled convict and who was attending a small Middle Western college. She continually argued with herself and with the author, in whom she had confided, that in reality she belonged on the "other side of the railroad tracks" and that her life could be enormously simplified by acquiescing in this verdict and living accordingly. While in her case there was a tendency to dramatize her conflicts, nevertheless there was enough societal reinforcement of her self-conception by the treatment she received in her relationship with her father and on dates with college boys to lend it a painful reality. Once these boys took her home to the shoddy dwelling in a slum area where she lived with her father, who was often in a drunken condition, they abruptly stopped seeing her again or else became sexually presumptive.

Notes

1. Shaw, C., *The Natural History of a Delinquent Career*, Chicago, 1941, pp. 75–76. Quoted by permission of the University of Chicago Press, Chicago.

2. Brown, L. Guy, *Social Pathology*, 1942, pp. 44–45.

3. Allport, G., *Personality, A Psychological Interpretation*, 1947, p. 57.

4. Slavson, S. R., *An Introduction to Group Psychotherapy*, 1943, pp. 10, 229*ff.*

5. Murphy, G., *Personality*, 1947, p. 482.

6. Mead, G., "The Psychology of Punitive Justice," *American Journal of Sociology*, 23 March, 1918, pp. 577–602.

7. Evidence for fixed or inevitable sequences from predelinquency to crime is absent. Sutherland, E. H., *Principles of Criminology*, 1939, 4th ed., p. 202.

8. Sutherland seems to say something of this sort in connection with the development of criminal behavior. *Ibid.*, p. 86.

19 / Career Deviance

HOWARD S. BECKER

One of the most crucial steps in the process of building a stable pattern of deviant behavior is likely to be the experience of being caught and publicly labeled as a deviant. Whether a person takes this step or not depends not so much on what he does as on what other people do, on whether or not they enforce the rule he has violated. . . . First of all, even though no one else discovers the nonconformity or enforces the rules against it, the individual who has committed the impropriety may himself act as an enforcer. He may brand himself as deviant because of what he has done and punish himself in one way or another for his behavior. This is not always or necessarily the case, but may occur. Second, there may be cases like those described by psychoanalysts in which the individual really wants to get caught and perpetrates his deviant act in such a way that it is almost sure he will be.

In any case, being caught and branded as deviant has important consequences for one's further social participation and self-image. The most important consequence is a drastic change in the individual's public identity. Committing the improper act and being publicly caught at it place him in a new status. He has been revealed as a different kind of person from the kind he was supposed to be. He is labeled a "fairy," "dope fiend," "nut" or "lunatic," and treated accordingly.

In analyzing the consequences of assuming a deviant identity let us make use of Hughes' distinction between master and auxiliary status traits.[1] Hughes notes that most statuses have one key trait which serves to distinguish those who belong from those who do not. Thus the doctor, whatever else he may be, is a person who has a certificate stating that he has fulfilled certain requirements and is licensed to practice medicine; this is the master trait. As Hughes points out, in our society a doctor is also informally expected to have a number of auxiliary traits: most people expect him to be upper middle class, white, male, and Protestant. When he is not there is a sense that he has in some way failed to fill the bill. Similarly, though skin color is the master status trait determining who is Negro and who is white, Negroes are informally expected to have certain status traits and not to have others; people are surprised and find it anomalous if a Negro turns out to be a doctor or a college professor. People often have the master status trait but lack some of the auxiliary, informally expected characteristics; for example, one may be a doctor but be female or Negro.

Hughes deals with this phenomenon in regard to statuses that are well thought of, desired and desirable (noting that one may have the formal qualifications for entry into a status but be denied full entry because of lack of the proper auxiliary traits), but the same process occurs in the case of deviant statuses. Possession of one deviant trait may have a generalized symbolic value, so that people automatically assume that its bearer possesses other undesirable traits allegedly associated with it.

To be labeled a criminal one need only commit a single criminal offense, and this is all the term formally refers to. Yet the word carries a number of connotations specifying auxiliary traits characteristic of anyone bearing the label. A man who has been convicted of house-breaking and thereby labeled criminal is presumed to be a person likely to break into other houses; the police, in rouding up known offenders for investigation after a crime has been committed, operate on this premise. Further, he is considered likely to commit other kinds of crimes as well, because he has shown himself to be a person without "respect for the law." Thus, apprehension for one deviant act exposes a person to the likelihood that he will be regarded as deviant or undesirable in other respects.

There is one other element in Hughes' analysis we can borrow with profit: the distinction between master and subordinate statuses.[2] Some statuses, in our society as in others, override all other statuses and have a certain priority. Race is one of these. Membership in the Negro race, as socially defined, will override most other status considerations in most other situations; the fact that one is a physician or middle-class or female will not protect one from being treated as a Negro first and any of these other things second. The status of deviant (depending on the kind of deviance) is this kind of master status. One receives the status as a result of breaking a rule, and the identification proves to be more important than most others. One will be identified as a deviant first, before other identifications are made. The question is raised: "What kind of person would break such an important rule?" And the answer is given: "One who is different from the rest of us, who cannot or will not act as a moral human being and therefore might break other important rules." The deviant identification becomes the controlling one.

Treating a person as though he were generally rather than specifically deviant produces a self-fulfilling prophecy. It sets in motion several mechanisms which conspire to shape the person in the image people have of him.[3] In the first place, one tends to be cut off, after being identified as deviant, from participation in more conventional groups, even though the specific consequences of the particular deviant activity might never of themselves have caused the isolation had there not also been the public knowledge and reaction to it. For example, being a homosexual may not affect one's ability to do office work, but to be known as a homosexual in an office may make it impossible to continue working there. Similarly, though the effects of opiate drugs may not impair one's working ability, to be known as an addict will probably lead to losing one's job. In such cases, the individual finds it difficult to conform to other rules which he had no intention or desire to break, and perforce finds himself deviant in these areas as well. The homosexual who is deprived of a "respectable" job by the discovery of his deviance may drift into unconventional, marginal occupations where it does not make so much difference. The drug addict finds himself forced into other illegitimate kinds of activity, such as robbery and theft, by the refusal of respectable employers to have him around.

When the deviant is caught, he is treated in accordance with the popular diagnosis of why he is that way, and the treatment itself may likewise produce increasing deviance. The drug addict, popularly considered to be a weak-willed individual who cannot forego the indecent pleasures afforded him by opiates, is treated repressively. He is forbidden to use drugs. Since he cannot get drugs legally, he must get them illegally. This forces the market underground and pushes the price of drugs up far beyond the current legitimate market price into a bracket that few can afford on an ordinary salary. Hence the treatment of the addict's deviance places him in a position where it will probably be necessary to resort to deceit and crime in order to support his habit.[4] The behavior is a consequence of the public reaction to the deviance rather than a consequence of the inherent qualities of the deviant act.

Notes

1. Everett C. Hughes, "Dilemmas and Contradictions of Status," *American Journal of Sociology*, L (March, 1945), 353–359.

2. *Ibid.*

3. See Marsh Ray, "The Cycle of Abstinence and Relapse Among Heroin Addicts," *Social Problems*, 9 (Fall, 1961), 132–140.

4. See *Drug Addiction: Crime or Disease?* Interim and Final Reports of the Joint Committee of the American Bar Association and the American Medical Association on Narcotic Drugs (Bloomington, Indiana: Indiana University Press, 1961).

Part 3 / Becoming Deviant

In Part 1, I made some general statements about the way deviant categories arise and the way violators of these categories may be reacted to. In Part 2, I explored some of the major theories and perspectives that serve to explain why actors may commit deviant acts. In this part of the book, I will deal more systematically with reactions that may bring about early stages of deviant careers—careers which may ultimately become subject to institutional control and regulation (Part 4).

In the general introduction, a distinction was made between the initiation of the labeling ceremony in a private domain and initiation in the public domain. I also noted how those engaged in deviant pursuits attempt to manage their behavior and attitudes in such a way as to avoid detection by socially significant "straights," especially formal agents of social control. This avoidance clearly indicates that not only is there some potentially stigmatizing or discreditable feature of their biography, but detection is frequently associated with a range of personal and social costs. As an example, the drug pusher runs the risk of being sanctioned by the courts. It is conceivable, of course, that the pusher may never experience any direct contact with the social-control apparatus. He or she would remain what I have termed a noninstitutional deviant. Still, the pusher is aware of the potentially damaging nature of his or her activities and realizes that if authorities became aware of those activities, that knowledge could be used to initiate some type of institutional career.

In the analysis of strategies for information control and management, it is useful, therefore, to think in terms of actor *and* audience response. The pusher, in an effort to protect his or her self-image and identity cluster, as well as to reduce the odds of being officially designated as a deviant, may employ certain strategies (e.g., denying to self and others that he or she is a pusher). Similarly, those who must deal with actual or potential deviance often invoke various types of coping or accommodative strategies. A wife, for example, may try to accommodate herself to her husband's increasingly violent behavior. If she is successful, the deviance will remain primarily a matter of private knowledge, regulation, and management—although the wife herself may consider her husband to be deviant. If, on the other hand, the wife's accommodative strategies (e.g., attempts at neutralization or rationalization) fail, she may find it necessary to bring in third parties (e.g., social-control agents like the police) to regulate her husband's behavior. Not only have the wife's "tolerance limits" been exceeded in this case, but behavior that had been managed in the private setting now becomes subject to institutional control. And the husband may be typed, processed, and responded to as an involuntary mental patient.

The selections that follow explore the ways in which strategies for management and accommodation operate in private settings. The initial two selections deal primarily with how actors attempt to manage and control potentially discrediting information about themselves. The remaining selections illustrate how audiences respond to deviant or increasingly bizarre behavior on the part of significant and generalized others. These articles offer excellent illustrations of the usefulness of many of the basic concepts and processes introduced in Parts 1 and 2. For example, Ferraro and Johnson, in their analysis of spouse battering, rely very heavily on Sykes and Matza's neutralization techniques.

Joseph W. Schneider and Peter Conrad, in their article "In the Closet with Illness: Epilepsy, Stigma Potential and Information Control," provide an interesting account of how people attempt to manage what they view as discreditable information about themselves. These writers focus on a sample of eighty epileptics, none of whom has a history of long-term institutionalization. The researchers, in their reliance on the metaphor of the closet, initially advance the concept of "stigma potential" to emphasize the fact that epilepsy is a trait which causes one's identity to be discredited. Characterizing the stigma as "potential," they argue, rests on two basic assumptions: (1) that knowledge of the attribute (i.e., epilepsy) be limited to a few people, and (2) that if the trait were to become more widely known, significant changes in self, along with various controls of behavior, might result. Schneider and Conrad cite several examples that underscore the stigma potential of epilepsy (e.g., being discriminated against in the area of employment and being prohibited from marrying in some states). The authors then assert that stigma is not an automatic result of possessing some discreditable trait. Rather, the significance of " 'having' epilepsy is a product of a collective definitional process"—one in which the actor and others participate. A discreditable trait or performance becomes relevant to self only if it is perceived as such by the actor. How might the potentially stigmatized feel that others think about them, and how might others react to disclosure? Schneider and Conrad note that our understanding of an actor's *perception of stigma* is limited. They then discuss various strategies relative to concealment and disclosure (i.e., whether, and under what conditions, one will come out of the closet or not). For example, parental training regarding the stigma of epilepsy is often very important. Not only do parents frequently serve as coaches but, as they do so, the children learn how to deal with the fact that they are potentially discreditable. Other people also teach the importance of concealment. The authors end by discussing the strategies of selective concealment and instrumental telling.

" 'Shooting Up': Autobiography of a Heroin Addict," published anonymously, offers a first-person account of how a white, middle-class female became an addict. It also illustrates how she attempted to convince herself and others of her nondeviance, or nonaddiction. Although she reports having used the drug for a considerable period of time, she does not view herself as an addict. Rather, she types herself as an occasional user. Such a conception helps to keep her self-image and identity intact. Other justifications and rationalizations are used to support her belief that she is not an addict. For example, she claims that she does not experience withdrawal symptoms like other addicts, and when she uses heroin, she only does so to deal with stress and a tight schedule. Still, it is evident that she is very concerned with protecting her public identity; this concern is especially apparent from the comments on her hospitalization experience. Not only was she infuriated that a psychiatrist was brought in and a written record created, but she even plotted how she might steal the records and burn them. Upon release, she bemoaned the fact that her marijuana smoking friends were putting her down for wanting to use heroin. In her words: "They were really beginning to make me feel like a deviant."

"The Adjustment of the Family to the Crisis of Alcoholism," by Joan K. Jackson, provides an excellent account of how family members, particularly wives, try to adjust to a husband's alcoholism. Jackson's article offers a fruitful examination of how the accommodative process actually works. A wife may at first deny that a drinking problem exists by rationalizing it away, and she may be successful in her attempts. However, it may happen that not only does the drinking become progressively worse, but a family crisis develops. The wife may then decide that there is no real hope for the marriage and leave. Jackson maintains that even though many wives do leave their husbands, they frequently return; their return is often prompted by an increased understanding of alcoholism and by the need to lessen their feelings of guilt at leaving a sick man. When a wife returns, she will attempt to reorganize the family, while still relying upon accommodative strategies as necessary.

Kathleen J. Ferraro and John M. Johnson, in "How Women Experience Battering: The Process of Victimization," present some recent evidence on the battering of women. The accounts of 120 battered women provide the major data source. The researchers are concerned specifically with locating those conditions that keep women locked in abusive relationships. What they discover is that instead of seeking help or escaping, most women initially rationalize the violence that is perpetrated upon them by their husbands. Ferraro and Johnson cite several reasons why battered women resort to rationalization. The main one involves the relative lack of institutional, legal, and cultural supports. Thus, practical and social constraints, when coupled with the factors of commitment and love, prompt the use of rationalizations. Ferraro and Johnson, in extending Sykes and Matza's "techniques of neutralization," develop a six-category typology of rationalizations. Each woman used at least one of these techniques, and some used more than one. In terms of the specific rationalizations, women who invoke "the denial of victimization" technique often blame themselves, thereby neutralizing the spouse's responsibility. Some felt that if they had been more passive or conciliatory, the violence could have been avoided. Rationalizations may be effective for some; however, when battered women cease to rationalize and begin to see themselves as victims of abuse, the process of feeling victimized begins. The researchers discuss six catalysts that bring about this redefinition of abuse (e.g., a change in the level of abuse, a change in resources, and a change in the visibility of violence). Ferraro and Johnson conclude with a discussion of what they term the emotional career of victimization; they also comment on the aftermath of leaving.

"The Psychological Meaning of Mental Illness in the Family," by Marion Radke Yarrow, Charlotte Green Schwartz, Harriet S. Murphy, and Leila Calhoun Deasy, offers a vivid description of how behavior that is managed initially in a private setting ultimately becomes the object of institutional control. The case of the thirty-five-year-old cab driver serves as an excellent illustration of this process. The husband began to act bizarrely, and the wife tried, in various ways, to adjust to his behavior. She sought, in addition, to explain to herself—and to others—what might have motivated or produced the changes (job difficulties, for instance). As her husband's behavior became more violent, however, the wife found it necessary to bring in agents of social control. The time when the husband became the object of institutional processing marked the beginning of an involuntary, or institutional, career.

It should be noted that as family members seek to adjust to the increasingly maladaptive behavior of a relative, they frequently display a reluctance to impute pathology to him or her. The wife's initial refusal to characterize her husband as mentally ill illustrates this point. A similar response was evident in the study by Jackson. Most of us would find it difficult to admit to ourselves and others that we are living with "weirdos" or "deviants," or that we, in some way, may have contributed to the deviance.

Edwin M. Lemert's work "Paranoia and the Dynamics of Exclusion" also provides some insight into the way in which behavior that occurs in a private domain is reacted to by others. The focus is on an institutional setting and not the family. Lemert's research not only provides a concrete illustration of how people may respond to perceived deviants; it illustrates how a sequence of negative interaction (i.e., Lemert's selection, Part 2) may gradually produce feelings of paranoia. The humming of the tune "Dragnet" when the "institutional deviant" approached offers an excellent example of this. Lemert argues that interactional processes like this only served to produce a gradual estrangement between the involved parties. He does not imply that the initial "paranoid" behavior may have been produced by the negative reactions—it is clear that it may have developed out of some psychopathology—but he suggests that the reactions of others played a major role in exacerbating the subject's feelings of paranoia. In this regard, Lemert contends that the notion of a "paranoid pseudocommunity" does not seem to apply. This is apparent from the subject's observations and feelings that certain members were actually conspiring against him—feelings that were supported by actual incidents. The subject thus appeared to have a keen grasp of social reality. Lemert's article also provides a useful alternative to explaining how *selected* cases of paranoia may arise. In this situation it appears that a personal crisis, when compounded by a sequence of negative interaction, can produce paranoia.

20 / In the Closet with Illness: Epilepsy, Stigma Potential and Information Control

JOSEPH W. SCHNEIDER
PETER CONRAD

The metaphor of the closet has been used frequently to discuss how people avoid or pursue "deviant" identities. Formulated originally in the homosexual subculture, to be "in the closet" has meant to be a secret or covert homosexual. Sociologists have adopted the notion of "coming out" of the closet to describe the development of a gay identity, focusing on self-definition and "public" disclosure as important elements of identity formation (Dank, 1971; Humphreys, 1972; Warren, 1974; Ponse, 1976). Kitsuse (1980) recently has extended the concept of coming out to refer to the "social affirmation of the self" for a wide variety of disvalued groups, including feminists, elderly people, blacks, prostitutes, marijuana users, American Nazis, and many others. In arguing against an "oversocialized" view of deviants encouraged by some narrow labeling interpretations, Kitsuse suggests that increasing numbers of disvalued people in American society have "come out" to affirm their identities as legitimate grounds for the dignity, worth and pride they believe is rightfully theirs.

This link between the closet metaphor and the development of identity is premised, however, on the assumption that in "coming out" there is indeed something to come out to; that there are some developed or developing social definitions that provide the core of this new, open and proud self. Certainly in the case of homosexuality, abandoning the closet of secrecy and concealment was facilitated greatly by the availability of a public identity as "gay and proud." But what of those disvalued by some attribute, performance, or legacy for whom there is no alternate new and proud identity? And what of those for whom even the existence of some "old" and "spoiled" identity may be questionable? In such cases where there may be no clear identity to move from or to, the closet metaphor may seem to lack insight and hence be of little use. We believe, however, that this metaphor taps a more fundamental sociological problem that may, but need not, be linked to the formation of identity.

In this paper we argue that the metaphor of the closet, entry into

228

and exit from it, may be used to focus on the more general sociological problem of how people attempt to manage what they see as discreditable information about themselves. We draw on depth interview data from a study of people with epilepsy—a stigmatized illness (see also Schneider and Conrad, 1979). We try to see how people attempt to maintain favorable or at least neutral definitions of self, given a condition for which no "new" readily available supportive identity or subculture yet exists, and which most of the time—except for the occurrence of periodic seizures—is invisible. By extending the metaphor of the closet to describe this situation, we hope both to increase its analytic utility and learn more about how people manage nondeviant yet stigmatized conditions.[1]

Our sample of 80 people is divided roughly equally by sex, ranging in age from 14 to 54. Most of the respondents come from a metropolitan area of the midwest and none have a history of long-term institutionalization for epilepsy. Interviews were conducted over a two and a half year period beginning in mid-1976, and respondents were selected on the basis of availability and willingness to participate. We used a snowball sampling technique, relying on advertisements in local newspapers, invitation letters passed anonymously by common acquaintances, and names obtained from local social agencies, self-help groups, and health workers. No pretense to statistical representativeness is intended nor was it sought. Due to official restrictions and perceived stigma associated with epilepsy, a population listing from which to draw such a sample does not exist. Our intention was to develop a sample from which theoretical insights would emerge (see Glaser and Strauss, 1967).

We will try here to provide an "insider's" view[2] of 1) how people with epilepsy themselves define their condition as undesirable and discreditable, and, hence, grounds for being "in the closet"; and of 2) how they attempt to manage this discreditable information in such a way as to protect their reputations and rights as normal members of society. We first discuss epilepsy as a potentially stigmatized condition, then move to illustrations of how people perceive the stigma of epilepsy and adopt various strategies of concealment and (paradoxically) selective disclosure, all directed toward protecting what they believe to be a threatened self.

THE STIGMA POTENTIAL OF EPILEPSY

We suggest the concept "stigma potential" to emphasize the significance of epilepsy as an attribute discreditable to one's personal identity (cf. Goffman, 1963: 157). Description of the stigma as "potential" rests on two assumptions: 1) that knowledge of one's epilepsy be limited to relatively few others, and 2) that if it were to become more widely known, significant redefinition of self, accompanied by various restrictions and regulation of conduct, might well follow. Although Goffman suggests that possession of such discreditable attributes weighs heavily and shamefully on one's own definitions of self, whether others have the same knowledge or not, we prefer to make that an empirical question. Like Goffman's discreditable person, Becker's (1963, 1973) secret or potential deviant recognizes his or her own acts, qualities and characteristics, *and* is aware of certain relevant prohibitions in the larger cultural and social setting. Given this knowledge, the potential deviant is one who concludes that there is at least some probability that disclosure would lead to discrediting and undesirable consequences. Becker is more equivocal on the issue of self-derogation and shame, requiring only that the actor be aware that rules do exist which may be applied and enforced if others become aware of the hidden practice or attribute. Although shame is an important phenomenon, it is not necessary to the rise of information control strategies. It is of both theoretical and practical interest that epilepsy is an attribute that would seem to create precisely this kind of potentially deviant or stigmatized person.

Like leprosy and venereal disease, epilepsy is an illness with an ancient associated stigma. Furthermore, epileptic seizures—which can range from nearly imperceptible "spacing out" to the more common, dramatic and bizarre grand mal convulsions—constitute violations of taken-for-granted expectations about the competence of actors in social settings, and are thus likely candidates for becoming "deviant behaviors." Although physicians have been defining and treating it for centuries (Temkin, 1971), epilepsy has long been associated with disreputability, satanic possession, and evil (Lennox and Lennox, 1960). Nineteenth century medical and psychiatric research, including that of Maudsley and Lombroso, suggested a causal link between epilepsy and violent crime[3] and encouraged myths about the relation of epilepsy, violent behavior and mental illness. This research supported placing epileptics in colonies and later special hospitals, excluding them from jobs, from entering the United States as immigrants, and sometimes even from marrying and having children.

The advent of anticonvulsant medications (e.g., phenobarbital in 1912 and Dilantin in 1938) allowed for greater medical control of seizures, enabling epileptics to live more conventional lives. Modern medical conceptualizations of epilepsy as a seizure disorder produced by "intermittent electrochemical impulses in the brain" (HEW-NIH, 1975) are far removed from the earlier morally-tinged interpretations. But historical residues of the deviant status of epilepsy remain central to the condition's current social reality. The stigma potential of epilepsy is well-documented. In a fairly recent review of the literature, Arangio (1975, 1976) found that stigma was still pervasive. It was manifested in various forms of social discrimination: difficulty in obtaining a driver's license; until 1965, prohibitions (in some states) against marrying; discrimination in obtaining employment (e.g., until 1959 epileptics were not hired for federal civil service positions); difficulties in obtaining all types of insurance; laws (in nine states) that permit sterilization of epileptics under some conditions; and laws (in 17 states) that allow for institutionalization of epileptics (Arangio, 1975). Researchers using intermittent Gallup poll data over the 25-year period 1949 to 1974 found a decrease in attitudinal prejudice toward epileptics, although 20 percent of the population in 1974 still maintained that epileptics should not be employed (Caveness *et al.*, 1974).

Such attitudes and official regulations are, of course, not lost on people with epilepsy. A recent nationwide survey found that one quarter of all epileptics do not tell their employers about epilepsy, and half indicated that having epilepsy created problems in getting a job (Perlman, 1977). While these and other "objective" aspects of prejudice and discrimination toward people with epilepsy have been documented, the ways in which such features of the larger cultural and social world are given meaning in people's subjective experience is less accessible and relatively unexplored.

THE PERCEPTION OF STIGMA

Stigma is by no means an automatic result of possessing some discreditable attribute. The significance of "having" epilepsy is a product of a collective definitional process in which the actor's perspective occupies a central place. As suggested earlier, a discreditable attribute or performance becomes relevant to self only if the individual perceives it as discreditable, whether or not such perceptions are actually applied by others to self or simply considered as a relevant "object" in the environment that must be taken into account. The actor has an important part in the construction of the meaning of epilepsy and of illness generally. It is of course logically possible that people otherwise deemed "ill" are unaware of what their conditions mean to the others with whom they interact: for example, a person surprised by sympathetic reactions to his or her disclosure of cancer, or a young "tough" who in polite society wears venereal disease as a badge of sexual prowess.

Most sociological work on stigma assumes that the stigmatized learn the meaning of their attribute or performance primarily through direct exposure to rejection and disapproval from others. Less understood is the place of the *perception of stigma*—of what the putatively stigmatized think others think of them and "their kind" and about how these others might react to disclosure. This brings us back to the situation of Goffman's discreditable actor, but makes actors' definitions central and problematic. Such actor definitions of epilepsy provide the foundation on which the stigma of epilepsy is constructed.

Over and over in our interviews, people with epilepsy told us that they "have" something that others "don't understand," and that this lack of understanding and knowledge of "what epilepsy is" is a fundamental source of what they see as an actual or potentially negative reaction. They believe that what little information others have about epilepsy is probably incorrect and stereotypical, sometimes incorporating elements of madness and evil. Adjectives such as "frightened" and "scared" were used to describe others' views of epilepsy. One woman, whose epilepsy had been diagnosed at middle age and who had lost a teaching job because of seizures at work, said:

> Well, I understand it now and *I'm* not afraid of it. But most people are unless they've experienced it, and so you just don't talk to other people about it, and if you do, never use the word "epilepsy." The word itself, I mean job-ways, insurance-ways . . . anything, the hang-ups there are on it. There's just too much prejudice so the less said about it the better.

One man compared others' ignorance and fear of epilepsy to similar reactions to leprosy: "The public is so ill educated toward an epileptic. It's like someone with leprosy walking into a room. You see a leper and you run because you're afraid of it." And another woman spoke of epilepsy's "historical implications":

> The fact of having epilepsy. It isn't the seizures. I think they are a very minor part of it. Its implications are so *enormous.* The historical implications of epilepsy are fantastic. I'm lucky to have been born when I was. If I was born at the beginning of this century I would have been discarded . . . probably locked away somewhere.

In these and similar ways, people recognize that ignorance and fear taint public images of epilepsy. They then take such recognitions into account in their own strategies and decisions about how to control such discrediting information.

Seizures in social situations are an important aspect of this discrediting perception of epilepsy. Seizures might be seen as sociologically akin to such involuntary *faux pas* as breaking wind or belching. Farts or belches, however, are reasonably familiar and normalized in middle-class society, but people with epilepsy believe that others ordinarily consider seizures as beyond the boundaries of undesirable but nevertheless "normal" conduct. One woman suggested seizures are "like having your pants fall down" in public. Another described how she believed others see seizures: "I can't use the word 'horrible,' but they think . . . it's *ugly*. It is. It's strange. It's something you're not used to seeing." People with epilepsy believe that others see the actual behaviors associated with seizures—including unconsciousness, violent muscle contractions, falling to the ground, or simply being "absent" from the social scene—as objective grounds for a more fundamental, "essential" disreputability. The stigma was described this way by another woman:

> It's one of those fear images; it's something that people don't know about and it has strong negative connotations in people's minds. It's a bad image, something scary, sort of like a beggar; it's dirty, the person falling down and frothing at the mouth and jerking and the bystanders not knowing what to do. It's something that happens in public which isn't "nice."

As these data suggest, aside from the question of shame or self-labeling, people who have epilepsy perceive the social meanings attached to it and to seizures as threats to their status as normal and competent members of society.

COACHES FOR CONCEALMENT: LEARNING TO BE DISCREDITABLE

How do people construct these views of others' perceptions? As we suggested, conventional sociological wisdom has emphasized direct disvaluing treatment by others. While this interactive experience is undoubtedly important to study, our data strongly suggest that people with epilepsy also learn such views from significant and supportive others, particularly from parents. Parental training in the stigma of epilepsy is most clear for people who were diagnosed when they were children, but stigma coaches were also identified by those who were diagnosed when they were adults.[4]

Our data indicate that the more the parents convey a definition of epilepsy as something "bad," and the less willing they are to talk about it with their children, the more likely the child is to see it as something to be concealed. One thirty-four year old woman had maintained a strategy of tightly controlled secrecy from the time she was diagnosed as having epilepsy at age fourteen. She recalled her parents' reaction:

> Complete disbelief. You know, "We've never had anything like that in our family." I can remember that was very plainly said, almost like I was something . . . something was wrong. They did not believe it. In fact, we went to another doctor and then it was confirmed.

These parents proceeded to manage their daughter's epilepsy by a combination of silence and maternal "coaching" on how to conceal it from others. When asked if she told her husband of her epilepsy before they were married, the same woman said:

> I talked to Mom about it. She said, "Don't tell him because some people don't understand. He may not understand. That's not something you talk about." I asked her, "Should I talk to him about passing out?" She said, "Never say 'epilepsy.' It's not something we talk about."

She had learned her "lesson" well and concealed her illness for almost twenty years.

Family silence about epilepsy can itself be a lesson in stigma. One middle-aged woman who was just beginning to "break through" (cf. Davis, 1961) such silence, said that her parents had never told her she had epilepsy: "They just told me I suffered from fainting fits." She had filled this vacuum of silence by concluding that she must be "going mad." Throughout her childhood, and even in her present relationship with her parents, epilepsy had been "brushed under the carpet": "It's not nice to talk about those things." Like sexual variety in the late nineteenth century, epilepsy was obviously something "bad" because it was something "people just didn't (i.e., shouldn't) talk about."

Parents are not the only coaches for secrecy. Close associates, friends, and even professionals sometimes suggest concealment as a strategy for dealing with epilepsy, particularly in circumstances where it is believed to be a disqualifying characteristic. One woman described such advice by a physician-medical examiner who said he "had to" fire her from a teaching job because of her seizures: "He advised me to lie about it. He said, 'If you don't miss work from it and it's not visible to anybody, lie about it.' And I've been doing that since and I've been able to work since."

As the literature on subcultures makes clear, stigmatized people can learn practical survival strategies from others' experience. A supportive subculture surrounding epilepsy is only in its infancy, as is true for most illnesses,[5] but various self-help groups do exist through which people with epilepsy may learn relevant coping skills (see Borman et al., 1980). In the absence of a developed subculture for people like themselves, some people with epilepsy learn the importance of concealment from people with other illnesses. As one woman said of her diabetic husband's experience:

> He didn't know. He hadn't gone through this [or] met other diabetics. He didn't know how to carry out a lie. One of the things that we learned, again from the diabetes, as how [to] lie if they asked for a urine sample. We now have met, through the rap sessions, people who said, "You bring somebody else's urine!" Well, that's a pretty shocking thing to have to do. Yeah, there are times when you gotta lie.

The importance of others as coaches for concealment is clear. Through this "diabetes underground" her husband learned how to lie, then taught it to her.

Some significant others, however, including some parents, adopt strategies of openness, honesty and neutralization. Parents who define their child's epilepsy "just like any other medical problem" and "certainly nothing to be ashamed of" apparently encourage their children to have a much more neutral view and a more open informational control strategy. One successful businessman credited his parents with managing epilepsy so as to minimize it and prevent him from using it as a "crutch" or "excuse":

> The parents of an epileptic child are the key to the whole ball of wax, in recognizing that you have a problem in the family but not to let that control the total actions and whole livelihood and whole future of the family. Accept it and go about doing what has to be done to maintain an even keel.

The themes of "taking epilepsy in stride," not "using" it as a "cop-out" are reminiscent of the cautions against the temptation to use medical excuses which Parsons (1951) analyzed (cf. Waitzkin and Waterman, 1974). They were common to the accounts given to us by people who seemed to portray their epilepsy as "no big thing," partly from concern that such comments might be interpreted by others as requests for "sympathy" and "special treatment." Parents who cautioned against such "special pleading" uses of epilepsy also typically were recalled as having taught their children the values of self-reliance, independence and achievement—as another way of overcoming an emphasis on epilepsy and its significance. Learning that epilepsy need not be a barrier to personal or social acceptance led individuals to be more "out" of than "in" in the closet of epilepsy; learning to believe that epilepsy was a shameful flaw encouraged, understandably, the development of just the opposite strategy.

STRATEGIES OF SELECTIVE CONCEALMENT: THE CLOSET OF EPILEPSY HAS A REVOLVING DOOR

Most discussions of the self and the "closet" assume that one can only be in or out, and that being out must follow a period of being in. As we learned more about how people experience epilepsy, we realized that such a view of the closet of epilepsy was much too simple. Sometimes people conceal their epilepsy, sometimes they do not, and the same persons can be both "open" and "closed" during the same period in their lives. In short, both concealment and disclosure proved to be quite complex and selective strategies of information management.

A part of the "wisdom" of the world of epilepsy is that there are some people you can tell about your illness and others you cannot (cf. Goffman, 1963). Even the most secretive (and twelve of our respondents said we were the first people they had told about their epilepsy except for their physician and immediate family) had told at least several other people about their condition. Close friends and family members are perhaps the most clear instance of "safe others," but "people I feel comfortable with" and those who "won't react negatively to epilepsy" are also sometimes told. Such persons are often used to test reactions: "I think the first couple of times I mentioned it was with my very closest friends to sort of test the water and when it wasn't any problem, then I began to feel freer to mention it."

The development of more diffuse disclosure or "coming out" seemed contingent on how these early disclosures went. Just as perceived "positive" results may encourage people to come out more, perceived "negative" consequences from trial disclosures may encourage a return to concealment as the predominant way to control personal and social impacts. As one woman put it:

> I tried to get a driver's license when I was 18 or 19, after I was married. We were living in Mississippi and I put it on [the form] that I was epileptic, only because I was afraid if I pass out and I'm drivin' a car, well, that's dangerous. I took the thing up there and they said, "Epileptics can't—you have to have a doctor's thing." We moved about two months later to California. I got my driver's license and didn't put it down.

Later on she made another attempt at disclosure, this time on an application to live in a college dormitory. After being disqualified from living on campus and then declining a scholarship, she decided that secrecy was the only strategy by which she could minimize the risk of rejection and differential treatment. In retrospect, she concluded: "I don't know if maybe I wasn't testing . . . at the time, you know, well, is it okay? If things had been different, maybe I could have talked about it." When asked if she discussed epilepsy with new people she meets, another woman spoke specifically of this "risk":

> It depends. I still find it hard, but I'm trying to. I have to trust somebody a lot before I'll tell them in terms of a friendship basis. All my close friends know, but in terms of my work, forget it. This is a risk I can't take after the previous experience. I still have great in-built fears about losing a job from it. I'm not ready to put myself at that risk.

An upwardly-mobile young administrator said he lost his driver's license as a result of disclosing his epilepsy. He recalled that experience and what he had "learned" from it: "I started out tryin' to be honest about it and got burned. So I gave up bein' honest about it in that circumstance." Although this man did disclose his epilepsy to a wide variety of others, including his employer, he said he regularly lied about it on driver's license forms.

Such data clearly suggest that people can and do maintain carefully segregated and selective strategies of managing the stigma potential of epilepsy. Some situations were considered considerably more "high risk" than others. In employment, for example, concealment, including lying on initial employment applications, was thought to be the best general strategy. Because they thought there would be reprisals if their employers subsequently learned of their epilepsy, respondents who advocated such concealment typically said they adopted a monitoring or "see how it's going" approach to possible later disclosure. If they saw approval in others' reactions to them during initial contacts, they could attempt disclosure. One young woman who said she had not had a seizure for 19 years and took no medication was still very sensitive about her "past" when applying for a job:

> Well, employers are the only thing I haven't been open with. On an application, I will not write it. If I feel I have a chance for a job and I'm gonna make it, I'll bring it up. But to put it on that application—because employers, they look at it, they see that thing checked; it just gives me a feeling that they don't give you a chance.

Although she said she never had experienced discriminatory treatment in employment, this woman said she usually waits "until I get into that interview and sell myself first. Then I'll come out and say, 'There's one more point. . . .'" Another respondent said he would wait until "I have my foot in the door and they said, 'Hey, he's doing okay'" before disclosing his epilepsy to employers. People who had tried this strategy of gradual disclosure after employer approval of their work were often surprised that others made so little of their condition. As a result of such experiences they proceeded to redefine some aspects of their own "theories" of others' reactions to epilepsy.

Finally, concealing epilepsy—staying in the closet—was believed important in situations where others might be predisposed to criticize. One woman, who said she was open to friends, commented that she wouldn't want others "in the neighborhood" to know. She explained: "At this point I'm not involved in quarrels. I would think that if I got into a quarrel or feuding situation, it [the epilepsy] would be something that would be used against me." The same view of epilepsy as ammunition for critics was expressed by a man who defined his work as "very political." He thought that if others learned of his epilepsy, they would "add that on as an element of my character that makes [me] undesirable." Sometimes this "closing ranks" against adversaries can even exclude those who otherwise would be told. One woman said that because her brother married a woman "I don't particularly care for," she had decided simply not to tell him of her diagnosis. Her sister-in-law was "the type that would say, you know, 'You're crazy because you have it,' or 'There's something wrong with you.' And she would probably laugh." Even a physician may be seen more as a gatekeeper than an advocate and counselor. One man expressed this theme in many of our interviews quite clearly:

> If he is going to go running to the state and tell the state every time I have a seizure, I don't feel I can be honest with that doctor. He is not keeping his part of the bargain. Everything on my medical records is supposed to be sacred.

Taken together, these data suggest that the process of information management used by people with epilepsy is much more complex than the now-familiar metaphor of being either "in or out of the closet" would lead us to believe. They also indicate that, in strategies of disclosure and concealment of potentially stigmatizing attributes, being out of or in the closet of *epilepsy* may often have much less to do with one's "identity" than with the more practical matter of preventing others from applying limiting and restrictive rules that disqualify one from normal social roles. Epilepsy is something that is hidden at some times and in some places and disclosed quite readily at other times and in other places. Such disclosure and concealment appear contingent upon a complex interaction of one's learned perceptions of the stigma of epilepsy, actual "test" experiences with others before and/or after disclosure, and the nature of the particular relationships involved.

INSTRUMENTAL TELLING: DISCLOSING AS A MANAGEMENT STRATEGY

Information management may include disclosure as well as concealment, even when the information is potentially discreditable. Except for the respondents who adopted rigidly secretive strategies, the people we spoke to said they "usually" or "always" told certain others of their epilepsy under certain circumstances. In this final section we discuss two types of such telling that emerged in our data: telling as "therapy" and "preventive telling." Both involve disclosure but, like concealment, are conscious attempts to mitigate the potentially negative impact of epilepsy on one's self and daily round.

Telling as Therapy

Disclosing feelings of guilt, culpability, and self-derogation can be cathartic, as we know from a variety of social science research. Particularly for those who have concealed what they see as some personal blemish or flaw, such telling can serve a "therapeutic" function for the self by sharing or diffusing the burden of such information. It can free the energy used to control information for other social activities. Such relief, however, requires a properly receptive audience: that is, listeners who are supportive, encouraging, empathetic, and nonjudgmental. Such occasions of telling and hearing cannot only be cathartic, they also can encourage people with epilepsy to define their condition as a nonremarkable and neutral facet of self, perhaps even an "interesting" one, as one man told us. This sort of "telling as therapy" is akin to what Davis (1961) described as the relief associated with breaking through the collectively created and negotiated silence surrounding the physical disabilities of polio victims when they interacted with normals.

Such therapeutic telling seems instrumental primarily in its impact on the actor's self-definition: at the minimum, it simply externalizes what is believed to be significant information about self that has been denied one's intimates and associates. Many of the people we interviewed, in recalling such experiences of "coming out" to select and safe audiences, emphasized the importance of talk as therapy. One woman said of such talking: "It's what's got me together about it [the epilepsy]." And a man recalled how telling friends about epilepsy allowed him to minimize it in his own mind:

> I think in talking to them [friends] I would try to convince myself that it didn't have to be terribly important. Now that I think more about it, I was probably just defiant about it: "I ain't gonna let this Goddamned thing get in my way, period."

For a final example, one of the few respondents, who in keeping with her mother's careful coaching had told virtually no one, insightfully suggested how she might use the interview itself as grounds for redefining her epilepsy and self:

> It just seems so weird now that I've—because I'm talking to you about it, and I've never talked to anybody about it. It's really not so bad. You know it hasn't affected me that much, but no one wants to talk about it. . . .[Talking about epilepsy] makes me feel I'm really not so bad off. Just because I can't find answers to those questions, cuz like I think I feel sorry for myself. I can sit around the house and just dream up all these things, you know, why I'm persecuted and [all].

Such selective disclosure to supportive and nonjudgmental others can thus help "banish the ghosts" that flourish in secrecy and isolation. It allows for feedback and the renegotiation of the perception of stigma. Through externalizing what is believed to be a potentially negative feature of self, people with epilepsy *and* their audiences can redefine this attribute as an "ordinary" or "typical" part of themselves (Dingwall, 1976). As we have already indicated, however, this strategy appears to be effective primarily among one's intimates and close friends. When facing strangers or those whose reactions cannot be assumed supportive, such as prospective employers, the motor vehicle bureau, or virtually any bureaucracy's application form, such openness can be set aside quickly.

Preventive Telling

Another kind of instrumental telling we discovered in our data could be called "preventive": disclosure to influence others' actions and/or ideas toward self and toward epileptics in general. One variety of such preventive telling occurs when actors think it probable that others, particularly others with whom they share some routine, will witness their seizures. The grounds cited for such disclosure are that others then "will know what it is" and "won't be scared." By "knowing what it is," respondents mean others define "it"—the epilepsy and seizure—as a *medical* problem, thereby removing blame and responsibility from the actor for the aberrant conduct in question. The actors assume that others should not be "frightened" if they too learn that "it" is a medical problem.

To engage such anticipatory preventive telling is to offer a kind of "medical disclaimer" (cf. Hewitt and Stokes, 1975) intended to influence others' reactions should a seizure occur. By bringing a blameless, beyond-my-control medical interpretation to such potentially discrediting events, people attempt to reduce the risk that more morally disreputable interpretations might be applied by naive others witnessing one's seizures. One young woman recalled that she felt "great" when her parents told her junior high teachers about epilepsy, because "I'd rather have them know than think I was a dummy or something . . . or think I was having . . . you know, *problems*." Reflecting the power of medical excuses (as well as a relative hierarchy of legitimacy among medical excuses), a middle-aged man who described himself as an "alcoholic" told of how he would disclose epilepsy to defuse others' complaints about his drinking:

> I'd say, "I have to drink. It's the only way I can maintain. . . I have seizures you know" . . . and this kind of thing. People would then feel embarrassed. Or you'd say, "I'm epileptic," then they'd feel embarrassed and say, "Oh, well, gee, we're sorry, that's right. We forgot about that."

Such accounts illustrate the kind of social currency that medical definitions possess in general and in particular with respect to epilepsy. As with all currency, however, its effectiveness as a medium of acceptable exchange rests on its mutual validation by those who give and receive it, what others in fact think of such accounts remains largely unknown.

Beyond providing a medical frame of reference through which others may interpret seizures, such preventive telling may also include specific instructions about what others should do when seizures do occur. Because people with epilepsy believe others are almost totally ignorant of what seizures are, they similarly assume that others have little idea of how to react to seizures. By providing what in effect are directions for others to follow, people who do preventive telling believe they are protecting not only their body but their self. As the young administrator we quoted earlier put it:

> Down the road, I'll usually make a point to tell someone I'm around a lot because I know that it's frightening. So I will, partly for my own purposes, tell them I've got it; if I have one [seizure] that it's nothing to worry about. And don't take me to the hospital even if I ask you to. I always tell people that I work with because I presume I'll be with them for some long period of time. And I may have a seizure and I want them to know what *not* to do, in particular.

Through such telling, people solve some of the problems that a seizure represents for naive others. While these others then have the task of carrying out such instructions—which typically are "do nothing," "make me comfortable," "don't call the ambulance," and "keep me from hurting myself"—the authority, and therefore responsibility, for such reaction rests with the individual giving the instructions.

Disclosure of one's epilepsy may depend also on the anticipation of rejection at some subsequent telling or disclosure occasion. "Coming out" to those who appear to be candidates for "close" relationships is a strategy for minimizing the pain of later rejection. As one man said, "If they're going to leave [because of epilepsy] better it be sooner than later." Another spoke of such telling as a "good way of testing" what kind of friend such persons would be. "Why go through all the trauma of falling in love with someone if they are going to hate your guts once they find out you're an epileptic?"

We discovered that people also disclose their epilepsy when they feel it necessary or important to "educate" others. While this strategy is sometimes mediated and supported through participation in various self-help groups, some individuals initiated it themselves. One young man who became active in a local self-help group described his "rap" on epilepsy as follows:

It's a good manner, I use it quite a bit. I'll come through and say epilepsy is a condition, not a disease. I can throw out all the statistics. I usually say most people are not in wheelchairs or in bed because of epilepsy, they're walking the streets just like I am and other people. Anything like that to make comparisons, to get a point across.

Another respondent, who believed she had benefited greatly by an early talk with a veteran epileptic, spoke of the importance of such education: "That's why I think it is important to come out of the closet to some extent. Because once people have met an epileptic and found out that it's a *person* with epilepsy, that helps a lot." Exposure to a person who "has epilepsy" but is conventional in all other ways may stimulate others to redefine their image of "epileptics."

CONCLUSION

Illness is an individualizing and privatizing experience. As Parsons (1951) argued, occupants of the sick role are not only dissuaded from "enjoying" the exemptions associated with their state but are segregated and separated from other sick people. When individuals desire to be "normal" and lead conventional lives the potential of stigma is isolating; persons fear disclosure of discreditable information and may limit their contacts or connections with others. As Ponse observes, "The veils of anonymity are often as effective with one's own as with those from whom one wishes to hide. Thus, an unintended consequence of secrecy is that it isolates members from one another" (1976:319). Persons with stigmatized illnesses like epilepsy, and perhaps with other illness as well, are doubly insulated from one another, at least in one very important sense. Because there is no illness subculture they are separate, alone and unconnected with others sharing the same problems (for an unusual exception, see Gussow and Tracey, 1968). And this very desire to lead conventional and stigma-free lives further separates and isolates them from each other. It is not surprising that the vast majority of people with epilepsy we interviewed did not know a single other epileptic.

Returning to our metaphor of the closet, we can now see that the potential of stigma certainly leads some people to create the closet as a secret and safe place. And usually, whether with homosexuality or epilepsy, people are in the closet alone. There are important differences, however. Few people in the closet with epilepsy even have any idea where other closets may be. Because there is usually no supportive subculture (a few recent and important self-help groups are notable exceptions) there is no place for a person with epilepsy to get insider information or to test the possible effects of coming out. Since most people with epilepsy want to be considered conventional people with a medical disorder, there is little motivation to come out and develop an epileptic identity. It is little wonder, then, that the closet of epilepsy has a revolving door.

To summarize: for those who possess some discreditable feature of self, some generally hidden "fact" or quality, the disclosure of which they believe will bring undesired consequences, the attempt to control information is a major strategy. We have described several ways people with epilepsy engage in such management work. Our data have suggested that the idea of being "in the closet" and that of being a "secret deviant" need to be extended to incorporate the complex reality of how people very selectively disclose or withhold discreditable information about themselves. Finally, we have shown how disclosing can serve the same ends as concealing. In addition, we suggest that sociological explorations into the experience of illness may well lend new dimensions to old concepts and give us greater understanding of the ways people manage such discomforting and vulnerable parts of their lives.

References

Anspach, Renee R.
   1979   "From stigma to identity politics: Political activism among the physically disabled and former mental patients." Social Science and Medicine 13A: 766–73.
Arangio, Anthony J.
   1975   Behind the Stigma of Epilepsy. Washington, D.C.: Epilepsy Foundation of America.
Becker, Howard S.
   1976   "The Stigma of Epilepsy." American Rehabilitation 2 (September/ October) 4–6.
   1963   Outsiders. New York: Macmillan.
   1973   "Labeling theory reconsidered." Pp. 177–208 in Howard S. Becker, Outsiders, New York: Free Press.
Borman, Leonard D., James Davies and David Droge
   1980   "Self-help groups for persons with epilepsy." In B. Hermann [ed.], A Multidisciplinary Handbook of Epilepsy. Springfield, Ill.: Thomas.
Caveness, W. F., H. Houston Merritt and G. H. Gallup, Jr.
   1974   "A survey of public attitudes towards epilepsy in 1974 with an indication of trends over the past twenty-five years," Epilepsia 15:523–36.
Conrad, Peter and Joseph W. Schneider
   1980   Deviance and Medicalization: From Badness to Sickness. St. Louis, Missouri: Mosby.
Dank, Barry M.
   1971   "Coming out in the gay world." Psychiatry 34 (May): 180–97

Davis, Fred
  1961 "Deviance disavowal: The management of strained interaction by the visibly handicapped." Social Problems 9 (Fall): 120–32.
Dingwall, Robert
  1976 Aspects of Illness. New York: St. Martin's.
Fabrega, Horacio, Jr.
  1972 "The study of disease in relation to culture." Behavioral Science 17:183–200.
  1979 "The ethnography of illness." Social Science and Medicine 13A:565–76.
Freidson, Eliot
  1966 "Disability as social deviance." Pp. 71–99 in M. Sussman [ed.], Sociology and Rehabilitation. Washington, D.C.: The American Sociological Association.
  1970 Profession of Medicine. New York: Dodd, Mead.
Glaser, Barney G. and Anselm L. Strauss
  1967 The Discovery of Grounded Theory. Chicago: Aldine.
Goffman, Erving
  1963 Stigma. Englewood Cliffs, N.J.: Prentice-Hall.
Gussow, Zachary, and George S. Tracey
  1968 "Status, ideology and adaptation to stigmatized illness: A study of leprosy." Human Organization 27 (4):316–25.
Hewitt, John P. and Randall Stokes
  1975 "Disclaimers." American Sociological Review 40:1–11.
Humphreys, Laud
  1972 Out of the Closets. Englewood Cliffs, N.J.: PrenticeHall.
Idler, Ellen L.
  1979 "Definitions of health and illness in medical sociology." Social Science and Medicine 13A:723–31.
Kitsuse, John I.
  1980 "Coming out all over: Deviants and the politics of social problems." Social Problems 28, 1.
Lennox, Gordon W. and Margaret A. Lennox
  1960 Epilepsy and related disorders, Volume I, Boston: Little, Brown
Mark, Vernon H. and Frank R. Ervin.
  1970 Violence and the Brain. New York: Harper & Row.
Parsons, Talcott
  1951 The Social System, New York: Free Press.
Perlman, Leonard G.
  1977 The Person With Epilepsy: Life Style, Needs, Expectations. Chicago: National Epilepsy League.
Ponse, Barbara
  1976 "Secrecy in the lesbian world." Urban Life 5 (October)313–38.
Schneider, Joseph W. and Peter Conrad
  1979 "Medical and sociological typologies: The case of epilepsy." Unpublished manuscript, Drake University, Des Moines, Iowa.
Strauss, Anselm L. and Barney G. Glaser
  1975 Chronic Illness and the Quality of Life, St. Louis, Missouri: Mosby.

Temkin, Oswei
  1971   The Falling Sickness, Second edition, Baltimore, Maryland: Johns
          Hopkins Press.
U.S. Department of Health Education and Welfare—National Institute of
Health
  1975   The NINCDS Epilepsy Research Program. Washington, D.C.: U.S.
          Government Printing Office.
Waitzkin, H.K. and B. Waterman
  1974   The Exploitation of Illness in Capitalist Society. Indianapolis:
          Bobbs-Merrill.
Warren, Carol A.B.
  1974   Identity and Community in the Gay World. New York: Wiley.
West, Patrick B.
  1979a   "Making sense of epilepsy." Pp. 162–69 in D. J. Osborne, M.M.
          Gruneberg and J.R. Eiser (eds.), Research in Psychology and Medi-
          cine, Volume 2, New York: Academic.
  1979b   "An investigation into the social construction and consequences
          of the label epilepsy." Sociological Review 27:719–41.

Notes

1. The moral parallel between illness and deviance has been well-recognized in the sociological literature. Parsons (1951) first noted that illness and crime are analytically similar because they both represent threats to effective role performance and are "dysfunctional" for society, calling forth appropriate mechanisms of social control. Freidson (1966, 1970) addressed this moral parallel more directly, by arguing that both illness and deviance are disvalued and disvaluing attributes variously attached to actors and situations believed to challenge preferred and dominant definitions of appropriate conduct and "health." More recently, Dingwall (1976) has advocated a phenomenological, insider's approach to illness as lived experience. He suggests that illness might be considered deviance (1) to the extent that it involves behavior perceived by others as "out of the ordinary" or unusual, and (2) if sufficient intentionality or willfulness can be attributed to the ill/deviant actor for the conduct in question (see also Conrad and Schneider, 1980). While we stop short of concluding that epilepsy is "deviant," it seems clear from our data that it is stigmatized, at least in the eyes of those who have it.

2. While there is a relative imbalance of sociological "insider" accounts of being deviant, such work is even more rare for the experience of illness. We have few sociological studies of what it is like to be sick, to have cancer, diabetes, schizophrenia, heart disease, and so on (for exceptions see Davis, 1961; Gussow and Tracey, 1968; Strauss and Glaser, 1975). This may be due in part to the historic dominance of professional medical definitions of health and illness. We agree with Dingwall (1976), Fabrega (1972, 1979), and Idler (1979), that more research is needed into how these and other illnesses are experienced as social phenomena.

3. For a more current version of the argument linking the biophysiology of the brain and violence, see Mark and Ervin (1970).

4. See West's (1979a, b) discussion of 24 British families containing a child with epilepsy and how parents managed negative stereotypes of epilepsy in light of their child's diagnosis.

5. For an interesting discussion of some exceptions, see Anspach's (1979) analysis of the "identity politics" of the physically disabled and former mental patients. As we suggest, the availability of a new and positive identity is crucial to the development of the kind of politics Anspach describes.

21 / "Shooting Up": Autobiography of a Heroin Addict

ANONYMOUS

An autobiography implies gross egocentricity, as if I thought I were a terribly interesting person or something; but after considering the alternatives, this, nevertheless, seems to be the most valuable approach to my subject. If I were to restrict my discourse to general statements about the addict groups I've known, my ideas would have wider applicability, but the paper would be nothing more than a superficial description of addict subcultures such as has been arrived at a dozen times already by sociologists through interviews with inmates. By writing subjectively, I can give a better description of what shooting-up feels like. All the objective descriptions I have read don't get anywhere close to the reality. No wonder professionals have such a hard time explaining heroin use if the best reason they can think of is euphoria or simply "pleasurable effects." The biggest disadvantage of the autobiographical approach is that I am not a typical case; therefore, I'm explaining little except my own case. I will specify what is atypical about my case:

I am a [white] university student who has achieved some small success in school: I'm close to graduation and usually get A's. And I am from an upper-middle class background: both my parents are professionals; I was raised in the North End; I attended private schools. This is a big contrast from most hypes I know. They're exceptional if they got through high school, and most of them were raised in Eastside, which is the worst slum in Smogsville. To give you some idea of what Eastside is like, you can go down there any night and see drunks in the street and girls looking for a pickup—they seem to be promiscuous by about age thirteen. I don't think I'm exaggerating when I say that the major leisure-time activity of young guys is stealing. You can buy smack on almost every block, or just cruise around for a few minutes until you run into someone on the street you know can make connections. I have never met anyone from Eastside who didn't use smack. Incidentally, no one in Smogsville except policemen and people from the adjacent lower-class neighborhoods have ever heard of Eastside. People from Eastside have a strong identification with their neighborhood and use the term among themselves, but they don't use it to outsiders because they know you won't know what area they're talking about. It's just a few square blocks, practically a community in itself.

Second, I'm atypical in that I've been using smack for almost a year and haven't gotten strung out. This is unusual. Most of the hypes only last a few months on the street before they go to jail for awhile. In short, my pattern of use is different.

The obvious question now becomes how a straight-looking girl from the North End ever managed to get familiar with Eastside, considering that Eastside is a closed society and people down there don't even know how to talk to someone from the middle-class world, and they automatically dislike them besides. To answer that question is to tell how she started using smack.

I learned Eastside and smack from a boyfriend who grew up there. Unless a girl wanted to change identities and become one of them herself, which is to say become a scuzz, the only way she could get in would be through a boyfriend. I met the guy on a farm in Oregon. I was the cook and he was a farmhand. I was up there because I was on the road and he was up there because he busted out of juvy hall and had relatives in Fallsville. I'd been traveling around the country for a couple of years, but that's another story. Because of a fortuitous combination of circumstances I ended up back here in school, the guy followed, turned himself in, did about a year, and got out with the intention of turning middle-class. He and I and a buddy of his from Eastside used to go around together for a couple of nights a week, usually not doing much except getting loaded—smoking marijuana or maybe dropping reds or rainbows—none of which I much liked except that it was a rather different social activity.

Then the buddy got a girlfriend who was a hype from way back. She was 28, an ex-hustler, and a veteran of many habits, especially coke. I never knew anyone who took so much dope. All she cared about was getting loaded and that's all she ever did. My boyfriend and I often dropped by their pad after the library closed. One night they had just bought some smack and offered us some. My boyfriend demurred but I said, "Hell, yes, I want some," just because that's about the only thing I'd never done. Everyone was rather surprised at my willingness (there was another hype there with really awful tracks on his arms), but they shrugged, advised me that I might heave or get sick since it was my first time, discussed who should fix me up (I can't remember which one they decided on), and described the procedure to me. One guy took off his belt and tied me off, another cooked the stuff and hit me.

The rush was terrific. I wasn't expecting it. The others were asking me if I felt it yet, since they hadn't been sure how much to give me and thought they were erring on the short side instead of the heavy side. They gave me plenty, though, because I stood up, maybe to un-kink or flex my arm or something, since finding a vein on my arm takes some probing, and when the rush did hit me it practically knocked me off my feet. My head reeled so I could hardly even sit up, let alone stand or walk. I hadn't expected such an overwhelming ex-perience, but I thought it was fun, a really wild sensation. The others were checking, asking me if I felt okay, and I assured them I felt bet-ter than fine. My attitude was like, "Wow, this stuff sure does it to ya! Spectacular."

I suppose I might have been a little worried if anyone else acted like there was something to be worried about, but they were all very casual about shootin' up, like they did it all the time. Their mood was happy and light, and as soon as the rush passed and I could be aware of something besides my body, then my mood was happy and light, too. Mostly, I was having fun. It was a big adventure. I kept thinking how daring I was. The only one that wasn't too happy was my boy-friend. He didn't think I ought to be taking any smack and he was nervous just being around the stuff. He got jumpy every time he was around something that could put him back in jail because he hadn't been out long enough to feel comfortable or secure on the streets.

I was very high for several hours. After the rush, smack feels a little like reds. I feel talkative and warm towards the people I'm with. I like everything and everybody. I dry heaved a couple of times, but it passed. In retrospect, I guess I was nodding. I think I would recog-nize the feelings as such now. Nodding means spells of floating; surges of sensation flow through the body and for a few moments you can't think, only feel. Everything is suspended while the person is absorbed in his body. To an observer it looks like he's falling asleep—and if he's had too much he might almost pass out. (Just a little bit more than the passing-out stage is an O.D. or overdose.) After awhile I just settled down to a super-relaxed state and went home and went to sleep. I was still loaded the next day. This has often happened to me if I take a really big hit. It takes a day or so to wear off. The biggest effects of the wearing-off stage are a pleasant weakness, slowness, and numbness. You can't feel your feet touch the ground; walking feels like springing along; every movement is a sensation—again, floating is the closest analogy.

I went to school in the morning, preoccupied with what I was feel-ing, self-conscious, and tickled because I knew I looked the same as I always did: there I was, going among ordinary people and activities as if I were part of it all, when really I was experiencing everything on a different plane, in a new mode. I got a kick out of dissembling, acting straight; like I was playing a trick on everybody.

I didn't think I'd ever use smack again. I thought it was a chance incident. I was kind of proud of my distinction. How many girls from my background have run into the things I have. (But I see now that kids nowadays, especially middle-class kids, know a whole lot about dope.) But a couple of weeks later one of the hypes I knew wanted to borrow a hundred bucks to make up enough to buy a piece and go into business. I lent it to him, got the money back within a week, and a couple of balloons for my cut. Incidentally, getting any money back from a hype is a rare occurrence. A balloon is literally a balloon, like kids play with, only it has a spoon of smack in it. It costs $25 and yields about 10 good hits for someone like me who doesn't have a habit. Someone with a bad habit might get two or three hits out of it.

About the same time I got an apartment out in the sticks, very safe. Within a few weeks the couple I first shot up with were both using heavy. They had to give up their apartment and move in with his family since they were spending all their money on smack. The girl was the big force behind our increasing use. She was always engineering a buy. They needed a place to shoot, and I had an ideal place. So at least once a week they came up and they always brought me a hit. We got into kind of a routine where they'd come every weekend and babysit while I worked. I don't think we especially liked each other, but we got along, and anyway, we had a reciprocal arrangement worked out: my apartment for their smack. I liked to get loaded every weekend and if I couldn't I was frustrated and mad.

After a few weeks I got serum hepatitis and quit using for about six weeks because I was just too sick to want it. Besides, I was taking 20 units of course work at school and it was all I could do to keep functioning. I was exhausted all the time and knew that if I used any drugs it would be my ruin. I didn't have any opportunities to shoot during that time anyway because my people had gotten badly strung out and couldn't spare any stuff. They quit coming over also because they heard I had hepatitis. Also, we'd had a falling out over an imagined insult (the girl was wearing one of those mod floppy outfits and I though they were pajamas).

But during midterm week of first quarter, my boyfriend by chance had some stuff. We shot up and it was sure nice. I realized what a beautiful feeling I'd been missing. I was ready to start shooting regularly again, like once a week, and my boyfriend always seemed to make sure to have the stuff for me. He must have sensed that the only use he was to me was as a connection, and he'd settle for anything. I got so disgusted with him I got rid of him once anyway for two weeks, smack or no smack. He begged and pleaded to see me for just a few minutes, though, and was tactful enough to bring a fix. So that period of abstinence didn't last long.

Our sources of free smack ran dry about this time, since all our people were desperately strung out, down, raunched out, and writing checks for a living. I started sending my boyfriend to buy smack and I spent $50 in two or three weeks. Putting out that much money really hurt and I firmly resolved I'd never spend another cent. By this time our people were in jail and I figured that was the end of that episode of my life. I'd seen enough of it. Simultaneously, I realized I was getting hepatitis again. I went and had the lab tests run, and of course I was right. I still fixed up once, though, because I felt terrible and didn't want to study. I got sick so fast that I couldn't even make it back to the doctor. He'd told me to come back in a week because he thought I just had a little touch of infectious hepatitis. But when I got up enough strength to go—five or six days after my first visit—they put me in the hospital.

The doctors couldn't figure out what was wrong with me. The tests showed my liver was 90 percent destroyed and people just don't get that sick from infectious hepatitis. They don't get infectious hepatitis twice in five months either. They never thought of serum hepatitis— I look so much like an average housewife. They must have thought I had cancer because they were going to do a biopsy. I was exasperated. Those ding-a-ling doctors would have run round in circles forever, so I just told the specialist what I had. I don't see how they could have failed to notice the marks on my arms or realize that my illness was following the typical serum hepatitis pattern. (I knew all about it because I looked it up in a medical textbook.) I guess they had a preconception of what a hype looked like, and I didn't fit the picture, so they were nonplussed. Their minds couldn't maneuver outside of the categories they had set up. Then, when I told them I was using the needle they swung to the other extreme and tried to type me as an addict. I had a hard time convincing them that I wasn't undergoing withdrawal. I don't see how they could have a dumb notion like that either, because kicking causes aching bones, cramping muscles, especially in the legs, and severe pain, and they could see perfectly well that I wasn't in any pain at all.

Anyway, now that they knew what I had they still didn't know how to react. I had the impression that they'd never seen anyone who'd used heroin before. The doctor didn't even know what questions to ask. I didn't want to be asked any questions anyway. I just wanted to lie there so I could get out in a few days. But it wasn't so easy. They called in a psychiatrist, which infuriated me. I talked to her nicely enough though—small talk, because I certainly wasn't going to answer any personal questions so she could get enough on me to work up some construct about some kind of psychological problem. The implications of calling in a psychiatrist were plain and I was outraged.

That insult still galls me. I still wish that there was some way I could get those hospital records, especially the record of the shameful fact that there was a psychiatric consultation, and burn them. I've even planned how I might do it, and I still might carry it through. My experiences in the hospital are a good illustration of Goffman's mortification concepts. I had to fight practically every day for my status and dignity as a full person.

To carry on with the story, I was in the hospital almost a month last quarter, but I still carried 12 units and got all A's. I also had an abortion, which is off the subject but may be pertinent. About twenty minutes after I was discharged I got home and found my boyfriend slumped over the sink with the needle still in his arm, O.D.'d. I had already been trying to get rid of him for months, especially because of the black eye and fat lip he'd given me. This time, I decided to make it final. I wasn't going to need any more connections anyway. So I went and got the neighbors and called the cops. The neighbor man revived him somewhat and he left before the police got there, and I haven't seen him since. His sister called me two weeks ago, all upset because he was kicking and his groans were driving her crazy.

My resolution not to shoot lasted a week or so. I was taking a course in criminology and every time I came across references in my readings to heroin I wished I had some. I had looked up my old friends and met a lot of new ones, all of whom smoked marijuana, so I tried to get to like that. It was all right, but what I really wanted was some smack. Everyone I knew was running me down for even considering it, and always asking: "You're not going to use any more of that stuff, are you?" They were really beginning to make me feel like a deviant. So I pretended I'd never use it again, even though I knew I would if I got a chance. (Looking back, my encounter with an official agency— as represented by those authority figures, the doctors—and the existence of that incriminating record, were making me think of myself as a heroin user, even though objectively I know my use is marginal and insignificant in my identity makeup.)

Six weeks after I got out of the hospital I got a chance. I managed to get a new kit so as to eliminate the risk of hepatitis. I shot reds occasionally. I accidentally ran into a local hype I knew and he scored a balloon for me. It was lousy stuff, cut with *brown* sugar, if you can imagine that, and it felt like it was cut with strychnine, too. That's no joke. I've heard of cutting it with strychnine. I've had some of the symptoms too—muscle spasms, vomiting of blood, etc.

A dealer friend of mind said that there wasn't any use in my getting burned, so he introduced me to some reliable people. I think he gets a percentage and that's why he'll score for me now, whereas I knew better than to even ask him a few weeks ago.

My friends know I use occasionally, but they used to think I was crazy to do it, so I don't shoot around anyone and I keep my mouth shut about it when I do. (They must be beginning to accept it nonchalantly because my most vociferous critic got me two new points yesterday.)

A couple of weeks ago I got infected veins. My arm was really a mess. I knew I had to get some penicillin because I was going to start a new job and I couldn't even move my arm. I lucked out and got a doctor who gave me the prescription without writing anything in the file—I'm very uneasy about the written evidence against me that already exists. Incidentally, I also had to tell this doctor what I had because he couldn't guess just by looking at my arms. He gave me an emotional lecture about a patient who had died of an overdose, and the nurse almost cried because she knew the story. It was a terrific scene. I suppose it was humorous because they made such a big deal over it, when I'm such a small-scale user as to hardly count as a user. I also perceive, just as I'm writing this all down, that people's reactions are making me feel more like a deviant now than when I really was using a lot of stuff. And compared to the hypes I knew, I was straight even back then. On the other hand, back then the constant awareness of living a secret life with drugs was a strain. I feel like I'm living a big lie in either of these opposite situations.

My infection has cleared up within this past week. I can see now that the main vein in my right arm is collapsed. That's from shooting reds; I'll never shoot another. However, I fully intend to use a little heroin whenever I feel I need it—every week or two.

Now that I've given a brief rundown on past history, I'll give a prognosis. The obvious question is *why*. I like to think I can give an honest, if not reasonable, answer. I think I need it. It hinges on what heroin does for me, which is something most users seem unable to articulate. Smack is functional for me. It's enabled me to reach a balance, to maintain stability in an upsetting situation. It's enabled me to get along satisfactorily in a state of prolonged, latent crisis. I am consciously unhappy in almost everything I'm doing. I've had the urge to break out for the last two years. (By break out, I mean jump in my car and go to New Mexico or Idaho or someplace.) With the occasional help of drugs, I've been able to keep my nose to the grindstone, act like a study machine instead of a person, and forego all but the most cursory social contacts. I have a very tight schedule and (besides indulging in fattening snacks and candy) drugs are the only gratification I allow myself. When I feel very uptight, instead of winding up until my mental and emotional functions start going haywire, I take a couple of hours to get loaded.

I get loaded preferably with a group of close friends, but I also often use heroin late at night by myself when I lay aside my books an hour or so early. The reason I use heroin, instead of having a drink or using a soft drug like grass, is simple. First, I used to be a heavy drinker, but my liver is shot and I ought to avoid liquor, so that avenue is closed. Second, heroin is by far the most effective drug for the purpose. Pills tear a person's body up. I know from long and unhappy experience. I dread the occasions when I have to take pills, like when I've got to stay up and cram through a paper, or when I've got to go to work after I've already been working all day. I dread the comedown more than from smack. I know when I take pills that I'll feel like hell the next day. Grass is all right, but I don't want a hallucinogen when I'm trying to relax. Somebody asked me not long ago what I wanted to do, expecting me to outline my career plans, but I simply answered, "Split." Symbolically, that's what I did every time I smoked. But my trips were beginning to lose their significance and their efficacy as a stopgap measure. I used to think some of my sessions were shortcut preliminary steps in the self-actualization process, like Jungian analysis or client-centered therapy. But instead of getting valuable introspection, I was getting only trivial thoughts. I smoked frequently for two months and I'm thoroughly sick of it. I'm going to get rid of my stash.

In contrast, the effects of heroin are purely physical, real, sensual, not artifacts of the personality. The most apt description is to draw a comparison to sex. Indeed, smack and sex are very alike. I'll expand on this: both sex and smack are body-centered; they relieve tension equally well; they are equally self-submerging and totally involving—one yields all one's awareness, one's very being, to physical sensations. I once read a quote from a woman addict: "It's like sex. You wouldn't dream that you could get so much pleasure from your own body." I think she hit on a simile that has often been overlooked. At first glance this seems perverted. Since there is only one party, it might seem more closely analogous to masturbation than sex. But it's only by a stretch of the imagination that orgasm can be seen as anything but one-sided, and the health bugs and body-building freaks are just as guilty of over-valuing their bodies. Further support for the notion that smack is an alternative means of gratifying the common physical drives is the fact that sex and smack are mutually exclusive. It is impossible to make love while loaded. There are never exceptions. Non-users arrive at this same idea intuitively with the oft heard comment, "I'll get my highs on sex." In my own case, I am consciously aware that smack serves as a substitute for sex. I say this with some embarrassment because it is so blatantly narcissistic, but I admit it nevertheless. I am necessarily doing without sex because I've learned that casual sex is worse than useless and it takes months to cultivate a good relationship. I don't spend as many hours with all the people I know put together as it would take to get to know someone well enough for good sex. I just don't have that kind of time. I think this lack in my life would disturb me, would actually become disruptive, if I didn't get loaded.

Instead of all this emphasis on the supposed social incompetence of addicts (they can't hold jobs, bear responsibility, stand pressure, and so on), someone ought to hypothesize sexual adequacy as the determining variable—and by extension, the capacity for love (a sociologist would probably make up some ridiculous term like "ability to form strong affective relationships").

Besides physical gratification, immersion in sex or smack is also the greatest and most effective of removal activities (as Goffman uses the concept). For awhile one is completely out of his workaday situation. I'd like to get out of mine altogether, but since I can't, occasional release stretches out my endurance limit a little farther to the future. I don't understand why escape is culturally defined as base and castigated as a sign of weakness and personal failure when *everyone* has a favorite escape activity. People all express a need to "get away from it all for awhile," so they take vacations or go skiing or to the races or something. Drugs are considered an unnatural escape hatch, virtually perverted. I can say one thing in defense of drugs: shooting up is a more positive activity than vegetable-like, impassive abandonment to the TV; at least it's personal instead of vicarious experience, and one is processing the stimuli and reacting instead of surrendering all functioning.

This brings me to the crux of my involvement with heroin, or with drugs in general: any mode of experience is better than none.

I know that drugs are dangerous, and heroin most of all, and I'd rather be living a healthy life. But how can I live a healthy life in Southern California? I work in a shady business and in the other sphere of my life, school, I exist as a computer, methodically incorporating vast quantities of data, relating, reorganizing, or regurgitating it on demand. Considering that I am absolutely trapped in my unhappy situation, it's a wonder I don't undergo some kind of massive rebellious emotional upheaval or personality disintegration.

On these grounds I object to the characterization of drug users as psychic weaklings. I've stood a whole lot in my time. Those who really can't cope use drugs not for the reasons I do, as a temporary alleviating measure, but as a terminal measure—suicide.

It might be fruitful if I described the last time I shot up, which was almost a week ago. I intended to postpone my little ritual until after midterms, but I just couldn't study another page. I was so restless that my muscles were twitching and I looked up after every line. I was sick of sitting in the same chair cramming my tired brain. Something big and important was happening in the world, the Cambodian crisis, and I wanted to join the student community and get out and do something. But I didn't know how to act like a member of the student community—I'm older and have had different kinds of experiences, and we have little in common—and I couldn't spare the study time anyway. But it was just no use studying.

I finally quit fighting it and shot up. Within moments I felt as if I'd been transported to a realm of peace. Surges of relaxation coursed through me and every trace of agitation, mental or physical, dispersed. I felt tremendously relieved. The only idea in my head was "what a blessed feeling." I had been at the explosion point and now I was totally quiescent. I'd been so tense I almost ached and now I felt warm, loose, and tingly. I just sat there and enjoyed the sensation for about twenty minutes or half an hour, and then opened my book and read calmly for the rest of that afternoon and for every afternoon since.

Since writing this paper is having something of a cathartic effect, and since I've allowed myself two dinner dates this week with very nice guys which I expect to enjoy thoroughly, I don't think I'll build up such a level of frustration and tension again for many days.

22 / The Adjustment of the Family to the Crisis of Alcoholism

JOAN K. JACKSON

... Over a 3-year period, the present investigator has been an active participant in the Alcoholics Anonymous Auxiliary in Seattle. This group is composed partly of women whose husbands are or were members of Alcoholics Anonymous, and partly of women whose husbands are excessive drinkers but have never contacted Alcoholics Anonymous. At a typical meeting one-fifth would be the wives of Alcoholics Anonymous members who have been sober for some time; the husband of another fifth would have recently joined the fellowship; the remainder would be equally divided between those whose husbands were "on and off" the Alcoholics Anonymous program and those whose husbands had as yet not had any contact with Alcoholics Anonymous.

At least an hour and a half of each formal meeting of this group is taken up with a frank discussion of the current family problems of the members. As in other meetings of Alcoholics Anonymous the questions are posed by describing the situation which gives rise to the problem and the answers are a narration of the personal experiences of other wives who have had a similar problem, rather than direct advice. Verbatim shorthand notes have been taken of all discussions, at the request of the group, who also make use of the notes for the group's purposes. Informal contact has been maintained with past and present members. In the past 3 years 50 women have been members of this group.

The families represented by these women are at present in many different stages of adjustment and have passed through several stages during the past few years. The continuous contact over a prolonged period permits generalizations about processes and changes in family adjustments.

In addition, in connection with research on hospitalized alcoholics, many of their wives have been interviewed. The interviews with the hospitalized alcoholics, as well as with male members of Alcoholics Anonymous, have also provided information on family interactions.

256

Further information has been derived from another group of wives, not connected with Alcoholics Anonymous, and from probation officers, social workers and court officials.

The following presentation is limited insofar as it deals only with families seeking help for the alcoholism of the husband. Other families are known to have solved the problem through divorce, often without having attempted to help the alcoholic member first. Others never seek help and never separate. There were no marked differences between the two groups seeking help, one through the hospital and one through the A.A. Auxiliary. The wives of hospitalized alcoholics gave a history of the family crisis similar to that given by women in the Auxiliary.

A second limitation is that only the families of male alcoholics are dealt with. It is recognized that the findings cannot be generalized to the families of alcoholic women without further research. Due to differences between men and women in their roles in the family as well as in the pattern of drinking, it would be expected that male and female alcoholics would in some ways have a different effect on family structure and function.

A third limitation is imposed for the sake of clarity and brevity: only the accounts of the wives of their attempts to stabilize their family adjustments will be dealt with. For any complete picture, the view of the alcoholic husband would also have to be included.

It must be emphasized that this paper deals with the definitions of the family situations by the wives, rather than with the actual situation. It has been noted that frequently wife and husband do not agree on what has occurred. The degree to which the definition of the situation by the wife or husband correlates with actual behavior is a question which must be left for further research.

The families represented in this study are from the middle and lower classes. The occupations of the husbands prior to excessive drinking include small business owners, salesmen, business executives, skilled and semiskilled workers. Prior to marriage the wives have been nurses, secretaries, teachers, saleswomen, cooks, or waitresses. The economic status of the childhood families of these husbands and wives ranged from very wealthy to very poor.

Method

From the records of discussions of the Alcoholics Anonymous Auxiliary, the statements of each wife were extracted and arranged in a time sequence. Notes on informal contacts were added at the point in the sequence where they occurred. The interviews with the wives of hospitalized alcoholics were similarly treated. These working records on individual families were then examined for uniformities of behavior and for regularities in changes over time.

The similarities in the process of adjustment to an alcoholic family member are presented here as stages of variable duration. It should be stressed that only the similarities are dealt with. Although the wives have shared the patterns dealt with here, there have been marked differences in the length of time between stages, in the number of stages passed through up to the present time, and in the relative importance to the family constellation of any one type of behavior. For example, all admitted nagging, but the amount of nagging was variable.

When the report of this analysis was completed it was read before a meeting of the Auxiliary with a request for correction of any errors in fact or interpretation. Corrections could be presented either anonymously or publicly from the floor. Only one correction was suggested and has been incorporated. The investigator is convinced that her relationship with the group is such that there would be no reticence about offering corrections. Throughout her contact with this group her role has been that of one who is being taught, very similar to the role of the new member. The overall response of the group to the presentation indicated that the members individually felt that they had been portrayed accurately.

The sense of having similar problems and similar experiences is indicated also in the reactions of new members to the Auxiliary's summarization of the notes of their discussions. Copies of these summaries are given to new members, who commonly state that they find it a relief to see that their problems are far from unique and that there are methods which successfully overcome them.

Statement of the Problem

For purposes of this presentation, the family is seen as involved in a cumulative crisis. All family members behave in a manner which they hope will resolve the crisis and permit a return to stability. Each member's action is influenced by his previous personality structure, by his previous role and status in the family group, and by the history of the crisis and its effects on his personality, roles and status up to that point. Action is also influenced by the past effectiveness of that particular action as a means of social control before and during the crisis. The behavior of family members in each phase of the crisis contributes to the form which the crisis takes in the following stages and sets limits on possible behavior in subsequent stages.

Family members are influenced, in addition, by the cultural definitions of alcoholism as evidence of weakness, inadequacy, or sinfulness; by the cultural prescriptions for the roles of family members; and by the cultural values of family solidarity, sanctity, and self-sufficiency. Alcoholism in the family poses a situation defined by the culture as shameful but for the handling of which there are no prescriptions which are effective or which permit direct action not in conflict with other cultural prescriptions. While in crises such as illness or death the family members can draw on cultural definitions of appropriate behavior for procedures which will terminate the crisis, this is not the case with alcoholism in the family. The cultural view has been that alcoholism is shameful and should not occur. Only recently has any information been offered to guide families in their behavior toward their alcoholic member and, as yet, this information resides more in technical journals than in the media of mass communication. Thus, in facing alcoholism, the family is in an unstructured situation and must find the techniques for handling it through trial and error.

STAGES IN FAMILY ADJUSTMENT TO AN ALCOHOLIC MEMBER

The Beginning of the Marriage

At the time marriage was considered, the drinking of most of the men was within socially acceptable limits. In a few cases the men were already alcoholics but managed to hide this from their fiancées. They drank only moderately or not at all when on dates and often avoided friends and relatives who might expose their excessive drinking. The relatives and friends who were introduced to the fiancée were those who had hopes that "marriage would straighten him out" and thus said nothing about the drinking. In a small number of cases the men spoke with their fiancées of their alcoholism. The women had no conception of what alcoholism meant, other than that it involved more than the usual frequency of drinking, and they entered the marriage with little more preparation than if they had known nothing about it.

Stage 1. Incidents of excessive drinking begin and, although they are sporadic, place strains on the husband-wife interaction. In attempts to minimize drinking, problems in marital adjustment not related to the drinking are avoided.

Stage 2. Social isolation of the family begins as incidents of excessive drinking multiply. The increasing isolation magnifies the importance of family interactions and events. Behavior and thought become drinking-centered. Husband-wife adjustment deteriorates and tension rises. The wife begins to feel self-pity and to lose her self-confidence as her behavior fails to stabilize her husband's drinking. There is an attempt still to maintain the original family structure, which is disrupted anew with each episode of drinking, and as a result the children begin to show emotional disturbance.

Stage 3. The family gives up attempts to control the drinking and begins to behave in a manner geared to relieve tension rather than achieve long-term ends. The disturbance of the children becomes more marked. There is no longer an attempt to support the alcoholic in his roles as husband and father. The wife begins to worry about her own sanity and about her inability to make decisions or act to change the situation.

Stage 4. The wife takes over control of the family and the husband is seen as a recalcitrant child. Pity and strong protective feelings largely replace the earlier resentment and hostility. The family becomes more stable and organized in a manner to minimize the disruptive behavior of the husband. The self-confidence of the wife begins to be rebuilt.

Stage 5: The wife separates from her husband if she can resolve the problems and conflicts surrounding this action.

Stage 6: The wife and children reorganize as a family without the husband.

Stage 7: The husband achieves sobriety and the family, which had become organized around an alcoholic husband, reorganizes to include a sober father and experiences problems in reinstating him in his former roles.

Stage 1. Attempts to Deny the Problem

Usually the first experience with drinking as a problem arises in a social situation. The husband drinks in a manner which is inappropriate to the social setting and the expectations of others present. The wife feels embarrassed on the first occasion and humiliated as it occurs more frequently. After several such incidents she and her husband talk over his behavior. The husband either formulates an explanation for the episode and assures her that such behavior will not occur again, or he refuses to discuss it at all. For a time afterward he drinks appropriately and drinking seems to be a problem no longer. The wife looks back on the incidents and feels that she has exaggerated them, feels ashamed of herself for her disloyalty and for her behavior. The husband, in evaluating the incident, feels shame also and vows such episodes will not recur. As a result, both husband and wife attempt to make it up to the other and, for a time, try to play their conceptions of the ideal husband and wife roles, minimizing or avoiding other difficulties which arise in the marriage. They thus create the illusion of a "perfect" marriage.

Eventually another inappropriate drinking episode occurs and the pattern is repeated. The wife worries but takes action only in the situations in which inappropriate drinking occurs, as each long intervening period of acceptable drinking behavior convinces her that a recurrence is unlikely. As time goes on, in attempting to cope with individual episodes, she runs the gamut of possible trial and error behaviors, learning that none is permanently effective.

If she speaks to other people about her husband's drinking, she is usually assured that there is no need for concern, that her husband can control his drinking and that her fears are exaggerated. Some friends possibly admit that his drinking is too heavy and give advice on how they handled similar situations with their husbands. These friends convince her that her problem will be solved as soon as she hits upon the right formula for dealing with her husband's drinking.

During this stage the husband-wife interaction is in no way "abnormal." In a society in which a large proportion of the men drink, most wives have at some time had occasion to be concerned, even though only briefly, with an episode of drinking which they considered inappropriate (7). In a society in which the status of the family depends on that of the husband, the wife feels threatened by any behavior on his part which might lower it. Inappropriate drinking is regarded by her as a threat to the family's reputation and standing in the community. The wife attempts to exert control and often finds herself blocked by the sacredness of drinking behavior to men in America. Drinking is a private matter and not any business of the wife's. On the whole, a man reacts to his wife's suggestion that he has not adequately controlled his drinking with resentment, rebelliousness, and a display of emotion which makes rational discussion difficult. The type of husband-wife interaction outlined in this stage has occurred in many American families in which the husband never became an excessive drinker.

Stage 2. Attempts to Eliminate the Problems

Stage 2 begins when the family experiences social isolation because of the husband's drinking. Invitations to the homes of friends become less frequent. When the couple does visit friends, drinks are not served or are limited, thus emphasizing the reason for exclusion from other social activities of the friendship group. Discussions of drinking begin to be sidestepped awkwardly by friends, the wife, and the husband.

By this time the periods of socially acceptable drinking are becoming shorter. The wife, fearing that the full extent of her husband's drinking will become known, begins to withdraw from social participation, hoping to reduce the visibility of his behavior, and thus the threat to family status.

Isolation is further intensified because the family usually acts in accordance with the cultural dictate that it should be self-sufficient and manage to resolve its own problems without recourse to outside aid. Any experiences which they have had with well-meaning outsiders, usually relatives, have tended to strengthen this conviction. The husband has defined such relatives as interfering and the situation has deteriorated rather than improved.

With increasing isolation, the family members begin to lose perspective on their interaction and on their problems. Thrown into closer contact with one another as outside contacts diminish, the behavior of each member assumes exaggerated importance. The drinking behavior becomes the focus of anxiety. Gradually all family difficulties become attributed to it. (For example, the mother who is cross with her children will feel that, if her husband had not been drinking, she would not have been so tense and would not have been angry.) The fear that the full extent of drinking may be discovered mounts steadily; the conceptualization of the consequences of such a discovery becomes increasingly vague and, as a result, more anxiety-provoking. The family feels different from others and alone with its shameful secret.

Attempts to cover up increase. The employer who calls to inquire about the husband's absence from work is given excuses. The wife is afraid to face the consequences of loss of the husband's pay check in addition to her other concerns. Questions from the children are evaded or they are told that their father is ill. The wife lives in terror of the day when the children will be told by others of the nature of the "illness." She is also afraid that the children may describe their father's symptoms to teachers or neighbors. Still feeling that the family must solve its own problems, she keeps her troubles to herself and hesitates to seek outside help. If her husband beats her, she will bear it rather than call in the police. (Indeed, often she has no idea that this is even a possibility.) Her increased isolation has left her without the advice of others as to sources of help in the community. If she knows of them, an agency contact means to her an admission of the complete failure of her family as an independent unit. For the middle-class woman particularly, recourse to social agencies and law enforcement agencies means a terrifying admission of loss of status.

During this stage, husband and wife are drawing further apart. Each feels resentful of the behavior of the other. When this resentment is expressed, further drinking occurs. When it is not, tension mounts and the next drinking episode is that much more destructive of family relationships. The reasons for drinking are explored frantically. Both husband and wife feel that if only they could discover the reason, all members of the family could gear their behavior to making drinking unnecessary. The discussions become increasingly unproductive, as it is the husband's growing conviction that his wife does not and cannot understand him.

On her part, the wife begins to feel that she is a failure, that she has been unable to fulfill the major cultural obligations of a wife to meet her husband's needs. With her increasing isolation, her sense of worth derives almost entirely from her roles as wife and mother. Each failure to help her husband gnaws away at her sense of adequacy as a person.

Periods of sobriety or socially acceptable drinking still occur. These periods keep the wife from making a permanent or stable adjustment. During them her husband, in his guilt, treats her like a queen. His behavior renews her hope and rekindles positive feelings toward him. Her sense of worth is bolstered temporarily and she grasps desperately at her husband's reassurance that she is really a fine person and not a failure and an unlovable shrew. The periods of sobriety also keep her family from facing the inability of the husband to control his drinking. The inaccuracies of the cultural stereotype of the alcoholic—particularly that he is in a constant state of inebriation— also contribute to the family's rejection of the idea of alcoholism, as the husband seems to demonstrate from time to time that he can control his drinking.

Family efforts to control the husband become desperate. There are no culturally prescribed behavior patterns for handling such a situation and the family is forced to evolve its own techniques. Many different types of behavior are tried but none brings consistent results; there seems to be no way of predicting the consequences of any action that may be taken. All attempts to stabilize or structure the situation to permit consistent behavior fail. Threats of leaving, hiding his liquor away, emptying the bottles down the drain, curtailing his money, are tried in rapid succession, but none is effective. Less punitive methods, as discussing the situation when he is sober, baby-ing him during hangovers, and trying to drink with him to keep him in the home, are attempted and fail. All behavior becomes oriented around the drinking, and the thought of family members becomes obsessive on this subject. As no action seems to be successful in achieving its goal, the wife persists in trial-and-error behavior with mounting frustration. Long-term goals recede into the background and become secondary to just keeping the husband from drinking today.

There is still an attempt to maintain the illusion of husband-wife-children roles. When father is sober, the children are expected to give him respect and obedience. The wife also defers to him in his role as head of the household. Each drinking event thus disrupts family functioning anew. The children begin to show emotional distur-bances as a result of the inconsistencies of parental behavior. During periods when the husband is drinking the wife tries to shield them from the knowledge and effects of his behavior, at the same time drawing them closer to herself and deriving emotional support from them. In sober periods, the father tries to regain their favor. Due to experiencing directly only pleasant interactions with their father, considerable affection is often felt for him by the children. This affection becomes increasingly difficult for the isolated wife to toler-ate, and an additional source of conflict. She feels that she needs and deserves the love and support of her children and, at the same time, she feels it important to maintain the children's picture of their father. She counts on the husband's affection for the children to motivate a cessation of drinking as he comes to realize the effects of his behavior on them.

In this stage, self-pity begins to be felt by the wife, if it has not entered previously. It continues in various degrees throughout the succeeding stages. In an attempt to handle her deepening sense of inadequacy, the wife often tries to convince herself that she is right and her husband wrong, and this also continues through the following stages. At this point the wife often resembles what Whalen (5) de-scribes as "The Sufferer."

Stage 3. Disorganization

The wife begins to adopt a "What's the use?" attitude and to accept her husband's drinking as a problem likely to be permanent. Attempts to understand one another become less frequent. Sober periods still engender hope, but hope qualified by skepticism; they bring about a lessening of anxiety and this is defined as happiness.

By this time some customary patterns of husband-wife-children interaction have evolved. Techniques which have had some effec-tiveness in controlling the husband in the past or in relieving pent-up frustration are used by the wife. She nags, berates or retreats into silence. Husband and wife are both on the alert, the wife watching for increasing irritability and restlessness which mean a recurrence of drinking, and the husband for veiled aspersions on his behavior or character.

The children are increasingly torn in their loyalties as they become tools in the struggle between mother and father. If the children are at an age of comprehension, they have usually learned the true nature of their family situation, either from outsiders or from their mother, who has given up attempts to bolster her husband's position as father. The children are often bewildered but questioning their parents brings no satisfactory answers as the parents themselves do not understand what is happening. Some children become terrified; some have increasing behavior problems within and outside the home; others seem on the surface to accept the situation calmly.[1]

During periods of the husband's drinking, the hostility, resentment and frustrations felt by the couple is allowed expression. Both may resort to violence—the wife in self-defense or because she can find no other outlet for her feelings. In those cases in which the wife retaliates to violence in kind, she feels a mixture of relief and intense shame at having deviated so far from what she conceives to be "the behavior of a normal woman."

When the wife looks at her present behavior, she worries about her "normality." In comparing the person she was in the early years of her marriage with the person she has become, she is frightened. She finds herself nagging and unable to control herself. She resolves to stand up to her husband when he is belligerent but instead finds herself cringing in terror and then despises herself for her lack of courage. If she retaliates with violence, she is filled with self-loathing at behaving in an "unwomanly" manner. She finds herself compulsively searching for bottles, knowing full well that finding them will change nothing, and is worried because she engages in such senseless behavior. She worries about her inability to take constructive action of any kind. She is confused about where her loyalty lies, whether with her husband or her children. She feels she is a failure as a wife, mother and person. She believes she should be strong in the face of adversity and instead feels herself weak.

The wife begins to find herself avoiding sexual contact with her husband when he has been drinking. Sex under these circumstances, she feels, is sex for its own sake rather than an indication of affection for her. Her husband's lack of consideration of her needs to be satisfied leaves her feeling frustrated. The lack of sexual responsiveness reflects her emotional withdrawal from him in other areas of family life. Her husband, on his part, feels frustrated and rejected; he accuses her of frigidity and this adds to her concern about her adequacy as a woman.[2]

By this time the opening wedge has been inserted into the self-sufficiency of the family. The husband has often been in difficulty with the police and the wife has learned that police protection is available. An emergency has occurred in which the seeking of outside help was the only possible action to take; subsequent calls for aid from outsiders do not require the same degree of urgency before they can be undertaken. However, guilt and a lessening of self-respect and self-confidence accompany this method of resolving emergencies.

The husband intensifies these feelings by speaking of the interference of outsiders, or of his night in jail.

In Stage 3 all is chaos. Few problems are met constructively. The husband and wife both feel trapped in an intolerable, unstructured situation which offers no way out. The wife's self-assurance is almost completely gone. She is afraid to take action and afraid to let things remain as they are. Fear is one of the major characteristics of this stage: fear of violence, fear of personality damage to the children, fear for her own sanity, fear that relatives will interfere, and fear that they will not help in an emergency. Added to this, the family feels alone in the world and helpless. The problems, and the behavior of family members in attempting to cope with them, seem so shameful that help from others is unthinkable. They feel that attempts to get help would meet only with rebuff, and that communication of the situation will engender disgust.

At this point the clinical picture which the wife presents is very similar to what Whalen (5) has described as "The Waverer."

Stage 4. Attempts to Reorganize in Spite of the Problems

Stage 4 begins when a crisis occurs which necessitates that action be taken. There may be no money or food in the house; the husband may have been violent to the children; or life on the level of Stage 3 may have become intolerable. At this point some wives leave, thus entering directly into Stage 5.

The wife who passes through Stage 4 usually begins to ease her husband out of his family roles. She assumes husband and father roles. This involves strengthening her role as mother and putting aside her role as wife. She becomes the manager of the home, the discipliner of the children, the decision-maker; she becomes somewhat like Whalen's (5) "Controller." She either ignores her husband as much as possible or treats him as her most recalcitrant child. Techniques are worked out for getting control of his pay check, if there still is one, and money is doled out to her husband on the condition of his good behavior. When he drinks, she threatens to leave him, locks him out of the house, refuses to pay his taxi bills, leaves him in jail overnight rather than pay his bail. Where her obligations to her husband conflict with those to her children, she decides in favor of the latter. As she views her husband increasingly as a child, pity and a sense of being desperately needed by him enter. Her inconsistent behavior toward him, deriving from the lack of predictability inherent in the situation up to now, becomes reinforced by her mixed feelings toward him.

In this stage the husband often tries to set his will against hers in decisions about the children. If the children have been permitted to stay with a friend overnight, he may threaten to create a scene unless they return immediately. He may make almost desperate efforts to gain their affection and respect, his behavior ranging from getting them up in the middle of the night to fondle them to giving them stiff lectures on children's obligations to fathers. Sometimes he will attempt to align the males of the family with him against the females. He may openly express resentment of the children and become belligerent toward them physically or verbally.

Much of the husband's behavior can be conceptualized as resulting from an increasing awareness of his isolation from the other members of the family and their steady withdrawal of respect and affection. It seems to be a desperate effort to regain what he has lost, but without any clear idea of how this can be accomplished—an effort to change a situation in which everyone is seen as against him; and, in reality, this is becoming more and more true. As the wife has taken over control of the family with some degree of success, he feels, and becomes, less and less necessary to the ongoing activity of the family. There are fewer and fewer roles left for him to play. He becomes aware that members of the family enjoy each other's company without him. When he is home he tries to enter this circle of warmth or to smash it. Either way he isolates himself further. He finds that the children discuss with the mother how to manage him and he sees the children acting on the basis of their mother's idea of him. The children refuse to pay attention to his demands: they talk back to him in the same way that they talk back to one another, adding pressure on him to assume the role of just another child. All this leaves him frustrated and, as a result, often aggressive or increasingly absent from home.

The children, on the whole, become more settled in their behavior as the wife takes over the family responsibilities. Decisions are made by her and upheld in the face of their father's attempts to interfere. Participation in activities outside the home is encouraged. Their patterns of interaction with their father are supported by the mother. Whereas in earlier stages the children often felt that there were causal connections between their actions and their father's drinking, they now accept his unpredictability. "Well," says a 6-year old, "I'll just have to get used to it. I have a drunken father."

The family is more stabilized in one way but in other ways insecurities are multiplied. Pay checks are received less and less regularly. The violence or withdrawal of the father increases. When he is away the wife worries about automobile accidents or injury in fights, which become more and more probable as time passes. The husband may begin to be seriously ill from time to time; his behavior may become quite bizarre. Both of these signs of increasing illness arouse anxiety in the family.

During this stage hopes may rise high for father's "reform" when he begins to verbalize wishes to stop drinking, admits off and on his inability to stop, and sounds desperate for doing something about his drinking. Now may begin the trek to sanitariums for the middle-class alcoholic, to doctors, or to Alcoholics Anonymous. Where just the promise to stop drinking has failed to revive hope, sobriety through outside agencies has the ability to rekindle it brightly. There is the feeling that at last he is "taking really constructive action." In failure the discouragement is deeper. Here another wedge has been inserted into the self-sufficiency of the family.

By this time the wedges are many. The wife, finding she has managed to bring some semblance or order and stability to her family, while not exactly becoming a self-assured person, has regained some sense of worth which grows a little with each crisis she meets successfully. In addition, the very fact of taking action to stabilize the situation brings relief. On some occasion she may be able to approach social agencies for financial help, often during a period when the husband has temporarily deserted or is incarcerated. She may have gone to the family court; she may have consulted a lawyer about getting a restraining order when the husband was in a particularly belligerent state. She has begun to learn her way around among the many agencies which offer help.

Often she has had a talk with an Alcoholics Anonymous member and has begun to look into what is known about alcoholism. If she has attended a few Alcoholics Anonymous meetings, her sense of shame has been greatly alleviated as she finds so many others in the same boat. Her hopes rise as she meets alcoholics who have stopped drinking, and she feels relieved at being able to discuss her problems openly for the first time with an audience which understands fully. She begins to gain perspective on her problem and learns that she herself is involved in what happens to her husband, and that she must change. She exchanges techniques of management with other wives and receives their support in her decisions.

She learns that her husband is ill rather than merely "ornery," and this often serves to quell for the time being thoughts about leaving him which have begun to germinate as she has gained more self-confidence. She learns that help is available but also that her efforts to push him into help are unavailing. She is not only supported in her recently evolved behavior of thinking first of her family, but now this course also emerges from the realm of the unconceptualized and is set in an accepted rationale. She feels more secure in having a reason and a certainty that the group accepts her as "doing the right thing." When she reports deviations from what the group thinks is the "right way," her reasons are understood; she receives solid support but there is also pressure on her to alter her behavior again toward the acceptable.

Blaming and self-pity are actively discouraged. In group discussions she still admits to such feelings but learns to recognize them as they arise and to go beyond them to more productive thinking.

How much her altered behavior changes the family situation is uncertain, but it helps her and gives her security from which to venture forth to further actions of a consistent and constructive type, constructive at least from the point of view of keeping her family on as even a keel as possible in the face of the disruptive influence of the husband. With new friends whom she can use as a sounding board for plans, and with her growing acquaintance with the alternatives and possible patterns of behavior, her thinking ceases to be circular and unproductive. Her anxiety about her own sanity is alleviated as she is reassured by others that they have experienced the same concern and that the remedy is to get her own life and her family under better control. As she accomplishes this, the difference in her feelings about herself convinces her that this is so.

Whether or not she has had a contact with wives of Alcoholics Anonymous members or other wives who have been through a similar experience and have emerged successfully, the very fact of taking hold of her situation and gradually making it more manageable adds to her self-confidence. As her husband is less and less able to care for himself or his family, she begins to feel that he needs her and that without her he would be destroyed. Such a feeling makes it difficult for her to think of leaving him. His almost complete social isolation at this point and his cries for help reinforce this conviction of being needed.

The drinking behavior is no longer hidden. Others obviously know about it, and this becomes accepted by the wife and children. Already isolated and insulated against possible rejection, the wife is often surprised to find that she has exaggerated her fears of what would happen were the situation known. However, the unpredictability of her husband's behavior makes her reluctant to form social relationships which could be violently disrupted or to involve others in the possible consequences of his behavior.

Stage 5. Efforts to Escape the Problems

Stage 5 may be the terminal one for the marriage. In this stage the wife separates from her husband. Sometimes the marriage is re-established after a period of sobriety, when it appears certain that the husband will not drink again. If he does revert to drinking, the marriage is sometimes finally terminated but with less emotional stress than the first time. If the husband deserts, being no longer able to tolerate his lack of status in his family, Stage 6 may be entered abruptly.

The events precipitating the decision to terminate the marriage may be near-catastrophic, as when there is an attempt by the husband to kill the wife or children, or they may appear trivial to outsiders, being only the last straw to an accumulation of years.

The problems in coming to the decision to terminate the marriage cannot be underestimated. Some of these problems derive from emotional conflicts; some are related to very practical circumstances in the situation; some are precipitated by the conflicting advice of outsiders. With several children dependent on her, the wife must decide whether the present situation is more detrimental to them than future situations she can see arising if she should leave her husband. The question of where the money to live on will come from must be thought out. If she can get a job, will there be enough to provide for child care also while she is away from home? Should the children, who have already experienced such an unsettled life, be separated from her to be cared for by others? If the family still owns its own home, how can she retain control of it? If she leaves, where can she go? What can be done to tide the family over until her first earnings come in? How can she ensure her husband's continued absence from the home and thus be certain of the safety of individuals and property in her absence? These are only a small sample of the practical issues that must be dealt with in trying to think her way through to a decision to terminate the marriage.

Other pressures act on her to impede the decision-making process. "If he would only stay drunk till I carry out what I intend to do," is a frequent statement. When the husband realizes that his wife really means to leave, he frequently sobers up, watches his behavior in the home, plays on her latent and sometimes conscious feelings of her responsibility for the situation, stresses his need for her and that without her he is lost, tears away at any confidence she has that she will be able to manage by herself, and threatens her and the children with injury or with his own suicide if she carries out her intention.

The children, in the meantime, are pulling and pushing on her emotions. They think she is "spineless" to stay but unfair to father's chances for ultimate recovery if she leaves. Relatives, who were earlier alienated in her attempts to shield her family but now know of the situation, do not believe in its full ramifications. They often feel she is exaggerating and persuade her to stay with him. Especially is this true in the case of the "solitary drinker." His drinking has been so well concealed that the relatives have no way of knowing the true nature of the situation. Other relatives, afraid that they will be called on for support, exert pressure to keep the marriage intact and the husband thereby responsible for debts. Relatives who feel she should leave him overplay their hands by berating the husband in such a manner as to evoke her defense of him. This makes conscious the positive aspects of her relationship with him, causing her to waver in her decision. If she consults organized agencies, she often gets conflicting advice. The agencies concerned with the well-being of the family may counsel leaving; those concerned with rehabilitating the husband may press her to stay. In addition, help from public organizations almost always involves delay and is frequently not forthcoming at the point where she needs it most.

The wife must come to terms with her own mixed feelings about her husband, her marriage and herself before she can decide on such a step as breaking up the marriage. She must give up hope that she can be of any help to her husband. She must command enough self-confidence, after years of having it eroded, to be able to face an unknown future and leave the security of an unpalatable but familiar past and present. She must accept that she has failed in her marriage, not an easy thing to do after having devoted years to stopping up the cracks in the family structure as they appeared. Breaking up the marriage involves a complete alteration in the life goals toward which all her behavior has been oriented. It is hard for her to rid herself of the feeling that she married him and he is her responsibility. Having thought and planned for so long on a day-to-day basis, it is difficult to plan for a long-term future.

Her taking over the family raises her self-confidence but failure to carry through on decisions undermines the new gains that she has made. Vacillation in her decisions tends to exasperate the agencies trying to help her, and she begins to feel that help from them may not be forthcoming if she finally decides to leave.

Some events, however, help her to arrive at a decision. During the absences of her husband she has seen how manageable life can be and how smoothly her family can run. She finds that life goes on without him. The wife who is working comes to feel that "my husband is a luxury I can no longer afford." After a few short-term separations in which she tries out her wings successfully, leaving comes to look more possible. Another step on the path to leaving is the acceptance of the idea that, although she cannot help her husband, she can help her family. She often reaches a state of such emotional isolation from her husband that his behavior no longer disturbs her emotionally but is only something annoying which upsets daily routines and plans.

Stage 6. Reorganization of Part of the Family

The wife is without her husband and must reorganize her family on this basis. Substantially the process is similar to that in other divorced families, but with some additions. The divorce rarely cuts her relationships to her husband. Unless she and her family disappear, her husband may make attempts to come back. When drunk, he may endanger her job by calls at her place of work. He may attempt violence against members of the family, or he may contact the children and work to gain their loyalty so that pressure is put on the mother to accept him again. Looking back on her marriage, she forgets the full impact of the problem situation on her and on the children and feels more warmly toward her husband, and these feelings can still be manipulated by him. The wide circulation of information on alcoholism as an illness engenders guilt about having deserted a sick man. Gradually, however, the family becomes reorganized.

Stage 7. Recovery and Reorganization of the Whole Family

Stage 7 is entered if the husband achieves sobriety, whether or not separation has preceded. It was pointed out that in earlier stages most of the problems in the marriage were attributed to the alcoholism of the husband, and thus problems in adjustment not related directly to the drinking were unrecognized and unmet. Also, the "sober personality" of the husband was thought of as the "real" personality, with a resulting lack of recognition of other factors involved in his sober behavior, such as remorse and guilt over his actions, leading him to act to the best of his ability like "the ideal husband" when sober. Irritation or other signs of growing tension were viewed as indicators of further drinking, and hence the problems giving rise to them were walked around gingerly rather than faced and resolved. Lack of conflict and lack of drinking were defined as indicating a perfect adjustment. For the wife and husband facing a sober marriage after many years of an alcoholic marriage, the expectations of what marriage without alcoholism will be are unrealistically idealistic, and the reality of marriage almost inevitably brings disillusionments. The expectation that all would go well and that all problems be resolved with the cessation of the husband's drinking cannot be met and this threatens the marriage from time to time.

The beginning of sobriety for the husband does not bring too great hope to the family at first. They have been through this before but are willing to help him along and stand by him in the new attempt. As the length of sobriety increases, so do the hopes for its permanence and efforts to be of help. The wife at first finds it difficult to think more than in terms of today, waking each morning with fear of what the day will bring and sighing with relief at the end of each sober day.

With the continuation of sobriety, many problems begin to crop up. Mother has for years managed the family, and now father again wishes to be reinstated in his former roles. Usually the first role re-established is that of breadwinner, and the economic problems of the family begin to be alleviated as debts are gradually paid and there is enough left over for current needs. With the resumption of this role, the husband feels that the family should also accept him at least as a partner in the management of the family. Even if the wife is willing to hand over some of the control of the children, for example, the children often are not able to accept this change easily. Their mother has been both parents for so long that it takes time to get used to the idea of consulting their father on problems and asking for his decisions. Often the father tries too hard to manage this change overnight, and the very pressure put on the children toward this end defeats him. In addition, he is unable to meet many of the demands the children make on him because he has never really become acquainted with them or learned to understand them and is lacking in much necessary background knowledge of their lives.

The wife, who finds it difficult to conceive of her husband as permanently sober, feels an unwillingness to let control slip from her hands. At the same time she realizes that reinstatement of her husband in his family roles is necessary to his sobriety. She also realizes that the closer his involvement in the family the greater the probability of his remaining sober. Yet she remembers events in the past in which his failure to handle his responsibilities was catastrophic to the family. Used to avoiding anything which might upset him, the wife often hesitates to discuss problems openly. At times, if she is successful in helping him to regain his roles as father, she feels resentful of his intrusion into territory she has come to regard as hers. If he makes errors in judgment which affect the family adversely, her former feelings of being his superior may come to the fore and affect her interaction with him. If the children begin to turn to him, she may feel a resurgence of self-pity at being left out and find herself attempting to swing the children back toward herself. Above all, however, she finds herself feeling resentful that some other agency achieved what she and the children could not.

Often the husband makes demands for obedience, for consideration and for pampering which members of the family feel unable to meet. He may become rather euphoric as his sobriety continues and feel superior for a time.

Gradually, however, the drinking problem sinks into the past and marital adjustment at some level is achieved. Even when this has occurred, the drinking problem crops up occasionally, as when the time comes for a decision about whether the children should be permitted to drink. The mother at such times becomes anxious, sees in the child traits which remind her of her husband, worries whether these are the traits which mean future alcoholism. At parties, at first, she is watchful and concerned about whether her husband will take a drink or not. Relatives and friends may, in a party mood, make the husband the center of attention by emphasizing his nondrinking. They may unwittingly cast aspersions on his character by trying to convince him that he can now "drink like a man." Some relatives and friends have gone so far as secretly to "spike" a nonalcoholic drink and then cry "bottoms up!" without realizing the risk of reactivating patterns from the past.

If sobriety has come through Alcoholics Anonymous, the husband frequently throws himself so wholeheartedly into A.A. activities that his wife sees little of him and feels neglected. As she worries less about his drinking, she may press him to cut down on these activities. That this is dangerous, since A.A. activity is correlated with success in Alcoholics Anonymous, has been shown by Lahey (9). Also, the wife discovers that, though she has a sober husband, she is by no means free of alcoholics. In his Twelfth Step work, he may keep the house filled with men he is helping. In the past her husband has avoided self-searching; and now he may become excessively introspective, and it may be difficult for her to deal with this.

If the husband becomes sober through Alcoholics Anonymous and the wife participates actively in groups open to her, the thoughts of what is happening to her, to her husband and to her family will be verbalized and interpreted within the framework of the Alcoholics Anonymous philosophy and the situation will probably be more tolerable and more easily worked out.

SUGGESTIONS FOR FURTHER RESEARCH

The above presentation has roughly delineated sequences and characteristics of family adjustment to an alcoholic husband. A more detailed delineation of the stages is required. The extent to which these findings, based on families seeking help, can be generalized to other families of alcoholics needs to be determined, and differences between these families and others specified. Consideration should be given to the question of correspondence between the wife's definition of the situation and that which actually occurs.

Further research is needed on the factors which determine the rate of transition through the stages, and on the factors which retard such a transition, sometimes to the extent that the family seems to remain in the same stage almost permanently. In the group studied, the majority passed from one stage to the next but took different lengths of time to make the transition. Those wives whose husbands have been sober a long time had all passed through all the stages. None of the long-term members remained in the same stage throughout the time that the group was under study.

Other problems which require clarification are: (a) What are the factors within families which facilitate a return to sobriety or hamper it? (b) What variations in family behavior are determined by social class? (c) What problems are specific to the different types of drinking patterns of the husband—for example, the periodic drinker, the steady drinker, the solitary drinker, the sociable drinker, the drinker who becomes belligerent, and the drinker who remains calm? There are indications in the data gathered in the present study that such specific problems arise.

SUMMARY

The onset of alcoholism in a family member has been viewed as precipitating a cumulative crisis for the family. Seven critical stages have been delineated. Each stage affects the form which the following one will take. The family finds itself in an unstructured situation which is undefined by the culture. Thus it is forced to evolve techniques of adjustment by trial and error. The unpredictability of the situation, added to its lack of structure, engenders anxiety in family members which gives rise to personality difficulties. Factors in the culture, in the environment, and within the family situation prolong the crisis and deter the working out of permanent adjustment patterns. With the arrest of the alcoholism, the crisis enters its final stage. The family attempts to reorganize to include the ex-alcoholic and makes adjustments to the changes which have occurred in him.

It has been suggested that the clinical picture presented by the wife to helping agencies is not only indicative of a type of basic personality structure but also of the stage in family adjustment to an alcoholic. That the wives of alcoholics represent a rather limited number of personality types can be interpreted in two ways, which are not mutually exclusive.

(a) That women with certain personality attributes tend to select alcoholics or potential alcoholics as husbands in order to satisfy unconscious personality needs;

(b) That women undergoing similar experiences of stress, within similarly unstructured situations, defined by the culture and reacted to by members of the society in such a manner as to place limits on the range of possible behavior, will emerge from this experience showing many similar neurotic personality traits. As the situation evolves some of these personality traits will also change. Changes have been observed in the women studied which correlate with altered family interaction patterns. This hypothesis is supported also by observations on the behavior of individuals in other unstructured situations, in situations involving conflicting goals and loyalties, and in situations in which they were isolated from supporting group interaction. It is congruent also with the theory of reactions to increased and decreased stress.

Notes

1. Some effects of alcoholism of the father on children have been discussed by Newell (8).
2. It is of interest here that marriage counselors and students of marital adjustment are of the opinion that unhappy marriage results in poor sexual adjustment more often than poor sexual adjustment leads to unhappy marriage. If this proves to be true, it would be expected that most wives of alcoholics would find sex distasteful while their husbands are drinking. The wives of the inactive alcoholics report that their sexual adjustments with their husbands are currently satisfactory; many of those whose husbands are still drinking state that they enjoyed sexual relationships before the alcoholism was established.

References

1. Mowrer, H. R. A psychocultural analysis of the alcoholic. Amer. Sociol. Rev. 5:546–557, 1940.
2. Bacon, S. D. Excessive drinking and the institution of the family. In: Alcohol, Science and Society; Lecture 16. New Haven; Quarterly Journal of Studies on Alcohol; 1945.
3. Baker, S. M. Social case work with inebriates. In: Alcohol, Science and Society; Lecture 27. New Haven; Quarterly Journal of Studies on Alcohol; 1945.
4. Futterman, S. Personality trends in wives of alcoholics. J. Psychiat. Soc. Work 23:37–41, 1953.
5. Whalen, T. Wives of alcoholics: four types observed in a family service agency. Quart. J. Stud. Alc. 14:632–641, 1953.
6. Price, G. M. A study of the wives of 20 alcoholics. Quart. J. Stud. Alc. 5:620–627, 1945.
7. Club and Educational Bureaus of Newsweek. Is alcoholism everyone's problem? Platform, N.Y., p. 3, Jan. 1950.
8. Newell, N. Alcoholism and the father-image. Quart. J. Stud. Alc. 11: 92–96, 1950.
9. Lahey, W. W. A Comparison of Social and Personal Factors Identified with Selected Members of Alcoholics Anonymous. Master's Thesis; University of Southern California; 1950.

23 / How Women Experience Battering: The Process of Victimization

KATHLEEN J. FERRARO
JOHN M. JOHNSON

On several occasions since 1850, feminists in Britain and the United States have initiated campaigns to end the battering of women by husbands and lovers, but have received little sympathy or support from the public (Dobash and Dobash, 1979). Sociologists systematically ignored the existence of violence against women until 1971, when journal articles and conferences devoted to the topic of domestic violence began to appear (Gelles, 1974; O'Brien, 1971; Steinmetz and Straus, 1974). Through the efforts of grass-roots activists and academics, battering has been recognized as a widespread social problem (Tierney, 1982). In 1975 a random survey of U.S. families found that 3.8 percent of women experienced severe violence in their marriage (Strauss *et al.*, 1980). The National Crime Survey of 1976 found that one-fourth of all assaults against women who had ever been married were committed by their husbands or ex-husbands (Gacquin, 1978). Shelters providing services to battered women in the United States have not been able to keep pace with requests for assistance (Colorado Association for Aid to Battered Women, 1978; Ferraro, 1981a; Roberts, 1981; Women's Advocates, 1980).

Although the existence of violence against women is now publicly acknowledged, the experience of being battered is poorly understood. Research aimed at discovering the incidence and related social variables has been based on an operational definition of battering which focuses on the violent act. The Conflict Tactic Scales (CTS) developed by Straus (1979), for example, is based on the techniques used to resolve family conflicts. The Violence Scale of the CTS ranks eight violent behaviors, ranging in severity from throwing something at the other person to using a knife or gun (Straus, 1979). The scale is not designed to explore the context of violent actions, or their meanings for the victim or perpetrator. With notable exceptions (Dobash and Dobash, 1979), the bulk of sociological research on battered women has focused on quantifiable variables (Gelles, 1974, 1976; O'Brien, 1971; Steinmetz, 1978; Straus, 1978).

Interviews with battered women make it apparent that the experi-

277

ence of violence inflicted by a husband or lover is shocking and confusing. Battering is rarely perceived as an unambiguous assault demanding immediate action to ensure future safety. In fact, battered women often remain in violent relationships for years (Pagelow, 1981).

Why do battered women stay in abusive relationships? Some observers answer facilely that they must like it. The masochism thesis was the predominant response of psychiatrists writing about battering in the 1960s (Saul, 1972; Snell *et al.*, 1964). More sympathetic studies of the problem have revealed the difficulties of disentangling oneself from a violent relationship (Hilberman, 1980; Martin, 1976; Walker, 1979). These studies point to the social and cultural expectations of women and their status within the nuclear family as reasons for the reluctance of battered women to flee the relationship. The socialization of women emphasizes the primary value of being a good wife and mother, at the expense of personal achievement in other spheres of life. The patriarchal ordering of society assigns a secondary status to women, and provides men with ultimate authority, both within and outside the family unit. Economic conditions contribute to the dependency of women on men; in 1978 U.S. women earned, on the average, 58 percent of what men earned (U.S. Department of Labor, 1980). In sum, the position of women in U.S. society makes it extremely difficult for them to reject the authority of men and develop independent lives free of marital violence (Dobash and Dobash, 1979; Pagelow, 1981).

Material and cultural conditions are the background in which personal interpretations of events are developed. Women who depend on their husbands for practical support also depend on them as sources of self-esteem, emotional support, and continuity. This paper looks at how women make sense of their victimization within the context of these dependencies. Without dismissing the importance of the macro forces of gender politics, we focus on inter- and intrapersonal responses to violence. We first describe six techniques of rationalization used by women who are in relationships where battering has occurred. We then turn to catalysts which may serve as forces to reevaluate rationalizations and to initiate serious attempts at escape. Various physical and emotional responses to battering are described, and finally, we outline the consequences of leaving or attempting to leave a violent relationship.

THE DATA

The data for this study were drawn from diverse sources. From July, 1978 to September, 1979 we were participant observers at a shelter

Table 1 / Demographic Characteristics of Shelter Residents During First Year of Operation (*N* = 120)

Age		Education	
–17	2%	Elementary school	2%
18–24	33%	Junior high	8%
25–34	43%	Some high school	28%
35–44	14%	High school graduate	43%
45–54	6%	Some college	14%
55+	1%	College graduate	2%
		Graduate school	1%
Ethnicity		*Number of Children*	
White	78%	0	19%
Black	3%	1	42%
Mexican-American	10%	2	21%
American Indian	8%	3	15%
Other	1%	4	2%
		5+	1%
		Pregnant	7%
Family Income		*Employment Status*	
–$5,000	27%	Full time	23%
$ 6,000–10,000	36%	Part time	8%
$11,000–15,000	10%	Housewife	54%
$16,000+	10%	Student	5%
No response*	17%	Not employed	8%
		Receiving welfare	2%

*Many women had no knowledge of their husbands' income.

for battered women located in the southwestern United States. The shelter was located in a suburban city of a major urban center. The shelter served five cities as well as the downtown population, resulting in a service population of 170,000. It was funded primarily by the state through an umbrella agency concerned with drug, mental health, and alcoholism problems. It was initially staffed by paraprofessionals and volunteers, but since this research it has become professionalized and is run by several professional social workers.

During the time of the research, 120 women passed through the shelters; they brought with them 165 children. The women ranged in age from 17 to 68, generally had family incomes below $15,000, and did not work outside the home. The characteristics of shelter residents are summarized in Table 1.

We established personal relationships with each of these women, and kept records of their experiences and verbal accounts. We also tape-recorded informal conversations, staff meetings, and crisis phone conversations with battered women. This daily interaction with shelter residents and staff permitted first-hand observation of feelings and thoughts about the battering experience. Finally, we taped interviews with 10 residents and five battered women who had left their abusers without entering the shelter. All quotes in this paper are taken from our notes and tapes.

In addition to this participant study, both authors have been involved with the problem of domestic violence for more than 10 years. In 1976–77, Ferraro worked as a volunteer at Rainbow Retreat, the oldest shelter still functioning in the United States. In 1977–78, we both helped to found a shelter for battered women in our community. This involvement has led to direct contact with hundreds of women who have experienced battering, and many informal talks with people involved in the shelter movement in the United States and Europe.

The term battered woman is used in this paper to describe women who are battered repeatedly by men with whom they live as lovers. Marriage is not a prerequisite for being a battered woman. Many of the women who entered the shelter we studied were living with, but were not legally married to, the men who abused them.

Rationalizing Violence

Marriages and their unofficial counterparts develop through the efforts of each partner to maintain feelings of love and intimacy. In modern, Western cultures, the value placed on marriage is high; individuals invest a great amount of emotion in their spouses, and expect a return on that investment. The majority of women who marry still adopt the roles of wives and mothers as primary identities, even when they work outside the home, and thus have a strong motivation to succeed in their domestic roles. Married women remain economically dependent on their husbands. In 1978, married men in the United States earned an average of $293 a week, while married women earned $167 a week (U.S. Department of Labor, 1980). Given these high expectations and dependencies, the costs of recognizing failures and dissolving marriages are significant. Divorce is an increasingly common phenomenon in the United States, but it is still labeled a social problem and is seldom undertaken without serious deliberations and emotional upheavals (Bohannan, 1971). Levels of commitment vary widely, but some degree of commitment is implicit in the marriage contract.

When marital conflicts emerge there is usually some effort to negotiate an agreement or bargain, to ensure the continuity of the relationship (Scanzoni, 1972). Couples employ a variety of strategies, depending on the nature and extent of resources available to them, to resolve conflicts without dissolving relationships. It is thus possible for marriages to continue for years, surviving the inevitable conflicts that occur (Sprey, 1971).

In describing conflict-management, Spiegel (1968) distinguishes between "role induction" and "role modification." Role induction refers to conflict in which "one or the other parties to the conflict agrees, submits, goes along with, becomes convinced, or is persuaded in some way" (1968:402). Role modification, on the other hand, involves adaptations by both partners. Role induction seems particularly applicable to battered women who accommodate their husbands' abuse. Rather than seeking help or escaping, as people typically do when attacked by strangers, battered women often rationalize violence from their husbands, at least initially. Although remaining with a violent man does not indicate that a woman views violence as an acceptable aspect of the relationship, the length of time that a woman stays in the marriage after abuse begins is a rough index of her efforts to accommodate the situation. In a U.S. study of 350 battered women, Pagelow (1981) found the median length of stay after violence began was four years; some left in less than one year, others stayed as long as 42 years.

Battered women have good reasons to rationalize violence. There are few institutional, legal, or cultural supports for women fleeing violent marriages. In Roy's (1977:32) survey of 150 battered women, 90 percent said they "thought of leaving and would have done so had the resources been available to them." Eighty percent of Pagelow's (1981) sample indicated previous, failed attempts to leave their husbands. Despite the development of the international shelter movement, changes in police practices, and legislation to protect battered women since 1975, it remains extraordinarily difficult for a battered woman to escape a violent husband determined to maintain his control. At least one woman, Mary Parziale, has been murdered by an abusive husband while residing in a shelter (Beverly, 1978); others have been murdered after leaving shelters to establish new, independent homes (Garcia, 1978). When these practical and social constraints are combined with love for and commitment to an abuser, it is obvious that there is a strong incentive—often a practical necessity—to rationalize violence.

Previous research on the rationalizations of deviant offenders has revealed a typology of "techniques of neutralization," which allow offenders to view their actions as normal, acceptable, or at least justifiable (Sykes and Matza, 1957). A similar typology can be constructed for victims. Extending the concepts developed by Sykes and Matza, we assigned the responses of battered women we interviewed to one of six categories of rationalization: (1) the appeal to the salvation ethic; (2) the denial of the victimizer; (3) the denial of injury; (4) the denial of victimization; (5) the denial of options; and (6) the appeal to higher loyalties. The women usually employed at least one of these techniques to make sense of their situations; often they employed two or more, simultaneously or over time.

1) *The appeal to the salvation ethic:* This rationalization is grounded in a woman's desire to be of service to others. Abusing husbands are viewed as deeply troubled, perhaps "sick," individuals, dependent on their wives' nurturance for survival. Battered women place their own safety and happiness below their commitment to "saving my man" from whatever malady they perceive as the source of their husbands' problems (Ferraro, 1979a). The appeal to the salvation ethic is a common response to an alcoholic or drug-dependent abuser. The battered partners of substance-abusers frequently describe the charming, charismatic personality of their sober mates, viewing this appealing personality as the "real man" being destroyed by disease. They then assume responsibility for helping their partners to overcome their problems, viewing the batterings they receive as an index of their partners' pathology. Abuse must be endured while helping the man return to his "normal" self. One woman said:

> I thought I was going to be Florence Nightingale. He had so much potential; I could see how good he really was, and I was going to 'save' him. I thought I was the only thing keeping him going, and that if I left he'd lose his job and wind up in jail. I'd make excuses to everybody for him. I'd call work and lie when he was drunk, saying he was sick. I never criticized him, because he needed my approval.

2) *The denial of the victimizer:* This technique is similar to the salvation ethic, except that victims do not assume responsibility for solving their abusers' problems. Women perceive battering as an event beyond the control of both spouses, and blame it on some external force. The violence is judged situational and temporary, because it is linked to unusual circumstances or a sickness which can be cured. Pressures at work, the loss of a job, or legal problems are all situations which battered women assume as the causes of their partners' violence. Mental illness, alcoholism, and drug addiction are also viewed as external, uncontrollable afflictions by many battered women who accept the medical perspective on such problems. By focusing on factors beyond the control of their abuser, women deny their husbands' intent to do them harm, and thus rationalize violent episodes.

> He's sick. He didn't used to be this way, but he can't handle alcohol. It's really like a disease, being an alcoholic. . . . I think too that this is what he saw at home, his father is a very violent man, and alcoholic too, so it's really not his fault, because this is all he has ever known.

3) *The denial of injury:* For some women, the experience of being battered by a spouse is so discordant with their expectations that they simply refuse to acknowledge it. When hospitalization is not required—and it seldom is for most cases of battering[1]—routines quickly return to normal. Meals are served, jobs and schools are attended, and daily chores completed. Even with lingering pain, bruises, and cuts, the normality of everyday life overrides the strange, confusing

memory of the attack. When husbands refuse to discuss or acknowledge the event, in some cases even accusing their wives of insanity,
women sometimes come to believe the violence never occurred. The
denial of injury does not mean that women feel no pain. They know
they are hurt, but define the hurt as tolerable or normal. Just as individuals tolerate a wide range of physical discomfort before seeking
medical help, battered women tolerate a wide range of physical
abuse before defining it as an injurious assault. One woman explained her disbelief at her first battering:

> I laid in bed and cried all night. I could not believe it had happened, and I
> didn't want to believe it. We had only been married a year, and I was
> pregnant and excited about starting a family. Then all of a sudden, this!
> The next morning he told me he was sorry and it wouldn't happen again,
> and I gladly kissed and made up. I wanted to forget the whole thing, and
> wouldn't let myself worry about what it meant for us.

4) *The denial of victimization:* Victims often blame themselves for
the violence, thereby neutralizing the responsibility of the spouse.
Pagelow (1981) found that 99.4 percent of battered women felt they
did not deserve to be beaten, and 51 percent said they had done nothing to provoke an attack. The battered women in our sample did not
believe violence against them was justified, but some felt it could
have been avoided if they had been more passive and conciliatory.
Both Pagelow's and our samples are biased in this area, because they
were made up almost entirely of women who had already left their
abusers, and thus would have been unlikely to feel major responsibility for the abuse they received. Retrospective accounts of victimization in our sample, however, did reveal evidence that some women
believed their right to leave violent men was restricted by their participation in the conflicts. One subject said:

> Well, I couldn't really do anything about it, because I did ask for it. I knew
> how to get at him, and I'd keep after it and keep after it until he got fed up
> and knocked me right out. I can't say I like it, but I shouldn't have nagged
> him like I did.

As Pagelow (1981) noted, there is a difference between provocation
and justification. A battered woman's belief that her actions angered
her spouse to the point of violence is not synonymous with the belief
that violence was therefore *justified.* But belief in provocation may
diminish a woman's capacity for retaliation or self-defense, because it
blurs her concept of responsibility. A woman's acceptance of responsibility for the violent incident is encouraged by an abuser who continually denigrates her and makes unrealistic demands. Depending
on the social supports available, and the personality of the battered
woman, the man's accusations of inadequacy may assume the status
of truth. Such beliefs of inferiority inhibit the development of a notion of victimization.

5) *The denial of options:* This technique is composed of two elements: practical options and emotional options. Practical options, including alternative housing, source of income, and protection from an abuser, are clearly limited by the patriarchal structure of Western society. However, there are differences in the ways battered women respond to these obstacles, ranging from determined struggle to acquiescence. For a variety of reasons, some battered women do not take full advantage of the practical opportunities which are available to escape, and some return to abusers voluntarily even after establishing an independent lifestyle. Others ignore the most severe constraints in their efforts to escape their relationships. For example, one resident of the shelter we observed walked 30 miles in her bedroom slippers to get to the shelter, and required medical attention for blisters and cuts to her feet. On the other hand, a woman who had a full-time job, had rented an apartment, and had been given by the shelter all the clothes, furniture, and basics necessary to set up housekeeping, returned to her husband two weeks after leaving the shelter. Other women refused to go to job interviews, keep appointments with social workers, or move out of the state for their own protection (Ferraro, 1981b). Such actions are frightening for women who have led relatively isolated or protected lives, but failure to take action leaves few alternatives to a violent marriage. The belief of battered women that they will not be able to make it on their own—a belief often fueled by years of abuse and oppression—is a major impediment to [acknowledgment] that one is a victim and taking action.

The denial of *emotional* options imposes still further restrictions. Battered women may feel that no one else can provide intimacy and companionship. While physical beating is painful and dangerous, the prospect of a lonely, celibate existence is often too frightening to risk. It is not uncommon for battered women to express the belief that their abuser is the only man they could love, thus severely limiting their opportunities to discover new, more supportive relationships. One woman said:

> He's all I've got. My dad's gone, and my mother disowned me when I married him. And he's really special. He understands me, and I understand him. Nobody could take his place.

6) *The appeal to higher loyalties:* This appeal involves enduring battering for the sake of some higher commitment, either religious or traditional. The Christian belief that women should serve their husbands as men serve God is invoked as a rationalization to endure a husband's violence for later rewards in the afterlife. Clergy may support this view by advising women to pray and try harder to please their husbands (Davidson, 1978; McClinchey, 1981). Other women have a strong commitment to the nuclear family, and find divorce

repugnant. They may believe that for their children's sake, any marriage is better than no marriage. One woman we interviewed divorced her husband of 35 years after her last child left home. More commonly women who have survived violent relationships for that long do not have the desire or strength to divorce and begin a new life. When the appeal to higher loyalties is employed as a strategy to cope with battering, commitment to and involvement with an ideal overshadows the mundane reality of violence.

CATALYSTS FOR CHANGE

Rationalization is a way of coping with a situation in which, for either practical or emotional reasons, or both, a battered woman is stuck. For some women, the situation and the beliefs that rationalize it, may continue for a lifetime. For others, changes may occur within the relationship, within individuals, or in available resources which serve as catalysts for redefining the violence. When battered women reject prior rationalizations and begin to view themselves as true victims of abuse, the victimization process begins.[2]

There are a variety of catalysts for redefining abuse; we discuss six: (1) a change in the level of violence; (2) a change in resources; (3) a change in the relationship; (4) despair; (5) a change in the visibility of violence; and (6) external definitions of the relationship.

1) *A change in the level of violence:* Although Gelles (1976) reports that the severity of abuse is an important factor in women's decisions to leave violent situations, Pagelow (1981) found no significant correlation between the number of years spent cohabiting with an abuser and the severity of abuse. On the contrary: the longer women lived with an abuser, the more severe the violence they endured, since violence increased in severity over time. What does seem to serve as a catalyst is a sudden change in the relative level of violence. Women who suddenly realize that battering may be fatal may reject rationalizations in order to save their lives. One woman who had been severely beaten by an alcoholic husband for many years explained her decision to leave on the basis of a direct threat to her life:

> It was like a pendulum. He'd swing to the extremes both ways. He'd get drunk and beat me up, then he'd get sober and treat me like a queen. One day he put a gun to my head and pulled the trigger. It wasn't loaded. But that's when I decided I'd had it. I sued for separation of property. I knew what was coming again, so I got out. I didn't want to. I still loved the guy, but I knew I had to for my own sanity.

There are, of course, many cases of homicide in which women did not escape soon enough. In 1979, 7.6 percent of all murders in the United States where the relationship between the victim and the offender was known were murders of wives by husbands (Flanagan *et al.*, 1982). Increases in severity do not guarantee a reinterpretation of the situation, but may play a part in the process.

2) *A change in resources:* Although some women rationalize co-habiting with an abuser by claiming they have no options, others begin reinterpreting violence when the resources necessary for escape become available. The emergence of safe homes or shelters since 1970 has produced a new resource for battered women. While not completely adequate or satisfactory, the mere existence of a place to go alters the situation in which battering is experienced (Johnson, 1981). Public support of shelters is a statement to battered women that abuse need not be tolerated. Conversely, political trends which limit resources available to women, such as cutbacks in government funding to social programs, increase fears that life outside a violent marriage is economically impossible. One 55-year-old woman discussed this catalyst:

> I stayed with him because I didn't want my kids to have the same life I did. My parents were divorced, and I was always so ashamed of that. . . .Yes, they're all on their own now, so there's no reason left to stay.

3) *A change in the relationship:* Walker (1979), in discussing the stages of a battering relationship, notes that violent incidents are usually followed by periods of remorse and solicitude. Such phases deepen the emotional bonds, and make rejection of an abuser more difficult. But as battering progresses, periods of remorse may shorten, or disappear, eliminating the basis for maintaining a positive outlook on the marriage. After a number of episodes of violence, a man may realize that his victim will not retaliate or escape, and thus feel no need to express remorse. Extended periods devoid of kindness or love may alter a woman's feelings toward her partner so much so that she eventually begins to define herself as a victim of abuse. One woman recalled:

> At first, you know, we used to have so much fun together. He has kind've, you know, a magnetic personality; he can be really charming. But it isn't fun anymore. Since the baby came, it's changed completely. He just wants me to stay at home, while he goes out with his friends. He doesn't even talk to me, most of the time. . . .No, I don't really love him anymore, not like I did.

4) *Despair:* Changes in the relationship may result in a loss of hope that "things will get better." When hope is destroyed and replaced by despair, rationalizations of violence may give way to the recognition of victimization. Feelings of hopelessness or despair are the basis for some efforts to assist battered women, such as Al-Anon.[3] The director of an Al-Anon organized shelter explained the concept of "hitting bottom":

> Before the Al-Anon program can really be of benefit, a woman has to hit bottom. When you hit bottom, you realize that all of your own efforts to

control the situation have failed; you feel helpless and lost and worthless and completely disenchanted with the world. Women can't really be helped unless they're ready for it and want it. Some women come here when things get bad, but they aren't really ready to be committed to Al-Anon. Things haven't gotten bad enough for them, and they go right back. We see this all the time.

5) *A change in the visibility of violence:* Creating a web of rationalizations to overlook violence is accomplished more easily if no intruders are present to question their validity. Since most violence between couples occurs in private, there are seldom conflicting interpretations of the event from outsiders. Only 7 percent of the respondents in Gelles' (1979) study who discussed spatial location of violence indicated events which took place outside the home, but all reported incidents within the home. Others report similar findings (Pittman and Handy, 1964; Pokorny, 1965; Wolfgang, 1958). If violence does occur in the presence of others, it may trigger a reinterpretation process. Battering in private is degrading, but battering in public is humiliating, for it is a statement of subordination and powerlessness. Having others witness abuse may create intolerable feelings of shame which undermine prior rationalizations.

> He never hit me in public before—it was always at home. But the Saturday I got back (returned to husband from shelter), we went Christmas shopping and he slapped me in the store because of some stupid joke I made. People saw it, I know, I felt so stupid, like, they must all think what a jerk I am, what a sick couple, and I thought, 'God, I must be crazy to let him do this.'

6) *External definitions of the relationship:* A change in visibility is usually accomplished by the interjection of external definitions of abuse. External definitions vary depending on their source and the situation; they either reinforce or undermine rationalizations. Battered women who request help frequently find others—and especially officials—don't believe their story or are unsympathetic (Pagelow, 1981; Pizzey, 1974). Experimental research by Shotland and Straw (1976) supports these reports. Observers usually fail to respond when a woman is attacked by a man, and justify nonintervention on the grounds that they assumed the victim and offender were married. One young woman discussed how lack of support from her family left her without hope:

> It wouldn't be so bad if my own family gave a damn about me. . . .Yeah, they know I'm here, and they don't care. They didn't care about me when I was a kid, so why should they care now? I got raped and beat as a kid, and now I get beat as an adult. Life is a big joke.

Clearly, such responses from family members contribute to the belief among battered women that there are no alternatives and that they must tolerate the abuse. However, when outsiders respond with unqualified support of the victim and condemnation of violent men, their definitions can be a potent catalyst toward victimization. Friends and relatives who show genuine concern for a woman's well-being may initiate an awareness of danger which contradicts previous rationalizations.

> My mother-in-law knew what was going on, but she wouldn't admit it. . . . I said, 'Mom, what do you think these bruises are?' and she said 'Well, some people just bruise easy. I do it all the time, bumping into things.'. . . And he just denied it, pretended like nothing happened, and if I'd said I wanted to talk about it, he'd say, 'life goes on, you can't just dwell on things.'. . . But this time, my neighbor *knew* what happened, she saw it, and when he denied it, she said, 'I can't believe it! You know that's not true!'' . . . and I was so happy that finally, somebody else saw what was goin' on, and I just told him then that this time I wasn't gonna' come home!

Shelters for battered women serve not only as material resources, but as sources of external definitions which contribute to the victimization process. They offer refuge from a violent situation in which a woman may contemplate her circumstances and what she wants to do about them. Within a shelter, women meet counselors and other battered women who are familiar with rationalizations of violence and the reluctance to give up commitment to a spouse. In counseling sessions, and informal conversations with other residents, women hear horror stories from others who have already defined themselves as victims. They are supported for expressing anger and rejecting responsibility for their abuse (Ferraro, 1981a). The goal of many shelters is to overcome feelings of guilt and inadequacy so that women can make choices in their best interests. In this atmosphere, violent incidents are reexamined and redefined as assaults in which the woman was victimized.

How others respond to a battered woman's situation is critical. The closer the relationship of others, the more significant their response is to a woman's perception of the situation. Thus, children can either help or hinder the victim. Pizzey (1974) found adolescent boys at a shelter in Chiswick, England, often assumed the role of the abusing father and themselves abused their mothers, both verbally and physically. On the other hand, children at the shelter we observed often became extremely protective and nurturing toward their mothers. This phenomenon has been thoroughly described elsewhere (Ferraro, 1981a). Children who have been abused by fathers who also beat their mothers experience high levels of anxiety, and rarely want to be reunited with their fathers. A 13-year-old, abused daughter of a shelter resident wrote the following message to her stepfather:

> I am going to be honest and not lie. No, I don't want you to come back. It's not that I am jealous because mom loves you. It is [I] am afraid I won't live to see 18. I did care about you a long time ago, but now I can't care, for the simple reason you['re] always calling us names, even my friends. And an-

other reason is, I am tired of seeing mom hurt. She has been hurt enough in her life, and I don't want her to be hurt any more.

No systematic research has been conducted on the influence children exert on their battered mothers, but it seems obvious that the willingness of children to leave a violent father would be an important factor in a woman's desire to leave.

The relevance of these catalysts to a woman's interpretation of violence vary with her own situation and personality. The process of rejecting rationalizations and becoming a victim is ambiguous, confusing, and emotional. We now turn to the feelings involved in a victimization.

THE EMOTIONAL CAREER OF VICTIMIZATION

As rationalizations give way to perceptions of victimization, a woman's feelings about herself, her spouse, and her situation change. These feelings are imbedded in a cultural, political, and interactional structure. Initially, abuse is contrary to a woman's cultural expectations of behavior between intimates, and therefore engenders feelings of betrayal. The husband has violated his wife's expectations of love and protection, and thus betrayed her confidence in him. The feeling of betrayal, however, is balanced by the husband's efforts to explain his behavior, and by the woman's reluctance to abandon faith. Additionally, the political dominance of men within and outside the family mediate women's ability to question the validity of their husband's actions.

At the interpersonal level, psychological abuse accompanying violence often invokes feelings of guilt and shame in the battered victim. Men define violence as a response to their wives' inadequacies or provocations, which leads battered women to feel that they have failed. Such character assaults are devastating, and create long-lasting feelings of inferiority (Ferraro, 1979b):

> I've been verbally abused as well. It takes you a long time to . . . you may say you feel good and you may . . . but inside, you know what's been said to you and it hurts for a long time. You need to build up your self-image and make yourself feel like you're a useful person, that you're valuable, and that you're a good parent. You might think these things, and you may say them. . . .I'm gonna prove it to myself.

Psychologists working with battered women consistently report that self-confidence wanes over years of ridicule and criticism (Hilberman and Munson, 1978; Walter, 1979).

Feelings of guilt and shame are also mixed with a hope that things will get better, at least in the early stages of battering. Even the most violent man is nonviolent much of the time, so there is always a basis for believing that violence is exceptional and the "real man" is not a threat. The vascillation between violence and fear on the one hand, and nonviolence and affection on the other was described by a shelter resident:

> First of all, the first beatings—you can't believe it yourself. I'd go to bed, and I'd cry, and I just couldn't believe this was happening. And I'd wake up the next morning thinking that couldn't of happened, or maybe it was my fault. It's so unbelievable that this person that you're married to and you love would do that to you but yet you can't leave either because, ya' know, for the other 29 days of the month that person loves you and is with you.

Hope wanes as periods of love and remorse dwindle. Feelings of love and intimacy are gradually replaced with loneliness and pessimism. Battered women who no longer feel love for their husbands but remain in their marriages enter a period of emotional dormancy. They survive each day, performing necessary tasks, with a dull depression and lack of enthusiasm. While some battered women live out their lives in this emotional desert, others are spurred by catalysts to feel either the total despair or mortal fear which leads them to seek help.

Battered women who perceive their husbands' actions as life-threatening experience a penetrating fear that consumes all their thoughts and energies. The awareness of murderous intent by a presumed ally who is a central figure in all aspects of her life destroys all bases for safety. There is a feeling that death is imminent, and that there is nowhere to hide. Prior rationalizations and beliefs about a "good marriage" are exploded, leaving the woman in a crisis of ambiguity (Ridington, 1978).

Feelings of fear are experienced physiologically as well as emotionally. Battered women experience aches and fatigue, stomach pains, diarrhea or constipation, tension headaches, shakes, chills, loss of appetite, and insomnia. Sometimes, fear is expressed as a numbed shock, similar to rape trauma syndrome (Burgess and Holmstrom, 1974), in which little is felt or communicated.

If attempts to seek help succeed, overwhelming feelings of fear subside, and a rush of new emotions are felt: the original sense of betrayal re-emerges, creating strong feelings of anger. For women socialized to reject angry feelings as unfeminine, coping with anger is difficult. Unless the expression of anger is encouraged in a supportive environment, such women may suppress anger and feel only depression (Ball and Wyman, 1978). When anger is expressed, it often leads to feelings of strength and exhilaration. Freedom from threats of violence, the possibility of a new life, and the unburdening of anger create feelings of joy. The simple pleasures of going shopping, taking children to the park, or talking with other women without fear of criticism or punishment from a husband, constitute amazing freedoms. One middle-aged woman expressed her joy over her new-ly acquired freedom this way:

> Boy, tomorrow I'm goin' downtown, and I've got my whole day planned out, and I'm gonna' do what *I* wanna' do, and if somebody doesn't like it, to *hell* with them! You know, I'm having so much fun, I should've done this years ago!

Probably the most typical feeling expressed by women in shelters is confusion. They feel both sad and happy, excited and apprehensive, independent, yet in need of love. Most continue to feel attachment to their husbands, and feel ambivalent about divorce. There is grief over the loss of an intimate, which must be acknowledged and mourned. Although shelters usually discourage women from contacting their abusers while staying at the shelter, most women do communicate with their husbands—and most receive desperate pleas for forgiveness and reconciliation. If there is not strong emotional support and potential material support, such encouragement by husbands often rekindles hope for the relationship. Some marriages can be revitalized through counseling, but most experts agree that long-term batterers are unlikely to change (Pagelow, 1981; Walker, 1979). Whether they seek refuge in shelters or with friends, battered women must decide relatively quickly what actions to take. Usually, a tentative commitment is made, either to independence or working on the relationship, but such commitments are usually ambivalent. As one woman wrote to her counselor:

> My feelings are so mixed up sometimes. Right now I feel my husband is really trying to change. But I know that takes time. I still feel for him some. I don't know how much. My mind still doesn't know what it wants. I would really like when I leave here to see him once in a while, get my apartment, and sort of like start over with our relationship for me and my baby and him, to try and make it work. It might. It kind of scares me. I guess I am afraid it won't. . . .I can only hope this works out. There's no telling what could happen. No one knows.

The emotional career of battered women consists of movement from guilt, shame, and depression to fear and despair, to anger, exhilaration, and confusion. Women who escape violent relationships must deal with strong, sometimes conflicting, feelings in attempting to build new lives for themselves free of violence. The kind of response women receive when they seek help largely determines the effects these feelings have on subsequent decisions.

References

Arendt, Hannah
  1963   On Revolution. New York: Viking
Ball, Patricia G., and Elizabeth Wyman

1978 "Battered wives and powerlessness: What can counselors do?" Victimology 2(3–4):545–552.
Beverly
1978 "Shelter resident murdered by husband." Aegis, September/October :13.
Bohannan, Paul (ed.)
1971 Divorce and After. Garden City, New York: Anchor.
Burgess, Ann W., and Linda Lytle Holmstrom
1974 Rape: Victims of Crisis. Bowie, Maryland: Brady.
Colorado Association for Aid to Battered Women
1978 Services to Battered Women. Washington, D.C.: Office of Domestic Violence, Department of Health, Education and Welfare.
Davidson, Terry
1978 Conjugal Crime, New York: Hawthorn.
Dobash, R. Emerson, and Russell P. Dobash
1979 Violence Against Wives. New York: Free Press.
Ferraro, Kathleen, J.
1979a "Hard love: Letting go of an abusive husband." Frontiers 4(2)16–18.
1979b "Physical and emotional battering: Aspects of managing hurt." California Sociologist 2(2)134–149.
1981a "Battered women and the shelter movement." Unpublished Ph.D. dissertation, Arizona State University.
1981b "Processing battered women." Journal of Family Issues 2(4): 415–438.
Flanagan, Timothy J., David J. van Alstyne, and Michael R. Gottfredson (eds.)
1982 Sourcebook of Criminal Justice Statistics: 1981. U.S. Department of Justice, Bureau of Justice Statistics, Washington, D.C.: U.S. Government Printing Office.
Gacquin, Deidre A.
1978 "Spouse abuse: Data from the National Crime Survey." Victimology 2:632–643.
Garcia, Dick
1978 "Slain women 'lived in fear.' " The Times (Erie, Pa.) June 14:B1.
Gelles, Richard J.
1974 The Violent Home, Beverly Hills: Sage.
1976 "Abused wives: Why do they stay?" Journal of Marriage and the Family 38 (4):659–668.
Graham, Hugh Davis, and Ted Robert Gurr (eds.)
1979 Violence in America. Beverly Hills: Sage.
Gurr, Ted Robert
1970 Why Men Rebel. Princeton, N.J.: Princeton University Press.
Hilberman, Elaine
1980 "Overview: The 'wife-beater's wife' reconsidered." American Journal of Psychiatry 137 (11):1336–1347.
Hilberman, Elaine, and Kit Munson
1978 "Sixty battered women." Victimology 2(3–4):460–470.
Johnson, John M.
1981 "Program enterprise and official cooptation of the battered wom-

en's shelter movement." American Behavioral Scientist 24(6):827–842.

McGlinchey, Anne
  1981 "Woman battering and the church's response." Pp. 133–140 in Albert R. Roberts (ed.), Sheltering Battered Women. New York: Springer.

Martin, Del
  1976 Battered Wives. San Francisco: Glide.

National Crime Survey Report
  1980 Intimate Victims. Washington, D.C.: U.S. Department of Justice.

O'Brien, John E.
  1971 "Violence in divorce-prone families." Journal of Marriage and the Family 33(4): 692–698.

Pagelow, Mildred Daley
  1981 Woman-Battering, Beverly Hills: Sage.

Pittman, D.J. and W. Handy
  1964 "Patterns in criminal aggravated assault." Journal of Criminal Law, Criminology, and Police Science 55(4): 462–470.

Pizzey, Erin
  1974 Scream Quietly or the Neighbors Will Hear. Baltimore: Penguin.

Pokorny, Alex D.
  1965 "Human violence: A comparison of homicide, aggravated assault, suicide, and attempted suicide." Journal of Criminal Law, Criminology, and Police Science 56 (December):488–497.

Ridington, Jillian
  1978 "The transition process: A feminist environment as reconstitutive milieu." Victimology 2(3–4): 563–576.

Roberts, Albert R.
  1981 Sheltering Battered Women. New York: Springer.

Roy, Maria (ed.)
  1977 Battered Women. New York: Van Nostrand.

Saul, Leon J.
  1972 "Personal and social psychopathology and the primary prevention of violence." American Journal of Psychiatry 128 (12):1578–1581.

Scanzoni, John
  1972 Sexual Bargaining. Englewood Cliffs, N.J.: Prentice-Hall.

Shotland, R. Lance, and Margret K. Straw
  1976 "Bystander response to an assault: When a man attacks a woman." Journal of Personality and Social Psychology 34(5):990–999.

Snell, John E., Richard Rosenwald, and Ames Robey
  1964 "The wifebeater's wife: A study of family interaction." Archives of General Psychiatry 11 (August):107–112.

Spiegel, John P.
  1968 "The resolution of role conflict within the family." Pp. 391–411 in N.W. Bell and E. F. Vogel (eds.), A Modern Introduction to the Family. New York: Free Press.

Sprey, Jetse
  1971 "On the management of conflict in families." Journal of Marriage and the Family 33(4):699–706.

Steinmetz, Suzanne K.

1978   "The battered husband syndrome." Victimology 2(3–4):499–509.
Steinmetz, Suzanne K., and Murray A. Straus (eds.)
1974   Violence in the Family. New York: Harper & Row.
Straus, Murray A.
1978   "Wife beating: How common and why?" Victimology 2(3–4):443–458.
1979   "Measuring intrafamily conflict and violence: The conflict tactics(CT) scales." Journal of Marriage and the Family 41(1):75–88.
Straus, Murray A., Richard J. Gelles, and Suzanne K. Steinmetz
1980   Behind Closed Doors: Violence in the American Family. Garden City: Doubleday.
Sykes, Gresham M., and David Matza
1957   "Techniques of neutralization: A theory of delinquency." American Sociological Review 22 (6):667–670.
Tierney, Kathleen J.
1982   "The battered women movement and the creation of the wife beating problem." Social Problems 29(3):207–220.
U.S. Department of Labor
1980   Handbook of Labor Statistics. Washington, D.C.: U.S. Government Printing Office.
Vaughan, Sharon Rice
1979   "The last refuge: Shelter for battered women." Victimology 4(1):113–150.
Walker, Lenore E.
1979   The Battered Woman. New York: Harper & Row.
Warrior, Betsy
1978   Working on Wife Abuse. Cambridge, Mass.: Betsy Warrior.
Wolfgang, Marvin E.
1958   Patterns in Criminal Homicide. New York: John Wiley.
Women's Advocates
1980   Women's Advocates: The Story of a Shelter. St. Paul, Minnesota: Women's Advocates.

Notes

1. National crime survey data for 1973–76 show that 17 percent of persons who sought medical attention for injuries inflicted by an intimate were hospitalized. Eighty-seven percent of injuries inflicted by a spouse or ex-spouse were bruises, black eyes, cuts, scratches, or swelling (National Crime Survey Report, 1980.

2. Explanation of why and how some women arrive at these feelings is beyond the scope of this paper. Our goal is to describe feelings at various stages of the victimization process.

3. Al-Anon is the spouse's counterpart to Alcoholics Anonymous. It is based on the same self-help, 12-step program that A.A. is founded on.

24 / The Psychological Meaning of Mental Illness in the Family

MARIAN RADKE YARROW
CHARLOTTE GREEN SCHWARTZ
HARRIET S. MURPHY
LEILA CALHOUN DEASY

The manifestations of mental illness are almost as varied as the spectrum of human behavior. Moreover, they are expressed not only in disturbance and functional impairment for the sick person but also in disruptive interactions with others. The mentally ill person is often, in his illness, a markedly deviant person, though certainly less so than the popular stereotype of the "insane." One wonders what were the initial phases of the impact of mental illness upon those within the ill person's social environment. How were the disorders of illness interpreted and tolerated? What did the patients, prior to hospitalization, communicate of their needs, and how did others— those closest to the ill persons—attempt, psychologically and behaviorally, to cope with the behavior? How did these persons come to be recognized by other family members as needing psychiatric help?

This paper presents an analysis of cognitive and emotional problems encountered by the wife in coping with the mental illness of the husband. It is concerned with the factors which lead to the reorganization of the wife's perceptions of her husband from a *well* man to a man who is mentally sick or in need of hospitalization in a mental hospital. The process whereby the wife attempts to understand and interpret her husband's manifestations of mental illness is best communicated by considering first the concrete details of a single wife's experiences. The findings and interpretations based on the total sample are presented following the case analysis.

ILLUSTRATIVE CASE

Robert F., a 35-year-old cab driver, was admitted to Saint Elizabeth's Hospital with a diagnosis of schizophrenia. How did Mr. F. get to the mental hospital? Here is a very condensed version of what his wife told an interviewer a few weeks later.

Mrs. F. related certain events, swift and dramatic, which led directly to the hospitalization. The day before admission, Mr. F. went shopping with his wife, which he never had done before, and expressed worry lest he lose her. This was in her words, "rather strange." (*His behavior is not in keeping with her expectations for him.*) Later that day, Mr. F. thought a TV program was about him and that the set was "after him." "Then I was getting worried." (*She recognizes the bizarre nature of his reactions. She becomes concerned.*)

That night, Mr. F. kept talking. He reproached himself for not working enough to give his wife surprises. Suddenly, he exclaimed he did have a surprise for her—he was going to kill her. "I was petrified and said to him, 'What do you mean?' Then, he began to cry and told me not to let him hurt me and to do for him what I would want him to do for me. I asked him what was wrong. He said he had cancer. . . . He began talking about his grandfather's mustache and said there was a worm growing out of it." She remembered his watching little worms in the fish bowl and thought his idea came from that. Mr. F. said he had killed his grandfather. He asked Mrs. F. to forgive him and wondered if she were his mother or God. She denied this. He vowed he was being punished for killing people during the war. "I thought maybe . . . worrying about the war so much . . . had gotten the best of him. (*She tries to understand his behavior. She stretches the range of normality to include it.*) I thought he should see a psychiatrist . . . I don't know how to explain it. He was shaking. I knew it was beyond what I could do . . . I was afraid of him . . . I thought he was losing his normal mental attitude and mentality, but I wouldn't say that he was insane or crazy, because he had always bossed me around before . . ." (*She shifts back and forth in thinking his problem is psychiatric and in feeling it is normal behavior that could be accounted for in terms of their own experience.*) Mr. F. talked on through the night. Sometime in the morning, he "seemed to straighten out" and drove his wife to work. (*This behavior tends to balance out the preceding disturbed activities. She quickly returns to a normal referent.*)

At noon, Mr. F. walked into the store where his wife worked as a clerk. "I couldn't make any sense of what he was saying. He kept getting angry because I wouldn't talk to him. . . . Finally, the boss' wife told me to go home." En route, Mr. F. said his male organs were blown up and little seeds covered him. Mrs. F. denied seeing them and announced she planned to call his mother. "He began crying and I had to promise not to. I said, . . . 'Don't you think you should go to a psychiatrist?' and he said, 'No, there is nothing wrong with me.' . . .

Then we came home, and I went to pay a bill . . ." (*Again she considers, but is not fully committed to, the idea that psychiatric help is needed.*)

Back at their apartment, Mr. F. talked of repairing his cab while Mrs. F. thought of returning to work and getting someone to call a doctor. Suddenly, he started chasing her around the apartment and growling like a lion. Mrs. F. screamed, Mr. F. ran out of the apartment, and Mrs. F. slammed and locked the door. "When he started roaring and growling, then I thought he was crazy. That wasn't a human sound. You couldn't say a thing to him . . ." Later, Mrs. F. learned that her husband went to a nearby church, created a scene, and was taken to the hospital by the police. (*Thoroughly threatened, she defines problem as psychiatric.*)

What occurred before these events which precipitated the hospitalization? Going back to their early married life, approximately three years before hospitalization, Mrs. F. told of her husband's irregular work habits and long-standing complaints of severe headaches. "When we were first married, he didn't work much and I didn't worry as long as we could pay the bills." Mrs. F. figured they were just married and wanted to be together a lot. (*Personal norms and expectations are built up.*)

At Thanksgiving, six months after marriage, Mr. F. "got sick and stopped working." During the war he contracted malaria, he explained, which always recurred at that time of year. "He wouldn't get out of bed or eat. . . . He thought he was constipated and he had nightmares. . . . What I noticed most was his perspiring so much. He was crabby. You couldn't get him to go to a doctor. . . . I noticed he was nervous. He's always been a nervous person. . . . Any little thing that would go wrong would upset him—if I didn't get a drawer closed right. . . . His friends are nervous, too. . . . I came to the conclusion that maybe I was happy-go-lucky and everyone else was a bundle of nerves. . . . For a cab driver, he worked hard—most cab drivers loaf. When he felt good, he worked hard. He didn't work so hard when he didn't." (*She adapts to his behavior. The atypical is normalized as his type of personality and appropriate to his subculture.*)

As the months and years went by, Mrs. F. changed jobs frequently, but she worked more regularly than did her husband. He continued to work sporadically, get sick intermittently, appear "nervous and tense" and refrain from seeking medical care. Mrs. F. "couldn't say what was wrong." She had first one idea, then another, about his behavior. "I knew it wasn't right for him to be acting sick like he did." Then, "I was beginning to think he was getting lazy because there wasn't anything I could see." During one period, Mrs. F. surmised he was carrying on with another woman. "I was right on the verge of going, until he explained it wasn't anyone else." (*There is a building up of deviant behavior to a point near her tolerance limits. Her interpretations shift repeatedly.*)

About two and a half years before admission, Mrs. F. began talking to friends about her husband's actions and her lack of success in getting him to a doctor. "I got disgusted and said if he didn't go to a doctor, I would leave him. I got Bill (the owner of Mr. F.'s cab) to talk to him. . . . I begged, threatened, fussed . . ." After that, Mr. F. went to a VA doctor for one visit, overslept for his second appointment and never returned. He said the doctor told him nothing was wrong.

When Mr. F. was well and working, Mrs. F. "never stopped to think about it." "You live from day to day. . . When something isn't nice, I don't think about it. If you stop to think about things, you can worry yourself sick. . . He said he wished he could live in my world. He'd never seem to be able to put his thinking off the way I do . . ." (*Her mode of operating permits her to tolerate his behavior.*)

Concurrently, other situations confronted Mrs. F. Off and on, Mr. F. talked of a coming revolution as a result of which Negroes and Jews would take over the world. If Mrs. F. argued that she didn't believe it, Mr. F. called her "dumb" and "stupid." "The best thing to do was to change the subject." Eighteen months before admission, Mr. F. began awakening his wife to tell of nightmares about wartime experiences, but she "didn't think about it." Three months later, he decided he wanted to do something besides drive a cab. He worked on an invention but discovered it was patented. Then, he began to write a book about his wartime experiences and science. "If you saw what he wrote, you couldn't see anything wrong with it. . . . He just wasn't making any money." Mrs. F. did think it was "silly" when Mr. F. went to talk to Einstein about his ideas and couldn't understand why he didn't talk to someone in town. Nevertheless, she accompanied him on the trip. (*With the further accumulation of deviant behavior, she becomes less and less able to tolerate it. The perceived seriousness of his condition is attenuated so long as she is able to find something acceptable or understandable in his behavior.*)

Three days before admission, Mr. F. stopped taking baths and changing clothes. Two nights before admission, he awakened his wife to tell her he had just figured out that the book he was writing had nothing to do with science or the world, only with himself. "He said he had been worrying about things for ten years and that writing a book solved what had been worrying him for ten years." Mrs. F. told him to burn his writings if they had nothing to do with science. It was the following morning that Mrs. F. first noticed her husband's behavior as "rather strange."

In the long prelude to Mr. F.'s hospitalization, one can see many of the difficulties which arise for the wife as the husband's behavior no longer conforms and as it strains the limits of the wife's expectations for him. At some stage the wife defines the situation as one requiring help, eventually psychiatric help. Our analysis is concerned primarily with the process of the wife's getting to this stage in interpreting and responding to the husband's behavior. In the preceding case are many reactions which appear as general trends in the data group. These trends can be systematized in terms of the following focal aspects of the process:

1. The wife's threshold for initially discerning a problem depends on the accumulation of various kinds of behavior which are not readily understandable or acceptable to her.
2. This accumulation forces upon the wife the necessity for examining and adjusting expectations for herself and her husband which permit her to account for his behavior.
3. The wife is in an "overlapping" situation, of problem — not problem or of normal — not normal. Her interpretations shift back and forth.
4. Adaptations to the atypical behavior of the husband occur. There is testing and waiting for additional cues in coming to any given interpretation, as in most problem solving. The wife mobilizes strong defenses against the husband's deviant behavior. These defenses take form in such reactions as denying, attenuating, balancing and normalizing the husband's problems.
5. Eventually there is a threshold point at which the perception breaks, when the wife comes to the relatively stable conclusion that the problem is a psychiatric one and/or that she cannot alone cope with the husband's behavior.

These processes are elaborated in the following analysis of the wives' responses.

METHOD OF DATA COLLECTION

Ideally, to study this problem one might like to interview the wives as they struggled with the developing illness. This is precluded, however, by the fact that the problem is not "visible" until psychiatric help is sought. The data, therefore, are the wives' reconstructions of their earlier experiences and accounts of their current reactions during the husband's hospitalization.

It is recognized that recollections of the prehospital period may well include systematic biases, such as distortions, omissions and increased organization and clarity. As a reliability check, a number of wives, just before the husband's discharge from the hospital, were asked again to describe the events and feelings of the prehospital period. In general, the two reports are markedly similar; often details are added and others are elaborated, but events tend to be substantially the same. While this check attests to the consistency of the wives' reporting, it has, of course, the contamination of overlearning which comes from many retellings of these events.

THE BEGINNINGS OF THE WIFE'S CONCERN

In the early interviews, the wife was asked to describe the beginnings of the problem which led to her husband's hospitalization. ("Could you tell me when you first noticed that your husband was different?") This question was intended to provide an orientation for the wife to reconstruct the sequence and details of events and feelings which characterized the period preceding hospitalization. The interviewer provided a minimum of structuring in order that the wife's emphases and organization could be obtained.

In retrospect, the wives usually cannot pinpoint the time the husband's problem emerged. Neither can they clearly carve it out from the contexts of the husband's personality and family expectations. The subjective beginnings are seldom localized in a single strange or disturbing reaction on the husband's part but rather in the piling up of behavior and feelings. We have seen this process for Mrs. F. There is a similar accumulation for the majority of wives, although the time periods and kinds of reported behavior vary. Thus, Mrs. Q. verbalizes the impact of a concentration of changes which occur within a period of a few weeks. Her explicit recognition of a problem comes when she adds up this array: her husband stays out late, doesn't eat or sleep, has obscene thoughts, argues with her, hits her, talks continuously, "cannot appreciate the beautiful scene," and "cannot appreciate me or the baby."

The problem behaviors reported by the wives are given in Table 1. They are ordered roughly; the behaviors listed first occurred primarily, but not exclusively, within the family; those later occurred in the more public domain. Whether the behavior is public or private does not seem to be a very significant factor in determining the wife's threshold for perceiving a problem.

There are many indications that these behaviors, now organized as a problem, have occurred many times before. This is especially true where alcoholism, physical complaints or personality "weaknesses" enter the picture. The wives indicate how, earlier, they had assimi-

Table 1 / Reported Problem Behavior at Time of the Wife's Initial Concern
and at Time of the Husband's Admission to Hospital

Problem Behavior	INITIALLY		AT HOSPITAL ADMISSION	
	PSYCHOTICS	PSYCHO-NEUROTICS	PSYCHOTICS	PSYCHO-NEUROTICS
	N	N	N	N
Physical problems, complaints, worries	12	5	7	5
Deviations from routines of behavior	17	9	13	9
Expressions of inadequacy or hopelessness	4	1	5	2
Nervous, irritable, worried	19	10	18	9
Withdrawal (verbal, physical)	5	1	6	1
Changes or accentuations in personality "traits" (slovenly, deceptive, forgetful)	5	6	7	6
Aggressive or assaultive and suicidal behavior	6	3	10	6
Strange or bizarre thoughts, delusions, hallucinations and strange behavior	11	1	15	2
Excessive drinking	4	7	3	4
Violation of codes of "decency"	3	1	3	2
Number of Respondents	23	10	23	10

lated these characteristics into their own expectations in a variety of
ways: the characteristics were congruent with their image of their
husbands, they fitted their differential standards for men and women
(men being less able to stand up to troubles), they had social or
environmental justifications, etc.

When and how behavior becomes defined as problematic appears
to be a highly individual matter. In some instances, it is when the wife
can no longer manage her husband (he will no longer respond to her
usual prods); in others, when his behavior destroys the status quo
(when her goals and living routines are disorganized); and, in still
others, when she cannot explain his behavior. One can speculate that
her level of tolerance for his behavior is a function of her specific
personality needs and vulnerabilities, her personal and family value

systems and the social supports and prohibitions regarding the husband's symptomatic behavior.

INITIAL INTERPRETATIONS OF HUSBAND'S PROBLEM

Once the behavior is organized as a problem, it tends also to be interpreted as some particular kind of problem. More often than not, however, the husband's difficulties are not seen initially as manifestations of mental illness or even as emotional problems (Table 2).

Table 2 / Initial Interpretations of the Husband's Behavior

Interpretation	PSYCHOTICS N	PSYCHONEUROTICS N
Nothing really wrong	3	0
"Character" weakness and "controllable" behavior (lazy, mean, etc.)	6	3
Physical problem	6	0
Normal response to crisis	3	1
Mildly emotionally disturbed	1	2
"Something" seriously wrong	2	2
Serious emotional or mental problem	2	2
Number of Respondents	23	10

Early interpretations often tend to be organized around physical difficulties (18% of cases) or "character" problems (27%). To a very marked degree, these orientations grow out of the wives' long-standing appraisals of their husbands as weak and ineffective or physically sick men. These wives describe their husbands as spoiled, lacking will-power, exaggerating little complaints and acting like babies. This is especially marked where alcoholism complicates the husband's symptomatology. For example, Mrs. Y., whose husband was chronically alcoholic, aggressive and threatening to her, "raving," and who "chewed his nails until they almost bled," interprets his difficulty thus: "He was just spoiled rotten. He never outgrew it. He told me when he was a child he could get his own way if he insisted, and he is still that way." This quotation is the prototype of many of its kind.

Some wives, on the other hand, locate the problem in the environment. They expect the husband to change as the environmental crisis subsides. Several wives, while enumerating difficulties and concluding that there is a problem, in the same breath say it is really nothing to be concerned about.

Where the wives interpret the husband's difficulty as emotional in nature, they tend to be inconsistently "judgmental" and "understanding." The psychoneurotics are more often perceived initially by their wives as having emotional problems or as being mentally ill than are the psychotics. This is true even though many more clinical signs (bizarre, confused, delusional, aggressive and disoriented behavior) are reported by the wives of the psychotics than of the psychoneurotics.

Initial interpretations, whatever their content, are seldom held with great confidence by the wives. Many recall their early reactions to their husbands' behaviors as full of puzzling confusion and uncertainty. Something is wrong, they know, but, in general, they stop short of a firm explanation. Thus, Mrs. M. reports, "He was kind of worried. He was kind of worried before, not exactly worried. . . ." She thought of his many physical complaints; she "racked" her "brain" and told her husband, "Of course, he didn't feel good." Finally, he stayed home from work with "no special complaints, just blah," and she "began to realize it was more deeply seated."

CHANGING PERCEPTIONS OF THE HUSBAND'S PROBLEM

The fog and uneasiness in the wife's early attempts to understand and cope with the husband's difficulties are followed, typically, by painful psychological struggles to resolve the uncertainties and to change the current situation. Usually, the wife's perceptions of the husband's problems undergo a series of changes before hospitalization is sought or effected, irrespective of the length of time elapsing between the beginnings of concern and hospitalization.

Viewing these changes macroscopically, three relatively distinct patterns of successive redefinitions of the husband's problems are apparent. One sequence (slightly less than half the cases) is characterized by a progressive intensification; interpretations are altered in a definite direction—toward seeing the problem as mental illness. Mrs. O. illustrates this progression. Initially, she thought her husband was "unsure of himself." "He was worried, too, about getting old."

These ideas moved to: "He'd drink to forget. . . . He just didn't have the confidence. . . . He'd forget little things. . . . He'd wear a suit weeks on end if I didn't take it away from him. . . . He'd say nasty things." Then, when Mr. O. seemed "so confused," "to forget all kinds of things . . . where he'd come from . . . to go to work," and made "nasty, cutting remarks all the time," she began to think in terms of a serious personality disturbance. "I did think he knew that something was wrong . . . that he was sick. He was never any different this last while and I couldn't stand it any more. . . . You don't know what a relief it was. . . ." (when he was hospitalized). The husband's drinking, his failure to be tidy, his nastiness, etc., lose significance in their own right. They move from emphasis to relief and are recast as signs of "something deeper," something that brought "it" on.

Some wives whose interpretations move in the direction of seeing their husbands as mentally ill hold conceptions of mental illness and of personality that do not permit assigning the husband all aspects of the sick role. Frequently, they use the interpretation of mental illness as an angry epithet or as a threatening prediction for the husband. This is exemplified in such references as: "I told him he should have his head examined," "I called him a half-wit," "I told him if he's not careful, he'll be a mental case." To many of these wives, the hospital is regarded as the "end of the road."

Other wives showing this pattern of change hold conceptions of emotional disturbance which more easily permit them to assign to their husbands the role of patient as the signs of illness become more apparent. They do not as often regard hospitalization in a mental hospital as the "last step." Nevertheless, their feelings toward their husbands may contain components equally as angry and rejecting as those of the wives with the less sophisticated ideas regarding mental illness.

A somewhat different pattern of sequential changes in interpreting the husband's difficulties (about one-fifth of the cases) is to be found among wives who appear to cast around for situationally and momentarily adequate explanations. As the situation changes or as the husband's behavior changes, these wives find reasons and excuses but lack an underlying or synthesizing theory. Successive interpretations tend to bear little relation to one another. Situational factors tend to lead them to seeing their husbands as mentally ill. Immediate, serious and direct physical threats or the influence of others may be the deciding factor. For example, a friend or employer may insist that the husband see a psychiatrist, and the wife goes along with the decision.

A third pattern of successive redefinitions (slightly less than one-third of the cases) revolves around an orientation outside the framework of emotional problems or mental illness. In these cases, the wife's specific explanations change but pivot around a denial that the husband is mentally ill.

A few wives seem not to change their interpretations about their husband's difficulties. They maintain the same explanation throughout the development of his illness, some within the psychiatric framework, others rigidly outside that framework.

Despite the characteristic shiftings in interpretations, in the group as a whole, there tend to be persisting underlying themes in the individual wife's perceptions that remain essentially unaltered. These themes are a function of her systems of thinking about normality and abnormality and about valued and devalued behavior.

THE PROCESS OF RECOGNIZING THE HUSBAND'S PROBLEM AS MENTAL ILLNESS

In the total situation confronting the wife, there are a number of factors, apparent in our data, which make it difficult for the wife to recognize and accept the husband's behavior in a mental-emotional-psychiatric framework. Many cross-currents seem to influence the process.

The husband's behavior itself is a fluctuating stimulus. He is not worried and complaining all of the time. His delusions and hallucinations may not persist. His hostility toward the wife may be followed by warm attentiveness. She has, then, the problem of deciding whether his "strange" behavior is significant. The greater saliency of one or the other of his responses at any moment of time depends in some degree upon the behavior sequence which has occurred most recently.

The relationship between husband and wife also supplies a variety of images and contexts which can justify varied conclusions about the husband's current behavior. The wife is likely to adapt to behavior which occurs in their day to day relationships. Therefore, symptomatic reactions which are intensifications of long-standing response patterns become part of the fabric of life and are not easily disentangled as "symptomatic."

Communications between husband and wife regarding the husband's difficulties act sometimes to impede and sometimes to further the process of seeing the difficulties within a psychiatric framework. We have seen both kinds of influences in our data. Mr. and Mrs. F. were quite unable to communicate effectively about Mr. F.'s problems. On the one hand, he counters his wife's urging that he see a doctor with denials that anything is wrong. On the other hand, in his own way through his symptoms, he tries to communicate his problems

. . . but she responds only to his verbalized statements, taking them at face value.

Mr. and Mrs. K. participate together quite differently, examining Mr. K.'s fears that he is being followed by the F.B.I., that their house has been wired and that he is going to be fired. His wife tentatively shares his suspicions. At the same time, they discuss the possibility of paranoid reactions.

The larger social context contributes, too, in the wife's perceptual tug of war. Others with whom she can compare her husband provide contrasts to his deviance, but others (Mr. F.'s nervous friends) also provide parallels to his problems. The "outsiders," seeing less of her husband, often discount the wife's alarm when she presses them for opinions. In other instances, the friend or employer, less adapted to or defended against the husband's symptoms, helps her to define his problem as psychiatric.

This task before the wife, of defining her husband's difficulties, can be conceptualized as an "overlapping" situation (in Lewin's terms), in which the relative potencies of the several effective influences fluctuate. The wife is responding to the various sets of forces simultaneously. Thus, several conclusions or interpretations of the problem are simultaneously "suspended in balance," and they shift back and forth in emphasis and relief. Seldom, however, does she seem to be balancing off clear-cut alternatives, such as physical versus mental. Her complex perceptions (even those of Mrs. F. who is extreme in misperceiving cues) are more "sophisticated" than the casual questioner might be led to conclude.

Thus far, we have ignored the personally threatening aspects of recognizing mental illness in one's spouse, and the defenses which are mobilized to meet this threat. It is assumed that it is threatening to the wife not only to realize that the husband is mentally ill but further to consider her own possible role in the development of the disorder, to give up modes of relating to her husband that may have had satisfactions for her and to see a future as the wife of a mental patient. Our data provide systematic information only on the first aspect of this problem, on the forms of defense against the recognition of the illness. One or more of the following defenses are manifested in three-fourths of our cases.

The most obvious form of defense in the wife's response is the tendency to *normalize* the husband's neurotic and psychotic symptoms. His behavior is explained, justified or made acceptable by seeing it also in herself or by assuring herself that the particular behavior occurs again and again among persons who are not ill. Illustrative of this reaction is the wife who reports her husband's hallucinations and assures herself that this is normal because she herself heard voices when she was in the menopause. Another wife responds to her husband's physical complaints, fears, worries, nightmares, and delusions with "A lot of normal people think there's something wrong when there isn't. I think men are that way; his father is that way."

When behavior cannot be normalized, it can be made to seem less severe or less important in a total picture than an outsider might see it. By finding some grounds for the behavior or someting explainable about it, the wife achieves at least momentary *attenuation* of the seriousness of it. Thus, Mrs. F. is able to discount partly the strangeness of her husband's descriptions of the worms growing out of his grandfather's mustache when she recalls his watching the worms in the fish bowl. There may be attenuation, too, by seeing the behavior as "momentary" ("You could talk him out of his ideas.") or by rethinking the problem and seeing it in a different light.

By *balancing* acceptable with unacceptable behavior or "strange" with "normal" behavior, some wives can conclude that the husband is not seriously disturbed. Thus, it is very important to Mrs. R. that her husband kissed her goodbye before he left for the hospital. This response cancels out his hostile feelings toward her and the possibility that he is mentally ill. Similarly, Mrs. V. reasons that her husband cannot be "out of his mind" for he had reminded her of things she must not forget to do when he went to the hospital.

Defense sometimes amounts to a thorough-going *denial*. This takes the form of denying that the behavior perceived can be interpreted in an emotional or psychiatric framework. In some instances, the wife reports vividly on such behavior as repeated thoughts of suicide, efforts to harm her and the like and sums it up with "I thought it was just a whim." Other wives bend their efforts toward proving the implausibility of mental illness.

After the husband is hospitalized, it might be expected that these denials would decrease to a negligible level. This is not wholly the case, however. A breakdown of the wives' interpretations just following the husband's admission to the hospital shows that roughly a fifth still interpret the husband's behavior in another framework than that of a serious emotional problem or mental illness. Another fifth ambivalently and sporadically interpret the behavior as an emotional or mental problem. The remainder hold relatively stable interpretations within this framework.

After the husband has been hospitalized for some time, many wives reflect on their earlier tendencies to avoid a definition of mental illness. Such reactions are almost identically described by these wives: "I put it out of my mind—I didn't want to face it—anything but a mental illness." "Maybe I was aware of it. But you know you push things away from you and keep hoping." "Now you think maybe you should have known about it. Maybe you should have done more than you did and that worries me."

DISCUSSION

The findings on the perceptions of mental illness by the wives of patients are in line with general findings in studies of perception. Behavior which is unfamiliar and incongruent and unlikely in terms of current expectations and needs will not be readily recognized, and stressful or threatening stimuli will tend to be misperceived or perceived with difficulty or delay.

We have attempted to describe the factors which help the wife maintain a picture of her husband as normal and those which push her in the direction of accepting a psychiatric definition of his problem. The kind and intensity of the symptomatic behavior, its persistence over time, the husband's interpretation of his problem, interpretations and defining actions of others, including professionals, all play a role. In addition, the wives come to this experience with different conceptions of psychological processes and of the nature of emotional illness, itself, as well as with different tolerances for emotional disturbance. As we have seen, there are also many supports in society for maintaining a picture of normality concerning the husband's behavior. Social pressures and expectations not only keep *behavior* in line but to a great extent *perceptions* of behavior as well.

There are implications of these findings both for those who are working in the field of prevention of mental illness and early detection of emotional disturbance as well as for the rehabilitation worker. They suggest that to acquaint the public with the nature of mental illness by describing psychotic behavior and emphasizing its non-threatening aspect is, after all, an intellectualization and not likely to be effective in dealing with the threatening aspects of recognizing mental illness which we have described. Further, it is not enough simply to recognize the fact that the rehabilitation of patients is affected by the attitudes and feelings of the family toward the patient and his illness. Perhaps a better acceptance of the patient can be developed if families who have been unable to deal with the problem of the illness are helped to work through this experience and to deal with their difficulties in accepting the illness and what remains of it after the patient leaves the hospital.

25 / Paranoia and the Dynamics of Exclusion[1]

EDWIN M. LEMERT

One of the few generalizations about psychotic behavior which sociologists have been able to make with a modicum of agreement and assurance is that such behavior is a result or manifestation of a disorder in communication between the individual and society. The generalization, of course, is a large one, and, while it can be illustrated easily with case history materials, the need for its conceptual refinement and detailing of the process by which disruption of communication occurs in the dynamics of mental disorder has for some time been apparent. Among the more carefully reasoned attacks upon this problem is Cameron's formulation of the paranoid pseudocommunity (1).

In essence, the conception of the paranoid pseudocommunity can be stated as follows:[2]

Paranoid persons are those whose inadequate social learning leads them in situations of unusual stress to incompetent social reactions. Out of the fragments of the social behavior of others the paranoid person symbolically organizes a pseudocommunity whose functions he perceives as focused on him. His reactions to this *supposed community* of response which he sees loaded with threat to himself bring him into open conflict with the actual community and lead to his temporary or permanent isolation from its affairs. The "real" community, which is unable to share in his attitudes and reactions, takes action through forcible restraint or retaliation *after* the paranoid person "bursts into defensive or vengeful activity" (1).

That the community to which the paranoid reacts is "pseudo" or without existential reality is made unequivocal by Cameron when he says:

"As he (the paranoid person) begins attributing to others the attitudes which he has towards himself, he unintentionally organizes these others into a functional community, a group unified in their supposed reactions, attitudes and plans with respect to him. He in this way organizes individuals, some of whom are actual persons and some only inferred or imagined, into a whole which satisfies for the time being his immediate need for explanation but which brings no assurance with it, and usually serves to increase his tensions. The community he forms not only fails to correspond to any organization shared by others but actually contradicts this consensus.

More than this, the actions ascribed by him to its personnel are not actually performed or maintained by them; *they are united in no common undertaking against him"* (1). (Italics ours.)

The general insightfulness of Cameron's analysis cannot be gainsaid and the usefulness of some of his concepts is easily granted. Yet a serious question must be raised, based upon empirical inquiry, as to whether in actuality the insidious qualities of the community to which the paranoid reacts are pseudo or a symbolic fabrication. There is an alternative point of view, which is the burden of this paper, namely that, while the paranoid person reacts differentially to his social environment, it is also true that "others" react differentially to him and this reaction commonly if not typically involves covertly organized action and conspiratorial behavior in a very real sense. A further extension of our thesis is that these differential reactions are reciprocals of one another, being interwoven and concatenated at each and all phases of a process of exclusion which arises in a special kind of relationship. Delusions and associated behavior must be understood in a context of exclusion which attenuates this relationship and disrupts communication.

By thus shifting the clinical spotlight away from the individual to a relationship and a process, we make an explicit break with the conception of paranoia as a disease, a state, a condition, or a syndrome of symptoms. Furthermore, we find it unnecessary to postulate trauma of early childhood or arrested psychosexual development to account for the main features of paranoia—although we grant that these and other factors may condition its expression.

This conception of paranoia is neither simple *a priori* theory nor is it a proprietary product of sociology. There is a substantial body of writings and empirical researches in psychiatry and psychology which question the sufficiency of the individual as primary datum for the study of paranoia. Tyhurst, for example, concludes from his survey of this literature that reliance upon intrapsychic mechanisms and the "isolated organism" have been among the chief obstacles to fruitful discoveries about this disorder (18). Significantly, as Milner points out, the more complete the investigation of the cases the more frequently do unendurable external circumstances make their appearance (13). More precisely, a number of studies have ended with the conclusions that external circumstances—changes in norms and values, displacement, strange environments, isolation, and linguistic separation—may create a paranoid disposition in the absence of any special character structure (15). The recognition of paranoid reactions in elderly persons, alcoholics, and the deaf adds to the data generally consistent with our thesis. The finding that displaced persons who withstood a high degree of stress during war and captivity subsequently developed paranoid reactions when they were isolated in a foreign environment commands special attention among data requiring explanation in other than organic or psychodynamic terms (7, 10).

From what has been said thus far, it should be clear that our formulation and analysis will deal primarily with what Tyhurst (18) calls paranoid patterns of behavior rather than with a clinical entity in the classical Kraepelinian sense. Paranoid reactions, paranoid states, paranoid personality disturbances, as well as the seldom-diagnosed "true paranoia," which are found superimposed or associated with a wide variety of individual behavior or "symptoms," all provide a body of data for study so long as they assume priority over other behavior in meaningful social interaction. The elements of behavior upon which paranoid diagnoses are based—delusions, hostility, aggressiveness, suspicion, envy, stubbornness, jealousy, and ideals of reference—are readily comprehended and to some extent empathized by others as social reactions, in contrast to the bizarre, manneristic behavior of schizophrenia or the tempo and affect changes stressed in manic-depressive diagnoses. It is for this reason that paranoia suggests, more than any other forms of mental disorder, the possibility of fruitful sociological analysis.

DATA AND PROCEDURE

The first tentative conclusions which are presented here were drawn from a study of factors influencing decisions to commit mentally disordered persons to hospitals, undertaken with the cooperation of the Los Angeles County Department of Health in 1952. This included interviews by means of schedules with members of 44 families in Los Angeles County who were active petitioners in commitment proceedings and the study of 35 case records of public health officer commitments. In 16 of the former cases and in seven of the latter, paranoid symptoms were conspicuously present. In these cases family members and others had plainly accepted or "normalized" paranoid behavior, in some instances longstanding, until other kinds of behavior or exigencies led to critical judgments that "there was something wrong" with the person in question, and, later, that hospitalization was necessary. Furthermore, these critical judgments seemed to signal changes in the family attitudes and behavior towards the affected persons which could be interpreted as contributing in different ways to the form and intensity of the paranoid symptoms.

In 1958 a more refined and hypothesis-directed study was made of eight cases of persons with prominent paranoid characteristics. Four of these had been admitted to the state hospital at Napa, California, where they were diagnosed as paranoid schizophrenic. Two other cases were located and investigated with the assistance of the district attorney in Martinez, California. One of the persons had previously been committed to a California state hospital, and the other had been held on an insanity petition but was freed after a jury trial. Added to these was one so-called "White House case," which had involved threats to a President of the United States, resulting in the person's commitment to St. Elizabeth's Hospital in Washington, D.C. A final case was that of a professional person with a history of chronic job difficulties, who was designated and regarded by his associates as "brash," "queer," "irritating," "hypercritical," and "thoroughly un-likeable."

In a very rough way the cases made up a continuum ranging from one with very elaborate delusions, through those in which fact and misinterpretation were difficult to separate, down to the last case, which comes closer to what some would call paranoid personality disturbance. A requirement for the selection of the cases was that there be no history or evidence of hallucinations and also that the persons be intellectually unimpaired. Seven of the cases were of males, five of whom were over 40 years of age. Three of the persons had been involved in repeated litigations. One man published a small, independent paper devoted to exposures of psychiatry and mental hospitals. Five of the men had been or were associated with organi-zations, as follows: a small-town high school, a government research bureau, an association of agricultural producers, a university, and a contracting business.

The investigations of the cases were as exhaustive as it was possible to make them, reaching relatives, work associates, employers, attor-neys, police, physicians, public officials and any others who played significant roles in the lives of the persons involved. As many as 200 hours each were given to collecting data on some of the cases. Written materials, legal documents, publications and psychiatric histories were studied in addition to the interview data. Our procedure in the large was to adopt an interactional perspective which sensitized us to sociologically relevant behavior underlying or associated with the more apparent and formal contexts of mental disorder. In particular we were concerned to establish the order in which delusions and social exclusion occur and to determine whether exclusion takes con-spiratorial form.

THE RELEVANT BEHAVIOR

In another paper (8) we have shown that psychotic symptoms as described in formal psychiatry are not relevant bases for predictions about changes in social status and social participation of persons in whom they appear. Apathy, hallucinations, hyperactivity, mood swings, tics, tremors, functional paralysis or tachychardias have no intrinsic social meanings. By the same token, neither do such imputed attributes as "lack of insight," "social incompetence" or "defective role-taking ability" favored by some sociologists as generic starting points for the analysis of mental disorders. Rather, it is behavior which puts strain on social relationships that leads to status changes: informal or formal exclusion from groups, definition as a "crank," or adjudication as insane and commitment to a mental hospital (8). This is true even where the grandiose and highly bizarre delusions of paranoia are present. Definition of the socially stressful aspects of this disorder is a minimum essential, if we are to account for its frequent occurrence in partially compensated or benign form in society, as well as account for its more familiar presence as an official psychiatric problem in a hospital setting.

It is necessary, however, to go beyond these elementary observations to make it pre-eminently clear that strain is an emergent product of a relationship in which the behaviors of two or more persons are relevant factors, and in which the strain is felt both by ego and *alter* or *alters*. The paranoid relationship includes reciprocating behaviors with attached emotions and meanings which, to be fully understood, must be described cubistically from at least two of its perspectives. On one hand the behavior of the individual must be seen from the perspective of others or that of a group, and conversely the behavior of others must be seen from the perspective of the involved individual.

From the vantage of others the individual in the paranoid relationship shows:

1. A disregard for the values and norms of the primary group, revealed by giving priority to verbally definable values over those which are implicit, a lack of loyalty in return for confidences, and victimizing and intimidating persons in positions of weakness.

2. A disregard for the implicit structure of groups, revealed by presuming to privileges not accorded him, and the threat or actual resort to formal means for achieving his goals.

The second items have a higher degree of relevancy than the first in an analysis of exclusion. Stated more simply, they mean that, to the group, the individual is an ambiguous figure whose behavior is uncertain, whose loyalty can't be counted on. In short, he is a person who can't be trusted because he threatens to expose informal power structures. This, we believe, is the essential reason for the frequently encountered idea that the paranoid person is "dangerous" (4).

If we adopt the perceptual set of ego and see others or groups through his eyes, the following aspects of their behavior become relevant:

1. the spurious quality of the interaction between others and himself or between others interacting in his presence;

2. the overt avoidance of himself by others;
3. the structured exclusion of himself from interaction.

The items we have described thus far—playing fast and loose with the primary group values by the individual, and his exclusion from interaction—do not alone generate and maintain paranoia. It is additionally necessary that they emerge in an interdependent relationship which requires trust for its fulfillment. The relationship is a type in which the goals of the individual can be reached only through cooperation from particular others, and in which the ends held by others are realizable if cooperation is forthcoming from ego. This is deduced from the general proposition that cooperation rests upon perceived trust, which in turn is a function of communication (11). When communication is disrupted by exclusion, there is a lack of mutually perceived trust and the relationship becomes dilapidated or paranoid. We will now consider the process of exclusion by which this kind of relationship develops.

THE GENERIC PROCESS OF EXCLUSION

The paranoid process begins with persistent interpersonal difficulties between the individual and his family, or his work associates and superiors, or neighbors, or other persons in the community. These frequently or even typically arise out of bona fide or recognizable issues centering upon some actual or threatened loss of status for the individual. This is related to such things as the death of relatives, loss of a position, loss of professional certification, failure to be promoted, age and physiological life cycle changes, mutilations, and changes in family and marital relationships. The status changes are distinguished by the fact that they leave no alternative acceptable to the individual, from whence comes their "intolerable" or "unendurable" quality. For example: the man trained to be a teacher who loses his certificate, which means he can never teach; or the man of 50 years of age who is faced with loss of a promotion which is a regular order of upward mobility in an organization, who knows that he can't "start over"; or the wife undergoing hysterectomy, which mutilates her image as a woman.

In cases where no dramatic status loss can be discovered, a series of failures often is present, failures which may have been accepted or adjusted to, but with progressive tension as each new status situation is entered. The unendurability of the current status loss, which may appear unimportant to others, is a function of an intensified commitment, in some cases born of an awareness that there is a quota placed on failures in our society. Under some such circumstances, failures have followed the person, and his reputation as a "difficult person" has preceded him. This means that he often has the status of a stranger on trial in each new group he enters, and that the groups or organizations willing to take a chance on him are marginal from the standpoint of their probable tolerance for his actions.

The behavior of the individual—arrogance, insults, presumption of privilege and exploitation of weaknesses in others—initially has a segmental or checkered pattern in that it is confined to status-committing interactions. Outside of these, the person's behavior may be quite acceptable—courteous, considerate, kind, even indulgent. Likewise, other persons and members of groups vary considerably in their tolerance for the relevant behavior, depending on the extent to which it threatens individual and organizational values, impedes functions, or sets in motion embarrassing sequences of social actions. In the early generic period, tolerance by others for the individual's aggressive behavior generally speaking is broad, and it is very likely to be interpreted as a variation of normal behavior, particularly in the absence of biographical knowledge of the person. At most, people observe that "there is something odd about him," or "he must be upset," or "he is just ornery," or "I don't quite understand him" (3).

At some point in the chain of interactions, a new configuration takes place in perceptions others have of the individual, with shifts in figure-ground relations. The individual, as we have already indicated, is an ambiguous figure, comparable to textbook figures of stairs or outlined cubes which reverse themselves when studied intently. From a normal variant the person becomes "unreliable," "untrustworthy," "dangerous," or some with whom others "do not wish to be involved." An illustration nicely apropos of this came out in the reaction of the head of a music department in a university when he granted an interview to a man who had worked for years on a theory to compose music mathematically:

> When he asked to be placed on the staff so that he could use the electronic computers of the University *I shifted my ground* ... when I offered an objection to his theory, he became disturbed, so I changed my reaction to "yes and no."

As is clear from this, once the perceptual reorientation takes place, either as the outcome of continuous interaction or through the receipt of biographical information, interaction changes qualitatively. In our words it becomes *spurious*, distinguished by patronizing, evasion, "humoring," guiding conversation onto selected topics, underreaction, and silence, all calculated either to prevent intense interaction or to protect individual and group values by restricting access to them. When the interaction is between two or more persons in the individual's presence it is cued by a whole repertoire of subtle expressive signs which are meaningful only to them.

The net effects of spurious interaction are to:

1. stop the flow of information to ego;
2. create a discrepancy between expressed ideas and affect among those with whom he interacts;
3. make the situation or the group image an ambiguous one for ego, much as he is for others.

Needless to say this kind of spurious interaction is one of the most difficult for an adult in our society to cope with, because it complicates or makes decisions impossible for him and also because it is morally invidious.[3]

The process from inclusion to exclusion is by no means an even one. Both individuals and members of groups change their perceptions and reactions, and vacillation is common, depending upon the interplay of values, anxieties and guilt on both sides. Members of an excluding group may decide they have been unfair and seek to bring the individual back into their confidence. This overture may be rejected or used by ego as a means of further attack. We have also found that ego may capitulate, sometimes abjectly, to others and seek group re-entry, only to be rejected. In some cases compromises are struck and a partial reintegration of ego into informal social relations is achieved. The direction which informal exclusion takes depends upon ego's reactions, the degree of communication between his interactors, the composition and structure of the informal groups, and the perceptions of "key others" at points of interaction which directly affect ego's status.

ORGANIZATIONAL CRISIS AND FORMAL EXCLUSION

Thus far we have discussed exclusion as an informal process. Informal exclusion may take place but leave ego's formal status in an organization intact. So long as this status is preserved and rewards are sufficient to validate it on his terms, an uneasy peace between him and others may prevail. Yet ego's social isolation and his strong commitments make him an unpredictable factor; furthermore the rate of change and internal power struggles, especially in large and complex organizations, means that preconditions of stability may be short lived.

Organizational crises involving a paranoid relationship arise in several ways. The individual may act in ways which arouse intolerable anxieties in others, who demand that "something be done." Again, by going to higher authority or making appeals outside the organization, he may set in motion procedures which leave those in power no other choice than to take action. In some situations ego remains relatively quiescent and does not openly attack the organization. Action against him is set off by growing anxieties or calculated motives of associates—in some cases his immediate superiors. Finally, regular organizational procedures incidental to promotion, retirement or reassignment may precipitate the crisis.

Assuming a critical situation in which the conflict between the individual and members of the organization leads to action to formally exclude him, several possibilities exist. One is the transfer of ego from one department, branch or division of the organization to another, a device frequently resorted to in the armed services or in large corporations. This requires that the individual be persuaded to make the change and that some department will accept him. While this may be accomplished in different ways, not infrequently artifice, withholding information, bribery, or thinly disguised threats figure conspicuously among the means by which the transfer is brought about. Needless to say, there is a limit to which transfers can be employed as a solution to the problem, contingent upon the size of the organization and the previous diffusion of knowledge about the transferee.

Solution number two we call encapsulation, which, in brief, is a reorganization and redefinition of ego's status. This has the effect of isolating him from the organization and making him directly responsible to one or two superiors who act as his intermediators. The change is often made palatable to ego by enhancing some of the material rewards of his status. He may be nominally promoted or "kicked upstairs," given a larger office, or a separate secretary, or relieved of onerous duties. Sometimes a special status is created for him.

This type of solution often works because it is a kind of formal recognition by the organization of ego's intense commitment to his status and in part a victory for him over his enemies. It bypasses them and puts him into direct communication with higher authority who may communicate with him in a more direct manner. It also relieves his associates of further need to connive against him. This solution is sometimes used to dispose of troublesome corporation executives, high-ranking military officers, and academic *personae non gratae* in universities.

A third variety of solutions to the problem of paranoia in an organization is outright discharge, forced resignation or non-renewal of appointment. Finally, there may be an organized move to have the individual in the paranoid relationship placed on sick leave, or to compel him to take psychiatric treatment. The extreme expression of this is pressure (as on the family) or direct action to have the person committed to a mental hospital.

The order of the enumerated solutions to the paranoid problem in a rough way reflects the amount of risk associated with the alternatives, both as to the probabilities of failure and of damaging repercussions to the organization. Generally, organizations seem to show a good deal of resistance to making or carrying out decisions which require expulsion of the individual or forcing hospitalization, regardless of his mental condition. One reason for this is that the person may have power within the organization, based upon his position, or monopolized skills and information,[4] and unless there is a strong coalition against him the general conservatism of administrative judgments will run in his favor. Herman Wouk's novel of *The Caine Mutiny* dramatizes some of the difficulties of cashiering a person from a position of power in an essentially conservative military organization. An extreme of this conservatism is illustrated by one case in which we found a department head retained in his position in an organization even though he was actively hallucinating as well as expressing paranoid delusions.[5] Another factor working on the individual's side is that discharge of a person in a position of power reflects unfavorably upon those who placed him there. Ingroup solidarity of administrators may be involved, and the methods of the opposition may create sympathy for ego at higher levels.

Even when the person is almost totally excluded and informally isolated within an organization, he may have power outside. This weighs heavily when the external power can be invoked in some way, or when it automatically leads to raising questions as to the internal workings of the organization. This touches upon the more salient reason for reluctance to eject an uncooperative and retaliatory person, even when he is relatively unimportant to the organization. We refer to a kind of negative power derived from the vulnerability of organizations to unfavorable publicity and exposure of their private lives that are likely if the crisis proceeds to formal hearings, case review or litigation. This is an imminent possibility where paranoia exists. If hospital commitment is attempted, there is a possibility that a jury trial will be demanded, which will force leaders of the organization to defend their actions. If the crisis turns into a legal contest of this sort, it is not easy to prove insanity, and there may be damage suits. Even if the facts heavily support the petitioners, such contests can only throw unfavorable light upon the organization.

THE CONSPIRATORIAL NATURE OF EXCLUSION

A conclusion from the foregoing is that organizational vulnerability as well as anticipations of retaliations from the paranoid person lay a functional basis for conspiracy among those seeking to contain or oust him. Probabilities are strong that a coalition will appear within the organization, integrated by a common commitment to oppose the paranoid person. This, the exclusionist group, demands loyalty, solidarity and secrecy from its members; it acts in accord with a common scheme and in varying degrees utilizes techniques of manipulation and misrepresentation.

Conspiracy in rudimentary form can be detected in informal exclusion apart from an organizational crisis. This was illustrated in an office research team in which staff members huddled around a water cooler to discuss the unwanted associate. They also used office telephones to arrange coffee breaks without him and employed symbolic cues in his presence, such as humming the Dragnet theme song when he approached the group. An office rule against extraneous conversation was introduced with the collusion of supervisors, ostensibly for everyone, actually to restrict the behavior of the isolated worker. In another case an interview schedule designed by a researcher was changed at a conference arranged without him. When he sought an explanation at a subsequent conference, his associates pretended to have no knowledge of the changes.

Conspiratorial behavior comes into sharpest focus during organizational crises in which the exclusionists who initiate action become an embattled group. There is a concerted effort to gain consensus for this view, to solidify the group and to halt close interaction with those unwilling to completely join the coalition. Efforts are also made to neutralize those who remain uncommitted but who can't be kept ignorant of the plans afoot. Thus an external appearance of unanimity is given even if it doesn't exist.

Much of the behavior of the group at this time is strategic in nature, with determined calculations as to "what we will do if he does this or that." In one of our cases, a member on a board of trustees spoke of the "game being played" with the person in controversy with them. Planned action may be carried to the length of agreeing upon the exact words to be used when confronted or challenged by the paranoid individual. Above all there is continuous, precise communication among exclusionists, exemplified in one case by mutual exchanging of copies of all letters sent and received from ego.

Concern about secrecy in such groups is revealed by such things as carefully closing doors and lowering of voices when ego is brought under discussion. Meeting places and times may be varied from normal procedures; documents may be filed in unusual places and certain telephones may not be used during a paranoid crisis.

The visibility of the individual's behavior is greatly magnified during this period; often he is the main topic of conversation among the exclusionists, while rumors of the difficulties spread to other groups, which in some cases may be drawn into the controversy. At a certain juncture steps are taken to keep the members of the ingroup continually informed of the individual's movements and, if possible, of his plans. In effect, if not in form, this amounts to spying. Members of one embattled group, for example, hired an outside person unknown to their accuser to take notes on a speech he delivered to enlist a community organization on his side. In another case, a person having an office opening onto that of a department head was persuaded to act as an informant for the nucleus of persons working to depose the head from his position of authority. This group also seriously debated placing an all-night watch in front of their perceived malefactor's house.

Concomitant with the magnified visibility of the paranoid individual, come distortions of his image, most pronounced in the inner coterie of exclusionists. His size, physical strength, cunning, and anecdotes of his outrages are exaggerated, with a central thematic emphasis on the fact that he is dangerous. Some individuals give cause for such beliefs in that previously they have engaged in violence or threats, others do not. One encounters characteristic contradictions in interviews on this point, such as: "No, he has never struck anyone around here—just fought with the policemen at the State Capitol," or "No, I am not afraid of him, but one of these days he will explode."

It can be said parenthetically that the alleged dangerousness of paranoid persons storied in fiction and drama has never been systematically demonstrated. As a matter of fact, the only substantial data on this, from a study of delayed admissions, largely paranoid, to a mental hospital in Norway, disclosed that "neither the paranoiacs nor paranoids have been dangerous, and most not particularly troublesome" (14). Our interpretation of this, as suggested earlier, is that the imputed dangerousness of the paranoid individual does not come from physical fear but from the organizational threat he presents and the need to justify collective action against him.[6]

However, this is not entirely tactical behavior—as is demonstrated by anxieties and tensions which mount among those in the coalition during the more critical phases of their interaction. Participants may develop fears quite analogous to those of classic conspirators. One leader in such a group spoke of the period of the paranoid crisis as a "week of terror," during which he was wracked with insomnia and "had to take his stomach pills." Projection was revealed by a trustee who, during a school crisis occasioned by discharge of an aggressive teacher, stated that he "watched his shadows," and "wondered if all would be well when he returned home at night." Such tensional states, working along with a kind of closure of communication within the group, are both a cause and an effect of amplified group interaction which distorts or symbolically rearranges the image of the person against whom they act.

Once the battle is won by the exclusionists, their version of the individual as dangerous becomes a crystallized rationale for official action. At this point misrepresentation becomes part of a more deliberate manipulation of ego. Gross misstatements, most frequently called "pretexts," become justifiable ways of getting his cooperation, for example, to get him to submit to psychiatric examination or detention preliminary to hospital commitment. This aspect of the process has been effectively detailed by Goffman, with his concept of a "betrayal funnel" through which a patient enters a hospital (5). We need not elaborate on this, other than to confirm its occurrence in the exclusion process, complicated in our cases by legal strictures and the ubiquitous risk of litigation.

THE GROWTH OF DELUSION

The general idea that the paranoid person symbolically fabricates the conspiracy against him is in our estimation incorrect or incomplete. Nor can we agree that he lacks insight, as is so frequently claimed. To the contrary, many paranoid persons properly realize that they are being isolated and excluded by concerted interaction, or that they are being manipulated. However, they are at a loss to estimate accurately or realistically the dimensions and form of the coalition arrayed against them.

As channels of communication are closed to the paranoid person, he has no means of getting feedback on consequences of his behavior, which is essential for correcting his interpretations of the social relationships and organization which he must rely on to define his status and give him identity. He can only read overt behavior without the informal context. Although he may properly infer that people are organized against him, he can only use confrontation or formal inquisitorial procedures to try to prove this. The paranoid person must provoke strong feelings in order to receive any kind of meaningful communication from others—hence his accusations, his bluntness, his insults. Ordinarily this is non-deliberate; nevertheless, in one complex case we found the person consciously provoking discussions to get readings from others on his behavior. This man said of himself: "Some people would describe me as very perceptive, others would describe me as very imperceptive."

The need for communication and the identity which goes with it does a good deal to explain the preference of paranoid persons for formal, legalistic, written communications, and the care with which many of them preserve records of their contacts with others. In some ways the resort to litigation is best interpreted as the effort of the individual to compel selected others to interact directly with him as equals, to engineer a situation in which evasion is impossible. The fact that the person is seldom satisfied with the outcome of his letters, his petitions, complaints and writs testifies to their function as devices for establishing contact and interaction with others, as well as "setting the record straight." The wide professional tolerance of lawyers for aggressive behavior in court and the nature of Anglo-Saxon legal institutions, which grew out of a revolt against conspiratorial or star-chamber justice, mean that the individual will be heard. Furthermore his charges must be answered; otherwise he wins by default. Sometimes he wins small victories, even if he loses the big ones. He may earn grudging respect as an adversary, and sometimes shares a kind of legal camaraderie with others in the courts. He gains an identity through notoriety.

REINFORCEMENT OF DELUSION

The accepted psychiatric view is that prognosis for paranoia is poor, that recoveries from "true" paranoia are rare, with the implication that the individual's delusions more or less express an unalterable pathological condition. Granting that the individual's needs and dispositions and his self-imposed isolation are significant factors in perpetuating his delusional reactions, nevertheless there is an important social context of delusions through which they are reinforced or strengthened. This context is readily identifiable in the fixed ideas and institutionalized procedures of protective, custodial, and treatment organizations in our society. They stand out in sharpest relief where paranoid persons have come into contact with law enforcement agencies or have been hospitalized. The cumulative and interlocking impacts of such agencies work strongly to nurture and sustain the massive sense of injustice and need for identity which underlie the delusions and aggressive behavior of the paranoid individual.

Police in most communities have a well-defined concept of cranks, as they call them, although the exact criteria by which persons are so judged are not clear. Their patience is short with such persons: in some cases they investigate their original complaints and if they conclude that the person in question is a crank they tend to ignore him thereafter. His letters may be thrown away unanswered, or phone calls answered with patronizing reassurance or vague promises to take steps which never materialize.

Like the police, offices of district attorneys are frequently forced to deal with persons they refer to as cranks or soreheads. Some offices delegate a special deputy to handle these cases, quaintly referred to in one office as the "insane deputy." Some deputies say they can spot letters of cranks immediately, which means that they are unanswered or discarded. However, family or neighborhood quarrels offer almost insoluble difficulties in this respect, because often it is impossible to determine which of two parties is delusional. In one office some complainants are called "fifty-fifty," which is jargon meaning that it is impossible to say whether they are mentally stable. If one person seems to be persistently causing trouble, deputies may threaten to have him investigated, which, however, is seldom if ever done.

Both police and district attorney staffs operate continuously in situations in which their actions can have damaging legal or political repercussions. They tend to be tightly ingrouped and their initial reaction to outsiders or strangers is one of suspicion or distrust until they are proved harmless or friendly. Many of their office procedures and general manner reflect this—such as carefully recording in a log book names, time, and reason for calling of those who seek official interviews. In some instances a complainant is actually investigated before any business will be transacted with him.

When the paranoid person goes beyond local police and courts to seek redress through appeals to state or national authorities, he may meet with polite evasion, perfunctory treatment of his case or formalized distrust. Letters to administrative people may beget replies up to a certain point, but therafter they are ignored. If letters to a highly placed authority carry threats, they may lead to an investigation by security agencies, motivated by the knowledge that assassinations are not unknown in American life. Sometimes redress is sought in legislatures, where private bills may be introduced, bills which by their nature can only be empty gestures.

In general, the contacts which the delusional person makes with formal organizations frequently disclose the same elements of shallow response, evasion or distrust which played a part in the generic process of exclusion. They become part of a selective or selected pattern of interaction which creates a social environment of uncertainty and ambiguity for the individual. They do little to correct and much to confirm his suspicion, distrust and delusional interpretations. Moreover, even the environment of treatment agencies may contribute to the furtherance of paranoid delusion, as Stanton and Schwartz have shown in their comments on communication within the mental hospital. They speak pointedly of the "pathology of communication" brought about by staff practices of ignoring explicit meanings in statements or actions of patients and reacting to inferred or imputed meanings, thereby creating a type of environment in which "the paranoid feels quite at home" (17).

Some paranoid or paranoid-like persons become well known locally or even throughout larger areas to some organizations. Persons and groups in the community are found to assume a characteristic stance towards such people—a stance of expectancy and preparedness. In one such case, police continually checked the whereabouts of the man and, when the governor came to speak on the courthouse steps, two officers were assigned the special task of watching the man as he stood in the crowd. Later, whenever he went to the state capitol, a number of state police were delegated to accompany him when he attended committee hearings or sought interviews with state officials.[7] The notoriety this man acquired because of his reputed great strength in tossing officers around like tenpins was an obvious source of pleasure to him, despite the implications of distrust conveyed by their presence.

It is arguable that occupying the role of the mistrusted person becomes a way of life for these paranoids, providing them with an identity not otherwise possible. Their volatile contentions with public officials, their issuance of writings, publications, litigations in *persona propria*, their overriding tendency to contest issues which other people dismiss as unimportant or as "too much bother" become a central theme for their lives, without which they would probably deteriorate.

If paranoia becomes a way of life for some people, it is also true that the difficult person with grandiose and persecutory ideas may fulfill certain marginal functions in organizations and communities. One is his scapegoat function, being made the subject of humorous by-play or conjectural gossip as people "wonder what he will be up to next." In his scapegoat role, the person may help integrate primary groups within larger organizations by directing aggressions and blame towards him and thus strengthening feelings of homogeneity and consensus of group members.

There are also instances in which the broad, grapeshot charges and accusations of the paranoid person function to articulate dissatisfactions of those who fear openly to criticize the leadership of the community, organization, or state, or of the informal power structures within these. Sometimes the paranoid person is the only one who openly espouses values of inarticulate and politically unrepresented segments of the population (12). The "plots" which attract the paranoid person's attention—dope rings, international communism, monopolistic "interests," popery, Jewry, or "psychopoliticians"—

often reflect the vague and ill-formed fears and concerns of peripheral groups, which tend to validate his self-chosen role as a "protector." At times in organizational power plays and community conflicts his role may even be put to canny use by more representative groups as a means of embarrassing their opposition.

THE LARGER SOCIO-CULTURAL CONTEXT

Our comments draw to a close on the same polemic note with which they were begun, namely, that members of communities and organizations do unite in common effort against the paranoid person prior to or apart from any vindictive behavior on his part. The paranoid community is real rather than pseudo in that it is composed of reciprocal relationships and processes whose net results are informal and formal exclusion and attenuated communication.

The dynamics of exclusion of the paranoid person are made understandable in larger perspective by recognizing that decision making in America social organization is carried out in small, informal groups through casual and often subtle male interaction. Entree into such groups is ordinarily treated as a privilege rather than a right, and this privilege tends to be jealously guarded. Crucial decisions, including those to eject persons or to reorganize their status in larger formal organizations, are made secretly. The legal concept of "privileged communication" in part is a formal recognition of the necessity for making secret decisions within organizations.

Added to this is the emphasis placed upon conformity in our organization-oriented society and the growing tendency of organization elites to rely upon direct power for their purposes. This is commonly exercised to isolate and neutralize groups and individuals who oppose their policies both inside and outside of the organization. Formal structures may be manipulated or deliberately reorganized so that resistant groups and indivuduals are denied or removed from access to power or the available means to promote their deviant goals and values. One of the most readily effective ways of doing this is to interrupt, delay or stop the flow of information.

It is the necessity to rationalize and justify such procedures on a democratic basis which leads to concealment of certain actions, misrepresentation of their underlying meaning and even the resort to unethical or illegal means. The difficulty of securing sociological knowledge about these techniques, which we might call the "controls behind the controls," and the denials by those who use them that they exist are logical consequences of the perceived threat such knowledge and admissions become to informal power structures. The epiphenomena of power thus become a kind of shadowy world of our culture, inviting conjecture and condemnation.

CONCLUDING COMMENT

We have been concerned with a process of social exclusion and with the ways in which it contributes to the development of paranoid patterns of behavior. While the data emphasize the organizational forms of exclusion, we nevertheless believe that these are expressions of a generic process whose correlates will emerge from the study of paranoia in the family and other groups. The differential responses of the individual to the exigencies of organized exclusion are significant in the development of paranoid reactions only insofar as they partially determine the "intolerable" or "unendurable" quality of the status changes confronting him. Idiosyncratic life history factors of the sort stressed in more conventional psychiatric analyses may be involved, but equally important in our estimation are those which inhere in the status changes themselves, age being one of the more salient of these. In either case, once situational intolerability appears, the stage is set for the interactional process we have described.

Our cases, it will be noted, were all people who remained undeteriorated, in contact with others and carrying on militant activities oriented towards recognizable social values and institutions. Generalized suspiciousness in public places and unprovoked aggression against strangers were absent from their experiences. These facts, plus the relative absence of "true paranoia" among mental-hospital populations, leads us to conclude that the "pseudocommunity" associated with random aggression (in Cameron's sense) is a sequel rather than an integral part of paranoid patterns. They are likely products of deterioration and fragmentation of personality appearing, when and if they do, in the paranoid person after long or intense periods of stress and complete social isolation.

References

1. Cameron, N., "The Paranoid Pseudocommunity," *American Journal of Sociology*, 1943, 46, 33–38.
2. Cameron, N., "The Paranoid Pseudocommunity Revisited," *American Journal of Sociology*, 1959, 65, 52–58.
3. Cumming, E., and J. Cumming, *Closed Ranks*, Cambridge, Mass.: Harvard Press, 1957, Ch. VI.
4. Dentler, R. A., and K. T. Erikson, "The Functions of Deviance in Groups," *Social Problems*, 1959, 7, 102.

5. Goffman, E., "The Moral Career of the Mental Patient," *Psychiatry*, 1959, 22, 127 ff.
6. Jaco, E. G., "Attitudes Toward, and Incidence of Mental Disorder: A Research Note," *Southwestern Social Science Quarterly*, June, 1957, p. 34.
7. Kine, F. F., "Aliens' Paranoid Reaction," *Journal of Mental Science*, 1951, 98, 589–594.
8. Lemert, E., "Legal Commitment and Social Control," *Sociology and Social Research*, 1946, 30, 33–338.
9. Levenson, B., "Bureaucratic Succession," in *Complex Organizations*, A. Etzioni, (ed.), New York: Holt, Rinehart and Winston, 1961, 362–395.
10. Listivan, I., "Paranoid States: Social and Cultural Aspects," *Medical Journal of Australia*, 1956, 776–778.
11. Loomis, J. L., "Communications, The Development of Trust, and Cooperative Behavior," *Human Relations*, 1959, 12, 305–315.
12. Marmor, J., "Science, Health and Group Opposition" (mimeographed paper), 1958.
13. Milner, K. O., "The Environment as a Factor in the Etiology of Criminal Paranoia," *Journal of Mental Science*, 1949, 95, 124–132.
14. Ödegard, Ö., "A Clinical Study of Delayed Admissions to a Mental Hospital," *Mental Hygiene*, 1958, 42, 66–77.
15. Pederson, S., "Psychological Reactions to Extreme Social Displacement (Refugee Neuroses)," *Psychoanalytic Review*, 1946, 36, 344–354.
16. Sapir, E., "Abnormal Types of Speech in Nootka," *Canada Department of Mines, Memoir 62*, 1915, No. 5.
17. Stanton, A. H., and M. S. Schwartz, *The Mental Hospital*, New York: Basic Books, 1954, 200–210.
18. Tyhurst, J. S., "Paranoid Patterns," in A. H. Leighton, J. A. Clausen, and R. Wilson, (eds.), *Exploration in Social Psychiatry*, New York: Basic Books, 1957, Ch. II.

Notes

1. The research for this paper was in part supported by a grant from the California State Department of Mental Hygiene, arranged with the assistance of Dr. W. A. Oliver, Associate Superintendent of Napa State Hospital, who also helped as a critical consultant and made the facilities of the hospital available.

2. In a subsequent article Cameron (2) modified his original conception, but not of the social aspects of paranoia, which mainly concern us.

3. The interaction in some ways is similar to that used with children, particularly the *"enfant terrible."* The function of language in such interaction was studied by Sapir (16) years ago.

4. For a systematic analysis of the organizational difficulties in removing an "unpromotable" person from a position see (9).

5. One of the cases in the first study.

6. *Supra*, p. 3.

7. This technique in even more systematic form is sometimes used in protecting the President of the United States in "White House cases."

Part 4 / Institutional Deviance

In Part 3, I described how deviant behavior may initially be managed in a private setting. The material that was presented demonstrated how such behavior may become subject to regulation by a social-control agent or agency. (The case of the thirty-five-year-old cab-driver who threatened to kill his wife, cited in "The Psychological Meaning of Mental Illness in the Family," provided such an illustration.) When such regulation occurs, the actor's behavior is screened by the institution and its staff, and a label may be placed on him or her. The individual then becomes an institutional deviant, expected thereafter to conform to the institution's definition of the label. Some people will accept this labeling. In this event, not only does the person's public identity (how others view him or her) mesh with personal identity (how the person views himself or herself), but we can speak of the secondary, or career, deviant. Other deviants, however, will reject the label and attempt to structure and present to others a nondeviant image of self. The selections in this part explore such possibilities as these; they also illustrate clearly how institutional careers are initiated and perpetuated. Throughout the following discussion of the various articles, the "organizational paradigm," which was presented in the general introduction, is applied.

Typing by Agents of Social Control

I have argued previously that it is difficult to understand deviance unless we first analyze the institution or organization out of which a specific social-control agent operates. It is particularly important to know how the existing theory of the office (working ideology), existing deviant categories, and diagnostic stereotypes are applied to clients.

The selection by Lewis A. Mennerick, "Social Typing and the Criminal Justice System," provides further elaboration of this thesis. Mennerick notes initially that criminal justice personnel are afforded a great deal of discretion. He also points out that previous researchers concerned with discretion have, instead of examining the similarities among the various occupations involved (e.g., police officer, court worker), tended to analyze each subsystem separately. Not only is this a limited strategy, but it fails to enhance our understanding of how staff members, in applying labels pertaining to social types, may actually help to initiate and perpetuate selected deviant careers.

Mennerick, who approaches this subject from an occupational perspective, offers some needed insight into this process. He examines the ways in which criminal justice workers employ social typologies in the decision-making process. A basic part of his thesis is that a range of concerns affects the forms of typification employed. In his beginning analysis of the social typing of clients, Mennerick makes an important point: when formal role prescriptions are insufficient, service workers resort to social typing (e.g., "stereotypes," "typifications," "normal crimes," or "non-normal accounts"). The assignment of social types serves as a handy substitute for not really knowing the person; this labeling process also helps to structure and make sense out of any interactional encounter. Mennerick argues that criminal justice workers are under continuous pressure to "reify their clients" (i.e., to type them and treat them as objects). He then proceeds to describe some of the occupational concerns that affect the typing of clients by the police, court workers, and correctional personnel.

As an illustration, Mennerick, in drawing upon the work of C. A. Hartjen, notes that the police profession can be characterized by five basic "occupational concerns": danger, authority, efficiency, hostility, and suspicion. Thus when an officer encounters a citizen, he or she must assess the situation in terms of these concerns. Is, for example, the individual a "tough guy" or not? If he is, then not only will the client be typed as being dangerous but the officer will act differently (e.g., he or she may exercise more caution or force). Similarly, court personnel, like the police and other criminal justice personnel, also employ social-type labeling. Unlike the police, however, court workers seem most concerned with efficiency. Mennerick also suggests that the theory of the office is predicated on the assumption that all defendants are guilty. Thus, in most cases, processing becomes very perfunctory and routinized. Mennerick concludes by outlining some of the career and normative concerns that have a bearing on the type of diagnostic stereotype employed. For example, in terms of career enhancement, police prefer "safe" arrests to "risky" ones, while prosecutors prefer "convictions" to "acquittals." Similarly, parole officers prefer "sincere clients" to "dangerous people."

Roger Jeffery, in "Normal Rubbish: Deviant Patients in Casualty Departments," presents a specific account of how medical patients are initially typed by physicians. His observations are based on data gathered at three Casualty departments in an English city. Jeffery finds that two major categories exist for the evaluation of potential patients: good or interesting, and bad or rubbish. Those patients who were classified as "good" usually met one of three criteria: (1) they offered doctors a chance to practice skills necessary for passing their examinations, (2) they allowed staff members to practice their skills, and (3) they tested the general competence of the staff. In effect, "good" patients fell within the realm of expectations associated with the medical profession and its practitioners. The "rubbish" did not fit these molds.

Of interest in Jeffery's statement that, unlike the category of "good patient," the category of "rubbish" was generated by the staff members themselves. Further, the workers possessed definite notions as to what "normal rubbish" looked like; they also felt that they could predict features relating to a patient's past life, his or her behavior within the department, and his or her behavior outside the facility. These expected traits, Jeffery points out, were used to guide treatment, as well as to shunt patients into standard career lines. He then describes the various categories of "rubbish," particularly in terms of how the occupants are perceived, responded to, and treated by the medical personnel. Four major categories of "normal rubbish" are noted: trivia, drunks, those suffering from an overdose, and tramps. For example, it is believed that tramps can be recognized by their rotten clothing, bad smell, untrustworthiness, and abusive behavior. Jeffery offers some case material in support of such conceptions. He then outlines the various justifications that medical personnel use to legitimate their handling of the "rubbish," and ends by describing how the staff may punish people in this category (e.g., by delaying medical treatment).

Once a person has been initially identified as a deviant or potential deviant, he or she frequently becomes subject to institutional control and scrutiny. The article by Thomas J. Scheff and Daniel M. Culver, "The Societal Reaction to Deviance: Ascriptive Elements in the Psychiatric Screening of Patients in a Midwestern State," offers a vivid account of what may happen to those actors brought involuntarily before a psychiatric screening board.

Scheff and Culver note that most patients are incarcerated. Even though many patients did not meet the minimal criteria for admission, twenty-four out of the twenty-six cases examined were committed. Scheff and Culver explain this finding by arguing that the theory of the office is predicated solidly upon the "presumption of mental illness," at least as far as it relates to the involuntary patient. Thus, when such patients come before the board, they are almost invariably committed; this suggests that the commitment decision has already been made, with the psychiatrists seeming merely to go through the motions. This approach is apparent from the brief examinations given, the type of questions asked, and the comments offered by various psychiatric personnel. By committing a patient, Scheff and Culver reason, the psychiatrists are confirming the mental institution's expectations of how the involuntary actor should be typed. They are also able to deal with any ambiguity that may arise concerning a person's condition; they thereby remove the threat of negative public reaction that could result if such patients were released.

Social-Control Agents, Corruption, and the Amplification of Deviance

As was noted in the general introduction, very little direct attention has been given to the decision-makers who label behavior as deviant; as a result, most of them can operate with relative impunity. This is especially apparent in terms of how those viewed as "rubbish," and involuntary patients are frequently treated. Accordingly, a systematic and ongoing analysis is needed in order to clarify how social-control agents, both formal (e.g., police) and informal (e.g., teachers), conduct themselves, as well as how they arrive at their decisions. The evidence points to the need for a heightened degree of monitoring and accountability, and also indicates that some significant structural-organizational changes are in order (e.g., eradicating the involuntary career line and doing away with the "rubbish" career route). In studying the decision-making processes involved, one must also entertain the very real possibility that the decision-makers themselves, as well as their organizations, may become involved in deviant pursuits. They may, additionally, contribute to rule-breaking on the part of social actors—an event that can lead to institutional typing, sanctioning, and treatment. The pieces in Part 4 explore possibilities such as these. Here, the primary concern is with those contingencies that may give rise to the *beginning* stages of a deviant career for actors, agents, and organizations.

Lawrence W. Sherman, in "Three Models of Organizational Corruption in Agencies of Social Control," is concerned with analyzing those conditions under which social-control agencies adopt deviant goals and become organizationally corrupt. He begins by discussing whether organizations can be viewed as real moral actors. Sherman argues that since the actions of organizations are real, they can be labeled as conforming to or deviating from moral norms. He then offers a definition of organizational corruption as it exists in agencies of social control. Sherman defines corruption as "the illegal misuse of public authority in accordance with operative organizational goals for the private gain of social control agents or others participating in the agency's dominant administrative coalition." Given the existence of organizational corruption, a basic question presents itself: Why do some social-control agencies and not others adopt goals consistent with corruption, or even adopt corruption itself as a goal?

Sherman, in using concepts from the sociology of formal organizations, advances three basic models to explain the corruption: (1) cooptation of subjects of control, (2) capture by external exploiters of control, and (3) domination by internal exploiters of control. For example, a basic pattern associated with Model 1 is allowing the regulated to become members of the policy-making board. As an illustration, Sherman cites some of the practices of federal regulatory agencies (e.g., Security and Exchange Commission employees accepting free trips and hotel rooms from the industry groups they police), as well as practices of local police departments (e.g., detectives using burglar-informants to gather evidence against others). Sherman concludes his discussion of the models by advancing three hypotheses that he feels could be used to predict how corruption might arise. His third hypothesis, a derivative of Model 3, is stated as follows: "The more sheltered social control agencies are from dependence on outsiders, the more likely it is that organizational corruption will arise, if at all, through internal domination by sellers of enforcement decisions." The Knapp Commission's report offers an excellent illustration of this process.

Gary T. Marx, in "Ironies of Social Control: Authorities as Contributors to Deviance Through Escalation, Nonenforcement and Covert Facilitation," also focuses on social-control apparatuses and their agents. His thesis is that social control can contribute to, or even generate, rule-breaking behavior. Marx then discusses three situations under which this can occur: (1) escalation, (2) nonenforcement, and (3) covert facilitation. Escalation, for example, refers to the situation where agents, in taking enforcement action, unintentionally encourage rule-breaking. As an illustration, police involvement in family disturbances can give rise to violations of the law where none were imminent and can lead to police and citizen injuries. Similarly, high-speed chases can produce tragic results. People may be injured, killed, or charged with manslaughter—persons who, in the absence of the chase, might not have been charged with any offense. Marx also comments on how post-apprehension escalation may work. Of interest here are the ways in which authorities may, because of their reactions, make additional law violations more likely. Nonenforcement, the second situation covered by Marx, occurs when authorities, by taking no enforcement action, intentionally permit rule-breaking.

As an example, Marx describes how the police, in return for information, not only may treat an informant leniently but may let him or her go free. This interdependent or exchange system, Marx maintains, is very highly developed in the case of the drug scene. Covert facilitation, the third situation discussed by Marx, occurs when agents, by taking hidden or deceptive enforcement action, intentionally encourage rule-breaking. Marx offers many illustrations of this (e.g., using decoys, pursuing "dirty tricks" campaigns, planting "lost" wallets near selected police, offering bribes to police officers and other officials).

"Police Corruption in New York City," by the Knapp Commission, provides a more graphic and concrete account of the gratuities afforded police officers in New York City. These gratuities ranged from free meals to free goods to cash payments. Of significance is the commission's observation that such practices were accepted by both the police and the citizenry, with these people feeling that no real corruption was involved. For example, many businessmen claimed that they offered gratuities in an effort to "promote good will." The report goes on to describe corrupt policemen as being either "grass-eaters" or "meat-eaters." The majority of those accepting payoffs are grass-eaters: they accept gratuities and solicit small payments (e.g., five-, ten-, and twenty-dollar payments); however, they do not aggressively seek to obtain such payments. The meat-eaters, by contrast, spend much of their work time seeking out and locating situations that will bring them handsome financial returns (e.g., gambling and narcotics enterprises). In some cases, the payoff is in the thousands. The piece concludes with a discussion of those factors influencing the type and source of corruption. The most important factor, the commission claims, is the officer's character. For example, will he buck the system and refuse corruption money, or will he go along with the system? Other variables include an officer's branch, where he is assigned, his actual duty assignment and his rank. With regard to sources of payoffs, organized crime is the biggest; this is followed by legitimate business. Throughout, one comes to feel that if a subculture of corruption and graft exists, many officers will be recruited and socialized into it.

Sanctioning and Treatment

Once individuals have been typed and screened, they frequently become subject to institutional sanctioning and treatment. Such processing increases the probability that a person will eventually become a career deviant, particularly in the manner described by Lemert (Part 2).

"Court Processing of Delinquents" by Robert M. Emerson, provides an account of how juvenile courts are likely to react to those juveniles who violate deviant categories. An important finding concerns the role of juveniles relative to court personnel. In particular, attempts are made, throughout the "denunciation" ceremony, to discredit the youths' "moral character" and to show that in spite of opportunities to reform, the juveniles still kept "messing up." This is the conception that the probation officer frequently conveys to the judge—a conception that the judge will later use in rendering a decision. Emerson also notes that, given the marginal status of juveniles and their general lack of resources, it is virtually impossible to structure an effective "counterdenunciation."

Jacqueline P. Wiseman, in "Court Responses to Skid Row Alcoholics," describes the process of "platoon sentencing" whereby 50 to 250 men are sentenced within a very short period of time. Wiseman's classification of social types and probable sentences provides an excellent illustration of how institutional stereotypes relating to skid row alcoholics are actually applied. For example, the alcoholic who is gravely ill is frequently given a suspended sentence and taken to a hospital. Of interest, too, is the way corrupt personnel, many of whom are ex-alcoholics, attempt to present a specific image of the alcoholic to the judge. Wiseman further points out that if the alcoholic is slated for institutional treatment, his behavior becomes regulated by some "people-changing institution" (e.g., an alcoholic ward or hospital). Furthermore, the alcoholic becomes subject to a different theory of the office (and associated institutional stereotypes) and a different set of institutional expectations. He or she is also expected to act in accordance with the new status, and failure to do so may result in the application of various types of institutional sanctions.

"Characteristics of Total Institutions," by Erving Goffman, provides a general overview of what, for example, the officially adjudicated alcoholic or deviant can expect to encounter in the treatment situation. Goffman presents a rough typology of five groups of "total institutions." The actual examples range from homes for the aged and the blind to prisons and monasteries. A central feature of such institutions is the breakdown of barriers regulating the sleep, work, and play of inmates. This is accomplished most effectively by conducting all aspects of the clients' life "in the same place and under the same authority," as well as tightly regulating all aspects of the daily routine. Associated with such strategies is the "stripping process," in which all features of the inmates' personal identity and being are removed. Goffman terms this procedure the "mortification of the self." Inmates may react to the institutional experience by withdrawing, turning rebellious, becoming colonizers, or turning into converts of the system. Even though these variations in adjustments are made, Goffman contends that most inmates are probably concerned with "playing it cool"; this frequently means that they will become involved in various aspects of the inmate culture.

Effects of Institutional Processing

I have argued previously that the labeling ceremony or institutional processing can be viewed from two major perspectives: the institution's or the actor's. Thus far, not only have the selections dealt with processing from the institution's perspective, but very little direct focus has been given to the actor's perceptions and responses. If, however, we are to approach a more complete understanding of the effects of various types of processing, then we must try to assume the role of individuals who are affected. Erving Goffman's work "The Moral Career of the Mental Patient" represents what many would consider to be a classic attempt to do so.

Goffman is concerned with analyzing the *moral career* of the mental patient, particularly in terms of how patients perceive and respond to their treatment. Of major concern, then, is the impact of the ward experience upon *self*. He points out initially, as indicated especially in the work by Yarrow et al. (Part 3), and Scheff and Culver (Part 4), that very few patients come willingly to the hospital. Rather, many arrive as a result of family or police action. (In this sense, then, the article further substantiates the discussion of the way in which behavior in private domains may become regulated by some institution.) Goffman argues that the prepatient career can be analyzed in terms of an "extrusory model." What this means in essence is that the patient initially has certain relationships and rights; however, at admission, he or she ends up with very few. Throughout Goffman's insightful analysis, one can obtain an excellent understanding of how the actor's public identity becomes transformed into a "deviant" identity—in this case, that of a mental patient. Important to this process are such phenomena as the "alienative coalition" and the "betrayal funnel." Goffman argues further that "the last step in the prepatient career can involve his realization—justified or not—that he has been deserted by society and turned out of relationships by those closest to him." At this stage the patient may begin to orient himself to the "ward system." Some patients may, for example, accept the "sick role" and develop a set of rationalizations to "explain" their hospitalization. Such strategies enable the patient to regain and sustain a certain semblance of self—a self that has been subjected to a frontal assault by the institution, its personnel, family members and relatives, and, frequently, other patients. With his or her acceptance of this label, the individual begins to take on the identity of the secondary, or career, deviant.

Unlike Goffman, Richard D. Schwartz and Jerome H. Skolnick, in their article "Two Studies of Legal Stigma," are concerned with the effects of processing upon the *actors* themselves. These writers analyze how *social observers*—that is, third parties and witnesses—may react to the *ex*-criminal or *ex*-deviant. Specifically, in the first study the researchers examine the effects that a criminal record may produce upon the probability of obtaining employment. Potential employers were asked if they would hire four categories of applicants, the only difference among them being whether or not they possessed a criminal label. The findings clearly indicate that contact with a stigmatizing institution or agency (i.e., the criminal justice system) significantly reduces the chances of being hired. This is apparent from the observation that only one subject with a record of conviction received a positive response, as compared with three positive responses for those without a letter from a judge, six responses for those acquitted with a letter, and nine for those with no record.

Significant, then, is the finding that even though subjects were acquitted, they still, as a group, would experience a reduction in their chances of obtaining jobs. The second study examined the effects that a malpractice suit produced upon the practices of doctors. Of the fifty-eight doctors interviewed, fifty-two reported no adverse effects upon their practices, and five of the remaining six said that their practices had actually improved as a result of the suit. The reactions in these two studies are not so much a function of the particular criminal or deviant category violated as of the status and attributes of the offenders. Obviously doctors, when compared with skilled workers, possess a higher degree of status and respect in our society; they also possess more power and resources. The research also underscores the irreversibility characteristic of a deviant label. Specifically, institutions are most efficient in stamping people with labels, while the reverse process of institutional delabeling, if it exists, is extremely inefficient. As a result, actors, audiences, and third parties continually impute a host of negative attributes to those who have experienced contact with "stigmatizing" programs and institutions.

"Being Different: The Autobiography of Jane Fry, a Transsexual," by Robert Bogdan, provides a first-person account of what it means to occupy the transsexual role. Jane begins by recounting some of her experiences with her family, friends, and institutional agents. Of interest are her statements regarding her three years of psychotherapy, a period during which most of her time was spent trying to locate the psychological reasons behind her preference for transsexualism. Not only did such efforts fail, but she bemoans the fact that the psychiatrists and doctors regard her as fitting into particular molds. Jane then offers some useful distinctions among transsexualism, homosexuality, and transvestism. She goes on to describe some of the structural barriers that reduce the possibility that an operation (i.e., in this case male-to-female surgery) will be tried. The major problems involve the high cost and the difficulty of locating doctors who will perform the surgery. Throughout the selection, it becomes increasingly obvious that Jane must continually grapple with a host of self-image and identity problems. In her words: "The biggest problem I face is dealing with society in a way that it accepts me and I can accept myself."

26 / Social Typing and the Criminal Justice System

LEWIS A. MENNERICK

INTRODUCTION

The present paper seeks to expand our understanding of the criminal justice system by examining the system from an occupational perspective. The work of criminal justice personnel, while guided generally by legal statutes and administrative rules, is also characterized by extensive discretion which workers exercise in their daily interaction with clients. Frequently, previous research on discretion in decision making has tended to examine each occupation or sub-system separately, often ignoring similarities among the various occupations—police officer, court worker, prison guard—within the system. The present paper views these occupations within the broader context of *service occupations* and examines the ways in which workers employ *social typologies* of their clients based on *occupational concerns, career concerns,* and *normative concerns* as part of the decision-making process. Such typing assists workers in structuring worker-client encounters, thereby facilitating daily work activities.

Through the review and synthesis of descriptions and analyses of the activities of criminal justice system workers, this paper demonstrates that various forms of typification/categorization play a crucial role in constructing the social world of criminal justice workers. In the analysis that follows, I first elaborate on the characterization of criminal justice system personnel as service workers and on the concept of social type. I then discuss basic dimensions that underlie the typing process and ways in which criminal justice system workers employ typologies. Further, although the thrust of the argument is that typing is functional in that it facilitates the workers' interaction with offenders, thereby facilitating day-to-day work activities, I also discuss how such typing can also be dysfunctional both for the worker and for the client.

SERVICE OCCUPATIONS WITHIN THE CRIMINAL JUSTICE SYSTEM

The criminal justice system encompasses a variety of service occupations, including police officer, prosecutor, public defender, judge, probation officer, prison guard/correctional officer, and parole agent. While certain insights can be gained by viewing these workers as members of distinct occupations, it is useful to focus on their common characteristic. That is, such workers engage directly in service-oriented activities. Service occupations, as Becker has observed, are characterized by relatively "direct and personal contact" between workers and clients, thus providing clients the opportunity to exert significant influence on the work scene and to cause potential conflict in the worker-client relationship (Becker, 1963:82; Mennerick, 1974). That police and corrections system personnel confront a work scene often characterized by conflict, fear, hostility and/or uncertainty has been well documented (see, for example: Bayley and Mendelsohn, 1968:88–106; Guenther and Guenther, 1974; Hartjen, 1972; Jacobs and Retsky, 1975; McNamara, 1967:168–169; Reiss and Bordua, 1967:26, 47; Skolnick, 1966: 42–54; Weinberg, 1942; Westley, 1953:35; Wilson, 1970:20, 33, 39). Likewise, the potential for conflict and uncertainty also exists as prosecutors, defense attorneys, and judges interact with defendants. The central thesis of this paper, then, is that criminal justice workers, like other service workers, frequently employ social typologies of their clients as one means of ordering their work environment. Social typing assists service workers in attempting to cope with clients who tend to be variable and unpredictable and with a work scene often characterized by uncertainty (see Mennerick, 1974:398; Hasenfeld and English, 1974:13–14, 282).

Before examining the process of typing more closely, it is important to note, for clarity, that the clientele of criminal justice system workers can be viewed as two-fold. *One* clientele is the community at large which workers serve by performing social control activities. However, the present paper focuses primarily on the *second* clientele, which consists of those individuals who are singled out as criminal offenders and processed within the criminal justice system.

SOCIAL TYPING OF CLIENTS

As is the case with other roles in society, certain expectations and obligations are implicit in the role of service worker and client. However, when formal role prescriptions fail to supply enough information to guide worker-client interaction, social types frequently provide the necessary information that is otherwise lacking (Mennerick,

Table 1 / Social Typing and Coping with Clients

Service workers confront clients	→ →	Workers anticipate potential conflict	→ →	Workers utilize client typologies	→ →	Workers employ tactics or strategems to cope with different types of clients

1974:398). Referring to social types in a more general context, Klapp describes them as a "substitute for really knowing the person." Thus, they allow people to fill the void between mere knowledge of the other's formal status and intimate acquaintance with him (Klapp, 1958:674; also see Klapp, 1971; Strong, 1943, 1946).[1] Further, as will become evident later, whereas the social type can be viewed as a "substitute for really knowing the person," the "normal crime" and "normal" and "non-normal accounts" can be viewed as substitutes for really knowing in detail the specific criminal offense which was committed and the individual alleged to have committed it. Thus, whether reference be to "social types," "stereotypes," "typifications," "normal crimes," or "non-normal accounts," the key issue in the present analysis is that the process of typing contributes significantly to the ordering of social interaction (see McKinney, 1969: 1–2).[2]

For service workers, social typing assists in ordering the workers' expectations of client behavior and thereby constitutes one means of bring greater structure to an often uncertain work scene. Once clients are typed, the worker is usually in a better position to employ tactics to deal with them. Table 1 illustrates this process in summary form (Mennerick, 1974:400). Thus, the process of typing is functional for criminal justice system workers in the sense that it assists them in orienting their behavior. Typing is a mechanism that permits workers to "know" the kinds of clients with whom they are dealing, thereby alerting them to the various problems particular types of clients may pose. Further, typing is not a solitary event. Rather, whereas offenders are typed initially by the police, they continue to be typed and re-typed in various ways by workers throughout the criminal justice system.

TYPOLOGICAL DIMENSIONS

Because of occupational constraints—namely, the fact [that] clients can influence their work activity in important ways—criminal justice workers constantly confront the potential for conflict, stress, and uncertainty in interactions with clients. Further, conflict and uncertainty are often exacerbated by organizational constraints, including the need to process large numbers of clients and to respond to community interests. Thus, criminal justice system personnel confront continuing pressures to reify their clients, that is, to type offenders and to treat them as objects rather than as unique individuals. Such typing is based on at least three major dimensions: (1) *occupational concerns* that reflect the day-to-day problematics of managing the work scene, (2) *career concerns* that relate to workers' attempts to maintain or enhance their occupational position, and (3) *normative concerns* focusing on the desire that "justice" be served and moral standards be maintained.

Before proceeding, it is important to note that I do not assert that this list of major concerns is exhaustive or that all concerns (and their more specific manifestations) are of equal importance to all workers in each of the three sub-systems—the police, the court, and the corrections system—within the broader criminal justice system. Rather, while some concerns are shared by workers throughout the criminal justice system, other concerns are more prominent in certain sub-systems than others. Further, although these concerns can be viewed independently, they often overlap and intermesh.

Occupational Concerns

Occupational concerns reflect those issues that, from the workers' perspective, are central to the carrying out of daily work activities. Some concerns, including those related to "danger" and "suspicion," can be viewed as intrinsic to particular occupations, such as that of police officer. Still other concerns—"efficiency" and "maintenance of order," for example—can be viewed as occupational concerns that also correspond to the formal and informal goals of the organizations within which the workers are situated. In short, occupational concerns reflect commonly agreed upon job-related-issues that workers consider important. Thus, criminal justice personnel type clients in part at least according to the worker's perceptions of the situation— perceptions which, in turn, are grounded in occupational concerns.[3]

The Police: The typing of clients is an important mechanism in police decision-making as it relates to police encounters with citizens. For example, Clayton Hartjen argues that police officers engaged in stereotyping in deciding "how and when to intervene" with citizens and that such typing is based on five important *"occupational concerns"* that policemen tend to share: danger, authority, efficiency, hostility, and suspicion. Thus, police seek clues that allow them to categorize people and events. It is through the process of typing that police order reality and bring structure to their day-to-day work (Hartjen, 1972:66–71). As but one example, police officers frequently employ typing when intervening in disputes or arguments among citizens. More specifically, Wilson (1970:33) comments that when confronting such situations, the police officer "tests the participants—who is the 'tough guy,' who has the beef, who is blustering, who is dangerous?" Thus, it is clear that police officers who, for example, type individuals or situations as dangerous will behave differently, as in exercising greater caution or exerting more force, than if the situation were perceived as nonthreatening. More generally, then, police utilize typologies and their work-scene behavior varies according to the particular definition of the situation employed.

The Courts: The issues of danger, hostility, suspicion, and authority may be of occasional concern to court personnel as when defendants demonstrate disrespect for the judge or fail to follow the defense counsel's advice. However, upon entering the court system, the citizen's status is re-defined, and his ability to control the situation is greatly reduced. Indeed, court procedures frequently become routinized and court personnel often operate on the assumption that all defendants are guilty. Thus, within the courts, occupational concerns focus on the major issue of efficiency. Court workers, in turn, commonly typify or categorize defendants (and their cases) in ways that will assist in the rapid and smooth handling of cases and in the optimal utilization of available resources. Such typing, based on the concern for efficiency, facilitates the work of court personnel and contributes to the system's effectiveness. In examining this process, I will concentrate primarily on prosecutors, public defenders, and judges.

In many jurisdictions, the courts tend to be overburdened with both prosecutors and defense attorneys subjected to considerable pressure to persuade criminal defendants to accept negotiated pleas of guilty so as to expedite the court docket (Chambliss and Seidman, 1971:401–403; also see for example: Kaplan, 1973:230–231; President's Commission, 1967:31–32; Sudnow, 1965:264). Yet, prosecutors typically possess extreme discretionary power and both legal and extra-legal considerations often enter into the decision-making process (see Chambliss and Seidman, 1971:396–399; Cole, 1970; Hartjen, 1978:131; Kalmanoff, 1976: 209–210, 214–216; Kaplan, 1973:230–238; Neubauer, 1974; Rosett and Cressey, 1976:96). Daudistel and his colleagues (1979:133–134), for example, suggest that "prosecutors develop conceptions of the 'normal' criminal" and that such conceptions may influence charging decisions. Myers and Hagan (1979:440), in turn, refer to " 'strong case typification,' " arguing that prosecutors type criminal cases "in terms of their prior experience with cases that have been pursued successfully to conviction and sentencing."

Typing also occurs among public defenders. As Sudnow points out, public defenders review each defendant's case to establish its similarity to or divergence from other cases. Thus, cases are evaluated in relation to characterizations of what Sudnow refers to as "normal crimes." When confronting normal crimes, public defenders and prosecutors share a "common orientation to allowable reductions" and develop "unstated recipes for reducing original charges to lesser offenses" (Sudnow, 1965:258–269; also see Swigert and Farrell, 1977). Chambliss and Seidman (1971:407) note further that the public defender relies on the prosecutor to define the situation and accepts the prosecutor's "view of the defendant" to enhance efficiency.

Finally, like other court workers, judges also employ typologies related to efficiency. Frequently, "typical cases" come to be processed in a routinized manner (see Mileski, 1971:498). For example, in the traffic court studied by Brickey and Miller, the judge tended to be unresponsive to defendants who offered "normal accounts," that is, unsatisfactory excuses for their behavior. In contrast, the occasional defendant who offered a "non-normal account" (such as he violated the speed limit due to an emergency) was instructed to plead not guilty. Such typing allowed the judge to screen out the "guilty," thereby lessening the number of defendants requiring a trial and increasing the court's efficiency (Brickey and Miller, 1975:690–696).

For prosecutors, defense counsel, and judges, such forms of social typing facilitate work activities and thereby increase efficiency.

Corrections: Workers in the corrections systems share concerns similar to those of the police discussed earlier.[4] However, on the work scene, these concerns often combine and are manifested in the overriding occupational concern that order and control be maintained over convicted offenders. Social typing reflecting these concerns occurs throughout the corrections system and contributes to the *maintenance of order* and ultimately to the facilitation of work. Several illustrations document the point.

John Irwin (1977:29–30) points out, for example, that prison administrators responded to the increasing political organizing of inmates that began in the 1960s by developing "a conceptual category of 'revolutionary.'" Prison personnel then employed various measures to locate and deal with those inmates so designated. Similarly, Doran's (1977:440–60, 63) analysis of decision making by prison adjustment center classification committees reveals that in making its evaluations, the committee tends to employ stereotypical categories which, in turn, assist the committee in deciding how the inmate is to be handled.

Prison guards also develop and employ social types based on the concern that order and control be maintained. For example, Jacobs and Retsky (1975:26–27; also see Heffernan, 1972:63, 161; Giallombardo, 1966:81; Guenther and Guenther, 1974:44–47, 49–50) comment that guards differentiate between "good" and "bad" inmates depending upon the inmate's willingness to "conform to authority." Still other types, such as the "rat" or the "snitcher," are derived from informal inmate roles. Yet, these inmate-types, by providing the staff with information on fellow inmates, also assist workers in maintaining control (see Giallombardo, 1966:107–108; Heffernan, 1972:131).

The decision making of parole boards, which frequently confront heavy caseloads (Orland, 1975:135), also may be influenced by social typing of inmates. Carroll and Mondricko's (1976) study of parole board decision making, for example, suggests a form of stereotyping in which different criteria were applied to white inmates and to black inmates. Finally, McCleary points out that parole officers confront several routine work-related problems, the major one being that of "controlling parolees." Generally, then, parole officers may employ types—such as "dangerous men" and "noncriminals"—based largely on assessments of the amount of "trouble" parolees may cause the worker (McCleary, 1978:103–128; also see Irwin, 1970:189). Thus, typing plays an important role in assisting workers throughout the corrections system, in maintaining a more orderly work scene.

Career Concerns

As emphasized in the preceding discussion, occupational concerns reflect various aspects of the work scene (including the concern for efficiency) that are important on an immediate, day-to-day basis. Thus, typing based on such concerns contributes to the routinization of interaction with clients, thereby assisting workers in "getting the job done." However, still other forms of typing are based on what I will refer to as *career concerns.* Career concerns reflect aspects of the work scene that have broader and usually longer-run implications. Specifically, such concerns call special attention not merely to the day-to-day effectiveness of workers but to the common desire for *career maintenance* and/or *career enhancement.*

On the one hand, such concerns indicate the personal (often taken-for-granted) goal of maintaining one's current position. In simplest terms, workers maintain their position—maintain the status quo—by demonstrating competence or by concealing incompetence. Service workers, including criminal justice system personnel, frequently confront clients and situations that have the potential to threaten the worker's position in various ways, as in making the worker appear to lack sound judgment or to lack the ability to control the situation. Thus, it is important that workers be able to identify and either avoid or cope with those situations that might call their ability into question. Typing, then, is one mechanism that assists workers in differentiating between those clients whose actions may be problematic and those who pose no threat. Indeed, the consequences for workers who cannot identify and deal with such clients may range from informal reprimands by their superiors to termination. The workers' concern, then, does not necessarily focus on efficiency per se. In some cases, criminal justice workers can maintain their current position with a modicum of efficiency. Rather, regardless of the actual level of competence, a crucial factor is that workers learn to avoid or to cope with the kinds of "mistakes" that increase their visibility and require their superiors or others in influential positions to respond. And it is in this respect that social typing comes into play as a mechanism for assisting workers in carrying out their tasks and in maintaining their position.

Career enhancement, in contrast, reflects the desire not merely to maintain but to improve one's occupational standing, as in receiving informal recognition from peers and superiors, increasing job satisfaction, being promoted to a higher position, or procuring merit salary raises. Although various factors can come into play, establishing a "good track record" is one important element. Thus, in the case of career enhancement, occupational concerns and career concerns frequently intermesh, as reflected in typing related to the concern for efficiency and maintenance of order.

Several examples will illustrate how criminal justice workers—police and court personnel, in particular—employ social types based on career concerns.

The Police: Police officers are especially sensitive to the types of clients who can either hinder or enhance the officer's career. For example, Bayley and Mendelsohn (1968:105, 101–105) indicate that police officers differentiate among citizens depending upon "whether they are likely to pose a threat to their careers by making contact difficult or by exposing them to censure." Concerns regarding career maintenance are also implicit in Lundman's finding that "to protect themselves against potential mistakes, police officers classify arrests along a continuum from safe to risky." Thus, "safe" arrests involve minor offenses and offenders who lack the power to cause problems by drawing attention to either the policeman or the department (Lundman, 1974:137–238). However, social types can also have positive career implications, as in the "good pinch," an arrest characterized as being "politically clear" and as being a likely source of "esteem" for the police officer (Westley, 1953:35–36; also see Skolnick, 1966:162).

The Courts: Typing by court workers relates both to the occupational concern for efficiency, as discussed earlier, and also to concerns for career maintenance or enhancement. More specifically, utilization of the guilty plea and effectiveness in processing cases contribute to the success and efficiency of workers and are rewarded by both fellow workers and superiors (Chambliss and Seidman, 1971:400, 402; Rosett and Cressey, 1976:90, 128, 132). Thus, in determining which cases to pursue, prosecutors are concerned in part, at least, with their professional (and political) reputation, both with co-workers and with the public at large, which may be enhanced by gaining convictions (Chambliss and Seidman, 1971:403; Kaplan, 1973:232). Similarly, Sudnow (1965:261) points out that "knowledge of the properties of offense types of offenders" is the measure of the public defender's competence. Typing, in turn, assists judges in routinizing decision making and reducing the number of not-guilty pleas, thereby both increasing the court's efficiency and serving the judge's "self-interest" by facilitating his work load (Brickey and Miller, 1975; also see Mileski, 1971). Finally, typing by probation officers—implicit in the formulation of "conceptions" of the offender's "character or personality" and the reason for violating the law—reflects their concern that probationers assigned to them not cause supervision problems (Irwin, 1970:42–43). Indeed having to oversee troublesome clients can have very negative career implications for the officer.

Corrections: To some extent at least, corrections personnel also differentiate among offenders in terms of the ways in which they affect the worker's career. In the case of parole agents, for example, some types—such as "sincere clients" who willingly accept parole officers as counselors—may reduce alienation by providing a form of satisfaction (or job enhancement) not found in routine "bookkeeping chores" (McCleary, 1978:106, 120–124). For prison guards the accurate typing of certain inmates as "escape risks" or "trouble-makers" may contribute to career maintenance and may also be a source of recognition. However, overall, social typing based on career concerns appears to be less common among corrections workers. In the end, typing tends to be based more often on other concerns, such as those related to control and order, rather than on concerns for maintaining or enhancing one's career. For prison guards, at least, this may be a reflection of the need to manage a potentially volatile work scene on a daily basis with little prospect, even in the long run, of career improvement through promotion within the system (see Jacobs and Retsky, 1975:10).

Normative Concerns: Justice and Morality

Criminal justice personnel also type offenders based on normative concerns which focus specifically on the workers' conceptions of what constitutes "justice" and on their conceptions of "good" moral character. The concern that justice be served refers generally to the belief that law violators should be apprehended, convicted, and controlled. However, on a more specific level, it refers to the concern that the degree of reaction be commensurate with the circumstances of the particular crime and/or the particular offender. While social typing is one mechanism that assists workers in meting out justice, workers also type offenders in relation to the workers' standards of morality. Thus, like other service workers, criminal justice personnel often confront clients whose moral standards or values and subsequent behavior differ from the workers' conception of correctness (see Becker, 1952:461; Mennerick, 1974:405–406). Concerns relating to workers' perceptions of what is "just" and what is morally acceptable are particularly salient among criminal justice workers in that such workers, ideally, are the upholders of law and order. They personify what is defined *officially* as "right" and "just."

At this point, the issue is not whether such workers in fact do serve justice (as opposed to actually denying justice) or whether such workers represent the only standards of morality. Rather, the issue is that criminal justice personnel have acquired the power to impose their own conceptions of justice and of how the system should operate. They have acquired the power to set themselves up as exemplars of what is morally correct and to evaluate their clients' moral character against those standards. Thus, I am not arguing that criminal justice workers serve justice in an absolute sense or that their assessments of moral acceptability are in fact correct. To do so would raise many issues, both empirical and ideological, which are beyond the scope of this analysis. Instead, I assert that such workers function in terms of their *own* conceptions of justice and morality and in the process type clients in relation to those conceptions. Such typing, then, represents the *workers' perceptions* of what is right and just and assists workers in carrying out their duties in ways they consider appropriate.

The Police: Social typing based on the officer's desire that justice be served often involves different types of law-abiding citizens as well as different types of offenders. Thus, conceptions of citizens who are generally law-abiding may be refined further to include some citizens who never cause problems and others who occasionally require a mild warning. The point that the police differentiate even among those defined as criminal is illustrated by Reiss and Bordua (1967:37–38; also see Cicourel and Kitsuse, 1968:131–132, Piliavin and Briar, 1964; Skolnick, 1966:71–90), who comment that "many police see two broad classes of violators—those who deserve to be punished and those who do not." Thus, from one police officer's perspective, justice is served as he differentiates among citizens and makes judgments as to the appropriate action that should be taken in dealing with particular types.

Both criminals and law-abiding citizens also are typed in relation to the policeman's standards of morality. Such typing takes several forms. First, morally-based typing includes the differentiation among various segments of the population without necessary reference to specific violations of the law: for example, the distinction between "normal" citizens and skid-row residents who are perceived as lacking the ability "to live 'normal' lives" (Bittner, 1967:705). Second, decisions regarding when and how the law is enforced, even among those who are guilty, reflect conceptions of both justice and morality. For example, Skolnick points out that while some offenders tend "to receive extra consideration," others such as the "stud" who is unemployed and "owes a debt to society," violate the policeman's moral code and deserve to go to jail (Skolnick, 1966:85–86; also see Bayley and Mendelsohn, 1968:70–71). Finally, moral distinctions are even made among victims of crime, as when police officers differentiate in terms of the victim's " 'legitimacy' " (Wilson, 1970:27; also see Bittner, 1967: 707; Daudistel, et al., 1979:98–107).

The Courts: Social typing related to serving justice also occurs among court personnel. Rosett and Cressey, for example, argue that courthouse workers "develop shared conceptions of what are acceptable, right and just ways of dealing with specific kinds of offenses, suspects and defendants" (Rosett and Cressey, 1976:90–92, 104–113; also see Daudistel, et al., 1979:210–217; Sudnow, 1965:262–263). Like the police, court workers' conceptions of justice and morality may also overlap. Daudistel, Sanders, and Luckenbill (1979:188), for example, comment that court personnel may view evidence differently depending upon their assessment of the defendant's "character" and that some cases are dismissed not only because of inadequate evidence but also because the defendants "do not deserve to be punished." However, most commonly, typing based on assessments of the defendant's moral character is reflected in the *assumption* by prosecutors, public defenders, and judges that the defendant is guilty (see, for example: Brickey and Miller, 1975:696, Mileski, 1971:491; Rosett and Cressey, 1976:109, 126; Sudnow, 1965:269). Having been so defined, the defendant is then processed in accordance with that definition.

Corrections: The prison guard, in determining whether or not to "write up" an inmate who has violated an institutional rule, may base the decision in part on his perception of the inmate and on whether the inmate really "deserves" to be disciplined. Typing also may occur in parole agent decision making pertaining to parole revocation. However, it is likely that serving justice is less significant for corrections workers than for other criminal justice system personnel. To a great extent, both formal and informal justice related definitions of offenders have already been well established by police and court personnel. Thus, corrections workers function more as executors of justice than as determiners of what is just. Even prison adjustment center classification committees, as Doran (1977:46–47) notes, adhere to the "overriding assumption" that the inmates with whom they are dealing "must in fact be guilty."

In contrast, typing based on conceptions of the offender's moral character occurs throughout the corrections system. Such typing, stressing the offender's moral inferiority or degeneracy, is found among prison administrators (see Irwin, 1977:38), prison guards (see Jacobs and Retsky, 1975:24–26; Giallombardo, 1966:82; Heffernan, 1972:97; Weinberg, 1942:721), and among treatment workers including psychiatric and educational personnel (see Powelson and Bendix, 1951:82; Mennerick, 1971:26–31). Further, conceptions of certain inmates as "militants" (see Carroll and Mondrick, 1976) and conceptions of parolees as being "less honest" (see Irwin, 1970:182) reflect both the concern for order and control and judgments by parole boards and parole agents as to the moral character of certain types of offenders.

Normative Concerns and the Facilitation of Work

Typing based on normative concerns related to conceptions of justice can be viewed, superficially at least, as a means of achieving the publicly proclaimed goal of "justice." However, such typing, like typing based on occupational and career concerns, also contributes to the facilitation of work. It is a mechanism that enhances certain aspects of organizational efficiency. More specifically, by employing typologies based on their own conceptions of justice, workers can more readily distinguish between those clients who from the workers' perspective "merit" the system's attention and those who do not. Through such typing, the client need no longer be dealt with as a unique individual but rather can be processed as but one more instance of a broader social category.

Likewise, a superficial examination of typing based on assessments of moral character suggests that such typing simply reflects the workers' perceptions of offenders as deviating in significant ways from the workers' own values and moral standards. Yet, even morally-based typing facilitates the work of criminal justice personnel. The case of corrections workers illustrates the point. First, by morally discrediting their clients, corrections personnel no longer need to treat them with the same consideration as they would a client whom they view as morally correct (cf. Goffman, 1963:8–9). Thus, for example, correctional officers can handle inmates "en masse" and parole agents can merely assume that it is the parolee who is not telling the truth (See

Giallombardo, 1966:82, 90; Irwin, 1970:182). Second, the typing of offenders as morally inferior also facilitates the activities of corrections workers by maintaining or increasing social distance, by reinforcing the workers' own "self-esteem," and by justifying the sometimes unconscionable ways in which offenders are treated (see Goffman, 1961:87; Irwin, 1977:38; Jacobs and Retsky, 1975:24; Powelson and Bendix, 1951:85).

DISCUSSION AND CONCLUSION

In the present paper, I have argued that criminal justice system workers share an important characteristic, that of being members of service occupations. Because of the potential for conflict, stress, and uncertainty in interactions with clients, criminal justice personnel confront continuing pressures to type clients. Social typing helps bring structure to this potentially amorphous work scene by providing a means by which workers can order their expectations of client behavior. It alerts workers to the "kinds" of clients with whom they are dealing and to the problems that certain types of clients can cause. Social typing by criminal justice workers, in turn, reflects various issues including *occupational concerns, career concerns,* and *normative concerns.*

However, from the preceding analysis, it is clear that each of these concerns (and their more specific manifestations, as in the concern over danger, for example) are not of equal significance to workers in each of the three sub-systems. Further, it is important to note that in addition to variation among the sub-systems, the prominence of concerns may vary within each sub-system. Thus, just as "styles" of work may differ among police departments, prosecutors' offices, and judges, the significance ascribed to particular concerns also may vary. Some variation is situational. To illustrate, whereas policemen are always aware of the potential for danger, those working in cities or districts where, for example, racial/ethnic intergang "warfare" is common may be expecially sensitized to this concern. Other variations occur over time. For example, prison guards, while always aware of the potential for inmate disturbances, may consider danger and the need to maintain control more important occupational concerns during periods (such as the late 1960s and early 1970s) when political organizing and inmate riots are occurring with relative frequency throughout the country. In the end, however, the key issue is that workers do employ typologies of their clients based on those *concerns,* which in that time and place are *relevant,* and that such typing is instrumental in facilitating the work of criminal justice personnel.

Three points remain. First, social typing is a central feature of everyday life and, as I have argued, is especially important in contributing to the smooth functioning of the criminal justice system. However, whether typing contributes to *justice* for the individual defendant and for the larger community, as opposed to merely serving the system, remains to be determined empirically. Certainly, social typing—stereotyping, in particular—often carries negative connotations. Yet, some characteristics of persons can be predicted from other characteristics. To the extent that social typing is based on social characteristics that have predictive value, one can argue that typing constitutes a very sensible mechanism for decision making: a mechanism that facilitates both the criminal justice system and the broader desire that justice be served.

However, the typing process is not always as trouble-free or accurate as the preceding would seem to indicate. Indeed, while typing is frequently functional, it may also be dysfunctional for the worker as when the cues upon which he relies to formulate the type are ambiguous or contradictory, resulting in the mistyping of and consequent inappropriate response to clients. Further, as Hartjen (1972:77–81) stresses, in the case of the police, such typing may, in fact, also cause additional problems as, for example, when citizens fail to perceive the situation in terms consistent with the officer's stereotypes. Certainly, much additional research is required for a better understanding of the implications of the typing process for the worker *and* for the client, both when the typing is accurate and when clients are mistyped (see Mennerick, 1974).

Finally, although I have stressed the ways in which typing assists criminal justice personnel, I also assert that such typing may be dysfunctional for workers in an existential sense. That is, as the work tasks become routinized, emphasis is on processing clients as objects and workers become insensitive to clients as individuals—as fellow human beings. Likewise, the consequences for the client, who typically lacks power in relation to the justice system, may be devastating in that typing assures that clients will not be treated as people, but merely as social categories.

References

Bayley, D.H., and H. Mendelsohn
    1968   Minorities and the Police: *Confrontation in America*. New York: Free Press.
Becker, H.S.
    1952   "Social class variations in the teacher-pupil relationship." *Journal of Educational Sociology* 25:451–465.
    1963   *Outsiders: Studies in the Sociology of Deviance*. New York: Free Press.

Bittner, E.
   1967 "The police on skid-row: a study of peace keeping." *American Sociological Review* 32:699–715.
Brickey, S.L., and D.E. Miller
   1975 "Bureaucratic due process: an ethnography of a traffic court." *Social Problems* 22:688–697.
Carroll, L., and M.E. Mondrick
   1976 "Racial bias in the decision to grant parole." *Law and Society Review* 11:93–107.
Chambliss, W.J., and R.B. Seidman
   1971 *Law, Order, and Power.* Reading, Mass.: Addison-Wesley.
Cicourel, A.V., and J.I. Kitsuse
   1968 "The social organization of the high school and deviant adolescent careers." Pp. 124–135 in E. Rubington and M.S. Weinberg (Eds.), *Deviance: The Interactionist Perspective.* New York: Macmillan.
Cole, G.F.
   1970 "The decision to prosecute." *Law and Society Review* 4:331–343.
Daudistel, H.C., W.B. Sanders, and D.F. Luckenbill
   1979 *Criminal Justice: Situations and Decisions.* New York: Holt, Rinehart and Winston.
Doran, R.E.
   1977 "Organizational stereotyping: the case of the adjustment center classification committee." Pp. 41–68 in D.F. Greenberg (Ed.), *Corrections and Punishment.* Beverly Hills: Sage.
Giallombardo, R.
   1966 *Society of Women: A Study of a Women's Prison.* New York: Wiley.
Goffman, E.
   1961 *Asylums: Essays on the Social Situation of Mental Patients and Other Inmates.* Garden City: Doubleday.
   1963 *Stigma: Notes on the Management of Spoiled Identity.* Englewood Cliffs, N.J.: Prentice-Hall.
Guenther, A.L., and M.Q. Guenther
   1974 "Screws vs. thugs." *Society* 11:42–50.
Hartjen, C.A.
   1972 "Police-citizen encounters: social order in interpersonal interaction." *Criminology* 10:61–84.
   1978 *Crime and Criminalization,* second edition. New York: Holt, Rinehart and Winston/Praeger.
Hasenfeld, Y., and R.A. English
   1974 *Human Service Organizations: A Book of Readings.* Ann Arbor: University of Michigan Press.
Heffernan, E.
   1972 *Making It in Prison: The Square, the Cool, and the Life.* New York: Wiley-Interscience
Irwin, J.
   1970 *The Felon.* Englewood Cliffs, N.J.: Prentice-Hall.
   1977 "The changing social structure of the men's prison." Pp. 21–40 in D.F. Greenberg (Ed.), *Corrections and Punishment.* Beverly Hills: Sage.

Jacobs, J.B. and H.G. Retsky
  1975 "Prison guard." *Urban Life: A Journal of Ethnographic Research* 4:5–29.
Kalmanoff, A.
  1976 *Criminal Justice: Enforcement and Administration.* Boston: Little, Brown.
Kaplan, J.
  1973 *Criminal Justice: Introductory Case Materials.* Mineola, N.Y.: Foundation Press.
Klapp, O.E.
  1958 "Social types: process and structure." *American Sociological Review* 23:674–678.
  1971 *Social Types: Process, Structure and Ethos* (Collected Studies). San Diego: Aegis.
Lundman, R.J.
  1974 "Routine police arrest practices: a commonweal perspective." *Social Problems* 22:127–141.
McCleary, R.
  1978 *Dangerous Men: The Sociology of Parole.* Beverly Hills: Sage.
McKinney, J.C.
  1969 "Typification, typologies, and sociological theory." *Social Forces* 48:1–12.
McNamara, J.H.
  1967 "Uncertainties in police work: the relevance of police recruits' background and training." Pp. 163–252 in D.J. Bordua (Ed.), *The Police: Six Sociological Essays.* New York: Wiley.
Mennerick, L.A.
  1971 "The county jail school: problems in the teacher-student relationship." *Kansas Journal of Sociology* 7:17–33.
  1974 "Client typologies: a method of coping with conflict in the service worker-client relationship." *Sociology of Work and Occupations* 1:396–418.
  1980 "Client typologies and worker autonomy: the case of correctional system personnel," unpublished.
Mileski, M.
  1971 "Courtroom encounters: an observation study of a lower criminal court." *Law and Society Review* 5:473–538.
Myers, M.A., and J. Hagan
  1979 "Private and public trouble: prosecutors and the allocation of court resources." *Social Problems* 26:439–451.
Neubauer, D.
  1974 "After the arrest: the charging decision in prairie city." *Law and Society Review* 8:495–517.
Orland, L.
  1975 *Prisons: Houses of Darkness.* New York: Free Press.
Piliavin, I., and S. Briar
  1964 "Police encounters with juveniles." *American Journal of Sociology* 70:206–214.

Powelson, H., and R. Bendix
  1951 "Psychiatry in prison." *Psychiatry* 14:73–86.
President's Commission on Law Enforcement and Administration of Justice
  1967 *Task Force Report: The Courts.* Washington, D.C.: U.S. Govern-
         ment Printing Office.
Reiss, A.J., Jr., and D.J. Bordua
  1967 "Environment and organization: a perspective on the police." Pp.
         25–55 in D.J. Bordua (Ed.), *The Police: Six Sociological Essays.* New
         York: Wiley.
Rosett, A. and D.R. Cressey
  1976 *Justice by Consent: Plea Bargains in the American Courthouse.*
         Philadelphia: Lippincott.
Skolnick, J.H.
  1966 *Justice Without Trial: Law Enforcement in Democratic Society.*
         New York: Wiley Science Editions.
Strong, S.M.
  1943 "Social types in a minority group: formulation of a method." *Ameri-
         can Journal of Sociology* 48:563–573.
  1946 "Negro-white relations as reflected in social types." *American Jour-
         nal of Sociology* 52:23–30.
Sudnow, D.
  1965 "Normal crimes: sociological features of the penal code in a public
         defender office." *Social Problems* 12:255–276.
Swigert, V.L., and R.A. Farrell
  1977 "Normal homicides and the law." *American Sociological Review*
         42:16–32.
Weinberg, S.K.
  1942 "Aspects of the prison's social structure." *American Journal of Soci-
         ology* 47:717–726.
Westley, W.A.
  1953 "Violence and the police." *American Journal of Sociology* 59:34–
         41.
Wilson, J.Q.
  1970 *Varieties of Police Behavior.* New York: Atheneum. Originally pub-
         lished by Harvard University Press, 1968.

Notes

1. As discussed elsewhere (Mennerick, 1980), this need not preclude the possibility that particular clients with whom the worker is relatively well acquainted also may
be subject to being typed.

2. In recent years, the terms "social type" and "stereotype" have been used interchangeably with greater frequency; and, indeed, some authors refer to "stereotypes"
instead of "social types" in describing workers' conceptions of clients. However,
whereas "stereotyping" often has been characterized as being inaccurate or as reflecting prejudice, typing is used in the present context as a neutral concept (see Klapp,
1958:675). Thus, whether the particular types employed by workers are accurate or
whether they reflect bias remains to be determined empirically, not merely assumed.
Finally, whereas typing is the explicit focus of some authors cited in the following

analysis, it is implicit in the work of still others whose original emphasis was on different issues.

3. See Hartjen (1972) for a more detailed discussion of occupational concerns and stereotyping as they relate to the police.

4. The utilization of social types by corrections workers is examined in much more detail, using a somewhat different framework, in another manuscript (see Mennerick, 1980).

27 / Normal Rubbish: Deviant Patients in Casualty Departments

ROGER JEFFERY

ENGLISH CASUALTY DEPARTMENTS

Casualty departments have been recognised as one of the most problematic areas of the NHS since about 1958, and several official and semi-official reports were published in the following years, the most recent being a House of Commons Expenditure Committee Report.[1] The greatest public concern is voiced when departments are closed permanently, or over holiday weekends, because of shortages of staff.[2] The major criticisms have been that Casualty departments have to operate in old, crowded, and ill-equipped surroundings, and that their unpopularity with doctors has meant that the doctors employed as Casualty Officers are either overworked or of poor quality. 'Poor quality' in this context seems to mean either doctors in their pre-registration year, or doctors from abroad. The normal appointment to the post of Casualty Officer (CO) is for six months, and many doctors work this period only because it is required for those who wish to sit the final examinations for FRCS. Although consultants have in general played very little part in the running of casualty departments (which is one reason for their poor facilities) there has been dispute over whether they should be the responsibility of orthopaedic or general surgeons: some hospitals have appointed physicians as consultants-in-charge.[3] These problems with the doctors have apparently not affected the nursing staff and in general Casualty seems to be able to attract and keep enough nurses.

The reasons for the unpopularity of Casualty work amongst doctors have usually been couched either in terms of the poor working conditions, or in terms of the absence of a career structure within Casualty work. Most Casualty staff are junior doctors; very rarely are appointments made above the level of Senior House Officer, and there are very few full-time consultant appointments. Other reasons which are less frequently put forward, but seem to underlie these objections relate more to the nature of the work, and in particular to the notion that the Casualty department is an interface between hospital and community. Prestige amongst doctors is, at least in part, related to the distance a doctor can get from the undifferentiated mass of patients, so that teaching hospital consultancies are valued because they are at the end of a series of screening mechanisms.[4] Casualty is one of these screening mechanisms, rather like general practitioners in this repect. However, they are unusual in the hospital setting in the freedom of patients to gain entrance without having seen a GP first; another low prestige area similar in this respect is the VD clinic. One of the complaints of the staff is that they are obliged, under a Ministry of Health circular, to see every patient who presents himself; and having been seen, the chances are high that the patient will then be treated. The effect of this openness is that there is a great variety of patients who present themselves, and this has hindered the development of a speciality in Casualty work. There is a Casualty Surgeons' Association, and some appointments include 'Traumatic Surgery', but it is obvious that these cover only a small selection of the patients seen in Casualty, as has been recognised by the employment of physicians as well. Casualty has been unsuited to the processes of differentiation and specialisation which have characterised the recent history of the medical profession, and this helps to explain the low prestige of the work, and the low priority it has received in hospital expenditure.

The material on which this paper is based was gathered at three Casualty departments in an English City. The largest was in the city centre, the other two were suburban; of the seven months of field work, $4\frac{1}{2}$ were in the city centre. These departments would appear to be above average in terms of the criteria discussed above: all were fully staffed; only two of the seventeen doctors employed during the fieldwork period were immigrant; all were senior house officers, and one department had a registrar as well; and the working conditions were reasonable. The data presented came from either fieldwork notes or tape-recorded, open-ended interviews with the doctors.

TYPIFICATIONS OF PATIENTS

As Roth[5] and Strong and Davis[6] have argued, moral evaluation of patients seems to be a regular feature of medical settings, not merely amongst medical students or in mental hospitals. As Gibson[7] and Godse[8] have both pointed out, social and moral evaluations are important for the treatment given to patients defined as 'overdoses' and those defined as drunk or drug-dependent, and in the English Casualty departments I studied these categories were of considerable salience to the staff. In general, two broad categories were used to evaluate patients good or interesting, and bad or rubbish. They were sometimes used as if they were an exhaustive dichotomy, but more generally appeared as opposite ends of a continuum.

> (CO to medical students) If there's anything interesting we'll stop, but there's a lot of rubbish this morning.
> We have the usual rubbish, but also a subdural haemorrhage.
> On nights you get some drunken dross in, but also some good cases.

In most of this paper I shall be discussing the category of rubbish, but I shall first deal with the valued category, the good patients.

GOOD PATIENTS

Good patients were described almost entirely in terms of their medical characteristics, either in terms of the symptoms or the causes of the injury. Good cases were head injuries, or cardiac arrests, or a stove-in chest; or they were RTA's (Road Traffic Accidents). There were three broad criteria by which patients were seen to be good, and each related to medical considerations.

(i) If they allowed the CO to practice skills necessary for passing professional examinations. In order to pass the FRCS examinations doctors need to be able to diagnose and describe unusual conditions and symptoms. Casualty was not a good place to discover these sorts of cases, and if they did turn up a great fuss was made of them. As one CO said, the way to get excellent treatment was to turn up at a slack period with an unusual condition. The most extreme example of this I witnessed was a young man with a severe head injury from a car accident. A major symptom of his head injury was the condition of his eyes, and by the time he was transferred to another hospital for neurological treatment, twelve medical personnel had looked into his eyes with an ophthalmoscope, and an *ad hoc* teaching session was held on him. The case was a talking point for several days, and the second hospital was phoned several times for a progress report.[9] Similar interest was shown in a man with gout, and in a woman with an abnormally slow heart beat. The general response to cases like this can be summed up in the comments of a CO on a patient with bilateral bruising of the abdomen:

> This is fascinating. It's really great. I've never seen this before.

(ii) If they allowed staff to practice their chosen speciality. For the doctors, the specific characteristics of good patients of this sort were fairly closely defined, because most doctors saw themselves as future specialists—predominantly surgeons. They tended to accept, or con-

form to, the model of the surgeon as a man of action who can achieve fairly rapid results. Patients who provided the opportunity to use and act out this model were welcomed. One CO gave a particularly graphic description of this:

> But I like doing surgical procedures. These are great fun. It just lets your imagination run riot really (laughs) you know, you forget for a moment you are just a very small cog incising a very small abscess, and you pick up your scalpel like anyone else (laughs). It's quite mad when you think about it but it's very satisfying. And you can see the glee with which most people leap on patients with abscesses because you know that here's an opportunity to do something.

Another one put it like this:

> Anything which involves, sort of, a bit of action . . . I enjoy anything which involves bone-setting, plastering, stitching, draining pus.

For some CO's, Casualty work had some advantages over other jobs because the clientele was basically healthy, and it was possible to carry out procedures which showed quick success in terms of returning people to a healthy state.

In two of the hospitals much of this practical action was carried out by the senior nurses, and the doctors left them the more minor surgical work. These nurses too were very pleased to be able to fulfil, even if in only a minor way, the role of surgeon, and found it very rewarding.

(iii) If they tested the general competence and maturity of the staff. The patients who were most prized were those who stretched the resources of the department in doing the task they saw themselves designed to carry out—the rapid early treatment of acutely ill patients. Many of the CO's saw their Casualty job as the first in which they were expected to make decisions without the safety net of ready advice from more senior staff. The ability to cope, the ability to make the decisions which might have a crucial bearing on whether a patient lived or died, this was something which most staff were worried about in advance. However, they were very pleased with patients who gave them this experience. The most articulate expression of this was from a CO who said:

> I really do enjoy doing anything where I am a little out of my depth, where I really have to think about what I am doing. Something like a bad road traffic accident, where they ring up and give you a few minutes warning and perhaps give you an idea of what's happening . . . And when the guy finally does arrive you've got a rough idea of what you are going to do, and sorting it all out and getting him into the right speciality, this kind of thing is very satisfying, even though you don't do very much except perhaps put up a drip, but you've managed it well. And I find that very pleasing. It

might be a bit sordid, the fact that I like mangled up bodies and things like this, but the job satisfaction is good.

Good patients, then, make demands which fall squarely within the boundaries of what the staff define as appropriate to their job. It is the medical characteristics of these patients which are most predominant in the discussions, and the typifications are not very well developed. Indeed, unpredictability was often stressed as one of the very few virtues of the Casualty job, and this covered not only the variability in pressure—sometimes rushed off their feet, sometimes lounging around—but also the variability between patients, even if they had superficial similarities. This is in marked contrast to 'rubbish'.

RUBBISH

While the category of the good patient is one I have in part constructed from comments about 'patients I like dealing with' or 'the sort of work I like to do', 'rubbish' is a category generated by the staff themselves. It was commonly used in discussions of the work, as in the following quotes:

It's a thankless task, seeing all the rubbish, as we call it, coming through.

We get our share of rubbish, in inverted commas, but I think compared with other Casualty departments you might find we get less rubbish.

I wouldn't be making the same fuss in another job—it's only because it's mostly bloody crumble like women with insect bites.

I think the (city centre hospital) gets more of the rubbish—the drunks and that.

He'll be tied up with bloody dross down there.

Rubbish appeared to be a mutually comprehensible term, even though some staff members used other words, like dross, dregs, crumble or grot. There appeared to be some variation in the sorts of cases included under these terms, but I shall argue later that these differences related to the differential application of common criteria, rather than any substantive disagreement.

In an attempt to get a better idea of what patients would be included in the category of rubbish I asked staff what sorts of patients they did not like having to deal with, which sorts of patients made them annoyed, and why. The answers they gave suggested that staff had developed characterisations of 'normal' rubbish—the normal suicide attempt, the normal drunk, and so on—which they were thinking of when they talked about rubbish.[10] In other words, staff felt able to predict a whole range of features related not only to his medical condition but also to his past life, to his likely behaviour inside the Casualty department, and to his future behaviour. These expected features of the patient could thus be used to guide the treatment (both socially and medically) that the staff decided to give the patient. Thus patients placed in these categories would tend to follow standard careers, as far as the staff were concerned, in part because of their common characteristics and in part because they were treated as if they had such common characteristics. The following were the major categories of rubbish mentioned by staff.

(i) *Trivia.* The recurring problem of Casualty departments, in the eyes of the doctors, has been the 'casual' attender. In the 19th century the infirmaries welcomed casual attenders as a way of avoiding the control of the subscribers, but since before the inauguration of the N.H.S. there have been frequent complaints about the patients who arrive without a letter from their GP and with a condition which is neither due to trauma nor urgent.[11]

For the staff of the Casualty departments I studied, normal trivia banged their heads, their hands or their ankles, carried on working as usual, and several days later looked into Casualty to see if it was all right. Normal trivia drops in when it is passing, or if it happens to be visiting a relative in the hospital. Trivia 'didn't want to bother my doctor'. Normal trivia treats Casualty like a perfunctory service,[12] on a par with a garage, rather than as an expert emergency service, which is how the staff like to see themselves.

> They come in and say 'I did an injury half an hour ago, or half a day ago, or two days ago. I'm perfectly all right, I've just come for a check-up.'

> (Trivia) comes up with a pain that he's had for three weeks, and gets you out of bed at 3 in the morning.

Trivia stretches the boundaries of reasonable behaviour too far, by bringing for advice something which a reasonable person could make up his own mind about. Trivia must find Casualty a nice place to be in, else why would they come? For trivia, Casualty is a bit of a social centre: they think 'It's a nice day, I might as well go down to Casualty.' By bringing to Casualty conditions which should be taken to the G.P., trivia trivialises the service Casualty is offering, and lowers its status to that of the G.P.

(ii) *Drunks.*[13] Normal drunks are abusive and threatening. They come in shouting and singing after a fight and they are sick all over the place, or they are brought in unconscious, having been found in the street. They come in the small hours of the night, and they often have to be kept in until morning because you never know if they have been knocked out in a fight (with the possibility of a head injury) or whether they were just sleeping it off. They come in weekend after weekend with the same injuries, and they are always unpleasant and awkward.

> They keep you up all hours of the night, and you see them the next day, or in out-patients, and they complain bitterly that 'the scar doesn't look nice' and they don't realise that under there you've sewn tendons and nerves, that they're bloody lucky to have a hand at all.

> The person who comes along seeking admission to a hospital bed at 2 o'clock in the morning and he's rolling around and is incomprehensible, and one's got other much more serious cases to deal with but they make such a row you've got to go to them.

(iii) Overdoses.[14] The normal overdose is female, and is seen as a case of self-injury rather than of attempted suicide. She comes because her boy-friend/husband/parents have been unkind, and she is likely to be a regular visitor. She only wants attention, she was not seriously trying to kill herself, but she uses the overdose as moral blackmail. She makes sure she does not succeed by taking a less-than-lethal dose, or by ensuring that she is discovered fairly rapidly.

> In the majority of overdoses, you know, these symbolic overdoses, the sort of '5 aspirins and 5 valiums and I'm ill doctor, I've taken an overdose'.

> By and large they are people who have done it time and time again, who are up, who have had treatment, who haven't responded to treatment.

> Lots of the attempts are very half-hearted. They don't really mean it, they just want to make a bit of a fuss, so that husband starts loving them again and stops going drinking.

> Most of the people I've met, they've either told someone or they have done it in such a way that someone has found them. I think there's very few that really wanted to, you know.

(iv) Tramps. Normal tramps can be recognised by the many layers of rotten clothing they wear, and by their smell. They are a feature of the cold winter nights and they only come to Casualty to try to wheedle a bed in the warm for the night. Tramps can never be trusted: they will usually sham their symptoms. New CO's and young staff nurses should be warned, for if one is let in one night then dozens will turn up the next night. They are abusive if they don't get their way: they should be shouted at to make sure they understand, or left in the hope that they will go away.

(Tramps are) nuisance visitors, frequent visitors, who won't go, who refuse to leave when you want them to.

(Tramps are) just trying to get a bed for the night.

These four types covered most of the patients included in rubbish, or described as unpleasant or annoying. There were some other characterisations mentioned less frequently, or which seemed to be generated by individual patients, or which seemed to be specific to particular members of staff. 'Nutcases' were in this uncertain position: there were few 'typical' features of psychiatric patients, and these were very diffuse. Nutcases might be drug addicts trying to blackmail the CO into prescribing more of their drug by threatening to attempt suicide if they do not get what they want; but in general they are just 'irrational' and present everyone with insoluble problems. Since Casualty staff tended to be primarily surgical in orientation they had little faith in the ability of the psychiatrists to achieve anything except to remove a problem from the hands of Casualty. 'Smelly', 'dirty' and 'obese' patients were also in this limbo. Patients with these characteristics were objected to, but there was no typical career expected for these patients: apart from the one common characteristic they were expected to be different.

As Sudnow[15] suggests, staff found it easier to create typical descriptions if they had to deal with many cases of that sort. However, it was not necessary for any one member of staff to have dealt with these cases, since the experiences of others would be shared. 'Rubbish' was a common topic of general conversations, and in this way staff could find out not only about patients who had come in while they were off duty, but also about notable cases in the past history of the department. The register of patients would also contain clues about the classification of patients this way—staff frequently vented their feelings by sarcastic comments both on the patient's record card and on the register. Again, the receptionists tended to be a repository for information of this kind, partly because they and the senior nurses had worked longest in the departments. In the departments I studied this common fund of knowledge about patients was sufficient to recognise regular visitors and tramps: other departments were reputed to keep 'black books' to achieve the same purpose.

The departments thus varied in the categories of patients typified under rubbish. The city centre hospital had all types, but only one of the suburban hospitals had tramps in any number, and neither of them had many drunks. Overdoses and trivia were, it seems, unavoidable. Comments on drunks and tramps in the suburban hospitals tended to stress their infrequency and staff had difficulty in typing them. As one CO at a suburban hospital said about drunks,

Some are dirty, but so are some ordinary people. Some are clean. Some are aggressive, some are quiet. Some are obnoxious. It's the same with ordinary people.

The features of rubbish which are attended to are not the strictly medical ones—they are left as understood. These non-medical features were not essential parts of any diagnosis, since it is not necessary to know that a man is a drunk or a tramp to see that he has cut his head. Similarly, the medical treatment of an overdose does not depend on the intentions of the patient, nor on the number of previous occasions when an overdose has been taken. The features which were attended to were more concerned with the ascription of responsibility or reasonableness. However, the staff could find out these features of patients in the course of the routine questions asked in order to establish a diagnosis.[16] Thus the questions 'when did this happen?' and 'how did this happen?' provide information not only relevant to the physical signs and symptoms which can be expected, but also to the possibility that this is trivia. 'How many pills did you take?' establishes not only the medical diagnosis but also the typicality of the overdose. Similarly, questions designed to find out whether or not the patient will follow the doctor's orders (to change the dressing, or to return to the outpatients clinic) will affect not only the orders the doctor will give but will also provide evidence about the typicality of the tramp or drunk.

RULES BROKEN BY RUBBISH

In their elaboration of *why* certain sorts of patients were rubbish, staff organised their answers in terms of a number of unwritten rules which they said rubbish had broken. These rules were in part concensual, and in part ideological. Thus some patients negotiated their status with staff in terms of these rules, while other patients rejected these rules and argued for rights even though in the eyes of the staff, they might not deserve them. In so far as they were ideological, these rules can be seen as attempts by medical staff to increase their control over their clientele, so that they could spend more time on 'good' patients. The rules which the staff were trying to enforce can be seen as the obverse of professionalisation, in two senses. First, they are the obverse of attempts to specialise and to build up specialised knowledge, which implies that some areas will be excluded. Secondly, they are the obverse of attempts to increase control over the clientele, which implies that those who cannot be controlled should be excluded.[17] These rules, then, can be seen as the criteria by which staff judged the legitimacy of claims made by patients for entry into the sick role, or for medical care. I have organised them on lines similar to the classic discussion by Parsons of the sick role.[18]

These rules can also be seen as specifications of 'conventionality' and 'theoreticity', to use McHugh's terms,[19] which help to underline the continuity between his work and Parsons's. For McHugh, conventionality is an assessment that a given act 'might have been otherwise'—someone has failed to follow a rule in a situation when the normal grounds for failure (accident, coercion, miracle) are absent. Theoreticity refers to the assessment that an actor 'knows what he is doing'.

These, then, are rules inductively generalised from accounts given by staff.

a) Patients must not be responsible, either for their illness or for getting better: medical staff can only be held responsible if, in addition, they are able to treat the illness.

The first half of this rule was broken by all normal rubbish. Drunks and tramps were responsible for their illnesses, either directly or indirectly. Drunks will continue to fall over or be involved in fights because they are drunk, and they are responsible for their drunkenness. Tramps are responsible for the illnesses like bronchitis which are a direct result of the life the tramp has chosen to lead. Normal overdoses knew what they were doing, and chose to take an overdose for their own purposes. Trivia *chose* to come to Casualty, and could be expected to deal with their illnesses themselves. All normal rubbish had within their own hands the ability to affect a complete cure, and since there was little the Casualty staff could do about it, they could not be held responsible to treat the illnesses of normal rubbish. Comments which reflected this rule included,

> I don't like having to deal with drunks in particular. I find that usually they're quite aggressive. I don't like aggressive people. And I feel that, you know, they've got themselves into this state entirely through their own follies, why the hell should I have to deal with them on the NHS? So I don't like drunks, I think they are a bloody nuisance. I don't like overdoses, because I've got very little sympathy with them on the whole, I'm afraid.
> (Q: Why not?)
> mm well you see most of them don't mean it, it's just to draw attention to themselves, you see I mean they take a non-lethal dose and they know it's not lethal.

> I do feel that tramps could have been helped, and have been helped and have rejected it. So often I feel this is brought on by themselves.

> People who create a lot of trouble because of their own folly.

If patients can be held responsible, then the staff feel they have no moral obligation to treat them, though the legal obligation may remain. However, responsibility is not easily assigned. Thus some staff find it very difficult to decide about responsibility in psychiatric cases, and they express ambivalence over whether or not tramps, drunks and overdoses are 'really ill' in their underlying state. As one CO said, he did not mind treating

> Anyone who is genuinely ill—I'm not talking about the psychiatric types I suppose, they're genuinely ill but the thing is I don't really understand psychiatric illness.

The staff normally felt uncertain about the existence of an illness if there was no therapy that they, or anyone else, could provide to correct the state, and it would seem that this uncertainty fostered frustration which was vented as hostility towards these patients. One example of this was in the comments on overdoses, and the distinctions made between those who really tried to commit suicide (for whom there is some respect) and the rest (viewed as immature calls for attention). This seems to be behind the following comments:

> And I mean, certainly with overdoses, and sometimes you feel, if they are that determined, why not let them put themselves out of their misery.

> I think it's all so unnecessary, you know, if you are going to do the job, do it properly, don't bother us!

> It's the same I'm sure in any sphere, that if you're doing something and you're treating it and—say you're a plumber and the thing keeps going wrong because you haven't got the right thing to put it right, you get fed up with it, and in the end you'd much rather hit the thing over the . . . hit the thing with your hammer. Or in this case, to give up rather than go on, you know, making repeated efforts.

Similar feelings were expressed about drunks:[20]

> They're jolly difficult people to deal with, there's no easy answer. Unlike someone who's got something you can put right. With them, the thing that's wrong is much more difficult to put right.

> You know that whatever you do for them is only 5% of their problem, and you're not really approaching the other 95% or touching it.

b) Patients should be restricted in their reasonable activities by the illnesses they report with.

This rule has particular point in a Casualty department, and trivia who have been able to delay coming to the department most obviously break this rule. This is implicit in the comments already reported about trivia. However, there is another aspect to this rule, which refers to the discussion of the relationship between deviance and illness, which I shall return to later. This is the requirement that the

activities being followed should be reasonable, and the obvious offenders against this rule are the tramps. It applies also to other sorts
of patients, who may be attributed one deviant trait ('hippy type')
which then places them in the position of being an 'illegitimate aspir-
er to the sick role' as a generalisation from one deviant trait to a deviant character. Comments which applied [to] this role included:

> I also like some patient relationships, providing the patient is a co-opera-
> tive, pleasant, useful human being. I am afraid I get very short, very an-
> noyed, with neurotic patients and with patients who I think are just drop-
> outs from society really—it's a horrible thing to say—not worth helping.

> If a man has led a full productive life, he's entitled to good medical atten-
> tion, because he's put a lot into society.

> (Tramps) put nothing in, and are always trying to get something out.

Obviously the Protestant Ethic of work is alive and well in Casualty
departments.

c) Patients should see illness as an undesirable state.

The patients who most obviously offend against this rule are the
overdoses and the tramps. The overdoses are seen to want to be ill in
order to put moral pressure on someone, or to get attention. Tramps
want to be ill in order to get the benefits of being a patient—a warm
bed and warm meals. Trivia are also suspected of being neurotic or
malingering, in order to explain why they come, as in the following
comments:

> In fact you get entirely indifferent, you think that everyone's neurotic,
> you just don't care. You just say 'you haven't got a fracture mate, you can't
> sue me, I haven't missed anything.' And that's all you think about, getting
> them out.

d) Patients should co-operate with the competent agencies in trying to get well.

The major non-co-operative patients were the drunks and the
overdoses. Drunks fail to be co-operative by refusing to stay still
while being sutured or examined, and overdoses fight back when a
rubber tube is being forced down their throats so that their stomachs
can be washed out. These are both cases where patients *refuse* to cooperate, rather than being unable to co-operate, as would be the case
for patients in epileptic or diabetic fits. Similarly, they refuse to cooperate in getting 'well' because they cannot be trusted to live their
lives in future in such a way that they would avoid the same injuries.
The normal overdose, after all, is one who has been in time and time
again, as is the normal drunk. Other patients may also offend against
this rule, like skinheads who were hurt in a fight and said they were
going to get their own back on their enemies:

We're wasting everybody's time by X-raying that bloke because he's only going to do it again.

However, it was noticeable that if recurrent injuries were a result of what the staff regarded as reasonable activities (such as playing rugby) similar hostility was not provoked. In general, then, patients had a duty to live their lives in order to avoid injury, to remain well, and patients who did not do this were not worth helping.

These four rules, then, seemed to cover the criteria by which normal rubbish was faulted. It can be seen that each of them required quite fine judgement about, for example, whether a patient was uncooperative by choice or because of some underlying illness. Discussions of dirty patients included an attempt to find out if they were ill and could not clean themselves, and an abusive tramp had his behaviour reinterpreted when he later had a fit—his abuse was put down to the effects of the tension preceding the fit. In other cases there was evidence of negotiation between patients and staff over how the patient was to be classified. Patients would provide evidence which did not match the normal pattern for rubbish. Certainly the staff treated differently patients who demonstrated they were abnormal overdoses or tramps. For example, respect was shown to the man who took an overdose, then slashed his wrists when he came into Casualty and finally drowned himself in the bathroom of the Casualty ward. Lesser respect was accorded to others who also made serious attempts to kill themselves. Overdoses who demonstrated that they were unlikely to repeat the behaviour were also treated better, like a thirty-year old social worker who brought himself in and then actively assisted with the washout proceedings. Again, the clean, well-spoken tramp who had diabetes which he kept under control was helped to get somewhere other than the Salvation Army hostel to sleep for the night. Though I did not interview patients about this, there is impressionistic evidence that patients were aware of the rules which staff tried to impose, and attempted to organize their interactions with staff in order to put up a good front in terms of those rules. This was certainly the case with patients who negotiated for abnormal status, and was perhaps true for other patients. Patients with relatively minor ailments would frequently stress the accidental nature of the injury, their reasons for assessing it as serious, the reasonableness for their activities at the time of the accident, and their desire to get back to work.

PUNISHMENT

Rubbish could be punished by the staff in various ways, the most important being to increase the amount of time that rubbish had to spend in Casualty before completing treatment. In each hospital there were ways of advancing and retarding patients so that they were not seen strictly in the order in which they arrived. Good patients, in general being the more serious, could be seen immediately by being taken directly to the treatment area, either by the receptionist or by the ambulanceman. Less serious cases, including the trivia, would go first to a general waiting area. Patients there were normally left until all serious cases had been dealt with. However, during relatively busy periods these arrangements only permitted rather gross division of cases, so that the general area would also include many patients who were not regarded as trivia, and would usually contain some 'good' patients as well. In slack periods this technique was more finely used, so that if the nurse or receptionist was sure that the patient was rubbish she could delay calling the doctor.

However, the staff could also delay treatment for overdoses, tramps and drunks in a more selective fashion. Patients in these categories could be taken to relative backwaters and shut into rooms so that they could be ignored until the staff were prepared to deal with them. Sometimes staff employed a deliberate policy of leaving drunks and tramps in the hope that they would get annoyed at the delay and take their own discharge.

The other forms of punishment used were verbal hostility or the vigorous restraint of unco-operative patients. Verbal hostility was in general fairly restrained, at least in my presence, and was usually less forthright than the written comments made in the 'medical' notes, or the comments made in discussions with other staff. Vigorous treatment of patients was most noticeable in the case of overdoses, who would be held down or sat upon while the patient was forced to swallow the rubber tube used. Staff recognised that this procedure had an element of punishment in it, but defended themselves by saying that it was necessary. However, they showed no sympathy for the victim, unlike cases of accidental self-poisoning by children. Drunks and tramps who were unco-operative could be threatened with the police, who were called on a couple of occasions to undress a drunk or to stand around while a tramp was treated.

Punishment was rarely extended to a refusal to see or to treat patients, except for a few tramps who came to the department but never got themselves registered, merely sitting in the warm for a while, and for some patients who arrived in the middle of the night and were persuaded by the staff nurse to come back later. The staff were very conscious of the adverse publicity raised whenever patients were refused treatment in Casualty departments, and they were also worried by the medico-legal complications to which Casualty departments are prone, and this restrained their hostility and the extent of the delay they were prepared to put patients to. A cautionary tale was told to emphasise the dangers of not treating rubbish properly, concerning a tramp who was seen in a Casualty department and discharged. A little later the porter came in and told the CO that the tramp had collapsed and died outside on the pavement. The porter then calmed the worries of the CO by saying 'It's all right sir, I've turned him round so that it looks as though he was on his way *to* Casualty.'

DEVIANCE AND ILLNESS

What I have argued so far is that Casualty staff classify patients broadly into good and rubbish patients. The features of good patients which are attended to are medical in character, whereas rubbish is described in predominantly social terms. In addition, there are typical sorts of rubbish which are picked out for particular comment, the normal trivia, normal overdoses, normal tramps and normal drunks. Staff justify their hostile typifications of those patients by arguing that they have broken most of the rules which should govern who is a legitimate aspirant for entry into patienthood. Other patients who break one or more of these rules also evoke hostile responses in staff, but are not typified in the same way. Patients who break these rules are likely to be penalised, if possible by being kept waiting longer than necessary, but the threat of legal problems ensures that they will get some diagnosis and treatment. On these grounds it seems clear to me that these patients are seen as deviant, in that they are given an unflattering label, are seen to break rules, and are liable to punishment. While I would be happy to leave the matter there, in one respect at least the discussion so far is inadequate. This results from the attempt by several sociologists of medicine to treat illness, and the sick role, as themselves deviant, whereas I have implied that illness is not deviant, only those who make illegitimate claims to be allowed entry to the sick role or to patienthood are deviant. Therefore it is necessary to consider the debate about the relationship between illness and deviance, though I cannot in the space available give full justice to it.

There are two alternative ways of dealing with my material which leave no contradiction between my discussion and that of those who see the sick role as deviance. The first is that of Bagley, who would regard rubbish as 'counter-deviance,' that is, deviance from the deviant role of sickness.[21] This seems to me to be an unnecessary creation of a new term, one which seems to have few if any uses outside medical sociology and which begs the original question of why sickness should be seen as deviance at all. The second way of avoiding contradications might be to argue that doctors do not regard sickness as deviance because they are largely cut off from the rest of society—they share a sub-universe of meanings which is separate from those of the rest of society.[22] This would allow for sickness in the wider society to be seen as deviance, and for the attitudes and behavior of doctors to be irrelevant to this question. *A priori* it seems implausible that the extent of separation between the world of the medical staff could be so divorced from that of the rest of society, or that the attitudes of those staff could be reasonably regarded as irrelevant, though this seems to be the position which Freidson holds.[23] Neither of these solutions, then, seem adequate enough to allow me to avoid looking more closely at the prior agrument about sickness and deviance.

Rather than recapitulate all contributions to this debate I shall relate my material to the position recently taken by Dingwall.[24] He uses McHugh's analysis to argue that illness makes an actor vulnerable to *prima facie* charges of conventionality, because it involved the breaking of rules which are applied to all competent members of a society. However, any specific illness may or may not make an actor vulnerable to a charge of theoreticity, depending on whether or not he is able to deny any charges that he is wilfully ill, or responsible in other ways for his condition. Illness is thus 'clearly deviance' by the first criterion, but a matter of negotiation by the second criterion. Dingwall's attempt to separate the two criteria in this way seems rather misleading, since it is the application of both criteria together which will lead actors to level charges of deviance (or not); but in general, this argument takes us much further than earlier discussions, focussed at different levels.

If, then, we accept Dingwall's argument that the study of the moral status of illness should start with the study of its ascription in everyday settings, the evidence I have presented suggests that illness is a morally ambiguous condition. It makes actors vulnerable to charges of deviant behaviour, but the resolution of those charges depends on negotiation, and is contextually specific. Part of the work done by Casualty staff is the production of deviance as the obverse of the production of legitimate illness. The special characteristics of Casualty departments perhaps make these processes more obvious than elsewhere, but they are probably a general feature of medical encounters.

Notes

1. See for example, the British Orthopedic Association, 'Memorandum on Accident Services', *Journal of Bone and Joint Surgery*, Vol. 41B, No. 3, 1959, pp. 457–63; Nuffield Provincial Hospitals Trust, *Casualty Services and their Setting*, London,

O.U.P., 1960; and House of Commons Expenditure Committee, 4th Report, *Accident and Emergency Services*, London H.M.S.O. 1974. A fuller survey of this literature can be found in H. Gibson, *Rules, Routines and Records*, Ph.D. thesis, Aberdeen University, 1977.

2. See e.g. the summary in *World Medicine*, February 1972, p. 11.

3. Reported in the Expenditure Committee Report, *op. cit.* pp. xii–xiii.

4. This is similar to Freidson's distinction between client control and colleague control: see E. Freidson, *Patients' Views of Medical Practice*, New York, Russell Sage Foundation, 1961.

5. J. Roth, 'Some Contingencies of the Moral Evaluation and Control of Clientele: The case of the Hospital Emergency Service', *A.J.S.* Vol. 77, No. 5, March 1972. The studies of medical students which are relevant are: H. Becker *et al., Boys in White*, Chicago, University of Chicago Press, 1961; and R. K. Merton *et al.* (eds), *The Student Physician*, Cambridge, Harvard University Press, 1957.

6. P. Strong and A. Davis, 'Who's who in paediatric encounters: morality, expertise and the generation of identity and action in medical settings', in A. Davis (ed), *Relationships between doctors and patients*, Westmead, Teakfield, 1978, pp. 51–2.

7. H. Gibson, op. cit., chapter 9.

8. A. H. Godse, 'The attitudes of Casualty staff and ambulancemen towards patients who take drug overdoses' *Social Science and Medicine*, Vol. 12, 5A, September 1978, pp. 341–6.

9. This case, while not as spectacular as one reported by Sudnow, does suggest a general level of depersonalisation in British teaching hospitals rather higher than in American hospitals. See D. Sudnow, *Passing On*, New York, Prentice-Hall 1968.

10. I am using normal in the sense that Sudnow uses, in D. Sudnow, 'Normal Crimes', *Social Problems*, Vol. 12, Winter 1965.

11. This topic recurs in the reports referenced in note 1 above, and in most of the research reports on casualty case-loads in the medical press. In an attempt to discourage casual attenders the Ministry of Health changed the title of the departments from 'Casualty' to 'Accident and Emergency' during the 1960s. However, most of the staff continued to call it Casualty (and I have followed their usage) and there is no evidence that the change of name has altered the nature of the case-load.

12. See E. Goffman, *Asylums*, Harmondsworth, Penguin, 1968, especially the section 'Notes on the Vicissitudes of the Tinkering Trades'.

13. Gibson (op. cit. pp. 164–86) discusses the ways in which 'drunk' fails as a medical category since a wide variety of careers and treatments are associated with drunk patients, which tends to support the argument that this is essentially a moral category.

14. Godse (op. cit.) suggests that there is generalised hostility towards all drug overdoses, but he elaborates his discussion with respect to three types. One of these—deliberate suicide attempts or gestures—fails to distinguish between what I call 'normal' overdoses and those believed by the staff to be serious suicide attempts. Gibson (op. cit. pp. 186–94) also reports that staff presumed that most, if not all, cases of self-poisoning were seen as acts of self-injury, wilfully and directly caused, rather than as attempts to commit suicide.

15. Sudnow, 'Normal Crimes', op. cit.

16. P. Strong and A. Davis, op. cit., p. 52.

17. The research of a similar kind carried out by the author in Pakistan, doctors were both less interested in good patients and less bothered by rubbish; similarly, they had less autonomy over their working conditions.

18. T. Parsons, *The Social System*, New York, The Free Press, 1951. Although Parsons never says where he developed the sick role model from, it is plausible that it comes from his discussions with doctors in his Boston study, and from his course in psychotherapy (see his footnote 2, pp. 428–9). If so, and if we reformulate the sick role in the way that I have, this may overcome some of the problems which have been pointed out by other writers: for example, the inapplicability of the sick role to chronic illness. That is, there is indeed a preference by doctors for an illness which is temporary, transitory and curable, and part of the reason for the low prestige of work with geriatric or chronic patients is that doctors are uneasy dealing with patients who do not conform to this pattern.

19. P. McHugh, 'A commonsense conception of deviance', in H. P. Drietzel (ed.), *Recent Sociology No. 2*, New York, Crowell Collier Macmillan, 1968.

20. Similar uncertainty has been reported from America amongst a general population and amongst social workers. See H. A. Mulford and D. E. Miller, 'Measuring Community Acceptance of the Alcoholic as a Sick Person', *Quarterly Journal of Studies in Alcoholism*, Vol. 25, June 1964; and H. P. Chalfont and R. A. Kurtz, 'Alcoholics and the Sick Role: Assessments by Social Workers', *Journal of Health and Social Behaviour*, Vol. 12, March 1971.

21. C. Bagley, 'The Sick Role, Deviance and Medical Care', *Social and Economic Administration*, Vol. 4, 1971.

22. This is the sort of argument made by Becker *et al.*, op. cit., in discussing the sources of negative evaluations by medical students.

23. E. Freidson, *Profession of Medicine*, New York, Dodd Mead, 1970. He advances similar arguments in 'Disability and Deviance', in M. B. Sussman, (ed), *Sociology and Rehabilitation*, Washington DC, ASA 1966.

24. R. Dingwall, *Aspects of Illness*, London, Martin Robertson, 1976.

28 / The Societal Reaction to Deviance: Ascriptive Elements in the Psychiatric Screening of Mental Patients in a Midwestern State

THOMAS J. SCHEFF
DANIEL M. CULVER

The case for making the societal reaction to deviance a major independent variable in studies of deviant behavior has been succinctly stated by Kitsuse:

> A sociological theory of deviance must focus specifically upon the interactions which not only define behaviors as deviant but also organize and activate the application of sanctions by individuals, groups, or agencies. For in modern society, the socially significant differentiation of deviants from the non-deviant population is increasingly contingent upon circumstances of situation, place, social and personal biography, and the bureaucratically organized activities of agencies of control.[1]

In the case of mental disorder, psychiatric diagnosis is one of the crucial steps which "organizes and activates" the societal reaction, since the state is legally empowered to segregate and isolate those persons whom psychiatrists find to be committable because of mental illness.

Recently, however, it has been argued that mental illness may be more usefully considered to be a social status than a disease, since the symptoms of mental illness are vaguely defined and widely distributed, and the definition of behavior as symptomatic of mental illness is usually dependent upon social rather than medical contingencies.[2] Furthermore, the argument continues, the status of the mental patient is more often an ascribed status, with conditions for status entry external to the patient, than an achieved status with conditions for status entry dependent upon the patient's own behavior. According to this argument, the societal reaction is a fundamentally important variable in all stages of a deviant career.

The actual usefulness of a theory of mental disorder based on the societal reaction is largely an empirical question: to what extent is entry to the status of mental patient independent of the behavior or "condition" of the patient? The present paper will explore this question for one phase of the societal reaction: the legal screening of persons alleged to be mentally ill. This screening represents the official phase of the societal reaction, which occurs after the alleged deviance has been called to the attention of the community by a complainant. This report will make no reference to the initial deviance or other situation which resulted in the complaint, but will deal entirely with procedures used by the courts after the complaint has occurred.

The purpose of the description that follows is to determine the extent of uncertainty that exists concerning new patients' qualifications for involuntary confinement in a mental hospital, and the reactions of the courts to this type of uncertainty. The data presented here indicate that, in the face of uncertainty, there is a strong presumption of illness by the court and the court psychiatrists.[3] In the discussion that follows the presentation of findings, some of the causes, consequences and implications of the presumption of illness are suggested.

The data upon which this report is based were drawn from psychiatrists' ratings of a sample of patients newly admitted to the public mental hospitals in a Midwestern state, official court records, interviews with court officials and psychiatrists, and our observations of psychiatric examinations in four courts. The psychiatrists' ratings of new patients will be considered first.

In order to obtain a rough measure of the incoming patient's qualifications for involuntary confinement, a survey of newly admitted patients was conducted with the cooperation of the hospital psychiatrists. All psychiatrists who made admission examinations in the three large mental hospitals in the state filled out a questionnaire for the first ten consecutive patients they examined in the month of June, 1962. A total of 223 questionnaires were returned by the 25 admission psychiatrists. Although these returns do not constitute a probability sample of all new patients admitted during the year, there were no obvious biases in the drawing of the sample. For this reason, this group of patients will be taken to be typical of the newly admitted patients in Midwestern State.

The two principal legal grounds for involuntary confinement in the United States are the police power of the state (the state's right to protect itself from dangerous persons) and *parens patriae* (the State's right to assist those persons who, because of their own incapacity, may not be able to assist themselves.)[4] As a measure of the first ground, the potential dangerousness of the patient, the questionnaire contained this item: "In your opinion, if this patient were released at the present time, is it likely he would harm himself or others?" The psychiatrists were given six options, ranging from Very Likely to Very Unlikely. Their responses were: Very Likely, 5%; Likely, 4%; Somewhat Likely, 14%; Somewhat Unlikely, 20%; Unlikely, 37%; Very Unlikely, 18%. (Three patients were not rated, 1%).

As a measure of the second ground, *parens patriae*, the questionnaire contained the item: "Based on your observations of the patient's behavior, his present degree of mental impairment is:

None_____   Minimal_____   Mild_____   Moderate_____
Severe_____"   The psychiatrists' responses were: None, 2%; Minimal, 12%; Mild, 25%; Moderate, 42%; Severe, 17%. (Three patients were not rated, 1%).

To be clearly qualified for involuntary confinement, a patient should be rated as likely to harm self or others (Very Likely, Likely, or Somewhat Likely) and/or as Severely Mentally Impaired. However, voluntary patients should be excluded from this analysis, since the court is not required to assess their qualifications for confinement. Excluding the 59 voluntary admissions (26% of the sample), leaves a sample of 164 involuntary confined patients. Of these patients, 10 were rated as meeting both qualifications for involuntary confinement, 21 were rated as being severely mentally impaired, but not dangerous, 28 were rated as dangerous but not severely mentally impaired, and 102 were rated as not dangerous nor as severely mentally impaired. (Three patients were not rated.)

According to these ratings, there is considerable uncertainty connected with the screening of newly admitted involuntary patients in the state, since a substantial majority (63%) of the patients did not clearly meet the statutory requirements for involuntary confinement. How does the agency responsible for assessing the qualifications for confinement, the court, react in the large numbers of cases involving uncertainty?

On the one hand, the legal rulings on this point by higher courts are quite clear. They have repeatedly held that there should be a presumption of sanity. The burden of proof of insanity is to be on the petitioners, there must be a preponderance of evidence, and the evidence should be of a "clear and unexceptionable" nature.[5]

On the other hand, existing studies suggest that there is a presumption of illness by mental health officials. In a discussion of the "discrediting" of patients by the hospital staff, based on observations at St. Elizabeth's Hospital, Washington, D.C., Goffman states:

[The patient's case record] is apparently not regularly used to record occasions when the patient showed capacity to cope honorably and effectively with difficult life situations. Nor is the case record typically used to provide a rough average or sampling of his past conduct. [Rather, it extracts] from his whole life course a list of those incidents that have or might have had "symptomatic" significance. ... I think that most of the information gathered in case records is quite true, although it might seem also to be true that almost anyone's life course could yield up enough denigrating facts to provide grounds for the record's justification of commitment.[6]

Mechanic makes a similar statement in his discussion of two large mental hospitals located in an urban area in California:

In the crowded state or county hospitals, which is the most typical situation, the psychiatrist does not have sufficient time to make a very complete psychiatric diagnosis, nor do his psychiatric tools provide him with the equipment for an expeditious screening of the patient . . .

In the two mental hospitals studied over a period of three months, the investigator never observed a case where the psychiatrist advised the patient that he did not need treatment. Rather, all persons who appeared at the hospital were absorbed into the patient population regardless of their ability to function adequately outside the hospital.[7]

A comment by Brown suggests that it is a fairly general understanding among mental health workers that state mental hospitals in the U.S. accept all comers.[8]

Kutner, describing commitment procedures in Chicago in 1962, also reports a strong presumption of illness by the staff of the Cook County Mental Health Clinic:

Certificates are signed as a matter of course by staff physicians after little or no examination . . . The so-called examinations are made on an assembly-line basis, often being completed in two or three minutes, and never taking more than ten minutes. Although psychiatrists agree that it is practically impossible to determine a person's sanity on the basis of such a short and hurried interview, the doctors recommend confinement in 77% of the cases. It appears in practice that the alleged-mentally-ill is presumed to be insane and bears the burden of proving his sanity in the few minutes allotted to him . . .[9]

These citations suggest that mental health officials handle uncertainty by presuming illness. To ascertain if the presumption of illness occurred in Midwestern State, intensive observations of screening procedures were conducted in the four courts with the largest volume of mental cases in the state. These courts were located in the two most populous cities in the state. Before giving the results of these observations, it is necessary to describe the steps in the legal procedures for hospitalization and commitment.

STEPS IN THE SCREENING OF PERSONS ALLEGED TO BE MENTALLY ILL

The process of screening can be visualized as containing five steps in Midwestern State:

1. The application for judicial inquiry, made by three citizens. This application is heard by deputy clerks in two of the courts (C and D), by a court reporter in the third court, and by a court commissioner in the fourth court.

2. The intake examination, conducted by a hospital psychiatrist.

3. The psychiatric examination, conducted by two psychiatrists appointed by the court.

4. The interview of the patient by the guardian *ad litem*, a lawyer appointed in three of the courts to represent the patient. (Court A did not use guardians *ad litem*.)

5. The judicial hearing, conducted by a judge.

These five steps take place roughly in the order listed, although in many cases (those cases designated as emergencies) step No. 2, the intake examination, may occur before step No. 1. Steps No. 1 and No. 2 usually take place on the same day or the day after hospitalization. Steps No. 3, No. 4, and No. 5 usually take place within a week of hospitalization. (In courts C and D, however, the judicial hearing is held only once a month.)

This series of steps would seem to provide ample opportunity for the presumption of health, and a thorough assessment, therefore, of the patient's qualifications for involuntary confinement, since there are five separate points at which discharge could occur. According to our findings, however, these procedures usually do not serve the function of screening out persons who do not meet statutory requirements. At most of these decision points, in most of the courts, retention of the patient in the hospital was virtually automatic. A notable exception to this pattern was found in one of the three state hospitals; this hospital attempted to use step No. 2, the intake examination, as a screening point to discharge patients that the superintendent described as "illegitimate," i.e., patients who do not qualify for involuntary confinement.[10] In the other two hospitals, however, this examination was perfunctory and virtually never resulted in a finding of health and a recommendation of discharge. In a similar manner, the other steps were largely ceremonial in character. For example, in court B, we observed twenty-two judicial hearings, all of which were conducted perfunctorily and with lightning rapidity. (The mean time of these hearings was 1.6 minutes.) The judge asked each patient two or three routine questions. Whatever the patient answered, however, the judge always ended the hearings and retained the patient in the hospital.

What appeared to be the key role in justifying these procedures was played by step No. 3, the examination by the court-appointed psychiatrists. In our informal discussions of screening with the judges and other court officials, these officials made it clear that although the statutes give the court the responsibility for the decision to confine or release persons alleged to be mentally ill, they would rarely if ever take the responsibility for releasing a mental patient without a medical recommendation to that effect. The question which is crucial, therefore, for the entire screening process is whether or not the court-appointed psychiatric examiners presume illness. The remainder of the paper will consider this question.

Our observations of 116 judicial hearings raised the question of the adequacy of the psychiatric examination. Eighty-six of the hearings failed to establish that the patients were "mentally ill" (according to the criteria stated by the judges in interviews).[11] Indeed, the behavior and responses of 48 of the patients at the hearings seemed completely unexceptionable. Yet the psychiatric examiners had not recommended the release of a single one of these patients. Examining the court records of 80 additional cases, there was still not a single recommendation for release.

Although the recommendation for treatment of 196 out of 196 consecutive cases strongly suggests that the psychiatric examiners were presuming illness, particularly when we observed 48 of these patients to be responding appropriately, it is conceivable that this is not the case. The observer for this study was not a psychiatrist (he was a first year graduate student in social work) and it is possible that he could have missed evidence of disorder which a psychiatrist might have seen. It was therefore arranged for the observer to be present at a series of psychiatric examinations, in order to determine whether the examinations appeared to be merely formalities or whether, on the other hand, through careful examination and interrogation, the psychiatrists were able to establish illness even in patients whose appearance and responses were not obviously disordered. The observer was instructed to note the examiners' procedures, the criteria they appeared to use in arriving at their decision, and their reaction to uncertainty.

Each of the courts discussed here employs the services of a panel of physicians as medical examiners. The physicians are paid a flat fee of ten dollars per examination, and are usually assigned from three to five patients for each trip to the hospital. In court A, most of the examinations are performed by two psychiatrists, who went to the hospital once a week, seeing from five to ten patients a trip. In court B,

C and D, a panel of local physicians was used. These courts seek to arrange the examinations so that one of the examiners is a psychiatrist, the other a general practitioner. Court B has a list of four such pairs, and appoints each pair for a month at a time. Courts C and D have a similar list, apparently with some of the same names as court B.

To obtain physicians who were representative of the panel used in these courts, we arranged to observe the examinations of the two psychiatrists employed by court A, and one of the four pairs of physicians used in court B, one a psychiatrist, the other a general practitioner. We observed 13 examinations in court A and 13 examinations in court B. The judges in courts C and D refused to give us the names of the physicians on their panels, and we were unable to observe examinations in these courts. (The judge in court D stated that he did not want these physicians harassed in their work, since it was difficult to obtain their services even under the best of circumstances.) In addition to observing the examinations by four psychiatrists, three other psychiatrists used by these courts were interviewed.

The medical examiners followed two lines of questioning. One line was to inquire about the circumstances which led to the patient's hospitalization, the other was to ask standard questions to test the patient's orientation and his capacity for abstract thinking by asking him the date, the President, Governor, proverbs, and problems requiring arithmetic calculation. These questions were often asked very rapidly, and the patient was usually allowed only a very brief time to answer.

It should be noted that the psychiatrists in these courts had access to the patient's record (which usually contained the Application for Judicial Inquiry and the hospital chart notes on the patient's behavior), and that several of the psychiatrists stated that they almost always familiarized themselves with this record before making the examination. To the extent that they were familiar with the patient's circumstances from such outside information, it is possible that the psychiatrists were basing their diagnoses of illness less on the rapid and peremptory examination than on this other information. Although this was true to some extent, the importance of the record can easily be exaggerated, both because of the deficiencies in the typical record, and because of the way it is usually utilized by the examiners.

The deficiencies of the typical record were easily discerned in the approximately one hundred applications and hospital charts which the author read. Both the applications and charts were extremely brief and sometimes garbled. Moreover, in some of the cases where the author and interviewer were familiar with the circumstances involved in the hospitalization, it was not clear that the complainant's testimony was any more accurate than the version presented by the patient. Often the original complaint was so paraphrased and condensed that the application seemed to have little meaning.

The attitude of the examiners toward the record was such that even in those cases where the record was ample, it often did not figure prominently in their decision. Disparaging remarks about the quality and usefulness of the record were made by several of the psychiatrists. One of the examiners was apologetic about his use of the record, giving us the impression that he thought that a good psychiatrist would not need to resort to any information outside his own personal examination of the patient. A casual attitude toward the record was openly displayed in 6 of the 26 examinations we observed. In these 6 examinations, the psychiatrist could not (or in 3 cases, did not bother to) locate the record and conducted the examination without it, with one psychiatrist making it a point of pride that he could easily diagnose most cases "blind."

In his observations of the examinations, the interviewer was instructed to rate how well the patient responded by noting his behavior during the interview, whether he answered the orientation and concept questions correctly, and whether he denied and explained the allegations which resulted in his hospitalization. If the patient's behavior during the interview obviously departed from conventional social standards (e.g., in one case the patient refused to speak), if he answered the orientation questions incorrectly, or if he did not deny and explain the petitioners' allegations, the case was rated as meeting the statutory requirements for hospitalization. Of the 26 examinations observed, eight were rated as Criteria Met.

If, on the other hand, the patient's behavior was appropriate, his answers correct, and he denied and explained the petitioners' allegations, the interviewer rated the case as not meeting the statutory criteria. Of the 26 cases, seven were rated as Criteria Not Met. Finally, if the examination was inconclusive, but the interviewer felt that more extensive investigation might have established that the criteria were met, he rated the cases as Criteria Possibly Met. Of the 26 examined, 11 were rated in this way. The interviewer's instructions were that whenever he was in doubt he should avoid using the rating Criteria Not Met.

Even giving the examiners the benefit of the doubt, the interviewer's ratings were that in a substantial majority of the cases he observed, the examination failed to establish that the statutory criteria were met. The relationship between the examiners' recommendations and the interviewer's ratings are shown in the following table. The interviewer's ratings suggest that the examinations established that the statutory criteria were met in only eight cases, but the examiners recommended that the patient be retained in the hospital

Table 1 / Observer's Ratings and Examiners' Recommendations

Observer's Ratings		CRITERIA MET	CRITERIA POSSIBLY MET	CRITERIA NOT MET	TOTAL
Examiners'	Commitment	7	9	2	18
Recommendations	30-day Observation	1	2	3	6
	Release	0	0	2	2
	Total	8	11	7	26

in 24 cases, leaving 16 cases which the interviewer rated as uncertain, and in which retention was recommended by the examiners. The observer also rated the patient's expressed desires regarding staying in the hospital, and the time taken by the examination. The ratings of the patient's desire concerning staying or leaving the hospital were: Leave, 14 cases; Indifferent, 1 case; Stay, 9 cases; and Not Ascertained, 2 cases. In only one of the 14 cases in which the patient wished to leave was the interviewer's rating Criteria Met.

The interviews ranged in length from five minutes to 17 minutes, with the mean time being 10.2 minutes. Most of the interviews were hurried, with the questions of the examiners coming so rapidly that the examiner often interrupted the patient, or one examiner interrupted the other. All of the examiners seemed quite hurried. One psychiatrist, after stating in an interview (before we observed his examinations) that he usually took about thirty minutes, stated:

"It's not remunerative. I'm taking a hell of a cut. I can't spend 45 minutes with a patient. I don't have the time, it doesn't pay."

In the examinations that we observed, this physician actually spent 8, 10, 5, 8, 8, 7, 17, and 11 minutes with the patients, or an average of 9.2 minutes.

In these short time periods, it is virtually impossible for the examiner to extend his investigation beyond the standard orientation questions, and a short discussion of the circumstances which brought the patient to the hospital. In those cases where the patient answered the orientation questions correctly, behaved appropriately, and explained his presence at the hospital satisfactorily, the examiners did not attempt to assess the reliability of the petitioner's complaints, or to probe further into the patient's answers. Given the fact that in most of these instances the examiners were faced with borderline cases, that they took little time in the examinations, and that they usually recommended commitment, we can only conclude that their decisions were based largely on a presumption of illness. Supplementary observations reported by the interviewer support this conclusion.

After each examination, the observer asked the examiner to explain the criteria he used in arriving at his decision. The observer also had access to the examiner's official report, so that he could compare what the examiner said about the case with the record of what actually occurred during the interview. This supplementary information supports the conclusion that the examiner's decisions are based on the presumption of illness, and sheds light on the manner in which these decisions are reached:

1. The "evidence" upon which the examiners based their decision to retain often seemed arbitrary.

2. In some cases, the decision to retain was made even when no evidence could be found.

3. Some of the psychiatrists' remarks suggest prejudgment of the cases.

4. Many of the examinations were characterized by carelessness and haste.

The first question, concerning the arbitrariness of the psychiatric evidence, will now be considered.

In the weighing of the patient's responses during the interview, the physician appeared not to give the patient credit for the large number of correct answers he gave. In the typical interview, the examiner might ask the patient fifteen or twenty questions: the date, time, place, who is President, Governor, etc., what is 11x10, 11x11, etc., explain "Don't put all your eggs in one basket," "A rolling stone gathers no moss," etc. The examiners appeared to feel that a wrong answer established lack of orientation, even when it was preceded by a series of correct answers. In other words, the examiners do not establish any standard score on the orientation questions, which would give an objective picture of the degree to which the patient answered the questions correctly, but seem at times to search until they find an incorrect answer.

For those questions which were answered incorrectly, it was not always clear whether the incorrect answers were due to the patient's "mental illness," or to the time pressure in the interview, the patient's lack of education, or other causes. Some of the questions used to establish orientation were sufficiently difficult that persons not mentally ill might have difficulty with them. Thus one of the examiners always asked, in a rapid-fire manner: "What year is it? What year was it seven years ago? Seventeen years before that?" etc. Only two of the five patients who were asked this series of questions were able to answer it correctly. However, it is a moot question whether a higher percentage of persons in a household survey would be able to do any better. To my knowledge, none of the orientation questions that are used have been checked in a normal population.

Finally, the interpretations of some of the evidence as showing mental illness seemed capricious. Thus one of the patients, when asked, "In what way are a banana, an orange, and an apple alike?" answered, "They are all something to eat." This answer was used by the examiner in explaining his recommendation to commit. The observer had noted that the patient's behavior and responses seemed appropriate and asked why the recommendation to commit had been made. The doctor stated that her behavior had been bizarre (possibly referring to her alleged promiscuity), her affect inappropriate ("When she talked about being pregnant, it was without feeling,") and with regard to the question above:

> She wasn't able to say a banana and an orange were fruit. She couldn't take it one step further, she had to say it was something to eat.

In other words, this psychiatrist was suggesting that the patient manifested concreteness in her thinking, which is held to be a symptom of mental illness. Yet in her other answers to classification questions, and to proverb interpretations, concreteness was not apparent, suggesting that the examiner's application of this test was arbitrary. In another case, the physician stated that he thought the patient was suspicious and distrustful, because he had asked about the possibility of being represented by counsel at the judicial hearing. The observer felt that these and other similar interpretations might possibly be correct, but that further investigation of the supposedly incorrect responses would be needed to establish that they were manifestations of disorientation.

In several cases where even this type of evidence was not available, the examiners still recommended retention in the hospital. Thus, one examiner, employed by court A stated that he had recommended 30-day observation for a patient whom he had thought *not* to be mentally ill, on the grounds that the patient, a young man, could not get along with his parents, and "might get into trouble." This examiner went on to say:

> We always take the conservative side. [Commitment or observation] Suppose a patient should commit suicide. We always make the conservative decision. I had rather play it safe. There's no harm in doing it that way.

It appeared to the observer that "playing safe" meant that even in those cases where the examination established nothing, the psychiatrists did not consider recommending release. Thus in one case the examination had established that the patient had a very good memory, was oriented and spoke quietly and seriously. The observer recorded his discussion with the physician after the examination as follows:

> When the doctor told me he was recommending commitment for this patient too (he had also recommended commitment in the two examinations held earlier that day) he laughed because he could see what my next question was going to be. He said, "I already recommended the release of two patients this month." This sounded like it was the maximum amount the way he said it.

Apparently this examiner felt that he had a very limited quota on the number of patients he could recommend for release (less than two percent of those examined).

The language used by these physicians tends to intimate that mental illness was found, even when reporting the opposite. Thus in one case the recommendation stated: "No gross evidence of delusions or hallucinations." This statement is misleading, since not only was there no gross evidence, there was not any evidence, not even the slightest suggestion of delusions or hallucinations, brought out by the interview.

These remarks suggest that the examiners prejudge the cases they examine. Several further comments indicate prejudgment. One physician stated that he thought that most crimes of violence were committed by patients released too early from mental hospitals. (This is an erroneous belief.)[12] He went on to say that he thought that all mental patients should be kept in the hospital at least three months, indicating prejudgment concerning his examinations. Another physician, after a very short interview (8 minutes), told the observer:

> On the schizophrenics, I don't bother asking them more questions when I can see they're schizophrenic because *I know what they are going to say.* You could talk to them another half hour and not learn any more.

Another physician, finally, contrasted cases in which the patient's family or others initiated hospitalization ("petition cases," the great majority of cases) with those cases initiated by the court:

> The petition cases are pretty *automatic.* If the patient's own family wants to get rid of him you know there is something wrong.

The lack of care which characterized the examinations is evident in the forms on which the examiners make their recommendations. On most of these forms, whole sections have been left unanswered. Others are answered in a peremptory and uninformative way. For example, in the section entitled Physical Examination, the question is asked: "Have you made a physical examination of the patient? State fully what is the present physical condition," a typical answer is "Yes. Fair," or, "Is apparently in good health." Since in none of the examinations we observed was the patient actually physically examined, these answers appear to be mere guesses. One of the examiners used regularly in court B, to the question "On what subject or in what way is derangement now manifested?" always wrote in "Is mentally ill." The omissions, and the almost flippant brevity of these forms, together with the arbitrariness, lack of evidence, and prejudicial character of the examinations, discussed above, all support the observer's conclusion that, except in very unusual cases, the psychiatric examiner's recommendation to retain the patient is virtually automatic.

Lest it be thought that these results are unique to a particularly backward Midwestern State, it should be pointed out that this state is noted for its progressive psychiatric practices. It will be recalled that a number of the psychiatrists employed by the court as examiners had finished their psychiatric residencies, which is not always the case in many other states. A still common practice in other states is to employ, as members of the "Lunacy Panel," partially retired physicians with no psychiatric training whatever. This was the case in Stockton, California, in 1959, where the author observed hundreds of hearings at which these physicians were present. It may be indicative of some of the larger issues underlying the question of civil commitment that, in these hearings, the physicians played very little part; the judge controlled the questioning of the relatives and patients, and the hearings were often a model of impartial and thorough investigation.

DISCUSSION

Ratings of the qualifications for involuntary confinement of patients newly admitted to the public mental hospitals in a Midwestern state, together with observations of judicial hearings and psychiatric examinations by the observer connected with the present study, both suggest that the decision as to the mental condition of a majority of the patients is an uncertain one. The fact that the courts seldom release patients, and the perfunctory manner in which the legal and medical procedures are carried out, suggest that the judicial decision to retain patients in the hospital for treatment is routine and largely based on the presumption of illness. Three reasons for this presumption will be discussed: financial, ideological, and political.

Our discussions with the examiners indicated that one reason that they perform biased "examinations" is that their rate of pay is determined by the length of time spent with the patient. In recommending retention, the examiners are refraining from interrupting the hospitalization and commitment procedures already in progress, and thereby allowing someone else, usually the hospital, to make the effective decision to release or commit. In order to recommend release, however, they would have to build a case showing why these procedures should be interrupted. Building such a case would take much more time than is presently expended by the examiners, thereby reducing their rate of pay.

A more fundamental reason for the presumption of illness by the examiners, and perhaps the reason why this practice is allowed by the courts, is the interpretation of current psychiatric doctrine by the examiners and court officials. These officials make a number of assumptions, which are now thought to be of doubtful validity:

1. The condition of mentally ill persons deteriorates rapidly without psychiatric assistance.
2. Effective psychiatric treatments exist for most mental illnesses.
3. Unlike surgery, there are no risks involved in involuntary psychiatric treatment: it either helps or is neutral, it can't hurt.
4. Exposing a prospective mental patient to questioning, cross-examination, and other screening procedures exposes him to the unnecessary stigma of trial-like procedures, and may do further damage to his mental condition.
5. There is an element of danger to self or others in most mental illness. It is better to risk unnecessary hospitalization than the harm the patient might do himself or others.

Many psychiatrists and others now argue that none of these assumptions are necessarily correct.

1. The assumption that psychiatric disorders usually get worse without treatment rests on very little other than evidence of an anecdotal character. There is just as much evidence that most acute psychological and emotional upsets are self-terminating.[13]
2. It is still not clear, according to systematic studies evaluating psychotherapy, drugs, etc., that most psychiatric interventions are any more effective, on the average, than no treatment at all.[14]
3. There is very good evidence that involuntary hospitalization and social isolation may affect the patient's life: his job, his family affairs, etc. There is some evidence that too hasty exposure to psychiatric treatment may convince the patient that he is "sick," prolonging what might have been an otherwise transitory episode.[15]
4. This assumption is correct, as far as it goes. But it is misleading because it fails to consider what occurs when the patient who does not wish to be hospitalized is forcibly treated. Such patients often become extremely indignant and angry, particularly in the case, as often happens, when they are deceived into coming to the hospital on some pretext.

5. The element of danger is usually exaggerated both in amount and degree. In the psychiatric survey of new patients in state mental hospitals, danger to self or others was mentioned in about a fourth of the cases. Furthermore, in those cases where danger is mentioned, it is not always clear that the risks involved are greater than those encountered in ordinary social life. This issue has been discussed by Ross, an attorney:

A truck driver with a mild neurosis who is "accident prone" is probably a greater danger to society than most psychotics; yet, he will not be committed for treatment, even if he would be benefited. The community expects a certain amount of dangerous activity. I suspect that as a class, drinking drivers are a greater danger than the mentally ill, and yet the drivers are tolerated or punished with small fines rather than indeterminate imprisonment.[16]

From our observations of the medical examinations and other commitment procedures, we formed a very strong impression that the doctrines of danger to self or others, early treatment, and the avoidance of stigma were invoked partly because the officials believed them to be true, and partly because they provided convenient justification for a pre-existing policy of summary action, minimal investigation, avoidance of responsibility and, after the patient is in the hospital, indecisiveness and delay.

The policy of presuming illness is probably both cause and effect of political pressure on the court from the community. The judge, an elected official, runs the risk of being more heavily penalized for erroneously releasing than for erroneously retaining patients. Since the judge personally appoints the panel of psychiatrists to serve as examiners, he can easily transmit the community pressure to them, by failing to reappoint a psychiatrist whose examinations were inconveniently thorough.

Some of the implications of these findings for the sociology of deviant behavior will be briefly summarized. The discussion above, of the reasons that the psychiatrists tend to presume illness, suggests that the motivations of the key decision-makers in the screening process may be significant in determining the extent and direction of the societal reaction. In the case of psychiatric screening of persons alleged to be mentally ill, the social differentiation of the deviant from the non-deviant population appears to be materially affected by the financial, ideological, and political position of the psychiatrists, who are in this instance the key agents of social control.

Under these circumstances, the character of the societal reaction appears to undergo a marked change from the pattern of denial which occurs in the community. The official societal reaction appears to reverse the presumption of normality reported by the Cummings as a characteristic of informal societal reaction, and instead exaggerates both the amount and degree of deviance.[17] Thus, one extremely important contingency influencing the severity of the societal reaction may be whether or not the original deviance comes to official notice. This paper suggests that in the area of mental disorder, perhaps in contrast to other areas of deviant behavior, if the official societal reaction is invoked, for whatever reason, social differentiation of the deviant from the non-deviant population will usually occur.

CONCLUSION

This paper has described the screening of patients who were admitted to public mental hospitals in early June, 1962, in a Midwestern state. The data presented here suggest that the screening is usually perfunctory, and that in the crucial screening examination by the court-appointed psychiatrists, there is a presumption of illness. Since most court decisions appear to hinge on the recommendation of these psychiatrists, there appears to be a large element of status ascription in the official societal reaction to persons alleged to be mentally ill, as exemplified by the court's actions. This finding points to the importance of lay definitions of mental illness in the community, since the "diagnosis" of mental illness by laymen in the community initiates the official societal reaction, and to the necessity of analyzing social processes connected with the recognition and reaction to the deviant behavior that is called mental illness in our society.

Notes

1. John I. Kitsuse, "Societal Reaction to Deviant Behavior: Problems of Theory and Method," *Social Problems*, 9 (Winter, 1962), pp. 247–257.

2. Edwin M. Lemert, *Social Pathology*, New York: McGraw-Hill, 1951; Erving Goffman, *Asylums*, Chicago: Aldine, 1962.

3. For a more general discussion of the presumption of illness in medicine, and some of its possible causes and consequences, see the author's "Decision Rules, Types of Error and Their Consequences in Medical Diagnosis," *Behavioral Science*, 8 (April, 1963), pp. 97–107.

4. Hugh Allen Ross, "Commitment of the Mentally Ill: Problems of Law and Policy," *Michigan Law Review*, 57 (May, 1959), pp. 945–1018.

5. This is the typical phrasing in cases in the *Dicennial Legal Digest*, found under the heading "Mental Illness."

6. Goffman, *op. cit.*, pp. 155, 159.

7. David Mechanic, "Some Factors in Identifying and Defining Mental Illness," *Mental Hygiene*, 46 (January, 1962), pp. 66–75.

8. Esther Lucile Brown, *Newer Dimensions of Patient Care*, Part I, New York: Russell Sage, 1961, p. 60, fn.

9. Luis Kutner, "The Illusion of Due Process in Commitment Proceedings," *Northwestern University Law Review*, 57 (Sept. 1962), pp. 383–399.

10. Other exceptions occurred as follows: the deputy clerks in courts C and D appeared to exercise some discretion in turning away applications they considered improper or incomplete, at step No. 1; the judge in Court D appeared also to perform some screening at step No. 5. For further description of these exceptions see "Rural-Urban Differences in the Judicial Screening of the Mentally Ill in a Midwestern State." (In press)

11. In interviews with the judges, the following criteria were named: Appropriateness of behavior and speech, understanding of the situation, and orientation.

12. The rate of crimes of violence, or any crime, appears to be less among ex-mental patients than in the general population. Henry Brill and Benjamin Maltzberg, "Statistical Report Based on the Arrest Record of 5354 Ex-patients Released from New York State Mental Hospitals During the Period 1946–48." Mimeo available from the authors; Louis H. Cohen and Henry Freeman, "How Dangerous to the Community Are State Hospital Patients?", *Connecticut State Medical Journal*, 9 (Sept. 1945), pp. 697–700; Donald W. Hastings, "Follow-up Results in Psychiatric Illness," *Amer. Journal of Psychiatry*, 118 (June 1962), pp. 1078–1086.

13. For a review of epidemiological studies of mental disorder see Richard J. Plunkett and John E. Gordon, *Epidemiology and Mental Illness*. New York: Basic Books, 1960. Most of these studies suggest that at any given point in time, psychiatrists find a substantial proportion of persons in normal populations to be "mentally ill." One interpretation of this finding is that much of the deviance detected in these studies is self-limiting.

14. For an assessment of the evidence regarding the effectiveness of electroshock, drugs, psychotherapy, and other psychiatric treatments, see H. J. Eysenck, *Handbook of Abnormal Psychology*, New York: Basic Books, 1961, Part III.

15. For examples from military psychiatry, see Albert J. Glass, "Psychotherapy in the Combat Zone," in *Symposium on Stress*, Washington, D.C., Army Medical Service Graduate School, 1953, and B. L. Bushard, "The U.S. Army's Mental Hygiene Consultation Service," in *Symposium on Preventive and Social Psychiatry*, 15–17 (April 1957), Washington, D.C.: Walter Reed Army Institute of Research, pp. 431–43. For a discussion of essentially the same problem in the context of a civilian mental hospital, cf. Kai T. Erikson, "Patient Role and Social Uncertainty—A Dilemma of the Mentally Ill," *Psychiatry*, 20 (August 1957), pp. 263–275.

16. Ross, *op. cit.*, p. 962.

17. Elaine Cumming and John Cumming, *Closed Ranks*, Cambridge, Mass: Harvard University Press, 1957, 102; for further discussion of the bipolarization of the societal reaction into denial and labeling, see the author's "The Role of the Mentally Ill and the Dynamics of Mental Disorder: A Research Framework," *Sociometry*, 26 (December, 1963), pp. 436–453.

29 / Three Models of Organizational Corruption in Agencies of Social Control

LAWRENCE W. SHERMAN

One of Sutherland's greatest contributions to the sociological study of crime was his conception of organizations as deviant actors. Yet for almost forty years this contribution was all but ignored. Partly because Sutherland (1940, 1949) was inconsistent and contradictory in his use of the concept (Shapiro, 1976), and partly because sociologists of crime have been preoccupied with explaining the behavior of individuals, Sutherland's critics have been able to discredit the concept of deviant organizations as "economic anthropomorphism" (Geis, 1962). Bloch and Geis, for example, flatly pronounce that, "For the purposes of criminological analysis, ... corporations cannot be considered persons" (1970:306). This narrow position not only ignores a major problem for inquiry into such central criminological concerns as violence and theft (Schrager and Short, 1978), it also ignores one of the most consequential shifts in the social structure of Western societies over the past several centuries: the emergence of organizations as the most powerful "persons" in society (Coleman, 1973, 1974).

In recent years, however, a growing number of sociologists have either employed or implied the concept of organizations as criminal or deviant actors, in both conceptual discussions (Reiss, 1966; Wheeler, 1976; Ermann and Lundman, 1978; Schrager and Short, 1978; Shover, 1978) and in research on such problems as consumer fraud in auto repairs (Leonard and Weber, 1970), police corruption (Sherman, 1978; Lundman, 1979) and occupational safety violations (Pearson, 1978). The concept of organizational deviance has become more widely accepted, but it has rarely been treated as a variable. Very little of the existing work on organizational deviance has attempted to explain why some organizations and not others engage in deviant conduct, or why some commit more deviant acts than others. The one theoretical framework that has been employed to answer this question, strain theory, was adapted from the individual level of explanation (Merton, 1968; Chapter VI), and it often fits the facts it is used to explain; but the strain theory explanations have been necessarily confined to organizational deviance involving the use of illegitimate means to achieve societally legitimate goals. *Organizational deviance involving the adoption of societally illegitimate organizational goals has yet to be explained.* The apparently growing social problem of corporations that lose money or go bankrupt through planned internal or external exploitation, religious organizations that deprive their members of liberty and life, and other organizations that *invert* (and not just displace) their manifest socially approved goals still await sociological examination as a general phenomenon.

One fertile area for developing theories of why organizations adopt deviant goals is the broad category of agencies of official social control, defined as those organizations empowered by society to deprive people and organizations of their material wealth, their liberty or their lives.[1] The extensive literature on the corruption of social control agencies provides some basic descriptive material in which patterns of the adoption of deviant goals may be observed. After defining social control corruption and distinguishing its individual from its organizational forms, I present three models of the processes by which social control agencies adopt corrupt gain as an organizational goal and suggest some hypotheses about the conditions under which each model typically occurs. First, however, the unavoidable threshold issue that has stymied so much work on organizational deviance must be addressed: whether organizations are real actors.

ARE ORGANIZATIONS REAL, MORAL ACTORS?

The long dominant sociological view of organizations is that they have no reality apart from the existence of their members (Simon, 1964). More recent sociological discussions of organizations, however, speak of "the reality of organizations . . . as independent of their members" (Aldrich, 1979:2) derived from their ability to generate the actions of individuals (Hall, 1977:23–27), so that strictly organizational factors account for part of the behavior of individuals at all times in organizations. In this restated position in a very old debate (cf. Warriner, 1956), organizations can be said to act when individual agents (cf. Coleman, 1974) of the organization act under the influence of organizational factors. Since their actions are real, organizations can logically be labeled as conforming to or deviating from moral norms.

Whatever the philosophic objections might be to treating organizations as moral actors (e.g., Rawls, 1971:505), organizations are clearly defined as real in modern society. The legal system, for example, while struggling with several competing theories of how corporations are morally responsible for their acts, leaves no doubt that organizations are indeed to be held morally responsible for their acts, leaves no doubt that organizations are indeed to be held morally responsible; juries have even convicted corporations of crimes while acquitting individual corporate officers for the same offenses (Harvard Law Review, 1979b). Journalistic treatments and everyday language follow this conception. As Cohen (1966:21) points out, even philosophers and sociologists, when not engaged in disputing the reality of organizations, "do not doubt that the gas company" overcharged them or that "the university is not paying them what they are worth." The fact that much action in modern society is organizational action suggests that a conception of organizations as moral actors ought, at the least, to be admitted to the sociological floor for discussion; and the first question might well be why some organizations become corrupt.

DEFINING ORGANIZATIONAL CORRUPTION

The definitions of corruption in government vary widely among social scientists. Some definitions center on public office, while others use market situations or conceptions of the public interest, and other elements (Heidenheimer, 1970:4–6). The narrower category of corruption in agencies of social control may be most usefully defined in relation to the authority of public office (Goldstein, 1975:3–5; Sherman, 1978:30), but all of the definitions include the element of private gain (usually financial, although power, prestige and perquisites could be included) for individuals who exercise that authority. Those individuals include both the officials in whom the authority is formally vested and others who control those officials by participating in the agency's dominant administrative coalition.

As Thompson (1967:128) defines it, the dominant coalition is a process (not an entity) in which certain individuals powerful enough to participate in any given decision determine the operative organizational goals:

> Almost inevitably this includes organizational members, but it may also incorporate significant outsiders. . . . In this view, organizational goals are established by individuals—but interdependent individuals who collectively have sufficient control of organizational resources to commit them in certain directions and withhold them from others (1967:128).

Corrupt acts by agents of social control may thus be defined as *the illegal misuse of public authority by social control agents resulting in private gain for the agents or others participating in the agency's dominant coalition.* This definition admittedly suffers from ambiguity about the key terms of "misuse" and its "resulting" in private gain. The term "misuse" opens the definition to a variety of conceptions of the public interest, and the term "result" belies the often complex causal connection between official decisions and private gain. A regulatory official, for example, who makes a decision favorable to a private corporation's interest and takes a highly paid position with that company five years later illustrates both problems. The example also illustrates the inadequacy of relying on official rules for a definition since the behavior in question is generally construed as perfectly legal and proper, but the broad legal definitions of bribery could conceivably be used to punish the behavior as illegal (see generally, Harvard Law Review, 1979a).

This definition explicitly rejects a definition of corruption as illicit attainment of organizational gain. The violation of laws in order to preserve or enhance the power or domain of an organization is an important social problem, and one which is often found in agencies of social control. But it is a distinct problem, with possibly distinct causes, from the problem of illicit attainment of individual gain.

The boundaries of a definition of corruption are no more or less clearly defined than the boundaries of definitions of all crime and deviance.[2] Yet the definition of corruption probably enjoys more consensus than the choice of criteria for distinguishing organizational deviance from individual deviance in organizations. Several definitions of organizational deviance have been suggested, but none of them has been widely adopted.

One definition of organizational deviance suggests that four characteristics would have to be present in order for social control corruption to be organizational rather than individual (Ermann and Lundman, 1978:7–9); the actions must be: (1) supported by the internal operating norms of an organization; (2) justified to new organizational members through a process of socialization inculcating those norms; (3) supported by fellow workers in the organization; and (4) supported by the dominant administrative coalition of the organization. This definition of organizational deviance repeats Sutherland's error of confusing elements of causation with the elements of the behavior itself (Shapiro, 1976). Operating norms (which can vary widely from one organizational unit to the next), organizational socialization into a deviant activity, and peer group support may all help to explain why organizational deviance occurs, but those characteristics are neither necessary nor useful for distinguishing organizational from individual deviance. All three characteristics apply to crimes committed *against* organizations by their employees, such as systematic employee theft (Mars, 1973), as well as to crimes committed by employees on *behalf of* their organizations, such as price-fixing (Geis, 1977). Only the fourth element of this definition (support by the dominant coalition) is essential for distinguishing deviance committed by individuals as representatives of the organization from deviance committed by individuals as personal actors.

Another definition relies only on the support of the organization's dominant coalition to determine whether deviance is organizational or individual (Sherman, 1978:4–5), a position consistent with at least one legal theory (Harvard Law Review, 1979b:1250–1251). Whether a deviant act is committed against, within, or on behalf of an organization is thus defined by the operative or "real" goals of the organization, as distinct from the manifest or formal goals, and not by the nature of the act itself. Under this definition, employee theft from the organization, for example, would be individual deviance committed against the organization as long as the organization's operative goal set by the dominant coalition is to maximize profits (or for governmental and nonprofit agencies, to keep down costs). But where employee theft is consistent with an operative organizational goal of maintaining internal harmony through "informal rewards" (Dalton, 1959: Chapter 7; Conklin, 1977:68) or of exploiting the organization's resources for the personal benefit of organizational employees (Raw *et al.*, 1972), then it would constitute organizational deviance. The objective behavior is the same, but the different operative goals set by the dominant coalition define the consequences of the behavior for the organization's interests differently at any given point in time.

When an individual acts "on behalf" of an organization, then, he or she is acting in accordance with the dominant coalition's operative goals. Thus it might seem appropriate to employ Shover's definition of organizational crime:

> . . . criminal acts committed by individuals or groups of individuals . . . during the normal course of their work as employees of organizations, which they intend to contribute to the achievement of goals or other objectives thought to be important for the organization as a whole, some subunit within the organization, or their own particular duties (1978:39).

It is difficult or impossible, however, to assess an individual's intent, even with direct observation of behavior, either sociologically (Shapiro, 1976) or in a criminal prosecution (Schrager and Short, 1978:409–410). It is possible to observe communications from the dominant coalition to organizational members, and to observe whether the member's behavior is consistent with those messages. A more practicable operational definition of organizational crime, then, is:

> Illegal acts of omission or commission committed by an individual or a group of individuals in a legitimate formal organization in accordance

with the operative goals of the organization, which have a serious physical or economic impact on employees, consumers or the general public (Schrager and Short, 1978:411–412).

Rather than asking who benefits, the latter definition is more concerned with who is harmed and how much, something that is much easier to assess. The virtue of this definition, however, is also its failing. By including only clear cut cases of such serious harm as the Buffalo Creek Mining Disaster (Erikson, 1976), the definition excludes many deviant and criminal[3] acts which actually cause physical or economic harm to no one, either because they do not have the potential to do so or because they did not have that result. Many forms of corruption in social control agencies would be excluded by the Schrager and Short definition. Police bribe-taking to allow gambling is a clear example: a bribe taken by a Food and Drug Administration official to approve a new drug that had not been adequately tested but which did not turn out to have harmful effects would be another. But the criterion of serious harm is only relevant to the definition of deviant acts *per se;* it does not affect their distinction between individual and organizational action on the basis of operative organizational goals.

Three of the four definitions of organizational deviance (Ermann and Lundman, 1978; Schrager and Short, 1978; Sherman, 1978), then, rely on the concept of operative organizational goals set by the dominant administrative coalition to distinguish individual and organizational action, and the fourth definition (Shover, 1978) implies a similar distinction. By combining this distinction with the admittedly provisional definition of social control corruption suggested above, organizational corruption in agencies of social control may be defined as *the illegal misuse of public authority in accordance with operative organizational goals for the private gain of social control agents or others participating in the agency's dominant administrative coalition.*

THEORIES OF ORGANIZATIONAL DEVIANCE

Given this definition of organizational corruption, the central problem is why some social control organizations and not others adopt operative goals consistent with corruption, or even adopt corruption itself as an operative goal. This is a very different problem from the one addressed by existing theories of specific types of organizational deviance, most of which are confined to strain theory explanations of the organizational use of societally illegitimate means in accordance with societally legitimate organizational goals. For business organizations, the usual problem for explanation is why some and not others break the law in order to achieve the societally legitimate goal of making a profit (Lane, 1953; Leonard and Weber, 1970; Farberman, 1975; Geis, 1977; Sonnenfeld and Lawrence, 1978).[4] For government organizations, the usual problem for explanation is why some and not others break the law in attempting to achieve such legitimate public interest goals as maintaining order (Marx, 1972).

None of these theories, however, can explain why a corporation would abandon the goal of profit making in order to milk corporate assets for the personal gain of organizational employees, or why a nursing home would abandon the goal of providing health care to the elderly in order to enrich its owners, or why a police department would abandon the goal of enforcing the law in favor of the goal of profiting from the sale of nonenforcement. Nor, for that matter, can the traditional theories of goal displacement, in which "an instrumental value becomes a terminal value" (Merton, 1968:253) or the imperatives of organizational survival "may lead to unanticipated consequences resulting in a deflection of original goals" (Selznick, 1949:259), explain the adoption of deviant goals. The displacement of one societally legitimate goal with another, such as the Tennessee Valley Authority's substitution of private land development for its original goal of conservation through public ownership, may enhance rather than threaten an organization's survival; but that is not necessarily the case for the adoption of a societally illegitimate goal. Even if the adoption of that goal enhances short-term prospects for survival and growth, in the long run it may make the organization vulnerable to punishment and even destruction.

The problem of organizational corruption in official agencies of social control is unlike any other problem for which theories have already been suggested, and is part of a larger gap in the sociology of organizational deviance. As a problem of organizational behavior, it may be better understood with three concepts taken from the sociology of formal organizations: co-optation, capture and shelter. Each of these concepts provides the basis for a model of how social control agencies become organizationally corrupt.

MODEL I: CO-OPTATION OF SUBJECTS OF CONTROL

One common pattern of social control corruption is co-optation: the participation of the subjects of social control in the policy-making process of the agency. Corruption in federal regulatory agencies is most often described in this manner, but local police departments sometimes fit this pattern as well. The colloquial usage of the concept implies that the subjects of control, threatened by the possibility that the control agencies will force them to cease their activity, "co-opt" the control agency by making control agents identify with the interests of the subjects of control. This imagery underlies the conventional interpretation of such behavior as Securities and Exchange Commission employees accepting free trips and hotel rooms from securities industry groups (Conklin, 1977:123) or the "revolving door" through which employees of regulated industries move into regulatory agency employment and back again, as did more than half of the people appointed to nine of the federal regulatory agencies during 1970–75 (Burnham, 1975). Such "links" between the regulated and the regulators are said to reduce the effectiveness of the control process (Conklin, 1977:123, Skolnick, 1978:159–167).

Both the concept of co-optation and this model of social control corruption are actually much more subtle than the conventional imagery. As Selznick (1949:13) originally defined it, "co-optation is the process of absorbing new elements into the leadership or policy-determining structure of an organization as a means of averting threats to its stability or existence," with the consequence that the organization's character, role and operative goals may be modified. It is not the social control agencies which are co-opted; the regulators may pose a threat to the existence of the regulated, but there is little evidence that, for example, the Mafia families or other businesses absorb social control agents into their leadership structures. Rather, in this model the reverse is true: the regulated pose a threat to the regulators, and the regulators absorb the regulated into their policy-making process of regulation.

To have the regulated threaten the regulators when the power of societally legitimated coercion is on the side of the regulators may be counter-intuitive, but it makes sense from a sociological view of organizations. The regulated's threat derives from the organizational imperatives of the regulators. In order to accomplish (or appear to accomplish, through the production of enforcement statistics) their formal goal of regulation, the regulators may require expertise or information that is available only from the regulated (Wheeler, 1976). If the regulated withhold the information, expertise, or other resources that regulators require for accomplishing their formal goals, they may threaten the stability or survival of the regulators (Leavitt *et al.*, 1978:271). In order to be assured of the resources for accomplishing their formal goals, the regulators may absorb the regulated into their policy-making structure. Once absorbed, however, the regulated may not only displace the formal goals of the regulators, they may also invert them completely, inducing the social control agency to adopt the deviant goal of selling its enforcement power.

Local police detectives, for example, have always depended on burglars for the information necessary to arrest other burglars and to recover stolen property (Skolnick, 1966:126–137). In order to accomplish these legitimate formal goals, detectives develop close personal relationships with burglars—not unlike, in some respects, the relations of federal regulatory agents and those they regulate. Through these relationships, (which Thompson, 1967:35, describes as "contracting," not "co-opting") the burglars help, in a sense, to make enforcement policy, through such decisions as who will be arrested and who will not. The burglar-informants are often made to feel that they are a part of the police department (Skolnick, 1966: 130). The fact that the detectives overlook their minor misdeeds (Westley, 1970:39) does not constitute misuse of public authority for private gain, so the relationship itself cannot be termed corrupt. Sometimes such relationships can go further, with detectives "licensing" burglars to operate in certain territories without fear of arrest in exchange for cash payments (Steffens, 1931:222–223; Sutherland, 1937:117) or even helping burglars to plan burglaries in order to split the reward for recovery of the stolen goods (Laurie, 1970:214). Where such actions are in accordance with the operative goals of the social control agency (our criterion for distinguishing organizational and individual behavior), they constitute organizational corruption. The legitimate formal goal of arresting burglars may still be operative, but it takes second place to the illegitimate goal of profit through the sale of nonenforcement.

Similarly, when the Securities and Exchange Commission (SEC) was founded in 1934 to develop and enforce corporate financial reporting standards, its principal goal was to help stabilize the economy by preventing price manipulation and ruinous speculation, and by providing investors with reliable information. The financial community in general, and the accounting profession in particular, was so opposed to the SEC that it threatened to go on "strike" by halting capital investment and refusing to file audits (Chatov, 1975). In order to appear to be ensuring that investors receive reliable information, the SEC gave up its public mandate to develop corporate financial reporting standards to the private sector. Moreover, the SEC has also depended on the accounting and financial sector for expertise, a dependence reflected in the ancient principle that "it takes a thief to catch a thief." Just as the famous thief Eugene Francois Vidocq was hired in restoration France to establish the first centralized Criminal Investigation Division of the French Police and staff it with criminals (Stead, 1957:94), President Roosevelt and his successors have appointed corporate lawyers and accountants to both the staff and the Commissionerships of the SEC. Whether the "revolving door" of employment between the SEC and the private sector means that every

SEC decision is made with a view to private gain is subject to debate, but there are those who would label such behavior as organizational corruption.

That it is often the regulated who threaten the regulators is further supported by the history of other federal independent regulatory agencies. The standard assumption that the regulatory agencies were all created to control deviance in a recalcitrant industry may only be true for some of the agencies, such as the Interstate Commerce Commission (Chatov, 1975:97; but see Stone, 1975:107; and Skolnick, 1978:166). Many others were created with the active support of the industries themselves in order to insure predictability and stable profits (Conklin, 1977:122). Both the Civil Aeronautics Board and the Federal Communications Commission, for example, have been described as having been "established by the regulated industries to operate a cartel in their behalf, and both have behaved according to the expectations of their creators, restricting entry and maintaining prices and industry profits" (Chatov, 1975:97).

Similarly, some gangsters have been able to use local police departments to guarantee themselves a monopoly on the local vice and gambling industries. Dependent on gangsters such as "Wincanton's" Irv Stern (Gardiner, 1970:23) for campaign contributions necessary to get elected, Mayors and City Council members sometimes allow the gangsters to set law enforcement policy and to choose top police officials. The high police officials then misuse their public authority for their own personal gain (in payoffs from the gangsters), but lower level officers may be compelled to misuse their public authority for the personal gain of the elective officials and their police superiors, not themselves (Gardiner, 1970:25; Sherman, 1978:36). The elective officials' dependence on campaign contributions leads them to co-opt the gangsters who then make corruption an operative organizational goal of the police department.

MODEL II: CAPTURE BY EXTERNAL EXPLOITERS OF CONTROL

A second pattern of social control corruption is capture: the exploitation of the agency's authority for the financial gain of outsiders who control significant resources of the agency. Unlike the co-optation of gambling organizations and airlines which use social control agencies as tools to restrict competition and to maintain price levels, politicians capture social control agencies to use them as marketable commodities. While some politicians may be so dependent on one source of campaign contributions (such as "Wincanton's" gangster boss, Irv

Stern) that they are forced to co-opt that source, others may have a variety of sources of campaign funds interested in the policies and practices of the social control agencies under the control of elective officials. Under those conditions, politicians need not co-opt anyone; they can sell control policy to the highest bidder, sometimes even on a case by case basis.

The exploitation of control power for the financial gain of politicians is only possible when the politicians have "captured" the control agency (Thompson, 1967:30, 37). That is, it is only when the politicians—either elective officials or party leaders (or any other environmental actors controlling organizational resources, for that matter)—have such complete power to constrain almost any action by the social control agency that the captors can market those actions. Not all social control agencies are captives of their environments. Some of them, including all of those described below under Model III, have a good deal of autonomy and insulation from environmental domination. Others may generally operate without interference, but they have the potential for capture whenever elective officials or others choose to interfere. Still others are directed on almost a day to day basis by elective and political party officials.

The basic tool of capture is control over jobs, both how many there will be and who will fill them. Enforcement personnel comprise the vital resource of social control agencies, and the loyalties of the personnel selected can do much to shape the character of those organizations. Where this resource is largely under the control of the agency itself, capture seems to be very rare. Where it is under the control of another autonomous agency, such as a civil service commission, capture also seems rare. But where elective and party officials obtain direct control over personnel, capture of the social control agency appears to be quite common.

The classic case of selling the law enforcement decisions of a captive social control agency is the politically-dominated corrupt police department. As described by Royko (1972), Fogelson (1977) and Sherman (1978), these police departments vary somewhat in the precise form of their political domination, but in all of them some aspects of the personnel process are controlled by outsiders and are used to influence enforcement decisions. In the nineteenth century police departments Fogelson (1977) describes, the political machines determined every aspect of every police officer's career, from hiring to assignment and promotion. In Sherman's (1978:35) study of the contemporary "Central City" Police Department, however, only promotions and assignments (and not hiring) were found to be under political control; and his study of the Oakland Police Department of the early 1950s found only assignment to be subject to political influence. Nevertheless, in each of these cases, patrol officers were or-

dered by their superiors to ignore law violations at certain vice establishments that paid the politicians controlling the police departments for the privilege to operate without police interference.[5]

While some police departments may be under the day to day direction of political figures for corrupt purposes, other social control
agencies may only occasionally be captured for corrupt exploitation.
In the U.S. Justice Department, for example, few antitrust prosecution decisions seem to be influenced by attempts of the President or
his party leaders to sell the decisions to the organizations they threat-
en. Yet during the antitrust prosecution of International Telephone
and Telegraph for its acquisition of the Hartford Fire Insurance
Company, former President Nixon did just that: he directly ordered
the (presidentially appointed) Attorney General not to prosecute the
case, and negotiated a sizable campaign contribution from I.T.T. at
about the same time (New York Times, 1974). Similar campaign contributions to the Nixon administration in return for aid in the federal
prosecution of the contributor occurred with the S.E.C. (Sale,
1977:248) and other regulatory agencies, although the evidence of
direct capture of the decision-making process by the President is less
clear in those cases.

Even without blatant sale of particular decisions, of course, Presidents and their political aides can sell regulatory authority to regulated industries. When Nixon aide Herbert Kalmbach solicited corporate contributions for the 1972 campaign, he allegedy forced the corporations to give much more than they had planned by threatening
to use the regulatory agencies against their interests (New York
Times, 1973). Whether all such threats could have been implemented may be open to some question, given the civil service selection
and tenure of regulatory agency employees (though not of the commissioners or board members); but judging by the Nixon administration's apparently successful capture of the National Transportation
Safety Board—by installing what one career civil servant described
as the "the White House Mafia, the guys who were put in these agencies to get rid of people like me" (Berger, 1977:244)—the threats may
well have been deliverable. If *any* of the enforcement decisions were
influenced by the campaign contributions, then that behavior clearly
constituted organizational corruption.

MODEL III: DOMINATION BY INTERNAL
EXPLOITERS OF CONTROL

The political capture of social control agencies would not surprise the
good-government reformers of the progressive era, whose solution to
that problem was to insulate the agencies from political influence as

much as possible. What would surprise them, however, is that even highly autonomous agencies of social control have adopted deviant goals and become organizationally corrupt. The dominant administrative coalitions of these "sheltered" (Thompson, 1967:152) organizations[6] have been taken over by organizational members who support the goal of personally profiting from the sale of law enforcement decisions. Where organizational members do not have to compete with outside captors, they may take advantage of the opportunity to exploit the power of official control of their own personal gain.

Certain police departments provide a classic example of this pattern. They also show how the autonomy necessary for this process of becoming corrupt need not be entirely formal or legal in nature. In New York City, for example, the historically corrupt police department has apparently been free from political capture for the sale of law enforcement decisions since Mayor O'Dwyer was almost indicted during a gambling payoff scandal in the early 1950s (Mockridge and Prall, 1954). The department went right on selling enforcement immunity for the gain of its own members, however, even after the political involvement ceased (Knapp, 1972). Even during the heyday of Tammany Hall, for that matter, the New York police were able to attain a fair amount of autonomy from political capture, apparently keeping the lion's share of the graft within the department (Steffens, 1931:248).

The Cincinnati Police Department would surprise the progressives even more. Restructured according to their ideal plan to provide almost complete isolation from politics, that department provided for civil service selection and promotion up to and including the rank of chief. Even the City Manager cannot remove the police chief except for cause, a structure that has been strongly endorsed by the International Association of Chiefs of Police (1976). For years, Cincinnati was widely reputed in police circles to have one of the most honest police departments in the country (Reppetto, 1970), a fact attributed to its great autonomy. In 1975, however, nine police officers alleged that a police chief had been selling arrest immunity to a number of vice establishments and directing enforcement policy accordingly (New York Times, 1975); the chief was later convicted on related criminal charges. The chief apparently imposed deviant operative goals on the organization despite its apparent climate of integrity and (or perhaps because of) its great autonomy.

The federal-level law enforcement agencies, such as the Federal Bureau of Investigation and the Drug Enforcement Agency, have also experienced the same pattern of organizational corruption. Renowned for the high "quality" and college education of their agents as well as their general freedom from political interference, federal police agencies are often thought of as being above corruption. Yet that is far from true. The federal Drug Enforcement Agency has had a continuing problem of organizational corruption since the 1930s (Epstein, 1977:104–105). Similar problems have been found in the U.S. Immigration and Naturalization Service (New York Times, 1973). In one of the most extreme cases of organizational autonomy in federal law enforcement, the Federal Bureau of Investigation (which makes all its own personnel decisions internally) has recently lost its corruption-free image in a series of allegations from FBI agents (Crewdson, 1979; New York Times, 1979).

Internal domination by exploiters of control is not confined to police agencies. Civil service building inspectors in New York City, working without any political control, developed an almost universal practice of extorting bribes for issuing certificates of occupancy (Shipler, 1972), for which the majority of the building inspectors working in Manhattan between 1972 and 1974 were indicted (Ranzal, 1974). Grain inspectors officially licensed by the U.S. Department of Agriculture have developed a pattern of taking bribes to overlook violations (Robbins, 1975). Wherever organizations combine regulatory powers and a relatively sheltered system of organizational control from within, the potential for this pattern of corruption seems to be present.

PREDICTING THE MODELS

These three models demonstrate that there are a variety of conditions under which social control agencies adopt deviant operative goals and become organizationally corrupt. The brief illustrative material presented here probably identifies only a few of the possible conditions, and certainly fails to identify all of the necessary conditions of each model. As a first step towards explaining organizational corruption in social control agencies, however, three hypotheses can be induced from the models:

H_1: The more social control agencies depend upon their subjects to accomplish their formal goals, the more likely it is that organizational corruption will arise, if at all, through co-optation of the subjects of control.

H_2: The more vulnerable social control agencies' personnel decisions are to external manipulation, the more likely it is that organizational corruption will arise, if at all, through external capture of the agencies for the sale of enforcement decisions.

H_3: The more sheltered social control agencies are from dependence on outsiders, the more likely it is that organizational corruption will arise, if at all, through internal domination by sellers of enforcement decisions.

None of these hypotheses can predict *whether* a social control agency will become organizationally corrupt; they merely predict the model by which corruption would occur if it did arise. Indeed, hypotheses 2 and 3, if used to predict corruption, would lead to contradictory predictions: both an open system (H_2) and a closed system (H_3) will lead to organizational corruption. What is missing from both the hypotheses and the models is specification of the conditions under which threatened agencies do *not* corruptly co-opt their subjects of control, under which agencies with externally controlled personnel decisions are *not* captured by politicians, and under which highly autonomous agencies are *not* dominated by internal exploiters of regulatory authority. The concepts taken from the sociology of organizations help us understand why each of the models occur, but they do not explain why corruption does not occur when the conditions of each model are present.

The additional conditions needed to predict whether a social control agency will become corrupt might be drawn from a variety of types of explanation of crime borrowed from the individual level of analysis: differences in deterrence (Gibbs, 1975), opportunities to commit crime (Wilkins, 1965), or perhaps even the strength of organizational bonds to conventional social norms (Hirschi, 1969). Alternatively, explanations of organizational goal setting stressing the political economy of organizations (Zald, 1970) and organizational conflict (Pfeffer, 1978) might be applied, although this explanatory perspective is even further away from being a theory than are explanations of individual criminality (Perrow, 1972).

Whatever direction theories of the organizational adoption of deviant operative goals may take, there would seem to be two priorities for theory construction. First, criminological concepts that apply only to the individuals must be separated from those appropriate for both levels of analysis. Sutherland once pointed out (in the unfair context of attempting to discredit psychoanalytic theory as an explanation of any crime) that it is unlikely that "the crimes of the Ford Motor Company are due to the Oedipus Complex, or those of the Aluminum Company of America to an Inferiority Complex" (1949:257). Yet there are many concepts used to explain individual crime, from commitment to stigma, which may well be applicable at the organizational level as well. The second task for theory construction is to identify those concepts which are only applicable at the organizational level of analysis. With more attention to such distinctively organizational issues as control of resources, conflicts over goals and the formation of dominant coalitions, as well as to the relevant explanations of individual crime, we may begin to understand the causes as well as the forms of organizational deviance.

References

Aldrich, Howard E.
   1979   Organizations and Environments. Englewood Cliffs, N.J.: Prentice-Hall.
Berger, Dan
   1977   "Lethal smokescreen," Pp. 238–249 in J. D. Douglas and J. D. Grant (eds.), Official Deviance. Philadelphia: J.B. Lippincott.
Black, Donald
   1979   "Comment: Common sense in the sociology of law." American Sociological Review 44(1):18–27.
Bloch, Herbert A. and Gilbert Geis
   1970   Man, Crime and Society. New York: Random House.
Burnham, David
   1975   "Duality of appointments to U.S. agencies scored." The New York Times, November 7:14.
Chatov, Robert
   1975   Corporate Financial Reporting: Public or Private Control? New York: Free Press.
Cohen, Albert K.
   1966   Deviance and Control. Englewood Cliffs, N.J.: Prentice-Hall.
Coleman, James S.
   1973   "Loss of power." American Sociological Review 38:1–17.
   1974   Power and the Structure of Society. New York: W. W. Norton.
Conklin, John E.
   1977   'Illegal But Not Criminal': Business Crime in America. Englewood Cliffs, N.J.: Prentice-Hall.
Crewdson, John M.
   1979   "Former FBI agent tells investigators of widespread abuse and corruption." New York Times, January 20:8.
Dalton, Melville
   1959   Men Who Manage. New York: J. W. Wiley.
Epstein, Edward J.
   1977   Agency of Fear: Opiates and Political Power in America. New York: G. P. Putnam.
Erikson, Kai T.
   1976   Everything in Its Path: Destruction of Community in the Buffalo Creek Flood. New York: Simon and Schuster.
Ermann, M. David and Richard Lundman (eds.)
   1978   Corporate and Governmental Deviance: Problems of Organizational Behavior In Contemporary Society. New York: Oxford University Press.
Farberman, Harvey

1975   "A criminogenic market structure: The automobile industry." Sociological Quarterly 16:438–57.

Fogelson, Robert
1977   Big City Police. Cambridge: Harvard University Press.

Gardiner, John A.
1970   The Politics of Corruption: Organized Crime in an American City. New York: Russell Sage Foundation.

Geis, Gilbert
1962   "Toward a delineation of white collar offenses." Sociological Inquiry 32 (Spring): 159–171.
1977   "The heavy electrical equipment antitrust cases of 1961." Pp. 117–
[1967] 132 in G. Geis and R. F. Meier (eds.), White Collar Crime: Offenses in Business, Politics and the Professions. New York: Free Press.

Gibbs, Jack
1975   Crime, Punishment, and Deterrence. New York: Elsevier.

Goldstein, Herman
1975   Police Corruption: A Perspective on Its Nature And Control. Washington, D.C.: Police Foundation.

Gottfredson, Michael R. and Michael J. Hindelang
1979a   "A study of the behavior of law." American Sociological Review 44(1):3–18.
1979b   "Response: Theory and research in the sociology of law." American Sociological Review 44(1):27–37.

Hall, Richard H.
1977   Organizations: Structure and Process (2d. ed.). Englewood Cliffs, N.J.: Prentice-Hall.

Harvard Law Review
1979a   "Campaign contributions and federal bribery law." Harvard Law Review 92(2):451–469.
1979b   "Corporate crime: Regulating corporate behavior through criminal sanctions." Harvard Law Review 92(6):1227–1375.

Heidenheimer, Arnold J.
1970   Political Corruption: Readings in Comparative Analysis. New York: Holt, Rinehart and Winston.

Hirschi, Travis
1969   Causes of Delinquency. Berkeley: University of California Press.

International Association of Chiefs of Police
1976   The Police Chief Executive Report. Washington, D.C.: U.S. Law Enforcement Assistance Administration.

Knapp, Whitman et al.
1972   Report of the Commission to Investigate Allegations of Police Corruption and the City's Anti-Corruption Procedures. New York: Braziller.

Lane, Robert E.
1977   "Why businessmen violate the law." Pp. 102–111 in G. Geis and R. Meier (eds.), White Collar [1953] Crime. New York: Free Press.

Laurie, Peter
1970   Scotland Yard: A Personal Inquiry. London: The Bodley Head.

Leavitt, Harold J., William R. Dill and Henry B. Eyring
    1978   "Rulemakers and referees." Pp. 259–277 in M. D. Ermann and R. J. Lundman (eds.), Corporate and Governmental Deviance. New York: Oxford University Press.
Leonard, William N. and Marvin Glenn Weber
    1977   "Automakers and dealers: A study of criminogenic market forces." Pp. 133–148 in G. Geis and [1970] R. Meier (eds.), White Collar Crime. New York: Free Press.
Levett, Alan E.
    1975   "Centralization of city police in the nineteenth century United States." Doctoral dissertation, Department of Sociology, University of Michigan.
Lundman, Richard
    1979   "Police misconduct as organizational deviance." Law and Policy Quarterly 1(1):81–100.
Mars, Geralds
    1973   "Hotel pilferage: A case study in occupational theft." Pp. 200–210 in Malcolm Warner (ed.), Sociology of the Workplace: An interdisciplinary Approach. London: Allen and Unwin.
Marx, Gary T.
    1972   "Civil disorder and the agents of social control." Pp. 75–97 in Gary T. Marx (ed.). Muckraking Sociology. New Brunswick, N.J.: Transaction Books.
Merton, Robert K.
    1968   Social Theory and Social Structure, New York: Free Press.
Mockridge, Norton and Robert H. Prall
    1954   The Big Fix. New York: Henry Holt.
New York Times
    1979   "Ex-agent, alleging cover-up, sues FBI." Feb. 18:23.
    1975   "Jury indicts chief." Dec. 19:20.
    1974   "Kleindienst admits misdemeanor." May 17:1.
    1973   "Airline discloses illegal donation." July 7:1.
    1973   "Justice officials find corruption rife." May 21:1.
Parisi, Anthony J.
    1979   "Oil giants are worrying all the way to the bank." New York Times, March 11:3–1, 11.
Pearson, Jessica S.
    1978   "Organizational response to occupational injury and disease: The case of the uranium industry." Social Forces 57(1):23–41.
Perrow, Charles
    1972   Complex Organizations: A Critical Essay. Glenview, Ill.: Scott, Foresman.
Pfeffer, Jeffrey
    1978   "The micropolitics of organizations." Pp. 29–50 in Marshall W. Meyer and Associates, Environments and Organizations. San Francisco: Jossey-Bass.
Ranzal, Edwards
    1974   "City report finds building industry infested by graft." New York Times, November 8:1.

Raw, Charles, Godfrey Hodgson and Bruce Page
  1972   Do You Sincerely Want to Be Rich? Bernard Kornfeld and I.O.S.:
         An International Swindle. Newton Abbot: Readers Union.
Rawls, John
  1971   A Theory of Justice. Cambridge, Mass.: Harvard University Press.
Reiss, Albert J., Jr.,
  1966   "The study of deviant behavior: Where the action is." The Ohio
         Valley Sociologist 32:1–12.
Reppetto, Thomas A.
  1970   "Changing the system: Models of municipal police organization."
         Doctoral dissertation, Harvard University.
Robbins, William
  1975   "Europe grain men press complaints." The New York Times, June
         6:1, 36.
Royko, Mike
  1972   Boss: Richard J. Daley of Chicago. London: Paladin.
Sale, Kirkpatrick
  1977   "The world behind Watergate." Pp. 240–252 in G. Geis and R.
         Meier (eds.), White Collar Crime. New York: Free Press.
Schrager, Laura Shill and James F. Short, Jr.
  1978   "Toward a sociology of organizational crime." Social Problems
         25(4):407–419.
Selznick, Philip
  1949   TVA and the Grass Roots: A Study in the Sociology of Formal Orga-
         nization. Berkeley: University of California Press.
Shapiro, Susan
  1976   "A background paper on white collar crime." Unpublished manu-
         script, Yale University.
Sherman, Lawrence W.
  1978   Scandal and Reform: Controlling Police Corruption. Berkeley: Uni-
         versity of California Press.
Shipler, David K.
  1972   "Study finds $25 million yearly in bribes is paid by city's construc-
         tion industry." The New York Times, June 26: 1, 26.
Shover, Neal
  1978   "Defining organizational crime." Pp. 37–40 in M. D. Ermann and
         R. J. Lundman (eds.), Corporate and Governmental Deviance. New
         York: Oxford University Press.
Simon, Herbert A.
  1964   "On the concept of organizational goal." Administrative Science
         Quarterly 9(1):1–22.
Skolnick, Jerome H.
  1966   Justice Without Trial: Law Enforcement in Democratic Society.
         New York: Wiley.
  1978   House of Cards: The Legalization and Control of Casino Gambling.
         Boston: Little, Brown.
Sonnenfeld, Jeffrey and Paul R. Lawrence
  1978   "Why do companies succumb to price-fixing?" Harvard Business
         Review 56(4):145–157.

Stead, Philip John
  1957   The Police of Paris. London: Staples.
Steffens, Lincoln
  1931   Autobiography. New York: Harcourt, Brace.
Stone, Christopher D.
  1975   Where the Law Ends: The Social Control of Corporate Behavior.
          New York: Harper & Row.
Sutherland, Edwin H.
  1937   The Professional Thief. Chicago: University of Chicago Press.
  1940   "White collar criminality." American Sociological Review 5:1–12.
  1945   "Is 'white collar crime' crime?" American Sociological Review 10
          (April): 132–139.
  1949   White Collar Crime. New York: Holt, Rinehart and Winston.
Tappan, Paul
  1947   "Who is the criminal?" American Sociological Review 12 (Febru-
          ary):96–102.
Thompson, James D.
  1967   Organizations in Action. New York: McGraw-Hill.
Warriner, Charles K.
  1956   "Groups are real: A reaffirmation." American Sociological Review
          21 (5):549–554.
Westley, William A.
  1970   Violence and the Police. Cambridge, Mass.: Massachusetts Institute
          of Technology Press.
Wheeler, Stanton
  1976   "Trends and problems in the sociological study of crime." Social
          Problems 23 (5):525–534.
Wilkins, Leslie T.
  1965   Social Deviance. London: Tavistock.
Zald, Mayer N.
  1970   Organizational Change: The Political Economy of the YMCA. Chi-
          cago: University of Chicago Press.

Notes

1. While it is often observed that organizations cannot be put in jail, they can be deprived of life (Coleman, 1974).

2. For evidence that problems of definition are still very much alive, see the exchange between Black (1979) and Gottfredson and Hindelang (1979a,b) with regard to victimization data.

3. By excluding illegal behavior that does not have a serious physical or economic impact, Schrager and Short solved the persistent problem of whether to call acts punishable by merely civil penalties "crime" (Sutherland, 1945; Tappan, 1947). In the process, however, they have allowed their own value judgment about impact to determine what will be labeled a crime, thereby violating the principle evident in their injunction not to "label some legal actions as criminal on moral grounds" (1978:412). Instead, they opted to use moral grounds to label some criminal actions as noncriminal.

4. The legitimacy of profit making, of course, is by no means universal, and a deviant label is now often applied to "excessive" profit levels, such as those of the oil companies (Parisi, 1979) during the energy crisis of 1973. But the idea of profit itself, it

seems, is still far from being defined as deviant by a majority of the American public.

5. A question beyond the scope of this paper is the nature of the process by which organizations are captured. In the case of urban police departments, however, the answer is very simple: they were created as captive organizations by the white Anglo-Saxon Protestant political machines which first established them to control the newer immigrants (Levett, 1975). The more interesting question, perhaps, is the nature of the process by which police departments were successfully liberated from external capture (see Fogelson, 1977; Sherman, 1978).

6. These organizations are, of course, still open to a variety of influences, but they are sheltered from direct external control of personnel promotions and assignments.

30 / Ironies of Social Control: Authorities as Contributors to Deviance Through Escalation, Nonenforcement and Covert Facilitation

GARY T. MARX

Many current theoretical approaches to deviance causation tend to neglect a crucial level of analysis: the specific interactive context within which rule breaking occurs. Anomie (Merton, 1957) and subcultural theorists (Sutherland and Cressey, 1974) and combinations of these approaches (Cloward and Ohlin, 1960) tend to focus on rather abstract initial group properties such as opportunity structures and norms, rather than on the interactive group processes out of which behavior emerges. Those questioning the mechanistic force of such variables nevertheless stress the independence of the deviant as a maker of choices (Matza, 1966).

Even when attention is given to situational aspects of rule breaking, as with some functionalists, the focus tends to be too mechanistic. In what can be called the trampoline model of social control (Homans, 1950; Parsons, 1951), norm violations lead to reparative social control responses. Social controllers are thought to be in a relentless struggle with autonomous criminals, who freely choose to violate the law, and who always do what they are charged with having done. The systemic and reciprocal effects become most apparent *after* the deviance appears. In contrast (and closer to the perspective to be developed here), theorists such as Reiss (1951) and Hirschi (1969) see social control as an important variable in the production of deviance. However, they argue that it is the absence of social control that helps to explain deviance. I shall argue that its *presence* does too.

Whatever merit the above approaches may have for dealing with various aspects of deviance, they must be supplemented by a theoretical perspective which focuses on the immediate context of the rule infraction. Such a perspective must at least take as an empirical question the degree of autonomy in the actions of the rule violator, and whether people actually do what they are charged with having done.

413

In current theories the deviant is seen either as autonomous or as a pawn of broad social and cultural forces. Most interpretations tend to reify the categories of authority and "criminal" and to draw the line between them too sharply. They miss the interdependence that may exist between these groups and the extent to which authorities may induce or help others to break the law, be involved in law breaking themselves, or create false records about others' supposed law breaking. Conversely, the extent to which those engaged in illegal activities may be contributing to social order is also ignored. Here I focus on some neglected aspects of the role of authorities in law violations.

The idea that authorities may play a role in generating deviance is not new. Clearly, the labeling perspective has focused attention on the role of authorities—for example, the work of Tannenbaum (1938), Kitsuse (1962), Becker (1963), Wilkins (1965), Scheff (1966), Lemert (1951, 1972) and Hawkins and Tiedeman (1975). In such work, authorities have been seen to "create" deviance by defining some of a wide range of behavior as illegal, using their discretion about which laws will then be most actively enforced, and singling out some of those who violate these laws for processing by the criminal justice system. Subsequent restrictions on the behavior of those processed as deviants, such as their being singled out for special attention by authorities, and subsequent changes in their self-images, are thought to result in their becoming even more involved in deviant activities.

These are not, however, the roles that authorities play in creating deviance on which I wish to focus. Much of the labeling argument is true by definition; that which isn't seems plausible enough and has the easy virtue of overlapping with the underdog world view of many who hold it, though systematic research in its support cannot be said to be overwhelming (Manning, 1973; Wellford, 1975; Gove, 1980). Yet even if subsequent evidence suggests that labeling as such does not, on balance, amplify deviance and even deters it, I think a strong case can still be made for the important role of authorities.

I do begin at an abstract level with what I see to be a fundamental insight of the labeling perspective: the possible irony of social controllers creating what they set out to control. But then I emphasize a different set of factors. In spite of its calling attention to the role of authorities, the emphasis in the labeling approach is usually placed on what authorities do to others already known or thought to be deviant. Its main concern is with secondary rather than primary deviance. Its usual focus is not on the behavior of control agents before or during the rule breaking, nor on the degree of autonomy in the actions of the rule breaker. Nor is its usual focus even on whether the deviance actually occurred, preferring instead, in Rains' (1975: 10) words, "to describe the full process of imputation without regard for warrant." But here I will deliberately focus on infraction—on some of the ways in which it is shaped or induced by prior or concomitant actions of authorities, and on some of the causes involved.[1]

Situations where social control contributes to, or even generates, rule-breaking behavior include these three ideal types:

A) Escalation (by taking enforcement action, authorities unintentionally encourage rule breaking).
B) Nonenforcement (by strategically taking *no enforcement action,* authorities intentionally permit rule breaking).
C) Covert facilitation (by taking *hidden or deceptive enforcement action,* authorities intentionally encourage rule breaking).

These are analytic distinctions. In a given empirical instance all may be present.

In much of the rest of the paper I discuss these types of social control. I use examples from criminal justice situations primarily, but believe the processes are also evident in other social settings, such as the school, family and work.

Documents and published accounts are major sources. However, I have also drawn on interviews and observations made over a seven-year period in 18 U.S. police departments while studying community police patrols, community service officers, civilian police planners, and performance measures, plus those made during a year spent studying English and French police. My initial interest in the topic grew out of work done for the Kerner Commission in 1968 on police behavior in civil disorders.

ESCALATION

The clearest cases of authorities contributing to rule breaking involve escalation. As with facilitation, authorities' intervention is conducive to deviance. However, secrecy need not be involved (the facilitation can be overt), and the final consequence is generally not consciously, or at best publicly, sought by controllers when they initially enter the situation.[2] It is not simply that social control has no effect, rather that it can amplify. (In the language of cybernetics, this is a case of deviation amplifying feedback [Cf. Maruyama, 1963]—in everyday language, snowballing or mushrooming.) In escalation the very process of social control directly triggers violations. In urging that attention be focused on the deviant act as such, Cohen has written:

> The history of a deviant act is a history of an interaction process. The antecedents of the act are an unfolding sequence of acts contributed by a set of actors (1965:9).

Nowhere is this logic clearer than in the case of escalation. Five major analytic elements of escalation are:

1) An increase in the *frequency* of the original violations.
2) An increase in the *seriousness* of violations, including the greater use of violence.
3) The appearance of *new* categories of violators and/or victims (without a net diminution of those previously present).
4) An increase in the commitment, and/or skill and effectiveness of those engaged in the violation.
5) The appearance of violations whose very definition is tied to social control intervention.

Escalation may stem from initial or postapprehension enforcement efforts.

Police involvement in family conflict, crowd, and automobile chase situations can contribute to violations when none were imminent, or it can increase the seriousness of these situations. In responding to challenges to their authority or to interpersonal conflict situations, preemptive police actions (euphemistically called by some with a sardonic smile, "constructive coercion" and "preventive violence") may lead to further violence.

A three-year study of police-citizen incidents in New York City notes that "the extent to which the handling of relatively minor incidents such as traffic violations or disorderly disputes between husbands and wives seemed to create a more serious situation than existed prior to the police attempt to control the situation" (McNamara, 1967). Family disturbance calls are an important source of police injuries to citizens and vice versa. Bard has similarly observed that "there is more than ample evidence that insensitive, untrained, and inept police management of human problems is a significant breeding ground for violence" (1971:3). Certain styles of intervention are likely to provoke aggressive responses.

An English policeman characterized the 1960s' riot control behavior of American police in some cities as "oilin' the fire." Police responses to crowd situations offer many examples of escalation (Marx, 1970; Stark, 1972). Provocative overreaction (referred to by another English policeman as "cracking a nut with a sledgehammer") can turn a peaceful crowd into a disorderly one. In the 1967 riot in New Haven, for example, a small group of angry but as yet law-abiding blacks marched in the street—to be met by police tear gas; this then provoked a small riot. Or in Detroit a small riot emerged during the Poor People's March when, during a meeting in a large hall, police inside the building tried to push people outside, at the same time that mounted police outside were trying to push people back inside. Such police reactions and subsequent arrests may occur in the most benign of circumstances, such as at sporting events or concerts.

High-speed chases offer another all too tragic example. They result in injuries, in death, and often in manslaughter charges against persons who, in the absence of the chase, might have faced minimal or no charges. For example, in a Boston suburb, a car being chased by two police cruisers at speeds of 95 miles an hour killed a footpatrolman. The young driver of the car was subsequently charged not only with speeding but with manslaughter. The same day a 15-year-old youth facing manslaughter charges hung himself in a jail in a nearby town. He was arrested the week before, following a high-speed chase in which his car killed two people (*Boston Globe,* November 21, 1975). The high-speed chase, perhaps because of the risks and emotions involved and the denial of police authority, also figures disproportionately in situations where prisoners are abused. The escalation here has second-order effects, coming to involve new offenders (police themselves) as well as new offenses (e.g., assault and denial of civil rights).

One consequence of strong enforcement actions can be to change the personnel and social organization of those involved in illegal activities. For example, stepped-up enforcement efforts with respect to heroin and cocaine appear to have moved the drug traffic away from less sophisticated and skilled local, often amateur, groups to more highly skilled, centralized, better organized criminal groups (Young, 1971; Sabbag, 1976; Adler *et al.,* forthcoming). The greater skill and sophistication of those now drawn into the activity may mean the development of new markets. Increased risks may mean greater profits, as well as incentives to develop new consumers and markets. The more professional criminals are more likely to be able to avoid prosecution and are in a better position to induce police corruption.

Increased corruption, a frequent escalatory consequence of stepped-up enforcement efforts, is one of a number of second-order forms of illegality which may indirectly appear. Even attacking corruption may generate other problems. Thus, following reform efforts in one city (Sherman, 1978: 257), police morale declined and citizen complaints went up sharply, as did police use of firearms. In Boston a recent increase in high-speed chases and attendant offenses and injuries is directly traceable to an order to enforce traffic laws more stringently. Another second-order effect can be seen in the monopoly profits which may accrue to those who provide vice in a context of strong enforcement pressures. These profits can be invested in still other illegal activities. Thus, some of the tremendous profits earned by organized crime groups that emerged during prohibition, and the skills developed then, went into gambling, labor racketeering and narcotics. Violence may increase among criminal groups contending for new monopoly profits. Their monopoly may also have been aided by informing on competitors. The increased cost of the product they provide may mean increased illegality on the part of customers facing higher prices (Schur, 1965). A link between drug addiction and street crime, for example, has often been argued.

Authorities may directly provide new resources which have unintended effects. Part of the increased homicide rates in the 1970s, for example, particularly among minority youths, has been attributed to vastly augmented amounts of federal "buy" money for drugs. This increased the opportunity for youths to become informers, and some of them were subsequently killed. The drugs, stolen goods, money, weapons, and tips sometimes given to informers and others who aid police may be used in subsequent crimes. A more benign resource may be the youth workers sent to work with gangs in their environment. Some of the detached street-worker programs, aimed at reducing gang delinquency, may have actually increased it: by strengthening identification with the gang, they made it more cohesive and encouraged new recruits (Klein, 1969). Klein observes that the assumed advantages of group work with gangs are "mythical," and he advocates abandoning standard detached worker programs. In Chicago, antipoverty funds for self-help programs among gangs offered resources, opportunities and incentives which created a context for fraud, extortion and violence (Short, 1974).

Contemporary American law has evolved an increasing number of crimes which emerge solely as an artifact of social control intervention. These emerge incidentally to efforts to enforce other laws. If authorities had not taken action, the offense would not have been committed. Resisting arrest or assaulting an officer are familiar examples. The prosecution of white-collar crimes offers a different example.

Prosecutors who initially set out to make cases of corruption, fraud, or food and drug violatons may be unable to prove the targeted crime, yet still be able to prosecute for perjury or obstruction of justice. The latter violations become possible only after an investigation begins, and can exist regardless of the quality of evidence for the case the prosecutor originally hoped to make.

More routine are white-collar offenses involving the violation of requirements imposed on citizens to aid in the investigation of still other crimes. In and of themselves the violations need not produce social harm. In the effort to detect and sanction infractions the criminal justice system can promote crimes because of its own need for information. Failing to file reports or filing a false statement to the U.S. government are examples. Failure to file an income tax form is a crime even if one owes no taxes.[3]

Most of the escalation examples considered here have involved the initial enforcement effort and one point in time. The work of Wilkins (1965) and that of Lemert (1951, 1972) call attention to postapprehension escalation and a person's "career" as a deviant. Wilkins sees a spiraling interactive process whereby rule breaking leads to sanctioning, which then leads to more serious rule breaking, which in turn leads to more serious sanctioning and so on. Lemert focuses on how people may change their lives and self-conceptions in response to being formally processed, punished, stigmatized, segregated or isolated. To the extent that their lives and identities come to be organized around the facts of their publicly labeled deviance, they are secondary deviants.

However, postapprehension escalation can occur without an accelerating spiral or changes in self-image. Having been apprehended for one offense, or identified as a rule violator, can set in motion actions by authorities that make additional violations more likely. For one thing, contact with the criminal justice system may alter one's status (e.g., to probationer, inmate or parolee) so that one is guilty of a misdemeanor or felony for acts that would be legally inoffensive if committed by others. In addition, being placed in such statuses may provide actors with inducements to the comission of a crime, either by way of opportunity or pressure, to which others are not exposed.

Among the most poignant and tragic examples of escalation are those that emerge from the application of the initial sanction. Prisoners, such as George Jackson, who are sent up at a young age for a short term, then who find their sentences continually lengthened because of their behavior in prison, are clear examples. According to one study, only 6 of 40 offenses punishable in one state prison would be misdemeanors or felonies if done outside (Barnes and Teeters, 1959, as cited in Lemert, 1972: 81). Similarly, violation of some of the regulations faced by those on parole or probation can send them to prison, but the same acts are not illegal when done by others.

For those not yet in prison, the need to meet bail and expensive legal fees can exert pressure to obtain such funds illegally. Clarence Darrow reported the case of a young thief who wanted the famous lawyer to defend him. Darrow asked if he had any money. The young man said, "No," and then with a smile said he thought he could raise some by that evening. An undercover narcotics detective (more taken by the seeming stupidity of those he arrests than of the system that generates their behavior) reports, "I even make buys again from guys who I've arrested and come right back out to make some fast bread for their expenses in court" (Schiano, 1974: 93). There seems to be the possibility of infinite regress here.

Escalation is of course only one form that the interdependence and reciprocal influences among rule breakers and enforcers can take. It is treated here because of its irony. A more common form is probably displacement (without a significant increase or decrease in infractions). Displacement may occur with respect to other types of rule breaking, rule breakers, victims, place and procedure (Reppetto, 1975a).

Social control actions may unintentionally generate functional alternatives. The relationship between controllers and controlled may often be characterized as a movable equilibrium. As in sports or any competitive endeavor, new strategies, techniques and resources may give one side a temporary advantage, but the other side tends to find ways to neutralize, avoid or counter them. The action may become more sophisticated, practitioners more skilled, and the nature of the game may be altered—but the game does not stop. A saying among Hong Kong drug dealers in response to periodic clampdowns captures this nicely: "Shooting the singer is no way to stop the opera."

NONENFORCEMENT

In nonenforcement, the contribution of authorities to deviance is more indirect than with escalation or covert facilitation. Rule breaking does not expand unintentionally and authorities do not set people up and covertly facilitate it. Instead, those involved in nonenforcement relationships (e.g., with police) may break rules partly because they believe they will not be appropriately sanctioned. Here we have an exchange relationship between police and offenders. Offenders perform services for police; in return they are allowed to break rules and may receive other benefits.

When it is organized and specialized, nonenforcement is the most difficult of the three forms of interdependence to identify empirically. As a strategy it is often illegal and is more likely to be hidden. One does not find conditions for its use spelled out in policy manuals. Indeed the opposite is more apt to be true. In prohibiting nonenforcement, training and policy guidelines often go to great lengths to point out its dangers. Police are sworn to uphold the law: not to do so may involve them in malfeasance, aiding and abetting a felon, compounding a felony, perjury, and a host of other violations. Some anticorruption policies are from one perspective antinonenforcement policies. They seek to create conditions that will work against collusive nonenforcement relations; at the same time the realities of the police job are such that it emerges as a major fact of police life.

Obtaining reliable information on this process is difficult. Police sometimes deny its existence, and almost always deny its possible criminogenic implications, while their critics may exaggerate them. The existence of nonenforcement cannot be denied, although given the absence of systematic research, there is much room for disagreement about its extensiveness and its net consequences.[4] My purpose here is to analyze it as an ideal-typical category which sometimes has crime-generative effects.

Nonenforcement may literally involve taking no enforcement action, passing on information regarding police and criminal activities (including tips on raids), using improper procedures that will not stand up in court, offering ineffective testimony, helping a person facing charges to obtain leniency, giving gifts of contraband, and taking enforcement action against competitors. While there is sometimes overlap, we can differentiate "self-interested nonenforcement" involving traditional police corruption from "principled nonenforcement"—of most interest here—where police actions are thought to serve broader organizational goals.[5] Nonenforcement or leniency can be an important resource that authorities offer to those engaged in rule breaking whose cooperation they need. It is protected by the legitimate discretion in the police role and the United States' comparatively high standards of proof and rules of evidence required for conviction.

Police may adopt a policy of nonenforcement with respect to 1) informants who give them information about the law breaking of others and/or help in facilitating the controlled commission of a crime; 2) vice entrepreneurs who agree to keep their own illegal behavior within agreed upon bounds; 3) individuals who either directly regulate the behavior of others using resources police lack or means they are denied, or who take actons desired by authorities but considered too politically risky for them to undertake.

A former director of the FBI states, "Without informants we're nothing" (*New York Times*, April 16, 1974). The informant system, central to many types of law enforcement, is a major source of nonenforcement. Informants can offer police a means of getting information and making arrests that cannot come from other sources, given strictures against electronic surveillance, search and seizure, coercion, and the difficulty of infiltration. In return the system can work to the advantage of rule breakers. In the words of an FBI agent known for his ability to cultivate informants among those in organized crime:

> They [informants] worked with agents because it was profitable for them: They avoided prison, got reduced sentences or parole for friends and relatives, maybe enjoyed some revenge against guys who had betrayed them, and picked up informer fees and some very substantial sums in the way of

rewards paid by insurance companies delighted to refund five percent in return for saving the ninety-five percent liability (Villano, 1977:103).

The system can be used by both police and informants as a form of institutionalized blackmail. Potentially damaging action such as arrest or denouncement of someone as an informant or offender is withheld as long as the cooperation sought is forthcoming.

The tables can also get turned, as the informant manipulates the control agent into corrupt activities (or merely acquieses in the agent's desire for these). For example, in the case of drugs, the exchange of immunity or drugs for information can, in a series of incremental changes, lead to joint marketing and other criminal ventures (Commission, 1972). The nonenforcement may become mutual and the balance of power shift. The informant not only controls the flow of information but could even threaten exposure, which may entail greater risk for the police officer than for the drug dealer (Moore, 1977; Karchmer, 1979).

Where the informant is involved in the controlled commission of a crime, social control actions may generate rule breaking in two ways. Criminogenic effects may be present because police ignore illegal activities of the informant. But they may also be present because informants covertly facilitate the rule breaking of others. Informants facing charges or desiring drugs, for example, may have strong incentives to facilitate others' deviance.[6]

Louis Tackwood, an informant for the Los Angeles Police Department for ten years, worked first in traditional crime and later in radical politics. He appears to have committed numerous crimes, yet never to have been sentenced. He recalls:

> I never worried about getting caught. It was the idea of the money, the free crime. Here's a cat, a person, who like me has been successful in forming several organizations for crime. Here are the police officers telling me, hey, we want you to work for us. Two things went through my mind then—money and I got a free hand to do anything I want to do (Citizens Commitee and Tackwood, 1973:24).

In more muted terms, a former commander of detectives in Chicago hints at how the informant system in a context of secrecy and specialization may work at cross-purposes:

> The burglary detectives may be inclined to "pass" a junkie with a small amount of drugs if he can turn up stolen property, while the narco squad will forget a few nickel and dime burglaries in return for cooperation in apprehending a major peddler. Homicide investigators looking for information on a murder will view a busy prostitute only as a source of information (Reppetto, 1976b).

People often become informants while in jail, or facing arrest. Sentencing may be deferred for a period of time while the informant "works off" the charges (for example, see Cloyd, 1979). In some police circles this is known as "flipping" or "turning" a man. With respect to drug enforcement, in some cities a point system is used whereby the informant receives one point for each marijuana purchase and two points for the purchase of harder drugs. If the informant earns a fixed number of points, such as ten, charges will be dropped. There is no doubt considerable variation *among* departments and *within*. Accounts such as that offered by Tackwood are perhaps best treated as ideal-typical illustrations.

The practice of police foregoing prosecution in return for information is more common than granting the informant a wild license to burglarize. Even here, the prior knowledge that one may be able to trade information for leniency can be conducive to law violations. Individuals sometimes manage to avoid arrest by falsely claiming that they are informants.

The exchange system is most highly developed for drugs. Something of a *de facto* license to deal may be offered ("you don't look too close at him"). To be useful the informant must be close to or involved in capering. In commenting on large transactions a detective observes, "Any junk dealer that you work with as an informant is moving junk when you're working with him. It has to be. You can't waste time chasing after some churchgoing Mary. If he's selling onions, what's he gonna tell you? The only way he can know what's coming down is if he's doing business." In this case the arrangement was "one for three." "For every load he gives you, he moves three." The rationale is clearly stated (Grosso and Rosenberg, 1979:55): "If he gives us one, it's one we wouldn't have had otherwise, right?"

The system occasionally is reproduced as a means of internal control. The Knapp Commission (1972) in New York offered leniency to corrupt police in return for their cooperation in catching other police. See Schecter and Phillips (1974), Daley (1978), and Grosso and Rosenberg (1979) for some of the ambiguities surrounding this procedure.

Certain occupational categories such as the fence have historically involved the informant's role (Klockars, 1974). The fence may offer information to the police, can return stolen goods—and in the case of thief takers, such as Jonathan Wild, even directly apprehend thieves, while receiving a degree of immunity and police help in regulating their clientele and employees.

The major vice control strategy at the turn of the century was one of containment, and it is still important. In what would only seem a contradiction to the outside observer, late nineteenth century police in many cities had written rules governing how houses of prostitution and gambling were to be run, though these were clearly illegal. Some vice entrepreneurs took pride in the honest quality of the services they provided. The very extensive Lexow hearings (Senate Committee, 1895) on the New York police show how they systematically licensed gambling, prostitution and police activities (Steffens, 1957, offers a classic discussion).

In return for noninterference from police (often further bought by the payment of bribes), vice entrepreneurs may agree to engage in self-policing and operate with relative honesty (i.e., run orderly disorderly houses), restrict their activities to one type of vice, stay in a given geographical area, and run low-visibility operations. By favoring certain vice operators and cooperating with them to keep others out, police may introduce a degree of control and stability into what would otherwise be a chaotic cutthroat situation. Establishing a peaceful racket organization may also be seen as a way of not alienating a local community that demands vice activities (Whyte, 1967). The goal becomes compromises reached through negotiation and regulation, rather than elimination of the activity.

Instead of being offered as a reward for self-regulation, nonenforcement may also be extended for regulating others. The literature on prisons gives many examples of the role selected prisoners play in maintaining order. Concessions, some clearly illegal, may be given to key prisoners in return for their regulating the behavior of others through questionable means (Sykes, 1958; Cloward *et al.*, 1960).

These represent cases where full control is technically impossible. Authorities need the continuing support of at least some of those they wish to control, and they are willing to pay a price for it. In other cases authorities may be capable of repressive action but prefer to delegate it because it is seen as too risky for them to undertake directly. For example, in 1963 the FBI experienced strong pressure to find the killer of civil rights leader Medgar Evers. They had learned the names of some of those involved and had the murder weapon, but could not obtain evidence on who fired the shot. Under FBI direction, an active burglar and fence kidnapped and threatened to kill a key figure in the plot, and was able to obtain a signed statement identifying the murderer. In return, the cooperative burglar was "the beneficiary of the best the Bureau could do for him"—he avoided a long prison sentence for armed robbery and kept $800 in cash stolen from the man's wallet (Villano, 1977).

Vigilante-type groups offer another example. Police may look the other way and essentially delegate certain enforcement rights to a group that wishes to take action that police might like to take but are unwilling to. The summary justice of the southern lynch mob, and group violence against blacks, were often conspicuous because of the lack of a restraining police presence. Until recently in many areas of the South, police (when not themselves members) ignored or gave encouragement to the Klan. The weak, if not openly supportive, attitude of many southern leaders in the face of discrimination and white violence significantly encouraged the Klan. This greatly hampered the federal effort to enforce civil rights laws and protect civil rights workers. With respect to traditional offenses, it has been claimed that in some urban minority areas police have been less than diligent in investigating the murders of drug pushers supposedly carried out by vigilantes seeking to rid their communities of pushers.

Still another type of nonenforcement can originate in some criminals' possession of unique skills, or even in their having the same enemies as authorities do. The fact that organized crime and the United States government have had some common enemies (Mussolini in Italy, and Castro in Cuba) has sometimes led to cooperation between them. In Italy local mafiosi were active in the underground and provided the Allies with intelligence for the invasion of Sicily. As the Allies then moved on to the Italian mainland, anti-Fascist mafia were appointed to important positions in many towns and villages. The French liner *Normandie* was burned in New York, just before it was to become an Allied troop ship. Following this incident, the government sought the aid of mob-controlled longshoremen, truckers and guards as help against waterfront sabotage and infiltration during World War II.[7] Help was received from Joe (Socks) Lanza on the East Side and Lucky Luciano on the West Side. Just what the government offered in return is less clear, although Luciano's cooperation won him, at the least, a transfer to more comfortable prison quarters near Albany (Talese, 1972: 206).

Recent reports of connections between the CIA and the underworld may simply be the continuation of an old American tradition. The CIA with its "executive action program" designed to "eliminate the effectiveness of foreign leaders" also delegated some of its dirty work (such as assassination efforts directed against Castro and Lumumba) to underworld figures. In Castro's case organized crime figures were thought to have "expertise and contacts not available to law-abiding citizens." They also had a motive which it was thought would take attention away from sponsorship of the U.S. government. According to one estimate (Schlesinger, 1978), Castro's coming to power cost organized crime $100 million a year. Outsiders were used by the CIA to avoid having "an Agency person or government person get caught" (Select Committee, 1975: 74).

A former bank robber and forger involved in the unsuccessful plot to assassinate Lumumba was given plastic surgery and a toupee by the CIA before being sent to the Congo. This man was recommended by the Chief of the CIA's Africa Division as a "field operative" because "if he is given an assignment which may be morally wrong in the eyes of the world, but necessary because his case officer ordered him to carry it out, then it is right, and he will dutifully undertake appropriate action for its execution without pangs of conscience. In a word, he can rationalize all actions" (Select Committee, 1975: 46). It appears that in extreme cases one crucial element which agents of social control may obtain in such exchange relationships is a psychopathic personality not inhibited by conventional moral restraints.

In a related example in Indochina, the U.S. took over the French policy of ignoring (or even encouraging) the growing of and trafficking in opium, in return for anticommunist activities. According to McCoy (1972), the CIA provided planes and military equipment used by Laotian Hill tribes to ship opium to Saigon, where it was then processed into heroin (see also Chambliss, 1977).

Still another type of strategic nonenforcement, one not involving exchanges, happens when authorities fail to take action about a violation they know is planned, or in progress, until the violation is carried out. This permits arrest quotas to be met and can lead to heavier charges, greater leverage in negotiations, better evidence, and a higher level of offender arrest. For example, an experienced cocaine smuggler, who could easily identify "amateurs" in the business, argues that federal agents always waited for such persons to be arrested before talking to them. He notes:

> Rather than walk up to someone obviously headed for trouble—where they might flash a badge and say, 'Get smart, kid, it's not going to work'— they will, as a matter of policy, allow him to risk his life with the local heavies, get a few snorts of pure, and walk into jail at the airport back home. Why prevent smuggling when you can punish it—isn't that what jails are for (Sabbag, 1977: 120)?

COVERT FACILITATION

The passive nonenforcement involving exchange relationships described above can be differentiated from a more active surreptitious role authorities may play as they (or their agents) directly enter into situations in order to facilitate rule breaking by others. The rule breaking that emerges from nonenforcement may be seen by authorities as an undesirable if perhaps necessary side effect. In the case of covert facilitation, authorities consciously seek to encourage rule breaking: getting someone to break the rule is the major goal. Both law and internal policy are often favorable to police facilitation of crime. This is a very old phenomenon. Eve, after all, was set up by the serpent. In the Bible she says, "The serpent beguiled me and I did eat." Indicating awareness of the paradoxical (provocative yet lawful) nature of the tactic, some police describe it as *lawful* entrapment. A not atypical policy manual of one police department contains a section on "permissible tactics for arranging the controlled commission of an offense." Police are told that they or their agents under appropriate conditions may:

A) affirmatively suggest the commission of the offense to the subject;
B) attempt to form a relationship with the subject of sufficient closeness to overcome the subject's possible apprehension over his trustworthiness;
C) offer the subject more than one opportunity to commit the offense;
D) create a continuing opportunity for the subject to commit the offense;
E) minimize the possibility of being apprehended for committing the offense.

For the purposes of this paper we identify at least three types of covert facilitation:

1) disguised police or their agents cooperating with others in illegal actions;
2) police secretly generating opportunities for rule breaking without being coconspirators;
3) police secretly generating motives for rule breaking without being coconspirators.

With respect to the "controlled commission of an offense," police or their agents may enter into relationships with those who don't know that they are police, to buy or sell illegal goods and services or to victimize others. The former is the most common. Agents of social control may purchase or sell drugs, pose as tourists seeking prostitutes, as prostitutes seeking customers, or as homosexuals seeking partners. They may pose as fences buying or selling stolen goods, as hit men taking a contract, as criminals trying to bribe prosecutors, and as entrepreneurs running pornographic bookstores. They may join groups that are (or become) involved in car theft, burglary or robbery. They may infiltrate political groups thought to be dangerous. The last decade reveals many examples of covert facilitation as authorities responded to widespread protest (Marx, 1974).

Both of the two other types of covert facilitation (deceptively creating opportunity structures or motives but without collusion) have a "give-them-enough-rope" quality. Police activity here is more passive and the deception is of a different order from that involved in the "controlled commission of an offense." Police do not directly enter into criminal conspiracies with their targets, and charges of entrapment would not be supported—but they do attempt to structure the world in such a way that violations are made more likely.

The use of decoys to draw street crime is a major form of police creation of opportunity structures. Police anticrime squads, increasingly in vogue, may disguise their members as old women, clerics, derelicts, tennis players and bike riders; they may use attractive police women in civilian clothes to induce robbery and assault, with other police watching from close by (Halper and Ku, 1976). Private guards posing as inattentive customers paying for small purchases with large bills routinely test cashier honesty. Plainclothed "security inspectors" may test employee vigilance by seeing if they can get away with shoplifting. There is almost no limit to the variety of attractive opportunities for property theft that can be generated. Other examples include leaving packages in a watched unmarked decoy car with its windows open, leaving expensive skis (which, when moved, emit an electronic signal audible only to guards) in a conspicuous place at ski resorts, and opening crates of expensive merchandise at airport storage terminals and dusting them with an invisible powder that can be seen only by an ultraviolet light machine that employees pass as they leave work (Marx, 1980).

Covert facilitation involving the creation of motives can be seen in many counterintelligence activities. Here the goal may be disruption and subversion (rather than strictly law enforcement). In "dirty tricks" campaigns, police may take clandestine actions in the hope of provoking factionalism and violence. In one extreme example, an FBI agent in Tucson, Arizona, instigated a series of bombings of a Mafia home and a business to encourage fighting among rival organized crime groups (Talese, 1972). In one of the more bizarre cases of the last decade, the FBI, in "Operation Hoodwink," sought to encourage conflict between the Communist Party and elements in organized crime (Donner, 1976). The FBI was also responsible for burning cars of leftist activists so that it appeared to be done by rival political groups (*New York Times*, July 11, 1976). Undercover agents operating on opposing sides apparently played an important role in the violent split that occurred between the Huey Newton and Eldridge Cleaver factions of the Black Panthers. Perhaps more common are efforts to make it appear that an individual involved in criminal or radical politics is an informant, by planting information or contriving leaks. The "informant" may then be subject to possible retaliatory violence. This may be done by a genuine informant as part of a strategy of subversion or to cast blame elsewhere if arrests are to be made where it will be obvious that an informant was present (Schiano and Burton, 1974; Villano, 1977).

Some of the trickery of uniformed police might also be classified here. In the following extreme example from Wambaugh (1975: 47), the power of the police office is used to generate a motive. A black bar known for heavy-drinking patrons is staked out. The plan is:

> . . . to find a drunk sleeping in his car in the parking lot at the rear and wake him gently telling him that he had better go home and sleep it off. Then they would wait down the street in the darkness and arrest the grateful motorist for drunk driving as he passed by.[8]

In a version of turnabout as fair play (at least to reform police executives), covert facilitation may also be turned inward in efforts to deal with corrupt police and assess police honesty. Tactics recently used by the New York City police include: planting illegally parked cars with money in them to see if police tow truck operators would steal it; planting "lost" wallets near randomly selected police to see if they would be turned in intact; offering bribes to arresting officers; putting through a contrived "open door" call to an apartment where marked money was prominently displayed to see if two officers under suspicion would steal it (they did); establishing phoney gambling operations to see if police sought protection money; and having an undercover officer pose as a pusher to see if other undercover narcotics agents paid out the full amount of "buy" money they claimed (*New York Times*, November 29, 1972 and December 28, 1973; Sherman, 1978).

Government lawyers, judges and congressmen may also be targets of such tactics. Thus Sante A. Bario, a federal drug agent, posed as Salvatore Barone, a Las Vegas underworld figure, and was "arrested" in a Queens bar for carrying two loaded pistols. He then offered an assistant district attorney under suspicion $15,000 and the "charges" were dismissed (as was the assistant D.A.; Lardner, 1977); Operation Abscam, part of a federal bribery investigation, involved undercover agents posing as Arab sheiks who offered money to congressmen in return for favors (*New York Times*, Feb. 4, 1980).

For convenience we have thus far treated three types of interdependence as if they were distinct empirically as well as analytically. However, there are deviance and social control situations in which each or several are present—or where they merge or may be temporally linked. One of the things rule breakers may offer to police in return for nonenforcement is aid in covertly facilitating someone else's rule breaking. The arrest that emerges out of this can involve escalation. For example, a drug informant's petty theft may be ignored (nonenforcement) in return for his making controlled buys (covert facilitation). The arrest growing out of this may lead to additional charges if the suspect is involved in a high-speed chase and fights with the arresting officers after they call him a name. Escalation may lead to a later policy of nonenforcement in those situations where authorities perceive that their intervention would in fact only make matters worse.[9] Stepped-up enforcement may also lead to nonenforcement by increasing opportunities for police corruption.

Notes

1. Other forms of interdependence treated in the larger work from which this article is drawn, but ignored here, include: 1) "cops as robbers," where authorities are self-interested rule breakers; 2) the falsely accused; 3) the efforts of citizens to provoke, bribe, or otherwise implicate police in their rule breaking.

2. Because of their intentionality, nonenforcement and covert facilitation are social control strategies; this cannot be said of escalation which is defined by its unintended consequences, though these may be present with the former as well. Sometimes, of course, police may follow a policy of deliberate provocation in the hope of encouraging escalation so that they can legally use force, bring heavier charges, or dispense "alley justice."

3. As Jack Katz has pointed out in a private communication, "Such laws reflect the fact that in a way large sections of our society are always under investigation for a crime."

4. Estimates of how widespread this is vary. A knowledgeable crime reporter (Plate, 1975: 103) observes, "the number of criminals actually licensed by police to make a living in this way is quite extraordinary." According to one estimate, 50 percent of those arrested by the old Federal Bureau of Narcotics were converted into "specialized employees" (McIntyre, 1967: 10–13).

5. Here we ignore the many other sources of nonenforcement such as lack of resources, intimidation, bureaucratic timidity, lack of belief in the rule, or compassion, as well as the suspension of law enforcement in order to have something to hold over a person should the need arise later.

6. A narcotics agent critical of this practice notes: They put such pressure on the informant that, in effect, you've got him by the nuts. That's even what they call it, "the nut," working off the nut, or the violation. The pressure [on the informant] is so great he'll manufacture information, make up some to get off the hook. It's just a perfect example of how law enforcement is maintaining the problem (Browning, 1976).

7. A more cynical interpretation is that Luciano actually arranged for the destruction of the *Normandie* as the prelude for his subsequently exchanging mob protection against future "foreign" sabotage (Gosch and Hammer, 1975).

8. This is mentioned because of its analytic significance. Far more common is the reverse: monitoring bars as they close and encouraging drunks not to drive, or even arranging transportation for them.

9. In the case of civil disorders, however, underreaction as part of a policy of nonenforcement can have the unintended consequence of encouraging the spread of disorder. The three largest civil disorders of the 1960s (Watts, Newark and Detroit) were all characterized by an initial period of police underreaction. Given the infraction-generating potential of both over- and underreaction, police often find themselves criticized no matter how they respond, and policies are cyclical.

31 / Police Corruption in New York City

THE KNAPP COMMISSION

GRATUITIES

By far the most widespread form of misconduct the Commission found in the Police Department was the acceptance by police officers of gratuities in the form of free meals, free goods, and cash payments. Almost all policemen either solicited or accepted such favors in one form or another, and the practice was widely accepted by both the police and the citizenry, with many feeling that it wasn't corruption at all, but a natural perquisite of the job.

Free Meals

The most universally accepted gratuity was the free meal offered to policemen by luncheonettes, restaurants, bars, and hotels. Despite the Commission's announced lack of interest in investigating instances of police free meals, investigators found it impossible to avoid noticing such instances while going about their private affairs or while engaged in investigating more serious matters.

Early in his administration Commissioner Murphy took a strong stand with respect to such freeloading and stirred up a good deal of animosity among rank and file policemen by inveighing against even a free cup of coffee.

The Commissioner's position was somewhat undermined by his handling of what was undoubtedly the most highly publicized free meal served to a New York policeman in recent years. Assistant Chief Inspector Albert Seedman—in March of 1972 when he was under active consideration for the post of Chief of Detectives—hosted a dinner for his wife and another couple at the New York Hilton. The bill for dinner, which came to $84.30 including tip, was picked up by the hotel. When the check for this meal was discovered by Commission investigators during the course of a routine investigation, a Commission attorney immediately brought it to the attention of Seedman, who had in the meantime been appointed the Chief of Detectives. Chief Seedman then explained that the hotel management had invited him to dine in return for performing a security check for the hotel—a service normally provided by the police at no charge. This information was turned over on a confidential basis to Commissioner Murphy, who relieved Chief Seedman of his command pending an inquiry.

A week later the Commissioner released a statement outlining a version of the affair which was significantly different from the one Chief Seedman had given our staff attorney. While he originally had ascribed the free meal (including tip) to an invitation from the hotel in specific recognition of services rendered, the statement released by the Commissioner indicated that he had gone with his friends to the hotel fully expecting to pay for the meal, had simply made "no fuss" when the management failed to present a bill, and had covered his embarrassment by leaving a "large tip." Having accepted Chief Seedman's revised version of the affair, Commissioner Murphy restored him to command of the division, announcing that he had committed no "serious wrongdoing."

This incident had a significant effect on the already cynical attitude of many policemen. It was difficult for police officers to take seriously Commissioner Murphy's stern warnings against receiving "any buck but a pay check," when they apparently did not apply to one of the Commissioner's top aides. Several police officers commented wryly to Commission investigators that at last a meaningful guideline had been established for free meals: "It's okay—up to $84.30."

In fact, of course, the average patrolman was found to eat nowhere near that well. Free meals were indeed available to almost all policemen throughout the City, but patrolmen rarely dined in style. Every patrolman knew which establishments on his beat provided free meals, and these were the places where he lunched each day. Uniformed policemen generally ate modest-priced meals in cafeterias, luncheonettes, restaurants, bars, or in the employee cafeterias of hotels. Commission employees observed countless uniformed patrolmen eating in such establishments, then leaving without paying and sometimes without even leaving a tip. Most often, no bill was even presented.

Many thousands of free meals were consumed by policemen each day and the sheer numbers created problems for the most popular eateries. Some luncheonettes which did a particularly heavy police business either offered a discount or charged policemen a token fee, most commonly $.50.

It was not only the policeman on patrol who felt that his lunches should be provided free. Numerous examples were reported to the Commission of officers in the station house sending radio cars to local restaurants to pick up meals for police officers whose duties prevented them from getting out on the street.

Nor were take-out orders always limited to food. Patrolman Phillips testified that it was not uncommon for policemen assigned to a radio car to pick up a "flute"—a Coke bottle filled with liquor—which they would deliver to the station house. In most instances, however, take-out orders involved the same sort of low-priced meals obtained by police officers on patrol. The Commission obtained a list used in one precinct house apparently setting out the dates on which certain eating places were to be approached for sandwiches, pizza, and other food to go.

The owner of one home-delivery food business which sold $2.00 fried chicken dinners found that his dinners were so popular with the police in his local precinct that they were ordering eighty to ninety dinners a week from him. This was substantially cutting into his profits, so he decided to start charging the police a nominal price of $.50 per dinner. This angered the police, who began issuing summonses to his delivery cars on every trip they made, resulting in $600 in summonses in one week. The owner called the Police Commissioner's office and explained his problem, and soon afterwards, he stopped receiving summonses. However, he had already dropped the $.50 charge per dinner.

Not all patrolmen were as restrained as the general run, and some were observed eating in rather fashionable establishments. Two patrolmen in particular confronted Commission investigators with a situation difficult to ignore by pulling up nightly to the back entrance of a fairly high-priced downtown restaurant located directly under the windows of the Commission's offices. The officers were served in their car by a uniformed waiter with a tray and a napkin draped over one arm.

Non-uniformed officers generally ordered less modest meals than uniformed patrolmen. Plainclothesmen, detectives, and high-level officers, who worked in civilian clothes instead of the conspicuous blue uniform, patronized a much wider selection of restaurants than the uniformed force, including many clearly in the luxury category. And the meals they ordered were often grandiose compared with the cafeteria-style food favored by uniformed men.

William Phillips, when assigned as a detective in a midtown precinct, regularly patronized, with other detectives, the very best restaurants, where he received gratis what he called "electric-chair meals." He reported that as he sipped the last drop of brandy after an enormous feast all he could think was "pull the switch, I'm ready to go!" Free meals of this sort, which in Phillips' case could add up to hundreds of dollars in one week, obviously presented a more serious but much less frequently encountered problem than the hot dog traditionally demanded by a patrolman from a vendor.

The owner of one of New York's finest French restaurants reported to the Commission that he was approached by policemen demanding free dinners. When he flatly turned them down, they took retaliatory action: The restaurant was located on a street where parking was illegal before 7:00 P.M., and the police began showing up every night at 6:55 to tow away cars belonging to patrons.

The Commission discovered that there was a certain etiquette among police officers concerning free meals in restaurants. In most precincts an officer could not eat free in a restaurant on another man's beat without first getting his permission. Officers also tried to time their free meals for restaurants' slow periods, to avoid taking up tables which might otherwise be used by paying customers. And thoughtful policemen in at least one precinct installed a wall chart containing a box for each eatery in the precinct, where officers made an appropriate entry every time they had a free meal, the idea being to keep track of the police traffic and spread the burden fairly. Also, some restaurants offered free meals only to officers in a position to do them a favor in return. At one luncheonette in the Bronx where a Commission attorney was dining with his wife, the waitress took a patrolman's order for food to go, then went to the manager and asked, "We don't charge him, do we?" The manager took one look at that officer and said, "You can charge that bastard as much as you like. It's only the ones from the Forty-Seventh [that we take care of]."

Hotels

The Commission's interest turned to hotels after a former hotel security officer came in with hotel records indicating that at least one hotel was paying off police in free meals, free rooms, and cash payments at Christmas. Commission investigators then interviewed security officers and general managers at ten major hotels in the City, all of whom flatly denied giving gratuities in any form to the police.

The Commission's next step was to subpoena personnel and records reflecting police gratuities from seven large hotels, two of which were among those questioned earlier. The result was a paper flood of meal checks, meal tickets, room records and hotel logs. An initial examination of these records showed that large numbers of policemen—as well as other public officials—were receiving gratuities from hotels, chiefly in the form of free meals. This practice was described in detail by security directors and managers who this time were subpoenaed for testimony under oath.

The pattern of free meals that emerged was similar to that the Commission had found in independent restaurants, with patrolmen generally eating in the hotels' employee dining rooms, coffee shops, or less expensive restaurants, and higher-ranking officers ordering lavish meals in the hotels' more expensive restaurants.

Records from several of the hotels showed that they each fed as many as 300 to 400 meals a month to policemen in their employee dining rooms, mostly to patrolmen in uniform. The value of these meals was usually under $2.00 each. To get free meals in the employee dining rooms, the policemen generally went to the security officer, where their uniforms—or in the case of non-uniformed officers, their shields—served as identification. They were either asked to sign the meal checks or hotel logs with their names and ranks or were given meal tickets to be turned in in the dining rooms. When the names given in the hotel checks and logs were checked against the precinct rosters, a sizable percentage of them proved to be false (including two uniformed officers identifying themselves as Whitman Knapp and Sydney Cooper, who was then chief of the Department's anti-corruption force).

In these same hotels, higher-ranking officers (sergeants, detectives, inspectors, lieutenants, captains, and one chief inspector) ate in the hotels' better restaurants, ordering the most expensive items on the menu, with the tab rarely coming to less than $20 per person in the larger midtown hotels. And the volume was substantial: over $500 a month at most hotels checked and $1,500 a month at the Statler-Hilton.

Hotels also were found to provide free rooms to police officers upon request. The ostensible reason for this was usually that the officer lived out of town and had to be in court early the following morning. In practice, however, policemen often took rooms when they were neither on official business nor scheduled to make a court appearance the following day. Occasionally, a group of them would book a free room for an afternoon in order to watch an important ball game on the TV provided by the hotel.

Free Drinks

In the course of its investigation into bars, Commission investigators could not help but observe numerous uniformed police officers imbibing free drinks—both on duty and off. Bar owners and policemen also told the Commission that it was common practice for bars to offer free drinks to policemen.

Three patrol sergeants in the Nineteenth Precinct regularly spent their entire tours going from one bar to another. While the behavior of patrolmen was less extreme, there was plenty of drinking on duty and off by them, too, with no evidence of any attempt by superiors to stop it. One example of a superior's laissez-faire attitude occurred in the presence of Commission investigators at an East Side bar. Three patrolmen, in uniform and on duty, were in the bar, one drinking a mixed drink, one a beer, and one coffee. The uniformed sergeant for the sector, who was on patrol and theoretically responsible for supervising the patrolmen, entered the bar, stayed for five minutes, then left. The patrolmen continued to drink during and after his visit.

Christmas Payments

Payments to police at Christmas by bars, restaurants, hotels, department stores, and other retail businesses have long been a police tradition. Although the Department has made efforts to halt the practice, at the time of the investigation it still continued. A particularly rigorous campaign was waged against the practice in December of 1971, with the reported result that officers collected their Christmas gratuities in January, after the campaign was over.

Christmas money was usually collected in a fairly organized fashion. Early in December, lists were made up at many precinct houses, division headquarters, and squad rooms, on which were entered the names of all the businesses in their jurisdiction from which the police expected Christmas payments. The list was then divided up among the various officers, each of whom was to go to the businesses on his list and collect. He either collected a flat fee to be divided up later at the station house by participating officers, or he presented a list, broken down to include the various officers.

Patrolman Phillips described how Christmas graft was collected when he was a detective in the Seventeenth Precinct some years ago:

> Well, Christmas was an organized operation, and the squad clerical men had the master Christmas list, which was kept locked up at all times. Each detective at Christmas time was given a list of between ten and fifteen establishments. The money was all brought in. It was divided equally among all the detectives in the squad. The lieutenant and sergeant had their own Christmas list. They did not participate in ours.

When asked how long the master list was, Patrolman Phillips said, "it was quite a long list, ten or fifteen yellow pages . . . [it contained] every hotel, almost every bar, every cabaret, and other business establishments in the Seventeenth Precinct." He said that the Christmas pad came to $400 or $500 per man in that precinct, not counting individual payments, which usually added another $200 or so. Phillips also reported that specific amounts were set aside for transmittal to higher ranking supervisors, right up to the Chief of Detectives. The Commission was unable to verify whether the money was actually transmitted.

The Christmas lists presented to hotels in particular were quite detailed, giving amounts to be paid to police officers of all ranks, up to and including the borough commander and Chief Inspector. (Again, the Commission obtained no direct proof that these monies were ever actually received by the officers named on the lists.) One Christmas list obtained from a large hotel set forth specific amounts to be given to each of the detectives assigned to the squad with jurisdiction over that hotel.

While lists of this sort reflected a practice as widespread as it was long-standing, the lists themselves could not always be accepted on face value since, as in the case of the detective list, they often reflected proposed rather than actual payments. During the Commission hearings the lieutenant in charge of the detective squad mentioned above requested and was given the opportunity to testify that he had never received the payment reflected on the list and the hotel personnel who provided the list acknowledged that not all payments on it were actually accepted.

The giving of gratuities to high-level police officers was a common practice. Former Chief Inspector Sanford Garelik acknowledged in executive testimony before the Commission that, as a field commander, he had received gratuities from businessmen with whom he came in contact in the course of his duties. Instead of returning these gifts or asking that they not be sent, he stated that he attempted to respond by giving return gifts of equal value.

Free Merchandise and Other Gifts

A number of merchants gave policemen gifts for services rendered and free merchandise. These included such items as free packages of cigarettes solicited by policemen from tobacco shops and grocery stores, free bags of groceries from retail stores, free service at dry cleaners and laundries, and free goods from factories and wholesalers. In his public testimony before the Commission Patrolman Droge stated that in one precinct in which he had served, police officers had used their tours to make the rounds of a bread factory, a frankfurter plant, and an ice cream plant, among others, stocking up on goods to take home. "I recall one police officer," said Droge, "who felt that if he didn't go home with a bag of groceries, then his tour wasn't complete."

Tips for Services Rendered

Policemen often accepted or solicited payments for services performed during their tours of duty. Some of these services were legitimate parts of their jobs, like guarding foreign diplomats, for which they should not have been tipped, and others were services which should have been performed by private guards rather than by City-paid policemen, like escorting supermarket managers to the bank.

Foreign consulates, many of which have city policemen assigned to guard them, have been known to offer gratuities to the police in various forms. Some would send cases of whiskey and champagne to precinct houses. Others made gifts of gold watches and money to various police officers.

When City marshals served eviction notices, they would notify the police, and when a car responded, the marshal paid $5 to the patrolmen in the car for handling the eviction.

When managers of many supermarkets and liquor stores were ready to take the day's receipts to the bank, they called the local precinct house and asked that a patrol car be sent over. The policemen in the car would then give the manager a ride to the bank, for which they received "anywhere from a couple of packs of cigarettes to $4.00."

Proprietors of check cashing services, who open up shop in the morning with large supplies of cash on hand, frequently had standing arrangements to have a patrol car waiting outside each morning when the proprietor came in.

Proprietors of burglarized stores and factories, if they arrived at the scene before the police did, paid $5 a man to each officer who showed up. However, if the police arrived first, they often helped themselves to merchandise.

Since our investigation, the Department has issued an order requiring that, when patrol cars manned by patrolmen reach the scene of a burglary before the sergeant gets there, the cars must be inspected by the sergeant before they leave the scene. Although this sounds like a sensible reform, a precinct commander and other police officers told the Commission that they felt the required procedure was demeaning and unlikely ever to be followed, as it would result in the public spectacle of a police supervisor searching for evidence of theft by patrolmen.

Comments

Almost to a man, legitimate businessmen questioned by the Commission about why they offered gratuities to the police claimed that they did so "to promote good will." Almost all expected to receive either extra or better service than that given to the general public, and many expected the police to overlook minor illegal acts or conditions.

Restaurants and bars expected police who dined and drank free to respond promptly if they were ever called in an emergency and to handle such calls with more discretion than usual. If the police ever had to arrest a man in one of the hotels which offered free meals and Christmas money, the management could be fairly confident that instead of charging into the dining room in the middle of dinner and making the arrest in full view of all the diners, the police would probably make the arrest much more discreetly.

Another benefit to bars, restaurants, and hotels was that patrons were allowed to park and double-park illegally in front of their establishments.

In many instances it is unfair to infer that payments of a gratuity necessarily reflected a shakedown by the police officer involved. A bar owner, restauranteur, or other businessman is usually most happy to have a police officer in or near his premises, and in a good many situations, payments—particularly Christmas gratuities—were made simply because the police officer became friendly with the local merchants in his patrol area. Gift giving, however, was very rarely a reciprocal matter in the sense of friends exchanging gifts on an equal basis. If, as in the case of some high-ranking officers, a return gift was made it was always in response to an original overture by someone who usually stood to gain by the presumed good will.

The fact is that the public by and large does not regard gratuities as a serious matter. While some may be offended by the occasionally arrogant way in which some police officers demand what they consider to be their due, most people are willing to allow a police officer who spends long hours providing protection for an area to stop in for a quick free meal or cup of coffee at an eating establishment which enjoys the benefit of his protection. Indeed, an investigation of hotels in New York conducted a few years ago by the New York County District Attorney came up with essentially the same evidence as that found by the Commission of hotels providing free meals and a prosecutorial judgment was apparently made not to pursue the matter even though criminal violations were involved.

Officers who participated in Ethical Awareness Workshops recently sponsored by the Department have reached an interesting conclusion. They felt that no police officer should ever accept a gratuity of any sort. Their reasoning was twofold: One, that even a series of small gratuities—like cups of coffee—would, in certain instances, affect an officer's performance of his duty, and two, that acceptance of gratuities is demeaning to a professional police officer. However, it is doubtful whether such standards could reasonably be imposed throughout the Department.

The general tolerance of gratuities both by policemen and by the public gives rise to the question whether some system should be developed whereby gratuities are specifically condoned as long as they are not excessive. At the time of our investigation, there was a *de facto* tolerance of such gratuities, and if the Department could institutionalize this approach by establishing realistic guidelines setting out what is and is not permissible it could at least remove the illegal atmosphere which may operate to condition policemen for more serious misconduct. Admittedly, the problem of drawing a line is a difficult one. If the Department should decide to permit policemen to accept free meals and goods, the Commission urges that all such gratuities be reported in memorandum books or on Daily Field Activity Reports, which should be reviewed daily by supervisory officers. Supervisory personnel could then be held responsible for insuring that such privileges were not abused.

Some areas do seem susceptible to an official regulatory approach. For example, there would seem to be no reason why the practice of hotels providing free rooms to police officers could not be officially sanctioned. If an officer is forced to work late hours in any area of the City far from his home and is expected to be on duty or in court early the following morning, it does not seem unreasonable that he be provided with a hotel room, on a space available basis, with the expense being paid for by the City. If such rooms are provided they should be duly reported and, where possible, approved in advance as part of a regular system.

Assuming that hotels and restaurants actually do not wish to provide free meals and rooms to police officers, it has been demonstrated that they are not forced to. At the time of the Commission hearings, under the glare of publicity, many of the big hotels announced that they would no longer provide such services.

GRASS-EATERS AND MEAT-EATERS

Corrupt policemen have been informally described as being either "grass-eaters" or "meat-eaters." The overwhelming majority of those who do take payoffs are grass-eaters, who accept gratuities and solicit five- and ten- and twenty-dollar payments from contractors, tow-truck operators, gamblers, and the like, but do not aggressively pursue corruption payments. "Meat-eaters," probably only a small percentage of the force, spend a good deal of their working hours aggressively seeking out situations they can exploit for financial gain, including gambling, narcotics, and other serious offenses which can yield payments of thousands of dollars. Patrolman William Phillips was certainly an example of this latter category.

One strong impetus encouraging grass-eaters to continue to accept relatively petty graft is, ironically, their feeling of loyalty to their fellow officers. Accepting payoff money is one way for an officer to prove that he is one of the boys and that he can be trusted. In the climate which existed in the Department during the Commission's investigation, at least at the precinct level, these numerous but relatively small payoffs were a fact of life, and those officers who made a point of refusing them were not accepted closely into the fellowship of policemen. Corruption among grass-eaters obviously cannot be met by attempting to arrest them all and will probably diminish only if Commissioner Murphy is successful in his efforts to change the rank and file attitude toward corruption.

No change in attitude, however, is likely to affect a meat-eater, whose yearly income in graft amounts to many thousands of dollars and who may take payoffs of $5,000 or even $50,000 in one fell swoop (former Assistant Chief Inspector Sydney Cooper, who had been active in anti-corruption work for years, recently stated that the largest score of which he had heard—although he was unable to verify it— was a narcotics payoff involving $250,000). Such men are willing to take considerable risks as long as the potential profit remains so large. Probably the only way to deal with them will be to ferret them out individually and get them off the force, and, hopefully, into prisons.

PADS, SCORES AND GRATUITIES

Corruption payments made to the police may be divided into "pad" payments and "scores," two police slang terms which make an important distinction.

The "pad" refers to regular weekly, biweekly, or monthly payments, usually picked up by a police bagman and divided among fellow officers. Those who make such payments as well as policemen who receive them, are referred to as being "on the pad."

A "score" is a one-time payment that an officer might solicit from, for example, a motorist or a narcotics violator. The term is also used as a verb, as in "I scored him for $1,500."

A third category of payments to the police is that of gratuities, which the Commission feels cannot in the strictest sense be considered a matter of police corruption, but which has been included here because it is a related—and ethically borderline—practice, which is prohibited by Department regulations, and which often leads to corruption.

Operations on the pad are generally those which operate illegally in a fixed location day in and day out. Illegal gambling is probably the single largest source of pad payments. The most important legitimate enterprises on the pad at the time of the investigation were those like construction, licensed premises, and businesses employing large numbers of vehicles, all of which operate from fixed locations and are subject to summonses from the police for myriad violations.

Scores, on the other hand, are made whenever the opportunity arises—most often when an officer happens to spot someone engaging in an illegal activity like pushing narcotics, which doesn't involve a fixed location. Those whose activities are generally legal but who break the law occasionally, like motorists or tow-truck operators, are also subject to scores. By far the most lucrative source of scores is the City's multimillion-dollar narcotics business.

FACTORS INFLUENCING CORRUPTION

There are at least five major factors which influence how much or how little graft an officer receives, and also what his major sources are. The most important of these is, of course, the character of the officer in question, which will determine whether he bucks the system and refuses all corruption money; goes along with the system and accepts what comes his way; or outdoes the system, and aggressively seeks corruption-prone situations and exploits them to the extent that it seriously cuts into the time available for doing his job. His character will also determine what kind of graft he accepts. Some officers, who don't think twice about accepting money from gamblers, refuse to have anything at all to do with narcotics pushers. They make a distinction between what they call "clean money" and "dirty money."

The second factor is the branch of the Department to which an officer is assigned. A plainclothesman, for example, has more—and different—opportunities than a uniformed patrolman.

The third factor is the area to which an officer is assigned. At the time of the investigation certain precincts in Harlem, for instance, comprised what police officers called "the Gold Coast" because they contained so many payoff-prone activities, numbers and narcotics being the biggest. In contrast, the Twenty-Second Precinct, which is Central Park, has clearly limited payoff opportunities. As Patrolman Phillips remarked, "What can you do, shake down the squirrels!" The area also determines the major sources of corruption payments. For instance, in midtown Manhattan precincts businessmen and motorists were major sources; on the Upper East Side, bars and construction; in the ghetto precincts, narcotics and numbers.

The fourth factor is the officer's assignment. For uniformed men, a seat in a sector car was considered fairly lucrative in most precincts, while assignment to stand guard duty outside City Hall obviously was not, and assignment to one sector of a precinct could mean lots of payoffs from construction sites while in another sector bar owners were the big givers.

The fifth factor is rank. For those who do receive payoffs, the amount generally ascends with the rank. A bar may give $5 to patrolmen, $10 to sergeants, and considerably more to a captain's bagman. Moreover, corrupt supervisors have the opportunity to cut into much of the graft normally collected by those under them.

SOURCES OF PAYOFFS

Organized crime is the single biggest source of police corruption, through its control of the City's gambling, narcotics, loansharking, and illegal sex-related enterprises like homosexual after-hours bars and pornography, all of which the Department considers mob-run. These endeavors are so highly lucrative that large payments to the police are considered a good investment if they protect the business from undue police interference.

The next largest source is legitimate business seeking to ease its way through the maze of City ordinances and regulations. Major offenders are construction contractors and subcontractors, liquor licensees, and managers of businesses like trucking firms and parking lots, which are likely to park large numbers of vehicles illegally. If the police were completely honest, it is likely that members of these groups would seek to corrupt them, since most seem to feel that paying off the police is easier and cheaper than obeying the laws or paying fines and answering summonses when they do violate the laws. However, to the extent police resist corruption, business interests will be compelled to use their political muscle to bring about revision of the regulations to make them workable.

32 / Court Processing of Delinquents

ROBERT M. EMERSON

A NOTE ON TOTAL DENUNCIATION

Consideration of the structural features of total denunciation provides additional insight into the processes of establishing moral character in the juvenile court. For a successful total denunciation must transcend routine denunciation by *foreclosing* all possible defenses and by *neutralizing* all possible sources of support.

Foreclosure of defenses available to the delinquent . . . has two related elements. First, in order to discredit moral character totally, it must be clearly demonstrated that the denounced delinquent has been given a great many "breaks" or "chances" which he has, however, rejected and spoiled. Such a demonstration is necessary to prove that the case is "hopeless," that the delinquent youth's character is so ruined as to preclude any possibility of reform. The role of the disregarded "chance" is clearly seen in the following case, where a probation officer convinces both judge and public defender to go along with his punitive recommendation by proving that the youth has received chances not even officially reported:

> Two escapees from reform school were brought into court on a series of new complaints taken out by the police. Public defender argued that these complaints should be dismissed and the boys simply returned to the school. The probation officer, however, argued strongly that the boys should be found delinquent on the new complaints (this would require reconsideration of their cases by the Youth Correction Authority, perhaps leading to an extension of their commitment). The probation officer described how one of his colleagues had worked hard on one of these cases earlier, giving the boy a great many chances, none of which did any good. The judge accepted the probation officer's recommendation.
>
> After the hearing, the public defender admitted that he felt the probation officer had been right, acknowledging the validity of his picture of the character of this boy: "I did not realize he was such a bastard. . . . Apparently one of the probation officers had given him a lot of breaks. He had him on so many cases that he should be shot."

444

Second, it must be made to appear that the delinquent himself "messed up" the chances that he had been given. It should be established not only that the youth misbehaved on numerous occasions, but also that he did so in full knowledge of the possible consequences and with no valid excuse or extenuating circumstances. In this way, responsibility or "fault" for the imminent incarceration must fall completely on the denounced delinquent. Any official contribution to the youth's "messing up" (e.g., an official's intolerance) must be glossed over so that the delinquent bears total blame.

Court probation is in fact constructed so that responsibility for "messing up," should it occur, unavoidably falls on the delinquent .... Probationers are constantly warned that they will be committed if there is any further misconduct, and they are given a number of "breaks" on this condition. As one probation officer commented about a youth who had been "given a break" by the judge: "This way, if he gets committed, he knows he has it coming." Furthermore, the constant warnings and lectures against getting into trouble that occur throughout probation tend to undermine in advance the possibility of defending subsequent misbehavior. For example, it is difficult for a youth to excuse a new offense as the product of peer group influence when he has continually been warned to stay away from "bad friends."

A second key element in a successful total denunciation is the neutralization of all possible sources of support. There are several components in this neutralization. First, the assessment of discredited and "hopeless" character must be made to appear as a general consensus among all those concerned in the case. A delinquent without a spokesman—with no one to put in a good word for him—stands in a fundamentally discredited position.

Here the stance taken by the delinquent's lawyer, normally a public defender, becomes crucial. A vigorous defense and pitch by a lawyer often might dispel the appearance of consensus and weaken the denunciation. This occurs very rarely, however, because of court cooptation of the public defender. Working closely with the probation staff, the public defender comes to share their values and indexes of success and failure in delinquency cases. Consequently, he will generally concur with the court's highly negative assessments of delinquent moral character. As a public defender noted in response to a question about how he usually handled his cases in the juvenile court:

> Generally I would find the probation officer handling the case and ask him: "What do you have on this kid? How bad is he?" He'll say: "Oh, he's bad!" Then he opens the probation folder to me, and I'll see he's got quite a record. Then I'll ask him, "What are you going to recommend?" He'll say,

"Give him another chance. Or probation. Or we've got to put him away."

But probation officers don't make this last recommendation lightly. Generally they will try to find a parent in the home, "someone who can keep him under control, someone who can watch him." But if the probation officer has given the kid a number of chances, it is a different story: "He's giving the kid chances and he keeps screwing up. . . . [Commitment will then be recommended.] And I say the kid deserves it. Before a kid goes away he's really got to be obnoxious—he will deserve it."

Adoption of probation standards for assessing delinquent character becomes crucial in total denunciation. The public defender is then in the position of arguing on behalf of a youth whose moral character has been totally discredited in his eyes and who he feels should indeed be committed. His courtroom defense will generally reflect this assessment. He will make only the most perfunctory motions of arguing that the delinquent be let off, and he will do so in a way that communicates an utter lack of conviction that this is a desirable course of action. Or, as in the following case, he will not even go through the motions of making a defense but will explicitly concur with the recommended incarceration and the grounds on which it rests:

A policeman told of finding an 11-year-old Negro boy in a laundry where a coin box had been looted. The officer reported that the boy had admitted committing the offense. Public defender waived cross-examination, and the judge found the youth delinquent.

Probation officer then delivered a rather lengthy report on the case. The boy had been sent to the Boys' Training Program and, while no great trouble, did not attend regularly. He had also recently been transferred to the Harris School and had been in trouble there. Probation officer recommended that the prior suspended sentence be revoked and the boy committed to the Youth Correction Authority.

Judge then asked the public defender if he had anything he wanted to say. Public defender: "The record more or less speaks for itself. He does not seem to have taken advantage of the opportunities the court has given him to straighten out." Then, after briefly reconferring with the probation officer, the judge ordered the commitment. Public defender waived the right of appeal.

Second, the denouncer must establish that in "messing up" and not taking advantage of the chances provided him, the denounced has created a situation in which there is *no other alternative open* but commitment to the Youth Correction Authority. In some cases, this may involve showing that the youth is so dangerous that commitment to the Authority is the only effective way he can be restrained; in others, demonstration that by his misbehavior the youth has completely destroyed all possible placements, including the one he has been in. It is only by dramatically showing in these ways that "there is nothing we can do with him" that the proposed commitment can be made to appear as an inevitable and objective necessity.

The fact that many total denunciations concentrate on proving that nothing else can be done with the case reflects the court's basic resistance to unwarrantable agency attempts to "dump" undesirable cases onto them for incarceration. The court feels that most of these institutions are too ready to give up on cases that from the court's point of view are still salvageable. To overcome this suspiciousness, the denouncer must not only present the youth's character as essentially corrupt and "hopeless," but also show that every effort has been made to work with him and every possible opportunity afforded him. The denouncer, in other words, must take pains to avoid appearing to be merely getting rid of a difficult and troublesome case simply to make his own work easier. This requires showing both that persistent efforts have been made to work with the case and that at the present time even extraordinary efforts cannot come up with anything as an alternative to incarceration.

A final aspect of demonstrating that there is no viable alternative to incarceration involves isolating the denounced delinquent from any kind of reputable sponsorship. In the usual case, where a parent acts as sponsor, successful total denunciation requires either that the parent be induced to denounce the youth and declare him fit only for incarceration or that the parent be discredited. In other cases, where the sponsor is a parental substitute, this sponsor must similarly be led to denounce the youth or be discredited. In this way, for example, sponsors who seek too aggressively to save delinquents considered overripe for commitment by other officials may encounter attacks on their motives, wisdom, or general moral character. This not only undermines the viability of any defense of character made by the sponsor, but also effectively isolates the delinquent by showing the unsuitability of his sponsorship as an alternative to commitment.

COUNTER-DENUNCIATION

As noted earlier, the courtroom proceeding routinely comes to involve a denunciation of the accused delinquent in the course of a confrontation between him and his accusers. This fact creates the conditions for the use of *counter-denunciation* as a defensive strategy. This strategy seeks to undermine the discrediting implications of the accusation by attacking the actions, motives and/or character of one's accusers.

The underlying phenomenon in counter-denunciation has been noted in a number of other contexts. McCorkle and Korn, for example, have analyzed the concept of the "rejection of the rejectors" as a defensive reaction to imprisonment (1964, p. 520). Similarly, Sykes and Matza explain the "condemnation of the condemners" in the process of neutralization in the following terms: "The delinquent shifts the focus of attention from his own deviant acts to the motives and behaviors of those who disapprove of his violations" (1957, p. 668). The concept of counter-denunciation, in contrast, focuses on the communicative work which accomplishes this shift of attention. Furthermore, it gains relevance as a defense against attempted character discrediting. Use of this strategy, however, is extremely risky in the court setting. While counter-denunciation may appear to the delinquent as a "natural" defense as he perceives the circumstances of his case, it tends to challenge fundamental court commitments and hence, even when handled with extreme care, often only confirms the denunciation.

It is striking that counter-denunciation has the greatest likelihood of success in cases where the complainant or denouncer lacks official stature or where the initiative rests predominantly with private parties who have clearly forced official action. Under these circumstances the wrongful quality of the offense can be greatly reduced if not wholly eliminated by showing that the initiator of the complaint was at least partially to blame for the illegal act. For example:

> A 16-year-old Negro boy, Johnny Haskin, was charged with assault and battery on two teenaged girls who lived near his family in a public housing project. Although a juvenile officer brought the case into court, he was clearly acting on the initiative of the two girls and their mother, for he had had no direct contact with the incident and did not testify about it. He simply put the two girls on the stand and let them tell about what happened. This was fairly confused, but eventually it appeared that Johnny Haskin had been slapping the younger sister in the hall of the project when the older girl had pulled him off. He had then threatened her with a knife. The girls admitted that there had been fighting in the hall for some time, and that they had been involved, but put the blame on Johnny for starting it. Mrs. Haskin, however, spoke up from the back of the room, and told about a gang of boys coming around to get her son (apparently justifying Johnny's carrying a knife). And Johnny himself denied that he had started the fighting, claiming that the younger girl had hit him with a bat and threatened him first.
>
> Judge then lectured both families for fighting, and placed Johnny on probation for nine months, despite a rather long prior record.

In this case, by establishing that the girls had also been fighting, the boy was at least partially exonerated. The success of this strategy is seen in the fact that the judge lectured both families, and then gave the boy what was a mild sentence in light of his prior court record.

Similarly, the possibility of discrediting the victim, thereby invalidating the complaint, becomes apparent in the following "rape" case:

> Two Negro boys, ages 12 and 13, had admitted forcing "relations" on a 12-year-old girl in a schoolyard, the police reported. After a full report on the incidents surrounding the offense, the judge asked the policemen: "What kind of girl is she?" Officer: "I checked with Reverend Frost [the girl's minister and the person instrumental in reporting this incident] and he said she was a good girl."

As the judge's query implies, the reprehensibility of this act can only be determined in relation to the assessed character of the girl victim. Had the police or the accused brought up evidence of a bad reputation or incidents suggesting "loose" or "promiscuous" behavior, the force of the complaint would have been undermined.

In the above cases, successful counter-denunciation of the complainants would undermine the moral basis of their involvement in the incident, thereby discrediting their grounds for initiating the complaint. But this merely shifts part of the responsibility for an offense onto the complaining party and does not affect the wrongful nature of the act per se. Thus, by denouncing the general character of the complainant and the nature of his involvement in the offense, the accused does not so much clear himself as diminish his guilt. If the offense involved is serious enough and the culpability of the complainant not directly related to the offense, therefore, this strategy may have little impact.

For example, in the homosexuality-tinged case of car theft described earlier ... both the accused and his father tried to support their contention that the car owner was lying by pointing to his discredited character. But the "victim's" homosexuality had no real connection with the act of stealing the car nor with the threatened physical violence it entailed, and hence did not affect the judge's evaluation of the act and of the delinquent's character. Under these circumstances, the soiled nature of the victim simply was not considered sufficiently extenuating to dissolve the reprehensibility of the act.[1]

In general, then, a successful counter-denunciation must discredit not only the general character of the denouncer but also his immediate purpose or motive in making the complaint. Only in this way can the counter-denunciation cut the ground out from under the wrongfulness of the alleged offense. For example:

> An 11-year-old Negro boy was charged with wantonly damaging the car of an older Negro man, Frankie Williams, with a BB gun. With the boy was his mother, a respectably dressed woman, a white lawyer, and a white couple who served as character witnesses.
>
> A juvenile officer brought the case in and then called Mr. Williams up to testify. The witness told of going outside to shovel his car out of the snow

several weeks previously and finding his windshield damaged in several places. He had noticed the boy at this time leaning out of the window of his house with a BB gun. Laywer then cross-examined, getting Williams to admit that he had been bickering with the family for some time, and that a year before the mother had accused him of swearing at her son and had tried to get a court complaint against him. (Judge ruled this irrelevant after Williams had acknowledged it.) Williams seemed flustered, and grew angry under the questioning, claiming that because of the boy's shooting he would not be able to get an inspection sticker for his car.

Juvenile officer then told judge that although he had not investigated the case, his partner reported that the marks on the windsheield were not consistent with a BB gun. Williams had also admitted that he had not looked for any BB pellets. On the basis of this evidence, the judge found the boy not delinquent. He then severely warned all parties in the case: "I'm going to tell you I do not want any more contests between these two families. Do you understand?"

Here, by showing that the complainant had both a selfish motive for complaining about his damaged windshield (to help get it repaired) and a grudge against the defendant and his family, as well as bringing out the lack of concrete evidence to substantiate the charge, the lawyer was able to get the complaint totally dismissed.

Similarly, the circumstances of the following case were such as to suggest initially that complaints had been taken out to intimidate or at least get even with boys against whom there was some resentment:

Two teenaged Negro boys were brought to court for breaking windows. Case was continued, and policeman gave the following account of what had happened. Several weeks previously there had been a disturbance and some windows broken in a middle class section of the city. There were six boys apparently involved, including these two. One of the occupants of the home had come out and begun shooting at the boys, who were on the other side of the street, "allegedly to protect his property." One of these two boys had been hit in the leg, and another man (apparently a passerby) had also been hit. The shooter, named Barr, "is now up before the grand jury" for this, but meanwhile had taken out complaints against these two boys. A private attorney representing the two accused then took over, explaining how his clients had just been summonsed to testify against Barr. Lawyer next questioned the cop about why complaints had been brought only against these two of the six boys, including the one who had been shot, and the other who had been a witness to the shooting. Cop replied that the other boys had been investigated, but there was nothing against them.

Here the boys' lawyer successfully established that the complaints against his clients had been initiated by the defendant in a related criminal action, suggesting an attempt to discredit in advance their testimony against him. The judge responded by continuing the case, releasing both boys to the custody of their parents, even though one had a long record.

Finally, successful counter-denunciation requires that the denounced provide a convincing account for what he claims is an illegitimate accusation. The court will reject any implication that one person will gratuitously accuse another of something he has not done. The youth in the following case can provide this kind of account:

> Five young boys were charged with vandalism and with starting a fire in a public school. Juvenile officer explained that he had investigated the incident with the school principal, getting two of the boys to admit their part in the vandalism. These two boys had implicated the other three, all of whom denied the charge.
>
> The judge then took over the questioning, trying to determine whether the three accused had in fact been in the school. In this he leaned heavily on finding out why the first two boys should lie. One of the accused, Ralph Kent, defended himself by saying he had not been at the school and did not know the boy who had named him. Judge asked how this boy had then been able to identify him. Kent replied that he had been a monitor at school, and one of his accusers might have seen him there. And he used to take the other accuser to the basement [lavatory] because the teacher would not trust him alone for fear he would leave the school.
>
> The two other boys continued to deny any involvement in the incident, but could provide no reason why they should be accused unjustly. The judge told them he felt they were lying, and asked several times: "Can you give me a good reason why these boys would put you in it?" Finally he pointed toward Kent and commented: "He's the only one I'm convinced wasn't there." He then asked Kent several questions about what he did as a monitor. When it came to dispositions, Kent was continued without a finding while the four other boys were found delinquent.

In this situation an accused delinquent was able to establish his own reputable character in school (later confirmed by the probation report on his school record), the discredited character of one of his accusers, and a probable motive for their denunciation of him (resentment toward his privileges and position in school) in a few brief sentences. It should be noted, however, that this successful counter-denunciation was undoubtedly facilitated by the fact that denouncers and denounced were peers. It is incomparably more difficult for a youth to establish any acceptable reason why an adult should want to accuse and discredit him wrongfully.

Counter-denunciation occurs most routinely with offenses arising out of the family situation and involving complaints initiated by parents against their own children. Here again it is possible for the child to cast doubt on the parents' motives in taking court action, and on the parents' general character:

> A Negro woman with a strong West Indian accent had brought an incorrigible child complaint against her 16-year-old daughter. The mother reported: "She never says anything to me, only to ask, 'Gimme car fare, gimme lunch

money.' . . . As for the respect she gave me I don't think I have to tolerate her!" The daughter countered that her mother never let her do anything, and simply made things unbearable for her around the house. She went out nights, as her mother claimed, but only to go over to a girl friend's house to sleep.

This case was continued for several months, during which time a probation officer worked with the girl and the court clinic saw mother and daughter. The psychiatrist there felt that the mother was "very angry and cold." Eventually an arrangement was made to let the girl move in with an older sister.

In this case the daughter was effectively able to blame her mother and her intolerance for the troubled situation in the home. But in addition, counter-denunciation may also shift the focus of the court inquiry from the misconduct charged to the youth onto incidents involving the parents. This shift of attention facilitated the successful counter-denunciation in the following case:

A 16-year-old white girl from a town some distance from the city was charged with shoplifting. But as the incident was described by the police, it become clear that this offense had occurred because the girl had run away from home and needed clean clothes. Police related what the girl had said about running away: She had been babysitting at home and was visited by her boyfriend, who had been forbidden in the house. Her father had come home, discovered this, and beaten her with a strap. (The girl's face still appeared somewhat battered with a large black-and-blue mark on one cheek, although the court session occurred at least three days after the beating.) She had run away that night.

The rest of the hearing centered not on the theft but on the running away and the incident which precipitated it. After the police evidence, the judge asked the girl: "How did you get that mark on your face?" Girl: "My father hit me." Judge: "With his fist?" Girl (hesitating): "Yes, it must have been his fist." Later in the proceeding, the judge asked the girl specifically why she had run away. She emphasized that she had not tried to hide anything; the kids had been up until eleven and the boy had left his bike out front. "I didn't try to hide it. I told them he'd been there."

With this her father rose to defend himself, arguing with some agitation: ". . . His clothes were loose. Her clothes were loose. Her bra was on the floor. . . . She was not punished for the boy being in the house, but for what she did." Girl (turning toward her father): "What about my eye?" Father: "She got that when she fell out of the bed (angrily, but directed toward the judge)." Girl (just as angrily): "What about the black and blue marks?" Father: "Those must have been from the strap."

The relatively high probability of successful counter-denunciation in cases arising from family situations points up the most critical contingency in the use of this protective strategy, the choice of an appropriate object. Denouncers with close and permanent relations with the denounced are particularly vulnerable to counter-denunciation, as the accusation is apt to rest solely on their word and illegitimate motives for the denunciation may be readily apparent. But again, where relations between the two parties are more distant, counter-denunciation has more chance of success where the denouncer is of more or less equivalent status with the denounced. Thus, the judge can be easily convinced that a schoolmate might unjustly accuse one from jealousy, but will reject any contention that an adult woman would lie about an attempted snatching incident.

While a denounced youth has a fair chance of successfully discrediting a complainant of his own age, and some chance where the complainant is a family member, counter-denunciations directed against officials, particularly against the most frequent complainants in the juvenile court, the police, almost inevitably fail. In fact, to attempt to counterattack the police, and to a lesser extent, other officials, is to risk fundamentally discrediting moral character, for the court recoils against all attacks on the moral authority of any part of the official legal system.

One reflection of this is the court's routine refusal to acknowledge complaints of *unfair* treatment at the hands of the police. On occasion, for example, parents complain that their children were arrested and brought to court while others involved in the incident were not. Judges regularly refuse to inquire into such practices:

> Two young Puerto Rican boys were charged with shooting a BB gun. After police testimony, their mother said something in Spanish, and their priest-translator explained to the judge: "What they've been asking all morning is why they did not bring the other two boys." The judge replied: "I can only deal with those cases that are before me. I can't go beyond that and ask about these other boys that are not here."

Similarly, in this same case the judge refused to inquire into a complaint of police brutality when the mother complained that one boy had been hit on the head, saying: "The question of whether he was injured is not the question for me right now."

But beyond this, the court will often go to great lengths to protect and defend the public character of the police when it is attacked during a formal proceeding. To accuse a policeman of acting for personal motives, or of dishonesty in the course of his duties, not only brings immediate sanctions from the court but also tends to discredit basically the character of the delinquent accuser. . . .

References

McCorkle, Lloyd W., and Richard Korn. 1964. "Resocialization Within Walls." In David Dressler (ed.), *Readings In Criminology and Penology.*

New York: Columbia University Press.

Sykes, Gresham M., and David Matza. 1957. "Techniques of Neutralization: A Theory of Delinquency." *American Sociological Review*, 22:664–70.

Note

1. Note, however, that even though this denunciation succeeded, the denouncer suffered both discrediting and penalty. Immediately after the delinquency case had been decided the police took out a complaint for "contributing to the delinquency of a minor" against him, based on his admitted homosexual activities with the youth. This "contributing" case was brought before the juvenile court later that same morning, complainant and accused changed places, and the first denouncer was found guilty, primarily from what he had revealed about his behavior earlier in establishing the delinquency complaint.

33 / Court Responses to Skid Row Alcoholics

JACQUELINE P. WISEMAN

     Matching sentences with men who plead guilty is thus the judge's true concern. This task must be handled within the pressures created by restricting drunk court to a morning session in one courtroom, regardless of the number of men scheduled to be seen that day.

Up until last year (when drunk arrests were temporarily reduced because of the large number of hippies and civil rights demonstrators in jail), 50 to 250 men were often sentenced within a few hours. Appearance before the judge was handled in platoons of five to 50. This meant the judge decided the fate of each defendant within a few short minutes. Thus judicial compassion attained assembly-line organization and speed.

As a court observer noted:

> The Court generally disposes of between 50 and 100 cases per day, but on any Monday there are 200 to 250 and on Monday mornings after holiday weekends the Court may handle as many as 350 cases. I would estimate that, on the average, cases take between 45 seconds and one minute to dispose of.[1]

Later, with drunk arrests drastically curtailed, the court handled no more than 50 cases in an average morning, and perhaps 125 on the weekends, according to the observer.[2] Right after a civil rights demonstration that resulted in many arrests, only 33 persons were observed in drunk court. This reduction in the quantity of defendants, however, did not appear to increase the length of time spent on each person. Rather, it seemed to reduce it. The observer noted the average length of time per person was 30 seconds, although the size of platoons was reduced from 50 to 15 or 20.

SENTENCING CRITERIA

How is the judge able to classify and sentence a large, unwieldy group of defendants so quickly? The answer is he utilizes social characteristics as indicators to signify drinking status—just as in an arrest situation the policeman looked for social characteristics to identify alcoholic trouble-making potential, combined with the arrestee's legal impotence. The effect is essentially the same: the men are objectified into social types for easy classification. In the case of the judge, the legal decision process must be more refined than for a policeman's arrest, no-arrest decision. Therefore, the judge's sentencing criteria are more complex, as they must include all possible decision combinations.

From court observations, plus interviews with court officers and judges, three primary criteria for typing defendants in drunk court emerge:

The General Physical Appearance of the Man   Is he shaky and obviously in need of drying out? Here, some of the judges ask the men to extend their hands before sentencing and decide the sentence on the degree of trembling.

Physical appearance may actually be the most potent deciding factor. As one court officer put it, when asked how the judges decide on a sentence:

> Primarily by appearance. You can tell what kind of shape they're in. If they're shaking and obviously need drying out, you know some are on the verge of the DT's so these get 10 to 15 days [in jail] to dry out. . . .

One of the seasoned judges said that his criteria were as follows:

> I rely on his record and also his "looks." Their "looks" are very important. I make them put their hands out—see if they are dirty and bloody in appearance.[3]

Past Performance   How many times have they been up before the court on a drunk charge before? A record of past arrests is considered to be indicative of the defendant's general attitude toward drinking. The longer and more recent the record, the greater the need for a sentence to aid the defendant to improve his outlook on excessive liquor consumption. (This is in some contradiction to the presumed greater need the man must have for drying out, since previous recent jailings mean that he could not have been drinking for long.)

The previous comment, plus the answer by a court officer to the question, "Who get's dismissed?" illustrates this criteria for sentencing:

> A person with no previous arrests [gets dismissed]. If they have had no arrests, then the judge hates for them to have a conviction on their record. *The more arrests they've had and the more recently they've had them, the more likely they are to get another sentence.* (Emphasis mine.) . . .

The Man's Social Position Does he have a job he could go to? Is he married? Does he have a permanent address, or will he literally be on the streets if he receives a dismissal?

For these data, dress is an all-important clue, age a secondary one. A man who looks down-and-out is more likely to receive a sentence than the well-dressed man. According to a court officer:

> If they look pretty beat—clothes dirty and in rags, then you figure that they need some help to stop drinking before they kill themselves. . . .

> If they're under 21 we usually give them a kick-out. If they are a business man or a lawyer we have them sign a civil release so they can't sue and let them go. . . .

An observer reports that a judge freed a young man with the following remarks:

> I am going to give you a suspended sentence and hope that this experience will be a warning to you. I don't want you to get caught up in this cycle. . . .

Transients form a category of their own and get a special package deal—if they will promise to leave town, they draw a suspended sentence or probation. The parallel between this practice and the police policy of telling some Skid Row drunks to "take a walk" need only be mentioned. The following interchanges are illustrative:

> *Judge:* I thought you told me the last time you were in here that you were going to leave Pacific City.

> *Defendant:* I was supposed to have left town yesterday. I just got through doing time.

> *Judge:* Go back to Woodland. Don't let me see you in here again or we are going to put you away. Thirty days suspended. . . .

> *Defendant:* I am supposed to leave with the circus tomorrow. If I don't go, I will be out of work for the whole season.

> *Judge:* You promised to leave three times before. Thirty days in the County Jail. . . .

By combining the variables of physical appearance, past performance, and social position, a rough description of social types expected in drunk court, and matching sentences for each type is shown in Table 1.

OTHER SENTENCING ASSISTANCE

Even with the aid of a simplified mental guide, the judge cannot be expected to assemble and assimilate sufficient material on each man, review it, mentally type the man, and then make a sentencing decision

Table 1 / Paradigm of Social Types and Sentences in Drunk Court

Social Type	Probable Sentence
A young man who drank too much: a man under 40, with a job, and perhaps a wife, who has not appeared in court before.	A kick-out or a suspended sentence.
The young repeater: same as above, but has been before judge several times (may be on way to being an alcoholic.)	Suspended sentence or short sentence (five–ten days) to scare him, or possible attendance at Alcoholism School.
The repeater who still looks fairly respectable. (Image vacillating between an alcoholic and a drunk.)	30-day suspended sentence, with possible attendance at Alcoholism School.
Out-of-towner (social characteristics not important as they have nonlocal roots.) Therefore not important as to whether overindulged, a chronic drunk, or an alcoholic.	Suspended sentence on condition he leave town. Purpose is to discourage him from getting on local loop and adding to taxpayer's load.
The middle-aged repeater who has not been up for some time. (May be an alcoholic who has relapsed.)	Suspended sentence with required attendance at Alcoholism School or given to custody of Christian Missionaries.
The derelict-drunk who looks "rough," i.e., suffering withdrawal, a hangover, has cuts and bruises, may have malnutrition or some diseases connected with heavy drinking and little eating; a chronic drunk; seedy clothing, stubble beard, etc.	30–60–90 day sentence depending on number of prior arrests and physical condition at time of arrest. (Has probably attended Alcoholism School already.)
The man who looks gravely ill (probably a chronic alcoholic).	County hospital under suspended sentence.

in less than a minute. Thus, it is not surprising that almost all drunk court judges employ the aid of one assistant and sometimes two court attachés who are familiar with the Row and its inhabitants. These men are known as court liaison officers. Because of personal familiarity with chronic drunkenness offenders, the liaison officers are able to answer questions about each accused person quickly and to recommend a case disposition. Such persons obviously operate as an informal screening board.

The most important court helper in Pacific City is a man who knows most of the Row men by sight and claims also to know their general outlook on alcohol and life. Known to the defendants as "the Rapper," this man often sits behind the judge and suggests informally who would benefit most from probation and assignment to Alcoholism School, who might need the "shaking-up" that jail provides, and who ought to be sent to alcoholic screening at City Hospital and perhaps on to State Mental Hospital. As each man is named, the Rapper whispers to the judge, who then passes sentence.[4]

In Pacific City, the man who was the Rapper for a period of time was an ex-alcoholic who could claim intimate knowledge of the chronic drunkenness offender because he had drunk with them. A relative of the Rapper was highly placed in city politics, and the Rapper made no secret of the fact that his appointment was politically engineered.[5] During the course of the study (several times in fact), the Rapper himself "fell off the wagon" and underwent treatment at Northern State Mental Hospital, one of the stations on the loop. While there, the Rapper told about his recent job with the court and how he helped the judge:

> Each man arrested has a card with the whole record on it. We would go over the cards before the case came up. We see how many times he's been arrested. I could advise the judge to give them probation or a sentence. Many times, the family would call and request a sentence. I would often arrange for them to get probation plus clothes and a place to stay at one of the halfway houses. Oh, I'll help and help, but when they keep falling off—I get disgusted.[6]

The Christian Missionaries also send a liaison man to the drunk court sessions. He acts as Rapper at special times and thereby also serves in an informal screening capacity. Sponsorship by this organization appears to guarantee that the defendant will get a suspended sentence. For instance, this interchange was observed in court several times:

> *Judge*, turning to Missionary representative: "Do you want him [this defendant]?" (Meaning, "Will you take him at one of your facilities?")
>
> *Missionary:* (Nods "Yes.")
>
> *Judge:* "Suspended sentence." . . .

Another observer discussed this arrangement with a veteran judge:

> *Interviewer: Isn't there any attempt made to consider the men for rehabilitation?*
>
> The men are screened by the Christian Missionaries usually. The Christian Missionaries send someone down to the jail who tries to help them. They

talk with the men and screen them. Nobody does the job that the Christian Missionaries do in the jails.

Interviewer: The Court abdicates the screening of defendants to the Christian Missionaries, then?

Not completely. We try to keep a record. Some of these men we can help but most we can't. I know by heart all of their alibis and stories.[7]

Another important informal court post is filled by an employee who is known to some of the men as "the Knocker." The job of the Knocker is to maintain the personal records of the men who appear before drunk court and to supply the judge with this information. A court observer reported the following:

The Knocker spoke to the judge in just about every case. However, I do not know what he said. He may just be reading to the judge the official records, or he may be giving his personal judgement about the possibility of the defendant being picked up again in the near future. One thing seems clear: the judge receives his information from the Knocker just before he hands out the sentence.

Sometimes it is difficult to distinguish the Knocker (who merely gives information to the judge) from the Rapper (who "suggests" the proper sentence.) In 1963, two of these court liaison officers worked together. An interview with one partner is quoted below:

Interviewer: What do you do?

Up here we act as a *combination district attorney and public defender.* We are more familiar with these guys than the judges are. The judges alternate. We have the previous arrest records. A lot of times, guys will give phony names. It may take us a while to catch up with them. We try to remember if we have seen a guy before. (Emphasis mine.)

Interviewer: How does a judge decide whether to sentence the men and if so, for how long?

We help him out on that. If a guy has been in three times in four weeks, they should get a minimum of 30 days. They need to dry out. You know, if a man has been arrested three times in four weeks, you ask yourself the question: "How many times has he been drunk that he wasn't arrested?" Also, you look at the condition of a man—he may even need hospitalization.

Interviewer: You mean you can tell whether a man ought to be sent to jail by looking at him?

Some of them look a lot more rough looking than others. You can tell they have been on a drunk for more than one day. They are heavily bearded. They have probably been sleeping in doorways or on the street. You can tell they have been on a long drunk. . . .

Thus perhaps the most revealing aspect of the sentencing procedure is the virtual absence of interest in the *charge* and the judge's role as spokesman for the court officer's decision. This may account for the fact the judge seldom discusses the case with the defendant, except in a jocular, disparaging way. . . . The following interchanges, which illustrate this attitude, were witnessed by observers:

> *Defendant:* I was sleeping in a basement when a man attacked me with a can opener.
>
> *Judge:* Did you also see elephants? . . .
>
> *Judge:* What is your story this time?
>
> *Defendant:* (As he begins to speak, Judge interrupts.)
>
> *Judge:* You gave me that line yesterday; 30 days in the County Jail. . . .

JUSTIFYING THE SENTENCING PROCESS

How does the municipal court judge, serving in drunk court sessions, allow himself to be a party to such extra-legal activities as platoon sentencing, the heavy reliance on advice from "friends of the court," and the utilization of extraneous social characteristics in setting the sentence? Why is there not a conflict with his self-image of judicial compassion for the individual and scrupulous attention to legal niceties?

For some judges, this conflict is resolved by falling back on the alcoholism-as-an-illness view of drunkenness, and by redefining many of the men who appear before him as *patients* rather than defendants. Thus, when asked to describe their duties, drunk court judges often sound like physicians dealing with troublesome patients for whom they must prescribe unpleasant but necessary medicine, rather than judges punishing men for being a public annoyance. As an example of this:

> I know that jail isn't the best place for these men, but we have to do something for them. We need to put them someplace where they can dry out. You can't just let a man go out and kill himself. . . .
>
> This is a grave and almost hopeless problem. But you have to try some kind of treatment. Often they are better off in jail than out on the street. . . .

The drunk court judges sometimes add the wish that the city provided a more palatable alternative to the County Jail, but then reiterate the view that it is better than no help at all.

Court attachés have essentially the same attitude:

> Some of these guys are so loaded that they will fall and break their skull if you don't lock them up. Half of these guys have no place to stay anyway except a dingy heap. They are better off in jail. . . .

The whole purpose of the law is to try to help them. It's for the protection of themselves and for others, that's the way the law reads. For example, say you're driving through here [Skid Row] and you hit a drunk. He could get killed and if you don't stop and render aid, you could become a criminal. . . .

Giving them 30 days in County Jail is sometimes a kindness. *You are doing them a favor, like a diabetic who won't take his insulin.* Sometimes you must hurt him to help him. (Emphasis mine.). . . .

Like the Skid Row police, the officers, the judge and his coterie are reinforced in their definition of the situation as clinical, and of themselves as diagnosticians and social internists, by the fact that relatives often call the court and ask that a man be given time in jail for his own good. The judge usually complies. Furthermore, as has been mentioned, there is at the jail a branch of the Out-Patient Therapy Center that was originally established to work for the rehabilitation of alcoholics. . . . Having this jail clinic allows the drunk court judge to say:

I sentence you to 30 days and I will get in touch with the social worker at the County Jail and she will help you.[8]

I sentence you to therapy with the psychologists at the County Jail. (Also reported by court observers.)

Creation of the Pacific City Alcoholism School also allows the judge to feel that he is fulfilling both judicial and therapeutic duties, giving the defendant a suspended sentence on the condition that he will attend the lecture sessions.

Where the name of the social worker or psychologist of Alcoholism School is not invoked as part of the sentence, an awareness of alcoholism as an illness is frequently used as an introductory statement to indicate the reasoning of the courts for giving a jail sentence.

We realize that you men are sick and need help. Any action I might take, therefore, should not in any sense be construed as punishment. Jail in this case is not a punitive measure, but to help you with your alcoholism problem.

However, the uneasiness of the judge with the jailing of alcoholics has other indicators. The captain of the County Jail, for instance, reports that inmates serving time for public drunkenness have only to write a letter requesting modification and it is almost automatically forthcoming, something not true for modification requests of prisoners convicted of other misdemeanors.[9]

That drunk court's methods and procedures of handling the Row men go against the judicial grain also seems to be indicated by the fact court officers claim a new judge must be "broken in" to drunk court before he operates efficiently. When the judge first arrives, he will sentence differently from an experienced judge and in the direction of greater leniency. This upsets the established pattern.

The result is he is taken in hand and guided to do "the right thing" by the veteran court aids. As one court aid put it:

> Most of the judges are pretty good—they rely on us. Sometimes you get a new judge who wants to do things his way. We have to break them in, train them. This court is very different. We have to break new judges in. It takes some of them some time to get adjusted to the way we do things.[10]

The high rate of recidivism of chronic drunkenness offenders leads some experts to question the value of jail as a cure for alcoholism or chronic drunkenness.[11] Publicly, at least, the judges appear to hold to the view that the current arrest and incarceration process *can* be helpful, but that often the alcoholic simply does not respond to "treatment" permanently and needs periodic "doses" of jail-therapy. As one judge put it:

> Some men have simply gone so far that you can't do anything for them. They are hopeless. All we can do is send them to jail to dry out from time to time.[12]

Notes

1. Frederic S. LeClercq, "Field Observations in Drunk Court of the Pacific City Municipal Court" (unpublished memorandum, 1966), p. 1.

2. These observations were made almost two years after LeClercq made his.

3. LeClercq, "Field Observations in Drunk Court," p. 12.

4. The use of a "Rapper" is apparently not a local phenomenon. Bogue notes it also in his study of the Chicago Skid Row. See Donald J. Bogue, *Skid Row in American Cities* (Chicago: University of Chicago, 1963), p. 414.

5. When the Rapper started drinking again, he was not replaced; rather, court officers and an official of the Christian Missionaries fulfilled his duties.

6. The Rapper was under treatment again for alcoholism at State Mental Hospital when he made this statement. . . . Kurt Lewin discusses this phenomenon of rejection of one's own (if they are a minority group of some type) in "Self-Hatred Among Jews," Chap. 12 of *Resolving Social Conflict* (New York: Harper Publishing Company, 1945).

7. LeClercq, "Field Observations in Drunk Court," p. 11.

8. Reported by inmate in County Jail on public drunkenness charge.

9. Source: Captain, County Jail.

10. LeClercq, "Field Observations in Drunk Court," p. 7.

11. As previously mentioned, the chief deputy of County Jail puts the number of recidivists at 85 percent of the total admissions in any one year. A small "loop," made by a chronic drunkenness offender who goes between municipal jail and Skid Row, has been well chronicled by Pittman and Gordon in *The Revolving Door* (Glencoe, Ill.: The Free Press, 1958).

12. Statement made by Municipal Judge from city near Pacific City.

34 / Characteristics of Total Institutions

ERVING GOFFMAN

INTRODUCTION

Total Institutions

Every institution captures something of the time and interest of its members and provides something of a world for them; in brief, every institution has encompassing tendencies. When we review the different institutions in our Western society we find a class of them which seems to be encompassing to a degree discontinuously greater than the ones next in line. Their encompassing or total character is symbolized by the barrier to social intercourse with the outside that is often built right into the physical plant: locked doors, high walls, barbed wire, cliffs and water, open terrain, and so forth. These I am calling total institutions, and it is their general characteristics I want to explore. This exploration will be phrased as if securely based on findings but will in fact be speculative.

The total institutions of our society can be listed for convenience in five rough groupings. *First*, there are institutions established to care for persons thought to be both incapable and harmless; these are the homes for the blind, the aged, the orphaned, and the indigent. *Second*, there are places established to care for persons thought to be at once incapable of looking after themselves and a threat to the community, albeit an unintended one: TB sanitoriums, mental hospitals, and leprosoriums. *Third*, another type of total institution is organized to protect the community against what are thought to be intentional dangers to it; here the welfare of the persons thus sequestered is not the immediate issue. Examples are: Jails, penitentiaries, POW camps, and concentration camps. *Fourth*, we find institutions purportedly established the better to pursue some technical task and justifying themselves only on these instrumental grounds: Army barracks, ships, boarding schools, work camps, colonial compounds, large mansions from the point of view of those who live in the servants' quarters, and so forth. *Finally*, there are those establishments designed as retreats from the world or as training stations for the religious: Abbeys, monasteries, convents, and other cloisters. This sublisting of total institutions is neither neat nor exhaustive, but the listing itself provides an empirical starting point for a purely denotative definition of the category. By anchoring the initial definition of total institutions in this way, I hope to be able to discuss the general characteristics of the type without becoming tautological.

Before attempting to extract a general profile from this list of establishments, one conceptual peculiarity must be mentioned. None of the elements I will extract seems entirely exclusive to total institutions, and none seems shared by every one of them. What is shared and unique about total institutions is that each exhibits many items in this family of attributes to an intense degree. In speaking of "common characteristics," then, I will be using this phrase in a weakened, but I think logically defensible, way.

Totalistic Features

A basic social arrangement in modern society is that we tend to sleep, play and work in different places, in each case with a different set of coparticipants, under a different authority, and without an overall rational plan. The central feature of total institutions can be described as a breakdown of the kinds of barriers ordinarily separating these three spheres of life. *First*, all aspects of life are conducted in the same place and under the same single authority. *Second*, each phase of the member's daily activity will be carried out in the immediate company of a large batch of others, all of whom are treated alike and required to do the same thing together. *Third*, all phases of the day's activities are tightly scheduled, with one activity leading at a prearranged time into the next, the whole circle of activities being imposed from above through a system of explicit formal rulings and a body of officials. *Finally*, the contents of the various enforced activities are brought together as parts of a single overall rational plan purportedly designed to fulfill the official aims of the institution.

Individually, these totalistic features are found, of course, in places other than total institutions. Increasingly, for example, our large commercial, industrial and educational establishments provide cafeterias, minor services and off-hour recreation for their members. But while this is a tendency in the direction of total institutions, these extended facilities remain voluntary in many particulars of their use, and special care is taken to see that the ordinary line of authority does not extend to these situations. Similarly, housewives or farm families can find all their major spheres of life within the same fenced-in area, but these persons are not collectively regimented and do not march through the day's steps in the immediate company of a batch of similar others.

The handling of many human needs by the bureaucratic organization of whole blocks of people—whether or not this is a necessary or effective means of social organization in the circumstances—can be taken, then, as the key fact of total institutions. From this, certain important implications can be drawn.

Given the fact that blocks of people are caused to move in time, it becomes possible to use a relatively small number of supervisory personnel where the central relationship is not guidance or periodic checking, as in many employer-employee relations, but rather surveillance—a seeing to it that everyone does what he has been clearly told is required of him, and this under conditions where one person's infraction is likely to stand out in relief against the visible, constantly examined, compliance of the others. . . .

In total institutions . . . there is a basic split between a large class of individuals who live in and who have restricted contact with the world outside the walls, conveniently called *inmates*, and the small class that supervises them, conveniently called staff, who often operate on an 8-hour day and are socially integrated into the outside world. Each grouping tends to conceive of members of the other in terms of narrow hostile stereotypes, staff often seeing inmates as bitter, secretive and untrustworthy, while inmates often see staff as condescending, highhanded and mean. Staff tends to feel superior and righteous; inmates tend, in some ways at least, to feel inferior, weak, blameworthy and guilty. Social mobility between the two strata is grossly restricted; social distance is typically great and often formally prescribed; even talk across the boundaries may be conducted in a special tone of voice. These restrictions on contact presumably help to maintain the antagonistic stereotypes. In any case, two different social and cultural worlds develop, tending to jog along beside each other, with points of official contact but little mutual penetration. It is important to add that the institutional plan and name comes to be identified by both staff and inmates as somehow belonging to staff, so that when either grouping refers to the views or interests of "the institution," by implication they are referring to the views and concerns of the staff.

The staff-inmate split is one major implication of the central features of total institutions; a second one pertains to work. In the ordinary arrangements of living in our society, the authority of the workplace stops with the worker's receipt of a money payment; the spending of this in a domestic and recreational setting is at the discretion of the worker and is the mechanism through which the authority of the workplace is kept within strict bounds. However, to say that inmates in total institutions have their full day scheduled for them is to say that some version of all basic needs will have to be planned for, too. In other words, total institutions take over "responsibility" for the inmate and must guarantee to have everything that is defined as essential "layed on." It follows, then, that whatever incentive is given for work, this will not have the structural significance it has on the outside. Different attitudes and incentives regarding this central feature of our life will have to prevail.

Here, then, is one basic adjustment required of those who work in total institutions and of those who must induce these people to work. In some cases, no work or little is required, and inmates, untrained often in leisurely ways of life, suffer extremes of boredom. In other cases, some work is required but is carried on at an extremely slow pace, being geared into a system of minor, often ceremonial payments, as in the case of weekly tobacco ration and annual Christmas presents, which cause some mental patients to stay on their job. In some total institutions, such as logging camps and merchant ships, something of the usual relation to the world that money can buy is obtained through the practice of "forced saving"; all needs are organized by the institution, and payment is given only after a work season is over and the men leave the premises. And in some total institutions, of course, more than a full day's work is required and is induced not by reward, but by threat of dire punishment. In all such cases, the work-oriented individual may tend to become somewhat demoralized by the system.

In addition to the fact that total institutions are incompatible with the basic work-payment structure of our society, it must be seen that these establishments are also incompatible with another crucial element of our society, the family. The family is sometimes contrasted to solitary living, but in fact the more pertinent contrast to family life might be with batch [block] living. For it seems that those who eat and sleep at work, with a group of fellow workers, can hardly sustain a meaningful domestic existence. Correspondingly, the extent to which a staff retains its integration in the outside community and escapes the encompassing tendencies of total institutions is often linked up with the maintenance of a family off the grounds.

Whether a particular total institution acts as a good or bad force in civil society, force it may well have, and this will depend on the suppression of a whole circle of actual or potential households. Conversely, the formation of households provides a structural guarantee that total institutions will not arise. The incompatibility between these two forms of social organization should tell us, then, something about the wider social functions of them both.

Total institutions, then, are social hybrids, part residential community, part formal organization, and therein lies their special sociological interest. There are other reasons, alas, for being interested in them, too. These establishments are the forcing houses for changing persons in our society. Each is a natural experiment, typically harsh, on what can be done to the self.

Having suggested some of the key features of total institutions, we can move on now to consider them from the special perspectives that seem natural to take. I will consider the inmate world, then the staff world, and then something about contacts between the two.

THE INMATE WORLD

Mortification Processes

It is characteristic of inmates that they come to the institution as members, already full-fledged, of a *home world*, that is, a way of life and a round of activities taken for granted up to the point of admission to the institution. It is useful to look at this culture that the recruit brings with him to the institution's door—his *presenting culture*, to modify a psychiatric phrase—in terms especially designed to highlight what it is the total institution will do to him. Whatever the stability of his personal organization, we can assume it was part of a wider supporting framework lodged in his current social environment, a round of experience that somewhat confirms a conception of self that is somewhat acceptable to him and a set of defensive maneuvers exercisable at his own discretion as a means of coping with conflicts, discreditings and failures.

Now it appears that total institutions do not substitute their own unique culture for something already formed. We do not deal with acculturation or assimilation but with something more restricted than these. In a sense, total institutions do not look for cultural victory. They effectively create and sustain a particular kind of tension between the home world and the institutional world and use this persistent tension as strategic leverage in the management of men. The full meaning for the inmate of being "in" or "on the inside" does not exist apart from the special meaning to him of "getting out" or "getting on the outside."

The recruit comes into the institution with a self and with attachments to supports which had allowed this self to survive. Upon entrance, he is immediately stripped of his wonted supports, and his self is systematically, if often unintentionally, mortified. In the accurate language of some of our oldest total institutions, he is led into a series of abasements, degradations, humiliations, and profanations of self. He begins, in other words, some radical shifts in his *moral career*, a career laying out the progressive changes that occur in the beliefs that he has concerning himself and significant others.

The *stripping processes* through which *mortification of the self* occurs are fairly standard in our total institutions. Personal identity equipment is removed, as well as other possessions with which the inmate may have identified himself, there typically being a system of nonaccessible storage from which the inmate can only reobtain his effects should he leave the institution. As a substitute for what has been taken away, institutional issue is provided, but this will be the same for large categories of inmates and will be regularly repossessed by the institution. In brief, standardized defacement will occur. . . . Family, occupational, and educational career lines are chopped off, and a stigmatized status is submitted. Sources of fantasy materials which had meant momentary releases from stress in the home world are denied. Areas of autonomous decision are eliminated through the process of collective scheduling of daily activity. Many channels of communication with the outside are restricted or closed off completely. Verbal discreditings occur in many forms as a matter of course. Expressive signs of respect for the staff are coercively and continuously demanded. And the effect of each of these conditions is multiplied by having to witness the mortification of one's fellow inmates. . . .

In the background of the sociological stripping process, we find a characteristic authority system with three distinctive elements, each basic to total institutions.

First, to a degree, authority is of the *echelon* kind. Any member of the staff class has certain rights to discipline any member of the inmate class. . . . In our society, the adult himself, however, is typically under the authority of a *single* immediate superior in connection with his work or under authority of one spouse in connection with domestic duties. The only echelon authority he must face—the police— typically are neither constantly nor relevantly present, except perhaps in the case of traffic-law enforcement.

Second, the authority of corrective sanctions is directed to a great multitude of items of conduct of the kind that are constantly occurring and constantly coming up for judgment; in brief, authority is directed to matters of dress, deportment, social intercourse, manners and the like. . . .

The third feature of authority in total institutions is that misbehaviors in one sphere of life are held against one's standing in other spheres. Thus, an individual who fails to participate with proper enthusiasm in sports may be brought to the attention of the person who determines where he will sleep and what kind of work task will be accorded to him.

When we combine these three aspects of authority in total institutions, we see that the inmate cannot easily escape from the press of judgmental officials and from the enveloping tissue of constraint. The system of authority undermines the basis for control that adults in our society expect to exert over their interpersonal environment and may produce the terror of feeling that one is being radically demoted in the age-grading system. On the outside, rules are sufficiently lax and the individual sufficiently agreeable to required self-discipline to insure that others will rarely have cause for pouncing on him. He need not constantly look over his shoulder to see if criticism and other sanctions are coming. On the inside, however, rulings are abundant, novel, and closely enforced so that, quite characteristically, inmates live with chronic anxiety about breaking the rules and chronic worry about the consequences of breaking them. The desire to "stay out of trouble" in a total institution is likely to require persistent conscious effort and may lead the inmate to abjure certain levels of sociability with his fellows in order to avoid the incidents that may occur in these circumstances.

It should be noted finally that the mortifications to be suffered by the inmate may be purposely brought home to him in an exaggerated way during the first few days after entrance, in a form of initiation that has been called *the welcome*. Both staff and fellow inmates may go out of their way to give the neophyte a clear notion of where he stands. As part of this *rite de passage*, he may find himself called by a term such as "fish," "swab," etc., through which older inmates tell him that he is not only merely an inmate but that even within this lowly group he has a low status.

Privilege System

While the process of mortification is in progress, the inmate begins to receive formal and informal instruction in what will here be called the *privilege system*. Insofar as the inmate's self has been unsettled a little by the stripping action of the institution, it is largely around this framework that pressures are exerted, making for a reorganization of self. Three basic elements of the system may be mentioned.

First, there are the house rules, a relatively explicit and formal set of prescriptions and proscriptions which lay out the main requirements of inmate conduct. These regulations spell out the austere round of life in which the inmate will operate. Thus, the admission procedures through which the recruit is initially stripped of his self-supporting context can be seen as the institution's way of getting him in the position to start living by the house rules.

Second, against the stark background, a small number of clearly defined *rewards or privileges* are held out in exchange for obedience to staff in action and spirit. It is important to see that these potential gratifications are not unique to the institution but rather are ones carved out of the flow of support that the inmate previously had quite taken for granted. On the outside, for example, the inmate was likely to be able to unthinkingly exercise autonomy by deciding how much sugar and milk he wanted in his coffee, if any, or when to light up a cigarette; on the inside, this right may become quite problematic and a matter of a great deal of conscious concern. Held up to the inmate as possibilities, these few recapturings seem to have a reintegrative effect, re-establishing relationships with the whole lost world and assuaging withdrawal symptoms from it and from one's lost self.

The inmate's run of attention, then, especially at first, comes to be fixated on these supplies and obsessed with them. In the most fanatic way, he can spend the day in devoted thoughts concerning the possibility of acquiring these gratifications or the approach of the hour at which they are scheduled to be granted. The building of a world around these minor privileges is perhaps the most important feature of inmate culture and yet is something that cannot easily be appreciated by an outsider, even one who has lived through the experience himself. This situation sometimes leads to generous sharing and almost always to a willingness to beg for things such as cigarettes, candy and newspapers. It will be understandable, then, that a constant feature of inmate discussion is the *release binge fantasy*, namely, recitals of what one will do during leave or upon release from the institution.

House rules and privileges provide the functional requirements of the third element in the privilege system: *punishments*. These are designated as the consequence of breaking the rules. One set of these punishments consists of the temporary or permanent withdrawal of privileges or abrogation of the right to try to earn them. In general, the punishments meted out in total institutions are of an order more severe than anything encountered by the inmate in his home world. An institutional arrangement which causes a small number of easily controlled privileges to have a massive significance is the same arrangement which lends a terrible significance to their withdrawal.

There are some special features of the privilege system which should be noted.

First, punishments and privileges are themselves modes of organization peculiar to total institutions. . . . And privileges, it should be emphasized, are not the same as prerequisites, indulgences or values, but merely the absence of deprivations one ordinarily expects one would not have to sustain. The very notions, then, of punishments and privileges are not ones that are cut from civilian cloth.

Second, it is important to see that the question of release from the total institution is elaborated into the privilege system. Some acts will become known as ones that mean an increase or no decrease in length of stay, while others become known as means for lessening the sentence.

Third, we should also note that punishments and privileges come to be geared into a residential work system. Places to work and places to sleep become clearly defined as places where certain kinds and levels of privilege obtain, and inmates are shifted very rapidly and visibly from one place to another as the mechanisms for giving them the punishment or privilege their cooperativeness has warranted. The inmates are moved, the system is not. . . .

Immediately associated with the privilege system we find some standard social processes important in the life of total institutions.

We find that an *institutional lingo* develops through which inmates express the events that are crucial in their particular world. Staff too, especially its lower levels, will know this language, using it when talking to inmates, while reverting to more standardized speech when talking to superiors and outsiders. Related to this special argot, inmates will possess knowledge of the various ranks and officials, an accumulation of lore about the establishment, and some comparative information about life in other similar total institutions.

Also found among staff and inmates will be a clear awareness of the phenomenon of *messing up*, so called in mental hospitals, prisons, and barracks. This involves a complex process of engaging in forbidden activity, getting caught doing so, and receiving something like the full punishment accorded this. An alteration in privilege status is usually implied and is categorized by a phrase such as "getting busted." Typical infractions which can eventuate in messing up are: fights, drunkenness, attempted suicide, failure at examinations, gambling, insubordination, homosexuality, improper taking of leave, and participation in collective riots. While these punished infractions are typically ascribed to the offender's cussedness, villainy, or "sickness," they do in fact constitute a vocabulary of institutionalized actions, limited in such a way that the same messing up may occur for quite different reasons. Informally, inmates and staff may understand, for example, that a given messing up is a way for inmates to show resentment against a current situation felt to be unjust in terms of the informal agreements between staff and inmates, or a way of postponing release without having to admit to one's fellow inmates that one really does not want to go.

In total institutions there will also be a system of what might be called *secondary adjustments*, namely, technics which do not directly challenge staff management but which allow inmates to obtain disallowed satisfactions or allowed ones by disallowed means. These practices are variously referred to as: the angles, knowing the ropes, conniving, gimmicks, deals, ins, etc. Such adaptations apparently reach their finest flower in prisons, but of course other total institutions are overrun with them too. It seems apparent that an important aspect of secondary adjustments is that they provide the inmate with some evidence that he is still, as it were, his own man and still has some protective distance, under his own control, between himself and the institution. . . .

The occurrence of secondary adjustments correctly allows us to assume that the inmate group will have some kind of a *code* and some means of informal social control evolved to prevent one inmate from informing staff about the secondary adjustments of another. On the same grounds we can expect that one dimension of social typing among inmates will turn upon this question of security, leading to persons defined as "squealers," "finks," or "stoolies" on one hand, and persons defined as "right guys" on the other. It should be added that where new inmates can play a role in the system of secondary adjustments, as in providing new faction members or new sexual objects, then their "welcome" may indeed be a sequence of initial indulgences and enticements, instead of exaggerated deprivations. Because of secondary adjustments we also find *kitchen strata*, namely, a kind of rudimentary, largely informal, stratification of inmates on the basis of each one's differential access to disposable illicit commodities; so also we find social typing to designate the powerful persons in the informal market system.

While the privilege system provides the chief framework within which reassembly of the self takes place, other factors characteristically lead by different routes in the same general direction. Relief from economic and social responsibilities—much touted as part of the therapy in mental hospitals—is one, although in many cases it would seem that the disorganizing effect of this moratorium is more significant than its organizing effect. More important as a reorganizing influence is the *fraternalization process*, namely, the process through which socially distant persons find themselves developing mutual support and common *counter-mores* in opposition to a system that has forced them into intimacy and into a single, equalitarian community of fate. It seems that the new recruit frequently starts out with something like the staff's popular misconceptions of the character of the inmates and then comes to find that most of his fellows have all the properties of ordinary decent human beings and that the stereotypes associated with their condition or offense are not a reasonable ground for judgment of inmates. . . .

Adaptation Alignments

The mortifying processes that have been discussed and the privilege system represent the conditions that the inmate must adapt to in some way, but however pressing, these conditions allow for different ways of meeting them. We find, in fact, that the same inmate will employ different lines of adaptation or tacks at different phases in his moral career and may even fluctuate between different tacks at the same time.

First, there is the process of *situational withdrawal*. The inmate withdraws apparent attention from everything except events immediately around his body and sees these in a perspective not employed by others present. This drastic curtailment of involvement in interactional events is best known, of course, in mental hospitals, under the title of "regression." . . . I do not think it is known whether this line of adaptation forms a single continuum of varying degrees of withdrawal or whether there are standard discontinuous plateaus of disinvolvement. It does seem to be the case, however, that, given the pressures apparently required to dislodge an inmate from this status, as well as the currently limited facilities for doing so, we frequently find here, effectively speaking, an irreversible line of adaptation.

Second, there is the *rebellious line*. The inmate intentionally challenges the institution by flagrantly refusing to cooperate with staff in almost any way. The result is a constantly communicated intransigency and sometimes high rebel-morale. Most large mental hospitals, for example, seem to have wards where this spirit strongly prevails. Interestingly enough, there are many circumstances in which sustained rejection of a total institution requires sustained orientation to its formal organization and hence, paradoxically, a deep kind of commitment to the establishment.

Third, another standard alignment in the institutional world takes the form of a kind of *colonization*. The sampling of the outside world provided by the establishment is taken by the inmate as the whole, and a stable, relatively contented existence is built up out of the maximum satisfactions procurable within the institution. Experience of the outside world is used as a point of reference to demonstrate the desirability of life on the inside; and the usual tension between the two worlds collapses, thwarting the social arrangements based upon this felt discrepancy. Characteristically, the individual who too obviously takes this line may be accused by his fellow inmates of "having found a home" or of "never having had it so good." Staff itself may become vaguely embarrassed by this use that is being made of the institution, sensing that the benign possibilities in the situation are somehow being misued. Colonizers themselves may feel obliged to deny their satisfaction with the institution, if only in the interest of sustaining the counter-mores supporting inmate solidarity. They may find it necessary to mess up just prior to their slated discharge, thereby allowing themselves to present involuntary reasons for continued incarceration. It should be incidentally noted that any humanistic effort to make life in total institutions more bearable must face the possibility that doing so many increase the attractiveness and likelihood of colonization.

Fourth, one mode of adaptation to the setting of a total institution is that of *conversion*. The inmate appears to take over completely the official or staff view of himself and tries to act out the role of the perfect inmate. While the colonized inmate builds as much of a free community as possible for himself by using the limited facilities available, the convert takes a more disciplined, moralistic, monochromatic line, presenting himself as someone whose institutional enthusiasm is always at the disposal of the staff. . . . Some mental hospitals have the distinction of providing two quite different conversion possibilities—one for the new admission who can see the light after an appropriate struggle and adopt the psychiatric view of himself, and another for the chronic ward patient who adopts the manner and dress of attendants while helping them to manage the other ward patients with a stringency excelling that of the attendants themselves. . . .

While the alignments that have been mentioned represent coherent courses to pursue, few inmates, it seems, carry these pursuits very far. In most total institutions, what we seem to find is that most inmates take the tack of what they call *playing it cool*. This involves a somewhat opportunistic combination of secondary adjustments, conversion, colonization and loyalty to the inmate group, so that in the particular circumstances the inmate will have a maximum chance of eventually getting out physically and psychically undamaged. Typically, the inmate will support the counter-mores when with fellow inmates and be silent to them on how tractably he acts when alone in the presence of the staff. Inmates taking this line tend to subordinate contacts with their fellows to the higher claim of "keeping out of trouble." They tend to volunteer for nothing, and they may even learn to cut their ties to the outside world sufficiently to give cultural reality to the world inside but not enough to lead to colonization. . . .

Culture Themes

A note should be added here concerning some of the more dominant themes of inmate culture.

First, in the inmate group of many total institutions there is a strong feeling that time spent in the establishment is time wasted or destroyed or taken from one's life; it is time that must be written off. It is something that must be "done" or "marked" or "put in" or "built" or "pulled." . . . As such, this time is something that its doers have bracketed off for constant conscious consideration in a way not quite found on the outside. And as a result, the inmate tends to feel that for the duration of his required stay—his sentence—he has been totally exiled from living. It is in this context that we can appreciate something of the demoralizing influence of an indefinite sentence or a very long one. We should also note that however hard the conditions of life may become in total institutions, harshness alone cannot account for this quality of life wasted. Rather we must look to the social disconnections caused by entrance and to the usual failure to acquire within the institution gains that can be transferred to outside life—gains such as money earned, or marital relations formed, or certified training received.

Second, it seems that in many total institutions a peculiar kind and level of self-concern is engendered. The low position of inmates relative to their station on the outside, as established initially through the mortifying processes, seems to make for a milieu of personal failure and a round of life in which one's fall from grace is continuously pressed home. In response, the inmate tends to develop a story, a line, a sad tale—a kind of lamentation and apologia—which he constantly tells to his fellows as a means of creditably accounting for his present low estate. While staff constantly discredit these lines, inmate audiences tend to employ tact, suppressing at least some of the disbelief and boredom engendered by these recitations. In consequence, the inmate's own self may become even more of a focus for his conversation than it does on the outside.

Perhaps the high level of ruminative self-concern found among inmates in total institutions is a way of handling the sense of wasted time that prevails in these places. If so, then perhaps another interesting aspect of inmate culture can be related to the same factor. I refer here to the fact that in total institutions we characteristically find a premium placed on what might be called *removal activities*, namely, voluntary unserious pursuits which are sufficiently engrossing and exciting to lift the participant out of himself, making [him] oblivious for the time to his actual situation. If the ordinary activities in total institutions can be said to torture time, these activities mercifully kill it.

Some removal activities are collective, such as ball games, woodwork, lectures, choral singing and card playing; some are individual but rely on public materials, as in the case of reading, solitary TV watching, etc. No doubt, private fantasy ought to be included too. Some of these activities may be officially sponsored by staff; and some, not officially sponsored, may constitute secondary adjustments. In any case, there seems to be no total intitution which cannot be seen as a kind of Dead Sea in which appear little islands of vivid, enrapturing activity.

Consequences

In this discussion of the inmate world, I have commented on the mortification process, the reorganizing influences, the lines of response taken by inmates under these circumstances, and the cultural milieu that develops. A concluding word must be added about the long-range consequences of membership.

Total institutions frequently claim to be concerned with rehabilitation, that is, with resetting the inmate's self-regulatory mechanisms so that he will maintain the standards of the establishment of his own accord after he leaves the setting. In fact, it seems this claim is seldom realized and even when permanent alteration occurs, these changes are often not of the kind intended by the staff. With the possible exception presented by the great resocialization efficiency of religious institutions, neither the stripping processes nor the reorganizing ones seem to have a lasting effect. No doubt the availability of secondary adjustments helps to account for this, as do the presence of counter-mores and the tendency for inmates to combine all strategies and "play it cool." In any case, it seems that shortly after release, the ex-inmate will have forgotten a great deal of what life was like on the inside and will have once again begun to take for granted the privileges around which life in the institution was organized. The sense of injustice, bitterness and alienation, so typically engendered by the inmate's experience and so definitely marking a stage in his moral career, seems to weaken upon graduation, even in those cases where a permanent stigma has resulted.

But what the ex-inmate does retain of his institutional experience tells us important things about total institutions. Often entrance will mean for the recruit that he has taken on what might be called a *proactive status*. Not only is his relative social position within the walls radically different from what it was on the outside, but, as he comes to learn, if and when he gets out, his social position on the outside will never again be quite what it was prior to entrance. . . . When the proactive status is unfavorable, as it is for those in prisons or mental hospitals, we popularly employ the term "stigmatization" and expect that the ex-inmate may make an effort to conceal his past and try to "pass."

35 / The Moral Career of the Mental Patient

ERVING GOFFMAN

Traditionally the term *career* has been reserved for those who expect to enjoy the rises laid out within a respectable profession. The term is coming to be used, however, in a broadened sense to refer to any social strand of any person's course through life. The perspective of natural history is taken: unique outcomes are neglected in favor of such changes over time as are basic and common to the members of a social category, although occurring independently to each of them. Such a career is not a thing that can be brilliant or disappointing; it can no more be a success than a failure. In this light, I want to consider the mental patient, drawing mainly upon data collected during a year's participant observation of patient social life in a public mental hospital,[1] wherein an attempt was made to take the patient's point of view.

One value of the concept of career is its two-sidedness. One side is linked to internal matters held dearly and closely, such as image of self and felt identity; the other side concerns official position, jural relations, and style of life, and is part of a publicly accessible institutional complex. The concept of career, then, allows one to move back and forth between the personal and the public, between the self and its significant society, without having overly to rely for data upon what the person says he thinks he imagines himself to be.

This paper, then, is an exercise in the institutional approach to the study of self. The main concern will be with the *moral* aspects of career—that is, the regular sequence of changes that career entails in the person's self and in his framework of imagery for judging himself and others.[2]

The category "mental patient" itself will be understood in one strictly sociological sense. In this perspective, the psychiatric view of a person becomes significant only in so far as this view itself alters his social fate—an alteration which seems to become fundamental in our society when, and only when, the person is put through the process of hospitalization.[3] I therefore exclude certain neighboring categories: the undiscovered candidates who would be judged "sick" by psychiatric standards but who never come to be viewed as such by themselves or others, although they may cause everyone a great deal of trouble;[4] the office patient whom a psychiatrist feels he can handle with drugs or shock on the outside; the mental client who engages in psychotherapeutic relationships. And I include anyone, however robust in temperament, who somehow gets caught up in the heavy machinery of mental hospital servicing. In this way the effects of being treated as a mental patient can be kept quite distinct from the effects upon a person's life of traits a clinician would view as psychopathological.[5] Persons who become mental hospital patients vary widely in the kind and degree of illness that a psychiatrist would impute to them, and in the attributes by which laymen would describe them. But once started on the way, they are confronted by some importantly similar circumstances and respond to these in some importantly similar ways. Since these similarities do not come from mental illness, they would seem to occur in spite of it. It is thus a tribute to the power of social forces that the uniform status of mental patient can not only assure an aggregate of persons a common fate and eventually, because of this, a common character, but that this social reworking can be done upon what is perhaps the most obstinate diversity of human materials that can be brought together by society. Here there lacks only the frequent forming of a protective group-life by ex-patients to illustrate in full the classic cycle of response by which deviant subgroupings are psychodynamically formed in society.

This general sociological perspective is heavily reinforced by one key finding of sociologically oriented students in mental hospital research. As has been repeatedly shown in the study of nonliterate societies, the awesomeness, distastefulness, and barbarity of a foreign culture can decrease in the degree that the student becomes familiar with the point of view to life that is taken by his subjects. Similarly, the student of mental hospitals can discover that the craziness or "sick behavior" claimed for the mental patient is by and large a product of the claimant's social distance from the situation that the patient is in, and is not primarily a product of mental illness. Whatever the refinements of the various patients' psychiatric diagnoses, and whatever the special ways in which social life on the "inside" is unique, the researcher can find that he is participating in a community not significantly different from any other he has studied.[6] Of course, while restricting himself to the off-ward grounds community of paroled patients, he may feel, as some patients do, that life in the locked wards is bizarre; and while on a locked admissions or convalescent ward, he may feel that chronic "back" wards are socially crazy places. But he need only move his sphere of sympathetic participation to the "worst" ward in the hospital, and this too can come into social focus as a place with a livable and continuously meaningful social world. This in no way denies that he will find a minority in any ward or patient group that continues to seem quite beyond the capacity to follow rules of social organization, or that the orderly fulfilment of normative expectations in patient society is partly made possible by strategic measures that have somehow come to be institutionalized in mental hospitals.

The career of the mental patient falls popularly and naturalistically into three main phases: the period prior to entering the hospital, which I shall call the *prepatient phase*; the period in the hospital, the *inpatient phase;* the period after discharge from the hospital, should this occur, namely, the *ex-patient phase.*[7] This paper will deal only with the first two phases.

THE PREPATIENT PHASE

A relatively small group of prepatients come into the mental hospital willingly, because of their own idea of what will be good for them, or because of wholehearted agreement with the relevant members of their family. Presumably these recruits have found themselves acting in a way which is evidence to them that they are losing their minds or losing control of themselves. This view of oneself would seem to be one of the most pervasively threatening things that can happen to the self in our society, especially since it is likely to occur at a time when the person is in any case sufficiently troubled to exhibit the kind of symptom which he himself can see. As Sullivan described it,

> What we discover in the self-system of a person undergoing schizophrenic changes or schizophrenic processes, is then, in its simplest form, an extremely fear-marked puzzlement, consisting of the use of rather generalized and anything but exquisitely refined referential processes in an attempt to cope with what is essentially a failure at being human—a failure at being anything that one could respect as worth being.[8]

Coupled with the person's disintegrative re-evaluation of himself will be the new, almost equally pervasive circumstance of attempting to conceal from others what he takes to be the new fundamental facts about himself, and attempting to discover whether others too have discovered them.[9] Here I want to stress that perception of losing one's mind is based on culturally derived and socially engrained stereotypes as to the significance of symptoms such as hearing voices, losing temporal and spatial orientation, and sensing that one is being followed, and that many of the most spectacular and convincing of these symptoms in some instances psychiatrically signify merely a temporary emotional upset in a stressful situation, however terrifying to the person at the time. Similarly, the anxiety consequent upon this perception of oneself, and the strategies devised to reduce this anxiety, are not a product of abnormal psychology, but would be exhibited by any person socialized into our culture who came to conceive of himself as someone losing his mind. Interestingly, subcultures in American society apparently differ in the amount of ready imagery and encouragement they supply for such self-views, leading to differential rates of *self*-referral; the capacity to take this disintegrative view of oneself without psychiatric prompting seems to be one of the questionable cultural privileges of the upper classes.[10]

For the person who has come to see himself—with whatever justification—as mentally unbalanced, entrance to the mental hospital can sometimes bring relief, perhaps in part because of the sudden transformation in the structure of his basic social situations; instead of being to himself a questionable person trying to maintain a role as a full one, he can become an officially questioned person known to himself to be not so questionable as that. In other cases, hospitalization can make matters worse for the willing patient, confirming by the objective situation what has theretofore been a matter of the private experience of self.

Once the willing prepatient enters the hospital, he may go through the same routine of experiences as do those who enter unwillingly. In any case, it is the latter that I mainly want to consider, since in America at present these are by far the more numerous kind.[11] Their approach to the institution takes one of three classic forms: they come because they have been implored by their family or threatened with the abrogation of family ties unless they go "willingly"; they come by force under police escort; they come under misapprehension purposely induced by others, this last restricted mainly to youthful prepatients.

The prepatient's career may be seen in terms of an extrusory model; he starts out with relationships and rights, and ends up, at the beginning of his hospital stay, with hardly any of either. The moral aspects of this career, then, typically begin with the experience of abandonment, disloyalty, and embitterment. This is the case even though to others it may be obvious that he was in need of treatment, and even though in the hospital he may soon come to agree.

The case histories of most mental patients document offense against some arrangement for face-to-face living—a domestic establishment, a work place, a semipublic organization such as a church or store, a public region such as a street or park. Often there is also a record of some *complainant*, some figure who takes that action against the offender which eventually leads to his hospitalization. This may not be the person who makes the first move, but it is the person who makes what turns out to be the first effective move. Here is the *social* beginning of the patient's career, regardless of where one might locate the psychological beginning of his mental illness.

The kinds of offenses which lead to hospitalization are felt to differ in nature from those which lead to other extrusory consequences—to imprisonment, divorce, loss of job, disownment, regional exile, noninstitutional psychiatric treatment, and so forth. But little seems known about these differentiating factors; and when one studies actual commitments, alternate outcomes frequently appear to have been possible. It seems true, moreover, that for every offense that leads to an effective complaint, there are many psychiatrically similar ones that never do. No action is taken; or action is taken which leads to other extrusory outcomes; or ineffective action is taken, leading to the mere pacifying or putting off of the person who complains. Thus, as Clausen and Yarrow have nicely shown, even offenders who are eventually hospitalized are likely to have had a long series of ineffective actions taken against them.[12]

Separating those offenses which could have been used as grounds for hospitalizing the offender from those that are so used, one finds a vast number of what students of occupation call career contingencies.[13] Some of these contingencies in the mental patient's career have been suggested, if not explored, such as socio-economic status, visibility of the offense, proximity to a mental hospital, amount of treatment facilities available, community regard for the type of treatment given in available hospitals, and so on.[14] For information about other contingencies one must rely on atrocity tales: a psychotic man is tolerated by his wife until she finds herself a boy friend, or by his adult children until they move from a house to an apartment; an alcoholic is sent to a mental hospital because the jail is full, and a drug addict because he declines to avail himself of psychiatric treatment on the outside; a rebellious adolescent daughter can no longer be managed at home because she now threatens to have an open affair with an unsuitable companion; and so on. Correspondingly there is an equally important set of contingencies causing the person to by-pass this fate. And should the person enter the hospital, still another set of contingencies will help determine when he is to obtain a discharge—such as the desire of his family for his return, the availability of a "manageable" job, and so on. The society's official view is that inmates of mental hospitals are there primarily because they are suffering from mental illness. However, in the degree that the "mentally ill" outside hospitals numerically approach or surpass those inside hospitals, one could say that mental patients *distinctively* suffer not from mental illness, but from contingencies.

Career contingencies occur in conjunction with a second feature of the prepatient's career—the *circuit of agents*—and agencies—that participate fatefully in his passage from civilian to patient status.[15]

Here is an instance of that increasingly important class of social system whose elements are agents and agencies, which are brought into systemic connection through having to take up and send on the same persons. Some of these agent-roles will be cited now, with the understanding that in any concrete circuit a role may be filled more than once, and a single person may fill more than one of them.

First is the *next-of-relation*—the person whom the prepatient sees as the most available of those upon whom he should be able to most depend in times of trouble; in this instance the last to doubt his sanity and the first to have done everything to save him from the fate which, it transpires, he has been approaching. The patient's next-of-relation is usually his next of kin; the special term is introduced because he need not be. Second is the *complainant*, the person who retrospectively appears to have started the person on his way to the hospital. Third are the *mediators*—the sequence of agents and agencies to which the prepatient is referred and through which he is relayed and processed on his way to the hospital. Here are included police, clergy, general medical practitioners, office psychiatrists, personnel in public clinics, lawyers, social service workers, school teachers, and so on. One of these agents will have the legal mandate to sanction commitment and will exercise it, and so those agents who precede him in the process will be involved in something whose outcome is not yet settled. When the mediators retire from the scene, the prepatient has become an inpatient, and the significant agent has become the hospital administrator.

While the complainant usually takes action in a lay capacity as a citizen, an employer, a neighbor, or a kinsman, mediators tend to be specialists and differ from those they serve in significant ways. They have experience in handling trouble, and some professional distance from what they handle. Except in the case of policemen, and perhaps some clergy, they tend to be more psychiatrically oriented than the lay public, and will see the need for treatment at times when the public does not.[16]

An interesting feature of these roles is the functional effects of their interdigitation. For example, the feelings of the patient will be influenced by whether or not the person who fills the role of complainant also has the role of next-of-relation—an embarrassing combination more prevalent, apparently, in the higher classes than in the lower.[17] Some of these emergent effects will be considered now.[18]

In the prepatient's progress from home to the hospital he may participate as a third person in what he may come to experience as a kind of *alienative coalition*. His next-of-relation presses him into coming to "talk things over" with a medical practitioner, an office psychiatrist, or some other counselor. Disinclination on his part may be met by threatening him with desertion, disownment, or other legal action, or by stressing the joint and explorative nature of the interview. But typically the next-of-relation will have set the interview up, in the sense of selecting the professional, arranging for time, telling the professional something about the case, and so on. This move effectively tends to establish the next-of-relation as the responsible person to whom pertinent findings can be divulged, while effectively establishing the other as the patient. The prepatient often goes to the interview with the understanding that he is going as an equal of someone who is so bound together with him that a third person could not come between them in fundamental matters; this, after all, is one way in which close relationships are defined in our society. Upon arrival at the office the prepatient suddenly finds that he and his next-of-relation have not been accorded the same roles, and apparently that a prior understanding between the professional and the next-of-relation has been put in operation against him. In the extreme but common case the professional first sees the prepatient alone, in the role of examiner and diagnostician, and then sees the next-of-relation alone, in the role of advisor, while carefully avoiding talking things over seriously with them both together.[19] And even in those nonconsultative cases where public officials must forcibly extract a person from a family that wants to tolerate him, the next-of-relation is likely to be induced to "go along" with the official action, so that even here the prepatient may feel that an alienative coalition has been formed against him.

The moral experience of being third man in such a coalition is likely to embitter the prepatient, especially since his troubles have already probably led to some estrangement from his next-of-relation. After he enters the hospital, continued visits by his next-of-relation can give the patient the "insight" that his own best interests were being served. But the initial visits may temporarily strengthen his feeling of abandonment; he is likely to beg his visitor to get him out or at least to get him more privileges and to sympathize with the monstrousness of his plight—to which the visitor ordinarily can respond only by trying to maintain a hopeful note, by not "hearing" the requests, or by assuring the patient that the medical authorities know about these things and are doing what is medically best. The visitor then nonchalantly goes back into a world that the patient has learned is incredibly thick with freedom and privileges, causing the patient to feel that his next-of-relation is merely adding a pious gloss to a clear case of traitorous desertion.

The depth to which the patient may feel betrayed by his next-of-relation seems to be increased by the fact that another witnesses his betrayal—a factor which is apparently significant in many three-party situations. An offended person may well act forbearantly and accom-modatively toward an offender when the two are alone, choosing peace ahead of justice. The presence of a witness, however, seems to add something to the implications of the offense. For then it is beyond the power of the offended and offender to forget about, erase, or suppress what has happened; the offense has become a public social fact.[20] When the witness is a mental health commission, as is some-times the case, the witnessed betrayal can verge on a "degradation ceremony."[21] In such circumstances, the offended patient may feel that some kind of extensive reparative action is required before witnesses, if his honor and social weight are to be restored.

Two other aspects of sensed betrayal should be mentioned. First, those who suggest the possibility of another's entering a mental hospi-tal are not likely to provide a realistic picture of how in fact it may strike him when he arrives. Often he is told that he will get required medical treatment and a rest, and may well be out in a few months or so. In some cases they may thus be concealing what they know, but I think, in general, they will be telling what they see as the truth. For here there is a quite relevant difference between patients and mediat-ing professionals; mediators, more so than the public at large, may conceive of mental hospitals as short-term medical establishments where required rest and attention can be voluntarily obtained, and not as places of coerced exile. When the prepatient finally arrives he is likely to learn quite quickly, quite differently. He then finds that the information given him about life in the hospital has had the effect of his having put up less resistance to entering than he now sees he would have put up had he known the facts. Whatever the intentions of those who participated in his transition from person to patient, he may sense they have in effect "conned" him into his present predicament.

I am suggesting that the prepatient starts out with at least a portion of the rights, liberties, and satisfactions of the civilian and ends up on a psychiatric ward stripped of almost everything. The question here is *how* this stripping is managed. This is the second aspect of betrayal I want to consider.

As the prepatient may see it, the circuit of significant figures can function as a kind of *betrayal funnel*. Passage from person to patient may be effected through a series of linked stages, each managed by a different agent. While each stage tends to bring a sharp decrease in adult free status, each agent may try to maintain the fiction that no further decrease will occur. He may even manage to turn the prepa-tient over to the next agent while sustaining this note. Further, through words, cues, and gestures, the prepatient is implicitly asked by the current agent to join with him in sustaining a running line of polite small talk that tactfully avoids the administrative facts of the situation, becoming, with each stage, progressively more at odds with these facts. The spouse would rather not have to cry to get the prepatient to visit a psychiatrist; psychiatrists would rather not have a scene when the prepatient learns that he and his spouse are being seen separately and in different ways; the police infrequently bring a prepatient to the hospital in a strait jacket, finding it much easier all around to give him a cigarette, some kindly words, and freedom to relax in the back seat of the patrol car; and finally, the admitting psychiatrist finds he can do his work better in the relative quiet and luxury of the "admission suite" where, as an incidental consequence, the notion can survive that a mental hospital is indeed a comforting place. If the prepatient heeds all of these implied requests and is reasonably decent about the whole thing, he can travel the whole circuit from home to hospital without forcing anyone to look directly at what is happening or to deal with the raw emotion that his situation might well cause him to express. His showing consideration for those who are moving him toward the hospital allows them to show consideration for him, with the joint result that these interactions can be sustained with some of the protective harmony characteristic of ordinary face-to-face dealings. But should the new patient cast his mind back over the sequence of steps leading to hospitalization, he may feel that everyone's *current* comfort was being busily sustained while his long-range welfare was being undermined. This realization may constitute a moral experience that further separates him for the time from the people on the outside.[22]

I would now like to look at the circuit of career agents from the point of view of the agents themselves. Mediators in the person's transition from civil to patient status—as well as his keepers, once he is in the hospital—have an interest in establishing a responsible next-of-relation as the patient's deputy or *guardian*; should there be no obvious candidate for the role, someone may be sought out and pressed into it. Thus while a person is gradually being transformed into a patient, a next-of-relation is gradually being transformed into a guardian. With a guardian on the scene, the whole transition process can be kept tidy. He is likely to be familiar with the prepatient's civil involvements and business, and can tie up loose ends that might otherwise be left to entangle the hospital. Some of the prepatient's abrogated civil rights can be transferred to him, thus helping to sustain the legal fiction that while the prepatient does not actually have his rights he somehow actually has not lost them.

Inpatients commonly sense, at least for a time, that hospitalization is a massive unjust deprivation, and sometimes succeed in convincing a few persons on the outside that this is the case. It often turns out to be useful, then, for those identified with inflicting these deprivations, however justifiably, to be able to point to the cooperation and agreement of someone whose relationship to the patient places him above suspicion, firmly defining him as the person most likely to have the patient's personal interest at heart. If the guardian is satisfied with what is happening to the new inpatient, the world ought to be.[23]

Now it would seem that the greater the legitimate personal stake one party has in another, the better he can take the role of guardian to the other. But the structural arrangements in society which lead to the acknowledged merging of two persons' interests lead to additional consequences. For the person to whom the patient turns for help—for protection against such threats as involuntary commitment—is just the person to whom the mediators and hospital administrators logically turn for authorization. It is understandable, then, that some patients will come to sense, at least for a time, that the closeness of a relationship tells nothing of its trustworthiness.

There are still other functional effects emerging from this complement of roles. If and when the next-of-relation appeals to mediators for help in the trouble he is having with the prepatient, hospitalization may not, in fact, be in his mind. He may not even perceive the prepatient as mentally sick, or, if he does, he may not consistently hold to this view.[24] It is the circuit of mediators, with their greater psychiatric sophistication and their belief in the medical character of mental hospitals, that will often define the situation for the next-of-relation, assuring him that hospitalization is a possible solution and a good one, that it involves no betrayal, but is rather a medical action taken in the best interests of the prepatient. Here the next-of-relation may learn that doing his duty to the prepatient may cause the prepatient to distrust and even hate him for the time. But the fact that this course of action may have had to be pointed out and prescribed by professionals, and be defined by them as a moral duty, relieves the next-of-relation of some of the guilt he may feel.[25] It is a poignant fact that an adult son or daughter may be pressed into the role of mediator, so that the hostility that might otherwise be directed against the spouse is passed on to the child.[26]

Once the prepatient is in the hospital, the same guilt-carrying function may become a significant part of the staff's job in regard to the next-of-relation.[27] These reasons for feeling that he himself has not betrayed the patient, even though the patient may then think so, can later provide the next-of-relation with a defensible line to take when visiting the patient in the hospital and a basis for hoping that the relationship can be re-established after its hospital moratorium. And of course this position, when sensed by the patient, can provide him with excuses for the next-of-relation, when and if he comes to look for them.[28]

Thus while the next-of-relation can perform important functions for the mediators and hospital administrators, they in turn can perform important functions for him. One finds, then, an emergent unintended exchange or reciprocation of functions, these functions themselves being often unintended.

The final point I want to consider about the prepatient's moral career is its peculiarly *retroactive* character. Until a person actually arrives at the hospital there usually seems no way of knowing for sure that he is destined to do so, given the determinative role of career contingencies. And until the point of hospitalization is reached, he or others may not conceive of him as a person who is becoming a mental patient. However, since he will be held against his will in the hospital, his next-of-relation and the hospital staff will be in great need of a rationale for the hardships they are sponsoring. The medical elements of the staff will also need evidence that they are still in the trade they were trained for. These problems are eased, no doubt unintentionally, by the case-history construction that is placed on the patient's past life, this having the effect of demonstrating that all along he had been becoming sick, that he finally became very sick, and that if he had not been hospitalized much worse things would have happened to him—all of which, of course, may be true. Incidentally, if the patient wants to make sense out of his stay in the hospital, and, as already suggested, keep alive the possibility of once again conceiving of his next-of-relation as a decent, well-meaning person, then he too will have reason to believe some of this psychiatric work-up of his past.

Here is a very ticklish point for the sociology of careers. An important aspect of every career is the view the person constructs when he looks backward over his progress; in a sense, however, the whole of the prepatient career derives from this reconstruction. The fact of having had a prepatient career, starting with an effective complaint, becomes an important part of the mental patient's orientation, but this part can begin to be played only after hospitalization proves that what he had been having, but no longer has, is a career as a prepatient.

THE INPATIENT PHASE

The last step in the prepatient's career can involve his realization— justified or not—that he has been deserted by society and turned out of relationships by those closest to him. Interestingly enough, the patient, especially a first admission, may manage to keep himself from coming to the end of this trail, even though in fact he is now in a locked mental hospital ward. On entering the hospital, he may very strongly feel the desire not to be known to anyone as a person who could possibly be reduced to these present circumstances, or as a person who conducted himself in the way he did prior to commitment. Consequently, he may avoid talking to anyone, may stay by himself when possible, and may even be "out of contact" or "manic" so as to avoid ratifying any interaction that presses a politely reciprocal role upon him and opens him up to what he has become in the eyes of others. When the next-of-relation makes an effort to visit, he may be rejected by mutism, or by the patient's refusal to enter the visiting room, these strategies sometimes suggesting that the patient still clings to a remnant of relatedness to those who made up his past, and is protecting this remnant from the final destructiveness of dealing with the new people that they have become.[29]

Usually the patient comes to give up this taxing effort at anonymity, at not-hereness, and begins to present himself for conventional social interaction to the hospital community. Thereafter he withdraws only in special ways—by always using his nickname, by signing his contribution to the patient weekly with his initial only, or by using the innocuous "cover" address tactfully provided by some hospitals; or he withdraws only at special times, when, say, a flock of nursing students makes a passing tour of the ward, or when, paroled to the hospital grounds, he suddenly sees he is about to cross the path of a civilian he happens to know from home. Sometimes this making of oneself available is called "settling down" by the attendants. It marks a new stand openly taken and supported by the patient, and resembles the "coming out" process that occurs in other groupings.[30]

Once the prepatient begins to settle down, the main outlines of his fate tend to follow those of a whole class of segregated establishments—jails, concentration camps, monasteries, work camps, and so on—in which the inmate spends the whole round of life on the grounds, and marches through his regimented day in the immediate company of a group of persons of his own institutional status.[31]

Like the neophyte in many of these "total institutions," the new inpatient finds himself cleanly stripped of many of his accustomed affirmations, satisfactions, and defenses, and is subjected to a rather full set of mortifying experiences: restriction of free movement; communal living; diffuse authority of a whole echelon of people; and so on. Here one begins to learn about the limited extent to which a conception of oneself can be sustained when the usual setting of supports for it are suddenly removed.

While undergoing these humbling moral experiences, the inpatient learns to orient himself in terms of the "ward system."[32] In public mental hospitals this usually consists of a series of graded living arrangements built around wards, administrative units called services, and parole statuses. The "worst" level involves often nothing but wooden benches to sit on, some quite indifferent food, and a small piece of room to sleep in. The "best" level may involve a room of one's own, ground and town privileges, contacts with staff that are relatively undamaging, and what is seen as good food and ample recreational facilities. For disobeying the pervasive house rules, the inmate will receive stringent punishments expressed in terms of loss of privileges; for obedience he will eventually be allowed to reacquire some of the minor satisfactions he took for granted on the outside.

The institutionalization of these radically different levels of living throws light on the implications for self of social settings. And this in turn affirms that the self arises not merely out of its possessor's interactions with significant others, but also out of the arrangements that are evolved in an organization for its members.

There are some settings which the person easily discounts as an expression or extension of him. When a tourist goes slumming, he may take pleasure in the situation not because it is a reflection of him but because it so assuredly is not. There are other settings, such as living rooms, which the person manages on his own and employs to influence in a favorable direction other persons' views of him. And there are still other settings, such as a work place, which express the employee's occupational status, but over which he has no final control, this being exerted, however tactfully, by his employer. Mental hospitals provide an extreme instance of this latter possibility. And this is due not merely to their uniquely degraded living levels, but also to the unique way in which significance for self is made explicit to the patient, piercingly, persistently, and thoroughly. Once lodged on a given ward, the patient is firmly instructed that the restrictions and deprivations he encounters are not due to such things as tradition or economy—and hence dissociable from self—but are intentional parts of his treatment, part of his need at the time, and therefore an expression of the state that his self has fallen to. Having every reason to initiate requests for better conditions, he is told that when the staff feels he is "able to manage" or will be "comfortable with" a higher ward level, then appropriate action will be taken. In short, assignment to a given ward is presented not as a reward or punishment, but as an expression of his general level of social functioning, his status as a person. Given the fact that the worst ward levels provide a round of life that inpatients with organic brain damage can easily manage, and that these quite limited human beings are present to prove it, one can appreciate some of the mirroring effects of the hospital.[33]

The ward system, then, is an extreme instance of how the physical facts of an establishment can be explicitly employed to frame the conception a person takes of himself. In addition, the official psychiatric mandate of mental hospitals gives rise to even more direct, even more blatant, attacks upon the inmate's view of himself. The more "medical" and the more progressive a mental hospital is—the more it attempts to be therapeutic and not merely custodial—the more he may be confronted by high-ranking staff arguing that his past has been a failure, that the cause of this has been within himself, that his attitude to life is wrong, and that if he wants to be a person he will have to change his way of dealing with people and his conceptions of himself. Often the moral value of these verbal assaults will be brought home to him by requiring him to practice taking this psychiatric view of himself in arranged confessional periods, whether in private sessions or group psychotherapy.

Now a general point may be made about the moral career of inpatients which has bearing on many moral careers. Given the stage that any person has reached in a career, one typically finds that he constructs an image of his life course—past, present, and future—which selects, abstracts, and distorts in such a way as to provide him with a view of himself that he can usefully expound in current situations. Quite generally, the person's line concerning self defensively brings him into appropriate alignment with the basic values of his society, and so may be called an *apologia.* If the person can manage to present a view of his current situation which shows the operation of favorable personal qualities in the past and a favorable destiny awaiting him, it may be called a *success story.* If the facts of a person's past and present are extremely dismal, then about the best he can do is to show that he is not responsible for what has become of him, and the term *sad tale* is appropriate. Interestingly enough, the more the person's past forces him out of apparent alignment with central moral values, the more often he seems compelled to tell his sad tale in any company in which he finds himself. Perhaps he partly responds to the need he feels in others of not having their sense of proper life courses affronted. In any case, it is among convicts, 'wino's,' and prostitutes that one seems to obtain sad tales the most readily.[34] It is the vicissitudes of the mental patient's sad tale that I want to consider now.

In the mental hospital, the setting and the house rules press home to the patient that he is, after all, a mental case who has suffered some kind of social collapse on the outside, having failed in some over-all way, and that here he is of little social weight, being hardly capable of acting like a full-fledged person at all. These humiliations are likely to be most keenly felt by middle-class patients, since their previous condition of life little immunizes them against such affronts; but all patients feel some downgrading. Just as any normal member of his outside subculture would do, the patient often responds to this situation by attempting to assert a sad tale proving that he is not "sick," that the "little trouble" he did get into was really somebody else's fault, that his past life course had some honor and rectitude, and that the hospital is therefore unjust in forcing the status of mental patient upon him. This self-respecting tendency is heavily institutionalized within the patient society where opening social contacts typically involve the participants' volunteering information about their current ward location and length of stay so far, but not the reasons for their stay—such interaction being conducted in the manner of small talk on the outside.[35] With greater familiarity, each patient usually volunteers relatively acceptable reasons for his hospitalization, at the same time accepting without open immediate question the lines offered by other patients. Such stories as the following are given and overtly accepted.

> I was going to night school to get a M.A. degree, and holding down a job in addition, and the load got too much for me.

> The others here are sick mentally but I'm suffering from a bad nervous system and that is what is giving me these phobias.

> I got here by mistake because of a diabetes diagnosis, and I'll leave in a couple of days. [The patient had been in seven weeks.]

> I failed as a child, and later with my wife I reached out for dependency.

> My trouble is that I can't work. That's what I'm in for. I had two jobs with a good home and all the money I wanted.[36]

The patient sometimes reinforces these stories by an optimistic definition of his occupational status: A man who managed to obtain an audition as a radio announcer styles himself a radio announcer; another who worked for some months as a copy boy and was then given a job as a reporter on a large trade journal, but fired after three weeks, defines himself as a reporter.

A whole social role in the patient community may be constructed on the basis of these reciprocally sustained fictions. For these face-to-face niceties tend to be qualified by behind-the-back gossip that comes only a degree closer to the 'objective' facts. Here, of course, one can see a classic social function of informal networks of equals: they serve as one another's audience for self-supporting tales—tales that are somewhat more solid than pure fantasy and somewhat thinner than the facts.

But the patient's *apologia* is called forth in a unique setting, for few settings could be so destructive of self-stories except, of course, those stories already constructed along psychiatric lines. And this destructiveness rests on more than the official sheet of paper which attests that the patient is of unsound mind, a danger to himself and others— an attestation, incidentally, which seems to cut deeply into the patient's pride, and into the possibility of his having any.

Certainly the degrading conditions of the hospital setting belie many of the self-stories that are presented by patients; and the very fact of being in the mental hospital is evidence against these tales. And of course, there is not always sufficient patient solidarity to prevent patient discrediting patient, just as there is not always a sufficient number of 'professionalized' attendants to prevent attendant discrediting patient. As one patient informant repeatedly suggested to a fellow patient:

If you're so smart, how come you got your ass in here?

The mental hospital setting, however, is more treacherous still. Staff has much to gain through discreditings of the patient's story— whatever the felt reason for such discreditings. If the custodial faction in the hospital is to succeed in managing his daily round without complaint or trouble from him, then it will prove useful to be able to point out to him that the claims about himself upon which he rationalizes his demands are false, that he is not what he is claiming to be, and that in fact he is a failure as a person. If the psychiatric faction is to impress upon him its views about his personal make-up, then they must be able to show in detail how their version of his past and their version of his character hold up much better than his own.[37] If both the custodial and psychiatric factions are to get him to cooperate in the various psychiatric treatments, then it will prove useful to disabuse him of *his* view of their purposes, and cause him to appreciate that they know what they are doing, and are doing what is best for him. In brief, the difficulties caused by a patient are closely tied to his version of what has been happening to him, and if cooperation is to be secured, it helps if this version is discredited. The patient must "insightfully" come to take, or affect to take, the hospital's view of himself.

Notes

1. The study was conducted during 1955–56 under the auspices of the Laboratory of Socio-environmental Studies of the National Institute of Mental Health. I am grateful to the Laboratory Chief, John A. Clausen, and to Dr. Winfred Overholser, Superintendent, and the late Dr. Jay Hoffman, then First Assistant Physician of Saint Elizabeths Hospital, Washington, D.C., for the ideal cooperation they freely provided. A preliminary report is contained in Goffman, "Interpersonal Persuasion," pp. 117–193; in *Group Processes: Transactions of the Third Conference*, edited by Bertram Schaffner: New York, Josiah Macy, Jr. Foundation, 1957. A shorter version of this paper was presented at the Annual Meeting of the American Sociological Society, Washington, D.C., August 1957.

2. Material on moral career can be found in early social anthropological work on ceremonies of status transition, and in classic social psychological descriptions of those spectacular changes in one's view of self that can accompany participation in social movements and sects. Recently new kinds of relevant data have been suggested by

psychiatric interest in the problem of "identity" and sociological studies of work careers and "adult socialization."

3. This point has recently been made by Elaine and John Cumming, *Closed Ranks*; Cambridge, Commonwealth Fund, Harvard Univ. Press, 1957; pp. 101–102. "Clinical experience supports the impression that many people define mental illness as 'That condition for which a person is treated in a mental hospital.' . . . Mental illness, it seems, is a condition which afflicts people who must go to a mental institution, but until they do almost anything they do is normal." Leila Deasy has pointed out to me the correspondence here with the situation in white collar crime. Of those who are detected in this activity, only the ones who do not manage to avoid going to prison find themselves accorded the social role of the criminal.

4. Case records in mental hospitals are just now coming to be exploited to show the incredible amount of trouble a person may cause for himself and others before anyone begins to think about him psychiatrically, let alone take psychiatric action against him. See John A. Clausen and Marian Radke Yarrow, "Paths to the Mental Hospital," *J. Social Issues* (1955) 11:25–32; August B. Hollingshead and Fredrick C. Redlich, *Social Class and Mental Illness*; New York, Wiley, 1958: pp. 173–174.

5. An illustration of how this perspective may be taken to all forms of deviancy may be found in Edwin Lemert, *Social Pathology*; New York, McGraw-Hill, 1951; see especially pp. 74–76. A specific application to mental defectives may be found in Stewart E. Perry, "Some Theoretic Problems of Mental Deficiency and Their Action Implications," *Psychiatry* (1954) 17:45–73; see especially p. 68.

6. Conscientious objectors who voluntarily went to jail sometimes arrived at the same conclusion regarding criminal inmates. See, for example, Alfred Hassler, *Diary of a Self-made Convict*; Chicago, Regnery, 1954; p. 74.

7. This simple picture is complicated by the somewhat special experience of roughly a third of ex-patients—namely, readmission to the hospital, this being the recidivist or "repatient" phase.

8. Harry Stack Sullivan, *Clinical Studies in Psychiatry*; edited by Helen Swick Perry, Mary Ladd Gawel, and Martha Gibbon; New York, Norton, 1956; pp. 184–185.

9. This moral experience can be contrasted with that of a person learning to become a marihuana addict, whose discovery that he can be 'high' and still 'op' effectively without being detected apparently leads to a new level of use. See Howard S. Becker, "Marihuana Use and Social Control." *Social Problems* (1955) 3:35–44; see especially pp. 40–41.

10. See footnote 2: Hollingshead and Redlich, p. 187, Table 6, where relative frequency is given of self-referral by social class grouping.

11. The distinction employed here between willing and unwilling patients cuts across the legal one, of voluntary and committed, since some persons who are glad to come to the mental hospital may be legally committed, and of those who come only because of strong familial pressure, some may sign themselves in as voluntary patients.

12. Clausen and Yarrow; see footnote 4.

13. An explicit application of this notion to the field of mental health may be found in Edwin M. Lemert, "Legal Commitment and Social Control," *Sociology and Social Research* (1946) 30:370–378.

14. For example, Jerome K. Meyers and Leslie Schaffer, "Social Stratification and Psychiatric Practice: A Study of an Outpatient Clinic," *Amer. Sociological Rev.* (1954) 19:307–310. Lemert, see footnote 5; pp. 402–403. *Patients in Mental Institutions*, 1941; Washington, D.C., Department of Commerce, Bureau of Census, 1941; p. 2.

15. For one circuit of agents and its bearing on career contingencies, see Oswald Hall, "The Stages of a Medical Career," *Amer. J. Sociology* (1948) 53:227–336.

16. See Cumming, footnote 3; p. 92.

17. Hollingshead and Redlich, footnote 4; p. 187.

18. For an analysis of some of these circuit implications for the inpatient, see Leila C. Deasy and Olive W. Quinn, "The Wife of the Mental Patient and the Hospital Psychiatrist." *J. Social Issues* (1955) 11:49–60. An interesting illustration of this kind of analysis may also be found in Alan G. Gowman, "Blindness and the Role of Companion," *Social Problems* (1956) 4:68–75. A general statement may be found in Robert Merton, "The Role Set: Problems in Sociological Theory," *British J. Sociology* (1957) 8:106–120.

19. I have one case record of a man who claims he thought *he* was taking his wife to

see the psychiatrist, not realizing until too late that his wife had made the arrangements.

20. A paraphrase from Kurt Riezler, "The Social Psychology of Shame," *Amer. J. Sociology* (1943) 48:458.

21. See Harold Garfinkel, "Conditions of Successful Degradation Ceremonies," *Amer. J. Sociology* (1956) 61:420–424.

22. Concentration camp practices provide a good example of the function of the betrayal funnel in inducing cooperation and reducing struggle and fuss, although here the mediators could not be said to be acting in the best interests of the inmates. Police picking up persons from their homes would sometimes joke good-naturedly and offer to wait while coffee was being served. Gas chambers were fitted out like delousing rooms, and victims taking off their clothes were told to note where they were leaving them. The sick, aged, weak, or insane who were selected for extermination were sometimes driven away in Red Cross ambulances to camps referred to by terms such as "observation hospital." See David Boder, *I Did Not Interview the Dead*; Urbana, Univ. of Illinois Press, 1949; p. 81; and Elie A. Cohen, *Human Behavior in the Concentration Camp*; London, Cape, 1954; pp. 32, 37, 107.

23. Interviews collected by the Clausen group at NIMH suggest that when a wife comes to be a guardian, the responsibility may disrupt previous distance from in-laws, leading either to a new supportive coalition with them or to a marked withdrawal from them.

24. For an analysis of these nonpsychiatric kinds of perception, see Marian Radke Yarrow, Charlotte Green Schwartz, Harriet S. Murphy, and Leila Calhoun Deasy, "The Psychological Meaning of Mental Illness in the Family," *J. Social Issues* (1955) 11:12–24; Charlotte Green Schwartz, "Perspectives on Deviance: Wives' Definitions of their Husbands' Mental Illness," *Psychiatry* (1957) 20:275–291.

25. This guilt-carrying function is found, of course, in other role-complexes. Thus, when a middle-class couple engages in the process of legal separation or divorce, each of their lawyers usually takes the position that his job is to acquaint his client with all of the potential claims and rights, pressing his client into demanding these, in spite of any nicety of feelings about the rights and honorableness of the ex-partner. The client, in all good faith, can then say to self and to the ex-partner that the demands are being made only because the lawyer insists it is best to do so.

26. Recorded in the Clausen data.

27. This point is made by Cumming, see footnote 3; p. 129.

28. There is an interesting contrast here with the moral career of the tuberculosis patient. I am told by Julius Roth that tuberculous patients are likely to come to the hospital willingly, agreeing with their next-of-relation about treatment. Later in their hospital career, when they learn how long they yet have to stay and how depriving and irrational some of the hospital rulings are, they may seek to leave, be advised against this by the staff and by relatives, and only then begin to feel betrayed.

29. The inmate's initial strategy of holding himself aloof from ratifying contact may partly account for the relative lack of group-formation among inmates in public mental hospitals, a connection that has been suggested to me by William R. Smith. The desire to avoid personal bonds that would give license to the asking of biographical questions could also be a factor. In mental hospitals, of course, as in prisoner camps, the staff may consciously break up incipient group-formation in order to avoid collective rebellious action and other ward disturbances.

30. A comparable coming out occurs in the homosexual world, when a person finally comes frankly to present himself to a "gay" gathering not as a tourist but as someone who is "available." See Evelyn Hooker, "A Preliminary Examination of Group Behavior of Homosexuals," *J. Psychology* (1956) 42:217–225; especially p. 221. A good fictionalized treatment may be found in James Baldwin's *Giovanni's Room*; New York, Dial, 1956; pp. 41–63. A familiar instance of the coming out process is no doubt to be found among prepubertal children at the moment one of these actors sidles *back* into a room that had been left in an angered huff and injured *amour-propre*. The phrase itself presumably derives from a *rite-de-passage* ceremony once arranged by upper-class mothers for their daughters. Interestingly enough, in large mental hospitals the patient sometimes symbolizes a complete coming out by his first active participation in the hospital wide patient dance.

31. See Goffman, "Characteristics of Total Institutions," pp. 43–84; in *Proceedings*

of the Symposium of Preventive and Social Psychiatry; Washington, D.C., Walter Reed Army Institute of Research, 1958.

32. A good description of the ward system may be found in Ivan Belknap, *Human Problems of a State Mental Hospital;* New York, McGraw-Hill, 1956; see especially p. 164.

33. Here is one way in which mental hospitals can be worse than concentration camps and prisons as places in which to "do" time; in the latter, self-insulation from the symbolic implications of the settings may be easier. In fact, self-insulation from hospital settings may be so difficult that patients have to employ devices for this which staff interpret as psychotic symptoms.

34. In regard to convicts, see Anthony Heckstall-Smith, *Eighteen Months;* London, Wingate, 1954; pp. 52–53. For 'wino's' see the discussion in Howard G. Bain, "A Sociological Analysis of the Chicago Skid-Row Lifeway;" unpublished M.A. thesis, Dept. of Sociology, Univ. of Chicago, Sept., 1950; especially "The Rationale of the Skid-Row Drinking Group," pp. 141–146. Bain's neglected thesis is a useful source of material on moral careers.

Apparently one of the occupational hazards of prostitution is that clients and other professional contacts sometimes persist in expressing sympathy by asking for a defensible dramatic explanation for the fall from grace. In having to bother to have a sad tale ready, perhaps the prostitute is more to be pitied than damned. Good examples of prostitute sad tales may be found in Sir Henry Mayhew, "Those that Will Not Work," pp. 210–272; in his *London Labour and the London Poor,* Vol. 4; London, Griffin, Bohn, and Cox, 1862. For a contemporary source, see *Women of the Streets,* edited by C. H. Rolph; London, Zecker and Warburg, 1955; especially p. 6. "Almost always, however, after a few comments on the police, the girl would begin to explain how it was that she was in the life, usually in terms of self-justification." Lately, of course, the psychological expert has helped out the profession in the construction of wholly remarkable sad tales. See, for example, Harold Greenwald, *Call Girl;* New York, Ballantine, 1958.

35. A similar self-protecting rule has been observed in prisons. Thus, Hassler, see footnote 6, in describing a conversation with a fellow-prisoner; "He didn't say much about why he was sentenced, and I didn't ask him, that being the accepted behavior in prison" (p. 76). A novelistic version for the mental hospital may be found in J. Kerkhoff, *How Thin the Veil: A Newspaperman's Story of His Own Mental Crack-up and Recovery;* New York, Greenberg, 1952; p. 27.

36. From the writer's field notes of informal interaction with patients, transcribed as near verbatim as he was able.

37. The process of examining a person psychiatrically and then altering or reducing his status in consequence is known in hospital and prison parlance as *bugging,* the assumption being that once you come to the attention of the testers you either will automatically be labeled crazy or the process of testing itself will make you crazy. Thus psychiatric staff are sometimes seen not as *discovering* whether you are sick, but as *making* you sick; and "Don't bug me, man," can mean, "Don't pester me to the point where I'll get upset." Sheldon Messenger has suggested to me that this meaning of bugging is related to the other colloquial meaning, of wiring a room with a secret microphone to collect information usable for discrediting the speaker.

36 / Two Studies of Legal Stigma

RICHARD D. SCHWARTZ
JEROME H. SKOLNICK

Legal thinking has moved increasingly toward a sociologically meaningful view of the legal system. Sanctions, in particular, have come to be regarded in functional terms.[1] In criminal law, for instance, sanctions are said to be designed to prevent recidivism by rehabilitating, restraining, or executing the offender. They are also said to be intended to deter others from the performance of similar acts and, sometimes, to provide a channel for the expression of retaliatory motives. In such civil actions as tort or contract, monetary awards may be intended as retributive and deterrent, as in the use of punitive damages, or may be regarded as a *quid pro quo* to compensate the plaintiff for his wrongful loss.

While these goals comprise an integral part of the rationale of law, little is known about the extent to which they are fulfilled in practice. Lawmen do not as a rule make such studies, because their traditions and techniques are not designed for a systematic examination of the operation of the legal system in action, especially outside the courtroom. Thus, when extra-legal consequences—e.g., the social stigma of a prison sentence—are taken into account at all, it is through the discretionary actions of police, prosecutor, judge, and jury. Systematic information on a variety of unanticipated outcomes, those which benefit the accused as well as those which hurt him, might help to inform these decision makers and perhaps lead to changes in substantive law as well. The present paper is an attempt to study the consequences of stigma associated with legal accusation.

From a sociological viewpoint, there are several types of indirect consequences of legal sanctions which can be distinguished. These include differential deterrence, effects on the sanctionee's associates, and variations in the degree of deprivation which sanction imposes on the recipient himself.

First, the imposition of sanction, while intended as a matter of overt policy to deter the public at large, probably will vary in its effectiveness as a deterrent, depending upon the extent to which potential offenders perceive themselves as similar to the sanctionee. Such

"differential deterrence" would occur if white-collar anti-trust violators were restrained by the conviction of General Electric executives, but not by invocation of the Sherman Act against union leaders.

The imposition of a sanction may even provide an unintended
incentive to violate the law. A study of factors affecting compliance
with federal income tax laws provides some evidence of this effect.[2]
Some respondents reported that they began to cheat on their tax
returns only *after* convictions for tax evasion had been obtained
against others in their jurisdiction. They explained this surprising
behavior by noting that the prosecutions had always been conducted
against blatant violators and not against the kind of moderate offenders which they then became. These respondents were, therefore,
unintentionally educated to the possibility of supposedly "safe" violations.

Second, deprivations or benefits may accrue to non-sanctioned individuals by virtue of the web of affiliations that join them to the
defendant. The wife and family of a convicted man may, for instance,
suffer from his arrest as much as the man himself. On the other hand,
they may be relieved by his absence if the family relationship has
been an unhappy one. Similarly, whole groups of persons may be
affected by sanctions to an individual, as when discriminatory practices increase because of a highly publicized crime attributed to a
member of a given minority group.

Finally, the social position of the defendant himself will serve to
aggravate or alleviate the effects of any given sanction. Although all
three indirect consequences may be interrelated, it is the third with
which this paper will be primarily concerned.

FINDINGS

The subjects studied to examine the effects of legal accusation on
occupational positions represented two extremes: lower-class unskilled workers charged with assault, and medical doctors accused of
malpractice. The first project lent itself to a field experiment, while
the second required a survey design. Because of differences in
method and substance, the studies cannot be used as formal controls
for each other. Taken together, however, they do suggest that the
indirect effects of sanctions can be powerful, that they can produce
unintended harm or unexpected benefit, and that the results are
related to officially unemphasized aspects of the social context in
which the sanctions are administered. Accordingly, the two studies
will be discussed together, as bearing on one another. Strictly speak-

ing, however, each can, and properly should, stand alone as a separate examination of the unanticipated consequences of legal sanctions.

Study I. The Effects of a Criminal Court Record on the Employment Opportunities of Unskilled Workers

In the field experiment, four employment folders were prepared, the same in all respects except for the criminal court record of the applicant. In all of the folders he was described as a thirty-two year old single male of unspecified race, with a high school training in mechanical trades, and a record of successive short term jobs as a kitchen helper, maintenance worker, and handyman. These characteristics are roughly typical of applicants for unskilled hotel jobs in the Catskill resort area of New York State where employment opportunities were tested.[3]

The four folders differed only in the applicant's reported record of criminal court involvement. The first folder indicated that the applicant had been convicted and sentenced for assault; the second, that he had been tried for assault and acquitted; the third, also tried for assault and acquitted, but with a letter from the judge certifying the finding of not guilty and reaffirming the legal presumption of innocence. The fourth folder made no mention of any criminal record.

A sample of one hundred employers was utilized. Each employer was assigned to one of four "treatment" groups.[4] To each employer only one folder was shown; this folder was one of the four kinds mentioned above, the selection of the folder being determined by the treatment group to which the potential employer was assigned. The employer was asked whether he could "use" the man described in the folder. To preserve the reality of the situation and make it a true field experiment, employers were never given any indication that they were participating in an experiment. So far as they knew, a legitimate offer to work was being made in each showing of the folder by the "employment agent."

The experiment was designed to determine what employers would do in fact if confronted with an employment applicant with a criminal record. The questionnaire approach used in earlier studies[5] seemed ill-adapted to the problem, since respondents confronted with hypothetical situations might be particularly prone to answer in what they considered a socially acceptable manner. The second alternative—studying job opportunities of individuals who had been involved with the law—would have made it very difficult to find comparable groups of applicants and potential employers. For these reasons, the field experiment reported here was utilized.

Some deception was involved in the study. The "employment agent"—the same individual in all hundred cases—was in fact a law student who was working in the Catskills during the summer of 1959 as an insurance adjuster. In representing himself as being both an adjuster and an employment agent, he was assuming a combination of roles which is not uncommon there. The adjuster role gave him an opportunity to introduce a single application for employment casually and naturally. To the extent that the experiment worked, however, it was inevitable that some employers should be led to believe that they had immediate prospects of filling a job opening. In those instances where an offer to hire was made, the "agent" called a few hours later to say that the applicant had taken another job. The field experimenter attempted in such instances to locate a satisfactory replacement by contacting an employment agency in the area. Because this procedure was used and since the jobs involved were of relatively minor consequence, we believe that the deception caused little economic harm.

As mentioned, each treatment group of twenty-five employers was approached with one type of folder. Responses were dichotomized: those who expressed a willingness to consider the applicant in any way were termed positive; those who made no response or who explicitly refused to consider the candidate were termed negative. Our results consist of comparisons between positive and negative responses, thus defined, for the treatment groups.

Of the twenty-five employers shown the "no record" folder, nine gave positive responses. Subject to reservations arising from chance variations in sampling, we take this as indicative of the "ceiling" of jobs available for this kind of applicant under the given field conditions. Positive responses by these employers may be compared with those in the other treatment groups to obtain an indication of job opportunities lost because of the various legal records.

Of the twenty-five employers approached with the "convict" folder, only one expressed interest in the applicant. This is a rather graphic indication of the effect which a criminal record may have on job opportunities. Care must be exercised, of course, in generalizing the conclusions to other settings. In this context, however, the criminal record made a major difference.

From a theoretical point of view, the finding leads toward the conclusion that conviction constitutes a powerful form of "status degradation"[6] which continues to operate after the time when, according to the generalized theory of justice underlying punishment in our society, the individual's "debt" has been paid. A record of conviction produces a durable if not permanent loss of status. For purposes of effective social control, this state of affairs may heighten the deterrent effect of conviction—though that remains to be established. Any such contribution to social control, however, must be balanced against the barriers imposed upon rehabilitation of the convict. If the ex-prisoner finds difficulty in securing menial kinds of legitimate work, further crime may become an increasingly attractive alternative.[7]

Another important finding of this study concerns the small number of positive responses elicited by the "accused but acquitted" applicant. Of the twenty-five employers approached with this folder, three offered jobs. Thus, the individual accused but acquitted of assault has almost as much trouble finding even an unskilled job as the one who was not only accused of the same offense, but also convicted.

From a theoretical point of view, this result indicates that permanent lowering of status is not limited to those explicitly singled out by being convicted of a crime. As an ideal outcome of American justice, criminal procedure is supposed to distinguish between the "guilty" and those who have been acquitted. Legally controlled consequences which follow the judgment are consistent with this purpose. Thus, the "guilty" are subject to fine and imprisonment, while those who are acquitted are immune from these sanctions. But deprivations may be imposed on the acquitted, both before and after victory in court. Before trial, legal rules either permit or require arrest and detention. The suspect may be faced with the expense of an attorney and a bail bond if he is to mitigate these limitations on his privacy and freedom. In addition, some pre-trial deprivations are imposed without formal legal permission. These may include coercive questioning, use of violence, and stigmatization. And, as this study indicates, some deprivations not under the direct control of the legal process may develop or persist after an official decision of acquittal has been made.

Thus two legal principles conflict in practice. On the one hand, "a man is innocent until proven guilty." On the other, the accused is systematically treated as guilty under the administration of criminal law until a functionary or official body—police, magistrate, prosecuting attorney, or trial judge or jury—decides that he is entitled to be free. Even then, the results of treating him as guilty persist and may lead to serious consequences.

The conflict could be eased by measures aimed at reducing the deprivations imposed on the accused, before and after acquittal. Some legal attention has been focused on pre-trial deprivations. The provision of bail and counsel, the availability of habeas corpus, limitations on the admissability of coerced confessions, and civil actions for false arrest are examples of measures aimed at protecting the rights of the accused before trial. Although these are often limited in effectiveness, especially for individuals of lower socioeconomic status, they at least represent some concern with implementing the presumption of innocence at the pretrial stage.

By contrast, the courts have done little toward alleviating the post-acquittal consequences of legal accusation. One effort along these lines has been employed in the federal courts, however. Where an individual has been accused and exonerated of a crime, he may petition the federal courts for a "Certificate of Innocence" certifying this fact.[8] Possession of such a document might be expected to alleviate post-acquittal deprivations.

Some indication of the effectiveness of such a measure is found in the responses of the final treatment group. Their folder, it will be recalled, contained information on the accusation and acquittal of the applicant, but also included a letter from a judge addressed "To whom it may concern" certifying the applicant's acquittal and reminding the reader of the presumption of innocence. Such a letter might have had a boomerang effect, by reemphasizing the legal involvement of the applicant. It was important, therefore, to determine empirically whether such a communication would improve or harm the chances of employment. Our findings indicate that it increased employment opportunities, since the letter folder elicited six positive responses. Even though this fell short of the nine responses to the "no record" folder, it doubled the number for the "accused but acquitted" and created a significantly greater number of job offers than those elicited by the convicted record. This suggests that the procedure merits consideration as a means of offsetting the occupational loss resulting from accusation. It should be noted, however, that repeated use of this device might reduce its effectiveness.

The results of the experiment are summarized in Table 1. The differences in outcome found there indicate that various types of legal records are systematically related to job opportunities. It seems fair to infer also that the trend of job losses corresponds with the apparent punitive intent of the authorities. Where the man is convicted, that intent is presumably greatest. It is less where he is accused but acquitted and still less where the court makes an effort to emphasize the absence of a finding of guilt. Nevertheless, where the difference in punitive intent is ideally greatest, between conviction and acquittal, the difference in occupational harm is very slight. A similar blurring of this distinction shows up in a different way in the next study.

Study II: The Effects on Defendants Of Suits for Medical Malpractice

As indicated earlier, the second study differed from the first in a number of ways: method of research, social class of accused, relationship between the accused and his "employer," social support available to accused, type of offense and its possible relevance to occupational adequacy. Because the two studies differ in so many ways, the reader is again cautioned to avoid thinking of them as providing a rigorous comparative examination. They are presented together only

Table 1 / Effect of Four Types of Legal Folder on Job Opportunities (in per cent)

	No record	Acquitted with letter	Acquitted without letter	Convicted	Total
	(N = 25)	(N = 25)	(N = 25)	(N = 25)	(N = 100)
Positive response	36	24	12	4	19
Negative response	64	76	88	96	81
Total	100	100	100	100	100

to demonstrate that legal accusation can produce unanticipated deprivations, as in the case of Study I, or unanticipated benefits, as in the research now to be presented. In the discussion to follow, some of the possible reasons for the different outcomes will be suggested.

The extra-legal effects of a malpractice suit were studied by obtaining the records of Connecticut's leading carrier of malpractice insurance. According to these records, a total of 69 doctors in the State had been sued in 64 suits during the post World War II period covered by the study, September, 1945, to September, 1959.[9] Some suits were instituted against more than one doctor, and four physicians had been sued twice. Of the total of 69 physicians, 58 were questioned. Interviews were conducted with the approval of the Connecticut Medical Association by Robert Wyckoff, whose extraordinary qualifications for the work included possession of both the M.D. and LL.B. degrees. Dr. Wyckoff was able to secure detailed response to his inquiries from all doctors contacted.

Twenty of the respondents were questioned by personal interview, 28 by telephone, and the remainder by mail. Forty-three of those reached practiced principally in cities, eleven in suburbs, and four in rural areas. Seventeen were engaged in general practice and forty-one were specialists. The sample proved comparable to the doctors in the State as a whole in age, experience, and professional qualifications.[10] The range was from the lowest professional stratum to chiefs of staff and services in the State's most highly regarded hospitals.

Of the 57 malpractice cases reported, doctors clearly won 38; nineteen of these were dropped by the plaintiff and an equal number were won in court by the defendant doctor. Of the remaining nineteen suits, eleven were settled out of court for a nominal amount, four for approximately the amount the plaintiff claimed and four resulted in judgment for the plaintiff in court.

The malpractice survey did not reveal widespread occupational harm to the physicians involved. Of the 58 respondents, 52 reported no negative effects of the suit on their practice, and five of the remaining six, all specialists, reported that their practice *improved* after the suit. The heaviest loser in court (a radiologist), reported the largest gain. He commented, "I guess all the doctors in town felt sorry for me because new patients started coming in from doctors who had not sent me patients previously." Only one doctor reported adverse consequences to his practice. A winner in court, this man suffered physical and emotional stress symptoms which hampered his later effectiveness in surgical work. The temporary drop in his practice appears to have been produced by neurotic symptoms and is therefore only indirectly traceable to the malpractice suit. Seventeen other doctors reported varying degrees of personal dissatisfaction and anxiety during and after the suit, but none of them reported impairment of practice. No significant relationship was found between outcome of the suit and expressed dissatisfaction.

A protective institutional environment helps to explain these results. No cases were found in which a doctor's hospital privileges were reduced following the suit. Neither was any physician unable later to obtain malpractice insurance, although a handful found it necessary to pay higher rates. The State Licensing Commission, which is headed by a doctor, did not intervene in any instance. Local medical societies generally investigated charges through their ethics and grievance committees, but where they took any action, it was almost always to recommend or assist in legal defense against the suit.

DISCUSSION

Accusation has different outcomes for unskilled workers and doctors in the two studies. How may these be explained? First, they might be nothing more than artifacts of research method. In the field experiment, it was possible to see behavior directly, i.e., to determine how employers act when confronted with what appears to them to be a realistic opportunity to hire. Responses are therefore not distorted by the memory of the respondent. By contrast, the memory of the doctors might have been consciously or unconsciously shaped by the wish to create the impression that the public had not taken seriously the accusation leveled against them. The motive for such a distortion might be either to protect the respondent's self-esteem or to preserve an image of public acceptance in the eyes of the interviewer, the profession, and the public. Efforts of the interviewer to assure his subjects of anonymity—intended to offset these effects—may have succeeded or may, on the contrary, have accentuated an awareness of the danger. A related type of distortion might have stemmed from a desire by doctors to affect public attitudes toward malpractice. Two conflicting motives might have been expected to enter here. The doctor might have tended to exaggerate the harm caused by an accusation, especially if followed by acquittal, in order to turn public opinion toward legal policies which would limit malpractice liability. On the other hand, he might tend to underplay extra-legal harm caused by a legally insufficient accusation in order to discourage potential plaintiffs from instituting suits aimed at securing remunerative settlements and/or revenge for grievances. Whether these diverse motives operated to distort doctors' reports and, if so, which of them produced the greater degree of distortion is a matter for speculation. It is only suggested here that the interview method is more subject to certain types of distortion than the direct behavioral observations of the field experiment.

Even if such distortion did not occur, the results may be attributable to differences in research design. In the field experiment, a direct comparison is made between the occupational position of an accused and an identical individual not accused at a single point in time. In the medical study, effects were inferred through retrospective judgment, although checks on actual income would have no doubt confirmed these judgments. Granted that income had increased, many other explanations are available to account for it. An improvement in practice after a malpractice suit may have resulted from factors extraneous to the suit. The passage of time in the community and increased experience may have led to a larger practice and may even have masked negative effects of the suit. There may have been a general increase in practice for the kinds of doctors involved in these suits, even greater for doctors not sued than for doctors in the sample. Whether interviews with a control sample could have yielded sufficiently precise data to rule out these possibilities is problematic. Unfortunately, the resources available for the study did not enable such data to be obtained.

A third difference in the two designs may affect the results. In the field experiment, full information concerning the legal record is provided to all of the relevant decision makers, i.e., the employers. In the medical study, by contrast, the results depend on decisions of actual patients to consult a given doctor. It may be assumed that such decisions are often based on imperfect information, some patients knowing little or nothing about the malpractice suit. To ascertain how much information employers usually have concerning the legal record of the employee and then supply that amount would have been a desirable refinement, but a difficult one. The alternative approach would involve turning the medical study into an experiment in which full information concerning malpractice (e.g., liable, accused but acquitted, no record of accusation) was supplied to potential patients. This would have permitted a comparison of the effects of legal accusation in two instances where information concerning the accusation is constant. To carry out such an experiment in a field situation would require an unlikely degree of cooperation, for instance by a medical clinic which might ask patients to choose their doctor on the basis of information given them. It is difficult to conceive of an experiment along these lines which would be both realistic enough to be valid and harmless enough to be ethical.

If we assume, however, that these methodological problems do not invalidate the basic finding, how may it be explained? Why would unskilled workers accused but acquitted of assault have great difficulty getting jobs, while doctors accused of malpractice—whether acquitted or not—are left unharmed or more sought after than before?

First, the charge of criminal assault carries with it the legal allegation and the popular connotation of intent to harm. Malpractice, on the other hand, implies negligence or failure to exercise reasonable care. Even though actual physical harm may be greater in malpractice, the element of intent suggests that the man accused of assault would be more likely to repeat his attempt and to find the mark. However, it is dubious that this fine distinction could be drawn by the lay public.

Perhaps more important, all doctors and particularly specialists may be immune from the effects of a malpractice suit because their services are in short supply.[11] By contrast, the unskilled worker is one of many and therefore likely to be passed over in favor of someone with a "cleaner" record.

Moreover, high occupational status, such as is demonstrably enjoyed by doctors,[12] probably tends to insulate the doctor from imputations of incompetence. In general, professionals are assumed to possess uniformly high ability, to be oriented toward community service, and to enforce adequate standards within their own organization.[13] Doctors in particular receive deference, just because they are doctors, not only from the population as a whole but even from fellow professionals.[14]

Finally, individual doctors appear to be protected from the effects of accusation by the sympathetic and powerful support they receive from fellow members of the occupation, a factor absent in the case of unskilled, unorganized laborers.[15] The medical society provides advice on handling malpractice actions, for instance, and referrals by other doctors sometimes increase as a consequence of the sympathy felt for the malpractice suit victim. Such assistance is further evidence that the professional operates as "a community within a community,"[16] shielding its members from controls exercised by formal authorities in the larger society.

In order to isolate these factors, additional studies are needed. It would be interesting to know, for instance, whether high occupational status would protect a doctor acquitted of a charge of assault. Information on this question is sparse. Actual instances of assaults by doctors are probably very rare. When and if they do occur, it seems unlikely that they would lead to publicity and prosecution, since police and prosecutor discretion might usually be employed to quash charges before they are publicized. In the rare instances in which they come to public attention, such accusations appear to produce a marked effect because of the assumption that the pressing of charges, despite the status of the defendant, indicates probable guilt. Nevertheless, instances may be found in which even the accusation of first degree murder followed by acquittal appears to have left the doctor professionally unscathed.[17] Similarly, as a test of the group protection hypothesis, one might investigate the effect of an acquittal for assault on working men who are union members. The analogy would be particularly instructive where the union plays an important part in employment decisions, for instance in industries which make use of a union hiring hall.

In the absence of studies which isolate the effect of such factors, our findings cannot readily be generalized. It is tempting to suggest after an initial look at the results that social class differences provide the explanation. But subsequent analysis and research might well reveal significant intra-class variations, depending on the distribution of other operative factors. A lower class person with a scarce specialty and a protective occupational group who is acquitted of a lightly regarded offense might benefit from the accusation. Nevertheless, class in general seems to correlate with the relevant factors to such an extent that in reality the law regularly works to the disadvantage of the already more disadvantaged classes.

CONCLUSION

Legal accusation imposes a variety of consequences, depending on the nature of the accusation and the characteristics of the accused. Deprivations occur, even though not officially intended, in the case of unskilled workers who have been acquitted of assault charges. On the other hand, malpractice actions—even when resulting in a judgment against the doctor—are not usually followed by negative consequences and sometimes have a favorable effect on the professional position of the defendant. These differences in outcome suggest two conclusions: one, the need for more explicit clarification of legal goals; two, the importance of examining the attitudes and social structure of the community outside the courtroom if the legal process is to hit intended targets, while avoiding innocent bystanders. Greater precision in communicating goals and in appraising consequences of present practices should help to make the legal process an increasingly equitable and effective instrument of social control.

Notes

1. Legal sanctions are defined as changes in life conditions imposed through court action.

2. Richard D. Schwartz, "The Effectiveness of Legal Controls: Factors in the Reporting of Minor Items of Income on Federal Income Tax Returns." Paper presented at the annual meeting of the American Sociological Association, Chicago, 1959.

3. The generality of these results remains to be determined. The effects of criminal involvement in the Catskill area are probably diminished, however, by the temporary nature of employment, the generally poor qualifications of the work force, and the excess of demand over supply of unskilled labor there. Accordingly, the employment differences among the four treatment groups found in this study are likely, if anything to be *smaller* than would be expected in industries and areas where workers are more carefully selected.

4. Employers were not approached in pre-selected random order, due to a misunderstanding of instructions on the part of the law student who carried out the experiment during a three and one-half week period. Because of this flaw in the experimental procedure, the results should be treated with appropriate caution. Thus, chi-squared analysis may not properly be utilized. (For those used to this measure, $p < .05$ for table 1.)

5. Sol Rubin, *Crime and Juvenile Delinquency*, New York: Oceana, 1958, pp. 151–156.

6. Harold Garfinkel, "Conditions of Successful Degradation Ceremonies," *American Journal of Sociology*, 61 (March, 1956), pp. 420–24.

7. Severe negative effects of conviction on employment opportunities have been noted by Sol Rubin, *Crime and Juvenile Delinquency*, New York: Oceana, 1958. A further source of employment difficulty is inherent in licensing statutes and security regulations which sometimes preclude convicts from being employed in their pre-conviction occupation or even in the trades which they may have acquired during imprisonment. These effects may, however, be counteracted by bonding arrangements, prison associations, and publicity programs aimed at increasing confidence in, and sympathy for, ex-convicts. See also. B. F. McSally, "Finding Jobs for Released Offenders," *Federal Probation*, 24 (June, 1960), pp. 12–17; Harold D. Lasswell and Richard C. Donnelly, "The Continuing Debate over Responsibility: An Introduction to Isolating the Condemnation Sanction," *Yale Law Journal*, 68 (April, 1959), pp. 869–99; Johs Andeneas, "General Prevention—Illusion or Reality?", *J. Criminal Law*, 43 (July–August, 1952), pp. 176–98.

8. 28 United States Code, Secs. 1495, 2513.

9. A spot check of one county revealed that the Company's records covered every malpractice suit tried in the courts of that county during this period.

10. No relationship was found between any of these characteristics and the legal or extra-legal consequences of the lawsuit.

11. See Eliot Freidson, "Client Control and Medical Practice," *American Journal of Sociology*, 65 (January, 1960), pp. 374–82. Freidson's point is that general practitioners are more subject to client-control than specialists are. Our findings emphasize the importance of professional as compared to client control, and professional protection against a particular form of client control, extending through both branches of the medical profession. However, what holds for malpractice situations may not be true of routine medical practice.

12. National Opinion Research Center, "Jobs and Occupations: A Popular Evaluation," *Opinion News*, 9 (Sept., 1947), pp. 3–13. More recent studies in several countries tend to confirm the high status of the physician. See Alex Inkeles, "Industrial Man: The

Relation of Status to Experience, Perception and Value," *American Journal of Sociology*, 66 (July, 1960), pp. 1–31.

13. Talcott Parsons, *The Social System*, Glencoe: The Free Press, 1951, pp. 454–473; and Everett C. Hughes, *Men and their Work*, Glencoe: The Free Press, 1958.

14. Alvin Zander, Arthur R. Cohen, and Ezra Scotland, *Role Relations in the Mental Health Professions*, Ann Arbor: Institute for Social Research, 1957.

15. Unions sometimes act to protect the seniority rights of members who, discharged from their jobs upon arrest, seek re-employment following their acquittal.

16. See William J. Goode, "Community Within A Community: The Professions," *American Sociological Review*, 22 (April, 1957), pp. 194–200.

17. For instance, the acquittal of Dr. John Bodkin Adams after a sensational murder trial, in which he was accused of deliberately killing several elderly women patients to inherit their estates, was followed by his quiet return to medical practice. *New York Times*, Nov. 24, 1961, p. 28, col. 7. Whether the British regard acquittals as more exonerative than Americans is uncertain.

37 / Being Different: The Autobiography of Jane Fry, a Transsexual

ROBERT BOGDAN

Being referred to as a "transsexual" doesn't bother me too much. I would rather be thought of as a person first, but it doesn't make me angry because that's what I am. A transsexual is a person who wishes to change sexes and is actively going about it. Which is exactly what I am doing.[1]

I have the physical organs of a man, but I feel that I am a woman. For a long time I fought these feelings, but I don't anymore. I take female hormones and dress and live as a woman, and I have for two years. I understand my transsexualism for what it is. Basically, it boils down to this: What is a person? Is a person what he is on the inside? Or what he is on the outside? I know what I am on the inside, a female. There is no doubt there. I could spend 50 years of my life trying to change, but I doubt if that would do anything. I know what I am. I like it, and I don't want to change. The only thing I want to change is my body, so that it matches what I am. A body is like a covering; it's like a shell. What is more important? The body or the person that is inside?

As you will read, I went for three years of psychotherapy and I couldn't find anything in my childhood to pin this thing down on, nothing that would be different from your background or anybody else's. Sure, if you look hard enough into my childhood you would find things, just like if I looked into yours I could find things, if I wanted to. You might say that there were psychological reasons for my state if my father was a superdrunk, or if my mother made me sleep with her, or if she wanted a girl so much she dressed me in girls' clothes; but there was nothing like that. My father said to me once that there were a few males on his side of the family way back that were fairly feminine. I don't know whether heredity is part of it or not. For sure, my father isn't feminine.

I spent three years searching for psychological reasons and other kinds of reasons, because I was expected to. I'm not interested in reasons anymore. I don't give a damn what caused it. God could have poked his finger in my belly button and said, "You're going to think of yourself as a girl," and that could have caused it. All I want to do is get it fixed. I just want to be myself. But in order to get it fixed you have to convince God knows how many people that you're sane, convince people that you really want the operation, find someone to do it, and come up with the money.

I stopped looking for reasons two years ago. Every doctor you see gives you a different explanation, and you just come to the point of knowing that they just don't know what the hell they are talking about. One thing that I did learn in meeting all the doctors is that you have to give a little—pretend a little. Any one of them can kill you physically or emotionally. They can put the dampers on everything. If they decide that I am totally insane because I want to be a female, who knows what they can do. I nod when they tell me their theories now. You have got to learn to give and take, which I took some time in learning.

Before I go on and tell you about the operation and transsexualism and the hassle involved in that, let me tell you a little about the way I look at life and analyze myself. There is this story I heard once about Freud that pretty much sums it up. He was at a meeting with some colleagues, and he lit up this huge stogey. His colleagues around the table started snickering because of his writing about oral complexes and phallus symbols. Freud just looked at it and said, "Yes gentlemen. I know this is a phallic symbol but it is also a god damned good cigar." That's a good way to look at life. If it's enjoyable, do it as long as it doesn't harm anybody, and don't worry about analyzing everything. That is my philosophy. I am the only one responsible for what I do, and as long as I don't harm another human being mentally or physically, I'm being a good person. I think that I'm a good person because I operate according to my principles. I may break the law, but I'm not breaking my law which seems like the sensible one to me. I also think people should help each other, which I try to do. I think people should help me. They shouldn't sit down and try to analyze me, or try to figure out why I am the way I am or whether I am eligible for a sex change.

There are two laws that I know of that affect transsexuals—one the police can pick you up for. It's about impersonation. I don't know the actual law, but it was put on the books in the 1700s. The reason they had it was that farmers were dressing up as Indians in order to avoid paying taxes—some would even dress as women. So they passed this law not allowing people to dress up in public and to paint their faces. That's the law they now arrest transsexuals and transvestites on.

The other law keeps surgeons from doing the operation. That one comes from England. There was a war going on there and the people were trying to get out of the draft by cutting off their fingers and toes, and they would have a surgeon do it. So the law states that no surgeon can take away any part of your body that would make you ineligible for the draft. So cutting off my genitals is making me ineligible for the draft. I think the draft board could afford to lose a few, but anyway that's the law that the surgeons are afraid of. I've heard of a couple of times where doctors were ready to perform the operation and were notified by the DA that if they did they would press charges.

The doctors usually back off. They don't want to get involved. They don't have the time to get in a test case, and most of the time they don't want that kind of publicity. The hospitals especially don't like that kind of publicity. They don't get donations, I guess, if the public finds out they are doing sexual change operations. The board of directors and contributors jump down their throats for doing such an atrocious thing, and if the word gets out that a hospital is doing the surgery, they get besieged by transsexuals wanting to get one.

Most people don't know the difference between transvestites, homosexuals, and transsexuals, so I think I ought to clear that up before I go any further. Most people just lump them all together. I saw one Archie Bunker show on homosexuals that really pointed out how Americans think about people who have different sexual practices. People don't realize how prejudiced they are about homosexuality and transsexuality, because they aren't even at a point of knowing that it's something that you can be prejudiced about. They are so sure that the rest of the world is supposed to be the way they are that they don't even think the people who are different have an opinion. They just lump them all together as nuts or perverts. That's the way Archie was on this program.

Well, anyway, a transvestite only wants to dress like a woman. They don't want to go all the way and have an operation and live as a woman. The transsexual wants an operation. It's a difference in the way you think about yourself. The way of thinking of a transsexual is: "I am a female with a birth defect. I am a woman, but I have the organs of the other sex. I want to be a whole person again." The term is also used to refer to people who are physiologically women who want to be men. The way of thinking of a transvestite is: "I am a man, but I want to play the role of a female. I know that I am a male, but I get kicks out of dressing like a woman." The transvestite gets emotional gratification and psychological good feelings from dressing. A transsexual doesn't. There is an interest in clothing, but it's much like a woman's interest. No erotic stimulation or anything like that. Like, I am just as happy bumming around in a pair of jeans and a blouse as in some type of fancy low-cut gown with heels.

The difference between a homosexual and a transsexual or a transvestite is that the homosexual knows that he is a man, let's say, but he is sexually attracted to those of the same sex and has sex with them. He says: "I know that I am a man, but I want to have sex with a man." Some transvestites are not homosexuals, because they don't want sex. Transsexuals are not homosexuals because they don't want to have sex with those who are of the same sex as they are; they want sex with the opposite sex.

I used to be down on homosexuals. Homosexuals and transsexuals usually don't hit it off. I happened to relate well with a group a few years ago, and I was able to get over my prejudices and start seeing what we had in common rather than what we differed over. I found it easy to relate to this group, because what we had in common was that we were suppressed. We both share some of the dangers of being brutalized because of our beliefs. We can be picked up for impersonation, or for vagrancy, or anything else they want to pick us up for. We also share being made jokes of or beat up at any time. Like, just last week I had a seizure in the middle of the street, and someone called an ambulance. The first thing that I remember was being in the ambulance strapped to a stretcher. I looked up, and there are these two guys laughing and joking. One says to me, "Don't worry, *dearie.* We've got you figured out." I was so angry I almost couldn't control myself, but that is typical of what we have to watch out for.

When you're like me, you have always got to be on your guard that you don't get into a position that is going to get you into a jam. Like, I went downtown and picketed the recruiting center as part of the antiwar demonstration. I had decided that I was going to perform an act of civil disobedience with a group if they tried to clear us out of the road. But standing around down there, all of a sudden it hit me. If I get busted and get taken to jail, they might throw every charge in the book at me if they found out I was physically a man. I have to be more careful than anybody else that goes on a march like that. I went in the front of the parade in this particular march, carrying a banner—but that wasn't smart to do. If people were to ever find out and if it was in the papers, the reporters and the readers would zero in on the fact of what I was, and that would have blown the whole issue. Immediately, all the hard hats would go back to their favorite sayings: "Look at all those faggot queers with the long hair marching around. They got a real beauty out in front this time." People like me aren't sincere about those issues, according to them. We don't count.

It's hard for transsexuals, because you don't have many allies. I'm almost totally dependent on white, middle-class doctors to give me a fair shake. There are so few doctors that will see me, that I have to scrape to get what I want. They are in control. They told me that I have to conform to their standards or I don't get the operation.

I'm probably different from other transsexuals, but they probably think the same about themselves. One thing is that it is usually hard for transsexuals to talk about themselves, especially after the operation. I'm going to tell you a lot about myself. Talking about it opens up a lot of old wounds. I haven't had the operation, so it's a lot easier because the wounds are still in the open and I get new ones every day.

I don't think very many transsexuals have gone through three years of psychotherapy, as I have. Most phase it out after 50 sessions or so. I'm different, too, in that most transsexuals don't go to psychiatric hospitals. Why that is I don't know. Most transsexuals are also very introverted. They want to stay totally undercover, outside the public eye. They don't want to upset the apple cart. They have to keep low profiles so as to keep respectable. This is because they don't depend on each other so much as on their physicians.

Your doctor is the most important part of your life. He takes precedence over fathers and mothers, in some cases. That is the person who prescribes the hormones and may be able to help you get the operation. You've got to keep him happy. Doctors are gods to them. Which is why I don't think I get along too well with some doctors, because I don't think of them or treat them like God, not anymore anyway—I think they are as fucked up in some respects as me. When you talk to another transsexual, the first thing they will talk about is what their doctor is doing for them. I don't think it's healthy or that you can be a person, if your whole life is so dependent on someone else who can cut you off any time.

I am talking about the transsexuals I know. I haven't known that many. Maybe I've met a total of 30. There aren't too many in the United States. Dr. Benjamin's book says there are 100,000, or something like that, in the United States. Maybe I should just talk for myself.

The vast majority of transsexuals try to make it in the straight world, as the gay community calls it. The reason for that is because the operation is not very well advertised. I mean, you don't see many articles in popular magazines about it, so people don't know about it. People who are transsexuals and don't know about operations are trying to live the role that society says they have to. Like myself—everybody used to say, "You have got to be a little boy." I knew I wasn't, but they said I had to. As you will read in this book, I went into the Navy to try to be. I went into submarine service trying to be. I even got married trying to be. I underwent psychotherapy, but that didn't work either. Then I heard about the operation, and that's what I have been working toward ever since.

I am presently living in purgatory. A little between heaven and hell. I am working my way upwards, slowly, but when you have to fight the whole damn system single-handed, it's hard. Usually, you look for help and people turn their backs on you. I tell them what I want, and they say, "He's really a *sick* person." They don't get it through their heads that they are the ones that have made me sick and are keeping me sick. Most transsexuals have had hassles, but they don't have the hassles over being a transsexual; they have them over the way society fucks over them. After it fucks over you, it asks, "What can we do to help?" So to help they stick you into an institution for the mentally ill that gives you more hassles. It's a cycle. When I went into the VA psychiatric ward, I was in hell. Now that I am getting hormone shots and living and working as a female, it's purgatory. Once I get the operation, although I know it's not going to be perfect, it will kind of be like heaven. I am not going to say that the operation is going to cure everything—I don't consider it a cure-all. I have a lot of hassles to clear up, just like most people. It's not going to be a cure-all, but it will sure as hell get rid of many of the pressures and tensions I am under.

The cost of the operation is twice what it would be if it weren't so controversial. You feel that you're being taken advantage of. The cost in Casablanca is about $8000, and they go between $3500 and $5000 in other places. That is not the cost of the operation—that is just the surgeon's fees. That is not counting the anesthesiologist, the operating room, the recovery time, medication, and so on. Since when does a person get over $3500 for less than a day's work? What they do is remove parts of the male organ and use part of it to build a vagina. The vagina has the nerve endings from the penis and scrotum, so there are sexual feelings.

There are two doctors in the world today who are working toward perfecting the male-to-female surgery. One is a doctor in Casablanca; the other is in Tijuana. They have their own clinics with operating suites and the whole thing. They are both expensive. You have to deposit the right amount in their Swiss bank account prior to the operation. He gets out of paying the taxes and the hassle of taking that much through customs. These are the men who are doing most of the surgical research.

There are people in the United States doing research, but it is mostly statistical or psychological. A couple of places out West did some operations and have decided to wait between 12 and 20 years to find out the results before they do any more. Johns Hopkins did a lot, but I don't think they are doing any now either. They were supposed to be doing one every three months or so. There are other places here and there that do them, but it's hard to find out for sure who's doing them.

According to Dr. Benjamin, who studied over 100 people who had the operation, only one was considered unsatisfactory. They had all made a better adjustment to life than before the operation. The one that was unsatisfactory was a medical thing, not psychological. So the operation seems pretty foolproof. By the way, psychotherapy has never been known to "cure" a transsexual.

The reason the cost is so high is part of the old supply and demand thing. Transsexuals need one thing, the operation, and there is only a small group of doctors who will do it. If these people stick together in the price they charge, the only thing someone can do is pay their price. You can't very well boycott or picket, or stuff like that. There is no recourse but to pay it or not get it done.

People who do the operation have this informal rule, that in order to be eligible for it you have to be living as a female for two years. That includes working as a female. You also have to have a recommendation from a psychiatrist you have been seeing for two years. They say that, if you can work as a female successfully enough to make the money, then you'll make a good adjustment after the operation. It's the kind of a situation where you're so concerned about the operation that it's hard to concentrate on working—if you had the operation, you might settle down. Besides, it's almost impossible to get any kind of a job that pays enough for you to save on. The other thing is: Who is going to write you a recommendation in the first place to get a job, and what name are they going to put down, your old one or your new one? Also, what about when they ask you for your social security card and it has a man's name on it? Medicaid won't pay for it, and Blue Cross and Blue Shield get upset when you even suggest it. They consider it cosmetic surgery.

The operation is a vicious circle. I want to have the operation so bad that I am under great pressure and strain. The pressure makes it hard to find or keep a good job. The fact that you can't keep a job and that you're uptight is used as evidence that you're not sane. They tell you, "If you really wanted it, you could do it." I can see their reasoning, but I don't agree with it. I don't know what I can do about it though. They tell you getting the money is part of the therapy.

What people don't understand is that transsexuals, myself included, think of this whole operation in the same way you would think of having a wart removed, or having plastic surgery done on your nose. If you think your nose is ugly and you want it fixed, if it's bothering you, instead of worrying about it and while your head is thinking about it the way it is and all that stuff, you go out and get it fixed. That's the way I think of it, but most physicians don't. Most people are so uptight about sex in general, and about penises and vaginas, that they have to find something psychological to worry about. It's funny.

I don't know how you're taking this so far, but the majority of people hear about me and they automatically think I have problems—super head problems. Even if I don't have them, they think I'm crazy. You just try to avoid people like that. After I get to know people it works out. If I make them uptight, I leave.

People usually find out that I'm a transsexual not from me, but from my "friends." It makes me angry to have to explain it to people because, I don't know, how would you like to have to explain yourself to everyone you met? Explain how you think you're a man or a woman. Why the hell do I have to be explained? I mean to hell with the transsexualism, I'm a human being first, and female second, and a transsexual third. But people can't respond to it like that. Society doesn't want to know me as a human being. I have to be a transsexual first to do anything. It's almost, "Forget Jane Fry and let's talk about the transsexual." It's almost like when I went to get my appendix out. They were so much into looking at me as a transsexual that they didn't do anything about my appendix. When I was in the psychiatric hospitals, they concentrated so much on me being a transsexual that they weren't willing to help me with what I needed help with.

I have come to automatically distrust people because of this. I want to be accepted as a human being, and people won't do it; they make it so you can't be a human being. This combined with the operation being so hard to achieve that you have to concentrate on being a transsexual 24 hours a day instead of being a person. All your hopes ride on the operation, and that's what you keep striving for and that's what you fight for. So you think of it all the time, and people treat you like one all the time, and there you are.

It actually makes it more frustrating for me when people don't know about me before I meet them, because you have to jump over a hurdle—I have to explain more or less what I'm all about. Sometimes I blow people's minds intentionally. I get a horror or a fear reaction from people who are set in their ways, who haven't run across this kind of thing before.

Men get particularly uptight around me. They just don't know how to handle it. Some guys, the first time they see me, like all males who see a female, look at me as a female and then all of a sudden they find out; it blows their image of themselves. They say to themselves, "God, I must be queer." A lot of people seem to go through that, but I don't know what to do about it. I get along with women a lot better. They don't seem so threatened.

The biggest problem I face is dealing with society in a way that it accepts me and I can accept myself. I have done that to some extent, but I feel I'm kind of doing it the easy way by living on the fringes in the freak culture. Most of my friends are either students or hang out in the University section. People are much more open in their thinking—they don't care if you're different or not. It makes life a lot easier than if I was to try, say, to play the role of the supermiddle-class secretary that lives in the suburbs. The majority of transsexuals do that. They are superstraight. Maybe that's easy for them, dealing with it that way, but I just couldn't make it. By living on the fringe I don't have to face the head hassles they do every day. The majority of transsexuals don't have the time or energy left after fighting the hassles to understand what society is like. They are so busy trying to join in and at the same time fight it that they don't see what it's all about.

Being a transsexual, it seems like you're fighting all society and everybody in it. If you don't have psychological hang-ups after all that fighting, there is something wrong with you. I've got problems now, quite a few emotional hang-ups right now. It doesn't mean that I have to be locked up. I recognize them, but I also recognize the reason I got them. I spend half my time worrying about what society thinks, instead of worrying about me. So you have to end up with problems. Anybody can relate the emotional problems that I have now to my childhood and say that my transsexualism is the reason for it, but it's nothing about the transsexualism itself that causes hang-ups—it's fighting society.

This doctor told me that my father was a very violent man and in rejecting him I rejected masculinity and violence, so I had to be a female. I think that's bullshit. What he didn't stop to think was that I probably was a transsexual right from the beginning and I was so worried about the problems that it caused with others I didn't know how to relate to them. You get so wrapped up in your emotions that you can't relate.

I don't think my transsexualism is the direct cause of my emotional problems, but I have to let psychiatrists keep saying it is or else they won't treat me. I have got to get back on the road to getting my operation, so I have to see one. When I see a psychiatrist now, I just ignore it when they start rapping on about my transsexualism. If it gets too bad, I just won't see them anymore.

A lot of people can't even imagine the shit I go through. It's the same thing that they go through, except I go through it to a greater extent. They are forced to become one thing or the other; they have to conform to a certain set of standards, even though they don't think it fits them. With me it's just more obvious that's all. A normal guy, if he likes to cut flowers or wants to be a hairdresser or something like that, his masculinity is questioned and he has pressure on him not to do it. Or a woman who wants to drive a truck—it's the same thing. The male/female thing is just part of it. There are other roles we play too. Masks—that's what I call them. By the time a person is 20 years old you can't see the person for the masks. If someone tries to go against the masks, they are schizophrenic or something else. That's what they are called. That's what's on my medical records.

With the masks society tries to hide human sexuality. What I mean is that society has taken and stereotyped masculinity and femininity so you don't get a full and real picture of what it is. Everybody is trying to live up to the stereotype image.

It's hard to live away from the stereotype a little, but it is a thousand times harder to go away from it as radically as I have. I am doing what most people can't even think of, going from a man to a woman. My father's first comment when I told him was, "Why can't you pick an easier one, like being a homosexual?" Which makes a good point. At least if I was a homosexual, I would be the same sex, but to do something so obvious like changing dress and everything is something that you can't hide. Women who want to go to work are thought to be crazy—if a normal person wants to change roles, he has to fight a lot, but if he wants to change sex, that's a lot more.

I guess you can think of transsexualism as more or less a mask, too. Or it can be. I'm a transsexual, but people try to force me into a stereotype—they try to exaggerate the importance of what I am. It's a part of you, granted, but they make it more a part of you than it really is. I am trying not to make it that way. I'm trying not to fall into the slot, but I'm forced into it.

Note

1. Jane's definition of transsexualism closely parallels the one found in most modern dictionaries and those used by the professional community. Harry Benjamin, the doctor who first used the term, states, "The transsexual male or female is deeply unhappy as a member of the sex (or gender) to which he or she was assigned by the anatomical structure of the body, particularly the genitals. To avoid misunderstanding: this has nothing to do with hermaphroditism. The transsexual is physically normal (although occasionally underdeveloped). . . . True transsexuals feel that they belong to the other sex, they want to be and function as members of the opposite sex. . . ." (*The Transsexual Phenomenon*, New York: The Julian Press, 1966, p. 13)

Part 5 / Noninstitutional Deviance

In Part 4, I described how institutional careers may be initiated and perpetuated. The material in that section examined how various types of institutional processing may affect people. An equally important concern is the way in which noninstitutional careers may evolve. As noted earlier, such careers or activities generally arise as a result of the actor's own desires and needs; this means that frequently the actor plays an assertive role in moving into a particular type of activity, as well as consciously structuring and presenting a specific image of self to others. Often, too, as indicated in the general introduction, there may be a degree of overlap between institutional and noninstitutional careers. For instance, prostitutes, skid row alcoholics, homosexuals, and thieves may be arrested and thus pulled into, rather than intentionally entering, an institutional career. The selections in this part describe events such as these.

Structures and Organizational Components

"The Social Organization of Deviants" by Joel Best and David F. Luckenbill, provides an excellent framework for understanding the social organizations in which deviants become involved. The authors make an initial distinction between the social organization of *deviants* and the social organization of *deviance*. The former refers to the "patterns of relationships between deviant actors," while the latter refers to the "patterns of relationships between the various roles performed in deviant transactions." Best and Luckenbill elect to focus on the social organization of deviants. Deviant organizations, they reason, can vary along certain dimensions, most notably in terms of their sophistication (i.e., complexity, degree of coordination, and purposiveness). For example, with regard to complexity, organizations can have varying divisions of labor, degrees of stratification, and degrees of role specialization. Best and Luckenbill note that in terms of sophistication, deviants organize in identifiable ways. They discuss five organizational forms: loners, colleagues, peers, mobs, and formal organizations. Each of these forms can be analyzed relative to four variables (i.e., whether the deviants associate with each other, whether they engage in deviance together, whether there is an elaborate division of labor and whether activities extend over time and space). The authors describe various types of each organizational form. They then examine the consequences of organizing as loners, colleagues, peers, mobs, or formal organizations. Best and Luckenbill argue that the degree of sophistication of a deviant organization has consequences for deviants and social-control agents. Five propositions are advanced in support of this argument. The authors' second hypothesis is especially relevant for the next section on entering and learning about deviant cultures. Specifically, they hypothesize that "the more sophisticated the form of deviant organization, the more elaborate the socialization of its members." The underlying assumption here is that "neophyte deviants" not only must learn how to perform deviant acts and attain the appropriate skills and techniques, but they must also develop a *cognitive perspective* (e.g., learn the relevant rationalizations and language). As an illustration, loners do not depend on others for instruction, while pool hustlers do.

Thomas S. Weinberg and Gerhard Falk, in "The Social Organization of Sadism and Masochism," sensitize one to the fact that, if we are to make sense of the relationships occurring among social actors, as well as among different roles, then an initial effort must be made to flesh out the underlying organizational structure and its components. Like Best and Luckenbill, Weinberg and Falk are concerned primarily with the social organization of deviants; they focus on the subjects of sadism and masochism. The authors make a beginning claim that sociologists have generally neglected these topics as areas of study. This, they point out, may be attributable to the fact that the psychoanalytic model, with its emphasis on individual psychopathology, has predominated. Not only do Weinberg and Falk reject such a model, but they maintain that sadism and masochism can be more fully understood as sociological phenomena. In support of this, they argue that structurally the sadomasochists have developed a subculture and that the subculture can be characterized by a set of norms, a shared belief system, and a common language or argot. The researchers then describe how contacts are made with the subculture (e.g., through advertisements and through associations), as well as the type of functions that sadomasochistic organizations serve for their members. For example, such organizations provide members with information on sexual techniques, facilitate sexual and social contacts, and supply justifications useful for the normalization of attitudes and behaviors.

Entering and Learning Deviant Cultures

The statements by Best and Luckenbill and by Weinberg and Falk, indicate that deviant organizations can be characterized in terms of their relative degree of sophistication. Best and Luckenbill also highlight the fact that a person can gain initial entry to organizations through various channels. Once individuals gain entry, however, they must, if they elect to stay, learn the existing culture and traditions. A similar requirement exists with respect to the institutional deviant. Failure to meet expectations may result in such penalties as ostracism or exclusion from the group. (The general social-psychological processes involved in learning deviant cultures were highlighted in my discussion of the cultural transmission model in Part 2.) The initial selections in this part deal primarily with entry routes, while the latter ones offer specific illustrations of how actors become socialized into deviant or semi-deviant careers. In this respect, Heyl's research on the training of house prostitutes is especially insightful.

In the first selection, "Seekers and Saucers: The Role of the Cultic Milieu in Joining a UFO Cult," authors Robert W. Balch and David Taylor analyze the entry routes that a selected group of people used to become members of a UFO cult. The researchers begin by outlining the guiding philosophy of the organization. Balch and Taylor note that Bo and Peep's prescription for salvation was most rigorous. Stated rather simply, if the followers expected to enter the "next revolutionary high," they had to overcome their emotions and worldly attachments. Of significance, at least in terms of structure, is the observation that the cult was loosely organized—being held together primarily by the charismatic appeal of Bo and Peep, the leaders. Not only were contacts with the outside world limited but interaction with other members was also restricted. For example, when members went camping or traveled, the preferred arrangement was the partnership. The recruitment process itself was highly structured, with its most significant feature being the way in which interactions between members and potential recruits were deliberately limited.

Balch and Taylor point out that new members rarely established close affective ties with members prior to joining, nor did they do so after entering the cult. The researchers find this lack of affective ties remarkable, particularly in view of the literature that has emphasized the importance of this factor in the recruitment and conversion process. Balch and Taylor reason that social scientists have actually overemphasized the importance of such ties. They prefer instead a model that emphasizes the importance of the existing social milieu. If the seeker is part of a milieu where a movement's assumptions make sense, and if he or she defines joining as an extension of a spiritual quest, then joining prior to the establishment of any significant social ties makes sense. Balch and Taylor, in support of their thesis, describe the lifestyle of the followers prior to joining the cult and then examine the social world of the metaphysical seeker. Of interest are the observations indicating that a disproportionate number of the cultists were "remnants of the counterculture." Of interest, too, are Balch and Taylor's comments indicating that "conversion," as used in the traditional sense, had not taken place. There was no wholesale rejection of belief systems, nor was a person's identity rejected for a different identity. The authors conclude by reasoning that potential members of a cult require "strong social support from existing members when a radical substitution of belief systems is required."

As a corollary, the next two selections do, in fact, underscore the important role that group support plays in the restructuring of an actor's identity and belief system. "Becoming a Taxi-Dancer: The Significance of Neutralization in a Semi-Deviant Occupation," by Lawrence K. Hong and Robert W. Duff, offers a week-by-week analysis of how, once exposure to the occupation is gained, females become taxi-dancers. Of major concern to Hong and Duff is the effect that involvement in what some would consider to be semideviant occupation has upon the dancer's self-image. One way of dealing with threats or potential threats to one's identity is to develop an effective set of rationalizations. (This, it may be recalled, is a central feature of the cultural transmission model discussed in Part 2.) The researchers describe how this comes about. During the first week, for example, and through the encouragement of co-workers and the management, the women begin to internalize a set of "neutralization techniques" that can be used to legitimate their involvement in the profession. Thereafter, and especially during weeks two and three, the women begin to learn more and more of the appropriate techniques. By the fourth week, they have learned most of the existing techniques and have also become committed to the occupation— that is, they come to view themselves as taxi-dancers. Hong and Duff also discuss how women may gain entry, such as through contacts with other dancers, and they present some of the reasons why they may elect to become dancers, such as financial considerations.

Barbara Sherman Heyl, in "The Madam as Teacher: The Training of House Prostitutes," describes the socialization of house prostitutes. Heyl primarily focuses on the "female trainer-trainee relationship" that exists at the house level. Once a novice enters the house she becomes trained by the "madam." A major portion of the training involves instruction in the appropriate sexual techniques—fellatio, coitus, and "half and half." The newcomer is also taught the house rules (such as the amount of time to be spent with a customer and the specific sums of money to be charged for various types of sexual services), client management, and how to "hustle." Throughout this training, an attempt is made to effectively isolate the novice from her prior lifestyle and associations. This specific process is important in structuring an occupational identity as a "professional" (i.e., a view of self as a career prostitute). Heyl goes on to note that the house prostitute, unlike the call girl, must go through considerable training; this is primarily because of the structure of the profession. Specifically, established houses require close interaction among their participants and thus they hire only the trained prostitute. Like the Hong and Duff study, Heyl's offers an excellent application of the cultural transmission model discussed in Part 2. The research also graphically illustrates how the existing theory of the office and associated stereotypes become inculcated within the house prostitute—a process that may produce a career or secondary deviant.

Patterns and Variations

As is apparent from the preceding statements, deviant or semideviant occupations vary in terms of their sophistication and corresponding organizational structure. Quite clearly, the house prostitute, given the particular nature of the profession, is subjected to a more elaborate and intense degree of socialization than is the case with the call girl. This observation highlights the fact that even in the same profession, deviant organizations, activities, and pursuits take a wide variety of forms. The selections in this part explore some of these patterns.

Carol A. Whitehurst, in "Women and the Commission of Crime: A Theoretical Approach," focuses on patterns of crime for women and men. Her main concern is with demonstrating how sociological theories of deviance can be used to explain two basic facts: (1) "women's reported crime always has and continues to represent only a small proportion of men's reported crime," and (2) "the proportion of total reported crime committed by women has increased considerably since about 1960." Whitehurst offers some official data and then assesses the accuracy of the figures. For example, she points out (and rightfully so) that the FBI's *Uniform Crime Reports*—data sources that are often used to assess major trends in crime—are limited in many ways. For example, only arrest figures are included, certain categories of crime are not recorded, and the race and social class of the offender are not reported. By contrast, self-report data (i.e., data resulting from subjects' own reports of criminal or delinquent acts they have committed) frequently present a more accurate picture of crime. Such data support the same trends that are suggested by official statistics, although the patterns are less pronounced. Whitehurst entertains and dismisses most of the popular statements that have been advanced to explain patterns of female crime (e.g., economic motivations, increasing freedom and rising assertiveness, and the advent of the women's movement). She argues that the changes in female crime, as well as the rise of the women's movement, are reflective of larger social and economic changes. Whitehurst ends by examining how various theoretical perspectives (e.g., anomie, differential association, and social learning) can be used to obtain a more complete understanding of why women commit less crime and why women's crime has been rising.

"Road Hustlers," by Robert C. Prus and C. R. D. Sharper, offers an account of card and dice hustling—especially the ways in which newcomers become socialized into the various hustling roles. These authors make an initial distinction between professional and nonprofessional hustling crews, particularly in terms of the amount of training involved. For example, novices in a nonprofessional crew receive relatively little training, while those in a professional crew must go through an extensive apprenticeship. People involved with the professionals are subjected to learning experiences in four major areas: (1) they learn how to sharpen their "larceny sense," (2) they learn how to get along with fellow hustlers, (3) they acquire skills in specific hustling roles, and (4) they learn how to "make the nut," or reduce expenses while on the road. With regard to one's larceny sense, crew members expect their partners to take advantage of any situation that could make or save money for the crew; crew members also, in terms of impression management, expect members to "fit in" and "sustain identities conducive to manipulation." A number of hustling roles are available to novices and members. Prus and Sharper describe three: the mechanic, the shoot-up man, and the muscle man. Not only does the mechanic receive the most explicit tutelage but he is generally under the most pressure. Like the mechanic, the shoot-up man must also spend a great deal of time mastering his role. He learns how to mix with the crowd, encourages people to part with their money, and provides distractions when the mechanic is about to make a switch. The muscle-man role is, by contrast, less well-defined and is more apt to be associated with rough-hustle situations (i.e., amateur or less-polished hustles).

"Corporate Organization and Criminal Behavior," by Marshall B. Clinard and Peter C. Yeager, continues a major theme being developed in this part, particularly the idea that, like the "institutional deviant" in Part 4, the "noninstitutional deviant," if he or she is to be viewed analytically as a career deviant, must become inculcated with the existing working ideology or theory of the office. Clinard and Yeager are primarily concerned with corporate executives—powerful decision-makers who, like prostitutes and street hustlers, may engage in widespread criminal activities yet may escape detection. The authors, in their attempt to make sense out of patterns of corporate crime and to account for its origins, focus on the content of corporate normative systems. They note initially that corporate norms may conflict with ethical and legal norms; this appears likely when a corporation emphasizes profits above ethics and ignores its responsibility to the consumer, the community, and society. Clinard and Yeager cite several examples of what happened when corporate codes of conduct clashed with legal norms (e.g., the price-fixing conspiracy in the electrical industry). Not only can lawbreaking become an accepted pattern within a corporation, but the underlying normative system may be such that it actually *encourages* the commission of illegal acts. In the authors' words: "A corporation may socialize its members to normative systems conducive to criminality."

Of particular interest is the discussion of the making of a corporate criminal. An important factor in this process is the rather complete socializing or welding of the employee to the corporation. Such a process frequently weakens a person's ties with external groups and also produces what has been termed a bureaucratic "functionary"—a person who accepts orders and does the job. The authors conclude with a discussion of how executives may neutralize their illgal or unethical conduct. Clinard and Yeager point out that many executives can understand the illegal nature of their conduct yet are able to justify it, often by citing the pervasiveness of such activities. The example of the Harvard professor who trained his students to lie and misrepresent their positions in negotiations serves as an excellent case in point. The irony is that many of these students now occupy the positions of corporate president and chief executive officer. According to the quote from the *Wall Street Journal,* "It's a safe bet that . . . students will eventually get to practice what they learn."

The Effects of Deviant Careers

Involvement in activities, careers, and professions that are commonly viewed as deviant by others is not without its personal and social costs. If, for example, deviance becomes known, the actor may become stigmatized and subsequently discredited. Thus, those who engage in potentially discrediting behavior must manage their "front" in such a way as to avoid detection by socially significant "straights." The articles in this section, focus directly on the social actor, and particularly on the management strategies that may be invoked to protect a person's identity and self-image from erosion or outright destruction.

"The Social Integration of Peers and Queers," by Albert J. Reiss,

Jr., provides an account of how peers who engage in homosexual behavior protect their identity. Reiss notes initially that not only are the peers aware that they are engaging in what some would term deviant behavior, but they must also come to grips with any threats that their actions may have on their personal and public identities. One way this can be accomplished is to view the homosexual exchange as strictly a financial transaction. Reiss then describes the manner in which peers become recruited into the activity, as well as the content of the norms governing transactions. For example, one of the norms is that "the sexual transaction must be limited to mouth-genital fellation." Furthermore, "both peers and queers, as participants, should remain affectively neutral during the transaction." Reiss observes that breaches of the normative code by the adult fellator are frequently met with violence. Such violence (or the threat of violence) serves as an important instrument of social control as far as keeping the customer in line, and it also reduces the possibility that the peer will view himself as a homosexual, at least in the career sense.

Edwin M. Lemert, in "Role Enactment, Self, and Identity in the Systematic Check Forger," is concerned with how the occupation of forgery affects a person's identity. The evidence indicates that the check forger often experiences an identity crisis—a crisis arising primarily as a result of the activity itself. Specifically, not only is the forger constantly on the move, but he is unable to establish any meaningful relationships or contacts with others—contacts which are important in the structuring, presentation, and maintenance of a specific personal and public identity. This frequently means that the "self becomes amorphous." Lemert argues that given this particular condition of self, the forger often exhibits a sense of relief when arrested. The identity problem is partially solved as an identity is imputed to the forger, even though it is a deviant or criminal one. As Lemert points out, the check forger "is much like the actor who prefers bad publicity to none at all."

"Becoming a Hit Man: Neutralization in a Very Deviant Career," by Ken Levi, presents an account of how the professional murderer neutralizes a potentially discrediting feature of his biography. Levi begins by maintaining that, unlike the professional killer, the novice lacks "neutralizers" that are provided by the occupation and is therefore confronted with two basic problems: (1) overcoming his inhibitions, and (2) avoiding damage to his self-image. Levi, in providing insight into how these problems are managed, offers a number of distinctions between the organized and the independent murderer. The organized killer, for example, usually belongs to a syndicate, does not get paid on a contract basis, and often kills for revenge. Furthermore, the organized killer can neutralize his behavior through use of conventional rationalizations (e.g., the "appeal to higher loyalties"). The free-lance or independent murderer, by contrast, lacks most of these defenses and must therefore draw on other sources. Levi reasons that the role of independent murderer is itself composed of several components that (if a person is socialized into the role) can help guard against the possibility that the incumbent will impute a deviant identity to himself. Levi describes three main features of this role: (1) the contract, (2) reputation and money, and (3) skill. As an illustration, the contract is usually an unwritten agreement, arranged over the phone, between people who have no personal contact, and with the motive and victim being unknown. This type of arrangement protects the parties from the law and also enables the hit man to deny that anyone has been victimized. Similarly, by approaching the hit as "just a job," the killer can, as far as picking up another neutralization technique, deny wrongfulness or deny that anyone has been injured. The economic motive, Levi maintains, is an especially important career contingency; this motive, as noted above, was also of primary concern to the peers whom Reiss studied. Levi ends by offering a comparison of a killer's first hit with his subsequent ones. What becomes apparent is that not only were later hits neutralized effectively, but the killer appeared to experience little or no damage to self. He had become a career deviant.

38 / The Social Organization of Deviants

JOEL BEST
DAVID F. LUCKENBILL

Ethnographic research on particular social scenes provides data for general, grounded theories (Glaser and Strauss, 1967). For the study of deviance, field studies have supplied the basis for the development of general theories of the social psychology of deviance (Goffman, 1963; Lofland, 1969; Matza, 1969). However, while several reports about specific forms of deviance focus on social organization (Einstader, 1969; McIntosh, 1971; Mileski and Black, 1972; Shover, 1977; Zimmerman and Wieder, 1977), there is no satisfactory general theory of the social organization of deviance.

Sociologists of varying perspectives have debated the nature of social organization among juvenile delinquents, professional criminals, organized criminals and white-collar criminals. Others have developed typologies of deviants that include social organizational features (Clinard and Quinney, 1973; Gibbons, 1965, 1977; Miller, 1978). However, these treatments of social organization suffer from several flaws. First, they are often too narrow, focusing on a single type of deviance, such as burglary or, more broadly, crime. Second, they usually are content with describing the organizational forms of different types of deviance. They fail to locate such forms along a dimension of organization or examine the consequences of organizational differences for deviants and social control agents. Third, they typically confuse two different bases for analyzing social organization: a general theory must distinguish between the social organization of *deviants* (the patterns of relationships between deviant actors) and the social organization of *deviance* (the patterns of relationships between the various roles performed in deviant transactions).

In this paper, we present a framework for understanding the social organization of deviants.[1] By examining reports of field research, several forms of social organization are identified and located along a dimension of organizational sophistication. Then some propositions are developed regarding the consequences of organizational variation for deviants and social control agents. Finally, some implications for the study of social organization are considered.

530

FORMS OF DEVIANT ORGANIZATION

The social organization of deviants refers to the structure or patterns of relationships among deviant actors in the context of deviant pursuits. The social organization of deviants varies along a dimension of sophistication. Organizational sophistication involves the elements of complexity, coordination and purposiveness (cf. Cressey, 1972). Organizations vary in the complexity of their division of labor including the size of membership, degree of stratification, and degree of specialization of organizational roles. Organizations also vary in their coordination among roles including the degree to which rules, agreements, and codes regulating relationships are formalized and enforced. Finally, organizations vary in the purposiveness with which they specify, strive toward, and achieve their objectives. Forms of organization which display high levels of complexity, coordination, and purposiveness are more sophisticated than those forms with lower levels.

Research reports suggest that deviants organize in several identifiable ways along the dimension of sophistication. Beginning with the least sophisticated, we will discuss five forms: loners, colleagues, peers, mobs and formal organizations. These organizational forms can be defined in terms of four variables: 1) whether the deviants associate with one another; 2) whether they participate in deviance together; 3) whether their deviance requires an elaborate division of labor; and 4) whether their organization's activities extend over time and space (see Table 1). *Loners* do not associate with other deviants, participate in shared deviance, have a division of labor, or maintain their deviance over extended time and space. *Colleagues* differ from loners because they associate with fellow deviants. *Peers* not only associate with one another, but also participate in deviance together. In *mobs,* the shared participation requires an elaborate division of labor. Finally, *formal organizations* involve mutual association and participation, an elaborate division of labor, and deviant undertakings extended over time and space.

Table 1 / Characteristics of Different Forms of the Social Organization of Deviants

	Type of Organization				
Variable	LONERS	COLLEAGUES	PEERS	MOBS	FORMAL ORGANIZATIONS
Mutual association	−	+	+	+	+
Mutual participation	−	−	+	+	+
Division of labor	−	−	−	+	+
Extended organization	−	−	−	−	+

The descriptions of these forms of organization must be qualified in two ways. First, the forms are presented as ideal types. There is variation among the types of deviants within each form, as well as between one form and another. The intent is to sketch out the typical features of each form, recognizing that particular types of deviants may not share all of the features of their form to the same degree. Organizational sophistication can be viewed as a continuum, with deviants located between, as well as on, the five points. Describing a number of forms along this continuum inevitably understates the complexities of social life. Second, the descriptions of these forms draw largely from field studies of deviance in the contemporary United States, and attempt to locate the deviants studied along the dimension of organizational sophistication. A particular type of deviant can be organized in various ways in different societies and at different times. The references to specific field studies are intended to place familiar pieces of research within this framework; they are not claims that particular types of deviants invariably organize in a given way.

Loners

Some deviants operate as individuals. These loners do not associate with other deviants for purposes of sociability, the performance of deviant activities, or the exchange of supplies and information. Rather, they must supply themselves with whatever knowledge, skill, equipment and ideology their deviance requires. Loners lack deviant associations, so they cannot receive such crucial forms of feedback as moral support or information about their performance, new opportunities, or changes in social control strategies. They often enter deviance as a defensive response to private troubles (Lofland, 1969). Because their entry does not require contact with other deviants, as long as they can socialize themselves, loners frequently come from segments of the population which are less likely to be involved in the more sophisticated forms of deviance; it is not uncommon for loners to be middle-aged, middle-class or female. Because their deviance often is defensive, and because they lack the support of other deviants, loners' careers typically are short-lived. Examples of loners include murderers (Luckenbill, 1977), rapists (Amir, 1971), embezzlers (Cressey, 1953), check forgers (Lemert, 1967:99–134; Klein and Montague, 1977), physician narcotic addicts (Winick, 1961), compulsive criminals (Cressey, 1962), heterosexual transvestites (Buckner, 1970), amateur shoplifters (Cameron, 1964), some gamblers (Lesieur, 1977), and many computer criminals (Parker, 1976).[2]

Colleagues

Like loners, colleagues perform as individuals. Unlike loners, however, colleagues associate with others involved in the same kind of deviance. Colleagues thus form a simple group which provides important services for members. First, colleagues often socialize newcomers, providing training in deviant skills as well as an ideology which accounts for and justifies their deviance. Association also offers sociability among members with whom one's deviant identity need not be concealed: an actor can take down his or her guard without fear of discovery by agents of social control (Goffman, 1959, 1963). Also, association provides a source of information about ways to obtain deviant equipment, new techniques, new opportunities for engaging in deviance, and strategies for avoiding sanctioning. Colleagues learn and are held to a loose set of norms which direct conduct in both deviant and respectable activities. "Don't inform on a colleague" and "Never cut in on a colleague's score" exemplify such norms. The moral climate established by these expectations increases the stability of colleagues' social scene. At the same time, only some deviant activities and some people are suited for such a loose form of organization. A successful career as a colleague depends ultimately on the individual's performance when operating alone. As a result, newcomers often sample the scene and, when they encounter difficulties, drift away. Only the more successful colleagues maintain extended deviant careers. Some examples of colleagues include most prostitutes (Hirschi, 1962; Bryan, 1965, 1966), pimps (Milner and Milner, 1972), and pool hustlers (Polsky, 1967).

Peers

Like colleagues, peers associate with one another and benefit from services provided by their fellows. Peers are involved in the socialization of novices, considerable sociable interaction, and the maintenance of a loose, unwritten code of conduct to be followed by individuals who wish to remain in the peer group. Unlike colleagues, peers participate in deviant acts together; they are involved in deviant transactions at the same time and in the same place. In some cases, such mutual participation is required by the nature of the deviant activity. This is exemplified in the performance of homosexual acts, or in the "task force raids" where a collection of young men engages in simple acts of violence such as gang fighting or rolling drunks (Cressey, 1972). In other cases, mutual participation is required because peers form a network for supplying one another with essential goods and services, as found in the distribution of illicit drugs. In either event, peers interact basically as equals; there is a minimal division of labor and specialized roles are uncommon. Although individuals pass through these social scenes, peer groups often are quite stable, perhaps because peer groups solve structural problems within society for their members. Two common varieties of deviant peers are young people who have not yet entered integrated adult work roles, and those who frequent a deviant marketplace and depend on their contacts with one another for the satisfaction of illicit needs. Examples of peers include hobos (Anderson, 1923), homosexuals (Humphreys, 1970; Mileski and Black, 1972; Warren, 1974), group-oriented gamblers (Lesieur, 1977), swingers (Bartell, 1971), gang delinquents (Shaw, 1930; Matza, 1964; Rosenberg and Silverstein, 1969), motorcycle outlaws (Thompson, 1966), skid row tramps (Wiseman, 1970; Rubington, 1978) and illicit drug users (Blumer, 1967; Carey, 1968; Feldman, 1968; Stoddart, 1974).

Mobs

Mobs are small groups of professional or career deviants organized to pursue specific, profitable goals.[3] Their deviance requires the coordinated actions of members performing specialized roles—a more sophisticated division of labor than that found among peers. Thus, work is divided among confidence artists (the inside man and the outside man), pickpockets (the tool and the stall), or card and dice hustlers (the mechanic and the shootup man; Maurer, 1962, 1964; Prus and Sharper, 1977). Ordinarily, at least one of the roles in the mob is highly skilled, requiring considerable practice and training to perfect. This training (normally via apprenticeship), the need for on-the-job coordination, and the common practice of traveling from city to city as a mob lead to intensive interaction between mobsters. Elaborate technical argots develop, as well as elaborate codes specifying mobsters' obligations to each other.

Mobs have complex links to outsiders. They are organized to accomplish profitable yet safe crimes. McIntosh (1971) describes the historical shift from craft thieving, where mobs develop routine procedures for stealing relatively small sums from individuals, to project thieving, where larger amounts are taken from corporate targets using procedures specifically tailored to the particular crime. In either case, mob operations are planned and staged with an eye toward avoiding arrest. Also, mobs may attempt to neutralize the criminal justice system by bribing social control agents not to make arrests, "fixing" those cases where arrests take place, or making restitution to victims in return for dropped charges. Mobs also have ties to others who purchase stolen goods, provide legal services, and supply information and deviant equipment. Finally, a network of sociable and business contacts ties mobs to one another, enabling strategic information to spread quickly. These arrangements insure that mobs can operate at a consistently profitable level with minimal interference. Consequently, the careers of individual mobsters, as well as those of specific mobs, seem to be more stable than those of deviants organized in less sophisticated ways.[4] Examples of mobs are the groups of professional criminals specializing in confidence games (Sutherland, 1937; Maurer, 1962), picking pockets (Maurer, 1964), shoplifting (Cameron, 1964), armed robbery (Einstader, 1969; Letkemann, 1973), burglary (Shover, 1973) and card and dice hustling (Prus and Sharper, 1977).

Formal Organizations

Formal organizations of deviants differ from mobs in the scope of their actions.[5] Normally they involve more people, but, more importantly, their actions are coordinated to efficiently handle deviant tasks on a routine basis over considerable time and space. While mobsters work as a group in a series of episodic attacks, formal organizations are characterized by delegated responsibility and by routine and steady levels of productivity. In many ways, formal organizations of deviants share the features which characterize such respectable bureaucracies as military organizations, churches and business firms. They have a hierarchal division of labor, including both vertical and horizontal differentiation of positions and roles and established channels for vertical and horizontal communication. A deviant formal organization may contain departments for planning, processing goods, public relations and rule enforcement, with positions for strategists, coordinators, accountants, lawyers, enforcers, and dealers in illicit goods. There may be recruitment policies for filling these diversified positions, and entry into the organization may be marked by a ritual ceremony of passage. Formal organizations usually have binding, but normally unwritten, rules and codes for guiding members in organizational action, and these rules are actively enforced.

Formal organizations of deviants can make large profits by operating efficiently. At the same time, they must protect themselves from harm or destruction. As in less sophisticated forms of organization, loyal members are expected to maintain the group's secrets. In addition, deviant formal organizations attempt to locate power in the office, rather than in an individual charismatic leader. Although charismatic leadership obviously plays a part in some deviant formal organizations, the successful organization is able to continue operations when a leader dies or is arrested. Finally, deviant formal organizations typically invest considerable energy in neutralizing the criminal justice system by corrupting both high and low level officials. The scope and efficiency of their operations, their organizational flexibility, and their ties to agencies of social control make formal organizations of deviants extremely stable. Examples of such deviant formal organizations include very large urban street gangs (Keiser, 1969; Dawley, 1973), smuggling rings (Green, 1969), and organized crime "families" (Cressey, 1969; Ianni, 1972).

THE SIGNIFICANCE OF THE SOCIAL ORGANIZATION OF DEVIANTS

The identification and description of these different organizational forms permit a comparative analysis. What are the consequences of organizing as loners, colleagues, peers, mobs, or formal organizations? A comparison suggests that the sophistication of a form of deviant social organization has several consequences for both deviants and social control agents. Five propositions can be advanced.

I. *The more sophisticated the form of deviant organization, the greater its members' capability for complex deviant operations.* Deviant activities, like conventional activities, vary in their complexity. The complexity of a deviant operation refers to the number of elements required to carry it through; the more component parts to an activity, the more complex it is.[6] Compared to simple activities, complex lines of action demand more careful preparation and execution and take longer to complete. The complexity of a deviant activity depends upon two identifiable types of elements. First, there are the *resources* which the actors must be able to draw upon. Some activities require that the deviant utilize special knowledge, skill, equipment, or social status in order to complete the operation successfully, while simple acts can be carried out without such resources. Second, the *organization of the deviant transaction* affects an activity's complexity.[7] Some deviant acts can be accomplished with a single actor, while others require two or more people. The actors in a transaction can share a common role, as in a skid row bottle gang, or the transaction may demand different roles, such as offender and victim or buyer and seller. Furthermore, the degree to which these roles must be coordinated, ranging from the minimal coordination of juvenile vandals to the precision routines performed by mobs of pickpockets, varies among situations. The more people involved, the more roles they perform; and the more coordination between those roles, the more complex the deviant transaction's organization. The more resources and organization involved in a deviant operation, the more complex the operation is.

In general, deviants in more sophisticated forms of organization commit more complex acts.[8] The deviant acts of loners tend to be simple, requiring little in the way of resources or organization. Although colleagues work apart from one another, they generally share certain resources, such as shared areas. The hustlers' pool hall and the prostitutes' red light district contain the elements needed to carry out deviant operations, including victims and clients. Peers may interact in situations where they are the only ones present, performing complementary or comparable roles, as when two people engage in homosexual intercourse or a group of motorcycle outlaws makes a "run." Peers also may undertake activities which involve nonmembers, as when members of a delinquent gang rob a passerby. The activities carried out by mobs involve substantially more coordination among the members' roles. In an armed robbery, for instance, one member may be assigned to take the money, while a second provides "cover" and a third waits for the others in the car, ready to drive away on their return. Finally, the activities of formal organizations tend to be particularly complex, requiring substantial resources and elaborate organization. Major off-track betting operations, with staff members at local, district and regional offices who carry out a variety of clerical and supervisory tasks on a daily basis, represent an exceedingly complex form of deviance.

The relationship between the sophistication of organization and the complexity of deviant activities is not perfect. Loners can engage in acts of considerable complexity, for example. The computer criminal who single-handedly devises a complicated method of breaking into and stealing from computerized records, the embezzler who carries through an elaborate series of illicit financial manipulations, and the physician who juggles drug records in order to maintain his or her addiction to narcotics are engaged in complex offenses requiring substantial resources. However, these offenses cannot be committed by everyone. These loners draw upon resources which they command through their conventional positions, turning them to deviant uses. The computer criminal typically is an experienced programmer, the embezzler must occupy a position of financial trust, and the physician has been trained in the use of drugs. Possessing these resources makes the loner's deviance possible. Thus, the more concentrated the resources necessary for a deviant operation, the less sophisticated the form of organization required. However, when resources are not concentrated, then more sophisticated forms of organization are necessary to undertake more complex deviant operations.

Sophisticated forms of deviant organization have advantages beyond being able to undertake complex operations by pooling resources distributed among their members. Some deviant activities require a minimal level or organization; for example, homosexual intercourse demands the participation of two parties. In many other cases, it may be possible to carry out a deviant line of action using a relatively unsophisticated form of organization, but the task is considerably easier if a sophisticated form of organization can be employed. This is so because more sophisticated forms of deviant organization enjoy several advantages: they are capable of conducting a larger number of deviant operations; the operations can occur with greater frequency and over a broader range of territory; and, as discussed below, the members are better protected from the actions of social control agents. Of course, sophisticated organizations may engage in relatively simple forms of deviance, but the deviant act is often only one component in a larger organizational context. Taking a particular bet in the policy racket is a simple act, but the racket itself, handling thousands of bets, is complex indeed. Similarly, a murder which terminates a barroom dispute between two casual acquaintances is very different from an execution which is ordered and carried out by members of a formal organization, even though the two acts may appear equally simple. In the latter case, the killing may be intended as a means of maintaining discipline by demonstrating the organization's ability to levy sanctions against wayward members.

II. *The more sophisticated the form of deviant organization, the more elaborate the socialization of its members.* Neophyte deviants need to acquire two types of knowledge: 1) they must learn how to perform deviant acts, and how to gain appropriate *skills and techniques;* 2) they must develop a *cognitive perspective,* a distinctive way of making sense of their new, deviant world (cf. Shibutani, 1961: 118–127). Such a perspective includes an ideology which accounts for the deviance, the individual's participation in deviance, and the organizational form, as well as a distinctive language for speaking about these and other matters.

As forms of deviant organization increase in sophistication, socialization becomes more elaborate. Loners do not depend upon other deviants for instruction in deviant skills or for a special cognitive perspective; they learn through their participation in conventional social scenes. Murderers, for instance, learn from their involvement in conventional life how to respond in situations of interpersonal conflict, and they employ culturally widespread justifications for killing people (Bohannon, 1960; Wolfgang and Ferracuti, 1967). Embezzlers learn the technique for converting a financial trust in the course of respectable vocational training, adapting justifications such as "borrowing" from conventional business ideology (Cressey,1953). In contrast, colleagues teach one another a great deal. Although pool hustlers usually know how to shoot pool before they enter hustling, their colleagues provide a rich cognitive perspective, including a sense of "we-ness," some norms of behavior, a system for stratifying the hustling world, and an extensive argot (Polsky, 1967).[9] Peers receive similar training or, in some cases, teach one another through a process of emerging norms (Turner, 1964). Juvenile vandals, for example, can devise new offenses through their mutually constructed interpretation of what is appropriate to a particular situation (Wade, 1967). Sometimes, the knowledge peers acquire has largely symbolic functions that affirm the group's solidarity, as when a club of motorcycle outlaws devises a written constitution governing its members (Reynolds, 1967:134–136). In mobs and formal organizations, the cognitive perspective focuses on more practical matters; their codes of conduct specify the responsibilities members have in their dealings with one another, social control agents and others. Greater emphasis is also placed on the acquisition of specialized skills, with an experienced deviant coaching an apprentice, frequently over an extended period of time.

Two circumstances affect the socialization process in different forms of deviant organization. First, the sophistication of the organization affects the scope and style of the training process. The amount of training tends to increase with the sophistication of the organization. The skills required to perform deviant roles vary, but there is a tendency for more sophisticated forms of organization to incorporate highly skilled roles. Further, the more sophisticated forms of organization often embody cognitive perspectives of such breadth that the deviant must acquire a large body of specialized knowledge. In addition, the socialization process tends to be organized differently in different forms of deviant organization. While loners serve as their own agents of socialization, and colleagues and peers may socialize one another, mobs and formal organizations almost always teach newcomers through apprenticeship to an experienced deviant. Second, the socialization process is affected by the newcomer's motivation for entering deviance. Loners, of course, choose deviance on their own. In the more sophisticated forms, newcomers may ask for admission, but they often are recruited by experienced deviants. While peers may recruit widely, as when a delinquent gang tries to enlist all of the neighborhood boys of a given age, mobs and formal organizations recruit selectively, judging the character and commitment of prospective members and sometimes demanding evidence of skill or prior experience. For loners, entry into deviance frequently is a defensive act, intended to ward off some immediate threat. Peers, on the other hand, often are using deviance to experience stimulation; their deviance has an adventurous quality (Lofland, 1969). In contrast, mobs and formal organizations adopt a more professional approach: deviance is instrumental, a calculated means of acquiring economic profits.[10] These differences in the scope of socialization, the way the process is organized, and the neophyte's motivation account for the relationship between sophistication of organization and the elaborateness of the socialization.

III. *The more sophisticated the form of deviant organization, the more elaborate the services provided its members.* Every social role poses practical problems for its performers. In some cases these problems can be solved by providing the actors with supplies of various sorts. Actors may require certain *equipment* to perform a role. They may also need *information* about their situation in order to coordinate their behavior with the ongoing action and successfully accomplish their part in an operation. One function of deviant social organization is to solve such practical problems by supplying members with needed equipment and information. More sophisticated forms of social organization are capable of providing more of these services.

Deviants differ in their requirements for equipment. Some need little in the way of equipment; a mugger may be able to get by with a piece of pipe. In other cases, deviants make use of specialized items which have few, if any, respectable uses (e.g., heroin or the booster boxes used in shoplifting).[11] Most loners require little equipment. When specialized needs exist, they are met through conventional channels accessible to the deviants, as when a physician narcotic addict obtains illicit drugs from hospital or clinic supplies. Colleagues also supply their own equipment, for the most part, although they may receive some assistance; pool hustlers, for example, provide their own cues, but they may rely on financial backers for funding. Peers adopt various patterns toward equipment. In some cases, peer groups develop to facilitate the distribution and consumption of deviant goods, such as illicit drugs. In other instances, peers use equipment as a symbol of their deviant status, as when gang members wear special costumes. The equipment used by mobsters is more utilitarian; many of their trades demand specialized tools, for safecracking, shoplifting and so forth. In addition to a craftsman's personal equipment, the mob may require special materials for a specific project. Norms often exist that specify the manner in which these equipment purchases will be financed. In still other instances, some mobsters with expensive pieces of equipment may cooperate with several different mobs who wish to make use of them (such as the "big store" which is centrally located for the use of several confidence mobs). Formal organizations also have extensive equipment requirements. Because their operations extend over considerable time, formal organizations may find it expedient to invest in an elaborate array of fixed equipment. Off-track bookmaking, for example, may involve the purchase or rental of offices, desks, calculators, computer lines, special telephone lines, office supplies and automobiles. Special staff members may have the responsibility for maintaining this equipment (Bell, 1962:134). In addition, some formal organizations are involved in producing or distributing deviant equipment for the consumption of other deviants; drug smuggling offers the best example.

Deviants need information in order to determine their courses of action. To operate efficiently, they need to know about new opportunities for deviant action; to operate safely, they need to know about the movements of social control agents. The more sophisticated forms of organization have definite advantages in acquiring and processing information. Loners, of course, depend upon themselves for information; opportunities or threats outside their notice cannot be taken into account. Colleagues and peers can learn more by virtue of their contacts with the deviant "grapevine," and they may have norms regarding a member's responsibility to share relevant information. In mobs, information is sought in more systematic ways. In the course of their careers, mobsters develop perceptual skills, enabling them to "case" possible targets (Letkemann, 1973). In addition, some mobs rely on outsiders for information; spotters may be paid a commission for pointing out opportunities for theft. A formal organization can rely upon its widely distributed membership for information and its contacts with corrupted social control agents.

The degree to which deviants need special supplies varies with the requirements of their operations, the frequency with which they interact with victims or other nondeviants, and their visibility to social control agents. Supplies other than equipment and information may be required in some instances. However, for most supply problems, sophisticated forms of social organization enjoy a comparative advantage.

IV. *The more sophisticated the form of deviant organization, the greater its members' involvement in deviance.* Complex deviant operations require planning and coordinated action during the deviant act. Socialization and supply also involve interaction among an organization's members. More sophisticated forms of deviant organization, featuring complex operations and elaborate socialization and supply, are therefore more likely to involve intensive social contact with one's fellow deviants. Furthermore, because deviants face sanctions from social control agents and respectable people, their contacts with other deviants are an important source of social support. The differences in the ability of forms of social organization to provide support for their members have important social psychological consequences for deviants' careers and identities.

The dimensions of deviant careers vary with the form of deviant organization. Longer deviant careers tend to occur in more sophisticated forms of organization. For naive loners, deviance can comprise a single episode, a defensive act to ward off an immediate threat. For systematic loners, and many colleagues and peers, involvement in deviance is limited to one period in their life. Prostitutes grow too old to compete in the sexual marketplace, delinquents move into respectable adult work roles, and so forth. Members of mobs and formal organizations are more likely to have extended careers. Where the roles are not too physically demanding, deviance can continue until the individual is ready to retire from the work force (Inciardi, 1977). Deviant careers also vary in the amount of time they demand while the individual is active; some kinds of deviance take up only a small portion of the person's hours, but other deviant roles are equivalent to full-time, conventional jobs. Although the relationship is not perfect, part-time deviance is associated with less sophisticated forms of deviant organization.[12]

Social organization is also related to the relative prominence of the deviant identity in the individual's self-concept. Individuals may view their deviance as tangential to the major themes in their lives, or as a central focus, an identity around which much of one's life is arranged. The latter pattern is more likely to develop in sophisticated forms of deviant organization, for, as Lofland (1969) points out, several factors associated with deviant social organization facilitate the assumption of deviant identity, including frequenting places populated by deviants, obtaining deviant equipment, and receiving instruction in deviant skills and ideology. These factors also would appear to be associated with the maintenance of deviance as a central identity. Loners seem especially adept at isolating their deviance, viewing it as an exception to the generally conventional pattern their lives take. This is particularly true when the deviance was initially undertaken to defend that conventional life style from some threat. Even when an individual is relatively committed to deviance, normal identities can serve as an important resource. In his discussion of the World War II underground, Aubert (1965) notes that normal identities served to protect its members. In the same way, an established normal status shields the deviant from the suspicion of social control agents and, if the members refrain from revealing their conventional identities to one another, against discovery brought about by deviant associates who invade their respectable lives. Such considerations seem to be most important in middle-class peer groups organized around occasional lesiure-time participation in a deviant marketplace, such as homosexuality and swinging.[13] Other deviants, particularly members of mobs and formal organizations, may associate with their fellows away from deviant operations, so that both their work and their sociable interaction take place among deviants. This is also true for peer groups that expand into "communities" and offer a wide range of services to members. Active members of urban gay communities can largely restrict their contacts to other homosexuals (Harry and Devall, 1978; Wolf, 1979). In these cases there is little need to perform conventional roles, aside from their obvious uses as concealment, and the deviant identity is likely to be central for the individual.

The degree to which an individual finds a deviant career and a deviant identity satisfying depends, in part, on the form of deviant organization of which he or she is a part. As in any activity, persons continue to engage in deviance only as long as the rewards it offers are greater than the rewards which could be obtained through alternative activities. The relevant rewards vary from one person to the next and from one type of deviance to another; a partial list includes money, physical and emotional satisfaction, valued social contacts and prestige. Because the relative importance of these rewards varies with the individual, it is impossible to measure the differences in rewards between forms of deviant organization. There is some evidence that monetary profits are generally higher in more sophisticated forms of deviant organization. While an occasional loner can steal a very large sum through an embezzlement or a computer crime, most mobs can earn a reasonably steady income, and rackets run by formal organizations consistently bring in high profits. A more revealing measure of satisfaction is career stability; members of more sophisticated forms of deviant organization are more likely to remain in deviance. Loners' careers are short-lived, even when they are involved in systematic deviance. Lemert's (1967) account of the failure of professional forgers to remain at large suggests that the lack of social support is critical. As noted above, persons frequently drift out of their roles as colleagues and peers when other options become more attractive. The long-term careers of members of mobs and formal organizations suggest that these forms are more likely to satisfy the deviant.[14]

V. *The more sophisticated the form of deviant organization, the more secure its members' deviant operations.* The social organization of deviants affects the interaction between deviants and social con-

trol agents. This relationship is complicated because increased sophistication has consequences which would seem to make social control efforts both easier and more difficult. On the one hand, the more
sophisticated the deviant organization, the greater its public visibility and its chances of being subject to social control actions. Because
more sophisticated forms of organization have more complex deviant operations, there are more people involved with the organization as members, victims, customers and bystanders. Therefore,
there are more people capable of supplying the authorities with information about the identities, operations, and locations of organizational members. On the other hand, more sophisticated forms of organization are more likely to have codes of conduct requiring their
members to be loyal to the organization and to maintain its secrets.
Further, more sophisticated forms of organization command resources which can be used to protect the organization and its members from social control agents. While highly sophisticated organizations find it more difficult to conceal the fact that deviance is taking
place, they often are more successful at shielding their members
from severe sanctions. This relationship becomes apparent through a
review of the problems members of different organizational forms
have in coping with social control.

Loners' operations are relatively insecure, for they must provide
their own protection. Many loners depend upon isolating their deviance; the isolated alcoholic drinks at home, and the physician addict
uses narcotics in private. Such physical isolation facilitates secrecy of
operations and a degree of stability, but the secrecy is shattered easily. Because loners employ limited, conventional channels of information about social control practices they can fall prey to surreptitious
methods of social control: sudden spot-checks of narcotic prescriptions may uncover the physician's addiction, and unexpected audits
to check computer transactions may foil the computer criminal.
Even without surreptitious control practices, ignorance or gaffes can
expose loners' secretive operations. In attending to the loner's appearance, behavior or life style, others may observe signs of his or her
involvement in deviance. In some cases, loners perform in the presence of respectable persons; others may witness the loner's hallucina-
tory behavior or be the target of a street robbery. Given knowledge
of a loner's involvement in deviance, others can mobilize the appropriate authorities. Such mobilization brings a likelihood of apprehension and legal processing because loners must rely on their personal,
often limited, resources to combat social control efforts. A naive loner may have enough social margin to call upon respectable relatives
or friends for support (Wiseman, 1970:233), but those with a record
of systematic deviance are especially vulnerable, as Bittner's (1967)

research on the processing of the lower-class mentally ill demonstrates.

Colleagues' and peers' operations are also insecure. To be sure, colleagues and peers have access through their organizational networks to better information about social control practices. Consequently, they can adjust their operations more effectively to avoid apprehension and legal processing. Colleagues and peers also share codes of conduct which help insure the secrecy of member's identities, activities and locations. Despite such advantages, these deviants encounter conditions rendering their deviant operations insecure. First, colleagues and peers pursue deviant activities which generally are more visible than those undertaken by loners. In some cases, they must make themselves accessible to clients, as found with prostitutes and pool hustlers. In others, they enter public places to contact and trade with other deviants, as when homosexuals exchange sexual services in tearooms, or when drug dealers and buyers do business on streetcorners or in alleys. In still other cases, their resources are so limited that they cannot command private places, as found with skid row tramps and delinquent gangs (Werthman and Piliavin, 1967). Second, while loners operate alone, colleagues and peers associate with others. Hence, the number of people aware of the members' involvement in deviance can be considerably larger, so that individuals may develop a reputation—they may become known for their deviance. Third, colleagues and peers have limited organizational resources with which to manage social control efforts. Even when members feel an obligation to help an arrested comrade, they rarely are able to do more than arrange for bail.

Mobsters' operations are more secure than those of loners, colleagues or peers. Because mobs engage in routine theft, more people are aware of members' identities, activities and locations, including victims, tipsters, fences, fixers, lawyers, and members of other mobs. To offset this visibility, mobs have several features facilitating security. First, mobs organize their operations so as to pose minimal dangers to themselves. In some cases, mobs include roles oriented toward protecting deviant operations from outsiders. For instance, burglars who post a lookout and robbers who have a driver waiting in a running car have anticipated some threatening contingencies. In other cases, the nature of the relationship with the victim offers additional protection; because confidence games call for dishonesty on the part of the mark, fewer victims go to the police. Second, members learn and employ specialized skills to accomplish deviant operations safely. Learning to "case" potential targets and to identify operations which can be managed safely and profitably, and perfecting specialized deviant skills (such as the deft manipulation of the pickpocket), provide insurance for the future. Third, although they possess damaging information about one another, mobsters share a code of conduct which offers some protection for the deviants. These codes warn against revealing the mob's secrets to outsiders and affirm the responsibilities of members toward those deviants who are captured by social control agents. Fourth, the organization supplies resources for managing social control efforts. Where possible, mobs attempt to corrupt social control agents in order to ward off arrests. If members are captured, the mob may have contacts with corrupted agents who can "fix" the case's outcome; the mob may compensate the victim in return for dropping criminal charges, or it may try to influence the testimony of witnesses. Because they are prepared to counter social control agents, mobsters' operations are relatively secure.

Finally, formal organizations are characterized by considerable security. It is possible to trace the histories of some specific formal organizations over several decades; they endured in spite of personnel turnover, succession of leadership, mergers with other organizations, and conflict with other deviant groups and social control agents (Nelli, 1976). Because these organizations touch the lives of so many people, including victims, customers, bystanders, lawyers, politicians, police officers and members of the media, their existence is no secret. Nonetheless, their members enjoy reasonable safety for several reasons. First, a binding code of conduct enjoins members from revealing organizational secrets, and violations of these rules may be punishable by violence. Some organizations even employ members who specialize in enforcing these rules. Second, formal organizations go to considerable lengths to protect members against social control efforts: they may maintain a network of informants who can warn of impending raids; they may employ their own lawyers to defend members who are arrested; and, by systematically corrupting social control agents at all levels of the control hierarchy, formal organizations can insure against aggressive law enforcement. Third, even when arrests occur, organizations can avoid serious damage. The hierarchal division of labor places the lowest ranking members in the positions most vulnerable to arrest. Because organizational leaders rarely commit public violations, law enforcement agencies find it difficult to compile evidence against them. Nor is the arrest of a ranking member enough to cripple an organization; it is easy enough to move another member into the captured deviant's slot in the structure of the organization. The failure of social control agents to destroy several well-known formal organizations reflects some of the advantages of organizational sophistication.

Because forms of deviant organization differ in their vulnerability to social control, control agents must adapt their tactics to fit the form of organization if they hope to apprehend deviants. The structure of the offense has well-established effects on social control: where agents can count on victims to bring cases to their attention, social control tactics can be reactive; but the absence of a complainant forces agencies to adopt proactive tactics. Whether they are pursuing reactive or proactive tactics, control agents must devote more resources to apprehending deviants as the sophistication of the deviant organization increases. Organizational sophistication carries advantages—greater loyalty among members, mechanisms for enforcing such loyalty, better information about control agents' plans and movements, operations designed to minimize risk, and so on—which social control agents must overcome before the deviants can be captured. Thus, in dealing with deviant formal organizations, social control agents must bring extraordinary resources to bear. For instance, in order to protect them from the organization's revenge, members who defect and inform on their fellows may be institutionalized in specially guarded settings or given new identities and set up in legitimate careers in new cities. Special task forces of agents may be established and permitted to work independently of the police and other ordinary agents who are thought to have been corrupted. Or, where deviants cannot be prosecuted for their "real" crimes, agents may attempt to compile evidence for ancillary violations, such as income tax evasion. In spite of such control strategies, deviant formal organizations have proven able to withstand attack for decades.

CONCLUSION

Deviants can be arrayed along a dimension of organizational sophistication. We have focused on five forms of organization: loners, colleagues, peers, mobs and formal organizations. The level of organizational sophistication has important consequences for deviants and social control agents; the complexity of deviant operations, the type of socialization and services provided deviants, the members' involvement in deviance, and the security from social control depend, in part, on the form of deviant organization. The social organization of deviants affects the texture of deviant life; a comparison of field studies reporting on similar types of deviance, such as the various forms of theft, reveals different patterns in the members' routines where organizational differences exist.

The analysis of the social organization of deviants can be extended in two directions. First, the dimension of organizational sophistication can serve as the basis for developing a generalized grounded theory of social organization. Second, the impact of social structure on the social organization of deviants deserves systematic investigation.

The dimension of organizational sophistication developed in this paper could be applied to conventional occupations.[15] For reasons noted below, it is difficult to identify many respectable occupations filled by loners—an unpublished writer, laboring on a manuscript, can serve as one example. In contrast, many respectable careers, including those of doctors, lawyers and other professionals, are organized as relations among colleagues. Ignoring relationships with supervisors, interaction within work groups in factories and farm labor resembles the contacts between deviant peers.[16] The staff in a small store or office works as a mob. And, of course, bureaucracies and other legitimate formal organizations can be easily identified. If an analysis similar to this one—but made among forms of respectable organization—were to compare complexity of operation, patterns of socialization, supply, member involvement, and security from external threats, it could lead to a more general statement about the effects of organizational sophistication on members and relevant audiences (Glaser and Strauss, 1967).

While analogies can be drawn between deviant and respectable forms of organization, the two should be distinguished. They occupy very different positions in the larger social structure. Deviant activities are subject to sanctioning by social control agents, therefore secrecy forms a key theme in the lives of deviants. While conventional workers may want to conceal some details of their work from competitors (who might steal their secrets) and outsiders (who might be shocked by backstage revelations), relatively few respectable occupations require workers to totally conceal their involvement in their careers. Hence the scarcity of respectable loners—virtually every worker is openly linked to the larger social web. Moreover, these ties are affirmed in written documents—licenses, contracts, government regulations, deeds of ownership, company rules and the like. Deviants are far less likely to commit their activities to a written record because they operate outside the larger institutional network. The advantage is the preservation of secrecy, but there are also disadvantages: written records can increase efficiency, particularly in complex organizations of some scope, and links to the institutional order provide respectable organizations with some protections which deviants must do without. Finally, respectable workers are likely to have relationships in which they produce, as well as consume. Some deviants (e.g., robbers), who exploit victims without providing compensating goods or services, can be seen as consistently performing a role as consumer. Workers who produce have stronger ties to the social network; a producer must be visible if someone is to purchase his or her wares. Thus, secrecy is both necessary to the deviant and a consequence of his or her role as an exploiter. In spite of their similarities, deviant and respectable forms of organization are distinguished by their need for secrecy, their use of written records, and their involvement in production.

The structural context within which deviants organize also warrants investigation. Clearly, the social organization of deviants is affected by the larger social structure (cf. Miller, 1978). However, precisely what structural conditions are significant and how they operate to shape deviant organization have been largely ignored in the investigation of deviance.

Studying the conditions under which a particular organizational form develops offers a means of linking the social organization of deviants to the social structure. One method of studying this process is the systematic analysis of historical materials. Although several historical case studies of the invention and vindication of deviant labels and the establishment of social control agencies exist, less has been written about the development or decline of organizational forms (cf. O'Donnell, 1967; McIntosh, 1971; Nelli, 1976; Best, 1977; O'Malley, 1979). A theory linking social structure to deviant organization might focus on structural opportunities, social control and structural supports. Because more sophisticated organizational forms feature routinized and profitable deviance, their development requires sufficient opportunities for deviance. Mobs of professional thieves call for a stable supply of lucrative victims, for example, and formal organizations involved in gambling require a large and stable supply of customers. Changes in structurally constrained opportunities should have consequences for the deviants' organization. Similarly, the organization of social control agencies is consequential. Where control resources are sufficient to allow for effective control within an area, less sophisticated forms of organization may decrease—for they do not have the resources to neutralize control efforts—and more sophisticated forms of organization may increase. Finally, more sophisticated organizational forms are likelier to flourish where there are structural supports. Structural supports include the command of a geographical area (such as the 19th-century urban rookery), the presence of persons who provide services to deviants (such as fences), and the sponsorship of others (such as the peasants who supported the social bandit, or the merchants and government officials who supported the pirate). Structural opportunities, social control, and structural supports constitute important elements in the structural context of the social organization of deviants.

References

Amir, Menachem
1971 Patterns in Forcible Rape. Chicago: University of Chicago Press.

Anderson, Nels
  1923   The Hobo. Chicago: University of Chicago Press.
Aubert, Vilhelm
  1965   The Hidden Society. Totowa, N.J.: Bedminster.
Bartell, Gilbert
  1971   Group Sex. New York: New American
Bell, Daniel
  1962   The End of Ideology. Revised edition. New York: Collier.
Best, Joel
  1977   "Licensed to steal: Toward a sociology of English piracy, 1550–
         1750." Paper presented at the Naval History Symposium, Annapo-
         lis.
Bittner, Egon
  1967   "Police discretion in apprehending the mentally ill." Social Prob-
         lems 14:278–292.
Blau, Peter M. and W. Richard Scott
  1962   Formal Organizations. San Francisco: Chandler.
Blumer, Herbert
  1967   The World of Youthful Drug Use. Berkeley: University of Califor-
         nia Press.
Bohannon, Paul
  1960   African Homicide and Suicide. Princeton: Princeton University
         Press.
Bryan, James H.
  1965   "Apprenticeships in prostitution." Social Problems 12: 287–297.
  1966   "Occupational ideologies and individual attitudes of call girls." So-
         cial Problems 13: 441–450.
Buckner, H. Taylor
  1970   "The transvestic career path." Psychiatry 33: 381–389.
Cameron, Mary Owen
  1964   The Booster and the Snitch. New York: Free Press.
Carey, James T.
  1968   The College Drug Scene. Englewood Cliffs, N.J.: Prentice-Hall.
Clinard, Marshall B. and Richard Quinney
  1973   Criminal Behavior Systems: A Typology. Second edition. New
         York: Holt, Rinehart and Winston.
Cressey, Donald R.
  1953   Other People's Money. New York: Free Press.
  1962   "Role theory, differential association, and compulsive crimes." Pp.
         443–467 in Arnold M. Rose (ed.), Human Behavior and Social Pro-
         cesses. Boston: Houghton Mifflin.
  1969   Theft of the Nation. New York: Harper & Row.
  1972   Criminal Organization. New York: Harper & Row.
Dawley, David
  1973   A Nation of Lords. Garden City, N.Y.: Anchor.
Einstader, Werner J.
  1969   "The social organization of armed robbery." Social Problems 17:
         64–83.

Feldman, Harvey W.
   1968   "Ideological supports to becoming and remaining a heroin addict."
          Journal of Health and Social Behavior 9: 131–139.
Gibbons, Don C.
   1965   Changing the Lawbreaker. Englewood Cliffs, N.J.: Prentice-Hall.
   1977   Society, Crime, and Criminal Careers. Third edition. Englewood
          Cliffs, N.J.: Prentice-Hall.
Glaser, Barney G. and Anselm L. Strauss
   1967   The Discovery of Grounded Theory. Chicago: Aldine.
Goffman, Erving
   1959   The Presentation of Self in Everyday Life. Garden City, N.Y.: An-
          chor.
   1963   Stigma. Englewood Cliffs, N.J.: Prentice-Hall.
Green, Timothy
   1969   The Smugglers. New York: Walker.
Harry, Joseph and William B. DeVall
   1978   The Social Organization of Gay Males. New York: Praeger.
Hirschi, Travis
   1962   "The professional prostitute." Berkeley Journal of Sociology 7: 33–
          49.
Humphreys, Laud
   1970   Tearoom Trade. Chicago: Aldine.
Ianni, Francis A. J.
   1972   A Family Business. New York: Sage.
Inciardi, James A.
   1975   Careers in Crime. Chicago: Rand McNally.
   1977   "In search of the class cannon." Pp. 55–77 in Robert S. Weppner
          (ed.), Street Ethnography. Beverly Hills, Calif.: Sage.
Keiser, R. Lincoln
   1969   The Vice Lords. New York: Holt, Rinehart and Winston.
Klein, John F. and Arthur Montague
   1977   Check Forgers. Lexington, Mass.: Lexington.
LeMasters, E. E.
   1975   Blue-Collar Aristocrats. Madison, Wis.: University of Wisconsin
          Press.
Lemert, Edwin M.
   1967   Human Deviance, Social Problems, and Social Control. Englewood
          Cliffs, N.J.: Prentice-Hall.
Lesieur, Henry R.
   1977   The Chase. Garden City, N.Y.: Anchor.
Letkemann, Peter
   1973   Crime as Work. Englewood Cliffs, N.J.: Prentice-Hall.
Lofland, John
   1979   Deviance and Identity. Englewood Cliffs, N.J.: Prentice-Hall.
Luckenbill, David F.
   1977   "Criminal homicide as a situated transaction." Social Problems 25:
          176–186.
Matza, David

1964   Delinquency and Drift. New York: Wiley.
1969   Becoming Deviant. Englewood Cliffs, N.J.: Prentice-Hall.
Maurer, David W.
1939   "Prostitutes and criminal argots." American Journal of Sociology 44: 346–350.
1962   The Big Con. New York: New American.
1964   Whiz Mob. New Haven, Conn.: College and University Press.
McIntosh, Mary
1971   "Changes in the organization of thieving." Pp. 98–133 in Stanley Cohen (ed.), Images of Deviance. Baltimore, Maryland: Penguin.
Mileski, Maureen and Donald J. Black
1972   "The social organization of homosexuality." Urban Life and Culture 1: 131–166.
Miller, Gale
1978   Odd Jobs: The World of Deviant Work. Englewood Cliffs, N.J.: Prentice-Hall.
Milner, Christina and Richard Milner
1972   Black Players. Boston: Little, Brown.
Nelli, Humbert
1976   The Business of Crime. New York: Oxford University Press.
O'Donnell, John A.
1967   "The rise and decline of a subculture." Social Problems 15: 73–84.
O'Malley, Pat
1979   "Class conflict, land and social banditry: Bushranging in nineteenth century Australia." Social Problems 26: 271–283.
Parker, Donn B.
1976   Crime by Computer. New York: Scribner's.
Petersilia, Joan, Peter W. Greenwood and Marvin Lavin
1978   Criminal Careers of Habitual Felons. Santa Monica, Calif.: Rand.
Polsky, Ned
1967   Hustlers, Beats, and Others. Chicago: Aldine.
Prus, Robert C. and C.R.D. Sharper
1977   Road Hustler. Lexington, Mass.: Lexington.
Reynolds, Frank
1967   Freewheelin' Frank. New York: Grove.
Rosenberg, Bernard and Harry Silverstein
1969   Varieties of Delinquent Experience. Waltham, Mass.: Blaisdell.
Rubington, Earl
1978   "Variations in bottle-gang controls." Pp. 383–391 in Earl Rubington and Martin S. Weinberg (eds.), Deviance: The Interactionist Perspective. Third edition. New York: Macmillan.
Shaw, Clifford R.
1930   The Jack Roller. Chicago: University of Chicago Press.
Shibutani, Tamotsu
1961   Society and Personality. Englewood Cliffs, N.J.: Prentice-Hall.
Shover, Neal
1977   "The social organization of burglary." Social Problems 20: 499–514.
Stoddart, Kenneth
1974   "The facts of life about dope." Urban Life and Culture 3: 179–204.

Sutherland, Edwin H.
　1937　The Professional Thief. Chicago: University of Chicago Press.
Thompson, Hunter S.
　1966　Hell's Angels. New York: Ballantine.
Turner, Ralph H.
　1964　"Collective behavior." Pp. 382–425 in Robert E. L. Faris (ed.),
　　　　Handbook of Modern Sociology. Chicago: Rand McNally.
Wade, Andrew L.
　1967　"Social processes in the act of juvenile vandalism." Pp. 94–109 in
　　　　Marshall B. Clinard and Richard Quinney (eds.), Criminal Behavior
　　　　Systems: A Typology. New York: Holt, Rinehart and Winston.
Warren, Carol A. B.
　1974　Identity and Community in the Gay World. New York: Wiley.
Werthman, Carl and Irving Piliavin
　1967　"Gang members and the police." Pp. 56–98 in David J. Bordua
　　　　(ed.), The Police. New York: Wiley.
Winick, Charles
　1961　"Physician narcotic addicts." Social Problems 9: 174–186.
Wiseman, Jacqueline P.
　1970　Stations of the Lost. Englewood Cliffs, N.J.: Prentice-Hall.
Wolf, Deborah G.
　1979　The Lesbian Community. Berkeley: University of California Press.
Wolfgang, Marvin E. and Franco Ferracuti
　1967　The Subculture of Violence. London: Tavistock.
Zimmerman, Don H. and D. Lawrence Wieder
　1977　"You can't help but get stoned." Social Problems 25: 198–207.

Notes

1. A second paper, in preparation, will discuss the social organization of deviance.

2. Following Lemert (1967), loners can be subdivided into naive loners, for whom deviance is an exceptional, one-time experience, and systematic loners, whose deviance forms a repeated pattern. Lemert's analysis of the problems confronting systematic check forgers, who have trouble maintaining a deviant identity with little social support, suggests that systematic loners may have particularly unstable careers.

3. The term "mob," as it is used here, is drawn from the glossary in Sutherland: "A group of thieves who work together; same as 'troupe' and 'outfit' " (1937: 239; cf. Maurer, 1962,1964). A more recent study uses the term "crew" (Prus and Sharper, 1977).

4. Although the mob is able to accomplish its ends more efficiently, the same tasks are sometimes handled by loners. For example, see Maurer (1964: 166–168) and Prus and Sharper (1977:22).

5. Our use of the term "formal organization" is not meant to imply that these organizations have all of the characteristics of an established bureaucracy. Rather, "formal" points to the deliberately designed structure of the organization—a usage consistent with Blau and Scott (1962:5).

6. The complexity of a deviant activity must be distinguished from two other types of complexity. First, the definition of organizational sophistication, given above, included the complexity of the division of labor among the deviants in a given organizational form as one criterion of sophistication. Second, the complexity of an activity should not be confused with the complexity of its explanation. A suicide, for example, can be easily accomplished, even though a complex social-psychological analysis may be required to explain the act.

7. This point illustrates the distinction, made earlier, between the social organization of deviance (the pattern of relationships between the roles performed in a deviant transaction) and the social organization of deviants (the pattern of relationships between deviant actors). The former, not the latter, affects an activity's complexity.

8. In most cases, loners do not possess the resources required for more than one type of complex deviance; physicians, for instance, are unable to commit computer thefts. In contrast, members of more sophisticated forms of organization may be able to manage several types of operations, as when a mob's members shift from picking pockets to shoplifting in order to avoid the police, or when an organized crime family is involved in several different rackets simultaneously (Maurer, 1964; Ianni, 1972: 87–·106).

9. Within a given form of organization, some cognitive perspectives may be more elaborate than others. While pool hustlers have a strong oral tradition, founded on the many hours they share together in pool halls, prostitutes have a relatively limited argot. Maurer (1939) argues that this is due to the restricted contact they have with one another during their work.

10. Here and elsewhere, colleagues represent a partial exception to the pattern. Colleagues resemble members of mobs and formal organizations in that they adopt an instrumental perspective, view deviance as a career, are socialized through apprenticeship to an experienced deviant, and accept deviance as a central identity. While peers have a more sophisticated form of organization, their mutual participation in deviance is based on their shared involvement in an illicit marketplace or leisure-time activity. In contrast, colleagues usually are committed to deviance as means of earning a living.

Yet, because colleagues share a relatively unsophisticated form of organization, they labor under restrictions greater than those faced by mobs and formal organizations. Socialization is of limited scope; call girls learn about handling money and difficult clients, but little about sexual skills (Bryan, 1965). The code of conduct governing colleagues is less encompassing and less binding than those for more sophisticated forms, and the deviance of colleagues is usually less profitable. The absence of the advantages associated with organizational sophistication leads colleagues, despite their similarities to mobs and formal organizations, into an unstable situation where many individuals drift away from deviance.

11. Sometimes such equipment is defined as illicit, and its possession constitutes a crime.

12. Two reasons can be offered to explain this relationship. If a type of deviance is not profitable enough to support the individual, it may be necessary to take other work, as when a pool hustler moonlights (Polsky, 1967). Also, many loners have only a marginal commitment to deviance and choose to allocate most of their time to their respectable roles. This is particularly easy if the form of deviance requires little time for preparation and commission.

13. Swingers meeting new couples avoid giving names or information which could be used to identify them (Bartell, 1971:92–95); and Humphreys (1970) emphasizes that many tearoom participants are attracted by the setting's assurance of anonymity.

14. During their careers, deviants may shift from one organizational form or one type of offense to another. The habitual felons interviewed by Petersilia et al. (1978) reported that, while many of their offenses as juveniles involved more than one partner (presumably members of a peer group), they preferred to work alone or with a single partner on the crimes they committed as adults. The most common pattern was for juveniles who specialized in burglaries to turn to robbery when they became adults.

15. Letkemann (1973), Inciardi (1975) and Miller (1978) have tried to locate some forms of criminal activity within the frameworks developed by sociologists of work and occupations.

16. Just as many deviant peer groups focus around leisure-time activities, some respectable leisure scenes, such as the tavern and bowling alley, are populated by peers (LeMasters, 1975).

39 / The Social Organization of Sadism and Masochism

THOMAS S. WEINBERG
GERHARD FALK

INTRODUCTION

Sadism and masochism, the giving and receiving of pain for erotic gratification, have been largely neglected as areas for sociological study. As two recent papers point out, descriptions of the social aspects of this behavior are virtually nonexistent in the professional literature (Spengler, 1977; Weinberg, 1978). The apparent lack of interest in studying sadomasochistic behavior from a sociological perspective may be attributable to its having been traditionally examined from a psychoanalytic model. The influence of such writers as Krafft-Ebing (1932) and Sigmund Freud (1938) may have been to obscure the social aspects of this behavior by defining it solely in terms of individual pathology. Inasmuch as sociologists have until quite recently ignored sadomasochism, descriptions of its social aspects have been largely left to journalists (e.g., Coburn, 1977; Halpern, 1977; Smith and Cox, 1979a and 1979b). This is unfortunate, because these journalistic observations are neither systematic nor theoretical.

In this paper we present, in a preliminary way, some sociological observations drawn from an ongoing research project, which began in December 1977. Our focus is on the ways in which contacts are made among participants in the sadomasochistic (S&M) world, sadomasochistic organizations, and other subcultural supports for and influences upon this behavior. We are primarily concerned with heterosexual sadomasochism, an area that has been less examined than the homosexual S&M world. Although there are some points of contact between these two S&M subcultures, and even though some individuals may participate in both and define their sexuality in a flexible way, the two worlds remain distinct. The homosexual S&M world is much more visible, with many large cities having at least one so-called leather bar. As Spengler (1977) has noted, only homosexual sadomasochists appear to be approachable for study. Heterosexual

555

sadomasochists are extremely reluctant to be interviewed or studied in any way.

METHODS

Given the difficulties in contacting a large sample of sadomasochists,[1] our conclusions must remain tentative. Our data consist of a few formal and informal interviews with men engaging in S&M behavior and with prostitutes, or "dominatrixes," specializing in "female domination." Like Spengler, we found it impossible to question sadomasochistically oriented women who were not involved in prostitution. Our only information about such women comes indirectly through conversations with their husbands, who were themselves involved in sadomasochism. Additional sources of information on the social organization of sadomasochism comes from advertisements, flyers, magazines, and literature produced by sadomasochistic organizations.

Our contacts with respondents were made through answering advertisements placed in S&M contact magazines. We presented ourselves as professional sociologists who were interested in understanding the S&M subculture. Respondents generally wished to remain anonymous; they used pseudonyms and preferred to make contacts on the telephone rather than in person. Other contacts were made fortuitously through people who knew the nature of the study.[2]

SOCIOLOGICAL STUDIES OF SADOMASOCHISM

The few studies of sadism and masochism in the sociological literature point out that S&M is a well established subculture characterized by publications, a market economy, and its own argot. Howard S. Becker (1963), for instance, estimated that one catalog devoted to sadomasochistic fetishism, which he had examined, contained between 15 and 20 thousand photographs for sale; and he therefore concluded that the dealer "did a land-office business and had a very sizable clientele" (1963:20–21). Becker further emphasized the importance of some sort of sadomasochistic subculture in developing deviant motivations through providing people with the appropriate conceptual linguistic tools:

> Deviant motivations have a social character even when most of the activity is carried on in a private, secret, and solitary fashion. In such cases, various media of communication may take the place of face-to-face interaction in inducting the individual into the culture. The pornographic pic-

tures I mentioned earlier were described to prospective buyers in a stylized language. Ordinary words were used in a technical shorthand designed to whet specific tastes. . . . One does not acquire a taste for "bondage photos" without having learned what they are and how they may be enjoyed (Becker, 1963:31).

John Gagnon (1977) notes the existence of clubs for heterosexuals interested in sadomasochism:

The formalization of the sadomasochistic aspects of the gay community has been paralleled by the creation of "clubs" for heterosexual masochists and sadists. Such sites offer opportunities for people with common sexual preferences to meet. Where once the problems of meeting were solved through word of mouth and through advertisements of various sorts, there is now a more public "velvet underground" in various cities which offers an opportunity for more interaction, and the creation of a local sadomasochistic culture. The city in this case provides for sexual minorities what it provided for literary minorities in the past (Gagnon, 1977:329).

A questionnaire study by Andreas Spengler (1977) of sadomasochistic West German men, however, casts doubt upon the importance of sadomasochistic clubs for making sexual contacts, at least for heterosexual men. He found that these heterosexual men were not so well integrated into a sadomasochistic subculture as were bisexual and homosexual men. Fewer heterosexual men participated in sadomasochistic parties, had an acquaintance with like-minded people, or were successful in receiving responses to advertisements placed in sadomasochistic publications. Prostitution was a more important sadomasochistic outlet for heterosexual men than it was for the other respondents. Spengler explains this finding by noting that there are few (nonprostitute) women who participate in the sadomasochistic subculture. Observations of sadomasochistic clubs and parties by journalists (e.g., Halpern, 1977; Smith and Cox, 1979a) who note a heavy preponderance of men and the presence of professional dominatrixes at these functions tend to support Spengler's findings. Spengler's "unsystematic impression" is that "nearly all the subcultural groups among heterosexual sadomasochists exist in cooperation with prostitutes (1977:455)" and that one of the functions of these heterosexually oriented sadomasochistic subcultures for their members is to maintain the fiction that prostitutes are "really" passionately involved in the sadomasochistic encounter.

Thomas S. Weinberg (1978) emphasizes the importance of sadomasochistic organizations in developing and disseminating apologias, attitudes, and ideologies supportive of sadomasochism that enable their members to justify their sexual desires. He points out the importance of fantasy and theatricality in the sadomasochistic world and examines the ways in which "frameworks" and "keys" delimiting and cuing sadomasochistic episodes are developed through the use of a shared subcultural argot.

Joann S. DeLora and Carol A. B. Warren (1977) believe that there is a general acceptance of "the milder forms of sadistic or masochistic pleasure" in American culture (1977:366), and they note the existence of "sadomasochistic games by couples as a part of their lovemaking rituals" (1977:267). This does not, however, necessarily mean that either sadomasochistic behavior or sadomasochistic subcultures are widespread in this society.

MAKING CONTACTS IN THE SUBCULTURE

There are a number of ways in which sadomasochistic contacts are made. These include placing or responding to advertisements in contact magazines and other publications, finding partners through participation in other subcultural settings such as bars or swingers' clubs or through participation in prostitution. Some contacts occur by chance; others develop through encounters in sadomasochistic organizations (Weinberg, 1978).

Advertisements

The most common means of reaching other S&M devotees appears to be the use of advertisements in sadomasochistic contact magazines. Spengler (1977) found that these ads were the most frequently used way of finding partners and that only 7% of his sample had never placed one. The advertisements contained in contact magazines are usually organized by region, with the advertiser identified only by a code number. The ads state the preferences, requirements, and so forth of their placers. Some of the ads are accompanied by photographs, purportedly of the advertisers.

Placing and Responding to Advertisements: Procedures for placing ads and responding to them are similar in all of these magazines. In order to place an ad, one submits a fee ranging from about $5 to $10 and certifies to being over the age of 21. Some publications also require that advertisers subscribe to the publication at an additional cost of $10 or more. In order to respond to an ad, some magazines require that one be a subscriber or a member of a club sponsored by the publisher. Responding to an ad costs $1–$2 per letter. The letters are placed in stamped envelopes with the advertisers' code numbers on them. All of the envelopes are then put into a larger envelope, which also contains the publisher's fee. The publisher then addresses the coded envelopes to the advertisers and thus assures their anonymity. Our experience with this process indicates that the publishers at least do forward the letters if it is at all possible and even go so far as to return undeliverable letters at their own expense. Many of the advertisers also appear to be legitimate. When we sent letters to advertisers in our region, we received responses from some of these people. However, we are still attempting to increase our sample through these informants, an obviously difficult undertaking.

Most of the ads found in S&M contact magazines are supposedly placed by women, the majority of whom are self-described "dominants." The men tend to be "submissives" (Weinberg, 1978). This appears to be the most commonly occurring combination in North American S&M culture. Part of the explanation for the large representation of female advertisers may be that women are usually not charged a fee for advertising, that many of the female advertisers are prostitutes ("Seeks very rich slaves only"; "Photos, used lingerie for sale"; "Correspondence welcome but I expect compensation for my time") and that the purchasers of these magazines are predominantly males seeking dominant females.

According to some of our respondents, they sometimes place ads in the "personals" columns of local newspapers. These ads are disguised as inquiries for "pen pals." Since swingers also use the same kinds of ads ("Modern couple desires couples as pen pals"; "Couple, 30, desires discreet pen pals") it is difficult to ascertain whether an ad is a swingers' advertisement or an S&M inquiry. Both use similar code words such as "modern" or "discreet" to indicate a sexual interest. Infrequently, an S&M advertiser will include a phrase such as "interested in English culture" to indicate a preference for being whipped.

Advertisements and the Communication of Fantasy: Many of the advertisements found in contact magazines illustrate a major aspect of the sadomasochistic subculture; it is, to a large degree, a fantasy world. One cannot fully understand the organization of the S&M scene unless the central importance of the expression of fantasy for its participants is recognized. The subculture serves to segregate the sexual fantasy needs of its members from other aspects of their lives. This is often accomplished by setting up a particular theatrical situation, frequently aided by props and costumes of various kinds, in which the participants don new identities and act out different parts. Popular situations include, for example, the naughty schoolboy who is reprimanded (i.e., verbally degraded) and physically punished by the female school teacher, and the patient who is given an enema by a nurse. The importance of fantasy (and its components of hostility) is apparent in the following ads drawn from contact publications:

1. Blonde Dominatrix dressed in rubber or leather costume. Seeks experienced or novice slaves who believe in Dominant Female Superiority. I'm well qualified in B&D, watersports, humiliation, petticoat training and have equipment built by slaves.
2. Tall, cruel, Creole Beauty seeks Dominant Male partner to assist her in controlling & disciplining her many slaves. Come be my King so we can play King & Queen. Do not answer if you are not sincere and generous. Letter, photo & phone gets you a surprising quick reply. This is for dominants only, have too many slaves now.
3. Beautiful Dominatrix, 24. A true sophisticate of the bizarre and unusual. I have a well equipped dungeon in my luxurious home. You will submit to prolonged periods of degradation for my pleasure. Toilet servitude a must. I know what you crave and can fulfill your every need.
4. Very pretty 30 yr old female has fantasies about receiving hand-spankings on bare behind. I've never allowed myself to act out any of the fantasies. Is there anyone out there who'd like to correspond with me about their fantasies or experiences with spanking?
5. Cruel husband seeking experienced dominant man to assist in training petite, shy, young wife. Eager to watch her transformed from shy, personal, sex slave to slut. Presently serving me and friend in humiliation, verbal abuse, deep throat, GR., golden shower, lewd dancing, nude posing, public display. Prefer man with extensive movie/erotica collection, over 50, obese with a fetish for petite, young girls or hung Black. Also those with aggressive Bi-partners or trained pets.

These ads, as is apparent, contain coded messages. The language of S&M serves to indicate to potential respondents the advertisers' expectations and the sorts of roles and relationships they are looking for. For example, "B&D" (Bondage and Discipline) refers to tying up or restraining a person, along with the possibility of some sort of physical punishment. "Watersports" refers to urination. "Petticoat training" indicates cross-dressing. "Toilet servitude" (or, sometimes, "toilet training") refers to the handling of feces, being defecated upon, or to coprophagia. The abbreviation "GR" stands for "Greek," an indication that the advertiser is interested in anal intercourse. "Golden shower" is code for being urinated upon, sometimes with the inclusion of urolagnia.

Participation in the sadomasochistic subculture also often develops out of contacts made in other "deviant" sexual scenes, such as the swinging subculture, gay bars, and prostitution. Interestingly, some of the same people who advertise in the S&M contact magazines of one publisher also advertise in the swinging publications of another, using the same picture but with a somewhat different advertisement.

Prostitution and S&M Contacts: Prostitution is an important source of sexual contacts for sadomasochistically oriented men (DeLora and Warren, 1977; Spengler, 1977; Weinberg, 1978). Prostitutes have written autobiographical descriptions of their participation in this behavior (Hollander, 1972; Von Cleef, 1974). Many professional dominatrixes advertise not only in sadomasochistic contact publications, but also in sex-oriented publications such as *Screw.* Our interviews with professional prostitutes who specialize in "Houses of Domination" indicate a highly developed skill in S&M. Prostitutes with whom we have spoken pointed out that specializing in sadomasochism is far more lucrative than conventional prostitution.[3] Fees range from $35 to $45 for half an hour, and from $50 to $100 or more for an hour's session. A number of prostitutes advertise "No Straight Sex, S&M and TV (i.e., transvestitism) only" and do not, they claim, have sexual intercourse with their clientele. Apart from the development of special skills and the creation of fantasy scenarios, professional dominatrixes appear to differ little from women engaged in conventional prostitution. Like the more usual forms of prostitution, sadomasochistic specialists practice their trade in houses of prostitution, massage parlors (Evening Tribune, 1980), and as individual entrepreneurs.

Chance Contacts

Some contacts are made accidentally. One respondent told us, for example, that he was approached and engaged in conversation by a number of men who were attracted by his wife's leather coat and high leather boots, although she had not purposely worn them to advertise her interest in S&M. One way to encourage such approaches, then, is to display symbols commonly accepted in the sadomasochistic subculture. This does not appear to be a very common practice among heterosexual devotees of S&M, apart from their participation in S&M parties, although participants in the homosexual leather scene frequently wear symbols such as colored handkerchiefs or strategically located key chains to advertise their preferences.

Initial Meetings: Determining Compatibility

When contacts are first made among sadomasochists, they follow a format similar to the initial sizing up which occurs among swingers (Bartell, 1971; Palson and Palson, 1972). This is not surprising; some informants have told us that they were introduced to sadomasochism through swinging. Typically, two couples may go out to dinner and spend relatively little time discussing their sexuality. Rather, the purpose of their meeting is to discover, in a nonthreatening situation, whether they are comfortable with each other and socially compatible. One respondent who is a business executive noted that social compatibility is important because sexual activity takes up a relatively small amount of an evening's time and "you have to have something to talk about with the other couple." His group consists of other professionals such as dentists and attorneys.

Since the S&M scene demands absolute trust and confidence in another person, especially if one may be bound helplessly and gagged, this initial meeting is a critical one. Only after people have built up a certain amount of trust do they proceed to engage in sadomasochistic activities.

Before an actual scene occurs, the participants in it discuss their needs, fantasies, fears, and what they are and are not willing to do. What ultimately occurs during a scene is the outcome of this discussion, in which the original thoughts are somewhat modified, then subjected to a bargaining process by which the verbalized desires of the partner are accommodated. This accommodation appears to be necessary because the participants wish to carry their imagination into action by convincing their partner that their wishes are reasonably compatible. Unless there is agreement, there probably will not be mutual gratification. Contrary to the popular notion that the sadist is in command of this situation, S&M devotees often assert that it is the masochist who controls the scene, because it is his or her fantasies that the sadist acts out.

S&M ORGANIZATIONS AND THEIR FUNCTIONS

There are a number of formally organized sadomasochistic clubs and numerous informal groups of sadists and masochists throughout this country. For the purpose of this discussion, we will classify them roughly into the following categories, based upon what seem to be their primary activities: (1) discussion or consciousness-raising groups; (2) publishing organizations; (3) sex clubs; and (4) theatrical companies.[4]

Discussion or Consciousness-raising Groups

The Till Eulenspiegel Society[5] in New York City describes itself as a "discussion and consciousness-raising group," the objective of which is "to promote better understanding and self-awareness of these (sa-domasochistic) drives so that they may be enjoyed as a part of a full sex life, rather than set aside out of fear or guilt." The society explicitly denies being "in any sense a sex club or swingers' organization." During the Eulenspiegel's weekly meetings, members discuss their feelings and behavior and occasionally are given demonstrations and lectures by sadomasochistic experts. Although Eulenspiegel does not appear to propagandize to the larger society nor to lobby for legal change, it does seem to resemble in some of its avowed purposes other minority organizations, such as those studied by Yearwood and Weinberg (1979). Despite the Eulenspiegel Society's denial that it is a sex club, it does, in fact, sponsor parties at which sadomasochistic behavior occurs (Halpern, 1977).

Publishing Organizations

The House of Milan, located in Los Angeles, publishes a number of contact magazines *(Latent Image, Aggressive Gals, Bitch Goddesses)* that serve to facilitate communication among S&M devotees throughout the country. They also publish magazines for those who enjoy simply reading about female domination, spanking, transvestitism, rubber fetishes, and so on. This organization gives parties occasionally, which are advertised in its contact publications.

1. Dictor Enterprises in Philadelphia publishes a sadomasochistic contact magazine called *Amazon*. The aim of this magazine, according to its former publisher, Malibu Publications, is to "provide the average person with a publication that reveals S&M/B&D as a normal form of sexual activity and alleviates any feelings of guilt and/or perversion arising from long held misconceptions." To this end, the magazine includes not only contact ads, but also a question and answer column written by "a clinical psychologist with long, widely varied experience in sex therapy and family counseling," a section containing news about new publications, other organizations, films of interest to S&M devotees, sources of products, news of upcoming events, and the like, fiction involving sadomasochistic interests and behavior, cartoons, and commercial advertisements for other clubs, films, and sexual devices.

Sex Clubs

Chateau 19 is an "on-premise S&M club" (Smith and Cox, 1979a) in New York City. Its twice weekly sessions are open to the public. For an admission fee ($7.50 for men, $2.50 for women, including two drinks) one is free to participate in any of the night's activities. Smith and Cox (1979a) reported that there was a wide range in the ages of the club's habitues, with most being between the ages of 25 and 35. From their description, Chateau 19 appears to be very similar to other on-premise impersonal sex clubs such as Plato's Retreat in New York City, San Francisco's Sutro Bath House, and gay baths found throughout the country.

Theatrical Companies

Sadomasochistic fantasies have been brought "out of the closet" by an organization known as "The Project." The Project, which calls itself a "research team," was founded in the early 1970s by a New York City radio personality. It has been featured on talk shows on the three major television networks and has been written about in a number of popular culture and sexually oriented newspapers and magazines. Performers in The Project travel throughout the state to churches, colleges, single groups, private parties, and various social organizations, acting out for a fee, fantasies that they have collected through "hundreds of interviews and thousands of letters." The program of one of their productions, called "Another Way to Love," included the following S&M scenarios:[6]

1. " 'The Beauty of Looking Beastly': An authentic psychosexual fairy tale wherein the 'ugliest man in the world' lives his most beautiful moment" (a scene in which a man is publicly humiliated by a beautiful woman who forces him to wear a collar and leash and a mask hiding his face).
2. " 'I'm the Haughtiest Girl in the Whole USA': Wherein a fetishistic 'judge' who specializes in 'justice' for pretty girls convicted of pretty-girl crimes liquifies his toughest prisoner into a splash pool of humiliation by getting to the bottom of her evil" (a scene in which a man dressed as a monk puts a woman into stocks, forcing her to publicly confess her crime of "haughtiness," and then tortures her by tickling her bare feet).
3. " 'Bottoms up!': A peek into the bedroom of an earnest young wife who endeavors to redesign her color scheme by pestering, plaguing, and provoking her posterior decorator" (a spanking fantasy).
4. " 'Paul(a)': Wherein the fantacist awakens her husband to a galaxy of life changes most profound" (a scene in which a woman, dressed in a translucent black body suit, high heeled boots, and armed with a whip, forces her husband to dress up in a French maid's uniform, complete with female undergarments and a wig).

The list of organizations described above is in no sense exhaustive; however, it does serve to illustrate the variety of more formally developed associations found within the sadomasochistic subculture. Although the purposes of these organizations appear to vary widely, from enterprises designed to make a profit for their owners to those, like Eulenspiegel, that exist to help sadomasochists accept their inclinations, they nevertheless serve similar functions for persons interested in S&M. First, they all provide the possibilities of sexual outlets, either through direct participation as in Chateau 19 or in the parties given by other organizations, through the opportunity to make connections with similarly inclined people by advertising in contact magazines such as *Amazon,* or through the use of these magazines to stimulate sexual fantasies. Second, all of these organizations serve to disseminate information about sadomasochism to their members, enabling them to learn new techniques, develop new interests, and find out about events, news, and so forth relevant to their needs. Third, all of the sadomasochistic organizations develop and communicate, either explicitly or implicitly, justifications and apologias enabling people to accept their feelings and behavior as perfectly normal. Fourth, by providing these special settings, justifications, and the appropriate linguistic tools, they enable people to segregate their sadomasochistic needs and behavior from other areas of their lives.

CONCLUSIONS

Although sadomasochism has traditionally been studied as an individual psychopathology, in many instances this behavior is a group phenomenon. A variety of sadomasochistic groups and organizations facilitate contacts among members, teach new techniques and behaviors, and serve to normalize individuals' attitudes, interests, and sexual activities. A more comprehensive understanding of sadomasochism requires that it be examined within a broader social context, rather than remain limited to a study of individual case histories. When this is done, some alternative ways of thinking about sadomasochism emerge. For example, S&M may serve recreational as well as sexual needs for its devotees. One journalist (Coburn, 1977:45) speculates that a new sort of S&M "chic" has been developing in this country, and she cites recent popular magazine articles, popular music, billboard advertisements, and so forth, all with S&M motifs as evidence for this speculation. Sadomasochistic themes also appear in recent movies (e.g., "Myra Breckenridge," "The Opening of Misty Beethoven," and "Wholly Moses!" among others) and in novels. Another way of looking at sadomasochism is in terms of economics. Sadomasochistic publications are filled with ads from manufacturers of expensive wearing apparel, devices, equipment, and so forth. There seems to be a lucrative business in magazines, movies, sex clubs, prostitution, and the like, all aimed at a sadomasochistic market.

References

Bartell, Gilbert D.
  1971   Group Sex. New York: Signet Books.
Becker, Howard S.
  1963   Outsiders: Studies in the Sociology of Deviance. New York: Free
         Press.
Coburn, Judith
  1977   "S&M." New Times 8 (Feb. 4);43–50.
DeLora, Joann S., and Carol A.B. Warren
  1977   Understanding Sexual Interaction. Boston: Houghton-Mifflin.
Evening Tribune (San Diego)
  1980   "Parlor operator sentenced." (Jan. 23):B-6.
Freud, Sigmund
  1938   The Basic Writings of Sigmund Freud. (A.A. Brill, trans. and ed.).
         New York: Modern Library.
Gagnon, John
  1977   Human Sexualities, Glenview, Ill.: Scott, Foresman.
Halpern, Bruce
  1977   "Spanks for the memory." Screw 420 (March 21):4–7.
Hollander, Xaviera
  1972   The Happy Hooker. New York: Dell.
Krafft-Ebing, R.V.
  1932   Psychopathia Sexualis. New York: Physicians' and Surgeons' Book
         Company.
Palson, Charles and Rebecca Palson
  1972   "Swinging in wedlock." Transaction/Society 9 (Feb.):28–37.
Smith, Howard and Cathy Cox
  1979a   "Scenes: s&m in the open." Village Voice 24(Jan. 15):24.
  1979b   "Scenes: dialogue with a dominatrix." Village Voice 24 (Jan.
          29):19–20.
Spengler, Andreas
  1977   "Manifest sadomasochism of males: results of an empirical study."
         Archives of Sexual Behavior 6:441–56.
Von Cleef, Monique
  1971   The House of Pain. Secaucus, N.J.: Lyle Stuart.
Weinberg, Thomas S.
  1978   "Sadism and masochism: sociological perspectives." Bulletin of the
         American Academy of Psychiatry and the Law 6:284–95.
Yearwood, Lennox and Thomas S. Weinberg
  1979   "Black organizations, gay organizations: sociological parallels." Pp.
         301–16 in Martin P. Levine (ed.), Gay Men: The Sociology of Male
         Homosexuality. New York: Harper.

Notes

1. Spengler (1977:442) acknowledges this problem when he states, "Extreme difficulties exist in questioning sadomasochists. Heterosexual sadomasochists live undercover; their groups are cut off from the outside world. . . . Anonymity is one of the special norms of sadomasochistic subcultures."

2. One such chance contact occurred when one of the writers happened to casually mention the study to a former student whom he met one day in the student union. A few hours later, he was surprised by a telephone call from this man, who told him that he had spoken to a friend who might be interested in discussing sadomasochism. About an hour later, the writer received a call from his student's friend, a young woman who had been a prostitute, dominatrix, and madame in a house of female domination. Over a lengthy lunch the next day, this woman and the writer discussed his work in sadomasochism. She was particularly concerned about his personal reasons for the study (was he really a policeman, or a voyeur, or a sadomasochist attempting to use the research for his own sexual purposes?) and spent the time probing his motivations. Apparently convinced that he had no ulterior motives, understood people in deviant lifestyles, and could be trusted, she became an invaluable resource for contacts and information about the S&M world.

3. Some quotations from our interviews with dominatrixes are reproduced elsewhere (Weinberg, 1978: especially pp. 286–287). The transcript of a fascinating interview with a professional prostitute specializing in S&M appears in Smith and Cox (1979b).

4. There are, of course, any number of ways in which these organizations could be classified such as according to whether they are profit or nonprofit enterprises, whether they serve to facilitate sexual contacts and in what specific ways they do this, whether they are politically oriented and so on.

5. The organization takes its name from a figure in German folklore who is said to have carried heavy loads up mountains because it felt so good when he put these burdens down and thus acknowledged his presumably masochistic tendencies.

6. The writers first became aware of the existence of The Project when one of them saw an advertisement for one of its productions in a Buffalo, New York, homophile publication. He attended the performance, which was held in the Buffalo Gay Community Services Center, in March 1976. The show consisted of a half-dozen scenarios, four of which are described above, performed by a male and a female actor. This was followed by a discussion period, during which the audience could ask the actors questions. In addition to its prerehearsed shows, The Project also acts out individuals' private fantasies at its own location in New York City. The individual, who pays a fee for this service, does not participate in the performance of his own fantasy, however, but remains strictly an observer. The Project does not appear to have been conceived solely as a profit-making venture for its creator, however. At the conclusion of its two Buffalo performances, the actors made a donation of several hundred dollars to support the activities of the Gay Center. Considering the low cost of admission to the performances ($3 for a Sunday matinee and $3.50 for that evening's show), the fairly small attendance, and travel expenses, The Project does not seem to have made very much money during its visit.

40 / Seekers and Saucers: The Role of the Cultic Milieu in Joining a UFO Cult

ROBERT W. BALCH
DAVID TAYLOR

During the early 1970s there was a resurgence of religious interest in the United States. Especially popular were the cults and sects which either drew their inspiration from non-Western religious traditions or rejected the moral relativism of the established Christian churches. Some of these groups, especially the Unified Family and the Children of God, grew so rapidly and transformed their members so completely that they were accused of "brainwashing" and "psychological kidnapping."

One of the most notorious cults captured national attention during the fall of 1975 when over 30 people suddenly disappeared in Oregon after attending a lecture about flying saucers. At the meeting, a middle-aged man and woman who called themselves Bo and Peep offered their audience eternal life in the "literal heavens." Bo and Peep—or the Two, as their followers called them—claimed to be members of the kingdom of heaven who had taken human bodies to help mankind overcome the human level of existence.[1]

Bo and Peep's prescription for salvation was rigorous. In order to enter the "next evolutionary kingdom," their followers had to abandon their friends, families, jobs, and material possessions. They traveled around the country in small "families," camping and generally leading a spartan existence. Bo and Peep told them they would be taken to heaven in UFOs if they could overcome all their human emotions and worldly attachments—a process they called Human Individual Metamorphosis. The name referred to a "chemical and biological change" that would transform their followers into new creatures with indestructible bodies.

Bo and Peep's UFO cult was one of the remarkable religious success stories of the mid-seventies. Within seven months after their first meeting in Los Angeles, the Two may have attracted as many as 150 followers.[2] The figure is noteworthy, because over 100 of them were recruited in just four meetings held in California, Oregon, and Colorado. The Oregon meeting is not only significant because of the national publicity it received, but because approximately 35 people decided to join afterwards. Most remarkable of all is that the Two rarely gave prospective members more than a week to make up their minds, and, when someone did, it was usually after less than six hours' contact with either the Two or any of their followers. The media speculated about brainwashing, and some ex-members got national coverage themselves when they accused the Two of "mind control." However, the accusation is not only sensational, but incorrect. In the following pages we argue that the decision to join Bo and Peep's UFO cult can only be understood in terms of the unique point of view of the metaphysical seeker, whose outlook is shaped by a religious underworld variously known as the cultic milieu (Campbell, 1972), the occult social world (Buckner, 1965), or the metaphysical subculture (Balch and Taylor, 1976b).

DATA COLLECTION

Shortly after Bo and Peep's Oregon meeting, we joined the UFO cult as hidden observers.[3] During the next seven weeks we traveled with several different families, observing and taking part in every aspect of their daily lives. Six months later we interviewed 31 ex-members in Arizona, California, Florida, Montana, and Oregon. Locating former members proved to be a difficult task, requiring extensive travel and a considerable amount of detective work. Using simple "snowball" sampling—each informant suggesting additional contacts—we eventually located 37 ex-members, six of whom preferred not to discuss their experiences. Although we did use an interview schedule, all interviews were informal and followed whatever format our respondents preferred. On the basis of the data we collected about cult members during the participant-observer phase of our study, we are confident that our sample is representative of the cult's membership.

Most members of the cult were in their early twenties, although their ages ranged from 14 to 58. There were roughly equal numbers of males and females when we joined, but, for reasons still unclear, a greater number of men was recruited during the time we observed the cult. A large minority had attended college, and the younger members were indistinguishable from college students anywhere in the United States. Their median occupational status was rather low, reflecting the cult's overall youthfulness and the fact that most members had changed jobs frequently, preferring not to be tied down to a routine that would limit their personal freedom.

SOCIAL ORGANIZATION OF THE UFO CULT

The UFO cult was a loosely organized collection of seekers that depended on the charismatic appeal of Bo and Peep to hold it together. The Two and their followers traveled around the country holding public meetings to tell other seekers about their message. They moved every few days, camping out as they went. Encounters with the outside world were limited to a few highly structured situations. In order to survive, they asked for food, gasoline, and money at stores and churches, but their contact with outsiders was limited to asking for help. Only rarely did members explain who they were or mention Bo and Peep. Members also had contact with outsiders during public meetings. After the message had been presented, by either Bo and Peep or some of their followers, anyone in the audience could approach members of the cult to have his questions answered. However, the interaction was limited to discussing the message, and the answers given by members of the cult were often so stereotyped that they sounded like tape-recordings.

In order to speed up the metamorphic process, Bo and Peep assigned each of their followers a partner, usually a person of the opposite sex. The partnership was the basic unit of social organization. Its purpose was to develop "friction" and, ultimately, awareness of the human qualities each person had to overcome. Although partners were supposed to stay together 24 hours a day, sexual relationships and even friendships were discouraged. They were not only "too human," but they prevented the "friction" that would accelerate the metamorphosis.

Bo and Peep camped with their followers until a month after the Oregon meeting. Then, for reasons still unclear, they went into seclusion, explaining that they would return just before the spaceships came. They never set a date, however, and most of their followers never saw them again. Before they left, the Two divided the cult into several "families" of about 14 members each. Each family was headed by two spokesmen—a partnership appointed by Bo and Peep. However, their duties were never very well defined, and most members preferred a democratic arrangement where everyone had an equal voice. The spokesmen may have been appointed by the Two, but they were still earthly seekers like everyone else. Within a few weeks most spokesmen either had been replaced, or their position had been eliminated altogether.

Each family was completely autonomous, traveling almost constantly, going wherever it felt it was being led. Family members held public meetings of their own as they traveled. Most of them were small, but a few attracted audiences of several hundred people, and some of them were surprisingly successful, even without the charismatic presence of the Two. A meeting in northern Arizona produced nine new members, eight of them from a town with less than 500 people. Another meeting in Berkeley, California, recruited as many as 20. But generally these meetings produced nothing more than catcalls and insults, or at best interested questions. During their random movements across the country, families rarely kept in touch with each other, and after the press lost interest in Bo and Peep's odyssey, many families had no way of learning anything about other members of the UFO cult.

Despite the importance of partnerships and families, the UFO cult was highly individualistic, a feature consistent with the individual nature of Bo and Peep's metamorphic process. Each member of the cult had to establish a direct psychic connection with a member of the next level, a process the Two called "tuning in." Bo and Peep instructed each of their followers to devote "100 per cent of his total energy" to "the process," which left no time for mundane activities like reading, singing, listening to the radio, or socializing with friends.

While traveling, the preferred arrangement was one partnership per vehicle, to prevent unnecessary social interaction. Although the rule was frequently violated, partners were expected to set up their camp away from other members of their family, and to keep to themselves except during family meetings. Aside from a brief period when members tuned in together before meetings, there was an absence of ritual in the UFO cult. Even this had its origins in Bo and Peep's desire to keep idle conversation to a minimum before meetings got underway. The Two even told their followers not to help each other with everyday jobs like fixing cars and putting up tents. They claimed that helping was not only an "energy drain" for the helper, but denied the person being helped an opportunity to confront and overcome his human nature—whether anger, frustration, fear, or overdependence on others.

Although we have referred to Bo and Peep's following as a cult, the group had a strong sectarian flavor (see Balch and Taylor, 1977). According to Wallis (1974, 1975a, 1975b), the fundamental criterion of the sect is "epistemological authoritarianism." Unlike the leaders of most cults, who recognize many equally valid paths to the top of the spiritual mountain, the Two claimed authoritative and privileged access to the Truth. In a flyer they prepared for prospective members, Bo and Peep were quite specific about the uniqueness of their message:

> This is no spiritual, philosophic, or theoretical path to the top of the mountain. It is a *reality;* in fact it is the *only* way *off* the top of the mountain.

The cult's other sectarian features, e.g., its self-enforced separation from the world, make sense in light of the fact that Bo and Peep claimed to have the only path to true salvation.[4]

BECOMING A MEMBER OF THE UFO CULT

The recruitment process in the UFO cult was highly structured, and varied little even after Bo and Peep disappeared. If members felt that their connection at the next level wanted them to hold a meeting, they would find a suitable place and put up posters announcing the meeting, usually in "head shops," in health food stores, and around college campuses. After the Two disappeared, speakers for each meeting were selected by other members of the group. During the meeting itself they would be flanked by members of their family, who were called "buffers" because they absorbed the negative energy projected by hostile members of the audience.

The entire presentation generally took 15 or 20 minutes, but in one meeting we observed that the message was delivered in only three minutes. After a lengthy question-and-answer period, those who were sincerely interested in learning more about the message would be invited to a follow-up meeting, usually held in another place on the following day. These people would be asked to leave their names and phone numbers so that they could be contacted later that night. During the first meeting, the location of the follow-up would be kept secret to prevent curiosity seekers from showing up the next day. The follow-up meeting was usually more informal. The message would be restated, and the "prospective candidates" would have a chance to ask any additional questions that had not been answered the day before. At no time during our observations did we see members of the cult try to convince the audience using "hard-sell" tactics that Bo and Peep's message was true.

Within a few days of the follow-up meeting, those who were ready to join were told the location of a "buffer camp" where the socialization of new members would occur. Indoctrination in the buffer camp was very low-key, consisting of informal discussions around the campfire with Bo and Peep, and once in a while a private audience with them in their tent. After the Two disappeared, family spokesmen took over the job of socializing the new members, but the nature of the process remained the same. Rather than being subjected to intense social pressure and eventual demands for public commitment, new members were encouraged to spend as much time as they could alone with their partners, getting in tune with the next level. Interaction between new and old members was generally confined to informal discussions around the campfire, when the newcomers were encouraged to ask questions and express their doubts and anxieties. Some of these meetings were spent in almost complete silence, as members sat quietly around the fire tuning in, baking potatoes, or just watching the stars.

The most significant feature of Bo and Peep's recruitment strategy was the way it limited interaction between members of the cult and potential recruits. Virtually all such interaction was confined to stereotyped encounters at the two public meetings described above. When a prospective member decided to join, leaving behind his friends, family, and career, he did so on the basis of only a few hours of highly structured interaction with members of the group. Under these circumstances, new recruits almost never established close affective ties with members of the cult before they joined. Furthermore, during those two public meetings, the candidate learned very little about the cult's day-to-day existence. Since the Two believed that everyone had to decide on the basis of the message alone, they often refused to answer practical questions like "What do you eat?" and "Where do you get your money?"

Even after a seeker decided to join, he got very little social support from members of the cult. The buffer camp was usually located a day's drive away from the meeting place, and new members had to get there on their own as a test of their commitment. In one case prospective members were given four days to reach a post office 800 miles away, where they found directions to the buffer camp scribbled in the Zip Code book. Nine people decided to join that day, and all of them got to the camp on time and became members of the group.

The absence of affective ties with members of the cult is especially remarkable considering the importance of this factor in the sociological literature on recruitment and conversion. In their influential study of the "Divine Precepts" cult, Lofland and Stark (1965) argue that "cult affective bonds" are a necessary condition for joining. Yet Bo and Peep could recruit as many as 35 people at once without satisfying this condition.

Lofland and Stark (1965) distinguish between verbal and total converts, with verbal converts defined as those who profess belief and are accepted by core members, but take no active part in the everyday life of the cult. According to Lofland and Stark, "intensive interaction" is necessary to transform the verbal convert into a total convert, who is behaviorally as well as ideologically committed to the movement. They define intensive interaction as "concrete, daily, and even hourly accessibility" to other members which overcomes any remaining uncertainty about the truth of the cult's message (Lofland and Stark, 1965:873).

Although becoming a member of a deviant religious group is usually seen as the end-product of a long process of social interaction, the entire process in the UFO cult was compressed into a few days. When new members arrived at the buffer camp, they had already made a substantial behavioral commitment to the cult. While some members had little to lose by joining, others left behind good jobs, homes, and even small children. Many new members began telling others about the message even before they reached the buffer camp. The zeal of these "instant converts" often exceeded the enthusiasm of the older members who greeted them at the campground.

We would not deny the importance of intensive interaction in strengthening the commitment of new members, but its role has been exaggerated. New members of the UFO cult were most likely to drop out during the first week after they joined, usually because of loneliness or their inability to cut themselves off from friends and relatives in the outside world. But the attrition rate for new members is high in most cults and sects, even those that do provide their fledgling recruits with strong social support (e.g., Zablocki, 1971).

THE SOCIAL WORLD OF THE METAPHYSICAL SEEKER

We believe that social scientists have overemphasized the importance of cult affective bonds in recruiting new members, because of the dominant conception of the cult as a *deviant* religious organization. For example, Yinger (1970:279) refers to cults as "religious mutants, extreme variations on the dominant themes by means of which men struggle with their problems." Because cults are deviant groups in a skeptical rationalistic society, many social scientists have assumed that the people who join them require a tremendous amount of social support to draw them in and insulate them from a hostile disbelieving world. However, if the seeker lives in a social milieu where the movement's assumptions make sense, and if he defines joining as the logical extension of his spiritual quest, then it is easy to understand how he could join a "deviant" religious cult without first establishing social ties with those who already belong. We will begin our discussion by characterizing the life style of Bo and Peep's followers before they joined the cult. Then we will explore the social world of the metaphysical seeker, showing how that style of life is an integral part of a cultic milieu where joining a cult is not only tolerated, but often encouraged.

The Protean Style of the Metaphysical Seeker

In his discussion of the "protean man," Lifton (1970) describes the dilemmas confronting men and women in postindustrial society. In response to "historical dislocation" and the "flooding of imagery" produced by rapid change and mass communication, Lifton argues that modern man has adopted a protean style, named for the Greek mythical figure, Proteus, who could change his form at will.

> The protean style of self-process is characterized by an interminable series of experiments and explorations—some shallow, some profound—each of which may be readily abandoned in favor of still new psychological quests. [Lifton, 1970:319]

The description seems to fit members of the UFO cult very well, especially their "strong ideological hunger" (Lifton, 1970:319) and pattern of shifting allegiances.

Before joining Bo and Peep, members of the UFO cult had organized their lives around the quest for truth. Most described themselves as spiritual seekers. After listing all her previous spiritual "trips," a woman who joined the cult when we did remarked: "Until I started talking to you, I never realized how much shit I'd been into." The woman, then 21, said she ran away from home at age 15 "to find the truth," and she had been searching ever since. An older member aptly characterized their perennial quest as a "bumper car ride through a maze of spiritual trips."

True to the protean style, most members of the cult moved frequently and had relatively few material possessions and social commitments. Their emotional ties with the conventional American style of life were generally weak. Hardly any of them had ever voted, and most of them were uninformed and unconcerned about contemporary social and political issues. A disproportionate number were remnants of the counterculture who preferred to avoid commitments that would unduly restrict their personal freedom. One man captured the protean flavor of his life when we asked him what he had given up to follow the Two:

> I gave up a lot to come on this trip, man. I gave up my record collection, a set of tools, my old lady. But it's not the first record collection I've given up, and it's not the first set of tools. And I've had eight old ladies.

Although a significant number of cult members had given up good jobs and comfortable homes to join the cult, most had not. For some of the younger members, the material aspects of life in the cult were not very different from what they had experienced before they joined. For example, one new member had just dropped out of the Christ Family, a small sect that wandered barefoot from town to town, begging for its food and lodging. For him the transition to Bo and Peep's nomadic UFO cult was easy. Many others had been traveling around the country with backpacks or in remodeled vans, rarely staying anywhere for more than a few weeks at a time.

Even those who made substantial material sacrifices to join were not strongly attached to their possessions. A member who joined after selling his house for five dollars explained: "For me it was easy. I'm single. I just had some property to which I never felt any attachment anyway." Some of those who appeared to have made the greatest sacrifice had been gradually divesting themselves of their material possessions long before they met the Two. In one instance publicized by the Oregon press, a middle-aged couple supposedly abandoned their house and family to join the cult. Actually one of their sons came with them, and, even before they ever heard of Bo and Peep, they had quit their jobs, sold their home, and moved into a commune, where they were living when they decided to join.

The protean style of Bo and Peep's followers is important, because weak attachments to extracult relationships and activities make one available for membership. Other things being equal, a man with a good job, a family, and a respectable position in the community is less likely to join a flying saucer cult than a single male living alone or in a commune, with few material possessions and a strong penchant for change and excitement. To a great extent, the reason is the different degree of social constraint in each person's life.

The Role of the Seeker in the Cultic Milieu

Although the protean style fits most members of the UFO cult, we must avoid the trap of relating macroscopic structural conditions to the microscopic world of individuals without specifying the intermediate links in the causal chain. From Lipton's description of the protean man, it would seem that individuals respond to the structural dislocations of our time as if they were social isolates, completely out of touch with other alienated members of our anomic society. However, alienation is a collective phenomenon. As Zygmunt (1972:256) points out, men tend to become "alienated together."

Before they joined, members of the UFO cult shared a metaphysical world-view in which reincarnation, disincarnate spirits, psychic powers, lost continents, flying saucers, and ascended masters are taken for granted. This world-view, which Ellwood (1973) calls the "alternative reality," has a long history in the United States. It is perpetuated by a cultic milieu that exists in virtually every large community in the country. This milieu consists of a loosely integrated network of seekers who drift from one philosophy to another in search of metaphysical truth. We have entitled this section "The Role of the Seeker" because the concept of role places the individual seeker squarely in this social milieu. Within the metaphysical social world, the seeker is not disparaged as a starry-eyed social misfit. Instead, he is respected because he is trying to learn and grow. Members of the cultic milieu tend to be avid readers, continually exploring different metaphysical movements and philosophies (Buckner, 1965; Campbell, 1972; Mann, 1955). Whether in a tipi in the Oregon woods or a mansion in Beverly Hills, their evenings are often spent with friends and acquaintances discussing metaphysical topics like psychic research, flying saucers, or Sufi mysticism. A significant part of their lives is devoted to the pursuit of intellectual growth, however undisciplined that may be in conventional academic terms.

There is a common expression in metaphysical circles: "There are many paths to the top of the mountain." The seeker believes the quest for Truth is a highly individual process. As a long-time seeker in the UFO cult put it: "It looks to me like we're all trying to find the way. But what works for me, what's a test for me, may not mean shit to you." The long climb to the top of the mountain is usually a zig-zag course, as the seeker tries one path after another on the way up, always open to new ideas and alternatives.

Like Lifton's protean man, the seeker has a processual identity which changes continuously throughout his life. To stop exploring is to stop growing. Life is seen as an infinite series of "growth experiences," and the language of personal growth, like Christians' concept of humility, can be used to cope with almost any crisis. No matter how much he had given up to follow Bo and Peep, every one of the ex-members we interviewed defined his membership in the cult as a good growth experience. While a cynic might argue that this is nothing more than a convenient rationalization for a stupid mistake, it is clear that the quest for growth is part of the seeker's vocabulary of motives (Mills, 1940) that is learned and shared in the cultic milieu.

Many members of the UFO cult received strong support and encouragement from their friends when they considered joining the cult. Even many of those whose friends and relatives were very skeptical reported that no one tried to hold them back: "They told me, if that's what you feel you have to do, then you had better do it. It doesn't matter what we think."

Although it should be obvious, it is also worth noting that seekers get married, have children, and socialize their sons and daughters into the cultic milieu. As one member, whose mother was an avid follower of Edgar Cayce, told us, "I was raised on this stuff." The youngest member of the UFO cult was an extremely bright boy of 14 who had joined the cult with his parents. For over a year before hearing the message, he had read extensively about mysticism, psychic phenomena, health foods, and spiritual healing. He had been socialized into the occult social world, and the role of the seeker, even before he had the chance to experience the unsettling social dislocations described by Lifton.

The social nature of the alternative reality suggests that we need to reformulate the conventional image of the seeker. Our conception of the personally *disoriented* searcher "floundering about among religions" (Lofland and Stark, 1965: 869, 870) should be replaced with an image of one who is socially *oriented* to the quest for personal growth. Seekership constitutes a social identity that is positively valued by the individual and his significant others.

A closer look at the alternative reality of the metaphysical social world can help us understand how the Two could recruit so many followers in such a short time without providing prospective members with affective bonds to the group.

Bo and Peep's Appeal to Subcultural Values

Although Bo and Peep's message sounded bizarre to practically everyone who read about it in the newspapers, it was firmly grounded in the metaphysical world-view. Bo and Peep put together an eclectic mixture of metaphysics and Christianity that many seekers found appealing because it integrated a variety of taken-for-granted beliefs, including flying saucers, reincarnation, Biblical revelations, and the physical resurrection of Jesus. (See Balch and Taylor, 1977, for a more complete explanation of the cult's belief system.) One of the Oregon recruits described his reaction to the message this way: "There were so many truths, man. I listened to Bo's rap, and I'm thinking, yeah, I've heard that before. He told me a lot of things I already knew, but he put them all together in a way I'd never thought of."

Despite its roots in the taken-for-granted beliefs of the cultic milieu, Bo and Peep's message had many unique features, e.g., the physical nature of the metamorphic process and role of UFOs in transcending the human level of existence. Yet, as Wallis (1974, 1975a, 1975b) points out, the cultic milieu is epistemologically individualistic, acknowledging many paths to spiritual enlightenment. In the metaphysical social world anything is possible. As one of our informants reminded us, it was not too long ago that Buck Rogers, spaceships, and ray guns were science fiction. Since then we have put men on the moon and sent a spaceship to Mars, and laser-beams are now being contemplated as military weapons. In a world that changes as rapidly as ours, he said, one cannot afford to close one's mind to any possibility, even spaceships from heaven. Not many seekers were completely convinced by the Two when they heard the message, and many remained skeptical as long as they belonged to the cult, but they set aside their doubts. Another ex-member captured the openness of the metaphysical seeker when he explained that the "willing suspension of disbelief" is an essential part of any genuine spiritual quest.

Although Bo and Peep claimed that their metamorphic process

was the only way of getting to heaven, whenever they spoke to an audience they couched the absolutism of their message in language designed to appeal to the open-minded tolerance of the seeker. They agreed that there were many equally valid paths to the top of the mountain, but they added that only a UFO could get the seeker *off* the mountain into the kingdom of heaven that lies far beyond this planet.

In spite of the cult's sectarian characteristics, even Bo and Peep's "process" was a direct outgrowth of the epistemological individualism of the cultic milieu. The Two called their process Human Individual Metamorphosis to emphasize the uniqueness of each individual's transformation. The psychic connection established with the next level was unique for every member of the cult, and no two individuals had the same attachments to overcome. Nor would they require the same experiences to complete their metamorphosis. As members were so fond of saying: "The process is an individual thing."

Bo and Peep also appealed directly to the value of personal growth. It was a central part of their cosmology. According to the Two, Earth is only one of many "gardens" throughout the universe that supports life. All life forms are in a constant state of flux, evolving slowly but steadily to higher levels of consciousness. The Two compared Earth to a school, and mankind to its students. As human beings advance through a procession of lifetimes, they learn from their experiences, moving up through the grades from kindergarten to graduation time.

Bo and Peep said that by abandoning his past and making a connection with the next level, the seeker could accelerate his growth to the point where he would actually convert himself into an androgenous being. Even at the next level, there is no finality or perfection as there is in the Christian's heaven—only more growth. They said that not even God is perfect, because perfection means stagnation. As one member put it succinctly: "Growth is life."

The Subcultural Basis of the Motivation to Join

The value placed on personal growth in the metaphysical social world helps account for the motivation to join the UFO cult. The prevailing image of the religious seeker is a social misfit who experiences one crisis after another before he finally joins a cult or a sect in order to cope with his problems. There is no doubt that most members of the UFO cult had experienced "psychic deprivation" (Glock, 1964) before they joined. In a typical account, a young woman described the spiritual vacuum of her life before Bo and Peep: "I could get high so many ways—drugs, music, scenery, people—but I still felt an emptiness. I never felt that fullness, that rock-bottom solidness I was looking for."

However, most social scientific studies of cults are overly reductionistic in their focus on the personal problems of cult members. They ignore the extent to which psychic deprivation is generated by the role of the seeker. One of Lofland and Stark's (1965) subjects aptly described the seeker's dilemma when she said: "The more I search, the more questions I have." The top of the spiritual mountain is an elusive goal, continually receding the higher the seeker climbs. The seeker is supposed to grow by asking for tests and learning from his experiences, but growth is subjective and hard to define. As one member explained: "You never know if you pass a test." In short, the motivation to continue searching is built into the role.

As the seeker goes through life, he is attuned to signs that might give his quest some direction. An axiom of the alternative reality is that nothing happens by pure coincidence. Things happen because they are meant to, and it is the seeker's job to ferret out the hidden meaning in everyday events that might reveal his role in the cosmic plan.

Most of the ex-members we interviewed reported a series of coincidences just before they joined which convinced them that Bo and Peep's message was true. Consider the case of a 22-year-old woman who joined in a small Arizona community where she had been living for several months. She had been feeling restless and thought about moving on but she had no particular destination in mind. Then one night during a violent thunderstorm, a lightning bolt suddenly lit up her room while she was asleep. As she sat up with a start, only half awake, she had a fleeting vision of an open doorway suspended in the air directly in front of her. At the time the meaning of the vision escaped her, but a week later she met two members of the UFO cult who told her about an open doorway in the heavens that would allow them to leave the planet aboard UFOs. The coincidence of her restlessness, the vision, and the sudden opportunity to join the UFO cult was compelling evidence that she was meant at least to take a closer look at Bo and Peep's message.

The seeker is understandably open to metaphysical teachers who might be able to clarify some of the confusion surrounding his spiritual quest and accelerate his growth. In the world of metaphysics there is a premium on hidden wisdom, whether Kabbalistic lore, tales of astral visits with ascended masters, or messages from benevolent space brothers. Metaphysics is the study of things beyond the realm of normal human experience, and the more obscure the hidden mysteries, the more the seeker needs a teacher.

Whether consciously or not, metaphysical teachers often maintain their authority by exploiting the seeker's insecurity. A skillful teacher can effectively suppress the open expression of doubt by implying that his students will comprehend his obscure metaphysical teachings according to their level of spiritual awareness. Like the villagers in the story of the emperor's new clothes, not many students are willing to risk revealing their ignorance by challenging a man they and their fellow seekers consider a master of the hidden mysteries.

Bo and Peep played on the insecurity of the seeker in much the same way. They compared their followers to twelfth graders who were about to "graduate from the planet" because they had evolved as far as they could in their present human form. Supposedly the rest of mankind was unable to understand their message because it was still plodding along through the other 11 grades.

The Absence of Conversion in the UFO Cult

Members of the UFO cult were not converts in the true sense of the word. Conversion, according to Travisano (1970: 600–601), refers to the "radical reorganization of identity, meaning, and life. . . . In conversion, a whole new world is entered, and the old world is transformed through reinterpretation. The father sees his bachelorhood as youthful fun; the convert sees his as debauchery." However, members of the UFO cult did not undergo a serious rupture of identity when they became "total converts" to Bo and Peep's message. Instead, they defined "the process" as a logical extension of their spiritual quest.

Unlike members of more sectarian organizations such as some Jesus movement group who define their lives before "accepting Christ" in very negative terms (Richardson et al., 1972), Bo and Peep's followers tended to look favorably on their pasts. The following remark is typical: "This information clarified everything we had been into before. It's like the next logical step."

The continuity between participation in the UFO cult and the role of the seeker in the cultic milieu stood out most clearly when members became disillusioned with the process and considered dropping out. Their disillusionment was accompanied by discernible changes in their everyday speech. Many words, phrases, and conversational topics unique to the UFO cult began to disappear from their talk. They stopped talking about UFOs and the physical nature of the metamorphic process, and began to emphasize how they had grown from their experience in the cult.

In a manner consistent with the protean style, most ex-members of the UFO cult insisted that Bo and Peep, however misguided they appeared in retrospect, had accelerated their spiritual growth by helping them overcome their mundane attachments:

> The most important thing is the process of becoming. Don't get hung up on the future. Just let it be. It doesn't matter what you call it—the process is the path, the way, the Tao. All the great teachers were saying the same thing—Jesus, Lao Tzu, Buddha, the Two. . . . The process is whatever you want it to be as long as you're free of attachments.

Paradoxically, the openness that allowed so many seekers to suspend their doubts and follow the Two also facilitated the process of dropping out. For example, one ex-member recalled something his partner told him just before he decided to leave the cult:

> He said over and over again just before I left the trip: "We have to keep an open mind about this thing, man. The Two may not be who they say they are, but that's not important. The Two aren't important."

His comment is significant for two reasons. First, it illustrates the seeker's protean adaptability. It was fairly common for members to argue, just before they left the cult, that Bo and Peep were no longer important. The Two had merely brought them some useful information, and now that they had learned all they could from the process, it was time to move on, to overcome even their attachment to Bo and Peep. Second, his comment reflects the common belief that even a charlatan may have something to offer. A reporter once asked a member what he would think if Bo and Peep's message turned out to be a hoax. "Then I will still have grown," he replied.

For most of Bo and Peep's followers, then, becoming a member of the UFO cult did not constitute the rejection of one identity for another. Instead, their decision to follow the Two was a *reaffirmation* of their seekership. Whenever one identity grows naturally out of another, causing little disruption in the lives of those involved, the term "conversion" is inappropriate. Perhaps prospective members of a religious cult only need strong social support from existing members when a radical substitution of belief systems is required.

CONCLUSION

While there is no way of knowing how successful Bo and Peep would have been with different recruitment methods, it is clear that the absence of social interaction between members and would-be recruits is not necessarily a fatal omission in recruiting members to a contemporary religious movement. However deviant it might appear to the outside world, a religious cult is not necessarily deviant within the social world of the metaphysical seeker. Even if it were, there are powerful norms that encourage an open-minded assessment of deviant beliefs and discourage condemning others for doing what they think is best for themselves. When a religious seeker also has few social commitments and material possessions, most of the major restraints against joining a deviant religious cult are absent. To a great extent, even the motivation to join such a group is generated by social-psychological forces operating in the cultic milieu.

The curious pattern of recruitment in Bo and Peep's UFO cult underscores the importance of studying religious cults in their social and cultural context. The process of becoming a member may vary greatly depending on the social milieu from which a cult draws its members, and the extent to which membership requires a transformation of one's social identity in that milieu.

References

Balch, R.W. and D. Taylor (1977) 'The metamorphosis of a UFO cult: a study of organizational change." Paper read at the annual meeting of the Pacific Sociological Association, Sacramento, California.

——(1976a) "Salvation in a UFO." Psychology Today 10: 58–66, 106.

——(1976b) "Walking out the door of your life: becoming a member of a contemporary UFO cult." Paper read at the annual meeting of the Pacific Sociological Association, San Diego, California.

Barkun, M. (1974) Disaster and the Millennium. New Haven, CT: Yale Univ. Press.

Buckner, H. T. (1965) "The flying saucerians: an open door cult," pp. 223–230 in M. Truzzi (ed.) Sociology and Everyday Life. Englewood Cliffs, NJ: Prentice-Hall.

Campbell, C. (1972) "The cult, the cultic milieu, and secularization," pp. 119–136 in M. Hill (ed.) A Sociological Yearbook of Religion in Britain, Vol. 5. London: SCM Press.

Ellwood, R. S., Jr.(1973) Religious and Spiritual Groups in Modern America. Englewood Cliffs, NJ: Prentice-Hall.

Festinger, L., H. W. Riecken, and S. Schachter (1956) When Prophecy Fails. Minneapolis: Univ. of Minnesota.

Glock, C. Y. (1964) "The role of deprivation in the origin and evolution of religious groups," pp. 24–36 in R. Lee and M. E. Marty (eds.) Religion and Social Conflict. New York: Oxford Univ. Press.

Goffman, E. (1959) Presentation of.Self in Everyday Life. Garden City, NY: Doubleday.

Lifton, R. J. (1970) "Protean man," pp. 311–331 in R. J. Lifton (ed.) History and Human Survival. New York: Random House.

Lofland, J. (1966) Doomsday Cult. Englewood Cliffs, NJ: Prentice-Hall.

——and R. Stark (1965) "Becoming a world-saver: a theory of conversion to a deviant perspective." Amer. Soc. Rev. 30:862–875.

Mann, W. E. (1955) Sect, Cult and Church in Alberta. Toronto: Univ. of Toronto Press.

Mills, C. W. (1940) "Situated actions and vocabularies of motive." Amer. Soc. Rev. 5: 904–913.

Richardson, J. T., R. B. Simmonds, and M. W. Harder (1972) "Thought reform and the Jesus movement." Youth and Society 4: 185–200.

Travisano, R. V. (1970) "Alternation and conversion as qualitatively different transformations," pp. 594–606 in G. P. Stone and H.A. Farberman (eds.) Social Psychology Through Symbolic Interaction. Waltham, MA: Xerox.

Wallis, R. (1975a) "Scientology: therapeutic cult to religious sect." Sociology 9: 89–100.

———(1975b) "The cult and its transformation," pp. 35–49 in R. Wallis (ed.) Sectarianism. New York: John Wiley.

———(1974) "Ideology, authority, and the development of cultic movements." Social Research 41: 299–327.

Yinger, J. M. (1970) The Scientific Study of Religion. New York: Macmillan.

Zablocki, B. (1971) The Joyful Community. Baltimore, MD: Penguin.

Zygmunt, J. F. (1972) "Movements and motives: some unresolved issues in the psychology of social movements." Human Relations 25: 449–467.

Notes

1. Before their "awakening," the Two apparently led rather ordinary lives. Bo, who was 44 at the time of the Oregon meeting, had been a music professor at a university in Texas, and later a choir director for an Episcopal church. Peep, 48, had been a professional nurse. After meeting in a Texas hospital in 1972, they opened a short-lived metaphysical center specializing in astrology, spiritual healing, theosophy, and comparative religions, where they first began to suspect their higher purpose on the planet. During the next three years they spent much of their time traveling together, deliberately isolating themselves from the rest of the world in order to learn more about their mission. It was not until the spring of 1975 that they recruited their first followers at a private meeting in Los Angeles.

2. Estimating the size of Bo and Peep's following at any given time is hazardous, because members were scattered across the country in small families, and no one, not even the Two, kept track of the number of people recruited. While estimates of the cult's size at the peak of its popularity range up to 1,500, there were probably never more than 200 members, and 150 is probably more realistic. These figures are based on our own calculations as well as estimates made by members themselves.

3. Although we were aware of the ethical objections to covert observation, we decided to join the cult as hidden observers for pragmatic and methodological reasons. Pragmatically there was no other way to study the cult effectively, because although members spoke freely with reporters, they generally limited their comments to the "party line" dictated by the Two. We believed the only way we could get accurate data about the cult was to join it ourselves. Our judgment was supported by the sharp contrast we observed between daily life in the cult and the way members presented themselves to the outside world (Balch and Taylor, 1976a).

The pragmatic considerations that led to our joining as hidden observers dovetailed nicely with our ethnographic methodological orientation. As Barkun (1974:43) points out in his recent study of millenarian movements, research that offers an "inside" perspective is all too rare in the study of religious cults. The works of Festinger et al. (1956) and Lofland and Stark (1965; Lofland, 1966) are conspicuous exceptions. They are notable not only because they are unusual, but because of the significant contributions they have made to the study of religious movements.

In addition to allowing us to enter the "backstage region" of the cult (Goffman, 1959), we believed our decision to join as hidden observers would enable us to see the world through the eyes of Bo and Peep's followers as no other method could. Several months later, when we more openly interviewed members who had dropped out of the cult, our "inside" knowledge of the group's beliefs, organization, and membership helped us focus our questions and contributed to the excellent rapport we enjoyed with our respondents. As one ex-member said of another social scientist who had tried unsuccessfully to study the cult: "He didn't even know what questions to ask."

It is worth noting that we encountered no hostility when we revealed our "true" identities prior to each interview, and no one refused to be interviewed because of the deception. In fact, we were asked to contribute a chapter to a book about the cult that is being written by several ex-members.

4. At this writing the UFO cult still exists, and its sectarian features are more pronounced than ever before. Bo and Peep rejoined the remnants of their following sometime during the early months of 1976. Since their return, the cult has stopped recruiting and has become very secretive, disappearing almost entirely from the public view. These changes are described in Balch and Taylor (1977).

41 / Becoming a Taxi-Dancer: The Significance of Neutralization in a Semi-Deviant Occupation

LAWRENCE K. HONG
ROBERT W. DUFF

Taxi-dancing, which was one of the most common forms of masculine recreation in the 1920s and 1930s (Cressey, 1932; Nye, 1973), has been regaining its popularity in recent years (Hong and Duff, 1976). In Los Angeles, for example, the number of taxi-dance halls has more than doubled in the last few years; increasing from three in 1971 to eight today. Other American cities where taxi-dance halls may be found include New York, Detroit, and Honolulu. Hundreds of taxi-dance halls may also be found in Asian cities such as Hong Kong, Tokyo, and Manila. The revival of taxi-dance halls in the United States can be partially attributed to an expansion of their functions in recent years. Though supplying female partners for dancing purpose is still their chief function, there is a growing emphasis in the taxi-dance halls of the 1970s toward promoting a "social club" atmosphere. Comfortable sitting areas are provided in the dance halls for customers and hostesses to converse and share nonalcoholic refreshments. Customers are also encouraged to play pool and other games with the dance hostesses. Once a week and on special days, such as Valentine's Day and New Year's Eve, buffet dinners are also served in the dance halls to enhance the convivial atmosphere of the clubs.

Customers are delighted with the new approach adopted by the dance halls. With the increased opportunity to socialize with the hostesses, they find it easier to act out their fantasies and satisfy their needs for romantic involvement. Working as a dance hostess is an unconventional venture for most of the women. First of all, the reality of the job requires the simulation of a romantic relationship between the hostess and the customers. It is obvious that this type of pseudo-relationship is in direct contradiction to both the past and the present ideologies pertaining to female-male relations. Furthermore, the job also runs against some traditional normative expectations, because it requires intimate interactions with customers who may be very different from the hostess in terms of age, race, and cultural background (see Hong and Duff, 1976). Also, the public attitude today still views taxi-dancing as a form of activity bordering on prostitution, in spite of the fact that the occupation is approved by local ordinances.

Who are these women who become taxi-dancers? How do they avoid self-esteem damage? How do they overcome the traditional normative barriers with respect to age and race? How do they protect themselves from the possible negative reactions of friends and relatives?

Based on published reports pertaining to other semi-deviant and deviant occupations (Pittman, 1971; Saulutin, 1971; Riege, 1969; Lopata and Noel, 1967; Bryan, 1965, 1966), we initiated the study with the expectation that taxi-dancers, similar to workers in related occupations, may utilize some forms of justification to neutralize the unpleasantness of their job. However, we felt the previously published comments on the use of justifications are too scanty to allow making reliable inferences on their applicability to taxi-dancers. Furthermore, they are also ambiguous on the role of neutralization in occupational socialization. Hence, we studied the taxi-dancers in Los Angeles, hoping that our research would result in more adequate answers to these (aforementioned) questions.

METHODS

The material of this study was obtained by means of participant observation and intensive interviews. We observed and interviewed more than 70 dance hostesses in Los Angeles over a four year period. We approached the hostesses as customers and were able to develop excellent rapport with them. After about six months from the onset of the study, one of the authors became so well acquainted with a number of the hostesses that he was able to maintain informal social contacts with them outside the dance halls.

In gathering the information, two methods of sampling were employed. The first method is similar to a panel survey design: we chose a number of newly hired hostesses, starting from their first day on the job, and informally interviewed each of them over an average period of two months, with 18 months being the longest. During the first two weeks, the hostesses were interviewed every two or three days. In the subsequent weeks, the interviews were conducted at four or five day intervals. During the entire study period, the hostess' interactions with her customers, other hostesses, and the management were also carefully observed. This method of interview and observation was applied to six different groups of taxi-dancers at different times. The size of the groups ranged from three to five.

Since the first method was too costly in terms of money and time for a large sample, a second method of sampling approximating the cohort survey design was also employed. Slightly more than half of the hostesses were interviewed once or twice and divided into different cohorts according to the length of time they had been on the job. Thus, by comparing the different cohorts, we were able to assess their attitudes and other behaviors over time without having to track the same individuals for an extended period.

In analyzing the data, we compared relevant information from our interviews with Sykes and Matza's (1957) neutralization techniques. In the remainder of this paper, we shall present the findings and the typical responses of the interviewees.

FINDINGS

Recruiting the Hostesses

Young women are recruited to work in the dance halls through newspaper advertisements and the personal efforts of women currently employed as hostesses. Due to the high turnover rate for hostesses, "want-ads" to recruit new women appear in the classified sections of the local newspapers almost every day. However, only about half the hostesses are recruited through the newspapers. Almost an equal number are recruited by women already employed in the dance halls. Many hostesses, after having developed a positive attitude toward their occupation, are eager recruiters; they want their friends and relatives to work with them.

Most of the women hired are young (18 to 25), white, divorced or separated, and have finished high school. They generally come from a working class or lower middle class background. Judging from these personal characteristics, it is evident that they have been purposely selected. The dance hall managers prefer young, white, and unattached women because they can attract more customers, for obvious reasons. Furthermore, they want to hire women of at least lower middle or working class background who have at minimum a high school education to insure that their hostesses possess the types of conversational skills and demeanor that are conducive to nurturing the romantic fantasies of the customers.

For women who want to become taxi-dancers, the main attraction is money. The hostesses are guaranteed $2.00 to $2.50 an hour plus an additional amount for the time they spend with customers. The customers are charged at a rate of $.15 per minute from the time they "check out" a hostess to the time they "check in"; the hostess receives about 50% of this charge as her commission. On average, a hostess can make between $3.60 to $5.40 an hour, which is substantially more than what she can receive from a conventional job.

Typically, a woman seeking employment in a taxi-dance hall knows very little about the job; the revival of taxi-dancing is too recent for the various aspects of this work-role to have become popular knowledge, and she is too young to have any knowledge of its controversial past. During the employment interview, the job is briefly described to her by the manager or the owner. The description typically is vague and accentuates the positives:

> This job is like going to a party every night. If you like to dance and talk to people, this job is perfect for you. The girls sit over there and the customers come over to ask them to dance. You will meet people from all over the world. If you don't like a particular customer, you don't have to dance with him. It is just like in a party, if you don't like a guy, you don't have to dance with him. You'll be paid the same for sitting and talking with a customer as for dancing with him. This is really a fun job.

Those who are personally recruited by friends and relatives are not likely to possess much more information about the job than those who respond to the newspaper want-ads, because their friends and relatives would not have recruited them if they disliked the job. Therefore, almost all the women entering the taxi-dancing career have only a very superficial knowledge of its activities and demands.

Confronting the Reality

During the first day on the job, many hostesses immediately find out that the job is psychologically stressful. The majority of these women, due to their social and educational backgrounds, are conventional in their values and attitudes. They share the dominant values of the outside society and their particular age group with respect to female-male relationships. Hence, they find it intensely uncomfortable when their customers are interested not only in social dancing but also in romantic and/or sexual involvement. Almost invariably the new hostess has some early negative experiences with customers who aggressively demand forms of sexual contact on the dance floor. Oftentimes this is part of a ritual "testing out" of the new hostess by one or more of the regular customers.

Compounding the problem is the disparity in age, race, and cultural background between the hostesses and the customers. Almost half the clientele of the dance halls are foreign-born Mexicans, Chinese, and Filipinos. Although many customers are white, these are usually much older than the hostesses. As a consequence of her early negative experiences coupled with what she discovers about the nature of the clientele, it is not uncommon to find a new hostess feeling depressed during her first week on the job.

Some of the new hostesses may turn down customers whom they had found to be unpleasant from previous occasions. When this occurs too often or when she shows signs of depression, the management will try to console her by jokingly pointing out the intrinsic rewards of her work. She is informed that her job is like "a social worker or a counselor" trying to help these "lonely men who are far away from home" or "who are unhappy with their wives." Similar psychological support also comes from her coworkers, especially if they include friends or relatives who were instrumental in recruiting her.

In our view, the encouragements provided by the management and the coworkers are the first step in a very important socialization process leading the woman to accept her work role as a taxi-dancer. Consciously or unconsciously, the management and her coworkers (which may include friends or relatives) are beginning to supply the new hostess with "justifications" to continue working in the dance hall. As we shall see later, these justifications can be best described as "neutralization techniques" (Sykes and Matza, 1957; Ball, 1966; Priest and McGrath, 1970; Dunford and Kunz, 1973; Rogers and Buffalo, 1974; Friedman, 1974) because it is through the learning of the justifications that the new hostess eventually comes to accept her job. The internalization of these justifications, which becomes intensified during the second and third weeks, appears to be a precondition helping to make the taxi-dancer role acceptable to the young woman.

However, it must be pointed out that many new hostesses have become so depressed and disgusted with the job that they simply quit after the first week. Some of them would leave sooner (and a few do), if the pay period was not on a weekly basis. From our four years of observation, we estimate at least one-fourth of the new hostesses do not return to work after the first week. For those who remain, the next two weeks become the most crucial period in learning to accept the taxi-dancer role.

Learning to Neutralize

About 75% of the new hostesses survive the first week. However, as they enter the second week of their work in the taxi-dance hall, they are still uncertain about whether or not they want the job. But, as compared to those who have left, they feel less depressed about the job, and their attitudes toward the customers are mixed rather than totally negative. It must be mentioned that this mixed feeling does not necessarily represent a progressive change on their part; many of the hostesses have this attitude to begin with. In fact, it was this mixed feeling that had prevented them from quitting work after the first week. When asked about her feeling toward her job, a hostess in her second week of work commented:

> I don't know. You meet a lot of different people in this job. Some are very nice, but some are weird. You have to know how to handle yourself. Sometimes you get a good customer and it is great. Last night, this man just sat and talked with me for hours. He was really nice. If all my customers were like him, it'd be all right.

During the second week, the new hostess also begins to know the management and other hostesses better, and feels more at ease in interacting with them. This is an important development in her socialization process which paves the way for her to learn more "neutralization techniques." Though she was introduced to the techniques during her first week at work, it is in the second and third weeks that she begins to learn most of the techniques through repeated interactions with management and co-workers. It should be noted that hostesses who were recruited by friends and relatives usually have a slight head start on learning the neutralization techniques because their friends or relatives are likely to expose them to a large variety of techniques as early as the first week. Thus, with the additional help from the management and other hostesses, these hostesses tend to master the variety of neutralization techniques much faster than those who were recruited by other means.

The management always attempts to promote a casual and relaxed atmosphere in the dance hall. When business is not busy, the hostesses usually sit around in small groups and chat. Generally, the talks revolve around daily activities and news items of interest to them. But, when a new hostess is present in the group, the conversation inevitably turns to her attitude toward the job and the customers. The new hostess may also have questions concerning the job that she wants to ask the other hostesses. It is in such informal gatherings that the new hostess is exposed to a variety of neutralization techniques.

In addition to being exposed to the "claim of benefits" technique (Friedman, 1974) mentioned earlier—i.e., the idea that the taxi-dancer role is philanthropic—the new hostess is also exposed to other neutralization techniques such as "denial of injury," "denial of victim," and "denial of responsibility" (see Sykes and Matza, 1957; Ball, 1966; Priest and McGrath, 1970; Dunford and Kunz, 1973; Rogers and Buffalo, 1974; Friedman, 1974). For example, the "denial of injury" technique was clearly implied in a conversation between a new hostess and her coworkers overheard by one of the authors. One of the more experienced hostesses, in trying to soothe the guilt feeling of a novice who thought she was leading her customers on by playing along with their romantic interests, commented: "Don't feel bad about it. I do it all the time. They know about it. They are not that foolish." In other words, the new hostess was being informed, albeit erroneously, that the customers were not actually emotionally involved, and that they were aware that the hostesses were feigning involvement as part of the game. Therefore, nobody was hurt in the game, and she should not feel guilty about it. In the same conversation, another hostess, who had been working there for at least six months, injected a comment that can be most appropriately classified as "denial of victim":

> They deserve it. I don't care. All they want is to get you to bed with them. This guy dances with me all the time, and asks me to go to breakfast with him after work. I know what he wants, but he is not going to get anything from me.

In the second comment, the hostess was implying that the customer was the transgressor rather than the victim, and therefore deserving of injury. She was not concerned about hurting the feelings of her customer because he was the wrong-doer.

The "denial of responsibility" is also a common neutralization technique used by the hostesses. A new hostess who feels the job is demeaning is likely to be reminded by her coworkers that "every job is the same." "As long as there are men around, they will proposition you. It doesn't matter whether you work in an office, a factory, or a dance hall." In other words, since there are no alternatives, the hostess is not personally accountable for choosing a job that she finds to be degrading.

At first these justifications are casually passed on to a novice by the experienced hostesses ostensibly as a means of helping her to resolve immediate moral dilemmas, but once they are internalized, they become an effective mechanism that can be activated in the future to render inoperative those internal and external restraints that may pull her away from the taxi-dancing career. At any rate, by the end of the third week, many new hostesses are well versed in the neutralization techniques. When they are asked about their job, inevitably they will respond in terms of justifications.

It is important to point out that the use of neutralization techniques alone is not sufficient to make a new hostess committed to her work. During the second seek, she is still evaluating her job—balancing its benefits (mainly income) with its cost (mainly emotional stress). The utilization of neutralization techniques undoubtedly has helped her in reducing the costs and thus enhancing the potential rewards of the job. But, if the amount of income does not meet her expectations (due to paucity of customers), she is not likely to keep the job for too long, in spite of the reduced psychological cost as a result of neutralization. Similarly, some new hostesses may find the stress of the job so intolerable, either because of failure to internalize the neutralization techniques, or in spite of internalizing them, that they quit the job regardless of the amount of income. In short, neutralization appears to be a necessary factor but not a sufficient factor in influencing the occupational commitment of the taxi-dancers.

Acquiring Steady Customers

There is always competition for the "better" steady customers: those who treat the hostess more like a date, are less sexually aggressive, of higher socioeconomic status, and pay for long periods of time. Frictions between hostesses may result from attempts to steal, or "move in on," a good steady customer. The new hostess is at a disadvantage when she enters into this competition. Many of the more desirable customers are already into steady relationships with the established hostesses. As a result, the new hostess' initial experiences are often with some of the least desirable of the dance hall regulars, including some of the most sexually aggressive. On the other hand, she does have one advantage—she is new. A new face and personality always attract attention in the dance hall, and a new hostess can successfully steal a steady customer from an experienced hostess if she has mastered certain tactics.

These tactics entail the development of an *impression* to each customer that their relationship is exclusive. She argues to each that he is the "only one that really interests" her. "The others are all just part of the job." They "mean nothing" to her. In other words, she must cultivate the romantic interest of the customers by "leading them on." These are, at the same time, the tactics that the experienced hostesses employ to keep their steady customers, and the tactics that the new hostesses must master in order to acquire a steady clientele.

However, it should be emphasized that aggressively stealing, or "moving in on" the steady customers of an established hostess is not a common means by which the new hostess secures her steadies. There are many other customers, including regulars, who do not have steady partners. Usually, it is from this group that the new hostess attempts to recruit her clientele. In addition, the tactic of "leading on" customers, so prevalent among the hostesses, actually insures that a certain turnover of customers will take place. Most customers sooner or later become suspicious of their hostess' performance. Her continual verbal reassurance of fidelity is in constant contradiction to the visual evidence which the customer must confront as he observes her with other steadies. Also, most steady customers are finally frustrated when their relationship never develops beyond the confines of the dance hall; though sometimes a hostess will allow the relationship to extend outside the hall in order to hold a restless but highly desirable customer, or because she has actually become personally interested in the man. In general, however, new hostesses are seen as offering "new possibilities" to the customer who is becoming suspicious, frustrated, or simply bored with his steady hostess, or who has lost his steady partner because she has quit her job.

A few new hostesses learn to apply the tactics of "leading on" the customers as early as the first week on the job. From the perspective of the taxi-dancing profession, these women are "naturals": they do not acquire the tactics from the dance halls but seem to possess exceptional interpersonal skills even before they are taxi-dancers. Most of the new hostesses, however, learn the tactics from the more experienced hostesses! Normally, one would expect the established hostesses to guard the secrets of their success, especially from their potential competitors. But, surprisingly, this is not the case. In fact, they are eager to discuss their tactics with other hostesses, especially the new ones.

Without prying into the psyche of the established hostesses, it is difficult to assess their motives for divulging their secrets. But, a number of hypotheses are possible. First, the hostess may have a compulsion to confess in order to purge herself of the guilt feelings which arise from her leading customers on (cf. Friedman, 1968 on the scatological rites of burglars). This hypothesis would also imply partial failure in the use of neutralization techniques. A second hypothesis may be that the established hostess is attempting to assert her social status by boasting of her exploits with the customers in front of the other hostesses, especially the new ones. Finally, a third interpretation is also possible. The established hostesses may be doing it for self-protection. By sharing her trade secrets with the new hostesses, she may make them feel indebted to her and refrain from "moving in on" her steady customers. Some evidence tends to support the third hypothesis: we do not recall finding any new hostess moving in on the steady clientele of an established hostess, if the latter is friendly to the new hostess starting from her first week on the job.

Enjoying the Work

Upon entering the fourth week of her career, a taxi-dancer usually finds the job sufficiently rewarding to keep it for an indefinite period of time; she is not interested in looking for another job at least in the foreseeable future. Apparently, she has internalized enough justifications to neutralize much of the unpleasantness of the job; she is also likely to have acquired a number of steady customers to keep the job financially rewarding.

From the fourth week onward, there is also a noticeable decrease in her verbalization of justifications. When asked about her job, she is likely to say: "I like it," "It's fun," or "It's an easy job." She also begins to show enthusiasm in her work as indicated by acts in her interactions with coworkers and customers such as smiling, giggling, touching, offering cigarettes and chewing gum, greeting by saying "hi," and saying "see you" when leaving.

Perhaps, the most revealing indications of her new attitude are her willingness to recruit friends and relatives to work as taxi-dancers, and her emerging status consciousness within the dance hall. It is reasonable to assume that unless she sees some positive features in it, she will not ask her friends and relatives to work with her. She would be courting potential damage to her self-esteem by exposing her world of work to her friends and relatives, if she believed that taxi-dancing was demeaning or degrading. Some elements of self-fulfilling prophecy are also at work here: while her emerging positive attitude may lead her to recruit friends and relatives, having friends and relatives working with her may, in turn, legitimize her work and make her attitude toward her job more positive.

Her new attitude can also be seen in her development of status consciousness. She begins to speak with pride about the fact that she has steady customers, that her customers spend a long period of time with her, and that they are the better ones—i.e., they are nice, educated, have a good job, and, most important, do not "grab and grind."

The hostess is extremely proud of herself, if her customers begin to come in to see her on a regular schedule—with time and day prearranged—as determined by *her convenience*. Tardiness and absences on the part of customers are at their own risks; her time will have to be paid even though the customers are not physically present. She is now at the pinnacle of her career, and enjoys it immensely. However, it should be added that even for the successful taxi-dancer, her career will seldom extend for more than two or three years. There are a variety of reasons for this. The hostesses belong to a transient age group. Like other workers in the same age category, they are highly mobile. Many marry and retire. Some find a better job. Some move from the Los Angeles area. Only a few see the job as a long-term endeavor.

DISCUSSION AND SUMMARY

Studies of deviant and semi-deviant occupations, such as call girls (Bryan, 1965, 1966), strippers (Saulutin, 1971), dance instructresses (Lopata and Noel, 1967; Riege, 1969), masseuses (Verlarde and Warlick, 1973), and male prostitutes (Pittman, 1971), have consistently reported that workers in these occupations use justifications to explain or to defend their occupational behaviors. The present study also finds the same tendency among the taxi-dancers. Moreover, we find that the learning of justifications plays a significant role in the occupational socialization of the taxi-dancers. Without learning the various justifications to neutralize the unpleasantness of the job, the novice is not likely to commit herself to the taxi-dancing career. Typically, a taxi-dancer goes through the following process in her occupational socialization which is highlighted by her learning of the neutralization techniques.

(1) The First Week. Before starting her work in the taxi-dance hall, a new hostess knows very little about the job she is about to work. During the job interview, she is given the impression that the job is easy and fun. However, on the first day of her work, she is shocked to find out that many customers have amorous interests in her, and may make sexual advances toward her. Compounding the problem is that many of the customers are either foreign born or older whites. Being young, white, high school educated, and working class in background, she finds it difficult to reconcile her conventional values with the unconventional behaviors in the dance hall. She feels depressed. The management and other hostesses console her by jokingly pointing out the intrinsic values of her work—i.e., she is helping out the "lonely men" and "unhappy husbands." If she has friends or relatives working in the same place, they will take a major role in consoling her too. This is the beginning of her exposure to the neutralization techniques.

(2) The Second and Third Weeks. During the next two weeks, the new hostess is still evaluating her job—balancing its financial benefit with its emotional cost. She is still unsure about the job. But, now she becomes exposed to more neutralization techniques as she interacts more frequently with the management and other hostesses. Besides the "claim of benefit" technique, she is also exposed to others which can be best described as "denial of injury," "denial of victim," and "denial of responsibility" techniques. By the end of the third week, she has a tendency to respond in terms of "neutralization techniques" when asked about her job. If she is recruited by friends or relatives, they may introduce her to these techniques as early as the first week.

(3) The Fourth Week and Beyond. As she enters the fourth week, the hostess is likely to have made a positive resolution about her job. It is apparent that she has neutralized much of the unpleasantness of the job, and found the balance of benefit and cost in favor of keeping the job. She is likely to have acquired the tactics of "leading her customer on," thus enabling her to secure a steady clientele. Gradually, she begins to use fewer neutralization responses, when asked about her job. Instead she begins to use more positive responses such as "I like it," "It is fun," and so on. Her new positive attitude toward

her job is also revealed in her interactions with coworkers, her pride in her customers, and her status consciousness. She shows a genuine interest and enjoyment in her work.

In view of the findings of this study, it appears that the use of justifications by workers in the semi-deviant and deviant occupations may have far greater significance than what had been previously recognized. Former studies seldom pay attention to the role justifications played in occupational socialization. This oversight may be attributed to the method of data collection used in these studies. All the former studies cited in this paper obtained their information by interviewing subjects at one point in time after they had been established in their occupations. On the other hand, we used a longitudinal approach. We interviewed and observed panels of subjects over a period of time beginning from their early days in the profession, and also cohorts of subjects representing various lengths of tenure on the job. Thus, we were able to discover that the justifications were learned, and that they were being used as neutralization techniques with the effect of facilitating commitment to the job.

In conclusion, we would like to emphasize that the use of neutralization techniques is not limited to semi-deviant and deviant occupations. For example, Friedman (1974) has observed that these techniques are also employed by workers in legitimate occupations, such as salesmen and contest interviewers. Future research, therefore, may want to look into the process of learning and the significance of neutralization techniques in other occupations, including the legitimate ones.

References

Ball, R. (1966) "An empirical exploration of neutralization theory." Criminologica 4 (August): 22–32.

Bryan, J. (1966) "Occupational ideologies and individual attitudes of call girls." Social Problems 13 (Spring): 441–450.

———. (1965) "Apprenticeships in prostitution." Social Problems 12 (Winter): 287–297.

Cressey, P. (1932) The Taxi-Dance Hall. Chicago: Univ. of Chicago Press.

Dunford, F. and P. Kunz (1973) "The neutralization of religious dissonance." Rev. of Religious Research 15 (Fall): 2–9.

Friedman, A. (1968) "The scatological rites of burglars." Western Folklore 27 (July): 171–179.

Friedman, N. (1974) "Cookies and contests: notes on ordinary occupational deviance and its neutralization." Sociological Symposium 11 (Spring): 1–9.

Hong, L. and R. Duff (1976) "Gentlemen's social club: revival of taxi-dancing in Los Angeles." J. of Popular Culture 9 (Spring): 827–832.

Lopata, H. and J. Noel (1967) "The dance studio—style without sex." Trans-Action (January/February): 10–17.

Nye, R. (1973) "Saturday night at the paradise ballroom: or, dance halls in the twenties." J. of Popular Culture 7 (Summer): 14–22.

Pittman, D. (1971) "The male house of prostitution." Trans-Action 8 (March/April): 21–27.

Priest, M. and J. McGrath III (1970) "Techniques of neutralization: young adult marijuana smokers." Criminology 8 (August): 185–194.

Riege, M. (1969) "The call girl and the dance teacher: a comparative analysis." Cornell J. of Social Relations 4 (Spring): 58–70.

Rogers, J. and M. Buffalo (1974) "Neutralization techniques." Pacific Soc. Rev. 17 (July): 313–331.

Saulutin, M. (1971) "Stripper morality." Trans-Action 9 (June): 12–27.

Sykes, G. and D. Matza (1957) "Techniques of neutralization: a theory of delinquency." Amer. Soc. Rev. 26 (December): 664–670.

Verlarde, A. and M. Warlick (1973) "Massage parlours: the sensuality business." Society 11 (November/December): 63–74.

42 / The Madam as Teacher: The Training of House Prostitutes

BARBARA SHERMAN HEYL

Although the day of the elaborate and conspicuous high-class house of prostitution is gone, houses still operate throughout the United States in a variety of altered forms. The business may be run out of trailers and motels along major highways, luxury apartments in the center of a metropolis or run-down houses in smaller, industrialized cities. (Recent discussions of various aspects of house prostitution include: Gagnon and Simon, 1973:226–7; Hall, 1973: 115–95; Heyl, 1974; Jackson, 1969:185–92; Sheehy, 1974:185–204; Stewart, 1972; and Vogliotti, 1975:25–80.) Madams sometimes find themselves teaching young women how to become professional prostitutes. This paper focuses on one madam who trains novices to work at the house level. I compare the training to Bryan's (1965) account of the apprenticeship of call girls and relate the madam's role to the social organization of house prostitution.

Bryan's study of thirty-three Los Angeles call girls is one of the earliest interactionist treatments of prostitution. His data focus on the process of entry into the occupation of call girl and permit an analysis of the structure and content of a woman's apprenticeship. He concluded that the apprenticeship of call girls is mainly directed toward developing a clientele, rather than sexual skills (1965:288, 296–7). But while Bryan notes that pimps seldom train women directly, approximately half of his field evidence in fact derives from pimp-call girl apprenticeships. Thus, in Bryan's study (as well as in subsequent work on entry into prostitution as an occupation) there is a missing set of data on the more typical female trainer-trainee relationship and on the content and process of training at other levels of the business in nonmetropolitan settings. This paper attempts to fill this gap.

I. ANN'S TURN-OUT ESTABLISHMENT

A professional prostitute, whether she works as a streetwalker, house prostitute, or call girl, can usually pick out one person in her past who "turned her out," that is, who taught her the basic techniques and rules of the prostitute's occupation.[1] For women who begin working at the house level, that person may be a pimp, another "working girl," or a madam. Most madams and managers of prostitution establishments, however, prefer not to take on novice prostitutes, and they may even have a specific policy against hiring turn-outs (see Erwin (1960:204–5) and Lewis (1942:222)). The turn-out's inexperience may cost the madam clients and money; to train the novice, on the other hand, costs her time and energy. Most madams and managers simply do not want the additional burden.

It was precisely the madam's typical disdain for turn-outs that led to the emergence of the house discussed in this paper— a house specifically devoted to training new prostitutes. The madam of this operation, whom we shall call Ann, is forty-one years old and has been in the prostitution world twenty-three years, working primarily at the house level. Ann knew that pimps who manage women at this level have difficulty placing novices in houses. After operating several houses staffed by professional prostitutes, she decided to run a school for turn-outs partly as a strategy for acquiring a continually changing staff of young women for her house. Pimps are the active recruiters of new prostitutes, and Ann found that, upon demonstrating that she could transform the pimps' new, square women into trained prostitutes easily placed in professional houses, pimps would help keep her business staffed.[2] Ann's house is a small operation in a middle-sized, industrial city (population 300,000), with a limited clientele of primarily working-class men retained as customers for ten to fifteen years and offered low rates to maintain their patronage.

Although Ann insists that every turn-out is different, her group of novices is remarkably homogeneous in some ways. Ann has turned out approximately twenty women a year over the six years while she has operated a training school. Except for one Chicano, one black and one American Indian, the women were all white. They ranged in age from eighteen to twenty seven. Until three years ago, all the women she hired had pimps. Since then, more women are independent (so-called "outlaws"), although many come to Ann sponsored by a pimp. That is, in return for being placed with Ann, the turn-out gives the pimp a percentage of her earnings for a specific length of time. At present eighty percent of the turn-outs come to Ann without a long-term commitment to a pimp. The turn-outs stay at Ann's on the average of two to three months. This is the same average length of time Bryan (1965:290) finds for the apprenticeship in his call-girl study. Ann seldom has more than two or three women in training at any one time. Most turn-outs live at the house, often just a large apartment near the older business section of the city.

II. THE CONTENT OF THE TRAINING

The data for the following analysis are of three kinds. First, tape recordings from actual training sessions with fourteen novices helped specify the structure and content of the training provided. Second, lengthy interviews with three of the novices and multiple interviews with Ann were conducted to obtain data on the training during the novice's first few days at the house before the first group training sessions were conducted and recorded by Ann. And third, visits to the house on ten occasions and observations of Ann's interaction with the novices during teaching periods extended the data on training techniques used and the relationship between madam and novice. In addition, weekly contact with Ann over a four-year period allowed repeated review of current problems and strategies in training turn-outs.

Ann's training of the novice begins soon after the woman arrives at the house. The woman first chooses an alias. Ann then asks her whether she has ever "Frenched a guy all the way," that is, whether she has brought a man to orgasm during the act of fellatio. Few of the women say they have. By admitting her lack of competence in a specialized area, the novice has permitted Ann to assume the role of teacher. Ann then launches into instruction on performing fellatio. Such instruction is important to her business. Approximately eighty percent of her customers are what Ann calls "French tricks." Many men visit prostitutes to receive sexual services, including fellatio, their wives or lovers seldom perform. This may be particularly true of the lower- and working-class clientele of the houses and hotels of prostitution (Gagnon and Simon, 1973:230). Yet the request for fellatio may come from clients at all social levels; consequently, it is a sexual skill today's prostitute must possess and one she may not have prior to entry into the business (Bryan, 1965:293; Winick and Kinsie, 1971:180, 207; Gray, 1973:413).

Although Ann devotes much more time to teaching the physical and psychological techniques of performing fellatio than she does to any other sexual skill, she also provides strategies for coitus and giving a "half and half"—fellatio followed by coitus. The sexual strategies taught are frequently a mixture of ways for stimulating the client sexually and techniques of self-protection during the sexual acts. For example, during coitus, the woman is to move her hips "like a go-go dancer's" while keeping her feet on the bed and tightening her inner thigh muscles to protect herself from the customer's thrust and full penetration. Ann allows turn-outs to perform coitus on their backs only, and the woman is taught to keep one of her arms across her chest as a measure of self-defense in this vulnerable position.

After Ann has described the rudimentary techniques for the three basic sexual acts—fellatio, coitus, and "half and half"—she begins to explain the rules of the house operation. The first set of rules concerns what acts the client may receive for specific sums of money. Time limits are imposed on the clients, roughly at the rate of $1 per minute; the minimum rate in this house is $15 for any of the three basic positions. Ann describes in detail what will occur when the first client arrives: he will be admitted by either Ann or the maid; the women are to stand and smile at him, but not speak to him (considered "dirty hustling"); he will choose one of the women and go to the bedroom with her. Ann accompanies the turn-out and the client to the bedroom and begins teaching the woman how to check the man for any cuts or open sores on the genitals and for any signs of old or active venereal disease. Ann usually rechecks each client herself during the turn-out's first two weeks of work. For the first few days Ann remains in the room while the turn-out and client negotiate the sexual contract. In ensuing days Ann spends time helping the woman develop verbal skills to "hustle" the customer for more expensive sexual activities.

The following analysis of the instruction Ann provides is based on tape recordings made by Ann during actual training sessions in 1971 and 1975. These sessions took place after the turn-outs had worked several days but usually during their first two weeks of work. The tapes contain ten hours of group discussion with fourteen different novices. The teaching tapes were analyzed according to topics covered in the discussions, using the method outlined in Barker (1963) for making such divisions in the flow of conversation and using Bryan's analysis of the call girl's apprenticeship as a guide in grouping the topics. Bryan divides the content of the training of call girls into two broad dimensions, one philosophical and one interpersonal (1965: 291–4). The first emphasizes a subcultural value system and sets down guidelines for how the novice *should* treat her clients and her colleagues in the business. The second dimension follows from the first but emphasizes actual behavioral techniques and skills.

The content analysis of the taped training sessions produced three major topics of discussion and revealed the relative amount of time Ann devoted to each. The first two most frequently discussed topics can be categorized under Bryan's dimension of interpersonal skills; they were devoted to teaching situational strategies for managing clients. The third topic resembles Bryan's value dimension (1965: 291–2).

The first topic stressed physical skills and strategies. Included in this category were instruction on how to perform certain sexual acts and specification of their prices, discussion of particular clients, and instruction in techniques for dealing with certain categories of clients, such as "older men" or "kinky" tricks. This topic of physical skills also included discussion of, and Ann's demonstration of, positions designed to provide the woman maximum comfort and protection from the man during different sexual acts. Defense tactics, such as ways to get out of a sexual position and out of the bedroom quickly, were practiced by the novices. Much time was devoted to analyzing past encounters with particular clients. Bryan finds similar discussions of individual tricks among novice call girls and their trainers (1965:293). In the case of Ann's turn-outs these discussions were often initiated by a novice's complaint or question about a certain client and his requests or behavior in the bedroom. The novice always received tips and advice from Ann and the other women present on how to manage that type of bedroom encounter. Such sharing of tactics allows the turn-out to learn what Gagnon and Simon call "patterns of client management" (1973:231).

Ann typically used these discussions of bedroom difficulties to further the training in specific sexual skills she had begun during the turn-out's first few days at work. It is possible that the addition of such follow-up sexual training to that provided during the turn-out's first days at the house results in a more extensive teaching of actual sexual skills than that obtained either by call girls or streeetwalkers. Bryan finds that in the call-girl training—except for fellatio—"There seems to be little instruction concerning sexual techniques as such, even though the previous sexual experience of the trainee may have been quite limited" (1965:293). Gray (1973:413) notes that her sample of streetwalker turn-outs were rarely taught specific work strategies:

> They learned these things by trial and error on the job. Nor were they schooled in specific sexual techniques: usually they were taught by customers who made the specific requests.

House prostitution may require more extensive sexual instruction than other forms of the business. The dissatisfied customer of a house may mean loss of business and therefore loss of income to the madam and the prostitutes who work there. The sexually inept streetwalker or call girl does not hurt business for anyone but herself; she may actually increase business for those women in the area should dissatisfied clients choose to avoid her. But the house depends on a stable clientele of satisfied customers.

The second most frequently discussed topic could be labeled: client management—verbal skills. Ann's primary concern was teaching what she calls "hustling." "Hustling" is similar to what Bryan terms a "sales pitch" for call girls (1965:292), but in the house setting it takes place in the bedroom while the client is deciding how much to spend and what sexual acts he wishes performed. "Hustling" is de-

signed to encourage the client to spend more than the minimum rate.[3]
The prominence on the teaching tapes of instruction in this verbal
skill shows its importance in Ann's training of novices.

On one of the tapes Ann uses her own turning-out experience to
explain to two novices (both with pimps) why she always teaches
hustling skills as an integral part of working in a house.

Ann as a Turn-out[4]

Ann: Of course, I can remember a time when I didn't know that I was
supposed to hustle. So that's why I understand that it's difficult to
learn to hustle. When I turned out it was $2 a throw. They came in.
They gave me their $2. They got a hell of a fuck. And that was it.
Then one Saturday night I turned *forty four* tricks! And Penny [the
madam] used to put the number of tricks at the top of the page and
the amount of money at the bottom of the page—she used these
big ledger books. Lloyd [Ann's pimp] came in at six o'clock and he
looked at that book and he just *knew* I had made all kinds of money.
Would you believe I had turned forty-two $2 tricks and two $3
tricks—because two of 'em got generous and gave me an extra
buck! [Laughs] I got my ass whipped. And I was so tired—I
thought I was going to die—I was 15 years old. And I got my ass
whipped for it. [Ann imitates an angry Lloyd:] "Don't you know
you're supposed to ask for more money?!" No, I didn't. Nobody
told me that. All they told me was it was $2. So that is learning it the
hard way. I'm trying to help you learn it the *easy* way, if there is an
easy way to do it.

In the same session Ann asks one of the turn-outs (Linda, age
eighteen) to practice her hustling rap.

Learning the Hustling Rap

Ann: I'm going to be a trick. You've checked me. I want you to carry it
from there. [Ann begins role-playing: she plays the client; Linda,
the hustler.]

Linda: [mechanically] What kind of party would like to have?

Ann: That had all the enthusiasm of a wet noodle. I really wouldn't *want*
any party with that because you evidently don't want to give me
one.

Linda: What kind of party would you *like* to have?

Ann: I usually take a half and half.

Linda: Uh, the money?

Ann: What money?

Linda: The money you're supposed to have! [loudly] 'Cause you ain't
gettin' it for free!

Ann: [upset] Linda, if you *ever*, ever say that in my joint . . . Because
         that's fine for street hustling. In street hustling, you're going to
         have to hard-hustle those guys or they're not going to come up with
         anything. Because they're going to *try* and get it for free. But when
         they walk in here, they *know* they're not going to get it for free to
         begin with. So try another tack—just a little more friendly, not
         quite so hard-nosed. [Returning to role-playing:] I just take a half
         and half.
Linda: How about fifteen [dollars]?
Ann: You're leading into the money too fast, honey. Try: "What are you
         going to spend?" or "How much money are you going to spend?"
         or something like that.
Linda: How much would you like to spend?
Ann: No! Not "like." 'Cause they don't *like* to spend anything.
Linda: How much *would* you like to spend?
Ann: Make it a very definite, positive statement: "How much are you
         going to spend?"

Ann considers teaching hustling skills her most difficult and important task. In spite of her lengthy discussion on the tapes of the rules
and techniques for dealing with the customer sexually, Ann states that
it may take only a few minutes to "show a girl how to turn a trick." A
substantially longer period is required, however, to teach her to hustle. To be adept at hustling, the woman must be mentally alert and
sensitive to the client's response to what she is saying and doing and
be able to act on those perceptions of his reactions. The hustler must
maintain a steady patter of verbal coaxing, during which her tone of
voice may be more important than her actual words.

In Ann's framework, then, hustling is a form of verbal sexual aggression. Referring to the problems in teaching novices to hustle, Ann
notes that "taking the aggressive part is something women are not
used to doing; particularly young women." No doubt, hustling is
difficult to teach partly because the woman must learn to discuss
sexual acts, whereas in her previous experience, sexual behavior and
preferences had been negotiated nonverbally (see Gagnon and Simon, 1973:228). Ann feels that to be effective, each woman's "hustling
rap" must be her own—one that comes naturally and will strike the
clients as sincere. All of that takes practice. But Ann is aware that the
difficulty in learning to hustle stems more from the fact that it involved
inappropriate sex-role behavior. Bryan concludes that it is precisely
this aspect of soliciting men on the telephone that causes the greatest
distress to the novice call girl (1965:293). Thus, the call girl's income
is affected by how much business she can bring in by her calls, that is,
by how well she can learn to be socially aggressive on the telephone.
The income of the house prostitute, in turn, depends heavily on her
hustling skills in the bedroom. Ann's task, then, is to train the novice,

who has recently come from a culture where young women are not expected to be sexually aggressive, to assume that role with a persuasive naturalness.

Following the first two major topics—client management through physical and verbal skills—the teaching of "racket" (prostitution world) values was the third-ranking topic of training and discussion on the teaching tapes. Bryan notes that the major value taught to call girls is "that of maximizing gains and minimizing effort, even if this requires transgressions of either a legal or moral nature" (1965:291). In her training, however, Ann avoids communicating the notion that the novices may exploit the customers in any way they can. For example, stealing or cheating clients is grounds for dismissal from the house. Ann cannot afford the reputation among her tricks that they risk being robbed when they visit her. Moreover, being honest with clients is extolled as a virtue. Thus, Ann urges the novices to tell the trick if she is nervous or unsure, to let him know she is new to the business. This is in direct contradiction to the advice pimps usually give their new women to hide their inexperience from the trick. Ann asserts that honesty in this case usually means that the client will be more tolerant of mistakes in sexual technique, be less likely to interpret hesitancy as coldness, and be generally more helpful and sympathetic. Putting her "basic principle" in the form of a simple directive, Ann declares: "Please the trick, but at the same time get as much money for pleasing him as you possibly can." Ann does not consider hustling to be client exploitation. It is simply the attempt to sell the customer the product with the highest profit margin. That is, she would defend hustling in terms familiar to the businessman or sales manager.

That Ann teaches hustling as a value is revealed in the following discussion between Ann and Sandy—a former hustler and long-time friend of Ann. Sandy, who married a former trick and still lives in town, has come over to the house to help instruct several novices in the hustling business.

Whores, Prostitutes and Hustlers

Ann: [To the turn-outs:] Don't get up-tight that you're hesitating or you're fumbling, within the first week or even the first five years. Because it takes that long to become a good hustler. I mean you can be a whore in one night. There's nothing to that. The first time you take money you're a whore.

Sandy: This girl in Midtown [a small, Midwestern city] informed me—I had been working there awhile—that I was a "whore" and she was a "prostitute." And I said: "Now what the hell does that mean?" Well the difference was that a prostitute could pick her customer and a whore had to take anybody. I said: "Well honey, I want to tell you something. I'm neither one." She said: "Well, you *work*." I said: "I know, but I'm a *hustler*. I make *money* for what I do."

Ann: And this is what I turn out—or try to turn out—hustlers. Not prostitutes. Not whores. But hustlers.

For Ann and Sandy the hustler deserves high status in the prostitution business because she has mastered a specific set of skills that, even with many repeat clients, earn her premiums above the going rate for sexual acts.

In the ideological training of call girls Bryan finds that "values such as fairness with other working girls, or fidelity to a pimp, may occasionally be taught" (1965:291–2); the teaching tapes revealed Ann's affirmation of both these virtues. When a pimp brings a woman to Ann, she supports his control over that woman. For example, if during her stay at the house, the novice breaks any of the basic rules—by using drugs, holding back money (from either Ann or the pimp), lying or seeing another man—Ann will report the infractions to the woman's pimp. Ann notes: "If I don't do that and the pimp finds out, he knows I'm not training her right, and he won't bring his future ladies to me for training." Ann knows she is dependent on the pimps to help supply her with turn-outs. Bryan, likewise, finds a willingness among call-girls' trainers to defer to the pimps' wishes during the apprenticeship period (1965:290).

Teaching fairness to other prostitutes is particularly relevant to the madam who daily faces the problem of maintaining peace among competing women at work under one roof. If two streetwalkers or two call girls find they cannot get along, they need not work near one another. But if a woman leaves a house because of personal conflicts, the madam loses a source of income. To minimize potential negative feelings among novices, Ann stresses mutual support, prohibits "criticizing another girl," and denigrates the "prima donna"—the prostitute who flaunts her financial success before the other women.

In still another strategy to encourage fair treatment of one's colleagues in the establishment, Ann emphasizes a set of rules prohibiting "dirty hustling"—behavior engaged in by one prostitute that would undercut the business of other women in the house. Tabooed under the label of "dirty hustling" are the following: appearing in the line-up partially unclothed; performing certain disapproved sexual positions, such as anal intercourse; and allowing approved sexual extras without charging additional fees. The norms governing acceptable behavior vary from house to house and region to region, and Ann warns the turn-outs to ask about such rules when they begin work in a new establishment. The woman who breaks the work norms in a house, either knowingly or unknowingly, will draw the anger of the other women and can be fired by a madam eager to restore peace and order in the house.

Other topics considered on the tapes—in addition to physical skills, "hustling" and work values—were instruction on personal hygiene and grooming, role-playing of conversational skills with tricks on topics not related to sex or hustling ("living room talk"), house rules not related to hustling (such as punctuality, no perfume, no drugs), and guidelines for what to do during an arrest. There were specific suggestions on how to handle personal criticism, questions and insults from clients. In addition, the discussions on the tapes provided the novices with many general strategies for becoming "professionals" at their work, for example, the importance of personal style, enthusiasm ("the customer is always right"), and sense of humor. In some ways these guidelines resemble a beginning course in salesmanship. But they also provide clues, particularly in combination with the topics on handling client insults and the emphasis on hustling, on how the house prostitute learns to manage a stable and limited clientele and cope psychologically with the repetition of the clients and the sheer tedium of the physical work (Hughes, 1971:342–5).

III. TRAINING HOUSE PROSTITUTES—A PROCESS OF PROFESSIONAL SOCIALIZATION

Observing how Ann trains turn-outs is a study in techniques to facilitate identity change (see also Davis, 1971 and Heyl, 1975, chapter 2). Ann uses a variety of persuasive strategies to help give the turn-outs a new occupational identity as a "professional." One strategy is to rely heavily on the new values taught the novice to isolate her from her previous life style and acquaintances. Bryan finds that "the value structure [taught to novice call girls] serves, in general, to create in-group solidarity and to alienate the girl from 'square' society" (1965:292). Whereas alienation from conventional society may be an indirect effect of values taught to call girls, in Ann's training of house prostitutes the expectation that the novice will immerse herself in the prostitution world ("racket life") is made dramatically explicit.

In the following transcription from one of the teaching tapes, the participants are Ann (age thirty-six at the time the tape was made), Bonnie (an experienced turn-out, age twenty-five) and Kristy (a new turn-out, age eighteen). Kristy has recently linked up with a pimp for the first time and volunteers to Ann and Bonnie her difficulty in adjusting to the racket rule of minimal contact with the square world—a rule her pimp is enforcing by not allowing Kristy to meet and talk with her old friends. Ann (A) and Bonnie (B) have listened to Kristy's (K) complaints and are making suggestions. (The notation 'B-K' indicates that Bonnie is addressing Kristy.)

Kristy's Isolation from the Square World

B-K: What you gotta do is sit down and talk to him and weed out your friends and find the ones he thinks are suitable companions for you—in your new type of life.

K-B: None of them.

A-K: What about *his* friends?

K-A: I haven't met very many of his friends. I don't like any of 'em so far.

A-K: You are making the same mistake that makes me so goddamned irritated with square broads! You're taking a man and trying to train *him*, instead of letting the man train you.

K-A: What?! I'm not trying to train him, I'm just. . . .

A-K: All right, you're trying to force him to accept your friends.

K-A: I don't care whether he accepts them or not. I just can't go around not talking to anybody.

A-K: "Anybody" is your old man! He is your world. And the people he says you can talk to are the people that are your world. But what you're trying to do is force your square world on a racket guy. It's like oil and water. There's just no way a square and a racket person can get together. That's why when you turn out you've got to change your mind completely from square to racket. And you're still trying to hang with squares. You can't do it.

Strauss' (1969) concept of "coaching" illuminates a more subtle technique Ann employs as she helps the novice along, step by step, from "square" to "racket" values and life style. She observes carefully how the novice progresses, elicits responses from her about what she is experiencing, and then interprets those responses for her. In the following excerpt from one of the teaching tapes, Ann prepares two novices for feelings of depression over their newly-made decisions to become prostitutes.

Turn-out Blues

Ann: And while I'm on the subject—depression. You know they've got a word for it when you have a baby—it's called "postpartum blues." Now, I call it "turn-out blues." Every girl that ever turns out has 'em. And, depending on the girl, it comes about the third or fourth day. You'll go into a depression for no apparent reason. You'll wake up one morning and you'll say: "Why in the hell am I doing this? Why am I here? I wanna go home!" And I can't do a thing to help you. The only thing I can do is leave you alone and hope that you'll fight the battle yourself. But knowing that it will come and knowing that everybody else goes through it too, does help. Just pray it's a busy night! So if you get blue and you get down, remember: "turn-out blues"—everybody gets it. Here's when you'll decide whether you're going to stay or you're gonna quit.

Ann's description of "turn-out blues" is a good example of Strauss' account (1969:111–2) of how coaches will use prophecy to increase their persuasive power over their novices. In the case of "turn-out blues," the novice, if she becomes depressed about her decision to enter prostitution, will recall Ann's prediction that this would happen and that it happens to all turn-outs. This recollection may or may not end the woman's misgivings about her decision, but it will surely enhance the turn-out's impression of Ann's competence. Ann's use of her past experience to make such predictions is a form of positive leverage; it increases the probability that what she says will be respected and followed in the future.

In Bryan's study the call girls reported that their training was more a matter of observation than direct instruction from their trainer (1965:294). Ann, on the other hand, relies on a variety of teaching techniques, including lecturing and discussion involving other turn-outs who are further along in the training process and can reinforce Ann's views. Ann even brings in guest speakers, such as Sandy, the former hustler, who participates in the discussion with the novices in the role of the experienced resource person. "Learning the Hustling Rap," above, offers an example of role-playing—another teaching technique Ann frequently employs to help the turn-outs develop verbal skills. Ann may have to rely on more varied teaching approaches than the call-girl trainer because: (1) Ann herself is not working, thus her novices have fewer opportunities to watch their trainer interact with clients than do the call-girl novices; and (2) Ann's livelihood depends more directly on the success of her teaching efforts than does that of the call-girl trainer. Ann feels that if a woman under her direction does not "turn out well," not only will the woman earn less money while she is at her house (affecting Ann's own income), but Ann could also lose clients and future turn-outs from her teaching "failure."[5]

The dissolution of the training relationship marks the end of the course. Bryan claims that the sharp break between trainer and trainee shows that the training process itself is largely unrelated to the acquisition of a skill. But one would scarcely have expected the trainee to report "that the final disruption of the apprenticeship was the result of the completion of adequate training" (1965:296). Such establishments do not offer diplomas and terminal degrees. The present study, too, indicates that abrupt breaks in the training relationship are quite common. But what is significant is that the break is precipitated by personal conflicts exacerbated by both the narrowing of the skill-gap between trainer and trainee and the consequent increase in the novice's confidence that she can make it on her own. Thus, skill acquisition counts in such an equation, not in a formal sense ("completion of adequate training"), but rather in so far as it works to break down the earlier bonds of dependence between trainer and trainee.

IV. THE FUNCTION OF TRAINING AT THE HOUSE LEVEL OF PROSTITUTION

Bryan concludes that the training is necessitated by the novice's need for a list of clients in order to work at the call-girl level and not because the actual training is required to prepare her for such work. But turn-outs at the house level of prostitution do not acquire a clientele. The clients are customers of the house. In fact, the madam usually makes sure that only she has the names or phone numbers of her tricks in order to keep control over her business. If Ann's turn-outs (unlike call girls) do not acquire a clientele in the course of their training, why is the training period necessary?

Although Ann feels strongly that training is required to become a successful hustler at the house level, the function served by the training can be seen more as a spin-off of the structure of the occupation at that level: madams of establishments will often hire only trained prostitutes. Novices who pose as experienced hustlers are fairly easily detected by those proficient in the business working in the same house; to be found out all she need do is violate any of the expected norms of behavior: wear perfume, repeatedly fail to hustle any "over-money" or engage in dirty hustling. The exposure to racket values, which the training provides, may be more critical to the house prostitute than to the call girl. She must live and work in close contact with others in the business. Participants in house prostitution are more integrated into the prostitution world than are call girls, who can be and frequently are "independent"—working without close ties to pimps or other prostitutes. Becoming skilled in hustling is also less important for the call girl, as her minimum fee is usually high, making hustling for small increments less necessary. The house prostitute who does not know how to ask for more money, however, lowers the madam's income as well—another reason why madams prefer professional prostitutes.

The training of house prostitutes, then, reflects two problems in the social organization of house prostitution: (1) most madams will not hire untrained prostitutes; and (2) the close interaction of prostitutes operating within the confines of a house requires a common set of work standards and practices. These two factors differentiate house prostitution from call-girl and streetwalking operations and facilitate this madam's task of turning novices into professional prostitutes. The teaching madam employs a variety of coaching techniques to train turn-outs in sexual and hustling skills and to expose them to a set of occupational rules and values. Hers is an effort to prepare women with conventional backgrounds for work in the social environment of a house of prostitution where those skills and values are expected and necessary.

References

Becker, Howard S.
  1970 Sociological Work. Chicago: Aldine.
Barker, Roger G. (ed.)
  1963 The Stream of Behavior: Explorations of its Structure and Content. New York: Appleton-Century-Crofts.
Bryan, James H.
  1965 "Apprenticeships in prostitution." Social Problems 12 (Winter): 287–97.
  1966 "Occupational ideologies and individual attitudes of call girls." Social Problems 13 (Spring): 441–50.
Davis, Nanette J.
  1971 "The prostitute: Developing a deviant identity." Pp. 297–332 in James M. Henslin (ed.), Studies in the Sociology of Sex. New York: Appleton-Century-Crofts.
Erwin, Carol
  1960 The Orderly Disorderly House. Garden City, N.Y.: Doubleday.
Faulkner, Robert R.
  1974 "Coming of age in organizations: A comparative study of career contingencies and adult socialization." Sociology of Work and Occupations 1 (May): 131–73.
Gagnon, John H. and William Simon
  1973 Sexual Conduct: The Social Sources of Human Sexuality. Chicago: Aldine.
Gray, Diana
  1973 "Turning-out: A study of teenage prostitution." Urban Life and Culture 1 (January): 401–25.
Hall, Susan
  1973 Ladies of the Night. New York: Trident Press.
Heyl, Barbara S.
  1974 "The madam as entrepreneur." Sociological Symposium 11 (Spring): 61–82.
  1975 "The house prostitute: a case study." Unpublished Ph.D. dissertation, Department of Sociology, University of Illinois-Urbana.
Hughes, Everett C.
  1971 "Work and self." Pp. 338–47 in The Sociological Eye: Selected Papers. Chicago: Aldine-Atherton.
Jackson, Bruce
  1969 A Thief's Primer. Toronto, Ontario: Macmillan.

Kinsey, Alfred C., Wardell B. Pomeroy and Clyde E. Martin
   1948 Sexual Behavior in the Human Male. Philadelphia: W.B. Saunders.
Lewis, Gladys Adelina (ed.)
   1942 Call House Madam: The Story of the Career of Beverly Davis. San
      Francisco: Martin Tudordale.
Polsky, Ned.
   1969 Hustlers, Beats and Others. Garden City, N.Y.: Doubleday.
Ross, H. Laurence
   1959 "The 'Hustler' in Chicago." Journal of Student Research 1: 13–19.
Sheehy, Gail
   1974 Hustling: Prostitution in Our Wide-Open Society. New York: Dell.
Stewart, George I.
   1972 "On first being a john." Urban Life and Culture 1 (October): 255–74.
Strauss, Anselm L.
   1969 Mirrors and Masks: The Search for Identity. San Francisco: Sociology
      Press.
Vogliotti, Gabriel R.
   1975 The Girls of Nevada. Secaucus, New Jersey: Citadel Press.
Winick, Charles and Paul M. Kinsie
   1971 The Lively Commerce: Prostitution in the United States. Chicago:
      Quadrangle Books.

Notes

1. This situation-specific induction into prostitution may be contrasted with the "smooth and almost imperceptible" transition to the status of poolroom "hustler" noted by Polsky (1969:80–1).

2. In the wider context of the national prostitution scene, Ann's situation reflects the "minor league" status of her geographical location. In fact, she trains women from other communities who move on to the more lucrative opportunities in the big city. See the stimulating applications of the concept of "minor league" to the study of occupations in Faulkner (1974).

3. The term "hustling" has been used to describe a wide range of small-time criminal activities. Even within the world of prostitution, "hustling" can refer to different occupational styles; see Ross' description of the "hustler" who "is distinguished from ordinary prostitutes in frequently engaging in accessory crimes of exploitation," such as extortion or robbery (1959:16). The use of the term here is thus highly specific, reflecting its meaning in Ann's world.

4. The indented sections (for example, "Ann as a Turn-out" and "Learning the Hustling Rap") are transcriptions from the teaching tapes. Redundant expressions have been omitted, and the author's comments on the speech tone or delivery are bracketed. Words underlined indicate emphasis by the speaker.

5. These data bear only on the skills and values to which Ann *exposes* the turn-outs; confirmation of the effects of such exposure awaits further analysis and is a study in its own right. See Bryan's (1966) study of the impact of the occupational perspective taught by call-girl trainers on the individual attitudes of call girls. See Davis (1971:315) for a description of what constitutes successful "in-service training" for streetwalkers.

43 / Women and the Commission of Crime: A Theoretical Approach

CAROL A. WHITEHURST

Because theories of deviant behavior have generally ignored women's crime, they have been considered theories less of deviant behavior than of male deviant behavior.[1] This oversight, which
illustrates the larger problem of the invisibility of women in much of
social science, underscores the need for a feminist analysis of crime
not based on the white, middle-class male model (see Smith, 1974;
Daniels, 1975; Millman and Kanter, 1975). Very few theorists have
asked why women commit (or don't commit) crimes; those who have
posed this question have often based their answers on biological or
psychological assumptions, offering little or no evidence to support
their contentions. An often-cited example is Otto Pollack's argument
that women actually commit as much crime as men, but are addicted
to crimes that are easily concealed and seldom reported (Pollack,
1950).

This paper will explore how sociological theories of deviance can
help explain women's commission of crime in light of two important
facts: (1) women's reported crime always has represented only a
small proportion of men's reported crime, and (2) the proportion of
total reported crimes committed by women has increased considerably since about 1960.

WOMEN'S CRIME AS A PROPORTION OF MEN'S CRIME

In 1980, men accounted for over 80 percent of all arrests for serious
crimes.[2] However, for total violent crimes,[3] the proportions were 90
percent male, and 10 percent female. For property crimes,[4] the proportions were 78.5 percent male and 21.5 percent female. The
crimes women were most likely to commit (other than prostitution)
relative to men, were fraud, forgery and counterfeiting, larceny-
theft, and embezzlement. Those crimes that women were least likely
to commit (other than rape) relative to men, were burglary, weapons

614

Table 1 / Women's Arrests as Percentages of All Crimes in Three
Categories, 1955–1980

	Serious Crimes	Violent Crimes	Property Crimes
1955	9.12	12.03	8.36
1960	10.95	11.77	10.76
1965	14.37	11.41	14.99
1970	18.04	10.50	19.71
1980	19.10	10.00	21.50

Source: Adapted from Uniform Crime Reports (Washington D.C.: Federal Bureau of
   Investigation, U.S. Department of Justice, 1980), Table 27; and from Eileen B.
   Leonard, Women, Crime and Society (New York: Longman, 1982), p. 27.

carrying and possession, robbery, sex offenses other than prostitution, vandalism, and motor vehicle theft.

THE INCREASE IN WOMEN'S CRIME SINCE 1960

Between 1960 and 1972, total female arrests increased far more than
male. According to the F.B.I's Uniform Crime Reports (UCR), there
was a 159.4 percent increase in male commission of robbery, and a
277.2 percent increase for females; for larceny, there was an 82.3
percent increase for males and a 303.2 percent increase for females.
Overall, male property crimes increased 71.9 percent while female
rates increased 281.5 percent. However, because women start from a
much smaller base, these statistics are misleading. It is more useful to
examine the increase in the proportion of total arrests. Table 1 shows
the increases from 1955 through 1980.

While total serious crimes increased, this was accounted for entirely by an increase in property rather than violent crimes, mostly occurring during the 1960s and early 1970s. Increases have been greater for juvenile girls than for adult women, and self-report studies indicate that differences in crime commission for juveniles are smaller
than arrest figures indicate (Cernkovich and Giordano, 1979; Hindelang, 1973).

ACCURACY OF FIGURES

The UCR figures represent only arrests, not actual commission of
crime. Since actual crimes represent many times the number of arrests, these figures represent reactions to crime, not crime itself. The
UCR figures are limited in a number of other ways: data provided by
law enforcement agencies are voluntary and therefore not necessari-

ly representative (Chapman, 1980: 58–59); many categories of crime, such as the majority of corporate crimes, are not included at all; figures are affected by demographic changes, such as the baby-boomers reaching the peak "at risk" years during the 1960s and 1970s, when crime rates rose the fastest; and figures are affected by changes in definitions and statutes in the criminal justice and police systems.

As examples of the last point, Chapman (1980) points out that arrest rates are affected by changed definitions of crime. Defining narcotics use as a crime and classifying female drug users as criminals contribute to a "female crime wave." After 1972 the $50 minimum for larceny was eliminated; this change contributed to much higher rates of larceny. Some crimes committed frequently by women, such as welfare fraud and shoplifting, have become more vigorously prosecuted (Chapman, 1980; Steffensmeier, 1980). Finally, as Feinman (1980) points out, the period of fastest increases in rates of crime for (primarily young) women was also the period when substantial numbers of "at risk" men were being sent to Vietnam. This factor increased the proportion of women offenders relative to men. As Chapman has said, trends in female criminality "may reflect greater changes in reporting, arrest, prosecution, and sentencing than in actual behavior" (1980:28).

It may be that female crime or arrest rates are more accurate now than in the past because of improved collection methods and a decline in "chivalry," or preferential treatment for women. The "chivalry" argument is that the perception of women as less aggressive and less likely to break the law has benefited women. Police didn't like to arrest women; judges, prosecutors, and juries didn't like to convict them; and women were less likely than men to be sent to prison if convicted (Simon, 1979). While there is some truth to this argument, actually only certain women have benefited from "chivalry" for some crimes. For crimes considered "unacceptable" for women (e.g., violent crimes and crimes of "sexual misconduct"), treatment has often been harsher for women (Chapman, 1980; Jones, 1980). In addition, it is only middle- and upper-class women, the least likely to come into contact with the criminal justice system, who have benefited from preferential treatment (Klein, 1976). As Feinman (1980) points out, the lower-class woman has never been accorded the "Madonna" aspect of the Madonna-whore duality.

Far more black and minority poor women than middle-class white women are arrested, and a majority of institutionalized women are from racial minorities, are poor, and are convicted of nonviolent crimes (Babcock, 1973). The typical American female criminal is young, black, and poor; has limited education and skills; is the head of a household and a mother; and is imprisoned most often for larceny or a drug offense (Chapman, 1980:60; Glick and Neto, 1977). Preferential treatment actually seems to be accorded more on the basis of class and race than on the basis of gender.

It may also be that chivalry is becoming a thing of the past. Most current studies tend to support the idea of a changing attitude within the criminal justice system, usually depending on the offense and the age of the offender. Crites's (1976) analysis of California data found evenhanded treatment for women and men in court, and Simon (1975) found similar proportions of women and men convicted in court. Kramer and Kempinen (1978) reported that the slight preferential treatment they found in 1970 had disappeared by 1975. They also found lighter sentences for women in 1970 and 1975, but smaller sex differences in 1975. The researchers felt that this was not necessarily because of a decline in chivalry, but was partly because of courts' increasing reluctance to prosecute on anything other than legal grounds or sentencing guidelines, which they attributed to the civil rights movement. Less frequent sentencing may also reflect lesser seriousness of the offenses.

Although arrest data are less clear, there are some indications that "Law enforcement agencies, responding to increased pressure from victims, are taking a more aggressive role in arresting women offenders" (Feinman, 1980:17; see also Steffensmeier, 1980). In another study, the decision of police to arrest was found to be influenced by demeanor and type of offense, not the sex of the offender (Moyer and White, 1979). Ward et al. (1980) found that 80 percent of women charged in robberies were accessories or partners, and more recent studies tend to reach similar conclusions (Klein and Kress, 1976; Simon, 1979). Studies conducted by the Federal Bureau of Prisons in 1973–1975 concluded that most women prisoners had been convicted for drug offenses, larceny-theft, and forgery—crimes that were, for the most part, fairly minor (Feinman, 1980:27).

Steffensmeier (1980) argues that women's crime rates have increased for a number of reasons, including greater likelihood that female suspects would be reported, greater suspicion and surveillance, increased pressure for equal application of the law, and a trend toward greater professionalism and universalistic standards among police. Steffensmeier also points out that crackdowns on welfare fraud and a trend toward computerized record-keeping and improved methods of detecting fraud recidivists would tend to increase female relative to male arrests for fraud.

Self-report data show smaller gaps between female and male crime than do official arrest records, which would tend to indicate some continuing tendency toward preferential treatment for some women for some crimes. However, the gap is smaller for juveniles, blacks, and lesser offenses (Cernkovich and Giordano, 1979; Hindelang, 1973; Shover et al., 1979; Smith, 1979; Smith and Visher, 1980).

Thus, most studies would suggest that males continue to commit more crimes, especially serious ones, than do females; that the gap between females and males is smaller than is indicated by arrest rates; and that women's and girls' arrest rates are increasingly reflecting their actual commission of crime.

ETIOLOGY OF CRIME

Since the vast majority of women's reported crimes are property crimes, current researchers tend to conclude that women's crime is largely economically motivated. Rans (1975) found some general correlation between economic need and crime, and found that historically higher crime rates for women have been associated with inflation, unemployment, and greater family responsibilities. U.S. prison admissions for women peaked from 1931 to 1935 (during the depths of the Depression), from 1961 to 1963 (a period of economic recession), and during the 1970s (a period of instability in the economy with rising unemployment) (Chapman, 1980:63). Crime may be seen as an economic alternative for some poor women (Klein, 1976). Steffensmeier (1980) sees the large increases in arrests of women for larceny-theft as resulting from marketing consumption trends and the worsening economic position of many women in the United States; this author points out that women are increasingly required to support themselves and others and that poverty is increasingly a female problem. Feinman (1980:20) explains that women's economic situation has deteriorated since 1960—the gap in earnings has increased, more women are poor heads of households, and more women lost their jobs first in the recession of 1974–1975.

Widom and Stewart (1977) concluded that in cross-national comparisons, higher female arrest rates were associated with lower levels of economic differentiation by sex (e.g., equal pay laws), but lower female arrest rates were associated with female involvement in the labor force, college education, and having female legislators. Widom and Stewart concluded, "it is possible that [legal] equality without actual equality is related to high female crime rates, while a combination of legal and actual equality is related to lower female crime rates." Thus, if the increases in crime rates for women reflect actual changes in behavior, they indicate that more women are poor, single, and heads of households.

While it has been argued that women's expanding work opportunities would result in more white-collar crime because of greater opportunity to commit such crimes (Simon, 1975), there seems to be little support for this idea. The crimes that have increased substantially for women are larceny-theft, primarily shoplifting (Steffensmeier, 1978, estimated that 70–80 percent of female larceny arrests were for shoplifting), and fraud/embezzlement, which reflects largely welfare[5] and credit card fraud, the passing of bad checks, and lower-echelon embezzlement (Glick and Neto, 1977; Steffensmeier, 1978, 1980). It has been estimated that only about 1 percent of embezzlement cases are prosecuted in criminal courts, and these mainly are those at lower levels (Feinman, 1980:363). Feinman concluded that some of the increases in embezzlement during the 1960s and 1970s may have occurred because greater numbers of women were bank tellers, cashiers, payroll clerks, and so on. There is little evidence that lucrative white-collar crimes committed by females have increased. As Norland and Shover (1977) have observed, no clear-cut pattern of change in women's criminality is yet observable. (See also Bruck, 1975; Klein and Kress, 1976; Rans, 1975; Simon, 1979; Steffensmeier, 1978; Weis, 1976.)

It has also been argued that the increasing freedom of women and their increased aggressiveness would result in higher rates of violent crime (Adler, 1975). Adler attributed this not to the women's movement per se, but to the fact that women were smarter, were shrewder, and had bigger ideas. She argued that lessened restrictions and sex role expectations for women, along with increased demands for assertiveness and more varied opportunities, would loosen social control and allow women's behavior to become like that of men. This argument assumes that women's roles, expectations, and socialization have been rapidly approaching equality with those of men, which is certainly debatable (see Baldwin, 1983; Leonard, 1982), and that female liberation equates with norm-violating, aggressive behavior. However, it is not violent crime that has increased for women relative to men. Walter Miller (1973) found little or no support for the claim that female criminality, in general or in connection with gang activity, was either more prevalent or more violent than in the past. Judges and attorneys interviewed by Rita Simon in 1975 reported that the women they were seeing were no different from those they had seen five to six years earlier (Simon, 1979).

Simon (1975) had suggested that women might actually commit less violent crime because of reduced frustration over their roles. She argued that as women's employment and educational opportunities expand, their feelings of being victimized and exploited decrease and their motivation to kill becomes muted (Simon, 1977). However, as Steffensmeier (1980) points out, female violence has neither declined relative to male violence, as Simon predicted, nor increased faster, as Adler predicted.

THE WOMEN'S MOVEMENT

There are several major difficulties in suggesting that the women's movement has led to an increase in female crime, in part because it is not a variable than can be operationalized (see Campbell, 1981:236). Secondly, if the women's movement were to blame, the greatest increases in female crime should have occurred in the past ten or twelve years (since about 1970), while actually the greatest changes occurred during the 1960s and have recently leveled off (Bartel, 1979; Gora, 1979; Steffensmeier and Steffensmeier, 1980). Specific aspects of the women's movement are not much more successful as explanations for the rise in female crime. Greater female participation in the labor force has mostly benefited white middle-class adult women, whereas the typical offender is poor, from a minority group, and young. Bartel (1979) found that increased labor force participation was negatively related to female crime.

The largest increases in the commission of crimes from 1960 to 1975 were among women under age eighteen who were mostly not in the labor force (Chapman, 1980:52). Opportunities have improved little for women, especially for women whose offenses are reflected in the statistics. If most women's crimes are committed out of economic need, greater opportunities could reduce rather than increase crime. On the other hand, if women's occupational opportunities at upper levels actually expand substantially, there could be an increase in this type of crime, although not necessarily, because of women's "vastly different historical, social, and economic experiences" (Leonard, 1982: 182).

The "masculination" or increased aggressiveness of women because of the women's movement is not supported as a cause of crime because women's crimes are not violent but are still considered to be extensions of the traditional female role (Chapman, 1980; Crites, 1976; Klein and Kress, 1976; Smart, 1976; Steffensmeier, 1978; Weis, 1976). Further, there is little or no evidence that the women's movement has had any substantial effect on socialization practices (Baldwin, 1983). Finally, there is no support for the idea that feminist ideology or pro-feminist attitudes are related to female crime. Adler (1975) found many female offenders vocally opposed any association with the women's movement, and came from lower strata that traditionally recognize male domination and superiority. Widom (1979) found that female offenders were significantly less pro-feminist than non-offenders, and James and Thornton (1980) found that girls' positive attitudes toward feminism had little influence on their delinquent involvement; any effect at all was negative. Jones (1980:320) found that battered women who killed their husbands either ignored or opposed feminism. Giordano and Cernkovich (1979) found little or no association between liberated attitudes and self-reported delinquency in girls, and Bruck (1975) reported meeting no women offenders who felt any association with the women's movement or feminism at the time of their crimes.

Female college students reporting fewer nonviolent offenses were slightly more likely to subscribe to feminist ideology than those who reported more such offenses, and self-perceived "masculinity" in girls was moderately related to "fun crimes" (e.g., joyriding), but negatively related to feminism (Eve and Edmonds, 1978). Leventhal (1977) found that incarcerated women were more likely than female college students to support traditional female roles, and they had less positive attitudes toward the women's movement and feminism. Women's crime has risen in many countries where the women's movement has made no progress at all (Widom and Stewart, 1977). Steffensmeier (1980:1098) concluded, "The movement appears to have had a greater impact on changing the image of the female offender than [on] the types of criminal offenses that she is likely to commit." Available data indicate no connection between female crime and feminism, and any recognition of women's changed capacities or needs seems to have no political or ideological content (Adler, 1975).

It would seem to be more useful to argue that changes in female crime and the emergence of the women's movement both express larger social and economic changes. Datesman and Scarpitti (1980:3) argue that the women's movement cannot be seen as a direct cause of female crime, although it may have contributed to changes in how women are handled in the criminal justice system. These researchers also point out that women may now be more likely to adopt the "male" role as supporters of themselves and their children. However, the ideology of the women's movement itself is unrelated or negatively related to female crime. Until recently there has been little attempt to try systematically to explain women's deviance from the standpoint of established theories of deviant behavior. However, as others have recently pointed out (Crites, 1976; Leonard, 1982), some insights from these theories may help to develop a broader theoretical approach to male and female deviance.

THEORIES

Anomie theory, as developed by Merton (1938), seems to suggest that if goals are held out equally to men and women, then women should experience greater discrepancies and be more norm-violating (Harris, 1977). However, if we assume that women have not been socialized into the same goals of occupational and material success, then women may experience less means-ends discrepancy and thus less deviance (Campbell, 1981:69; Harry and Sengstock, 1977; Leonard, 1982; Steffensmeier, 1978). However, as women's goals shift from finding a husband and having children toward occupational and economic goals, crimes to achieve these should also increase, unless legal means for achieving them increase accordingly (Campbell, 1981:77–79; Datesman et al., 1975; Harry and Sengstock, 1977; Sandhu and Allen, 1969).

Subcultural, social role, social learning, socialization and differential association theories have in common the idea that females and males have fundamentally different subcultures and learn different values, expectations, aspirations and roles through a process of socialization in groups. Leonard (1982:137) suggests that violence, strength, and toughness are not avenues of status for girls, and Morris (1964) found that girls experienced a relative absence of subcultural supports for and more stringent disapproval of delinquency. Because of differential socialization, girls have been found to be more conformist (Bardwick and Douvan, 1971; Maccoby and Jacklin, 1980; Thomas and Weigart, 1971), to have fewer skills necessary for criminal activity (Hoffman-Bustamente, 1973), to be more obedient and nonaggressive (Block, 1978; Lewis, 1972), and to receive an excess of definitions unfavorable to crime (Jensen, 1972). Girls also spend less time in groups and on the streets, and have fewer friends supportive of delinquent behavior (Campbell, 1981:64; Giordano, 1978; James and Thornton, 1980; Jensen and Eve, 1976; Simons et al., 1980). Thus, the low incidence of female crime and crimes typical of women can partly been seen as representing female subcultural values and role expectations (Crites, 1976; Heidensohn, 1968; Klein, 1976; Leonard, 1982; Morris, 1964; Rosenblum, 1975; Shover et al., 1979).

Social control or bonding theories suggest that parental supervision and control are negatively related to delinquency, and that girls tend to be more controlled and bonded than boys (Sutherland and Cressey, 1974: 130; Thomas and Weigart, 1971). Girls who are less bonded to parents or who perceive little benefit from adherence to conventional norms are somewhat more likely to violate norms (Andrew, 1976; Campbell, 1981: 80; James and Thornton, 1980; Jensen and Eve, 1976; McCord, 1979; Shover et al., 1979; Simons et al., 1980; Smith, 1979).

Labeling or societal reaction theory suggests that those most likely to be labeled are those with the least power to resist. This viewpoint overlooks the effects of positive labeling, which has benefited non-poor white women, thus modifying rather than amplifying female deviance (Campbell, 1981:81; Heidensohn, 1968; Thorsell and

Klemke, 1979). However, societal reaction to women can change with a change in women's image, and this new attitude toward women's potential for crime and violence can further be reflected in higher female crime rates (Jones, 1980; Leonard, 1982:85).

Conflict theories and radical criminology have been criticized for their failure to deal adequately with the position of women (Klein and Kress, 1976), but Campbell (1981:73) describes how radical criminologists have analyzed delinquency among youth subcultures in terms of the fads and fashions of their social strata. Girls preoccupied with appearance are particularly susceptible to the demands for consumption, which may lead to the typical female crime of shoplifting. Conflict approaches could develop a structural context in which the interaction of class, race, and sex roles could be analyzed to understand crime.

Although theories of deviant behavior have not generally been applied to women, they can be useful in understanding both the traditional patterns and recent changes in women's crime. Crime is best seen as an expression of structural changes in the economy, opportunities, societal values, and changing roles and relationships. These theories can be useful in understanding both women's and men's crimes.

References

Adler, Freda. *Sisters in Crime* (New York: McGraw-Hill, 1975).

Adler, Freda, and Rita Simon. *The Criminology of Deviant Women* (Boston: Houghton Mifflin, 1979).

Andrew, J. M. "Delinquency, Sex, and Family Variables." *Social Biology*, 23 (1976):168–171.

Babcock, Barbara Allen. "Introduction: Women and the Criminal Law." *American Criminal Law Review*, 11 (Winter 1973):291–294.

Baldwin, Janice I. "The Effects of Women's Liberation and Socialization on Delinquency and Crime." *Humboldt Journal of Social Relations*, 10 (Spring 1983): forthcoming.

Bardwick, Judith, and Elizabeth Douvan. "Ambivalence: The Socialization of Women." In Vivian Gornick and Barbara K. Moran, *Woman in Sexist Society* (New York: Basic Books, 1971), pp. 225–241.

Bartel, Ann P. "Women and Crime: An Economic Analysis." *Economic Inquiry*, 17 (January 1979):29–51.

Block, Jeanne H. "Another Look at Sex Differences in the Socialization Behavior of Mothers and Fathers." In Julia Sherman and Florence L. Denmark, eds., *Psychology of Women: Future Directions of Research* (New York: Psychological Dimensions, 1978).

Bruck, Connie. "Women Against the Law." *Human Behavior* (December 1975):24–33.

Campbell, Anne. *Girl Delinquents* (New York: St. Martin's Press, 1981).

Cernkovich, Stephen, and Peggy Giordano. "A Comparative Analysis of Male and Female Delinquency." *Sociological Quarterly*, 20 (Winter 1979):131–145.

Chapman, Jane Roberts. *Economic Realities and the Female Offender* (Lexington, Mass.: Lexington Books, 1980).

Crites, Laura. "Women Offenders: Myth Vs. Reality," in Crites, *The Female Offender* (Lexington, Mass.: Lexington Books, 1976), pp. 33–44.

Daniels, Arlene Kaplan. "Feminist Perspectives in Sociological Research," In Marcia Millman and Rosabeth Moss Kanter, *Another Voice: Perspectives on Social Life and Social Science* (New York: Anchor Books, 1975), pp. 340–380.

Datesman, Susan, and Frank Scarpitti. "The Extent and Nature of Female Crime." In Susan Datesman and Frank Scarpitti, *Women, Crime and Justice* (New York: Oxford University Press, 1980), pp. 3–64.

Datesman, Susan, Frank Scarpitti, and Richard Stephenson. "Female Delinquency: An Application of Self and Opportunity Theories." *Journal of Research in Crime and Delinquency*, 12 (July 1975): 107–123.

Eve, Raymond A., and Kreelene R. Edmonds. "Women's Liberation and Female Criminality, or 'Sister, Will You Give Me Back My Dime?' " Paper presented at meeting of the National Society of Social Problems, San Francisco, Calif., September 1978.

Feinman, Clarice. *Women in the Criminal Justice System* (New York: Praeger, 1980).

Giordano, Peggy. "Girls, Guys and Gangs: The Changing Social Context of Female Delinquency." *Journal of Criminal Law and Criminology*, 69 (Spring 1978):126–132.

Giordano, Peggy, and Stephen A. Cernkovich. "On Complicating the Relationship Between Liberation and Delinquency." *Social Problems*, 26 (April 1979):467–481.

Glick, Ruth, and Virginia Neto. *National Study of Women's Correctional Programs* (Washington D.C.: National Institute of Law Enforcement and Criminal Justice, 1977).

Gora, J. G. "A Cohort Analysis of Trends in Crime Seriousness, 1929–1976." Paper presented at meeting of the American Society of Criminology, Philadelphia, Pa., November 1979.

Harris, Anthony R. "Sex and Theories of Deviance: Toward a Functional Theory of Deviant Type-Scripts," *American Sociological Review*, 42 (February 1977) 3–15.

Harry, Joseph, and Mary C. Sengstock. Comment on Harris's (*American Sociological Review*, February 1977) "Attribution, Goals and Deviance." *American Sociological Review*, 43 (April 1977):278–280.

American Sociological Review, 43 (April 1977):278–280.

Heidensohn, Frances. "The Deviance of Women: A Critique and an Inquiry." *The British Journal of Sociology*, 19 (June 1968):160–175.

Hindelang, Michael J. "Causes of Delinquency: A Partial Replication and Extension." *Social Problems*, 20 (1973):271–287.

Hoffman-Bustamente, Dale. "The Nature of Female Criminality." *Issues in Criminology*, 8 (Fall 1973):117–136.

James, Jennifer, and William Thornton. "Women's Liberation and the Female Delinquent." *Journal of Research in Crime and Delinquency*, 17 (1980):230–244.

Jensen, Gary F. "Parents, Peers, and Delinquent Action: A Test of the Differential Association Perspective." *American Journal of Sociology*, 78 (November 1972):562–575.

Jensen, Gary F., and Raymond Eve. "Sex Differences in Delinquency: An Examination of Popular Sociological Explanations." *Criminology*, 13 (February 1976):427–448.

Jones, Ann. *Women Who Kill* (New York: Holt, Rinehart and Winston, 1980).

Klein, Dorie. "The Etiology of Female Crime: A Review of the Literature." In Laura Crites, *The Female Offender* (Lexington, Mass.: Lexington Books, 1976), pp. 5–31.

Klein, Dorie, and June Kress. "Any Woman's Blues: A Critical Overview of Women, Crime and the Criminal Justice System." *Crime and Social Justice*, 1 (1976):34–49.

Kramer, John H., and Cynthia Kempinen, "Erosion of Chivalry? Changes in the Handling of Male and Female Defendants from 1970 to 1975." Paper presented at convention of the Society for the Study of Social Problems, San Francisco, Calif., September 1978.

Leonard, Eileen B. *Women, Crime and Society: A Critique of Theoretical Criminology* (New York: Longman, 1982).

Leventhal, Gloria. "Female Criminality: Is 'Women's Lib' to Blame?" *Psychological Reports*, 41 (December 1977):1179–1182.

Maccoby, Eleanor, and Carol Nagy Jacklin. "Sex Differences in Aggression: A Rejoinder and Reprise." *Child Development*, 51 (December 1980):964–980).

McCord, Joan. "Some Child-Rearing Antecedents of Criminal Behavior in Adult Men." *Journal of Personality and Social Psychology*, 37 (September 1979):1477–1486.

Merton, Robert K. "Social Structure and Anomie." *American Sociological Review*, 3 (October 1938):672–682.

Miller, Walter B. "The Molls." *Society*, 11 (November–December 1973). Reprinted in Susan Datesman and Frank Scarpitti, *Women, Crime and Justice* (New York: Oxford University Press, 1980), pp. 238–248.

Millman, Marcia, and Rosabeth Moss Kanter (eds.). *Another Voice: Feminist Perspectives on Social Life and Social Science* (New York: Anchor Books, 1975).

Morris, Ruth. "Female Delinquency and Relational Problems." *Social Forces*, 43 (October 1964):82–89.

Moyer, Imogene, and Garland F. White. "Police Processing of Female Offenders." Paper presented at annual meeting of the Academy of Criminal Justice Sciences, 1979.

Norland, Stephen, and Neal Shover. "Gender Roles and Female Criminality: Some Critical Comments." *Criminology*, 15 (May 1977):87–104.

Pollack, Otto. *The Criminality of Women* (Philadelphia: University of Pennsylvania Press, 1950).

Rans, Laurel. "Women's Arrest Statistics." *Woman Offender Report* (March–April 1975).

Rosenblum, Karen. "Female Deviance and the Female Sex Role: A Preliminary Investigation." *British Journal of Sociology,* 26 (June 1975):169–185.

Sandhu, H. S., and D. E. Allen. "Female Delinquency, Goal Obstruction and Anomie." *Canadian Review of Sociology and Anthropology,* 6 (1969): 107–110.

Shover, Neal, Stephen Norland, Jennifer James, and William E. Thornton, "Gender Roles and Delinquency," *Social Forces,* 58 (September 1979):162–175.

Simon, Rita James. "A Look to the Future." In Freda Adler and Rita Simon, *The Criminology of Deviant Women* (Boston: Houghton Mifflin, 1979), pp. 6–9.

Simon, Rita James. *Women and Crime* (Lexington, Mass.: D.C. Heath, 1975).

Simon, Rita James. "Women and Crime in Israel" In Simha Landau and Leslie Sibba, *Criminology in Perspective* (Lexington, Mass: D.C. Heath, 1977), Chap. 7.

Simons, Ronald L., Martin G. Miller, and Stephen M. Aigner, "Contemporary Theories of Deviance and Female Delinquency: An Empirical Test." *Journal of Research in Crime and Delinquency,* 17 (January 1980):42–53.

Smart, Carol. *Women, Crime and Criminology: A Feminist Critique* (London: Routledge and Kegan Paul, 1976).

Smith, Dorothy E. "Women's Perspective as Radical Critique of Sociology." *Sociological Inquiry,* 44 (1974):7–13.

Smith, Douglas A. "Sex and Deviance: An Assessment of Major Sociological Variables." *Sociological Quarterly,* 20 (Spring 1979):183–196.

Smith, Douglas, and Christy A. Visher, "Sex and Involvement in Deviance/ Crime: A Quantitive Review of the Empirical Literature." *American Sociological Review,* 45 (August 1980):691–701.

Steffensmeier, Darrell J., "Crime and the Contemporary Woman: An Analysis of Changing Levels of Female Property Crime, 1960–1975." *Social Forces,* 57 (December 1978):566–584.

Steffensmeier, Darrell J. "Sex Differences in Patterns of Adult Crime, 1965–77: A Review and Assessment." *Social Forces,* 58 (June 1980):1080–1108.

Steffensmeier, Darrell J., and Renee Steffensmeier, "Trends in Female Delinquency." *Criminology,* 18 (1980):62–185.

Sutherland, Edwin H., and Donald R. Cressey. *Criminology* (New York: J. B. Lippincott, 1974).

Thomas, Darwin L., and Andrew J. Weigart. "Socialization and Adolescent Conformity to Significant Others: A Cross-National Analysis." *American Sociological Review,* 36 (October 1971):835–847.

Thorsell, Bernard, and Lloyd W. Klemke, "The Labeling Process: Reinforcement and Deterrent?" In Delos H. Kelly, ed., *Deviant Behavior: Readings in the Sociology of Deviance* (New York: St. Martin's Press, 1979), pp. 654–664.

Ward, David, Maurice Jackson, and Renee Ward. "Crimes and Violence by Women." In Susan Datesman and Frank Scarpitti, *Women, Crime and Justice* (New York: Oxford University Press, 1980), pp. 171–191.

Weis, Joseph G. "Liberation and Crime: The Invention of the New Female Criminal." *Crime and Social Justice,* 6 (Fall–Winter 1976):17–27.

Widom, Cathy Spatz. "Female Offenders: Three Assumptions About Self-

Esteem, Sex-Role Identity, and Feminism." *Criminal Justice and Behavior,* 6 (1979):365–382.

Widom, Cathy Spatz, and Abigail Stewart. "Female Criminality and the Changing Status of Women." Paper presented at annual meeting of the American Society of Criminology, Atlanta, Ga., November 1977.

Notes

1. Simons, Miller, and Aigner (1980) found that all the theories they tested (labeling, control, anomie, and differential association), with the possible exception of anomie theory, applied equally well to girls and boys.

2. Serious crimes include murder and non-negligent manslaughter, aggravated assault, rape, robbery, burglary, larceny-theft, motor vehicle theft, and arson (Crime Index Total).

3. Violent crimes include murder and non-negligent manslaughter, aggravated assault, rape, and robbery.

4. Property crimes include burglary, larceny-theft, motor vehicle theft, and arson.

5. Feinman (1980:17) reports that, according to the (October 5, 1978), ACLU *News* welfare fraud accounted for 34 percent of all women arrested for fraud in 1976.

44 / Road Hustlers

ROBERT C. PRUS
C. R. D. SHARPER

While some learning takes place in a rough hustle, the most extensive apprenticeship period begins on contact with professional crews. In contrast to the haphazard operations of the nonprofessionals, professional crews have a rather sophisticated modus operandi to which they will expect any newcomer to adjust readily. Additionally, while the ability to manipulate game equipment is important in a rough hustle, persons who encounter professional crews discover that not only is there much more complexity to manipulating equipment than they ever imagined but also find that other skills and qualities are considered more important in professional circles, where the ability to manipulate cards or dice is rather commonplace and taken more for granted.

Maybe you are trying to get up in the world and you want to get in with a crew that's solid, or that knows what they are doing, and you may have the skill to do it. Sure they might accept you, but they will still treat you as a novice or an apprentice. Learning the ropes with them is tough, because they are very secretive. They are not going to show you their bread-and butter moves or take you to their best parties. They may figure that you might not last too long, so it's tough, but I guess what overcomes it is determination on the part of the apprentice. If you just keep insisting that you want to learn and are willing to take all the shit, if you kind of overlook it and you show them that you are determined to get into it, then they will gradually open up to you. Like I say, it's tough, but learning the ropes with these people is great, because they're professionals and you learn the right way of doing things.

Not only does the learning of attitudes and techniques conducive to card and dice hustling begin long before a person becomes involved with professional hustlers, but clearly what one has learned prior to his contacts with professional hustlers influences their assessments of his usefulness to them. From the crew's perspective, the more compatible a newcomer's existing attitudes and talents with the crew's life-style, the more valuable he is to them. The newcomer is expected to fit into the crew's operations; and, although the tutelage of newcomers is much more extensive than that which occurs in a rough hustle, it is not defined as a central role by current crew members. Thus, much of the learning comes about either incidentally, as the newcomer learns by "hanging around" practicing hustlers, or through being criticized in post-facto "coaching." In general, whatever specific tutelage a newcomer receives is designed primarily to protect or assist the crew in its activities. Accordingly, the preferred pupil is one who learns quickly and independently—one who is dedicated and who simply doesn't make mistakes.

People who connect with professional crews are subjected to learning experiences along four themes. First, there is the sharpening of one's "larceny sense"—the learning of attitudes and techniques conducive to general forms of theft and fraud. Second, there is learning to get along with fellow hustlers—learning to deal with them as equals, and learning how to avoid being exploited by one's co-workers. Third, one finds role-specific learning, in which they acquire skills in particular hustling roles (for example, mechanic, shoot-up man). Finally, there is learning how to "make the nut"—finding ways to reduce expenses while hustling on the road. It should be noted that these types of learning occur more or less concurrently and more or less continuously throughout one's career. Further, while hustlers in varying degrees may acquire some of these same qualities while bouncing around in a rough hustle, the extent and intensity of the learning experience potentially available in professional crews are so much greater than one is otherwise likely to encounter. Within a single professional crew, one is able to experience a much more diversified, concentrated, and refined set of operations than one might while working with a variety of nonprofessional crews.

LARCENY SENSE

Consistent with a general thief orientation, crew members are expected to be observant and sensitive to situational occurrences. It is expected that they will either possess or develop larceny sense, that they be opportunistic, taking the fullest advantage of every situation in which to save or make the crew or themselves some money. From the crew's perspective, two qualities are important vis-à-vis opportunism: attitudes favorable to theft and the capacity for impression management.

Defining hustling in a business context, crew members expect their partners to capitalize on every opportunity to make money for the crew. While individual members may "feel sorry" for a sympathy-arousing or likable target, within the crew one finds considerable support for defining any other player as "a sucker," someone to be beaten for his money:

When I first got involved in hustling, my attitudes were less calloused. I might be at a stag of some sort and say some fellow is losing a little money. Through the course of the evening, talking back and forth, you find out that maybe he just got married, or that he has some kids and here he's writing checks and I would slow down. If you pull something like this with a crew, the other guys will want to know what the hell you are doing! They're waiting for you to take him and you're saying, "Well gee, the guy doesn't have much money." You would get the worst tongue lashing! The position they take is that "You can't have feelings on the road." And it's true, if you start saying to yourself, "Well, maybe I better not beat this guy or that guy," you would soon be out of business or at least you would really cut down on your profits.

When a crew is on the road, they have no feelings for the other players. They say, "Well, if the sucker doesn't blow it to you, he's going to blow it to somebody else, so you might as well take him for his money. He's going to lose it one way or the other. If they don't blow it on cards, they will spend it at the race track, or on chicks, or throw it in stocks; one way or another, they will blow their money, and you might as well have the money as anyone else." After a while, you find that you have no feelings for the other players. When I first started out, I had some feelings for the people I was beating, but later on I didn't, because then you think, "This is my money." You get to feel that it's your money and that you are beating them for it. You also realize that you have expenses, and maybe you're trying to provide for a family. So you think, "If I'm going to dedicate my life to hustling, I might as well do it right. Forget about them, just worry about myself."

You can't make money every day in hustling, there's always slack days, so when the good days come around, you better forget about feeling sorry for them, just put your head down and make the money. You also learn that if the guy you are feeling sorry for starts winning some of his money back, he's not going to feel sorry for you. So, you might as well beat him for as much as you can, and just forget about it. He would take you for your money and probably laugh at you, so you might as well beat him for his money. If you didn't, the other crew members would consider you a sucker! . . .

I remember one time when I had just started working with this one top crew. We were playing poker and there was this cripple there. He was deformed and on crutches, but the guy loved to play poker. Anyway we started to beat him and I felt sorry for the guy. I said, "Leave the guy alone, he's crippled." They looked at me and said "Are you kidding? His money is just as good as anyone else's!" You see, I wasn't ready to go in there and cheat him, to give the guy a good hand. My guys sensed it and they were getting a little hot. They pulled me aside and said, "Now, look, beat this guy!" Who knows how much money he had on him, he had a stack of twenties. So, even a cripple, if you can beat him, you do it.

Priests, we beat priests, oh yeah, they're good, they dig in their pockets and blow their money as gracefully as anyone else. When I was just starting out, I would say, "I'm a Catholic, I can't beat this priest." Like, I had been an altar boy. So later, when I was with this crew and the first time a priest came and got into the game, I wasn't manipulating towards him. These guys sensed it and let me know they weren't happy with me. It ended up that we really took advantage of him, it was like a circus. There's been monks, priests, brothers, we've beaten. Who knows where they get the money. We have beaten priests quite a few times at conventions. You may be at some sort of convention and he may be a prof at some university. They may be friends with somebody, and they get together and pretty soon, he gets in the game and he's the guy to beat. Women, it's the same thing. Sometimes you don't want to beat a woman, but you might as well, you can't afford to have feelings about the people you are going to beat. . . .

Now, say I was with a crew and noticed that a new man was tightening up with a cripple or a priest or whatever, and he didn't want to take advantage of him, I would give him shit! Just like I got shit. You have to, because you can't afford to feel sorry for people. Like you'll hear these sob stories over the table. The guy may go to the toilet and sure enough the guys will be saying "Gee, he can't afford to lose all that money. He's got this to pay, or that to pay." Maybe he owns a business and everyone knows he is going broke, but he doesn't know how to control his gambling. You hear this sort of thing at the table, but if you slow down, it will definitely get in your way. You have enough on your mind in a game without trying to protect this or that guy from losing. . . .

If you don't have this larceny sense it's going to be rough on you, because you are going to be in conflict all the time, not only with yourself, but with the crew. . . .It's like when they started me on boosting, if you don't boost, they are going to take you for a sucker. "If something is laying there, pick it up, it's money to you! What's the matter with you! Don't you understand that's money in your pocket?" I've had a lot of lectures like that. It's not that I've been an angel, but hustling pool or cards or craps seemed different than stealing from a store.

It took me a while to overcome the fear of jail or just the fear of getting caught. Embarrassment was a big thing to me, "Imagine me stealing something and getting caught," type of thing. Sure, a lot of half-assed hustlers know about boosting, but to get them out doing it is a different matter. They will beat the suckers and cheat you on your share, but they might be scared to death to steal something or roll a motel. Anyway, with repetition you lose the fear of getting caught. You just come to accept the fact that you're in that subculture and you just don't get embarrassed, it's your work, and you have to accept it. Once you accept that, things are easier. Because you can't start putting people you work with in different categories, like, "He's a son of a bitch. He's a rotten bastard." You can't do that. You're all the same, you're all thieves. You are all in that category, so you might as well accept it. The sooner you learn it, the better off you are. Nobody is a nice guy on the road, I don't care who, nobody is! Given the chance, some of your partners will probably steal money from you; you don't know, so you have to be on the ball all the time and do as they do.

A second and more subtle aspect of larceny sense is that of impression management: to be able to assume and sustain identities conducive to manipulation; that one be capable of "fitting in" and, thus, take full advantage of the situation. From the crew's perspective it is important that all the members be able to associate readily with a wide variety of persons; anyone unable to mix with the clientele is unlikely to last with a professional crew:

Socializing is a big thing in hustling. You have to be able to get along with the suckers and treat them well. You want them to think that you're a decent guy. You have to establish trust. Then you can get in there and work on them, manipulate them around. If you go to a party you have to look like you belong. You know, drink a little, joke a little. They are there to have a good time and if you're too serious, they might get suspicious. Like years ago, I might have one beer the whole evening, but then I would get shit, because even the suckers say, "Well, what are you here for, just to gamble?" They want to drink and enjoy themselves, you know, and here I am with one drink for the whole night. So, I'd go to the bar and bring back ginger ale, with a little whiskey in it, but even then they like to see you be as they are. In other words, if you want to win my money, you do what I do. They might have some silly excuse like, "I've been drinking and you're not, you're taking advantage." You can get pulled up if you just sit there, not drinking and joking with them. If it seems that all you are interested in is the money, then, they kind of wonder, "What does this guy do?" . . .
*   The main thing is to be able to relate to people and be rather incon-*

*spicuous. If you look like the average citizen and you can communi-
cate with people, you have a better chance of making it in hustling. I
don't know how you learn to do this, I guess by watching the other
guys and through your own experiences. You get accustomed to it.
Like now, it doesn't seem to bother me if I go to a party with a bunch
of lawyers, doctors, or factory workers. It was difficult at first, but
then you learn, people are people. When you get talking with a guy
and they are with a bunch of guys together, they are not going to
relate to you with the terminology they might use if they were profs
at a university or doctors, they are going to relate as guys, so you can
relate to them.*

*Now, if you have no gift of gab, whatsoever, believe me it will be a
handicap because you can't go to a party or a banquet or some sort of
function without communicating with these people. If you are standing there like a bump on a log, people want to know who you
are.... You can't just go in there and win their money and not say
anything. Some hustlers spend a lot of time reading newspapers.
They like to be able to talk about the news. Then if you go to a party,
you can talk about sports or community events or what's happening
in the country today. Now, a lot of players want to talk about sports
or women, but if they want to talk about politics or news events, you
can talk about that too. If you can talk about the things that they're
interested in, they will be more willing to accept you....*

*Now, these professionals we've been talking about, they can all
mix with people. At a party, they all seem like good natured fellows,
with the gift of gab. They all look respectable, anyone of them could
be, let's say, a lawyer, or businessman, an executive of some sort, you
really wouldn't know, they could fit in anywhere. But that's what it
takes, if you want to con people around, you have to get them to accept you.... Now, if you have a new man who has difficulties mixing with people, you let him know that socializing with the suckers is
a big thing in hustling. If he can't manage that, you pretty well have
to let him go.*

INTERNAL RELATIONS

The second area of apprenticeship is that of learning how to deal
with one's fellow hustlers. From the prospect's perspective this
means being able to establish himself as an integral member of the
crew; for in many respects, this is a period of testing at which time
the crew attempts to ascertain the prospect's suitability as a "regular." As the newcomer to the team, the prospect is likely to encounter some advice and extensive criticism. If he has worked his way up

through the ranks and has attained a reputation as a capable performer, he may resent being treated as an inferior. The existing regulars, on the other hand, want the most competent performer they can find and they are concerned with "here-and-now" production. They envision this time as one in which the new man has to show them that he is "worth his salt." And, unless the new man is extremely proficient, they are likely to feel that he is costing them money and are not reluctant to let him know his performance could have been improved. Thus, any prospect who is unable to sustain some verbal abuse, is quite simply, unlikely to remain with the crew. As the criticisms will come early in one's contact with the crew, a termination may effectively preclude other learning experiences.

The second form of testing involves what might be termed "shortcaking." Viewing themselves as having more seniority, having more investments, and doing more of the work, regular members of the crew will frequently give the prospect less than an equal share of an evening's winnings. Again, a prospect unable/unwilling to make some concessions to the existing group of regulars is unlikely to "make the grade":

They justify it like this. They have more seniority, they have more material, they have put more time into it, they have invested more money, and they are risking more than the newcomer. The ideal is that equals get equal shares, right. But the newcomer is not seen as an equal, so to them it seems fair. Now, if you were to go to a spot and win, say, six or seven hundred dollars and there are four of you, well they probably wouldn't take any money. But, say the crew went to a spot and won six or seven thousand, well then they might take fifteen hundred dollars off the top to split between themselves. Now, the newcomer is no wiser and if you hand him a thousand dollars, he's liable to kiss your ass. . . .

I remember my first thousand, boy was I surprised! It was thirteen hundred and I thought, "Gee, this is great!" I thought hustling was the greatest thing in the world. You just couldn't get me away from it. But you see on scores like that they might steal a lot of money from you and you wouldn't realize it until you learn a little more about their norms. When you start seeing them do this to other newcomers, then you start thinking back, "Yeah, that's what they did to me.". . . It's pretty well standard procedure when it's a newcomer, but, if a man is worth the money, you give it to him, and that's the way they work.

But a newcomer is at a disadvantage, even if he knows that he is getting shortcaked, he can't say too much. He has to prove himself to them. And if he's making good money, he pretty well has to charge his losses to experience, the cost of his education, you might say. . . .You might start to challenge these guys, but it's pretty rough if you're just starting with them. You have to win the confidence of one or two of the guys, so that someone would be willing to stand up for you in the crew. But they are going to think of you as a novice and until you have more experience or more equipment and can show them that you're worth as much as they are, you can expect them to take these edges. At the same time, though, you have to show them that you are aware of what they're doing, otherwise they will define you as a sucker too!

HUSTLING ROLES

Although one may, on a limited-talent basis alone, expect to find some division of labor among partners in a rough hustle, professional crews seem much more consciously oriented to specific game roles. And, while people who become connected with professional crews are generally recruited on the basis of specific talents, over time most of those who remain with professional crews develop a multiplicity of talents. As there is no systematic progression involved in learning these various hustling skills, each will be discussed as a separate specialization.

The Mechanic

The mechanic, whose job it is to manipulate game equipment, will have the most explicit tutelage. It is, however, most unlikely that he will have learned all his moves from any one instructor; and it is even less likely that he will have learned to manipulate from fellow crew mechanics, as most mechanics are relatively secretive about their talents. Thus, one finds that those who become mechanics generally have worked with a variety of other hustlers who, over time, may disclose various techniques which, taken together, result in a growing collection of moves. While some of these moves are taught as a consequence of personal liking or concerns with building a stronger crew, hustlers may build more extensive repertoires by reciprocating tutelage of moves with other hustlers.

Although most hustlers are able to do some manipulations, it takes a great deal of time and practice to acquire the skills and reputation of a mechanic, and this person may spend most of his spare time over a period of months practicing a single move. It is not merely the number of moves a mechanic possesses that defines game success, but the smoothness with which these are introduced:

When I was starting out, I tried to pick up some ideas from other hustlers I met and mostly practiced out of books. But I found that there's no way you can learn from a book. Unless you experience the move yourself, maybe from watching someone make it or, better still, have someone watching over your shoulder, "That's right, now practice that," you're in trouble. But I was doing it on hearsay and fumbling through. But each move takes practice, you have to stay with it, many many hours in front of the mirror....

Some of these rough hustlers are so sloppy that you can't imagine how they can get by without something happening. But I guess if you just keep your head down and do your job, you're supposed to make money. But I was lucky, I met this one fellow who seemed to take a liking to me and he showed me a few moves. He would show me a move and I would go and practice it, then later I would ask him, "Am I doing this right? How does this look?" He was the most helpful of all the people I met. Very few hustlers would ever take their time to help you like that. They don't want to teach you anything that might make you as good as them....

Now, say you have a new man on the crew, maybe a shoot-up man or a muscle man, well then you might show them a few simple things, like a false cut or a false shuffle, so that you could prearrange the deck and let them deal. Say that there's only one mechanic in the game. Naturally, every time I deal, my partner wins, so it would be nice if he dealt and one of us would win too. What I might do while we are playing, is to go through the deck and prearrange it in the course of play. Then I'll set them down in front of him and they're all ready to deal. So if he can false shuffle and I false cut, then that would be nice. But you don't go much further than that....

Now if you connect with some rough hustlers, you pretty well say, "Don't do anything, my partner and I will do everything!" Unless you know the guy's a terrific mechanic, you tell him just to play his regular game. They seldom have enough time to really get into the mechanics of it. They are just guys who have maybe marked cards, or they might hold out cards. So you tell them, "Just sit there and win the money and let me take care of the mechanics." That's all they have to do. But you try to keep your manipulations to a minimum. Because the more you monkey with the deck, the more the other players will look at you. It's funny, but these locals, they think you can pull cards out of your hand or something. They figure that every time you deal, they're supposed to win. You have to explain to them, that they can't win every time you deal, that they just have to take their time and play basic poker. You see, they want to win it all at once, but you have to grind it out, shoot up the pot and take your time.

That's another part of being a mechanic, you have to learn how and when to make your moves. . . . But you really never stop learning and even when you think you're on top of it, you still have to practice and watch your moves. Like sometimes your partners might tell you to slow down on your deal. Sure enough, I would be concentrating on the game and just whip those cards out on the table. "Just deal like a sucker," they might say, so you slow down and make sure you are holding the deck sort of sloppy like. You try to reduce suspicion throughout the game, you try to keep the suckers happy.

In addition to mastering the moves and acquiring a sense of timing, prospective mechanics also have to learn to handle the pressure associated with that game role. The mechanic is the one doing the manipulations and if any search takes place, he is the one likely to be found with the implicating gambling equipment. Of all the persons involved in the game, the mechanic typically is under the most pressure. Thus, although one does not learn confidence in the same way one learns technical skills, it is a vital aspect of the mechanic's role. While past experiences in successfully passing as a regular player provide mechanics with some assurance in an ongoing game situation, confidence also tends to increase with the belief that one has several workable moves (offering situational versatility) and that one is working with a crew that can handle accusations and provide some protection from player indignation.

The Shoot-Up Man

Although a central requirement of the shoot-up man is that he have a respectable appearance, enabling him to "look good winning the money," considerable effort is required to master the role. In their public relations capacity, shoot-up men are expected to mix with the clientele and to make them feel at ease during the game, thus encouraging the patrons to part with their money while remaining good sports. If a person is being recruited specifically for this role, better-than-average social skills are considered a prerequisite. A good shoot-up man will also provide distractions when he anticipates the mechanic making switches. If these diversions are discreet, they afford the mechanic an increased level of safety and, thus, increase his confidence and ability to control the game. While the shoot-up man will have much less explicit tutelage than the mechanic, a good shoot-up man is considered an invaluable component of a professional crew, and one finds a great deal of difference in the operations of a professional and someone whose role it is to "win the money" in a rough hustle:

The differences are almost unbelievable. In a rough hustle, the man sits back and thinks all he has to do is win the money in a game. In a professional crew, the shoot-up man is not only a public relations man before the game, but he may also start the game going. Then, during the game, he works as hard as anybody. He is constantly mixing with the people, cooling them out, enticing them, conning them around. And, he provides shade for the mechanic. He knows when you are going to make a move, "Excuse me," he says or maybe he orders a drink; a good shoot-up man is a big help to a mechanic, he can take a lot of the heat off you. These amateurs sit back and you might have to tell them if you can imagine this, not to stare at you! And usually with someone in a rough hustle, you have to do all the work. They give you no assistance; they think all they have to do is win the money.

The Muscle Man

Relatively few muscle men work themselves into professional crews "through the ranks." In part, this reflects the lesser likelihood of rough hustling partnerships involving a muscle man and, in part, it reflects the different expectations associated with muscle men in professional and rough-hustle situations. First, although professional crews will work more difficult games and are more determined to "squeeze" every dollar they can out of every game, they are also much more adept at avoiding physical confrontations. To them, a muscle man represents a form of insurance, in the event things get rough. However, as they expect to be able to cool out indignant targets, they also feel that someone who provides muscle should do so inconspicuously and should be able to function in a broader game capacity (for example, shoot-up man or elementary mechanics). Consequently, they are oriented toward a middle-aged, respectably appearing, bigger man who can relate to the other players but who could also stand up to an irate player if necessary. While the professional crews, with their greater structure and duration, are more likely to plan overtly to include someone of this nature in their group, the intention is to provide protection for the crew members, particularly the mechanic who, by virtue of the equipment, is in a disadvantageous position.

Although one might expect to find more muscle men in a rough hustle, the relatively transitory quality of rough-hustle partnerships operates against this. However, when used in rough hustle crews, muscle men tend to be more obvious (intimidating) and are more likely to have had prior records for assault, robbery, and so forth. Muscle men in a rough hustle, thus, come much closer to fitting the popular stereotype of the "big lug" associated with gamblers as depicted in the media. Professional crews have no desire to become connected with these rougher people.

While professional crews prefer muscle men able to double as shoot-up men, they will occasionally involve a man specifically for his muscle effect when they anticipate a rough party. If this happens and if the crew finds the new man congenial and feels he has potential, it is he to whom the most extensive training is directed. First, he will be encouraged and coached on how to remain inconspicuous. In conjunction with this, he will be directed to relax and socialize with the patrons. If the man seems able and dedicated, he will be instructed on how and when to win the money and how to assist the mechanic by helping him squeeze into tight spots when other players are jammed around the (typically, dice) game or providing distractions at opportune times. Finally, he will be instructed in elementary moves designed to assist the crew in their operations. If a newcomer with this sort of physical strength is able to make this transition, the other crew members, recognizing the security he represents, are likely to consider him a valuable addition.

Making the Nut

Whereas all card/dice hustlers face the problem of having sufficient equipment and suitable attire, those hustlers who spend more time on the road face additional expenses relating to lodging and food bills, travel costs, and phone expenses. For example, a crew of four men could easily spend $50 to $100 a day on food and lodging alone, and if one were to multiply this by one hundred nights on the road, it becomes quite evident that these costs alone could amount to a small fortune in a year's time. Operating with some structure and duration, and from a general thief orientation, it should not be surprising to see professional crews finding ways of "making the nut," minimizing the expenses associated with road hustling. In contrast to persons in legitimate businesses, road hustlers are unlikely to deduct these job-related expenses from whatever income taxes they might be paying. Any expenses incurred on the road are, thus, seen as coming directly out of their pockets and cutting directly into their "take-home pay." Further, insofar as they have no guarantee that any party will work out successfully, it is highly desirable that the expenses or "the nut" be kept to a minimum lest expenditures exceed gains and the venture result in a direct personal loss. This ability to "keep the nut down" further differentiates the professional from the rough hustler:

The professional will use whatever means he can to hold the nut down and they know how to minimize expenses. Now you don't really notice it when you're in a rough hustle, but after, you just become so aware of it. Like, if you go someplace with a nonprofessional crew, you just see those expenses build up. First they go to a motel, and you know they pay. They are worried that not paying will get them caught, they always have the fear in them. Then, if they get on the phone and make a long-distance call, they put in money. But, when you go with a professional crew, you see all this saving of money. It is a little risky, but if they didn't do it, I could just imagine all the money they would have to spend. Also, these professionals very seldom pay for a meal and you always eat well, because you go to a nice place. You go to a place where the middle-class or the upper-class people go. You go there and eat, and act like they do, you just don't pay. So, it's fine. Now, a nonprofessional crew may go to a truck stop or a mediocre restaurant and pay for their food. If you eat two or three times a day and you stay at a motel, you can really shoot up the nut, and that's not counting your gas or your calls. . . .

But, you see, you don't start learning these things until you are working with top people. And they are very secretive about their operations. If they accept you, you can learn by hanging around, but they don't associate with these rough hustlers any more than they have to, and then, they don't want to tell them or show them anything. . . . I'll give you an idea of how smooth they are. When I first started going on the road with these guys, I must have been working with them for a month before I realized that they were rolling hotels. They did it so well, it looked so natural. In the morning they would say, "Okay boys, let's leave." They wouldn't say anything to me, and I would ask, "Who is paying for this?" Then, they would act like nice guys, "Well, I'll get it today." So now, you feel like you want to get it, so you get your money out and say, "I'll get it." And they are there, "Oh no, it's okay."

Looking back I know that I paid for meals and they rolled the restaurant but what are you going to do? Go back and say, "Give me my money back!" For about a month I didn't catch on, then when you get to a real shitty place, you catch on. You see them hemming and hawing and stalling around. You wonder what they are doing, so you watch and you see what's going on. Now, once you find out on your own, then they open up to you. But, it's not like they're going to say, "Well, this is what we're going to do. . . ." They don't do that, it's basically learn as you go. And, the more you learn, the more your status goes up. If they see that you are getting hep, your chances of staying with that crew are a lot better. After a while you realize that they are doing this constantly and it's a normal thing for them to do. Rolling restaurants, rolling motels, and boosting is the thing to do for a hustler; no one looks down on you for doing it. In fact, it's their norm. You're a sucker if you don't! . . . But you see it's a world of difference. These amateurs or nonprofessionals will think nothing of gypping you on your share, but when it comes to rolling a restaurant, they're afraid. . . .

Another way of keeping the nut down is through boosting. You do what you can to hold that nut down, so boosting's a big thing with professionals. It varies from crew to crew. Some crews might spend any free time they have boosting. Other crews will boost mostly for their own needs and when the opportunity is there. Like almost any hustler would think you're a sucker if you have the opportunity and don't take whatever it is. Because most things you can unload, maybe to another hustler, or a sucker, or maybe a fence. But, it's different than with full-time thieves. Sure, they're better at it, but for a hustler it's like gravy when he can get something for nothing. A guy stealing for a living also has to take more chances. A hustler will only boost when the situation looks good. You know, if he sees that opportunity. And then, you usually have someone to round for you, to distract the clerk. You also watch what you steal. Like, if there's only one thing on a counter and you take it, it's likely to be missed, but if there's three or four items, it's safer. And you close up spaces, you don't leave a big empty space. . . .

But this boosting thing, it's something that you learn. When I first saw these guys doing it, I wondered, "How in the hell are they doing it?" You see a guy come out with a big camera, you wonder, "How in the world did he ever get it out?" Or you may see a guy walk out with a bike, or a lawn mower, "How do they do it?" You learn these things; it seemed a natural procedure of the guys on the road. They didn't really go into boosting as a business, it was just something they did. They might just be waiting around for the party to start, maybe browsing around the mall in the afternoon, and it isn't that they have to take it, but they do. And, they feel, "Well, I got something here worth a little bit of money, if nothing happens at the party, at least I've got something to fall back on. . . ."

So, between what you or the others in the crew can boost and these fences or thieves you meet, you can get most anything you might want, say in the way of watches, radios, small appliances, and especially clothes and shoes. You can get, let's say, good or top quality items at half price or less and that really helps keep the expenses down. . . . You also run into pickpockets and there again, if you want to take the chance, you can get credit cards and complete sets of I.D. cards. Once you get connected with these professionals, these opportunities just seem to open up, you keep learning about more angles and more gaffs.

Given the illegal nature of one's hustling activities and the rather stringent demands of one's partners, a relatively rapid and complete adjustment to hustling is required if one is to make the grade as a professional. Additionally, lacking the formal structure of many training programs, it is incumbent upon the novice to acquire this facility with a minimum of direct instruction. Not only does the increasing mastery of the field enhance game performance and promote crew earnings, but as novices become more sensitive to the complexities of hustling and acquire subsequent skills in this area, they are drawn increasingly into hustling as a way of life.

45 / Corporate Organization and Criminal Behavior

MARSHALL B. CLINARD
PETER C. YEAGER

The cultural environment within which the modern American corporation operates may actually encourage or discourage criminal or deviant behavior. Some corporations appear to be more legally ethical in their business operations. In research conducted in connection with this [essay], it was found that approximately 40 percent of the largest U.S. manufacturing corporations were not charged with a law violation by any of the twenty-five federal agencies during 1975 and 1976. . . . Some of the *Fortune* 500, such as the Digital Equipment Corporation, have a reputation for high ethical standards (*Wall Street Journal*, October 24, 1977). Many corporations, for example, appear not to have made illegal political contributions to the Nixon campaign or to have been charged with violations connected with foreign payments. . . . On the other hand, some corporations have been charged with numerous violations of various types. . . .

Corporate norms of doing business may conflict with one or several ethical or legal norms. The interplay among corporate norms of unethical behavior, societal norms, and law violations may run throughout a given corporation and be present in much of the decisionmaking (Clark and Hollinger, 1977). Businessmen are subject to contradictory expectations—a universalistic one (as citizen) and a particularistic one (as businessman)—with the obligation to the firm generally guiding behavior. A corporation that emphasizes profits above business ethics and ignores corporate responsibility to the community, the consumer, or society is likely to have difficulty complying with legal norms. The policies of some corporations can encourage the "criminal tendencies" of particular executives. For example, the persons involved in the electrical price-fixing case of the 1960s found illegal activity "an established way of life" when they began their jobs (Geis, 1973, p. 109).

In this connection, it has been suggested that we should begin our studies of why corporations break the law by learning more about why different corporations, like different political administrations, appear to become permeated with their own particular attitudes and stands in relation to law obedience and good citizenship generally (Stone, 1975, p. 237). Stone has referred to the "culture of a corporation," which is an entire constellation of attitudes and forces, some of which contribute to illegal behavior. Those factors contributing to illegal behavior include

> a desire for profits, expansion, power; desire for security (at corporate as well as individual levels); the fear of failure (particularly in connection with shortcomings in corporate innovativeness); group loyalty identification (particularly in connection with citizenship violations and the various failures to "come forward" with internal information); feelings of omniscience (in connection with adequate testing); organizational diffusion of responsibility (in connection with the buffering of public criticism); corporate ethnocentrism (in connection with limits in concern for the public's wants and desires). (Stone, 1975, p. 236)

In a follow-up of Baumhart's mid-1950s survey of corporate ethics, Brenner and Molander (1977) found that superiors continued to be ranked as the primary influence in unethical decisionmaking. About half of those surveyed in the 1977 study thought that their superiors frequently did not wish to know how results were obtained as long as they achieved the desired outcome: "Respondents frequently complained of superiors' pressure to support incorrect viewpoints, sign false documents, overlook superiors' wrongdoing, and do business with superiors' friends" (p. 60).

Under conditions such as these the use of sanctions to accomplish compliance with law is but one of the various forces operating within a corporation encouraging or opposing violations of law. The success of law enforcement

> ultimately depends upon its consistency with and reinforcement from other vectors—the organization's rules for advancement and reward, its customs, conventions, and morals. If the law is too much at odds with these other forces, its threats will make the employees more careful to cover their tracks before it makes them alter their institutionally supportive behavior. (Stone, 1975, p. 67)

Woodmansee, writing in 1975, illustrated what happens when corporate codes of conduct clash with legal norms.

> General Electric has been charged with price fixing and other monopoly practices not only for its light bulbs, but for turbines, generators, transformers, motors, relays, radio tubes, heavy metals, and lightning arresters. At least 67 suits have been brought against General Electric by the Antitrust Division of the Justice Department since 1911, and 180 antitrust suits were brought against General Electric by private companies in the early 1960s alone. General Electric's many trips to court hardly seem to have "reformed" the company; in 1962, after 50 years' experience with Gener-

al Electric, even the Justice Department was moved to comment on "General Electric's proclivity for frequent and persistent involvement in antitrust violations." And there have been new suits in the years since 1962. (p. 52)

Lawbreaking can become a normative pattern within a corporation, with or without pressure for profits or from the economic environment. In confidential interviews with a number of board chairmen and chief executive officers of very large corporations, a consensus emerged that the top management, particularly the chief executive officer, sets [the] ethical tone. The president and chief executive officer of a large manufacturing corporation noted that "by example and holding a tight rein a chief executive . . . can set the level of ethical or unethical practices in his organization. This influence can spread throughout the organization." As another high executive pointed out, price fixing or kickbacks must be "congenial to the climate of the corporation." Still another board chairman said, "Some corporations, like those in politics, tolerate corruption."

DIFFUSION OF ILLEGAL BEHAVIOR WITHIN INDUSTRIES

Corporate wrongdoing sometimes reflects the normative structure of a particular industry. That is, criminal behavior by the corporation and its executives often is the result of the diffusion of illegal practices and policies within the industry (Sutherland, 1949, p. 263). Frequently it is not the corporate organization itself that must be examined but the corporation's place in the industry (Riedel, 1968, p. 94).

In a recent analysis of some old data on restraint of trade collected by Sutherland during the 1930s and 1940s for his study of corporate crime, Cressey (1976) found that generally corporations in the same industry have similar rates of recidivism. "For example, neither of the two mail-order houses included in Sutherland's study were repeaters of the restraint of trade offense—Sears Roebuck had no adverse decisions against it, and Montgomery Ward had only one. But all three motion-picture companies had high recidivism rates—Paramount and Warner Brothers each had twenty-one, and Loew's had twenty-two. Two dairy companies, Borden and National Dairy Products, had middle-range rates of seven and eight" (pp. 216–217). A study of price fixing reported that this offense is more likely to occur when the companies deal with a homogeneous product line (Hay and Kelley, 1974). Relying on his studies of corporate crime in the Federal German Republic, Tiedemann (1974, 1976) concluded that much of this activity is a response to competition in certain industries. For example, 50 percent of all scrap imports in the European Coal and Steel Community were found to be faked: one-third of the subsidized scrap metal was nonexistent. In 1978 almost all Mercedes establishments in Germany, as well as their clients, were charged with having changed the contract dates on motor cars and trucks so that they could get the high subsidies paid by the German government in 1976 in an effort to stimulate the national economy (*Frankfurter Allgemeine Zeitung*, November 17, 1978).

The atmosphere thus becomes one in which participants . . . learn the necessary values, motives, rationalizations, and techniques favorable to particular kinds of crimes. A corporation may socialize its members to normative systems conducive to criminality. The head of the Enforcement Division of the SEC has said: "Our largest corporations have trained some of our brightest young people to be dishonest" (*New York Times Magazine*, September 25, 1976, p. 58). Diffusion of industry practices was evident in the electrical price fixing conspiracy of the 1960s in the manner in which the corporation representatives arranged meetings far from the home offices of the corporations, used code names in meetings of representatives of the corporations, sent mail in plain envelopes rather than business envelopes, used public telephones to avoid wiretaps, and falsified accounts to conceal their meeting places (Herling, 1962). Although large aircraft manufacturers commonly made foreign payoffs, particularly in Japan, Lockheed is generally believed to have set the pace. As the chairman of the board testified before a Senate subcommittee, "If you are going to win it is necessary." Still, officials of the Northrop Corporation, "which, like Lockheed, made similar payments through a special subsidiary company established in Switzerland to handle the financing," told the subcommittee, Senator Church said, that "*they learned how to do that from Lockheed*" (Shaplen, 1978, p. 54).

The role of industry ethics in law violations is shown in a widespread price conspiracy that resulted in the indictment of twenty-three carton manufacturing corporations and fifty of their executives in 1976 (United States of America, Plaintiff, v. Alton Box Board Company, et al., Defendants, Criminal Action No. 76, CR 199, U.S. District Court, Northern District of Illinois, Eastern Division. All references and quotes are from court documents). Included were International Paper Company, Container Corporation of America, Packaging Corporation of America, Weyerhauser, Diamond International Corporation, and Alton Box. American industry and consumers depend enormously on goods packaged in folding cartons, and in terms of corporate annual sales (over $1 billion), number of defendants, duration of the conspiracy (1960 to 1974), and number of transactions involved, this case represents one of the most flagrant violations of the Sherman Antitrust Act in the law's eighty-six-year history. In the indictment the conspirators were charged with the following crimes:

1. Disclosing to other members of the conspiracy the price being charged or to be charged for a particular folding carton to the buyer of that folding carton, with the understanding that the other members of the conspiracy would submit a noncompetitive bid, or no bid, on that folding carton to that buyer.
2. Agreeing with other members of the conspiracy who were supplying the same folding carton to a buyer on the price to be charged to that buyer.
3. Agreeing with other members of the conspiracy on increases in list prices of certain folding cartons.

Shortly after being indicted, all but one of the corporate executives pleaded guilty; later some tried to change their pleas to nolo contendere, an effort that was vigorously opposed by the government. According to the government statement,

> These defendants were not engaged in a short-term violation based on sudden market pressures; price-fixing was their way of doing business. The participants demonstrated a knowing, blatant disregard for antitrust laws. One grand jury witness testified that during a six-year period he personally engaged in thousands of price-fixing transactions with competitors which were illegal.[1] This illegal conduct was carried on in all parts of the country by all management levels in the billion-dollar folding-carton industry. The thousands upon thousands of exchanges of prices with competitors, the dozens upon dozens of meetings with competitors were done with a single purpose and design—to eliminate price competition in this industry. (Government's Statement of Reasons and Authorities in Opposition to Defendants' Motions to Plead *Nolo Contendere, United States v. Alton Box Board Company,* Criminal Action No. 76 CR 199 [May 7, 1976] at 10-11)

One executive of a large corporation stated: "The meetings and exchange of price information were well known to the senior management and in the industry as a whole." Another stated: "Meetings of competitors were a way of life in the folding carton industry."

Community standards can also encourage wrongdoing in an industry. Some businessmen may be able to justify illicit behavior if they see it as conforming to community norms (Chibnall and Saunders, 1977). Discussing the variations in obedience to laws by a group of manufacturing companies within the shoe industry, Lane (1953) concluded that "the [community's] attitude toward the law, government, and the morality of illegality" (p. 160) is highly influential. Even though the companies he studied were in the same industry and were subject to the same laws, variation in law disobedience was great. In Haverhill, Massachusetts, 7 percent of the companies were in violation, while in Auburn, Maine, 44 percent were. Lane concluded that such differences might be explained by the home community's attitudes about the importance of law and government and its tolerance of illegal behavior.

THE EXECUTIVE IN THE CORPORATION: THE MAKING OF A CORPORATE CRIMINAL

In their well-known analysis of large-scale organization, March and Simon (1958) developed a theory to explain how employees can be induced to make decisions that are correct from the standpoint of an organization such as a corporation. Basically, they claimed that the organization's elite controls the premises of decisionmaking for subordinates by setting priorities and regulating the flow of communication; thus, top officials manipulate subordinates' assessments of situations in a system of unobtrusive control (cf. Perrow, 1972, pp. 152–157).

In his discussion of the nature of corporations, Drucker (1972, p. 40) affirmed that a natural tendency exists in every large-scale organization to discourage initiative and encourage conformity. A primary means of fostering conformity in corporations is through the training of persons who are likely to hold positions of responsibility. Studies have been made in detail of how corporations lead new managers through an initiation period designed to weaken their ties with external groups, including their own families, and encourage a feeling of dependence on and attachment to the corporation (Madden, 1977; Margolis, 1979). Outside connections are reduced, and a club mentality is bred through overwork, frequent transfers, which inhibit attachment to local communities, and provisions for recreational and educational needs during leisure time. Co-workers and higher-ups become "significant others" in the individual's work and social life. "Briefly, this all suggests that organization members can be socialized to accept the goal structure of the organization" (Meier, 1975, p. 10). After interviews with corporate executives, Margolis (1979) concluded that executive transfers to other communities play a key role in the psychological initiation of managers. By last-minute assignments and out-of-town work the priority of the corporation is established. Not surprisingly, recruiters of top executives claim that corporations tend to hire "our kind of person" in terms of managerial style and family commitments, which might interfere with corporate responsibilities, "physical appearance, and personal habits" (*Wall*

Street Journal, September 19, 1979). In an advertisement in the *Wall Street Journal* (September 20, 1979), the president of Solfan Corporation bluntly noted: "The job of personnel director at our company is not for everyone. I know because this year I have already had two men in this position. It wasn't for them. If your family or your 'life-style' or your kid's boy scout experience is more important to you than your job, then this isn't for you."

Ability to socialize employees so thoroughly into the corporate world insures one of the main characteristics of bureaucratic organizations described by Max Weber: "The very nature of a bureaucracy, as Weber so well demonstrated, is to make the *individual dispensable*" (Stone, 1975, p. 65). In this sense, the corporation is constructed not of persons but of roles and positions that it has created and defined and therefore over which it has control. This permits individual movement into and out of the corporation without a disruption of activity; the only function of persons is to carry out the activities that belong to those positions they hold (Coleman, 1978, p. 26).

The end product in many cases is what has been called a "functionary" in other contexts, "a new kind of man who in his role of serving the organization is morally unbounded. . . . His ethic is the ethic of the good soldier: take the order, do the job" (Howton, 1969, pp. 5–6). Given the outcomes desired at the higher levels, generally the employee neither questions these ends nor his use of the most efficient or quickest means of achieving them. In his examination of the electrical price-fixing conspiracy, Cook (1966) discussed at length the mentality of the organizational man that encouraged illegal behavior throughout the entire industry: "They were men who surrendered their own individualities to the corporate gods they served. Though they knew that their acts were illegal, not to say unethical, though the shady maneuvering at times affronted their sense of decency, not one found it possible to pronounce an unequivocal 'no' " (p. 38). Similarly, in a case involving the side effects of an anticholesterol drug HE/14 several pharmaceutical corporation executives were convicted of lying about animal studies testing the drug's effects: "No one involved expressed any strong repugnance or even opposition to selling the unsafe drug. Rather they all seemed to drift into the activity without thinking a great deal about it" (Carey, 1978, p. 384).

In his study of the electrical industry price-fixing conspiracy, Geis (1967) discussed a theme common to many studies of individuals involved in corporate crime. That is, the individual has been trained in the illegal behavior as a part of his occupational role. Schrager and Short (1978) believe that individual personality becomes unimportant; criminal behavior stemmed more from the roles they were expected to fulfill than from individual pathology (p. 410).

Some of the testimony in the folding carton price conspiracy specifically indicated how an individual executive learns to use price fixing as an accepted business practice in the industry. One corporate executive said: "Each was introduced to price-fixing practices by his superiors as he came to that point in his career when he had price-fixing responsibility." Another testified as follows:

Q.: Mr. DeFazia, how were you informed that discussing prices was part of your job?

A.: I don't think I was ever really told it was part of my job. I think it was just something I sort of worked right into. That was Mr. Cox's responsibility back in those years. I was young, I was still a green kid, I just picked it right up from working along with him.

Q.: Mr. Cox provided guidance to you? Kind of discussed?

A.: No. We worked in the same office. I guess you just pick it up. I don't know how you would want to say it, just like learning your ABC's, you hear it repeated so often that it's just part of your daily activity.

Lockheed's special review committee established to investigate foreign and domestic illegal payments and practices reported to the SEC in 1976 that senior corporate management was responsible for this strategy. Accountants as well as other employees, however, were aware of the devious methods used in securing, recording, and transferring money to foreign sources for bribes: "Employees learned not to question deviations from standard operating procedures and practices. Moreover, the Committee was told by several witnesses that employees who questioned foreign marketing practices damaged their claims for career advancement." A similar committee for the 3M Company reported to the SEC in 1976 . . . : "We felt that employees should have asked more questions and should have challenged their supervisors more, but realistically, the internal control systems did not provide a means or an atmosphere for challenges to executives at the level of president, chairman of the board, and chief executive officer" (p.31). And yet another review committee, this time of J. Ray McDermott and Co., in a 1977 report to the SEC . . . stated that the corporation . . .

has retained the atmosphere of a privately held company. Employees from senior management on down have taken the position that "the boss's word is law." The critical issue, even in questionable payments, was whether the boss was aware and approved the transaction. . . . Employees who balked at orders from the boss were likely to be fired (p. 6).

Pressures often exist at all levels of the corporation to promote attitudes and behaviors conducive to corporate goals regardless of means. At the lower and middle levels, the corporate actors are encouraged to develop a short-term perspective that "leads them to believe the future is now," thereby producing an overemphasis on corporate objectives and short-run advantages (Madden, 1977, p. 60). Some characterize this process in terms of a great moral struggle between the individual and the "massed corporate hierarchy"—"a man can be crushed and beaten and forced into actions against which his ethical sense rebels" by a hierarchy "supreme in its power and a law unto itself" (Cook, 1966, p. 72). It is far more likely, however, that this process is subtle, and the individual, in the course of his work, gradually comes to identify with the main goals and ideology of the corporation: "If operative goals take on qualities of normative requirements for organizational behavior, and if these norms conflict with those of the legal order, then corporate crime may be indigenous to organizational processes" (Meier, 1975, p. 10).

It would be a mistake to imagine a scenario in which the corporation's directors or highest officers generate these pressures for the lower levels without being affected themselves. Like other social organizations, corporations have inherent socialization pressures that are passed on through the generations. Corporate executives assume roles into which they are duly socialized by the structure and nature of work and the status system, as are lower level employees. Socialization is therefore structural and cultural. Executives are subject, in fact, to the same kinds of indoctrination into the corporate mind as employees at lower levels—through their associations with others who play similar roles, through their training and education, and through their isolation from potentially countervailing influences (Henning, 1973, p. 158). Drucker (1972) noted that executives' contacts outside business tend to be restricted to persons of similar background if not those who work for the same organization. And the very insistence upon loyalty and the restriction of competing interests characteristic of the army [are] typical of corporations: "Hence executive life not only breeds a parochialism of the imagination comparable to the 'military mind' but places a considerable premium on it" (p. 81).

One does not have to picture a corporation composed of automatons marching to the same beat in order to understand how individuals as corporate actors could participate in activities that they might never consider outside the corporate environment.[2] Motivations besides the ones discussed here range from altruistic loyalty to the corporate good to outright self-interest. Many involved in illegal corporate activities regard their acquiescence and active participation as necessary in order to keep their jobs, although they may have no illusions about the illegal and immoral nature of their behavior. A former high-ranking General Motors executive, John Z. DeLorean, contended, for example, that the company knew about the safety problems of the Corvair before production began but failed to take remedial action: "Claims DeLorean: 'Charlie Chayne, vice president of engineering, along with his staff, took a very strong stand against the Corvair as an unsafe car long before it went on sale in 1959. He was not listened to but [was] instead told in effect: "You're not a member of the team. Shut up or go looking for another job" ' " (*Time*, November 19, 1979, p. 85). The decisionmakers were "not immoral men," said DeLorean, but he claimed that they were operating in a business atmosphere in which all was reduced to costs, profit goals, and production deadlines, an atmosphere in which approval was given to a product that the individuals acting alone would not have considered approving (Wright, 1979).

Executives' Rationalizations

A variety of justifications are available to those executives who are confronted with doubt or guilt about illegal or unethical behavior; these justifications allow them to neutralize the negative connotations of their behavior. In an examination of a famous case of business corruption and bribery in England, Chibnall and Saunders (1977) pointed out that an individual can fully understand the illegal nature of his actions but can justify them by citing the pervasiveness of such practices in the business world. There is considerable evidence that business executives believe that unethical practices are common. A *Harvard Business Review* survey found that four out of five executives maintained that at least some generally accepted practices in their industries were unethical, and when asked whether they thought that other executives would violate a code of ethics if they knew they would not be caught, four out of seven replied affirmatively (Baumhart, 1961). Studies made in 1976 by Uniroyal and a University of Georgia professor found that 70 percent of Uniroyal managers and 64 percent of a random sample of corporate managers perceived company pressure on personal ethics. "Most managers believed that their peers would not refuse orders to market off-standard and possibly dangerous products (although an even larger majority insisted they would personally reject such orders), and a majority thought young managers automatically go along with superiors to show loyalty" (Madden, 1977, p. 66). Confidential interviews with top officials, usually chief executive officers, of fifty-seven of the largest U.S. corporations in 1975 indicated that they felt unethical behavior was widespread in industry and, for the most part, had to be accepted as part of daily business (Silk and Vogel, 1976). Business results and the survival of the corporation inevitably came before personal ethics: "If we wait until all businessmen are ethical before we start our sales job, we will never get started" (p. 228). Moreover, there was great reluctance to criticize other businessmen for illegal actions. Finally, the behavior was legitimized through the good intentions of the actors and through its consequences; that is, no one was actually harmed, the firm benefited, and customer needs were served.

The issue of morals and corporate conduct became a topic of discussion in 1979 when it was reported that a Harvard Business School professor, in his business decisionmaking course, trained students to misrepresent their positions in negotiations and other business dealings (*Wall Street Journal*, January 15, 1979). Students found that hiding certain facts, bluffing, and even outright lying got them a better deal and, in part, a better grade. The course was designed to teach budding businessmen to negotiate in the "real world," in which "lying"—or "strategic misrepresentation"—is resorted to in some cases. As the article in the *Wall Street Journal* commented, "It's a safe bet that . . . students will eventually get to practice what they learn." (According to surveys by the school, 14 percent of its alumni are presidents or chief executive officers of their firms, and 19 percent of the top three officers of all *Fortune* 500 companies are Harvard Business School graduates.)

References

Baumhart, Raymond C., (1961) "How Ethical Are Businessmen?" *Harvard Business Review* 39 (July–August): 5–176.

Brenner S. N., and E. A. Molander (1977). "Is the Ethics of Business Changing?" *Harvard Business Review* 55 (January–February): 59–70.

Carey, James T. (1978). *Introduction to Criminology.* Englewood Cliffs: Prentice-Hall.

Chibnall, S., and P. Saunders (1977). "Worlds Apart: Notes on the Social Reality of Corruption." *British Journal of Sociology* 28 (June): 138–153.

Clark, John P. and Richard Hollinger (1977). "On the Feasibility of Empirical Studies of White-Collar Crime," in Robert F. Meier (ed.), *Theory in Criminology: Contemporary Views.* Beverly Hills: Sage.

Cook, Fred J. (1966). *The Corrupted Land: The Social Morality of Modern America.* New York: Macmillan.

Cressey, Donald R. (1976). "Restraint of Trade, Recidivism, and Delinquent Neighborhoods." In James F. Short, Jr. (ed.), *Delinquency, Crime, and Society.* Chicago: University of Chicago Press.

Drucker, Peter F. (1972). *Concept of the Corporation.* Revised edition. New York: Mentor.

Geis, Gilbert (1967). "White Collar Crime: The Heavy Electrical Equipment Antitrust Cases of 1961." In Marshall B. Clinard and Richard Quinney (eds.), *Criminal Behavior Systems: A Typology.* New York: Holt, Rinehart & Winston.

——— (1973). "Deterring Corporate Crime." In Ralph Nader and Mark J. Green (eds.), *Corporate Power in America,* New York: Grossman.

Hay, George and Daniel Kelley (1974). "An Empirical Survey of Price-fixing Conspiracies." *Journal of Law and Economics* 17 (April):13–39.

Henning, Joel F. (1973). "Corporate Social Responsibility: Shell Game for the Seventies?" In Ralph Nader and Mark J. Green (eds.), *Corporate Power in America*, New York: Grossman.

Herling, John (1962). *The Great Price Conspiracy: The Story of the Antitrust Violations in the Electrical Industry*. Washington, D.C.: Luce.

Howton, F. W. (1969). *Functionaries*. Chicago: Quadrangle.

Lane, Robert E. (1953). "Why Businessmen Violate the Law." *Journal of Criminal Law, Criminology and Police Science* 44 (July): 151–165. Reprinted in Gilbert Geis and Robert R. Meier (eds.), *White-Collar Crime: Offenses in Business, Politics, and the Professions*. Revised edition. New York: Free Press.

Madden, Carl (1977). "Forces Which Influence Ethical Behavior." In Clarence Walton (ed.), *The Ethics of Corporate Conduct*. Englewood Cliffs: Prentice-Hall.

March, J., and H. Simon (1958). *Organizations*. New York: Wiley.

Margolis, D. R. (1979). *The Managers: Corporate Life in America*. New York: Morrow.

Meier, Robert F. (1975). "Corporate Crime as Organizational Behavior." Address presented at the American Society of Criminology meeting. November.

Perrow, Charles (1972). *Complex Organizations: A Critical Essay*. Chicago: Scott, Foresman.

Riedel, Marc (1968). "Corporate Crime and Interfirm Organization: A Study of Penalized Sherman Act Violations." *Graduate Sociology Club Journal* 8: 74–97.

Schrager, Laura S., and James R. Short, Jr. (1978). "Toward a Sociology of Organizational Crime." *Social Problems* 25 (No.4): 407–419.

Securities and Exchange Commission Report (1977). Lockheed Aircraft Corporation, Internal Audit, Form 8K (May).

——— (1977). J. Ray McDermott. Report of the Audit Committee, Board of Directors, Form 8K (May).

——— (1975). Minnesota Mining and Manufacturing. Report of the Special Agent to the Board of Directors, Form 8K (October).

Shaplen, Robert (1978). "Annals of Crime: The Lockheed Incident." *New Yorker* (January 23):48–74, (January 30):78–91.

Silk, L. Howard, and David Vogel (1976). *Ethics and Profits: The Crisis of Confidence in American Business*. New York: Simon and Schuster.

Stone, Christopher (1975). *Where the Law Ends: The Social Control of Corporate Behavior*. New York: Harper & Row.

Sutherland, Edwin H. (1949). *White Collar Crime*. New York: Holt.

Tiedemann, Klaus (1974). *Subventions: Kriminalität in der Bundesrepublik*. Reinbek bei Hamburg: Rowohlt.

Woodmansee, John (1975). *The World of a Giant Corporation: A Report from the GE Project*. Seattle: North Country.

Wright, J. Patrick (1979). *On a Clear Day You Can See G.M.* Detroit: Wright Enterprises.

Notes

1. Illegal telephone calls between corporate executives were frequent. As one conspirator put it concerning price increases of cartons sold to the frozen food industry, "If there was a need for an increase he would call the others, see if [the] . . . percentage increase that he proposed was acceptable to them and if it was, then all the companies would move in the general area of the same percentage."

2. "Some may even find covert activity exciting, as noted in the case of Equity Funding. In this environment of fun, excitement, and do-as-you're-told corporate loyalty, the law's threats are simply no guarantee that people are going to comply. Indeed, what is worse, I have a strong suspicion—shared by others who have represented corporate clients in their tangled affairs—that being on the edge of the law can even lend a tingle of 007 intrigue to the life of middle-level corporate operatives" (Stone, 1975, p. 69).

46 / The Social Integration of Queers and Peers

ALBERT J. REISS, JR.

An attempt is made in this paper to describe the sexual relation between "delinquent peers" and "adult queers" and to account for its social organization. This transaction is one form of homosexual prostitution between a young male and an adult male fellator. The adult male client pays a delinquent boy prostitute a sum of money in order to be allowed to act as a fellator. The transaction is limited to fellation and is one in which the boy develops no self-conception as a homosexual person or sexual deviator, although he perceives adult male clients as sexual deviators, "queers" or "gay boys."

. . .

THE DATA

Information on the sexual transaction and its social organization was gathered mostly by interviews, partly by social observation of their meeting places. Though there are limitations to inferring social organization from interview data (particularly when the organization arises through behavior that is negatively sanctioned in the larger society), they provide a convenient basis for exploration.

Sex histories were gathered from 18.6 per cent of the 1008 boys between the ages of 12 and 17 who were interviewed in the Nashville, Tennessee, SMA for an investigation of adolescent conforming and deviating behavior. These represent all of the interviews of one of the interviewers during a two-month period, together with interviews with all Nashville boys incarcerated at the Tennessee State Training School for Boys.

. . .

HOW PEERS AND QUEERS MEET

Meetings between adult male fellators and delinquent boys are easily made, because both know how and where to meet within the community space. Those within the common culture know that contact can be established within a relatively short period of time, if it is wished. The fact that meetings between peers and queers can be made easily is mute evidence of the organized understandings which prevail between the two populations.

There are a large number of places where the boys meet their clients, the fellators. Many of these points are known to all boys regardless of where they reside in the metropolitan area. This is particularly true of the central city locations where the largest number of contact points is found within a small territorial area. Each community area of the city, and certain fringe areas, inhabited by substantial numbers of lower-class persons, also have their meeting places, generally known only to the boys residing in the area.

Queers and peers typically establish contact in public or quasi-public places. Major points of contact include street corners, public parks, men's toilets in public or quasi-public places such as those in transportation depots, parks or hotels, and "second" and "third-run" movie houses (open around the clock and permitting sitting through shows). Bars are seldom points of contact, perhaps largely because they are plied by older male hustlers who lie outside the peer culture and groups, and because bar proprietors will not risk the presence of under-age boys.

There are a number of prescribed modes for establishing contact in these situations. They permit the boys and fellators to communicate intent to one another privately despite the public character of the situation. The major form of establishing contact is the "cruise," with the fellator passing "queer-corners" or locations until his effort is recognized by one of the boys. A boy can then signal—usually by nodding his head, a hand gesticulation signifying OK, following, or responding to commonly understood introductions such as "You got the time?"—that he is prepared to undertake the transaction. Entrepreneur and client then move to a place where the sexual activity is consummated, usually a place affording privacy, protection and hasty exit. "Dolly," a three-time loser at the State Training School, describes one of these prescribed forms of making contact:

> "Well, like at the bus station, you go to the bathroom and stand there pretendin' like . . . and they're standin' there pretendin' like . . . and then they motions their head and walks out and you follow them, and you go someplace. Either they's got a car, or you go to one of them hotels near the depot or some place like that . . . most anyplace."

Frequently contact between boys and fellators is established when the boy is hitchhiking. This is particularly true for boys' first contacts of this nature. Since lower-class boys are more likely than middle-class ones to hitch rides within a city, particularly at night when such contacts are most frequently made, they perhaps are most often solicited in this manner.

The experienced boy who knows a "lot of queers" may phone known fellators directly from a public phone, and some fellators try to establish continued contact with boys by giving them their phone numbers. However, the boys seldom use this means of contact for reasons inherent in their orientation toward the transaction, as we shall see below.

We shall now examine how the transaction is facilitated by these types of situations and the prescribed modes of contact and communication. One of the characteristics of all these contact situations is that they provide a *rationale* for the presence of *both* peers and queers in the *same* situation or place. This rationale is necessary for both parties, for were there high visibility to the presence of either and no ready explanation for it, contact and communication would be far more difficult. Public and quasi-public facilities provide situations which account for the presence of most persons since there is relatively little social control over the establishment of contacts. There is, of course, some risk to the boys and the fellators in making contact in these situations since they are generally known to the police. The Morals Squad may have "stake-outs," but this is one of the calculated risks, and the communication network carries information about their tactics.

A most important element in furnishing a rationale is that these meeting places must account for the presence of delinquent boys of essentially lower-class dress and appearance who make contact with fellators of almost any class level. This is true despite the fact that the social settings which fellators ordinarily choose to establish contact generally vary according to the class level of the fellators. Fellators of high social class generally make contact by "cruising" past streetcorners, in parks, or the men's rooms in "better" hotels, while those from the lower class are likely to select the public bath or transportation depot. There apparently is some general equation of the class position of boys and fellators in the peer-queer transaction. The large majority of fellators in the delinquent peer-queer transaction probably are from the lower class ("apes"). But it is difficult to be certain about the class position of the fellator clients since no study was made of this population.

The absence of data from the fellator population poses difficulties in interpreting the contact relationship. Many fellators involved with delinquent boys do not appear to participate in any overt or covert homosexual groups, such as the organized homosexual community of the "gay world."[1] The "gay world" is the most visible form of organized homosexuality since it is an organized community, but it probably encompasses only a small proportion of all homosexual contact. Even among those in the organized homosexual community, evidence suggests that the homosexual members seek sexual gratification outside their group with persons who are essentially anonymous to them. Excluding homosexual married couples, Leznoff and Westley maintain that there is ". . . a prohibition against sexual relationships within the group . . ."[2] Ross indicates that young male prostitutes are chosen, among other reasons, for the fact that they protect the identity of the client.[3] Both of these factors tend to coerce many male fellators to choose an anonymous contact situation.

It is clear that these contact situations not only provide a rationale for the presence of the parties to the transaction but a guarantee of anonymity. The guarantee does not necessarily restrict social visibility as both the boys and the fellators may recognize cues (including, but not necessarily, those of gesture and dress) which lead to mutual role identification.[4] But anonymity is guaranteed in at least two senses: anonymity of presence is assured in the situation and their personal identity in the community is protected unless disclosed by choice.

There presumably are a variety of reasons for the requirement of anonymity. For many, a homosexual relationship must remain a secret since their other relationships in the community—families, business relationships, etc.—must be protected. Leznoff and Westley refer to these men as the "secret" as contrasted with the "overt" homosexuals,[5] and in the organized "gay world," they are known as "closet fags." For some, there is also a necessity for protecting identity to avoid blackmail.[6] Although none of the peer hustlers reported resorting to blackmail, the adult male fellator may nonetheless hold such an expectation, particularly if he is older or of high social class. Lower-class ones, by contrast, are more likely to face the threat of violence from adolescent boys since they more often frequent situations where they are likely to contact "rough trade." The kind of situation in which the delinquent peer-queer contact is made and the sexual relationship consummated tends to minimize the possibility of violence.

Not all male fellators protect their anonymity; some will let a boy have their phone number and a few "keep a boy." Still, most fellators want to meet boys where they are least likely to be victimized, although boys sometimes roll queers by selecting a meeting place where by prearrangement, their friends can meet them and help roll the queer, steal his car, or commit other acts of violence. Boys generally know that fellators are vulnerable in that they "can't" report their victimization. Parenthetically, it might be mentioned that these boys are not usually aware of their own institutional invulnerability to arrest. An adolescent boy is peculiarly invulnerable to arrest even when found with a fellator since the mores define the boy as exploited.[7]

Situations of personal contact between adolescent boys and adult male fellators also provide important ways to *communicate intent* or to carry out the transaction *without* making the contact particularly visible to others. The wall writings in many of these places are not without their primitive communication value, e.g., "show it hard," and places such as a public restroom provide a modus operandi. The entrepreneur and his customer in fact can meet with little more than an exchange of non-verbal gestures, transact their business with a minimum of verbal communication and part without a knowledge of one another's identity. In most cases, boys report "almost nothing" was said. The sexual transaction may occur with the only formal transaction being payment to the boy.

INDUCTION INTO THE PEER-QUEER TRANSACTION

The peer-queer culture operates through a delinquent peer society. Every boy interviewed in this study who voluntarily established contacts with fellators was also delinquent in many other respects. The evidence shows that contact with fellators is an institutionalized aspect of the organization of lower-class delinquency oriented groups. This is not to say that boys outside these groups never experience relationships with adult male fellators: some do, but they are not participants in groups which sanction the activity according to the prescribed group standards described below. Nor is it to say that all delinquent groups positively sanction the peer-queer transaction since its distribution is unknown.

How, then, do lower-class delinquent boys get to meet fellators? Most boys from the lowest socioeconomic level in large cities are prepared for this through membership in a delinquent group which has a knowledge of how to make contact with fellators and relate to them. This is part of their common culture. Often, too, the peer group socializes the boy in his first experiences or continuing ones with fellators. The behavior is apparently learned within the framework of differential association.

The peer group actually serves as a school of induction for some of its members. The uninitiated boy goes with one or more members of his peer group for indoctrination and his first experience. Doy L., a lower-class boy at a lower-class school and a two-time loser at the State Training School, explains how he got started:

I went along with these older boys down to the bus station, and they took me along and showed me how it was done . . . they'd go in, get a queer, get blowed and get paid . . . if it didn't work right, they'd knock him in the head and get their money . . . they showed me how to do it, so I went in too.

In any case, boys are socialized in the subcultural definitions of peer-queer relations by members of their group and many apply this knowledge when an opportunity arises. Within the group, boys hear reports of experiences which supply the cultural definitions: how contacts are made, how you get money if the queer resists, how much one should expect to get, what kind of behavior is acceptable from the queer, which is to be rejected and how. Boys know all this *before* they have any contact with a fellator. In the case of street gangs, the fellators often pass the neighborhood corner; hence, even the preadolescent boy learns about the activity as the older boys get picked up. As the boy enters adolescence and a gang of his own which takes over the corner, he is psychologically and socially prepared for his first experience, which generally occurs when the first opportunity presents itself. Lester H. illustrates this; his first experience came when he went to one of the common points of convergence of boys and fellators—The Empress Theatre—to see a movie. Lester relates:

I was down in the Empress Theatre and this gay came over and felt me up and asked me if I'd go out . . . I said I would if he'd give me the money as I'd heard they did, and I was gettin' low on it . . . so he took me down by the river and blowed me.

In a substantial number of cases, a brother introduces the boy to his first experience, much as he introduces him to other first experiences. Jimmie M. illustrates this pattern. Jimmie describes how he was led into his first heterosexual experience:

When I was almost 14, my younger brother said he'd screwed this woman and he told me about it, so I went down there and she let me screw her too.

His induction into the peer-queer transaction also occurred through his younger brother:

Well, my younger brother came home and told me this gay'd blowed him and he told me where he lived . . . And, I was scared to do it, but I figured I'd want to see what it was like since the other guys talked about it and my brother'd done it. So I went down there and he blowed me.

Not all boys belonging to groups which sanction peer hustling accept the practice. Some boys reject the peer-queer transaction while retaining membership in the group. It is not too surprising that such exceptions occur. Although in most delinquent groups some forms of sex activity confer status, it is rarely an absolute requisite for participation in such groups. Some boys in gangs which frequently gang shag, for example, refuse to participate in these activities. "I don't like my meat that raw" appears to be an acceptable "out." Exemption appears possible so long as the boy is acceptable in all, if not most, other respects. A lower-class delinquent boy apparently doesn't "chicken-out" or lose his "rep" if he doesn't want to engage in sex behaviors which most of his peers practice. (The same condition may hold for other practices, such as the use of narcotics.) Jerry P. from a lower-class school is in a group where all the other boys go with fellators; but he refuses to become involved, though he goes so far as to ride in the car with one of the gang's "regular queers." Jerry is in a gang which often gets picked up by a well known "local gay," a David B. Jerry admits: "I ride with B. a lot, but he's never done anything to me; I just can't go for that." When asked how he knew B. was a queer, he replied, "Oh, all the guys say so and talk about doin' it with him. . . . I could, but I just don't want to." Joe C., at a school which crosscuts the class structure, was asked if he had any other kind of sex experiences. His reply shows his rejection of his peer group's pattern of behavior with fellators. "You mean the queers?" "Uh huh." "I don't go with any. Most of my friends queer-bait, but I don't." A friend of his, Roy P., also rejects the activity: "Ain't no sense in queer-baitin'; I don't need the money that bad."

The impression should not be gained that most lower-class boys who are solicited by fellators accept the solicitation. A majority of all solicitations are probably refused when the initial contact is made unless several other conditions prevail. The first is that the boy must be a member of a group which permits this form of transaction, indoctrinates the boy with its codes and sanctions his participation in it. Almost all lower-class boys reported they were solicited by a queer at least once. A majority refused the solicitation. Refusal is apparently easy since boys report that queers are seldom insistent. There apparently is a mutual willingness to forego the transaction in such cases, perhaps because the queer cannot afford the risk of exposure, but perhaps also because the probability of his establishing contact on his next try is sufficiently high so that he can "afford" to accept the refusal. Looked at another way, there must be a set of mutual gains and expectations for the solicitation to be accepted and the transaction to proceed. Boys who refuse to be solicited are not vulnerable for another reason: they usually are members of groups which negatively sanction the activity. Such groups generally "bug" boys who go out with fellators and use other techniques of isolation to discourage the transaction. There also are gangs which look upon queers as "fair game" for their aggressive activity. They beat them, roll, and otherwise put upon them. A third condition that must prevail is that the boy who accepts or seeks solicitation from fellators must view the offer as instrumental gain, particularly monetary gain (discussed below).

There are boys, however, particularly those who are quite young, who report a solicitation from a man which they were unable to refuse but which they subsequently rejected as neither gratifying nor instrumentally acceptable. It is these boys who can be said to be "exploited" by adult fellators in the sense that they are either forced into the act against their will, or are at least without any awareness of how to cope with the situation. One such instance is found in the following report:

> This guy picked me up down at Fourth and Union and said he was going over to East Nashville, so I got in . . . but he drove me out on Dickerson Pike. (What'd he do?) . . . Well, he blowed me and it made me feel real bad inside . . . but I know how to deal with queers now . . . ain't one of 'em gonna do that to me again . . . I hate queers. . . . They're crazy.

There is an important admission in the statement, "But I know how to deal with 'em now." The lower-class boy as he grows older learns how to deal with sexual advances from fellators. Boys exchange experiences on how they deal with them and it becomes quite difficult to "exploit" a lower-class boy who is socialized in a peer group. It is perhaps largely the very young boy, such as the one in the case above, or those isolated from peer groups, who are most vulnerable to solicitation without previous preparation for it.

Lower-class boys, as we have seen, have the highest probability of being in situations where they will be solicited by fellators. But, *the lower-class boy who is a member of a career-oriented gang which positively sanctions instrumental relationships with adult male fellators and which initiates members into these practices, and a boy who at the same time perceives himself as "needing" the income which the transaction provides, is most likely to establish personal contact with adult male fellators on a continuing basis.*

It is suggested that the peer-queer transaction is behavior learned through differential association in delinquent gangs. This cannot be demonstrated without resort to a more specific test of the hypothesis. But, as Sutherland has pointed out, "Criminal behavior is partially a function of opportunities to commit special classes of crimes. . . . It is axiomatic that persons who commit a specific crime have the opportunity to commit that crime. . . . While opportunity may be partially a function of association with criminal patterns and of the specialized techniques thus acquired, it is not entirely determined in this manner, and consequently differential association is not a sufficient cause of criminal behavior."[8] Middle-class boys are perhaps excluded from the peer-queer transaction as much through lack of opportunity to commit this special class of crime in their community of exposure as through any criterion of differential association. The structure of the middle-class area is incompatible with the situational requirements for the peer-queer transaction.

NORMS GOVERNING THE TRANSACTION

Does the peer society have any norms about personal relations with fellators? Or, does it simply induct a boy into a relationship by teaching him how to effect the transaction? The answer is that there appear to be several clear-cut norms about the relations between peers and queers, even though there is some deviation from them.

The first major norm is that *a boy must undertake the relationship with a queer solely as a way of making money; sexual gratification cannot be actively sought as a goal in the relationship.* This norm does not preclude a boy from sexual gratification by the act; he simply must not seek this as a goal. Put another way, a boy cannot admit that he failed to get money from the transaction unless he used violence toward the fellator and he cannot admit that he sought it as a means of sexual gratification.

The importance of making money in motivating a boy to the peer-queer transaction is succinctly stated by Dewey H:

> This guy in the Rex Theatre came over and sat down next to me when I was 11 or 12, and he started to fool with me. I got over and sat down another place and he came over and asked me, didn't I want to and he'd pay me five bucks. I figured it was *easy money* so I went with him . . . I didn't do it before that. That wan't too long after I'd moved to South Nashville. I was a pretty good boy before that . . . not real good, but I never ran with a crowd that got into trouble before that. But, I met a lot of 'em there. (Why do you run with queers?) It's *easy money* . . . like I could go out and break into a place when I'm broke and get money that way . . . but that's harder and *you take a bigger risk* . . . with a queer it's *easy money.*

Dewey's comments reveal two important motivating factors in getting money from queers, both suggested by the expression, "easy money." First, the money is easy in that it can be made quickly. Some boys reported that when they needed money for a date or a night out, they obtained it within an hour through the sexual transaction with a queer. All a boy has to do is go to a place where he will be contacted, wait around, get picked up, carried to a place where the sexual transaction occurs, and in a relatively short period of time he obtains the money for his service.

It is easy money in another and more important sense for many of these boys. Boys who undertake the peer-queer transaction are generally members of career-oriented delinquent groups. Rejecting the limited opportunities for making money by legitimate means or finding them inaccessible, their opportunities to make money by illegitimate means may also be limited or the risk may be great. Theft is an available means, but it is more difficult and involves greater risk than the peer-queer transaction. Delinquent boys are not unaware of the risks they take. Under most circumstances, delinquents may calculate an act of stealing as "worth the risk." There are occasions, however, when the risk is calculated as too great. These occasions occur when the "heat" is on the boy or when he can least afford to run the risk of being picked up by the police, as is the case following a pickup by the police, being put on probation or parole, or being warned that incarceration will follow the next violation. At such times, boys particularly calculate whether they can afford to take the risk. Gerald L., describing a continuing relationship with a fellator who gave him his phone number, reflects Dewey's attitude toward minimizing risk in the peer-queer transaction: "So twic'd after that when I was gettin' real low and couldn't risk stealin' and gettin' caught, I called him and he took me out and blowed me." Here is profit with no investment of capital and a minimum of risk in social, if not in psychological, terms.

The element of risk coupled with the wish for "easy money" enters into our understanding of the peer-queer relationship in another way. From a sociological point of view, the peer-queer sexual transaction occurs between two major types of deviators—"delinquents" and "queers." Both types of deviators risk negative sanctions for their deviant acts. The more often one has been arrested or incarcerated, the more punitive the sanctions from the larger social system for both types of deviators. At some point, therefore, both calculate risks and seek to minimize them, at least in the very short run. Each then becomes a means for the other to minimize risk.

When the delinquent boy is confronted with a situation in which he wants money and risks little in getting it, how is he to get it without working? Illegitimate activities frequently provide the "best" opportunity for easy money. These activities often are restricted in kind and number for adolescents and the risk of negative sanctions is high. Under such circumstances, the service offered a queer is a chance to make easy money with a minimum of risk.

Opportunities for sexual gratification are limited for the adult male fellator, particularly if he wishes to minimize the risk of detection in locating patrons, to avoid personal involvement and to get his gratification when he wishes it. The choice of a lower-class male, precisely because of his class position somewhat reduces the risk. If the lower-class male also is a delinquent, the risk is minimized to an even greater degree.

This is not to say that the parties take equal risks in the situation. Of the two, the fellator perhaps is less able to minimize his risk since he still risks violence from his patron, but much less so if a set of expectations arise which control the use of violence as well. The boy is most able to minimize his risk since he is likely to be defined as "exploited" in the situation if caught.

Under special circumstances, boys may substitute other gratifications for the goal of money, provided that these gratifications do not include sexual gratification as a major goal. These special circumstances are the case where an entire gang will "make a night (or time) of it" with one or more adult male fellators. Under these circumstances, everyone is excepted from the subcultural expectations about making money from the fellator because everyone participates and there is no reason for everyone (or anyone) to take money. For the group to substitute being given a "good time" by a "queer" for the prescribed financial transaction is, of course, the exception which proves the rule.

Several examples of group exemption from the prescribed norm of a financial gain were discovered. Danny S., leader of the Black Aces, tells of his gang's group experiences with queers: "There's this one gay who takes us to the Colonial Motel out on Dickerson Pike . . . usually it's a bunch of us boys and we all get drunk and get blowed by this queer . . . we don't get any money then . . . it's more a drinking party." The Black Aces are a fighting gang and place great stress on physical prowess, particularly boxing. All of its members have done time more than once at the State Training School. During one of these periods, the school employed a boxing instructor whom the boys identified as "a queer," but the boys had great respect for him since he taught them how to box and was a game fighter. Danny refers to him in accepting terms: "He's a real good guy. He's fought with us once or twice and we drink with him when we run into him. . . . He's taken us to Miter Dam a coupla times; he's got a cabin up there on the creek and he blows us. . . . But mostly we just drink and have a real good time." These examples illustrate the instrumental orientation of the gang members. If the expense of the gang members getting drunk and having a good time are borne by a "queer," each member is released from the obligation to receive cash. The relationship in this case represents an exchange of services rather than that of money for a service.

The second major norm operating in the relationship is that *the sexual transaction must be limited to mouth-genital fellation. No other sexual acts are generally tolerated.*[9] The adult male fellator must deport himself in such a way as to re-enforce the instrumental aspects of the role relationship and to insure affective neutrality.[10] For the adult male fellator to violate the boy's expectation of "getting blowed," as the boys refer to the act, is to risk violence and loss of service. Whether or not the boys actually use violent means as often as they say they do when expectations are violated, there is no way of knowing with precision. Nevertheless, whenever boys reported they used violent means, they always reported some violation of the subcultural expectations. Likewise, they never reported a violation of the subcultural expectations which was not followed by the use of violent means, unless it was clearly held up as an exception. Bobby A. expresses the boys' point of view on the use of violent means in the following exchange: "How much did you usually get?" "Around five dollars; if they didn't give that much, I'd beat their head in." "Did they ever want you to do anything besides blow you?" "Yeh, sometimes . . . like they want me to blow them, but I'd tell them to go to hell and maybe beat them up."

Boys are very averse to being thought of in a queer role or engaging in acts to fellation. The act of fellation is defined as a "queer" act. Most boys were asked whether they would engage in such behavior. All but those who had the status of "punks" denied they had engaged in behavior associated with the queer role. Asking a boy whether he is a fellator meets with strong denial and often with open hostility. This could be interpreted as defensive behavior against latent homosexuality. Whether or not this is the case, strong denial could be expected because the question goes counter to the subcultural definitions of the peer role in the transaction.

A few boys on occasion apparently permit the fellator to perform other sexual acts. These boys, it is guessed, are quite infrequent in a delinquent peer population. Were their acts known to the members of the group, they would soon be defined as outside the delinquent peer society. Despite the limitation of the peer-queer sexual transaction to mouth-genital fellation, there are other sexual transactions which the peer group permits members to perform under special circumstances. They are, for example, permitted to perform the *male* roles in "crimes against nature," such as in pederasty ("cornholing" to the boys), bestiality (sometimes referred to as buggery) and carnal copulation with a man involving no orifice (referred to as "slick-legging" among the boys) provided that the partner is roughly of the same age and not a member of the group and provided also that the boys are confined to the single-sex society of incarcerated delinquent boys. Under no circumstances, however, is the female role in carnal copulation acceptable in any form. It is taboo. Boys who accept the female role in sexual transactions occupy the lowest status position among delinquents. They are "punks."

The third major norm operating on the relationship is that *both peers and queers, as participants, should remain affectively neutral during the transaction.* Boys within the peer society define the ideal form of the role with the fellator as one in which the boy is the entrepreneur and the queer is viewed as purchasing a service. The service is a business deal where a sexual transaction is purchased for an agreed upon amount of money. In the typical case, the boy is neither expected to enjoy nor be repulsed by the sexual transaction; mouth-genital fellation is accepted as a service offered in exchange for a fee. It should be kept in mind that self-gratification is permitted in the sexual act. Only the motivation of sexual gratification in the transaction is tabooed. But self-gratification must occur without displaying either positive or negative affect toward the queer. In the prescribed form of the role relationship, the boy sells a service for profit and the queer is to accept it without show of emotion.

The case of Thurman L., one of three brothers who are usually in trouble with the law, illustrates some aspects of the expected pattern of affective neutrality. Thurman has had a continuing relationship with a queer, a type of relationship in which it would be anticipated that affective neutrality would be difficult to maintain. This relationship continued, in fact, with a 21 year old "gay" until the man was "sent to the pen." When queried about his relationship with this man and why he went with him, Thurman replied:

> Don't know . . . money and stuff like that I guess. (What do you mean? . . . stuff like that?) Oh, clothes. . . . (He ever bought you any clothes?) Sure, by this one gay. . . . (You mind being blowed?) No. (You like it?) Don't care one way or the other. I don't like it, and I don't not like it. (You like this one gay?) Nope, can't say that I liked anythin' about him. (How come you do it then?) Well, the money for one thing. . . . I need that. (You enjoy it some?) Can't say I do or don't.

More typical than Thurman's expression of affective neutrality is the boy who accepts it as "OK" or, "It's all right; I don't mind it." Most frequent of all is some variant of the statement: "It's OK, but I like the money best of all." The definition of affective neutrality fundamentally requires only that there be no positive emotional commitment to the queer *as a person.* The relationship must be essentially an impersonal one, even though the pure form of the business relationship may seldom be attained. Thus, it is possible for a boy to admit self-gratification without admitting any emotional commitment to the homosexual partner.

Although the peer group prescribes affective neutrality toward the queer in the peer-queer transaction, queers must be regarded as low prestige persons, held in low esteem, and the queer role is taboo. The queer is most commonly regarded as "crazy, I guess." Some boys take a more rationalistic view: "They're just like that, I guess" or, "They're just born that way." While there are circumstances under which one is permitted to like a particular fellator, as in the case of all prejudices attached to devalued status, the person who is liked must be the exception which states the rule. Though in many cases both the boy and the fellator are of very low class origins, and in many cases both are altogether repulsive in appearance, cleanliness and dress by middle-class standards, these are not the standards of comparison used by the boys. The deviation of the queers from the boy's norms of masculine behavior places the fellator in the lowest possible status, even "beneath contempt." If the fellator violates the expected affective relationship in the transaction, he may be treated not only with violence but with contempt as well. The seller of the service ultimately reserves the right to set the conditions for his patrons.

Some boys find it difficult to be emotionally neutral toward the queer role and its occupants; they are either personally offended or affronted by the behavior of queers. JDC is an instance of a boy who is personally offended by their behavior; yet he is unable to use violence even when expectations governing the transaction are violated. He does not rely very much on the peer-queer relationship as a source of income. JDC expresses his view: "I don't really go for that like some guys; I just do it when I go along with the crowd. . . . You know. . . . That, and when I do it for money. . . . And I go along. . . . But . . . I hate queers. They embarrass me." "How?" "Well, like you'll be in the lobby at the theatre, and they'll come up and pat your ass or your prick right in front of everybody. I just can't go for that—not me." Most of the boys wouldn't either, but they would have resorted to violent means in this situation.

Two principal types of boys maintain a continuing relationship with a known queer. A few boys develop such relationships to insure a steady income. While this is permitted within peer society for a short period of time, boys who undertake it for extended periods of time do so with some risk, since in the words of the boys, "queers can be got too easy." The boy who is affectively involved with a queer or his role is downgraded in status to a position, "Ain't no better'n a queer." There are also a few boys affectively committed to a continuing relationship with an adult male homosexual. Such boys usually form a strong dependency relationship with him and are kept much as the cabin boys of old. This type of boy is clearly outside the peer society of delinquents and is isolated from participation in gang activity. The sociometric pattern for such boys is one of choice into more than one gang, none of which is reciprocated.

Street-hustlers are also downgraded within the peer society, generally having reputations as "punk kids." The street-hustler pretty much "goes it alone." Only a few street-hustlers were interviewed for this study. None of them was a member of an organized delinquent group. The sociometric pattern for each, together with his history of delinquent activity, placed them in the classification of non-conforming isolates.

A fourth major norm operating on the peer-queer relationship serves as a primary factor in stabilizing the system. This norm holds that *violence must not be used so long as the relationship conforms to the shared set of expectations between queers and peers.* So long as the fellator conforms to the norms governing the transaction in the peer-queer society, he runs little risk of violence from the boys.

The main reason, perhaps, for this norm is that uncontrolled violence is potentially disruptive of any organized system. All organized social systems must control violence. If the fellator clients were repeatedly the objects of violence, the system as it has been described could not exist. Most boys who share the common expectations of the peer-queer relationship do not use violent means unless the expectations are violated. To use violence, of course, is to become affectively involved and therefore another prescription of the relationship is violated.

It is not known whether adult male fellators who are the clients of delinquent entrepreneurs share the boys' definition of the norm regarding the use of violence. They may, therefore, violate expectations of the peer society through ignorance of the system rather than from any attempt to go beyond the set of shared expectations.

There are several ways the fellator can violate the expectations of boys. The first concerns money: refusal to pay or paying too little may bring violence from most boys. Fellators may also violate peer expectations by attempting to go beyond the mouth-genital sexual act. If such an attempt is made, he is usually made an object of aggression as in the following excerpt from Dolly's sex history:

> (You like it?) It's OK. I don't mind it. It feels OK. (They ever try anything else on you?) They usually just blow and that's all. (Any ever try anything else on you?) Oh sure, but we really fix 'em . . . throw 'em out of the car. . . . Once a gay tried that and we rolled him and threw him out of the car. Then we took the car and stripped it (laughs with glee).

Another way the fellator violates a boy's expectations is to introduce considerable affect into the relationship. It appears that affect is least acceptable in two forms, both of which could be seen as "attacks on his masculinity." In one form, the queer violates the affective neutrality requirement by treating the adolescent boy as if he were a girl or in a girl's role during the sexual transaction, as for example, by speaking to him in affectionate terms such as "sweetie." There are many reasons why the feminine sex role is unacceptable to these lower-class boys, including the fact that such boys place considerable emphasis on being "tough" and masculine. Walter Miller, for example, observes that:

. . . The almost compulsive lower class concern with "masculinity" derives from a type of compulsive reaction-formation. A concern over homosexuality runs like a persistent thread through lower class culture—manifested by the institutionalized practice of "baiting queers," often accompanied by violent physical attacks, an expressed contempt for "softness" or frills, and the use of the local term for "homosexual" as a general pejorative epithet (e.g., higher class individuals or upwardly mobile peers are frequently characterized as "fags" or "queers").[11]

Miller sees violence as part of a reaction-formation against the matriarchal lower-class household where the father often is absent. For this reason, he suggests, many lower-class boys find it difficult to identify with a male role, and the "collective" reaction-formation is a cultural emphasis on masculinity. Violence toward queers is seen as a consequence of this conflict. Data from our interviews suggests that among career-oriented delinquents, violation of the affective-neutrality requirement in the peer-queer relationship is at least as important in precipitating violence toward "queers." There are, of course, gangs which were not studied in this investigation which "queer-bait" for the express purpose of "rolling the queer."

The other form in which the fellator may violate the affective neutrality requirement is to approach the boy and make suggestive advances to him when he is with his age-mates, either with girls or with his peer group when he is not located for "business." In either case, the sexual advances suggest that the boy is not engaged in a business relationship within the normative expectations of the system, but that he has sexual motivation as well. The delinquent boy is expected to control the relationship with his customers. He is the entrepreneur "looking" for easy money or at the very least he must appear as being merely receptive to business; this means that he is receptive only in certain situations and under certain circumstances. He is not in business when he is with girls and he is not a businessman when he is cast in a female role. To be cast in a female role before peers is highly unacceptable, as the following account suggests:

> This gay comes up to me in the lobby of the Empress when we was standin' around and starts feelin' me up and callin' me Sweetie and like that . . . and, I just couldn't take none of that there . . . what was he makin' out like I was a queer or somethin' . . . so I jumps him right then and there and we like to of knocked his teeth out.

The sexual advance is even less acceptable when a girl is involved:

> I was walkin' down the street with my steady girl when this gay drives by that I'd been with once before and he whistles at me and calls, "hi Sweetie." . . . And, was I mad . . . so I went down to where the boys was and we laid for him and beat on him 'til he like to a never come to . . . ain't gonna take nothin' like that off'n a queer.

In both of these instances, not only is the boys' masculinity under attack, but the affective neutrality requirement of the business transaction is violated. The queer's behavior is particularly unacceptable, however, because it occurs in a peer setting where the crucial condition is the maintenance of the boy's status within the group. A lower-class boy cannot afford to be cast in less than a highly masculine role before lower-class girls nor risk definition as a queer before peers. His role within his peer group is under threat even if he suffers *no* anxiety about masculinity. Not only the boy himself but his peers perceive such behavior as violating role expectations and join him in violent acts toward the fellator to protect the group's integrity and status.

If violence generally occurs only when one of the major peer norms has been violated, it would also seem to follow that *violence is a means of enforcing the peer entrepreneurial norms of the system.* Violence or the threat of violence is thus used to keep adult male fellators in line with the boy's expectations in his customer role. It represents social control, a punishment meted out to the fellator who violates the cultural expectation. Only so long as the fellator seeks gratification from lower-class boys in a casual pick-up or continuing relationship where he pays money for a "blow-job," is he reasonably free from acts of violence.

There is another, and perhaps more important reason for the use of violence when the peer defined norms of the peer-queer relationship are violated. The formally prescribed roles for peers and queers are basically the roles involved in all institutionalized forms of prostitution, the prostitute and the client. But in most forms of prostitution, whether male or female, the hustlers perceive of themselves in hustler roles, and furthermore the male hustlers also develop a conception of themselves as homosexual whereas *the peer hustler in the peer-queer relationship develops no conception of himself either as prostitute or as homosexual.*

The fellator risks violence, therefore, if he threatens the boy's self-conception by suggesting that the boy may be homosexual and treats him as if he were.

Violence seems to function, then, in two basic ways for the peers. On the one hand, it integrates their norms and expectations by controlling and combatting behavior which violates them. On the other hand, it protects the boy's self-identity as nonhomosexual and reinforces his self-conception as "masculine."

The other norms of the peer society governing the peer-queer transaction also function to prevent boys in the peer-queer society from defining themselves as homosexual. The prescriptions that the goal is money, that sexual gratification is not to be sought as an end in the relationship, that affective neutrality be maintained toward the fellator and that only mouth-genital fellation is permitted, all tend to insulate the boy from a homosexual self-definition. So long as he conforms to these expectations, *his "significant others" will not define him as homosexual;* and this is perhaps the most crucial factor in his own self-definition. The peers define one as homosexual not on the basis of homosexual *behavior* as such, but on the basis of participation in the homosexual *role*, the "queer" role. The reactions of the larger society, in defining the *behavior* as homosexual is unimportant in their own self-definition. What is important to them is the reactions of their peers to violation of peer group norms which define roles in the peer-queer transaction.

. . .

Notes

1. See, for example, Maurice Leznoff and William A. Westley, "The Homosexual Community," *Social Problems,* 4 (April, 1956), pp. 257–263.

2. *Ibid.,* p. 258.

3. H. Laurence Ross, "The 'Hustler' in Chicago," *The Journal of Student Research,* 1 (September, 1959), p. 15.

4. The cues which lead to the queer-peer transaction can be subtle ones. The literature on adult male homosexuality makes it clear that adult males who participate in homosexual behavior are not generally socially visible to the public by manner and dress.

5. Maurice Leznoff and William A. Westley, *op. cit.,* pp. 260–261.

6. Ross notes that, failing in the con-man role, some hustlers resort to extortion and blackmail since they provide higher income. See Ross, *op. cit.,* p. 16. Sutherland discusses extortion and blackmail of homosexuals as part of the practice of professional thieves. The "muzzle" or "mouse" is part of the role of the professional thief. See Edwin Sutherland, *The Professional Thief,* Chicago: University of Chicago Press, 1937, pp. 78–81.

7. Albert J. Reiss, Jr., "Sex Offenses: The Marginal Status of the Adolescent," *Law and Contemporary Problems,* 25 (Spring, 1960), pp. 322–324 and 326–327.

8. Albert Cohen, Alfred Lindesmith and Karl Schuessler (editors), *The Sutherland Papers,* Bloomington, Indiana: The University of Indiana Press, 1956, p. 31.

9. It is not altogether clear why mouth-genital fellation is the only sexual act which is tolerated in the peer-queer transaction. The act seems to conform to the more "masculine" aspects of the role than do most, but not all possible alternatives. Ross has suggested to me that it also involves less bodily contact and therefore may be less threatening to the peers' self-definitions. One possible explanation therefore for the exclusiveness of the relationship to this act is that it is the most masculine alternative involving the least threat to peers' self-definition as nonhustler and nonhomosexual.

10. Talcott Parsons in *The Social System* (Glencoe: The Free Press, 1951, Chapter III) discusses this kind of role as ". . . the segregation of specific instrumental performances, both from expressive orientations other than the specifically appropriate rewards and from other components of the instrumental complex." (p. 87).

11. Walter Miller, "Lower-Class Culture as a Generating Milieu of Gang Delinquency," *The Journal of Social Issues,* 14 (1958), No. 3, p. 9.

47 / Role Enactment, Self, and Identity in the Systematic Check Forger

EDWIN M. LEMERT

. . .

Check forgery, in contrast to crimes such as assault, robbery, or burglary, is distinguished by its low social visibility. At the time the bogus check is passed there is nothing in the act which reveals that it is deviant or criminal. No special tools or equipment are needed for the crime, as with burglary, nor is any special setting required for the action, as is true with the "store" or the front of a bank, where the confidence man activates his fraudulent enterprises. Furthermore, there are few or no cues in interaction which give feedback to the forger from the victim nor from his own overt responses to indicate that he is behaving contrary to expectations; only later does the act become so defined and then never in direct interaction between the forger and his victim. Here is deviant behavior whose manifest or "existential" qualities do not differentiate or identify the person as a deviant.

Studies of the characteristics of check forgers based upon samples of those in jails, prisons, or on probation show considerable heterogeneity. However, it can be said that in general they more nearly resemble the general middle-class population than they do the populations of jails and prisons. They tend to be native white in orgin, male, and much older than other criminals when they commit their first crimes—somewhere in their late 20's or early 30's. Their intelligence averages much higher than that of other criminals and they equal or surpass the general population in years of education completed. Skilled, clerical, professional, and managerial occupations are at least as fully represented among forgers as in the general population, perhaps more so. An impressive small minority have come from prestigeful, wealthy families, or those in which siblings have achieved social eminence, although considerable discounting of forgers' claims on this point is necessary. A high percentage of forgers have been long-time residents in the communities in which they committed their first offenses, but relatively few have lived in so-called "delin-quency areas." Forgers are less likely than other criminals to have had a record of delinquency in their youth.

Prior socialization as delinquents or criminals is insufficient to ex-plain the crimes of a large percent, or even the majority, of persons who pass bad checks. Many have acquired and lived a considerable part of their early adult lives according to conventional middle-class morality. Typically they tend to express aversion to the idea of using violence in interpersonal dealings for whatever purpose. At the same time it must be said that an occasional person comes into forgery via the criminal route—the "short" con man turned forger, or the "old pro" burglar fallen on hard times, who has turned to passing bad checks for a livelihood.

Little effort has been made at systematic personality assessment of check forgers. Yet detectives have for a long time looked upon them as a distinctive criminal type; particularly those designated as profes-sionals.[1]

> The professional forger is a man of great ability, and naturally a cunning and suspicious sort of individual. Cautious in extreme, he likes to work in secret, and probably never more than two of his most intimate compan-ions know what he is about until counterfeits he has produced are ready to be put into circulation. He never permits anyone to watch him at work.

Probation officers, prison workers, and parole officers often describe check forgers with such adjectives as "impulsive," "dependent," "lacking ego strength," "unstable," and "immature." In most in-stances these are reifications of the criminal act itself, more in the nature of invidious labels than separately defined variables demon-strable in case histories of the forgers.

Check forgers with long records who end in prison or those who pass through diagnostic centers are sometimes termed "compul-sive"; some observers speak of their having a "disease," underscoring a common belief, "once a check forger always a check forger." Such statements also tend to be circular deductions and serve little useful purpose for analysis or research in the absence of definitions which separate them from the fact of recidivism. Nevertheless, these adjec-tives indicate that law enforcement people and prison staff members do in some way differentiate check forgers from other convicted criminals, especially in regard to a kind of cyclical pattern and inev-itability in their actions.

Check forgers themselves also provide cues and verbalizations which can be inferentially useful for the analysis of their behavior. In jail and prison they often are apathetic toward their predicaments and they seem less inclined than other prisoners to rationalize their behavior. First offenders frequently express continuing deep perplexity about their motivations; some speak of the "other me" as responsible for the check passing; some refer to themselves as "Dr. Jekyll and Mr. Hyde"; and some say that they "must be crazy." Such statements may also come from those with long criminal histories, from those who are also "check artists," as well as first offenders. Systematic check forgers seldom have the "businessman" ideology which was attributed to professional thieves by Sutherland.[2]

Check forgery is associated with a wide variety of personal and social contingencies, the nature of which has been dealt with elsewhere in a theory of naïve, i.e., criminally unsophisticated check forgery.[3] Some forgers pass worthless checks only once and quit; others, casual offenders, intersperse periods of stable employment with check writing sorties quickly followed by arrest. Some people imprisoned for bad checks are alcoholics who have unwisely passed worthless checks during a drinking spree, drug addicts "supporting a habit," or gamblers desperately trying to cover losses. The comments which follow are directed not to check forgers in general but to those who have a commitment to check forgery, who develop a system of passing bad checks, and who live according to the dictates of this system as they progressively perceive them. The characteristics of this system have been described in some detail in a previous article.[4] It is only necessary to recapitulate that committed check forgers typically work alone and while they develop a criminal behavior system, it is an individual system. It is neither the same nor the equivalent of professional crime, for it lacks social organization, occupational orientation, careful planning, common rules, a code of behavior, and a special language. In the present context the concern is with the exigencies from which the systems develop and the sociopsychological consequences of the adaptations making up the systems. These revolve around pseudonymity, mobility, and seclusiveness.

PSEUDONYMITY

Once a check forger passes a series of worthless checks, the central fact of his existence becomes the threat of arrest. The business community through the police is strongly organized against the check forger, and when his checks appear, a number of procedures are activated. The more checks he has outstanding the more intensified and widespread are the efforts to apprehend him. Nearly all of these procedures have to do with identification, for once the check forger is identified as working in an area, apprehension and arrest quickly follow. Consequently if he is to survive as a forger he must develop and use techniques which prevent his identification.

Other criminals anticipate and adapt to the threat of arrest through anonymity, e.g., the burglar who works at night, or the bank robbers who work swiftly, sometimes wearing masks, which will confuse witnesses and make subsequent identification difficult or impossible. The confidence man manipulates his victims so that they often remain unaware they have been duped, or so that they fear to go to the police. The check forger cannot use these alternatives as a defense against arrest because he must work during daylight hours and face large numbers of victims who require identification before they will cash his checks. While the forger might "cool out" a few victims in the manner of the con man, he can't psychologically disarm them all, nor can he employ the "fix" with any great degree of success. The district attorney usually has stacks of checks in evidence and numerous complainants ready to testify against him when he is arrested. The check forger by necessity relies upon pseudonyms as the preferred solution of his technical problem.

In a very literal sense the check forger becomes a real life actor, deliberately assuming a variety of roles and identities which both facilitate the cashing of checks and conceal his former or, if preferred, his "real" identity. Thus he may become a spurious customer in a supermarket, a guilty husband purportedly buying his wife a gift, an out-of-town real estate buyer, a corporation executive seeking to set up a branch office, an army officer on leave, or even an investigator for the Department of Internal Revenue.

The systematic forger's problem is the selection or fabrication of roles rather than the learning of new roles. His role models are occupational or leisure time roles of conventional society. Their distinctive quality is their high degree of superficiality.[5] While they require some acting ability, it is of a low order and easily learned. Such roles, as Goffman[6] suggests, are easily put together in response to situational cues from "bits and pieces of performances" which are already in the repertoire of most people.

Some negative learning is done by forgers in jail or prison, in the sense of things not to do, through listening to the stories of other check criminals. This is reflected in an adage followed by some, of "never try another man's stunt." While check forgers are responding to what they expect of others and what others expect of them, they do so in order to maintain deception and avoid arrest. Their behavior is fundamentally more in the nature of strategy or a swiftly moving game than it is a formal or constituted pattern. In this sense it is generically similar to that of the confidence man, representing, however, a lower order of creativity and strategy.

MOBILITY

While the check man employs pseudonyms to avoid exposure when passing his worthless checks, he cannot simply don a different or innocuous identity afterward; he must move on, out of the vicinity of his crime or crimes. This, of course, can be said for other kinds of crimes, but mobility is more or less "built in" the check forger's situation largely because he preys upon resident businessmen, rather than on transients, as do pickpockets or con men.[7] His mobility is shaped by continual awareness of the time required to deposit checks, clear them, and communicate notification of non-payment to law enforcement and business protective agencies. In large part his daily activities are geared to the tempo and rhythms of banking and business, which demarcate the length of time he can pass checks and remain in a given area, ending in a critical interval during which danger of arrest is ubiquitous.[8] Experienced check forgers develop an almost intuitive sense of these points in time which punctuate their periodic movements.

The movements of the systematic check passer take on a circularity of action and motivation in the sense that their mobility begets more mobility. When queried as to why they stay on the move, check forgers usually explain that it is expensive to travel, and also that if they are to impress their businessmen-victims they must appear to have a bank account appropriate to the checks they cash.[9]

> When you're moving around like that you've got to put up a front and look the part. You can't cash checks if you look seedy. How can I impress a clerk that I'm a businessman with a fat bank account if I don't have good quality clothes and stay in better hotels and drive an expensive make of car (rented).

The result of their high levels of expenditure is that forgers usually cash numerous checks in order to defray costs of constant travel and to maintain their prosperous style of life. The local "spreads" of checks stir strong indignation in the business community and quickly mobilize law enforcement people, sensing of which becomes the forger's motivation to move frequently. This suggests one of the main reasons why some check forgers speak of being caught up in something they can't stop.

SECLUSIVENESS

The vulnerability of the forger to recognition and identification impels him away from unnecessary contacts with other persons. Furthermore he must, if he is to remain free from arrest, keep himself from progressive involvement in social relationships, for with intimate interchange of experiences there comes the danger of inadvertent as well as deliberate exposure by others. Free and unguarded interaction, even with persons whom he likes and trusts, becomes an indulgence.

The forger's seclusiveness, in large part a learned response of wariness, is reinforced by his high mobility, which necessarily makes his contacts and interactions of short-lived variety; he simply does not have the time to build up close relationships with the people he meets. His relationships or social activities tend to be those which he can enter and leave quickly, with a minimum of commitment; the roles he enacts apart from the passing of his checks are for the most part casual in nature. In addition to this role selectivity he learns to avoid specific forms of behavior likely to lead beyond casual interaction.

The forger often meets people in settings where drinking is expected behavior, yet he must take care not to drink to the point of intoxication for fear of letting slip revealing or inconsistent facts about himself. If he gets drunk he is likely to do it alone, but this is risky, too, for he might be picked up on a drunk charge and be exposed by a routine fingerprint check. If the forger gambles it is likely to be at a crowded race track or casino, not at a friendly poker game.

The preference for seclusiveness puts its stamp upon the sexual participation of the forger. He is more limited than other criminals in seeking erotic pleasures; for he seldom has a common law wife or a regular traveling companion. Prostitutes are not in keeping with his pseudonyms of respectability, and association with them may lead to unwanted brushes with the police. When he picks up a girl he is apt to be discriminating in his choice, and typically he will treat her lavishly, but seldom will he give her his true name. In this role, as in others, he remains an actor, although at times the temptation to be otherwise is great.

THE EXTRINSIC NATURE OF CHECK FORGERS' REWARDS

Systematic check forgers are properly described by themselves and by others familiar with their ways as people who like to live fast and well. The money which flows into their hands is spent freely, often with refined taste on clothes, food, drink, travel, and entertainment. Their satisfactions are limited to those which can be had from conspicuous expenditure and display, or those which stem from the honorific qualities of assumed names, titles, or identities which a generous supply of money makes possible in our society. The attendant rewards are the result of automatic or unreflective deference cued by external or immediately recognizable symbols of high economic status. Even the sexual rewards of forgers have much of this quality.

The status pleasures of forgers are further tempered by the fact that they cannot and dare not, for any length of time, assume specific identities of those who are in high positions in a particular local community. They can be rich cattlemen from Texas, but not a particular, known, rich cattleman from Texas. They may use specific identities or impersonations of this sort to pass checks (known as "high powered") but if they are wise they will not register as such persons later at a local hotel.

Some of the rewards which forgers seek arise out of context of private meanings which can be understood only in terms of idiosyncratic life history factors. Thus for some reason they may have disliked bankers or credit managers, and they derive a particular zest or satisfaction from foisting bad checks on these people or on those who work for them. Unfortunately, the rigorous exactions of their criminal technology leave few opportunities for the indulgence in these more subtle gratifications. Furthermore, they have no way of making public these private psychic triumphs, for they have no audience. At best they can only laugh silently later over their beer or pre-dinner cocktail.

THE GROWTH OF ANXIETY

An unavoidable conclusion seems to be that the more successfully the forger plays his role the greater becomes his anxiety. The more checks he has outstanding the greater is his perception of the danger of arrest, and hence the greater his necessity to move on and devise new identities which conceal his previous behavior. The mounting sense of strain is made real to the forger by occasional "close calls" in which he barely escapes identification and arrest. As the anxiety magnifies it is reflected in jumpiness, stomach upsets, and other physical disturbances. A few check forgers develop acute symptoms, such as stomach ulcers.

> My routine ran like this: I usually picked my city, then after I arrived I opened a savings account with cash. That's on Monday. On Tuesday I deposited some checks to my account, no good, of course. Wednesday I deposited another check and then drew out part of the account in cash. Then I left town. I worked this all over California, depositing maybe $50,000 altogether in I don't know how many banks. I suppose I got about $10,000 in cash. By this time the ulcers kicked up and I laid off in a resort.

Anxiety serves to amplify the suspiciousness of the forger; in some instances it is aggravated into a paranoid-like state, called the "bull horrors" by professional criminals. This is what it implies—abnormal fear of the police. In this state any unusual behavior of a victim, or a chance knock on a hotel room door, may be taken by the forger to mean that he has been discovered or that detectives have arrived to arrest him. At this point it is clear that the symbolic process has been affected; anxiety has begun to distort or interfere with the forger's ability to take over or realistically appraise the responses of others to his actions.

Cooler or highly experienced forgers may be able to objectify the sources of their anxiety and symbolize it in the jargon of the professional criminal as "heat." As one forger put it, "The checks get hot, not me." As a solution to their psychic problems some forgers take a vacation, or "lay off at a resort." In this setting they continue to use a pseudonym but refrain from passing checks during the interim. This has the merit of reducing anxiety attributable to the fear of being recognized by victims or police, but it does not solve what by now has usually become an identity problem. In any event, contingencies or the need for more money are apt to cut short these palliative respites.

PERSONAL CRISIS

Detectives, police, and the check forgers themselves all agree that arrest is inevitable for the person who persists in passing bad checks for any length of time. A few check men manage to evade detection for several years, and one is known to have foiled the FBI for ten years, but these are the rare exceptions which prove the rule. Efficiently organized police work and fortuitous events undeniably have much to do with the forger's ultimate downfall, but from the point of view adopted here, these are constant factors with which he contends. That with which he is unable to cope is a kind of massive personal crisis which inheres in the prolonged enactment of his spurious roles.

That the forger reaches a dead end in his motivation can be inferred from the circumstances and attendant behavior at the time of the arrest. While a number of systematic forgers are apprehended entirely by chance or by police efforts, an impressive number of others engineer their own downfalls. For example, some phone the police or a parole officer and tell them where they can be found. Closely akin are those who foreclose their current criminal careers rather simply by remaining where they are, knowing full well that police or detectives will soon catch up with them, to find them in a resigned mood awaiting their arrival.[10] Still other forgers, like fabled animals wending back to their mythical graveyard to die, return to their home community, there either to court arrest or to arrange for the inevitable in familiar surroundings. In more complex cases an otherwise accomplished check man makes a mistake, knowing at the time that it is a mistake which probably will land him in jail or prison.

> After a weekend of drinking and sleeping with this girl I had known before, I woke up in my room at the Mark Hopkins with a hangover and no money left. I had one check left from those I had been passing in the city. It was over two weeks since I had started passing this series and knew I shouldn't try to cash this one. But I did anyway—and now here I am at Folsom.

When queried as to reasons for their sometimes open, sometimes oblique surrenders to detectives or other law enforcement agents, check forgers frequently refer to a cumulative state of apathy or sense of psychic exhaustion,[11] expressed in such statements as the following:

> After that I began to appreciate what a heck of a job it is to pass checks.

> In Seattle I got just plain tired of cashing checks.

> The thrill I got from passing checks was gone.

> I reached a point where I didn't care whether I stayed in Balboa or went to jail.

> It's the same thing over and over again; you get tired of running.

> It gets to be more and more of an effort.

> You have a sense of being caught in something you can't stop.

One meaning that can be readily assigned to such statements is that, assuming satisfactions or rewards of the forger's activities remain unchanged or constant, their costs of acquisition in terms of effort and expenditure of psychic energy (anxiety) increase to a prohibitive point. What started out as "easy" check passing becomes more and more work, or sheer labor, until that game is no longer worth the effort.

A second, less apparent implication of the sense of apathy which finally overwhelms the highly mobile check forger was suggested by a thoughtful older inmate of San Quentin prison, who had in his lifetime been both con man and a notorious utterer of very large checks. His interpretation was simply that during the course of a check passing spree, "You come to realize that kind of life has a false structure to it." This in sociological terms speaks of the inherent difficulty of establishing and maintaining identity by reference to purely extrinsic rewards. To admit this is for the forger in effect to admit that the roles he plays, or his way of life, make impossible a stable identity or the validation of a self ideal. An excerpt from an older published autobiography of a forger states the problem clearly.[12]

> I could not rid myself of the crying need for the sense of security which social recognition and contact with one's fellows, and their approval furnishes. I was lonely and frightened and wanted to be where there was someone who knew me as I had been before.

At best the forger can seek to use his affluence to buy from others the approval and recognition important to a sense of personal worth. But persons endowed with the intelligence and insight of a systematic check criminal quickly perceive the spurious qualities of such esteem, founded as it is only upon his generosity.

> Sure, you get big money. But it's easy come, easy go. You start out on Monday morning with a stack of checks. Maybe it's hard to get started, but after the first check it's easier. You work all week and by Thursday or Friday you have a pocketful of money. Then you pick up a girl and hit the bars and night spots. You have plenty of quick pals to pat you on the back and help you spend that money. Pretty soon it's Monday morning and you wake up with a hangover and empty pockets. You need more money so you start again.

While conspicuous expenditures on goods and services are important means of locating a person with reference to others, close observation of interaction reveals that these are necessary rather than sufficient factors for the purpose. They become most significant when they establish position in a *particular* group within a stratum or social category. The forger, by choice, enacts the form but not the substance of social roles. He lacks, avoids, or rejects contact with reference groups which could validate these roles or fix an underlying identity. He cannot particularize his social interaction, hence has no way of getting appreciation as a separate person. Appreciations must remain superficial imputations to the persons whose real or hypothetical identities he assumes.[13] Apart from the lack of opportunity to do so, the forger dares not put too much of what he regards as his "true self" into these identities; he cannot readily convert them and make them his own either in part or whole. To particularize his interaction to such an end would disclose his essential difference from others, i.e., his commitment to living by passing bogus checks and deceiving others. This disclosure, of course, would destroy the identities or assign him the criminal identity which he does not desire.

When put into a time perspective, the forger's interplay of role and identity has a dialectical quality. The forger sets out on his check writing and passing journey with an initial sense of fulfillment which is exciting or even exhilarating. This is related to the ease of passing checks and the sense of enjoyment of things he has always wanted but could not afford, or to the enactment of roles which on the surface at least are perceived as in keeping with the self-ideal he holds. There is also an awareness of fulfilling or satisfying some of the more highly subjective values previously alluded to. The sense of fulfillment undoubtedly varies from forger to forger in degree and content, depending upon whether he has been in jail, on probation, in prison, or on parole. However, it is present in any case.[14]

The passage of time brings no lasting respite to the fast moving check passer and the tendency is for his anxiety to mount to higher and higher levels. His attempts to cope with this anxiety at most are palliative and may lead to secondary anxieties which are added to his basic anxiety. Reference has already been made to "laying off in a resort" and to the ephemeral nature of the surcease it provides. In addition this may become risky if he is tempted to overstay or to depart from his system.

Some forgers who acutely sense the organized hue and cry against them or who realize that "they are hot" may try to reduce their tensions by "dropping down" to less hazardous methods. Instead of passing payroll checks, checks on accounts of actual persons, or large personal checks, they may cash small checks in supermarkets or drugstores. This is safer, but it is infinitely more labor and less productive. It may mean a jail rather than a prison sentence if the forger is caught, but this merely offers a choice between the lesser of two evils.

> In Minneapolis things began to get real rough. I had trouble getting name cards of businessmen to make my system work and I had this feeling that the FBI was around. Anyway, I had to cash $25 checks in supermarkets and it was damned hard work nearly all day just to get enough to live on, let alone play the horses.
>
> I'm a thief—a paperhanger. I go for high-powered cashiers' checks of $85 to $100. But you won't find any of that high-powered stuff on my record. When I feel the heat is on I drop down to personal checks. Then if I get arrested it is on a less serious charge.

There are, of course, status degradation implications in having to descend to "small time" personal checks. In extreme cases a check man may be driven to engage in forms of petty crime or activities even more compromising to his sense of self-respect. This is apparent in the apologetic tone of the following tersely expressed account of a passage in the life of a long-time check man in jail awaiting the outcome of his trial.

You have to understand that I'm an old man and I'm so well known that if my checks appear most detectives in the state can tie them to me. I've got to be smart and I have to lay off when things get hot. Once I was living with a pimp and his broad who were both on drugs. It was costing them $40 a day just for the stuff. I went out with the girl at night to help her hustle. Actually I was just doing them a good turn for letting me live with them. Naturally the police didn't come looking for me in places where she hustled, but I kept out of sight as much as possible just the same.

A not uncommon means chosen by check forgers for relief from tension is to increase their alcohol intake, a tendency which has led to some confusion in crime literature between alcoholics who pass checks to get liquor and the bona fide check man. The association between intoxication and felt anxiety and the instrumental quality of liquor for the latter is made vividly clear in the following:

You asked me if my drinking pattern changed and I can say yes—definitely. I even remember where—in Cincinnati. It was there that my system really began to pay off and I cashed several $400 and $500 checks in the banks. Ordinarily I had one, or at most, two, highballs or a couple of beers before dinner. That night I remember it went up to four drinks, plus a bottle of wine with dinner and liqueur afterwards. I went around in a fog that evening and most nights thereafter.

The urgent need of some forgers to find relief for their troubled inner selves is shown in the willingness to drink liquor despite long established or culturally ingrained attitudes favoring sobriety. Such was the case of a Jewish check forger:

In reality I am not a drinking man; I dislike any kind of beer or whiskeys, and the only time I actually drink is when I'm in trouble, meaning exactly, when I write bad checks. I become very troubled, even though I haven't as yet been apprehended, but I am troubled because I know deep down in my heart that my life of freedom will be short-lived, so to forget my trouble I start drinking. I might add that the first drink tastes like castor oil, and after the first I can tolerate it. When I sober up again I become troubled because of the bogus checks I wrote . . . and, as a fool would figure, I just say to myself I might as well go write checks till I get caught.

While intoxication provides some temporary relief for the troubled forger he knows that it is risky. Furthermore, passing bad checks the next morning with a hangover can be a harrowing experience, which some forgers say, they have never quite forgotten.

The other significant change which comes with passing time in the criminal cycle of the check forger lies in the meaning or function of the rewards of his labors. The zest and satisfaction originally gained from his large affluence declines. The same is true for such idosyncratic "thrills," whatever their psychic derivation, he may have originally felt in passing the checks themselves. Whatever reference value they may have had at one time, they are now diminished in their function for delimiting identity and validating self. If the interpretation advanced here is correct, the decline persists until a critical "turning point" is reached, and arrest occurs.

. . .

THE FORGER'S AVERSION TO CRIMINAL ASSOCIATIONS

It may be protested that the experiences and feelings of the systematic check forger are but similar to those of any person who lives outside the law and plagues society with a long series of crimes. While there is some surface truth in this, it also has to be noted that professional thieves follow hazardous criminal lives yet still manage their occupationally induced anxieties and solve their identity problems. The comparison becomes even more pointed when it is limited to con men, who closely resemble check forgers in their necessary assumption of fictitious identities and in their vulnerability to exposure by victims. Furthermore, con men experience high anxiety levels, fed by the additional probability of exploitation or "shakedowns" by police and detectives if they are recognized.[15]

A significant difference between the check forger and the con man is that the latter retains a locus of the self by means of intimate interaction with other con men.[16] Identity is further maintained by interaction with lesser criminals, and, paradoxically, through accommodative relationships with police.[17] Gambling, drinking, and sexual byplay for the con man tend to take place in the context of primary groups. As such they appear to be more efficient means for relaxing tensions and are less likely than with the forger to generate secondary anxieties. In some cases con men have been able to integrate their criminal forays with a relatively stable family life.

The comparison adumbrated here is intended less to apotheosize the con man than to point up the query as to why check men do not follow his bent and enter into associations with other check criminals or with other types of criminals in their leisure-time pursuits thereby acquiring a criminal identity. In part the answer to this already has been given; such intimacies are contrary to the perceived dictates of the forger's criminal behavior system. The spectre of the stool pigeon who can ruin him with one phone call is never far from the check man's mind, but a loose-tongued male companion in crime, or an angry erstwhile girlfriend can be equally dangerous to him.

It may be that the learned aversions of the check man to close human associations rests upon some kind of pre-criminal personality attributes or selective factors which operate in the recruitment to careers of check passing. This is suggested by the forger's frequent designation of himself as a "lone wolf," which in a number of cases is consistent with a history of family alienation or with a history of marginal participation in social groups. From this perspective, recruits to systematic check forgery of necessity would have to be isolate types in order to survive long enough to perfect a system or become anything more than amateurs or casual offenders. Unfortunately, separating learned aversion from predisposition requires kinds of data difficult or impossible to obtain.

Much firmer and less speculative ground for explanation of the check forger's disinclination for criminal colleagues or playfellows is at hand in the middle-class backgrounds of many forgers and their lack of acquaintance with criminal ways until they come to late adulthood. From such facts it can be inferred, as well as demonstrated by verbalizations of the forgers, that their values or orientation remain conventional, "middle class." Put into more specific context, they retain an image of themselves as "nice" persons, of "good" antecedents, or even of refinement, who, as they sometimes phrase it, "wouldn't have the guts to commit any other kind of crime." Associations with other criminals thus become distasteful for them, or even threatening in that they would validate a contradictory, rejected version of the self.

This interpretation is quite consistent with the seclusiveness which carries over into the forger's jail or prison behavior, and his tendency, whenever he can manage it, to occupy intermediary roles on the peripheries of the formal and informal groups in the prison. Examples are the role of a prison runner or that of a bookie in a contraband betting pool.

Such analysis strongly suggests that the problem of the systematic check forger is a special case of self-role conflict, or, more simply, a constantly aggravating moral dilemma. This requires the assumption of something like Sarbin's[18] "constancy principle," i.e., a cognitive structure (the self) tends to maintain its organization despite forces directed toward changing it. From this vantage, the forger's crisis results from the retention of a cognitive picture of himself as essentially a "good" person, but playing social roles in a way which violates the expectation of honesty in money matters. The disjunctive relation between the two structures, self and role, gives rise to the perturbations within the organism which are experienced as anxiety.

While this straightforward explanation is attractive, nevertheless it is difficult to reconcile it with the fact that although some forgers experience guilt and remorse, many do not—at least not in any form which can be demonstrated through interview or case history materials. Furthermore, the small minority of systematic forgers with a history of delinquency or of crime beginning in their late teens display the same suspiciousness and avoidance of contacts with other criminals as is found among those who have been categorized as "middle class." Nor is the personal crisis any less exacerbated in the former when it occurs.

For the class of systematic forgers with prior criminal sophistication the roots of dilemma are quite different, revolving about the low or dubious status which check passers hold in the eyes of other criminals. In many ways they are like the nouveau riche, or the "lower-upper" class in a New England town, envied because of their ready possession of money but suspect because of the source of their money.

Check passing is not viewed as a highly skilled criminal vocation[19] and the frequent prison sojourns of forgers implies the lack of any effective solution to the problem of ultimate arrest. The demeanor of forgers can be irritating to less well-educated criminals; in prison they are sometimes disliked because, as one burglar inmate acidly commented, "They like to pretend to be someone they ain't." Back of such attitudes is a vague distrust of the forger, a disapproval of his tendency to try to "con" others inside of the prison as he does on the outside.

It may be that there is a more generalized moral problem for all systematic forgers; the threat of exposure or designation as a "phony" may be the common dilemma which cuts across the psyche of the middle-class forger as well as one who is the product of early criminal socialization. Being a "phony," i.e., defining one's self in terms of a status while lacking the qualifications for the status, may be, as Goffman[20] claims, the "great cardinal sin." Nevertheless, there is good reason to believe that systematic forgers successfully protect themselves from the degradational implications of "phoniness." This they do less through rationalization or other psychodynamic mechanisms than they do by means of selective social participation and managed presentation of the self, which limit organismic involvement in role enactment.

That guilt is seldom more than of marginal importance for the forger so long as he doesn't become "too involved" and so long as he avoids victimizing those with whom he more closely identifies seems clear from the following.

The only times I felt bad was with the "nice people." Usually when I was with people who liked me and I them, I stopped passing checks, or if I did,

I was careful to see that nothing I did could harm them in any way. In Alabama when I went to church with my "friends" I put a check in the collection, but I made sure that it was good, so that they would not be publicly embarrassed later.

Many of the so-called "nice people" who come into the forger's life never learn that he is a "phony" person, or if they do, it is after he has left town. Consequently there is seldom any direct or immediate validation of the stigma. Guilt remains largely retrospective and remote for the forger, without social reinforcement. He "leaves the field" before it can be generated in social interaction.

IDENTITY CRISES AND NEGATIVE IDENTITY

The foregoing argues strongly that the personal crisis of the systematic forger stems less from a moral dilemma than it does from the erosion of identity. So conceived, his problem resides in a neutral component or dimension of the self, namely the sense of separateness and relationship to others, which is assumed to have its own consequences for behavior apart from substantive social value, "good or bad," assigned to it.[21] In a sense the forger fails because he succeeds; he is able to fend off or evade self-degradative consequences of his actions but in so doing he rejects forms of interaction necessary to convert his rewards in positive, status-specific self-evaluations. In time he reaches a point at which he can no longer define himself in relation to others on any basis. The self becomes amorphous, without boundaries; the identity substructure is lost. Apathy replaces motivation, and in phenomenological terms, "life" or "this way of life" is no longer worth living. This is the common prelude to the forger's arrest.

There is, of course, an adaptive aspect to the psychic surrender which precedes or attends the forger's almost casual entry into legal custody, which can be seen quite clearly in the sense of relief which is experienced at the time and also later in jail. From a moral perspective, the forger is "being brought to justice"; He "pays his debt to society." However, from the perspective of this chapter, his apathy or carelessness and subsequent arrest function to end his anxiety which is the subjective aspect of the organized "hue and cry" of modern crime detection. More importantly, they solve his identity problem; arrest immediately assigns the forger an identity, undesirable though it may be, as a jail or prison inmate. In effect, he receives or chooses a *negative identity*,[22] which despite its invidious qualities, is nearest and most real to him. At this juncture he is much like the actor who prefers bad publicity to none at all, or the youth who is willing to be a scapegoat for the group rather than not be part of the group at all.

. . .

Notes

1. Thomas Byrnes, *Professional Criminals of America* (New York: Cassell & Co., 1886), p. 12.
2. Edwin H. Sutherland, *The Professional Thief* (Chicago: University of Chicago Press, 1947), Chap. VI.
3. Edwin M. Lemert, "An Isolation and Closure Theory of Naïve Check Forgery," *Journal of Criminal Law and Criminology*, 44 (1953), 296–307.
4. Edwin M. Lemert, "The Behavior of the Systematic Check Forger," *Social Problems*, 6 (1958), 141–149.
5. One forger reported using 285 names during his career. He also argued that the less documentary identification used the less suspicion aroused in the victim. Leonard Hart, "You're a Sucker If You Cash My Check," *Colliers*, February 7, 1953.
6. Erving Goffman, *The Presentation of the Self in Everyday Life* (New York: Doubleday Anchor, 1959), pp. 72ff.
7. Sheldon Messinger thoughtfully suggests that this factor prevents the forger from setting up accommodative relationships with police which are the basis of the fix, by which professional thieves protect themselves—personal communication.
8. In one case, a forger traced his itinerary for the author. It covered a nine-month period, during which he worked in 25 cities between Oakland, California, and Atlanta, Georgia, never remaining longer than two weeks in each.
9. This is only partially revealing of the motivation of the forger; it will become apparent that he also needs large amounts of money to underwrite the kinds of recreation or activities he pursues to relieve his tensions and sense of loneliness.
10. One check man, who spent much of his free time in bars, sensed that bartenders had been alerted to his presence in the area. He brought about his arrest in a bar simply by talking a little louder than was his custom. The owner overheard him and phoned the police.
11. An appropriate descriptive term for this state is not easily found. It resembles the indifference to the threat of death which appeared among some inmates of Nazi concentration camps, as a response to "provisional detention without a time limit." See Bruno Bettelheim, "Individual and Mass Behavior in Extreme Situations," *Journal of Abnormal and Social Psychology*, 38 (1948), 434; Elie Cohen, *Human Behavior in the Concentration Camp* (New York: W. W. Norton & Company, Inc., 1953), p. 129. The reaction also suggests the idea of a "breaking point" or limits of effective response under stress. See Eli Ginzberg, *et al.*, *The Ineffective Soldier* (New York: Columbia University Press, 1959). Something of "acute depersonalization" also seems involved. See Paul Schilder, *The Image and Appearance of the Human Body* (London: Kegan Paul, Tench, Trubner and Co., 1935).
12. Roger Benton, *Where Do I Go From Here* (New York: L. Furman, 1936), p. 80.
13. Mills' concept of "status cycles" may be enlightening here. Like the white-collar worker on vacation, the forger seeks to create a "holiday image of self." The difference, of course, is that there is cultural sanction for the former but not for the forger's holiday image, financed as it is by fraudulent means. C. Wright Mills, *White Collar* (New York: Oxford University Press, 1951), p. 258.
14. One female forger described feelings analogous to sexual orgasm which followed cashing checks in stores.
15. See David Maurer, *The Big Con* (New York: Bobbs-Merrill Company, Inc., 1940). The comparison is best regarded as an historical one, for it is doubtful whether big con games, and con men of the sort described by Maurer, have existed for several decades.

16. While late nineteenth-century check forgers worked in groups, they usually split up after passing a large check on a bank. See Lemert, "Behavior of the Systematic Check Forger," *op. cit.*

17. The best evidence of this is the distinctive names, used by con men in the past, e.g., The Yellow Kid Weil, The Boone Kid Whitney, and The High Ass Kid. Maurer, *op. cit.*

18. Theodore Sarbin, "Role Theory," in *Handbook of Social Psychology*, ed. G. Lindzey (Cambridge: Cambridge University Press, 1954), Chap. 6.

19. ". . . they all (thieves and professional criminals) assume an air of superiority in the presence of the lowly 'short story writer,' as the bum check artist is known in the underworld." Sutherland, *op. cit.*, pp. 76–78.

20. Erving Goffman, "On Cooling Out the Mark," *Psychiatry*, 15 (1952), 451–63.

21. A conception approximating this distinction can be found in D. L. Burham, "Identity Definition and Role Demand in Hospital Careers of Schizophrenic Patients," *Psychiatry*, 24 (1961), 96–122.

22. Erik H. Erikson, "The Problem of Ego Identity," in *Identity and Anxiety*, ed. M. R. Stein, *et al.* (New York: Free Press of Glencoe, Inc., 1960), pp. 60–62.

48 / Becoming a Hit Man: Neutralization in a Very Deviant Career

KEN LEVI

Our knowledge about deviance management is based primarily on behavior that is easily mitigated. The literature dwells on unwed fathers (Pfuhl, 1978), and childless mothers (Veevers, 1975), pilfering bread salesman (Ditton, 1977), and conniving shoe salesmen (Friedman, 1974), bridge pros (Holtz, 1975), and poker pros (Hayano, 1977), marijuana smokers (Langer, 1976), massage parlor prostitutes (Verlarde, 1975), and other minor offenders (see, for example, Berk, 1977; Farrell and Nelson, 1976; Gross, 1977). There is a dearth of deviance management articles on serious offenders, and no scholarly articles at all about one of the (legally) most serious offenders of all, the professional murderer. Drift may be possible for the minor offender exploiting society's *ambivalence* toward his relatively unserious behavior (Sykes and Matza, 1957). However, excuses for the more inexcusable forms of deviant behavior are, by definition, less easily come by, and the very serious offender may enter his career with few of the usual defenses.

This article will focus on ways that one type of serious offender, the professional hit man, neutralizes stigma in the early stages of his career. As we shall see, the social organization of the "profession" provides "neutralizers" which distance its members from the shameful aspects of their careers. But for the novice, without professional insulation, the problem is more acute. With very little outside help, he must negate his feelings, neutralize them, and adopt a "framework" (Goffman, 1974) appropriate to his chosen career. This process, called "reframing," is the main focus of the present article. Cognitively, the novice must *reframe his experience* in order to enter his profession.

THE SOCIAL ORGANIZATION OF MURDER

Murder, the unlawful killing of a person, is considered a serious criminal offense in the United States, and it is punished by extreme penalties. In addition, most Americans do not feel that the penalties are extreme enough (Reid, 1976: 482). In overcoming the intense stigma associated with murder, the hit man lacks the supports available to more ordinary types of killers.

Some cultures allow special circumstances or sanction special organizations wherein people who kill are insulated from the taint of murder. Soldiers at war, or police in the line of duty, or citizens protecting their property operate under what are considered justifiable or excusable conditions. They receive so much informal support from the general public and from members of their own group that it may protect even a sadistic member from blame (Westley, 1966).

Subcultures (Wolfgang and Ferracuti, 1967), organizations (Maas, 1968), and gangs (Yablonsky, 1962) that unlawfully promote killing can at least provide their members with an "appeal to higher loyalties" (Sykes and Matza, 1957), if not a fully developed set of deviance justifying norms.

Individuals acting on their own, who kill in a spontaneous, "irrational" outburst of violence can also mitigate the stigma of their behavior.

> I mean, people will go ape for one minute and shoot, but there are very few people who are capable of thinking about, planning, and then doing it [Joey, 1974: 56].

Individuals who kill in a hot-blooded burst of passion can retrospectively draw comfort from the law which provides a lighter ban against killings performed without premeditation or malice or intent (Lester and Lester, 1975: 35). At one extreme, the spontaneous killing may seem the result of a mental disease (Lester and Lester, 1975: 39) or dissociative reaction (Tanay, 1972), and excused entirely as insanity.

But when an individual who generally shares society's ban against murder, is fully aware that his act of homicide is (1) unlawful, (2) self-serving, and (3) intentional, he does not have the usual defenses to fall back on. How does such an individual manage to *overcome his inhibitions* and *avoid serious damage to his self-image* (assuming that he does share society's ban)? This is the special dilemma of the professional hit man who hires himself out for murder.

RESEARCH METHODS

Information for this article comes primarily from a series of intensive interviews with one self-styled "hit man." The interviews were spread over seven, tape-recorded sessions during a four-month period. The respondent was one of fifty prison inmates randomly sampled from a population of people convicted of murder in Metropolitan Detroit. The respondent told about an "accidental" killing, involving a drunken bar patron who badgered the respondent and finally forced his hand by pulling a knife on him. In court he claimed self-defense, but the witnesses at the bar claimed otherwise, so they sent him to prison. During the first two interview sessions, the respondent acted progressively ashamed of this particular killing, not on moral grounds, but because of its "sloppiness" or "amateurishness." Finally, he indicated there was more he would like to say. So, I stopped the tape recorder. I asked him if he was a hit man. He said he was.

He had already been given certain guarantees, including no names in the interview, a private conference room, and a signed contract promising his anonymity. Now, as a further guarantee, we agreed to talk about him in the third person, as a fictitious character named "Pete," so that none of his statements would sound like a personal confession. With these assurances, future interviews were devoted to his career as a professional murderer, with particular emphasis on his entry into the career and his orientation toward his victims.

Was he reliable? Since we did not use names, I had no way of checking the veracity of the individual cases he reported. Nevertheless, I was able to compare his account of the hit man's career with information from other convicted murderers, with police experts, and with accounts from the available literature (Gage, 1972; Joey, 1974; Maas, 1968). Pete's information was generally supported by these other sources. As to his motive for submitting to the interview, it is hard to gauge. He apparently was ashamed of the one "accidental" killing that had landed him in prison, and he desired to set the record straight concerning what he deemed an illustrious career, now that he had arrived, as he said, at the end of it. Hit men pride themselves on not "falling" (going to jail) for murder, and Pete's incarceration hastened a decision to retire—that he had already been contemplating, anyway.

A question might arise about the ethics of researching self-confessed "hit men" and granting them anonymity. Legally, since Pete never mentioned specific names or specific dates or possible future crimes, there does not seem to be a problem. Morally, if confidentiality is a necessary condition to obtaining information about serious offenders, then we have to ask: Is it worth it? Pete insisted that he had retired from the profession. Therefore, there seems to be no "clear and imminent danger" that would justify the violation of confidentiality, in the terms set forth by the American Psychological Association (1978: 40). On the other hand, the *possibility* of danger does exist, and future researchers will have to exercise their judgment.

Finally, hit men are hard to come by. Unlike more lawful killers, such as judges or night watchmen, and unlike run-of-the-mill murderers, the hit man (usually) takes infinite care to conceal his identity. Therefore, while it is regrettable that this paper has only one case to report on, and while it would be ideal to perform a comparative analysis on a number of hit men, it would be very difficult to obtain such a sample. Instead, Pete's responses will be compared to similar accounts from the available literature. While such a method can never produce verified findings, it can point to suggestive hypotheses.

THE SOCIAL ORGANIZATION OF PROFESSIONAL MURDER

There are two types of professional murderers: the organized and the independent. The killer who belongs to an organized syndicate does not usually get paid on a contract basis, and performs his job out of loyalty and obedience to the organization (Maas, 1968: 81). The independent professional killer is a freelance agent who hires himself out for a fee (Pete). It is the career organization of the second type of killer that will be discussed.

The organized killer can mitigate his behavior through an "appeal to higher loyalties" (Sykes and Matza, 1957). He also can view his victim as an enemy of the group and then choose from a variety of techniques available for neutralizing an offense against an enemy (see, for example, Hirschi, 1969; Rogers and Buffalo, 1974). But the independent professional murderer lacks most of these defenses. Nevertheless, built into his role are certain structural features that help him avoid deviance ascription. These features include:

(1) *Contract.* A contract is an unwritten agreement to provide a sum of money to a second party who agrees, in return, to commit a designated murder (Joey, 1974: 9). It is most often arranged over the phone, between people who have never had personal contact. And the victim, or "hit," is usually unknown to the killer (Gage, 1972: 57; Joey, 1974: 61–62). This arrangement is meant to protect both parties from the law. But it also helps the killer "deny the victim" (Sykes and Matza, 1957) by keeping him relatively anonymous.

In arranging the contract, the hired killer will try to find out the difficulty of the hit and how much the customer wants the killing done. According to Pete, these considerations determine his price. He does not ask about the motive for the killing, treating it as none of his concern. Not knowing the motive may hamper the killer from morally justifying his behavior, but it also enables him to further deny the victim by maintaining his distance and reserve. Finally, the contract is backed up by a further understanding.

> Like this guy who left here (prison) last summer; he was out two months before he got killed. Made a mistake somewhere. The way I heard it, he didn't finish filling a contract [Pete].

If the killer fails to live up to his part of the bargain, the penalties could be extreme (Gage, 1972: 53; Joey, 1974: 9). This has the ironic effect that after the contract is arranged, the killer can somewhat "deny responsibility" (Sykes and Matza, 1957), by pleading self-defense.

(2) *Reputation and Money.* Reputation is especially important in an area where killers are unknown to their customers, and where the less written, the better (Joey, 1974: 58). Reputation, in turn, reflects how much money the hit man was commanded in the past.

> And that was the first time that I ever got 30 grand . . . it's based on his reputation. . . . Yeah, how good he really is. To be so-so, you get so-so money. If you're good, you get good money [Pete].

Pete, who could not recall the exact number of people he had killed, did, like other hit men, keep an accounting of his highest fees (Joey, 1974: 58, 62). To him big money meant not only a way to earn a living, but also a way to maintain his professional reputation.

People who accept low fees can also find work as hired killers. Heroin addicts are the usual example. But, as Pete says, they often receive a bullet for their pains. It is believed that people who would kill for so little would also require little persuasion to make them talk to the police (Joey, 1974: 63). This further reinforces the single-minded emphasis on making big money. As a result, killing is conceptualized as a "business" or as "just a job." Framing the hit in a normal businesslike context enables the hit man to deny wrongfulness, or "deny injury" (Sykes and Matza, 1957).

In addition to the economic motive, Pete, and hit men discussed by other authors, refer to excitement, fun, game-playing, power, and impressing women as incentives for murder (Joey, 1974: 81–82). However, none of these motives are mentioned by all sources. None are as necessary to the career as money. And, after awhile, these other motives diminish and killing becomes only "just a job" (Joey, 1974: 20). The primacy of the economic motive has been aptly expressed in the case of another deviant profession.

> Women who enjoy sex with their customers do not make good prostitutes, according to those who are acquainted with this institution first hand. Instead of thinking about the most effective way of making money at the job, they would be doing things for their own pleasure and enjoyment [Goode, 1978: 342].

(3) *Skill.* Most of the hit man's training focuses on acquiring skill in the use of weapons.

> Then, he met these two guys, these two white guys ... them two, them two was the best. And but they stayed around over there and they got together, and Pete told [them] that he really wanted to be good. He said, if [I] got to do something, I want to be good at it. So, they got together, showed him, showed him *how to shoot....* And gradually, he became good. ... Like he told me, like when he shoots somebody, he always goes for the head; he said, that's about the best shot. I mean, if you want him dead then and there.... And these two guys showed him, and to him, I mean, hey, I mean, he don't believe nobody could really outshoot these two guys, you know what I mean. *They know everything you want to know about guns, knives, and stuff like that* [Pete].

The hit man's reputation, and the amount of money he makes depends on his skill, his effective ability to serve as a means to *someone else's ends.* The result is a focus on technique.

> Like in anything you do, when you do it, you want to do it just right.... On your target and you hit it, how you feel: I hit it! I hit it! [Pete].

This focus on technique, on means, helps the hit man to "deny responsibility" and intent (Sykes and Matza, 1957). In frame-analytic terms, the hit man separates his morally responsible, or "principal" self from the rest of himself, and performs the killing mainly as a "strategist" (Goffman, 1974: 523). In other words, he sees himself as a "hired gun." The saying, "If I didn't do it, they'd find someone else who would," reflects this narrowly technical orientation.

To sum up thus far, the contract, based as it is on the hit man's reputation for profit and skill, provides the hit man with opportunities for denying the victim, denying injury, and denying responsibility. But this is not enough. To point out the defenses of the professional hit man is one thing, but it is unlikely that the *novice* hit man would have a totally professional attitude so early in his career. The novice is at a point where he both lacks the conventional defense against the stigma of murder, *and* he has not yet fully acquired the exceptional defenses of the professional. How, then, does he cope?

THE FIRST TIME: NEGATIVE EXPERIENCE

Goffman defines "negative experience" as a feeling of disorientation.

> Expecting to take up a position in a well-framed realm, he finds that no particular frame is immediately applicable, or the frame that he thought was applicable no longer seems to be, or he cannot bind himself within the frame that does apparently apply. He loses command over the formula-

tion of viable response. He flounders. Experience, the meld of what the current scene brings to him and what he brings to it—meant to settle into a form even while it is beginning, finds no form and is therefore no experience. Reality anomically flutters. He has a "negative experience"—negative in the sense that it takes its character from what it is not, and what it is not is an organized and organizationally affirmed response [1974: 387–379].

Negative experience can occur when a person finds himself lapsing into an old understanding of the situation, only to suddenly awaken to the fact that it no longer applies. In this regard, we should expect negative experience to be a special problem for the novice. For example, the first time he killed a man for money, Pete supposedly became violently ill:

> When he [Pete], you know, hit the guy, when he shot the guy, the guy said, 'You killed me' . . . something like that, cause he struck him all up here. And what he said, it was just, I mean, *the look right in the guy's eye*, you know. I mean he looked like: *why me?* Yeah? And he [Pete] couldn't shake that. Cause he remembered a time or two when he got cut, and all he wanted to do was get back and cut this guy that cut him. And this here. . . . No, he just could not shake it. And then he said that at night-time he'll start thinking about the guy: like he shouldn't have looked at him like that. . . . I mean actually [Pete] was sick. . . . He couldn't keep his food down, I mean, or nothing like that. . . . [It lasted] I'd say about two months. . . . Like he said that he had feelings . . . that he never did kill nobody before [Pete].

Pete's account conforms to the definition of negative experience. He had never killed anyone for money before. It started when a member of the Detroit drug world had spotted Pete in a knife fight outside an inner city bar, was apparently impressed with the young man's style, and offered him fifty dollars to do a "job." Pete accepted. He wanted the money. But when the first hit came about, Pete of course knew that he was doing it for money, but yet his orientation was revenge. Thus, he stared his victim in the *face*, a characteristic gesture of people who kill enemies for revenge (Levi, 1975: 190). Expecting to see defiance turn into a look of defeat, they attempt to gain "face" at the loser's expense.

But when Pete stared his victim in the face, he saw not an enemy, but an innocent man. He saw a look of: "Why me?" And this *discordant* image is what remained in his mind during the weeks and months to follow and made him sick. As Pete says, "He shouldn't have looked at him like that." The victim's look of innocence brought about what Goffman (1974: 347) refers to as a "frame break":

> Given that the frame applied to an activity is expected to enable us to come to terms with all events in that activity (informing and regulating many of them), it is understandable that the unmanageable might occur,

an occurrence which cannot be effectively ignored and to which the frame cannot be applied, with resulting bewilderment and chagrin on the part of the participants. In brief, a break can occur in the applicability of the frame, a break in its governance.

When such a frame break occurs, it produces negative experience. Pete's extremely uncomfortable disorientation may reflect the extreme dissonance between the revenge frame, that he expected to apply, and the unexpected look of innocence that he encountered and continued to recall.

SUBSEQUENT TIME: REFRAMING THE HIT

According to Goffman (1974: 319), a structural feature of frames of experience is that they are divided into different "tracks" or types of information. These include, "a main track or story line and ancillary tracks of various kinds." The ancillary tracks are the directional track, the overlay track, the concealment track, and the disattend track. The disattend track contains the information that is perceived but supposed to be *ignored*. For example, the prostitute manages the distasteful necessity of having sex with "tricks" by remaining "absolutely . . . detached. Removed. Miles and miles away" (1978: 344). The existence of different tracks allows an individual to define and redefine his experience by the strategic placement of information.

Sometimes, the individual receives outside help. For example, when Milgram in 1963 placed a barrier between people, administering electric shocks, and the bogus "subjects" who were supposedly receiving the shocks, he made it easier for the shockers to "disattend" signs of human distress from their hapless victims. Surgeons provide another example. Having their patients completely covered, except for the part to be operated on, helps them work in a more impersonal manner. In both examples, certain crucial information is stored away in the "concealment track" (Goffman, 1974: 218).

In other cases help can come from guides who direct the novice on what to experience and what to block out. Beginning marijuana smokers are cautioned to ignore feelings of nausea (Becker, 1953: 240). On the other hand, novice hit men like Pete are reluctant to share their "experience" with anyone else. It would be a sign of weakness.

In still other cases, however, it is possible that the subject can do the reframing *on his own*. And this is what appears to have happened to Pete.

And when the second one [the second hit] came up, [Pete] was still thinking about the first one. . . . Yeah, when he got ready to go, he was thinking

> about it. *Something changed.* I don't know how to put it right. Up to the moment that he killed the second guy now, he waited, you know. Going through his mind was the first guy he killed. He still seeing him, still see the *expression on his face.* Soon, the second guy walked up; I mean, it was like just his mind just *blanked out* for a minute, everything just blanked out. . . . Next thing he know, he had killed the second guy. . . . *He knew what he was doing,* but what I mean, he just didn't have nothing on his mind. Everything was wiped out [Pete].

When the second victim approached, Pete says that he noticed the victim's approach, he was aware of the man's presence. But he noticed none of the victim's personal features. He did not see the victim's face or its expression. Thus, he did not see the very thing that gave him so much trouble the first time. It is as if Pete had *negatively conditioned* himself to avoid certain cues. Since he shot the victim in the head, it is probable that Pete saw him in one sense; this is not the same kind of experience as a "dissociative reaction," which has been likened to sleep-walking (Tanay, 1972). Pete says that, "he knew what he was doing." But he either did not pay attention to his victim's personal features at the time of the killing, or he blocked them out immediately afterward, so that now the only aspect of his victim he recalls is the victim's approach (if we are to believe him).

After that, Pete says that killing became *routine.* He learned to view his victims as "targets," rather than as people. Thus, he believes that the second experience is the crucial one, and that the disattendance of the victim's personal features made it so.

Support from other accounts of hit men is scant, due to a lack of data. Furthermore, not everything in Pete's account supports the "reframing" hypothesis. In talking about later killings, it is clear that he not only attends to his victims' personal features, on occasion, but he also derives a certain grim pleasure in doing so.

> [the victim was] a nice looking woman. . . . She started weeping, and [she cried], 'I ain't did this, I ain't did that' . . . and [Pete] said that he shot her. Like it wasn't nothing . . . he didn't feel nothing. It was just money [Pete].

In a parallel story, Joey, the narrator of the *Killer,* also observes his victim in personal terms.

> [The victim] began to beg. He even went so far as to tell us where he had stashed his money. Finally, he realized there was absolutely nothing he could do. He sat there quietly. Then, he started crying. I didn't feel a thing for him [1974: 56].

It may be that this evidence contradicts what I have said about reframing; but perhaps another interpretation is possible. Reframing may play a more crucial role in the original redefinition of an experience than in the continued maintenance of that redefinition. Once Pete has accustomed himself to viewing his victims as merely targets, as "just money," then it may be less threatening to look upon them as persons, once again. Once the "main story line" has been established, discordant information can be presented in the "overlay track" (Goffman, 1974: 215), without doing too much damage. Indeed, this seems to be *the point* that both hit men are trying to make in the above exerpts.

THE HEART OF THE HIT MAN

For what I have been referring to as "disattendance" Pete used the term "heart," which he defined as a "coldness." When asked what he would look for in an aspiring hit man, Pete replied,

> See if he's got a whole lot of heart . . . you got to be cold . . . you got to build a coldness in yourself. It's not something that comes automatically. Cause, see, I don't care who he is, first, you've got feelings [Pete].

In contrast to this view, Joey (1974: 56) said,

> There are three things you need to kill a man: the gun, the bullets, and the balls. A lot of people will point a gun at you, but they haven't got the courage to pull the trigger. It's as simple as that.

It may be that some are born with "heart," while others acquire it in the way I have described.

However, the "made rather than born" thesis does explain one perplexing feature of hit men and other "evil" men whose banality has sometimes seemed discordant. In other aspects of their lives they all seem perfectly capable of feeling ordinary human emotions. Their inhumanity, their coldness, seems narrowly restricted to their jobs. Pete, for example, talked about his "love" for little children. Eddie "The Hawk" Ruppolo meekly allowed his mistress to openly insult him in a public bar (Gage, 1972). And Joey (1974: 55) has this to say about himself:

> Believe it or not, I'm a human being. I laugh at funny jokes, I love children around the house, and I can spend hours playing with my mutt.

All of these examples of human warmth indicate that the cold heart of the hit man may be less a characteristic of the killer's individual personality, than a feature of the professional framework of experience which the hit man has learned to adapt himself to, when he is on the job.

DISCUSSION

This article is meant as a contribution to the study of deviance neutralization. The freelance hit man is an example of an individual who, relatively alone, must deal with a profound and unambiguous stigma in order to enter his career. Both Pete and Joey emphasize "heart" as a determining factor in becoming a professional. And Pete's experience, after the first hit, further indicates that the inhibitions against murder-for-money are real.

In this article "heart"—or the ability to adapt to a rationalized framework for killing—has been portrayed as the outcome of an initial process of reframing, in addition to other neutralization techniques established during the further stages of professionalization. As several theorists (see, for example, Becker, 1953; Douglas, 1977; Matza, 1969) have noted, people often enter into deviant acts first, and then develop rationales for their behavior later on. This was also the case with Pete, who began his career by first, (1) "being willing" (Matza, 1969), (2) encountering a frame-break, (3) undergoing negative experience, (4) being willing to try again (also known as "getting back on the horse"), (5) reframing the experience, and (6) having future, routine experiences wherein his professionalization increasingly enabled him to "deny the victim," "deny injury," and "deny responsibility." Through the process of reframing, the experience of victim-as-target emerged as the "main story line," and the experience of victim-as-person was downgraded from the main track to the disattend track to the overlay track. Ironically, the intensity of the negative experience seemed to make the process all the more successful. Thus, it may be possible for a person with "ordinary human feelings" to both pass through the novice stage, and to continue "normal relations" thereafter. The reframing hypothesis has implications for other people who knowingly perform stigmatized behaviors. It may be particularly useful in explaining a personal conversion experience that occurs despite the relative absence of deviant peer groups, deviant norms, extenuating circumstances, and neutralization rationales.

References

American Psychological Association (1978) Directory of the American Psychological Association. Washington, DC: Author.

Becker, H. (1953) "Becoming a marijuana user." Amer. J. of Sociology 59: 235–243.

Berk, B. (1977) "Face-saving at the singles dance." Social Problems 24, 5: 530–544.

Ditton, J. (1977) "Alibis and aliases: some notes on motives of fiddling bread salesmen." Sociology 11, 2: 233–255.

Douglas, J., P. Rasmussen, and C. Flanagan (1977) The Nude Beach. Beverly Hills: Sage.

Farrell, R., and J. Nelson (1976) "A causal model of secondary deviance; the case of homosexuality." Soc. Q. 17: 109–120.

Friedman, N. L. (1974) "Cookies and contests: notes on ordinary occupational deviance and its neutralization." Soc. Symposium (Spring): 1–9.

Gage, N. (1972) Mafia, U.S.A. New York: Dell.

Goffman, F. (1974) Frame Analysis. Cambridge, MA: Harvard Univ. Press.

Goode, E. (1978) Deviant Behavior: An Interactionist Approach. Englewood Cliffs, NJ: Prentice-Hall.

Gross, H. (1977) "Micro and macro level implications for a sociology of virtue—case of draft protesters to Vietnam War." Soc. Q. 18, 3: 319–339.

Hayano, D. (1977) "The professional poker player: career identification and the problem of respectability." Social Problems 24 (June): 556–564.

Hirschi, T. (1969) Causes of Delinquency. Berkeley: Univ. of California Press.

Holtz, J. (1975) "The professional duplicate bridge player: conflict management in a free, legal, quasi-deviant occupation." Urban Life 4, 2: 131–160.

Joey (1974) Killer: Autobiography of a Mafia Hit Man. New York: Pocket Books.

Langer, J. (1976) "Drug entrepreneurs and the dealing culture." Australian and New Zealand J. of Sociology 12, 2: 82–90.

Lester, D., and G. Lester (1975) Crime of Passion: Murder and the Murderer. Chicago: Nelson-Hall.

Levi, K. (1975) Icemen. Ann Arbor, MI: University Microfilms.

Maas, P. (1968) The Valachi Papers. New York: G. P. Putnam.

Matza, D. (1969) Becoming Deviant. Englewood Cliffs, NJ: Prentice-Hall.

Pfuhl, E. (1978) "The unwed father: a non-deviant rule breaker." Soc. Q. 19: 113–128.

Reid, S. (1976) Crime and Criminology. Hinsdale, IL: Dryden Press.

Rogers, J., and M. Buffalo (1974) "Neutralization techniques: toward a simplified measurement scale." Pacific Soc. Rev. 17, 3: 313.

Sykes, G., and D. Matza (1957) "Techniques of neutralization: a theory of delinquency." Amer. Soc. Rev. 22: 664–670.

Tanay, E. (1972) "Psychiatric aspects of homicide prevention." Amer. J. of Psychology 128: 814–817.

Veevers, J. (1975) "The moral careers of voluntarily childless wives: notes on the defense of a variant world view." Family Coordinator 24, 4: 473–487.

Verlarde, A. (1975) "Becoming prostituted: the decline of the massage parlor profession and the masseuse." British J. of Criminology 15, 3: 251–263.

Westley, W. (1966) "The escalation of violence through legitimation." Annals of the American Association of Political and Social Science 364 (March) 120–126.

Wolfgang, M., and F. Ferracuti (1967) The Subculture of Violence. London: Tavistock.

Yablonsky, L. (1962) The Violent Gang. New York: Macmillan.

Part 6 / Changing Deviance

Part 4 offered materials that demonstrate how a person's public identity becomes transformed into a "deviant" identity. Central to this process is the "status denunciation ceremony," in which a collective effort is made to place an institutional tag upon a person. This status-conferring process was especially evident in those articles dealing with the involuntary processing and incarceration of clients as mental patients. The articles also helped to underscore the fact that the institutional deviant has relatively little to say about his or her processing. It has been emphasized, too, that the identity-transformation process is generally rather routine.

How the labeled deviant actually perceives and responds to institutional processing is often difficult to judge. As we have seen, some will accept the label, while others will either reject or ignore it. The individual's response is critical in the alteration of a deviant identity—that is, in moving from a deviant to a nondeviant status, with the deviant label being removed during the process of change. For example, if an individual rejects an institutional label, he or she can expect to encounter various types of difficulties. The plight of McMurphy (discussed in the general introduction) offers an illustration of this. Not only did he reject the "sick role," but his resistance, when viewed from the institution's perspective, was taken as a sign that he needed help. In this instance, the prognosis for change—again from the institution's viewpoint (i.e., its theory of the office and associated diagnostic stereotypes)—was extremely poor. A patient may, however, accept the label and act in accordance with institutional expectations. Such patients thus become willing parties in the transformation process.

Even if individuals decide to conform to social norms, they will most certainly encounter numerous structural and individual barriers—barriers which often reduce the probability that they will elect to change their behavior. The ex-deviant, as I have noted in the general introduction, frequently experiences difficulty finding housing and employment, primarily because others, in general, continue to react to the person as a deviant. Institutional processing is very systematic and efficient in tagging individuals as deviants. The reverse process, however, is anything but systematic and efficient. Specifically, there are few, if any, institutional mechanisms that can be used to systematically remove deviant labels (and the associated stigma) from individuals. Thus, deviants are often left to fend for themselves. Obviously, giving ex-cons a bit of money and a suit of clothes, without helping them to deal with potential structural barriers (such as having to indicate they are ex-cons on job applications) and individual problems (such as feelings of low self-esteem) is not going to do much by way of "rehabilitating" them. A viable model of change, or "rehabilitation," must incorporate a concern for both individual and structural factors. Even this, however, is not enough.

Clearly, if the underlying images, conceptions, and categories of deviance are altered (as discussed in Part 1), then the picture of deviance and the deviant must undergo some corresponding changes. Analytically, it is useful to think in terms of the transformation of deviant categories, as well as the transformation of actors and structures. As an example, certain crimes may become decriminalized, and acts that were formerly perceived as deviant may become acceptable. The selections in this part explore possibilities such as these. The initial two pieces analyze how the content of prevailing conceptions and categories may be transformed. The next two selections examine how actors may attempt to transform their deviant identity. The final selections illustrate some of the ways in which deviant organizations, decision-makers, and structures can be controlled, sanctioned, or even altered.

Deviant Conceptions and Categories

A central theme in Part 1 was the idea that the reactions of social observers provide acts with meanings—that is, indicate whether the acts are deviant or nondeviant. (Duster's analysis of how drug usage became criminalized offered an excellent account of this.) In "From Deviant to Normative: Changes in the Social Acceptability of Sexually Explicit Material," Charles Winick details how behavior that once was labeled as deviant has become relabeled positively. He is concerned specifically with documenting those factors and conditions that produced a "transformation of previously deviant sexual content in popular arts and media into relative acceptability." Winick describes five major sources of change: (1) larger social forces, (2) court decisions and other statements, (3) the content of the arts, (4) the functions served by sex-oriented material, and (5) the future. For example, in terms of larger social forces, he discusses how shifting sex roles and morality have produced greater acceptance of sexually explicit materials. Winick also comments on how disaffection with government, as well as disasters and recessions, have brought about changes in the perceived acceptability of sex-oriented materials. Equally significant changes have been produced by a series of court decisions. As far as what the future holds, Winick reasons that most of the popular trends are unlikely to reverse themselves. In fact, various types of advertising (e.g., ads that emphasize eroticism) will probably reinforce the trends. This does not, however, mean that the acceptance of such materials is complete. Not only are many Americans uncomfortable about the spread of sex-oriented material, but pockets of resistance have developed in various communities.

Patricia A. Adler and Peter Adler, in "Tinydopers: A Case Study of Deviant Socialization," offer another account of how an existing deviant or criminal category can undergo significant change. The authors focus on "tinydopers"—that is, marijuana-smoking children between the ages of 0–8 years. Adler and Adler are concerned initially with outlining those societal conditions that produced a "moral passage," or transformation of marijuana's social and legal status from criminalization to relative legitimization. The authors are also interested in demonstrating what is likely to happen when smoking spreads to one of society's most sacred groups, children. The researchers present a five-stage model of social change which they feel captures the diffusion and legitimization of marijuana. For example, during Stage I (the 1940s), the "carriers" or users were what Adler and Adler term "stigmatized outgroups" (blacks). By Stage II (the 1950s), usage had spread to "ingroup deviants" (e.g., jazz musicians) who identified with the stigmatized outgroups. From there, usage spread to such "avant-garde ingroup members" as college students (Stage III, the 1960s), to such "normal ingroup members" as the middle class (Stage IV, the 1970s), and finally to such "sacred groups" as children (Stage V, from 1975 on). Adler and Adler maintain that the spread of deviance to Stage V can produce social revulsion and can trigger attempts to ban the behavior by children; this appears to be the case with respect to the tinydopers. Throughout, one can obtain an excellent feel for the moral passage of marijuana. Of interest, too, are the ways in which parents manage a potentially discrediting feature about their child. Some, for example, are concerned that their tinydoper will tell others and thus take certain precautions; other parents are relatively unconcerned.

Deviant Actors

As I have suggested, noninstitutional deviants (e.g., drug addicts and prostitutes) and institutional deviants (e.g., mental patients and delinquents) who elect to change their deviant behavior can expect to encounter a range of structural and individual roadblocks—roadblocks that may ultimately produce a relapse or further deviance. Jacqueline P. Wiseman, in "Alcoholics and the Transformation of Deviant Identity," documents some of the barriers that skid row alcoholics can expect to encounter when they leave the institutional role and try to assume a conventional role in society. Wiseman initially points out that not only is the institutional experience of a contrived or artificial nature, but, unlike the middle-class alcoholic, the skid row alcoholic is "not returning to any niche being held for him in society." The alcoholic thus has difficulty finding employment, as well as acceptable living quarters. He also experiences trouble staying sober, and doing so often means avoiding old acquaintances and surroundings; this in turn frequently means spending a great deal of time alone. Wiseman contends that there are only three ways an alcoholic can move off skid row: (1) by becoming a member of an institution, (2) by becoming involved in "alcoholic rehabilitation as a profession," or (3) by dying.

Like Wiseman, John Irwin—in his article "Reentry"—outlines some of the problems that ex-deviants must deal with. His attention is given to ex-convicts. He speaks of problems in three areas: (1) "getting settled down," (2) overcoming obstacles to "doing good," and (3) dealing with the parole agency and its restrictions. Irwin concentrates on the first set of problems—that is, getting settled down. He maintains intitially that there is little societal awareness of what reentry actually entails. This general blindness, he reasons, is related to the many formal and informal stereotypes that are used to characterize the ex-convict. For example, the ex-convict, when compared with other returnees (e.g., veterans), may be typed and responded to as being "emotionally disturbed," "sociopathic," or "potentially dangerous." Others may label him or her as being a person of "low moral worth." Being situated in the parole status itself can produce strains and reactions that the parole agent may take as signs that the parolee has failed. Further, the agent frequently sees failure in terms of the existing stereotypes—he or she regards the parolee as morally unworthy or as incapable of adapting to the parole status. Irwin then describes various other problems relating to settling down (e.g., withstanding the initial impact of release, learning how to live as a civilian, and dealing with the parole agency). His comments on how the disorganizing experiences of reentry affect a person's self-concept are insightful. For example, not only does the person who is released often find himself in a strange environment, but he frequently experiences anxiety, frustration, and depression.

Deviant Organizations, Decision-Makers, and Structures

As is evident throughout this book, it is the social actor—and usually a person who is relatively powerless—who becomes selected out and processed as a deviant by some type of people-processing or people-changing institution. As I have already argued, it is the actor who must alter behavior. Placing the burden for change exclusively upon the individual, however, effectively means that the decision-makers and their organizations escape scrutiny. And yet, there is solid evidence pointing to the need for such examinations. In Part 4, Scheff and Culver's data on the perfunctory treatment of involuntary mental patients, as well as Jeffery's study of the indifferent handling of "rubbish," offer excellent cases in point. Policywise, an important message is also contained in research such as Scheff and Culver's: if an institution's underlying organizational structrue (i.e., its theory of the office, diagnostic stereotypes, career lines, and staff socializing procedures) remains unaltered, then selected categories of clients can expect to be typed and treated in a routinized, stereotypical, and uncaring fashion. Predictably, if Scheff and Culver's involuntary mental patients continue to be processed on the basis of a working ideology that presumes mental illness, we can expect that these patients will be committed. Similarly, if low-income and minority students continue to be processed in accordance with a theory of the office that presumes differential ability, we can expect failure, dropouts, and youth deviance. This need for focusing on underlying structures and ideologies applies not only to such formal, bureaucratic entities as the mental institution and the school, but to other types of groupings and organizations as well. Watson's description of the content of the outlaw motorcyclist subculture (Part 2), Sherman's analysis of organizational corruption (Part 4), Best and Luckenbill's discussion of the social organization of deviants (Part 5), Heyl's characterization of the training of house prostitutes (Part 5), and Clinard and Yeager's depiction of corporate crime (Part 5) offer but a few examples underscoring the need for focusing on underlying organizational structures. In terms of a more specific illustration, if the values and associated normative configurations of the outlaw motorist subculture remain intact, recruits, once socialized, will exhibit the expected behavior and attitudes. If, however, significant change is to occur on the part of the motorcyclists, it must come initially from an overhauling of those components (values and norms) that are inculcated within the individual. The same applies with respect to those who process mental patients, disadvantaged students, and other perceived "societal misfits." Clearly, a different theory of the office, once effectively ingrained within the decision-makers, would produce changes in client processing. As an example, if educators and counselors were to presume that *all* students have strong abilities, the need for sorting, categorizing, or stratifying students would be reduced substantially. Thus, in the analysis of change, attention must be given not only to the social actor but to the decision-makers, their institutions, and the underlying theories of the office.

James H. Frey, in "Controlling Deviant Organizations: Scientists as Moral Entrepreneurs," discusses the role that a "whistle blower,"— in this case, a scientist—can play in controlling private corporations, government agencies, and decision-makers. Whistle blowers are individuals who, in an attempt to assuage their conscience, alert social-control agents to the deviance they have observed. Blowing the whistle, Frey notes, is an act of moral entrepreneurship. He is concerned specifically with describing those conditions which determine the extent and type of moral entrepreneurship that may arise. Frey also outlines the role of the scientist in this process. As illustrations of the utility of this concept, he initially cites various examples of corporate/organizational deviance and then outlines some difficulties involved in trying to sanction the lawbreakers. Frey offers a table in which he outlines the visibility and risk of several types of moral entrepreneurship (i.e., internal versus external exposure). For example, full public disclosure produces high visibility and maximum risk to the whistle blower. Another table deals with the direction of exposure with regard to what Frey terms the "knowledgeability of the target" (i.e., a "naive" target as opposed to a "knowing" target). By way of illustration, an employee, in an effort to enhance his or her status with an organization, may, upon discovering deviant or illegal practices, try to blackmail a corporate official. Frey concludes with an analysis of specific conditions that affect moral entrepreneurship (e.g., the general environment, or experience factors).

In "Policing Physicians: Practitioner Fraud and Abuse in a Government Medical Program," Henry N. Pontell, Paul D. Jesilow, and Gilbert Geis also focus on decision-makers, in the case, physicians involved in the apparent defrauding and abusing of California's Medicaid program (Medi-Cal). Like Frey, these researchers underscore the difficulties involved in detecting, defining, and sanctioning physicians who have been engaged in fraud. These difficulties, the authors reason, may be due in part to the nature of the medical profession itself. Not only do doctors enjoy a high status in our society, but even when "shady acts" are uncovered, they are able to define the deviance in a different light. The lack of effective detection and prosecution may also be related to the fact that physicians are seen as providing crucial services—services that may be curtailed upon conviction or sanctioning of a doctor. The researchers outline some of the structural features that invite fraud. One of the major vehicles for fraud and abuse is the "fee for service" nature of Medi-Cal. As an example, the government may be billed for services not rendered, or the bill may be "upgraded" (i.e., the bill is for more services than the physician provided). The authors end with an analysis of actual enforcement attempts. The results exhibit a very clear pattern: most efforts to police physicians fail.

The last selection ("Rehabilitating Social Systems and Institutions") is from my recent book *Creating School Failure, Youth Crime, and Deviance.* I initially describe how legislators, practitioners, professionals, and others, with their rather strict and exclusive focus on the individual, help to perpetuate what I have termed a "medical-clinical-individualistic" model of change and treatment. I then offer evidence demonstrating how such a model frequently affects the social actor, who may elect to alter his or her behavior. Most significantly, people become caught between two worlds—the conforming and the nonconforming. Not only does this dilemma give rise to a great deal of anxiety and self-debate, but the actor soon learns that neither world is likely to change much. Thus, "the individual must weigh the costs and benefits that may ensue by virtue of involvement with one culture as opposed to another." Frequently—and due to such factors as peer pressure, as well as unsatisfactory experiences with former friends and family members—the actor will exhibit a relapse. Defining failure in *individual* terms and not in *structural-organizational* terms is associated with other serious limitations; most notably, this viewpoint protects the real culprits from scrutiny and analysis. In support of this thesis, I conclude with an analysis of how the educational system, by virtue of the way it is structured organizationally (i.e., its use of ability groups, tracks systems, and career lines), actually builds and perpetuates deviant careers for particularly vulnerable categories of students, such as black and low-income pupils. I also outline how, with the inculcation of a different theory of the office within educators, parents, and others, changes could be produced. These ideological and organizational alterations have implications for the rehabilitation of any social system or institution.

49 / From Deviant to Normative: Changes in the Social Acceptability of Sexually Explicit Material

CHARLES WINICK

In 1963, Ralph Ginzburg was fined $42,000 and sentenced to five years in prison for publishing the magazine *Eros,* which a federal judge had found to be obscene. In 1976, Ginzburg found some copies of the magazine in a warehouse and donated all of them to the American Civil Liberties Union, which announced its intention to sell them at public auction. In 13 years, what was once obscene had become tame; what had been deviant was now accepted. Any such substantial change in public morality is likely to be overdetermined, and the shift from sex prohibition to sexual script in the arts is no exception.

One of the relationships between deviance and social change, which is the subject of this paper, is the normalization of behavior which had previously been frowned upon. Beginning in the 1950s, increasing during the 1960s, and approaching new levels of explicit expression in the 1970s, sex-oriented media and art content that had formerly been regarded as deviant became relatively acceptable, as a result of a variety of kinds of social change.

Over the last 20 to 30 years, there has been a vast expansion of the audiences for sex-oriented materials in all of the arts and media of mass communication. Complementarily and simultaneously, there has been greater explicitness in the manner in which sexual material is presented in many different formats. The changes in content during this period are more dramatic than the analogous changes occurring in the previous two centuries of American history. Sex content that was once proscribed is now almost prescribed for many media and art forms.

The alteration in perception of what constitutes acceptability would appear to represent almost a case history of how material that was once labeled deviant has been relabeled positively. However, social scientists have seldom addressed themselves to identifying either the dimensions of the change in sex-related material or the reasons for its development. Some social philosophers, like Sorokin (1956), have decried what has happened but very few have attempt-

712

ed to understand why it occurred. It is reasonable to speculate that the changes in content reflect pushes from audiences and pulls from the arts and media and are the end products of deep-rooted social and institutional trends.

On the level of mass psychology, the Nuremberg Trials and the coming into our awareness of the Holocaust, by the late 1940s, probably helped to make us more willing to accept other previously hidden aspects of human behavior. A related residue of World War II was the reluctant recognition that some national leaders, like Adolf Hitler, had been quite mad. If our leaders had been so disturbed, perhaps some of the givens of our society might be reevaluated and found to be irrelevant to current society. A loss of confidence in leadership could lead to an erosion of confidence in values which had been taken for granted.

The Nuremberg and other post-World War II disclosures affected many Americans still recovering from the depression. [They exhibited] anxiety about communism, concern about the impact of automation and the technocratic state, and [were] receptive to the loneliness and vulnerability of existentialism. Such challenges to the integrity of self provided the background for a considerable range of shifts in social and community life that have facilitated a movement toward hedonism and privatization. The most obvious change has been a decline in the work week and a sharp increase in the time available for leisure. Early retirement is a growing trend that provides more leisure for older persons. Persons with increased leisure often use it in order to give more time to consumption of the media and popular arts.

Private satisfaction rather than public participation has become a growing feature of American life. Sennett (1977) has suggested some reasons for our general loss of interest in public life. Previously, Karl Mannheim (1950) had explained how legitimation had been eroded and meaning lost from many activities. On the basis of his analysis of data from the Detroit Area Study, Lenski (1961) questioned whether Max Weber's concept of the Protestant Ethic could fruitfully be applied to contemporary American society. The Protestant Ethic was probably a group of characteristics which were important at a particular time in history but which no longer are part of one constellation. Most notably, asceticism has surely ceased to be a significant part of American national character. Many television stations, newspapers, magazines and other media now have "life style" editors who regularly report on the new good life, the life of enjoyment.

One analysis posits hedonism as the appropriate ideological companion to the loss of legitimacy and meaning from our declining and alienating institutions (Etzioni, 1972). Hedonism seems to complement critiques of society as oppressive.

Recent decades have seen an intensive scrutiny of our social and moral values. The turbulence of a period of racial conflict, assassinations of national leaders, new communal living arrangements, questioning of the nulcear family and other existing life styles, disclosures of deceit and chicanery by high government officials, Watergate, youth rebellion, widespread drug use, substantial increases in the crime rate, the Vietnam War, decriminalization of abortion, and other extraordinary events led to a very searching examination of major institutions.

As work has become less satisfying, it appeared less rewarding in terms of deeper needs, values, and relationships and increasingly functioned as a source of money with which to enjoy the leisure that was a central locus of gratification. Many kinds of work lead to atonie, or a lack of resonance with reality (Winick, 1964). Workingmen's taverns no longer provide discussions of industrial or political issues but rather an opportunity for gaiety and frivolity (Cavan, 1966; Le Masters, 1975).

Marxists have argued that the source of social relations, culture, and ideology has shifted to a mass culture of consumerism (Alt, 1976). This trend has involved a privatization of daily existence mediated by new forms of popular culture, many aspects of which have increasingly expressed sex-oriented themes.

All of the social critiques noted above may have some etiological relevance. In order to explore some other causal contributors to the change and to document its parameters, some reasons for, and explication of, the details of the transformation of previously deviant sexual content in popular arts and media into relative acceptability will be discussed below under five headings: larger social forces, court decisions and other statements, content of the arts, functions served by sex-oriented material, and the future.

LARGER SOCIAL FORCES

A number of larger social forces have contributed to the changing climate for sex-oriented materials during the last few decades. They include a disaffection with government, disasters and recessions, the role of youth, perceptual and emotional isostasy, the importance of looking, and shifting sex roles and morality.

Disaffection With Government

The upsurge of interest in all aspects of sex during the 1960s was one of many responses to the loss of interest in government. As people became less confident in government, they increasingly moved to more private satisfactions.

Many citizens' feeling of cynicism and powerlessness are reflected in a survey conducted with a national sample (New York Times, 1976). Of the respondents, 55% agreed with the statement that "public officials don't care much about what people like me think." Almost three-fifths (59%) felt that government "is pretty much run for a few big interests."

A direct measure of withdrawal of interest from participation in political life was the very low degree of voter interest in the 1976 Presidential election, which provided a clear-cut choice between candidates. Only 53% of the citizens over 18 actually voted, which was the poorest turnout since 1948. The single most frequently cited reason for not voting, in postelection polls, was a lack of confidence in government.

Media reflect and reinforce such underlying feelings. During 1976, a number of successful films (*The Parallax View, Marathon Man, Three Days of the Condor, The Next Man*) dealt with a dread but unnameable government-linked conspiracy of vast magnitude, usually involving torture, poisoning, and murder. The popularity of such films suggests the public's readiness to accept a paranoid view of government, a view that was certainly reinforced by the FBI, CIA, and Watergate scandals.

Congressmen who had been linked to sexual or personal scandals generally won reelection in 1976. Their reelection implies the extent to which the general public had grown to accept irregular behavior in its elected officials and had decreased expectations of its political leadership.

Corruption in the institutions of American life had been foreshadowed in many pre-Watergate media, most remarkably in the character played by Burt Lancaster in the movie *The Sweet Smell of Success* (1957). As many people were turned off government by such films and by real events, they increasingly turned inward. Transcendental meditation, yoga, Zen, interest in Eastern religions, Esalen seminars, EST, Arica, autogenic relaxation, biofeedback, and many other methods for expanding personal satisfactions became very popular (Smith, 1976).

Disasters and Recessions

Americans have, in recent decades, been assured that they faced several kinds of imminent disaster and economic catastrophe. Advised that his insolent chariot (Keats, 1958) was unsafe at any speed (Nader, 1965), a representative organization man (Whyte, 1956) who was a member of a lonely crowd (Reisman, 1969) had to confront the limits to growth (Meadows, 1972). Told to think about the unthinkable (Kahn, 1964), he faced a crisis in black and white (Silberman, 1964) while his children confronted a crisis in the classroom (Silberman, 1971) or even death at an early age (Kozol, 1970). Future shock (Toffler, 1970) awaited those hardy enough to survive.

Many television shows, articles, and books have relentlessly warned Americans that they were hurrying, or at least slouching, into catastrophe. We can anticipate that persons living under a threat are especially likely to cope with anxiety via sexual outlets, like the men and women in the Decameron who distracted themselves by revelry in a large country house during the plague. We know that in previous times of social upheaval, like Restoration England, Germany in the latter part of the 18th century and the Weimar Republic, and America after World War I, there was an increase in the range of acceptable sexual behavior and the availability of such material in the popular arts.

For three decades, more and more problems have surfaced in this country and a number of them have been related to our several periods of concentrated economic difficulties, which it is customary to describe euphemistically as "recessions" or, more recently, as "stagflation." Beginning in 1973, the United States became aware, however reluctantly, that it was entering an economic depression that was the worst since the 1930s. Sexual gratification is especially important during such a time. When loss of a job, participation in marginal work, or anxiety about losing a job may cause people to become atonic and question their worth, the ability to express oneself sexually becomes particularly important (Winick, 1964). Such gratification may be derived from sexually oriented media, which can present fantasy or other vicarious experiences in a controllable and nonthreatening manner.

Just how gratifying a sexual fantasy may be can be inferred from the case of Sultan Shah-riyar, in the Thousand and One Nights. The sultan killed every woman with whom he made love. Knowing this, Scheherezade told so interesting a story that the sultan wanted her to finish it on the following night. She would always stop the tale at its most provocative moment. For a thousand nights, the stories about love were so gratifying to the sultan that he fell asleep every morning without having had intercourse—but fully satisfied. Fiction and movies similarly may present sexual provocation, pleasure without any potential letdown, for their audiences.

Anxiety has become pervasive because of problems like inflation, decreasing availability of oil and other sources of energy, food shortages, awareness of corruption, environmental pollution, threat of war in the Middle East, and a pervasive helplessness in the face of larger realities that, for the first time, many Americans feel they can no longer control.

Observing sexual activity on the screen and in books and magazines may, in fantasy, give the viewer a sense of fulfillment which could be particularly important for persons with misgivings about the directions that society is taking and when other kinds of achievement are becoming less available.

During the Great Depression of the 1930s, for some of the same reasons that have made them so appealing today, a number of sexually oriented pictorial materials were very popular. At that time, such content could not be sold openly but enjoyed a substantial covert popularity. Sexualized versions of popular comic strips like Mutt and Jeff and Tillie the Toiler had widespread distribution, and stag films were shown very frequently at many kinds of gatherings. With the end of the depression, and the beginning of World War II with its unifying national goals, such sex-oriented materials became less important. They became salient again in the 1950s, with the Korean War, McCarthyism, and other divisive movements. The conflict-riddled decade of the 1960s witnessed their full flourishing.

The Role of Youth

Mass media and the popular arts are perhaps more influential over young people, particularly adolescents and young adults, than over any other age group. The media and arts offer role models, methods for making contact with the world outside, vehicles of socialization, a current vocabulary of emotion, a social context for courtship, pleasant ways of spending leisure time to an age group which has such time, a continuing subject for conversation, subjects for hobbies and fan clubs, symbols of achievement, publicized exemplars of masculinity and femininity, training in consumer behavior, and objects of fantasy. Such attractions of the arts and media have been so important in recent decades because the American population has been relatively young, with a current median age of 28.9.

Among the larger social attitudes feeding the interest in media expressions of sexuality is the dramatic increase in educational levels during the last two decades. Millions of young people, born in the post-World War II baby boom, made education a major growth industry. Even in 1976, with widespread questioning about the utility of college education, over ten million students were enrolled in colleges and universities. The more education people have, the more extensive is their moviegoing and other media consumption and the more varied are their sex interests likely to be. A major finding of the first Kinsey (1948) report was that there was a positive and high correlation between education and range of sexual expression.

Increases in education have also often been linked with questioning the traditional values of a society. For many youths, the first opportunity for radicalization comes from colliding with society's restrictions on sexual expression. When they begin to question the rationale for various sexual restraints, they may also scrutinize the reasons for other kinds of limitations. Many young people identified with poet William Blake, who had, some 200 years earlier, argued that repression was the major political problem of the day and that society's goal should be freedom, the chief symbol of which was sexual freedom.

The more education a person has, the greater the likelihood of seeing a sexually oriented film. In the General Social Survey, college graduates were twice as likely to have seen an X-rated film during the year as those with less than a high school education (National Opinion Research Center, 1976). When a new opportunity for experience presents itself, college graduates are more likely than persons with less schooling to respond positively to the opportunity for innovation.

The increase in education among young people is additionally relevant because the movie audience is very young, with 73% of all movie admissions provided by persons between 12 and 29, who constitute only 39% of the United States population. Seven out of ten of frequent moviegoers, defined as those who attend movies at least twice a month, are under 30 (Newspaper Advertising Bureau, 1974). The youthful population is, especially in the last several years, the most sexually emancipated part of the population.

Yankelovich (1974), in the most ambitious recent study of the attitudes of young people, concluded that the more liberal casual sexual attitudes which had been confined to a minority of college students in the late 1960s had spread to mainstream college youth as well as mainstream working-class youth by the early 1970s, in a remarkably abrupt transition. The new code of sexual morality centered on the acceptability of nonmarital sex.

One reason for youths' interest in sex in films is that they are responding to the decline of rites of passage (Winick, 1968). Consider how little ceremonial observance there is of a teenager's getting a driver's license, one of the most significant changes in status. The decline of age-graded experiences, and in ceremonies and benchmarks of social life, has led many people to seek ritualistic satisfaction elsewhere. The ritualistic aspects of sex in movies may appeal to this need.

Young people have also been the primary audience for rock and roll music, a significant part of which is concerned with love and sex. Thus, Ray Charles' famous record of "I Got A Woman" is an account of coitus. In fact, "rock" etymologically connotes entrance of the penis into the vagina and "roll" refers to the organs' interaction (Winick, 1970a). Some famous performers, like Jim Morrison and Chuck Berry, would masturbate their guitars. The popularity of rock and roll among youth since 1953 coincides with the period within which movies and other media have become heavily sexualized.

Sex in rock music reached new candor in the 1970s. Andrea True, previously known as an actress in sex-oriented movies, recorded a major hit record of the decade called "More, more, more" ("how do ya like it . . . more, more, more"). "Love to Love You Baby" is 17 minutes of the title phrase, along with sexually explicit gasps and moans, repeated by Donna Summers, the "queen of sex rock." Another recent successful record, "Lady Marmalade," by the Labelle group, repeated the refrain, "Voulez-vous coucher avec moi?"

Identification of youths with such rock music is unusually intense because the composers, performers, and often record company executives involved in the music are likely to be young. In contrast, the composers, performers, and producers of the pre-rock, pre-1950s popular music of the "June-moon" type were likely to be older than its youthful consumers. Older composers like Cole Porter, George Gershwin, Jerome Kern, and Irving Berlin wrote from a European tradition; rock composers are super-contemporary and "now."

The success of sex-related rock records among young people is important for many reasons. One reason is the relationship between competition and sex. Wherever young people turn, they see many others competing for the same goals, such as school grades or jobs. Some have dealt with this competition by drug use or "dropping out" and others retreat into hedonism. Interest in sexually oriented media may represent another escape from competition and demands for accomplishment.

Also, particularly among young adults, notions of fun, communication, and pleasure have entered importantly into thinking about the recreational aspects of sex. At the same time, the procreational possibilities of sex are lesser sources of anxiety because of the development of laparoscopy as a simple technique for sterilization and significant advances in contraceptive technology represented by the pill and IUD. The pleasurable spectator pastime of watching sex in films and print materials fits in with young people's recreational outlook and the desire to improve their sexual-communicative skills.

Jet planes and charter flights have dramatically expanded opportunities for travel and helped to expose many young people to different approaches to sexuality in other countries. Moviegoers are twice as likely as nonmoviegoers to have made an airplane trip in the last three years (Newspaper Advertising Bureau, 1974). Many travelers to Europe have doubtless observed the more casual attitudes toward prostitution and sex in the arts in many countries and transferred such attitudes to their expectations in America.

Perceptual and Emotional Isostasy

The notion of perceptual and emotional isostasy may help to explain the popularity of media sex-related content. In geology, the principle of isostasy expresses the way in which the earth's high reliefs are compensated by variations in the density of materials extending below the surface. Highs and lows, in effect, balance each other. In economics, the analogous concept of countervalence has been used in order to express the manner in which a strong force, such as an aggressive corporation, is met by a competitive element, such as the consumer movement (Galbraith, 1956).

We suggest that there is an isostasy of the audience's responses to mass media, a reciprocal relationship between the number and severity of the country's problems and the amount of time which it devotes to media, and particularly to movies. Another way of expressing this notion is that the worse times become, the better will movie attendance be. The peak of moviegoing was reached during the Great Depression of the 1930s. 1974—the year of the energy crisis, a recession, Watergate, President Nixon's resignation, and a threat of war in the Middle East—was also the year in which American moviegoers spent more money at the box office ($1.9 billion) than ever before. Two escapist films—*The Sting* and *The Exorcist*—far outpaced the other films.

The notion of isostasy not only applies to the frequency of moviegoing; it also helps to explain why sexually oriented content is so popular in movies and other popular arts. All the media are likely to emphasize war, crime, and other violence-oriented materials. As a result, many consumers of the arts are seeking a balancing experience that is pleasurable. During the last decade, sexually oriented materials have increasingly provided such a pleasurable experience.

Another factor is the audience's response to television fare. There can be no doubt about the growing sophistication of television content, or about the heavy involvement of Americans with television. Viewing has continued to increase fairly steadily, reaching a current average of 45 hours weekly per household. Now that 98% of American homes possess television and 70% own color television, there has been a tremendous increase in exposure to sound pictures. As a result, there has been a revolution of rising expectations in terms of visual stimuli, and sexuality in the movies represents an effort to compete with the bombardment of free stimuli from television.

The increase in visual sophistication has been coterminous with a sharp decline in illusions about other aspects of American life. Race, international relations, and personal morality are some of the areas of social living in which traditional beliefs are becoming less binding. Attitudes toward sex are always closely intertwined with other attitudes. Greater acceptance of new options in various aspects of social life has been both cause and effect of the greater acceptance of sex reality in visual media.

The Importance of Looking

Looking may provide sexual satisfaction even if the object of the looking does not seem to be sexual. Interview studies with persons who witnessed but did not report crimes of violence involving women victims, as in the 1964 murder of Kitty Genovese in New York City, indicated that many derived a parasexual response from witnessing the event (Winick, 1968). Thirty-eight persons heard Miss Genovese being murdered but none of them called the police. In studies of similar witnesses to a crime who did not report it, a recurrent finding is that seeing such events is so provocative that the excitation takes precedence over summoning law enforcement authorities. In a less extreme term, this kind of sexual gratification from looking, or optical lubricity, can be found in the general population.

One expression of Americans' continuing interest in sexual gratification by looking is provided by our continuing enthusiasm for burlesque, which became more popular in the United States before World War II than ever before in any other country. Every town of more than 100,000 was likely to have its own burlesque theater (Gorer, 1937). Burlesque was and is unique in providing a visual satisfaction complete in itself, in contrast to other cultures which provided erotic spectacles as a prelude to direct sexual activity. In Mediterranean seaport cabarets, for example, there is a long tradition of erotic dancing, but the performers are available for subseqent sexual relations.

After a brief hiatus in the 1940s, burlesque made a comeback in the 1950s, with over 200 theaters now presenting it. Burlesque is expanding because it offers sex without the risk of obscenity prosecutions. Our desire to look without touching also expresses itself in the popularity of topless waitresses. There is probably no other country in the world where such waitresses could go about their business, confident that men would not try to touch them. There are topless bars all over America; New York City, for example, has 225 such bars.

Some patrons find sexual looking more satisfying than alcoholic beverages and it may be more profitable for cabarets to have the former than the latter. When the Supreme Court ruled, in 1972, that First Amendment rights may be curtailed in California clubs that served liquor and also presented what the Court called "bacchanalian revelries," a number of the clubs chose to give up their liquor license rather than abandon their topless or bottomless shows.

Shifting Sex Roles and Morality

In the 1960s, the women's liberation movement became a significant force in terms of women's rights to self-expression of all kinds, including sexual satisfaction. Although some feminists have complained that sexually explicit magazines, books, and movies derogate women, respondents to the General Social Survey who had a high score on a scale of female equality were twice as likely as those with a low equality score to have seen an X-rated film (National Opinion Research Center, 1976). We may speculate that sexually explicit films and the women's movement both represent a form of social change and that there is a generalized responsiveness to the new, as in the marketing concept of the "tryer" or "upscale" purchaser.

In some ways, the most important change in attitudes toward sexual behavior occurred in women. As women increasingly entered the labor force and became economically self-sufficient, they were less likely to accept older ideologies like the double standard for sex, whereby what was prohibited for women was approved for men. Concern about overpopulation and families' need for wives' incomes to cope with inflation led to less children and contributed to women's assumption of roles outside the home, a trend which was enormously enhanced by the availability of the birth control pill after 1961.

Magazines that addressed themselves to sexually liberated women became very popular. *Cosmopolitan,* which had been facing bankruptcy when it carried conventional features on homemaking, recipes, and other service content, became enormously successful after it began, in the 1960s, concerning itself with women's sexual satisfaction and pleasures. Its editor had previously been known as the author of a "how-to" book on *Sex and the Single Girl* (Brown, 1962).

The women's movement spawned a new dimension in sexually oriented materials. Magazines *Playgirl* and *Viva,* which began publication in 1973, are directed to women and show extensive photographs of nude men. A typical issue of *Viva* ("the international magazine for women") contains a pictorial feature on "crotch watching, the only female spectator sport," and ten different photographs of nude men (Anonymous, 1975). A new literature of sexual awareness for women became very popular, with books which provided details on masturbatory techniques (Dodson, 1975) and self-pleasure (Barbach, 1975) emerging as best sellers.

One effect of women's liberation has been to increase the proportion of women attending sexually oriented movies. Jokes about "the raincoat crowd" attending such movies are largely historical, now that couples represent so large a proportion—almost half, in many theatres—of their audiences. The increased attendance of women at erotic theatrical events can also be inferred from the near-disappearance of the word "striptease," which was common in the 1930s when women stripped for audiences of men, but which is less used today when so many couples attend the performances of what is now called "exotic dancing."

The women's movement could only become institutionalized, via *MS* magazine and the National Organization of Women, after the country began to face the consequences of the unisex trend. During the 1960s, when unisex moved from being a pejorative adjective to a positive description, many Americans experienced uneasiness about what constituted masculinity and femininity, and questioned if such concepts still had any utility. There is little doubt that some persons were eager audiences for sexually oriented films and fiction because the latter's sex roles were unequivocal and clear-cut and thus reassuring. In fiction and movies, men were men, women were women, and they knew how to express their gender via sexual behavior.

At the same time, discussions of sexual ethics tended to stress the interpersonal nature of the sexual situation rather than absolutes or doctrinal considerations. During the last two decades, situation ethics became a significant component of discussions about morality. Situation ethics were generally set forth as the right and good thing being whatever is the most living thing in a situation (Fletcher, 1966). In terms of sex, the notion that a wide range of behavior was normal was accepted by a large porportion of the population, which demanded freedom for the individual to satisfy his needs, desires, and tastes as he sees fit. The notion of "sexual minorities" as persons with unusual interests who are entitled to the same kind of protection as other minority groups was accepted fairly widely (Ullerstam, 1966). The propositions that sex is a significant part of happiness, and that sex should be approached with openness, encouraged the treatment of varieties of sexual expression in films, books, and magazines.

The idea that a person has value in and of himself, apart from possessions or accomplishments, has been assuming salience since the 1960s. This concept relates to sex in that sexual interaction increasingly is seen as one kind of self-expression. Movies and other popular arts provide an opportunity to see sexual interactions, not unlike one's own, elevated to the status of art. Furthermore, our increasing technocracy and bureaucracy tend to downgrade individuality, the loss of which may be seen as a kind of spiritual death. Equating sex with aliveness tends to make sex in the arts a testament to the individual's struggle to affirm his or her importance.

Such affirmation became more important as conventional marriage appeared to pose increasing problems and the divorce rate began climbing in the 1950s. Sexual expression in the popular arts represented an outlet for "getting off" impulses or feelings which could not be expressed in marriage. Tacit recognition of such a safety valve function could have been one reason that so many social institutions, by the 1950s, seemed to be reinforcing the growing acceptance of sex in the arts.

Freedom in the arts was reinforced by the new freedom of clothing, beginning in the late 1950s. Clothes as a way of concealing the body gave rise to clothes as a way of revealing it. Greater candor about the body via clothes facilitated and reflected sexual candor in the arts and media. As guilt and shame were less likely to be related to revealing the body, they were also less likely to be associated with sexual expression in behavior and the public arts.

COURT DECISIONS AND OTHER STATEMENTS

In addition to social trends, there were pronouncements, from some important agencies of social control, on the subject of the kind of sex-related content that is and is not acceptable in the popular arts. They included court decisions, the report of the Commission on Obscenity and Pornography, and other writings.

Court Decisions

Between 1957 and 1969, under Chief Justice Earl Warren, the U.S. Supreme Court issued a number of decisions which liberalized the nation's attitudes toward sexually oriented materials and thereby effected significant social change (Fahringer and Brown, 1973–1974). The Warren court probably achieved more social change than did legislatures, in obscenity as well as other areas. In U.S. v. Roth (1957), the Court created the formula of "whether to the average person applying contemporary community standards, the dominant theme of the material, taken as a whole, appeals to the prurient interest" as the test of obscenity. Scienter, or the seller's knowledge of material's content, was said by the Court to be a required constitutional predicate to an obscenity conviction (Smith v. California, 1959).

In Jacobellis v. Ohio (1964), the Court set forth the concept of a national community standard and two years later added the requirement that material must be "utterly without redeeming value" to be obscene (Memoirs v. Attorney General, 1966). In Redrup v. New

York (1967), the Court said that materials that were not pandered, sold to minors, or foisted on unwilling audiences, were constitutionally protected. The Warren Court's last important opinion on obscenity was Stanley v. Georgia (1969), which found that mere possession of obscenity in a person's home was not criminal.

On June 21 and 24, 1973, the Court, now dominated by appointees of President Nixon and headed by Warren Burger, announced major decisions on obscenity (Miller v. California, 1973; Paris Adult Theatre, 1973), which discarded the Roth test. The Court now held that, to be obscene, the work must depict, in a patently offensive way, sexual conduct specifically defined by the applicable state law; lack serious literary, artistic, political, or scientific value; and appeal to the prurient interest of the average person, applying contemporary community standards. The Court also held that the prosecution did not have to produce proof on the issue of obscenity and that there was no national community standard.

Each community was free to clarify what its standards were. In New York State courts, "community" has been defined as the whole state, while in adjacent New Jersey, it means the individual county, and in federal prosecutions, it is generally construed as the geographic area serviced by each of the 90 courts. What is obscene in one "community" may not be obscene in the very next "community."

Because the 1973 decisions clearly favored the prosecution and because of uncertainty over what "community" standards would be observed, it was originally thought that the 1973 decisions would brake the expansion of the production of sex-oriented materials. However, exactly the opposite seems to have taken place, in the case of both hard- and soft-core materials. Hard-core involves erection, coital penetration, oragenitalism, and closeups of genitalia. Soft-core may involve the presentation of "ultimate sexual acts" but the organs are not shown, there is no erection, no closeups of penetration, and the activity may be simulated.

Expansion of the number of areas willing to permit hard- and soft-core material has occurred, even though the 1973 decisions are more stringent than previous Supreme Court rulings and leading erotica publishers Mike Thevis and William Hamling were convicted of selling obscene materials and given substantial prison sentences. There is considerable public and prosecutional apathy toward obscenity, which may be seen as a "victimless crime," requiring large sums of taxpayers' money to be spent pursuing convictions that are increasingly difficult to obtain. Burt Pines, city attorney of Los Angeles, noted in 1974 that the city, after spending $500,000 in unsuccessful efforts to convict the movie *Deep Throat*, had abandoned the case.

Other prosecutors have been more successful. For example, a number of persons were convicted in Memphis in 1976 of conspiracy to violate the federal obscenity laws by distributing *Deep Throat* in Memphis, and in 1977 Larry Flynt was convicted of engaging in organized crime for publishing *Hustler*. These convictions appear, however, to have been the result of atypical local political conditions. Overall, the number of prosecutions since the 1973 decisions has declined. Although the decisions facilitate a prosecutor's task, there has been no increase in convictions. Defense attorneys now try harder to win an acquittal during a trial because they expect to be less successful in winning an appeal from a conviction.

Recent cases in many different states have invloved the introduction into evidence of polls which tend to show that the majority of an area's citizens feel that it is acceptable for media to show actual or pretended sex acts and that adults should have the right to see such materials, if they want to do so. In a 1976 survey conducted in the heartland community of Hamilton County, Ohio, for example, 74% of the respondents felt that adults had the right to see publications depicting nudity and sex.

A number of states, such as Oregon, Vermont, New Jersey, New York, and Indiana, had their obscenity statutes declared unconstitutional during the 1970s. For varying periods of time, therefore, such states had no obscenity prosecutions. Many persons noted that the total absence of obscenity prosecutions seemed to have no measurable effect on the quality of life in the affected states and this awareness further downgraded the salience of obscenity as a social problem. In a 1970 survey, the Commission on Obscenity and Pornography (1970) had found that only 2% of the nation's population felt that obscenity was a "serious problem." It ranked 14th out of 14 problems cited.

By the late 1950s, many state legislatures were liberalizing laws on homosexuality, sodomy, fornication, and other kinds of sexual activity. The National Gay Activists Task Force, sparked by prominent educators, scientists, and artists, urged legislatures to implement more open attitudes toward gays. "Homosexual" increasingly was used as an adjective connoting a tendency rather than as a noun denoting an unalterable condition, especially after the American Psychiatric Association had officially changed its classification of homosexuality, in 1974, from a disease to a sexual option which did not imply pathology. Such highly publicized official actions helped to create a more accepting attitude toward sex in the media and arts.

Report of Commission on Obscenity and Pornography

Another contributor to the dramatic change in the climate of acceptance for sexually oriented materials was the final report of the Commission on Obscenity and Pornography (1970), which concluded that sexually explicit materials had no harmful effect. The Commission's report recommended that federal and state obscenity laws, in terms of adults, be repealed. Although the subsequent dismissal of the report by President Nixon and the U.S. Senate was briefly publicized, the dismissal had less impact than the fact that a federal commission considering the effects of sex-oriented print and visual materials had found them harmless. The report served to alert many Americans to the issue of obscenity. The Commission was unable to find any valid and acceptable definition of obscenity and recommended that the term be abandoned; its report used the terms "sexually explicit" and "sexually oriented" materials.

Publishers, moviemakers, writers, and artists generally interpreted the report as a green light to expand content. Some publishers and producers took advantage of the ambiguous or seemingly favorable legal situation after 1970 in order to introduce previously prohibited sexual content. The new freedom was expressed both in soft- and hard-core films for general release, magazines, books, and "comix."

During the 1960s, there were several prominent literary critics, like Paul Goodman (1961), Stanley Edgar Hyman (1966), Peter Michelson (1966), Susan Sontag (1966), and Kenneth Tynan (1968), who wrote widely discussed essays in favor of sex-oriented materials, calling attention to their positive aspects. These essays contributed to a climate of acceptance for such materials in a number of different art forms, which began to reflect increasing candor and openness. Sontag's (1966) widely discussed "The Pornographic Imagination" was particularly influential in arguing that some sexually explicit works, like Pauline Réage's famous 1954 novel *The Story of O*, reach the level of literature, and she defended the artist's right to arouse the audience sexually. A number of these critics argued that we expect to respond to a work of art, but society does not want the audience to respond sexually to a work of sex-oriented art, and that such a double standard is unrealistic.

Beginning in the 1960s and into the 1970s, a number of nonliterary but very popular writers helped to provide an ideology of rejection of technocratic society and enthusiasm for self-expression and hedonism. Theodore Roszak (1969) urged his readers to resist "technocratic totalitarianism." Charles Reich (1970) viewed consciousness expansion as a harbinger of revolution. William I. Thompson (1972) saw increased hedonism and depoliticalization on the horizon. Although such writers did not address themselves specifically to sex-oriented materials, their best-selling books were often perceived to be expressing a message of free sexual expression. Reich (1976), however, actually later made the specific connection between rejection of modern technology and sexual freedom.

CONTENT OF THE ARTS

All of the arts, high as well as popular or mass communications, have participated in extraordinary liberalization of sex-related content which would have been considered deviant or even illegal only a few decades ago. The changes, which can be seen most clearly in films, books, magazines, and theatre, represent the expression and outcome of the complex political, sociological, economic and psychological forces noted above.

Films

One of the most remarkable changes in sexually oriented content is its penetration of conventional Hollywood films which are directed to the general public. Since the early 1960s, sexual activity increasingly tends to be shown on the screen rather than implied. During the 1950s, sexual intercourse had been suggested in films by various metaphors. The director would move the camera away from the couple to some symbolic parallel activity: crashing waves hitting a shore (*From Here to Eternity,* 1954), fireworks (*To Catch a Thief,* 1955), rearing stallions (*Not as a Stranger,* 1955), a train entering a tunnel (*North by Northwest,* 1959).

Such indirect expressions of sexual activity were necessary for films made under the Motion Picture Association Production Code, observance of which was necessary for a film to get a seal of approval. Getting a seal was an either-or matter, and a film without a seal was likely to be denounced by religious groups and spurned by the majority of theaters. There were rigid prohibitions against sexually explicit content when the industry Code was in effect.

Through the decade of the 1950s, "love goddesses" like Jane Russell, Jayne Mansfield, and Marilyn Monroe were making increasingly blatant appeals, as movies tried to offer what was not available on television. By the end of the decade, in *Room at the Top* (1959), when Susan asked Joe, "Wasn't it super?" she was probably the first movie heroine who admitted that she enjoyed making love. *The Pawnbroker* (1965) was the first Hollywood Code-approved film to show bare breasts.

In 1964, *The Carpetbaggers* added a new dimension of dialogue that clearly communicated sexual content without showing it on the screen ("What do you want to see on your honeymoon, darling?" "Lots and lots of lovely ceilings"). Similarly provocative dialogue, sexy titles, magazine spreads of near-nude scenes from films, and daring advertising copy combined to make many community elements feel that the Production Code had lost its ability to regulate movie content.

The major Hollywood studios, which had long opposed any introduction of a system of classifying films like England's—U (unrestricted), A (adult must accompany child under 16), and X (no one under 16 allowed)—finally realized that such a system was the only alternative to censorship. Adoption of the rating system in 1968 provided movie makers with new freedom because material not suitable for children could be identified as such.

Attitudes changed so rapidly that two years after the rating system began in 1970, the X-rated *Midnight Cowboy,* which featured a homosexual assault and heterosexual seduction, received the Academy Award as the year's best film. And hard-core movies became so popular that two of them—*Devil in Miss Jones* and *Deep Throat*—were, respectively, the sixth and eleventh most successful films of 1973, in terms of box office receipts. *Last Tango in Paris,* a soft-core film starring Marlon Brando and with anal intercourse as part of its extensive sexual content, was the year's third most successful film.

Deep Throat soon became a landmark because it was the first hard-core movie to get national distribution, as a result of publicity originating in a widely discussed obscenity trial in New York City. The $25,000,000 profit which the film earned—on an investment of $25,000—encouraged other producers to make hard-core films, which were readily distributed. Because it dealt with a woman's quest for sexual satisfaction, it was hailed as an expression of women's liberation, just as Erica Gavin had previously been applauded in the soft-core film *Vixen* (1968) because of her "take charge" qualities.

Deep Throat was particularly important in obtaining acceptance for other sex-oriented films. It created "porno chic," was the first such film to attract many couples, and a major media event, seen by many famous "square" celebrities. Linda Lovelace, the star, was interviewed widely and achieved a fame unapproached by any previous performers in sexually explicit films. The film's humor provided an escape value by permitting audiences to feel at ease while watching the sexual material. *Deep Throat* was discussed positively in major media like *The New York Times.* Its title became a verb, and a phrase from the movie—"different strokes for different folks"—entered the general language. And when *Deep Throat* became a camp success, seeing it became almost obligatory for many people who would not ordinarily have seen such a movie.

Another 1973 hard-core film which profited from publicity was *Behind the Green Door,* which starred Marilyn Chambers, who had previously been featured as the model on the package of Ivory Snow. The incongruity between the purity connotations of Ivory Snow and the ravishment of the actress in the film helped to attract huge audiences. Audience fantasies about the movie's content were probably enhanced by Miss Chambers' remaining mute throughout a considerable range of sexual activity.

He and She (1971), *Censorship in Denmark* (1970), and *History of the Blue Movie* (1971) were widely shown sexually explicit documentaries. *Mona* (1969), which dealt with a woman who engaged in oral sex in order to preserve her virginity till marriage, was typical of many fellatio-oriented films. *The Lovers,* which clearly suggested oral sex, had been upheld as not obscene by the Supreme Court as long ago as 1959.

Because the Swedish film *I Am Curious, Yellow* (1968) linked extensive sexual activity with the young heroine's quest for a better life, it received extensive discussion as a realistic and honest representation of contemporary youth. By 1968, a number of major Hollywood theatrical films were dealing frankly with homosexuality *(The Fox, The Sergeant, The Detective)*.

Contributing to the trend toward expansion of the limits of candor were some famous directors who made very successful and widely discussed films which contained sexual innovations. Michelangelo Antonioni, then generally regarded as the world's premier director, showed two nude women seducing a man in the very influential *Blow-Up* (1967). In *The Damned* (1970), Luchino Visconti presented incest. The film's sadomasochism was anticipated in Luis Bunuel's *Belle de Jour* (1967) and its transvestism had been a significant element of Federico Fellini's *I Vitelloni,* as long ago as 1953. These directors were so famous that their presenting such sex content encouraged other film makers to follow suit.

The first closeups of the sexual organs during coitus in a nationally distributed film could be seen in *Pornography in Denmark* (1970), a widely shown documentary. Around 1971, film makers began routinely showing coitus on the screen, fellatio could often be seen in 1972, bestiality figured in some 1973 movies (e.g., *Animal Lover*), and dominance-submission was prominent in 1974 titles (e.g., *Defiance*).

There may be a lag of just several months between a previously taboo sexual activity being shown in "adult" movies and its appearance in conventional Hollywood movies that go into general release. Thus, the first conventional film concerned with dominance-submission was *The Night Porter* (1974), a major studio production directed by Liliana Cavani and with two prominent stars (Dirk Bogarde and Charlotte Rampling), rated R. The heroine wears chains, steps on broken glass, enjoys being punched and nicked with glass by her lover, and smears his body with jam before she crawls on him for coitus.

She is married to another man and had previously met her sadistic lover when he was an officer of a Nazi prison camp in which she was a prisoner. The film's huge commercial and critical success led to many more dominance-submission movies in the following year, both hard-core *(The Story of Joanna)* and soft-core *(The Story of O)*.

The year 1975 also saw the enormous success of *Shampoo*, in which Julie Christie uses the most popular slang words for fellatio as she dives under a table in order to perform fellatio on Warren Beatty. In the same film, Beatty also has sexual intercourse with a mother and her daughter, within ten minutes of each other. The mother is married to one of Beatty's business associates.

No star of sexually explicit films enjoys as established a reputation as Warren Beatty. Up to the early 1970s, the performers in such films were essentially anonymous, using fanciful names, e.g., Bob Superstud. Today, acceptance of hard-core films is so widespread that they have developed their own stars, women like Linda Lovelace, Darby Lloyd Rains, Tina Russell, Marilyn Chambers, Georgina Spelvin, and men like Jamie Gillis, Harry Reems, Johnny Holmes, and Marc Stevens. Each of these performers is sufficiently well-known to have published an autobiography and attracted substantial followings. They are regularly interviewed in leading publications and their films are given comparative ratings equivalent to the four-star system used by some newspapers, as in *Screw's* percentile Peter-Meter and *Hustler's* erection ratings.

Another dimension of acceptance has been provided by Hollywood unions. In 1975, for the first time, Screen Actors Guild members appeared in a hard-core film *(Sometimes Sweet Susan)*, insuring reasonable rehearsal time and equitable salaries. Since then, more performers from television and "straight" movies have been appearing in hard-core films.

New audiences may be attracted as some hard-core films devote proportionately less footage to showing actual sex. In *Memories within Miss Aggie* (1974), a highly praised film made by Gerard Damiano, the director of *Deep Throat*, only about one-fifth of the film shows sexual activity, whereas most hard-core films devote much more of their footage to sex. Some members of the audience may find the sex more acceptable if there is less of it, just as many fans now enjoy the considerable amount of hard-core humorous content. The humor, as in *Deep Throat* and the French import *Pussy Talk* (1975), serves to ease the adaptation of some audience members to actual sex scenes.

Through the 1960s, sex-oriented films had generally been made in 16 millimeter prints. By the end of the decade, it was not uncommon for such films to be made in the more expensive 35 millimeter, with its superior clarity and detail. At the same time, budgets for such films began to escalate. By the 1970s, budgets of several hundred thousand dollars per film were reported. Such budgets permitted more time, a range of settings, name performers, and other contributors to the quality of the product.

As one result of such changes, there has been an increase in the number of theaters showing sex-oriented films. Since 1973, more theaters than ever before—over 1,100—now show hard-core movies and about 4,500 run soft-core, out of approximately 14,650 theaters in the United States. The only states not showing hard-core films are Arkansas, Kansas, Missouri, Oklahoma, and Tennessee, in addition to the District of Columbia. Within a state, not all cities will show hard-core materials. In Texas, for example, Houston will and Dallas will not show such films, while in Massachusetts, Boston refuses but Gloucester is willing to do so. To accommodate such differences, a hard-core movie is often also made in soft-core version.

Most of the theaters which began showing sexually oriented films were not newly built but were already in existence in suburban shopping centers or metropolitan areas and found such films to be more profitable than traditional features. Admission prices were substantially higher than for traditional films so that the theater could show a profit more easily. There was a steady supply of sex-oriented films and more (212) were actually made in a representative year (1975) than conventional theatrical films (208).

The near-exponential growth of sex-oriented movies in the last decade could reflect one additional factor: the unique ability of movies to appeal to the primary process—the unconscious—in a multidimensional manner. A movie can communicate directly with the unconscious of members of the audience sitting in a darkened theater by presenting a visual and auditory image, as it might be experienced in a dream or fantasy. For example, in *Naked Came the Stranger* (1975), the heroine follows her husband to the apartment where he is engaging in sexual activity with another woman. The heroine listens, outside the door, to the sounds of lovemaking inside the apartment. She raises her dress—she is wearing no underwear—and masturbates herself in rhythm to the sounds coming from the other side of the door. She continues to do so while several strangers walk down the stairs to go past her. The audience knows that such a scene would not take place in "real" life, although on an unconscious level its members enjoy and identify with the "action."

The unique power of movies to present similar intersensory material facilitates the ability of an audience to enter fully into sexual activity on the screen, on the unconscious level, and merge with it. Seeing a film in a darkened theater, with other people, maximizes involvement. To the extent that movies have been able to reflect the primary process rather than the secondary process of reality testing, they have offered a gratification that is very appealing to many people.

Books and Theater

There has been a major change in the quality and certainly the quantity of consumer-oriented books on sex. How-to books like *Sex Without Guilt* (Ellis, 1957), *The Sensuous Woman* (J., 1969), and *The Joy of Sex* (Comfort, 1972) sold millions of copies and helped to make the notion of sexual interest more acceptable. Such books are direct and factual and far removed from the euphemisms and poetic language of Van de Velde (1930), whose book had, for several decades, been the country's leading sex manual.

During the late 1950s and 1960s, fiction classics which had been unavailable in the United States *(Lady Chatterley's Lover, Memoirs of a Woman of Pleasure, Tropic of Cancer)* were published here after the Supreme Court delcared them to be not obscene. New writers like Frank Newman, Marcus Van Heller, Marco Vassi, Terry Southern, Larry Townsend, and Alex Trocchi were, at the same time, writing books that were much franker, wittier, and presented a broader range of sexual content than the euphemisms of previous years (e.g., "his manhood throbbed").

In the late 1960s, there was an expansion of paperback fiction for "adults only," which is available not only in specialized book stores but at newsstands and regular book stores. Over 30 publishers specialize in such books, each of which is constructred around a number of sex episodes with transition pages of nonsexual activity. The sex ratio, which is the number of pages devoted to sex in relation to the number of pages in the whole book, went from .29 in 1967 to .47 in 1969. In 1972, it jumped to .61 and was .63 in 1974, based on a representative sample of 428 titles (Smith, 1974). In books appearing after 1970, there are increases in the incidence of fellatio, cunnilingus, and anal intercourse.

The enormous publicity accorded the books by Masters and Johnson (1966, 1970) and other scientists continued the process of general acceptance of research on sex, a process which had begun with the first Kinsey (1948) book. The respectability given to sex research by such scientists had a ripple effect which extended to sex in mass media. Such changes in book content are important because regular moviegoers are much more likely to be book buyers than nonmoviegoers (Newspaper Advertising Bureau, 1974). And, of course, movies often derive from books.

The content of books is related to what is shown in theaters, and live theater has become much more sexually expansive since the Folies Bergère first used nudity in Paris in 1918 and London's Windmill Theatre featured static nude scenes in the 1950s. The American stage has not been the same since *Hair* (1967) presented nude men and women together in a famous scene.

Although ballet dancers like Mikhail Baryshnikov and Rudolf Neureyev are huge popular successes, there are complex relationships between a high art like classical ballet and more mass-oriented arts. But it is probably no coincidence that a nude ballet was performed at New York's Metropolitan Opera House, the showcase of Lincoln Center, for the first time in 1976. The ballet, Flemming Flindt's "The Triumph of Death," was danced by the Royal Danish Ballet, one of the world's leading classical troupes.

Various nonballet stage successes also helped to broaden the scope of what was acceptable. New approaches and content tend to get to movies from two to three years after they first appear on the stage and reach television in around five years, in a kind of trickle-down effect.

Famous writers like Jules Feiffer, Joe Orton, and Kenneth Tynan contributed skits to *Oh, Calcutta* (1969), a nude stage review that was deliberately designed to stimulate the audience sexually. It ran four years in New York and was successful in many other cities. In 1974, the nude sexual musical *Let My People Come* opened in New York and ran for three years. "Come in My Mouth" was a representative song from the show. In the play *Futz* (1967), a young man is in love with a sow. Billy the Kid, a character in *The Beard* (1967), buries his head beneath the skirts of Jean Harlow and licks her to orgasm. In *Fortune and Men's Eyes* (1967), there is a nude homosexual rape scene.

The existential playwrights in France had provided a new legitimacy for dominance-submission on the stage. In plays that were very influential in the United States, famous writers like Jean-Paul Sartre (*Les Séquestres d'Altona,* 1959), Albert Camus (*Caligula,* 1944), and especially Jean Genet (*Les Noirs,* 1958) presented sadism as a complex and important dimension of behavior.

It was hardly surprising that by 1970 the most popular play in New York was called *The Dirtiest Show in Town.*

Magazines

The modern era of sex in American magazines began in 1934 with the publication of *Esquire.* Its Petty and Vargas drawings of girls conveyed the notion of sex as fun. During the 1940s, Robert Harrison issued a number of picture magazines *(Flirt, Whisper, Eyeful)* primarily directed to lonely servicemen and featuring photographs and drawings of women in semi-undress.

None of Harrison's magazines showed photographs of women's breasts. One reason for the ability of *Playboy* to provide an attractive alternative to the realities of the 1950s, and the blandness of the first Eisenhower Administration, was its daring in running such photographs. From the first issue in 1953, circulation rose slowly but steadily to 2,000,000 ten years later. Its real growth came in the 1960s, when it reached 5,500,000 circulation. The great increase during the decade in the number of college students, many of whom embraced Hugh Hefner's "Playboy Philosophy" of sexual gratification for its own sake, helped expand the magazine's readership. To many "young urban males," the magazine seemed to implement countercultural attitudes like a liberal view of psychotropic drug use. When so much of America was coming apart because of the Vietnam War and other problems of the 1960s, *Playboy* offered sexual freedom as the centerpiece of a life style which would be further implemented via a huge corporate network of resorts, night clubs, television programs, book clubs, and a book publishing firm.

A key feature of *Playboy* was, and is, the nude centerfold. Typically, the model would be shown fully dressed and going about her regular business (e.g., sitting in the stacks of Harvard's Widener Library, carrying out her assignments as a graduate student of Sanskrit), then she would be presented nude and in bed, and finally shown fully dressed once more, shopping for groceries. The reader could thus, in fantasy, undress her and then dress her again. This opportunity to strip a woman in the pages of the magazine was an innovation which surely contributed to its enormous success. A related interest in peeping was probably responsible for the magazine's peak, the 6,500,000 copies of the November 1976 issue, feature Jimmy Carter's candid views on lust and sex.

In 1969, *Penthouse* began publication, showing the female pubic hair which had previously been airbrushed in *Playboy*. By 1976, *Penthouse* was selling 4,400,000 copies per month. Former madam Xaviera Hollander regularly replies to correspondence from readers.

Oui was started by *Playboy* to attract young people who wanted "harder" material. *Gallery*, which features amateur erotic photographs of "the girl next door," and *Club*, concentrating on the female posterior, each have a circulation of 1,000,000. *Players* is written for the black male. *Chic* stresses quality paper and photography. *Cheri* is the news magazine of sex. *Swank, Genesis, Cavalier, Club* and *High Society* are other successful magazines for men that are heavily sex-oriented.

Perhaps the most spectacular success of any recent sex-oriented magazine was that of *Hustler,* which began in 1974 and featured color photographs of the female genitals, original humor, an antiwar policy frequently enunciated by provocative editor Larry C. Flynt "the newsstand is the poor man's art gallery" and 16-page, life-size foldouts of nude models.

Some 35 other sex-oriented magazines for men seem to be flourishing at the present time. What is most extraordinary about their number is that each one appears to expand the market without taking away readers from its predecessors. Never before in any country have there been so many magazines for men featuring photographs of nude women.

In 1968, *Screw* commenced publication as a weekly celebration of sex and wittily irreverent guide to consumers of sex-oriented materials, and many other sex tabloids have since appeared and flourished. The editor of *Screw,* Al Goldstein, became a courageous national spokesman for sexual freedom in the arts, whose ideas were adopted by many others.

During the 1960s, as one outgrowth of the Free Speech Movement at the University of California, underground weekly newspapers like the *Los Angeles Free Press* and *East Village Other* began carrying "comix," or outspoken sex-oriented comic strips. Robert Crumb, a cartoonist, put out the first issue of *Zap,* a magazine that dealt humorously but explicitly and often kinkily with sex. Other "comix" magazines, like *Snatch, Suck, Jiz, Ball,* and *Fetish Times,* appeared and flourished. A representative feature, in the first issue of *Snatch,* was Crumb's "Adventures of Andy Hard-on." The "comix" had become so institutionalized that in May 1976 a special "dirty comics" convention was held at the Berkeley campus of the University of California.

FUNCTIONS SERVED BY SEX-ORIENTED MATERIAL

One reason for the enormous increase in sex-oriented media materials is a sense that they may not only be a source of entertainment and pleasure but might serve a variety of other positive personal and social functions. Discussion of such functions was facilitated by the considerable publicity given the many studies sponsored by the Commission on Obscenity and Pornography (1970). In addition to the more generalized social gratifications discussed previously, sex-oriented content may meet informational, personality, and other needs.

There has been growing awareness that films and other media provide an opportunity to explore and indirectly experience sex situations which, in real life, might be less accessible. A man may see a bondage relationship, for example, which he has never actually had and thereby facilitate an expression of his fantasy while not risking it in his everyday life.

Sex-oriented content may offer an important avenue of expression for persons who, for whatever reasons, have no partner for sex activity. Such content not only gives a fantasy release, it also may provide considerable detailed information that is not otherwise available. Interviews conducted for the Commission on Obscenity and Pornography indicated that a considerable proportion of consumers of sexually explicit movies and publications derived information about sex organs and positions from seeing sexual activity on the screen and were seeking satisfaction of a healthy curiosity about various aspects of sex (Winick, 1970b). Couples may find that their ability to communicate with one another about sexual matters may be enhanced by looking at such materials together. Various sexual positions are shown so clearly that some psychotherapists recommend specific films or publications to patients, with considerable success. Pictures or movies can present details of appearance and interaction that are simply not as communicable in any other way.

Magazines like *Forum* and *Sexology* have flourished because they answered readers' detailed questions on various aspects of sexual behavior. However, it is much easier for a person seeking information to buy a movie ticket or a book and not face the possible embarrassment of submitting his or her name in a letter to a magazine, which will answer the letter in words rather than pictures.

Seeing a sexually explicit film or other picture may cut through defenses which a patient has erected to verbal communication in an individual psychotherapy or group therapy situation. People who may have harbored feelings of guilt or anxiety about some sexual practices often feel less guilty or anxious after seeing such practices in a book or magazine or on a movie screen. Similarly, cartoons have been used by psychotherapists with patients whose verbosity is self-defeating and who need a pictorial vocabulary of emotion that is more accessible than words (Kadis and Winick, 1973).

For some persons, there is an element of connoisseurship in attending sexually oriented movies. Like other movie buffs, they compare actors with their performance in previous films, seek evidence of a director's style, look for production values and unusual settings, relate the sexual behavior to the personality style, respond to the manner in which transitions are handled, evaluate the music, and otherwise critically view the film. Such dimensions have assumed increasing importance as sexually oriented films are being shown in more theaters, have larger budgets, and enjoy increasing acceptance by the public.

A number of students of sex offenders believe, on the basis of an-amnestic data from the offenders on their earlier experiences, that exposure to sex-oriented materials could be a useful preparation for adult sexual functioning. Sex offenders often report relative inexperience with erotic materials, perhaps reflecting a deprived sexual environment which is an indicator of atypical and inadequate sexual socialization. The decline in such crimes as sexual molestation in Denmark, after the 1967 legalization of sexually explicit materials, suggests that such materials may drain off, in a socially harmless way, impulses which could otherwise involve antisocial expression (Committee on Obscenity and Pornography, 1970).

The continuing debate over sex-oriented materials has identified a number of other functions they serve and needs they meet. Increasingly, sex therapy centers and other "square" institutions are exploring newer methods of using such content in educational and therapeutic settings.

THE FUTURE

How are the trends of the last few decades likely to fare in the future? Most of the large-scale social factors that have led to the current popularity of sex-oriented popular arts are unlikely to reverse themselves. Furthermore, artistic freedoms that have been gained are seldom ever given back. In the past, however, there has often been a cyclical pattern of sexual freedom in the arts, so that the excesses of the Reformation theater in England were subsequently balanced by the repression of the Victorian era.

Some organizations, like Morality in Media, are resisting the expansion of sex-oriented materials. Questions have been raised about the long-term effects on the quality of life in American communities of so much sex-related content (Cline, 1974). Although a number of earlier commentators had been concerned about sex-oriented materials leading to sex crimes, the largest study of sex offenders found no such connection (Gebhard, 1965).

Even though active opposition to the spread of sex-oriented materials is sporadic, it would be wrong to assume that acceptance of such content is complete. Many Americans undoubtedly feel ambivalent or uncomfortable about the proliferation of sex in the arts. In some quarters, there is uneasiness about the ultimate effects of making public that which had previously been so private.

The consequences for sex roles, morality, and the family of so much sex in the public arts are not clear. It is also uncertain how exposure to such content affects actual sexual behavior—whether consumption of these materials is a stimulant or serves to drain off libidinal energy which might otherwise go into sexual interaction, or whether one or another outcome is particularly likely with specific kinds of audiences. Another possibility is that continued contact with sex-related content may lead to satiation and boredom, once the mystery and tension are removed from the presentation of sex. The boredom may extend to sexual activity as well as its presentation in the arts.

A number of communities have sought to control the spread of sex-oriented popular arts. One way in which communities are dealing with the sexual explosion in the arts is to have a European kind of "zoned-in" segregated district where such materials are freely available. In Boston, the area popularly known as the Combat Zone is reserved for adult entertainment, including bookstores and movies. Detroit has used the "zoned-out" dispersal approach to zoning in order to scatter the distribution of such places. American communities will doubtless continue to attempt to cope with sex-oriented content in the arts, in ways that reflect local problems and conditions.

The producers of such materials will probably try to continue to expand their market and use new technology, like cable television, pay TV, and videodiscs, to disseminate new formats which are not subject to any voluntary self-regulation. There is enough ambiguity in the ability of the Federal Communications Commission to regulate cable television so that *Deep Throat* has been presented on cable. We may expect that in any such unclear situation, some entrepreneurs will be willing to take risks in order to attract audiences and make money.

Rivalry between movies and television is likely to continue and to spur each medium to try to be more daring than the other. Theatrical movies attempted to attract consumers in the 1950s by presenting much more sex-oriented material than television was then able to show. In retaliation, television soap operas in the 1960s became much more liberal in terms of sex content, and other kinds of programs followed suit. The opening week of the most successful new series of the 1975–1976 television season, *Mary Hartman, Mary Hartman,* involved the arrest of an exhibitionist who was the heroine's grandfather. The heroine complained bitterly, in the same week, that her husband no longer had sexual intercourse with her. In order to counter such material, contemporary movies present more sex, to which television will again reply, and the cycle shows no sign of abating.

Another reason for expecting at least the temporary continuation of current trends is the commercial and marketing libidinization of youth. The most popular doll in American history was the Barbie, a sexy preadolescent whose play consisted of dates with her boy friend

Ken. During the 1960s, twenty million such mannequin dolls were sold annually (Winick, 1968). Nine out of ten American girls in the 5-to-10 age bracket own at least one Barbie. The girls who play with Barbie, Dawn, and their successors can rehearse sexual fantasies during very impressionable years. Such girls, when they become adults, may be ready to accept and perhaps even extend the trends noted above. Small wonder that women have so clearly been the leaders in the "sexual revolution."

Continuation of current directions is also likely to be reinforced by the growing erotization of advertising (Key, 1976). Television advertising is subject to the constraints of the Television Code, but print media are not so regulated. Some $35 billion a year is spent on advertising in America in a typical year, and its use of sex appeals has been increasing steadily. Sex in advertising helps to maintain an awareness of sex and to legitimate related content in entertainment media. A comparison of the sexual content of advertising in the 1970s (Winick, 1973) as compared with the 1940s (McLuhan, 1948) is almost startling in terms of how much more daring its content has become. The pervasiveness of advertising, with the representative American exposed to over 500 messages daily, gives such changes in its themes a unique power.

Advertising is a key contributor to the furniture of the American mind. Its importance, in the context of sex-oriented art and media materials, is that so many of our attitudes derive from and are influenced by advertising. The "sexual revolution" of our time is essentially attitudinal, and the public's willingness to explore more open attitudes is one reason for the expansion of the market for sex-oriented content.

One irony of the attitudinal revolution is that it is occurring in America, the exemplar of capitalism, while revolutionary countries like China are puritanical and repressive. Not too long ago, sexual freedom in the arts used to be associated with revolution and anarchism. Today, with American movies showing sexual intercourse with a fish *(Fireworks Woman)* and a man sucking his own penis *(Every Inch A Lady)*, and similar content in other media, the leading capitalist country now permits what would be anathema in the Communist countries.

In this country, demographic considerations could be especially important in the future. The fertility rate of American women has been declining dramatically, from 122.7 per 1,000 women aged 15 to 44 in 1957 to 65.7 per 100,000 in 1976. At the same time, there has been a steady decline in the death rate, so that the population is getting older. Since many of the trends which fed the interest in sex-oriented materials were related to the needs of young people, it is possible that the increase in age of the American population will modify the attitudes toward such materials in the popular arts. If other social changes of the last several decades are equally inconsistent with the trends of the next few decades, the future role of sex in the arts could be different.

References

Alt, J. (1976). "Beyond class: The decline of industrial labor and leisure." Telos, 28(summer):55–80.

Anonymous (1975). "Crotch watching." Viva, 2(4):12–20.

Barbach, L.G. (1975). For yourself. New York: Doubleday.

Brown, H.G. (1962). Sex and the single girl. New York: Bernard Geis.

Cavan, S. (1966). Liquor license: An ethnography of bar behavior. Chicago: Aldine.

Cline, V.B. (1974). Where do you draw the line? Provo: Brigham Young University Press.

Comfort, A. (1972). The joy of sex. New York: Crown.

Commission on Obscenity and Pornography (1970). Final report. Washington, D.C.: U.S. Government Printing Office.

Dodson, B. (1975). Liberating masturbation. New York: Bodysex Designs.

Ellis, A. (1957). Sex without guilt. New York: Lyle Stuart.

Etzioni, A. (1972). "The search for political meaning." The Center Magazine, 5(2):2–8.

Fahringer, H.P., and Brown, M.J. (1973–1974). "The rise and fall of Roth—A critique of the recent Supreme Court obscenity decisions." Kentucky Law Journal, 62(3):731–768.

Fletcher, J. (1966). Situation ethics: The new morality. Philadelphia: Westminster Press.

Galbraith, J.K. (1956). American capitalism: The concept of countervailing power. Boston: Houghton Mifflin.

Gebhard, P.H., et al. (1965). Sex offenders. New York: Harper & Row.

Goodman, P. (1961). "Pornography, art and censorship." Commentary, 32 (November): 203–212.

Gorer, G. (1937). Hot strip tease. London: Cresset Press.

Hyman, S.E. (1966). "In defense of pornography," in Standards. New York: Horizon.

J. (1969). The sensuous woman. New York: Lyle Stuart.

Jacobellis v. Ohio (1964). 378 U.S. 184.

Kadis, A.L., and Winick, C. (1973). "The cartoon as therapeutic catalyst." Pp. 106–123 in H.H. Mosak (ed.), Alfred Adler: His influence on psychology today. Park Ridge, N.J.: Noyes Press.

Kahn, H. (1964). Thinking about the unthinkable. New York: Avon.

Keats, J. (1958). The insolent chariot. Philadelphia: Lippincott.

Key, W.B. (1976). Media sexploitation. Englewood Cliffs, N.J.: Prentice-Hall.

Kinsey, A.C., et al. (1948). Sexual behavior in the human male. Philadelphia: Saunders.

Kozol, J. (1970). Death at an early age. New York: Bantam.

Le Masters, E.E. (1975). Blue collar aristocrats. Madison: University of Wisconsin.

Lenski, G. (1961). The religious factor. Garden City, N.Y.: Doubleday.

Mannheim, K. (1950). Freedom, power, and democratic planning. London: Routledge and Kegan Paul.

Masters, W.H., and Johnson, V.E. (1966). Human sexual response. Boston: Little Brown.

———(1970). Human sexual inadequacy. Boston: Little Brown.

McLuhan, H.M. (1948). The mechanical bride. New York: Vanguard.

Meadows, D.R. (1972). The limits to growth. Washington: Universe Books.

Memoirs v. Attorney General of Massachusetts (1966). 383 U.S. 413.

Michelson, P. (1966). "An apology for pornography," The New Republic, 155(December 10):21–24.

Miller v. California (1973). 413 U.S. 15.

Nader, R. (1965). Unsafe at any speed. New York: Grossman.

National Opinion Research Center, University of Chicago (1976). General social survey. Chicago: Author.

New York Times (1976). November 16.

Newspaper Advertising Bureau (1974). Movie going and leisure time. New York: Author.

Paris Adult Theatre (1973). 413 U.S. 49.

Redrup v. New York (1967). 386 U.S. 767.

Reich, C.A. (1970). The greening of America. New York: Random House.

———(1976). The sorcerer of Bolinas Reef. New York: Random House.

Reisman, D. (1969). The lonely crowd. New Haven: Yale University Press.

Roszak, T. (1969). The making of a counter-culture. New York: Doubleday.

Sennett, R. (1977). The fall of public man. New York: Knopf.

Silberman, C.E. (1964). Crisis in black and white. New York: Random House.

———(1971). Crisis in the classroom. New York: Random House.

Smith, A. (1976). Powers of mind. New York: Random House.

Smith, D.D. (1974). "Sex and sex roles in 'adult only' paperback fiction." Paper presented at the annual meeting of the American Association for Public Opinion Research, May 1974.

Smith v. California (1959). 361 U.S. 147.

Sontag, S. (1966). Styles of radical will. New York: Farrar, Straus, and Giroux.

Sorokin, P.A. (1956). American sex revolution. Boston: Sargent.

Stanley v. Gerogia (1969). 394 U.S. 557.

Thompson, W.I. (1972). At the edge of history. New York: Harper & Row.

Toffler, A. (1970). Future shock. New York: Random House.

Tynan, K. (1968). "Dirty books can stay." Esquire 70(October):168–170.

Ullerstam, L. (1966). The erotic minorities. New York: Grove.

United States v. Roth (1957). 354 U.S. 476.

Van De Velde, T.H. (1930). Ideal marriage. New York: Covici, Friede.

Whyte, W.H., Jr. (1956). The organization man. New York: Simon and Schuster.

Winick, C. (1964). "Atonie: The psychology of the unemployed and the marginal worker." Pp. 269–286 in G. Fisk, (ed.), The frontiers of management psychology. New York: Harper & Row.

————(1968). The new people. New York: Bobbs Merrill.

————(1970a). A study of consumers of explicitly sexual materials, Commission on Obscenity and Pornography. Technical papers, vol.iv:245–262.

————(1970b). "Sex and dancing." Medical Aspects of Human Sexuality, 4(9):122–132.

————(1973). "Sex and advertising." Pp. 162–167 in R.J. Glessing and W.P. White (eds.), Mass media: The invisible environment. Chicago: Science Research Associates.

Yankelovich, D. (1974). The new morality. New York: McGraw-Hill.

50 / Tinydopers: A Case Study of Deviant Socialization

PATRICIA A. ADLER
PETER ADLER

Marijuana smoking is now filtering down to our youngest generation; a number of children from 0–8 years old are participating in this practice under the influence and supervision of their parents. This phenomenon, *tinydoping,* raises interesting questions about changes in societal mores and patterns of socialization. We are not concerned here with the desirability or morality of the activity. Instead, we will discuss the phenomenon, elucidating the diverse range of attitudes, strategems and procedures held and exercised by parents and children.

An examination of the history and cultural evolution of marijuana over the last several decades illuminates the atmosphere in which tinydoping arose. Marijuana use, first located chiefly among jazz musicians and ghetto communities, eventually expanded to "the highly alienated young in flight from families, schools and conventional communities" (Simon and Gagnon, 1968:60. See also Goode, 1970; Carey, 1968; Kaplan, 1971; and Grinspoon, 1971). Blossoming in the mid-1960's, this youth scene formed an estranged and deviant subculture offsetting the dominant culture's work ethic and instrumental success orientation. Society reacted as an angry parent, enforcing legal, social and moral penalties against its rebellious children. Today, however, the pothead subculture has eroded and the population of smokers has broadened to include large numbers of middle class and establishment-oriented people.

Marijuana, then, may soon take its place with alcohol, its "prohibition" a thing of the past. These two changes can be considered movements of moral passage:

> *Movements to redefine behavior may eventuate in a moral passage, a transition of the behavior from one moral status to another ... What is attacked as criminal today may be seen as sick next year and fought over as possibly legitimate by the next generation. (Gusfield, 1967:187. See also Matza, 1969; Kitsuse, 1962; Douglas, 1970; and Becker, 1963 for further discussions of the social creation of deviance.)*

Profound metamorphoses testify to this redefinition: frequency and severity of arrest is proportionately down from a decade ago; the stigma of a marijuana-related arrest is no longer as personally and occupationally ostracizing; and the fear that using grass will press the individual into close contact with hardened criminals and cause him to adopt a deviant self-identity or take up criminal ways has also largely passed.

The transformation in marijuanas's social and legal status is not intrinsic to its own characteristics or those of mood-altering drugs in general. Rather, it illustrates a process of becoming socially accepted many deviant activities or substances may go through. This research suggests a more generic model of social change, a sequential development characteristic of the diffusion and legitimation of a formerly unconventional practice. Five stages identify the spread of such activities from small isolated outgroups, through increasing levels of mainstream society, and finally to such sacred groups as children.[1] Often, however, as with the case of pornography, the appearance of this quasi-sanctioned conduct among juveniles elicits moral outrage and a social backlash designed to prevent such behavior in the sacred population, while leaving it more open to the remainder of society.

Most treatments of pot smoking in the sociological literature have been historically and sub-culturally specific (see Carey, 1968; Goode, 1970; Grupp, 1971; Hochman, 1972; Kaplan, 1971; and Simon and Gagnon, 1968), swiftly dated by our rapidly changing society. Only Becker's (1953) work is comparable to our research since it offers a generic sequential model of the process for becoming a marijuana user.

The data in this paper show an alternate route to marijuana smoking. Two developments necessitate a modification of Becker's conceptualization. First, there have been many changes in norms, traditions and patterns of use since the time he wrote. Second, the age of this new category of smokers is cause for reformulation. Theories of child development proposed by Mead (1934), Erikson, (1968) and Piaget (1948) agree that prior to a certain age children are unable to comprehend subtle transformations and perceptions. As we will see, the full effects and symbolic meanings of marijuana are partially lost to them due to their inability to differentiate between altered states of consciousness and to connect this with the smoking experience. Yet this does not preclude their becoming avid pot users and joining in the smoking group as accepted members.

Socialization practices are the final concern of this research. The existence of tinydoping both illustrates and contradicts several established norms of traditional childrearing. Imitative behavior (see Piaget, 1962), for instance, is integral to tinydoping since the children's desire to copy the actions of parents and other adults is a primary motivation. Boundary maintenance also arises as a consideration: as soon as their offspring can communicate, parents must instruct them in the perception of social borders and the need for guarding group activities as secret. In contrast, refutations of convention include the introduction of mood-altering drugs into the sacred childhood period and, even more unusual, parents and children get high together. This bridges, often to the point of eradication, the inter-generational gap firmly entrenched in most societies. Thus, although parents view their actions as normal, tinydoping must presently be considered as deviant socialization.

METHODS

Collected over the course of 18 months, our data include observations of two dozen youngsters between the ages of birth and eight, and a similar number of parents, aged 21 to 32, all in middle-class households. To obtain a complete image of this practice we talked with parents, kids and other involved observers (the "multiperspectival" approach, Douglas, 1976). Many of our conversations with adults were taped but our discussions with the children took the form of informal, extemporaneous dialogue, since the tape recorder distracts and diverts their attention. Finally, our study is exploratory and suggestive; we make no claim to all-inclusiveness in the cases or categories below.

THE KIDS

The following four individuals, each uniquely interesting, represent many common characteristics of other children and adults we observed.

"Big Ed": The Diaperdoper—Big Ed derives his name from his miniature size. Born three months prematurely, now three years old, he resembles a toy human being. Beneath his near-white wispy hair and toddling diapered bottom, he packs a punch of childish energy. Big Ed's mother and older siblings take care of him although he often sees his father who lives in a neighboring California town. Laxity and permissivenesss characterize his upbringing, as he freely roams the neighborhood under his own and other children's supervision. Exposure to marijuana has prevailed since birth and in the last year he advanced from passive inhalation (smoke blown in his direction) to

active puffing on joints. Still in the learning stage, most of his power is expended blowing air into the reefer instead of inhaling. He prefers to suck on a "bong" (a specially designed waterpipe), delighting in the gurgling sound the water makes. A breast fed baby, he will go to the bong for oral satisfaction, whether it is filled or not. He does not actively seek joints, but Big Ed never refuses one when offered. After a few puffs, however, he usually winds up with smoke in his eyes and tearfully retreats to a glass of water. Actual marijuana inhalation is minimal; his size renders it potent. Big Ed has not absorbed any social restrictions related to pot use or any awareness of its illegality, but is still too young to make a blooper as his speech is limited.

Stephanie: The Social Smoker—Stephanie is a dreamy four-year old with quite good manners, calm assurance, sweet disposition and a ladylike personality and appearance. Although her brothers are rough and tumble, Stephanie can play with the boys or amuse herself sedately alone or in the company of adults. Attendance at a progressive school for the last two years has developed her natural curiosity and intelligence. Stephanie's mother and father both work, but still find enough recreational time to raise their children with love and care and to engage in freqent marijuana smoking. Accordingly, Stephanie has seen grass since infancy and accepted it as a natural part of life. Unlike the diaperdoper, she has mastered the art of inhalation and can breathe the smoke out through her nose. Never grasping or grubbing for pot, she has advanced from a preference for bongs or pipes and now enjoys joints when offered. She revels in being part of a crowd of smokers and passes the reefer immediately after each puff, never holding it for an unsociable amount of time. Her treasure box contains a handful of roaches (marijuana butts) and seeds (she delights in munching them as snacks) that she keeps as mementos of social occasions with (adult) "friends." After smoking, Stephanie becomes more bubbly and outgoing. Dancing to records, she turns in circles as she jogs from one foot to the other, releasing her body to the rhythm. She then eats everything in sight and falls asleep—roughly the same cycle as adults, but faster.

When interviewed, Stephanie clearly recognized the difference between a cigarette and a joint (both parents use tobacco), defining the effects of the latter as good but still being unsure of what the former did and how the contents of each varied. She also responded with some confusion about social boundaries separating pot users from non-users, speculating that perhaps her grandmother did smoke it but her grandfather certainly did not (neither do). In the words of her father: "She knows not to tell people about it but she just probably wouldn't anyway."

Josh: The Self-gratifier—Everyone in the neighborhood knows Josh. Vociferous and outgoing, at age five he has a decidedly Dennis-the-Menace quality in both looks and personality. Neither timid nor reserved, he boasts to total strangers of his fantastic exploits and talents. Yet behind his bravado swagger lies a seeming insecurity and need for acceptance, coupled with a difficulty in accepting authority, which has led him into squabbles with peers, teachers, siblings and parents.

Josh's home shows the traditional division of labor. His mother stays home to cook and care for the children while his father works long hours. The mother is always calm and tolerant about her youngster's smart-alec ways, but his escapades may provoke an explosive tirade from the father. Yet this male parent is clearly the dominating force in Josh's life. Singling Josh out from his younger sister and brother, the father has chosen him as his successor in the male tradition. The parent had himself begun drinking and smoking cigarettes in his early formative years, commencing pot use as a teenager, and now has a favorable attitude toward the early use of stimulants which he is actively passing on to Josh.

According to his parents, his smoking has had several beneficial effects. Considering Josh a "hyper" child, they claim that it calms him down to a more normal speed, often permitting him to engage in activities which would otherwise be too difficult for his powers of concentration. He also appears to become more sedate and less prone to temper tantrums, sleeping longer and more deeply. But Josh's smoking patterns differ significantly from our last two subjects. He does not enjoy social smoking, preferring for his father to roll him "pinners" (thin joints) to smoke by himself. Unlike many other tiny-dopers, Josh frequently refuses the offer of a joint saying, "Oh that! I gave up smoking that stuff." At age five he claims to have already quit and gone back several times. His mother backs this assertion as valid; his father brushes it off as merely a ploy to shock and gain attention. Here, the especially close male parent recognizes the behavior as imitative and accepts it as normal. To others, however, it appears strange and suggests surprising sophistication.

Josh's perception of social boundaries is also mature. Only a year older than Stephanie, Josh has made some mistakes but his awareness of the necessity for secrecy is complete; he differentiates those people with whom he may and may not discuss the subject by the experience of actually smoking with them. He knows individuals but cannot yet socially categorize the boundaries. Josh also realizes the contrast between joints and cigarettes down to the marijuana and tobacco they contain. Interestingly, he is aggressively opposed to tobacco while favoring pot use (this may be the result of anti-tobacco cancer propaganda from kindergarten).

Kyra: The Bohemian—A worldly but curiously childlike girl is seven-year-old Kyra. Her wavy brown hair falls to her shoulders and her sun-tanned body testifies to many hours at the beach in winter and summer. Of average height for her age, she dresses with a maturity beyond her years. Friendly and sociable she has few reservations about what she says to people. Kyra lives with her youthful mother and whatever boyfriend her mother fancies at the moment. Their basic family unit consists of two (mother and daughter), and they have travelled together living a free life all along the West Coast and Hawaii. While Josh's family was male dominated, this is clearly female centered, all of Kyra's close relatives being women. They are a bohemian group, generation after generation following a hip, up-to-the-moment, unshackled lifestyle. The house is often filled with people, but when the visitors clear out, a youthful, thrillseeking mother remains, who raises this daughter by treating her like a sister or friend. This demand on Kyra to behave as an adult may produce some internal strain, but she seems to have grown accustomed to it. Placed in situations others might find awkward, she handles them with precocity. Like her mother, she is being reared for a life of independence and freedom.

Pot smoking is an integral part of this picture. To Kyra it is another symbol for her adulthood; she enjoys it and wants to do it a lot. At seven she is an accomplished smoker; her challenge right now lies in the mastery of rolling joints. Of our four examples, social boundaries are clearest to Kyra. Not only is she aware of the necessary secrecy surrounding pot use, but she is able to socially categorize types of people into marijuana smokers and straights. She may err in her judgment occasionally, but no more so than any adult.

STAGES OF DEVELOPMENT

These four and other cases suggest a continuum of reactions to marijuana that is loosely followed by most tinydopers.

From birth to around 18 months a child's involvement is passive. Most parents keep their infants nearby at all times and if pot is smoked the room becomes filled with potent clouds. At this age just a little marijuana smoke can be very powerful and these infants, the youngest diaperdopers, manifest noticeable effects. The drug usually has a calming influence, putting the infant into a less cranky mood and extending the depth and duration of sleep.

After the first one and a half years, the children are more attuned to what is going on around them: they begin to desire participation in a "monkey see, monkey do" fashion. During the second year, a fascination with paraphernalia generally develops, as they play with it and try to figure it out. Eager to smoke with the adults and older children, they are soon discouraged after a toke (puff) or two. They find smoking difficult and painful (particularly to the eyes and throat)—after all, it is not easy to inhale buring hot air and hold it in your lungs.

But continual practice eventually produces results, and inhalation seems to be achieved somewhere during the third or fourth year. This brings considerable pride and makes the kids feel they have attained semi-adult status. Now they can put the paraphernalia to work. Most tinydopers of this age are wild about "roach clips," itching to put their joints into them as soon as possible after lighting.

Ages four and five bring the first social sense of the nature of pot and who should know about it. This begins as a vague idea, becoming further refined with age and sophistication. Finally, by age seven or eight kids have a clear concept of where the lines can be drawn between those who are and aren't "cool," and can make these distinctions on their own. No child we interviewed, however, could verbalize about any specific effects felt after smoking marijuana. Ironically, although they participate in smoking and actually manifest clear physical symptoms of the effects, tinydopers are rationally and intellectually unaware of how the drug is acting upon them. They are too young to notice a change in their behavior or to make the symbolic leap and associate this transformation with having smoked pot previously. The effects of marijuana must be socially and consensually delineated from non-high sensations for the user to fully appreciate the often subtle perceptual and physiological changes that have occurred. To the youngster the benefits of pot smoking are not at all subtle: he is permitted to imitate his elders by engaging in a social ritual they view as pleasurable and important; the status of adulthood is partially conferred on him by allowing this act, and his desire for acceptance is fulfilled through inclusion in his parents' peer group. This constitutes the major difference in appreciation between the child and adult smoker.

PARENTS' STRATEGIES

The youth of the sixties made some forceful statements through their actions about how they evaluated the Establishment and the conventional American lifestyle. While their political activism has faded, many former members of this group still feel a strong commitment to smoking pot and attach a measure of symbolic significance to it. When they had children the question then arose of how to handle the drug vis-á-vis their offspring. The continuum of responses they developed ranges from total openness and permissiveness to various measures of secrecy.

Smoking Regularly Permitted—Some parents give their children marijuana whenever it is requested. They may wait until the child reaches a certain age, but most parents in this category started their kids on pot from infancy. These parents may be "worried" or "unconcerned."

Worried—Ken and Deedy are moderate pot smokers, getting high a few times a week. Both had been regular users for several years prior to having children. When Deedy was pregnant she absolutely refused to continue her smoking pattern.

I didn't know what effect it could have on the unborn child. I tried to read and find out, but there's very little written on that. But in the Playboy Advisor there was a article: they said we advise you to stay away from all drugs when you're pregnant. That was sort of my proof. I figured they don't bullshit about these types of things. I sort of said now at least somebody stands behind me because people were saying, "You can get high, it's not going to hurt the baby."

This abstinence satisfied them and once the child was born they resumed getting high as before. Frequently smoking in the same room as the baby, they began to worry about the possible harmful effects this exposure might have on his physical, psychological and mental development. After some discussion, they consulted the family pediatrician, a prominent doctor in the city.

I was really embarrassed, but I said, "Doctor, we get high, we smoke pot, and sometimes the kid's in the room. If he's in the room can this hurt him? I don't want him to be mentally retarded." He said, "Don't worry about it, they're going to be legalizing it any day now—this was three years ago—it's harmless and a great sedative."

This reassured them on two counts: they no longer were fearful in their own minds, and they had a legitimate answer when questioned by their friends.[2]

Ken and Deedy were particularly sensitive about peer reactions:

Some people say, "You let your children get high?!" They really react with disgust. Or they'll say, "Oh you let your kids get high," and then they kind of look at you like, "That's neat, I think." And it's just nice to be able to back it up.

Ken and Deedy were further nonplussed about the problem of teaching their children boundary maintenance. Recognizing the need to prevent their offspring from saying things to the wrong people, they were unsure how to approach this subject properly.

How can you tell a kid, how can you go up to him and say, "Well you want to get high, but don't tell anybody you're doing it"? You can't. We didn't really know how to tell them. You don't want to bring the attention, you don't want to tell your children not to say anything about it because that's a sure way to get them to do it. We just never said anything about it.

They hope this philosophy of openness and permissiveness will forestall the need to limit their children's marijuana consumption. Limits, for them, resemble prohibitions and interdictions against discussing grass: they make transgressions attractive. Both parents believe strongly in presenting marijuana as an everday occurrence, definitely not as a undercover affair. When asked how they thought this upbringing might affect their kids, Deedy offered a fearful but doubtful speculation that her children might one day reject the drug.

I don't imagine they'd try to abuse it. Maybe they won't even smoke pot when they get older. That's a big possibility. I doubt it, but hopefully they won't be that way. They've got potheads for parents.

Unconcerned—Alan and Anna make use of a variety of stimulants—pot, alcohol, cocaine—to enrich their lives. Considered heavy users, they consume marijuana and alcohol daily. Alan became acquainted with drugs, particularly alcohol, at a very early age and Anna first tried them in her teens. When they decided to have children the question of whether they would permit the youngsters to partake in their mood-altering experiences never arose. Anna didn't curtail her drug intake during pregnancy; her offspring were conceived, formed and weaned on this steady diet. When queried about their motivations, Alan volunteered:

What the hell! It grows in the ground, it's a weed. I can't see anything wrong with doing anything, inducing any part of it into your body anyway that you possibly could eat it, smoke it, intravenously, or whatever, that it would ever harm you because it grows in the ground. It's a natural thing. It's one of God's treats.

All of their children have been surrounded by marijuana's aromatic vapor since the day they returned from the hospital. Alan and

Anna were pleased with the effect pot had on their infants; the relaxed, sleepy and happy qualities achieved after inhaling pot smoke made child-rearing an easier task. As the little ones grew older they naturally wanted to share in their parents' activities. Alan viewed this as the children's desire to imitate rather than true enjoyment of any effects:

Emily used to drink Jack Daniels straight and like it. I don't think it was taste, I think it was more of an acceptance thing because that's what I was drinking. She was also puffing on joints at six months.

This mimicking, coupled with a craving for acceptance, although recognized by Alan in his kids, was not repeated in his own feelings toward friends or relatives. At no time during the course of our interview or acquaintance did he show any concern with what others thought of his behavior; rather, his convictions dominated, and his wife passively followed his lead.

In contrast to the last couple, Alan was not reluctant to address the problem of boundary maintenance. A situation arose when Emily was three, where she was forced to learn rapidly:

One time we were stopped by the police while driving drunk. I said to Emily—we haven't been smoking marijuana. We all acted quiet and Emily realized there was something going on and she delved into it. I explained that some people are stupid and they'll harm you very badly if you smoke marijuana. To this day I haven't heard her mention it to anyone she hasn't smoked with.

As each new child came along, Alan saw to it that they learned the essential facts of life.

Neither Alan nor Anna saw any moral distinction between marijuana smoking and other, more accepted pastimes. They heartily endorsed marijuana as something to indulge in like "tobacco, alcohol, sex, breathing or anything else that brings pleasure to the senses." Alan and Anna hope their children will continue to smoke grass in their later lives. It has had beneficial effects for them and they believe it can do the same for their kids:

I smoked marijuana for a long time, stopped and developed two ulcers; and smoked again and the two ulcers went away. It has great medicinal value.

Smoking Occasionally Permitted—In contrast to uninterrupted permissiveness, other parents restrict marijuana use among their children to specific occasions. A plethora of reasons and rationalizations lie behind this behavior, some openly avowed by parents and others not. Several people believe it is okay to let the kids get high as long as it isn't done to often. Many other people do not have any carefully thought-out notion of what they want, tending to make spur-of-the-moment decisions. As a result, they allow occasional but largely undefined smoking in a sporadic and irregular manner. Particular reasons for this inconsistency can be illustrated by three examples from our research:

1) *Conflicts between parents* can confuse the situtaion. While Stella had always planned to bring her children up with pot, Burt did not like the idea. Consequently, the household rule on this matter varied according to the unpredictable moods of the adults and which parent was in the house.

2) Mike and Gwen had trouble *making up their minds.* At one time they thought it probably couldn't harm the child, only to decide the next day they shouldn't take chances and rescind that decision.

3) Lois and David didn't waver hourly but had *changing ideas over time.* At first they were against it, but then met a group of friends who liked to party and approved of tinydoping. After a few years they moved to a new neighborhood and changed their lifestyle, again prohibiting pot smoking for the kids.

These are just a few of the many situations in which parents allow children an occasional opportunity to smoke grass. They use various criteria to decide when those permissible instances ought to be, most families subscribing to several of the following patterns:

Reward—The child receives pot as a bonus for good behavior in the past, present or future. This may serve as an incentive: "If you're a good boy today, Johnny, I may let you smoke with us tonight," or to celebrate an achievement already completed like "going potty" or reciting the alphabet.

Guilt—Marijuana can be another way of compensating children for what they aren't getting. Historically, parents have tried to buy their kids off or make themselves loved through gifts of money or toys but pot can also be suitable here. This is utilized both by couples with busy schedules who don't have time for the children ("We're going out again tonight so we'll give you this special treat to make it up to you") and by separated parents who are trying to compete with the former spouse for the child's love ("I know Mommy doesn't let you do this but you can do special things when you're with me").

Cuteness—To please themselves parents may occasionally let the children smoke pot because it's cute. Younger children look especially funny because they cannot inhale, yet in their eagerness to be like Mommy and Daddy they make a hilarious effort and still have a good time themselves. Often this will originate as amusement for the parents and then spread to include cuteness in front of friends. Carrying this trend further, friends may roll joints for the little ones or turn them on when the parents are away. This still precludes regular use.

Purposive—Giving marijuana to kids often carries a specific anticipated goal for the parents. The known effects of pot are occasionally desired and actively sought. They may want to calm the child down because of the necessities of a special setting or company. Sleep is another pursued end, as in "Thank you for taking Billy for the night; if he gives you any trouble just let him smoke this and he'll go right to bed." They may also give it to the children medicinally. Users believe marijuana soothes the upset stomach and alleviates the symptoms of the common cold better than any other drug. As a mood elevator, many parents have given pot to alleviate the crankiness young children develop from a general illness, specific pain or injury. One couple used it experimentally as a treatment for hyperactivity (see Josh).

Abstention—Our last category of marijuana smoking parents contains those who do not permit their children any direct involvement with illegal drugs. This leaves several possible ways to treat the topic of the adults' own involvement with drugs and how open they are about it. Do they let the kids know they smoke pot? Moreover, do they do it in the children's presence?

Overt—The great majority of our subjects openly smoked in front of their children, defining marijuana as an accepted and natural pastime. Even parents who withhold it from their young children hope that the kids will someday grow up to be like themselves. Thus, they smoke pot overtly. These marijuana smokers are divided on the issue of other drugs, such as pills and cocaine.

    a. *permissive*—One group considers it acceptable to use any drug in front of the children. Either they believe in what they are doing and consider it right for the kids to observe their actions, or they don't worry about it and just do it.

    b. *pragmatic*—A larger, practically oriented group differentiated between "smokable" drugs (pot and hashish) and the others (cocaine and pills), finding it acceptable to let children view consumption of the former group, but not the latter. Rationales varied for this, ranging from safety to morality:

Well, we have smoked hashish around them but we absolutely never ever do coke in front of them because it's a white powder and if they saw us snorting a white powder there goes the drain cleaner, there goes baby powder. Anything white, they'll try it; and that goes for pills too. The only thing they have free rein of is popping vitamins.

Fred expressed his concern over problems this might engender in the preservation of his children's moral fibre:

If he sees me snorting coke, how is he going to differentiate that from heroin? He gets all this anti-drug education from school and they tell him that heroin is bad. How can I explain to him that doing coke is okay and it's fun and doesn't hurt you but heroin is something else, so different and bad? How could I teach right from wrong?

c. *capricious*—A third group is irregular in its handling of multiple drug viewing and their offsrping. Jon and Linda, for instance, claim that they don't mind smoking before their child but absolutely won't permit other drugs to be used in his presence. Yet in fact they often use almost any intoxicant in front of him, depending on their mood and how high they have already become.

In our observations we have never seen any parent give a child in the tinydoper range any kind of illegal drug other than marijuana and, extremely rarely, hashish. Moreover, the treatment of pot has been above all direct and open: even those parents who don't permit their children to join have rejected the clandestine secrecy of the behind-closed-doors approach. Ironically, however, they must often adopt this strategy toward the outside world; those parents who let it be known that they permit tinydoping frequently take on an extra social and legal stigma. Their motivation for doing so stems from a desire to avoid having the children view pot and their smoking it as evil or unnatural. Thus, to de-stigmatize marijuana they stigmatize themselves in the face of society.

CONCLUSIONS

Tinydoping, with its combined aspects of understandably innovative social development and surprising challenges to convention, is a fruitful subject for sociological analysis. A review of historical and cultural forces leading to the present offers insight into how and why this phenomeon came to arise. Essentially, we are witnessing the moral passage of marijuana, its transformation from an isolated and taboo drug surrounded by connotations of fear and danger, into an increasingly accepted form of social relaxation, similar to alcohol. The continuing destigmatization of pot fosters an atmosphere in which parents are willing to let their children smoke.

Marijuana's social transition is not an isolated occurrence, however. Many formerly deviant activities have gradually become acceptable forms of behavior. Table 1 presents a general model of social

Table 1 / Sequential Model of Social Change: The Diffusion and Legitimization of Marijuana

Stage		Carriers	Marijuana
I	1940's	Stigmatized outgroup	Blacks
II	1950's	Ingroup deviants who identify with stigmatized outgroup	Jazz Musicians
III	1960's	Avant-garde ingroup members	College students and counterculture
IV	1970's	Normal ingroup members	Middle class
V	1975+	Sacred group	Children

change which outlines the sequential development and spread of a conduct undergoing legitimization.

Particular behaviors which first occur only among relatively small and stigmatized outgroups are frequently picked up by ingroup deviants who identify with the stigmatized outgroup. In an attempt to be cool and avante-garde, larger clusters of ingroup members adopt this deviant practice, often for the sake of non-conformity as well as its own merits. By this time the deviant activity is gaining exposure as well as momentum and may spread to normal ingroup members. The final step is its eventual introduction to sacred groups in the society, such as children.

Becker's (1953) research and theory are pertinent to historical stages I and II. More recently, Carey (1968) and Goode (1970) have depicted stage III. To date, sociologists have not described stage IV and we are the first to portray stage V.

The general value of this model can be further illustrated by showing its application to another deviant activity which has followed a similar progression: pornography. Initially a highly stigmatized practice engaged in by people largely hidden from public view, it slowly became incorporated into a wider cross-section of the population. With the advent of *Playboy*, mainstream media entered the scene, resulting in the present proliferation of sexually-oriented magazines and tabloids. Recently, however, this practice passed into stage V; a violent societal reaction ensued, with moralist groups crusading to hold the sacred period of childhood free from such deviant intrusions.

Tinydoping has not become broadly publicly recognized but, as with pornography, the widespread (collective) softening of attitudes has not extended to youngsters. Rather, a backlash effect stemming

from conventional morality condemns such "intrusions and violations of childhood" as repulsive. Thus, the spread of deviance to
Group V prompts social revulsion and renewed effort to ban the behavior by children while allowing it to adults.

These data also recommend a re-examination of sociological theories about marijuana use. Becker's (1953) theory is in some ways
timeless, illuminating a model of the actor which encompasses a dynamic processual development. It proposes an initiation process that
precedes bona fide membership in a pot smoking milieu. Minimally,
this includes: learning the proper techniques to ensure adequate
consumption; perception of the drug's unique effects; association of
these effects with the smoking experience, and the conceptualization of these effects as pleasurable. Symbolic *meaning* is crucial to
this schema: through a "sequence of social experiences" the individual continually reformulates his attitudes, eventually learning to
view marijuana smoking as desirable. The formation of this conception is the key to understanding the motivations and actions of users.

Accepting this model for the adult initiate, the present research
has explored an historically novel group (tinydopers), describing a
new route to becoming a marijuana user taken by these children. As
has been shown, tinydopers are unable to recognize the psychological and physiological effects of pot or to connect them with having
smoked. This effectively precludes their following Becker's model
which accords full user status to the individual only after he has successfully perceived the effects of the drug and marked them as pleasurable. Our research into child perception relied mostly on observation and inference since, as Piaget (1948) noted, it is nearly impossible to discover this from children; the conceptual categories are too
sophisticated for their grasp. That the marijuana affects them is certain: giddy, they laugh, dance and run to the refrigerator, talking ex-
citedly and happily until they suddenly fall asleep. But through observations and conversations before, during and after the intoxicated
periods, tinydopers were found to be unaware of any changes in
themselves.

Their incomplete development, perceptually, cognitively and in-
teractionally, is the cause of this ignorance. According to the socialization theories of Mead (1934), Erikson (1968), and Piaget (1948),
children of eight and under are still psychologically forming, gradually learning to function. Piaget particularly notes definitive cognitive
stages, asserting that conservation, transformation and classification
are all too advanced for the tinydoper age bracket. According to
Mead (see also Adler and Adler, 1979), the essence lies in their lack of
mature selves, without which they cannot fully act and interact competently. The ages 8–9 seem to be a decisive turning point as young

sters change in internal psychological composition and become capable of *reflecting* on themselves, both through their own eyes and those of the other. (Mead argues that this is possible only after the child has completed the play, game and generalized other stages and can competently engage in roletaking.) Hence, before that time they cannot genuinely recognize their "normal selves" or differentiate them from their "high selves." Without this perception, the effects of marijuana are held to those created by the parents, who frame the experience with their own intentional and unintentional definitions of the situation. Thus, tinydopers become marijuana users almost unconsciously, based on a decision made by others. Moreover, the social meanings they associate with its use are very different than those experienced by adult initiates.

How does this new practice correspond to conventional modes of childrearing? One traditional procedure we see re-affirmed is imitative behavior (see Piaget, 1962), through which the child learns and matures by copying the actions of significant adult models. Several of the illustrative cases chosen show particularly how directly the youngsters are influenced by their desire to behave and be like older family members and friends. They have two aspirations: wanting to be accorded quasi-adult status and longing for acceptance as members of the social group. Parents have corresponding and natural positive feelings about inculcating meaningful beliefs and values into their offspring. Teaching boundary maintenance is also a necessary adjunct to allowing tinydoping. Marijuana's continued illegality and social unacceptability for juveniles necessitate parents ensuring that information about pot smoking is neither intentionally nor accidentally revealed by youngsters. Children must early learn to differentiate between members of various social groups and to judge who are and are not appropriate to be told. This is difficult because it involves mixing positive and negative connotations of the drug in a complex manner. Valuable parallels for this contradictory socialization can be found in child use of alcohol and tobacco, as well as to families of persecuted religious groups (i.e. Marrano Jews in 15th century Spain, covert Jews in Nazi Germany and possibly Mormons in the 19th century). Members of these enclaves believed that what they were teaching their offspring was fundamentally honorable, but still had to communicate to the younger generation their social ostracization and the need to maintain some barriers of secrecy.

Juxtaposed to those aspects which reproduce regular features of socialization are the contradictory procedures. One such departure is the introduction of mood-altering intoxicants into the sacred childhood period. Tinydoping violates the barriers created by most societies to reserve various types of responsibilities, dangers and special pleasures (such as drugs and sex) for adults only. Yet perhaps the most unusual and unprecedented facet of tinydoping socialization observed is the intergenerational bridging that occurs between parent and child. By introducing youngsters into the adult social group and having them participate as peers, parents permit generational boundaries to become extremely vague, often to the point of nonexistence. Several cases show how children have come to look at parents and other adults as friends. This embodies extreme variance from cultures and situations where parents love and treasure their children yet still treat them unequally.

How then can tinydoping be compared to traditional childrearing practices and habits? Existing indicators suggest both similarity and divergence. The parents in this study consider marijuana a substance they overwhelmingly feel comfortable with, regard as something "natural" (i.e. Alan and Ann), and would like their progeny to be exposed to in a favorable light. To them, tinydoping represents a form of normal socialization within the context of their subcultural value system. From the greater society's perspective, however, the illegality of the behavior, aberration from conventional childrearing norms and uncertain implications for futurity combine to define tinydoping as deviant socialization.

References

Adler, Peter and Patricia A. Adler
    1979   "Symbolic Interactionism," in Patricia A. Adler, Peter Adler, Jack D. Douglas, Andrea Fontana, C. Robert Freeman and Joseph Kotarba, An Introduction to the Sociologies of Everyday Life, Boston: Allyn and Bacon.
Adler, Patricia A., Peter Adler and Jack D. Douglas
    Forthcoming   "Organized Crime: Drug Dealing for Pleasure and Profit," in Jack D. Douglas (ed.), Deviant Scenes, forthcoming.
Aries, Phillipe
    1965   Centuries of Childhood: A Social History of Family Life, New York: Vintage.
Becker, Howard S.
    1953   "Becoming a Marijuana User," American Journal of Sociology, 59, November.
    1963   Outsiders, New York: Free Press.
Carey, James T.
    1968   The College Drug Scene, Englewood Cliffs: Prentice-Hall.
Douglas, Jack D.
    1970   "Deviance and Respectability: The Social Construction of Moral Meanings," in Jack D. Douglas (ed.), Deviance and Respectability, New York: Basic Books.
    1976   Investigative Social Research, Beverly Hills: Sage.

Erikson, Erik
1968   Identity, Youth and Crisis, New York: Norton.
Goode, Erich
1969   Marijuana, New York: Atherton.
1970   The Marijuana Smokers, New York: Basic Books.
Grinspoon, Lester
1971   Marihuana Reconsidered, Cambridge: Harvard University Press.
Grupp, Stanley E. (ed.)
1971   Marihuana, Columbus, Ohio: Charles E. Merrill.
1973   The Marihuana Muddle, Lexington, Mass.: Lexington Books.
Gusfield, Joseph R.
1967   "Moral Passage: The Symbolic Process in Public Designations of
       Deviance," Social Problems, 15, II, Fall.
Hochman, Joel S.
1972   Marijuana and Social Evolution, Englewood Cliffs: Prentice-Hall.
Kaplan, John
1971   Marihuana: The New Prohibition, New York: Pocket.
Kitsuse, John I.
1962   "Societal Reactions to Deviant Behavior," Social Problems, 9,3,
       Winter.
Lyman, Stanford and Marvin B. Scott
1968   "Accounts," American Sociological Review, 33, 1.
1970   A Sociology of the Absurd, New York: Appleton-Century-Crofts.
Matza, David
1969   Becoming Deviant, Englewood Cliffs: Prentice-Hall.
Mead, George H.
1934   Mind, Self and Society, Chicago: The University of Chicago Press.
Piaget, Jean
1948   The Moral Judgment of the Child, New York: Free Press.
1962   Play, Dreams and Imitation in Childhood, New York: Norton.
Piaget, Jean and B. Inhelder
1969   The Psychology of the Child, New York: Basic Books.
Simon, William and John H. Gagnon
1968   "Children of the Drug Age," Saturday Review, September 21.
Sykes, Gresham and David Matza
1957   "Techniques of Neutralization," American Sociological Review, 22,
       December.

Notes

1. The period of childhood has traditionally been a special time in which developing adults were given special treatment to ensure their growing up to be capable and responsible members of society. Throughout history and in most cultures children have been kept apart from adults and sheltered in protective isolation from certain knowledge and pratices (see Aries, 1965).

2. Particularly relevant to these "justifications" is Scott and Lyman's (1968) anlaysis of accounts, as statements made to relieve one of culpability. Specifically, they can be seen as "denial of injury" (Sykes and Matza, 1957) as they assert the innocuousness of giving marijuana to their child. An "excuse" is further employed, "scapegoating" the doctor as the one really responsible for this aberration. Also, the appeal to science has been made.

51 / Alcoholics and the Transformation of Deviant Identity

JACQUELINE P. WISEMAN

RETURN VERSUS BREAKING-IN

In the atmosphere of the institution, with the clear, friendly, logical counsel of the average middle-class professional worker, exhortations to reenter society seem to make a great deal of sense. True, much hard work is demanded, but the plans suggested also appear to offer progress and the goal seems worthwhile. Middle-class nondrinkers seem like the world's happiest people from this vantage point.

When asked what he is going to do upon release from an institution, the Skid Row alcoholic typically says:

> I'm hoping to "make it" in the outside world this time. I'm really going to try and not drink and to get back on the track. . . .

> I'm going to try to get back into society. I know that I've been leading an aimless, useless life. It's really no kind of life for anyone, there on Skid Row. . . .

> I'm going to work on my problem. I'm going to try to get back on my feet and live with the respectable world again. . . .

The Skid Row drunk is encouraged in this stance while in the institution by the professional posture of friendship offered by his therapist and other patients. Psychologists and social workers attempt to "gain rapport" with the patient. The alcoholic is also a part of the pseudo-mutual interaction that is a sought characteristic of group therapy sessions. These institutionally-created social success experiences often make the Skid Row man feel quite capable of inserting himself into any desirable primary group in the "outside world."

It is easy to forget that the environment of friendship at the institution is *contrived*[1] for the express purpose of offering the alcoholic a warm, supportive (therapeutic) community, and that the professionals who do this are actually trained to utilize empathetic techniques as part of their jobs.[2] Mainstream society does not concern itself with

Table 1 / Social Characteristics of Skid Row Men
(As Indicated by Current Occupation)

Occupation *(in month preceding interview)*	Percent of Skid Row Men in Pacific City *(N = 2,582)*
General laborers and construction workers	12
Culinary workers	6
Sales and clerical	5
Hotel managers and clerks	2
Teamsters	4
Longshoremen and warehousemen	3
Seamen and stewards	3
Domestics	1
Other	15
Not reported	6
No employment in preceding month	43

Source: *Pacific City Urban Redevelopment Association Report* (1963).

being therapeutic, however, and the reaction of the man-on-the-street or the boss-on-the-job to the ex-alcoholic is often a cold wind that clears away the haze of such pretensions to easy acceptance. Thus there is minimum transfer of personal adjustment training from the institution to the outside world.[3] Often this is a reality shock of no mean proportions, one sufficient to send the recipient back to the warm unreality of alcohol.

Furthermore, the fact is that the Skid Row alcoholic is really not *returning* to any niche being held for him in society in the same sense that it often is for the middle class alcoholic.[4] Rather, the Skid Row man is trying to break into mainstream society *for the first time* and he usually must do this without the support of friends or relatives as "starters."[5]

Using current occupation as an indicator, Table 1 is quite suggestive of just how much social distance there is between middle-class society, in general, and the average Skid Row alcoholic's position upon release. (Note the absence of professional, semi-professional, managerial, and technical occupations, as well as skilled workers— the backbone of the middle class. Additionally, almost half of the Row men [43 percent] had *no* employment in the preceding month.) Furthermore, as was mentioned . . . , the Skid Row man is much more often a man of inadequate skills and education than a man who has "skidded," in the social mobility sense of the term, from a relatively high position down to the bottom of the barrel. A number of studies previously cited indicate many Skid Row alcoholics were never in any stratum of society but were "wanderers" or working or living in institution-like settings from early youth.[6] Others relinquished their social niche so long ago and so completely that they have no one waiting for them to "return." (The possible exception is among those men who still have parents living. But here the choice is not too attractive — living with [and possibly caring for] an aged parent.)[7]

DETAILS OF EXECUTING "THE PLAN"

The plan the Skid Row alcoholic is presented for his "return" to middle-class society is not only demanding, in the face of his social class and occupational limitations, but somewhat skimpy as to details. The plan emphasizes only a few of the needs that he must meet and problems he must overcome to lead any sort of satisfactory existence.

Getting a job, a room, and maintaining sobriety (partially through avoidance of drinking friends) is the gist of the plan, but these maxims do not offer a guide to fulfilling other needs and solving other problems without resorting to Skid Row tactics. What is he to do for social contact, contact with the opposite sex? How is he to get the job, the room, and avoid old friends? How can he change from a today-oriented, no-social-stake person to a future-oriented, middle-class person with margin? How is he to feel a *part* of this middle-class society?

Once the Skid Row alcoholic is "on the streets," the plan is not at all so logical or easy to follow as it seemed to be when presented to him in the institution. His framework for constructing meaning must shift from the professional formulas of the return to a society, which is substantially middle-class in concept, to that of the homeless man coping with day-to-day needs in a world that is alien and unfriendly.

This disjunction in viewpoint inside and outside the institution could easily account for the paucity of reasons offered by the Skid Row alcoholic for drinking excessively again, as well as his apparent insincerity about trying to stay dry. The Row men stop drinking while imbued with the rehabilitator's framework; they start drinking when they *see things differently* on the outside; they are at a loss to explain their lapse when they *return to the rehabilitation framework again*, for the decision to drink was not made within this framework.[8]

If these men were to give a detailed account of the framework that makes taking a drink seem like the most feasible thing to do at the time it is done, they would have to recount their life as experienced while trying to follow the reentry plan. In such a description, the following items are pertinent:

SOCIAL STRUCTURE AND EMPLOYMENT OPPORTUNITIES

Even in times of high employment, it is difficult for a Skid Row alcoholic who has made the loop to get a job. In part, this is because (as has been mentioned) his union membership has lapsed during drinking bouts, or he cannot get a job in his trade as an electrician, metal worker, or one of the other crafts because so much of this work is tied in with contracts demanding security clearance for all workers.

To be unbondable means that the Skid Row man cannot work on many jobs connected with the handling of money or expensive equipment. His status as an alcoholic (or ex-alcoholic) means he cannot work around heavy machinery because of high-risk insurance provisions. Add to this his age, his loss of current experience in his field, and the suspiciously long gaps in his job record (which are hard to explain in any case), and the picture of a virtually unemployable man emerges.

Here is what these men say about the agony of job hunting:

> I know what is going to happen. Everything will be going along all right until they find I didn't work for nine months. When they ask why, and I tell them I was in a mental institution for a drinking problem—that's all, brother. They say, "Don't call us, we'll call you." . . .

> I wish that someone would go in ahead of me and say, "Look, this guy is an ex-alcoholic, but he's okay now. He hasn't had a drink for some time and he's really trying to make it." That would clear the air, and then I could go in and talk about my abilities. . . .

> If I get the job by lying about the past, sure as shootin' they find out.[9] I've been told nine months later that my security clearance didn't work out and I would have to leave even though my work was okay. Now, I'm afraid to accept something for fear I'll just lose it. . . .

> My references are so old that there is no use using them. I don't have any recent ones because all the work I've been doing is in institutions. I was an orderly in the mental hospital and I'd like to work as an orderly now, but I don't dare tell where I got my experience. . . .

A final blow to his job-getting ability is his address and lack of telephone:

> Skid Row is a bad address to have to put down on job applications. Right away they suspect you. And you don't have a telephone either so they can get in touch with you. I sometimes offer to check back from time to time, but you can see they aren't impressed. . . .

What kind of employment can these men get?

The range is limited to menial jobs with low pay. Such jobs often do not involve the man's former skill, or if they do, they are combined with other, low-status tasks. Gardening and "landscaping" the grounds of the numerous colleges and universities that dot the Pacific City area is a major resource for placement of ex-alcoholics by rehabilitation agents. Custodial work or cafeteria jobs are also available at such institutions. Other non-profit institutions such as hospitals and rest homes hire these men as attendants or orderlies.

In Pacific City itself, the Row men must be willing to work as dishwashers, busboys and on other general clean-up jobs. If they are lucky, they may find employment as an elevator operator or night clerk in a cheap hotel. The Row men who were merchant seamen can try to get their papers reinstated and go back to sea.

If he gets a job, the Skid Row alcoholic finds himself torn between fear of failure and anger at what he conceives to be exploitation.

First of all, as his work experience recedes into dim memory, the Row man loses confidence in his abilities to hold a job. Mistakes and problems that cause a secure jobholder some uneasiness cause the ex-alcoholic trying to "make it" to endure true agony. As one man put it:

> You aren't "current" on your job anymore. You forget how to do it. You are certain that people are watching you and saying, "He can't handle it." . . .

Another Row man related the following as what he conceived to be *his failure*, and as the reason he ultimately resumed drinking:

> I had a good job in the filing department, it was arranged for me by the Welfare Home, and I was doing well when they put me in charge of six young high school drop-outs on a government project to train them for jobs. I couldn't get them to do anything! I worked and worked with them, but they weren't interested in learning. I felt like I was a failure as a supervisor. It made me so nervous I started taking tranquilizers, but they didn't really help, so one day I just walked out and went back to drinking. I couldn't handle that job. It was too much for me. . . .

Furthermore, the Skid Row man trying to stay dry usually feels he is treated differently than the rest of the employees. He is constantly reminded that he is lucky to have a job. He is often paid less than usually offered for the work.[10] He is asked to do things he does not think should be part of the job (such as mopping floors, when he was hired to do gardening). And he is expected to perform these extra tasks in good spirit. His experience is that if society wants him back at all . . . it is to exploit him. Often he does as he is told for a while, but the moment comes when anger at what he feels to be an injustice gets the better of him. Years of unemployment have not taught him the discipline of patience on the job, nor does he yet have enough social margin to make the cultivation of such forbearance seem worthwhile, being still "now" oriented. He quits, usually telling the boss off in the bargain (which means no recommendation for future job hunting), and the unemployment part of the cycle starts again.

PROBLEMS OF LIVING QUARTERS

The problems of living quarters, once the Row man is "outside" again, come up almost immediately. Based on the type of job he can get, the Row man can usually afford only a single room, perhaps with cooking privileges, and probably near or in Skid Row. As previously mentioned, a single man who is not well dressed has difficulty renting a room, even in parts of the city that cater to laboring-class families or to single professional men. This is why the reformed alcoholic usually is resigned to living in Skid Row or the Tenderloin, where he blends in better. However, he is living in a drinking culture again.

Skid Row men who are given welfare vouchers through arrangements with jail welfare workers, the Christian Missionaries, the Welfare Home, or on direct appeal to the Welfare office, are sent to Skid Row hotels, inasmuch as the budget for such aid is limited and cannot support numerous men in any but the cheapest of rooms.[11] Skid Row cafes are the only eating establishments that take Welfare food tickets. Thus with the aid of Welfare, the Skid Row man finds himself sent to Skid Row, a drinking culture, and told not to start drinking again.

An alternative housing arrangement is the halfway house. There are quite a few such establishments in Pacific City, but they are not popular with the Skid Row man. Halfway houses are, from his point of view, too much like an institution in their scheduling of meals, lights out, and required attendance at AA meetings. Furthermore, these facilities are used by the state parole board to place prison parolees because this solves some surveillance problems. These ex-convicts are avoided by the Skid Row alcoholic unless he has also done some "hard time." Finally, those Skid Row men who have jobs complain they are constantly "hit up" for money by those without jobs.[12] This combination of association with ex-cons and penniless peers makes the halfway house an atmosphere charged with suspicion, uneasiness, and coolness. As one Skid Row man explained it:

> There isn't much friendliness in a halfway house. You have to be careful who you speak to. Either they are broke and want to put the touch on you, or

they are ex-cons and will take advantage of you. As a result, every man sort of keeps to himself. It's a cold and suspicious place. . . .[13]

SOBRIETY AND SOCIABILITY

The resolution not to drink and to avoid old drinking companions means spending most free time alone. As many of these men said:

> I ate all my meals alone. Most of the time, I had to cook them in my room on my hot plate. About once a month, I could afford dinner out, but it's really no fun to eat out alone. . . .

> Sometimes, I'd go to an early movie, then home, read in bed a while and go to sleep. Those four walls really close in on you after a while. . . .

> I was trying to live on Valoda Street in Gadsen District of Pacific City [working class]. It was very lonesome. I finally went to Skid Row where you know everyone. I hadn't even had anything to drink, but was picked up for drunk. . . .

As previously mentioned, most Skid Row alcoholics do not seek support for their abstinence from liquor by attending local Alcoholics Anonymous meetings or by socializing at AA clubs. AA has never had much appeal for the lower-class alcoholic. It is primarily a middle-class organization, focused on helping ex-alcoholics regain their lost status. Skid Row alcoholics dislike what they refer to as "drunkalogs," in which members tell with relish just how low they had sunk while drinking. They dislike what they call the "snottiness" and "holier-than-thou" attitude of the reformed alcoholic (or "AA virgins" as they call them). The only reason Skid Row men go to AA is to convince another person (someone who would be impressed by such attendance) that they are really trying to lick the alcohol problem. As one put it:

> I plan to join AA. Then people will believe I'm not drinking. As it is now, if I get drunk for three days, they don't count it if I'm sober for three weeks. . . .

Other Skid Row men tell of going to AA meetings out of desperation for *any* companionship and for the refreshments served. After the meeting, they feel a very strong urge to drink so that life becomes a round of early evening AA sessions followed by late evening drinking, and morning hangovers:

> It got so that I just went to AA meetings and from there would get a bottle and go to my room and drink—usually Vodka, and then sober up in time for the next AA meeting. . . .

One might ask why the Skid Row alcoholic does not make friends with co-workers on his new job—if he has found one. The answer given by many of the men is that they have nothing in common with the average worker. Experiences on the loop seem to socialize the Row man so that he is unable to enjoy the company of those who do not share such experiences as living in institutions on the circle, fooling the authorities, panhandling, and general Skid Row adventures.[14] This is especially true if the Skid Row alcoholic has been placed in a gardening or groundskeeper job. His co-workers are seldom urban men, and the Skid Row man keenly misses the presence of the "city" and the men who have knowledge of its many-faceted underlife.[15]

Of new on-the-job acquaintances, the Skid Row drinker says:

> They don't speak my language. They are square-Johns. . . .

> I got so lonesome for someone who talked my language. You can't talk to some jerks. . . .

> I want to talk with someone who knows what I'm talking about. Some guys have never done nothing. . . .[16]

THE PROBLEM WITH WOMEN

A Skid Row man trying to "make it" back into society has a particularly complicated problem so far as women are concerned.

. . . The average Skid Row man is usually quite charming and has no trouble attracting female companions on the Row or partners at the State Mental Hospital. However, neither of these types of women is seen by the alcoholic as a good influence for a man who is attempting to stop drinking. What he wants, in his own words, is "a decent woman."

The problem is, though, that he is shy and awkward about pursuing a woman of this type. As one Skid Row man put it:

> It's been so long since I been around a decent woman, I don't know how to act. . . .

Furthermore, if the Skid Row man has recently been in jail, at the Christian Missionaries, in a non-coeducational halfway house, or spending his time in all-male company on the Row, he has lost practice in communicating with women. Wallace quotes one such man's insecurity about women:

> Now, how shall I ask one of these girls for a dance? No need of introductions, that much I knew. Which would be best, "C'mon kid, let's prance this out?" Or, "May I have this dance?" How I wished these girls were men. I could talk to men.[17]

Another worry is the lack of acceptable credentials.[18]

What can I offer a decent woman? I have no job and no prospects. If I go with a drinking woman, sure as shootin' I'll wind up drinking again. . . .

As noted, the Skid Row alcoholic does have some access to professional women who would like to mother him, but here he must relinquish any hope of being head of the house, and must settle instead for being sort of a house pet.

THE DAILY ROUTINE

What is the daily round like for this man who is trying to gain some social margin so as to get in and stay in the society depicted by the middle-class professional? The mundane experiences of this project form the framework within which the Skid Row man gives up and takes a drink.

A composite description might go something like this: rise early in a lonely room; breakfast fixed on a hot plate, eaten alone in the room, or eaten alone in a cheap restaurant; ride the bus to work (often quite a distance), because an alcoholic usually has lost his driver's license or cannot afford a car and cannot afford to live near work; work all day at a boring, menial, poorly paid job with dull, unsympathetic (to the alcoholic) co-workers and an unsympathetic (to the alcoholic) boss; return at night to eat dinner alone and watch television in the hotel lobby, or read, attempt to freshen his limited wardrobe, or go to bed, knowing a similar day awaits him tomorrow.

Although he may be seeing a welfare worker or a therapist on a regular basis, the dried-out chronic drunk trying to "make it" discovers his relationship with these professionals is not the same as it was in institutions, and he has no claim on their outside social time for informal friendship.

The solitary status of the Skid Row man also affects his opportunities for *experiencing* success. Success, like margin, is an attribute ascribed by others. The Skid Row man has no friends or relatives to reinforce his determination to "make it" or congratulate him on progress. No one (except for an occasional professional therapist) seems even aware of his efforts to prove worthiness. Respectable society is not an entity, and it neither hands out keys to the city nor certificates of social integration. It seems almost impossible for a Skid Row man to know when he has, indeed, "made it." Certainly, merely going through the motions of being respectable will not necessarily elicit immediate recognizable rewards.[19]

The agents of social control counsel "patience" and that "better things will eventually come." But patience means future-orientation, a psychological state of mind that is foreign to a man who has been operating for many years on here-and-now satisfactions.

The story that follows is typical. The man was first interviewed at the Welfare Home for Homeless Men and then seen about a month later, quite by chance, at County Jail. He explained his lapse this way:

> I got a job at the Green Pine Hotel in the suburbs as janitor. I was terribly lonesome. I had no friends. I was on the job there two weeks and then came down to the city. There's quite a few fellows I know around. I want to be with somebody I know once in a while. I liked the job, but I got lonesome. There's nothing to do and no one to talk to. If I had had companionship, it wouldn't have happened. You get lonesome in one room. . . .

Also revealing is the answer to the question, "How were things out there?", asked of a Skid Row alcoholic who had just returned to jail after two weeks of freedom. He replied:

> Pretty rough! Everything moves so fast. No one knows or cares if you are alive. You just don't fit in anywhere. . . .

GOING FULL CIRCLE: "AND THEN I DECIDED TO HELL WITH IT"

In contrast to a return to the society and reality suggested as a goal by professional rehabilitators, there exists also the Skid Row society with its instant warmth, friendliness, and general conviviality. Here, many of the friends of the job-holding Skid Row alcoholic are living on welfare and spending their time drinking, partying, and making out. The dole in Pacific City provides a standard of living probably only slightly lower than the pay of the first menial job available to the alcoholic just discharged from an institution. The room of the "unreformed drunk" may compare favorably with the room in which the struggling "ex-alcoholic" is living. The amount and quality of food each is able to obtain varies but little, even though the unreformed man may be getting part of his daily bread from missions and other charitable organizations.

Furthermore, having once made the loop and learned its machinations, the Skid Row alcoholic trying to "make it" knows that these institutions are always available to him. Compared to the way he is living while trying to make a comeback, some of the stations that he despised and feared at first seem pleasant in retrospect.[20] Old friends are certain to be in any institutions he should choose (or be sent to). Although "admission to society" is so nebulous as to defy definition or provide any feeling of belonging, admission to an institution is just the opposite. While progress toward the goal of reintegration into society is difficult to apprehend, progress in an institution is well marked. On the inside the alcoholic is often told if he has done well on a task, and may be given a higher status job; in therapy, he is praised for "being honest and not holding back"; at the Christian Missionaries he may be promoted to a better room or a larger gratuity; he may even have "institutional margin" on the basis of past performance.[21] Outside the loop station, in Skid Row society, there are the small triumphs of making out and sharing one's cleverness with friends over a bottle.

Thus where the road into respectable society is cold and lonely, Skid Row and the stations of the loop offer conviviality, feeling of accomplishment, as well as an opportunity to forget the struggle.[22] The Row man can stop seeking an idealized society at the end of the rainbow, stop leading a treadmill existence, and return to being seen by his most significant others as a real person again.[23]

An important character in the "Return of the Prodigal Son" story is the respectable brother who stayed at home and out of trouble. In a very true sense, he epitomizes the general attitude of the average citizen toward anyone who strays from the fold too long or too completely and then expects to be granted amnesty merely by some suffering and an apology.

When asked to come to the party given in honor of the returning prodigal son, the self-righteous brother was angry and said to his father:

> Lo, these many years do I serve thee, neither transgress I at any time thy commandment; and yet thou never gavest me a kid, that I might make merry with my friends; but as soon as this thy son was come, which hath devoured thy living with harlots, thou hast killed for him the fatted calf.
>
> Luke 15:29–30

To which the Skid Row alcoholic might reply, as he gives up the fight for acceptance in the rehabilitator's society and returns to Skid Row living and inevitably a loop institution:

> And then I decided to hell with it, and I started drinking again.

CYCLING OUT

Is there any way off the loop? Besides the few who stick it out long enough to get back sufficient social margin to reclaim a lost existence, what other ways are there for Skid Row men to escape?

There appear to be three major ways off Skid Row:

1. Become a live-in servant for an institution (or, once in a while, for a professional woman).

2. Go into alcoholic rehabilitation as a profession.

3. Die.

The first has been amply discussed. Ex-alcoholics may be found at many nonprofit institutions, especially hospitals and rest homes, for some small wages plus board and room. This becomes, then, their new way of life.

The second escape route has possibly been traveled successfully by more alcoholics than is generally known. During the course of this study, the number of ex-alcoholics in positions of agents of social control on the loop was astounding. Ex-alcoholics can be found in administrative positions in the Courts, County Jail, the City Hospital, the State Mental Hospital, Welfare Home for Homeless Men, and the Christian Missionaries.

Other ex-alcoholics are to be found making a career of operating Alcoholics Anonymous clubs, halfway houses, and therapy groups. The newest halfway house for men to be started under the sponsorship of the Pacific City Department of Public Health will be manned by ex-alcoholics.

The factors underlying the success of this maneuver to get off the loop may well center about the fact that "going into rehab work" converts what is a vice in the outside world (i.e., excessive drinking, institutionalization, familiarity with other alcoholics, and absence of recent job experience) into an employable virtue. Indeed, this idea has been formally accepted by many agencies concerned with reform and rehabilitation of deviants.[24] "It takes one to know and understand one" philosophy prevails. Paradoxically, however, the assumption an ex-alcoholic will be more understanding in working with alcoholics has not generally held true if we are to accept the testimony of the men they work with. Alcoholics complain that, "There's nothing colder than an ex-alcoholic," which suggests that once a man makes it to "the right side" he no longer empathizes with former buddies but rather identifies with the associates of his newly-established status—other agents of social control.[25]

Death is the third way off the loop. Six Row men died in Pacific City during the course of this study of such causes as acute alcoholism, cirrhosis of the liver, brutal beatings in an alley, a seizure, and an internal hemorrhage. Men who get off the loop permanently in this way have long ago given up the right for reentrance into society. After a few such attempts they unhesitatingly take a drink the moment they leave an institution. Such men can be roughly divided into two types—both of whom accept the consequences of the bridges they have burned and the lonely life that will be their future.

They are:

1. *The so-called institutionalized man*, the perennial and resigned

loop maker. This includes the chronic drunkenness offender who uses the jail as an emergency hotel in bad weather, the self-admitted State Hospital man who uses that institution for drying out and building up both physically and financially, and the mission rounder who, cursing the hand who feeds him, still goes back when forced by hunger and illness.

2. *The Welfare Skid Row man* who "graduates" to vouchers and settles down to living on what his check provides, plus what he can earn on pick-up jobs. He drinks heavily except on the days he has an appointment with his social worker. Intermittent institutionalizations keep him alive.

Both these types of Row men are trapped on the loop. Death is their only avenue of escape.

Notes

1. This is not to say that professional rehabilitation workers are not sincere in their feelings of friendship toward their patients or clients. It is rather that these friendships are not of the type to carry past quitting time, when the off-duty professional usually prefers the company of persons of his own educational and social background.

Alcoholics are not the only persons to mistake professional friendliness for the genuine thing. The following was overheard at County Jail between ex-state prison inmates who were discussing parole officers:

At least those guys who go by the book, you know what they are going to do. You don't overestimate their show of friendliness and get out of line and get slapped down. (Overheard while observing in the Jail.)

2. See, for instance, William Schofield, *Psychotherapy, the Purchase of Friendship* (Englewood Cliffs, N.J.: Prentice-Hall, 1964).

3. See Robert Rapaport, *Community as Doctor: New Perspectives on a Therapeutic Community* (London: Tavistock Publications, 1959; and Springfield, Illinois: Charles C. Thomas, 1960), for a discussion of the deliberate creation of a permissive, security-oriented atmosphere that is no doubt helpful in reducing anxieties in patients but bears little resemblance to the less well-planned outside world.

4. For the middle-class returnee, the problem is one of breaking down the counter-role relationships that were built up during the heavy drinking period when they were "irresponsible," according to middle-class standards. The middle-class ex-alcoholic's problems in overcoming the dependency relationships he helped to create have been well-chronicled. See Joan K. Jackson, "Family Structure and Alcoholism," *Mental Hygiene* (July 1959), 403–7. Jackson points out that "if the husband does stop drinking, he is usually permitted to exercise his family roles *only on probation.*" (Emphasis mine.)

5. At least, there usually are no relatives to whom he is willing or able to return. Sometimes this is by choice. As one man put it:

I got to straighten myself out *before* I go to see my family. I can't let them see me this way. . . .

Another said:

Most of us would starve rather than call our relatives. That relationship is *over.* . . .

6. This is not intended to suggest that the Skid Row alcoholic was not of some higher status before coming to Skid Row. By the very term "bottom of the barrel" Skid Row residents suggest they were higher at *some* time, at least in their own eyes. However, both Donald J. Bogue, in *Skid Row in American Cities* (Chicago: University

of Chicago Press, 1963), pp. 320–22, and Howard M. Bahr, *Homelessness and Disaffiliation* (New York: Columbia University Bureau of Applied Social Research, 1968), pp.
220–30, indicate that these men started out in the lower portion of the status continuum
and rose only slightly before losing status. As previously mentioned, skidding from high
status to Skid Row happens in only a few well-publicized cases.

Pittman and Gordon's study of the chronic police case inebriate produced the following socio-economic characteristics, scarecely indicative of middle-class status:

> Approximately . . .
> 90 percent are skilled and unskilled workers (as compared with 59 percent of the
> general population)
> 75 percent had only a grade school education (as compared with 41 percent of the
> general population)
> 85 percent had no permanent residence, lived at a mission or shelter, a hotel or
> shelter, a hotel or rooming house (as compared with 21 percent of the general
> population).

See David J. Pittman and C. Wayne Gordon, *Revolving Door* (Glencoe, Ill.: The Free
Press, 1958), Chap. 2, "The Sociocultural Profile," pp. 16–58.

Bogue, *Skid Row in American Cities*, pp. 13–14, reports that, "in comparison with the
adult population of the city of Chicago as a whole, the . . . Skid Row men are:

    a. Foreign born white or "other nonwhite" race (American Indian).
    b. Single, widowed, or divorced: half have never married.
    c. Middle-aged or older men, concentrated in the ages of 45–74.
    d. Very poorly educated, with more than one-fifth being "functionally illiterate"
       (having completed fewer than five years of elementary school).
    e. Unemployed. The unemployment rate among the Skid Row men was more than
       eight times that of the general population.
    f. Not in the labor force, with "unable to work" as the primary reason.
    g. Employed as wage or salary workers.
    h. Of extremely low income, with almost one-half living on less than $90 per month.
       Almost one-fourth of the men had received less than $500 in cash during the
       preceding year.

7. Agents of social control report a large proportion of Skid Row alcoholics keep in
contact (usually through correspondence) with their mothers. (Maintenance of this
mother-son tie is often cited by those Freudianly inclined group therapy leaders as
evidence many alcoholics have not passed the oedipus crisis successfully, are latently
homosexual as a result, and thus drink to forget the guilt attached to this perversion. Of
course, there are no comparative figures on the proportion of nonalcoholic males who
maintain contact with their mothers.)

8. The fact there are an infinite number of mental frameworks, and a given individual may use more than one on the same phenomena, was discussed in chapter 1 to
explain how Skid Row may be seen as both a disgusting and exciting place in which to
live.

The point is that motivation to act is not, as seen by conventional psychological
theory, the result of either inner personality characteristics or external cues alone but is
rather the result of the way in which the situation is defined by the actor. The "wisdom"
of a given plan of action is dependent upon the ground rules for such wisdom—that is,
the theoretical framework by which the ingredients of the situation are "understood."
When presumably intelligent individuals do things and later admit they "should have
known better," they are referring to the fact they are now viewing the action from
another, less sympathetic framework.

9. Joan Emerson has suggested the Skid Row alcoholic (often accused of being a
con-artist) apparently does not know how to lie sensibly in an employment interview
situation. He either lacks the middle-class job-seeker's training in fictionalizing his job
experience and covering up embarrassing spots with plausible excuses, or he has
become out of practice in such activity.

10. . . . Skid Row men are often exploited by employers who pay them below-
standard or state-minimum wages, taking advantage of their desperate need for work

and money. Bogue, in *Skid Row in American Cities*, p. 492, also noted this in his study of the Chicago Skid Row and incorporated the following into his recommendations for eliminating the area:

The minimum-wage laws are openly broken, both in spirit and in deed, along Skid Row. Some industries . . . manage to get their work done at rates as low as fifty cents an hour, by declaring the men . . . are independent operators. Skid Row hotels and restaurants also pay very low wages to night watchmen, janitors, and dishwashers. By making a tie-in arrangement between salary and room or board, the man gets paid less than the minimum wage, even when his pay check and benefits are given their combined cash value. . . . A careful review of minimum-wage compliance should be made of every hotel, restaurant, mission, employment agency, and firm known to employ numbers of Skid Row men.

11. It seems strange that Pacific City Welfare officials do not see any contradiction in returning an alcoholic to live in a Skid Row hotel after he has been dried out and his health rebuilt at their Welfare Home for Homeless Men. When I was first granted permission to interview men at the Welfare Home for Homeless Men, the director said, as he bemoaned the high rate of recidivism among alcoholics:

If you can tell us why, after all we try to do for these men, that they go right back to Skid Row and drinking, you will be doing a great service with your research project. . . .

12. Earl Rubington has done some of the few analyses of the problem of operating or living in a halfway house. (The tone of most literature on halfway houses reads like annual reports—glowingly successful.) Rubington outlines the problems faced by ex-alcoholic administrators in "Organizational Strains and Key Roles," *Administrative Science Quarterly*, 9, No. 4 (March 1965), 350–69, and the panhandling problems Skid Row alcoholics face within the halfway house itself. See "Panhandling and the Skid Row Subculture," paper read at 53rd Annual Meeting of the American Sociological Society (Seattle, Washington, August 28, 1958).

13. My limited visits to halfway houses seem to confirm this. They are *very* quiet and the atmosphere is "cold." At one co-educational house, men and women could not eat meals at the same table. There was little talking in either the lounge or the coffee room. The alcoholism units at State Mental Hospital were swinging places by comparison.

14. . . . these subjects constitute a substantial proportion of small talk among Skid Row men.

15. Howard M. Bahr has been engaged in some well-constructed tests of generally-accepted hypotheses concerning life on Skid Row with special emphasis on the area of socialization. His findings seem to indicate Skid Row men develop a rather strong attachment to Skid Row drinking companions, which aid in their identification with the Row and their feelings of alienation off the Row. See Howard M. Bahr and Stephen J. Langfur, "Social Attachment and Drinking in Skid Row Life Histories," *Social Problems*, 14, No. 4 (Spring 1967), 464–72. Also, see Howard M. Bahr, "Drinking, Interaction, and Identification: Notes on Socialization into Skid Row," *Journal of Health and Social Behavior*, 8, No. 4 (December 1967), 272–85.

16. The experience of being "on the other side" apparently does not leave a man unmarked psychologically and, paradoxically, although it is degrading, it is simultaneously a source of pride to have survived it. As a survivor, a man actually feels superior to those who have not had this experience, and this creates a chasm between deviants and non-deviants that may never be closed again. John Irwin, in his study, *The Felon* (Englewood Cliffs, N.J.: Prentice-Hall, 1970), speaks of "the enduring affinity" ex-convicts have for each other—others with the same experience. It is also said that drug addicts at Synanon still consider themselves "hipper" than the nonuser.

17. Samuel E. Wallace, *Skid Row as a Way of Life* (Totowa, N.J.: The Bedminister Press, 1965), p. 174.

18. George Orwell, in *Down and Out in Paris and London* (New York: Harcourt, Brace & World Company, 1933), p. 148, speaks of "the degradation worked in a man who knows that he is not even considered fit for marriage. . . . Cut off from the whole race of women, a tramp feels himself degraded to the rank of a cripple or a lunatic. No humiliation could do more damage to a man's self-respect."

19. Additionally, trying and failing to gain acceptance is much more ego-debilitating

than not trying at all. Like going through college rush week and not getting a bid from a sorority or fraternity, there is no longer any doubt about your social acceptance with a group deemed desirable. The Skid Row alcoholic, in his efforts to get back into society may also encounter a "reality shock" not intended by his rehabilitators — that of finding that he is socially undesirable to the society he seeks, regardless of his efforts to the contrary.

20. Before it happens, the thought of being sent to jail for drunkenness, or going to a mental hospital for "the cure," seems like one of the worst experiences that a man can have. However, when he finds he *can* survive it, going through the same thing again holds fewer terrors. At times he even feels strengthened by the experience. Jack Black, a confessed thief of all trades, explains this phenomenon in terms of his reactions to the whipping post (*You Can't Win* [New York: The Macmillan Co., 1927], p. 278):

> As a punishment, it's a success; as a deterrent it's a failure; if it's half and half, one offsets the other and there's nothing gained. The truth is I wouldn't have quit no matter how I was treated. The flogging just hardened me more, that's all. I found myself somewhat more determined. . . . I had taken everything they had in the way of violence and could take it again. Instead of going away in fear, I found my fears removed. *The whipping post is a strange place to gather fresh confidence and courage, yet that's what it gave me.* . . .

. . . Furthermore, while the quest for society is fraught with uncertainty, life in an institution offers security of rules and regulations plus provisions for all the exigencies of living which are a problematic struggle on "the outside."

21. Howard Bahr's analysis of the relationship of drinking and social disaffiliation to presumed "institutionalization" indicates that it is not the simple one-to-one relationship some persons have thought. Rather, it is a complicated, interactive process. Howard M. Bahr, "Institutional Life, Drinking, and Disaffiliation," a paper read at the 1968 annual meeting of the Society for the Study of Social Problems in Boston.

22. It could be the grinding monotony of regular but boring and often physically demanding work, the lack of desirable or interesting companions, and the bleakness of his living quarters contribute to a certain "flatness" of experience quite unlike the little adventures the Skid Row alcoholic has enjoyed both in institutions and on the Row. Just as soldiers returning from the war find civilian life flat at first so may the Skid Row man find the square life dull.

23. It is indeed a paradox that the Skid Row man must return to an *ad hoc* existence (where neither his past nor his future is seriously affected by present adventures) to feel he is accepted as a real person. Only on Skid Row, where times of pleasure are momentarily "sealed off" from their consequences, can he enjoy himself. When he is working at his low-status job and living his ascetic "attempting-to-make-it" life, he has all the burdens of responsibility to the past and cognizance of the future without any of the rewards.

24. See, for instance, National Institute of Mental Health, *Experiments in Culture Expansion*, Report of proceedings of a conference on "The Use of Products of a Social Problem in Coping with the Problem" (Norco, California, July 1963), and *Offenders as a Correctional Manpower Resource*, Report of a seminar convened by the Joint Commission on Correctional Manpower and Training (Washington, D.C., March 1968). Erving Goffman has called the phenomenon of the deviant using his stigma to advantage as "going into business for himself." "Twelfth-step work" in Alcoholics Anonymous and Synanon (for drug users) are other examples of this phenomenon.

25. An excellent description of the way in which the ex-alcoholic seeks to identify with agents of social control to the extent that he is actually rude to ex-drinking partners is to be found in Earl Rubington's "Grady 'Breaks Out': A Case Study of an Alcoholic's Relapse," *Social Problems*, 11, No. 4 (Spring 1964), 372–80. This phenomenon of upwardly mobile low-caste persons turning with vehemence upon those who were formerly "their own kind" has been noted by many sociologists and psychologists, and has been given many labels including "identification with the aggressor," and "self-hatred of one's membership in a despised group." . . .

52 / Reentry

JOHN IRWIN

The impact of release is often dramatic. After months of anticipation, planning, and dreaming, the felon leaves the confined, routinized, slow-paced setting of the prison and steps into the "streets" as an adult-citizen. The problems of the first weeks are usually staggering and sometimes insurmountable. Becoming accustomed to the outside world, coping with parole, finding a good job—perhaps finding any job—and getting started toward a gratifying life style are at least difficult and for many impossible.

When released, the convict can be seen to be proceeding along a narrow and precarious route, beset with difficult obstacles. If the obstacles are too difficult, if satisfaction and fulfillment [are] not forthcoming, and/or his commitment to straightening up his hand is too weak, he will be diverted from the straight path toward systematic deviance. He himself believes in the route's precariousness and the high probability of his failure, and this intensifies its precariousness. Many of the obstacles are, however, both very real and very difficult.

The reentry problems have been divided here, somewhat arbitrarily, into three areas which will be treated in separate chapters. The first area includes the problems that arise immediately upon release—problems which arise mainly because the ex-felon is suddenly transplated from one setting to another. These problems, which are experienced to some extent by all returnees (ex-servicemen, Peace Corps returnees, releasees from prisoner of war camps, etc.), are related to "getting settled down" and "getting on your feet." What is implied by these two phrases is that before serious enterprises can be undertaken, before plans can be put into action, or before any real satisfaction in life can be expected one must withstand some immediate disorienting experiences and become a functioning and viable civilian who at least has good clothing and a place to live.

The second group of problems is encountered after one is on his feet (that is, one has become reoriented and, with some degree of success, a functioning citizen) and now seeks to do more than just "get by." These can be viewed as the obstacles to "doing good" or obstacles to achieving a satisfying life style. Although the ex-convict to some extent shares this class of experiences with other returnees, the intensity of the experiences and some of their dimensions are uniquely his.

778

Finally, the last of the three problem areas includes those which arise because the ex-felon is under the supervision of the parole agency, which legally may impose restraints upon him, alter his life routine, and without any new legal action return him to prison.[1] To examine how the parolee copes with the parole agency, a careful analysis must be made of the parolee's relationship with the parole agent and of some of the important aspects of the parole system. This aspect will be treated in a separate chapter, although many of the problems are interrelated with those of the other two areas.

AWARENESS OF THE REENTRY PROBLEM

Before examining the separate aspects of the reentry experience itself, I would like to contrast briefly the awareness of the problem relative to other types of releasees with the ignorance of it relative to parolees and to explore some of the reasons for this ignorance in order to emphasize the importance of a better understanding of reentry in the case of the parolee.

The first systematic attention to the special problems incurred by a population returning to its former social setting was directed toward English veterans of World War II who were being repatriated from war prisons or being discharged from overseas duty.[2] Some attention was paid to the similar situation in America.[3] Recently, the reentry problems of the Peace Corps returnees have been causing considerable concern.[4]

In all these instances the adjustment problems are seen to be complex, involving extreme personal stress, psychological "symptoms," and problems of "resocialization," as well as the more obvious adjustment problems, such as locating employment.

In the case of the felon being released on parole, however, there seems to be little or no awareness of many facets of the impact of reentry.[5] A publication of the California Department of Corrections handed out to each man before release does have the following statements:

> You are going to get out. "The free world! The streets! The ever-loving bricks!" What do you expect? "The sky to split? Heavenly music to waft in four directions? Wide Open Arms to Greet Every Entrance?"
>   It Ain't
>   Like That!!
>   It Ain't
>   Like That
>   At All!!!
> The world has been rocking on all the time you've been in. Usually, few people actually know that you have been away.

No one is going to do all your planning for you. Chances are pretty good that you'll have to start from scratch in building a social life—any life.

Loneliness is one of the greatest problems facing a parolee. It may help if you give this a little thought before you jump out there. It won't be easy. Don't expect to swim in milk and honey.[6]

Generally, however, there is little indication either from the literature or from interviews of persons involved in dealing with parolees of the existence of any awareness of the broader aspects of the reentry problem. This general blindness seems to be related to formal and informal societal conceptions of the ex-convict. For instance, from one perspective the ex-convict is seen to be an erratic person—he is "emotionally disturbed," "sociopathic," "potentially dangerous," or "dependent." Therefore, any unusual behavior or any "symptoms," such as the actions that have been reported by "normal" returnees in other instances, would be attributed to the personality propensities of the ex-convict and not to the transitional experiences. From another perspective the ex-convict is seen as a person of low moral worth who is being granted the special privilege of early release provided he agrees to live up to certain minimum standards of behavior—the special parole regulations. He should be thankful for this privilege and should find no difficulty, if he has regained some worthiness, in responding by conducting himself properly. Failure to do so stems from his thanklessness and/or unworthiness. Finally, the legally restricted parole status of the ex-convict often obscures the true picture of the important experiences in the parolee's first days. In this status he is subject to special restrictions and is in contact with an agency which is supervising him and affording him certain kinds of help. Actions of the parolees which stem partly or wholly from other aspects of the reentry impact are often interpreted by observers, and the parolee himself, as reactions to the strains inherent in this status. For instance, any erratic behavior—any appearances of disorganization, frustration, irritability, or depression, or any of the behavior patterns which have been frequently observed to accompany other instances of reentry—can in the parolee's situation be attributed to his inability to adjust to the formal and informal expectations (some of which are ambiguous and conflicting) inherent in the parole status, to a personal conflict with the parole agent, or to difficulties which were incurred because of the parole status becoming known, such as employment difficulties or difficulties in establishing social ties. All of these can and often do contribute to the total range of problems that the parolee faces in reentering. Often, however, they are given undue weight, and they screen the more profound dimensions of the initial reentry problem.

The parole agent is often incapable of understanding the full scope of reentry because of characteristics of his position. . . . The agent must police and help—"work with"—the parolee. He stands between potentially hostile segments of the citizenry and the parolee; he must give assurances to the former that he is doing his best to see that a potentially dangerous person is under control and must attempt to force the latter to adhere to a system of rules and regulations which can be very restrictive and obstructive to his efforts to adjust. Because of these often conflicting demands and the parole agent's heavy case load and limited time, the task of surveillance is seldom accomplished to anyone's satisfaction.

In helping or "working with" the parolee, the agent must "set up a program." Setting up a program entails finding the parolee employment and housing—if the parolee does not have these himself—and placing him in special department programs such as an out-patient clinic, parole school, and group counseling. Some aspects of working with many parolees are difficult and never cease. Parolees are one of the least employable segments of American society. Many of them are unskilled, or members of racial minorities, and have virtually no work record. On top of this they are ex-convicts. For these persons the agent must find jobs or supply leads and exhort them to pursue these leads. Besides jobs the agent must see that the parolee, who has often exhausted his financial resources, has a place to sleep and money for food until he obtains work and receives a paycheck. Again he has limited resources to do this. There is a department fund from which he may draw money for meal tickets, hotel rent, and some spending money, but this fund is far from unlimited and is often exhausted toward the end of the fiscal year. This facet of "working with" the parolee can be frustrating and time-consuming for the agent.

Besides these two primary tasks, the agent has to fulfill many procedural duties. He must visit each man a specified number of times, make regular progress reports on each parolee, and write special violation or emergency reports in the event the parolee is arrested, absconds, or repeatedly breaks the conditions of his parole. Needless to say, the most troublesome parolees, who may be the parolees who are having the most difficulty with the reentry impact, greatly increase the parole agent's work load.

Because of the heavy burden of his duties and his position relative to potentially hostile segments of society, the parole agent tends to be limited in his ability to conceive of the full scope of the parolee's adjustment problems. He tends, because of the enormity of the parolee's problems which are related to his assigned task, to be aware only of those which bear directly on his duties and which are conceivable from the perspective underlying the official definition of his position. As he sees it, the problems that the parolee faces in leaving the institution and settling in the outside community are (1) maintaining financial support of himself and his dependents, which means finding and holding regular employment, any employment; (2) avoiding "trouble"—staying away from bad associates, locations which the parole agent feels are "trouble" areas, and situations which may cause "trouble," such as some common-law relationships; (3) cooperating with the parole agent—maintaining an attitude of respect, being available for interviews, taking the agent's advice, and coming to him with any major problems (but not too often, for then he becomes a burden); (4) obeying society's laws and the special conditions of parole. From the agent's viewpoint these interrelated problems, which alone present difficulty enough, constitute the totality of the parolee's adaptive problems. If he approaches an acceptable solution of these he will remain outside of prison and have a good relationship with the parole agent. This should satisfy the parolee. If he fails in the early stages of his parole, then the parole agent tends to see his failure in terms of the conceptions mentioned above: the parolee is an erratic person, morally unworthy, or incapable of adapting to the strains of the parole status. It is seldom that any weight is given to the reentry impact itself.

Of course there are exceptions to this. For instance, one agent counseling a member of my sample who had just served ten years in Folsom recognized that the man was "shook up" upon release. He told the man, who had been given a few hundred dollars by his mother, to go to his place of residence, which was ten miles outside of the center of San Francisco in a very small suburban community, and relax for a few weeks. He advised him to come to the city a couple of times a week and refamiliarize himself with the pace of things before trying to plunge into a full, adult-civilian routine. But this small glimmer of understanding is rare and even in this case could only be indulged because of the financial status of the parolee. In the majority of the cases of reentry I studied, there was a complete lack of understanding on the part of the parole agent of the reentry impact, and where there was some understanding the exigencies of the parole agent's tasks prevented the agent from giving special consideration to the parolee in view of this understanding.

GETTING SETTLED DOWN

Two important and related themes appeared in interviews of convicts about to be released on parole. First there was considerable optimism in their plans and expectations, and most revealed the belief that their chances were average or better to live outside without being brought back. It seems that at this point in their prison career, at its termination, they had acquired considerable real or feigned optimism. Most of them expressed the belief that making it is up to the individual, and now that they had decided to try to make it their chances were very good. Most who come back, they believed, don't want to make it. Only four of the sample expressed doubts about their chances of making it.[7]

The second theme was a widely expressed concern for "getting out and getting settled down." Whatever their long-range plans, the great majority indicated an immediate desire to "get their feet on the ground," to "get into a groove of some kind." Most indicated an awareness that they would be starting from scratch, from the bottom, that "the streets" would be strange at first and that before they could begin real progress toward any goals there would be a period during which they must familiarize themselves with the outside world, meet a lot of immediate exigencies, and build up a stock of material necessities—clothes, toiletries, funishings, etc.:

> I am going to move very slowly at first. I'm going to look twice to see if the light is green before crossing the street. I'm not going to look for a job right away. After this 7½ years I just want to get my feet into the earth again. I have a friend who is giving me a place to stay. He has some kids and some animals. I just want to relax and learn about these things again. Then I am going to get a job, any job, a dishwashing job. I don't care what work I do, because it is going to be the leisure time that counts. I'm going to find out what I want to do with my leisure time. (Taped interview, San Quentin, June 1966)

> I wanna get out and get to work. Then I wanna see my kids. As soon as I sees the parole officer I'm goin'a see my kids. I'm goin'a get a little room at first and then in a coupl'a weeks I'm goin'a look for an apartment with some extra rooms. Then I'm goin'a take it easy for awhile, get my hair fixed. I ain't goin'a look for no woman for awhile. I'm goin'a have to see about my driver's license and I wanna look around for a little car. I'm goin'a need a car to visit my kids, some of them are over in Oakland. I like the job I got, but I would like a little more money. I need some rent money, some furniture and some money for a car. (Taped interview, Soledad Prison, July 1966)

> First I just want to get a forty hour a week job. I don't care what it pays, if I just have a check coming in every week. Then I can plan on something. I can start working towards something. If I don't have no job, or if I just work one or two hours here and a couple of hours there, like last time, then I can't look ahead to nothing and I probably won't make it. (Taped interview, Soledad Prison, July 1966)

The ex-convict's attempts to settle down and to get his feet on the ground are, however, often thwarted by a barrage of disorganizing events which occur in the first days or weeks on the outside. In spite of his optimism, preparedness, and awareness of the experiences in store for him, the disorganizing impact on the personality of moving from one meaning world into another, the desperation that emerges when he is faced with untold demands for which he is ill prepared, and the extreme loneliness that he is likely to feel often prevent him from every achieving equilibrium or direction on the outside. Often a sincere plan to "make it" in a relatively conventional style is never actualized because of the reentry impact. Many parolees careen and ricochet through the first weeks and finally in desperation jump parole, commit acts which will return them to prison, or retreat into their former deviant world. Many others, though they do not have their plans destroyed and do not immediately fail on parole because of the experiences which accompany their return to the outside community, have their plans, their perspectives, and their views of self altered. At the very least, reentry involves strains which are painful and which deserve attention.

In exploring this phase of the entry phenomenon, the ex-convict as an individual or a type will not be considered. Identities and modes of adaptation to the prision milieu will be suspsended for the time being and reentry will be examined as a general phenomenon experienced by all parolees. Other instances of reentry or similar phenomena will also be examined in order to produce wider understanding of this transitional experience.

Withstanding the Initial Impact

The ex-convict moves from a state of incarceration where the pace is slow and routinized, the events are monotonous but familiar, into a chaotic and foreign outside world. The cars, buses, people, buildings, roads, stores, lights, noises, and animals are things he hasn't experienced at firsthand for quite some time. The most ordinary transactions of the civilian have dropped from his repertoire of automatic maneuvers. Getting on a streetcar, ordering something at a hog dog stand, entering a theater are strange. Talking to people whose accent, style of speech, gestures, and vocabulary are slightly different is difficult. The entire stimulus world—the sights, sounds, and smells—is strange.

Because of this strangeness, the intial confrontation with the "streets" is apt to be painful and certainly is accompanied by some disappointment, anxiety, and depression.

> I don't know, man, I was just depressed the first few days. It was nothing that I could put my finger on. (Field notes, San Francisco, September 1966)

The thing I remember was how lonely I was out there the first few weeks. (Interview, San Quentin, January 1967)

I mean, I was shook, baby. Things were moving too fast, everybody rushing somewhere. And they all seemed so cold, they had this up tight look. (Interview, San Quentin, July 1967)

My dad picked me up at the prison and we spent the day driving up to San Francisco. It was night by the time we got to the city, 'cause we stopped and ate and looked at the ocean on the way. Well he dropped me off at my brother's where I was going to stay and left. My dad and my brother don't particularly dig each other. It was late and my brother was in bed. He had this couch set up for me. It was right under a window and this apartment was up about five stories or so. Well, it was one of these drippy nights in San Francisco. The bay was pretty close and a fog horn was blasting out every minute or so. I laid down and tried to go to sleep. Man, it was weird. I was thinking, so this is the big day that I had waited so long for. Man, I was depressed and nervous. The whole thing was unreal. (Interview, San Francisco, June 1968)

These experiences are not unique to the return of the felon or unique to the reentry phenomenon. Travelers to foreign places usually experience similar feelings.[8] Often when one returns home after a short absence, there is an immediate reaction of disappointment, self-doubt, and meaninglessness.[9] The reports of other returnees reveal similar experiences.

Three Components of the Initial Impact: The released felon, as is the case with other persons who suddenly find themselves in a strange world, is disoriented by the new physical surroundings and social settings in different ways. First, the strangeness of the sensory experience unsettles him in a very subtle manner. He is usually proceeding to an urban center upon release, and the intensity and the quality of the new stimulus world can be overpowering. There is more noise and different types of noise. There are many more lights and colors, and there is a great deal more rapid motion:

The first thing I noticed was how fast everything moves outside. In prison everybody even walks slow. Outside everyone's in a hurry. (Field notes, San Francisco, September 1966)

The lights at night kind of got me. (Interview, San Quentin, January 1967)

The first time I started across the street, I remember, I was watching a car coming and I couldn't judge his speed very good. I couldn't tell if he was going to hit me or not. It was weird. (Interview, San Francisco, June 1968)

> Riding in the car was like riding in a boat. It was rolling back and forth. I
> got sick right away. (Interview, San Francisco, June 1968)

Usually the discomfort and the resultant disorientation is not explicitly identified and traced to its sources. The returnee often feels
an uneasiness which he can't identify or he feels a sense of "unreal-
ness"; that is, a feeling that he is not really experiencing this but it
witnessing it as an observer or he is dreaming it.

Second, he is disorganized because of his lack of interpretive
knowledge of the everyday, taken-for-granted outside world. Alfred
Schutz in discussing the situation of the stranger approaching a foreign social world describes a type of knowledge of everyday activity
that strangers do not possess:

> Any member born or reared within the group accepts the ready-made
> standardized scheme of the cultural pattern handed down to him by an-
> cestors, teachers and authorities as an unquestioned and unquestionable
> guide in all the situations which normally occur within the social world.
> This knowledge correlated to the cultural pattern carries its evidence in
> itself—or, rather, it is taken for granted in the absence of evidence to the
> contrary. It is a knowledge of trustworthy *recipes* for interpreting the so-
> cial world. . . .[10]

The ex-convict to some extent reenters the outside world as a stranger. He has been away and has forgotten many of the cultural patterns, and in the passage of time changes in these patterns have occurred. He too finds that immediate interpretive recipes which
smooth social functioning (and without which every encounter becomes a strained, embarrassing, and difficult trial) have been lost to
him and will have to be learned again:

> They were talking different and doing different things. I felt like a fool.
> (Interview, San Francisco, July 1966)

> The clerk asked me what I wanted and for a minute I couldn't answer her.
> It was like I didn't understand her. (Interview, San Francisco, June 1968)

Third, he is ill-prepared to function smoothly in interaction with
outsiders in the outside world because he has lost the vast repertoire
of taken-for-granted, automatic responses and actions. These are
what Schutz calls "recipes for handling things and men in order to
obtain the best results in every situation with a minimum of effort by
avoiding undesirable consquences."[11] Here again the ex-convict is
like the stranger. He has lost the ability to perform many ordinary
civilian skills which have no use in the prison world and, therefore,
are not practiced. For instance, he has not made change, boarded
streetcars and buses, paid fares, or bought movie tickets or items
across a store counter. He had done these things before prison, but

during the prison experience he lost his ability to perform these actions in the unthinking, spontaneous manner in which citizens perform them and expect others to perform them:

> On about the second day I'm out I get on this trolley and start fumbling in my pocket for money. There're a lot a people behind me trying to get on, but I can't figure out how much to put in the box. You know what, man, I don't know how to find out how much to put in the box. The driver's getting salty and I don't want to ask him cause I'm embarrassed, so you know what I do? I back off the fucking thing and walk fifteen blocks. (Interview, San Francisco, July 1966)

There is a process of escalation in actual interactional settings when it is discovered that one does not have these interpretative and behavior recipes. As soon as others who automatically assume that the stranger possesses the taken-for-granted knowledge and responses discover that he doesn't, they too become self-conscious, move from the level of taken-for-granted interpretations and responses, and start doubting the reliability of their own recipes and patterns.[12] The doubt and self-consciousness [are] fed back and forth, further disorganizing each member of the setting, especially the stranger who is aware that he is responsible for getting this confrontation off its firm foundation of the taken-for-granted social patterns. During several hours spent with a parolee on his first day outside, I witnessed the difficulty the simple act of purchasing a coke at a hot dog stand can present the unprepared "stranger." He went to the window and a young waitress brusquely asked him for his order. He was not able to reply immediately and when he did, his voice was not sure, his pronunciation not clear. The waitress, who appeared unsettled, didn't understand the order even though I did with ease. The second time she understood it and went to fill his order. When she returned, handed it to him and quoted the price, he was still unsettled. He did not have the money ready. After a brief hesitation, during which the waitress waited quietly but nervously, he started searching his pockets for money. He was especially slow at getting the money out of his pocket and could not rapidly pick either the right change or a larger sum to cover it which most people would do in this situation. He seemed to have to carefully consider these somewhat strange objects, cogitate on their relative value, weight this against the price quoted, and then find some combination of them which would be equal to or more than that price. He admitted afterwards that he had been very unnerved by this experience and had been having similar difficult experiences since his release.

Impact on the Self: How do these disorganizing experiences which all releasees seem to experience lead to the feelings of self-doubt, self-estrangement, and meaninglessness which they report? We must take a hard look at the relationship between these disorganizing experiences and the nature of self-conceptions and perspective to understand the reactions. Our conceptions of self—the definitions, values, beliefs, and meanings which constitute the design we recognize and act upon as our "self"—are interwoven into a fabric of a total world perspective—our meaning world. The patterns and designs of this world exist only in the interweavings of all the component strains; the self as a cohesive design exists only in the interweavings of meanings pertaining directly to the self and meanings of the world in general. But the fabric is never completed. Like Penelope's tapestry, it is constantly being unraveled and then rewoven daily in ongoing interactional settings. Our meanings of self and the world are being tested, supported, or reshaped within a situation in interaction with others who are engaged in the same process. In order for there to be a continuity of design in the fabric of perspective, there has to be some degree of continuity of familiarity in the setting. A radical change, a shift in setting, where the objects and meanings of the new setting are unfamiliar, interrupts the weaving—the maintenance of the patterns and designs. Not only does the world seem strange; the self loses its distinctiveness. Not only does the person find the new setting strange and unpredictable, and not only does he experience anxiety and disappointment from his inability to function normally in this strange setting, but he loses a grip on his profounder meanings, his values, goals, conceptions of himself.

In this situation, planned, purposeful action becomes extremely difficult. Such action requires a definite sense of self, a relatively clear idea of one's relation to other things, and some sense of one's direction or goals. All of these tend to become unraveled in a radical shift of settings.

Variations in the Initial Impact: Although all released felons experience this facet of the reentry problem to some degree, most endure it and reorient themselves and continue to act with some continuity and stability relative to their former definitions, conceptions and plans. The intensity of this shock varies from ex-convict to ex-convict. For instance, returning to a familiar setting helps to reduce the duration of the initial impact. I interviewed one parolee after he had been out for one week, who said that he had been slightly "shook up," but was over it now. His appearance and behavior supported this claim. This parolee had moved back into his parents' home, into his old room. The clothes he left were waiting for him; they only needed some minor alterations. His wife and child, although they had not gone back together, were visiting him and the family almost nightly.

He had succeeded in securing a desirable job. The familiarity of the setting, coupled with the removal of other obstacles, helped this person to quickly reestablish some continuity with a familiar world. For him the initial reentry impact was minimal. For others, especially those who are coming to a strange city where they have no friends, possibly no secure job, the disjointed experience is tremendous. I spent several hours on several occasions in the first week with another parolee. This person was born and raised in Colorado and lived in San Jose when he was sent to prison. This was his first stay in San Francisco, and he had no job upon release. During the prerelease interview he had impressed me as a person with exceptional control over his actions. He had definite plans and stated that he was determined not to do anything which would deter him from following them. On the outside, however, he admitted that he was extremely "shook." For the first four or five days he couldn't eat a meal; he tried several times but after several bites found he could not force any more food down his throat. When he finished his daily routine of job hunting, he couldn't stay in his room, so he walked the city for hours, sometimes late into the night. He reported having a great deal of trouble talking to people, even though he had fancied himself as outgoing and glib. He felt foolish when he tried to buy something in a store because he seemed to have difficulty taking the money out of his pocket and finding the correct amount of change. During these transactions he reports that "the saleslady was looking at me like I was some kind of idiot." This individual, in spite of the intensity of his reactions, maintained his self-control. He went through this period with detachment and amusement. He seemed to be operating on two levels. On one level he had lost grip of himself, of his reactions, his body and his feelings; but on the other level he was witnessing himself reacting in this abnormal fashion.[13] He said that he knew that he would eventually settle down "once I get a job and get a routine."

Others do not take this experience with such aloofness. One parolee with a long background of alcoholism told me in a prerelease interview that he had found a solution to his alcohol problem and would not be troubled with it this time on the outside. He further disclosed relatively specific immediate plans. A man in his forties who had finally overcome his "inferiority complex," he was going to report immediately to the union where there was a job waiting for him, join an Alcoholics Anonymous group and participate religiously, join one or two social clubs so that he might meet a woman his age whom he would marry and then begin "living a normal life." He was released by an oversight of the parole agent on July 3, a Sunday before the Fourth of July. It would be two days before he could report to the union or the parole agent. He wandered the streets of San

Francisco feeling "nervous," "depressed," "scared," and "lonely."
He walked into a Market Street bar and plunged into a two-day
"drunk." He sobered up enough on Tuesday to report to the parole
agent, fearful that he would be locked up immediately for violating
the conditions of his parole by drinking. The parole agent was not too
severe with him and after a "bawling out" directed him to report to
the union. The parolee, in somewhat better spirits, but still hung
over, left the parole office, cashed the check the agent had given
him—the remainder of his $60—and launched another "drunk." He
made his way to skid row, a milieu he was well acquainted with from
his former years of drinking. A week passed and his funds were depleted. He sobered up and contacted his parole agent, who placed
him in city jail for four days to "dry out." The agent picked him up
from the jail and after a conference with the district parole supervisor took him to the union where he secured a job. He had no money
for rent and the agent would not advance him any, but he found a
room in a Salvation Army hotel for derelict seamen. He lasted two
more weeks, during which time he worked and remained sober. But
then he quit his job and absconded. Although alcohol seems to be an
important factor in this man's failure, the initial shock of reentry certainly was instrumental in preventing him from reestablishing some
self-organization so that he might start executing the plans he had
made in prison. When I reminded him of these plans on four different occasions during his chaotic first month, he variously shrugged
them off, desperately assured me that he was going to begin following them, or didn't respond.

Meeting the Exigencies of Living as a Civilian

The ex-convict faces problems in simply meeting the bare requisites
of civilian life which are much more acute than the same class of
problems of other returnees. In the case of prisoner-of-war repatri-
ates, war veterans, and Peace Corps returnees, there is some indication of special employment difficulties. For instance, Peace Corps returnees have reported that employers were not eager to hire them
upon return; in fact, their Peace Corps experience might have been
detrimental to their employment potential.[14] In these cases, however, they are usually speaking about their employability at the professional or executive level, not simply finding a "job"—any job. And
after finding job difficulties many of the Peace Corps members found
grants, fellowships, and teaching assistantships open to them if they
returned to higher education (and so far 60 per cent have).[15] The
problem of the parolee is often finding any job or at least a job which
pays a living wage. In this as in other facets of meeting the exigencies

of the life of the citizen, the parolee faces special and extreme problems for which he is usually extremely unprepared.

At the time of this study, the parolee was released with one change of sports clothes—a low-priced sports coat, two sports shirts, a pair of slacks, two pairs of dress socks, and plain-toed black or brown shoes—and three sets of khaki, blue or white work clothes, a pair of work shoes, and two changes of underclothing. Theoretically he is allowed a flexible sum of money to pay his expenses until he draws his first paycheck. However, this always turned out to be $60, $20 of which he receives when he leaves the institution and the rest when he reports to the parole office. Many parolees have some supplementary funds (56 per cent of the seventy interviewed after a year stated they had extra money, but 70 per cent still had less than $100) from prison jobs that paid up to 10 cents an hour, from friends or other sources—pensions, bonds, or their own savings. The parolee, if his job requires, may request special funds to buy tools. Other than this, he is given transportation to the city where he is to be supervised on parole.

Employment: The initial and probably the biggest obstacle in this problem area is obtaining employment. In order to be released on parole in California, the convict must have financial support—employment, support from his family, friends, or from other sources—or have a good possibility of securing immediate employment through a union, the California State Employment Service, or a private employment agency. One of these alternatives must be approved by the parolee's prospective parole agent. To meet this requirement of release, the parolee does one of the following:

1. He obtains his job (on guarantee of support) while in the institution by contacting friends or relatives who locate employment for him, former employers, unions, or by corresponding directly with prospective employers. The latter is probably the least successful. Unless the parolee has some sought-after skill, it is very unlikely that employers will hire him without an interview. Only two in the sample of forty-one secured jobs by writing directly to employers—one with a fruit-packing company which does seasonal hiring and the other with a shoe-manufacturing company. Ten persons found jobs through their family, friends, or former employers.

2. If the prospective parolee is in contact with friends or relatives and wants to be sure of not being "overdue," he will sometimes have them set up a "shuck" job. Although they cannot find someone who will actually hire the parolee, they often have a friend who will make a fictitious offer of employment. In this case, by prior agreement with friends, relatives, or with the convict himself, some potential employer, possibly a relative or friend, promises to hire the man

upon release with no intention of doing so. This is done merely to fulfill the requirement that he have a job to be released. Once released the parolee reports to the agent that he was not hired because of some unforeseen change in the employer's situation, or possibly the parolee will keep up the fiction and use the job as a "front" while remaining unemployed unbeknownst to the agent.

3. If the person cannot find his own job, real or fictitious, then he must rely on the parole agent to find him a job or to approve his release without a job. The latter is becoming the most common pattern. Sixty-one percent of seventy parolees were released without immediate employment. If a person has support—for instance, if he is to live in the home of a relative or friend who will guarantee support until the parolee finds a job—the agent will usually approve his release with no job. The emerging pattern, however, is to release the parolee to some organization which guarantees placing him on some job within a reasonable length of time. The agent usually has contact with several unions, such as the culinary unions, which, unless the general employment situation is tight, will agree to place some parolees. Frequently the parolee is released to the California State Employment Service. In the last three years this agency has become officially active in parolee placement. Presently most state employment offices have a special counselor who is assigned to parolees. These counselors work closely with the parole agents. One agent expresses the present attitude toward placement in this way:

> The state has a huge bureaucracy primarily devoted to finding people jobs. Why shouldn't they find these guys jobs instead of me? My job's watching these guys—I'm not trained to find them jobs. Let the people who are trained do it and I will do what I am trained for. That way the taxpayers get the most for their money. (Interview, San Francisco District Parole Office, October 1966)

However, the California State Employment Service is not very effective in placing parolees. Only two of the seventy parolees stated that they received their first job through the CSES, and only seven stated that they received any help during the year from the CSES.

Although the emerging pattern is to release a person without a job when he has not found a job himself, some agents prefer that he be employed and are active in locating jobs for them. Four of seventy parolees were initially placed by their agents. One of these persons had completed a training course in sheet metal work in prison, was taken out for an interview before his release date, and then when the employer agreed to hire him was released early. The agent in this case had picked the parolee especially for this job because he wanted to "open up" a particular company to parolees. This agent, as is the case with some others, is actively placing parolees on desirable jobs.

Other agents prefer to tap another resource for releasing men. This practice was more prevalent in the past when the department requirement on men having a job was more stringent. Some agents have contacts with industries or small businesses which use parolees as a source of cheap labor, for example, car washes, Goodwill Industries, and many small restraurants. These jobs usually have extremely low pay and and/or undesirable working conditions. The agent cultivates these contacts because they serve as a last resort. He is able to place his least employable parolees through them. Often the agent receives other types of cooperation from such employers. They will keep him informed of the activities of the parolee and in this way the agent is able to increase his surveillance over him. The employers are served by having a source of cheap labor over which they have extra controls. The parolee is in the disadvantageous position of having few or no job resources, and often he is required to stay on the job by the agent.

The problem of earning a living doesn't end for the parolee upon release. Many of the jobs do not work out, are undesirable, or were fictitious, and many parolees have no jobs. Sometimes, the parolee and the agent must cope with the employment difficulties throughout the parolee's supervision. In the sample of seventy, 30 per cent were not employed at the end of the first year or when they had been returned to prison, and 54 per cent stated that they had a hard time finding, or never could find, a good job. The difficulties that many parolees have in securing desirable—and desirable by the most modest criteria—employment cannot be overemphasized. As previously mentioned, the parolee is one of the hardest to employ in our society. He is often low-skilled or has no skill, and he carries the stigma of the ex-felon and often the stigma of race. In spite of the highly publicized emphasis on trade training in California prisons, few men learn an employable trade during their sentences there. For instance, out of seventy, only 40 per cent received trade training in prison and only 27 per cent of the 40 per cent received two or more years' training. In a study conducted by a Regional Office within the Parole Division it was found that only 36 per cent of all parolees had received trade training in prison and that only 34 per cent of the 36 per cent were working in a field related to their training.[16] Interviews with employment counselors in the CSES revealed that the only training programs which they unanimously believed were suitably geared to the outside employment situation and gave adequate training were nursing, welding (there was one dissent here), sheet metal, auto mechanics, auto body and fender repair, and cabinet making.[17] The inmates interviewed before release reported that it is difficult to get into these programs. At San Quentin, which has a population ranging from 3,500 to 4,000, 316 men can participate in the trade-training programs at one time. Furthermore, there are special restrictions on some classes of convicts; e.g., older men and narcotics offenders are restricted from most programs. The fact is that most of the persons who enter the California prisons with no employable skill are leaving them in the same way.

Residence: Upon release, residence is a problem for some. A temporary residence will be found for all parolees who do not have an offer of residence with their families, friends, or in halfway houses. The agent, however, usually sends them to one of three or four low-priced hotels in the skid-row areas of the city. Some of these are very undesirable living places. They are used principally by winos and destitute pensioners. They are dirty and depressing. One parolee stated in a prerelease interview:

> The parole office put me in some hotel that had a bunch of winos in the lobby. I had to sneak in the back door because I didn't want anyone to see me walking in the place. This time I'm not goin'a let him stick me back in one of those places. (Taped interview, Soledad Prison, July 1966)[18]

The picture is not always so grim. Some hotels regularly used by the agency are not undesirable, and most agents allow the parolee to find his own room if he desires. Many of the parolees, with the aid of friends, other parolees, or organizations (such as the Seven Step organization in San Francisco) succeed in finding fairly desirable and cheap hotel lodgings.

Residence becomes a bigger concern if the parolee doesn't find a job immediately and does not have extra money to pay his rent beyond the first week. The $60 budget offered by the agency lasts him about one week. Then he is more or less on his own. The agency will supply rent slips for one of several hotels in the Bay Area for another week, almost all of which are skid-row hotels. From then on the parolee must find some other way to pay his rent. Sometimes the agent will refer him to charity organizations, such as the Salvation Army; but often by this time the parolee has given up, absconded, or returned to systematic deviance. This may mean he has turned to illegal means of making money or to other deviants for assistance—for lodging, money and companionship.

Clothing: Clothing becomes a growing concern after the first few days. The prison-issued clothes, especially the shirt, need to be washed or cleaned and pressed. If the parolee has no job and needs to present himself in a neat fasion for job interviews, this problem is acute. Many parolees either salvage some of their old clothes (which are usually conspicuously out of style) or use some of their extra funds for this purpose. But if the parolee does not have the extra resources, as was true of more than half of the sample of seventy, he is faced with a frustrating problem. After a few days, it becomes difficult for him to keep himself appearing neat and clean. This is likely to occur at a time when other worries are mounting and when the feeling of loneliness and self-estrangement are at their height.

The clothing problem does not go away in the first week or so. In order for a person to live the simplest social life, a minimum of clothes far beyond that which is issued to the parolee is required. In the first weeks or months many frustrating situations emerge and many activities are closed to the parolee because he does not have adequate clothing.

Transportation: Transportation can also be a serious obstacle to settling into a routine. For the majority of parolees it will be some time after release before they find it possible to own an automobile. They must have special permssion to drive, automobile liability and property damage insurance (which is very expensive for a parolee who is in a high-risk category), and permssion to own an auto. In the first weeks or months of their parole, they must depend on public transportation or friends or they must walk. Most of them are unfamiliar with the public transportation system and their first attempts to use it are difficult and at times embarrassing. Using public transporation for going back and forth to work is at times troublesome. For instance, one parolee in my sample who lives in San Francisco secured a job in Marin Country. To get to work he caught the bus at 6:30 A.M. and arrived home after 6:00 P.M. For those who do not secure work in the first few weeks and who run out of funds, the 15- or 25-cent bus fare becomes a very large sum. Walking then supplants riding.

"Talking Care of Business": Beyond these more obvious and specific exigencies there are more subtle activities at which the parolee is particularly inept and which interfere with his progress toward settling into a groove; these will be referred to as "taking caring of business." For instance, the ability to schedule one's time is lost in the slow-paced, routinized prison life. The convict is accustomed to having his life regulated by an assortment of bells, horns, whistles, and commands. Once outside he must relearn to parcel out his day for himself, but this is a skill that has many obscure contours and requires unnoticed resources (for instance an alarm clock) and a period of practice. For no other reason than being out of the habit of taking care of business, the parolee tends to forget appointments or times of appointments, to disobey minor laws—especially traffic and parking laws—to forget to pay fines, bills, and to meet many small citizen

obligations which are so routine to the average citizen that their performance is seldom even noticed and never considered problematic. But beyond simply forgetting these small civilian responsibilities, the parolee often has an "obstinate" posture toward the petty details and the petty rules of civilian life.

His failure to take care of business is usually attributed by "normal" citizen-observers—such as parole agents, who do not understand the full complexities of these acquired skills—to his "laziness," his lack of desire to succeed on parole, his lack of moral worth, or his psychological inadequacies.

There is a snowballing tendency in the problems in this area. A failure to meet one of them usually compounds the difficulties in meeting others. For instance, if the person does not have a job upon release or loses his job before he can earn money to buy some clothes, pay his rent, and form a base of security, as time passes and his funds diminish it becomes increasingly hard for him find new employment. His clothes become dirty and wrinkled. He sometimes cannot afford to use the public transportation system and he wears out the poorly made prison-issued shoes walking to look for work.

Agency Response

The response of the parole agency in the meantime is often unsympathetic and ineffectual. As the parolee accelerates down this spiral into desperation, he becomes a headache to the parole agent. Not only is he failing to obey the parole rules by not maintaining employment and conducting himself as a good citizen, he is increasingly seeking or threatening to seek aid from the parole agent—aid which the parole agent has limited resources to supply. For instance, the parole agent's job connections are few and soon exhausted, his financial resources likewise. He can advance money for hotel rent and meal tickets, but the agent is discouraged from doing this beyond the first week. There is a general feeling among agents and supervisors that a parolee, if given the chance, will abuse this service. The parolee, theoretically, may borrow cash sums, but in actuality loans are infrequently made. Twenty-two per cent of the seventy requested a loan and 14 per cent received one. (One agent stated that he hadn't made a loan in five years.) One reason for this may be that the agent must lend the money to the parolee out of his pocket and then be reimbursed by the state the next month. This imposition on the agent, coupled with the general agency opinion that parolees would sponge off the agency if they were allowed to borrow frequently, results in infrequent loans.

One parolee in my sample, whose job did not materialize because of the 1966 slump in building trades, worked sporadically for several months at odd-tile setting, painting, and construction jobs which he contracted on his own. He was not earning enough money to pay his bare expenses and was broke a considerable portion of the time. There was no governmental financial aid available for this man—he was not eligible for welfare or unemployment benefits. He did receive several cash loans from friends, but this source was limited. On one occasion he made a trip from Hayward where he resided to the parole agency in Oakland—a distance of twenty miles—using his last money for bus fare. He asked the agent for a small loan for additional carfare and phone calls. The agent refused, telling him that the fund was exhausted.

The parole agent very often tries to wash his hands of these troublesome cases who threaten to take up a great deal of his efforts and who constantly beseech aid which he does not have adequate resources to give. These nusiance cases—those who are having extreme difficulty in meeting the exigencies of life and who are caught in a snowballing descent toward disaster—are a major disconcerting factor in his employment duties, a factor he must learn to cope with. Some simply ignore the problem. Others increase their efforts to solve this problem by attempting to locate jobs for the men and find other resources for aid. I believe, however, that many agents cope with this threat to their peace of mind by taking on attitudes and beliefs that attribute the parolee's difficulties to the parolee's own weaknesses. He hasn't found a job or held a job because he is lazy, didn't try hard enough, doesn't want a job, is really hanging around with other criminals and doesn't want to work, has no intentions of working, and is really participating or planning to participate in some deviant activities and is just "shucking" the parole agent in telling him that he is trying to find work. Of course, from the perspective of the parole agent these accusations are somewhat valid in the case of some parolees. In many cases, however, they are false, and the agent uses them as screens to shield him from the disturbing plight of many parolees.

Notes

1. Virtually all California felons are released on parole; in 1966, the figure was 94 per cent. Consequently, . . . the terms parolee, release, and ex-felon are used almost interchangeably.

2. See, for example, A. T. M. Wilson, "The Serviceman Comes Home," *Pilot Papers*, Volume I, No. 2 (April 1946); A. Curle, "Transitional Communities and Social Reconnection: A Follow-up Study of the Civil Resettlement of British Prisoners of War," *Human Relations*, Vol. I, Part 1 (1947); P. H. Newman, "The Prisoner-of-War Mentality: Its Effect after Repatriation," *British Medical Journal* (1946); S. Davidson, "Notes on a Group of Ex-prisoners of War," *Bulletin of the Menninger Clinic*, No. 10

(1946); M. Jones, "Rehabilitation of Forces Neurosis Patients to Civilian Life," *British Medical Journal*, I (1946); and G. C. Pether, "The Returned Prisoner of War," *Lancet*, I (1945).

3. Roy Grinker and John Spiegel, *Men Under Stress* (New York: McGraw-Hill, Inc., 1945); George Pratt, *Soldier to Civilian* (New York: McGraw-Hill, Inc., 1944); Donald Becker, "The Veteran: Problem and Challenge," *Social Forces* (October 1946).

4. Julius Horwitz, "The Peace Corpsman Returns to Darkest America," *The New York Times Magazine* (October 24, 1965); Richard Stolley, "The Reentry Crisis," *Life Magazine* (March 9, 1965), pp. 98–100; "Culture Shock: Adjusting to Life Back Home," *Newsweek* (March 15, 1965), p. 30.

5. The one exception to this is the recent article by Elliot Studt, "The Reentry of the Offender into the Community," U.S. Department of Health, Education, and Welfare, No. 9002 (1967). Studt emphasizes reentry as status passage and describes the difficulties encountered because of unpreparedness to occupy outside social roles. The emphasis in the following chapters will not be on the social *roles*, but on other interactional dimensions, such as perspectives, identities, and meaning worlds.

6. *How to Live Like Millions*, California Department of Corrections Publication No. 272 (38135), p. 8.

7. In a recent study of parolees undertaken by social welfare students, this pre-release optimism was also detected. See Lanny Berry, *et al.*, "Social Experiences of Newly Released Parolees" (unpublished master's thesis, University of California, 1966). p. 68.

8. For a literate description by a traveler of this experience see H. M. Tomlinson, *The Face of the Earth* (New York: Dell Publishing Co., 1960), p. 34.

9. A character in Thomas Wolfe's *The Web and the Rock* (New York: Dell Publishing Co., 1960) gives us a good example of this situation (p. 350).

10. "The Stranger: An Essay in Social Psychology," *American Journal of Sociology* (May 1944), p. 501.

11. Ibid., p. 501.

12. Harold Garfinkel has conducted experiments in which students purposely encountered unprepared persons and refused to take for granted that which normally is. The unprepared persons usually indicated some disorganization, and the interaction could not be continued while the student persisted in doubting the taken-for-granted basis for the interaction. ("Studies of the Routine Grounds of Everyday Activities," *Social Problems* (Winter 1964), pp. 225–50.

13. Bruno Bettelheim describes a similar type of detachment from himself in his adjustment to a concentration camp in "Individual and Mass Behavior," *Journal of Abnormal Psychology* (October 1943), p. 431.

14. Stolley, "The Reentry Crisis," p. 105.

15. Ibid., p. 104.

16. "Caseload Inventory—Region II," 12, 31, 1967, California Department of Corrections Document (1967). On file in "Parole Action Study" files, Center for Study of Law and Society, University of California.

17. Wendy Harris, an interviewer hired by the Parole Action Study, conducted these interviews of employment counselors.

18. When this man was released on parole after this interview in July 1966, his parole agent placed him in a hotel on Third Street in San Francisco's skid-row section. This time the parolee "jumped" parole in the first week.

53 / Controlling Deviant Organizations: Scientists as Moral Entrepreneurs

JAMES H. FREY

INTRODUCTION

The names of Dale Console, Ernest Fitzgerald, Authur Tamplin, Fumio Matsuda, George Geary, Kermit Vanivier, Ronald Ostrander or Jacqueline Verrett probably do not strike a note of familiarity with many, even the most knowledgeable observers of political and economic affairs. Yet, if it were not for each of these individuals, great injustices, even to the point of being lethal, which occurred as the result of clandestine, often illegal, harmful activities by private corporations and government agencies would have gone unnoticed and unreported. Each is a "whistle blower." That is, these individuals, "believing that the public interest overrides the interest of the organization he serves, publicly 'blows the whistle' if the organization is involved in corrupt, illegal, fraudulent or harmful activity" (Nader, et al., 1972: vii). Despite the potential of considerable risk to job and career, each of these individuals could no longer justify to his/her conscience and ethical standards the behavior they were able to observe. By blowing the whistle, each individual engaged in an act of moral entrepreneurship. That is, they took it upon themselves, after assessing the costs and benefits, to alert law enforcement agents to the deviance thay had observed. The purpose of this paper is to describe some of the conditions which determine the extent and/or variations of moral entrepeneurship or whistle blowing that are possible and to outline a place for scientists in the phenomenon of "blowing the whistle."

The individuals described above had an additional basis for commonality beyond their moral entrepreneurship. Each was a scientist/professional.[1] They were physicists, doctors, lawyers, engineers, and research scientists. The role of scientists in organizations has been described in considerable detail elsewhere (Marcson, 1960; Kornhauser, 1960; Sorenson and Sorenson, 1974; Hall, 1968; Pelz and Andrews, 1966). The focus of this literature has been on the conflict posed by the juxtaposition of a dual authority structure, professional vs. organizational, and on the resolution of this conflict. The general perspective of scientists as apolitical and nonactivist also has support in the literature (Price, 1967; Storer, 1966). In fact, the tenets of value neutrality and disinterestedness have been the source of considerable conflict among scientists, particularly those of a "humanist" bent who assert the absurdity and impossibility of a completely objective stance to any problem. For a scientist to take a public political or moral stance represents (1) a breach of professional and scientific codes which suggest a severe separation of professional and citizen roles, and, (2) a violation of the demand by the organization to be loyal. The existence of these two demands places the scientist-/professional under significant cross-pressures which are not easily resolved.

In organizations, scientists, engineers, chemists, researchers could possibly be in the best position to initiate activities which would expose the deviance of an organization. The exposure would ultimately lead to a loss of that organization's legitimacy with its environment, and a subsequent change in organizational behavior. That is, because of the higher probability that professionals, as opposed to production workers, will have access to organizational "Guilty Knowledge," they are in a better position to engage in moral entrepreneurship by means of "Whistle-Blowing." Individuals like lawyer Gary Greenberg who exposed the Nixon Administration's plans to delay desegregation or Dr. Jacqueline Verrett who told the public of the Food and Drug Administration's ineffectual testing of foodstuffs containing cyclamates are examples of professionals who have engaged in moral entrepreneurship. Each could reveal the deviance only because they had access to relevant decision making and information.

However, just being in a professional category or being professionally trained is not enough to guarantee that moral entrepreneurship will take place. There are many forms of whistle blowing; each is the result of a combination of factors which make up a cost-benefit configuration. That is, a professional will participate in some form of moral entrepreneurship, e.g., testimony at a public hearing or clandestinely slip information to a newspaper, depending on his perception of the risks he must take when compared to the benefits he/she will accrue from the act. After a brief discussion of organizational deviance, I will try to show how moral entrepreneurship is not an either-or situation; rather, it is a complicated act requiring the consideration of many factors.

ORGANIZATION/CORPORATE DEVIANCE

It is a well-documented fact that contemporary society is dominated by large-scale organizations. These social systems have replaced the family and community to a large extent as the major vehicles of work, play, prayer, and production. In an industrialized society organizations seem to be the more efficient means to deliver goods and services to regional, national, and international markets. Promulgating maxims of efficiency, productivity, and goal achievement, organizations have increased in number and scope. The boundaries of many exceed national borders and more assets exist in company coffers than in the entire treasury of some countries. In the course of their development organizations have also violated civil, administrative and criminal law by engaging in acts which are harmful and deceptive. Organizations, as deviants, present particular problems for law enforcement agencies and criminologists. Acknowledging the guilt or innocence of an organization is more difficult than making the same determination for an individual; studying individuals is less complex than analyzing organizational activity.

Deviance by organizations is not to be limited to activity which is in violation of a criminal code. Rather, several conditions must exist. First, the violation of civil and administrative codes shall also be acknowledged as deviance. This is consistent with Clinard's (1979) conception in a recent study of corporate crime. Second, in order for any action to be defined as organizational deviance it must be in violation of societal norms or, at least, the expectations of some external regulator. Third, the deviant act must also be acknowledged and given support by policy makers within the organization. Finally, it must be learned to be appropriate when new members enter the organization (Ermann and Lundman, 1978). Thus, acts of organizational deviance must be committed in accordance with the operative goals of the organization. For example, organization will publicly state that their products are safe; yet, compromises of safety occur on the drawing board or the assembly line with the consent of management. Gofman's exposure of inferior radiation packaging and Geary's revelation that U.S. Steel was selling untested pipe are examples of exposure of deviant activities which obviously were known by management. Without access to decision-making at the operational level how is one to know of the deviance? Well, the "insider" scientist is often in a position to know, and to expose, the deviance.

Another point of clarification is necessary before continuing. For the sake of this discussion, organizational deviance and corporate crime will be treated as synonymous. Granted, deviant acts are committed by organizations which would not be defined as "corporate." The limitation is utilized here because the corporate form is most familiar and is the subject of a larger portion of the literature.

Still, there is a lot we do not know about corporate deviance. According to Clinard (1979), who has conducted one of the few empirically based studies of this phenomenon, we do not know (a) how many crimes a given business commits each year, (b) how well the corporation is policed, (c) the recidivism rate of deviant corporations, (d) the rate of deviance and its fluctuations, and (e) the socio-economic costs of corporate crime. There is a great deal of interest in corporate crime, but few effective research studies or analyses exist. This is partially due to the fact that criminologists are not trained to understand the intricacies of corporate managment and behavior. Also, it is easier to study the poor and downtrodden than the rich and powerful.

A system of ethics has not yet been developed which specifically applies to the relationship of organizations, and organizations to society. Statements on the social responsibility of corporate and other types of organizational entities seem to be public verbiage showing little relation to reality or being motivated by nothing more than a desire to maintain organizational survival and a good public relations image. Up to this point, pressure for instilling societal responsibility on organizations has come from external sources: regulators, pressure groups, market conditions, public opinion. These have not worked well (Schur, 1969; Ogren, 1973; Harvard Law School, 1976). These sources of pressure have failed primarily because they have always worked from a position of power imbalance which finds them at a resource disadvantage. For example, the Justice System lacks the money and manpower to thoroughly prosecute corporate entities for such activities as restraint of trade or price fixing. In a recent effort to prosecute American Telephone and Telegraph (AT&T) on campaign financing violations, the total budget to the anti-trust division of the Attorney General's Office did not come close to the $60 million AT&T was prepared to spend in defense of its position.

Even if an organization is convicted, the sanctions which are administered are minimal and rarely serve as a deterrent (Clinard, 1979). For example, IBM, a mulitmillion dollar data processing firm, was recently fined $5000 for making illegal campaign contributions of several million dollars. Ralph Nader, Common Cause, and other citizen action groups have exposed many abuses in organizational dealings with individuals. Yet, it seems that organizational deviance continues. If the answer to control cannot be found in sources of external pressure then reform possibilities may come from a second source—whistle blowing or moral entrepreneurship on the part of members, particularly in professional categories, of organizations. This paper will explore the relation of professionals in organizations to the activity of moral entrepreneurship, and will make the point that the "professionalization" of organizations may ultimately be the best source of controlling these units on behalf of society. Nader et al. (1972:7) state it this way:

> The willingness and ability of insiders to blow the whistle is the last line of defense ordinary citizens have against the denial of their rights and the destruction of their interests by secretive and powerful organizations.

THE SCIENTIST AS MORAL ENTREPRENEUR

Placing the scientist into the role of moral entrepreneur calls for a basic reorientation of the scientist to his role in society. Traditionally, scientists as well as professionals in other occupations have been trained to assume an objective or affectively neutral stance in their work and to the uses of their results. Their goals were explanation and prediction, not control (Ben-David, 1971). While science has always been restricted by economic, social, political, and religious constraints, the scientific community and professional associations have rarely acted to change the nature of these constraints. In the past, scientists and scientific associations have been active as external voices of concern and dissent (Goran, 1974). Many were active in Anti-Vietnam demonstrations against Dow Chemical, University Development Corporations and military agencies. Scientific groups have made recommendations on the subject of supersonic transports, cyclamates, and pesticides. These activities, however, were usually ignored and made little impact (Goran, 1974: 8). Similar activity by the scientists who works directly for nonacademic, governmental or industrial organizations has not been as prolific. Moral entrepreneurship is a new role in society for the scientist-professional employed by an organization. The possibility for professionals to fulfill this role within organizations is greater for them, than for other organizational members, because of their access to privileged and/or "guilty" information.

Our society is truly an "employee" society with most all work being organizationally based. Occupational trends show that the proportion of salaried professionals is on the rise. In 1962, 40 percent of all scientists were employed by business and industry. In 1974 that figure had grown to 60.3 percent (Bureau of Census, 1976). I suspect it is even higher today, particularly with academic employment less available and considerably less lucrative. This phenomenon has been described as resulting in a movement from the classic concept of professions which emphasize service to individuals in time of crisis, to a more contemporary connotation of professions as "technocratic" with the primary role of catering to system needs (Krause, 1971). At any rate, there is no question that a larger portion of professional work is now done in organizational settings.

WHISTLE BLOWING AND MORAL ENTREPRENEURSHIP

Whistle blowing can be defined as the protest of an employee who, believing that the public interest overrides the interest of the organization he serves, publicly exposes the organization's involvement in corrupt, illegal, fraudulent or harmful activity (Nader et al., 1972: 5). The employee, resolving that his societal allegiance supersedes his organizational allegiance, acts to inform outsiders or legal authorities of illegal or harmful acts by the corporation or agency in which he/she has a work role. Examples of illegal or harmful activity include age and racial discrimination, sale of adulterated products, price fixing, and other acts in restraint of trade (e.g., bribery).

Becker's (1963) concept of moral entrepreneurship is akin to that of whistle blowing. The former is viewed as deviance defining activity in which its participants are viewed as coming out of the tradition of crusading reformers engaged in rule creation or rule enforcement.[2] The rule creator is interested in the content of rules and feels that "nothing can be made right in the world until rules are made to correct it" (1963:48). Enforcement begins when those who want a rule enforced publicly bring the infraction to the attention of others. Moral entrepreneurship is also the result of personal motivation on the part of the entrepreneurs. That is, they see some advantage to exposing the deviance.

Neither Nader nor Becker explicitly discusses the relation of professional/scientist to whistle blowing or moral entrepreneurship. Nader, by implication, lumps all categories of employees into one classification for his discussion while Becker sees only a peripheral relation of professionals to deviance defining activity. They are only involved when called upon as experts to contribute their specialized knowledge in drawing up legislation or to lend their presumed prestige in support of certain legal actions (Becker, 1963). In other words, they serve only a supportive or political role which is consistent with the traditional function of the scientist.

A second deficiency of Nader's and Becker's discussions is their one-dimensional emphasis on the individual-psychological level of analysis, thereby neglecting structural variables. Nader refers to conscience and conscientiousness while Becker talks of personal interest and the private evaluation of rules. There are other environmental factors which influence a professional's choice on the extent to which he/she will participate in moral entrepreneurship. Granted, there is an interactional process which takes place prior to any act or subsequent acts of moral entrepreneurship. However, this processs is not only conditioned by socio-psychological factors, but also by factors present in the larger environment, the professional or occupational culture, and the structural conditions of the organizations.

One final distinction must be made with regard to whistle blowing and moral entrepreneurship. Moral entrepreneurship need not be simply an "either/or" or an "all or none" activity on the part of the scientist. That is, there are degrees of moral entrepreneurship which vary by the extent of visibility (i.e., known to be associated with deviance exposure) and the amount of information he/she is willing to give out. Watergate's "Deep Throat" gave considerable information but his identity was unknown. Henry Durham exposed Lockheed's mismanagement of its contracts for the C-5A military transport and was branded a "turncoat" and his life was actually threatened as a result of his assuming maximum visibility. Variation is also conditioned by the extent of access to regulators or those agencies which can stimulate rule enforcement activity. It is not enough to simply "know" of the deviance; a prospective whistle blower must also know who to contact in law enforcement in order to have something done about the illegal act. Not only must the whistle blower have support from enforcement agencies, but evidence of support from colleagues, professional associations, or the general public also contribute to whether or not an act of whistle blowing will take place. Finally, the extent of moral entrepreneurship varies by the perceived ratio of costs to benefits. Thus, the greater the visibility or publicly acknowledged association with exposing the deviance, the greater the potential personal and occupational costs or risks to the whistle blower.

Thus, on the one extreme, a professional may not be willing to expose deviant organizational practices at all, even if he is aware of their existence. On the other hand, he may do whatever is necessary to make full disclosure. An example of the latter is George E. Holt, a computer engineer, who exposed the government's efforts to develop a vast computer network designated as FEDNET. This system was to contain information on U.S. citizens. His disclosure was made in a letter to President Nixon. Even though the project was eventually scrapped, Holt, a veteran of 22 years of meritorious service in the General Services Administration, was fired from his job.

There are other alternatives to the polar extremes. For example, deviant activities may be discussed with one or two colleagues and only take the form of "beefing" and seeking minimal social support. A second form of "in house" exposure is bringing the awareness of deviance to one's supervisor or a person of influence in the organization who may be able to offer an explanation or make a change. This could be viewed as acting on the organization's behalf, that is, protecting the organization before others find out. It could be viewed as a potential source of blackmail (e.g., "promote me, or else"). This, however, is an assertive action establishing the relation to exposure activities and the result could be a label of "trouble maker" or even an eventual job loss. A third form of exposure activity involves sharing awareness with outsiders, without having the observer explicitly or publicly associated with the act. Jack Anderson's sources fit this mold. Very often this is how academicians, "free professionals" and news media get information on deviant organizational activities.[3] But, risk is extremely variable depending upon the recipient's effort to maintain the source's confidentiality. The key Watergate informant known as "Deep Throat" seems to have taken less risk than Butterfield, who made the original revelation on impropriety in the White House. If it were not for conduits of information existing between organizational members and media sources, a great deal would be lost in the way of public or scientific information. Exposure by this means has traditionally been a source of control on organizations. The target of the information has to be one which is viewed as being a source of regulation or have the ability to enforce sanctions on the whistle blower. Otherwise moral entrepreneurship is nothing more than thrill-seeking behavior. However, the risk is even greater in this type of moral entrepreneurship if discussed, for the professional has violated all canons of organizational loyalty by his disclosure to outsiders. Loyalty is highly valued in organizational settings with discretions often punishable by demotion or termination.

Thus, there are four categories of moral entrepreneurship beyond total nonparticipation. Two are internal categories, i.e., inter-colleague exposure and upward exposure; exposure to outsiders forms the base for the other two types. These are (1) clandestine exposure to media or regulatory sources and (2) full visibility, public disclosure. Table 1 presents these types along the dimensions of visibility and risk. It is possible to assert that these can be sequential steps eventually leading to full disclosure. The lateral or vertical dimensions also exhibit some variations depending on the seriousness of the whistle blowing and the goal of that act. That is, one may talk to peers about a deviant act only to obtain status in their eyes and the recipient peers may not know of your intent. On the other hand, exposure may be

Table 1 / Types of Moral Entrepreneurship by Visibility and Risk

Type of Moral Entrepreneural Activity	Visibility to Sanctioning Agent	Risk/Cost to Whistle-Blower
NONE	NONE	NONE
Internal: Intercolleague Exposure	Minimal	Minimal
Internal: Vertical Exposure To Superiors	Medium	High
External: Clandestine Exposure to Outsiders	Minimal	High, if caught Low, if anonymous
External: Full Public Disclosure	High	Maximal

directed at someone who knows of the deviance in order to enhance one's status in the organization. Table 2 provides some detail on these variations.

The remainder of the paper presents a discussion of how existence and operation of certain socio-cultural variables might affect the type and degree of moral entrepreneurship activity on the part of professionals in organizations.

CONDITIONS FOR MORAL ENTREPRENEURSHIP

Before delineating the conditions affecting moral entrepreneurship it is necessary to clarify just who qualifies as a "professional" in an organizational setting. A salaried, organizationally employed mem-

Table 2 / Direction of Exposure by Knowledgeability of Target

Direction	Naive Target	Knowing Target
Lateral	1. Beefing	1. Beefing
	2. Support for problem solving—what to do	2. Support for problem solving
	3. Status Charm—gossip	3. Claim to peer status
Vertical	1. Org. Loyalty—clean up before exposure	1. Org. Loyalty
	2. Status vehicle—undercut supervisor in hope of getting his position	2. Potential blackmail (Self or altruistic motivated)
		3. Claim to peer status

ber of an occupational category usually designated as professional by census categories, e.g., research scientist, engineer, accountant, lawyer, physician, is the subject of our analysis. The "free," self-employed professional is not of concern. Neither are we specifically concerned with someone who enters a system as a change agent to make administrative judgments to promote productivity. These figures will not ordinarily go through the stages of moral entrepreneurship inasmuch as their job is predefined as one who is to discover and eliminate deviance of any type. This analysis applies to the professional who depends on an organization, not clients, for financial remuneration.

The General Environment[4]

Economic alternatives, particularly job opportunities, make up perhaps the most crucial factor in moral entrepreneurship. In times of economic recession, when jobs are not readily available and unemployment, even among professional and white collar workers, is high, moral entrepreneurship is less likely to occur. For example, in 1970 unemployment among engineers was at an all time high. To expose organizational deviance at this time could have meant a job loss and unemployment. In the late 1960's when our economy was pumped up, moral entrepreneurship, particularly on campuses, was a common occurrence. The latter was not, however, always directed at the employing organization.

A second dimension of the general environment which is conducive to moral entrepreneurship is cultural or value support for such activity. Currently, there is a great deal of concern about violations of basic human rights by large scale organizations, particularly corporate and governmental systems. A low trust level currently exists between the general public and institutional representatives. This type of value climate is, therefore, supportive of deviance exposure. It is also to be noted that professional activity is ordinarily highly valued and this lends more credence to public statements by members of these occupations.

The existence of pressure groups and social movements to serve as vehicles of support for moral entrepreneurship makes up the political dimension of the general environment. Deviance exposure activity can find ready allegiance from organizations such as Common Cause, Nader's Raiders, the Committee for Effective Congress, and many consumer groups. There is also a great deal of legislation that can be alluded to by moral entrepreneurs for their support. Affirmative action, public disclosure, and civil rights legislation provided the substance and sanction for a moral enterprise of exposure. There was a time when individuals who wished to challenge organizational practices had no way to equalize resources, therefore power, but these agencies and the legislation provide such an access.

Pre-Professional Experience

This dimension is ordinarily not considered in discussions of professional socialization or activity. The literature seems to assume that a person enters professional training *tabula rasa* and that his attitudes toward life and work only take shape under the influence of professional socialization.[5] However, factors such as family background, social status, and experience in leadership may have an effect on the extent of moral entrepreneural activity. For example, most student protesters came from liberal families which promoted critical assessment of life and institutions. Since most professionals come from middle and upper class backgrounds placing a high value on education, it is highly possible that persons from these backgrounds will be more likely to engage in critical behavior. Blau and Scott (1962) have shown that professionals tend to be more critical than nonprofessionals of organizational practices.

There is not time to discuss in detail the influence of other factors in this category on the probability for moral entrepreneurship. However, the point needs to be made that pre-employment–preprofessionalization experiences can be factors in the decision to participate in exposing deviant organizational activities. It is also highly probable that it is in these pre-employment experiences that one learns the cost-benefit ratio for any type of independent activity. That is, he learns a value of investing in society and the risks or values involved in threatening that investment. In addition, the values and risks of collective orientation or self-interest may also be internalized during this experiential, learning phase of one's life.

Specific Environment: Professional-Occupational Factors

It is here that we must consider four major factors which must be present in the specific environment for moral entrepreneurship to take place. First, in the course of performing occupational tasks, there must be access to privileged information. That is, the deviant behavior must be visible to the professional or he/she could not expose it. Second, inter-organizational professional support available from colleagues (though they may not be willing to be party to the exposure) may be an important source for both moral and technical support. Third, there should be support emanating from the profession itself. That is, the larger professional body, e.g., American Association for the Advancement of Science (AAAS), needs to provide resource support for entrepreneurship. Where standards conflict the professional can often marshal wide social support to countenance criticism of or deviations from organizational policy. Such behavior is particularly troublesome for the bureaucracies due to the prestige of professionals both within and outside the structure. Currently, unionization of professionals, particularly teachers and now medical doctors, ultimately means the creation of a very potent force in support of moral entrepreneurship unless, as some maintain, unionization detracts from the image and status of professionals. If these supports are not present, deviance exposure is very risky and costly, unless anonymity can be maintained.

A final factor which must be considered in the professional environment is the degree to which the practitioner has internalized the professional norms of collective or service orientation and independence. High internalization makes it difficult to endure organizational activity which may be harmful to individuals. On the other hand, it is possible for organizational loyalty to become very significant thereby diminishing the probability of moral entrepreneural activity. In addition, if professional training moves from the "independent" model to the "organizational" model of performance, moral entrepreneurship will be less likely to occur. The latter promotes a higher role commitment to institutional loyalty than professional loyalty.[6] Organizations and professions adapt to each other to reduce the potential or actuality of conflict (Kornhauser, 1960). The degree to which the professional practitioner views these various adaptations as favorable, the less likely he is to expose organizational deviance. However, deviance exposure becomes more likely as the conflict of bureaucratic and professional standards and control structures increases. Thus, within an organization, structural conduciveness must exist for moral entrepreneurship to take place. This also includes access to privileged information as mentioned above.

Line-staff hostility and the degree to which professional activity is positively sanctioned, as through salary, attendance at meetings, and the degree of autonomy allowed, are also factors that affect the probability of moral entrepreneurship. Conversely, the greater the efforts at cooptation, particularly as expressed in organizational rewards, the less likely is deviance exposure by members of the professional staff.

The discussion above certainly does not represent an exhaustive discussion of factors that influence moral entrepreneural activity. Neither is it possible to empirically demonstrate a relation between the degree to which these factors are present and the type or extent

Figure 1 / Factors Influencing Moral Entrepreneurship

of moral entrepreneurship. Only what appear to be the most important facts are included in Figure 1, a graphic representation of the conceptual model emphasized here.

CONCLUSIONS

Certainly it also remains to empirically demonstrate the interrelationships among pre-professional experiences, specific environmental factors, general environmental factors, and the extent of moral entrepreneurship. The exposure of organizational deviance or the threat of exposure—given the known existence of environmental supports—can act as a deterrent on such organization activity. Certainly the reaction of the organization being accused of deviant behavior is a necessary component to making the accusation of deviance visible and meaningful. The adversary situation is conducive to full disclosure and ultimately retribution.

For the person who engages in entrepreneural activity, the cost may be high. On the other hand, sufficient environmental supports may ultimately be the source of yet greater benefits—maybe even hero worship, martyrship, or immortality. Since there seems to be little deterrence to organizational deviance at this time, with laws and sanctions virtually inoperative, internal moral entrepreneurial activity coupled with sufficient and environment resource support may be the necessary alternative for effective control. Perhaps people who make a public disclosure are ones who are so upset at the organization (either because of the deviance or for some unrelated activity) that the loss of their jobs is not perceived as a particularly great cost. A clean break with the organization may have positive personal value, which balances financial loss. Also, some do not go the full disclosure route unless they are confident that economic alternatives exist for them.

As is usually the case with sociological topics, more research is needed. However, the prediction of moral entrepreneurship should remain an empirical question. That is, research should *not* be done to determine the characteristics of those who are likely to engage in this type of behavior. If these traits could be acknowledged in advance, potential whistle blowers would never get hired, thereby eliminating or neutralizing a significant source of organization control.

References

Becker, Howard
   1963   *The Outsiders.* Glencoe, Ill.: The Free Press
Becker, Howard, Blanche Geer, Everett Hughes, and Anselm Strauss
   1961   *Boys in White: Student Culture in a Medical School.* Chicago: University of Chicago Press.
Ben-David, Joseph
   1971   *The Scientist's Role in Society.* Englewood Cliffs: Prentice-Hall.
Blau, Peter M., and W. R. Scott
   1962   *Formal Organizations.* San Francisco: Chandler.
Bureau of the Census
   1976   *Statistical Abstract of The United States.* U.S. Department of Commerce.
Clinard, Marshall
   1979   *Illegal Corporate Behavior.* U.S. Department of Justice.
Committee on Governmental Affairs
   1978   *The Whistleblowers.* Washington D.C.: Senate.
Harvard Law School
   1976   "Development in the law-corporate crimes regulating corporate behavior through criminal sanctions." *Harvard Law Review* 92: 1227–1377.
Ermann, M. David, and Richard J. Lundman
   1978   "Deviant acts by complex organizations: Deviance and social control at the organizational level of analysis." *The Sociological Quarterly* 19:55–67.
Goran, Morris
   1974   *Science and Anti-Science.* Ann Arbor: Ann Arbor Science Publishers, Inc.

Gouldner, Alvin
   1958 "Cosmopolitans and locals: Toward an analysis of latent social roles—I." *Administrative Science Quarterly* 2: 281–306.
Hall, Richard H.
   1972 *Organizations: Structure and Process.* Englewood Cliffs: Prentice-Hall.
   1968 "Professionalization and bureaucratization." *American Sociological Review* 33: 92–104.
Kornhauser, William
   1960 *Scientists in Industry.* N.Y.: Harper.
Krause, Elliot A.
   1971 *The Sociology of Occupations.* Boston: Little, Brown and Company
Marcson, Simon
   1960 *The Scientist in American Industry.* N.Y.: Harper.
Merton Robert L.
   1957 *Social Theory and Social Structure.* New York: Free Press.
Nader, Ralph, Peter Petkas, and Kate Blackwell (eds.)
   1972 *Whistle Blowing.* N.Y.: Grossman Publishers.
Ogren R. W.
   1973 "The ineffectiveness of the criminal sanction in fraud and corruption cases: Losing the battle against white collar crime." *American Criminal Law Review* 11: 959–988.
Pelz, Donald C., and F. M. Andrews
   1966 *Scientists in Organizations.* New York: Wiley & Sons.
Peters, Charles, and Taylor Branch
   1972 *Blowing the Whistle: Dissent in the Public Interest.* New York: Praeger.
Price, D. K.
   1967 *The Scientific Estate.* Cambridge, Mass.: Harvard University Press.
Schur, Edwin M.
   1969 *Our Criminal Society.* Englewood Cliffs: Prentice-Hall.
Sorenson, James E., and Thomas L. Sorenson
   1974 "The conflict of professionals in bureaucratic organizations." *Administrative Science Quarterly* 19: 98–106.
Stone, Christopher, D.
   1975 *Where the Law Ends.* N.Y.: Harper & Row.
Storer, Norman W.
   1966 *The Social System of Science.* N.Y.: Holt, Rinehart and Winston.

Notes

   1. For a detailed description of the trials and the tribulations of individuals who have engaged in whistle blowing, see Peters and Branch (1972) and Committee on Governmental Affairs (1978).

   2. While it is not the purpose to present a detailed analysis of Becker's concept of moral entrepreneurship, further distinctions can be made. It is true that moral entrepreneurs may create rules or stimulate rule enforcement. They may also serve to stifle rule enforcement or even act to have a rule repealed. Thirdly, exposure of deviant activity may not be strictly law-related but also apply to norm violation that is not

defined in statute. Perhaps, for example, the war protesters of the 1960's were moral entrepreneurs in their efforts to interrupt the government's war making and conscription powers.

3. It is possible that exposure to news media would call for even more commitment to the act of moral entreprenenurship than would exposure to fellow professionals in academia or in free-lance activities. Professional associations may provide a nexus for trust that does not exist between, for example, engineer and journalist. For the purposes of this paper the distinction will not be drawn since exposure to outsiders is the commonality that is of interest at this time. A more complete discussion of the function of professional reference groups for colleagues employed in organizational settings is presented by Blau and Scott (1962: 71–74). Little or no work is available on intra-organizational professional reference groups.

4. The distinction of general and specific environments comes from Hall (1972) in his discussion of organization-environment relations.

5. This seems to be the case of the most prominent works on professional socialization, those of Merton (1957) and Becker et al. (1961).

6. Gouldner's (1958) distinction of cosmopolitan and local makes sense here. The local, being more loyal to the organization, is less likely to create a fuss about any deviant organizational activities. He could easily neutralize his awareness by asserting that it is not part of his job or that he doesn't want to jeopardize a good thing.

54 / Policing Physicians: Practitioner Fraud and Abuse in a Government Medical Program

HENRY N. PONTELL
PAUL D. JESILOW
GILBERT GEIS

When professionals, such as doctors, violate laws designed to constrain their autonomy—laws that, in effect, tell them how to run their practices—at least three issues are raised. First, those charged with enforcing the laws have to develop tactics to combat the expertise of the professional. Second, punishing a law-violating professional may result in the withdrawal of a crucial service from innocent parties. Third, the intelligence and social standing of the errant professional, and his or her ability to cast shady actions in a decent light, make effective detection and prosecution of violations difficult—a problem common to white-collar crime in general.

This paper examines patterns of control over physicians who obtain funds from Medi-Cal, the state of California's Medicaid program. Medi-cal is the second largest health-care reimbursement system in the United States, second only to the state of New York's. We look at how authorities define and identify fraud and abuse, the obstacles that hinder the enforcement of laws, the problems associated with sanctions, and, especially, how professional values and the power of medical doctors influence the control process.

When physicians engage in fraud and abuse benefit programs they violate both professional norms and the law (Lanza-Kaduce, 1980). Their behavior fits the classification that Katz has labelled "pure" white-collar crime:

> In the purest "white-collar" crimes, white-collar social class is used: (1) to diffuse criminal intent into ordinary occupational routines so that it escapes unambiguous expression in any specific, discrete behavior; (2) to accomplish the crime without incident or effects that furnish presumptive evidence of its occurrence before the criminal has been identified; and (3) to cover up the culpable knowledge of participants through concerted action that allows each to claim ignorance (1979:435).

As we show, it is easy for physicians to "diffuse criminal intent into ordinary occupational routines" while participating in government medical benefit programs. Physicians as a professional group enjoy a high level of autonomy in practicing medicine, which makes the search for evidence of wrongdoing both difficult and complex. There may be little "culpable knowledge of participants" in physician fraud and abuse cases where only a single physician is involved. Moreover, information from patients does not provide substantial proof in most cases. One doctor, who was taped by undercover agents pretending to be interested in buying his business, highlighted most of these points when he explained how he would defend himself against accusations of wrongdoing:

> I don't remember—I don't even remember what I put down for 95 percent of my patients . . . you create doubts. Who can disprove it? The nurse? Do you think she can remember any better than you? You know the type of intellect patients have. . . . I never put down for a CBC [complete blood count] or a SED [sedimentation] rate . . . if I don't draw blood. They remember if you give an injection. I don't like going through the routine, but it must be done. . . . Even if they show you the worst piece of paper you ever wrote, there is no way to prove a thing (U.S. Congress: Senate, 1976:59).

STRUCTURAL FEATURES RELATED TO FRAUD

The structure, organization, and administration of Medicare/Medicaid[1] contain an implicit fiscal incentive for physicians to overtreat and overdiagnose. The fee-for-service nature of government benefit programs provides one example. Under this policy, the doctor is reimbursed according to a schedule established by the government. Fee-for-service reimbursement is a major vehicle for fraudulent and abusive practices, such as billing for services never rendered; "upgrading" (billing for a service more extensive than that actually provided); overtreating; "ping-ponging" (referring the patient to another physician when there is no need for additional work); scheduling unnecessary visits; and "ganging" (billing for services to members of the same family on the same day. This generally occurs when one member of a family is accompanied by another, usually a mother and child. The doctor also "treats" the individual who has come with the ill person, though there is no complaint, and submits a bill for both persons). The fee-for-service structure of medical practice, incorporated in the government-funded medical system, thus provides a "crime-facilitative environment" (Needleman and Needleman, 1979). If physicians were paid beforehand a stipulated sum for each patient on their roster, the profit from such practices would largely be eliminated.

Although the structure of the programs may encourage fraud among physicians, these incentives do not in themselves explain fraudulent practices. One doctor may cheat the government, while another may remain satisfied with a lower—but honest—income. Government regulations for benefit programs are themselves the predisposing factors, or raw materials, for fraud and abuse. One California physician defrauded the Medi-Cal program by treating many poor patients. Prior to the inauguration of Medi-Cal, he had rendered free services for those who could not afford to pay. Without Medi-Cal, he probably would have continued to offer free treatments.

Tension between the government and the medical profession over Medicaid/Medicare may go far in explaining patterns of fraud and abuse. Our interviews with doctors, as well as other studies (Davidson, 1982; Garner *et al.*, 1979; Jones and Hamburger, 1976; Stevens and Stevens, 1974), reveal widespread dissatisfaction with the repayment system. Physicians claim they receive from Medicare only one-half of what they would normally charge patients. They also complain of excessive red tape and paperwork involved in the government system.

Colombotos *et al.* (1975) found that just over half of a national sample of physicians favored national health insurance. The physicians overwhelmingly preferred that the program be administered by a private third party rather than the government, and three-quarters supported a fee-for-service form of reimbursement. Such attitudes are partly attributable to the ideology and norms of the medical profession, especially the desire to operate free of government intervention. But they also have implications for the frequency of abuse and fraud in benefit programs.

Many physicians have expanded beyond their office and hospital practice into other medical domains, including laboratories, pharmacies, medical supply stores, and nursing homes. The complexity and size of this world provides many opportunities for fraud (Meier and Geis, 1979). Hospitals performing a myriad of functions offer the most criminogenic structure.

In sum, it appears that strategies to control physicians in government medical benefit programs must deal with: (1) a fee-for-service system which invites fraud and abuse; (2) a professional environment in which physicians resent the lowered fees and additional red tape and paperwork necessary to receive reimbursement for treating the poor; and (3) a complex world of overlapping ownerships and financial involvement in medically related businesses that makes abuses and crimes difficult to detect, and, at the same time, renders it convenient for those involved to abuse the system by taking advantage of overlapping interests.

THE MEDI-CAL PROGRAM

This paper focuses on official interpretations of abuses in California's Medi-Cal program. The program was implemented in March 1966 by the California Legislature, in response to the availability of federal funds from the 1965 Title XIX amendments to the Social Security Act. The program was designed to provide health care and related services to recipients of public assistance and the elderly.

We interviewed Medi-Cal personnel and officials in the Bureau of Medical Quality Assurance, the state's medical licensing board, in 1981 and 1982. Official reports and case files provided numerical, procedural, and attitudinal information. Within the state's Department of Health Services, where Medi-Cal is administered, our interviews were concentrated most heavily in the Surveillance and Utilization Review (SUR) Branch of the Audits and Investigations Division. This office is responsible for the integrity of the Medi-Cal program. It plays a major role in detecting fraud and abuse by screening claims and determining billing patterns. This is accomplished, using computers, by comparing specific physicians to a norm established by other physicians in similar circumstances. When a large discrepancy exists and fraud is suspected, the SUR Branch refers the case to investigators who establish if a crime has been committed. If it has, the Medi-Cal Fraud Unit takes over. Located in the state's Department of Justice, this unit was established in July 1978, pursuant to Public Law 95–142, Section 17. It investigates crimes and, where it believes it is warranted, brings criminal charges against physicians.

The SUR Branch plays a major role in officially defining fraudulent and abusive practices by physicians (as well as other health care providers) in California; the unit also channels subsequent enforcement activity. SUR personnel operate in the belief that major losses to the Medi-Cal program are not due to fraud but rather to overutilization and abuse of the system. Thus, most sanctions against physicians involve administrative rather than criminal actions. The work of the SUR Branch, therefore, is central to the enforcement process.

The SUR Branch

The SUR Branch was established in 1977 with a mandate to "detect overutilization, abuse, and fraud of Medi-Cal providers and beneficiaries and to initiate appropriate corrective actions" (California Department of Health Services, 1978:1). It has two main organizational units for dealing with abuse by physicians. The Case Detection and Development Section (CDDS) identifies violations through case referrals from outside sources (patients, nurses, bookkeepers, physicians) and by computer reports which identify suspicious physicians. After an internal review of cases, commonly referred to as "desk work-ups," those believed to warrant further investigation are referred to one of two field office medical teams made up of a physician, nurse, and administrative analyst. These teams, which comprise the second organizational unit, visit the physician's office and examine his or her records to determine the necessity of services rendered, whether the services were of acceptable medical quality, and whether the physician's files meet Medi-Cal standards. Depending upon the results of this investigation, SUR officials can take any of the following actions: (1) warn the physician about incorrect billing; (2) demand reimbursement for overpayments; (3) establish a special claims procedure under which full documentation of services rendered must accompany all future bills; (4) demand that the physician seek the SUR's authorization before accepting non-emergency patients; (5) suspend the physician from the Medi-Cal program, the most difficult sanction to achieve; (6) refer the case to the Medi-Cal Fraud Unit for possible criminal prosecution; and (7) refer the case to the state licensing agency for possible disciplinary action. SUR officials said that such actions saved the Medi-Cal program about $4 million dollars in 1981, a figure equivalent to the SUR Branch's operating budget for that year.

Table 1 summarizes SUR Branch activities in 1981. On-site investigations were carried out on 49 physicians with individual practices, 31 optometrists, and 23 dentists. Of the 217 cases closed (where some final action was taken), only four—all of them against physicians—were referred for either program suspension or criminal investigation. Requests for recoupment of undocumented program payments was the most frequently applied form of control. The only other type of control used in 1981 was SPEAR (Special Payment Evaluation and Review) action.[2] Under this sanction, the doctor must send SUR officials full documentation of services performed over a specified level. If the physician does not comply, the Medi-Cal program is under no obligation to reimburse him or her for services. This tactic was usually reserved for physicians who did not heed warning letters, and who displayed blatant disparities in billing practices.

Setting Up Shop

Before the SUR Branch was established, the Audits and Investigation Division responded to complaints and referrals. These primarily in-

Table 1 / Summary of SUR Branch Activities, 1981

Provider Type	On-Site Review	Cases Closed*	Referral For Suspension/Investigation	Dollars Demanded	Spear Actions
Physician	49	52	4	508,001	24
Pharmacy	20	25	0	21,720	0
Optometry	31	64	0	7,231	1
Clinical Lab	4	11	0	71,493	0
Medical Clinic	11	9	0	224,654	1
Dental	23	20	0	32,609	0
Psychologist	2	3	0	0	0
Podiatry	1	2	0	17,117	0
Medical Group	12	7	0	8,260	0
Medical Lab	1	5	0	1,591,587	0
Total	156	217	4	$2,484,672	26

*Sometimes this category exceeds the number of on-site reviews due to the fact that some cases were opened during the previous year and thus represent carry-overs.

volved suspected criminal fraud. The division did not employ health professionals, which hampered its ability to detect less blatant abuses of the Medi-Cal program. With the creation of the SUR Branch, officials aimed more at "systematic detection" rather than the "hit and miss" approach used previously.

Both before, and during, the early operation of the SUR Branch, the state delegated the control function to Blue Cross and Blue Shield, the private health insurance programs, whose job it was to review billing patterns against "peer group norms." (This review procedure was adopted by the Medicare system, and is still in use.) With Blue Cross and Blue Shield in charge of reviewing billing, the state was omitted from detection and enforcement activities until 1978, when increased budget allocations allowed the state's Department of Health to assume responsibility for postpayment review and to provide new contract specifications for fiscal intermediaries. The Computer Sciences Corporation took over the responsibility of fiscal intermediary from Blue Cross and Blue Shield, and the SUR Branch assumed program control functions. With this major restructuring, the state substantially increased its involvement in the control of fraudulent and abusive practices.

Establishing Procedures

The relative power of the different health care professions, as well as the influence of the medical socieities, are both evident in the evolution of specific procedures used to detect fraud and abuse. Although random on-site audits were, at the time of this research, conducted in California for pharmacists and optometrists, for example, such reviews were ended for physicians in mid-1977, soon after the SUR Branch began functioning. Officials cited three reasons for this surveillance selectivity: (1) Initial attempts to use this tactic against physicians produced no results: nine randomly selected reviews uncovered no abuses of the program. (2) Organizational resources could be better deployed elsewhere. (3) "Medical societies objected to [on-site review] and strongly urged that it be used only where there is apparent cause" (California Department of Health Services, 1978:2).

Local medical societies neither strongly support nor greatly resent the activities of state control agencies. Most societies cooperate with authorities, though this is not always the case. One successful method employed early on by state officials for gaining the support of uncooperative medical societies was to present them with the most glaring and blatant cases of abuse by physicians in their geographic areas. Medical societies usually do not report suspected cases of fraud and abuse to authorities, though they sometimes counsel members who have administrative charges brought against them and refer them to legal assistance. The medical societies are notoriously reluctant to decertify physicians and rarely view even criminal violations of Medi-Cal regulations as grounds for removal from the profession. Nonetheless, investigators constantly court the medical societies; their cooperation, however lukewarm and marked by inertia, is regarded as necessary for the adequate operation of the Medi-Cal program.

Government control units need the cooperation of medical societies to inform physicians about program policies and guidelines and to help insure that regulations are taken seriously. Officials believe that if they "go too far" in regulating physicians in the program, they are likely to forfeit the support of medical societies, and that this would result in a lowered rate of participation by physicians in the Medi-Cal program. This in turn could further restrict the sources of health care for the population served by Medi-Cal. It could also raise costs, since patients would likely go for care to more expensive facilities, such as the emergency department of hospitals, if a Medi-Cal physician was not available.

Medi-Cal officials learned that they had to be very careful in working up allegations against physicians. The first few cases brought before an administrative hearing officer were turned away for lack of sufficient evidence. Without a foolproof case, officials found that court procedures proved futile, given the resources accused physicians can bring to their defense. Officials decided to pursue cases only in the most blatant instances of wrongdoing, and where full documentation was available.

ENFORCEMENT PATTERNS

Fraud and abuse are hard to identify in medicine because of the technical nature of the field, the different treatment styles of physicians, and the relative ease with which offenses may be covered up, given the privileges and status of physicians. Such privileges include a large amount of professional autonomy, which makes it difficult for officials to determine whether abuse or fraud actually took place. One high-ranking Medi-Cal official, himself a physician, said:

> Our major problem is not fraud in terms of dollars or impact on the program. Our major problem is abuse, and I would prefer to say that it's nonfraudulent abuse. That is, where a provider or physician does more tests than he would if the patient were paying the bill, it becomes very difficult in most cases to say what is or is not abuse. There is a tendency to practice medicine more as an ideal, more complete, more thorough when you are not inhibited by the patient's ability to withstand the cost (Personal interview).

No one has yet proven this proposition, nor has a general consensus been reached on what practicing medicine as an "ideal" means; at the same time, the foregoing quotation represents an important official stance concerning the control of Medi-Cal violations. That more acts are designated abuses rather than frauds likely has to do with the way official definitions affect enforcement activities. These definitions in turn can be influenced, both blatantly and subtly, by the power of the medical profession. For example, when officials responsible for producing evidence against physicians are themselves physicians, they are more prone to regard violations as abuses. This becomes especially pronounced when the officials learn that attempts to label acts as fraud without impregnable proof—where such level of proof is difficult to come by—will be fruitless.

Organizational Goals

The formal organizational goal of the SUR Branch is to assure the integrity of the Medi-Cal program. In some respects it is a policing institution which detects and sanctions improper activities. Because it oversees recoupment of excessive payments, it is also a revenue-producing system. And, insofar as it helps to redesign regulations and administrative methods of control, it is involved in planning and managerial efficiency.

The obstacles to pursuing cases of fraud and abuse help shape the SUR's official position in policing Medi-Cal. Officials did not see their most important function as punishing errant physicians but as recommending better management of the Medi-Cal program. They realized that to be effective they had to accommodate powerful professional groups which could be aroused by the threat of increased government control. Thus, the SUR Branch had to earn the acceptance of the medical societies. Not surprisingly, its administrative approach was designed "to prevent fraud and abuse rather than to merely punish it after it happens," an official said. He continued:

> We don't measure our success by how much money we get back for the state of California. We think that a large part of what we do should be educational and working with the profession to eliminate practices which should be eliminated. We're really not interested in putting all doctors behind bars, or sending them into bankruptcy. We're interested in correcting a situation where it needs correction and doing that in as professional a manner as we can, providing that we are not dealing with crooks. That's something else. They [crooked doctors] need everything we can throw at them. Most doctors are not crooks (Personal interview).

Even while adopting this basically non-punitive stance, officials expressed frustration with the nature of the organization of the medical profession and the vagueness of the basic goals of the control body. One administrator reflected the teleological uncertainty of his unit in the following terms:

> When we discover irregular practices that don't look like outright fraud, where there are practices which should be controlled or curbed so the program, the taxpayers, and the patients can be protected, we have to ask ourselves: "Well, what are we trying to accomplish? Are we here primarily to deprive them of their livelihood for a while, or are we here to get as much money back as we can? What are we here for? (Personal interview).

The Production of Fraud and Abuse

The serious practical difficulties in proving intent on the part of the physician in cases of fraud accounted in some measure for the higher proportion of abuses than frauds. Limited resources precluded any serious official attention to cases which might border on fraud, though blatant cases of fraud were sure to be met with formal action. Administrators, however, tried not to get involved in "the gray area of medical practice," the area where professional opinions could differ.

Charging for more complex and/or time-consuming services than were actually provided was the most frequent abuse uncovered. Such acts were not usually regarded as abuses, and almost never as frauds. Categories of treatment were vague, which made attempts to label such practices as fraud difficult. Even when the evidence seemed to clearly indicate that the doctor billed incorrectly for services, the matter may have become questionable later. Reliance on audits of patient records, for example, often proved unsatisfactory. An investigator explained why this was so:

> All we have to do is go into the office and we see something, a note, a two-liner, and maybe it's a brief one—and we say, "Doctor, you billed us for a big one, we paid for it, but we checked your records, and all they show is a brief one." And then the doctor says, "Look fellows, I'm too busy taking care of patients to spend all my time writing down a lot of crap for you bureaucrats. I've got to take care of these people." What he is saying is that he did a complete physical, but didn't have time to put it all down. Do you call that fraud? No way. How are you going to prove it?"

The same official added:

> It is a great challenge to say what is or is not abuse and/or fraud of the program. For example, we know of instances of "overuse," but how much of it is due to a physician's genuine desire to do whatever he or she can for a patient without any financial obstacles and how much of it is due to his or her personal desire to gain wealth? (Personal interview).

The legal dividing line between abuse and fraud, which officials were keenly aware of, is the legal doctrine of intent (Edwards, 1955). Establishing intent was virtually impossible in most Medi-Cal cases. Abuse was relatively easier to prove since no evidence of intent was necessary. Abuse itself, however, was not always as clearcut as first appeared. Computers sometimes alerted investigators to cases which in fact showed sound reason for departing from the usual pattern.

> You may, for example, find somebody who does far more opthamology consultations than anybody else and looks suspicious. But, you check into this and find the opthalmologist is the only one within two hundred miles. With good reason, you close that case [and go on to] something else (Personal interview).

On other occasions, what originally looked like potential fraud was ultimately designated an abuse. For example, a California psychiatrist, sanctioned for Medi-Cal abuse, was paid approximately $9 per patient for one-and-one-half hour sessions of group psychotherapy. He signed 16 false claims for services rendered as the provider; in fact, his wife, a psychiatric nurse, led the sessions. Taken before the licensing agency for discipline, the psychiatrist argued that he had performed the services, although he was not present, since his wife worked under his supervision. He claimed that he thought the rules permitted him to do this. The licensing agency rejected his defense and suspended his license. The administrative report suggested that the psychiatrist was unfamiliar with the agency's requirements of the Medi-Cal program.

> Medi-Cal bulletins sent to his office ... were discarded by respondent without reading them. Respondent did not deliberately seek to defraud Medi-Cal; he simply lacked interest and was indifferent in keeping abreast of Medi-Cal rules and regulations. He casually concluded that since his wife was a qualified psychiatric nurse and rendered group psychotherapy under his supervision, that he qualified as the Medi-Cal provider for billing purposes. It appears that respondent's indifference was due, in part, to the fact that Medi-Cal patients constituted a minor portion of his professional income (California Department of Consumer Affairs, 1979).

Physicians generally did not have to fear that SUR investigators would seek information from patients. An official explained why:

> We have some highly intelligent, sophisticated, and well-educated patients on Medi-Cal. Generally, though, they're medically unsophisticated, and it is very difficult for them to make these kinds of determinations. It's difficult for them to say whether they were in the office at all on a specific date, rather than how long the doctor saw them. Relying on the patients' memory is not too good (Personal interview).

Sanctions

Suspending a doctor from the Medi-Cal program for abuse was very difficult to accomplish. It usually took a year or more to prepare a case, another year or two for a hearing, and yet another year to allow for appeal. Officials had to be certain that their cases were airtight, given the amount of time and resources involved and the uncertainty of the outcome. Thus, only the most flagrant instances of abuse and/or carelessness were pursued. One official noted:

> We better have a very strong case. We discovered that through experience—we lost some. We've backed off some and we've won a couple. But it's extremely difficult. We produce very few program suspensions. It's a tough process. The courts are not always in agreement as far as overwhelming evidence (Personal interview).

For these reasons, program administrators emphasized actions that could be taken without formal legal proceedings. For example, a physician was sometimes asked to supply copies of records and other program reports to substantiate patient visits over a certain amount.

> That's our single most effective tool. It acts rapidly, gets the message across quickly, curbs the abuse, and protects the program (Personal interview).

Program officials believed that enforcement activities had had a substantial impact on the Medi-Cal program: they were at least partially effective in identifying fraud and abuse, and in earmarking millions of dollars for recoupment. Yet officials did not know whether their actions had deterred abuses by other physicians.

SUMMARY

The work of the SUR Branch in policing the Medi-Cal program reflects a variety of crosscurrents that bear upon its mission. For one, the very organization of the program invites fraud. The fee-for-service delivery system in California offers physicians the chance to amass considerable gain with little risk. Diagnostic tests that have not been performed can easily be billed to the state, as can a variety of other spurious costs. The professional background of the physician affords strong protection against discovery. If such discovery does occur, there are a range of defensive tactics to safeguard against effective sanctions.

An alternative to the existing program would be prepaid health services for Medi-Cal recipients. Under a prepaid program, the state would have fixed costs, and the onus would be on the practitioner to deliver services within the price range for which he or she has contracted with the government agency. The problem here, of course, is that any reduction in the quantity and quality of care redounds to tbe financial benefit of the practitioner. It is not unlikely that fraud and abuse under such circumstances would take the form of substandard delivery of services, much as was true at the turn of the century when county sheriffs were paid by the numbers of prisoners under their care and skimped on food for their charges in order to save funds.

Authorities charged with policing the Medi-Cal program exhibit a number of behaviors that can be tied to the structure of the program. They are, for one, caught between literal interpretation of their mandate to maintain the program's integrity, and the practical goal of keeping their powerful constituents at bay. They cannot offend the medical societies by moving too forcefully against too many practitioners. Otherwise, they would risk forfeiting the societies' help in circulating and endorsing Medi-Cal guidelines. Nor can they adopt tough investigative tactics that physicians might regard as a violation of personal autonomy; physicians might simply refuse to participate in the Medi-Cal program. The use of false identity cards by undercover investigators to police physicians—a practice known as "shopping"—is not encouraged in California, though it is common in other states.

The evidence needed to win a court conviction for a criminal offense inhibit prosecution in all but the most blatant kinds of Medi-Cal fraud. Physicians have wide discretion in regard to the way they practice medicine; and few of their peers are wont to state publicly that they regard a given referral or diagnosis as patently unacceptable. The element of intent, essential for criminal action, is extraordinarily difficult to prove beyond a resonable doubt.

The quality of medical care available to both the wealthy and the poor truly involves matters of life and death. Fraud and abuse in a medical benefit program likely deprive some persons of the satisfactory treatment that they otherwise would receive. To fully understand this phenomenon, research is needed into the traits and behaviors of individuals who violate Medicaid laws and regulations, and the success of various tactics that have been employed in an attempt to control such behavior.

References

California Department of Consumer Affairs
   1979   Licensing file. Bureau of Medical Quality Assurance.
California Department of Health Services
   1978   "Surveillance utilization and review: The first six months." Staff report. Mimeographed.

Colombotos, John, Corinne Kirchner, and Michael Millman
  1975 "Physicians view national health insurance: A national study."
       Medical Care 13:369–396.
Davidson, Stephen M.
  1982 "Physician participation in Medicaid: Background and issues."
       Journal of Health Politics, Policy, and Law 6:703–717.
Edwards, John L.
  1955 Mens Rea in Statutory Offenses. New York: St. Martin's.
Garner, Dewey D., Winston C. Laio, and Thomas R. Sharpe
  1979 "Factors affecting physicians' participation in a state Medicaid pro-
       gram." Medical Care 17:43–58.
Jones, Michael W., and Bette Hamburger
  1976 "A survey of physician participation in and dissatisfaction with the
       Medi-Cal program." Western Journal of Medicine 124:75–83.
Katz, Jack
  1979 "Legality and equality: Plea bargaining in the prosecution of
       white-collar and common crimes." Law and Society Review
       13:431–459.
Lanza-Kaduce, Lonn
  1980 "Deviance among professionals: The case of unnecessary surgery."
       Deviant Behavior 1:333–359.
Meier, Robert F., And Gilbert Geis
  1979 "The white-collar offender." Pp. 428–445 in Hans Toch (ed.), Psy-
       chology of Crime and Criminal Justice. New York: Holt, Rinehart,
       and Winston.
Needleman, Martin L., and Carolyn Needleman
  1979 "Organizational crime: Two models of criminogenesis." The Socio-
       logical Quarterly 20:517–539.
Stevens, Robert, and Rosemary Stevens
  1974 Welfare Medicine in America: A Case Study of Medicaid. New
       York: Free Press.
U.S. Congress: Senate
  1976 Fraud and Abuse Among Practitioners Participating in the Medic-
       aid Program. Subcommittee on Long-Term Care, Special Commit-
       tee on Aging. 94th Congress, 1st session, Washington, D.C.: U.S.
       Government Printing Office.

Notes

1. Medicare and Medicaid, established in 1966, comprise two separate government medical benefit programs. Medicare is a federally-funded, national health insurance program for the aged, while Medicaid is a grant-in-aid program for the indigent in which the federal government shares costs with the states, based on per-capita income. Services provided to Medicaid recipients vary slightly among the states, but must include physician, hospital, laboratory, nursing home, and clinic services. Eligibility is determined by either the state office which administers the program or by the federal Social Security Administration. Stevens and Stevens (1974) provide an excellent analysis of the development of the Medicaid program.

2. This name was changed to Special Claims Review, in 1982, after the SUR Branch decided that SPEAR sounded unnecessarily ominous.

55 / Rehabilitating Social Systems and Institutions

DELOS H. KELLY

One fact that should be apparent now is that as long as failure, criminal, and deviant values and traditions exist, we will obtain outcomes commensurate with these phenomena. Correlatively, getting tough on crime and delinquency, for example, will not begin to get the job done, primarily because . . . those normative structures, conditions, and environments that guarantee the continued production of perceived deviation will remain virtually unchanged. Predictably, then, individuals will become exposed to and recruited out to play the role of the school failure, the young criminal, and the deviant. And some willing or unwilling recruits will . . . participate at times or drop out, while others will become regular members. These are some of the inescapable and basic facts the practitioners must begin to come to grips with. Unfortunately, . . . the efforts of these individuals (as well as the legislators, the policy makers, the professionals, and others) often do nothing more than to help perpetuate a medical-clinical-individualistic model of change and treatment. Thus, instead of looking within society to explain deviation, they look within the individual. Thereafter, the individual is taught how to cope or perhaps even feel good about himself or herself. And for some, a strategy of this type may work. For most, however, the efforts not only fail but the individuals experience a relapse; this is certainly understandable and most predictable.

THE CLINICAL MODEL REVISITED, OR BLAMING THE INDIVIDUAL

What the practitioners and others do not seem to recognize is that behavior viewed as criminal or deviant to them may be perceived as being acceptable and *normal* to the individual. In fact, . . . nonconformity is often the demanded response on the part of a group member. It may be recalled, for example, that Miller's gang boys received positive sanctions and rewards when they acted in accordance with the "focal concerns" (e.g., fighting and getting into trouble). More-

over, failure to conform, Miller claimed, would have probably resulted in exclusion from the gang. Similarly, Reiss', Cohen's, and Hargreaves' delinquent males were expected to live up to the values and
normative systems they were immersed in. The same held for the
nudists, prostitutes, mental patients, and the like. Observations such
as these contain an underlying message: Efforts at change focused
exclusively upon the individual are usually doomed from the start,
mainly because the policy makers and the practitioners fail to recognize that most individuals are actually responding normally to their
own *immediate* world. Thus, and even though people are removed,
treated, or incarcerated, they do, upon their return, become a part of
that environment once again. Quite clearly, Weinberg's nudists, Bryan's prostitutes, Scheff's mental patients, and Wallace's skid rowers
may leave; however, they must, upon their return, conform to the
existing normative structure. In a very real sense, the labeled deviants, criminals, delinquents, failures, and others become caught between two worlds: the conforming and the nonconforming; this dilemma creates some obvious problems for individuals so situated. If,
for example, an actor elects to go straight, he or she runs the risk of
being defined as a deviant and perhaps even rejected by his or her
peers. On the other hand, conformity to group norms and values may
produce further contact with social control agencies. What this often
means is that the individual must weigh the costs and benefits that
may ensue by virtue of involvement with one culture as opposed to
another. Ray's (1961) research on abstinence and relapse cycles
among heroin addicts offers an excellent illustration of how these
processes frequently operate.

Ray (1961:133) notes initially that the social world of addiction, like
any other world (e.g., the world of nudism or prostitution), can be
characterized by its organizational and cultural elements (e.g., its argot or language, market, pricing system). Not only this but commitment to the addict world provides the member with a major status
and associated identity. Addiction, however, often means that the addict will come to assume or exhibit other secondary status features.
For example, as the habit grows, most efforts will be oriented toward
obtaining drugs. Thus one may become careless about his or her appearance and cleanliness, and this frequently means that non-addicts
will begin to label the addict as a "bum," "degenerate," or lacking
"will power." Of significance here, at least as far as the potential for
change is concerned, is Ray's (1961:134) observation that even
though the addict is *aware* that he or she is being judged in terms of
these secondary characteristics or definitions and may, therefore, try
to *reject* or shed the labels, it is virtually impossible to do so, primarily
because most interactions and institutional experiences operate in

such a manner as to ratify the labels or definitions that have been applied to the addict. In fact, incarceration in correctional and mental facilities plays a most important role in the ratification process, particularly in view of the fact that contacts with non-addicts and their values often produce significant changes in one's identity or view of self. Ray (1961:133) comments on how the inmate and others may react to institutionalization:

> The addict's incarceration in correctional institutions has specific meanings which he finds reflected in the attitudes toward him by members of non-addict society and by his fellow addicts. Additionally, as his habit grows and the demands for drugs get beyond any legitimate means of supply, his own activities in satisfying his increased craving give him direct experiential evidence of the criminal aspects of self. These meanings of self as a criminal become internalized as he begins to apply criminal argot to his activities and institutional experiences. . . .

In effect, the inmate often accepts the criminal label and begins to act accordingly (i.e, becomes a career criminal); this same type of situation exists relative to the mental institution. However, instead of promoting the ideology that the client is criminal, the operating assumption is that the addict is psychologically inadequate or deficient. Thus, attempts are made to treat the individual's mind, usually through the use of some kind of counseling or group therapy. Contacts with psychiatric or psychological personnel produce another effect: They remind the addict that the institution and its staff view him or her as being mentally ill. In the words of one addict (Ray, 1961:134):

> When I got down to the hospital, I was interviewed by different doctors and one of them told me, "you now have one mark against you as crazy for having been down here." I hadn't known it was a crazy house. You know regular people [non-addicts] think this too.

And like the criminal, the addict may eventually accept the identity that is being imputed to him or her. Acceptance of this new status, as well as its associated labels, does reduce the odds that a cure can be effected, primarily because the addict becomes further entrenched within the addict and other (perceived) deviant cultures (e.g., the inmate).

Even though the overall prognosis for change is certainly poor, some addicts will experience a cure (i.e., remain free of drugs). The most likely candidates are drawn from the ranks of those addicts who, for some reason (e.g., incarceration), begin to question their addict identity, as well as the values of the drug world. Ray (1961:134) has stated this most succinctly:

an episode of cure begins in the *private thoughts* of the addict rather than in his overt behavior. These deliberations develop as a result of experience in specific situations of interaction with *important others* that cause the addict to experienced social stress, to develop some feeling of alienation from or dissatisfaction with his present identity, and to call it into question and examine it in all of its implications and ramifications. In these situations the *addict engages in private self-debate* in which he juxtaposes the values and social relationships which have become immediate and concrete through his addicition with those that are sometimes only half remembered or only imperfectly perceived. [Italics mine.]

Such questioning or self-debate may begin because of some kind of institutional contact (e.g., confinement in a hospital or correctional facility). It may also occur as a result of what Ray (1961:135) has termed a "socially disjunctive experience" with other addicts (e.g., an addict may be sent to buy drugs but never returns). More typically, however, the analysis of self or introspection emerges by virtue of some type of interaction or experience with a non-addict and/or the non-addict world; these provide the major catalytic elements for change (Ray, 1961:135).

Once withdrawal has been completed and a decision has been made to abstain (i.e., to structure an abstainer identity), the former addict is confronted immediately with some serious identity and self-image problems. During this initial period, Ray (1961:136) maintains that the individual becomes locked in a "running struggle" with problems of social identity. He or she is not sure of self; however, certain expectations are held about the future and its possibilities. Thus, the early stages of a cure are often characterized by substantial ambivalence; this is produced by the abstainer's efforts to find out where he or she stands relative to the addict and non-addict groups. Such ambivalence or lingering uncertainty may, according to Ray (1961:136), manifest itself through the type of pronouns used in discussions of addicts and their world (e.g., the use of "we" and "they" to refer to non-addicts as opposed to addicts), as well as in terms of how the attempted abstainer speaks of self (e.g., he or she may preface a statement with "When I was an addict. . . .").

Whether a former addict will continue to remain abstinent is, however, problematic. And critical to the success of any cure appears to be the role played by significant others (e.g., family members, spouses, friends, etc.). As Ray (1964:136) puts it: ". . . . Above all, he appears to desire ratification by significant others of his newly developing identity, and in his interactions during an episode of abstinence he expects to secure it." Stated somewhat differently, if others are generally supportive and caring, the chances are much greater that an abstainer identity can be built and perhaps maintained. Probably most important to the successful completion of this process are the reactions of one's immediate family members. If, as a result of perceived positive changes on the part of the individual (e.g., obtaining and keeping a job, improving appearance, professing an allegiance to non-addict values), the family's attitudes undergo modification, the probability of a long-term cure appears more likely (Ray, 1961:136). At this point Ray (1961:137) stresses the fact that attitudinal changes, whether they occur on the part of the abstainer or the family, are usually not enough to produce a cure. Rather, professed commitment to the non-addict life style and its values "must be grounded in action." In other words, the abstainer must, in his or her interactions with the non-addicts, be allowed to actually occupy and play out the role of the non-addict; this not only helps to strengthen one's image as an abstainer but it also provides an opportunity whereby the non-addict values and perspectives can be learned and shared. Failure to satisfy this latter condition, it can be noted, increases the likelihood of a relapse. And a relapse is most apt to occur when the expectations held of self and others are not met. As Ray (1961:137) puts it:

> The tendency toward relapse develops out of the meanings of the abstainer's experiences in social situations when he develops an image of himself as socially different from non-addicts, and relapse occurs when he redefines himself as an addict. When his social expectations and the expectations of others with whom he interacts are not met, social stress develops and he is required to re-examine the meaningfulness of his experience in non-addict society and in so doing question his identity as an abstainer. This type of experience promotes a mental realignment with addict values and standards. . . .

Ray (1961:137) notes that relapse or re-addiction is most likely to occur during the initial period following physical withdrawal; this is the time in which the addict becomes actively engaged in the "running struggle" or battle with identity problems (i.e., he or she engages in a great deal of self-debate). Coupled with this is the fact that the addict identity, values, life style, and experiences are still most immediate, while these same elements of the non-addict world are often unclear or hazy. A situation such as this (i.e., pressing identity problems, familiarity with the addict world, and a corresponding unfamiliarity with the non-addict society), however, places the individual in an especially vulnerable position and, predictably, many former addicts or attempted abstainers will, as a result of pressure by other addicts, relapse. The possibility of this occurring appears no-

ticeably great when the social expectations and reactions of addicts
are such that the individual finds it virtually impossible to identify
with or even act out any significant non-addict roles. Other addicts
may, according to Ray (1961:137), dislike any attempt at presenting a
"square" image of self, and they may begin to view the individual as
being peculiar or strange. Thus, the perceived "deviant" will be
pressured to conform.

Ray (1961:138) makes an important point to the effect that relapse
is not necessarily due to one's associations. Rather, it is a function of
how the individual evaluates self relative to the social situations he or
she encounters. For example, some abstainers will have contacts
with former addicts and still maintain their abstainer identity, while
others will redefine themselves as addicts and move back into the
fold. Similarly, some ex-addicts will associate with non-addicts and
stay abstinent, while others will reject the abstainer role and then
reassume the addict role. Predicting which outcome is most likely is
difficult, however, if the abstainer is pressured by other addicts to
conform and if, further, he or she is not allowed to assume a non-
addict status, the probability of relapse is high. The same applies to
associations with non-addicts. In fact, unsatisfactory experiences with
non-addicts often contribute heavily to a lack of cure, and particularly those interactional situations and associated exchanges which operate in such a manner as to keep the individual locked into his or her
addict role (Ray, 1961:138). Stated more simply, the abstainer may
try to move from an addict to a non-addict status, and correspending-
ly, he or she expects others to accept, as well as ratify, the attempted
status change. And when this acceptance is not forthcoming (e.g., significant others may continue to refer to the individual in terms of his
or her prior addict identity and status), questions about one's identity
and status begin to emerge. Ray (1961:138–139) offers the comments
of an addict who experienced this type of treatment:

> My relatives were always saying things to me like "Have you really quit
> using that drug now?" and things like that. And I knew that they were
> doing a lot of talking behind my back because when I came around they
> would stop talking but I overheard them. It used to burn my ass.

A person such as this would probably be an excellent candidate for
relapse. Relapse itself entails movement back into the addict world.
It also involves some resocializing of the individual. In the words of
Ray (1961:139):

> [Reentry] requires a recommitment to the norms of addiction and limits
> the degree to which he may relate to non-addict groups in terms of the
> latter's values and standards. It demands participation in the old ways of

organizing conduct and experiences and, as a consequence, the readoption of the secondary status characteristics of addiction. He again shows a lack of concern about his personal appearance and grooming. Illicit activities are again engaged in to get money for drugs, and as a result the possibility of more firmly establishing the criminal aspect of his identity becomes a reality.

Thus, complete resocialization not only demands a recommitment to the values of the addict world but it also requires a redefinition of self as an addict.

What may not be recognized from research such as the preceding is that a medical-clinical-individualistic model of change is very much in evidence. Understandably, then, if a change in personal and public identity, attitudes, or behavior is to occur, it must come from within the individual. It is he or she who must make the move. And even if, because of some socially disjunctive experience or personal crisis, a person begins to question or redefine his or her present deviant identities, he or she must attempt to operate in two worlds: the conforming and the nonconforming; this produces some obvious difficulties relative to any attempt to structure and maintain a non-deviant personal and public identity. Not only will deviant peers often pressure the "deviant" to conform to their values and associated normative system, but similar requests or demands will be made by selected non-deviants. In fact, the responses of, as well as interactions with, generalized (e.g., hospital and correctional staff) and significant (e.g., family) others are an especially important ingredient in the success or failure of any attempted cure or rehabilitation. Are these others willing to alter their perceptions of the deviant (i.e., begin to view him or her as non-deviant or conformist)? Equally critical, is the labeled or perceived deviant allowed to actually occupy and act out the role of a non-deviant, or is he or she kept effectively locked into a deviant status? In most cases, the evidence on these matters exhibits a mistakenly clear pattern: Not only are people unwilling to modify their views and expectations of those deviants and/or ex-deviants who are trying to restructure their complement of identities, but the "straights" also fail to provide any realistic opportunities whereby the perceived "misfits" can learn, or perhaps even relearn, the conventional, non-deviant roles; this unwillingness or reluctance to change can be used to highlight the most basic flaw of virtually all treatment and change programs. Specifically, environments, values, and normative systems remain unchanged. What this means with respect to theory and practice is that the legislators, law enforcement personnel, practitioners, therapists, and others either generally neglect or else ignore those factors, conditions, and influences responsible for producing deviant outcomes and, instead, concentrate on the actor. And, predictably, failure becomes defined in *individual* terms and not in *structural-organizational* terms. Obviously, blaming the individual is a much easier task than blaming the system.

REHABILITATING SOCIAL SYSTEMS AND INSTITUTIONS

Unfortunately, blaming the individual does nothing more than to protect the real culprits. If . . . a student is designated as a potential failure or delinquent and placed in a non-academic or delinquent career line, that pupil will, in more cases than not, live up to such expectations. Yet, instead of charging the educators and their system with malfeasance, we indict the academic failure or "misfit" and build a case against him or her. And not only will the student be convicted, so to speak, but the guilty parties escape prosecution and conviction.

What people at all levels must begin to recognize, however, is that failure, alienation, delinquency, misconduct, dropout, and so on are guaranteed products of the school. Another way of saying this is that the educational system's underlying organizational structure is geared to produce these outcomes and others. . . . Thus, and most predictably students will be assigned to deviant career lines and they will, once social exhibit attitudes and behaviors commensurate with their status; this, as I have stressed, also applies to any other social system an actor may become a part of (e.g., the nudist or skid row culture). The point that must be emphasized at this stage is, therefore, basic, yet most fundamental: If school failure, youth crime, and deviance are to be reduced significantly, then the organizational structure of the educational system must be attacked and altered radically. Eliminating deviant career lines (e.g., low ability groups or tracks) would be an important and necessary first step. Changing the *content* of some of the values of the school's existing subcultures or social systems would constitute another. If, for example, the anti-academic values of Hargreaves' delinquent subculture were replaced with those of the academic, the patterns of school failure, misconduct, and petty delinquency would look much different. In fact, not only would there be a sharp reduction in outcomes such as these, but an educational environment with a *common* set of academic values would have been created. Altering the value structure in this manner would, however, require other basic changes. Most dramatically, educators, school administrators, and others would be required to question the presumed validity of the success–fail philosophy that guides their interactions with students. Stated more simply, instituting a common set of values would eliminate the need for deviant career lines and this strategy would, in turn, require the development of a new working ideology—one that is based upon *the presumption of ability.* Translating this official perspective (i.e., the belief that *all* children and students possess ability and can perform) into action would not be easy, nor necessarily successful, primarily because changes would be required at all levels, regardless of whether focus is given to educators, parents, or others. In effect, we are dealing with a problem with deep societal roots.

Even though the existing theory and evidence actually call for a total revamping or restructuring of society, the probability of this occurring in either the short- or long-run is, admittedly, most remote. Nor should one expect much to happen within the educational system. Not only is the success-fail philosophy embedded deeply within the organizational structure of the school, but the educators, the administrators, and the students have been indoctrinated with this ideology. Most parents, as I argued, have also been socialized to believe in the current educational philosophy (i.e., they follow the belief that some students have ability, while others have little or none). Thus, parents, like the educators, must be a part of any plan to change the present situation.

Given the prospects for change, then it becomes an easy task to advance the argument that nothing can be done about those conditions responsible for producing *careers* of failure, youth crime, and deviance. And most do, in fact, argue along these lines. Such reasoning is, however, faulty and, even more basic, it fails to address the cold, hard facts. In this respect, the evidence is crystal clear: Institutions, by virtue of the way they are structured and intersect with each other, are geared to produce our failures, our delinquents, and our young criminals. The most graphic representation of this would have to be my analysis of how the educational system builds, maintains, and perpetuates a variety of deviant careers and identities— careers and identities that are often reinforced, strengthened, and solidified by a range of social control agencies and their agents. What evidence of this type points to, once again, is the need for structural-organizational change.

If change is to come about, then I believe that it must begin with the educational system. Not only is this one of our basic institutions but most children spend at least ten years or more within the system; they also spend many hours each day in school. The same does not exist with respect to many families or the community. Thus, the school probably represents the most stable environment in which to impact; this should not be taken to mean that the family units or peer networks should be ignored. On the contrary, they must be involved. Ideally, changes in the structure and process of schooling should emanate out to these elements.

Although most educators find very little wrong with the way they go about educating students, I have argued that they and their organization actually help to create many of the problems they would like to get rid of. And the basic problem is structural in nature. Stated most bluntly, the educators, parents, and others have bought the script, along with all of its value-laden stereotypes. The script must be rewritten. Hence, my initial call for the introduction of an educational philosophy predicated upon the presumption of ability—a theory of the office or working ideology that would, as I pointed out, eliminate the need for such sorting machines as ability groups, tracks, and streams; this, in turn, would require the elimination of the diagnostic stereotypes that characterize the *deviant* or non-academic career lines. In a sense, the school and its agents must begin to make it extremely difficult for the student to fail.

A new ideology and its corresponding diagnostic stereotypes call for some obvious desocialization and resocialization of present, as well as future, educators; this could be accomplished through a variety of methods. For example, teachers and other educational personnel would be required to attend seminars or workshops where they could be educated in terms of how the school, by virtue of its action or inaction, can help in the production of deviant careers and identities. Also, future educators of all types would not receive their credentials or even be allowed to teach until they had completed a set of mandatory courses dealing with the basic issues, concepts, and processes outlined in this book (e.g., courses which sensitize them to the way in which conflicting perspectives, such as the clinical versus the social system, affect the identifying and processing of clients; how and why career lines and subcultures may originate; how teachers can perpetuate academic stereotypes; how teachers may initiate status degradation ceremonies; how teachers may destroy a student's identity and self-image, and so on).

Additional strategies could be provided (e.g., implementing a range of institutional sanctions that would be used to deal with those who fail to comply with the new working ideology); however, what needs to be stressed at this stage is that parents, peers, and others must also be desocialized and resocialized accordingly. Obviously, and as with respect to the educational arena, the probability of producing noticeable change is low. Still, the logic and evidence point to such a need.

One of the basic problems with most families is that they have placed too much faith in the educational system and its agents. The guiding assumption is that, somehow, the educators really know what is best for their children; this, I contend, is not only a fallacious view but actually does nothing more than to give free rein to the educators. Thus, and predictably, it should not be surprising to find them operating on the basis of stereotypic notions about ability—the very same stereotypes that are, as we have seen, used to select out students for placement in deviant career lines. The responses on the part of the parents and the educators are certainly understandable, particularly in view of the fact that both have, as a result of their formal and informal socializing experiences, been indoctrinated with the success-fail philosophy. A major outcome of this socialization is that parents, peers, students, and others are taught not to question the educational decision makers. . . . In effect, whenever a parent questioned a decision, he or she was "cooled out" by the counselor.

Parents, like the educators and all others, should be resocialized. And as a start, they must become aware and begin to question and challenge the presumed validity of the success-fail philosophy, as well as each and every decision that is rendered on the behalf of their children. Parents must also begin to recognize that they can have a direct say in terms of how their children are handled by the educational decision makers. The same applies with respect to students; they, too, must begin to heighten their "consciousness" and become aware of what is actually happening at the hands of the educators. As an illustration, and in the area of career decisions, options must be presented to all—options, I might add, that are not only available for all to achieve but options that are actually attainable. For example, pupils must be apprised of what it takes to become a doctor, lawyer, professor, dentist, and the like, and they must be encouraged to pursue options such as these if they so choose; this strategy would not produce a glut of professionals. Some students, once the requirements and the nature of the occupations are spelled out, will elect to follow other career routes. The point that must be emphasized, however, is that career options must be *genuine* options and the choice factor must be *real*. And to be effective, information relative to careers and the right of choice must be presented at the earliest possible stage. Waiting until the junior or senior year is often too late, and this is especially so for those who have been processed as non-college material. The educational and occupational prospects of these students have already been damaged seriously; this does not mean that these individuals should be written-off. Quite the contrary, they, too, like the educators and the parents, could be retrained and resocialized. Admittedly, the task would be onerous, primarily because we would be required to undo what has taken many years to produce. Another way of saying this is that it takes a great deal of time and effort to produce a *good* non-college-bound product, failure, drop-out, delinquent, criminal, and so on. Hence, we should not expect any instant cures or miracles.

SOME FINAL COMMENTS

Yet, and as I argued in my introductory comments, this is exactly what the people are looking for. Thus, demands are being made continually for more laws, longer sentences, more cells, and the like—demands that are predicated firmly upon the belief that if we really crack down on crime, this will solve the problem. Unfortunately, the call for the use of "quick-fix" or "band-aid" solutions or measures will not begin to get the job done. As an illustration, we can incarcerate more people for longer periods of time; however, this will only aggravate the situation, primarily because we will have an even greater number of individuals operating under the brunt of stigmatizing labels—labels that will certainly mitigate against the probability that one will elect to go straight; this, it may be recalled, was one of the basic messages offered by Ray's research. In effect, addicts found it very difficult to structure and maintain an abstainer identity, both in the personal and public sense. Not only did they experience difficulty with the other addicts but non-addicts continued to respond to them as addicts. Equally important, the attempted abstainer was not allowed to assume nor act out the non-addict role. And predictably, most relapsed and moved back into the addict world. The same situation holds for the rest of society's deviants or ex-deviants; they, too, may try to build a non-deviant personal and public identity, and a few will actually succeed in doing so. All, however, will soon learn that society does not look too kindly upon its deviators, and they will also come to realize that structures, environments, and traditions are relatively unchanging. And, as I have argued rather repeatedly, if change is to occur, it must come from within the individual. It is he or she who must be rehabilitated.

Probably the most curious, as well as perplexing, feature of such a position or argument concerns the failure of the proponents to recognize the fact that most behavior, however defined, emerges out of a group or social psychological context; this holds regardless of whether we are focusing on the family, the peer group, the gang, the skid row culture, the nudist society, or the homosexual subculture. Thus, an ideology such as the preceding (i.e., promoting the notion of individual failure, pathology, or deficiency) must be viewed as being eminently uninformed, unsubstantiated, and most unscientific. It also contains some potentially damaging, as well as dangerous, features. For example, when we get down to the point of actually doing something about failure, crime, or deviance, we stop being sociologists or social scientists and become psychiatrists, psychologists, or some other type of clinician. Henceforth, we neglect the value and normative systems of which one is or has been implicated in—the very same structures that have given definition and shape to the person's behavior, identities, and self-image—and go to work on the mind; this is a most unfortunate and unproductive strategy, and it becomes especially so when considered in the light of the logic, theory, and evidence pointing to the need for rehabilitating some social systems and institutions. The best illustrations in support of this need, at least as found in this book, would have to be the evidence indicating how the *disadvantaged* or *powerless* (broadly defined) are frequently perceived and responded to by our schools, our mental institutions, our police departments, our courts, and our parole units. It is not a pretty sight.

Promoting the ideology of individual failure or deficiency is associated with other, equally subtle and pernicious, effects. Most prominently, focusing in on the individual deflects our attention away from the real problems. If, for example, people buy the arguments—and many certainly do—that school failure is an individual problem, that gang behavior is a function of a disturbed psyche, or that homosexuality and prostitution are manifestations of some type of genetic or biological abnormality, then the search for the actual causes or origins of these behaviors stops; this, too, is an unfortunate state of affairs. In effect, and as I have also argued, blaming the individual is and continues to be a very handy and effective political smokescreen. If, for example, the politicians, educators, and law enforcement officials can blame the individual, then they do not have to deal with the basic fact that the schools can, by virtue of the way they dispense education, contribute very heavily to the production of careers in failure, dropout, crime, deviance, and so on; nor do they have to deal with the fact that gang activity, when analyzed in terms of the normative systems that produce and demand such behavior, is often viewed as normal behavior by its members. This should not be taken to mean that violence should be tolerated. It should not. What these statements do mean is that we *have* some good evidence available to us. Being able to develop and implement programs on the basis of this information is where the difficulty comes in. How many politicians, for example, are willing to indict the educational or law enforcement system? Concomitantly, how many would be willing to provide the necessary funds for the restructuring of the educational system, as well as for the retraining of educational personnel, parents, and others? Quite obviously, none, if they are concerned with enhancing their political careers, would dare to venture into these areas; these are politically hot issues. Yet, and as I have illustrated, changes are needed—changes that could, in fact, be made. And changes that would make a difference.

Finally, failure to address the structural-organizational sources of crime, delinquency, and deviance only gives further credence to a clinical-medical model of explanation; this, too, is associated with some detrimental consequences. Most significantly, it not only allows for the continued perpetuation of myths about the nature and extent of social deviance but, in a related sense, it also provides the basis upon which many irresponsible statements are made. Like my comments relative to the school, there is, however, a way out. As a start, people should not be allowed to make statements about crime until they have studied it thoroughly and begin to know something about it; this holds for the politicians, the social scientists, the practitioners, and others. As an illustration, campaigning on the basis of a "lock them up" or "get tough on crime" plank will certainly produce the votes; however, such a platform, even if translated into policy, will not make a substantial dent in crime. Crime, whatever its variety, is, as I have demonstrated, more complex than this. And the basic flaw with an ideology or mentality such as this is that it is much too simplistic and clinical in nature. It also, as I have stressed rather repeatedly, fails to incorporate a direct and systematic concern for those factors, conditions, and environments that have actually given shape to the behavior or behaviors under scrutiny. Structures thus remain intact. . . .

. . .

"Outlaw Motorcyclists: An Outgrowth of Lower Class Cultural Careers" by J. Mark Watson. *Deviant Behavior*, 2:31–48, 1980. Reprinted with permission of Hemisphere Publishing Corporation.

Selection from *Criminology*, 10th Edition, by Edwin H. Sutherland and Donald R. Cressey. Copyright © 1978 by J.B. Lippincott Company. Reprinted by permission of Harper & Row, Publishers, Inc.

"Techniques of Neutralization: A Theory of Delinquency" by Gresham M. Sykes and David Matza. *American Sociological Review*, 22 (1957), pp. 666–670. Reprinted by permission of The American Sociological Association.

"Social Structure and Anomie" by Robert K. Merton. *American Sociological Review*, 3 (1938), pp. 672–682. Reprinted by permission of The American Sociological Association.

Selection from *Delinquency and Opportunity* by Richard A. Cloward and Lloyd E. Ohlin. Reprinted with permission of Macmillan Publishing Company. © The Free Press, a Corporation, 1960.

"A Sociological Analysis of the Law of Vagrancy" by William J. Chambliss. *Social Problems*, 12:1 (Fall, 1964), pp. 67–77. Reprinted by permission of the author and The Society for the Study of Social Problems.

Selection from *The Rich Get Richer and the Poor Get Prison* by Jeffrey H. Reiman. Copyright © 1979 John Wiley & Sons, Inc. Reprinted by permission of John Wiley & Sons, Inc.

"Delinquency, Situational Inducements, and Commitment to Conformity" by Scott Briar and Irving Piliavin. *Social Problems*, 13:1 (Summer, 1965), pp. 35–45. Reprinted by permission of the authors and The Society for the Study of Social Problems.

Selection from *Causes of Delinquency* by Travis Hirschi. © 1969 by The Regents of the University of California, reprinted by permission of the University of California Press.

Selection from *Social Pathology* by Edwin M. Lemert. Reprinted by permission of McGraw-Hill Book Company, copyright © 1951.

"In the Closet with Illness: Epilepsy, Stigma Potential and Information Control" by Joseph W. Schneider and Peter Conrad. *Social Problems*, 28:1 (October, 1980), pp. 32–44. Reprinted by permission of the authors and The Society for the Study of Social Problems.

" 'Shooting Up': Autobiography of a Heroin Addict" from *Deviance: Field Studies and Self-Disclosure* by Jerry Jacobs with permission of Mayfield Publishing Company. Copyright © 1974 by Jerry Jacobs.

"The Adjustment of the Family to the Crisis of Alcoholism" by Joan K. Jackson. Reprinted by permission from *Quarterly Journal of Studies on Alcohol*, Vol. 15, pp. 562–586, 1954. Copyright by Journal of Studies on Alcohol, Inc., New Brunswick, NJ 08903.

"How Women Experience Battering: The Process of Victimization" by Kathleen J. Ferraro and John M. Johnson. *Social Problems*, 30:3 (February, 1983), p. 325–335. Reprinted by permission of the authors and The Society for the Study of Social Problems.

"The Psychological Meaning of Mental Illness in the Family" by Marian Radke-Yarrow, Charlotte Green Schwartz, Harriet S. Murphy, and Leila

Calhoun Deasy. *Journal of Social Issues,* Vol. XI, No. 4, pp. 12–24. Reprinted by permission of Plenum Publishing Corporation.

"Paranoia and the Dynamics of Exclusion" by Edwin M. Lemert. *Sociometry,* Vol. 25, 1962, p. 2–20. Reprinted by permission of The American Sociological Association.

"Social Typing and the Criminal Justice System" by Lewis A. Mennerick. Reprinted with permission from *California Sociologist,* 4:2 (Summer, 1981), pp. 135–154.

"Normal Rubbish: Deviant Patients in Casualty Departments" by Roger Jeffrey. *Sociology of Health and Illness,* Vol. 1, No. 1, 1979. Reprinted by permission of Routledge & Kegan Paul PLC.

"Ascriptive Elements in the Psychiatric Screening of Mental Patients in a Midwestern State" by Thomas J. Scheff with the Assistance of Daniel M. Culver. *Social Problems,* 11:4 (Spring, 1964), pp. 401–413. Reprinted by permission of the authors and The Society for the Study of Social Problems.

"Three Models of Organizational Corruption in Agencies of Social Control" by Lawrence W. Sherman. *Social Problems,* 27:4 (April, 1980), pp. 478–491. Reprinted by permission of the author and The Society for the Study of Social Problems.

"Ironies of Social Control: Authorities as Contributors to Deviance Through Escalation, Nonenforcement and Covert Facilitation" by Gary T. Marx. *Social Problems,* 28:3 (February, 1981), pp. 221–233. Reprinted by permission of the author and The Society for the Study of Social Problems.

Selection from *The Knapp Commission on Police Corruption.* Reprinted by permission of George Braziller, Inc., copyright © 1972.

Selection from *Judging Delinquents* by Robert M. Emerson. Reprinted by permission of the author and Aldine Publishing Company, copyright © 1969.

Selections from *Stations of the Lost* by Jacqueline P. Wiseman. Reprinted with permission of the author and The University of Chicago Press, copyright © 1970.

"Characteristics of Total Institutions" by Erving Goffman. Reprinted from *Symposium on Preventive Social Psychiatry,* Walter Reed Medical Center, Washington, DC, (April, 1957), pp. 15–17.

"The Moral Career of the Mental Patient" by Erving Goffman. *Psychiatry* (1959), 22: 123–42. Reprinted with permission of the William Alanson White Psychiatric Foundation.

"Two Studies of Legal Stigma" by Richard D. Schwartz and Jerome H. Skolnick. *Social Problems,* 10:2 (Fall, 1962), pp. 133–142. Reprinted by permission of the authors and The Society for the Study of Social Problems.

Selection from *Being Different: The Autobiography of Jane Fry* by Robert Bogdan. New York: John Wiley & Sons, 1974. Reprinted with permission of the author, copyright © 1974.

"The Social Organization of Deviants" by Joel Best and David F. Luckenbill. *Social Problems,* 28:1 (October, 1980), pp. 14–31. Reprinted by permission of the authors and The Society for the Study of Social Problems.

"The Social Organization of Sadism and Masochism" by Thomas S. Weinberg and Gerhard Falk. *Deviant Behavior,* 1:379–393, 1980. Reprinted with permission of Hemisphere Publishing Corporation.

"Seekers and Saucers: The Role of the Cultic Milieu in Joining a UFO Cult" by Robert W. Balch and David Taylor. *American Behavioral Scientist,* 20:6 (July/August, 1977), pp. 839–860. Copyright © 1977 by Sage Publications, Inc. Reprinted by permission of Sage Publications, Inc.

"Becoming a Taxi-Dancer: The Significance of Neutralization in a Semi-Deviant Occupation" by Lawrence K. Hong and Robert W. Duff. *Sociology of Work and Occupations,* 4:3 (August, 1977), pp. 327–342. Copyright © 1977 by Sage Publications, Inc. Reprinted by permission of Sage Publications, Inc.

"The Madam As Teacher: The Training of House Prostitutes" by Barbara Sherman Heyl. Reprinted from *Social Problems,* 24:5 (June, 1977), pp. 545–555. This article also appears unedited in *The Madam As Entrepreneur: Career Management in House Prostitution* by Barbara Sherman Heyl. New Brunswick, NJ: Transaction Books, 1979, pp. 113–128. Reprinted with permission.

"Women and the Commission of Crime: A Theoretical Approach" by Carol A. Whitehurst is an original article written for this edition.

Selection from *Road Hustlers* by Robert C. Prus and C.R.D. Sharper. Lexington, MA: Lexington Books, D.C. Heath and Company, copyright 1977, D.C. Heath and Company. Reprinted with permission of the publisher.

Selection from *Corporate Crime* by Marshall B. Clinard and Peter C. Yeager. Reprinted with permission of Macmillan Publishing Company. Copyright © 1980 by The Free Press, a Division of Macmillan Publishing Company.

"The Social Integration of Queers and Peers" by Albert J. Reiss, Jr. *Social Problems,* 9:2 (Fall, 1961). This is an edited version. Reprinted by permission of the author and The Society for the Study of Social Problems.

Selection from *Human Deviance, Social Problems, and Social Control* by Edwin M. Lemert. © 1967, pp. 119–132. Reprinted by permission of Prentice-Hall, Inc., Englewood Cliffs, NJ.

"Becoming a Hit Man: Neutralization in a Very Deviant Career" by Ken Levi. *Urban Life,* 10:1 (April, 1981), pp. 47–63. Copyright © 1981 by Sage Publications, Inc. Reprinted by permission of Sage Publications, Inc.

"From Deviant to Normative: Changes in the Social Acceptability of Sexually Explicit Material" by Charles Winick. *Deviance and Social Change,* Edward Sagarin ed. Beverly Hills: Sage, 1977. Copyright © 1977 by Sage Publications, Inc. Reprinted by permission of Sage Publications, Inc.

"Tinydopers: A Case Study of Deviant Socialization" by Patricia A. Adler and Peter Adler. *Symbolic Interaction,* 1:2 (Spring, 1978), pp. 90–105. Reprinted by permission of JAI Press, Inc.

Selection from *The Felon* by John Irwin. © 1970 by Prentice-Hall, Inc., Englewood Cliffs, NJ. Reprinted with permission.

"Controlling Deviant Organizations: Scientists as Moral Entrepreneurs" by James A. Frey. Reprinted with permission from *California Sociologist,* 4:2 (Summer, 1981), pp. 135–154.

"Policing Physicians: Practitioner Fraud and Abuse in a Government Medical Program" by Henry N. Pontell, Paul D. Jesilow, and Gilbert Geis. *Social*

Problems, 30:1 (October, 1982), pp. 117–125. Reprinted by permission of the authors and The Society for the Study of Social Problems.
"Rehabilitating Social Systems and Institutions" by Delos H. Kelly. Reprinted with permission of the author from *Creating School Failure, Youth Crime, and Deviance* by Delos H. Kelly. Los Angeles: Trident Shop, 1982. Copyright © 1982 by author.